AMERICAN DIPLOMACY

Revised and Expanded Edition

AMERICAN
DIPLOMACY

A History

ROBERT H. FERRELL

INDIANA UNIVERSITY

Revised and Expanded Edition

W . W . NORTON & COMPANY · INC · *New York*

For LILA *and* CAROLYN

Library of Congress Catalog Card No. 69-13018

Cartography by E. D. Weldon

SBN 393 09861 3

PRINTED IN THE UNITED STATES OF AMERICA

2 3 4 5 6 7 8 9 0

Contents

Illustrations

Maps

Preface

Any author seeking to account for the novelties in a revision of a book finds himself inclined to write the book anew in his preface. This book is much longer than the original edition; there is a new introductory chapter on the nature of diplomats and diplomacy. Topical chapters have been broken up and placed in the chronology. New material, particularly on the nineteenth century and the 1960's, adds half again as many chapters as there were in the First Edition. For the first time there are Contemporary Documents accompanying all but the initial chapter and illustrations appropriate to the text throughout. There are more maps, drawn for this edition by the noted cartographer E. D. Weldon, and thoroughly updated bibliographies at the end of each chapter. In sum, not a great deal of the original edition remains, except the hope of the author, expressed ten years ago, that readers will find the book stimulating. The subject has inherent interest. It is indeed the most important topic of public concern of the present day. In recent years much has happened; the last decade has seen the Cuban missile crisis and the Vietnam War—both considered in detail in the present edition, the Vietnam War in a full chapter.

Like the First Edition, this book seeks to offer analysis as well as narrative, in the hope that the author's opinions, freely ventured, will stir up the student and encourage him to think for himself about the purposes and achievements and the shortcomings of American policy and will encourage him to learn more than the factual details of foreign relations.

As before, many friends have helped with the work of research and writing. Raymond G. O'Connor reread the First Edition with great care and made suggestions for revision. G. Bernard Noble obtained statistics on personnel of the state department. George W. Pierson produced a marvelous poem from the Rochester *Democrat* relating the fate of the *Caroline*. Paolo Coletta validated a humorous story about William Jennings Bryan. Stanley J. Underdal provided the text of a manuscript letter by Senator William E. Borah describing a problem of peacemaking in 1919. Edward H. Buehrig offered information on the expense to the United States government of caring for the Palestinian refugees, and he read the chapter on the Middle East. For the reading of chapters I wish also to thank Vaclav Benes, George Brooks, Philip C. Brooks, Calvin D. Davis, Richardson Dougall, William M. Franklin, Ross Gregory, Jon Holstine, Ronald J. Jensen, Frank J. Merli, Bernard B. Perry, Gaddis Smith, Leo F. Solt, Ssu-yu Teng, George M. Waller, and Gordon Warren.

Lawrence S. Kaplan read and criticized the entire manuscript in detail, in a most helpful way.

May I also thank the very able editors of W. W. Norton & Company— Elissa Epel, whose editing at one point persuaded me that she was a Republican (which calumny she has since indignantly denied); James L. Mairs, whose sharp queries often led to rewriting; and Donald S. Lamm, whose encouragement has lightened every stage of the work.

R.H.F.

AMERICAN DIPLOMACY

Revised and Expanded Edition

The Tradition, the Men, the Mechanisms

Diplomacy is the application of intelligence and tact to the conduct of official relations between the governments of independent states . . . .
—Sir Ernest Satow, *A Guide to Diplomatic Practice*

1. *The American diplomatic tradition*

The diplomatic tradition of the government of the United States, the American way in international negotiation, is largely European in origin, and hence it is with the diplomacy of the Old World that the present volume must begin. Europeans sometimes have sought to make their American friends feel as if diplomacy is as American as apple pie, and the French ambassador to the United States at the turn of the twentieth century, Jules Jusserand, once told an American audience that diplomacy is the art of bringing home the bacon without spilling the beans. This may be true, but words, even American words, will not remove the European contribution to American diplomacy.

And so one begins with Europe. Sir Harold Nicolson in a little book entitled *Diplomacy*, published on the eve of the Second World War, has set out Europe's tradition in excellent fashion, and his classic account deserves summary in these pages. He opens with an epigram, or a marvelous theological reference, by remarking the theory that diplomacy goes back to time immemorial, that diplomacy is as old as man, that the first diplomats may have been the angels who served as *angeloi* or messengers between heaven and earth. Insofar as Europe's diplomacy derived from history rather than divinity, according to Sir Harold, it began with the

3

diplomats of ancient Greece, the best orators produced by individual city-states, who went to rival cities to argue the causes of their localities. The Roman empire's contribution was *jus gentium*, a primitive international law, a combination of custom and legality by which travelers and merchants conducted their affairs within the empire and which through a slow metamorphosis changed into what we now know as international law. Diplomats of medieval times were hardly envoys in the modern sense, although the Byzantine empire did introduce the role of the observer into diplomacy. The Byzantine envoys were spies, sent out to ascertain the feelings of tribes in outlying regions, hoping that with such intelligence their superiors in Constantinople would be able to give the gradually weakening empire a longer life. Diplomacy in medieval times otherwise was a chaotic procession of envoys and special negotiations between feudal authorities, hardly the negotiations which pass today as diplomacy.

Diplomacy as we know it came into being only in the early modern era when Venice sent permanent *ambassadors*—the word is of Italian origin —to the courts of other principalities. And from Venice the custom of permanent envoys spread to the new nation-states of Western Europe, these envoys taking the name of "diplomats" from the fact that the documents they carried were called diplomas, literally letters folded double.

By the end of the wars of Napoleon, diplomacy had become so important, its ordering so essential, that a rule of the great Congress of Vienna set out a listing of titles for diplomats: according to this rule the first in importance should be ambassadors, papal legates, and papal nuncios; second, envoys extraordinary and ministers plenipotentiary; third, ministers resident; fourth, chargés d'affaires. The Congress of Vienna also put a stop to the unseemly pushing and shoving which had gone on in royal anterooms as diplomats formed themselves into line for receptions and other occasions; before the time of the congress the ambassador representing the most illustrious nation of the Continent had gone first in line, and the other envoys had scrambled for position; after the congress the *doyen* or dean of the *corps diplomatique*—French was the traditional language of diplomacy until well into the nineteenth century—became the envoy with longest service in a given capital, and the other diplomats followed according to terms of service.

Such was the European tradition that American diplomats had to deal with, the long history of continental diplomacy, and they conducted much of their nation's business in accord with it. But there was one special part of the European tradition which Americans did not accept easily, for Europe's diplomats had acquired an unsavory reputation from the era of the Renaissance and the subsequent maneuverings of monarchies, a reputation for unscrupulousness. This portion of Europe's heritage was in full flower at the time of the American revolution and continued to bloom well beyond it.

French diplomatic theorists of the seventeenth and eighteenth centuries offered advices on all kinds of chicanery. La Bruyère placed among the qualities of the diplomat the art of knowing how to offer a bribe appropriately while also seeming ready to receive one.

He knows how to interest those with whom he treats, . . . neither does he wish to be thought unapproachable in the matter and permits a certain sensibility for his personal fortune to become apparent. In this way he attracts proposals which reveal to him the most secret views of the other side, their deepest designs, their final resource—and he profits by it.

According to La Bruyère the goal of the diplomat was "never to be deceived himself and always to deceive others." Theorists of other nations were not far behind the French. The Italian writer Bargaccia remarked that when Pythagoras was being asked when men most resembled the gods he answered "when they speak truth." Wisely, said Bargaccia, because nothing belonged so properly to God as truth. He then added that "in case of urgency or for a good reason" one might consent not to be so very godlike, and that there were many ways to speak the truth without revealing it, "for example when you include the lesser in the greater, as one would say, when having ten crowns, that he has two." In the diplomatic literature of Europe there are examples of this sort of advice almost without end, such as the remark of the writer Vera on the propriety of lying:

Blamable in a private man, it is excusable in public business, since it is impossible to manage government affairs well if one is unable to dissemble and feign. This ability is acknowledged as the true attribute of kings, and it has been observed long ago that one who does not know how to feign is inapt to reign.

To the diplomats of Europe the truth sometimes had its own attractions. "It is bad to break one's word without cause," said Frederick the Great. "It gives one the reputation of being a changeable and flighty man." The Earl of Stanhope used to say during his own ministry that he always imposed on the foreign ministers by telling them the naked truth, and as they thought it impossible to come from a statesman, they never failed to write information to their courts which was directly contrary to the assurances he gave them.

The American diplomatic tradition, one must say, has been far different from the European in regard to truth and falsehood. It has not often dispensed lies for reason of state. The American republic, a democracy, being in the New World with qualities of heart and mind apart from the Old, could never easily have taken on the deceitfulness of Europe's diplomatic tradition, and it did not. The Italian statesman Cavour once remarked in a famous mot which ensured his European reputation, "If we had done for ourselves what we have done for Italy, what scoundrels we would have been." No American could have said such a thing.

How important it is to explain the special American contribution to the world's diplomacy in the twentieth century, the way of behavior which has come to be known as Wilsonian because it first was set out in detail in President Woodrow Wilson's announcement of the Fourteen Points in January 1918. At the beginning of the war in Europe in 1914, the president had said that the United States "have not the distinction of being masters of the world but the distinction of carrying certain lights for the world that the world has never so distinctly seen before, certain guiding lights of liberty, and principle, and justice." It was in the American tradition of truthfulness that Wilson in 1918 announced as the first of his points the principle of "open covenants of peace, openly arrived at, after which there shall be no private international understandings of any kind but diplomacy shall proceed always frankly and in the public view." Wilson described his open diplomacy as the New Diplomacy, in opposition to the Old Diplomacy which perforce bore a large responsibility for causing the World War of 1914–1918. By the time he set out his doctrine it was clear that the diplomacy of courts and cabinets, especially its concomitant, the secret treaty, was completely discredited. The president expressed not merely American yearnings but those of people the world over for a diplomacy which in its practices would parallel the openness of democracy in domestic government. He managed to express this point in a manner which, if it antagonized countless statesmen at the time, and later became a butt of ridicule, caught the feelings of the day and the feelings of millions of people down to the present day, people who believe that diplomacy as an extension of domestic politics should have the same openness.

The American president in 1918 was not asking for what many of his critics claimed was so naive a policy of truth that it meant no discussions outside the public view. In Wilson's opinion, negotiation did not need to be entirely in the open. Just before the end of the war, when the Fourteen Points received a semi-official interpretation at the hands of two journalists attached to the American embassy in Paris, Frank I. Cobb and Walter Lippmann, to which the president unofficially lent his assent, there was careful explanation that diplomats might converse behind closed doors:

The phrase "openly arrived at" need not cause difficulty. In fact . . . the phrase was not meant to exclude confidential diplomatic negotiations involving delicate matters. The intention is that nothing which occurs in the course of such confidential negotiations shall be binding unless it appears in the final covenant made public to the world.

Nor was the president always in favor of truthfulness if the occasion demanded a shading of the truth. It is interesting that one time in conversation with his confidant, Colonel Edward M. House, Wilson said that a man was justified in lying if it involved the honor of a lady or an issue of public policy.

But generally speaking Wilson did infuse morality into the diplomacy of Europe, restating and reinforcing what had always been part of the American diplomatic tradition, to tell the truth. There have been exceptions to the rule; during the U-2 affair of 1960 the official spokesman of the state department was put into a position (he himself did not know the truth) where he denied flatly that the United States had violated Soviet Russia's air space, until the USSR produced proof of the opposite; for the most part American diplomats have adhered to the truth. Wilson's stand for truthfulness was both a notable and salutary move in support of better diplomacy throughout the world and has had a lasting effect down to the present time.

2. *American diplomats*

Envoys during the opening period of the nation's diplomacy, from the time of the revolution down to the famous declaration of President James Monroe in 1823, frequently were men of ability, capable of handling the most difficult affairs with aplomb. Never was a great nation better served than the United States during its early years. The diplomatic roster included that paragon of discretion, Benjamin Franklin. During the country's first negotiation of a treaty of peace, the peace of Paris of 1782–1783, Franklin was joined by those two other brilliant diplomats John Adams and John Jay. In the 1790's, and for some years thereafter, at The Hague and elsewhere, the greatest of all American diplomats, John Quincy Adams, represented his country. The delegation at Ghent in 1814 which produced the Peace of Christmas Eve, December 24, included J. Q. Adams, Henry Clay, and Albert Gallatin.

The lesser figures of this early era were almost their equals. William Short, who served in Paris, The Hague, and Madrid in the early 1790's, was an excellent individual, although poorly treated by the Spanish foreign minister of his day. Charles Cotesworth Pinckney, appointed minister to France in the latter 1790's, was a South Carolinian of ability. The later chief justice of the United States, perhaps the most illustrious man of the law in the nation's history, John Marshall, served as envoy to France in 1797, in company of Pinckney. Rufus King, the Federalist who under Presidents John Adams and Thomas Jefferson presided over the legation in London, was a person of quick discernment. The negotiator of the Louisiana Purchase (if one considers that the purchase was negotiated rather than offered hastily by Napoleon), Robert R. Livingston, was a political leader of long experience.

The early secretaries of state, too, were men not merely of political stature that gave them influence with Congress and the president and the electorate; they frequently possessed diplomatic experience as well. Several of the secretaries down to and including Henry Clay, who served under President J. Q. Adams from 1825 to 1829 (this was the famous or infamous "corrupt bargain"), had been envoys and negotiators abroad.

At about the time that General Andrew Jackson assumed the presidency in 1829, the period of diplomatic quality, of capacity and experience, came to an end. A deplorable drop in the abilities of American diplomats began, which lasted at least until the early twentieth century. In his first message to Congress, Jackson had announced that the duties of public office were not so complicated but that the man of judgment, the average man, the common man, could fulfill them. The president also announced that he believed it a disservice to the republic for individuals to continue in office seemingly without end—that rotation was not merely fair but prudent. "The duties of all public officers are, or at least admit of being made so plain and simple," he proclaimed, "that men of intelligence may readily qualify themselves for their performance; and I cannot but believe that more is lost by the long continuance of men in office than is generally to be gained by their experience." The day of Jackson's first inauguration was of course a memorable occasion in American history, when after the ceremonies on Capitol Hill his supporters from far and near, of stations high and low, raced as fast as their legs and other available conveyances would take them to attend a levee at the Executive Mansion. The pressure to get in was so great that the crowd broke doors, entered through the windows, stood on the fragile polished chairs, and swooped down upon the proffered refreshments. In Jackson's time and after, the excellent diplomatic representation of earlier years thus disappeared. Throughout the nineteenth century the abilities of American diplomats became ever less visible, and envoys of the United States abroad achieved depths of incompetence hardly explored by envoys of any first-rate power. The foreign service, if one could use that term, became a home away from home for political hacks and hangers-on who for reasons unassociated with diplomacy went out accredited to foreign lands.

Quite apart from the workings of the spoils system, this debacle in representation undoubtedly came about in some measure because after the War of 1812 and the Monroe Doctrine the people of the United States turned their energies inward to the grand business of assimilating the lands of their continent, stretching the national territory to the Pacific. The nations of Europe did not often seem obstacles to this expansion, although it is true enough that Secretary of State Daniel Webster had to deal with Lord Ashburton of England in 1842 in order to settle the northeastern boundary in Maine; in the event Webster dealt so incautiously that he gave away several million acres of land to which his country had good title. President James K. Polk in part made amends for this fiasco by concluding the treaty of 1846 with Great Britain setting out the boundary of the so-called Oregon country, in which the American nation probably received more land than it deserved. Polk came close to failure in this latter negotiation and almost allowed his supporters of All Oregon, the territory to the far northern latitude of 54°40', to get out of hand. He managed his treaty just in time, before the Mexican War broke out. But then he was able to arrange a grand addition to the national territory by war against weak Mexico, and Europe could do little but watch the growth of the American republic. For the rest of the nineteenth century, with sole exception of the Civil War era when there was danger of a British intervention, the envoys of the United States could spend most of their time watching subordinates stamping documents, sending a few leisurely reports to the secretary of state, and planning for the next local ball, dinner, reception, or fox hunt. For these ministers and ambassadors (the United States employed the latter dignity on a reciprocal basis for the major diplomatic stations beginning in 1893) it was an enjoyable experience to be a large American frog in a foreign puddle.

In addition to the spoils system and the preoccupation with territorial expansion, the unassailability of the nation's geographic position contributed to the failure of diplomatic representation throughout the middle and latter nineteenth century. Jusserand once said that America was geographically the most fortunate of nations, with weak neighbors to north and south, and on east and west nothing but fish. There could be little challenge to the national purpose. Hostility flourished abroad, and its traces are preserved in the yellowing pages of the thousands of travel accounts by Europeans of the nineteenth century who came, saw, and despised. Their feelings could have no result—the United States was too far away.

The American people in the nineteenth century had two diplomatic advantages other than geography. Great Britain dominated the world through its navy, and after the War of 1812 the British government became increasingly friendly to the United States. And for a hundred years after Waterloo, Europe was largely at peace. No great war convulsed the Continent from 1815 to 1914. For a long time Europe was exhausted from the wars of the French revolution and Napoleon. If the Franco-Prussian War of 1870–1871 was a sign of trouble, Bismarck's policy of peace prevailed for a generation thereafter. Even with that wily statesman's retirement, and the appearance of a series of clumsy German officials who unsettled Europe to the point of war, a safety valve existed at least for a while—extra-European expansion to Africa and the Middle and Far East. Peace prevailed until 1914.

For the United States in the nineteenth century there was no occasion for large diplomatic ideas, apart from the idea of continental expansion. As mentioned, diplomacy became a foreign form of officeholding. What diplomatic problems proved necessary to settle were arranged at the state department in Washington, by special foreign envoys who by-passed the regular, and regularly inept, American representation abroad. Some intelligent individuals managed to go abroad to represent their country, including a galaxy of novelists, poets, and historians who found diplomatic posing a helpful assistance to their literary pursuits—Washington Irving, Nathaniel Hawthorne, Henry Wadsworth Longfellow, John Lothrop Motley, George Bancroft, James Russell Lowell. The general level of American representatives was deplorable. During the hectic weeks after his election in 1860, Abraham Lincoln spent his time in Springfield talking with office seekers and kept a little book in which he wrote the names of deserving individuals who might fill this or that post abroad. To get the inept former Secretary of War Simon Cameron out of the way, he sent him to Russia in 1862, perhaps to another land where ineptness was appreciated. Lincoln was careful in his appointment to the London legation, nominating the astute Charles Francis Adams, the son of J. Q. Adams. To France, perhaps the next foreign capital of importance at that time, he at first sent a deserving politician, William L. Dayton, who died in Paris in 1864 under bizarre circumstances. One evening Dayton had gone to the apartment of a lady of questionable reputation, apparently to discuss an important matter, and while there had dropped dead. The minister's body was spirited back to the legation, whence Dayton's decease was announced to the authorities.

President Lincoln's postwar successor after the interim presidency of Andrew Johnson, Ulysses S. Grant, had no feeling for diplomacy and allowed the appointment to London of General Robert C. Schenck, who eventually resigned under a cloud, although a different cloud than had gathered over Dayton. Schenck had permitted himself to be made a director of a Utah silver-mining company, and the company used his name to promote the sale of its stock in Great Britain. When the company failed it took down with it the savings of many irate Britishers, and virtually forced Schenck's resignation. Meanwhile he had gained a reputation for introducing British society to the game of draw poker, and one of his pupils was the prince of Wales.

The worst of President Grant's appointments were to the consular service. Grant had a custom of sending importuning visitors over to the state department bearing signed presidential cards with such legends as, "I will be willing to give the bearer, Mr. Brewster, one of the best consulates now vacant. I have known Mr. B's family for many years, quite favorably." Secretary of State Hamilton Fish one day in 1873 asked the president:

"Do you really wish George S. Fisher of Georgia given a place?"

"Yes," exclaimed the president, "I want to get him out of the country."

"Well," said Fish, "La Guayra will do."

As the century drew to a close the diplomatic service became ever more inefficient. Terms of appointment coincided with changes in the presidency. Between the months of March and July 1877, Secretary of State William M. Evarts received seven thousand applications for positions. Wearied by the pushing for consulships, he proposed to carve on his office door: "Come ye disconsulate." Years later one of his successors, Secretary of State John Hay, admittedly given to exaggeration of things he did not like, advised Henry Adams that "the real duties of a Secretary of State seem to be three: . . . to fight claims upon us by other States; to press more or less fraudulent claims of our citizens upon other countries; to find offices for the friends of Senators where there are none." According to Hay, the passage of the Civil Service Act of 1883 had vastly complicated his life: "all other branches of the civil service are so rigidly provided for that the foreign service is like the topmost rock which you sometimes see in the old pictures of the Deluge. The pressure for a place in it is almost indescribable."

The office of secretary of state was itself not inviolate from political pressure, and it is fairly clear that President William McKinley's initial secretary of state, the senile John Sherman, received the first post in the McKinley cabinet because the president wished to obtain Sherman's Senate seat for his close friend Mark Hanna. Sherman's lament was that "They deprived me of the high office of Senator by the temporary appointment of Secretary of State."

When the First World War opened in 1914, the American ambassador in the most important European capital—and perhaps even President Wilson's first secretary of state, William Jennings Bryan—was grossly incompetent. Wilson once penciled the following comments on dispatches from his ambassador to Germany, James W. Gerard, an active Tammany politician and generous contributor to the Democratic Party treasury whom Wilson had named to the Berlin post after vowing that he never would stoop so low:

10 Sept. [1915]
Ordinarily our Ambassador ought to be backed up as of course, but—this ass? It is hard to take it seriously. W.

11 Sept. [1915]
Who can fathom this? I wish they would hand this idiot his passports! W.

As for Secretary Bryan, he may have done something about his education in world affairs following his visit to Constantinople a few years after the turn of the century. Journeying westward into Europe, he had talked while in the Turkish capital with a resident American diplomat, Lewis Einstein. When Einstein saw Bryan off at the railway station he mentioned that the American political leader would have an interesting journey through the Balkans. The future secretary of state looked puzzled for a moment and then asked, "What are the Balkans?"

In the early twentieth century a change at last appeared for the better, and a half-century later the foreign service was coming close to the standards of excellence of the old days, the era of the founding of the nation. Joseph C. Grew, who entered the service in 1906, was the last man admitted without examination. Theodore Roosevelt had heard that young Grew had shot a tiger in China under hazardous circumstances. "By jove," said TR, "I'll have to do something for that young man." Next day Grew became third secretary of embassy in Mexico City. The Rogers Act of 1924 put the foreign service on a careful basis of examination and promotion. At the end of the Second World War some of the *esprit* of the foreign service was lost by the transfer of temporary wartime personnel into the ranks of the service. Again in 1954 there was a large addition to the ranks of the service which in the short run may have watered down the quality; a special committee chaired by President Henry M. Wriston of Brown University that year produced a plan which amalgamated department personnel in Washington with the foreign service in the field, so that service officers thereafter had to spend part of their time in Washington at the department and vice versa. Ten years later, in 1964, President Johnson announced that some 900 individuals in the United States Information Agency henceforth would be "an integral part of the Foreign Service," and four years later Congress passed the enabling legislation. Matters came to such a pass that a former ambassador, James W. Riddleberger, created an uproar in 1968 by protesting in the *Foreign Service Journal* that the secretary of state and some other individuals had arranged for the rank of career minister to be conferred upon Assistant Secretary of State Joseph J. Sisco, even though Sisco had never served in the field. It seemed that the standards of the department were slipping back to where they had been before 1906. Nonetheless, despite such anomalies as the Sisco appointment, despite the many "lateral entries" into the foreign service in 1946, 1954, and 1968 by individuals who had not climbed the rungs of the service's ladder, it was possible to say that by the time of the administrations of Presidents Harry S. Truman, Dwight D. Eisenhower, John F. Kennedy, Lyndon B. Johnson, and Richard M. Nixon, the service truly had become a professional organization.

By the time of President Nixon, more than two-thirds of the ambassadorial appointments were going to career foreign service officers, a figure which compared encouragingly to the approximately fifty-per-cent career-officer appointments during the era of President Franklin D. Roosevelt. The sensitive Moscow embassy, beginning in 1952, had gone to a succession of Russian-speaking career men: George F. Kennan, Charles E. Bohlen, Foy D. Kohler, and Llewellyn Thompson. To be sure, the enormous expense of the embassies in London, Paris, Rome, and Madrid had continued to dictate that their holders should be men (or in the case of Mrs. Clare Boothe Luce, who served as ambassadress to Italy, women) of wealth, able to withstand the crushing expense of Fourth-of-July and other parties. Reportedly General James M. Gavin went in the hole $20,000 during the eighteen months he served as ambassador to Paris. The paper king James D. Zellerbach appears to have spent $200,000 to meet official representation costs during the five-year period he was in Italy. The wealthy John Hay Whitney at the Court of St. James's spent more than $100,000 annually above his allowance. And the rapid increase in the number of ambassadorial missions, caused by the growth of the family of nations—the birth of nations in the Middle East, Asia, and especially Africa—probably has not diminished the number of posts open to political appointment. The best a career officer might hope for would be to rise to the rank of career minister or career ambassador (the two special ranks above the numbered ranks in the foreign service beginning with FSO-8 and working up to FSO-1), after which he could take charge of some embassy in a small country with a bad climate and no scenery. Still, by and large, the foreign service dominated the ambassadorial appointments, and its officers held almost all the other positions from which they could control almost all the important work of their embassies. This was a change of major proportion from the situation that obtained before 1906.

Mistakes, mistakes—they could still happen in the political appointment of ambassadors. The roster of errors in fairly recent times is embarrassing to recall but perhaps worth setting out in a few details as a hortatory explanation for any college or university student thinking about the foreign service. Admittedly some of the better stories (the following are from books by two retired diplomats, Charles W. Thayer and Henry S. Villard) relate to the 1930's, a time fairly remote from the present day.

There was, for example, the Texas applicant who was asked if he would like to be minister to one of the Baltic nations. "Minister?" he asked incredulously. "Hell, I've never even been in a pulpit, let alone ordained." Nevertheless he accepted the post.

A patronage dispenser in Washington telephoned a deserving man in South Dakota to offer him an embassy in Europe. Unfortunately the man had a namesake in the same town, and the phone call reached the wrong person; not until the latter was on his way to his new embassy was the error discovered.

One office-seeker with a large family in comfortable circumstances asked for and received an embassy in a far-off primitive nation. When a friend inquired why he wanted to give up a comfortable life in Delaware for a squalid Asian city, the ambassador-designate replied blandly, "My psychiatrist recommended it."

Charles Thayer reports that an ambassador assigned to Yugoslavia boasted to friends that he was on his way to Czechoslovakia and constantly confused the Masaryks with the Karageorgevitches.

The Virginia horse-breeder Raymond R. Guest, confirmed as ambassador to Ireland, in response to a question from Senator George D. Aiken of Vermont undertook to explain Ireland's role in NATO.

In 1956 a senator asked the Ohio clothing tycoon Maxwell H. Gluck, chosen by President Eisenhower to represent the United States in Ceylon, to name the prime minister, Mr. Bandaranaike, of the country to which he was to be accredited. Gluck could not do so. There was a furor before Gluck did his homework and was appointed. "Gluck," the new ambassador said waggishly to reporters after his confirmation: "Gluck," he said. "It rhymes with luck." Lucky Gluck spent a year in Colombo, entertaining pleasantly, and when he departed he left an indelible impression on local sensibilities by allowing his wife to dispose of her surplus clothing at public auction.

All of these stories admittedly were exceptional cases. Most of the political appointees were a great deal more competent than the individuals mentioned above. And the career men were always present to back up any incompetent political appointee. By the near two-hundred-year mark of American national existence few individuals would have contended that a contribution of $21,500 to the Republican Party treasury was enough to purchase an embassy, even in Ceylon. "Diplomacy," the British envoy Satow once wrote, "is the application of intelligence and tact to the conduct of official relations between the governments of independent states . . . ." Most American envoys were measuring up to such requirements.

3. *The organization of American diplomacy*

One comes, lastly, to a brief discussion of the mechanism in Washington, the department of state, through which the American government regulates its missions abroad; and of the mechanism "in the field," the embassy—the center of negotiation abroad.

The twentieth-century department of state has evolved from the committee of secret correspondence established by Congress in 1775, which with a change of name to committee of foreign affairs in 1777 existed until 1781. Congress then chose a secretary for foreign affairs, first Robert R. Livingston and then, commencing in 1784, John Jay. Jay presided over a department of foreign affairs until the beginning of the new government under the Constitution in 1789, when the department of state was established. As the office was conceived, the secretary of state was first and foremost a secretary. He was keeper of the great seal and was expected to be busy stamping and certifying public documents of importance and unimportance. Foreign affairs were only a secondary concern. Soon the business of foreign policy encroached upon his duties with the seal, until that purpose almost has been forgotten.

For many years after its origin the department grew slowly. Its staff comprised only five individuals under the first secretary of state, Thomas Jefferson. By 1820 the working force had increased to 15; by 1909 to 210; by 1936 to 753; by 1950 to about 6,800. By the year 1968, as of May 31, the personnel of the department numbered 6,741. There were an additional 948 individuals elsewhere in the United States on such assignments as passport problems. The working force abroad, incidentally, totaled 19,273, of whom 12,347 were citizens of the countries in which missions were located. Of these thousands of persons in the United States and abroad, the members of the foreign service numbered 3,619 in Washington (on rotating, temporary assignment), 117 elsewhere in the United States, and 6,924 abroad. One should add that the above-mentioned totals did not include personnel in the department-allied agencies such as the Agency for International Development, or the Arms Control and Disarmament Agency, or the United States Information Agency.

The officers of the state department for a long time—well into the nineteenth century—comprised only the secretary and his principal assistant, who was known as the chief clerk—a title no one of importance in the twentieth century would consider sufficiently gratifying. It was the department's chief clerk, Nicholas Trist, who negotiated the Treaty of Guadalupe Hidalgo of 1848, to the chagrin of President Polk, as a subsequent chapter of the present volume will relate. The office of assistant secretary of state, created some years before the Civil War, began to flourish in the latter nineteenth century, until it stabilized with four assistant secretaries and continued on that basis into the early 1940's. The first undersecretary of state was appointed in 1918 during President Wilson's administration, the office going initially to the distinguished lawyer Frank L. Polk. For over a hundred years there was a considerable permanence among the officers of the department. The combined terms of service of three of them, all eventually assistant secretaries, William Hunter, Alvey A. Adee, and Wilbur J. Carr, lasted more than a century. Hunter came into the department in 1829 and exited in 1886; Adee arrived in 1878 and stayed on until 1924; Carr appeared in 1892 and remained until 1937.

Then occurred a dramatic change. The rapidly increasing diplomatic business of the 1930's and the Second World War produced a series of reorganizations of the department. Although each revision of the organizational chart was accompanied with talk of permanence and perfection, all of the revisions resulted in ever more people and titles, until now the department boasts not merely thousands of employees but an undersecretary and a dozen or so assistant secretaries. Each of the leading officers of the department, the secretaries and the assistant secretaries, has at least one deputy, because so often officials are not present in Washington but attending conferences in Ouagadougou or in flight between Washington and Ouagadougou.

Parenthetically one should point out that John Foster Dulles was not the first flying secretary of state. It was said of one of his predecessors, James F. Byrnes, that "the department fiddles while Byrnes roams." Dulles, of course, found the plane not merely a convenience but a temptation. His record in the years 1953–1959 was 559,988 miles. His successor of the 1960's, Dean Rusk, exceeded this record in less than five years after he took office. Rusk by mid-1966 also had traveled twice as much within the United States—160,868 miles compared to Dulles's 80,702 miles.

The department has become a behemoth. The present-day organizational chart would be unintelligible to Mr. Secretary Jefferson. The department's cable traffic is incredible, considering that at the turn of the century old Adee singlehandedly read everything that entered and wrote almost everything that went out. In the 1960's cable traffic was running to as many as 10,000 incoming and outgoing messages a day.

Headquarters of the department now is in one of the larger public buildings of Washington. The first secretary for foreign affairs under the Confederation, Livingston, required three rooms. By the time of the Civil War the department was housed in a three-story Georgian-style building, appropriately decorated with a portico. After the war when business still did not seem pressing, the department moved to a building formerly an orphan asylum, a shabby brick structure far out on Fourteenth Street, reached by an ill-paved road. It was in these surroundings that Secretary of State Fish in 1871 signed the Treaty of Washington with a distinguished British delegation. In the summer of 1875 the south wing of an ornate Victorian classic building was finished on the west side of the White House, and Secretary Fish moved into what became known as the State, War and Navy Building. At the outset it contained enough space for all three of those cabinet departments. The other departments eventually left, but State stayed on in that graceless building with the atmosphere of a Southern law office, with (as George Kennan long afterward remembered it) the cool dark corridors, high ceilings, swinging doors, black leather rocking chairs, brass cuspidors, and a grandfather's clock in the office of the secretary. The department moved out only in 1947, to what was designated as New State, a building which had housed the war department. Inside the entrance to New State was a grisly mural displaying the arts of war, which department housekeepers hurriedly covered with a curtain (it is still there, behind the curtain). In 1957–1961, New State received a massive addition that brought the building to its present size covering four square blocks, 11.8 acres. New State became a great rabbit warren of corridors—five miles of them—and offices and open-glassed staircases and three new entrances with flapping flags—the only sound heard above the Cadillacs of the ambassadors and their assistants purring up to the proper ambassadorial gates.

Inside the big building, the labyrinth, or behemoth, the structure which the newspaperman James Reston once said had about as much character as a chewing gum factory in Los Angeles, it is difficult to know what is going on, despite the businesslike efficiency of the employees even when they are "stepping out for coffee." The presumption is that as the elevator lights blink, and the white buttons inside the elevators beep, and men and women scurry along the corridors into and out of offices, and library-like trucks pass down the halls weighted with important-looking documents, something is happening which affects the diplomacy of the United

The State, War and Navy Building, shortly after completion.

New State, as it appears today.

States. The system of the department is not always understandable to outsiders. Sometimes the ambassadors do not know, although they suspect
that everything takes a long time. One of the postwar American envoys,
the witty Stanton Griffis, who gave to his diplomatic memoir the endearing title *Lying in State*, recalled the advice of Undersecretary of State
Robert A. Lovett:

Probably the most amusing picture of the State Department at work is the
comparison of its operations with the love life of elephants, a bon mot which
is attributed to Bob Lovett. The analogy is simple, but astonishingly true. It
falls into three phases of comparisons; the first, that all important business is
done at a very high level; secondly, that any developments are accompanied
by tremendous trumpeting; and thirdly, that if any results are accomplished,
the period required is from eighteen months to two years.

Inspiring such humor, the department labors on. It undoubtedly is
troubled by bureaucracy, although few organizations of size, public or
private, escape such problems.

The department is afflicted with other problems, or at least confusions,
notably the competition of other agencies of the government in the business of foreign affairs. By the time of the Second World War, the work
of diplomacy had spread far beyond the precincts of the department. The
wartime and postwar enlargement of American interests abroad saw diplomacy become part of the business of almost all of the cabinet departments. During the war, in the administration of President Roosevelt (who
was a very poor administrator) the secretaries of state, war, and navy
had gotten together and inaugurated what became known as SWNCC, the
state-war-navy co-ordinating committee. Already there was too much
business outside even this committee's jurisdiction, notably in the treasury
department under Secretary Henry Morgenthau, Jr. (SWNCC was in
part an effort to control Morgenthau). After the war, diplomacy passed
into the hands of departments and agencies, presidential and otherwise,
beyond number. When General George C. Marshall was appointed special
envoy to China in 1945 he could insist that all diplomatic business with
China pass through his office, and he managed to control things in the
case of China, for he had President Truman's full backing. His mission
was the only one of its era which could obtain such control. After Marshall became secretary of state in 1947, he found it impossible to close the
floodgates of his department, and he did not even try.

A special reason for the spreading of control away from the department of state has been the desire of some of the postwar presidents to
take foreign policy into their own hands, on the assumption that foreign

relations are too important to leave to the department of state. This situation is hardly novel. Many presidents have enjoyed being their own secretaries of state. But in recent years there has been almost a duplication of the state department within the executive offices of the president. John F. Kennedy set up a miniature state department under the supervision of McGeorge Bundy. Lyndon B. Johnson also relied on Bundy, and then on Walt W. Rostow, for advice on foreign relations, or to work up presidential hunches into formal advice. President Nixon reportedly is not going to use his principal White House assistant for foreign affairs, Henry Kissinger, in this manner. Nixon chose as his secretary of state a man of slight experience in foreign affairs, William P. Rogers, and the assumption is that the president is going to handle many international matters personally. If the president does so, he doubtless soon will create his own little state department within the executive offices, as did his predecessors.

Is the fragmentation of control over foreign policy a good thing? Does it bode ill for the future? The only answer to such queries is that, right or wrong, good or bad, the spreading of control of foreign relations away from the department of state may be as inevitable a development as anything in history—and some things in history do seem to have a glacier-like inevitability, even though the processes of history, in theory, are not supposed to be inevitable. No one to date has been able to stop this fragmenting of American diplomacy, however tidy it might seem to put all of American foreign relations under one cabinet department. Every now and then some pundit may announce to his readers or listeners that it is necessary—even vital, he will say—that the department of state pick up the chores of diplomacy which have gone beyond its control, so that the secretary of state again may become the sole channel of relations between the government of the United States and nations of the world. This is a great idea, but little more than that. Even the first secretary of state, Jefferson, found his political enemy Alexander Hamilton interfering with his diplomacy, and President George Washington did little to prevent it. Never have foreign relations been completely under control of the department of state. And, anyway, the "instant diplomacy" so often required in the nuclear age tends to throw the burden of decision almost immediately upon the president.

As for the posts abroad, the embassies, the places to which the department in Washington sends its advices and from which it receives information and sometimes other advices—what are the embassies like? what are they doing? what are some of their problems? Are they very models of administrative efficiency, even while bureaucracy chokes up the department at home and while the other cabinet departments and autonomous agencies continue to make their own foreign policies?

Time was when a mission abroad was a small affair, employing a few people—perhaps, as at the American legation in London during the Civil War, three clerks in addition to the minister. Minister Adams in 1861–1865 employed his son Henry as one of the clerks, without salary. A century and more later, no embassy even in a small country would operate in such a manner. American embassies in major capitals are now huge affairs with hundreds of employees, as many as a thousand each in London, Paris, and Rome. Even in the small stations, the United States now thinks big. The subcommittee on appropriations of the House of Representatives discovered in 1962 that sixteen people were conducting the affairs of the American embassy in Ouagadougou, a mud-hut town of 65,000 which is the capital of the Upper Volta Republic in Central Africa. The embassy in Usumbura, the capital of Burundi, opened with a staff of eighteen, which meant sixty Americans counting families and all—more foreigners than the Belgians used to run the country as a trusteeship.

There is, frankly, some question as to whether American embassy staffs are not too large for efficient operation. The British and French, admittedly not as rich as the Americans, run their posts on about a tenth the personnel. Large posts in African countries raise immediately the question in the minds of the local people, "Now, when do we get American aid?" In the more civilized capitals those questions do not occur, but sometimes others do. Former Ambassador Ellis Briggs tells the story of the time he took over the embassy in Czechoslovakia after the communists had seized control of the country in 1948. They suspected that the large American representation in Prague meant that espionage was going on, and in a rather direct way helped Briggs shape up what the ambassador considered an unwieldy staff. Upon taking control Briggs had found that he had eighty people, and wished as a start to reduce the staff to forty. He pointed out to the department in Washington that thirty-three of his eighty colleagues were Pentagon personnel, and that ten ought to suffice to watch military developments in Czechoslovakia. He asked Washington gently why a naval attaché was necessary, since Czechoslovakia had no navy, and suggested that the attaché might be appointed to Switzerland or Bolivia. "After six months, and an expenditure of effort on my part sufficient to have built, singlehanded, a bridge across the Vltava River," he managed to cut two people from his staff. Then the communists declared five-sixths of the embassy staff *persona non grata*. He had two weeks to make the reduction. The result, the remaining staff of thirteen Americans including the ambassador,

was the most efficient mission, with the highest morale, of any in which I have been privileged to serve. Everything that was needful or important was accomplished with a minimum of friction and delay. No longer was it necessary to refer matters to a "country team" or to an interagency committee. We had the perfect response whenever a crackpot order was received from Washington: we "regretted that with our reduced staff it was unfortunately not possible" to investigate the rumor that the hop louse was lousing up the hop crop in the Sudetenland.

For the most part there are the huge staffs in the embassies, and the size of the missions tends to make them impressive, at least to outsiders. And one must add that the buildings in which operations occur are also impressive. Prior to the twentieth century the legations and embassies of the United States were altogether unimpressive, and there were only a few buildings which belonged to the American government, having come into public possession through gift. Even while the governments of other powers maintained the most sedate buildings, especially in major capitals, the United States lagged behind notoriously, on the apparent theory that a republican form of government required simplicity even to the point of absurdity. When Walter Hines Page arrived in London in 1913 he found the American embassy an appalling place, almost demeaning for the ambassador to enter. "I knew that Uncle Sam had no fit dwelling there," he said helplessly.

Beginning in 1929, Congress made small appropriations to construct or buy embassies abroad, and after the Second World War the acquiring of suitable buildings abroad took on momentum. Some of the new buildings, as for instance the new American embassy in Delhi, are remarkable pieces of architecture, in every way worthy of the nation whose business is conducted inside. Others are not so remarkable and, as Charles Thayer has put it, "charming Old World settings have had their ancient atmosphere rudely jarred by the erection of a glass box on stilts." Although nothing, he hastened to add, was as poor taste as the architecture of the opposition —witness the university building which Premier Stalin presented to the Poles in Warsaw some years ago, "which looks like a thirty-story birthday cake."

For better or worse, the business of diplomacy is conducted from these glass boxes on stilts, from striking new edifices such as the Delhi embassy, or from the buildings of other days. Into the lobbies each morning push the American travelers, in search of advice or assistance, and sometimes just a—as they think it is always available—drink from the ambassador's private store of scotch. Every morning the turmoil begins, and the embassy staff seeks to control the tide until it ebbs in the late afternoon. During much of the time the ambassador, of course, may not even be on the premises. Most of his meals are diplomatic occasions, and he cannot eat quietly in the embassy cafeteria. Ambassador David K. E. Bruce has said that during his two years as ambassador in Paris he had exactly one meal with his family, and that was a breakfast. Or else the ambassador may be caring for the groups of congressmen who annually have been descending on the embassies abroad in ever increasing numbers. Occasionally a congressman's nightclub expeditions have made the news, as in the recent case of Adam Clayton Powell of New York. The mere presence of the congressmen, passing in and out, is a large drain on an ambassador's time. Ellis Briggs writes that at his last post, in the off-election year 1961, over two hundred members of the Senate and House visited between October and Christmas.

For the department of state, whether in its 120-odd embassies or in the gigantic establishment in Washington, the problems of organization are tremendous. There seems no end of suggestions as to how to organize the mechanisms at home and abroad, and it is far easier to offer the suggestions from the outside—say, for some college or university professor to tell the department how to run its business—than for an insider to grapple with the confusion and resolve it toward organization rather than chaos. Sometimes it must appear as if, whatever the proposal, it is safer for the department to live with what it knows than to chance chaos.

And, to be sure, all of this difficulty with mechanisms is apart from the daily crises of foreign affairs, the real business of the department of state.

ADDITIONAL READING

The literature of diplomatic speculation is huge, and it is not merely French but British and American. For the theory of diplomacy the inquiring student might well begin with a classic of the French school, *Stephen D. Kertesz, ed., François de Callières, *On the Manner of Negotiating with Princes* (Notre Dame, Ind., 1963). The editor of this reprinted English translation, a former Hungarian diplomat, has himself contributed an introductory essay much worth pondering. *Francis H. Herrick, trans., Albert Sorel, *Europe under the Old Regime* (Los Angeles, 1947) sets out what diplomacy was like in Europe before the revolution of 1789, a translation of the masterly opening section of Sorel's *L'Europe et la révolution française.* For the views of a twentieth-century Frenchman see the presidential address to the American Historical Association in 1921 by the long-time ambassador to the United States, Jules Jusserand, *The School for Ambassadors and Other Essays* (New York, 1925), pp. 3–61. A British view of diplomacy, a classic account, is *Sir Harold Nicolson, *Diplomacy* (2d ed., London, 1950). More recent lectures by Sir Harold have been published under the title of *The Evolution of Diplomatic*

* Asterisked titles indicate paperback editions.

Method (New York, 1955), with the paperback edition shortened to *The Evolution of Diplomacy;* commentaries herein do not repeat those in *Diplomacy* but are less interesting, more discursive. For an American Nicolson, somewhat outdated because its opening section deals with the Lebanon crisis of 1958, see Charles W. Thayer, *Diplomat* (New York, 1959). The leading present-day American commentator on diplomacy, George F. Kennan, published an extraordinarily able article some years ago, "The Future of Our Professional Diplomacy," *Foreign Affairs*, XXXIII (1954–1955), 566–586, in which he contended prophetically that the foreign service as he then knew it probably would continue to reflect the general weaknesses of American society—"an age committed to bigness, to over-organization, to de-personalization, to the collective rather than individual relationship." See also Seymour J. Rubin, "American Diplomacy: The Case for 'Amateurism,' " *Yale Review*, XLV (1955–1956), 321–335, which contends that the trained expert is best for today's foreign service, and that all the talk about professional diplomats is a misreading of the requirements of the twentieth century. Callières, Rubin writes, may be all right for the early eighteenth century, but not much for the twentieth. No one, he says, goes to Newton for physics today, or to Blackstone for law.

The mechanics of foreign relations appear in the standard work by Sir Ernest Satow, *A Guide to Diplomatic Practice* (4th ed., New York, 1957). For the history of American organizational efforts in Washington see Gaillard Hunt, *The Department of State of the United States: Its History and Functions* (New Haven, 1914); Graham H. Stuart, *American Diplomatic and Consular Practice* (2d ed., New York, 1952), and the same author's *The Department of State* (New York, 1949); William Barnes and John Heath Morgan, *The Foreign Service of the United States: Origins, Development, and Functions* (Washington, 1961); Warren F. Ilchman, *Professional Diplomacy in the United States, 1779–1939: A Study in Administrative History* (Chicago, 1961). American ambassadors and officers of the department in Washington sometimes blow off steam, or fondly recall steam, in books which have appeared almost without letup since the day when young James Monroe in 1797 asked Secretary of State Timothy Pickering for a room at the department where he could write his memoirs as minister to France. Among recent volumes are Andrew Berding, *Foreign Affairs and You!* (Garden City, N.Y., 1962), advice by a former assistant secretary of state; Ellis Briggs, *Farewell to Foggy Bottom: The Recollections of a Career Diplomat* (New York, 1964), delightfully written; *Robert D. Murphy, *Diplomat among Warriors* (Garden City, N.Y., 1964), relating a long career in the foreign service, but containing an opinion on the Berlin blockade (Murphy believes the US army should have run through a convoy) which raises questions about the author's judgment; Henry Serrano Villard, *Affairs at State* (New York, 1965), a fine memoir with much humor and perception; *Smith Simpson, *Anatomy of the State Department* (Boston, 1967), advertised by its publisher as "a hard-hitting inquiry," and which strikes out—"lashes," would be the better word—at the foreign service in a way with which both Villard and Briggs, cited above, would disagree.

Textbooks on American foreign relations are now exceedingly numerous, and if one were to list the volumes in print including those for "international relations" courses in political science departments the titles might run to half a hundred. The literature of political science, and the general state of the art of "IR" as understood by political science, appears in *William T. R. Fox, *The American Study of International Relations* (Columbia, S.C., 1968). For surveys of the history of American foreign relations there are many able volumes, including those by Thomas A. Bailey, *Ruhl J. Bartlett, Russell H. Bastert, Samuel Flagg Bemis, Nelson M. Blake and Oscar T. Barck, Jr., Wayne S. Cole, Jules Davids, Alexander De Conde, L. Ethan Ellis, Richard W. Leopold, Julius W. Pratt, *Richard W. Van Alstyne, William Appleman Williams. Dexter Perkins has published a small survey, *The Evolution of American Foreign Policy* (rev. ed., New York, 1966). David F. Trask has written a careful account of recent times, *Victory without Peace: American Foreign Relations in the Twentieth Century* (New York, 1968). Arthur A. Ekirch, Jr., offers suggestive essays, *Ideas, Ideals, and American Diplomacy* (New York, 1966). See also David F. Long, *The Outward View: An Illustrated View of United States Foreign Relations* (Chicago, 1963). Armin Rappaport is editing a group of books, the American Diplomatic History series, of which four have appeared: Max Savelle, *Origins of American Diplomacy* (New York, 1967); Foster Rhea Dulles, *Prelude to World Power: 1860–1900* (New York, 1968); Julius W. Pratt, *Challenge and Rejection: 1900–1921* (New York, 1967); Selig Adler, *The Uncertain Giant: 1921–1941* (New York, 1965). The New American Nation series edited by Richard B. Morris and Henry Steele Commager has a volume on American foreign relations in the twentieth century: *Foster Rhea Dulles, *America's Rise to World Power: 1898–1954* (New York, 1955). George F. Kennan's well-known and justly admired *American Diplomacy: 1900–1950* (Chicago, 1951) covers roughly the same period with much less detail.

Topical books include Paul H. Clyde and Burton F. Beers, *The Far East: A History of the Western Impact and the Eastern Response, 1830–1965* (Englewood Cliffs, N.J., 1966); Akira Iriye, *Across the Pacific: An Inner History of American-East Asian Relations* (New York, 1967); J. Bartlett Brebner, *North Atlantic Triangle: The Interplay of Canada, the United States and Great Britain* (New Haven, 1945), an interpretation making use of twenty-five volumes on the relations of Canada and the United States sponsored by the Carnegie Endowment for International Peace and edited by James T. Shotwell; *Samuel Flagg Bemis, *The Latin American Policy of the United States* (New York, 1943); H. C. Allen, *Great Britain and the United States* (New York, 1955). For their special views see Thomas A. Bailey, *The Man in the Street: The Impact of American Public Opinion on Foreign Policy* (New York, 1948); and Cushing Strout, *The American Image of the Old World* (New York, 1963). Bailey has updated his commentary for *The Man in the Street* in a sprightly new volume of essays and maxims, *The Art of Diplomacy: The American Experience* (New York, 1968).

The American secretaries of state are always of interest, from the time of the first acting secretary, John Jay, in 1789, and a summary view is *Alexander De Conde, *The American Secretary of State: An Interpretation* (New York, 1962). Detailed accounts appear in Samuel Flagg Bemis, ed., *The American Secretaries of State and Their Diplomacy* (10 vols., New York, 1927–1929). The original Bemis series ended with the tenure of Secretary Charles Evans Hughes (1921–1925), and eight new volumes now are appearing on the recent secretaries, under editorship of Bemis and the present writer, for which see commentary below at the ends of chapters beginning with Chapter Twenty-one. For short accounts of the secretaries commencing with John Hay see *Norman A. Graebner, ed., *The American Secretaries of State in the Twentieth Century* (New York, 1961).

The definitive texts of treaties, together with exhaustive (even to the patience of readers) commentaries, appear in David Hunter Miller, ed., *Treaties and Other International Acts of the United States of America* (8 vols., Washington, 1931–1948). Miller only managed to annotate the treaties to July 1863. For more recent treaties see the old and unreliable compilation by William M. Malloy, or the series on recent treaties now published by the United States government. Selections from the instructions (outgoing) and dispatches (incoming) of American secretaries and envoys, from the time of the revolution, appeared in contemporary and near-contemporary publications down to the year 1861, when the American government began publication of the distinguished series *Foreign Relations of the United States,* the best documentary series in the world, the first volume of which contained documents for the year 1861. As of the year 1969 this series has advanced, with increasing numbers of volumes, down to events for the year 1945—which year will require twelve volumes. See Richard W. Leopold, "The Foreign Relations Series: A Centennial Estimate," *Mississippi Valley Historical Review,* XLIX (1962–1963), 595–612. Special collections of documents on American foreign relations have been published by Ruhl J. Bartlett, *Thomas P. Brockway, *Robert A. Divine, *Perry E. Gianakos and Albert Karson, Dorothy B. Goebel, Norman A. Graebner, Manfred Jonas, *Armin Rappaport, and Daniel M. Smith. The present writer has published *Foundations of American Diplomacy* (New York, 1968) which takes the record through the year 1872, with a projected second volume to 1945 and a third to the present.

An exhaustive list of titles on American foreign relations to the year 1921, as those titles were published as of 1934, appears in Samuel Flagg Bemis and Grace G. Griffin, *Guide to the Diplomatic History of the United States: 1775–1921* (Washington, 1935). "Bemis and Griffin" now might seem to require emendation, but the literature has so expanded as to make such a book, or books, an impossible project. Several recent scholars have contemplated such a project, only to shudder and look for something else. The inquiring student must search out the annotated quarterly listings in the journal *Foreign Affairs* or the ten-year compilations which that journal publishes (*Foreign Affairs*

Bibliography [4 vols., New York, 1933–1964]). A general listing of titles in American history, without annotation, appears in *Oscar Handlin *et al.*, eds., *Harvard Guide to American History* (rev. ed., Cambridge, Mass., 1960). For its subject see David F. Trask, Michael C. Meyer, and Roger R. Trask, comps., *A Bibliography of United States-Latin American Relations since 1810: A Selected List of Eleven Thousand Published References* (Lincoln, Nebr., 1968).

The American Revolution

May the freedom and Independence of America endure until the sun grows dim with age and this earth returns to chaos.
—a toast to revolution, 1776

Almost two hundred years have passed since the American people took up arms and fought a long, bitter, and at length successful revolution against the mother country for their national independence. With lapse of time and the renewal in many ways and on numerous occasions—most recently in two World Wars—of ties and friendships between the United States and Great Britain, the peoples of the two principal English-speaking nations of the world have gladly forgotten the tensions of the revolutionary era. The latter twentieth century is much different in thought and action from the eighteenth. The average American today has little knowledge of the War for American Independence. He has read a few romantic accounts of guns flashing at Bunker Hill, of long lines of redcoats wavering and stumbling before entrenched sharpshooting patriots. He has little acquaintance with the causes of the revolution or the manner in which it was fought or, especially, of the way in which the historic revolt in America tied itself diplomatically to the contemporary combinations and collisions of European politics.

1. *America and the revenge of France*

The key to understanding the successful course of the American revolution, once fighting had broken out between patriots and British troops in 1775, is the fact of French assistance: the revolution would have failed without the alliance of the United States with monarchical France in 1778.

The reason for French assistance to the rebellious colonials in North America had little to do with future American greatness. No individuals in 1775–1783 could have foretold the phenomenal success of republican principles in the New World, the expansion of the United States from sea to sea, America's rise from the obscurity of colonial struggle against Great Britain to a position in the seventh decade of the twentieth century as the most powerful nation in the world. The French nation did not foresee, by momentary vision into the grand processes of history, that in the twentieth century the United States would itself fight to preserve French independence, that America would, a hundred times over, "repay the debt to Lafayette." No such notions moved French statecraft in the eighteenth century. To Europeans of the day the American revolution was little more than an obscure legal conflict between mother country and colonies, which had no importance in itself but presented Britain's principal opponent, France, with opportunity to revenge itself for the defeat suffered at the hands of the British during the recent Seven Years War.

The latter conflict was a notable affair, and in a very real sense it set in motion a train of events that gave Americans their independence. The Seven Years War was fought out mostly in Europe between France and Great Britain and ended in a peace of Paris of 1763 whereby Canada passed under British control, Louisiana went from France to Spain, and Spain gave Florida to Great Britain. For its day, this territorial settlement was drastic and contrary to the custom in European wars of the eighteenth century whereby victor nations were not to take undue advantage of the vanquished. Britain had come under the sway of the elder William Pitt, who had caught the vision of a large British empire, and Pitt had pursued the war beyond its customary bounds. The peace of 1763 was a harsh peace. For the French nation, cherishing the memory of France's greatness under the late king Louis XIV, it was an impossible peace. The French statesmen at once set about getting revenge against Britain, and out of this purpose came, eventually, American independence.

The French foreign minister during and after the Seven Years War, Étienne-François Duc de Choiseul, a wily diplomatic practitioner, devoted servant of the Bourbon monarchy and the interests of France, could not get the Seven Years War out of mind. Obsessed by what he considered the enormous wrong done to France by Britain in 1763, he laced his instructions to French ministers and ambassadors with angry sermons on British wickedness. The Seven Years War had begun, Choiseul asserted, when England "threw at its feet the most sacred rules of equity, the most inviolable maxims of the rights of nations." "All the powers of Europe were alarmed at the scandalous rupture." "Its purpose was to invade France's American colonies, drive France from that continent, and seize all its commerce there." "But even this did not bound its ambitions." "It proposed to seize all of Louisiana, to penetrate by this way to New Mexico, and thus open for itself gradually the road to all the Spanish possessions." Oliver Cromwell had dreams of the sort when that militant Puritan ruled England in the mid-seventeenth century. Indeed, Choiseul believed, the English of his own day would go further. "They would stifle our marine in its birth, rule the sea alone and without a rival." Choiseul told his frivolous sovereign, Louis XV, that England "is, and will ever be, the declared enemy of our power, and of your state. Her avidity in commerce, the haughty tone she takes in the world's affairs, her jealousy of your power, the intrigues which she has made against you, make us foresee that centuries will pass before you can make a durable peace with that country which aims at supremacy in the four quarters of the globe."

Filled with hatred of Britain's ambition, incapable of forgetting the peace of 1763, Choiseul in 1764 sent out to the American colonies the first of several French observers whom he instructed to examine the prospects of dissension between colonists and Great Britain. Hopefully, wishfully, he read the reports of his men in America. From all save one he read what he wanted to read, for the requirements of diplomatic reporting in monarchical France were not unlike those in present-day dictatorships, and perhaps even in democracies: diplomatic correspondents reported what their superiors liked to read, for such was the way to promotion and preferment, whereas the truth, if sour and unattractive, made only for trouble. All the reporters except one sent back word of agitated colonial feelings, of unrest, of colonial desires for independence, of imminent revolt. As for the Baron de Kalb who went out to America in 1767, that honest gentleman reported that while the colonies seethed with unrest and tensions, there was no colonial desire to break the ties with England. In irritation and disappointment Choiseul charged Kalb with superficiality and pronounced the baron's labors useless.

Kalb was right about the popular temper in the colonies. Despite British provocation, colonial sentiment for a complete separation from Britain remained wavering and unsure until July 1776, when the colonists at last abandoned all their ties by a declaration of independence. Prior to that time, from the close of the Seven Years War until the signing of the declaration, colonial hopes often burned brightly for reconciliation with Great Britain. When Benjamin Franklin was in London on colonial business in 1767 he wrote to his son that "that intriguing nation [France] would like very well to meddle on occasion, and blow up the coals between Britain and her colonies; but I hope we shall give them no opportunity." While French observers watched for a break between the American colonies and the mother country, while the Stamp Act of 1765 and the Townshend Duty Acts of 1767 and the Boston Massacre of 1770 marked a growing dissension, hope remained in both England and America that the troubles were only family troubles, capable of solution within the accustomed constitutional procedures of the English-speaking family. Americans as well as Englishmen cherished the principles of the common law—their rights to life, liberty, and property. The American colonies had been tied to Great Britain since 1607, and it seemed impossible that the common inheritance could not preserve peace.

Relations between the old country and the new had long been close. Englishmen on occasion had accustomed themselves to speak lightly, condescendingly, even harshly of Americans, but most thinking people in the homeland refused to take such sentiments seriously. That stentorian representative of English conservatism, Dr. Samuel Johnson, had expressed his opinion of Americans as early as the year 1769 when he told a friend, "Sir, they are a race of convicts, and ought to be thankful for anything we allow them short of hanging." The faithful Boswell, hearing of this remark, permitted himself a gentle difference with his master. Johnson's comment, Boswell wrote, lacked "that ability of argument, or that felicity of expression, for which he was, upon other occasions, so eminent. Positive assertion, sarcastical severity, and extravagant ridicule which he himself reprobated as a test of truth, were united in this rhapsody." And surely, the Boswells far outnumbered the Johnsons in eighteenth-century British appraisals of American character. The High Tories ranted, as they had done for decades and would continue for decades after, but the majority of Englishmen thought better of Americans, were proud of the growing American colonies, and sided with such men as William Pitt the Elder, and Edmund Burke, who saw positive good in the existence of three million thriving colonials across the Atlantic. America, Pitt once exclaimed, was "indeed, the fountain of our wealth, the nerve of our strength, the nursery and basis of our naval power." Britain at the time of the American revolution had itself a population of only about eight million, as opposed to the French population of sixteen million, and many Englishmen agreed with Burke that it was desirable to increase the race in America, if only as a counterbalance to French power.

Unfortunately the British government after 1763 lay in the hands of the enemies of a moderate colonial policy. The young George III, whom contemporaries dubbed the Patriot King, had determined to secure a personal ascendancy over Parliament, and by judicious bribery he did so. Not himself a reactionary, the king in his campaign to increase the power of monarchy in England forced himself into reliance upon the more reactionary factions of his realm, antagonizing the forces of liberty, the forces of moderation. Under the personal direction of the king there began after 1763 the heavy-handed effort of the British government to tax the colonials for the support of government in the New World. This rational purpose was pursued from London with little understanding for colonial feelings. The British wished the Americans to pay. The Americans did not want to pay. The British failed to enlist the sympathy and good will of their colonials, and the government in London blundered its way into the American revolution. If the landlords then in control of Parliament had increased the tax on land even slightly, there would have been no need to tax the colonies. This might have been the procedure at the moment, after which the government could have gingerly approached the colonial legislatures with moderate revenue schemes and, with sufficient tact, could probably have obtained colonial consent. The British government after 1763 chose instead to pursue an appallingly tactless course that drove the colonials to revolt and that inspired the watchful French government to begin a general European war against Great Britain for the purpose of humbling France's traditional foe.

2. *The beginning of the revolution*

In the years immediately after the Duc de Choiseul's retirement from the foreign office in 1770 there was a let-up in Britain's colonial troubles in America, which might have ended if the British government had calculated the temper of the colonists in America and shaped colonial legislation accordingly. Statesmanship in London in the half-decade after 1770 could easily have prevented further trouble by the colonists. Instead there came that crowning blunder of British colonial policy, the Tea Act of 1773, a subsidy for shipment of East India tea to the colonies. Colonial merchants, the shelves of their stores groaning under the weight of smuggled Dutch tea, raised an argument about the constitutionality of such legislation, and afterward in quick succession came the Boston tea party, the British "intolerable acts" of 1774 in reprisal, and the opening shots of revolution in the springtime of 1775 at Concord and Lexington.

A worthy successor to Choiseul, Charles Gravier Comte de Vergennes, meanwhile had come into the French foreign office in 1774. He took up the problems of colonial revolt at the place where Choiseul had left them. Vergennes found the foreign office archives full of letters, diaries, and special reports on the prospects of a revolt against Britain by the English-speaking colonies in the New World. The foreign minister, like his predecessor, held no love for the English. Britain, he believed, was "an enemy at once grasping, ambitious, unjust, and perfidious. The invariable and most cherished purpose in her politics has been, if not the destruction of France at least her overthrow, her humiliation, and her ruin." "It is our duty then to seize every possible opportunity to reduce the power and the greatness of England." Vergennes felt that civil war in the British colonies would not occur for some years, and so at the outset of his duties as foreign minister he leisurely contemplated North American affairs but concerned himself with what seemed to be the more immediate problems of European diplomacy. He found himself happily surprised when the revolution began in 1775. A cautious man, he waited to see how resolute the colonists would be, to see whether the revolt would become extensive and bitter enough to warrant France's open intervention. Whereupon there appeared before him an enterprising Frenchman, Pierre Augustin Caron de Beaumarchais, watchmaker, courtier, author of the *Marriage of Figaro* and the *Barber of Seville*, lover of intrigue and liberty.

Beaumarchais was the spirit of Benvenuto Cellini, reborn in the eighteenth century. He had first come to the attention of high French society when as a young watchmaker he produced a watch so small that it could be worn in a ring on a lady's finger. Knowing exactly what to do with such a gimcrack, he presented a watch ring to Mme. de Pompadour, mistress of Louis XV, and soon had orders for rings from all the courtiers of Versailles. Thereafter he engaged in a number of escapades. Early in 1776, anxious for more excitement and adventure, Beaumarchais offered a special proposition to Vergennes, namely, that France secretly assist the American revolution by sending munitions through a bogus firm, to be headed by himself and to be known as Roderique Hortalez and Company.

The scheme was a clever one, befitting the talents of its author. Beaumarchais would receive a gift of money from the French government, perhaps also from the Spanish government, and employ the funds to purchase arms and other necessary military equipment for dispatch direct to America. All this activity was to be under the guise of private commerce, the simple business venture of Hortalez and Company. Thus if the curious and alert British ambassador at Paris, Lord Stormont, made inquiries and complained that France was intervening in the private affairs of Great Britain, the French government could answer that Beaumarchais's operations were those of a private citizen with no connection with the government.

The idea appealed to Vergennes and the foreign minister lost no time in persuading his colleagues of the French cabinet to approve a secret gift to the Americans, via Beaumarchais, of 1,000,000 livres, about $200,-000. This took, one should add, some considerable persuading, for Louis

XVI was squeamish about the ethics of the Beaumarchais proposal. Moreover, the king's finance minister, Baron Turgot, predicted that the scheme would bankrupt France, and he was eventually proved right: the indirect aid turned after a while into direct aid; the cost of France's war against Britain by 1783 totaled perhaps 1,200,000,000 livres, emptied the French treasury, and helped bring on the French revolution in 1789. But Vergennes in 1776 could not look that far ahead. He overcame the opposition of Turgot and the king and in May of that year came to an arrangement with Beaumarchais before any American agent had set foot in France, indeed before the American declaration of independence. The king of Spain, Charles III, uncle of Louis XVI, matched this gift, sending Beaumarchais another million livres. Charles's foreign minister reasoned deviously that such a gift, keeping alive the war in the New World, might cause the Americans and British to exhaust each other. In ensuing months there were further French contributions to the company of M. Hortalez, some in the form of outright gifts from French government arsenals. Across the Atlantic, from France to the United States, came a life-giving stream of military articles that the Americans so sadly lacked—powder, guns, clothes, drums, fifes, medicines of every sort, surgical instruments, and even cannon with the Louis XVI monogram. Beaumarchais wrote to the Spanish ambassador in Paris, Count Aranda, that the first shipment by Hortalez and Company in the summer of 1776 consisted of 300 "thousands" of powder for cannon, 30,000 muskets, 3,000 tents, 200 cannon with full train, 27 mortars, 100,000 cannon balls, 13,000 bombs, clothing for 30,000 men.

It is impossible to overemphasize the importance of French support for the American revolution, for without the munitions sent to America in 1776 and 1777 the revolt would have collapsed. There was, to mention only one need of the revolutionary armies, an acute shortage of powder, so much so that on Christmas day, 1775, Washington wrote: "Our want of powder is inconceivable. A daily waste and no supply administers a gloomy prospect." Three weeks later no powder was to be had at all, and if the British could have learned this they might have marched out to Cambridge and destroyed the new colonial army, probably ending the revolution. Arrival of French powder shortly thereafter was of crucial importance to the American cause. According to a computation later made by an American historian, French powder comprised nine-tenths of the American supply during the early years of the revolution.

In addition to furnishing munitions of war, France in the first years of the revolution assisted American commerce upon the seas. That commerce faced grave dangers from British warships, and the French government did its best to prevent captures of American vessels. A French naval squadron was stationed off the Channel ports to discourage too close scrutiny of French roadsteads for American ships. Another squadron went out to the French West India Islands in May 1776, with instructions to protect "insurgent" vessels which, pursued by British warships, might seek asylum under the French flag. The government of Louis XVI allowed American privateers to operate from French harbors, equipping themselves there and bringing back prizes to be sold to the highest bidder. This accommodation was in complete contravention of France's duties as a neutral, for France had not yet declared war on the British. Vergennes time after time winked at the practices of American privateersmen and at assistance given them by French citizens and government officials. When the foreign minister was confronted by affidavits sworn on "the Holy Evangelists of Almighty God" that in the French islands British sailors captured by American privateers were being held in prison and dying by "inch-meal," he resorted to the baldest evasions, promises, and denials. The British ambassador on one occasion asked the French government to restore prizes brought in by American privateers. Vergennes answered, "You cannot expect us to take upon our shoulders the burden of your war; every wise nation places its chief security in its own vigilance." Stormont replied, "The eyes of Argus would not be too much for us." Vergennes, unperturbed, answered with unction, "And if you had those eyes, they would only show you our sincere desire of peace." Stormont ventured that French officers were hurrying to America to enlist in the rebel forces. "Yes," said Vergennes, "the French nation has a turn for adventure."

This was the state of affairs—virtually a recognition by France of American belligerency, though such a judicial distinction was then unknown in international law—when in the late autumn of 1777 a new development in the civil war between the British and their colonies brought French intentions into the open. For a number of months the ships of Beaumarchais had been landing supplies at Portsmouth, New Hampshire, whence the munitions were carried westward to the gathering forces of General Horatio Gates. When in the summer and autumn of 1777 the lumbering troops of General John ("Gentleman Johnny") Burgoyne came down from Canada, they encountered the French muskets and powder of Gates's forces. Burgoyne's surrender on October 17, 1777, was almost a French victory. The battle of Saratoga, most decisive battle of the revolution, persuaded France to support openly, with ships and troops, the new government of the United States.

3. *The French alliance*

By the time of Saratoga a number of American diplomats had been sent abroad, to use the successes of American arms to gain foreign support for the revolution. The special hope of this "militia diplomacy"—sending American diplomats to the principal courts of Europe, whether or not those courts desired to receive them—was to obtain recognition of the United States by the various nations. Recognition, and perhaps a loan or gift of arms.

At the beginning it had proved difficult to convince the American Congress, the second Continental Congress which in 1776 had turned itself into a national congress, that diplomatic representation abroad was necessary or even advisable. When John Adams first suggested to his congressional colleagues that the United States apply for assistance to Britain's enemies in Europe, he received "grimaces" and "convulsions" from the members, for whose nerves, already shaken by the emotional difficulties of cutting the ties of the British empire, the idea of sending diplomats abroad was too much. There was feeling in Congress that it would be unwise to employ such "foreign papists" as the French in American service. Still, hesitation could not stand in face of the evident need for foreign alliance. The members of Congress quailed at the prospect of war with England without the aid of France, and in 1776 Congress authorized dispatch of three representatives to the French court: Benjamin Franklin; Arthur Lee, previously the agent of Massachusetts in London; and Silas Deane, a wealthy and respected member of Congress from Connecticut. Deane and Lee were already in Paris, where Deane was having dealings with Beaumarchais on behalf of the American government.

Of these three American diplomats—the first accredited diplomats in the history of the United States—the most impressive and able, by far, was Benjamin Franklin. The diplomatic services rendered by Franklin to the revolution were, as events proved, invaluable. When Franklin arrived in Paris in December 1776 he met a welcome such as a king would have enjoyed. He was one of the two best-known men in the world during the latter eighteenth century, the other being Voltaire, but the aging American could not have dreamed that Frenchmen would find his presence so irresistible. He made the most of his opportunities. Frenchmen for some reason believed Franklin, a citizen of Philadelphia, to be a Quaker fresh from Penn's Woods, and the venerable scientist obliged them by dressing to the role. Three weeks after he had settled down, the police

Benjamin Franklin.

reported that "this Quaker wears the full costume of his sect. He has an agreeable physiognomy. Spectacles always on his eyes; but little hair—a fur cap is always on his head." Franklin found his benign features on snuff-box lids and medallions, and his pictures and busts were everywhere. These, so he wrote his daughter in 1779, "have made your father's face as well known as that of the moon. . . . It is said by learned ety-mologists that the name *Doll,* for the images children play with, is derived from the word Idol; from the number of dolls now made of him, he may be truly said, *in that sense* to be *i-doll-ized* in this country." *Le grand Franklin*—deist and freethinker, a Quaker in France —was a striking figure. The simplicity of his dress hid the fact that he was a wealthy man. The humility of his bearing, the modesty of his speech, shielded from French minds his subtle and refined intellect that could take the measure of any person of his generation, even the most mannered courtiers and diplomats of Europe.

Franklin moved in triumph through French society during the year 1777, the year which, as he knew, was a crucial one for American inde-pendence. He established cordial relations with Vergennes, and constantly importuned the foreign minister—though his skill in personal relations made his inquiries seem not at all like importuning—for loans to the United States (he had secured 18,000,000 livres by 1782). He also sought French recognition of the independence of the United States, and a treaty of alliance between France and the United States, such a treaty to be followed by military and naval assistance. Vergennes held off, despite the blandishments of the American Poor Richard, until news of Bur-

Franklin's reception at the Court of France, 1778.

goyne's defeat at Saratoga gave assurance that revolt in the New World was meeting with considerable success. A courier bearing word of the American victory arrived early in December 1777. The foreign minister sent his secretary to the American commissioners in Paris, offering congratulation and inviting the Americans to renew their offer of a treaty of alliance. He required a short time to draw the treaty, which he signed with the Americans on February 6, 1778.

There were in fact two treaties which Vergennes made with the Americans. The first, the treaty of alliance, announced the "liberty, sovereignty, and independence absolute and unlimited of the United States." Here was formal French recognition of American independence. There followed stipulations that in case of war between France and Britain the United States should have a free hand to conquer Canada and the Bermuda Islands, and that France might seize the British West Indies. Each nation guaranteed the territory of the other, a customary amenity in alliances. There was the important proviso, essential to any alliance, that neither nation would conclude a truce or peace with the foe without the other's consent. In a separate treaty of amity and commerce the two nations established in general terms their commercial relations, with a promise by each to adhere to specified principles of neutral rights in the event of future wars. These principles need not detain us at this point, as their importance appeared later when war broke out in Europe after the French revolution of 1789.

"No American should ever forget the alliance of 1778. No Frenchman ever will." This remark by the leading historian of the diplomacy of the American revolution, Samuel Flagg Bemis, well characterizes the most signal American diplomatic achievement of the eighteenth century. Without the alliance there could never have been American independence. Prior to 1778 the shipment of French munitions to the New World ensured survival of the revolutionary armies during their first clashes with the well-supplied British regulars and enabled the Americans to win the battle of Saratoga. After 1778 the open assistance of French ships and troops made possible the final triumph of American arms, the victory at Yorktown in 1781, in which more Frenchmen participated than Americans.

French help, as we have seen, came because of the traditional enmity of Frenchmen and Britishers, and more specifically because of the defeat of France in the Seven Years War. American diplomats were under no illusions as to the reason for French intervention in the American war for independence, and it was with full awareness of the circumstances that they courted French assistance. They knew that they were precipitating—for their own advantage, they hoped—a large-scale war in Europe, another war on the scale of the Seven Years War, or the previous War of the Austrian Succession (1740–1748), or the War of the Spanish Succession (1702–1713). They knew that with the treaty of alliance of February 1778 there would follow open conflict between France and Britain, that France would enlist the support of its traditional Bourbon ally Spain, that other nations of Europe, in particular Prussia and Austria, might use the occasion to settle their own quarrels. There would probably be a general European war, once France had declared itself in favor of the Americans, and American diplomats would have to snatch their country's independence out of this European turmoil. It was risky business for the United States. No nation in Europe cared greatly about the success of republican principles in the New World, and even the French ally might abandon the cause of American independence if circumstances made such a course desirable.

Hostilities in Europe began on June 17, 1778, when French and British naval forces drifted into a skirmish along the Channel coast. Almost at once American diplomatic representatives saw their country drawn into European politics because of the necessity of the alliance with France.

4. *The wiles of Europe*

Vergennes sought a formal connection between France and Spain, hoping that in the war with Britain he could gain the help of the Spanish fleet, which if grouped with the French fleet would give naval superiority against England. The Spanish backed and filled during most of the year 1778, and only in the following year decided to join the French.

France's negotiation with Spain proved unsuspectedly difficult and time-consuming, for several reasons. For one, the Spanish monarchy— despite its decline in vigor during the eighteenth century—cherished dreams of past importance, and the Spanish felt, not without justice, that the French had been too quick in calling the tune with the Americans. Vergennes had concluded his alliance with the United States too hastily, the Spanish believed; Spain had not been consulted with sufficient deference. One cannot altogether blame Vergennes in the matter. He had sought to obtain prior Spanish consent to his alliance with the Americans, and when the Spanish government dallied and procrastinated he had gone ahead and made his treaties. Having done this he found his task of bringing Spain into the war exceedingly difficult.

Two other factors explain why Spain at first sought to remain aloof from the conflict, despite all the alleged friendliness, the fond emotional attachments, of the Bourbon family compact. For one, the Spanish were worried that an independent nation established close to their colony of Louisiana might prove a military threat. Then too, there was the possibility of persuading the British to cede Gibraltar (which Britain had taken from Spain in 1704). The Spanish dealings over Gibraltar with the British took the peculiar form of a proposal of mediation, with Gibraltar as its price, between Great Britain and the Americans. The mediation would have been on the basis of *uti possidetis*, the war map of the moment, which favored the British inasmuch as they were in possession of good-sized portions of the American seaboard. The British, as we now can see, should have signed up with the Spanish, for they would have lost far less than they eventually did. Admittedly the Americans had an alliance with the French, which stipulated that there should be no separate peace by either ally until American independence had been recognized by Great Britain, and so one might argue that whatever arrangements Spain made with the British did not relieve France of the obligations of the alliance of 1778. Still, if the Spanish had pushed through an arrangement over America with the British government it would have been difficult for the French to fight on singlehandedly for American independence. The government of Louis XVI would have had to go back on its word, a not-unheard-of procedure in eighteenth-century European international relations. Spanish dickering with Britain had considerable danger for the future of the American republic, but fortunately the government of Lord North refused to listen to the propositions of the Spanish ambassador in London.

Spain's efforts to secure Gibraltar out of the Franco-American-British struggle were little more than blackmail of Britain during its time of trouble. As the Spanish foreign minister wrote to his ambassador in London in 1778, the British "must know that what we do not get by negotiation we know how to get with a club." The price of Spanish neutrality was "that pile of stones of Gibraltar." The Spanish ambassador in London said all this to Lord Stormont, the erstwhile ambassador in Paris who had become foreign secretary of the Lord North government. Stormont was not averse to the idea of buying Spain out of the war, but there were a number of difficulties in working out the purchase, a series of cessions between France, Spain, and England in the New and Old Worlds. In the course of the proposed roundabout exchange of Haiti, Corsica, Minorca, and Gibraltar all sorts of arrangements were necessary, and while the dickering went on in London, Vergennes managed to convince the Spanish court that it would be easier to get Gibraltar by coming into the war.

When the Madrid government in 1779 entered the European war against Britain, the Spanish did not adhere to the Franco-American alliance, which they could have done, but concluded a special Treaty of Aranjuez between themselves and the French, avoiding recognition of American independence.

How far was the Spanish court then willing to support American independence? Was not the king of Spain more interested in what the Americans could do for his kingdom, rather than he for their country? The king of Spain had supported Hortalez and Company, and later secretly advanced small sums to American agents in Europe. This was as far as the Spanish would go in the matter of American aid. Meanwhile they embroiled the Americans in a purely Spanish problem. At Aranjuez they bound the French to fight Britain until the interest of Spain in the war, capture of Gibraltar from the British, had been attained. The effect of this provision of the Treaty of Aranjuez upon the fortunes of the American revolution was obvious. The United States became bound, through the French alliance, to stay in the war until France was willing to conclude a peace. Having attached themselves to the French, the Americans found themselves attached, indirectly through Aranjuez, to Spanish purposes—Gibraltar. In a sense our independence had become chained, to use Bemis's word, to the Rock of Gibraltar.

European politics in those years between the 1779 Treaty of Aranjuez and the peace treaties signed at Paris in 1783 were alive with moves and countermoves, projects and counterprojects, each usually masking an ulterior purpose. Most of them, one should add, never came to anything and do not deserve discussion. They only illustrated the dissembling nature of European statecraft in the eighteenth century. If one were to look merely at the talk, not the action, of European monarchs and statesmen, he would assume that nothing but the highest principles were being followed by the chancelleries of France, Britain, Spain, Prussia, Austria, and Russia. Veiled by the words and the professions were purposes that pointed up the enmities, rather than friendships, of Europe, purposes that represented *raison d'état*, reason of state, rather than simple reasonableness. This was the accepted way of international dealing long before the time of Bismarck and Stalin.

Take for example the Hussey-Cumberland negotiations of 1779–1781. No sooner had the Spanish entered the conflict against Great Britain than another devious Spanish proposal was intimated to the government of George III, or British proposal to Spain—it was difficult to know, really, who was proposing what, for negotiations were so tentative and cautious. The chief of the Spanish secret service in England, an Irish priest named Thomas Hussey, took up negotiations with an English agent, Richard Cumberland, and Cumberland accompanied Hussey on a mission to Spain in hope that somehow a *quid pro quo* might be arranged and Spain leave the war.

To Vergennes's intense relief, nothing came of this project, although it is of interest to realize that the French foreign minister at this time, a moment of military difficulties for the anti-British coalition in both Europe and America, was not unwilling to conclude a truce on the basis of *uti possidetis* in hope of salvaging what he could from the war. Vergennes in a private memorandum of February 1781 considered carefully how he might get out of the war by a truce with England. "One may therefore presume to say," he wrote, "that the king would be lacking delicacy, that he would be giving the Americans just cause for complaint or at least distrust, if he should propose to Congress to sign a truce leaving the English what they possess on the continent. Therefore," the minister concluded rather deviously, such a suggestion would have to come from Austria and Russia, who were then proposing a mediation of the war, for "only the mediators, bound by no such ties, could make a proposition so painful to the United States."

The Austro-Russian mediation proposal of 1780–1781 is itself of considerable interest, revealing the intricacies of European international relations during the American revolution, the chesslike calculations of each state before it made a diplomatic move, the difficult problems through which the Americans had to think their way to achieve the independence of the United States.

Austria was an ally of France at the outbreak of war in America, and it was the purpose of French diplomacy to keep the Austrians from invoking the Austro-French defensive alliance in Europe, which the Austrian court could have done if it wished. Vergennes desired no European complications, no attempt by his Austrian ally to carve some petty European principality, while he proceeded with his grand design of obtaining American independence and, thereby, humbling Great Britain. Irrespective of French wishes, the Austrians took advantage of the death of the ruler to annex Bavaria in the winter of 1777–1778, thereby beginning a war with Frederick the Great of Prussia. The problem for France was to stop the dreary campaigns of the Kartoffelnkrieg, the Potato War, so-called because the ill-fed soldiers of Austria and Prussia spent the winter of 1778–1779 digging frozen potatoes. Mediation of the War of the Bavarian Succession was accomplished in 1779 by the French court acting with Russia. Whereupon the Austrian emperor, furious at this intervention in his affairs by a supposed ally, undertook to reciprocate the French favor, and offered to mediate between Britain and France. In this mediation effort Austria was joined by Russia. It happened that the offer from these two powers coincided with a low point in the military fortunes of the French and Americans, and, as we have seen, Vergennes was willing to accept a mediation if necessary, and believed that he saw a way out of the embarrassments of the Franco-American treaty by getting Austria and Russia to propose the *uti possidetis.*

Among the European projects of these years one should mention the armed neutrality of 1780, announced by the Russian empress Catherine the Great as a defense of the neutral rights of small powers. This scheme would have brought together the neutral navies of northern Europe, which in concert could have demanded the right to trade with Britain's enemies in all goods except those obviously useful as implements of war. The British had been denying the neutrals this right. In actuality the armed neutrality never got beyond the stage of a project, for no nation went so far as to support by force the proposal of the tsarina. Nevertheless the British government had some difficult moments contemplating what might happen if the neutral navies of the European powers marshaled themselves against the Royal Navy. The result would not have been pleasant, for in the late eighteenth century the Scandinavian nations maintained formidable navies, and if coupled with the Russian navy they might have secured a concert of power sufficient to take control of the seas from Great Britain. Happily for the English the armed neutrality came to nothing. It never emerged from the ideal to the real, proving to be naught, as Catherine herself described it, but an armed nullity.

During these European moves and countermoves—armed neutrality, Austro-Russian mediation, Hussey-Cumberland negotiations, Spanish mediation offer—the Netherlands entered into the war against Great Britain.

In the first hopeful months of militia diplomacy, Congress had sought recognition of independence of the United States from the Dutch Estates General; but the Dutch, knowing that recognition would invite British reprisals and probably war, refused to take any formal step in that direction. Meanwhile, in the Dutch West Indian island of St. Eustatius, a thriving trade in contraband goods arose between the Dutch and other European nations on the one hand and the Americans on the other. This trade, together with participation of Dutch vessels in the French coastal trade after France entered the war in 1778, led Great Britain to declare war on the Estates General in 1780. The British pretext was as flimsy as it could possibly have been. Britain declared war after a draft of a treaty between Holland and the United States, bearing only signs of unofficial discussion between an American agent and a representative of the burgomasters of Amsterdam, was pulled from the sea (it was found among some insufficiently weighted papers which the American envoy, Henry Laurens, threw overboard just before a British vessel took him prisoner). But with the beginning of hostilities Great Britain brought to an end the coastal trading by the Dutch with France, and early in 1781 Admiral Sir George Rodney descended on the island of St. Eustatius and sacked it as completely as any island had been sacked since the freebooting years of Drake and Raleigh on the Spanish Main.

The conquest of St. Eustatius was of more than passing interest in the history of the American revolution. The island, as mentioned, had been providing immense quantities of munitions to the Americans. Rodney himself said, with some exaggeration, that "This rock, of only six miles in length and three in breadth, has done England more harm than all the arms of her most potent enemies, and alone supported the infamous American rebellion." The Dutch free port, popularly known as Statia, had a mile-long street of warehouses for contraband goods. Here a privateer could arm for a cruise, and the smuggler could purchase false papers together with gunpowder in tea chests or rice barrels. Its loss to the patriot cause was serious. Admiral Rodney's triumph, however, was less than he at first believed, for the French recaptured much of his booty, including the admiral's personal haul of over half a million dollars in cash seized when the French came back to the island before the admiral's agent had moved the loot to safety. Then too, when Rodney sold his other acquisitions at a gigantic auction in the West Indies, many of them went to the American cause for far less than their value, a far lower price than the Americans had been paying for such supplies from St. Eustatius under Dutch rule. And there was a crowning disappointment in the St. Eustatius operation: by lingering at the island, engaged in gathering together his booty, Rodney failed to apprehend the fleet of the French admiral the Comte de Grasse, then in the West Indies. Grasse shortly thereafter supported an operation of French and American troops before the Virginian village of Yorktown, and the capture of Cornwallis's entire force of more than seven thousand men on October 19, 1781, marked the concluding battle of the revolutionary war.

It was good news to Benjamin Franklin at Passy, near Paris, when the word came of Yorktown. For Franklin the years had passed slowly after 1778. They were years of advancing age—the philosopher was seventy-five in 1781—and he had absented himself from the family circle in Philadelphia. He attended scientific meetings, pursued his huge correspondence with individuals all over Europe, flirted with Mme. Helvetius. He read avidly the reports from America. At long last came the defeat of Cornwallis and with it the possibility of peace.

5. *A lack of bienséance*

After Yorktown a peace party began to gain adherents in England. With the slowness of the war and lack of important British victories the opponents to the personal rule of George III in Britain took heart, and a strong feeling for peace emerged. The opposition managed to carry a resolution through the House of Commons, early in 1782, declaring enemies of their country all those who should advise or in any way attempt to prosecute an offensive war in America for the purpose of reducing the colonies to obedience by force. Lord North resigned as prime minister in March 1782. George III drew up a message of abdication, and was dissuaded only by the thought that through appointment of Lord Rockingham as North's successor he could work with the ministry not completely under control of his enemies. The Rockingham ministry decided to make peace with America, and Franklin in Paris received visits from a British emissary, an elderly philosopher and one-time slave trader named Richard Oswald. With this change of affairs everything was set for a triumph of American diplomacy under Franklin's guiding genius.

The problem was to get out of the war and, at the same time, maintain good faith with France. Americans had no desire to continue fighting for Spanish aims in Europe, but they were bound indirectly, via the Franco-American alliance, to the Treaty of Aranjuez. It was Franklin who found a way out of the inconveniences of the French alliance and at the same time managed to preserve a substantial amount of American good faith.

The first important move in negotiations to end the war was made by one of Franklin's colleagues, John Jay. Jay had been sent to Spain by Congress in a tactless effort to obtain Spanish recognition. According to Don José de Moñino y Redondo, the Count of Floridablanca, the Spanish foreign minister, Jay's "two chief points were: Spain, recognize our independence; Spain, give us more money." After the futilities of such a mission eventually impressed themselves upon Congress, Jay received a new appointment as commissioner, together with Franklin and John Adams, to negotiate peace with Great Britain. The three American commissioners, it soon appeared, were unlike in temperament and outlook. Franklin was full of equanimity and hope, trusting to time and the advantages of history. Adams was irascible, pugnacious, eager to force his presence upon the French court, desirous of defending every shred of American rights against France and all other powers on earth. He had arrived at Paris after a mission similar to Jay's, to the Dutch in 1780 upon their involvement in war with Britain. Jay was distrustful, suspecting intrigue by Vergennes to deprive the American nation of its independence. Jay in his suspicions came to believe that Vergennes was dealing behind the backs of the Americans, ready to abandon their cause as soon as the occasion proved convenient. When he heard that Vergennes's private secretary had gone off to London on a special mission he was sure that the French foreign minister was conniving to defraud the Americans, and he entered into confidential negotiations without consent of his fellow commissioners, with the British agent Oswald.

Franklin, on learning of Jay's negotiations, at first had misgivings about them, for such parleys contradicted the spirit if not the letter of the alliance with France, according to which neither France nor the United States was to conclude a peace or truce without the consent of the other. Even so, there was reason to allow continuance of Jay's conversations. Although Franklin put little faith in Jay's fear that Vergennes was negotiating privily with the British, the foreign minister had placed the American peace commissioners in a most awkward position because of a roundabout arrangement he had made with the American Congress through the French minister to the United States, the Chevalier de la Luzerne. The latter, by extraordinary diplomatic talents coupled with careful use of money, had acquired influence over the American government. He claimed, in a letter to Vergennes, to have procured the election of Robert R. Livingston as secretary for foreign affairs, and Livingston appears to have been grateful for this assistance and showed appreciation by appointing a French officer as his assistant. The minister to the United States had persuaded Congress to instruct the peace commissioners in Paris to negotiate with the British only under step-by-step consent of the French government. The single *sine qua non* in negotiations was American independence, and on all other matters—boundaries, navigation of the Mississippi, fishing rights off Newfoundland and Nova Scotia—the commissioners found themselves submitted to the advice of the French court.

This was a highly unsatisfactory state of affairs. "Blush, blush, America," an angry member of Congress wrote to John Adams. The devious French prompting of the commissioners at Paris, sent to Franklin, Jay, and Adams as a formal instruction from their government, so tied the hands of the commissioners that if they had followed their instructions they would have been little more than clerks of the French foreign minister. Vergennes believed that he had maneuvered himself into controlling the American commissioners. The commissioners, vigorous personalities in their own right, wished no such control. Franklin felt that the French deserved a modicum of bad faith, and was willing to carry on separate and secret negotiations with the British.

The result was a "preliminary treaty" between Great Britain and the United States signed on November 30, 1782.

Here, in truth, was what in all but name amounted to a separate peace. Once the British and Americans had come to agreement, if only in a preliminary treaty, what more was there to negotiate? In this treaty Great Britain recognized American independence; set the Canadian-American boundary (in part based on imaginary geographic features) as the St. Croix River dividing Maine and Nova Scotia, the St. Lawrence-Atlantic watershed divide, the forty-fifth parallel to the St. Lawrence and then to the Great Lakes and their connecting waterways to the Lake of the Woods and the Mississippi; recognized the American "liberty" to fish in the territorial waters of British North America; stipulated that British forces would evacuate American soil and waters "with all convenient speed"; validated all debts due creditors of either country by citizens of the other; and provided that Congress "earnestly recommend" to the state legislatures a restoration of loyalist rights and property. Vergennes was told about this treaty on the night before it was signed.

At the time the foreign minister said nothing. Two weeks later he registered formal complaint. Franklin in a classic reply admitted that in concluding virtually a separate peace the American commissioners may have shown a lack of propriety, a lack of *bienséance*, but protested that they meant no disrespect for the king of France. The astute American remarked his hope that "the great work" of peace would not now be ruined "by a single indiscretion of ours," adding: "The English, I just now learn, flatter themselves they have already divided us. I hope this little misunderstanding will therefore be kept a secret, and that they will find themselves totally mistaken." Vergennes, catching at once the hint that the Americans in case of continued French objection might turn to alliance with England, essayed no more criticism of the American preliminary treaty.

If Vergennes had chosen to insist upon the right of the French government to advise the American peace commissioners in all matters save independence, it is doubtful what might have been the final outcome of Franklin's private negotiations with the British. Perhaps Congress, under control of the French minister to the United States, would have reprimanded its commissioners in France and refused ratification of the preliminary treaty. Perhaps Franklin might have been able to gain the support of Congress notwithstanding the opposition of Vergennes.

Certainly the American minister's hope as expressed to Vergennes, that the little misunderstanding between the two allies be kept secret, was at once nullified, through no fault of Franklin. The sage of Passy's private secretary, Dr. Edward Bancroft, who had become secretary to the American peace commission, was a British spy and regularly sent reports to London of everything that concerned the American negotiations. Bancroft each week dispatched information to the British which he wrote in invisible ink between the lines of love letters addressed to "Mr. Richardson." The love letters he placed in a sealed bottle let down by a string into a hole in a tree on the south side of the Tuileries gardens. He must have sent the British foreign office a bottleful of information about the meeting between Franklin and Vergennes.

But was Franklin in reality going beyond the bounds of propriety in signing the preliminary treaty with Great Britain? In one of his Poor Richard almanacs there was a homely bit of advice, offered by Poor Richard to his readers: "When you come to a low place, stoop." Did Franklin stoop in 1782?

Actually he did not. Franklin's intelligence apparently had penetrated to the center of Vergennes's thinking on the business of peace, weeks before his meeting with the French foreign minister. Franklin had seen that Vergennes was growing weary of the connection with Spain. The war for Gibraltar had come almost to a standstill, with the repulsion of a combined French-Spanish force before the fortress, and with some notable English naval victories against the Bourbon allies. Spanish hopes of taking Gibraltar were becoming impossible of achievement, and Franklin in his separate peace with the British seems to have done exactly what Vergennes desired: he offered to the foreign minister an excuse to get out of the Spanish attachment. Vergennes could now say to the Spanish government that because the unfaithful Americans had negotiated separately with the British he was no longer able to keep his country in the war, despite his deepest, most sincere, most heartfelt desires for Spanish recapture of Gibraltar. The American impropriety of November 30, 1782, served French as well as American advantage.

At once the powers set about arranging a formal and final peace with Britain, which was signed at Paris in separate treaties by the United States, France, Spain, and the Netherlands, on September 3, 1783. In this final peace Great Britain relinguished to Spain the territory of Florida, which the British had taken from Spain in the Treaty of Paris of twenty years before.

In such wise, out of the combinations and collisions of European powers, the United States secured independence. Thirteen British colonies, which in 1763 were protesting in tones of gravity and conviction their attachment to the mother country, twenty years later had fought a successful revolution against Great Britain, invoked a hostile combination of European powers against the homeland, and obtained through wise and discreet diplomacy the independence of a new nation, the United States of America. American fortunes had changed completely within a single generation. At the time this change wrought little impression upon the powers of Europe, who concerned themselves not with distant revolts in a far-off hemisphere but with their own animosities and ambitions. The American revolt had provided an occasion for France's revenge on Britain, and for a new attempt by Spain to take back Gibraltar, and for an effort of Austria to annex Bavaria. Few individuals in Europe worried about the future of the nation across the Atlantic. That nation was a

republic and everyone knew that republics were by nature weak governments, prone to division and contention, incapable of expansion and
growth. The Americans, so Europeans thought, could have their new
form of government, since by their revolution they had served so ad-
mirably the purposes of Europe.

The American revolution, seen by Europeans as a convenient incident

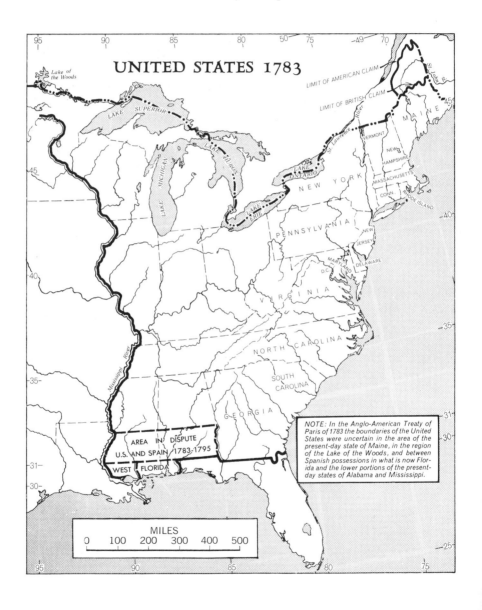

UNITED STATES 1783

NOTE: In the Anglo-American Treaty of
Paris of 1783 the boundaries of the United
States were uncertain in the area of the
present-day state of Maine, in the region
of the Lake of the Woods, and between
Spanish possessions in what is now Florida and the lower portions of the present-
day states of Alabama and Mississippi.

MILES
0   100   200   300   400   500

in the course of their own struggles, seen by Vergennes as a heaven-sent opportunity to humble the hated English, nonetheless was to prove itself of large importance, in two major respects. In the long perspective of history it marked the beginning of a new nation which would become the greatest in the world. It also placed before the peoples of Europe, as apart from their unsympathetic and indifferent governments, the example of a new nation dedicated to republican principles. The spirit of liberty would make startling changes in European life during the nineteenth and twentieth centuries.

A CONTEMPORARY DOCUMENT

[During the negotiation of the preliminary peace with Great Britain, Franklin together with his fellow commissioners proved willing to violate the instructions of Congress and negotiate without consulting the French court. Franklin nonetheless—unlike his fellow commissioners, Jay and especially John Adams—was not hostile to the court, and sought to explain himself in a letter of July 22, 1783, to Secretary Livingston. Source: Albert H. Smyth, ed., *The Writings of Benjamin Franklin* (10 vols., New York, 1905–1907), IX, 60–62.]

. . . Nothing was stipulated to [France's] Prejudice, and none of the Stipulations were to have Force, but by a subsequent Act of their own. I suppose, indeed, that they have not complain'd of it, or you would have sent us a Copy of the Complaint, that we might have answer'd it. I long since satisfi'd Comte de V. about it here. We did what appear'd to all of us best at the Time, and, if we have done wrong, the Congress will do right, after hearing us, to censure us. Their Nomination of Five Persons to the Service seems to mark, that they had some Dependence on our joint Judgment, since one alone could have made a Treaty by Direction of the French Ministry as well as twenty. . . .

I ought not, however, to conceal from you, that one of my Colleagues is of a very different Opinion from me in these Matters. He thinks the French Minister one of the greatest Enemies of our Country, that he would have straitned our Boundaries, to prevent the Growth of our People; contracted our Fishery, to obstruct the Increase of our Seamen; and retained the Royalists among us, to keep us divided; that he privately opposes all our Negotiations with foreign Courts, and afforded us, during the War, the Assistance we receiv'd, only to keep it alive, that we might be so much the more weaken'd by it; that to think of Gratitude to France is the greatest

of Follies, and that to be influenc'd by it would ruin us. He makes no
Secret of his having these Opinions, expresses them publicly, sometimes in presence of the English Ministers, and speaks of hundreds of
Instances which he could produce in Proof of them. None of which
however, have yet appear'd to me, unless the Conversations and Letter above-mentioned are reckoned such.

If I were not convinc'd of the real Inability of this Court to furnish the further Supplys we ask'd, I should suspect these Discourses
of a Person in his Station might have influenced the Refusal; but I
think they have gone no further than to occasion a Suspicion, that
we have a considerable Party of Antigallicans in America, who are
not Tories, and consequently to produce some doubts of the Continuance of our Friendship. As such Doubts may hereafter have a bad
Effect, I think we cannot take too much care to remove them; and
it is, therefore, I write this, to put you on your guard, (believing it
my duty, tho' I know that I hazard by it a mortal Enmity), and to
caution you respecting the Insinuations of this Gentleman against this
Court, and the Instances he supposes of their ill will to us, which I
take to be as imaginary as I know his Fancies to be, that Count de V.
and myself are continually plotting against him, and employing the
News-Writers of Europe to depreciate his Character, &c. But as
Shakespear says, "Trifles light as Air," &c. I am persuaded, however,
that he means well for his Country, is always an honest Man, often a
wise one, but sometimes, and in some things, absolutely out of his
senses. . . .

ADDITIONAL READING

For events national and international pertaining to the New World, the
best place to start is the voyages of Columbus, and here the student can find a
vastly readable account in *Samuel Eliot Morison's *Christopher Columbus:
Mariner* (Boston, 1955). Who other than this imaginative writer, America's
greatest historian, would think of how Columbus's discovery might have been
reported in the leading newspaper of Genoa if that city in 1493 had possessed
a popular press on the present-day American model:

GENOA MAN SEES NAKED NATIVES
FINDS GOLD IN RIVER SANDS
RICH STRIKE FOR KING OF SPAIN
Colombo with Three Ships Reaches Golden Islands Near India
Men Bear No Arms and Women Wear No Clothes
. . . The father of our distinguished fellow citizen is a retired wool
weaver living in the St. John Baptist ward. Contacted at his home, Mr.

Colombo was told the news. He said, "It does not surprise me at all. Chris was always a boy for the girls and the gold. I said he would come to no good, leaving Genoa and going to sea."

Christopher Columbus: Mariner is a condensation of a larger work, *Admiral of the Ocean Sea* (2 vols., Boston, 1942), that won the Pulitzer prize. Also worth reading are *Charles E. Nowell, *The Great Discoveries and the First Colonial Empires* (Ithaca, N.Y., 1954), *J. H. Parry, *Europe and a Wider World: 1415–1715* (London, 1949), and Arthur H. Buffinton, *The Second Hundred Years War: 1689–1815* (New York, 1929).

For the coming of the revolution there are many books, quite possibly more than for any other event in American history. The mercantile system of the mother country was one of the revolution's causes, and it appears in *Charles M. Andrews, *The Colonial Period of American History: England's Commercial and Colonial Policy* (New Haven, 1938). *Andrews's *The Colonial Background of the American Revolution* (New Haven, 1924) is of continuing interest. See also Thomas R. Adams, *American Independence: The Growth of an Idea* (Providence, R.I., 1965). A short survey is *Carl Ubbelohde, *The American Colonies and the British Empire: 1607–1763* (New York, 1968). The leading historian of the years immediately preceding the revolution, Lawrence Henry Gipson, has a volume in the New American Nation series, *The Coming of the Revolution: 1763–1775* (New York, 1954). The twelfth volume of Gipson's thirteen-volume work considers the crisis with an appropriate metaphor: *Britain Sails Into the Storm: 1770–1776* (New York, 1965).

The best single volume on the American revolution from the diplomatic point of view remains *Samuel Flagg Bemis, *The Diplomacy of the American Revolution* (New York, 1935), a thorough, well-written book that has become a classic. Its author is justly considered the dean of American diplomatic historians. See also the recent work by *Richard W. Van Alstyne, *Empire and Independence: The International History of the American Revolution* (New York, 1965), a volume in the America in Crisis series edited by Robert A. Divine. Supplemental are two earlier books, E. S. Corwin, *French Policy and the American Alliance of 1778* (Princeton, 1916) and Claude H. Van Tyne, *The War of Independence: American Phase* (Boston, 1929). Arthur Burr Darling, *Our Rising Empire* (New Haven, 1940) contains chapters on the revolution. Excellent general treatments are John C. Miller, *Triumph of Freedom: 1775–1783* (Boston, 1948); *Edmund S. Morgan, *The Birth of the Republic: 1763–89* (Chicago, 1956), a volume in the Chicago History of American Civilization series edited by Daniel J. Boorstin; and *John Richard Alden, *The American Revolution: 1775–1783* (New York, 1954), a volume in the New American Nation series.

The skulduggery of the revolution appears in Helen Augur, *The Secret War of Independence* (New York, 1955); *Carl Van Doren, *Secret History of the American Revolution* (New York, 1941); Samuel Flagg Bemis, *The Hussey-Cumberland Mission and American Independence* (Princeton, 1931); and the still-intriguing article by J. Franklin Jameson, "St. Eustatius in the

American Revolution," *American Historical Review*, VIII (1902–1903), 683–708. Jameson was one of the pioneers of American historical scholarship.

Three of Bemis's articles on the period are in his *American Foreign Policy and the Blessings of Liberty and Other Essays* (New Haven, 1962). For its special subject see *Durand Echeverria, *Mirage in the West: A History of the French Image in American Society to 1815* (Princeton, 1957).

A masterly account of the arranging of the peace is Richard B. Morris's *The Peacemakers* (New York, 1965). Morris has gone to the primary sources and restudied the entire maneuverings and negotiations leading to the peace of Paris of 1783. His book is a memorable contribution, the sort of volume which will be read long after the journeyman accounts have been forgotten. Not least of the qualities of his volume is its investigation into what happened to the peacemakers of 1782–1783, which allows the reader to see the irony of history when men of importance, even great men, pass into oblivion.

In the sense of affecting the world balance the United States was a world power from independence, and a great power some years before 1898. So argues Thomas A. Bailey, "America's Emergence as a World Power: The Myth and the Verity," *Pacific Historical Review*, XXX (1961), 1–16.

Biographies dealing with the revolution naturally center on Benjamin Franklin, the most famous American of the eighteenth century and the revolution's best diplomat. Carl Van Doren's *Benjamin Franklin* (New York, 1938) remains the leading work, although it doubtless will be replaced by accounts written from the voluminous Franklin papers now being published at Yale under the distinguished editorship of Leonard W. Labaree. Van Doren's book should be read with such books as Gerald Stourzh, *Benjamin Franklin and American Foreign Policy* (Chicago, 1954); *Verner W. Crane, *Benjamin Franklin and a Rising People* (Boston, 1954), a volume in the Library of American Biography series edited by Oscar Handlin; William B. Clark, *Ben Franklin's Privateers* (Baton Rouge, La., 1955). Georges Lemaitre, *Beaumarchais* (New York, 1946) provides a light sketch of that lighthearted character. Frank Monaghan, *John Jay* (New York, 1935) offers Jay in all his colors. For the equally colorful Adams see Page Smith's study based on the recently opened Adams papers, *John Adams* (2 vols., New York, 1962).

☆ *3* ☆

The Commerce of a New Nation

Harmony, liberal intercourse with all Nations, are recommended by policy, humanity and interest. But even our Commercial policy should hold an equal and impartial hand: neither seeking nor granting exclusive favours or preferences; consulting the natural course of things; diffusing and diversifying by gentle means the streams of Commerce, but forcing nothing; establishing with Powers so disposed; in order to give to trade a stable course, to define the rights of our Merchants, and to enable the Government to support them; conventional rules of intercourse, the best that present circumstances and mutual opinion will permit, but temporary, and liable to be from time to time abandoned or varied, as experience and circumstances shall dictate; constantly keeping in view, that 'tis folly in one Nation to look for disinterested favours from another; that it must pay with a portion of its Independence for whatever it may accept under that character; that by such acceptance, it may place itself in the condition of having given equivalents for nominal favours and yet of being reproached with ingratitude for not giving more.
—George Washington, Farewell Address, 1796

In the first dozen years after the signing of the Treaty of Paris of 1783 the United States negotiated commercial treaties with Great Britain and Spain, and these apparently prosaic achievements were major steps toward the fixing of American nationality. It was no easy task to regulate commerce with either of these countries, especially Great Britain. And commerce was of vital importance to the new United States, not merely because of the size of the merchant marine—second only to that of Britain—but because the new government under the Constitution, in force beginning in 1789, depended for its revenues on customs receipts.

1. *John Jay and Diego de Gardoqui*

The few years between the Treaty of Paris of 1783 and establishment of the new federal government have sometimes been described as the critical period in American history, a dubious appellation for the domestic politics of the United States, and likewise inaccurate for American foreign policy at that time. In domestic politics there was a somnolent era from 1783 to 1789. In foreign affairs the United States in the 1780's was so weak as to count for nothing in its occasional representations at the courts of Europe. The sole development in American diplomacy during the period which deserves any retelling was the abortive negotiations between John Jay, secretary for foreign affairs under the Confederation government, and the Spanish minister to the United States, Diego de Gardoqui.

Spain, one should add, was a weak power, far easier to deal with than Great Britain. Almost immediately after the American revolution had ended victoriously, the Spanish began to sense that a giant was arising in the New World. The Spanish ambassador to France during the revolution, Aranda, reportedly had written:

This federal republic is born a pigmy. A day will come when it will be a giant, even a colossus, formidable in these countries. Liberty of conscience, the facility for establishing a new population on immense lands, as well as the advantages of the new government, will draw thither farmers and artisans from all the nations. In a few years we shall watch with grief the tyrannical existence of this same colossus.

As secretary for foreign affairs John Jay was a transitional figure, in a time when American foreign relations passed from supervision by a committee of Congress to control by the department of state under a secretary of state in 1789. The committee of secret correspondence appointed in 1775 had supervised American diplomacy until, after a change of name, it went out of existence in 1781, with the appointment that year of the first secretary for foreign affairs, Robert R. Livingston. Livingston served until the end of the revolution, resigning in June 1783. The office went unfilled until Congress in May 1784 learned that Jay was returning from Paris after conclusion of the treaty of peace, and elected Jay as Livingston's successor on the same day this intelligence reached Philadelphia. The new secretary did not know of his appointment until his arrival back in the United States.

Jay was the best possible appointment for secretary in the year 1784. For one thing, his experience made him an easy choice. The only other Americans of large political reputation who possessed diplomatic experience, Franklin and John Adams, were still in Europe. Franklin was about to retire from diplomacy. He was an old man, and died a few years later, in 1790. Adams was to become minister to the Court of St. James's. Moreover, in addition to being experienced, the new secretary was an excellent administrator, as soon became evident in the manner in which he kept his business in order. Jay's opinions on European politics were not neutral. He had a fondness for the people of Great Britain. But he prudently kept this liking to himself. He also was careful not to show his distrust of the French, and of the Spanish. His defects of character were perhaps two. He was intensely proud of his abilities, as he knew that he was a competent and even brilliant manager and negotiator. (There was a touch in him of what a later generation would describe as egotism.) His other fault was that he was too often swayed by the opinions of his wife, whom he adored. Some years before becoming secretary for foreign affairs he had married Sarah Livingston, the daughter of the patriot governor of New Jersey. He was devoted to her, so much so that the Spaniard, Gardoqui, his adversary in negotiation in 1785–1786, sought to take advantage of Mrs. Jay's humors in order to influence him.

Don Diego was the son of the owner of the firm Gardoqui and Sons, which had managed the munitions shipment from Spain for the American cause during the revolution. Young Gardoqui spoke excellent English and had known Jay when the latter was the importuning, unrecognized American envoy to the court of Spain in 1779–1782. The king of Spain in sending Gardoqui had sought to obtain an advantage from the Spanish diplomat's former friendship. Gardoqui measured his American opponent with a care that deserves quoting in detail. He wrote back to his superior, the foreign minister Count Floridablanca, that

The American, Jay, who is generally considered to possess talent and capacity enough to cover in great part a weakness natural to him, appears (by a consistent behaviour) to be a very self-centered man, which passion his wife augments, because, in addition to considering herself meritoriously and being rather vain, she likes to be catered to and even more to receive presents. This woman, whom he loves blindly, dominates him and nothing is done without her consent, so that her opinion prevails, though her husband at first may disagree; from which I infer that a little management in dealing with her and a few timely gifts will secure the friendship of both, because I have reason to believe that they proceed resolved to make a fortune. He is not the only one in the country who has the same weakness, for there are many poor persons among the governing body, and I believe a skilful hand which knows how to take advantage of favourable opportunities, and how to give dinners and above all how to entertain with good wine, may profit without appearing to pursue them.

The minister entertained lavishly at a house in New York, and the Jays were often his guests. He gave special attention to Mrs. Jay and took her to dances and public festivities. He suggested to Floridablanca that the secretary for foreign affairs of the United States be presented with a handsome Spanish stallion. In due time Jay received a horse from Gardoqui, albeit not before the secretary asked for and obtained the consent of Congress for his acceptance of the gift. One might perhaps conclude that the amenities of the Spanish envoy did not hurt relations between Spain and the United States, and it is probably true that Jay was flattered by the attentions of an envoy of a country that during the American revolution had treated him poorly. Whether the secretary allowed Spanish entertainment to sway his judgment on matters of state appears doubtful.

The Jay-Gardoqui conversations of 1785–1786 were pre-eminently over commercial questions; in particular, the right of the Americans to navigate the Mississippi for the length of the river, despite the fact that in the vicinity of New Orleans the Spanish possessed both banks of the river. It was Jay's bad luck to get into a negotiation over the Mississippi at a time when it was almost impossible for an American negotiator to do anything advantageous about it.

The right of navigating the Mississippi was a question that went back in American history (not, of course, United States history) to the year 1763, when the British had won a war against the French and Spanish. The Floridas, East and West—which is to say present-day Florida, together with lower parts of the states of Alabama, Mississippi, and Louisiana (see map, p. 173)—passed from Spain to Britain. The king of France therefore ostentatiously gave the territory of Louisiana to the king of Spain, presumably to replace the land lost to the British, actually to get rid of what the French considered a white elephant. The king of Spain protested, for he was about to become land poor: "I say no, no, no, my cousin is losing altogether too much, I do not want him to lose anything in addition for my sake, and would to Heaven that I could do yet more for him." The French went ahead with their gift, with the result that the navigation of the Mississippi was shared after 1763 between the Spanish and British, the two nations holding territory bordering the river.

The Mississippi question had taken a new turn during and after the revolution, when the Congress and diplomatic envoys of the United States blandly assumed that there was an American right to navigate the Mississippi. The American claim to the navigation was hardly a good one. The trouble was that during the revolution, after Spanish entry into the war in 1779, the Spanish conquered the Floridas from the British. The entry of Spain into the war wiped out the arrangements of the Spanish-British treaty of 1763 which had stipulated joint rights to navigation of the Mississippi. For some reason, perhaps the age-old diplomatic procedure of giving away what one does not possess, the British in making peace with the United States in 1783 set out the right of the Americans to navigate the Mississippi. The British were much more careful in their treaty of 1783 with Spain, and said nothing about the river, which subject no longer properly could concern them. Anyway, the Americans had this British assurance, and in subsequent years sought to make the most of it. There was also an American argument out of the international law writers of the time who often contended that a nation possessing territory along the upper reaches of a river should have access through the river to its mouth.

These, then, were the slight diplomatic counters which John Jay sought to use with Gardoqui. It soon appeared that they were to no avail. In 1784, the year the king of Spain announced Gardoqui's appointment, thereby recognizing the American government, the Spanish governor at New Orleans upon direction from Madrid closed the river to American commerce. Gardoqui was not inclined to open it.

The Spanish government also claimed a boundary between American territory and West Florida a hundred miles north of the line on which Jay desired to fix it—Jay wished the thirty-first parallel. The Spanish had garrisoned Natchez. Moreover, they were intriguing with the Indians in the trans-Appalachian area. For Spain such intrigues were easy, as the authorities in New Orleans had only to say to the Indians the truth, namely, that Spain wished to have the tribes maintain themselves as a buffer against American western expansion; the Spanish did not covet Indian lands, and could make this fact clear to the natives. The Indians realized that the Americans, in dealing with representatives of the tribes, were seeking simply to end warfare in the western settlements, and that the next step after peace was likely to be removal, to the west of the Mississippi. The Americans wished to establish the boundary of their territory with the Spanish in West Florida so that they could deal more easily with the Indians.

The fundamental fact of the Jay-Gardoqui negotiations was not the series of conversations in New York but the fact that 50,000 American settlers had crossed the mountains in the first year after the Treaty of Paris, and by the autumn of 1785 they had their first small crops of tobacco and wheat which they wished to ship down-river, from the Ohio and Tennessee Rivers into the Father of Waters, and after transshipment at New Orleans these goods would go via ocean passage to the American east coast ports. It was far easier to ship goods by water from Pittsburgh to Philadelphia, all the way around, than to send the goods overland. The axle-breaking roads over the mountains were almost impassable for anyone other than individuals afoot or on horseback.

Perhaps by blandishment, far more likely by persuasion, and through Jay's failure to realize the force of American trans-Appalachian settlement in 1784, Gardoqui in 1785–1786 talked the secretary for foreign affairs into a proposed "forbearance" of use of the Mississippi, in exchange for a commercial treaty between the United States and Spain. The only difficulty, and it proved insurmountable, was that Jay was forced to go to Congress and ask amendment of his instructions for the negotiation. Congress had given Jay two points on which he could not yield: the boundary of thirty-one degrees, and use of the Mississippi. Jay told Congress frankly in 1786 that he thought a general treaty of commerce with Spain, which would allow American vessels and merchants a modest business with metropolitan Spain and with the empire, was preferable to sticking for navigation of the Mississippi when the United States had virtually no right—indeed none, though he did not say that—to demand access through a river controlled below the thirty-first parallel on both banks by Spain. Congress duly amended Jay's instructions. But the vote was close, with the southern states opposing the northern and middle states by vote of five against and seven in favor, Delaware "abstaining."

It seemed as if the wily Gardoqui might triumph. Instead Jay's good sense prevailed. He realized that according to the Articles of Confederation he would need the votes of nine states in Congress to consent to any treaty with a foreign nation. He would have had to work hard to secure such a vote, and the effort might well not be worth the cost. For there was an uproar of protest against the Jay Treaty of 1786. Charles Cotesworth Pinckney of South Carolina argued, regarding forbearance of the Mississippi, that if Congress was refusing to give in to the British occupation of the frontier posts north of the Ohio it should not give in to the Spanish over the right to navigate the Mississippi to the sea. James Monroe, at this time a young man, wrote to his philosopher friend Thomas Jefferson then in Paris that it was all a real estate deal: "these Eastern people," he said, wished to keep the population in the East so as to appreciate the vacant lands of New York and Massachusetts. Jay's closehanded negotiation also helped Monroe "have a conviction in my own mind that Jay has manag'd this negociation dishonestly." Pinckney of South Carolina thought the Confederation would break up if the Mississippi were closed as Jay suggested. Rufus King of New York, a supporter of more trade for his trade-minded state, thought the Confederation

would break up if the Mississippi were not closed and there were no commercial treaty with Spain. Jay sagaciously halted his negotiation and
played for time, as he had done with the Spanish government in his ill-
fated mission during the revolution. He sensed that a new government of
the United States, the outlines of which would become apparent during
the Philadelphia Convention of 1787, might create a stronger union and
enable some successor to negotiate more easily.

Out of the Jay-Gardoqui conversations of the mid-1780's came a proviso in the new Constitution that treaties must pass the Senate with a
margin of two-thirds. This provision would protect minorities such as the
South in regard, perhaps, to some new Jay Treaty.

2. The coolness of Britain

In retrospect, it would have been better if the government of Great
Britain had forgotten the rancors of the War of Independence, the seeming faithlessness of the Americans who not merely revolted against the
mother country but sought the support of the king of France against the
king of England. An opportunity of large proportions opened to the British government with the end of the American revolution, and at least some
Britons understood the possibilities of this short moment in history as
soon as the Americans had signed the preliminary peace of November
1782. In the person of the Britisher David Hartley, who negotiated for
several months with Franklin and the other peace commissioners in Paris
after signature of the preliminary peace, the new government of Charles
James Fox and Lord North (the wartime ministry of North had given
way in 1782 to that of the Earl of Rockingham, and Rockingham's death
the same year produced the Shelburne ministry and then the Fox-North
coalition) sought to remove the government of the United States from
French influence, even before signature of the final treaties of Paris by the
several belligerents in September 1783. But as Hartley talked day after day
with Franklin and the other Americans, the feelings of friendship in London lessened. Hartley, to his intense regret, was recalled. It was thereafter up to the Americans to approach the British on questions at issue
between the two governments. The Americans would have to be the
suitors, the suppliants.

The reason for the British change of mind was in large part of understanding that no special treaty of commerce would be necessary with the
Americans, once all the world was again at peace. The appearance in 1783
of a pamphlet by Lord Sheffield helped persuade the British of this fact.
The cheapness of British merchandise, Sheffield argued, would over-

whelm the American markets. The American government under the Confederation would be able to do nothing. Sheffield likened the power of the Confederation almost to a nullity.

It will not be an easy matter to bring the American states to act as a nation. They are not to be feared as such by us. It must be a long time before they can engage, or will concur in any material expense. . . . We might as well dread the effects of combinations among the German as among the American states, and deprecate the resolves of the Diet, as those of Congress.

Moreover, he contended, why allow American vessels (which could carry cargo more cheaply than British) to carry this trade across the Atlantic? Best to reserve the carrying of British merchandise for British ships. And time proved Sheffield correct. The first American census, taken in 1790, showed that nine-tenths of American imports came from Great Britain, mostly from England. All this without any reciprocity by the British, any Anglo-American treaty of commerce.

In considering why the British ministries beginning in 1782, composed of individuals who during the early part of the American revolution had been outspoken in support of the revolting colonists, failed to pursue a policy of *rapprochement*, and "sat still," one must probably examine a factor other than the arguments set out in Sheffield's pamphlet. Probably the onetime supporters of the rights of Americans discovered that it was easier to support the Americans in theory than in fact. In opposition to the king's friends led by North it was easy to stand for the rights of Englishmen in the New World. In office, Shelburne and the others proved more English than American.

On April 8, 1784, before proclamation of the final treaty of peace—indeed one day before George III proclaimed the treaty—the ministry of William Pitt the younger (which just had succeeded the Fox-North coalition), through the agency of the secretary of state for home affairs, Lord Sydney, sent instructions to the governor general of Canada not to withdraw the British garrisons then in the frontier posts north of the Ohio. The British would use those garrisons' presence on undeniably American soil to extract concessions from the United States. Sydney had at hand a convenient reason for delay, because the treaty of peace said that withdrawal of British troops from all places then under occupation should occur with "all convenient speed." The British government could ask for payment of the prerevolutionary debts owed by Americans to British subjects, and for indemnification of the loyalists whose property had been sequestered during the late war.

As far as amenities, rather than realities, of diplomacy were concerned, one might have thought that everything had been forgiven, for when John Adams, that arch-republican of the New World, came to England and applied for recognition at the Court of St. James's as the first American minister accredited to that court, he met with a reception that clearly was extraordinary. Adams recorded this historic event, his presentation to George III, in a long letter to Secretary Jay. Entering the king's chamber, he made the three reverences, one at the door, another about halfway, and a third before the presence, and then recited a formal speech, in the course of which he said that

I shall esteem myself the happiest of men, if I can be instrumental in recommending my country more and more to your Majesty's royal benevolence, and of restoring an entire esteem, confidence, and affection, or, in better words, the old good nature and the old good humor between people, who, though separated by an ocean, and under different governments, have the same language, a similar religion, and kindred blood.

Warmed to his discourse, the Massachusetts Adams concluded with the gracious formality of the eighteenth century: "I beg your Majesty's permission to add, that, although I have some time before been intrusted by my country, it was never in my whole life in a manner so agreeable to myself." Whereupon the king, trembling with emotion, replied:

The circumstances of this audience are so extraordinary, the language you have now held is so extremely proper, and the feelings you have discovered so justly adapted to the occasion, that I must say that I not only receive with pleasure the assurance of the friendly dispositions of the United States, but that I am very glad the choice has fallen upon you to be their minister.

The king thereupon invoked "the circumstances of language, religion, and blood" which, he said, should have "their natural and full effect."

During the audience the king had attempted what Adams considered a levity, saying laughingly that "there is an opinion among some people that you are not the most attached of all your countrymen to the manners of France." Adams put on as much gayety as he, an Adams, was capable of, and said: "That opinion, sir, is not mistaken; I must avow to your Majesty, I have no attachment but to my own country." The king replied, as quick as lightning: "An honest man will never have any other."

Then Adams retreated backward, making his last reverence at the door of the chamber, and left with the master of ceremonies, who shouted through the apartments down to the carriage, several stages of servants, gentlemen-porters, under-porters, roaring out like thunder as Adams went along, "Mr. Adams's servants, Mr. Adams's carriage," . . . . It was a great occasion.

But one occasion was not diplomacy. After months of frustration in dealing with the king's indifferent ministers, in the course of which the British made not the slightest move to appoint a minister to reside in the United States as a mark of respect to Adams's presence in London, the new American envoy at last decided that he could do nothing with the British government, and unceremoniously took his leave and went home to the New World in 1788.

When President Washington took over management of the country's affairs the next year, one of the first points of diplomacy was to try again with the British, and Washington sent Gouverneur Morris to see if the London government might prove more friendly than during the era of Adams. Morris had gone to France in 1788 to trade in tobacco, and was able easily to cross over to London and treat with the British as a special presidential agent. Morris actually was the first such presidential agent in American history, the first in a long line which was to include Colonel House under President Wilson and Harry Hopkins under President Franklin D. Roosevelt. Morris was a man of large affairs, a good talker, and a fast liver (his widow edited his diary drastically, and even after the editing it remains a remarkably racy document). He was also an editor, having brushed up the English of the Constitution of 1787. It must have seemed that such a man of parts could make his way with the British.

Gouverneur Morris did the best he could, which for a short time gave promise of results. His best, however, was not so much the result of his talents as the result of the Nootka Sound controversy of 1790 between Spain and Britain, which gave him an unexpected opportunity to press the British government. This controversy traced back to the original partition of the territories of the New World between the Spanish and Portuguese, first by Pope Alexander VI in 1493 and then the following year by the Treaty of Tordesillas which changed the meridian of division to a point 370 leagues west of the Cape Verde Islands and awarded Brazil to Portugal. There had been many changes after that, notably when the Spanish recognized English territorial possessions in 1670 and French in 1701. As mentioned, the French had given Louisiana to Spain in 1763, and the British lost the Floridas during the American revolution. But as late as the year 1790, almost three centuries after discovery of the New World, the Spanish still maintained pretensions under the right of discovery and the papal and treaty divisions of 1493–1494. Captain James Cook had inaugurated a trade between the fur regions of the Columbia River and China in his last voyage into the Pacific in 1774. A vessel bearing British traders had sailed into Nootka Sound on Vancouver Island in 1789, and the traders built a small ship and were about to set up a trading post. The

Spanish, recalling how the British had worked their way into a logging trade in Honduras by just such methods, sent a ship to the new settlement, captured the two British vessels, and took their crews in irons to Mexico.

It was a poor time for the Spanish to do such a thing—and, as it turned out, a fine time for a crisis so far as concerned the diplomacy of Gouverneur Morris. The British government in 1790 was still in charge of the "heaven-born" Pitt who had resented the actions of the Spanish during the American revolution so much that he had longed for an opportunity to get even. As Pitt's luck would have it, in 1790 Spain's ally France was in the toils of a revolution and unable to react to anything the British might do to the Spanish. Pitt sent the Spanish government an ultimatum. And Morris, in England, used the crisis to talk sharply to the prime minister, doubtless to Pitt's extreme annoyance. "We do not think it worth while to go to war with you for the [northern frontier] posts," Morris said he told Pitt, "but we know our rights and will avail ourselves of them when time and circumstances permit."

When the new secretary of state, Jefferson, heard of the Nootka crisis, he thought the time had arrived to solve at least the Spanish question, even perhaps to press the British to relinquish the frontier posts. In August 1790 he sent a special messenger with dispatches for Morris in London. The messenger had orders to continue to Lisbon and Madrid with papers for the American chargé in the Spanish capital, William Carmichael.

The possibility of hostilities between Britain and Spain alarmed President Washington and most of his advisers. Far from planning to seize the western posts, Washington worried that the British might conquer Spanish Louisiana by crossing neutral American soil in the west, from Canada. The British had no such intention, but Washington did not know that. He submitted to the cabinet the question of what the United States should do in case the British demanded transit. Should he say, "The United States is a nation, not a thoroughfare," in the manner in which, many years later, the Belgian King Albert allegedly answered a German ultimatum? Secretary Jefferson thought there should be no answer; if the British made the passage, wait to see what might come of it, he advised, keeping the issue alive until future events—perhaps that "chapter of accidents" which Jefferson so often looked forward to during his years in politics—and then decide whether to accept apologies or war. The vice president in the Washington administration, John Adams, advised refusal of passage, as well he might, remembering his recent treatment by the British government. Secretary of the Treasury Hamilton advised acquiescence to Britain and thought it advisable to go to war against Spain, seizing New Orleans.

It was an interesting discussion, but unfortunately all talk, for Spain accepted the British ultimatum before the Americans could do anything in the circumstances. As soon as the Nootka affair blew over, the British ministry ceased to converse with Gouverneur Morris.

Meanwhile the British had been playing with another American, Levi Allen, then in London seeking recognition for the "independent sovereign state" of Vermont, in the shape of a treaty of commerce. Imagine Vermont as a sovereign nation in the twentieth century, importing all its needs from the neighboring states loyal to the federal union, exporting only that commercial necessity, maple sugar.

3. Jay's Treaty

Getting along with the British was not easy. The great majority of American imports were coming from England despite the absence of a commercial treaty, and over half of these imports arrived in British ships. Parliament coolly had shut the West Indies and Canadian ports to American ships in 1784. Even the new Constitution seemed at first to offer little leverage with the British; despite the new form of government, the United States seemed almost doomed to impotence in negotiating with the former mother country. If the Nootka crisis had lasted longer, something might have been done, but it was over before it had gotten under way.

At the time of the crisis Secretary Jefferson actually was intrigued against by his opposite in the Washington cabinet, Hamilton—a state of affairs which showed the continuing difficulty of standing up to the British. Jefferson wished to discriminate against British commerce, in hope of obtaining a commercial treaty and entrance into the trade of the British West Indies and Canada. Hamilton opposed discrimination, claiming that the new government's revenues, and hence its very existence, rested on customs receipts, and that the year 1790 was no time to have a trade war when all the revolutionary debts, foreign and domestic, were just being refunded and, of course, had not yet been paid. Hamilton talked in New York with a certain Major Beckwith, who was an agent of the governor general of Canada, Lord Dorchester. Jefferson properly had stayed away from Beckwith, but Hamilton became the major's intimate. The secretary of the treasury—"Number 7" in Beckwith's cipher dispatches to Dorchester—gratuitously told the Britisher that when he, Beckwith, had anything important to convey to the American government, he should apply at the treasury department, because of the possible predilections of the secretary of state "elsewhere" (that is, for Britain's enemy France).

Fearing some sort of trade discrimination, the British at this time decided to send over their first minister. George Hammond, a young man of twenty-seven, arrived in November 1791. He soon became an intimate of Hamilton. Jefferson meanwhile found that Hammond had no powers to negotiate a treaty of commerce or indeed any other kind of treaty; all the minister could do was discuss. Hammond's instructions were to couple evacuation of the frontier posts with payment of the prewar debts, and to mediate between the hostile western Indians and the United States government, on the basis of setting up a "neutral, Indian, barrier state" in the territory north of the Ohio and east of the Mississippi, including if possible a strip along the northern border of the state of New York as far as the forts at the outlet of Lake Champlain. This plan was too much even for Hamilton.

But Hamilton found it impossible to keep his hand out of foreign affairs. The British minister, meditating on the details of his instructions, composed a long argument for the secretary of state, setting out what his government proposed to do for the new government in the New World. Never at a loss for words, Jefferson took up his pen and wrote in reply a treatise of about 17,000 words exclusive of footnotes and a formidable appendix. Hammond had told the British foreign secretary, Lord Grenville, that his memorial to Jefferson was a body of proof "so complete and substantial as to preclude the probability of cavil and contradiction." Then he received Jefferson's weighty dissertation. Hammond meanwhile had been pursuing the beautiful daughter of a Philadelphia merchant, and the blow from the secretary of state hurt all the more because the minister's mind was not altogether on diplomatic subjects. Hammond consulted Hamilton in his distress, and Hamilton said that Jefferson's note was far from a faithful representation of the sentiments of the administration and that President Washington had not even read it. This point was not true, but the damage was done.

At last, though, not too long after Hammond's arrival in the United States, the increasing difficulties of the European situation—what with France's political convulsions becoming ever more dangerous to the Continent's peace—gave the American government an opportunity for negotiation of a commercial treaty with Great Britain, the instrument which was to become known as Jay's Treaty. The French revolution had begun as a movement of the French people toward greater personal liberty, but the anatomy of revolution, as the historian Crane Brinton has written, always seems to require that revolts move toward increasing authoritarianism and even despotism, certainly toward excesses, until the time of eventual reaction. This crisis, ever since the point of reaction was reached in the French revolution, has received the name of the month in which it occurred in France, Thermidor (according to the revolutionary French calendar). There is also a tendency of revolutions to turn outward, from internal confusions to foreign war. Such was the case in France in 1792–1793. With the trial and execution of Louis XVI, all the great nations of Europe combined against revolutionary France, and the French themselves readily moved their troops against Europe in hope of revolutionizing the governments of neighboring territories. At first the British government watched the approach of the wars of the French revolution with nonchalance, not realizing what was coming. As Lord Bryce has written, "Men stood on the edge of stupendous changes, and had not a glimpse of even the outlines of those changes, not discerning the causes that were already in embryo beneath their feet, like seeds hidden under the snow of winter, which will shoot up under the April sunlight." War broke out in 1793. Soon all Europe was in arms. It was a good time, at last, for negotiation of a treaty with the British.

The British government simultaneously gave the Americans a new reason for a treaty of commerce, because executive orders of the British cabinet, known as orders in council, now interdicted much American commerce both in the New World and in Europe. Three orders in council in 1793–1794 restricted American vessels seeking trade with the warring nations. The order of November 6, 1793, announced that British warships should prize all vessels carrying supplies to or produce from any French colony. The British reasoned that France had opened its West Indian possessions to American carriers as an act of war upon Britain, so they invoked the so-called Rule of 1756, a British practice, attributed to that bygone year, which had stipulated that trade not open in time of peace should not be open in time of war. The British were not altogether accurate in their appraisal of what the French government was attempting. The French had opened their colonial ports to American shipping prior to 1793 and, with the advent to power of the Jacobins, were trying to exclude American shipping, to the advantage of French shipping. But it did not matter—as the British operated on the theory that any trade not available to British ships should not be available to vessels of the United States. The orders in council proceeded against the Americans on the assumption that it was good policy to hurt one's commercial rivals even if the rivals were not at war. As a result of the order in council of November 1793, dozens of American vessels were soon idle in the British West Indies, awaiting decision of local courts of admiralty. By March 1, 1794, about 250 United States merchant ships, most of them on direct passage from neutral to neutral ports, had been detained.

An order in council dated January 8, 1794, allowed not for seizure and condemnation of American ships trading with the French West Indies, but for detaining of vessels, pre-emption of cargoes of foodstuffs, and indemnification for freight. French property on board such ships was of course subject to capture.

It was a special point of American concern that the British were preempting cargoes of foodstuffs, one of the principal American exports. The Americans liked to believe that food should pass freely from nation to nation, whether at war or peace. Lord Grenville asserted, however, that the conflict now opening between Britain and France was different from all other wars. Here, perhaps, even if the point was at the expense of Americans, Grenville was making a sage observation. He claimed that the peculiar conditions pertaining to this new French war, the unusual mode of war employed by the enemy in "having armed almost the whole labouring class of the French Nation for the purpose of commencing and supporting hostilities against all the Governments of Europe," justified the British in seizing foodstuffs destined for such a nation in arms.

At this juncture came a new alarm. The governor general of Canada, Dorchester, made a speech to the Indians announcing on February 10, 1794, that the United States and Britain soon would be at war. He was reprimanded in July 1794, but the reprimand did not lessen the effect of his speech.

The reaction of the American government to this full confrontation with British power in 1793–1794 was the mission of John Jay, now chief justice of the supreme court, to England in 1794. And what a battery of problems Jay sought to resolve: the frontier forts, still occupied; the incessant British intrigue with the Indians in the northwest, the area north of the Ohio River, of which the Dorchester speech was only an outward indication; the continuing denial to Americans, since the end of the War of Independence, of the trade with the British West Indies and Canada; British conniving with the Vermont separatists; and, to be sure, the orders in council of 1793–1794 which were hindering American commerce, not least the order pre-empting foodstuffs carried on American vessels. The Americans also had a claim which, if valid enough in theory, was difficult in practice: they wished the return of slaves taken by British troops when the British evacuated New York and other ports at the end of the revolution. Because it was difficult to urge a return of slaves when the British were likely to remind the Americans of the ringing phrases in the Declaration of Independence, the Americans preferred to ask for compensation.

The Americans wanted a great deal from the government in London. The British were not asking for much, only payment of the prerevolutionary debts owed their merchants, and payment for property confiscated from the loyalists.

Jay arrived in London at a time when the British did not feel hard pressed enough to make concessions. The government knew that revenues from British goods entering American ports were sustaining the new federal union and necessary for its very survival. In addition Jay was hindered by the indiscretion of Hamilton to the British minister, Hammond. In the midst of Jay's dealings with the British, Hamilton gratuitously told Hammond that the United States would not join any league of armed neutrals in Europe, and thus gave away a possible threat—and Jay had few of them—which the chief justice might have used in London. But Hamilton's indiscretion was perhaps not as damaging as it at first seemed, for the British had a copy of the secret cipher by which Jay corresponded with the department of state and knew in advance what the Americans were prepared to do.

Jay's Treaty, signed on November 19, 1794, was negotiated in difficult circumstances, and for that reason alone was notable. The British pledged themselves to evacuate the frontier posts in territory around the Great Lakes. Britain promised to compensate the United States for spoliations on American shipping made since the outbreak of the European war. A mixed commission—half Britishers, half Americans—was to fix the amount of these damages while two other commissions were to close the gaps in the boundaries stipulated in the Treaty of Paris whereby the line between Maine and Canada and to the west of Lake Superior had remained uncertain. A fourth mixed commission was to determine a fair compensation for the private debts contracted and never paid by citizens of the United States prior to the Treaty of Paris. Jay's Treaty, incidentally, was something of an innovation in diplomacy in that it established so many mixed commissions to settle outstanding disputes. The United States in this way became a leader in what was to be a favorite nineteenth-century procedure of settlement between nations—arbitration.

In his treaty with Great Britain, John Jay failed to obtain recognition of American neutral rights, and this failure deserves a brief explanation. From the outset of the war in Europe in 1793 neutral rights, the right of a neutral to trade under specified rules with belligerents during wartime, were a major American concern because of the size of the merchant marine. The Americans were much interested in obtaining recognition of commercial rights from belligerents in any European war, and the more privileges accorded to American commerce the better. The problem was to obtain recognition of neutral rights from Britain, for the queen of the seas would be able to suppress any rights with which she was not in accord. Conversely, if the British approved wide commercial privileges for American traders, then the other nations of the world probably would agree to British trade definitions, and America's arrangements with Britain would by that fact become international law. The history of neutral rights is a complicated matter, but here it is enough to say that early in its history, actually in 1776 the United States established three principles of neutral rights for commercial treaties with foreign nations, and to these three principles added a fourth in 1784. The plan approved by Congress in 1776, the Plan of 1776 as it was called, stipulated first that free (that is, neutral) ships made free goods—that is, that the cargo of a neutral ship, with the exception of contraband, should not be subject to capture. Second was the principle that contraband should be narrowly defined, excluding foodstuffs and naval stores. Third was the idea that neutral ships had the right to trade between belligerent ports, that is, to take over a belligerent's carrying trade. To these principles the congressional Plan of 1784 added the notion that a blockade to be effective must involve "imminent danger" to vessels seeking to enter a blockaded port. After the United States concluded treaties in the 1780's in which Sweden and Prussia recognized the American interpretation of neutral rights, Jay during the negotiations with Great Britain sought to obtain a similar engagement, but met with prompt and unequivocal refusal. The American envoy was sorry not to have succeeded in this regard, but wrote home realistically that he could not expect the British to sign any agreement that would limit the effectiveness of their war with France. That Britain "at this period, and involved in war," he wrote, "should not admit principles, which would impeach the propriety of her conduct in seizing provisions bound to France, and enemy's property in neutral ships, does not appear to me extraordinary." He had managed to gain one concession: "The articles as they now stand secure compensation for seizures, and leave us at liberty to decide whether they were made in such cases as to be warranted by the *existing* law of nations." This concession was not enough for many of his countrymen, who observing Jay's failure to obtain recognition of American neutral rights were willing to believe that the envoy purposely had given away those rights to Great Britain.

If this accusation were not sufficient to discredit his negotiations, it was Jay's further ill luck that his treaty fell afoul of domestic politics in the United States. By the time that the Senate in 1795 undertook consideration of the treaty, American domestic politics were moving in a new course: political parties were appearing; lines were forming between the friends of France and those of Great Britain; the Hamiltonian Federalists, as they were coming to be called, stood forth in opposition to the Jeffersonian Republicans, to the complete disgust of President Washington who, like most of the founding fathers, had not anticipated appearance in the United States of political parties. Jay's Treaty turned out to be one of the issues on which parties took their separate stands. There was a great out-

John Jay hanged in effigy.

cry over the treaty. Jay, a Federalist, was hanged in effigy by some of the more enterprising Republicans, and other indignities were directed at the man who had dared to sign a treaty with Great Britain, the nation that was the enemy of France. Some nameless American reportedly wrote the following sentiments on a fence: "Damn John Jay! Damn every one that won't damn John Jay! Damn every one that won't put lights in his windows and sit up all night damning John Jay!" Whereupon Jay's Treaty passed the Senate, then dominated by Federalists, by a comfortable margin.

4. *Pinckney's Treaty*

In the same year that saw the passage of Jay's Treaty, 1795, the American special commissioner in Madrid, Thomas Pinckney, negotiated a commercial treaty with Spain, an agreement more favorable to the United States.

The Spanish had assumed in the mid-1780's that the government of the Confederation was so weak that it could not even take steps to begin repayment of debts foreign and domestic and thus might be willing to pay a high price to sign a treaty of commerce. But the Americans had refused to give up what they deemed the right of navigation of the Mississippi. During the Nootka Sound crisis Secretary Jefferson had believed that the moment to press the Spanish was at hand. But the crisis passed too quickly and Jefferson departed from office at the end of 1793. His successor Edmund Randolph soon perceived what proved to be a golden opportunity.

The reasons which persuaded the Spanish to sign what has become known as Pinckney's Treaty are not altogether clear to the present day. Two American scholars, Samuel Flagg Bemis and Arthur P. Whitaker, have gotten into what seems an unsolvable dispute over the matter. In a Pulitzer Prize-winning book published more than forty years ago, Bemis claimed that Pinckney's Treaty with Spain was a classic example of (to use the subtitle of Bemis's *Pinckney's Treaty*) America's advantage from Europe's distress, that the key to the diplomacy of the American treaty of 1795 was the decision of the Spanish government to change allies in the war which had broken out on February 1, 1793, between revolutionary France on the one side and the monarchical powers of Europe on the other. Pressed by the victories of France, the Spanish had decided to join their traditional ally France against their traditional enemy Great Britain. The Spanish government nonetheless feared the vengeance of the British. According to Bemis the Spanish did not know the terms of Jay's Treaty and thought that the Anglo-American commercial treaty might be a disguised alliance, perhaps with secret articles. Thus, the Spanish hoped to separate the Americans from the British by concluding a favorable commercial treaty. But, in Whitaker's view, it was frontier pressure upon Spain's New World possessions, the hopeless feeling of the Spanish government that the Americans were going to take the Floridas and probably Louisiana, that persuaded the Spanish to come to terms with Thomas Pinckney. Whitaker claims that the Spanish probably knew the terms of Jay's Treaty, and he has resorted to ship schedules and other technical scholarly proofs, including a Spanish-intercepted message between Pinckney and another American which appeared to "spill the beans" that Jay's Treaty was only a commercial treaty.

Perhaps the precise points of Spanish reasoning in regard to a treaty with the Americans may never be known. But surely it is difficult to measure "frontier influence," however real, whereas with certitude one can trace a series of grand events in European history which, considering the documented Spanish and American reactions, offer an explanation for Spain's concessions in Pinckney's Treaty.

The Spanish were about to change sides. When the French revolution turned outward in 1793 the Spanish found themselves in an awkward position. The monarchies of Europe had allied against the French, and this meant that the Spanish were allied to Great Britain, their enemy throughout the eighteenth century, not to mention earlier centuries. From the outset it was an uneasy relationship, and when the fortunes of war went against the Spanish, when the French began to give evidence that they were about to invade and conquer Spain from its own monarchical government, it was almost a natural thing that Spain would change sides. The Spanish monarchy was approaching so dissolute a condition anyway that such a tactic was easy. Floridablanca, who had come into power in 1777 and remained as foreign minister for fifteen years, had given way, just at the outbreak of the European war, to Don Manuel de Godoy, a flashy court adventurer who had impressed the queen of Spain with his many engaging qualities. For Godoy a change of loyalties was no problem at all.

The political habits of generations, and the willingness of a court favorite, combined to force the change at the first opportunity. The Spanish became almost indecently anxious to get out of the war against the murderers of Louis XVI. The British government did not help matters, either. When the British assisted the monarchists at Toulon in 1793 but then had to evacuate the port, they burned the nine French ships of the line and three frigates present at Toulon, rather than taking them out. Clearly the British preferred to shorten the power of France regardless of what political faction were involved. Immediately after Toulon the Spanish government began to seek ways to get loose from the British alliance. The Spanish minister at Copenhagen made peace overtures to the French minister in that city in February 1794.

Meanwhile the American government, far distant in its seat of power in Philadelphia, had decided that through patience and persuasion it might make a favorable treaty of commerce with the Spanish. The Americans apparently did not sense at first that European circumstances were about to favor them again, as at the time of Nootka, and that this time the crisis would last long enough for their purposes.

The Pinckney mission came about because Godoy had complained about the two Americans who at that time were representing the United States in Spain, William Carmichael and William Short. Exactly what it was about Carmichael and Short that bothered Godoy is difficult to say. Short soon replaced Carmichael, with whom he had been acting in commission. It may have been that Short knew more about Godoy's shifty maneuvering toward the French than Godoy liked. At any rate Godoy complained to Secretary Randolph that Short had not been "very circumspect." After the arrival of Pinckney, Short had a feverish interview with Godoy asking about the precise nature of the foreign minister's complaints. Godoy lied, disavowing the comment about Short not being circumspect. He said he had complained only about Short's former fellow commissioner, Carmichael, who by this time had died. Godoy wrote out a formal statement to that effect. He even said he preferred to negotiate with Short rather than Pinckney. Short thereupon resigned as envoy to Spain but stayed in Madrid and helped Pinckney.

Thomas Pinckney, the negotiator of 1795, was actually minister to Great Britain, and it must have been a point of some oddity to him that when Randolph sent him to Spain on special mission to negotiate a commercial treaty Pinckney was creating the same embarrassing position for Short as John Jay had done for him when Jay came to London on special mission in 1794. In the British capital Pinckney had not had much to do anyway, since relations with the British government had been carried on either, as in 1794, by Jay or, as then and earlier, by the British minister in Philadelphia, Hammond, and by the ardent American secretary of the treasury Hamilton, Hammond's too good friend. Pinckney fortunately was an able man, judicious and affable (so Spanish agents in Philadelphia described him in 1792 when he set out for London to be minister there). He had been born in 1750, educated at Westminster School in England, studied at Oxford and in France, trained for the law at the Inner Temple; but as a patriot he had returned to America in 1772, served as a major in the war, and been taken prisoner on the battlefield of Camden. He was a worthy minister to approach the Spanish over a treaty.

Pinckney did not leave London until late in the spring of 1795, and this delay was almost his undoing. Jay was waiting in London for an easier passage to the United States, hoping that while he waited he would receive his treaty back ratified by the president after consent of the Senate so that he could bring home the exchanged ratifications. Jay advised Pinckney not to set out for Madrid until the British treaty had been ratified. "In my opinion," he cautioned, "Mr. Pinckney should defer a certain Business until the treaty is ratified . . . ." Bemis has commented on this advice: "If the treaty had been ratified and its full terms known in Spain when Pinckney arrived there, as Jay had desired, it is doubtful whether he could have achieved such a successful ending of his Spanish mission."

Luck once more favored the United States. Pinckney arrived in Spain at the proper psychological moment, June 28, 1795. Prussia and the Netherlands had left the coalition against France. French armies in strength were passing through the Pyrenees into Spain. Godoy was anxiously and directly negotiating with the French through several channels, and terms of peace were rapidly taking shape. The Treaty of Basle was signed on July 22, 1795, secretly, but the courier bearing the document did not reach the Spanish capital until August 3. It was an ideal time to press the Spanish for a favorable treaty, though strangely enough Pinckney misread the international puzzle. He concluded that the Spanish would have their hands free upon making peace with the French, and might turn to the New World; hence the United States should make a treaty quickly with Spain. Godoy's reasoning doubtless was different. The problem was not freedom of maneuver after the French treaty, but the wrath of England which was likely to descend upon the perfidious Spanish in the form of the capture of Spanish Florida (so recently British), perhaps even Louisiana, not to mention Cuba and other colonial territories.

Godoy had another problem. He had hoped to obtain a treaty of alliance with France. Instead the French gave him only a treaty of peace. The Spaniard ostentatiously accepted the designation of Prince of the Peace from his grateful people, but the title was no substitute for a French alliance. His next best hope was alliance with the United States or, failing that, a commercial treaty with the new nation of the New World.

Acting quickly, if for the wrong reason, Pinckney and Short on October 27, 1795, concluded a marvelous treaty with Spain. Unlike the British treaty in 1794, the Spanish in 1795 affirmed the American principle of neutral rights. The treaty also recognized the boundary of the United States as set forth in the Treaty of Paris in 1783 with Britain: to the south the thirty-first parallel, to the west the Mississippi. And the Spanish granted the United States the right of navigation of the great river! A difficult part of the negotiation concerned the need of American traders of a place of deposit at New Orleans for goods passing down the Mississippi River on flatboats before they were transshipped to ocean-going vessels for the long voyage to the east coast. At one point in this discussion of "the right of deposit" Pinckney asked for his passports, a bold and daring step, and successful. Godoy capitulated. Pinckney accepted a mixed commission for adjudication of the spoliations of American ships and cargoes caused by Spanish cruisers in the war commencing in 1793, and Godoy consented to the privilege of deposit at New Orleans for a term of three years and agreed to continue it or provide another equal establishment elsewhere on the river.

Thus by the end of the eighteenth century the United States had not merely announced and secured from Great Britain its national independence; it had signed a series of commercial treaties—a matter of importance to a nation which possessed so large a merchant marine. First had come the commercial treaty with France, concluded at the same time as the alliance in 1778; then a wartime treaty with the Netherlands; subsequent treaties with Sweden, Prussia, and Morocco; Jay's Treaty, and Pinckney's. An impressive record.

These treaties of commerce, notably the treaties negotiated with Britain and Spain, accomplished a great deal in adjusting American foreign trade and in arranging the pattern of commerce after independence. Unfortunately the American record with commercial treaties looked more impressive on paper than it was in reality. Reflecting the world of words rather than action, the treaties proved not as durable as they had at first promised. By the time of Pinckney's Treaty, France and Britain, the two greatest powers of Europe, one predominantly a power on land and the other dominant on sea, had begun a series of wars that would turn the Continent into a theater of military operations, and likewise the seas, even the seas of the New World. The British raised coalitions against the French. The first had collapsed by 1795, but three more would follow. And in the course of this struggle no commercial pledges to a neutral power such as the United States were likely to deter Britain and France once they saw some advantage to their individual causes in changing the American arrangements. The people of the United States and their government wished only peace with the world, commerce with everyone, in time of peace but even, God forbid, in time of war. This outlook was to prove too theoretical for the era of the French revolution and, especially, for Napoleon, the man to whom the French nation soon thereafter confided management of its affairs.

A CONTEMPORARY DOCUMENT

[Jefferson enjoyed describing the benefits of peace, particularly the benefits of commerce during times of peace, and on December 16, 1793, he offered to Congress a report on "the nature and extent of the privileges and restrictions of the commercial intercourse of the United States with Foreign nations," together with suggestions for improvement. Source: Walter Lowrie and Matthew St. Clair Clarke, eds., *American State Papers: Foreign Relations* (6 vols., Washington, 1832–1859), I, 300–304.]

. . . Instead of embarrassing commerce under piles of regulating laws, duties, and prohibitions, could it be relieved from all its shackles in all parts of the world; could every country be employed in producing that which nature has best fitted it to produce, and each be free to exchange with others mutual surplusses for mutual wants, the greatest mass possible would then be produced of those things which contribute to human life and human happiness; the numbers of mankind would be increased, and their condition bettered. . . .

But should any nation, contrary to our wishes, suppose it may better find its advantage by continuing its system of prohibitions, duties, and regulations, it behooves us to protect our citizens, their commerce, and navigation, by counter prohibitions, duties, and regulations, also. Free commerce and navigation are not to be given in exchange for restrictions and vexations, nor are they likely to produce a relaxation of them.

Our navigation involves still higher considerations. As a branch of industry, it is valuable, but as a resource of defence, essential.

Its value, as a branch of industry, is enhanced by the dependence of so many other branches on it. In times of general peace, it multiplies competitors for employment in transportation, and so keeps that at its proper level; and in times of war, that is to say, when those nations who may be our principal carriers, shall be at war with each other, if we have not within ourselves the means of transportation, our produce must be exported in belligerent vessels, at the increased expense of war-freight and insurance, and the articles which will not bear that, must perish on our hands.

But it is as a resource of defence, that our navigation will admit neither neglect nor forbearance. The position and circumstances of the United States leave them nothing to fear on their land-board, and nothing to desire beyond their present rights. But on their sea-board, they are open to injury, and they have there, too, a commerce, which must be protected. This can only be done by possessing a respectable body of citizen-seamen, and of artists and establishments in readiness for ship-building.

Were the ocean, which is the common property of all, open to the industry of all, so that every person and vessel should be free to take employment wherever it could be found, the United States would certainly not set the example of appropriating to themselves, exclusively, any portion of the common stock of occupation. They would rely on the enterprise and activity of their citizens, for a due participation of the benefits of the seafaring business, and for keeping the marine class of citizens equal to their object. But if particular nations grasp at undue shares, and, more especially, if they seize on the means of the United States, to convert them into aliment for their own strength, and withdraw them entirely from the support of those to whom they belong, defensive and protecting measures become necessary on the part of the nation whose marine resources are thus invaded . . . .

ADDITIONAL READING

Arthur Burr Darling's *Our Rising Empire* (New Haven, 1940), covers this era in part, and is perhaps the best book with which to begin. See also the chapters in the fourth volume of Edward Channing's *A History of the United States* entitled *Federalists and Republicans, 1789–1815* (New York, 1917). Channing remains one of the most readable and instructive of historians, and his multivolume history is a monumental tribute to his genius and industry. A book dealing in part with diplomatic affairs is Merrill Jensen, *The New Nation: A History of the United States during the Confederation, 1781–1789* (New York, 1950). Alexander De Conde recounts part of this period's diplomacy in *Entangling Alliance: Politics and Diplomacy under George Washington* (Durham, N.C., 1958).

The Canadian concern appears in the detailed and scholarly book with the eighteenth-century title by A. L. Burt, *The United States, Great Britain, and British North America from the Revolution to the Establishment of Peace after the War of 1812* (New Haven, 1940). For Gouverneur Morris see Henry M. Wriston's *Executive Agents in American Foreign Relations* (Baltimore, 1929). The Nootka controversy and its relation to later policy is analyzed in John A. Logan, Jr., *No Transfer* (New Haven, 1961). The proclamation of neutrality has its explanation in Charles M. Thomas, *American Neutrality in 1793: A Study in Cabinet Government* (New York, 1931). Samuel Flagg Bemis has dealt with several topics of this era in his collected essays, *American Foreign Policy and the Blessings of Liberty* (New Haven, 1962), chapters 5–11. See also his *John Quincy Adams and the Foundations of American Foreign Policy* (New York, 1949) for the young Adams at The Hague, and later on mission to negotiate a commercial treaty with Prussia.

The treaty with Great Britain appears in *S. F. Bemis, *Jay's Treaty* (rev. ed., New Haven, 1962). *Joseph Charles, *The Origins of the American Party System* (Williamsburg, Va., 1956) has an essay on the treaty which is worth reading. Opposing each other in interpretation are *Bemis's *Pinckney's Treaty* (rev. ed., New Haven, 1960), and Arthur P. Whitaker's *The Spanish-American Frontier: 1783–1795* (Boston 1927).

For biographies see Frank Monaghan, *John Jay* (New York, 1935); John A. Carroll and Mary Wells Ashworth, *George Washington: First in Peace* (New York, 1957), the concluding volume of Douglas Southall Freeman's work completed after his death; and Page Smith's *John Adams* (2 vols., New York, 1962). For titles on Jefferson see the suggestions for additional reading at the end of chapter 5.

☆ *4* ☆

Neutrality and Quasi War

America is not SCARED.

—President John Adams to his son John
Quincy, 1797

In 1789, at the outset of the most dramatic revolution in modern world history, the French revolution, the troubles of revolutionary France seemed far removed from the problems of post-revolutionary America. The people of the United States had enjoyed a half-dozen years of peace after 1783. Actually there had been no serious fighting since the surrender of General Cornwallis at Yorktown in 1781. Like all peoples, the Americans immediately found their own concerns more important than those of their erstwhile allies in Europe, the French. The new federal government had begun to function in the spring of 1789, slowly getting underway. The most important problems of the country seemed domestic and primarily economic, remotely related to the comings and goings of the nations of the Continent. There was much talk about what the new government would do in assumption of the country's debts, domestic as well as foreign. Assumption of the state revolutionary debts was a large issue, which in 1789 the new secretary of the treasury, Hamilton, was about to resolve. The national credit appeared extremely important. The country was coming out of the economic doldrums of the mid-1780's, and that recovery too was important in the minds of the merchants and planters and small farmers who made up the American population.

What would Jefferson, the new secretary of state who took office in 1790, have to accomplish, other than to affix the great seal to documents of state—the duty which had given its name to his office? It was difficult to predict. He had a few minor concerns such as watching the consular convention of 1788 pass through the Senate—the first treaty to pass the

Senate—and cabinet discussions soon arose, frenzied for a short time, over the Nootka Sound affair. But the consular treaty passed, and the Nootka Sound affair passed. Jefferson might, so it seemed, complete the circle of his felicities (one of his favorite phrases) by watching over the routine correspondence of his office and spending time at his beloved plantation of Monticello. Business appeared as slow as the trips he frequently had to take from Monticello to New York and to Philadelphia, the two capitals of the federal government in the 1790's. The almost interminable fording of rivers and moving on horseback through sparsely settled country did not disturb the nation's first secretary of state, because affairs of state were hardly urgent.

There was some slight popular and diplomatic feeling that Jefferson's sojourn as American minister in France from 1785 to 1788 might have warped his sympathies in favor of the French. At the department of state he hired the writer and poet, Philip Freneau, as French translator, upon recommendation of James Madison. The salary was not much, $250 a year. Freneau hesitated to accept the appointment because he did not know the language. It was a fairly harmless political appointment. Madison felt that Freneau would be a good publicity manager for the secretary in matters other than foreign policy. As for Jefferson's feelings, reportedly so pro-French, one must quote the later appraisal of Pierre Adet, a French minister to the United States, who remarked, "Jefferson, I say, is American and, by that title, cannot be sincerely our friend. An American is the born enemy of all European peoples."

1. *Initial discussions*

At the beginning of the French revolution the revolutionary cause found much sympathy in the United States. Lafayette sent President George Washington the key to the Bastille, and lovers of freedom on both sides of the Atlantic rejoiced. Soon, however, Americans began to divide in their admiration of revolutionary France. Issues between factions in France touched issues in the United States. The French problem became acute for the United States with proclamation of the French republic on September 21, 1792, the execution of Louis XVI on January 21, 1793, and the dramatic declaration of war on February 1 against Great Britain, Spain, and the Netherlands.

The problem of American diplomacy at this juncture was an obvious one: what to do with the Franco-American alliance of 1778, still in effect in 1793. Should Americans rally to the side of France, as the French nation fifteen years before had come to the help of the infant United States? Or had the change of government in France ended the obligations under the treaty of 1778?

President Washington and his cabinet had few hesitations about issuing a declaration of neutrality in the war now opening in Europe, and on April 22, 1793, he duly did so. The president announced that the American nation would side with none of the belligerents but carry out the duties and expect recognition of the rights traditionally accorded by belligerents to neutrals in time of war.

Such was the decision of the moment, but the president knew that the moment soon might change and that he had better prepare himself and perhaps the country for some future invocation of the alliance by the government of France. He therefore had submitted to the cabinet on April 18, four days before announcing neutrality, a series of questions which he worded as acutely as he considered them important. After asking, almost as a formality, whether a proclamation should be published for the purpose of preventing interference by the citizens of the United States in the war between France and Britain, and what specifically such a proclamation should contain, Washington moved on in twelve additional questions as to what might well become problems of the future. He asked:

(1) Should the United States receive a minister from the French republic?

(2) If so, receive him with qualifications?

(3) Should the treaties made with the monarchy (amity and commerce, 1778; alliance, 1778; consular convention, 1788) apply to the republic?

(4) If it were possible to renounce or suspend the treaties, was it expedient?

(5) Would it be a breach of neutrality to consider the treaties still in operation?

(6) If the treaties were in operation, was the alliance's mutual guarantee of possessions in the New World—France guaranteeing American territory, the United States guaranteeing France's West Indian islands—applicable only if France were engaging in a defensive war in Europe?

(7) Was the present war in Europe defensive or of a mixed character?

(8) If the war were mixed in character, did the guarantee apply?

(9) What was the proper way to ensure the guarantee in the alliance?

(10) Should the United States under the treaties restrain British warships from use of American ports?

(11) If the regent of France—perhaps the head of a government in exile—sent a minister, should the United States recognize that envoy?

(12) Should the president convene Congress and, if so, what should he say to Congress?

The president's questions brought contradictory replies from Secretary of the Treasury Hamilton and Secretary of State Jefferson, and one must say that Hamilton's overlogical answer showed clearly how in diplomacy a wish might become father to a thought. The head of the treasury first asked the rhetorical question of whether the United States should honor the alliance, and his answer, a resounding "no," was complicated almost to the point of lacking conviction:

It is believed that they have an option to consider the operation of those treaties as suspended, and will have eventually a right to renounce them, if such changes shall take place as can *bona fide* be pronounced to render a continuance of the connections which result from them disadvantageous or dangerous.

The secretary argued from national interest—"In national questions, the general conduct of nations has great weight." He said it would be carrying a theory to the extreme "to pronounce that the United States are *under* an *absolute*, indispensable obligation." He called upon that arbiter of all questions, international, national, personal: prudence, he said, dictated delay. It was not necessary, he contended, to act at once. "It is putting too suddenly too much to hazard."

Secretary Jefferson had much the better of the argument, although he too came out in favor of delay and—proof that Jefferson was no doctrinaire—the importance of not pushing theories to an extreme. His remark on the generally binding nature of a treaty of alliance was a classic piece of reasoning of the sort that had passed into the Declaration of Independence seventeen years before:

I consider the people who constitute a society or nation as the source of all authority in that nation, as free to transact their common concerns by any agents they think proper, to change these agents individually, or the organisation of them in form or function whenever they please: that all the acts done by those agents under the authority of the nation, are the acts of the nation, are obligatory on them, & enure to their use, & can in no wise be annulled or affected by any change in the form of the government, or of the persons administering it. Consequently the Treaties between the U S. and France, were not treaties between the U S. & Louis Capet . . . .

After this piece of philosophy Jefferson moved slyly to his point. Having produced a feeling on the part of his readers that a national decision was a protean force, he added as if stating a truism that "I go further & deny that the most explicit declaration made at this moment that we acknolege [*sic*] the obligation of the treatys could take from us the right of noncompliance at any future time when compliance would involve us in great

& inevitable danger." With better justification than the above he concluded that in early 1793 it was not necessary, anyway, for the United States to anticipate so dire a situation, for the danger was neither extreme nor imminent nor even probable.

One may conclude from these logical exercises, fortunately unconnected to an extreme moment of danger, that almost at the outset the diplomacy of the new nation confronted the age-old problem of how to decide when a treaty no longer should be operable. No one has ever found a comfortable answer to this problem. The student of history need only recall the predicament into which Germany took itself in 1914 when by sending troops into Belgium, not merely did it violate the Belgian treaty of guarantee of 1839, but Chancellor Theodore von Bethmann Hollweg was honest enough to allegedly say to the British ambassador that the treaty was only "a scrap of paper." The Belgian treaty indeed was so old as to be virtually a scrap of paper, and the British and French themselves had contemplated violating it in case the Germans did not: Belgian territory in 1914 was too highly valuable to permit any seventy-five-year-old treaty to interfere with military movements. But Germany under Bethmann's leadership violated a solemn engagement under international law. The Germans were to pay dearly for the frankness of their violation, as the American government under President Wilson was enormously put out by this breach of the written word. The moot principle of international law, *rebus sic stantibus*, that treaties have effect only so long as conditions obtain under which the instruments were negotiated, has never found favor in the United States, and of course would be a chaotic principle if it ever were to gain acceptance. The observance of treaties creates continuing problems, among them the impossibility of taking an inconvenient treaty to court as private individuals may do in the case of inconvenient contracts and the need—apparently—for treaties to run in perpetuity unless the signatories agree to changes or unless one of the signatories ruptures the agreement by an act of war (in which case all mutual treaties automatically lapse). In the latter half of the twentieth century there are no better answers to these problems than were at hand for the rival purposes of Alexander Hamilton and Thomas Jefferson in the year 1793.

2. *Genêt, Fauchet, Adet*

Jefferson's point of view soon found expression in American politics through the actions of the new French minister to the United States, Edmond C. Genêt, who reached American soil on April 8, 1793, with a revolutionary mandate to obtain American co-operation as a benevolent neutral in the war.

Citizen Genêt, as he liked to be addressed, was a Frenchman of moderate revolutionary desires, a Girondin, filled with the spirit of liberty, equality, and fraternity, willing to do his best for his country in its time of danger from counterrevolutionary attack in Europe. He landed at Charleston, South Carolina, under instructions to win American aid and negotiate a new treaty of commerce, virtually a new alliance. Even before he had presented his credentials to President Washington he set about commissioning four privateers, and dispatched them to prey upon British vessels along the American coast.

But at this juncture the French minister ran into trouble. Moving northward from Charleston he found himself warmly greeted by fellow republicans of North America and must have come to believe that he would have no difficulty with the government, then located in the city of Philadelphia. Here he was disappointed, for Washington, who had already

Citizen Genêt.

issued a proclamation of neutrality on April 22, received him on May 18 with cool formality. Secretary Jefferson, acting under Washington's instructions, presented Genêt with a communication to the effect that grants of military commissions on American soil constituted an infringement of American sovereignty. Genêt was told that the privateers commissioned by him would have to leave American waters and could not send their prizes into American ports. Undaunted, the minister authorized the arming of *The Little Sarah*, a prize brought in by a French vessel, renamed her *La Petite Démocrate*, and threatened to send her to sea. Because the vessel was outfitting in the port of Philadelphia, the governor of

Pennsylvania sent an emissary to Genêt to persuade the French minister to detain the vessel. Genêt "flew in a great passion" and made it clear that he cared little for "old Washington" and that if necessary "he would appeal from the President to the People." The vessel sailed. Washington with the consent of his cabinet thereupon demanded Genêt's recall.

The minister might have gone home to the guillotine, had the Washington administration carried out its order, for Genêt's successor, Jean A. J. Fauchet, arrived in the United States in February 1794 with a warrant for Genêt's arrest and deportation to France, now under the control of Robespierre and the Jacobins. The American government congenially allowed the errant minister to remain in the New World. Genêt removed himself, "in retreat and silence," to a farm at Jamaica, Long Island, there to meditate upon "the great revolutions of the world" and to isolate himself "from the detestable intrigues of Courts and the discouraging cabals of nations." The "comet," as Hamilton had described him, disappeared from the political horizon, married the daughter of Governor George Clinton of New York, and lived happily ever after.

Because of the embarrassments of Genêt's mission, the United States decided to make clear its stand toward the European war, and in a neutrality act of June 1794, reinforcing the proclamation of neutrality made by Washington in April 1793, the government set forth its position. The act forbade citizens of the United States to enlist in the service of a foreign power and prohibited the fitting-out of armed vessels in American ports. The revolutionary government of France by this token should have known that it would be futile to invoke the alliance of 1778, but Genêt's successors, Fauchet and Pierre A. Adet, boldly continued his efforts to obtain assistance from the United States.

Jefferson resigned as secretary of state on the last day of December 1793. His successor, Edmund Randolph, soon got into difficulty with the new minister of France, Fauchet, and eventually was accused of treason in a murky plot the circumstances of which are difficult even today to clarify.

Randolph's disgrace occurred after some reported conversation with Fauchet came to the attention of the British government and, by a roundabout way, President Washington. Fauchet had sent dispatches back to Paris aboard a French vessel, the corvette *Jean Bart*, which was captured by the British man-of-war *Cerberus*. Just before the capture an officer threw a packet of papers overboard, but (reminiscent of Henry Laurens's similar effort, years before) the British fished it out. The papers went to Foreign Secretary Grenville, who already had conceived a dislike for Secretary Randolph. Among the papers was the famous dispatch Number 10 which contained Fauchet's recollection of conversation with the secretary of state. Fauchet reported confusedly on anti-Hamiltonian remarks supposedly made by Randolph. Grenville passed Number 10 to Hammond, who gave it to Hamilton's successor at the treasury, Oliver Wolcott, who passed it on to a fellow cabinet member, Secretary of War Timothy Pickering, who gave it to Washington.

It was a piece of ill luck that the dispatch should have gotten into the hands of Pickering. This tall, lean, cadaverous gentleman, a sort of "New England pickle," was to become Randolph's successor—but it does appear as if his concern over Randolph's loyalty had no relation to the possibility of a job opening. Pickering hardly trusted anyone other than himself, and he may on occasion have put his right hand up to watching the left. He was of a suspicious nature. Withal he was so transparently honest that Washington trusted him implicitly. Pickering was no radical and felt that revolutionary Frenchmen, if they ever died, were only one step removed from the lowest rung of hell, and if they were alive, it might be wise to hasten them along toward their future position. Washington was almost as suspicious of France. To him Pickering made good sense. And to Pickering, Fauchet's Number 10 was evidence of an awful plot.

Pickering was elated to get something on Randolph. He first wrote a letter of warning to Mount Vernon, of dark things seething beneath the surface of American foreign relations. Washington arrived in Philadelphia on August 11, 1795, and Pickering hastened to the president's house where he found him at the table. Cheerful and seemingly in good spirits, Randolph also was at the table. After taking a glass of wine the president soon rose and giving Pickering a wink went into another room. Pickering followed.

"What," said the president, "is the cause of your writing me such a letter?"

"That man in the other room," said Pickering, pointing toward where they had left Randolph, "is a traitor." In two or three minutes Pickering gave the president an intimation of what Fauchet in the intercepted dispatch had said of Randolph.

"Let us return to the other room," said the president, "to prevent any suspicion of our withdrawing."

Shortly after this furtive discussion the president ratified the treaty with England, Jay's Treaty. He then handed Fauchet's dispatch to Randolph with a request for an explanation. Randolph immediately resigned.

The secretary of state probably felt that if he could not have the confidence of the president it was impossible to remain as the principal officer of the cabinet, and Randolph never for a moment believed that he had been guilty of anything. He wrote a voluminous *Vindication* which he published in hope that his countrymen would believe him. From the

French minister, Fauchet, he obtained a certificate of his sterling qualities —a piece of bad judgment which does raise some question of naiveté. The more he protested the less convincing his case became. After all, he was contesting an issue with the president, who almost always in such cases has much more impressive credentials with the public and who by saying little or nothing usually can dominate the argument. One recalls the case many years later of Secretary of State William Jennings Bryan who found himself in a dispute with President Wilson and gave up his seal of office without even trying to vindicate himself, knowing that such a course would be futile. "I go out into the dark," Bryan said to some friends in 1915. "The President has all the prestige and power on his side . . . ." Such it was with Edmund Randolph, who retired in bitterness to his lands in Virginia and died in obscurity about the time of the War of 1812.

With his disappearance from Philadelphia the office of secretary of state went a-begging. The president offered it to four people—William Paterson of New Jersey, Thomas Johnson of Maryland, Charles Cotesworth Pinckney of South Carolina, and Patrick Henry. All refused. Finally he offered it to Pickering, who accepted the post.

The new secretary may well have disliked his position, as he openly claimed, but he stayed there until the year 1800 when his disloyalty to President John Adams became so patent that Adams expelled him from the secretaryship. Whatever the feeling about the job, Pickering did discover that it provided an excellent platform from which to make anti-French declarations. He liked to speak his mind. In his great old age in the year 1824 he wrote that "all my life long, I have been so accustomed freely to express my opinions, that some of my friends have occasionally regretted that I was so little reserved, that I did not conceal my sentiments, when, though correct, they might give offence; in a word, that I did not wear a mask." Perhaps, though, it was just as well that he was frank, as the successive French regimes of the 1790's showed little friendship for the nation across the Atlantic with which they were allied, and it was helpful for them to know from the secretary of state himself that they could no longer pursue any machinations through their ministers in America.

As secretary of state Pickering did his best to uphold American national dignity, and he was willing to act against the British as well as the French. Consider his trouble over the departure of the French envoy Fauchet. The Frenchman traveled to Newport, Rhode Island, and there went aboard the French frigate *Medusa*. Unfortunately the British ship-of-the-line *Africa* was lying outside of Newport, waiting for the *Medusa* to come out. The *Africa's* commander, Captain Rodman Home, was spending his idle hours stopping American ships and taking off seamen. The

Rhode Islanders were furious, and refused him the courtesies of the port. The captain drew up a peremptory letter to the British consul, to be laid before the state's governor:

I am resolved to be treated in the same manner, in all respects whatever, as they do those of the French republic [the United States, to be sure, had a consular convention with France]; and I am more plain in the nature of my present demands, as I have received a hint that, if I send my people on shore, while the Medusa lies at Newport, they will be considered as spies. In this case I want to say nothing. I am in full possession of every intelligence regarding that ship, which I want to be possessed of. And I require a written answer from the Governor of Rhode Island to these demands, and that without loss of time.

As if this were not complication enough, Fauchet's successor Adet demanded satisfaction of the Washington administration in Philadelphia because Fauchet's baggage, going by sea to Newport, was searched within American territorial waters by Captain Home's orders.

Pickering rose doughtily to the issue, whether presented by French or British officialdom. He dismissed the British consul who had transmitted Captain Home's "indecent and unjustifiable" letter which "grossly insulted" the governor of Rhode Island. He had the governor tell Home to leave within forty-eight hours or else he could have no more contact with the shore. As for Adet and the Fauchet baggage, Pickering did nothing, considering himself no baggage clerk. Everything then returned to normal when the French *Medusa*, Fauchet on board, escaped Newport in a dense fog.

Washington and Pickering had to put up with the most barefaced efforts by the new minister, Adet, to show popular and, so Adet hoped to demonstrate, official sentiment between the United States and revolutionary France. Adet's government instructed him to present the colors of France to the United States, together with a copy of a fraternal address from the Committee of Safety of the French National Convention. Washington chose New Year's Day, 1796, as a day appropriate for the solemn occasion. Adet presented the stand of colors and declared that

every citizen will receive, with a pleasing emotion, this flag, elsewhere the terror of the enemies of liberty, here the certain pledge of faithful friendship; especially when they recollect that it guides to combat men who have shared their toils, and who were prepared for liberty, by aiding them to acquire their own.

Washington wanted to quiet Adet with an excess of praise, hoping that the minister might become appropriately inactive. "To call your nation brave," said the conservative president, perhaps wincing, "were to pronounce but common praise." He proceeded:

Wonderful people! Ages to come will read with astonishment the history of your brilliant exploits! I rejoice that the period of your toils and of your immense sacrifices is approaching. I rejoice that the interesting revolutionary movements of so many years have issued in the formation of a constitution designed to give permanency to the great object for which you have contended. I rejoice that liberty, which you have so long embraced with enthusiasm—liberty, of which you have been the invincible defenders—now finds an asylum in the bosom of a regularly organized government;—a government, which being formed to secure the happiness of the French people, corresponds to the ardent wishes of my heart, while it gratifies the pride of every citizen of the United States by its resemblance to its own. On these glorious events, accept, Sir, my sincere congratulations.

When Pickering sent the French colors to the archives, Adet complained that "it has been decided that the French flag should be shut up among the archives," and said that France would look upon this act "as a mark of contempt or indifference." Pickering worked on his response for several days, and finally sent the minister a masterpiece explaining why, although France had put the American colors in the hall of the National Assembly, the American government had sent the French flag to the archives. In the latter estimable place, said Pickering, the colors of France would reside "with the evidences and memorials of our own freedom and independence." He also remarked, with a slight malevolence, that Adet should not try to foist off French customs on the Americans who had their own customs.

Adet could not keep his mouth shut, and soon was calling Pickering's attention to an almanac issued in Philadelphia which listed the diplomatic corps and gave first place to Great Britain instead of France. Adet demanded an apology so that he, Adet, could print the apology in the newspapers. Pickering replied that the United States government did not edit such things as local almanacs, and called attention to the *Massachusetts Register* for 1796 which put the French republic at the head of the list, and Great Britain at the foot.

Turning from almanacs and flags to the subject of Jay's Treaty, Adet in a new communication of November 15, 1796 got so far out of line that he could not continue as minister. He reproached the American government for friendliness with England. "Oh! Americans, covered with noble scars! Oh, you who have so often flown to death and to victory with French soldiers. . . . Let your government return to itself, and you will still find in Frenchmen faithful friends and generous allies." He had most of this manifesto published before the state department, to which he had addressed it as a note, could make a full translation. Adet said that his government had suspended his ministerial functions until the American government reformed its sentiments. Pickering and Adet were, so to speak, at pens' points. Pickering took him at his word, and business between them ceased.

By this time, and for such reasons as the above diplomacy, President Washington already had issued his Farewell Address. Less an address than a presidential manifesto, it was given out perhaps partly to secure the election of the president's chosen successor, John Adams. In the course of the Farewell Address, Washington said some truths about American foreign policy which were remembered long after any politics of the occasion had been forgotten. "Europe has a set of primary interests," he said, "which to us have none or a very remote relation. Hence she must be engaged in frequent controversies, the causes of which are essentially foreign to our concerns. Hence, therefore, it must be unwise in us to implicate ourselves by artificial ties in the ordinary vicissitudes of her politics or the ordinary combinations and collisions of her friendships or enmities."

Nowhere in this address, one should add, was the phrase "entangling alliances," which Jefferson first used in his inaugural of 1801. And Washington had not advised against American participation in the extraordinary affairs of Europe—he had counseled only against "ordinary combinations and collisions." This adjectival distinction was overlooked in subsequent references to the Farewell Address by political leaders and publicists, who sought for their own purposes to show that the first president of the United States was an isolationist and against any political contacts between his country and the nations of Europe.

Taken in the way in which Washington meant it, the Farewell Address was a memorable statement of American foreign policy. It set out his own achievement in foreign affairs. His leadership during a large European war had preserved the republic in strength and neutrality, despite the willingness of some Americans in 1793 and thereafter to take sides in a conflict that did not vitally concern them. The first president was a prudent man, and it fell to some of his successors to discover how incautious diplomacy could endanger American national existence.

3. The XYZ affair

In his Farewell Address, Washington asked his countrymen to stay clear of ordinary foreign entanglements, although he had not used those words, and his advice was well taken but soon forgotten. Political parties had been forming in his second administration, and by the time he was ready to leave office there was some question as to whether he could control the choice of his successor. The Hamiltonian Federalists were in essence the party of strong central government, and the Jeffersonians favored a more federal, less centralized, national regime. The parties also took stands on issues of foreign relations, the Hamiltonian Federalists often being pro-British, the Jeffersonian Republicans pro-French. Both sides injected into the electoral contest of 1796 their views on foreign affairs, and John Adams, whose views internationally might well be denominated pro-American, almost failed of election despite support by Washington. Adams had anticipated his election as an easy matter. In January 1796 he wrote lightly about it to his wife Abigail: "I am, as you say, quite a favorite. I am to dine today again. I am heir apparent, you know, and a succession is soon to take place." He added that "whatever may be the wish or the judgment of the present occupant, the French and the demagogues intend, I presume, to set aside the descent." He did not anticipate the bitterness of the struggle that year when not merely did he have to contend with the Jeffersonians but Hamilton supported Thomas Pinckney against him.

Charles-Maurice, Prince de Talleyrand.

As his luck would have it, Adams hardly had come into the presidency when a crisis arose with France.

The changing course of the French revolution explains this diplomatic crisis in 1797–1798. The revolution by this time had passed through the reign of terror and turned conservative, for the country had had enough of revolutionary turmoil. After Robespierre the direction of the French government came under a five-man executive known as the Directory, for which the minister of foreign affairs was the wily statesman Talleyrand. The Directory in due time was swept away by the revolutionary general from Corsica, Napoleon Bonaparte, who in 1797 was twenty-eight years old and engaged in a campaign in Italy. The revolution, thus, was in a period of transition at the time of the XYZ affair; the Directory was giving way to Bonaparte. French military prestige was rising in Europe.

Adams's initial diplomatic action, a decision to send a commission to France to adjust outstanding differences, stemmed from the problems of diplomatic representation which had confronted his predecessor Washington. Adet in Philadelphia had made himself impossible. Secretary Pickering and President Washington meanwhile had become much dissatisfied with the performance in Paris of the American minister, Jefferson's young confederate James Monroe. The minister gave the impression that he represented the American people rather than the Washington administration, and allowed the French government to believe that he, Monroe, did not altogether approve the course of the administration. Pickering had written a letter of censure to Monroe in June 1796, saying among other things: "You have here the sensations of the President in relation to the line of conduct you have pursued." In August he wrote Monroe that Charles Cotesworth Pinckney of South Carolina was going to replace him.

Monroe ever afterward bore Pickering a grudge, being certain that the lanky New Englander had cashiered him for the good of Great Britain. On getting back to the United States late in June 1797 he demanded justice from Pickering, asking a room and a clerk at the state department so he could make out his case. Pickering said this request might create an improper, inconvenient, unwise precedent. Monroe said he was entitled to the "blessings of an honest fame." He then published a long statement. Monroe's partisans said that Pickering was the Grand Vizir Timothy who took his principles of official conduct from Turkey.

Monroe's conduct had encouraged Pickering, who loved an argument anyway, to get up a long statement of American grievances toward France, which he nominally gave to Monroe's successor Pinckney but actually intended for publication in American newspapers. The instruction said that during the American revolution the French had acted at times for their own good; that France then had made "exertions to advance her own interest and secure her own safety." The peace negotiations in Paris had been a trap for the unwary Americans, "To keep us thus far dependent . . . to deprive the United States of an immense western territory, of the navigation of the Mississippi, and of the fisheries, except on our own coast." Pickering considered the cases of Genêt, Fauchet, and Adet seriatim. He appended copies of notes exchanged between himself and Adet. Dated January 16, 1797, and laid before Congress, the instruction was printed in a pamphlet of a hundred pages.

Pinckney had no chance to present this argument to the French government, which upon his arrival refused to receive him. He arrived before Monroe tardily set sail for the United States, and the French meanwhile gave the retiring minister a grand farewell reception. Pinckney demanded an explanation of his status in Paris. A few weeks later he was told that as a stranger remaining in Paris without permission he was rendering himself liable to arrest. He left for Holland. The rupture between France and the United States was complete, no ministers in either capital.

John Adams, now president, arranged to send a commission to treat with the French, and decided upon his commissioners and their instructions with care. He chose the commissioners with appreciation of American geography: C. C. Pinckney of South Carolina, John Marshall of Virginia, Elbridge Gerry of Massachusetts. Their politics were right, too: Pinckney and Marshall were Federalists; Gerry was a Jeffersonian, but a personal friend of Adams. The commissioners were instructed to modify the Franco-American treaty of commerce so as to make France's status exactly like that of Great Britain under Jay's Treaty. In other words, in case France were at war and the United States were a neutral, the American government was willing to give up its small-navy view of neutral rights so far as concerned issues with France. The United States was also willing to renounce the reciprocal guaranty contained in the eleventh article of the treaty of alliance of 1778, wherein France was to defend "the liberty, sovereignty and independence of the United States" while the United States was bound to defend "the possessions of France in America," which was to say, the French West Indies. The commissioners also were to put an end to the consular jurisdiction of France in American territory under the convention of 1788, prevent sale of French prizes in American ports, and get damages for French spoliations of American commerce during the war which had begun in 1793 and was still raging. Pinckney, Marshall, and Gerry arrived in Paris in the autumn of 1797, presented their credentials to Talleyrand on October 8, and learned that they would hear from him within a few days.

It was a most unfortunate time to begin a negotiation with revolutionary

France, for shortly after the commissioners presented themselves there came Napoleon's Treaty of Campo Formio with Austria on October 17, following the victories in Italy. French pride and arrogance received a tremendous lift. The spoils of war began enriching a country which but two years earlier had faced starvation.

Even before this news arrived in Paris, Talleyrand had begun to take advantage of the American envoys. A Swiss banker named Hottenguer —Mr. "X," so President Adams would denominate him in messages to Congress—appeared before the commissioners and in his private capacity asked according to "diplomatic usage" for $250,000 as a *douceur* for the Directory, as well as a loan to France, really a gift, of several million dollars. The French thus proposed an unblushing diplomatic holdup, albeit one not unusual in diplomatic practice in the eighteenth century. Mr. Bellamy, or "Y," a merchant of Hamburg, turned up, and said he was a confidential friend of Talleyrand; he said there should be a treaty with a secret clause providing for the loan to France (*"Il faut de l'argent—Il faut beaucoup d'argent"*). Bellamy proposed that the United States buy from France at twenty shillings in the pound 32,000,000 Dutch rescripts in florins, worth ten shillings in the pound. A few days later, on October 27, Hottenguer arrived with news of Campo Formio, and asked if that had not altered the situation? The Americans said it might have for France, but not for the United States. It was at this point that Pinckney

The XYZ Affair. A contemporary American cartoon showing the five-man French Directory demanding money from American Commissioners.

blurted out his famous "It is no; no; not a six-pence!"

Matters came to such a pass that a lady appeared, disclaimed any friendship with Talleyrand (hardly a believable pronouncement), and sought to tell Pinckney about the propriety of a loan. In the conversation she said that "We have a very considerable party in America who are strongly in our interest."

"Z," or Hauteval, told Gerry that Talleyrand was disappointed that he had not seen the Americans frequently "in their private capacities," and the foreign minister on April 3, 1798, sent a note to Gerry making an appointment for a conference, on the supposition that "Messrs. Pinckney and Marshall have thought it useful and proper to quit the territory of the republic." The messenger who delivered the note said that Gerry was to show it to Pinckney and Marshall. Pinckney left Paris for southern France, where he had some personal business. Marshall sparred with Talleyrand for an official dismissal and eventually obtained it. Gerry remained. The foreign minister on one occasion, with Gerry only as a witness (it never would have done to have had Pinckney and Marshall too), said that Bellamy's proposals were "just" and "might always be relied on." He had written out the plan himself for the Dutch florins, and then burned the paper.

Gerry, the lone Jeffersonian, slowly made a fool of himself. It would not be the only piece of foolishness attributed to him during his lifetime, as later when he was governor of Massachusetts the Jeffersonian legislature cut up electoral districts in the state in favor of their party and thereby created a cartographical monster known as a gerrymander. In 1798 he was a child in Talleyrand's hands. Although he had told the foreign minister that he could confer only informally, he gave the impression to outsiders that he was still representing the United States. Pickering instructed him to leave, though the instruction reached him weeks later. Gerry stayed until near the end of July, at which time he received a new instruction from Pickering censuring his behavior and giving him a peremptory recall. One of Gerry's contemporaries once wrote that Gerry always moved in a "thick fog of his own conjuration," and truer words were never spoken. Pickering, typically, came to detest Gerry. In a private letter the secretary of state wrote that Gerry had behaved with "disgraceful pusillanimity, weakness, duplicity and I think treachery."

While the Americans were treating in Paris, and the commissioners were being asked for a bribe and other arrangements, the French government was behaving in complete disregard of its engagements under the treaties of 1778. A proclamation from Paris on January 18, 1798, announced that during the European war then in progress the character of a neutral vessel would be determined by its cargo. This meant that every vessel loaded in whole or part with British merchandise was lawful prize, no matter who the owner; likewise every neutral vessel touching a British port except in stress of weather. Here was a prototype of Napoleon's later attempt to control European trade, the Continental System. It went much farther than British practice at the time.

Soon afterward President Adams learned of the attempted subornation of his envoys. He sent their dispatches to Congress in seven installments, at intervals from May 5, 1798, to January 18, 1799. But he kept the affair in his own hands, and prevented Pickering from taking it over—an eventuality which would have produced instant war. Not until everything had gone in to Congress did Pickering get an opportunity to write up a report. The secretary then prepared a composition "on the transactions relating to the United States and France" which after much editing Adams laid before Congress. Even after the editing the report contained severe characterizations, with much use of italics. As for the action of the French government: "In this way it determined to *fleece* us. In this way it gratified its *avarice and revenge*—and it hoped also to satiate its *ambition*."

Adams kept the affair in his own hands, but he could not prevent and indeed did not want to prevent measures looking toward a war between France and the United States; hence the phrase "quasi war" to describe the hostilities between the two countries in 1798–1800. The Federalists in Congress were anxious to fight. Where, and how, and also whether a war would serve the national interest, were questions they did not ask. Adams said thoughtfully that "At present there is no more prospect of seeing a French army here, than there is in Heaven." The Federalists professed to see French ambition everywhere. A series of measures, many of them Hamilton's, were enacted to raise an army and to authorize attacks by privateers and American warships upon French warships found preying upon American commerce. The treaties of 1778 and the consular convention of 1788 were abrogated unilaterally. Congress voted to authorize a navy department and set on foot measures to obtain frigates and other vessels. Fortunately several fine frigates were on hand. Congress in 1794 had authorized these frigates ostensibly against the Barbary pirates, actually against Great Britain and perhaps as a makeweight for Jay in his negotiation in London. The three frigates completed—the *Constitution*, the *United States*, and the *Constellation*—were models of the shipbuilding art. Joshua Humphreys, the Philadelphia Quaker who had been building ships for thirty years, advised that the vessels should be longer and broader of hull than any existing type, and yet not so high: this would allow for a spread of sail that made them especially fast, and gave room for nearly as many guns on one deck as ships of the usual frigate type could carry on two decks. These eighteenth-century "pocket battleships" gave a good account of themselves in the quasi war and later in the War of 1812. In the undeclared hostilities against the government of France there were several notable naval actions, including capture by the French of the American vessel *Retaliation* off Guadeloupe on November 20, 1798, capture of the French *L'Insurgente* by the American frigate *Constellation* on February 9, 1799, and the taking of *Le Berceau* by the *Boston* on October 12, 1800. The quasi war increased the American navy until it could boast a fleet of twenty-two ships mounting 456 guns, and carrying 3,484 men.

An army of 10,000 regulars was raised, and on July 2, 1798, President Adams nominated Washington as lieutenant general and commander-in-chief, an appointment unanimously confirmed the next day. Students of military history may find it of interest that Washington's appointment as lieutenant general was the last such ranking until a much more grave crisis in 1864 when President Abraham Lincoln nominated a little unimpressive man from Galena, Illinois, Ulysses S. Grant.

Congress took other action. In 1798 it passed the Alien and Sedition Acts, certainly not over Adams's opposition, to stop the geyser-like flow of foreign propaganda in the nation's newspapers and political intrigue of the kind used by the three ministers of France by then departed—and of a sort which France at that time was using to undermine regimes in Holland and the other neighboring states of Europe.

Then, in January 1799, Congress passed the Logan Act, in honor of the volunteer diplomacy of the Philadelphia Quaker, Dr. George Logan, who had gone to France during the preceding year to offer his good influences. He had had interviews with Talleyrand and the Directory and was acclaimed a "messenger of peace." Pickering was furious at this interference. The act stated that any individual citizen who represented his country without consent of the department of state was liable to a fine of $5,000 or imprisonment for one year, or both. One need hardly add that no one ever has been prosecuted under the Logan Act, still on the statute books. What a roster of distinguished names might have appeared in American prisons from 1799 until the present day! Logan, the cause of the Act of 1799, was elected to the Senate the next year.

All this was contrary to Talleyrand's expectation in originally asking the American commissioners for a bribe. The foreign minister had lived in the United States in 1794–1796 during the Jacobin era in his own country, and he knew the strength of the American republic. He did not wish to harass the Americans to the extent of war.

A war would have been unwelcome because of a scheme which had been maturing in his agile mind, an idea by which he hoped France might regain its great North American empire, lost since the peace of 1763.

Talleyrand knew about the work of a fellow Frenchman, General Victor Collot, whom Adet had commissioned to make a journey through the Ohio and Mississippi country to ascertain its worth. Collot in 1796 had passed overland to Pittsburgh, "the true Key of this frontier." He found the area "covered by mountains and passes without end, backed by the most astonishing navigation canal in the universe, by which all sorts of provisions and reinforcements can arrive." Pittsburgh, he wrote, "may truly be called impregnable." He moved on down the Ohio River, taking note of things, sizing up people, traveling with some rapidity so as to escape "the persecutions with which we were menaced by General Waine, who had received orders to arrest us." He stopped at Louisville, long enough to see the hero of yesteryear, George Rogers Clark, lying drunk in the streets. Evidently Collot did not tarry to confer with that "person of great military talents," the "rival, in short, of General Washington," when he should become sober. He went farther down the Ohio to its confluence with the Mississippi where he fell into the hands of a Captain Pike, presumably the later famous explorer Zebulon Pike. The captain did not know what to make of Collot's papers, all in French, and there was talk of sending the papers back to Philadelphia, but Pike let the Frenchman go, papers and all. It was thereafter a case of down the Mississippi and round to Philadelphia by sea. The general drew up a long report, enthusiastic in favor of French action. In the words of a fellow Frenchman,

The General insists . . . upon this: that France acquire Louisiana and the Floridas by negotiation and take Canada by force, because he believes firmly that this is the only means of holding the United States within pacific bounds, of breaking their exclusive ties with England, of keeping our colonies—supplying them ourselves with the produce of our soil, and finally of recovering in the two hemispheres the preponderance which the nature of things gives to us.

As matured in the mind of Talleyrand, the grand territory of Louisiana would be a large granary to feed the Negro labor in Santo Domingo (this French colony at the beginning of the nineteenth century included the entire island, the present-day states of Haiti and the Dominican Republic). Santo Domingo in turn would raise sugar to export to France, and for this project the foreign minister needed peace with the United States, not hostilities. The uproar in the United States over "XYZ" made him realize he had gone too far.

President Adams on June 21, 1798, had made known his condition of peace: "I will never send another minister to France without assurances that he will be received, respected, and honored, as the representative of a great, free, powerful, and independent nation." Talleyrand therefore dispatched Louis Pichon, a French diplomat with American experience, to The Hague as secretary of legation, to open a contact with the American minister there, William Vans Murray. Encouraged by Murray, Talleyrand at last sent a letter over his own signature to Pichon, for conveyance to President Adams, in which he used almost the identical words of Adams's condition of peace: he would receive American plenipotentiaries "with the respect due to the representatives of a free, independent, and powerful nation."

The receipt of this letter from The Hague placed John Adams in a quandary. The country was unified behind his administration in a desire to stand up to the French, and the Federalists had joined ranks with Adams. If he accepted the proffer of renewal of relations which Talleyrand lefthandedly had extended to him, he would stir the extremists in the Federalist Party to fury, give a new lease on life to the Jeffersonian Republicans, take a chance that Talleyrand upon the arrival of a new American mission in France would refuse anyway to see them and disavow the letter to Pichon. But Adams knew that his country needed peace above all else, for with time the sprawling United States could tie itself together, the bonds of economics and politics would with years bind the parts of the republic, and then—only then—could a statesman safely chance a foreign war. Adams knew also that statesmanship required him to send a new mission to France. In later years he expressed the desire to be remembered by the epitaph: "Here lies John Adams, who took upon himself the responsibility of the peace with France in the year 1800." To his everlasting credit he chose the path of statesmanship and announced to a startled country that he would send a new commission.

The new commissioners were Oliver E. Ellsworth and William R. Davie, together with William Vans Murry. As Ellsworth and Davie prepared to set forth to join Murray in Europe, the war took a turn unfavorable to France—Great Britain in 1799 raised up a second coalition (Russia, Austria, Portugal, Sardinia, Naples, the Ottoman empire). At first the allies seemed to carry everything. Then Napoleon broke up the second coalition by his victory at Marengo on June 14, 1800. The Americans thus were the more happy to make an arrangement abrogating the treaty of alliance of 1778, in return for which the United States abandoned claims for spoliations from France in the European war that had begun in 1793. This Treaty of Mortefontaine, signed September 30, 1800, was also the basis for reopening diplomatic relations between France and the United States.

Even in the making of peace the French used the Americans for their purposes in Europe. Napoleon had just defeated the second coalition and managed to abolish the Directory and place France under his personal control for ten years as first consul in what was called a Consulate form of government. The leader of France wished the neutrals of the Continent to join in another armed neutrality. He wanted to use the Treaty of Mortefontaine to advance this project. In the treaty the French insisted on a full-fledged statement reaffirming the principles of neutral rights as the Americans had understood them in their two treaty plans of 1776 and 1784; the American commissioners had been prepared to acknowledge with France the same interpretation of neutral rights as in Jay's Treaty, but the avowal of such practices did not suit the new French government. To lend dignity to the occasion with the Americans, looking to future membership in an armed neutrality, Napoleon arranged the signing of the treaty as part of a magnificent fete at Mortefontaine, Joseph Bonaparte's country estate. The first consul and his whole family attended the festivities.

The armed neutrality failed. Although in mid-December 1800, Sweden, Denmark, and Prussia signed separate conventions with Russia professing a "disinterested desire to maintain the inalienable rights of neutral nations," the league of armed neutrality broke up in the spring of 1801 because the murder of the Tsar Paul brought young Alexander I to the Russian throne, and he took his country out of the league. Also, in an unprecedented act toward a neutral nation, the British fleet on April 2, 1801, assaulted the Danes at Copenhagen and burned the Danish fleet.

For France the Treaty of Mortefontaine had led to nothing. But the Americans might well have realized, and if they did not understand they soon would, that whereas in September 1800 they had fitted into Napoleon's plans in a manner congenial to themselves—a treaty giving the United States everything it desired—the next turn of the wheel might not be so happy. With Napoleon in control almost anything could occur. The situation for Europe and the United States had become far more dangerous than during the 1790's.

A CONTEMPORARY DOCUMENT

[Pinckney, Marshall, and Gerry, in Paris to negotiate with the government of the Directory, reported their reception in the French capital, in some astonishment, to Secretary Pickering on October 22, 1797. Source: microfilm of the original document in the archives of the department of state. Walter Lowrie and Matthew St. Clair Clarke, eds., *American State*

Papers: Foreign Relations (6 vols., Washington, D.C., 1832–1859), II, 158–160, is the source usually cited for this famous dispatch, but is rather unreliable.]

. . . In the morning of October the eighteenth, Mr. Hubbard, of the House of Van Stophorts and Hubbard of Amsterdam called on general Pinckney and informed him that a Mr. Hottinguer who was in Paris and whom the Genl had seen at Amsterdam was a gentleman of considerable credit and reputation; that he had formerly been a banker . . . . [these dots are in the manuscript] at Paris, and had settled his [?] affairs with honor; that he had then formed connections in America, had married a [?] of that country; intended to settle there; was supported by some capital [?] houses in Holland; and that we might place great reliance on him.

In the evening of the same day, M. Hottinguer called on Genl Pinckney; and after having sat some time in a room full of company, whispered him that he had a message from M. Talleyrand to communicate when he was at leisure. General Pinckney immediately withdrew with him into another room; and when they were alone, M. Hottinguer said that he was charged with a business in which he was a novice; that he had been acquainted with M. Talleyrand in America; and that he was sure that he had a great regard for that country and its citizens; and was very desirous that a reconciliation should be brought about with France: that to effectuate that end, he was ready, if it was thought proper, to suggest a plan, confidentially, that M. Talleyrand expected would answer the purpose. Genl Pinckney said he should be glad to hear it. M. Hottinguer replied, that the Directory, and particularly two of the members of it, were exceedingly irritated at some passages of the President's speech, and desired that they should be softened; and that this step would be necessary previous to our reception: that besides this, a sum of money was required for the pocket of the Directory and ministers, which would be at the disposal of M. Talleyrand: and that a loan would also be insisted on. M. Hottinguer said if we acceded to these measures, M. Talleyrand had no doubt that all our differences with France might be accommodated. On enquiry, M. Hottinguer could not point out the particular passages of the speech that had given offence, nor the quantum of the loan, but mentioned that the douceur for the pocket was twelve hundred thousand livres,—about fifty thousand pounds sterling. Genl Pinckney told him, his colleagues and himself, from the time of their arrival here, had been treated with great slight and disrespect; that they earnestly wished for peace and reconciliation with France; & had been entrusted by their country with very great powers to obtain these ends, on honorable terms; that with regard to the propositions made, he could not even consider of them before he had communicated them to his colleagues; that after he had done so, he should hear from him. After a communication and consultation had, it was agreed that General Pinckney should call on M. Hottinguer, and request him to make his propositions to us all; and, for fear of mistake or misapprehension, that he should be requested to reduce the heads into writing. Accordingly, on the morning of October the nineteenth, General Pinckney called on M. Hottinguer, who consented to see his colleagues in the evening, and to reduce his propositions to writing. He said his communication was not immediately with M. Talleyrand, but thro' another gentleman, in whom M. Talleyrand had great confidence: this proved afterwards to be M. Bellamy, a native of Geneva, of the house of Bellamy Riccia and Company of Hamburg.

. . . Mr. Bellami stated to us explicitly and repeatedly that he was clothed with no authority; that he was not a diplomatic character; that he was not even a Frenchman; he was only the friend of M. Talleyrand, and trusted by him. That with regard to himself he had landed property in America, on which he hoped his children would reside; and that he earnestly wished well to the UStates. He then took out of his pocket a French translation of the President's speech, the parts of which, objected to by the Directory, were marked agreeably to our request to M. Hottinguer, and are contained in the exhibit A. Then he made us the second set of propositions . . . .

But, said he, gentlemen, I will not disguise from you, that this satisfaction, being made, the essential part of the treaty remains to be adjusted: "il faut de l'argent—il faut beaucoup d'argent." You must pay money—you must pay a great deal of money. He spoke much of the force, the honor, and the jealous republican pride of France; and represented to us strongly the advantages which we should derive from the neutrality thus to be purchased. He said that the receipt of the money might be so disguised as to prevent its being considered as a breach of neutrality by England; and thus save us from being embroiled with that power. . . .

He spoke of the respect which the Directory required, and repeated, that it would exact as much as was paid to the antient kings. We answered that America had demonstrated to the world, and especially to France, a much greater respect for her present government than for her former monarchy; and that there was no evidence of this disposition which ought to be required, that we were not ready to give. He said that we should certainly not be received; and seemed to shudder at the consequences. We told him that America had made every possible effort to remain on friendly terms with France; that she was still making them: that if France would not hear us, but would make war on the Ustates; nothing remained for us, but to regret the unavoidable necessity of defending ourselves. . . .

ADDITIONAL READING

For background on the relations of France and the United States in the latter 1790's see Edward Channing, *Federalists and Republicans, 1789–1815* (New York, 1917); Arthur Burr Darling, *Our Rising Empire* (New Haven, 1940); the two-volume study by Alexander De Conde, *Entangling Alliance* (Durham, N.C., 1958) and its sequel,* *The Quasi-War: The Politics and Diplomacy of the Undeclared War with France, 1798–1801* (New York, 1966). The attachment—or lack of it—of Americans for France appears in *Durand Echeverria, *Mirage in the West* (Princeton, 1957). Charles S. Hyneman examines *The First American Neutrality* (Urbana, Ill., 1934). Felix Gilbert looks to the origins of the American policy of isolation from the "ordinary" combinations and collisions of the European powers in *To the Farewell Address: Ideas of Early American Foreign Policy* (Princeton, 1961). Marshall Smelser notes a prime factor in American actions during the quasi war, *The Congress Founds the Navy: 1787–1798* (Notre Dame, Ind., 1959). For politics of this hectic time see *Manning J. Dauer, *The Adams Federalists* (Baltimore, 1953) and *Stephen G. Kurtz, *The Presidency of John Adams* (Philadelphia, 1957). Arthur A. Richmond has set out the complexities of "Napoleon and the Armed Neutrality of 1800: A Diplomatic Challenge to British Sea Power," *Journal of the Royal United Service Institution*, CIV (1959), 186–194.

Biographies include Albert J. Beveridge, *Life of John Marshall* (4 vols., Boston, 1916–1919), published during the senator's political retirement; Samuel Flagg Bemis, *John Quincy Adams and the Foundations of American Foreign Policy* (New York, 1949); Frederick B. Tolles, *George Logan of Philadelphia* (New York, 1953), on the wayward Quaker; Marvin R. Zahniser, *Charles Cotesworth Pinckney: Founding Father* (Chapel Hill, N.C., 1967); John A. Carroll and Mary Wells Ashworth, *George Washington: First in Peace* (New York, 1957); Page Smith, *John Adams* (2 vols., New York, 1962).

The Louisiana Purchase

There is on the globe one single spot, the possessor of which is our natural and habitual enemy. It is New Orleans, through which the produce of three-eighths of our territory must pass to market. and from its fertility it will ere long yield more than half of our whole produce, and contain more than half of our inhabitants.

—President Thomas Jefferson to Robert R. Livingston, 1802

Little more than two and one-half years elapsed between the signature of the Treaty of Mortefontaine on the last day of September 1800 and signature in early May 1803 (antedated to April 30) of three accords which together brought Louisiana into the national domain of the United States. A superficial student of history, observing the fête at Mortefontaine in celebration of the one treaty, might well have concluded that little but affection and co-operation had followed between one act and the second—that the *rapprochement* so much in evidence at the country house of Joseph Bonaparte had led to a further act of remorse by France in memory of the XYZ affair and other (if lesser) affronts. In actual fact, of course, the conclusion of the Treaty of Mortefontaine was followed one day later by signature in Spain of the secret Treaty of San Ildefonso between Spain and France providing for retrocession of Louisiana. Any friendship increased by the Franco-American treaty would be easily offset by news of this new one, once the Americans understood what their French friends had done. American relations with France thus began to plummet almost as soon as they had improved, and in all probability— who, to be sure, can know what might have happened in history?—they would have worsened into eventual war in the New World over Louisiana, had not the troubles of Europe forced or impelled Napoleon, now first consul of France, to sell Louisiana to the republic of the New World.

1. *The retrocession*

In the new equation of power and politics which opened with the end of the quasi war and beginning of the retrocession of Louisiana, the attitude of the new American president, Thomas Jefferson, would prove of great interest to the French, and indeed to Jefferson's own countrymen, many of whom believed that Jefferson was pro-French. It is quite possible that the Napoleonic scheme for taking back Louisiana might never have gotten under way if Napoleon had understood that Jefferson as president was no partisan of Napoleon's, whatever Jefferson's regard for Frenchmen. If Napoleon had measured Jefferson more correctly, had sensed the antagonism that existed behind the American philosopher's studied calm and measured official language of friendship and esteem, perhaps Louisiana would have remained Spanish until—cannot the student of history guess at least this much?—the American settlers in the 1820's and 1830's overwhelmed Spanish Louisiana on their way to Spanish Texas and California.

Instead Napoleon seems to have assumed that Jefferson, the erstwhile friend of France, was willing to abide and even support a new French empire in the New World.

Unfortunately for Napoleon and France, Jefferson had changed his mind about France from the doctrinaire liking and esteem he once had felt and protested on so many occasions. He had never liked the excesses of the revolution and indeed deplored them. The reaction of the Directory had bothered him, even though part of that reaction, the XYZ affair, had played into his hands when his Federalist opponents ill-advisedly established legislation such as the Alien and Sedition Acts, which pointed out to Jefferson's partisans how far the Federalists would go to preserve themselves in power. Jefferson seems to have changed his mind about France completely when, on November 9, 1799, the Directory gave way to the Consulate and after a short time to the dictatorship under Napoleon. The oligarchy of the Directory was almost as far removed from the principles of the French revolution as was the Consulate, but the person of the first consul was more obvious in his flaunting of the ideas of liberty, fraternity, and equality. Jefferson could not abide Napoleon.

The next chapter will show in some detail how the Federalists at the time of the embargo of 1807–1809, and later, claimed that Jefferson and the Jeffersonians were pro-French, the "lackeys" of Napoleon. Nothing could have been farther than the truth, though Jefferson as president could hardly announce his position in this regard.

The truth was that Jefferson as president sometimes seemed to side with the French, not because he admired the government of Napoleon, but because he feared the British and needed a counterforce. The key to his policy, as a recent historian, Lawrence S. Kaplan, has pointed out, was his distrust of the British. He believed that the government in London held little but malevolence for the United States and that, whenever the politics of Europe had settled down enough for the British navy to have a free hand in the New World, that hand would work to American disadvantage, probably bringing war, an extension of British possessions in Canada through conquest of French and Spanish colonies, and a reduction of American influence virtually to that of a colony. In 1802 during the negotiation over New Orleans or whatever (Jefferson at that time did not know) Spain had ceded to France, the American president occasionally tried to butter up the British chargé d'affaires, Edward Thornton. The effort was obvious even when Jefferson tried to exert his charm. Thornton wrote back to his superior in London, Lord Hawkesbury, that Jefferson seemed to tax his imagination "to supply the deficiency of his feeling." The president sometimes talked about concerting policy with the British government against the French, if need be. In a letter of 1802 he said that if France possessed New Orleans the United States would have to "marry the British fleet and nation." In March 1803 he instructed his two envoys to Napoleon, James Monroe and Robert R. Livingston, that if they were unable to buy New Orleans they should repair at once to London and conclude an alliance. He was talking, more than thinking, of action. His whole inclination stood against such a course.

Again, if Jefferson sometimes moved toward France during the era of Napoleon, he did so to set up a counter to the British. If he could have chosen his course, he would have consorted with neither French nor British and moved the United States out of the European balance of power, to isolation in the world across the Atlantic. He wrote as much to confidants in the first months of his presidency ("we shall haul off from European politics," he advised Stephen Sayre, February 16, 1801) and was to rejoice in the final triumph of this policy in the Monroe Doctrine.

As president beginning in March 1801, Jefferson could not remove his country from the balance of power on the Continent, even if he wished, for he hardly had taken office when the rumors of retrocession of Louisiana began to filter back from Europe. It soon became clear that he would have to do something about Louisiana, or at the least about New Orleans, and perhaps the Floridas if they too were passing to France.

The rumors of retrocession were believable because of the years of French intrigue over Louisiana. During the time of the monarchy the French minister in the United States in 1787–1789, Éléanore François Élie

Moustier, had sent a 330-page memoir to the foreign office outlining the importance of Louisiana to France. A few years later Citizen Genêt had sought to get a legion of American frontiersmen to go down the river from the American back country and seize New Orleans from Spain, which in Genêt's time was France's enemy. Citizen Adet in 1796 had sent Collot and an associate or two to explore the western country and report. And when Talleyrand became minister of foreign relations in July 1797, he already had in mind a colonial policy, perhaps because his wife had come from the East Indies, perhaps because during his exile in the United States he had seen the possibilities there. Talleyrand may also have been seeking a way to turn French interests from the traditional British antagonism, for despite the fact that the British government had expelled him to America, he harbored good feelings for the life in London; it is fair to say that Talleyrand always was essentially pro-British, despite his serving Napoleon's anti-British policies for many years. In any event, after Talleyrand came into the foreign office the French government began urging upon Spain the importance of a barrier territory to the Americans. The French also liked to point out that if the Spanish retroceded Louisiana there would be no loss of Spanish prestige, as would be entailed in an outright cession.

Talleyrand, as mentioned, appears to have dreamed of empire in the New World, a second New France, and after the war with England had ended with a truce in 1801 preceding the Treaty of Amiens of 1802, he was able for a short time to put this dream into operation. The initial step was to get back Louisiana; this work was well in course by the time the war ended with England. It might then be possible to separate the trans-Appalachian Americans from their east coast brethren—Talleyrand knew firsthand of the feeling between westerners and easterners. If he could bring trans-Appalachia into his New France, his country would control both banks of the Mississippi, Louisiana regaining its old boundaries from before the general European peace of 1763 when the English had managed to extend the boundaries of their North American colonies to the Mississippi River. Along with all this planning went the reconquest of Santo Domingo from the Negro chieftain Toussaint L'Ouverture who had taken over the island. In the revived French empire, Santo Domingo would raise sugar for export to Europe, and the Negroes there would live on flour and salted meat from Louisiana. Perhaps in a future war, or somehow through peace, all the domains of Spain and Britain would pass to France.

The scheming of the foreign minister, which required several years to mature after Talleyrand came to power in 1797, was interrupted by talk of Louisiana in the United States during the XYZ affair, when the Federalists had in mind a co-operation with the British navy and an attack on Louisiana—the British by sea, the Americans by land. During the American conflict with the Directory over the bribes asked by Talleyrand, the Spanish as allies of the French had ensured that their territory would be fair game.

Louisiana and the Floridas thus had been much talked about before news of the retrocession filtered back to President Jefferson in 1801–1802, and a forthright American diplomacy began to get some, if not all, of the territory ceded from Spain to France.

And the talk was becoming ever more important to American frontiersmen, who found the right of deposit at New Orleans essential to the value of their lands. Without the deposit it was impossible to send goods down the Mississippi for export. If the trans-Appalachian lands could produce nothing, they had no value.

The American frontier was beginning to encroach on the Spanish domains in the Floridas and in Louisiana well before the active diplomacy began in 1801 and resulted in the purchase of 1803. The American government in 1790 conducted its first census, and the result was startling, the more so if compared to the census returns of ten years later in 1800. The French chargé d'affaires in 1801, Louis Pichon (who had dealt with William Vans Murray at The Hague), wrote to Talleyrand on November 15 in regard to the new census:

All these developments, citizen minister, surpass imagination . . . and these wildernesses, hardly known thirty years ago, are already so peopled, sensing already so much their importance as to attract the attention of their neighbors and of the general Government. These considerations, citizen minister, are worthy of our attention.

By 1790 more than a hundred thousand Americans had passed over the mountains. They had scattered over a great area, and admittedly the estimated non-Indian population of the Northwest Territory in 1790 was only 3,000. But the census of 1800 revealed a population in Ohio alone of 45,365. In Georgia, still a frontier state, the populace had increased from 82,548 in 1790 to 161,414 in 1800. Kentucky rose from 73,677 to 220,955, Tennessee from 35,691 to 105,602. All this population growth was especially impressive if compared to the estimated population of West Florida and Louisiana under Spanish rule in 1800, which was 45,000. East Florida —present-day Florida—contained only 4,445 individuals in the year 1804, when the Americans already were in Louisiana.

The settlers were greatly increasing their use of the western waterways. New Orleans was becoming ever more important. Exportation of cotton increased from 243,000 pounds in 1799 to 20,000 bales—or 9,600,-000 pounds—in 1802. Trade on the river in 1803 was represented by 158 American vessels carrying 21,383 tons, as compared to 104 Spanish vessels carrying 9,573 tons, and three French schooners carrying 105 tons. Total value of exports that year was $2,158,000.

This was the scene, or imminent scene, when rumors of the retrocession began coming back to Washington. The American minister in London, the Federalist Rufus King—whom Jefferson had left in London to offset any feeling of the government there that the new administration would be pro-French—reported in a letter to Secretary Madison dated March 29, 1801, that Tuscany had been ceded from the French to the Spaniards, and that rumor had it that the *quid pro quo* was Louisiana and the Floridas. King's dispatch arrived in Washington on May 29, and in acknowledging the dispatch Madison mentioned similar reports arriving from other quarters. Alexander Hamilton sent word to the administration which he had received privately. The rumors continued, and eventually in November 1801 the British ministry gave King a copy of the treaty signed by Lucien Bonaparte and Godoy, according to which Louis, the young son-in-law of the king and queen of Spain, and titular prince of Parma, was to receive Tuscany as a sovereign kingdom, to be known as the kingdom of Etruria, with Florence as the capital. The Franco-Spanish treaty was dated March 21, 1801, and it arrived in Washington on February 18, 1802. The secret treaty of San Ildefonso, incidentally, does not seem to have circulated, and the United States government did not learn much about it until the time of the Louisiana treaty, when the French used the exact words of San Ildefonso to describe the bounds of the territory passing to the United States.

It is interesting that the British government was the agency through which definite word of the retrocession reached Jefferson. Rufus King was a loyal minister under the Republican administration, but as a Federalist he had an easy entree into official circles in London. And anyway, it was to British advantage to stir trouble between the United States and France. Moreover, the British were not enthusiastic about a replacing of Spain by France not merely in Louisiana but presumably in the Floridas, the latter location giving the French the ports of Mobile and Pensacola, which were altogether too close to British Caribbean possessions. Perhaps the ministry, passing the treaty of 1801 to King, thought he might renew the proposed co-operation of 1798, another Anglo-American plan for a descent upon Louisiana. In a discussion with the foreign secretary, Hawkesbury, Minister King said something, however, which must not have been altogether to Hawkesbury's liking. With care the American minister first quoted the remark of Montesquieu to the effect that God had permitted Turks and Spaniards to be in the world, to possess great empires with insignificance. He added that his government was unwilling to see the Floridas pass into possession of any nation except the United States.

Further support from the British government, however, proved impossible. The British were about to conclude the peace of Amiens with France and were not willing to allow Louisiana or the Floridas to jeopardize it. Minister Livingston in Paris wrote to King on March 10, 1802, "If any opening is given for pressing the business of Louisiana, I will meet you at Amiens at any time you will appoint to forward it." The treaty was signed on March 25, 1802, with no reference to Louisiana.

2. *Jeffersonian diplomacy*

Rufus King's letter of November 20, 1801, confirming the retrocession of Louisiana by enclosing the text of the Franco-Spanish treaty of 1801, arrived in Washington on February 18, 1802. Exactly two months later—perhaps speed did not seem necessary to Jefferson in the New World—the president indited the famous letter of April 18 to Minister Livingston in Paris, the letter he arranged for Pierre Samuel Du Pont de Nemours to carry to France, and which Jefferson left unsealed for Du Pont to read. In his best literary manner Jefferson sketched for Livingston (and Du Pont) what might happen if France possessed Louisiana. The retrocession of Louisiana to France, Jefferson wrote, "completely reverses all the political relations of the United States, and will form a new epoch in our political course." And then the famous comment: "There is on the globe one single spot, the possessor of which is our natural and habitual enemy. It is New Orleans, through which the produce of three-eighths of our territory must pass to market, and from its fertility it will ere long yield more than half of our whole produce, and contain more than half of our inhabitants." He followed this with the threat:

The day that France takes possession of New Orleans, fixes the sentence which is to restrain her forever within her low-water mark. It seals the union of two nations, who, in conjunction, can maintain exclusive possession of the ocean. From that moment, we must marry ourselves to the British fleet and nation. We must turn all our attention to a maritime force, for which our resources place us on very high ground; and having formed and connected together a power which may render reinforcement of her settlements here impossible to

France, make the first cannon which shall be fired in Europe the signal for the tearing up any settlement she may have made, and for holding the two continents of America in sequestration for the common purposes of the United British and American nations.

To Du Pont, Jefferson in a covering letter of April 25 then confided his desire for peace and his wish that the Franco-American, his friend of nearly twenty years, would impress the president's sentiments upon the French people and government:

I am thus open with you, because I trust that you will have it in your power to impress on that government considerations, in the scale against which the possession of Louisiana is nothing. In Europe, nothing but Europe is seen, or supposed to have any right in the affairs of nations; but this little event, of France's possessing herself of Louisiana, which is thrown in as nothing, as a mere makeweight in the general settlement of accounts,—this speck which now appears as an almost invisible point in the horizon, is the embryo of a tornado which will burst on the countries on both sides of the Atlantic, and involve in its effects their highest destinies. That it may yet be avoided is my sincere prayer; and if you can be the means of informing the wisdom of Bonaparte of all its consequences, you have deserved well of both countries. Peace and abstinence from European interferences are our objects, and so will continue while the present order of things in America remain uninterrupted.

It was shortly after writing Du Pont that the president allowed Secretary Madison, May 1, 1802, to instruct Livingston to ascertain the price for New Orleans and the Floridas. Jefferson, as mentioned, never considered seriously an alliance with Britain, though he was willing to threaten it in marvelous rhetoric that would resound through decades of American history down to the present day. Economics, peaceful persuasion: these, not war, were his weapons, and seldom (one can hardly name a similar occasion) even the literary threat of war. His mind turned easily to purchase.

Minister Livingston had arrived in France in December 1801 and, by the time President Jefferson had roused himself to the French threat to Louisiana, had been parleying with Talleyrand and Bonaparte for many months. He would so continue right down to the fateful Monday, April 11, 1803, when Talleyrand suddenly asked whether Livingston would like to purchase all of Louisiana. Livingston was a very able man. His enemies complained that he was slightly deaf by 1801–1803, and also possessed of aristocratic manners. But he had enjoyed a long career in the high affairs of American government. A quarter century before, he had taken a prominent part in the constitutional convention of the state of New York. He had been the first secretary for foreign affairs under the Confederation, from 1781 to 1783, when John Jay replaced him. He had been chancellor of New York from 1777 until 1801, when he went as minister to France. With this background he had undertaken his labors with the Consulate under Napoleon, and as soon as the rumors began that Louisiana had been retroceded, he commenced negotiation to find out whether the rumors were true and, if so, whether the retrocession had included the Floridas. On February 20, 1802, he had asked Talleyrand pointblank if East and West Florida, or either of them, were included in the cession by Spain to France. Talleyrand only equivocated, then and later, and the following written comment of March 13 was typical: "Do you doubt, sir, that the questions which concern the United States, the determination of which may affect their relations with France, will be examined with equal interest and attention?"

Livingston sought constantly to tell the French how worthless Louisiana was without the Floridas, and that Great Britain would not allow France to have the Floridas. New Orleans was nothing, he said, and likewise the upcountry: "a desert & an insignificant town." It was all a "distant wilderness" which could "neither add to her [France's] wealth nor to her strength." A longish memoir of August 10, 1802, entitled *Whether It Will Be Advantageous to France To Take Possession of Louisiana*, he reproduced in some twenty copies which through Joseph Bonaparte's good offices went to leading members of the government. Livingston flattered himself that the first consul read these memorials. Probably Napoleon did not, though he may have heard something of them from his brother Joseph. One cannot help wondering whether the strange places mentioned by Livingston, the odd-sounding towns and rivers, intrigued or impressed him with the far-off nature of this territory so much admired by the distant Americans. When the time came to be rid of the territory, the first consul easily could consign it all to the United States in exchange for gold.

In the course of his arguments about New Orleans and the Floridas, Livingston elaborated two points, one of which may have had some importance and the other of which undoubtedly did. He conceded that Louisiana was not a necessary territory for the United States, so long as the Americans possessed New Orleans and West Florida, but did suggest that it might be a wise move for the French to give the Americans the area north of the Arkansas, to form a buffer between the rest of French Louisiana, to the south, and British Canada. Livingston himself believed that the Floridas were more valuable than Louisiana and willingly would have traded the one for the other when he was about to receive Louisiana. His mention of upper Louisiana, the land above the mouth of the Arkansas, probably persuaded the French government that the Americans would take all Louisiana if opportunity presented. Livingston's other argument concerned the claims of his countrymen against France. According to the Treaty of Mortefontaine, France promised to conclude a separate agreement to settle the claims of American shippers for losses sustained during the maritime war—primarily the restitution of captured American vessels and payment for supplies. Livingston's estimate of the claims (much too low, it turned out) was 20,000,000 francs ($3,750,000). His harping on these claims finally convinced Napoleon's subordinates that the claims should be included somehow in the total price for Louisiana, as otherwise it would not be possible to allay American ill feeling toward France and thereby obtain American good will, as well as money from the selling of French real estate. At one point in the long discussion, Livingston bumptiously suggested to Talleyrand that the French exchange New Orleans and the Floridas for a settlement of the claims, with no extra money to France. Talleyrand quickly replied that "It is entirely opposed to the maxims of government adopted by the Republic to mingle important and delicate political relations with calculations of account and mere pecuniary interest." Livingston nonetheless had raised the claims issue, which entered the final settlement.

While the American minister was producing essays and arguments an event took place in the New World which lent urgency to a settlement with France: on October 16, 1802, the Spanish fiscal officer, or intendant, at New Orleans, Juan Ventura Moralès, closed the port to deposits of American goods in transit down the river. This was an outright violation of Pinckney's Treaty of 1795, which stipulated that the Spanish king would grant a place of deposit at New Orleans for three years and thereafter continue the privilege at New Orleans or provide an equivalent establishment elsewhere. Moralès averred that he had revoked the right of deposit on his own, but in fact the Spanish government in Madrid had put him up to it. Many years later a royal order of July 14, 1802, came to light in the Spanish archives, directing the intendant to put an end to the introduction and deposit of American merchandise at New Orleans. The order instructed Moralès not to justify himself by referring to the royal command, but to allege that after consulting the treaty of 1795, Pinckney's Treaty, he found that the limit of three years fixed by that convention forced him not to allow any more use of the deposit without express permission of the king. Just why the Spanish government so instructed Moralès, at a time when the retrocession was in process, is difficult to say. It is entirely possible that the French government had directed the Spanish to divest themselves of the deposit servitude, so that the territory might change hands without it. This was the instant interpretation which Americans placed upon the closure. No proof, however, has ever appeared as to French dictation to Spain in this regard. There is a wealth of circumstantial evidence to the contrary, leading to the conclusion that the closing of the port to American commerce was a purely Spanish measure. It seems to have been only a near coincidence of dates that Moralès closed the port on October 16, one day after the king of Spain gave the royal order for delivery of Louisiana to France. In the summer of 1802, the Spanish had pressed the French to give a guarantee that Louisiana would not be alienated and had refused to turn over the province until they obtained this guarantee, despite the Treaty of San Ildefonso of 1800 and the Godoy–Bonaparte Treaty of March 1801. The king of Spain dated his order to Moralès July 14. The French gave the requisite pledge, through their ambassador in Madrid, Gouvion St. Cyr, only on July 22. Whatever the inspiration, one must add, the French did quickly see their advantage. Talleyrand thanked the Spanish authorities for closing the Mississippi. The foreign minister wrote in explanation to General Charles Bernadotte, at that time designated as minister to the United States, "The difficulty of maintaining it [the closing of the Mississippi] will be less for us than would have been establishing it."

President Jefferson now had a crisis on his hands of far greater importance than merely receiving a copy of a treaty and writing, in response, a sharp and slyly open letter to Minister Livingston. When word of Moralès's action reached settlements in the American west, there was a near explosion of sentiment. Western congressmen learned what their position on this matter would have to be. It was clear that the Republican Party would have trouble if it did not do something. The Federalists were stirring, and a Federalist senator from Pennsylvania in February 1803 offered a resolution for an appropriation of $5,000,000 and a call-up of 50,000 militia to seize New Orleans and expel Spanish, French, all foreigners, leaving only Americans.

The result was appointment of James Monroe on special mission to the capitals of France and Spain. Jefferson must have taken a leaf from the diplomatic handbook of President Washington, for when the problems with Britain had risen to large proportions in 1794, the Federalist president had sent John Jay on special mission, during the course of which the political opposition had to remain quiet until Jay returned with his detested treaty. In those bygone days Jefferson had been hot in opposition. He might have argued in 1803 that the case was not the same. Perhaps not; but Monroe was his solution to the western clamor.

3. *Purchase*

Monroe was a promising choice for the special mission to France in 1803. He was an individual who would give heed to the wishes of Jefferson and Madison. There surely was no chance that Monroe would become independent and act contrary to their instructions. For years he had been a protégé, an *élève*, of Jefferson, and one of a small group of Virginia politicians whom Jefferson consulted on arcane political matters. In the mid-1790's he had gotten into trouble for what seemed to Secretary of State Pickering and even to other less biased observers a too-friendly attitude toward revolutionary France, and President Washington had recalled him. Although the personalities in France of that time were out of favor with Napoleon by 1803, the friendship for Frenchmen which Monroe once had evinced, together with his closeness to Jefferson, made him a likely envoy.

It is interesting to point out, as a sort of footnote, the trenchant observation about Monroe that appears in the fourth volume of Edward Channing's great work on the history of the United States. Just why Monroe displeased Channing is difficult to say, and it may be that the Harvard historian was seeking to shock his readers. But Channing's comment on Monroe's mission is worth quoting *in extenso*:

James Monroe was one of those men of persistent mediocrity from whom useful and attractive Presidents have been made. For years he had been in intimate relations with Jefferson and Madison . . . . Up to this time, Jefferson had had great confidence in Monroe's judgment. At the moment this was somewhat shaken. Monroe possessed a facility for poking into the personal affairs of great men. Having exploited the Hamilton–Reynolds scandal, he now had on his mind the connection between Mr. Jefferson and a certain Mrs. Walker. It may be that the time seemed rather opportune to get him out of the country. Certainly, neither his past history as a diplomatist nor his potential capacity for settling difficult problems could have marked him out as the best candidate for the extremely critical situation.

Whatever the reasoning for getting Monroe out of the country, Jefferson applied some fine words to his friend from Virginia in asking him to leave for France. "But some men," the president wrote, "are born for the public. Nature by fitting them for the service of the human race on a broad scale, has stamped with the evidences of her destination and their duty." He offered, and Monroe accepted, the princely salary, for those days, of $9,000 a year plus expenses.

Madison instructed Monroe, and through him, Minister Livingston as to what they might hope to obtain from the French. The instruction of March 2, 1803, made an interesting calculation of the worth to the secretary and president of the territories in question. Madison said they should estimate that the Floridas, together, were worth one-fourth of the value of New Orleans; and East Florida was worth one half of West Florida. Monroe took with him a draft for $2,000,000, but he might go higher. The president, Madison wrote, "has made up his mind to go as far as fifty millions of *livres tournois* [or francs—about $9,150,000], rather than to lose the main object." His price turned out to be slightly less than what Monroe and Livingston paid for the entire Louisiana territory. Neither the president nor the secretary envisioned anything more than New Orleans and perhaps the Floridas. Madison authorized the two envoys to guarantee, if necessary, the rest of the territory to the French. As a last resort they should content themselves with improving the right of deposit at New Orleans:

Should it be impossible to procure a complete jurisdiction over any convenient spot whatever, it will only remain to explain and improve the present right of deposit, by adding thereto the express privilege of holding real estate for commercial purposes, of providing hospitals, of having consuls residing there, and other agents who may be authorized to authenticate and deliver all documents requisite for vessels belonging to, and engaged in, the trade of the United States, to and from the place of deposit.

In the debates and conjectures of historians over the Louisiana Purchase, much observation has been made of the shortsightedness of Jefferson and Madison when instructing Monroe and Livingston—of how the two leading officials of the American government, certain that something might be arranged in a purchase with the French government, could have had no idea that they could get all of Louisiana, nor realized that the Floridas, so much talked about, would come to the United States easily in a treaty with Spain concluded in 1819 by John Quincy Adams. Jefferson's visage, which the twentieth-century sculptor Gutzon Borglum carved on a mountain in the American West presumably to depict the man who had arranged the purchase of Louisiana, should be erased, some people have argued, for Jefferson conceived of nothing of the sort and, instead, the chapter of accidents arranged the purchase. Should not the chapter of accidents be carved on Mount Rushmore? Perhaps the whole debate as to whether or not Thomas Jefferson, not to mention James Madison, deserved credit is unnecessary, for Jefferson never took any credit but admitted that the turn of events gave the United States the grand territory. The American president of 1803 at least had begun a negotiation with France, and if that negotiation had gone much farther than he had anticipated, it was not something for which he deserved blame, but at the least some credit, and maybe even his visage on a western mountain.

The instructions were modest, although in the wisdom of the time fairly expansive, and Monroe left for Paris on March 8. Jefferson and Madison could do little other than to await events.

The exact reasoning behind Napoleon's willingness to sell Louisiana to the United States may never be known, for the first consul did not write down his intimate thoughts at the time, and what record we have of his conversation is largely from the account of his then minister of the treasury, François Barbé-Marbois, published in 1829, many years after the events it describes. Marbois's memory of Napoleonic conversation appears unduly precise, given the fact that the treasury minister seems to have made few contemporary notes and surely was not taking a shorthand account or a tape recording. His narrative contains several comments which show wisdom after the fact and lead the reader to suspect that the author read events of the tumultuous quarter-century after 1803 into his book of 1829. Almost all one can do, then, is to reconstruct the political situation in France early in 1803, in January–April of that year, and seek to understand Napoleon's problems to presume from them why he acted the way he did.

His first and immediate problem as the new year dawned was the failure of his effort to subdue the rebellious Negroes in Santo Domingo. This Caribbean island of sugar and of coffee, indigo, and cotton seemed an immense prize. During the *ancien régime* the French had possessed only the western end of the island, present-day Haiti, but two-thirds of all France's foreign commerce had been with that part of the island. Before the French revolution, some 50,000 Frenchmen lived a life of luxury there, from the proceeds of the labor of half a million slaves. France had secured all of the island by treaty with Spain in 1795 and, as mentioned, Talleyrand—with the active support, even leadership, of Napoleon at least until January 1803—had planned to construct from Santo Domingo a new New France, together with Louisiana and the Caribbean remnants of the old French empire: Martinique, Guadeloupe, the lesser Indies. General Charles Leclerc, Napoleon's brother-in-law, had arrived in Santo Domingo early in 1802, with nearly 20,000 troops, and had taken Toussaint in a *ruse de guerre* and sent the Negro leader back to France where he died in prison early in 1803. But yellow fever consumed Leclerc and most of his troops. He was succeeded by General Donatien Rochambeau, a son of the count of that name who had commanded the

French troops at Yorktown twenty years before, and soon Rochambeau was in deep trouble, writing Napoleon that he would need 35,000 men on the island. The French government was uncertain of Rochambeau's abilities and feared that these troops too would be wasted, more quickly perhaps than their predecessors. Rochambeau was waging a savage guerrilla war against the Negroes, hanging, shooting, drowning, burning all he could catch. He hunted them down with fifteen hundred bloodhounds bought in Jamaica for more than a hundred dollars each. It was an impossible situation, and when news of Leclerc's death and the destruction of most of his troops reached Paris and was printed in the *Moniteur* of January 7, 1803, Napoleon must have shuddered.

Meanwhile the first consul had instructed his minister of the navy and colonies to prepare an expedition to occupy Louisiana. A contingent of perhaps 3,000 troops under command of General Claude Victor was making ready at the Dutch port of Helvoët Sluys, a small port southwest of Rotterdam. Napoleon's instructions to Victor were dated November 26, 1802, but for the remainder of the year his force failed to get out of harbor, as supplies had to come from Dunkirk and it also was necessary to prepare the transports. These delays proved fatal for the French occupation of Louisiana, providential for the United States. During part of January and all of February, Victor's troops were icebound.

Would Napoleon continue the war in Santo Domingo and send the expedition to Louisiana? To all appearances the plan of the dictator of France was to carry forward the island war as well as the proposed occupation. Part of Victor's troops were to disembark at Santo Domingo. He would send General Bernadotte to Washington as minister, to replace Chargé Pichon and, presumably, explain carefully to the Americans the pacific meaning of France's return to the North American continent. He had appointed a prefect, Pierre-Clément Laussat, to take over Louisiana. Early in January 1803, Napoleon instructed Victor, Bernadotte, and Laussat to leave as soon as they could.

Just how important the failure in Santo Domingo was for Napoleon's decision to sell is hard to say. George Dangerfield, in a recent book on Livingston, has pointed out that the failure made war in Europe inevitable: Bonaparte needed a new arena in which to recoup his losses. Such is Dangerfield's thesis. Marbois, in his memoir of 1829, said he felt that the death of Leclerc did not check or alter Napoleon's purposes. It may be, though, that there is not such opposition in these two interpretations as might appear, for if Napoleon had decided to resume war in Europe for other and sufficient reasons, he might then also have sought to bury his Caribbean defeat by selling Louisiana to the United States at the same time he resumed the European war.

Surely affairs in Europe were turning into crisis when the word came of the death of Leclerc. Livingston in Paris had observed in September 1802 that Britain was "very sour" about the peace of Amiens, and he was right, for the British had discovered that peace with Napoleon was a mistake. Napoleon chose to keep troops in the Netherlands and elsewhere, though he claimed that the troops in the Batavian Republic, as he called the Netherlands, were for dispatch to the New World. Some of them were. The British considered all of them a possible invasion force for the home islands. Indeed, the admiralty stationed warships off the Dutch coast. By holding troops in the Netherlands, Napoleon, incidentally, was not violating Amiens but his treaty with Austria, Lunéville. The British meanwhile chose to retain the island of Malta rather than give it back to France as Amiens stipulated. Technically the British were in violation of the peace of Amiens, rather than Napoleon. But the first consul's purposes seemed clear to the government in London and it kept its forces in Malta and its squadron blockading Victor's force at Helvoët Sluys. The British offered to trade Malta for an evacuation of the Netherlands. Napoleon refused.

A speech from the throne by George III in Parliament on March 1, 1803, referred to the suspicious nature of armaments in French and Dutch ports. One day after its content was communicated to the French government, a reply from Napoleon stated that the expedition preparing in the Dutch ports was destined for America, as everyone knew, but because of the message it had been recalled and would not proceed. Lord Hawkesbury apparently interpreted this reply as friendly. It was anything but that.

On March 12, 1803, during a reception in Madame Bonaparte's drawing room, Napoleon for his own good reasons cut the knot of European politics. In a famous scene he went up to the British ambassador and said (as reported by the astonished Livingston, to whom—because of his deafness —the ambassador immediately afterward repeated the conversation):

"I find, my lord, your nation wants war again."

"No sir," answered Lord Whitworth, "we are very desirous of peace."

"You have just finished a war of fifteen years," snapped Napoleon.

"It is true, sir, and that war was fifteen years too long."

"But you want another war of fifteen years."

"Pardon me, sir, we are very desirous of peace."

"*I must either have Malta or war.*"

"I am not prepared, sir, to speak on that subject, and I can only assure you, Citizen First Consul, that we wish for peace."

Within a few days the alarm spread through Europe.

Easter Sunday, April 10, 1803, appears to have been the day of decision in regard to Louisiana. Napoleon, after attending Mass, called together

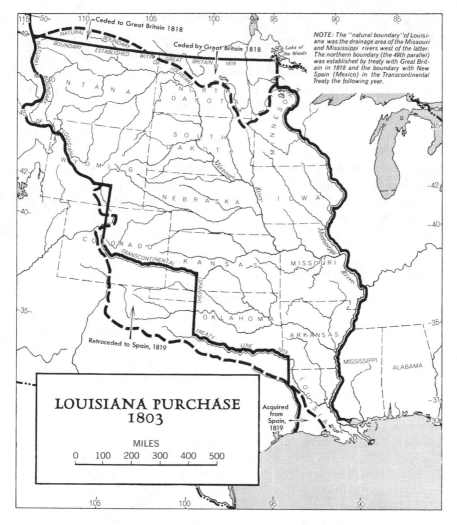

NOTE: The "natural boundary" of Louisiana was the drainage area of the Missouri and Mississippi rivers west of the latter. The northern boundary (the 49th parallel) was established by treaty with Great Britain in 1818 and the boundary with New Spain (Mexico) in the Transcontinental Treaty the following year.

Ceded to Great Britain 1818

Ceded by Great Britain 1818

Lake of the Woods

Retroceded to Spain, 1819

Acquired from Spain, 1819

LOUISIANA PURCHASE
1803

MILES
0   100   200   300   400   500

two of his ministers and (according to one of them, Marbois) explained his views about the New World territory. "I think," he began, "of ceding it to the United States. I can scarcely say that I cede it to them, for it is not yet in our possession. If, however, I leave the least time to our enemies, I shall only transmit an empty title to those republicans whose friendship I seek. . . . it appears to me that in the hands of this growing Power it will be more useful to the policy, and even to the commerce, of France than if I should attempt to keep it."

The next day Talleyrand, always the imperturbable negotiator even when making a complete *volte-face*, suddenly said in talk with Livingston about Louisiana: "What will you give for the whole?" The American minister was so startled as to be almost speechless.

Recovering poise, Livingston began the final negotiations for all of Louisiana, and had virtually made the arrangements by the time Monroe arrived on Wednesday. Some days passed in last-minute haggling over the price, Livingston attempting to beat down the French but with no success. He ran some chance of losing everything in this haggle for a few million dollars, but luck was with him. The treaty of cession was dated April 30, 1803, and the price was 60,000,000 francs, $11,250,000. The United States by a separate claims convention assumed the debts due from France to American citizens estimated at 20,000,000 francs, or $3,750,000, making $15,000,000 as the total price for Louisiana. On May 15, little more than two weeks after the Louisiana treaty, Great Britain declared war on France.

4. Jeffersonian scruples

When Livingston signed the treaty of cession on May 2, 1803, he was thoroughly aware of the importance of what he was doing. He rose and shook hands with Monroe and Marbois and made a statement for history. "We have lived long," he said, "but this is the noblest work of our lives." It was a statement of truth. On an occasion when people resort to banalities, Livingston had put the American achievement in truest terms.

The Federalists were not happy about giving credit to anyone for what they considered not merely an unconstitutional act but an enormous blow to their party fortunes. They carefully criticized Monroe. Jefferson probably solved the problem of who should have diplomatic credit when he wrote in a letter to Horatio Gates, the old victor of Saratoga, on July 11, 1803: "I find our opposition very willing to pluck feathers from Monroe, although not fond of sticking them into Livingston's coat. The truth is, both have a just proportion of merit; and were it necessary or proper, it would be shown that each has rendered peculiar services and of important value."

Napoleon seems to have been happy. At first annoyed that Marbois had taken 20,000,000 francs to pay claims of American citizens, he soon admitted that his minister of the treasury had obtained 10,000,000 more than Napoleon had asked (the first consul had told Marbois to get 50,-000,000; Marbois doubled the figure in his first conversation with Livingston, and then dropped to 60,000,000 plus American assumption of the claims). The first consul was not certain what might happen in the long future, but was willing to take his chances, so long as at the moment he had the money. He allegedly told Marbois—or so Marbois remembered —that

Perhaps it will also be objected to me that the Americans may in two or three centuries be found too powerful for Europe; but my foresight does not embrace such remote fears. Besides, we may hereafter expect rivalries among the members of the Union. The confederations that are called perpetual last only till one of the contracting parties finds it to its interest to break them.

Napoleon obtained his money, which seems to have been his chief concern. He was advanced good British gold, through the Dutch banking house of Hope and Company and the British house of Baring, in exchange for six per cent bonds of the United States, due in fifteen years. One-third of the principal was to be paid in 1819 and the remainder in the two following years. Alexander Baring, who years later would appear in the United States as Lord Ashburton to conclude a treaty over the Maine boundary, appeared in Paris in July 1803 after hostilities had broken out between France and Britain. He soon sailed to the United States to confer with Secretary of the Treasury Gallatin and bring back a portion of the bonds personally to England. Gallatin considered that Baring acquired the bonds at too low a figure, 78½, which did not accurately reflect the state of American public credit, but he enjoyed visiting with the amiable Englishman, and the transaction was soon done.

The British government looked benevolently upon the new addition to the territory of the United States, as its willingness to allow a gold payment to Napoleon clearly showed. It presumably was happy to ensure the neutrality of the United States in the war then opening. Another evidence of the British favoring the United States at this juncture in their European affairs was the conclusion of the King-Hawkesbury Treaty of May 12, 1803, which arranged for drawing the shortest line from the northwest point of the Lake of the Woods to the nearest source of the Mississippi; solving the problem of American debts to English creditors incurred prior to the revolution; other British claims; and claims of the United States for spoliations of American commerce during the previous British war with France. In this latter respect the treaty promised to accomplish what the mixed commissions under Jay's Treaty had failed to do.

It is worth pointing out that the King-Hawkesbury Treaty, if it had gone into effect, would have brought British territory into geographical contact with the Mississippi River, and by the old rule or supposed rule of international law which the Americans long had been urging upon the Spanish government, this contact would have given the British the right to free passage down the Mississippi. The King-Hawkesbury line from the Lake of the Woods to the great river assuredly would have reinforced the claim of Britain to navigation of the river as set out in the Anglo-

American treaty of peace of 1783. For this reason the Senate threw out article 5 of the treaty of 1803, which concerned drawing the line, and this senatorial advice persuaded the British to fail to ratify the treaty. A convention in 1818 with Great Britain (see below, chapter 7) arranged for a line from the Lake of the Woods south only to the forty-ninth parallel of latitude, and not farther south to the Mississippi. From the point of forty-nine degrees the line turned west along the parallel to the Rocky Mountains.

But to return to the Louisiana Purchase. The claims convention had been drawn with great rapidity, according with the rough estimate of Livingston that American claims totaled 20,000,000 francs or $3,750,000. It turned out that there were far more claims. Moreover, the French government was given a say in allocating the claims, so that into each contention for claims was introduced all the venality of the French treasury of the day. The year 1803 was still the era of Talleyrand—who, when in America, had so greatly admired Alexander Hamilton and could not understand why Hamilton had resigned from the treasury department because he could not live on his salary. Minister Livingston knew that the claims convention contained faults and defended his action by offering what to the present-day reader would sound like an extremely sensible opinion: "The moment was critical; the question of peace or war was in the balance; and it was important to come to a conclusion before either scale preponderated. I considered the convention as a trifle compared with the other great object, and as it had already delayed us many days, I was ready to take it under any form." He was to receive much criticism for the corrupt handling of the claims, one critic taunting him with "imbecility of mind and a childish vanity, mixed with a considerable portion of duplicity."

As the Federalist criticism of the purchase began to focus on specific points, two weaknesses quickly appeared in the negotiation (apart from the claims convention), which the opposition exploited for all they were worth. There was no certain definition of the boundaries of Louisiana. And the French had not given a clear title—in an agreement of 1802 with Spain they had pledged never to alienate Louisiana once it came into their possession.

The boundaries of Louisiana were highly unclear in the treaty of 1803. The French had insisted on using the language of the Treaty of San Ildefonso of 1800 concerning the boundaries: "Louisiana with the same extent that is now in the hands of Spain, and that it had when France possessed it, and such as it should be after the treaties subsequently entered into between Spain and other States." After the Americans insisted upon defining the purchase, Marbois asked Napoleon, and Napoleon had answered, "If an obscurity did not already exist, it would perhaps be good policy to put one there." Livingston went to Talleyrand for a definition, and the following colloquy occurred:

"What are the eastern bounds of Louisiana?"

"I do not know; you must take it as we received it."

"But what did you mean to take?"

"I do not know."

"Then you mean that we shall construe it our own way?"

"I can give you no direction. You have made a noble bargain for yourselves, and I suppose you will make the most of it."

Livingston thereupon presumed that the Floridas had come into United States possession, as well as Louisiana. At the beginning of the negotiation over Louisiana, he had written Madison that he would like to trade Louisiana (saving out New Orleans) for the Floridas but added that "Perhaps, however, I am too sanguine in my expectations: we will not, therefore, dispose of the skin till we have killed the bear." From this statement it is clear that the minister at first did not think the Floridas were coming in the same package as Louisiana. It was only after the negotiation that he began to believe the Floridas had come along, without Napoleon's knowing it, that Napoleon unwittingly had sold the Floridas to the United States.

The theory that Napoleon had bought something he did not know about, and sold it in the same state of mind, rested in the uncertainties of the description of San Ildefonso, but Livingston must have realized that his argument was weak, even though he urged Madison and Jefferson to take possession of West Florida as soon as possible, perhaps before taking formal possession of Louisiana. In this respect Jefferson showed better judgment, as he refused to make a diplomatic and military issue over so weak a claim. Besides, he felt it was unnecessary. "If we push them [the Spanish] strongly with one hand," he wrote his confidant John Breckenridge, August 12, 1803, "holding out a price in the other, we shall certainly obtain the Floridas, and all in good time." Jefferson allowed Monroe to go on to Madrid after finishing the negotiation in Paris, to treat in the Spanish capital for the Floridas—a mission which was an implicit recognition of the president's belief that they did not come along with Louisiana.

More important in the minds of the Federalists than the obscurities of the boundary description—and, after all, these obscurities did hold more possibilities for Republican than for Federalist successes—was the doubt about the title of Louisiana as Napoleon had sold the province. The Spanish had refused to complete the transaction with France until the French ambassador in July 1802 gave a written pledge that France would never alienate Louisiana ("I am authorized to declare to you in the name of the First Consul that France will never alienate it"). After all, the Spanish had prized Louisiana only as a barrier against the United States. Then the French had ceded the territory to Spain's pioneer enemies! Moreover, on May 27, 1803, the young king of Etruria died. To the Spanish by the summer of 1803 the entire transaction over Louisiana seemed both illegal and useless, and they lost no time in protesting both to Napoleon and to the United States. "This alienation," wrote the Spanish ambassador in Paris to Talleyrand,

not only deranges from top to bottom the whole colonial system of Spain, and even of Europe, but is directly opposed to the compacts and formal stipulations agreed upon between France and Spain, and to the terms of the cession in the treaty of Tuscany; and the King my master brought himself to give up the colony only on condition that it should at no time, under no pretext, and in no manner, be alienated or ceded to any other Power.

The Spanish minister in Washington, the Marqués de Casa Irujo, protested violently. The president chose not to look behind the title offered by France, and this seems the only course he could have taken, since he had dealt with not Spain but France. The Federalists considered this course dishonest.

The Federalist Party was the more accusatory of Jefferson after the purchase, because its members knew that the president was uncertain of the constitutionality of the procedure. The purchase contravened his dearest political principle, strict construction of the Constitution, and the Federalists knew it. Even before the purchase, when only New Orleans and the Floridas were being talked about, indeed on the day, January 10, 1803, that the Senate approved the nomination of Monroe, Attorney General Levi Lincoln submitted an ingenious proposal to change American boundaries, to annex the new land to an existing territory or state (such as Mississippi Territory, or Georgia). Jefferson, embarrassed at the purchase in prospect, grasped at this straw and showed the proposal to Gallatin, presumably deeming it worthy of attention. Gallatin, sooner than the president, had gotten over his strict constructionism and was contemptuous of Lincoln's legal quibble. "If the acquisition of territory is not warranted by the constitution," he said in a memorandum of January 13, "it is not more legal to acquire for one State than for the United States . . . ." Under Lincoln's construction, what could "prevent the President and Senate by treaty annexing Cuba to Massachusetts or Bengal to Rhode Island"? Jefferson then dropped his possible argument, but it was elaborated by his henchman in Congress, John Randolph—strict constructionist of strict constructionists—who argued that the country possessed unsettled boundaries at the time of adoption of the Constitution, that power to settle disputes as to limits was indispensable, and that it involved the power of extending boundaries. To such lengths were Jefferson and his supporters inclined to go, and the Federalists knew it.

The negotiation for New Orleans was probably undertaken—so Henry Adams has written with a perspicuity which commands belief—as an "inchoate act which would need express sanction from the States in the shape of an amendment to the Constitution." Jefferson hardly could face such supporters as John Breckenridge, whose Kentucky resolutions a bare five years earlier disputed such an act as presidential purchase of territory, without asking for an amendment. "Our peculiar security," the president wrote Wilson Cary Nicholas, "is in the possession of a written Constitution. Let us not make it a blank paper by construction. I say the same as to the opinion of those who consider the grant of the treaty-making power as boundless. If it is, then we have no Constitution." He wrote Breckenridge on August 12, 1803, that Congress, after consenting to the treaty and paying for it,

must then appeal to *the nation* for an additional article to the Constitution . . . . The Legislature, in casting behind them metaphysical subtleties and risking themselves like faithful servants, must . . . throw themselves on their country for doing for them unauthorized what we know they would have done for themselves had they been in a situation to do it.

But then Livingston in a dispatch hinted that Napoleon might change his mind on the pretext that, without a constitutional amendment, the United States government did not have the power to acquire territory. The president ceased to speak openly of an amendment; and after Congress in October–November 1803 consented to the treaty and appropriated the funds, little more was heard of the idea. John Quincy Adams, newly elected to the Senate, became impatient and on November 25 called on Secretary Madison with the draft of an amendment which he meant to propose. Madison thought it too full and suggested a simple declaration: "Louisiana is hereby admitted into this Union." That same day Adams moved for a committee, and not a single senator would second his motion. Louisiana had entered the union through the treaty power, without amendment.

There was a momentary problem of what to do with the assorted French- and Spanish-speaking population of Louisiana, and despite the proviso of the treaty, inserted, it was said, by Napoleon himself, that the inhabitants of Louisiana would become citizens of the United States, the president waited a while, trusting to what he described as the vast swarm of settlers who began almost immediately to move into the new territory.

Louisiana, as one might have expected, was the first state to be formed out of the purchase. But Jefferson was sensitive to Federalist fears of being outvoted by the new states in the territory of Louisiana, for the business of bringing in new states might work sometime to Republican disadvantage. The president, as mentioned, also had real constitutional scruples. So he thought that after he had made a state of the populated area below the latitude of the mouth of the Arkansas, he would create out of the rest an Indian enclave, a sort of "constabulary" to keep American settlers from spreading too far. The American people would cross the Mississippi in due time, advancing "compactly," laying off "range after range" of states beyond. Meanwhile the enclave or constabulary, or "Maré chausée," as he described it in a letter to his friend Du Pont, would "secure both Spain & us as to the mines of Mexico for half a century, and we may safely trust the provisions for that time to the men who shall live in it."

The final transfer of territory came on December 20, 1803, after the French had been in possession of Louisiana for all of twenty days. There was not much ceremony, for no French troops were present and only a handful of Americans. At noon the French flag was hauled down in New Orleans for the last time, and a patriotic sergeant of the Republican armies seized it and wrapped it around his body. The American flag slowly went up the pole, sticking for a while about halfway up. When it arrived at the top, a cheer came from the dozen or so Americans gathered in the square.

By this time Jefferson's exploring party under the leadership of William Clark and the president's private secretary, Meriwether Lewis, was en route across the new purchase, across the remaining Spanish territory, out to the Pacific to bring back information on the Indian tribes and the region's flora and fauna.

The Americans could thank their stars that they now were in Louisiana and the French were out, for they had seized the fleeting moment of the renewal of war in Europe to take advantage of the financial needs of the French first consul, and who could tell what Napoleon might have wished or done if another moment with its own requirements might have come upon him? Perhaps, as Jefferson so feared, the British would have taken New Orleans. When British forces did show up in front of the city in 1814 it was too late; Louisiana belonged to the American settlers who had thronged into the new lands.

For the statesmen of Europe the doubling of the territory of the American republic was an event to watch with concern and probably distaste, but other events were on their minds, and before long the exigencies of 1803 turned into the straitening circumstances of 1804 and the years thereafter. Indeed the year 1804, the year after the purchase, marked the beginning of a new era in Europe as Napoleon, already first consul for life, turned his dictatorship into an empire. In December of that year he induced the Pope to come to Paris to crown him, although at the crucial moment of the coronation he put the crown on his own head. Napoleon's pretensions were beginning to make enemies everywhere. But many years were to elapse before his downfall.

For the Americans, also, the swirl of events was to turn their minds to other things. Shortly after Napoleon's coronation, the war in Europe took a new course into a great duel between French land power and British sea power. In this new conflict the American republic would find itself once more involved in continental affairs, and this time it would be no quasi war after a case of attempted extortion, followed by a fête and a pleasant treaty. Nor would the new Anglo-French conflict allow the Americans to pick up another piece of imperial territory in the New World.

A CONTEMPORARY DOCUMENT

[Minister Livingston wrote long letters both to Secretary Madison and President Jefferson, and none of his letters is more interesting than his composition addressed to Madison and penned at midnight, April 13, 1803. Source: *State Papers and Correspondence bearing upon the Purchase of the Territory of Louisiana* (Washington, 1903), pp. 159–163.]

I have just come from the Minister of the Treasury. Our conversation was so important, that I think it necessary to write it, while the impressions are strong upon my mind; and the rather, as I fear shall not have time to copy and send this letter, if I defer it till morning.

By my letter of yesterday, you learned that the Minister [Talleyrand] had asked me whether I would agree to purchase Louisiana, &c. On the 12th, I called upon him to press this matter further. He then thought proper to declare that his proposition was only personal, but still requested me to make an offer; and, upon declining to do so, as I expected Mr. Monroe the next day, he shrugged up his shoulders, and changed the conversation. Not willing, however, to lose sight of it, I told him I had been long endeavoring to bring him to some point; but, unfortunately, without effect: that I wished merely to have the negotiation opened by any proposition on his part; and, with that view, had written him a note which contained that request, grounded upon my apprehension of the consequence of sending General Bernadotte without enabling him to say a treaty was begun. He told me he would answer my note, but that he must do it evasively, because Louisiana was not theirs. I smiled at this assertion, and told him I had seen the treaty recognizing it; that I knew the Consul had appointed officers to govern the country, and that he had himself told me that General Victor was to take possession; that, in a note written by the express order of the First Consul, he had told me that General Bernadotte was to treat relative to it in the United States, &c. He still persisted that they had it in contemplation to obtain it, but had it not. . . . I told him I should receive with pleasure any communication from him, but that we were not disposed to trifle; that the times were critical, and though I did not know what instructions Mr. Monroe might bring, I was perfectly satisfied that they would require a precise and prompt notice; that I was very fearful, from the little progress I had made, that my Government would consider me as a very indolent negotiator. He laughed, and told me that he would give me a certificate that I was the most importunate he had met with. . . .

This day Mr. Monroe passed with me in examining my papers; and while he and several other gentlemen were at dinner with me, I observed the Minister of the Treasury [Barbé-Marbois] walking in my garden. I sent out Colonel Livingston [son of the minister] to him; he told him he would return when we had dined. While we were taking coffee he came in; and, after being some time in the room, we strolled into the next room . . . as my house was full of company, he thought I had better call on him any time before 11 that night. He went away, and, a little after, when Mr. Monroe took leave, I followed him. He told me that he wished me to repeat what I had said relative to M. Talleyrand's requesting a proposition from me as to the purchase of Louisiana. . . . he said, that what I had told him led him to think that what the Consul had said to him on Sunday, at St. Cloud, (the day on which, as I told you, the determination had been taken to sell,) had more of earnest that he thought at the time. . . . The Consul told him . . . , 'Well, you have the charge of the treasury; let them give you one hundred millions of francs, and pay their own claims, and take the whole country.' . . . He earnestly pressed me to make some proposition that was so near the First Consul's as to admit his mentioning it to him. I told him that I would consult Mr. Monroe, but that neither he nor I could accede to his ideas on the subject. Thus, sir, you see a negotiation is fairly opened, and upon grounds which I confess I prefer to all other commercial privileges . . . . I speak now without reflection and without having seen Mr. Monroe, as it was midnight when I left the Treasury Office, and is now near 3 o'clock. It is so very important that you should be apprized that a negotiation is actually opened, even before Mr. Monroe has been presented [to the first consul], in order to calm the tumult which the news of war will renew, that I have lost no time in communicating it. We shall do all we can to cheapen the purchase; but my present sentiment is that we shall buy. . . .

ADDITIONAL READING

Arthur Burr Darling's *Our Rising Empire* (New Haven, 1940) is long on the background of the Louisiana Purchase; its pages and the chapter entitled "The Louisiana Procurement" in Channing's *Federalists and Republicans* (New York, 1917) are excellent introductions to the largest stroke of luck ever to come to statesmen of the United States. For a broad general view—social, economic, intellectual—of American life at the beginning of the new century, there is no better source than the first six chapters of Henry Adams's *History of the United States during the Administrations of Jefferson and Madison* (9 vols., New York, 1889–1891); these chapters have been reprinted as *The United States in 1800* (Ithaca, N.Y., 1955). In the multivolume edition Adams's description of the Louisiana Purchase is delightful. As one might expect, he allots no extra credit to Thomas Jefferson, who defeated his great-grandfather for the presidency. For the purchase see also E. Wilson Lyon's *Louisiana in French Diplomacy: 1759–1804* (Norman, Okla., 1934), the leading scholarly study and indeed the only study dealing in entirety with this great subject.

The European background appears well in *Herbert Butterfield, *Napoleon* (London, 1939), a short biography of about a hundred pages, a model of biographical writing. *Crane Brinton, *The Lives of Talleyrand* (New York, 1936) shows the life of that Napoleonic character. Talleyrand had what a later generation was fond of describing as style. Observing a Napoleonic parvenu, he quipped: "one sees that he is not used to walking on parquet." Napoleon's minister of the treasury appears in E. Wilson Lyon, *The Man Who Sold Louisiana: The Career of François Barbé-Marbois* (Norman, Okla., 1942). Marbois's book, *The History of Louisiana*, first published in France in 1829, was translated and published in Philadelphia the next year, and surely deserves reprinting today, as it remains a standard account.

The English acquiescence in the purchase occurred because of what Bradford Perkins has called *The First Rapprochement: England and the United States, 1795–1805* (Philadelphia, 1955). The second—or, as this same author describes it in a new book, the "great"—*rapprochement* occurred in the years at the beginning of the twentieth century when Americans and Britishers came together in sentimental attachment just before the First World War. For relations with England see also Robert Ernst, *Rufus King: American Federalist* (Chapel Hill, N.C., 1968); and Ralph W. Hidy, *The House of Baring in*

American Trade and Finance: English Merchant Bankers at Work, 1763–1861 (Cambridge, Mass., 1949).

The American background of the purchase is in *Durand Echeverria, Mirage in the West;* Arthur P. Whitaker, *The Mississippi Question: 1795–1803* (New York, 1934); Charles C. Tansill, *The United States and Santo Domingo: 1798–1873* (Baltimore, 1938); Ludwell L. Montague, *Haiti and the United States: 1714–1938* (Durham, N.C., 1940); Rayford W. Logan, *The Diplomatic Relations of the United States with Haiti: 1776–1891* (Chapel Hill, N.C., 1941).

The prime American figure in the sale, if not the negotiation, was President Jefferson, and to appreciate this many-faceted individual, this enigmatic American who sometimes seemed to think one thing, say another, write a third, and do a fourth, the best book remains *Gilbert Chinard, Thomas Jefferson: The Apostle of Americanism* (rev. ed., Boston, 1939). Multivolume biographies are Marie Kimball, *Jefferson* (3 vols., New York, 1943–1950), which will remain unfinished because of the death of the author; and Dumas Malone, *Jefferson and His Time* (Boston, 1948–   ), of which three volumes have appeared. Lawrence S. Kaplan, *Jefferson and France: An Essay on Politics and Political Ideas* (New Haven, 1967) is an extraordinarily astute portrayal of this part of Jefferson's life—his experience with France. Kaplan believes that the change of government from the Directory to a dictator destroyed Jefferson's faith in France, though not in its people. From that point onward he was cautious with Bonaparte, and even disliked him. But he saw the French as useful in holding off the British—whom he really distrusted. The Princeton University Press presently is undertaking a vast publication of all of Jefferson's correspondence, edited by Julian P. Boyd. This project, begun with federal funds during the presidency of another great American, Harry S. Truman, has been described by Mr. Truman as his most outstanding presidential accomplishment.

Biographies include Irving Brant's *James Madison: Secretary of State, 1800–1809* (Indianapolis, 1953), the fourth volume of a six-volume work, and especially George Dangerfield's *Chancellor Robert R. Livingston of New York: 1746–1813* (New York, 1960), an account of the leading negotiator of the purchase.

☆ **6** ☆

The War of 1812

No, sir, you must look for an explanation of her [Great Britain's] conduct in the jealousies of a rival. She sickens at your prosperity, and beholds in your growth—your sails spread on every ocean, and your numerous seamen—the foundations of a Power which, at no very distant day, is to make her tremble for naval superiority.

—Henry Clay to Congress, 1811

At the opening of the nineteenth century, the government of the United States could boast a record of accomplishment in policy, foreign and domestic. The nation had done well in foreign affairs. Foreign difficulties appeared to have resolved themselves, the new republic on the western side of the Atlantic had survived the troubles of its birth and early years of independence, it now was modestly established in the world family of nations. President Thomas Jefferson in his first administration ratified the Convention of 1800 ending the quasi war between the United States and France. He watched Britain and France make peace with each other at Amiens in 1802. The president looked for no immediate trouble from Europe. He indeed worked on a plan to lay up the navy. The frigates and gunboats could be put under the roof of a vast covered dock to be built on the shores of the Potomac.

Jefferson's first administration also marked a triumph in domestic politics. The election of 1800 had almost shattered the Federalist Party. And Louisiana ensured the Federalists' subordination to the Republicans; all the new states to come from the Louisiana territory would be Republican in politics. This fact was not lost to Jefferson, even during his constitutional qualms over annexation of the new domain, and he wrote frankly to his supporters about what Louisiana would mean for the party. Then too, not only had the Federalists suffered through annexation and, before that, in the presidential election of 1800, but every month seemed to mark a diminution in their numbers until by the end of the president's first term in March 1805, Jefferson's political opponents, once so powerful, were reduced to a few quarreling extremists in the northeastern part of the nation.

And yet there was something saddening about the United States, if one looked closely at the condition of the new country. How could the nation ever rise to a strength sufficient to make absolutely certain of its independence? Almost a century later, the historian Henry Adams would write poignantly about the American republic as Jefferson must have seen it:

Nearly every foreign traveller who visited the United States during these early years, carried away an impression sober if not sad. A thousand miles of desolate and dreary forest, broken here and there by settlements; along the seacoast a few flourishing towns devoted to commerce; no arts, a provincial literature, a cancerous disease of negro slavery, and differences of political theory fortified within geographical lines,—what could be hoped for such a country except to repeat the story of violence and brutality which the world already knew by heart, until repetition for thousands of years had wearied and sickened mankind? Ages must probably pass before the interior could be thoroughly settled; even Jefferson, usually a sanguine man, talked of a thousand years with acquiescence, and in his first Inaugural Address, at a time when the Mississippi River formed the Western boundary, spoke of the country as having "room enough for our descendants to the hundredth and thousandth generation." No prudent person dared to act on the certainty that when settled, one government could comprehend the whole; and when the day of separation should arrive, and America should have her Prussia, Austria, and Italy, as she already had her England, France, and Spain, what else could follow but a return to the old conditions of local jealousies, wars, and corruption which had made a slaughter-house of Europe?

The nation sprawled across a territory almost too big for it to fill. The country's nearly ten million people spread themselves over a land too vast, now increased by the enormous Louisiana Purchase. The District of Columbia was a symbol of American problems: the little capital of Washington with its string of houses down the length of the rutted path which was proudly called Pennsylvania Avenue, the partly finished Capitol (only its north wing was up), the Executive Mansion then rising down by the river, the primitive boarding houses crowded sometimes with four or five congressmen to a room. The scene inspired the Irish poet Thomas Moore to write disparagingly:

> In fancy now, beneath the twilight gloom,
> Come, let me lead thee o'er this "second Rome!"

Where tribunes rule, where dusky Davi bow,
And what was Goose-Creek once is Tiber now;
This embryo capital, where Fancy sees
Squares in morasses, obelisks in trees;
Which second-sighted seers, ev'n now, adorn
Where nought but woods and Jefferson they see,
Where streets should run and sages *ought* to be.

How could such an agglomeration as the United States stay together? Already, in the case of Jay's ill-fated proposition for a treaty with Spain in 1786, the country nearly had split, southern states against northern. What new issue might bring dissolution? Jefferson knew that as president he had to be careful not to accord favors to one section, lest another take umbrage. If domestic politics were fairly safe, might not some new crisis in foreign affairs prove the catalyst to disintegration? Despite pronouncements about the indissoluble nature of the Union, almost all of the country's early statesmen several times in their careers beheld the nation on the brink of disaster.

It was not fated that Jefferson during his presidency should complete the circle of his felicities. The European war had broken out again in May 1803, shortly after the Louisiana Purchase. For approximately two years the respective measures of the leading belligerents, Britain and France, did not weigh heavily on American commerce. But then, just after Jefferson commenced his second term, in the apparently golden year of 1805, came serious trouble. The Napoleonic wars in that year began to turn into a cataclysm which shook Europe to its foundations and eventually brought the United States into the fighting. There was no peace in Europe until 1815, long after Jefferson had retired to Monticello. His successor in the presidency, Madison, experienced almost two full terms of turmoil. As Jefferson and Madison knew so well, every tremor of the European balance of power during these critical years meant a potential or actual threat to American nationality. The United States had to move with each European change, hoping to avoid upsetting the balance and presenting to one of the major belligerents an opportunity to end the republican experiment in the New World.

Just before the war in Europe closed in 1815, the American government managed in the nick of time to conclude peace with Britain.

1. *America versus the European belligerents, 1803–1809*

What a spectacle, the wars of Napoleon! Here was a forerunner of the great world conflicts of the twentieth century. These wars ensured the subsequent hundred-year dominance of Great Britain in affairs of the Continent, and in the entire world when the age of imperialism took European civilization to all the continents and through all the oceans. The wars ensured the downfall of France, even though the French would be victorious in the World War of 1914–1918 and manage to emerge on the winning side in 1945. Never again after 1815 was France able by itself to turn all Europe into chaos. France had passed its peak, as had Spain two hundred years before. Future wars would lead either to defeat, as in 1870 when the French fought alone against the Prussians, or to victory only through a coalition.

A grand series of victories gave Napoleon continental supremacy but did not bring the defeat of the British navy. His huge empire, bristling with armament, never caught sight of its mortal enemy, those battered, black-hulled ships which stood off the coast and controlled the trade routes abroad. For all its victories, Napoleon's empire was like an animal in a net which, despite its writhing, succeeds only in drawing the net tighter.

In the course of this campaigning, the French found the cost mounting ever higher, the machine running at faster speed; despite the victories there seemed no final victory—only more agony on those slaughter-fields where to be wounded usually meant death as certainly as it meant death to be splintered with cannon-shot during some grand charge.

Life in Britain was more secure. During all the years of war—the wars of the French revolution as well as those of Napoleon—the British people lost only about 50,000 men, including casualties among Britain's German auxiliary troops. But trade suffered, and it was a time of poverty and hunger.

It was a frightful era in history, a convulsion of Europe which the United States might well have avoided.

Why, when war broke out in 1803, could not the United States have prevented being slowly drawn into the fighting, eventually entering the war on the side of France and against the mother country? Why did the United States, before having fully ensured its national survival, undertake a war against the greatest power in the world? The War of 1812 could and should have been avoided. It was not a necessary war and became inevitable only after diplomacy hardened around principle and changed, in fact, from diplomacy to dogmatic argument. There might have been no hostilities if during the decade preceding the outbreak of war the United States had fixed its attention upon what should have been its chief purpose, strengthening the foundations of its nationality, and pursued in foreign affairs a policy of accommodation instead of freedom of the seas.

The Americans, possessing a small navy and a large merchant marine, were seeking to trade in Europe at the height of the Napoleonic wars with any nation that would purchase their cargoes. The British government refused to allow such a free American wartime trade. The British were determined, first, to prevent assistance to Napoleonic France and, second, to permit as little competition as possible with British merchant shipping. The United States contended that international law sanctioned wartime trade by neutrals, in noncontraband goods, to belligerent ports not blockaded. The British challenged the freedom of the seas. Moreover, they approached the problem of neutral trade from the other end of the American argument, by extending their definition of blockade to include ports merely announced as blockaded: they imposed upon numerous French or French-controlled ports a paper blockade. The exigencies of Great Britain during a war against Napoleon Bonaparte stood in conflict with American principle. The royal navy had over six hundred ships of war, including 120 ships of the line and 116 frigates. The American navy numbered sixteen seaworthy vessels. For Americans, a war with Britain for the purpose of enforcing freedom of the seas was a quixotic undertaking.

The manner in which freedom of the seas led to war in 1812 thus forms a melancholy chapter in American history. Presidents Jefferson and Madison failed to make the most elementary calculations of American military weakness and British power, of the risks involved in war versus those involved in diplomatic accommodation. They chose to stand for a principle that was far from accepted in international practice, especially in the practice of Great Britain. Freedom of the seas set a standard that if followed would have limited the operations of belligerents in wartime, but it lacked acceptance by the British government, and this made it an impractical diplomatic principle for the American nation.

There was another principle at stake in the diplomacy that preceded the War of 1812, namely impressment of seamen from American ships by the British navy. This hateful practice figured amply in the diplomatic exchanges between Washington and London in the years before 1812, notably in the period 1803–1807, but it never became as important an issue as freedom of the seas. In regard to impressment the British government always refused to admit any rights by the American government. Lord Harrowby, the younger Pitt's foreign secretary, wrote to the British minister in Washington in 1804 that "the Pretension advanced by Mr. Madison that the American Flag should protect every Individual sailing under it on board of a Merchant Ship is too extravagant to require any serious Refutation." The problem of obtaining sailors for the British navy was a difficult one, admittedly, for when the war resumed in 1803 many sailors were needed and only the most heroic measures obtained them. The attractions of American service were such that British sailors deserted to American vessels in droves. The ship that brought the British minister to the United States in 1803 lost fourteen men by desertion. Nelson reported that 42,000 British sailors had deserted during the war that ended in 1801. The British were incensed by the lenient American naturalization laws, according to which—so said Lord St. Vincent, first lord of the Admiralty—"every Englishman . . . may be made an American for a dollar." Impressment, of course, was no novel policy, and had long been practiced by the British navy. For decades the press gangs had been recruiters for the navy, and statutes implying the right of the crown to make impressments had been in force since the time of Richard II. John Adams acquired fame in 1769 for defending Michael Corbet, who had thrown a harpoon into Lieutenant Panton and killed him in resistance of impressment. But whatever its antecedents, impressment took on new dimensions as an issue between the United States and Britain prior to the War of 1812. Approximately 9,000 bona fide American citizens were impressed from American ships before the War of 1812.

At the outset of the European war there was little trouble over what later became the prime bone of contention between London and Washington—neutral rights, freedom of the seas. In the first two years after rupture of the peace of Amiens there was little restriction of American commerce by the European belligerents. Tonnage expanded at a rate of about seventy thousand tons annually, a large increase if one realizes that the ordinary ocean-going vessel of the early nineteenth century carried a freight of about two hundred and fifty tons. The increased American tonnage was used for trade between belligerent ports in Europe, and especially for taking over the French and Spanish West India trade, normally carried by French and Spanish ships but now interrupted by the war. There was also a lively American competition for the British West India trade during these years. American-produced exports remained at about $42,000,000 annually, in the period 1803–1805. The value of foreign goods transshipped from American ports increased from $13,000,000 in 1803, to $36,000,000 in 1804, to $53,000,000 in 1805.

All was well for the first two years after renewal of the European war, but then came difficulty. The British government first cut off American carrying trade between the French and Spanish West Indies and Europe by a prize-court decision, the so-called *Essex* case of May 1805. The *Essex*, an American vessel, had sailed from Barcelona to Salem and had then been captured en route to Havana. The ship had paid import duties to the extent of $5,278 at Salem and received a drawback of $5,080 prior to clearing for Havana with the same cargo. The British admiralty judge, Sir William Grant, declared illegal the American practice of trading between the Spanish and French West Indies and Europe by touching at an intermediate American port and "neutralizing" the goods on board. According to Grant, produce carried on a broken voyage between two enemy ports had to pay a bona fide duty, else the shipper violated the Rule of 1756 that trade not open in time of peace was not open in time of war. The British considered American trading practices such as the *Essex* was engaging in as, to use the title of a contemporary pamphlet by the publicist James Stephen, *War in Disguise; or, the Frauds of the Neutral Flags.* In this pamphlet published the same year as the *Essex* decision, Stephen exposed in great detail the tricks, as he described them, by which the Americans hitherto had performed the daily miracle of transforming enemy into neutral commerce.

It is interesting to note that a corollary to the doctrine of continuous voyage announced in the *Essex* decision of 1805 was the doctrine of ultimate destination, evolved in the American Civil War, whereby Union warships stopped British vessels en route to Matamoras in Mexico, in knowledge that goods carried to Matamoras probably were for transshipment across the Rio Grande into Confederate-held Texas. Another presumption drawn from the *Essex* decision, totally unanticipated by Americans in 1805, was the doctrine of ultimate consumption, as applied by the British against the Germans early in the First World War and acquiesced in by the Americans in 1917–1918: according to this theory, if goods shipped by a neutral (before 1917, the United States) to a neutral (say, Denmark) allowed a subsequent Danish shipment of similar goods to Germany, the goods originally shipped into Denmark were liable to capture en route. Indeed, the enterprising British republished James Stephen's book in 1917. The historian president of the United States in 1917, Woodrow Wilson, must have observed this republication with misgiving.

To return to the war of a century earlier. In hope of obtaining concessions from the British government of 1805–1806, President Jefferson sent William Pinkney of Maryland to the British capital to assist the American minister, James Monroe, in straightening out these Anglo-American commercial difficulties through negotiating a treaty to replace the commercial articles of Jay's Treaty, due to expire twelve years after it was ratified in 1795. The British proved unco-operative. The treaty they negotiated seemed so insubstantial to President Jefferson that he refused to submit it to the Senate.

Meanwhile the war in Europe took a turn toward more rigorous measures between Britain and France and by both of them toward neutrals. The tempo of the war quickened when Britain at Trafalgar (October 21, 1805) obtained overwhelming mastery of the seas and Napoleon at

Austerlitz (December 2, 1805) gained near-complete ascendancy on the Continent. Napoleon on November 21, 1806, announced his famous Berlin Decree, declaring the British Isles in a state of blockade. The emperor forbade commerce and communication with his enemy, and authorized seizure and confiscation of any vessels that violated his instructions. He announced on December 17, 1807, in the Milan Decree that he would regard vessels searched by the British or obeying their maritime regulations as denationalized and liable to seizure and confiscation as British property. Not to be outdone, the British government in a series of orders in council during the year 1807 barred shipping from the coastal trade of France and France's allies, prohibited commerce with continental ports from which the British flag was excluded, and permitted only those neutral vessels which had first passed through a British port, and there paid customs duties, to call at "nonblockaded" continental ports.

One should perhaps remark, concerning the French decrees and British orders in council, that the theory behind the opposing measures was simple enough, although it can easily sound complicated. Neither the orders in council nor the Continental System, as Napoleon liked to describe his measures, aimed at actually cutting off supplies from the foe. They were primarily financial measures, by which each side sought to obtain a bloodless victory over the other. Napoleon allowed continental produce to be sold in England, to drain away British gold. The British in turn brought sugar, coffee, tobacco, and other articles to the Continent and hoped to force their manufactured goods upon the Continent—and to do so, if possible, with their own ships, and if that were impossible, then with neutral ships.

Within this pattern of belligerent measures and countermeasures the American merchant marine had to operate, and the choice open to American mariners was not attractive, for if they followed the rules of the British they were liable to capture by Napoleon, and if they followed the rules of the emperor they exposed themselves to British seizure. A ship, to be fully protected, had to have a set of false papers, verified by the oath of the captain. The Philadelphia merchant Stephen Girard took the precaution to have an extra person of French extraction aboard his ships, who could take command in event a French cruiser appeared. The situation was deeply humiliating to a small new nation such as the United States. Jefferson was saying in 1806 (according to the French minister in Washington who sent the following in a dispatch to his chief, Talleyrand) that "we have principles from which we shall never depart. Our people have commerce everywhere, and everywhere our neutrality should be respected. On the other hand, we do not want war, and all this is very embarrassing."

At last a vessel of the British navy outrageously attacked an American ship of war, an engagement impossible to overlook or forget. On June 22, 1807, the British ship *Leopard* attacked the *Chesapeake* and took off four men as deserters. To visit and search the public vessels of the United States was not a wholly new venture on the part of the British. The *Baltimore* had been searched near Havana in 1798, and seamen removed. The American "Gun Boat No. 6" was searched in 1805, and three seamen taken off. But the British *Leopard* had followed the American frigate out to sea, just beyond territorial waters, and assaulted the helpless vessel. The American ship was setting out for the Mediterranean for operations against the Barbary pirates, and its decks were piled high with gear. It became an epic of American valor, of how after the first broadside from the *Leopard*, the American crew brought up a hot coal from the galley to fire a gun at the hated British before the *Chesapeake* struck its colors and allowed the press crew to come abroad. At no time prior to 1812, even in the summer of that year, was public wrath so roused against the British as in the summer of 1807. Jefferson could have had war with Great Britain, had he not so desired peace.

Matters gradually reached a point where the president saw only one course of action conducive to American self-respect—a complete and self-imposed embargo upon American shipping to Europe. In essence this embargo meant an effort to force the British to remove their restrictions on neutral shipping, for the structure of American trade gave the United States a better chance of success with the British than with the French. "I never expected to be under the necessity of wishing success to Buonaparte," Jefferson said in 1807. "But the English being equally tyrannical at sea as he is on land, & that tyranny bearing on us in every point of either honor or interest, I say 'down with England' and as for what Buonaparte is then to do to us, let us trust to the chapter of accidents . . ." The British had been selling one-third of their manufactures to the United States. American foodstuffs were needed in the British West Indies. The American government apparently could exert a considerable economic pressure. Jefferson's program of economic coercion was the same sort of coercion which the American colonies had applied with some success against the British imperial system prior to the revolution, and there seemed little reason why such pressure would not work again.

The president signed the Embargo Act on December 22, 1807. Unfortunately, when it was repealed fifteen months later it had proved a complete failure. It enjoyed no success in forcing the belligerents to give up their commercial restrictions.

The reasons for the embargo's becoming a fiasco were numerous, and some of them complicated. Manufacturers of cotton and tobacco in Great

Britain were pressed, but simultaneously British shipowners were conveniently relieved of American competition. Moreover, at this time the ports of Spanish and Portuguese America were opened to British commerce. The people of Spain on May 2, 1808, rose up in revolt against their government, then under domination of Napoleon. The British army this same year landed in Portugal. Revolt in Spain and British action in Portugal enabled colonial authorities in the New World to open their ports to British and other foreign merchant ships, reversing the commercial policy of more than three centuries. The British being the chief trading nation on the seas in the year 1808, opening of the Latin American ports redounded to the benefit of British shippers just at the time that trade with the United States had closed.

Moreover, the American Embargo Act was outrageously violated by American citizens and thus much reduced in effectiveness. An amendment to the act passed in 1808 enabled vessels of the United States to sail in ballast for the purpose of bringing home property stored in European warehouses but belonging to American citizens. As Edward Channing has pointed out, eight hundred vessels went out on this errand, and only a small proportion returned home before March 1809 and expiration of the

The snapping turtle, or Ograbme (*embargo* spelled backward) takes after a man smuggling a barrel of tobacco to a British ship.

embargo. Whaling ships were permitted to clear under the embargo, and this led to trouble. One citizen of Boston took a ship out after whales, so he said, and carried for the job—perhaps as whale bait—five hundred casks of bacon. He returned from Halifax with one cask of whale oil and several hundred bales of Yorkshire woolens.

To violate the act by trading across the border to Canada was ridiculously easy, and many New Englanders used this opportunity. During the first year of the embargo 150,000 barrels of Yankee flour went to Eastport, Maine, whence they were carted over the border. The price of flour was $5 a barrel in the United States, $12 in Canada, and $25 in Jamaica. At the outset of the illicit trade to Canada it cost just 12½ cents to take a barrel over the line, and it was still easy to make out financially when transport rose in cost to $3. One man made $47 in a night, a large sum for the early nineteenth century. Not until the prohibition era a hundred years later was smuggling so profitable.

As if this sort of trouble were not enough for the harassed Jefferson administration seeking to enforce the embargo, another problem appeared: the embargo raised against the administration a serious political threat in the form of a revived Federalist Party. The Federalists made political capital out of the misfortunes consequent on the embargo. Most of their case was, of course, manufactured, for the embargo did not cause all the harm that the Federalists claimed. In Boston, for example, where to catch the eye of the electorate they established soup houses for starving sailors, it developed that no one was starving and no one needed Federalist soup—a canvass by the *Independent Chronicle* revealed that "the astonishing number of twenty-five daily apply for this excellent refreshment." Such failure did not restrain party warfare over the embargo, and the Federalists turned to circulating the old argument that Jefferson was in league with Napoleon—that the American president, acting as the lackey of the French emperor, had joined the Continental System.

The embargo, the Federalists said, capped Napoleon's restrictive measures in Europe. On a raft in the Niemen River at Tilsit, on June 25, 1807, Napoleon had met the tsar of Russia and obliged the tsar to enforce the French commercial system in all parts of his dominions and to help impose it on all of Europe. Up to that time the Berlin Decree had not been enforced. On Napoleon's return to Paris the seizures began. Confiscation became the rule in all Europe. The embargo then conveniently supplemented the Continental System by denying to the British the use of American neutral carriers to take English manufactures to European ports.

Federalists seized upon this apparent Franco-American co-operation and proclaimed to the people of New England and to anyone else who would listen, not excepting the British minister in Washington, that Jefferson had made a deal with the Tyrant of Europe. There arose the specter of Thomas Jefferson, the American Robespierre. The arch-Federalist Fisher Ames drew a sobering picture of the state of affairs of the American nation. "Our days," he wrote to a friend in early 1808, "are made heavy with the pressure of anxiety, and our nights restless with visions of horror. We listen to the clank of chains, and overhear the whispers of assassins. We mark the barbarous dissonance of mingled rage and triumph in the yell of an infuriated mob; we see the dismal glare of their burnings, and scent the loathsome steam of human victims offered in sacrifice." Ames's colleagues gloomily, and with an eye to the New England electorate, re-called the fate of the city states of Greece, the Roman republic, the communes of Italy, the republic of France.

For years afterward the Federalists were certain that their Republican enemies had conspired with the French prior to the War of 1812. Fisher Ames during the embargo had hoped that New England would secede from the Union. It may well be, as Samuel Eliot Morison has written, that in the early months of 1809 the people of maritime New England were in a state of mind which closely resembled that of the South in 1860. Had they seceded, so Morison says, Ames would have become a great sectional figure like John C. Calhoun, the prophet and champion of a lost cause, hero of the Daughters of the Northern Confederacy. The disaffec-tion of New England became so strong that in 1811 President Madison's secretary of state, Monroe, took interest in the tales of an Irish adventurer, William Henry, who had joined hands in an intrigue with a Frenchman named Soubiran, the self-styled Comte Edouard de Crillon. Henry claimed to have conclusive proof of the disloyalty of the New England Federalists. Monroe bought the "Henry papers" for the then enormous price of $50,000, the entire secret service fund at the disposal of the president. The papers were worthless. The Federalists were furious. To-ward the end of the subsequent war, in 1814, a group of these sectional dissidents convened at Hartford and talked themselves into a declaration which, fortunately for the Madison administration, appeared at the time of the peace of Ghent and slipped into oblivion. The Federalists croaked and muttered for years thereafter until other times and other issues at last occupied their imaginations. It was a strange course, near disloyalty, for a group of men who in their youth had been supporters of the Con-stitution of 1787.

2. The coming of the War of 1812

Jefferson during his second administration established the pattern for American response to the measures of the European belligerents. In defense of the principle of freedom of the seas and against the competing restrictive systems of Britain and France, the president elaborated an American system of economic coercion. The complete embargo as a feature of this system did not work as expected. Jefferson's political protégé and successor in the presidency, Madison, nonetheless determined to defend freedom of the seas in the same fashion as his mentor, through economic coercion, but changing from an embargo to other devices.

After the embargo, a number of American efforts toward economic coercion of Britain and France led finally to the War of 1812. The embargo gave way to a Nonintercourse Act on March 1, 1809, opening trade with all the world except Britain and France. This act, it was soon seen, was ineffective for extracting concessions from the belligerents. It was too easy to send ships to intermediate ports, and having neutralized goods there, one could transport them to Britain and France.

In the first weeks of operation of the Nonintercourse Act the new secretary of state, Robert Smith, concluded an agreement with the well-intentioned British minister, David M. Erskine, which played havoc with enforcement of American rights. Erskine promised to withdraw the orders in council of 1807 so far as the United States was concerned. President Madison then proclaimed a renewal of commercial intercourse with Britain. Several hundred shiploads of American provisions went out to the British Isles, whereupon the British foreign secretary, George Canning repudiated Erskine's agreement, as the minister had exceeded his instructions. Erskine had been instructed to withdraw the orders in council only if the president simultaneously would withdraw the interdiction of British warships in American ports, agree to the Rule of 1756, and have the Nonintercourse Act enforced against France by the British navy. Canning's move came after all the American merchantmen had arrived at British ports. The Americans were deprived of any counterweight to this British move. Just what was in the mind of Canning when, by a single letter of disavowal, he thrust aside an opportunity to secure friendship with the United States, is difficult to say. Despite his later friendliness with the American minister, Richard Rush, at the time of the Monroe Doctrine, he was known to have carried throughout his public career a hearty dislike of Americans. On their part the Americans never forgot what they deemed his perfidy in the Erskine affair of 1809.

After Minister Erskine, disgraced, went back to England, his place was taken by none other than the worst envoy the British could have sent to the United States: Francis James ("Copenhagen") Jackson. The new minister stayed only a short time, but his reputation preceded his arrival and remained long after his recall. Jackson had been the man who had gone with Lord Nelson to Copenhagen and treated with the Danes just before Nelson destroyed their fleet. Copenhagen Jackson was a rough character whom George III could not abide. The aging monarch reportedly received Jackson on one occasion with the remark that he was surprised that the prince royal had not kicked him downstairs. The new minister landed in Boston and made a triumphal tour of the capitals of Federalism en route to the village on the Potomac. There in October 1809 he was formally received by President Madison, and at once noted that Secretary of State Smith "had on a pair of dusty boots, and a round hat in his hand." Madison he discovered was a "rather mean-looking man," while the incomparable Dolley was "fat and forty, but not fair." After two weeks in Washington he was convinced that Americans "are all alike, except that some few are less knaves than others." Jackson got into a row with the president and departed for England via another triumphal tour of New England.

The Nonintercourse Act was to remain in effect only through the session of Congress which closed in the spring of 1810, and it was replaced by an act known as Macon's Bill Number 2, which must go down in history as one of the most ill-advised pieces of legislation ever to come out of the halls of Congress. The legislators were embarrassed over the task of providing a successor to the Nonintercourse Act. Congress fussed and fumed and debated in what Madison described as an "unhinged state." At last came Macon's Bill Number 1: American merchantmen might go wherever they wished; but American ports would be closed to merchantmen and warships of England and France; and this latter prohibition would end if either of the powers rescinded its decrees. The fault with Number 1 was that by the year 1810 British merchantmen seldom came to the United States, and French ships could come not at all. The proposal was hardly coercive. Congress turned to Number 2, which became law on May 1, 1810. It opened commerce of the United States with all the world, including Britain and France. If one of the belligerents repealed its commercial measures insofar as they affected the United States, the American government would apprise the other belligerent of the repeal and institute nonintercourse against that belligerent, should it not also repeal its restrictions.

Macon's Bill Number 2 was an attempt to auction off American support. Some critics then and later would say that it auctioned off American honor. Surely it was unbecoming to the dignity of an aspiring republic to try to sell support in this open way. The act's chief defect, though, apart from its embarrassing lack of scruple, was its attempt to be devious. As everyone knows, or eventually will learn, deviousness does not cover many situations, and there usually is much more to gain by openness—all this quite apart from the satisfaction an individual or a nation might derive from knowing a certain course is direct and clear. Deviousness invites deviousness, and unless the individual or nation has had much experience he, or it, is likely to come to grief.

Deviousness was not the best procedure with the Emperor Napoleon. With Macon's Bill Number 2, the Americans played into his hands. Words came cheaply to Napoleon, and he instructed his foreign minister of the moment, the Duc de Cadore, to make an announcement to the American minister in Paris, General John A. Armstrong. "I am authorized to declare to you, sir," Cadore wrote carefully, "that the decrees of Berlin and Milan are revoked, and that after the 1st of November [1810] they will cease to have effect; it being understood that [*bien entendu que*], in consequence of this declaration, the English shall revoke their orders in council, and renounce the new principles of blockade, which they have wished to establish; or that the United States, conformably to the act you have just communicated, shall cause their rights to be respected by the English." In a suitable literary wind-up to this spectacular pronouncement, Cadore assured Armstrong that "His Majesty loves the Americans. Their prosperity and their commerce are within the scope of his policy. The independence of America is one of the principal titles of glory to France. Since that epoch, the Emperor is pleased in aggrandizing the United States . . . ."

Any village lawyer could have seen the string which Cadore and his master Napoleon had attached to their revocation of the decrees. But President Madison, having observed Congress's deviousness with Macon's Bill Number 2, perhaps believing it was now time for himself to show guile, chose to ignore the qualification in the Cadore letter, to ignore the many instances of Napoleon's bad faith which had emblazoned themselves upon European history in the few short years of the emperor's career prior to 1810. The president gave the impression of accepting the Cadore letter at face value, and made a proclamation of it on November 2, 1810, in accord with the provisions of Macon's Bill Number 2. Congress on March 2, 1811, put into effect a nonintercourse policy against Great Britain.

The British refused to abandon their orders in council, and argued with the Americans that the French had not abandoned the Berlin and Milan Decrees. They pointed out that in dealing with Napoleonic France one had to have more assurance than words. As late as June 15, 1812, the British minister in Washington in his last communication to the American government stated that "If you can at any time produce a full and unconditional repeal of the French decrees . . . we shall be ready to meet you with a revocation of the orders in council." Madison remained adamant, choosing even at the risk of war to use Napoleon's promises to force concessions from the British. Congress in 1812 voted for war against Great

Britain, in defense of freedom of the seas.

The cause of the War of 1812—freedom of the seas—seems clear enough, despite an argument among historians which for years has swirled around American entry into war in 1812. At the time of the outbreak of the war, and throughout the nineteenth century, it was generally assumed that defense of neutral rights had brought the United States into the War of 1812. This still seems a convincing view, although for some years now it has been argued that other causes took the country to war: western desire for Canada, southern desire for the Floridas, western land hunger, frontier anger against British support of the Indians from Canada and Spain's inability to prevent Indian raids out of the Floridas, an agricultural depression in the West and South which stirred frontiersmen into ascribing their woes to Britain's restrictive maritime measures. Woodrow Wilson, a well-known scholar at the turn of the twentieth century, announced in 1902 that the causes of the War of 1812 were "singularly uncertain," and this argument as to what brought the war has gone on for more than sixty years.

A seeming paradox has encouraged some of the debate. In the voting in Congress for war in 1812, representatives from New England opposed American belligerency against Great Britain, while congressmen from the agricultural portions of the country, the West and South, voted in favor of war. This has led scholars to question the traditional view that the issue of freedom of the seas caused the war, for the West and South possessed almost no ocean shipping. In a pioneer work, *Expansionists of 1812*, Julius W. Pratt has concluded that because of opposition to war by New England the War of 1812 was in large part a western and southern war for Canada and the Floridas. Pratt's book on the origins of the War of 1812 was a masterly survey of its subject, in many ways representing American historical scholarship at its best, and it has inspired a generation of students. Even so, there does seem to be another explanation possible for the sectional vote on the war. Westerners and southerners had cotton, grain, and other products to sell in Europe, and they became aroused over Britain's restrictive maritime measures, against which by 1812 they were willing to go to war. The New England shippers, however, were able as late as 1812 to make considerable profits in trade, despite British restrictions, and opposed war.

Indeed, western and southern anger over Britain's maritime measures seems to have given rise to the talk in Congress in the years before 1812 about the possibility of conquering Canada and the Floridas. Reginald Horsman has shown in a brilliant study that Americans were interested in Canada chiefly because, given the weakness of the American navy, Canada was the only area in which they might effectively attack Great Britain.

Canada, Horsman contends (and part of his argument is a repetition of the thesis offered some years ago by A. L. Burt), was the means to an end, and the end was the freedom of the seas. As for the Floridas, owned by Britain's ally Spain, they were of some minor value as a further means of retaliation against the British, but their susceptibility to capture was of slight importance in bringing on the War of 1812. They figured in congressional debates, but they were being acquired piecemeal in the years after 1803. President Madison took part of West Florida in 1810 and most of the remaining part in 1812; after negotiation with the Spanish, East Florida (present-day Florida) was acquired in 1819. There was never much question but that the Floridas might be taken in entirety by means well short of war.

The thesis incautiously advanced by Louis M. Hacker, that land hunger was the reason for western interest in attacking Great Britain, has had a wide circulation but little acceptance. Perhaps it is incapable of proof one way or the other. Although western frontiersmen were always hungry for land, there was by 1812 much good land yet available in the Old Northwest—Indiana by 1812 had only a scattering of population, Michigan was virtually unoccupied outside of Detroit, Illinois was largely wilderness. It is difficult to show why 1812 was the year for this sort of war.

The Indian menace, much talked about prior to 1812, in recent years argued by some historians as a leading cause of the war, seems to have been a strictly secondary reason for war against Great Britain, although Governor William Henry Harrison of Indiana became so certain of the Indians' hostility that he provoked them into the famed battle of Tippecanoe on November 7, 1811. This battle, fought against the confederacy of Tecumseh and his brother the Prophet, resulted in nearly two hundred American casualties. Frontiersmen were persuaded that the British in Canada had been stirring up the Indians from the frontier trading post of Amherstburg, and they were determined to strike before the Indians became too strong, too well supplied with British powder and guns. Actually, while there is no question of the British supplying the Indians and even inciting them, the policy of the royal governors in Canada and their agents along the border was defensive—the government in London was concerned for the safety of Canada in event of hostilities with the United States, and Canadian authorities took precautionary measures. These measures were susceptible to misinterpretation by both the Americans and the Indians, for it was not easy to hand out weapons to the Indians and tell them at the same time that they were not to fight the Americans who all the while were encroaching on Indian lands. Still, British Indian policy in the crucial years before 1812 was defensive in intent. This fact appears to have been fairly well understood by congressional representatives of the American West and South, who in debate seldom failed to put Britain's maritime pretensions far ahead of their concern over British Indian policy.

The West and South were suffering from an agricultural depression by 1812, and here, as George Rogers Taylor has clearly shown, was an important if subsidiary reason for American entrance into the War of 1812. Although the economic distresses of the frontier region lay probably in lack of transportation, communication, and marketing and financial organization, it does seem possible that Britain's restrictive maritime measures added to western troubles. The frontiersmen felt that they did. They were ready to believe that the 1807 orders in council lay at the root of the agricultural depression.

But the prime reason for American entrance into the war against Great Britain in 1812 seems to have been the principle of the freedom of the seas, for without the rankling British commercial measures the United States would have stayed out of the war. In 1812 the war hawks, as John Randolph called them, were vastly exercised over freedom of the seas, and they equated it with American national honor. Their patriotism was roused by the rigid attitude of Great Britain on neutral rights. Hurt pride and roaring patriotism were marshaled behind freedom of the seas when the war-hawk Congress assembled in November 1811. The cry for war became irresistible. Such young men as Henry Clay and John C. Calhoun, from the West and South respectively, agitated with enormous effect for war. They were the new generation which had not known, but only heard of, the American revolution. They were brought up on a diet of British iniquity, they had heard from childhood about British outrages, they had observed in their early adult years the countless tragic instances when British boarding parties had seized American citizens, often from vessels just outside American ports, and sent them to forced service and frequently to death. Far less cautious than their aging revolutionary fathers, they exploded in indignation when Britain denied to the United States the freedom of the seas. The indignity was too much. They wanted war and got it.

In the last weeks of the year 1811 congressmen vied with each other in crying for war. The most dramatic call was sounded by the Speaker, Henry Clay. During a debate over the raising of the regular army to 25,-000 troops Clay descended from the chair and, beginning inauspiciously enough, soon launched into a short tirade which in eloquence is difficult to match in all the annals of American speechmaking. "What are we to gain by war . . . ?" the young war hawk inquired. In reply he would ask, What were we not to lose by peace? Commerce, character, a nation's best treasure, honor! He had, he said, no disposition to swell, or dwell, upon the catalog of injuries from England. Some people claimed a danger of French subjugation.

What are we required to do by those who would engage our feelings and wishes in her [Britain's] behalf? To bear the actual cuffs of her arrogance, that we may escape a chimerical French subjugation! We are invited, conjured to drink the potion of British poison actually presented to our lips, that we may avoid the imperial dose prepared by perturbed imaginations. We are called upon to submit to debasement, dishonor, and disgrace—to bow the neck to royal insolence, as a course of preparation for manly resistance to Gallic invasion! What nation, what individual was ever taught in the schools of ignominious submission, the patriotic lessons of freedom and independence?

Did the war hawks push the Madison administration into war? According to the owner of the *National Intelligencer*, Joseph Gales, the war men in Congress were in almost daily consultation with Monroe, who kept saying to them: "Gentlemen, *we must fight*. We are forever disgraced if we do not." Monroe's letters written in December 1811 support this point of view. As for President Madison, it seems clear that he had made up his own mind for war before he entered office in 1809. He had to wait until his countrymen agreed with him. If he delayed, appearing to outsiders to be weak and vacillating, he only followed his principle set out in the *Federalist* No. 10, that the governance of men consists of a timely calculating of the interests attaching to a given policy. By 1811–1812 he was coming to the moment of calculation. In the early summer of 1812 he willingly took the country into war. The vote in favor of war was overwhelming: in the House, 79 in favor, 49 against; in the Senate, 19 to 13.

In vain did some individuals point out that the nation was unprepared and altogether no match for Great Britain. "What!" Randolph had cried several years earlier during a congressional debate over war, "shall this great mammoth of the American forest leave his native element and plunge into the water in a mad contest with the shark?" To no avail. Americans did not need to fight the British navy—they could take Canada.

Curiously, if the war hawks had held off a little longer they could have obtained the freedom of the seas without a fight, for the British government by the spring of 1812 was willing to make large concessions. What had happened was that the manufacturing regions of England, like the American West and South, were in the throes of a depression. The depression apparently had been touched off by overspeculation in Latin American markets in 1808 and thereafter, although in its origins it went back to problems growing out of the industrial revolution and the war with France. Because of it the manufacturers were eager to regain trade with the United States and hoped that they could do so if the 1807 orders in council were repealed. The British position by 1812 defies easy explanation, but its broad outlines can be stated. As Horsman has established in his researches, a combination of British shipping interests and West India planters had urged the restrictive measures against American commerce which began in 1805 with the *Essex* decision. The shipping interests desired to cut off the lucrative American carrying trade with the Continent. The West India planters desired to prevent the Americans from carrying the produce of French and (until 1808) Spanish West India colonies to Europe, which there entered into competition with their own produce. The West India planters for a time hung back from joining the home shipping interests to cut off American trade, for they needed American foodstuffs to maintain their own specialized economies in the islands. But gradually it became apparent that the Americans were doing more damage in carrying French produce to Europe than they were assisting the British West Indies by bringing foodstuffs from the United States. The West India interests thereupon joined with shipping interests in England to demand restrictions on the Americans. Many Britishers meanwhile had been angered by the American demand for freedom of trade at a time when the mother country faced the most dire perils, and this feeling —coupled with hostility that went back to the American revolution and added to the demands of the West India planters and the shipping interests —brought the restrictive maritime policies.

This restriction was not to the advantage of Britain's manufacturing regions, in view of their large trade with the United States, and they objected from the outset. When Jefferson placed an embargo on American shipping in 1807 and closed American ports to foreign vessels, the British manufacturing interests took temporary relief by trading in the new Latin American markets. As time passed, those markets proved not as lucrative as they had first appeared. The Americans during these years failed to reopen trade with Britain, replaced the embargo with a Nonintercourse Act in 1809, allowed only a temporary commerce—for a few months in 1810— through Macon's Bill Number 2, and again closed commerce early in 1811. It became obvious that the American market was important and worth maintaining even at the expense of British concessions, and matters finally reached a point by early 1812 where the manufacturing interests in Britain, suffering intensely from the business depression, demanded withdrawal of the 1807 orders in council and obtained enough popular support to move the Tory ministry to action. The manufacturers reasoned that this would conciliate the United States, persuade the Americans to lift their nonintercourse with Britain, and give the Americans sufficient money from the continental trade to buy British products.

The irony of the situation is that by this time the effect of the orders in council had been virtually nullified—first via a system of licenses which had started in earnest in 1807 and which, although it reached its peak in 1810 (18,000 licenses were granted that year), had opened all sorts of possibilities for trade between Britain and the Continent; and secondly by an act of the tsar of Russia who, tiring of the Continental System, in 1810 opened the Baltic ports to trade. American exports to Russia rose from $12,000 in 1806 to $6,137,000 in 1811. As the year 1811 wore on, first American and then even British flotillas arrived in ballast from England to take back Russian naval stores. There were many other opportunities for enterprising American ship captains in the three years after repeal of the Embargo Act. Still the Americans persisted—that is, the Americans in the West and South persisted—in demanding withdrawal of the orders in council. The United States government under the Jeffersonian-Madisonian Republicans had so unwaveringly stated its diplomatic position, had nailed its principle of freedom of the seas so firmly to its diplomatic masthead, that by 1812 nothing less than a repeal of the orders would do. The British had to make this gesture to obtain withdrawal of the American trade embargo against Great Britain. The British government on June 16, 1812, announced suspension of its rules affecting American commerce. Lacking an Atlantic cable, the United States knew nothing of this long-sought-for move, and two days later on June 18, 1812, President Madison signed the declaration of war.

3. *The Peace of Ghent*

It was indeed a tremendously exciting and crucial moment in European and world history when the United States in 1812 rushed into the war against Britain. Napoleon on June 22 embarked on what he hoped would be the conquest of Russia, after which he would pass on to India by way of Persia. He planned to use the Russian army as an auxiliary force, after its defeat, and who can tell what might have happened to this dream of conquest if his troops had not been destroyed by the Russian winter? The United States entered the war at its most dramatic time, and during the summer and autumn of 1812 the same fears for the survival of Russia circulated throughout Europe as appeared again in 1941 when a new Napoleon sought to reach Moscow. Instead there came France's defeat. On the last day of 1812 John Quincy Adams at St. Petersburg set down in a letter to his mother the disaster that had befallen the Napoleonic armies. "Of the immense host with which six months since he invaded Russia," he wrote, "nine-tenths at least are prisoners or food for worms. They have been surrendering by ten thousands at a time, and at this moment there are at least one hundred and fifty thousand of them in the power of the Emperor Alexander. From Moscow to Prussia, eight hundred miles of road have been strewed with his artillery, baggage wagons, ammunition chests, dead and dying men, whom he has been forced to abandon to their fate . . . . In all human probability the career of Napoleon's conquests is at an end. France can no longer give the law to the continent. . . . A new era is dawning upon Europe." The American poet Joel Barlow, who as minister to France had followed Napoleon into Russia, was horrified at what he saw, as the subzero winter weather helped seal the defeat of the retreating Grand Army. Barlow was to die shortly of pneumonia in the harrowing cold of the Polish village of Zarnowiec near Cracow, and for that reason his "Advice to a Raven in Russia" is the more poignant:

> Imperial scavenger! but now you know,
> Your work is vain amid these hills of snow.
> His [Napoleon's] tentless troops are marbled through with frost
> And change to crystal when the breath is lost.
> Mere trunks of ice, tho limb'd like human frames,
> And lately warm'd with life's endearing flames.
> They cannot taint the air, the world impest,
> Nor can you tear one fiber from their breast.
> No! from their visual sockets as they lie,
> With beak and claws you cannot pluck an eye.
> The frozen orb, preserving still its form,
> Defies your talons as it braves the storm,
> But stands and stares to God, as if to know
> In what curst hands he leaves his world below.

This was the drama of the times, beside which the grievances of the American nation and its entrance and eventually its exit from the European war were small matters. Adams had not exaggerated the reports of French losses, for of the 600,000 men whom Napoleon took into Russia—the largest armed force ever assembled under one command up to that time—only 30,000 managed to escape back across the Niemen River in December 1812. Napoleon returned to Paris with a personal guard. By the end of 1812, France's entire position in Europe was on the verge of collapse.

The Americans were so divided in support of war, and so badly prepared for war, that it was fortunate that events were decided elsewhere. No war in American history, not even the war in Vietnam, has proved as unpopular as that which James Madison sought to wage. The New Englanders saw their commerce choked and the mother country "stabbed in the back" at a moment of peril. They wanted friendship with Britain, not war. No war in American history except the revolution saw such abysmal lack of preparation. The regular army of ten regiments, ill-equipped and half-filled, was commanded by senior officers whose military experience went back to the revolution. The troops of these incompetent commanders made a poor showing. As for the militia, the less said the better. Of the 694,000 men enrolled in the militia of the several states, fewer than 4,000 responded to Madison's call at the beginning of hostilities. Jefferson wrote to Monroe that American citizens were too prosperous "to be shot at for a shilling a day." Not until 1814 did the effective American fighting strength, militia and regular army combined, reach 35,000. The war hawk John C. Calhoun had boasted that within a month of the declaration of war upper Canada and a portion of lower Canada would be seized. He forgot the problem of raising an effective army. Also the problem of transportation. Control of the Great Lakes was likewise a requisite for success, and that task itself took far more time than the Americans had anticipated. There was no time left for Canada.

In a word, the national defenses in 1812 and even in 1814 were in a condition which could be described only as deplorable. Facing Great Britain, the Americans found themselves in a military position where, as the historian George Dangerfield has so ably put the state of affairs, the nation's sheer mass far outweighed its energy or capital. On the northern border the boundary between the United States and Canada lost itself in wilderness. There was no navy on the Great Lakes until Oliver Hazard Perry invented one out of the green woods of Lake Erie. Yet the possibilities of defense here were far better than on the Atlantic coast where numberless fine harbors and estuaries and rivers beckoned the ships of the British navy. The Americans had no defense against the depredations of that navy except a few valiant frigates, hopelessly outnumbered. Jefferson's cherished gunboats, the small craft in which he had placed so much hope for defense of the national coastline, proved of no value whatsoever. They could hardly stay in the water; a storm once had tossed one of those little vessels up, high and dry, into a cornfield. The only effective naval defenses were the sand reefs of North Carolina. The British possessed many bases close to American shores—Halifax, the Bermudas, Barbados, Jamaica—and from there could blockade as they pleased, ruining the fisheries of New England and the commerce of the eastern states, raiding to the very capital of the American nation. When in 1814 British forces marched inland to Washington, with the defending militia flying from the scene in disorder, they easily took control of the national capital. A British officer convened a mock session of Congress, and to his laughing fellow officers proposed from the dais, "Shall we burn the Yankee capital down?" After a rousing chorus of "Yeas" they did just that, setting fire to the Capitol and the Executive Mansion. The president escaped by crossing the Potomac in a small boat. Dolley Madison also joined the crowd heading for Virginia, and was seen emerging hastily from the Mansion carrying the portrait of George Washington.

British troops in Washington were a part of the larger forces sent to the New World in the spring of 1814, when after the first defeat of Napoleon (and before he returned from temporary exile on Elba) large forces became available. Wellington's soldiers, fortunately not under command of the Iron Duke, were split into two expeditions, one to come down from the St. Lawrence estuary to conquer the Champlain and Hudson Valleys, a second to attack the Atlantic seaboard and then move upon New Orleans and the Mississippi Valley.

It was an excellent piece of luck for the Americans that peace negotiations long since had begun. Almost from the start of the war, President Madison had sought to get out of it. He was a southerner and undoubted patriot. "Little Jemmy" was no weak-kneed supporter of the war, but he was a prudent man, more prudent than the westerners who had voted for war in 1811–1812, and he thought it advisable to get out if it could be done with honor for his country. In the summer of 1812 he empowered the American chargé d'affaires in London, Jonathan Russell, to propose an armistice, should such seem desirable. All Madison required was that the British suspend their orders in council against American shipping, suspend impressment, dismiss the impressed seamen, and abandon paper blockades. To be sure, it was odd that the Americans should have continued diplomatic relations during the war. Russell, fortunately, was right there in London. The chargé made two attempts, dealing with the difficult British foreign secretary, Lord Castlereagh. By the end of the summer the issue between the Americans and British had narrowed to impressment, but the British would not yield the point. As Castlereagh put it, in the stilted official language of the time, His Majesty's Government—still that of George III—"cannot consent to suspend the exercise of a right upon which the naval strength of the Empire mainly depends, until they are fully convinced that means can be devised and will be adopted, by which the object to be obtained by the exercise of that right can be effectually secured." By which he meant: the British needed seamen for the navy and were going to get them one way or another. Impressment became the sole *casus belli*.

Strangely, this discussion of impressment between Russell and Castlereagh in 1812 was the last occasion that subject was discussed until after the end of the war.

Russell's overture failed; but a proposal of peace came from another quarter, the tsar of Russia, and Madison made the most of it. The tsar's chargé in the United States, Daschkoff, offered mediation in the early spring of 1813. Madison was beginning to worry over the sullenness of New Englanders toward the war, and so he quickly accepted Daschkoff's proposition. The president appointed John Quincy Adams, Albert Gallatin, and James A. Bayard as ministers plenipotentiary to treat with British ministers similarly appointed. At this time he did not even know if the British would agree to the tsar's overture but appointed his commissioners anyway, and they (except Adams, already there as regular American minister) arrived in St. Petersburg in July 1813.

When the British first heard of the tsar's mediation offer, they turned it down, for they had no wish to submit their maritime principles to the scrutiny of a Baltic power notoriously unsympathetic to them. Then a series of European events began to change the minds of the ministers in London. With the abdication of Napoleon in 1814 the fourth coalition—it had taken four to defeat the French—began to disintegrate. As Dangerfield has written, "Vast flaws and cracks—political, economic, geographical, dynastic—appeared upon its surface, which, like some plaster hastily applied, had never been either smooth or convincing, and could not stand the seismic jarring of this sudden peace." Arguments were

A contemporary cartoon depicting Russian (the bear) attempts to mediate between America and the British.

raging at the peace conference assembled in Vienna. Ominous dissensions appeared within the coalition, many of them centering on the mercurial personality of the Russian tsar. The latter individual made a trip to London in 1814, preceded by his undiplomatic and malicious sister, and the Russian cause had been vastly confused by the fumbling uncertainties of these two royalties. The tsar tried to make himself popular in London at the very time that the prince regent (the "clown prince"), engaged in a row with his wife (he was trying to divorce her), was becoming greatly unpopular. One mistake led to another until the tsar had sown distrust throughout all the ranks of the British government, and even the opposition. The tsar admired Napoleon, and the British feared that he might reunite with Napoleon as he had done some years before, on the raft in the Niemen.

The security of the French capital was highly uncertain, as the Duke of Wellington found when he took up residence in Paris after Napoleon's abdication. Louis XVIII, the aging brother of the monarch guillotined in 1792, was now sitting on the restored throne. He had arrived in the baggage of the British army, and his new subjects found him hardly an object of admiration.

There were uncertainties, too, in North America, where the British military situation began to deteriorate. General Sir George Prevost with 11,000 men met defeat at Lake Champlain and Plattsburg on September 11, 1814. The British force which burned Washington was repulsed at Baltimore. The business of turning the United States into a self-supporting colony might have an attraction in theory but was not so easy in execution. It appeared as if a decisive victory might take a good deal of time.

The result was a British decision to make peace with the Americans, rather than "give Jonathan a good drubbing." Parliament now was out of sympathy with the idea of an American war and announced its sentiments in no uncertain terms. Members of the Commons envisioned a new-born commerce with the Americans. The Duke of Wellington, uneasy in Paris, also advised peace as quickly as possible, in letters to his highly placed friends in London. He even sent a cheerful note to the American peace commissioner Gallatin. The prime minister, Lord Liverpool, therefore advised Castlereagh, November 18, 1814:

I think we have been determined, if all other points can be satisfactorily settled, not to continue the war for the purposes of obtaining or securing any acquisition of territory. We have been led to this determination by the consideration of the unsatisfactory state of the negotiations at Vienna, and by that of the alarming situation of the interior of France. We have also been obliged to pay serious attention to the state of our finances . . . under such circumstances, it has appeared to us desirable to bring the American war if possible to a conclusion.

The British meanwhile had shifted the American peace negotiations to the Flemish city of Ghent, close to the Channel and away from the tsar.

When the British commissioners at Ghent started their parleys with the American negotiators, they asked for a peace with several conditions, including an Indian barrier state encompassing the area of the present states of Michigan, Wisconsin, Illinois, Indiana, and Ohio. This the American delegation refused. Next came a demand for peace on the principle of *uti possidetis,* the military situation of the moment, meaning that the British would have kept part of Maine along with other portions of American territory. The Americans held out for the *status quo ante bellum.* Their persistence, combined with British concern over the dissension in Vienna, the deteriorating military situation in Europe, the lack of a decisive military success in the New World, the attraction of a renewed American commerce, and the fragile state of the British exchequer, brought about what may be described as an American diplomatic victory. The American commissioners—Adams, Bayard, Gallatin, with the addition of Henry Clay and Jonathan Russell—eagerly accepted when offered the *status quo ante bellum.* They signed the peace at the residence of the British commissioners on Christmas Eve, 1814. John Quincy Adams, speaking for the delegation, remarked, "I hope it will be the last treaty of peace between

The Treaty of Ghent. (From Left to Right: Anthony St. John Baker, Henry Goulburn, William Adams, Admiral Lord Gambier, John Quincy Adams, Albert Gallatin, Christopher Hughes, James A. Bayard, Henry Clay, Jonathan Russell, and an unidentified man.)

Great Britain and the United States."

Henry Clay is reported later to have described the Treaty of Ghent as "a damned bad treaty," but the former war hawk signed it. He was relieved to be through the war, as was the Senate of the United States, which approved the treaty unanimously.

The Senate's task was eased by the fact that the treaty arrived in Washington almost simultaneously with news of General Andrew Jackson's glorious victory in New Orleans over General Pakenham. While the battle was fought almost two weeks after the conclusion of peace, its outcome led the unthinking to believe that the United States had won the war. Americans indeed emerged from the struggle not humbled but exultant. During the war years "Yankee Doodle" had virtually become a national anthem, and the verses sung to its strains were numerous and varied. "Brother Jonathan," hitherto the symbolic name for America, had lost place by 1815 to "Uncle Sam." And the British in their Chesapeake campaign unwittingly inspired a Washington attorney, Francis Scott Key, to write "The Star Spangled Banner," which (even though set to the tune of an old English drinking song, "Anacreon in Heaven," with a nearly impossible range for the average sober human voice) gave Americans a feeling for the symbolism of their flag. Key had gone out to the British fleet to arrange for the release of an American prisoner of war, Dr. William Beanes. Throughout the night of September 13–14, 1814, the two men had watched the fury of the bombardment and siege. At dawn Beanes asked if the flag was still there.

The peace of Ghent left several issues undecided. There was no mention of impressment, although the question had become academic with the end of the war in sight, and Great Britain never afterward resorted to the practice. No mention was made of freedom of the seas, in defense of which the United States had gone to war—but the issue of neutral rights could be safely left for time to resolve (when the United States later became involved in the Civil War and in two world wars, it proved convenient to forget neutral rights). At Ghent other issues had appeared: the northeast and northwest boundaries; control of armaments on the Great Lakes; fishing privileges off Newfoundland and Nova Scotia; British free navigation of the Mississippi. "The situation in which I am placed often brings to mind that in which you were situated in the year 1782 . . . ," J. Q. Adams wrote to his father in Quincy. "I am called upon to support the same interests, and in many respects, the same identical points and questions. . . . It is the boundary, the fisheries, and the Indian savages." Navigation of the Mississippi, prior to the heyday of river steamboats, did not seem too important to the British. They had no way to get down to the Mississippi from Canada without traversing American territory, and to obtain a right to go up the Mississippi was at the moment a dubious acquisition. The fishing privileges remained in an uncertain state until 1910, when they were amicably arbitrated. As for armaments on the Great Lakes, this problem received settlement in the Rush-Bagot Agreement of April 28–29, 1817, which, although it allowed a limited number of gunboats to both Canada and the United States on Lake Champlain and the Great Lakes, foreshadowed the total disarmament that was achieved shortly after the Civil War. The question of the boundaries, northeast and northwest, was left to mixed commissions under the terms of Ghent, but not finally settled until the 1840's (see below, chapter 9).

What can one conclude about the diplomacy of freedom of the seas that led to the War of 1812 and the Treaty of Ghent of 1814? Some writers have stressed that this controversy over neutral rights, together with the war that followed, brought Great Britain to the realization that at last the United States must be treated with dignity and respect. Doubtless an improved British acceptance of America and Americans did result from the War of 1812. Still, the British respect that America gained was an unintentional dividend. The war was not fought for general respect but for preservation of the principle of neutral rights, and in this sense it failed, as did also the diplomacy which ended in hostilities.

Surely American diplomacy toward the European belligerents, Britain and France, was not carefully and thoughtfully based on any realistic conception of the American national interest. It was not wise to risk the existence of the American nation for the abstract principle of freedom of the seas. If the European war had gone another way, if Napoleon had been victorious over Russia, or Russia had not challenged Napoleon, Britain might have fallen in 1812–1814. If Britain had failed, what would have been the judgment of history on the War of 1812 and its diplomatic preliminaries?

This is an interesting line of speculation. If Britain had lost, Napoleon could have reformed the British government and established himself and his brothers in Buckingham Palace. During his lifetime he might have controlled Europe and Asia from London to Peking. He could have sent a few frigates and divisions to the New World and taken care of the bumptious American democracy, an outpost of liberty threatening his autocratic imperial power.

Such visions seem not to have occurred to Thomas Jefferson and James Madison, either on the hilltop at Monticello or at the Executive Mansion in the District of Columbia. They never thought out their position on freedom of the seas, but luckily everything turned out all right.

A CONTEMPORARY DOCUMENT

[According to his own lights President Madison in his war message of June 1, 1812, carefully brought together the grievances against Great Britain. Source: James D. Richardson, ed., *A Compilation of the Messages and Papers of the Presidents: 1789—1897* (10 vols., Washington, D.C., 1896–1899), I, 499–505.]

. . . Without going back beyond the renewal in 1803 of the war in which Great Britain is engaged, and omitting unrepaired wrongs of inferior magnitude, the conduct of her Government presents a series of acts hostile to the United States as an independent and neutral nation.

British cruisers have been in the continued practice of violating the American flag on the great highway of nations, and of seizing and carrying off persons sailing under it, not in the exercise of a belligerent right founded on the law of nations against an enemy, but of a municipal prerogative over British subjects. . . .

The practice, hence, is so far from affecting British subjects alone that, under the pretext of searching for these, thousands of American citizens, under the safeguard of public law and of their national flag, have been torn from their country and from everything dear to them; have been dragged on board ships of war of a foreign nation and exposed, under the severities of their discipline, to be exiled to the most distant and deadly climes, to risk their lives in the battles of their oppressors, and to be the melancholy instruments of taking away those of their own brethren. . . .

British cruisers have been in the practice also of violating the rights and the peace of our coasts. They hover over and harass our entering and departing commerce. To the most insulting pretensions they have added the most lawless proceedings in our very harbors, and have wantonly spilt American blood within the sanctuary of our territorial jurisdiction. . . .

Under pretended blockades, without the presence of an adequate force and sometimes without the practicability of applying one, our commerce has been plundered in every sea, the great staples of our country have been cut off from their legitimate markets, and a destructive blow aimed at our agricultural and maritime interests. In aggravation of these predatory measures they have been considered as in force from the dates of their notification, a retrospective effect being thus added, as has been done in other important cases, to the unlawfulness of the course pursued. . . .

It has become, indeed, sufficiently certain that the commerce of the United States is to be sacrificed, not as interfering with the belligerent rights of Great Britain; not as supplying the wants of her enemies, which she herself supplies; but as interfering with the monopoly which she covets for her own commerce and navigation. She carries on a war against the lawful commerce of a friend that she may the better carry on a commerce with an enemy. . . .

Anxious to make every experiment short of the last resort of injured nations, the United States have withheld from Great Britain, under successive modifications, the benefits of a free intercourse with their market, the loss of which could not but outweigh the profits accruing from her restrictions of our commerce with other nations. And to entitle these experiments to the more favorable consideration they were so framed as to enable her to place her adversary under the exclusive operation of them. To these appeals her Government has been equally inflexible, as if willing to make sacrifices of every sort rather than yield to the claims of justice or renounce the errors of a false pride. . . .

There was a period when a favorable change in the policy of the British cabinet was justly considered as established. The minister plenipotentiary of His Britannic Majesty here proposed an adjustment of the differences more immediately endangering the harmony of the two countries. The proposition was accepted with the promptitude and cordiality corresponding with the invariable professions of this Government. A foundation appeared to be laid for a sincere and lasting reconciliation. The prospect, however, quickly vanished. The whole proceeding was disavowed by the British Government without any explanations which could at that time repress the belief that the disavowal proceeded from a spirit of hostility to the commercial rights and prosperity of the United States; and it has since come into proof that at the very moment when the public minister was holding the language of friendship and inspiring confidence in the sincerity of the negotiation with which he was charged a secret agent of his Government was employed in intrigues having for their object a subversion of our Government and a dismemberment of our happy union.

In reviewing the conduct of Great Britain toward the United States our attention is necessarily drawn to the warfare just renewed by the savages on one of our extensive frontiers—a warfare which is known to spare neither age nor sex and to be distinguished by features peculiarly shocking to humanity. It is difficult to account for the activity and combinations which have for some time been developing themselves among tribes in constant intercourse with British traders and garrisons without connecting their hostility with that influence and without recollecting the authenticated examples of such interpositions heretofore furnished by the officers and agents of that Government. . . .

Whether the United States shall continue passive under these progressive usurpations and these accumulating wrongs, or, opposing force to force in defense of their national rights, shall commit a just cause into the hands of the Almighty Disposer of Events, avoiding all connections which might entangle it in the contest or views of other powers, and preserving a constant readiness to concur in an honorable reestablishment of peace and friendship, is a solemn question which the Constitution wisely confides to the legislative department of the Government. In recommending it to their early deliberations I am happy in the assurance that the decision will be worthy the enlightened and patriotic councils of a virtuous, a free, and a powerful nation. . . .

ADDITIONAL READING

The literature of American diplomacy during the years 1803–1815 concentrates on the origins of the War of 1812, that most dismal war in the nation's history, the war which everyone now suspects the nation could have avoided with honor—despite the fact that leaders of that bygone era believed the war could not have been avoided with honor. The classic account is Henry Adams, *History of the United States during the Administrations of Jefferson and Madison* (9 vols., New York, 1889–1891). See also A. L. Burt, *The United States, Great Britain, and British North America* (New Haven, 1940). A recent general treatment, dull in prose and unsatisfactory in scholarship, is *Patrick C. T. White, *A Nation on Trial: America and the War of 1812* (New York, 1965), a volume in the America in Crisis series. *Harry L. Coles, *The War of 1812* (Chicago, 1965) is an excellent account of the origins (pp. 1–37) as well as the course of the war, together with the diplomacy of its conclusion (pp. 237–262); Coles's fine book is a volume in the Chicago History of American Civilization series. A rattling good tale is by Fred L. Engelman, *The Peace of Christmas Eve* (New York, 1962). Fine writing also appears in the first section of *George Dangerfield's *The Era of Good Feelings* (New York, 1952), on diplomacy during the war.

Maritime technicalities are set out in Alfred Thayer Mahan's *Sea Power in Its Relations to the War of 1812* (2 vols., Boston, 1905); F. E. Melvin, *Napoleon's Navigation System* (New York, 1919); E. F. Heckscher, *The Continental System* (Oxford, 1922); and Robert G. Albion and Jennie B. Pope, *Sea Lanes in Wartime: The American Experience, 1775–1942* (2d ed., Hamden,

Conn., 1968). The last is a thoroughgoing analysis, full of sharp reasoning. The Melvin and Heckscher volumes, appearing after the First World War and inspired by the maritime troubles of that conflict, differ in quality; the Melvin volume is a more careful study than that by Heckscher. The latter writer was an expert on mercantilism, the trade system of an earlier era. The account by Mahan is graced by that sailor-scholar's literary style and well-known theory that sea power constitutes the essence of national greatness.

An aging but still useful introduction to historical writing on the causes of the War of 1812 is Warren H. Goodman, "The Origins of the War of 1812: A Survey of Changing Interpretations," *Mississippi Valley Historical Review*, XXVIII (1941–1942), 171–186. Cited for over a quarter century for its commentary on the clash of interpretation, Goodman's article is a careful work, although it sidesteps in some of its conclusions. Interpretations of the War of 1812, other than the traditional view that violation of neutral rights brought on the war, are J. W. Pratt, *Expansionists of 1812* (New York, 1925); Louis M. Hacker, "Western Land Hunger and the War of 1812," *Mississippi Valley Historical Review*, X (1923–1924), 365–395; and George Rogers Taylor, "Agrarian Discontent in the Mississippi Valley preceding the War of 1812," *Journal of Political Economy*, XXXIX (1931), 471–505. Abbot Smith, "Mr. Madison's War," *Political Science Quarterly*, LVII (1942), 229–246, a beautifully written piece, contends that Madison tried to gather the interests together that wanted war, in the manner of the *Federalist* No. 10 where he had argued that the statesman's job was to deal with forces at hand. And so instead of pursuing his own policy in an active way, getting support for it by stirring up public opinion, he waited through two years of national indecision until he had support of the war hawks in 1811, whereupon he came out for war. Scholars recently have been arguing again over the origins of the War of 1812, and it is clear that what C. Vann Woodward described in an article of a few years ago as "the age of reinterpretation" is now upon us. The war's origins, however, have been getting some careful study, rather than theory or a juggling of interpretations. One of the important novelties of the new literature is an exploration of the English side of affairs, which appears in Reginald Horsman's *The Causes of the War of 1812* (Philadelphia, 1962) and in the first two volumes of Bradford Perkins's distinguished trilogy, *The First Rapprochement* (Philadelphia, 1955) and *Prologue to War: England and the United States, 1805–1812* (Berkeley, Calif., 1961). The war hawks have close attention in the volume by Roger Brown, *The Republic in Peril: 1812* (New York, 1964), and in a chapter of Norman K. Risjord's *The Old Republicans: Southern Conservatism in the Age of Jefferson* (New York, 1965). Victor Sapio, in a book to be published by the University of Kentucky Press, shows how an important state, Pennsylvania, reacted to the arguments for and against war; one of the problems of historical analysis of the American causes of the war is the disparate nature of the states in that era, and the need of scholars to get down into the fine print of local opinion rather than to take the views of leading journals and commentators, and Sapio does this brilliantly.

The American trade with Russia, which helped bring Napoleon's fateful decision to invade that nation, appears in Alfred W. Crosby, Jr., *America, Russia, Hemp, and Napoleon: American Trade with Russia and the Baltic, 1783–1812* (Columbus, Ohio, 1965).

See also *Durand Echeverria, *Mirage in the West* (Princeton, 1957); Lawrence S. Kaplan, *Jefferson and France* (New Haven, 1967); Louis Martin Sears, *Jefferson and the Embargo* (Durham, N.C., 1927); John A. Logan, Jr., *No Transfer* (New Haven, 1961); E. A. Cruikshank, *The Political Adventures of John Henry* (Toronto, 1936) and Samuel Eliot Morison, "The Henry-Crillon Affair of 1812," in *By Land and By Sea* (New York, 1953), concerning the expenditure by Secretary Monroe of the nation's entire secret service fund.

For the figures of the time see Samuel Flagg Bemis, *John Quincy Adams and the Foundations of American Foreign Policy* (New York, 1949), relating Adams's defection from the Federalist Party; Bernard Mayo, *Henry Clay: Spokesman of the New West* (Boston, 1937); Glyndon G. Van Deusen, *The Life of Henry Clay* (Boston, 1937); Irving Brant's *James Madison: Secretary of State* (Indianapolis, 1953), also *The President, 1809–1812* (Indianapolis, 1956), and *Commander in Chief, 1812–1836* (Indianapolis, 1961).

☆ 7 ☆

Era of Good Feelings

Great Britain, after vilifying us twenty years as a mean, low-minded, peddling nation, having no generous ambitions and no God but gold, had now changed her tone, and was endeavoring to alarm the world at the gigantic grasp of our ambition. . . . But it is very lately that we have distinctly seen this ourselves; very lately that we have avowed the pretension of extending to the South Sea; and until Europe shall find it a settled geographical element that the United States and North America are identical, any effort on our part to reason the world out of a belief that we are ambitious will have no other effect than to convince them that we add to our ambition hypocrisy.
—Secretary of State John Quincy Adams, diary, 1819

The time arrived when the entire Western world could settle down and relax in the quiet of peace. For Europe there had been almost constant war since 1789, the beginning of the French revolution. For the United States there had been an even longer time of troubles. Americans had gone through their own revolution and the uncertain period of federal government under the Articles of Confederation before being subjected to the rigors of the opposing belligerent systems of Europe during the wars of the French revolution and Napoleon. It was a time for rest. After the Treaty of Ghent, the diplomacy of the United States was a relaxed sort of negotiation, with far fewer than the usual perils and crises, and American diplomacy saw only four major developments: the defeat of the Barbary pirates (which was more military than diplomatic); conclusion of the Transcontinental Treaty of 1819; the announcement of the Monroe Doctrine; and recognition of the republics of Latin America. All four of these events marked the growing national consciousness of the American people. The Barbary pirates had been making trouble for a long time, and after the War of 1812 the United States sent two squadrons into the Mediterranean and overwhelmed them. The Transcontinental Treaty reflected a feeling that the boundaries of the republic should be precisely laid down against any possible foreign challenge as Americans moved westward into the new lands of the Louisiana Purchase. The Monroe Doctrine resulted from Americans' belief that it was well to draw a line between the New World and the Old, to let the powers of Europe know clearly and finally that their political systems were no longer welcome in the Western Hemisphere. The last development set out in the present chapter, recognition of Latin American independence, followed from the other acts of the era.

1. *Barbary pirates*

Difficulties with the piratical potentates of North Africa, the rulers of Morocco, Algiers, Tripoli, and Tunis, were a heritage of the treaty of peace with Great Britain in 1783: having detached itself from British protection during the revolution, the United States after 1783 had to make its own arrangements with the Barbary pirates without advantage of the British fleet. In the case of Morocco this was not too difficult, and, assisted by the good offices of Spain, the American government managed during the mid-1780's (when the Spanish were negotiating the Jay-Gardoqui Treaty) to obtain a Moroccan treaty without payment of tribute. The treaty was concluded in 1787 and cost $30,000 in presents, with no annual tribute. It proved a satisfactory arrangement, as the Moroccans kept their word. A few years later treaties followed with the other Barbary powers: Algiers, 1795; Tripoli, 1796; Tunis, 1797. These treaties were virtual confessions of American weakness. The treaty with the bey of Tunis gave slave-hunting rights, in an extraordinary way. According to its thirteenth article (the number may have been chosen for that reason), "If among the crews of merchant vessels of the United States there shall be found subjects of our enemies, they shall not be made slaves, on condition that they do not exceed a third of the crew; and when they do exceed a third, they shall be made slaves." The treaties bore dollar as well as human prices. The treaty with Algiers cost $642,500 in ransom money, presents, commissions and other charges, and the United States agreed to pay an annual tribute in naval stores to the value of $21,600. At the first opportunity the pirates were likely to violate the treaties.

The pirates of Algiers had been, and continued to be, especially troublesome. In the latter 1780's they had proved a deep embarrassment to the then American minister to France, Jefferson, who in vain had sought to persuade his country, under the weak Articles of Confederation, to ransom its citizens. By the year 1788, twenty-one United States citizens were in slavery, mostly in Algiers. At that time Congress could not negotiate a loan in Europe, for the Confederation government was not paying interest on outstanding loans. The individual states would not furnish money to rescue their own people. Secretary for Foreign Affairs Jay was not altogether eager to see the captives ransomed, however difficult their immediate condition of servitude, for Jay had written in 1785 about the reported declaration of war by Algiers: "This war does not strike me as a great evil. The more we are ill-treated abroad the more we shall unite and consolidate at home." If the attitude of Jay looked to a happier future, it did not help Jefferson in Paris, who was reduced to a stratagem more worthy of his ingenuity than of the dignity of his ministerial station. Jefferson publicly announced that he had no interest in the captives of Algiers, or at least could not find the funds to ransom them and hence could do nothing for them. Privately he dickered through the Mathurin Fathers who often had helped ransom slaves from the Algerines. He had to make the case of the American captives an act of mercy rather than a matter of international relations.

In the first years after the American revolution little help against Barbary came from the British government, and this was part of the American trouble. The British did not see much need to assist the United States against the pirates. Many Britishers felt that when the United States took itself out of the British commercial system by becoming independent it could not at the same time opt for the protection against Barbary accorded to imperial subjects. Anyway, if the pirates took American ships, there would be that many fewer vessels to compete with British commerce. Employing that expression applied to so many situations, Benjamin Franklin said wittily that if there were no Algiers it would have been worth England's while to have built one.

The newly independent United States did its best against the Barbary potentates, but the naval establishment was limited, and in the 1790's the constant threat of trouble with Britain or France interfering with American commerce kept the government from sending a force sufficient to overcome the pirates. Beginning in 1801 and until 1807, the United States maintained frigates in the Mediterranean; there were some small naval actions, and even an overland expedition to depose the pasha of Tripoli, led by the consul in Tunis, William Eaton. The measures taken were half-hearted and ill-starred.

Witness the capture by the pasha of Tripoli of the frigate *Philadelphia*, which had grounded on a shoal with its crew of more than three hundred men. The ship's physician, Dr. Jonathan Cowdery, described the treatment accorded to the crew:

We were taken on the 31st of October, 1803, and entirely robbed of property, even the greatest part of the clothes on our backs were taken from us. Our seamen were immediately put to hard labor, without mercy; and they have suffered much for the necessaries of life. Five have paid their last debt to nature [Nov. 7, 1804], and five have turned Turks. Myself and fellow officers were permitted to occupy the house where our Consul, Mr. Cathcart, resided while in Barbary.

Less than three months before this disaster the pasha, Yusuf, reportedly was demanding $500,000 and an annuity of $20,000. By January 1804, Commodore Edward Preble wrote that Yusuf's "asking price" for peace and ransom was $3,000,000. Yusuf might have stuck for his price, had not Lieutenant Stephen Decatur and a small band of followers burned the *Philadelphia* while the vessel lay under the batteries of Tripoli, a stroke which Lord Nelson characterized as "the most bold and daring act of the age." At last in June 1805, a treaty was signed, and Yusuf received $60,000 and released the *Philadelphia*'s prisoners.

In 1807, with British and French maritime measures tightening around American trade in the Atlantic, the Mediterranean naval vessels were withdrawn. It was in that unlucky year that the frigate *Chesapeake*, setting out for Barbary with decks laden with gear, was attacked by the *Leopard*.

Nothing was done about the pirates until after the War of 1812. Two squadrons formed in 1815, appropriately under Commodore William Bainbridge, who had captained the ill-fated *Philadelphia* years before, and Commodore Decatur, who also remembered the *Philadelphia*. Decatur got out first to the Mediterranean and forced the three rebellious rulers, the dey of Algiers and the beys of Tunis and Tripoli, into treaties, this time with indemnities paid to the Americans. The dey paid $10,000. The bey of Tunis paid $46,000. Decatur asked Yusuf of Tripoli for $30,000, and during negotiation aboard the *Guerriere*, the commodore kindly reduced the sum to $25,000. Commodore Bainbridge meanwhile arrived in the area and displayed his squadron at Algiers, Tunis, and Tripoli. It was the sort of diplomacy the pirates understood. The ruin of Barbary was complete when in 1816 an Anglo–Dutch fleet sortied against Algiers and blew up almost the entire Algerine fleet and a goodly portion of the city. The Barbary coast thereafter sank into a deep obscurity, to take on momentary importance only under entirely different circumstances: Morocco figured in the origins of the First World War, and then again in 1942, when the invasion of North Africa by the Anglo-American forces under General Dwight D. Eisenhower led to a meeting at Casablanca in January 1943 of the prime minister and the president, to plan the defeat of Germany, a nation that did not even exist in the heyday of Barbary pirates.

2. *The Transcontinental Treaty*

As for the Transcontinental Treaty of 1819, the second American action of the years after the War of 1812, it was, according to Samuel Flagg Bemis, the greatest diplomatic victory won by a single individual in the history of the United States. Had it not been for the tenacity, the diplomatic shrewdness, of John Quincy Adams, secretary of state under President Monroe, this treaty, which set the bounds between Spanish and American possessions, would have been signed in a far less advantageous form. Adams kept pressing the Spanish minister in Washington, Don Luis de Onís and when the Massachusetts statesman was finished, Don Luis had given up almost everything that he could.

The treaty of 1819 involved three major problems—the Floridas, Texas, and the boundary between the Louisiana Purchase and Spanish Mexico and California—and it is perhaps best to consider each problem separately.

The diplomatic argument over the Florida question is almost too complicated to recount, because only traces of the contentions of the early nineteenth century survive in the boundaries of the states of the Union. It is difficult to follow the talk about East and West Florida in the correspondence and the long diary-outlined conversations of J. Q. Adams and Onís. One writer has sought to drop it all into the dustbin of history by describing the dispute over the Floridas as "tiresome reiteration," the "higgling and splitting of hairs, partaking too much of the child's method of quarrelling." But set it out one must, for otherwise much of the negotiation of the Transcontinental Treaty makes no sense.

The problem of the Floridas as it lay between Adams and Onís was simple enough if put this way: the Americans claimed both East and West Florida as properly their own, though they were willing to secure their title by a treaty with Spain. Thereafter the whole problem turned into complexity.

Consider the claim of American ownership of West Florida. The Louisiana Purchase in 1803 had included a definition of the "colony or province of Louisiana, with the same extent that it now has in the hands of Spain, and that it had when France possessed it." The truth was that for many years, with exception of two decades after the Seven Years War when Great Britain possessed the Floridas, West Florida had been a part of Louisiana, and in this respect the Americans had a fairly decent case.

John Quincy Adams in old age. A daguerreotype by Matthew B. Brady, 1846.

In an arrangement made a hundred years before the Transcontinental Treaty, France and Spain, after a petty local war, had agreed in 1719 that the line between French Louisiana and Spanish Florida would be the Perdido River (the western boundary of the present-day state of Florida). When Louisiana passed from France to Spain in 1763, and Spanish Florida

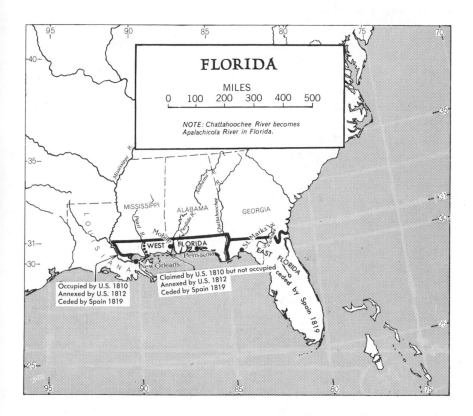

to Great Britain, the British also took the territory westward from the Perdido to the Mississippi River, except for the "island" of New Orleans. For administrative reasons the British named this strip West Florida, and extended its jurisdiction eastward as far as the Apalachicola River (with Pensacola, just to the east of the Perdido, as its capital). Then in 1783 the Spanish acquired what by that time had become known as "the Floridas," including not merely their erstwhile Florida (renamed East Florida, most of the present-day state), but the once (1719–1763) French strip together with the territory between the Perdido and the Apalachicola, which was now West Florida. The Spanish placed West Florida within the jurisdiction of Louisiana, where it remained until 1803. The Americans, one should add, did not find out about this Spanish administrative rearrangement, knowledge of which would have strengthened their case. In claiming that West Florida was a part of the purchase of 1803 they argued, of course, that between 1719 and the end of the Seven Years War most of West Florida (that is, eastward to the Perdido) had been a part of Louisiana and that this "historic" Louisiana, hence, was the Louisiana referred to in the treaty of 1803.

Napoleon could have straightened everything out in the treaty of cession but chose not to do so. Although the treaty of retrocession of 1800, under which Louisiana passed from Spain to France, contained the same ambiguous definition of the boundaries of Louisiana as appeared in the purchase treaty of 1803, it was pretty clear at the time that neither of the Floridas was passing to France along with Louisiana. In 1802, Napoleon still seems to have thought that West Florida was not a part of Louisiana, for in his instructions of that year to General Victor he stipulated that only the island of New Orleans be occupied. He did not say this to the Americans in 1803, but instead allowed them to use the purchase as a claim to West Florida. With a certain malice against Spain, Napoleon in ceding Louisiana to the United States left its boundaries unclear, and Talleyrand told Livingston to make the best of the bargain. The Americans therefore construed the treaty broadly, choosing to define Louisiana with its historic boundaries of 1719–1763. They could have defined its extent as during the era from the end of the Seven Years War to the peace of Paris of 1783 but of course chose not to do so. As mentioned, they did not know of West Florida's administrative reincorporation into Louisiana during the subsequent years of Spanish control.

Almost as soon as the ink had dried on the treaty of cession, Livingston began advising Secretary Madison to take West Florida. He reasoned that Napoleon did not even know what France had acquired and hence had sold it to the United States unwittingly. This piece of thought, which would be beyond the imagination even of a twentieth-century realtor, soon became common sense to the American people. Congress in 1804, the year after the purchase, passed the Mobile Act authorizing organization of the disputed territory as a United States customs district.

To pass an act of Congress was one thing and to take the territory something else: six years elapsed before the United States seized West Florida up to the Pearl River. In April 1812 the seized section became a part of the new state of Louisiana, and in May 1812 the section between the Pearl and the Perdido (including Mobile) became a part of Mississippi Territory.

The Americans concurrently elaborated an argument for East Florida, which if not based on the Louisiana Purchase was equally notable for its ingenuity. East Florida, so John Quincy Adams would argue after the War of 1812, should pass to the United States because Spain had failed to restrain the Indians from raiding into American territory, as provided in Pinckney's Treaty of 1795. Moreover, many Negroes, from several hundred to several thousand—the exact number was impossible to ascertain

—had taken refuge in East Florida, and the weak Spanish regime there had found it difficult to return them. During the Napoleonic wars Spanish ships had captured some American merchantmen, and French ships of war also had brought American merchantmen into Spanish ports; the American government, dreaming up a case against Spain which would justify taking East Florida, did not fail to mention these spoliations, Spanish and French. Then the Spanish intendant of Louisiana had closed the port of New Orleans to American commerce in 1802 and failed to offer another place of deposit. The Spanish government eventually countermanded the order. The Americans charged the losses of this act up to East Florida. During the War of 1812, the United States feared that the British might use the Floridas as a base and later accused the Spanish of co-operating with the British in the New World as they were doing in the Old. Another argument for East Florida.

Meanwhile life had become truly difficult for the Spanish monarchy— and the troubles in Spain could only help the Americans in their designs upon the Floridas. Charles IV abdicated in March 1808. His son reigned briefly as Ferdinand VII, but the French forced him to abdicate. Napoleon thereupon elected Joseph Bonaparte, but on May 2, 1808, the Spanish already had begun a revolt which spread through the peninsula and forced the French emperor to intervene in personal command of his troops, all to establish the *rey intruso*, the intruder king, Napoleon's brother Joseph. The presiding junta, like the Americans in their own revolution, sought outside help, making an alliance with Britain in January 1809 which set the scene for Wellington's Spanish campaigns. Together with the collapse the next year of the Continental System in the north, Napoleon was doomed, although few individuals realized what was happening. For the Americans it simply seemed a good time to appropriate West Florida to the Pearl, leaving to a later occasion such minor matters as a clear title.

The junta in 1809 sent Onís to the United States as its accredited representative, but the Madison administration let Onís wait until December 1815 before recognizing him. The situation admittedly was delicate. Madison probably would have preferred to recognize Joseph Bonaparte, but neither Joseph nor the junta was in assured control of all the country. Besides, the administration was observing the Jeffersonian watchword to await the European chapter of accidents.

Madison also may have observed that Onís was a tough customer. The American minister to Spain, George Washington Erving, later advised J. Q. Adams that Onís was "unaccommodating from temper, his views are limited, he is in a state of constant irritation, & is living as you say in the time of Ferdinand the Catholick [the patron of Columbus] & not in that of Ferdinand the 7th." Onís wrote reams of correspondence to his government about his problems. From 1809 to 1819 he sent 10,000 pages, a third of it of his own composition. And he liked to overawe even the verbose Americans with the written word. At one crucial moment he presented the state department with a historical memoir on the limits of Louisiana and Texas compiled by one Father José Antonio Pichardo; the memoir had 5,127 pages and thirty-one volumes.

Not much other than verbosity occurred over the Floridas and other Spanish–American issues until 1818 when General Jackson moved into action in a manner which animated American politics as well as foreign relations for months thereafter. On the fateful night of February 13, 1818, the *Napoléon des bois*, as the French minister in Washington dubbed him, was bivouacked with 3,000 troops on the bank of Big Creek, four miles from Hartford, Georgia, when he received a packet of mail including, Jackson afterward contended, a letter from Representative John Rhea transmitting President Monroe's "approval" of Jackson's suggestion to take Spanish Florida and, as Jackson's biographer Marquis James has described it, "let the diplomats sweep up the debris." James Monroe was to swear on his deathbed that he never had so commissioned Jackson. The Napoleon of the woods believed the opposite, unto his deathbed. What seems clear is that the administration understood Jackson's intentions toward the Floridas and unleashed him.

Off the "Gin-ral" went into East Florida where he took the town of St. Marks and then, plunging into a jungle that had hardly changed since the time of De Soto, moved for 107 miles to the village of Chief Boleck, known as Bowlegs. The chief and his people fled into the swamp, having been warned by a kindly seventy-year-old Scottish merchant named Alexander Arbuthnot. In the campaigning, Jackson captured the Scotsman and also an Englishman named Robert C. Ambrister. The former he ordered hanged, the latter shot. These, one should add, were not the only executions meted out by the dread Tennessean, who had a frontier habit of removing all obstacles in his path. His troops surged westward toward West Florida's capital, Pensacola. "The continued wading of water . . . ," he wrote, "first destroyed our horses, and next our shoes, the men are literanny [sic] barefoot." He attacked Pensacola on May 27, 1818. Next day the town surrendered. He seized the royal archives on May 29, appointed one of his colonels as military and civil governor, and announced immediate enforcement of the "revenue laws of the U. States." On May 30 he departed for Tennessee.

The administration had to do something—debris was everywhere. Onís hurled himself upon Washington like a thunderbolt, departing his summer retreat in Pennsylvania, and roused John Quincy Adams out of bed early one morning. The two men had three interviews in the next six days. He circulated his grievance in detail to the diplomatic corps. Monroe's cabinet met in almost daily session. Secretary of War Calhoun intimated that the Florida land schemes of two of Jackson's friends had inspired the general. President Monroe was beside himself with indecision. Adams alone defended the general and tactlessly asked his cabinet colleagues whether they wished to deal with Jackson as Elizabeth had dealt with Walter Raleigh—to have the benefit of his services and then abandon him? After three days of the argument Adams's hand trembled so much from fatigue that he had to neglect his diary. Monroe first tried to get Jackson to provide a better case. The president wrote the general that it would be necessary to establish that the posts were seized in retaliation for the misconduct of Spanish officers:

You must aid in procuring the documents necessary for this purpose. Those you sent . . . do not, I am satisfied, do justice to the cause. . . . Your letters to the [War] Department were written in haste, under the pressure of fatigue. . . . If you think it proper to authorize the secretary or myself to correct . . . passages, it will be done with care.

Jackson did not admire the drift of this letter, and refused to offer Monroe this way out; he said he could get up stronger evidence of Spanish rascality, but refused to allow any editing of his dispatches. For Monroe the only recourse was to face down the critics, foreign and domestic. He turned the job over to Adams. The secretary of state delivered himself of a manuscript which although directed nominally to Minister Erving in Madrid was more properly a manifesto. Adams had it printed in Washington long before it reached Erving. The secretary therein announced he was only setting out a "narrative of dark and complicated depravity" and that Spanish officials in the Floridas needed to answer for their sins, rather than General Jackson. It was a long document of several dozen pages, and the secretary appended a documentary annex of seventy-two items.

Even Adams's critics admitted the quality of his argument. Thomas Jefferson, who always considered the secretary a Federalist in Republican clothing, said the Erving note was "among the ablest compositions I have ever seen, both as to logic and style." The British minister in Washington, Charles Bagot, confessed that he "was not prepared for the direct and high handed defense of General Jackson. . . . There is however a Key which will explain this, and always will explain every measure of this Government viz:—Elections." Most important, Foreign Secretary Castlereagh reacted favorably to Jackson and Adams; Castlereagh refused, as he put it, to move a finger in the matter of Arbuthnot and Ambrister. The Spanish government would have no support from its ally Britain. The British gratuitously advised the Spanish to give in.

In the United States a drama of domestic politics nonetheless unfolded in which Henry Clay went over the water's edge in search of an issue by which he might defeat his fast-moving rival Jackson. Years before, Clay had spoken favorably of the occupation of West Florida and had favored the annexation of East Florida. Then Jackson had begun to eclipse him: when Clay was playing cards at Ghent in 1814, Jackson was preparing the defenses of New Orleans; while Jackson was resting on his laurels in Tennessee, President Monroe in 1817 passed over Clay and chose J. Q. Adams as "heir apparent," that is (in those times), secretary of state. The next year Jackson executed Arbuthnot, Ambrister, and two Indian "prophets," while occupying the Floridas. Clay could stand the competition no longer. He descended from the speaker's chair of the House of Representatives and began what proved to be a three-day speech in favor of several resolutions which would reprove the actions of General Jackson.

There followed one of the great scenes of American oratory. The House galleries filled to the rafters. Aisles were packed, cuspidors overturned. Gallant gentlemen refreshed ladies in the gallery by handing up oranges to them attached by handkerchiefs to long poles, and some people feared that the temporary building in which Congress met pending the rebuilding of the Capitol might collapse. It was the largest congressional spectacle since the trial of Aaron Burr.

Clay made a great speech. When he met Mrs. Samuel Harrison Smith, a member of the audience, after the first day of his remarks, he apologized for not having spoken longer, offering as his excuse that his voice had given out, that he had begun in too loud a tone and exhausted himself. He proved to be much exercised by the hanging of the Indian prophets Francis and Homollimico; he thought them some kind of religious leaders. "When did the all-conquering and desolating Rome ever fail to respect the altars and the gods of those whom she subjugated? Let me not be told that these prophets were imposters who deceived the Indians. They were *their* prophets." As for General Jackson, the primary source of irritation:

Recall to your recollections the free nations which have gone before us. Where are they now and how have they lost their liberties? If we could transport ourselves back to the ages when Greece and Rome flourished, and . . . ask a Grecian if he did not fear some daring military chieftain, covered with glory, some Philip or Alexander, would one day overthrow his liberties? No! no! . . . [he] would exclaim, we have nothing to fear for our heroes. . . . Yet Greece had fallen, Caesar passed the Rubicon.

Jackson himself arrived in Washington, resolved to "defeat these hellish machinations," and at the end of twenty-three days of congressional oratory, on February 8, 1819, the resolutions of censure failed. Some talk arose of a censure in the Senate, and the Jackson men countered with the rumor that the general often dealt with opponents by cutting off their ears.

The Jackson-Clay dispute thereupon simmered down, and the two rivals went their separate political ways. Some years later the Jeffersonian Republicans split into Whigs and Democrats, and Clay became a Whig and Jackson a Democrat.

The Floridas were only one of three territorial problems involved in the Transcontinental Treaty of 1819, even if by far the most important. After Jackson's diplomacy in Florida, and its support within both the United States and the British government, little remained for the Spanish but to solve their Florida and other arguments with the Americans as best they could.

The issue of Texas, the second area of dispute, went in their favor, although it was a small victory considering that the Spanish province of Mexico, to which Minister Onís had attached Texas, achieved independence in 1821. By ensuring Texas for Mexico, Onís unwittingly made possible the Mexican War which would lose Mexico an imperial domain far larger than Texas. At least Onís could salve his conscience that he had done his duty by Texas in 1819. His opponent Adams did not know that the minister's final instructions were to give up Texas if necessary. Adams tried for Texas, but Onís proved so resistant that the secretary demurred and accepted the line of the Sabine River, the western border of the present-day state of Louisiana, as the border between the Louisiana Purchase and Spanish Mexico. Adams still might have held out for Texas, but the cabinet, including Monroe, refused to back him. According to Adams's diary, even General Jackson believed the Floridas were more important than Texas, although Jackson was to forget this advice in the heat of the Texas annexation dispute of another day. As a member of Congress in his old age, Adams would hear much about his failure to obtain Texas, and the criticism rankled, for he had tried harder than the cabinet, harder than Monroe, harder than Jackson. Through an intermediary, Secretary of War George Bancroft, President James K. Polk on one occasion invited Congressman Adams to dinner, and Adams refused until such a time as Polk recanted a criticism of Adams's Texas diplomacy. The president angrily refused, and Adams died not long thereafter. Polk and

Adams belonged to different generations. To almost everyone in 1819, Texas had seemed an area only theoretically available for expansion. Even the rankest optimists of that day failed to foresee the flood of immigrants to Texas which began under private auspices in 1821.

The Transcontinental Treaty, an appellation awarded to the Adams-Onís Treaty by Samuel Flagg Bemis, is properly so called because of its attention to a third geographical problem, a trans-Mississippi boundary between Spanish possessions and the territory of the United States. Onís had good reason to try to fence off the Louisiana Purchase from Spain's Mexican lands, and his instructions from Madrid were explicit on that score. He and Adams duly argued out a line showing the western bounds of the purchase. As for the idea of extending this Spanish-American boundary to the Pacific, making the line transcontinental, putting in a

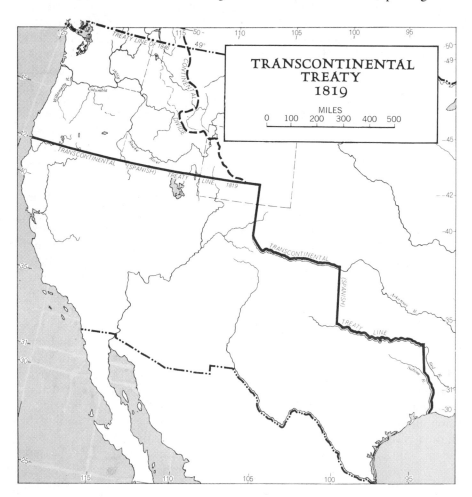

TRANSCONTINENTAL
TREATY
1819

MILES

0   100   200   300   400   500

final "jog" beyond the line of the Louisiana Purchase, out to the Pacific along the forty-second parallel, a line that would divide Spanish California from the then wild and largely uninhabited Oregon territory, this additional line of delineation was first suggested by Adams, in conversation with Onís in July 1818—actually during the cabinet crisis over the Jackson affair.

Just why Adams made this addition to what otherwise would not have been a transcontinental line is hard to say. In the United States at that time most people were as unconcerned about the fate of Oregon as about Texas; Oregon was no pressing issue. Adams later claimed with pride that the idea was his own. The distinguished historian of the Transcontinental Treaty, Philip C. Brooks, believes that John Jacob Astor perhaps prompted the secretary of state to include Oregon in the treaty line, although there is no certain record of Astor's intervention. Brooks believes that Astor may well have said something, as he was voluble on the subject. The great fur merchant reportedly had greeted Albert Gallatin on the latter's return from Ghent with the remark that the commissioners had left one thing undone: "You should have settled more definitely the question of the Columbia territory." Gallatin answered that their great-grandchildren would be the ones to talk about that. "If we live, Mr. Gallatin," was the reputed answer, "we shall see trouble about it in less than forty years." Astor in 1817 assembled a dinner party of a hundred persons to welcome J. Q. Adams home from the legation in England. Did he greet the new secretary of state with the same comments offered to Gallatin?

Perhaps the subject was in the air. That same year in which Adams broached to Onís the project of extending the Spanish-American frontier to the Pacific, 1818, the United States government had concluded a convention with the British government setting out the Anglo-American boundary from the Lake of the Woods out to the Rocky Mountains and thence to the Pacific in a "joint occupation" of Oregon. By "Oregon" the two parties meant the land now constituting the states of Oregon, Washington, Idaho, parts of Montana and Wyoming, and British Columbia. "Oregon" had no boundaries in the Convention of 1818, and Adams may well have thought it a good thing to fix the northernmost limit of Spanish territory so as to strengthen the American claim to Oregon which, frankly, was none too secure. It was in 1818 also that the British gave back the settlement at the mouth of the Columbia River which had been Astoria prior to its capture by H.M.S. *Racoon* during the War of 1812.

Wherever the idea came from, Adams transmitted it to Onís, with the result that the treaty included not merely the cession of the Floridas, with (unlucky article for Adams) Texas to remain as Spanish territory, but a steplike western boundary composed of rivers and parallels (see maps, pp. 173, 180) which took the Spanish-American frontier from the Gulf to the Pacific, crossing the Rocky Mountains westward to the ocean at the forty-second parallel, which now is the northern boundary of the state of California. Adams agreed that his own government would pay $5,000,000 worth of the claims by American citizens against Spain.

The Spanish government through Onís in Washington tried as best it could to avoid the inevitable, but Onís could do little against so redoubtable a diplomatic opponent as John Quincy Adams. Gradually he pressed Onís into agreement. Typical was his stand over article 2 of the proposed treaty, which stipulated that the king of Spain ceded to the United States "all the territories which belong to him, situated to the Eastward of the Mississippi, known by the name of East and West Florida." A comma placed between the word "territories" and the word "which" would have made clear the king of Spain's possession of West Florida. The secretary refused to admit that West Florida belonged to Spain. Adams would not give poor Onís a comma.

At the final stage of the negotiations he was debating with Onís the river boundaries, and although it was customary in diplomacy to take the mid-channel of rivers for boundaries Adams demanded the farthest edge. Monroe by this time was nervous, eager to close the negotiation for mid-channel of the boundary rivers. During a reception at the Executive Mansion, the president said to Onís: "I will do anything you want. I have had a personal esteem for you ever since the first day I dealt with you. Have a glass of wine with me." When the choleric Adams heard of this presidential indiscretion, he let Onís know that he, Adams, was negotiating the treaty. The secretary of state stood fast and obtained the farthest edge of the boundary rivers.

Adams and Onís signed the Transcontinental Treaty on Washington's birthday, 1819.

The secretary got into trouble with ratification of the treaty, for in reading one of Erving's dispatches from Madrid he had noticed the effective date of some skulduggery being arranged by Ferdinand VII. The United States had intended to sell the public lands of the Floridas and use the profit to meet the claims settlements. It was well known that the population of the territory had concentrated in a few towns, the rest of the area being public land. The king of Spain quietly deeded most of the public land of East Florida to three court favorites. Adams was able to show that one of the deeds was invalid, having been made after the expiration date for such acts as stipulated in the treaty. But the Duke of Alagón and the Count of Puñonrostro had good titles. The secretary had anticipated trouble and remarked in his diary that he was haunted by "a vague, general, and superstitious impression that this treaty was too great a blessing not to be followed shortly by something to alloy it." Of all people, the messenger of fate bringing this bad tidings to Monroe, who passed it to Adams, was Henry Clay. What a messenger! Adams's undoubted rival for the presidency upon Monroe's retirement. Monroe tried to make Adams feel better and said it was all the fault of Onís (who probably was innocent), and that if necessary Congress would authorize the seizure of all Florida territory and take Texas also for the expense of the seizure. Two years had to pass until a revolution in Spain enclosed the wily Ferdinand in a constitution, his government annulled the land grants, and the two governments in 1821 ratified the Transcontinental Treaty.

3. *The Monroe Doctrine*

Two years after ratification of the Transcontinental Treaty came the third event of the era of good feelings: in his annual message to Congress in December 1823, President Monroe announced the Monroe Doctrine.

The doctrine eventually became the most honored principle of American foreign policy, but strangely enough it was not considered of large importance at the time. It was not taken seriously outside the United States, and to Monroe himself it was little more than an expedient required by the diplomatic situation of the moment. Little further was heard from it until President Polk's first annual message to Congress in 1845. Interested in the fate of Oregon and California, concerned over possible machinations for these territories by Great Britain, Polk announced that Monroe's principles were "our settled policy, that no future European colony or dominion shall, with our consent, be planted or established on any part of the North American continent." Polk's emphasis upon North America, one should add, was unique with him. The doctrine of 1823 did not receive its name of Monroe Doctrine until 1852. Not until 1895 did an American president, Grover Cleveland, invoke it in the form originally announced by Monroe, *i.e.*, as applicable to the entire Western Hemisphere, and only in the twentieth century did it obtain recognition from the nations of the world.

Monroe's famous message to Congress assuredly did not contain much that was original. Throughout the latter eighteenth century there had been a feeling in America that the New World possessed institutions and a culture different from the Old, and Thomas Paine in his *Common Sense* easily had obtained agreement when he wrote that "It is the true interest of America to steer clear of European contentions, which she never can do, while, by her dependence on Britain, she is made the make-weight in the scale of British politics." John Adams along with other revolutionary patriots urged the same course, and later wrote, "we should separate ourselves, as far as possible and as long as possible, from all European politics and wars." The principle of nonentanglement broke down in 1778 because of the need for help against Great Britain, but the uneasiness of association with France became manifest in the peace negotiations. At one point in the negotiations in Paris occurred the conversation between Adams and the British emissary Oswald, in which the latter said that "You are afraid of being made the tools of the powers of Europe." Replied Adams: "Indeed I am. It is obvious that all the powers of Europe will be continually maneuvering with us, to work us into their real or imaginary balances of power. They will all wish to make of us a makeweight candle, while they are weighing out their pounds." Instances of this feeling that America should stay clear of European politics occurred time and again in the early diplomacy of the United States, one being Washington's neutrality proclamation of 1793. In the Farewell Address of 1796 there was the sensible inquiry, "Why, by interweaving our destiny with that of any part of Europe, entangle our peace and prosperity in the toils of European ambition, rivalship, interest, humor or caprice?" President Jefferson in his inaugural address of 1801 struck the familiar note: "peace, commerce and honest friendship with all nations, entangling alliances with none." Events in Europe after the Napoleonic wars called forth a restatement of this tradition of American detachment.

The course of European politics after Waterloo led to the Monroe Doctrine. The powers of the Continent had managed by the most profound exertions to defeat Napoleon, and the narrowness of their victory had impressed upon all of them the importance of maintaining their wartime coalition during the first uneasy years of peace. The powers commenced their conservative politics with the peace conference, the Congress of Vienna. The keynote of that conference in 1814–1815 was "legitimacy," a word advanced by Talleyrand, who had insinuated himself into the allied counsels to save his own country from further territorial spoilation. France now was back under the rule of a Bourbon, Louis XVIII. The Vienna conferees hoped to recreate the politics and borders of the Continent as in 1792, just before the French revolution had turned outward. Leaders of the great powers believed that, partly by thinking so and partly by judicious use of force, they could remove themselves and their nations from the nineteenth century back into the eighteenth, to the era when thrones and altars had not begun to shake and fall. They had waited a long time to reconstruct Europe on its prerevolutionary foundations and now were determined to do it.

What would be the guarantees of the peace settlement? By the Treaty of Chaumont of March 1814, formally renewed in the Treaty of Paris of November 1815, Austria, Russia, Prussia, and Great Britain bound themselves to the future convocation of diplomatic congresses for the preservation of peace and the *status quo*. This was the "concert of Europe," the Quadruple Alliance (and after the formal entry of France in 1818, the Quintuple Alliance).

The allies and the smaller nations also had an amorphous engagement, the celebrated Holy Alliance of September 1815, which solemnly declared the signatories'

fixed resolution, both in the administration of their respective states, and in their political relations with every other government, to take for their sole guide the precepts of that Holy Religion, namely, the precepts of justice, Christian charity, and peace, which, far from being applicable only to private concerns, must have an immediate influence on the councils of princes, and guide all their steps, as being the only means of consolidating human institutions and remedying their imperfections.

This injunction eventually achieved the signatures of all the rulers of Europe except the sultan of Turkey, the Pope, and the prince regent of Great Britain. It was impossible to ask the sultan, the Pope presumably did not need to sign, and the prince regent declared irritably that the principles of the alliance already guided his country. The United States received an invitation to join, and of course turned it down.

The Holy Alliance became a symbol of reaction, and many contemporary observers confused it with the Quadruple Alliance, although it was the latter grouping that sought to direct European affairs after 1815.

The Quadruple Alliance worked for a few years and then fell apart. At the outset the allies displayed little disagreement over postwar policy. The victory over Napoleon had been so narrow. But as the years went by the differences arose. Great Britain especially found its interests departing from those of the nations of the Continent. The problem was that the keeping of peace soon became not so much a question of subduing the rivalries of rulers as one of quieting the unrest of liberals. The latter were threatening their reactionary sovereigns with revolution. A series of disturbances commenced in Piedmont, Naples, Greece, and Spain. Accustomed to virtual independence during the war years, the provinces of Spain in the New World once more revolted and declared their independence. The British government under Lord Liverpool was no friend of revolution or liberalism, but its foreign secretary, Castlereagh, thought that the general policing of Europe was beyond the scope and ability of the concert of Europe and also contrary to British interests. The principal

European statesman, Prince Klemens von Metternich of Austria, disagreed. Metternich wished to hold down the lid on revolutionary disturbances. At Troppau in 1820 the statesmen of Austria, Russia, and Prussia, with British dissent, agreed that

States which have undergone a change of government due to revolution, the results of which threaten other states, ipso facto cease to be members of the European Alliance and remain excluded from it until their situation gives guaranties for legal order and stability. . . . If, owing to such alterations, immediate danger threatens other states, the powers bind themselves, by peaceful means, or if need be by arms, to bring back the guilty State into the bosom of the Great Alliance.

By the time a new conference opened in Verona in 1822 the British had become alarmed, and at Verona they duly separated themselves from their European allies.

Verona was the turning point of reaction in Europe and the immediate European event which inspired the Monroe Doctrine. The task of Metternich at Verona was a large one, putting down revolutions from the Near East to the Andes. The conference appeared adequate for the work at hand. Present were two emperors, three kings, three reigning grand dukes, a cardinal, a viceroy, three foreign secretaries, twenty ambassadors, and twelve ministers. The forces of reaction in Europe, facing the forces of revolution, seemingly would have no difficulty. At this juncture the British government moved out of the European concert of powers, and in the course of this exit the British foreign secretary, George Canning, sought to concert his policy with that of the United States and unintentionally prompted President Monroe to announce the doctrine of 1823.

Canning had come to the foreign office just before the Verona meeting and was eager to take Great Britain out of the coalition. The policy of intervention gave him a convenient excuse.

A further reason was the French invasion of Spain. After Verona the French had precipitately sent their army into Spain to restore that country to its monarch, Ferdinand VII, who was being humiliated by a revolutionary Constitutionalist government. The French prime minister, Comte Jean de Villèle, later said that he sent French troops to Spain to avoid invasion of Spain by Russian troops, for the tsar at that time had a million men under arms and was anxious to use them to put down revolution in Europe. Villèle's foreign minister, Vicomte François de Chateaubriand, believed that the reason for sending French troops to Spain was simply to suppress the revolution—but Chateaubriand, one suspects, was being emotional. Villèle was in charge of the French government and knew what he was about. At any rate, after this expedition there was desultory talk in French cabinet meetings about sending French princelings to the New World in the wake of French troops, to take over the governments of the revolting Spanish colonies. This talk had little chance of turning into action. Villèle never envisioned more than detachments of French troops, and there was no possibility of an expedition. All French measures were dependent upon Ferdinand VII assuming a reasonable attitude, but Ferdinand was the most unreasonable man in Europe—since he would never have been satisfied with anything less than absolute restoration of Spanish America to his personal rule; hence the French could hardly have seen their way clear to send an expedition to the New World. If by some miracle Ferdinand VII had changed his mind and the French sent an expedition, the British navy would have destroyed it en route, for Canning instructed the British ambassador in Paris on March 31, 1823, that he would not allow France to restore the Spanish colonies to Ferdinand VII. He apparently feared that under a restoration British commerce with the Spanish colonies might pass back to Spain.

Too, Canning wished to mitigate the effects of any aggrandizement of French power on the Continent. As he later boasted, "I resolved that if France had Spain, it should not be Spain 'with the Indies.' I called the New World into existence to redress the balance of the Old." When he sought American help in 1823 for his antirestoration policy he also seems to have desired to please the United States, which was Great Britain's largest customer, at this time taking one-sixth of Britain's foreign trade.

Canning moved to restrain the French, and the unanticipated result was the Monroe Doctrine. He approached the American minister in London, Richard Rush, on August 16, 1823, and on August 20 sent "unofficial and confidential" terms on which the United States and Britain could concert their policy toward any possible French intervention in the New World. "Nothing could be more gratifying to me," he wrote, "than to join with you in such a work, and I am persuaded, there has seldom, in the history of the world, occurred an opportunity when so small an effort of two friendly governments might produce so unequivocal a good and prevent such extensive calamities." Lacking instructions, Rush deferred agreement, but said that if Canning would recognize the independence of the revolted Spanish colonies he, Rush, would make an agreement with the foreign secretary even without instructions. Canning declined, vaguely mentioning a future recognition of the nations of Latin America. The French expedition in Spain took the last Constitutionalist stronghold, Cadiz, on September 30, 1823. Canning held a series of conversations early in October 1823 with the French ambassador, Prince Jules de Polignac, in which the two men agreed that France could not reconquer the Spanish colonies and return them to Spain: "any attempt to bring Spanish America again under its ancient submission to Spain must be utterly hopeless." Canning already had warned the French against such a move in March 1823. The American minister, Rush, did not learn from Canning of the so-called Polignac Memorandum—an account of the British position, given to Polignac on October 9—until November 24, and Canning did not communicate its essence to Rush until December 13. Meanwhile, and unaware of the British pressure on France, President Monroe made his own announcement.

Monroe did not understand the situation in Europe and believed that there was some danger of intervention by France in the New World. He had before him the examples of Spain, Naples, and Piedmont, where the continental allies had snuffed out revolutions. He knew there was talk of an invasion of Latin America. His secretary of state, Adams, sensed the true arrangement of forces in Europe, that there was never serious danger of a French expedition, that Canning had frustrated even the remote possibility of such an expedition, and it was Adams who urged Monroe and the cabinet to seize the occasion and make a unilateral statement of American principles. Upon Monroe's suggestion the statement was placed in the annual message to Congress in December 1823. Adams persuaded the president to cut out any acknowledgment in the message of the inde-

The Birth of the Monroe Doctrine; painting by Clyde O. Deland. (L to R.: John Quincy Adams, W. H. Crawford, William Wirt, President Monroe, John C. Calhoun, Daniel D. Tomkins, and an unidentified man.)

pendence of Greece, which Monroe wished to put in, and Adams also excised some presidential strictures on the French invasion of Spain. The resultant doctrine contained the following three essential points: non-colonization, "hands off" the New World, American abstention from the quarrels of Europe.

Noncolonization came from Adams's experience with Russian designs along the Pacific coast. The tsar in a mood of impetuosity had announced in a ukase of 1821 that Russia possessed sovereignty to Pacific coast territory and waters from Alaska south to the fifty-first parallel. This was an extension southward of the tsar's dominions, and Secretary Adams in a plucky note to the Russian minister in Washington in the summer of 1823 announced the principle of noncolonization, that "we should contest the right of Russia to *any* territorial establishment on this continent, and that we should assume distinctly the principle that the American continents are no longer subjects for any new European colonial establishments." As repeated in the Monroe Doctrine, this principle stated that "the American continents, by the free and independent condition which they have assumed and maintain, are henceforth not to be considered as subjects for future colonization by any European powers."

The second idea of the doctrine, hands off the New World, appeared in Monroe's message of 1823 as follows: "We owe it, therefore, to candor and to the amicable relations existing between the United States and those powers [of Europe] to declare that we should consider any attempt on their part to extend their system to any portion of this hemisphere as dangerous to our peace and safety."

In regard to abstention the president remarked that "In the wars of the European powers in matters relating to themselves we have never taken any part, nor does it comport with our policy so to do."

Such was the doctrine announced by President Monroe. As mentioned, the president did not consider it a large and special pronouncement but a prudent diplomatic move called forth by the state of European politics in the year 1823. He well knew that the British government would take care of its enforcement.

As for the European reaction to the doctrine, it was, quite naturally, one of surprise and disgust. If Lafayette in a typical remark of esteem for Americans thought the doctrine "the best little bit of paper that God had ever permitted any man to give to the World," the men who directed European affairs believed that the United States was taking credit for a British policy and doing so in an officious way. The powers found Monroe's principles monstrous, haughty, blustering, and arrogant. Metternich wrote the tsar that the new American act was another revolt, more un-provoked than and fully as audacious as the American revolution. It was an "indecent declaration," which cast "blame and scorn on the institutions of Europe most worthy of respect, on the principles of its greatest sovereigns, on the whole of those measures" necessary for preservation of society in the Old World. The tsarist government agreed, and informed the Russian minister in Washington that "the document in question . . . merits only the most profound contempt."

The doctrine thereupon passed into history and slumbered until the turn of the twentieth century when, under Grover Cleveland and Theodore Roosevelt, the European powers came to realize that the principles of Colonel Monroe were worthy of respect.

4. *Independence of Latin America*

A word remains to be said about recognition of the Latin American governments, proposed by Rush to Canning in the autumn of 1823. Recognition had been talked about for some years before the Rush-Canning conversations, and indeed there had been a vote on it in the House of Representatives in 1818. At that time Henry Clay had made a motion in the House for recognition of Buenos Aires (the United Provinces of the Rio de la Plata). Clay's resolve would have appropriated $18,000 for the salary and outfit of a minister. The resolution was technically proper, as under the Constitution the House had the right to appropriate money, although from the beginning of the federal government in 1789 the president personally had made the decision for recognition of new governments. But Clay's resolution threatened to embarrass the Monroe administration in 1818. Secretary of State John Quincy Adams was in the midst of the negotiation of the Transcontinental Treaty with Onís. By marshaling its supporters, the administration quashed Clay's proposal by a vote of 45 for, 115 against.

But by 1822, a year after ratification of the Transcontinental Treaty, different circumstances obtained, and Monroe decided upon recognition. The Latin American states had expelled the forces of Spain, with exception of a part of Peru still held by the royalists. José de San Martín, the liberator of the South, had taken its capital, Lima, and soon Simón Bolívar, the liberator of the North, would join him. Only the Caribbean possessions—Cuba, Puerto Rico, Santo Domingo—would remain faithful to Spain. On March 8, 1822, Monroe proposed to Congress an appropriation for missions to Buenos Aires, Colombia, Chile, Peru, and Mexico. Congress answered with $100,000 for "such missions to the independent nations on the American continent as the President might deem proper." Monroe signed the act on May 4.

Much to the disgust of Clay and certain other individuals, the president did not show an excess of enthusiasm for the independence of the new states. Secretary Adams likewise was not excited. Both men considered the neutrality of the United States more important than partisanship. Monroe felt that he was continuing Jefferson's policy, begun with the Spanish revolution of May 1808, of excluding European influence from America. In 1822 the president had not yet moved forward in his thinking to the exuberance of 1823. The Latin Americans were well aware of the cold wind blowing down from the north, and long before the year of United States recognition their representatives had departed from Washington. Only Manuel Torres, the representative of Colombia, remained, and he was permanently domiciled in Philadelphia, where he had resided for a quarter of a century. Monroe recognized his government first. Then came the turn of Mexico, which he recognized despite the fact that he thus was giving the national blessing to a native emperor, Iturbide, hardly a republican in sentiment. The United States recognized the three other nations of the group of five named in Monroe's message by sending ministers, to Buenos Aires and Chile in 1823 and to Peru in 1826. Central America and Brazil meanwhile were recognized in 1824. Brazil, incidentally, was another imperial government. These were the only Latin American nations recognized by the United States until 1830.

After Monroe had sent in his recognition message the British minister, Stratford Canning, had met Secretary Adams. Canning took the news of recognition lightly.

"So Mr. Adams," he said, "you are going to make honest men of them?"

"Yes, Sir," was the answer. "We proposed to your government to join us some time ago, but they would not, and now we shall see whether you will be content to *follow* us."

In Britain there was enormous opposition to such a course, which explains Canning's reluctance to meet Rush on the issue in 1823. The reactionary Tories of Lord Liverpool's government, while willing to allow Canning to detach Britain from the continental allies, were unwilling to assist by recognition the revolutionary governments in the New World. As events turned out, the British had to recognize the Latin American governments if they desired to continue trade in that region of the world. The British recognized Colombia, Mexico, and the United Provinces on December 31, 1824. It thereupon became the unpleasant duty of the Tory peer Lord Eldon as lord chancellor to read to Parliament on February 7, 1825, the king's speech affirming the government's decision to recognize. Eldon did so with a very bad grace. The king himself, George IV, declined to have anything to do with the speech. His Majesty said that he was suffering from a bad attack of gout and that, in any case, he had mislaid his false teeth.

In this manner ended an era in American diplomacy.

A CONTEMPORARY DOCUMENT

[Nowhere did the new national feelings of the post-1815 era appear more prominently than in the diary of John Quincy Adams. President Monroe's secretary of state saw the British minister, Stratford Canning, on January 27, 1821, and the result was a great argument. Source: Charles Francis Adams, ed., *Memoirs of John Quincy Adams, Comprising Portions of His Diary from 1795 to 1848* (12 vols., Philadelphia, 1874–1877), V, 249–252.]

The messenger of the Department announced Mr. Canning. I told the messenger to say to Mr. Canning that I would receive him in a few minutes. Mr. Eddy remained with me not more than five minutes longer; and Mr. Canning when he came in, as he sat down, took out his watch, and observed that it was forty minutes faster than the clock here. While he was speaking, the clock in the office struck one. I made no answer to his remark, which might be considered either as a complaint that he had been made to wait, or as an apology for having come before the time appointed. He proceeded to say that, conformably to the desire expressed by me yesterday, he had now come to have some further conversation upon the subject of our interview then.

There was in his manner an apparent effort of coolness, but no appearance of cheerfulness or good humor. I saw there was no relaxation from the tone he had yesterday assumed, and felt that none would on my part be suitable. I said he would recollect that our conference of this day was not at my desire. I had yesterday repeatedly expressed to him the opinion that if this discussion was to be further pursued it should be in writing. He had with some earnestness urged another conference, and when he requested me to fix the time I had told him that I was ready and willing to hear then anything that he had to say on the subject; that perhaps, under the excitement which he was then manifesting, he might himself prefer to resume the conversation some other day, and, if so, I would see him whenever it should be most agreeable to himself; he had then asked me to name a time, and I appointed this day at one o'clock.

He said, "Well, then, be it so." He then took from his pocket the National Intelligencer of yesterday, folded down to the column in which the proceedings of the House of Representatives were reported, and, referring to the statement that Mr. Floyd had reported a bill for the occupation of the Columbia River, said that was an indication of intentions in this Government which he presumed would leave no question of the propriety of his application to me.

I told him it was precisely that in which its greatest impropriety consisted. But I could only repeat what I had said to him yesterday, that I saw no use in continuing a discussion upon the propriety of his conduct or of mine.

He said he would most cheerfully consent to be the sacrifice, if that only was necessary to the harmony of the two countries; but that nothing could exceed his astonishment at the manner in which I had received his application of yesterday. He could assure me with the utmost sincerity that since the existence of this country as a nation there never had been a time when the British Government had been so anxiously desirous of preserving and cherishing the most perfect good understanding and harmony with this; but that at the same time they would not, on that account, yield one particle of their rights.

I told him I had no doubt of the correctness of his statement in both its parts, and I was happy to give him the same assurance on the part of this Government. It was the earnest wish of the President to preserve the most friendly relations with Great Britain; but he would maintain all the rights of the United States. And I would add, as my individual opinion, that any chicaning of our right to the mouth of Columbia River would assuredly not tend to promote that harmony between the two countries.

Mr. Canning again repeated his surprise at the tone and temper with which his application yesterday had been received. He said he had examined and re-examined himself, and had in vain enquired what could have been the cause of the asperity with which he had been treated by me.

"Sir," said I, "suppose Mr. Rush should be present at a debate in the House of Commons, and should hear a member in the course of a speech say something about the expediency of sending a regiment of troops to the Shetland Islands, or a new colony to New South Wales; suppose another member of Parliament should publish in a newspaper a letter recommending the same project; and suppose Mr. Rush should then go to Lord Castlereagh and formally allege those two facts as his motives for demanding whether the British Government had any such intentions; and, if answered that very probably they might, he should assume an imperious and tragical tone of surprise and talk about a violation of treaties: how do you think it would be received?"

He said that *now* he fully understood me, and could account for what had passed; this answer was perfectly explicit. But did I consider the cases as parallel?

"So far as any question of right is concerned," said I, "perfectly parallel."

"Have you," said Mr. Canning, "any *claim* to the Shetland Islands or New South Wales?"

"Have you any *claim*," said I, "to the mouth of Columbia River?"

"Why, do you not *know*," replied he, "that we have a claim?"

"I do not *know*," said I, "what you claim nor what you do not claim. You claim India; you claim Africa; you claim—"

"Perhaps," said he, "a piece of the moon."

"No," said I; "I have not heard that you claim exclusively any part of the moon; but there is not a spot on *this* habitable globe that I could affirm you do not claim; and there is none which you may not claim with as much color of right as you can have to Columbia River or its mouth."

"And how far would you consider," said he, "this exclusion of right to extend?"

"To all the shores of the South Sea," said I. "We know of no right that you have there."

"Suppose," said he, "Great Britain should undertake to make a settlement there, would you object to it?"

"I have no doubt we should," said I.

"But, surely," said Mr. Canning, "proof was made at the negotiation of the Convention of October, 1818, of the claims of Great Britain, and their existence is recognized in it."

"There was no proof," I said, "made of any claim, nor, to my knowledge, any discussion of claim. The boundary to the Stony Mountains was defined; westward of them Great Britain had no settlement whatever. We had one at the mouth of the Columbia, which, having been broken up during the war, was solemnly restored to us by the British Government, in fulfilment of a stipulation in the treaty of peace. We stipulated in the Convention that the ports and places on the Pacific Ocean should be open to both parties for ten years, and, taking all these transactions together, we certainly did suppose that the British Government had come to the conclusion that there would be neither policy nor profit in cavilling with us about territory on this North American continent."

"And in this," said he, "you include our northern provinces on this continent?"

"No," said I; "there the boundary is marked, and we have no disposition to encroach upon it. Keep what is yours, but leave the rest of this continent to us."

ADDITIONAL READING

For post-1815 diplomacy through 1823 and the Monroe Doctrine, the best introduction is *George Dangerfield, *The Era of Good Feelings* (New York, 1952), a masterful account written with grace and understanding. Dangerfield has contributed a volume to the New American Nation series, *The Awakening of American Nationalism: 1815–1828* (New York, 1965).

The Barbary pirates deserve a better literature than they have received. Scholars somehow have not caught the excitement of the burning of the *Philadelphia* and the other gallant engagements of that fighting time. C. O. Paullin examines the *Diplomatic Negotiations of American Naval Officers: 1778–1833* (Baltimore, 1912); R. W. Irwin looks coldly at *The Diplomatic Relations of the United States with the Barbary Powers: 1776–1816* (Chapel Hill, N.C., 1931). Louis B. Wright and J. H. Macleod do something more for their subject in *The First Americans in North Africa: William Eaton's Struggle for a Vigorous Policy against the Barbary Pirates, 1799–1805* (Princeton, 1945).

The Florida problem appears in Isaac J. Cox, *The West Florida Controversy, 1798–1813: A Study in American Diplomacy* (Baltimore, 1918). The definitive account of the Transcontinental Treaty is Philip C. Brooks, *Diplomacy and the Borderlands: The Adams-Onís Treaty of 1819* (Berkeley, Calif., 1939).

Recognition of the new Latin American nations by the United States has had several historians: John A. Logan, Jr., *No Transfer* (New Haven, 1961) deals in part with this problem; E. H. Tatum, Jr., *The United States and Europe: 1815–1823* (Berkeley, Calif., 1936) looks to the center of Latin America's problem; see also C. C. Griffin, *The United States and the Disruption of the Spanish Empire: 1810–1822* (New York, 1937); *Arthur P. Whitaker, *The United States and the Independence of Latin America: 1800–1830* (Baltimore, 1941); J. Fred Rippy, *Rivalry of the United States and Great Britain over Latin-America: 1808–1830* (Baltimore, 1929); William W. Kaufmann, *British Policy and the Independence of Latin America: 1804–28* (New Haven, 1951). The historian of the Monroe Doctrine is Dexter Perkins, who in addition to a general work, *A History of the Monroe Doctrine* (2d ed., Boston, 1955), has written three sequent volumes for the years 1823–1826 (Cambridge, Mass., 1927), 1826–1867 (Baltimore, 1933), and 1867–1907 (Baltimore, 1937).

Biographies include the indispensable *John Quincy Adams and the Foundations of American Foreign Policy* (New York, 1949) by Samuel Flagg Bemis; J. H. Powell, *Richard Rush, Republican Diplomat: 1780–1859* (Philadelphia, 1942); *Marquis James, *Andrew Jackson: The Border Captain* (Indianapolis, 1933); Bernard Mayo, *Henry Clay: Spokesman of the New West* (Boston, 1937); Glyndon G. Van Deusen, *The Life of Henry Clay* (Boston, 1937); and the last three volumes of Irving Brant's *James Madison*.

☆ **8** ☆

Manifest Destiny

A More Perfect Union embracing the entire North American Continent.
—Senator Daniel S. Dickinson, toast at the Jackson dinner, 1848

In the history of American diplomacy few ideas have been more important than "manifest destiny"—the belief of the people of the United States that the North American continent, despite prior claims by France, Spain, Russia, Great Britain, and Mexico, was destined to become American territory. This mystic conviction translated itself into reality in the years from the beginning of the nineteenth century to the end of the Civil War. French claims to North America vanished with the Louisiana Purchase of 1803. Spanish claims received settlement in the Adams-Onís Transcontinental Treaty of 1819, after which Spain's lands contiguous to the United States passed under control of the new government of Mexico. Russia's claims to Pacific territory withdrew northward to Alaska in a Russian-American agreement of 1824. British claims to Oregon territory disappeared in a treaty signed in 1846. And by 1848 Mexico's claims to Texas, New Mexico, and California were no more. "Away, away with all those cobweb tissues of rights of discovery, exploration, settlement, continuity, etc.," cried the New York editor, John L. O'Sullivan, who in the year 1845 coined the phrase "manifest destiny." It was, O'Sullivan claimed, "the right of our manifest destiny to overspread and to possess the whole of the continent which Providence has given us for the development of the great experiment in liberty and federative self-government entrusted to us."

O'Sullivan believed that the United States should not confine its territorial ambitions to the continent of North America: "Its floor shall be as a hemisphere—its roof the firmament of the star-studded heavens, and its congregation an Union of many Republics, comprising hundreds of happy millions . . . governed by God's natural and moral law of equality." Such hopes, of course, were never to be realized, and manifest destiny in its more practical vision limited itself to North America.

Two questions might arise at this point, the first of which can be stated as follows: Was manifest destiny nothing but imperialism, an American brand of a well-known nineteenth-century European practice? The nineteenth century was the age of imperialism in Europe, and although European nations undertook their vast colonial conquests in the latter part of the century, whereas the United States pursued its manifest destiny and continental ambition in earlier years, still it might well seem that there was little difference between imperialism and manifest destiny.

In actual fact there was a considerable difference. Manifest destiny was not imperialism if the latter term is properly defined as "rule over alien peoples." There were few Indians in the American West, hardly any at all if compared to the millions of inhabitants of Africa and the hundreds of millions of Asians. It is true that American policy toward the Indians frequently adhered to the frontier maxim that the only good Indians were dead Indians, and it is true that new diseases brought by the settlers decimated the Indians. But in view of the few Indians in the United States one must say that only in an extremely legalistic sense was the American nation imperialist during the early nineteenth century.

A second question in connection with manifest destiny concerns specifically the Mexican War: Was not this war, one of the most important chapters in American territorial expansion, a war of aggression—did not Americans pick a quarrel in 1846 with a weak and divided Mexico for the purpose of despoiling the Mexicans of New Mexico and California, and could not one therefore say that manifest destiny, at least as avowed in 1846–1848, was only an excuse for a war of conquest?

The reader, having noticed the opening paragraphs of this chapter, can see that the author does not believe manifest destiny was thus an excuse, but this argument, often made, deserves investigation. Many Americans have felt embarrassment because their country went to war against a feeble sister republic of the New World and took from her a large expanse of territory. Present-day psychologists would perhaps diagnose this feeling as a guilt complex, the persistent belief of many good-hearted and well-intentioned citizens of the United States that their country in the mid-nineteenth century had not lived up to minimum standards of behavior. This lingering guilt complex, over a hundred years after the event, becomes the more intense when one realizes that the nation in the twentieth century could not possibly give back to Mexico the territories won in 1846–1848. It might therefore be advantageous to look back to the details of Mexican-American relations in the early nineteenth century, to see whether the Mexican War was in fact a war of aggression, a war of conquest pure and simple, the sort of war which the government and people of the United States would condemn in the twentieth century, against which Americans have fought two world wars and accepted the possibility of a third, a war in which the idea of manifest destiny was only a sort of rationalizing veneer.

1. *Mexico and the Texas revolution*

At the turn of the nineteenth century the lands of Mexico belonged to Spain, and it was only after some years of uncertainty during the Napoleonic wars, after reconquest of Mexico by Spain at the end of the wars, that Mexico in 1821 became an independent nation. Twenty-five years of independence followed before the government in Mexico City had to face war with the United States.

The tasks of the Mexican government in its early years were, by any standard, large. The lands of Mexico began in Central America, at the border of Guatemala. Mexican territory reached eastward through Yucatan, northward through the isthmus of Tehuantepec to spread like a gigantic fan across twelve hundred miles of virgin territory from the Sabine River in the east to California in the west. Over these distances the government in Mexico City had to exert its authority, distances that in the early nineteenth century rendered the far reaches of the country much more remote from the Mexican capital than Fairbanks or Honolulu are from Washington, D.C. today. The task of administering the territory of Mexico from the capital in Mexico City was therefore almost impossible. The northern Mexican provinces of Texas, New Mexico, and California were distinctly separated by geography from the populous region about Mexico City and were oriented economically to the United States. From the Nueces River to the Rio Grande was a desert tract. South of the Rio Grande for hundreds of miles there was almost no cultivation. Westward for hundreds of miles stretched sheer wilderness and desert.

Was there any chance that with time Mexico might have peopled its northern empire? Not unless time were reckoned in terms of several decades, perhaps a century or more, and even this might not have sufficed. Some six million Indians and half-castes lived in Mexico—no one knows, of course, just what the population really was—and controlling this ignorant and poverty-stricken mass were only some 60,000 Spanish-speaking and Spanish-descended persons who were the government officials and landholders and priests and army officers. Nearly all of the 60,000 Spanish lived in the area now embraced within the republic of Mexico.

They had little desire to migrate to the northern provinces, Texas and New Mexico and California. They remained in their comfortable towns and ranches, and only a trickle of people from Mexico proper entered the upper territories. This trickle could do little when the Yankee flood began coming across the Sabine shortly after signature of the Transcontinental Treaty in 1819.

One cannot stress sufficiently the point that Texas and the other northern territories of Mexico were virtually empty lands, lacking Mexican settlers, and because of distance, lacking almost any control from Mexico City.

Mexican establishments in California, like those in Texas, were pitiful in their poverty and unimportance. If in Texas there were only about three thousand Mexicans of Spanish origin in the 1830's, there were little more than four thousand in California, a mere handful consisting chiefly of priests and monks about the missions, soldiers employed to keep the Indians submissive, and a few large landowners and cattle raisers. In California the area of Mexican control never extended north of San Francisco, nor inland beyond the coastal area. The first Mexican settlers had come at about the time of the American revolution, and few settlers followed them. Certainly there could be no comparison between the Mexican attempt to settle California and the effort by Englishmen a hundred and fifty years earlier to settle the province of New England, for in the Great Migration of 1630–1642 some 16,000 Englishmen from the Old World came there, to say nothing of simultaneous English migrations to other parts of America.

Aside from the difficulty of holding the northern territories, there was the more serious problem of the debility and incompetence of the Mexican government. The revolution against Spain had broken out in 1810, and the Mexicans triumphed conclusively over the forces of their mother country in 1821. In the next year a military adventurer, Agustín de Iturbide, made himself emperor of Mexico with the title of Augustus I. After a short time he fell from power, went abroad, returned, and was shot. The Mexicans in 1824 established a federal constitution on the United States model, and this constitution managed to stay in effect for five years, after which another military leader, Bustamante, subverted it and took office for three years. He was displaced by Antonio López de Santa Anna, the prince of Mexican adventurers, who was in and out of power several times in the next two decades. There was no peace in Mexico before 1877 when General Porfirio Díaz took the reins of government and held them with absolute authority until 1911, after which came a new time of trouble for government in Mexico.

It was nominally the effort of Santa Anna in 1835 to centralize the

Mexican government that led to a revolt in Texas in 1835–1836, but behind the constitutional issue lay the weakness of Mexican control in Texas, the thinness of Mexican settlement, and—above all—the fact that in fifteen years preceding the Texas revolution some thirty thousand Americans had moved into the Mexican province.

Land hunger had drawn American settlers to Texas during the years after the first group arrived in 1821 under the guidance of the *empresario* Stephen F. Austin. Austin had contracted with the Mexican government for many thousands of acres of land in return for bringing in families of settlers. The families paid about ten cents an acre for their land, with liberal arrangements of credit, at a time when inferior land was selling in the United States for $1.25 cash. The United States government, following a financial panic in 1819, had tightened its land policy, and the Bank of the United States, then the principal bank of credit in the country, had drastically reduced its loans and raised its rates of interest, so that settlers seeking cheap lands were driven by force of circumstance to accept the propositions of such men as Stephen Austin. Few of these early American settlers in Texas stopped to inquire as to the type of government they would encounter in their new country. Even the demand of Mexican authorities that they become converts to Catholicism did not disturb their consciences, and they accepted the forms of Catholicism as easily as they

Santa Anna.

accepted other Mexican laws exercised through the Texas organs of the Mexican government—always provided that government, law, and religion did not interfere with their wholehearted search for cheap land.

Naturally the carefree attitude and abandon with which settlers moved into Texas changed when, after a few years, prosperity permitted leisure for thought and consideration. What in early days had proved acceptable began to irk. Especially the effects of frontier religious revivals must be considered, as Methodist and Baptist and Presbyterian preachers took up superintendence over the souls of American frontiersmen. Settlers also remembered their old allegiance to the United States. When General Andrew Jackson took office as president of the United States in 1829, a wave of enthusiasm and hope rose in the American West. No frontier settlement, even in Mexican Texas, could forget that the "Ginral" was a man of the people. Meanwhile life kept improving. "Within four miles of me," wrote one Texas settler in the mid-1830's, "there are more than one thousand inhabitants, chiefly new emigrants, and within the same distance we have four small stores, two blacksmith shops and two schools. We have a dancing frolick every week and preaching allmost [sic] every Sunday."

In a bare decade and a half more settlers came to Texas than in centuries of Spanish administration. This was the inescapable statistic of the Texas situation by the time of the Texas revolution. By the early 1830's the American settlers outnumbered the Spanish-Mexican population by ten to one. Mexican administrators in Mexico City and in Texas took alarm. The Americans had been fairly happy under the short-lived constitution of 1824, the easy requirements of which were laxly enforced. The processes of Mexican government had not touched them to any important extent. But when the government of Santa Anna sought in 1835 to tighten the administration in Texas, trouble began which might have been foreseen from the moment the first American immigrants entered Texas in 1821. It was not foreseen, and by 1835 time had run out on Mexican claims to Texas. There followed during the winter and early spring of 1835–1836 the chief events of the Texas revolution.

Some settlers in Texas had risen in November 1835 and in an unorganized but effective fashion had expelled the few Mexican soldiers and administrators then present on Texan soil. To quell this rebellion, Santa Anna led a large army of 3,000 men into Texas and began his assault with the famous attack on the Alamo. There the rapacious Mexican leader isolated 188 Americans under Colonel William B. Travis and raised from the cathedral the black flag of No Quarter. For seven or eight days the Texans held out, issuing a defiant call for help to "all Americans in the world." But no help arrived, and the Mexican troops closed in on the defenders and slaughtered them to the last man. The Alamo, to indulge in an understatement, incited Texans to fury. "Thermopylae had her messenger of defeat—the Alamo had none," roared General Edward Burleson when he heard the news of the tragedy. Foolishly Santa Anna followed up this slaughter by an even larger carnival at Goliad, where he shot down more than 300 American prisoners in cold blood. News of these massacres spread terror among thousands of the Texas settlers, and as Santa Anna advanced there began a wild flight to the border of the United States, the Sabine River. A long, suffering procession of refugees, women and children and Negro slaves, struggled to reach American territory. The exodus took place in cold weather, with incessant rain. Fortunately Santa Anna shortly thereafter met his downfall when General Sam Houston caught him encamped in a trap. Houston had only to attack. This the Texan leader vigorously did, to the embarrassment of the Head of the Mexican State, who at the crucial moment was taking a siesta. With the Battle of San Jacinto on April 21, 1836, the capture of Santa Anna and dispersal of his army, Texas became independent.

One should perhaps point out, in discussing the Texas revolution, that it was in the main a revolt fought by volunteers from the United States. Of the approximately 700 men killed in action or massacred as prisoners by the Mexicans in the spring of 1836, less than a fifth had lived in Texas at the beginning of hostilities in the autumn of 1835. Companies of Americans descended the Mississippi as soon as news of the revolt arrived in the United States, and these forces, thinly disguised as emigrants, fought the revolution. Volunteers came from all over the United States, traveling even from Maine. The emigrants from Maine vowed solemnly that they would "fite or dye" for Texan liberty. American neutrality laws, of course, should have prevented this interference in the Texas revolution, for according to international law it is not permissible for citizens of a country to organize military companies on their own soil and travel as a unit to another country engaged in war. Two years after the Texas revolution, in 1838, when the Canadians had a large-scale revolt against British rule and when organized military units from the United States sought to interfere in the hostilities between the British government and its colonials, the United States hastily passed a stringent neutrality statute, which showed that American neutrality during the Texas revolt had been something less than proper.

As for the meaning of Texan independence for the continental expansion of the United States, the precise manner in which the events of 1835–1836 fitted into the course of manifest destiny, this was not immediately apparent in 1836. The Texans after their revolution made a desultory effort to be independent and obtained recognition by several foreign states, including the United States, Great Britain, and France. Some nine years elapsed before March 1, 1845, when the American Congress by joint resolution annexed Texas to the United States.

To the Texans of today—many of whom, like the inhabitants of present-day California, have spent most of their lives in other localities but have acquired a pride in their adopted state—the period of independence was a demonstration of Texan prowess before the entire world, after which the people of Texas joined the union. Actually the Texan republic was a feeble affair, which ran up a huge debt and almost from fear of bankruptcy joined the American union. The republic lived anything but a serene existence. In the days when the Mexicans were carrying everything before them in the spring of 1836, the head of the Yanqui rebels in Texas—the newly installed rebel governor—and his council were at loggerheads, trading recriminations rather than seeking ways of halting the foe. The governor at one point sent a message denouncing his council as Judases, scoundrels, wolves, and parricides. The council responded by branding the charges as "false and unfounded," condemning the language as "low, blackguardly and vindictive, and disgraceful to the office from which it emanated." Such were some of the difficulties of Texas independence.

Until annexation in 1845 there was sentiment for maintaining independence and refusing annexation to the United States. Part of this feeling based itself on the injunctions of the British agent in Texas, a naval captain named Charles Elliot, who advised the Texans to trust to the good offices and support of Great Britain. His scheme found some support in England, where the ministries occasionally saw in Texas a place to obtain raw cotton, and to which they could export manufactured goods without paying a tariff as in the United States. The British agent managed to offer the Texans early in 1845—when the United States had agreed, upon Texan approval, to annexation—a treaty by Mexico recognizing Texan independence and providing a settlement of the Mexico-Texas boundary. This boundary had remained in dispute since the revolution and the Mexicans were still nominally at war with the Texans. But the British scheme came to naught, for the Texan Congress in the early summer of 1845 accepted all but unanimously the proffer of annexation to the United States.

2. *The annexation of Texas*

Annexation of Texas by the United States, accomplished in 1845, had been a diplomatic problem long before Texan independence. It had arisen far earlier than the need to deal with Texan patriots and with the suggestions of the British resident agent. Interest of the United States in Texas

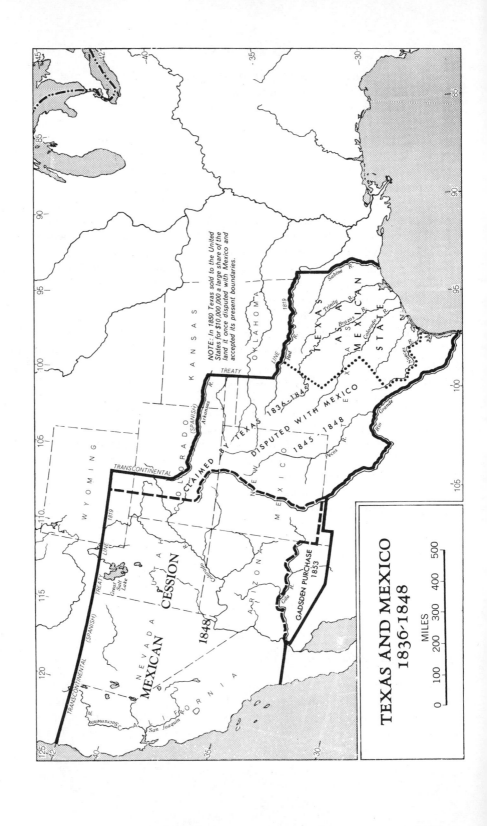

TEXAS AND MEXICO
1836-1848

NOTE: In 1850 Texas sold to the United States for $10,000,000 a large share of the land it once disputed with Mexico and accepted its present boundaries.

MEXICAN CESSION 1848

CLAIMED BY TEXAS 1836-1845

DISPUTED WITH MEXICO 1845-1848

GADSDEN PURCHASE 1853

MILES
0   100   200   300   400   500

went back at least to the time of the Louisiana Purchase in 1803, and it is safe to say that for a quarter of a century and more before Jefferson's fortunate bargain there had been a feeling of "our rising empire," a belief that the United States—as successor to the titles under the colonial charters which had granted lands from sea to sea—would itself reach from Atlantic to Pacific as generations of pioneers struck out into the West. In 1803, one may be sure, the vision of Texas under American settlement and sovereignty seemed realizable only in the remote future. The Texas question, despite the western explorations of Lewis and Clark and Zebulon Pike, seemed highly academic. Jefferson himself had believed that it would require a hundred generations, maybe more, to fill the West.

American ambitions, it is fair to say, changed with startling rapidity in the years after the War of 1812. John Quincy Adams in 1819 reluctantly agreed with Don Luis de Onís that the Sabine River would form part of the western boundary of the Louisiana territory. At the moment, Monroe's entire cabinet and General Andrew Jackson agreed that the Sabine was the best boundary that the United States could get. The Sabine boundary turned out to be a mistake, for within months after signature of the Adams-Onís Transcontinental Treaty opinions began to change. Jackson in patriotic old age asserted that he never agreed to the Sabine. Other patriots found themselves declaiming that the Sabine boundary was a fraud. John Quincy Adams had to defend his choice of the Sabine for the rest of his long life.

During his presidential administration Adams had sought to buy Texas from Mexico, but to no avail, perhaps because the New Englander was only willing to offer the paltry price of a million dollars. His secretary of state, Henry Clay, used every possible argument to make the proud and newly independent Mexicans sell their northern province, even pointing out that if Texas were ceded to the United States the capital of Mexico would be situated nearer the center of the country. Nothing came of such negotiation.

Andrew Jackson turned to a sharper diplomacy, and his minister to Mexico City, Colonel Anthony Butler, made persistent efforts to acquire Texas and did not shy from proposals to his chief that the United States bribe Mexican political leaders. This idea was not completely foolish. It was not uncommon for many Mexican political leaders of the early nineteenth century to accept bribes in one form or another, and Butler was only being realistic when he wrote to Jackson in 1831 that "As the influence of money is as well understood and as readily conceded by these people as any under Heaven, I have no doubt of its doing its office." The general scrawled on the back of one such letter, "A. Butler. What a Scamp." The scamp remained in Mexico City from 1829 to 1836, and we may be sure that Butler kept busy during that time, hatching one plot after another. The historian of Texas annexation and of the Mexican War, Justin H. Smith, later wrote of Butler that he "was a national disgrace . . . personally a bully and a swashbuckler, ignorant at first of the Spanish language and even the forms of diplomacy, shamefully careless about legation affairs, wholly unprincipled as to methods, and by the open testimony of two American consuls openly scandalous in conduct." Be that as it may, Butler busied himself after what many Americans considered the grandly national business of getting Texas from the Mexicans.

The Texan revolution of 1835–1836 made no change in American policy. Andrew Jackson, consummate politician that he was, refused during his second administration to sponsor admission of Texas to the union. Desiring annexation, he refrained from making political capital of it, for fear that the Texas question if propelled into politics would reopen the slavery question, uneasily adjourned by the Compromise of 1820. Northern congressional leaders were certain that Texas upon admission to the union would be a slave state, and this would raise the inconvenient issue of balance of slave versus free states in the Senate, which then was exactly even, thirteen slave and thirteen free. Especially they thought of what might happen if Texas upon annexation should split itself into five or ten slave states, for this would ruin any hope of maintaining the sectional balance. Jackson was aware of northern feeling on this matter. The most obtuse statesman—which Jackson assuredly was not—could hardly remain ignorant of the rising feeling between North and South. Jackson moved gingerly and with complete impartiality of action, if not of feeling, when the Texans in 1836 declared their independence. At one point Sam Houston asked the general if Texas, desperately in need of money, might have a share in distribution of surplus revenue from the treasury. Jackson commented on this request: "The writer did not reflect that we have a treaty with Mexico, and our national faith is pledged to support it. The Texans before they took the step to declare themselves Independent which has aroused all Mexico against them ought to have pondered well —it was a rash and premature act, our neutrality must be faithfully maintained." Giving as excuse for his inaction the existence of a treaty between his country and Mexico, and the proprieties of international intercourse, Jackson had in mind the delicate political situation in the United States.

With the refusal of the Jackson administration to annex Texas after San Jacinto, relations between the two sovereign English-speaking states of North America settled down to a brief and quiet interlude. Jackson recognized Texas independence eleven months after San Jacinto, four months longer than the American government had waited to recognize

Mexico after its successful revolution against Spain in 1821. The Mexicans nonetheless protested American recognition of Texas and refused themselves to recognize Texan independence, a policy in which they persisted to the bitter end. Events continued in this course—Texan independence, American recognition, Mexican nonrecognition—until President John Tyler in 1844 sponsored in the Senate a treaty of annexation, and failing in that effort resorted early in 1845 to a joint resolution of annexation.

There is no point in detailing the fortunes and misfortunes of the Tyler treaty of 1844 which failed in the Senate. The treaty failed not because of antislavery or proslavery agitation but because the Senate split along partisan lines, with southern Whigs voting against the treaty. There followed the presidential election of 1844, an election which many students later would describe as one of the three American elections turning on a question of foreign affairs—the other two being 1796 and 1920. The election of 1844 was a confused contest, as are most contests for the American presidency, and the winning candidate James K. Polk appears to have won not so much because he came out for annexation of Texas as because the national balance between Whigs and Democrats was just about even anyway and luck favored Polk in the electoral college. Whatever the confusion involved in electing Polk, who incidentally was the first "dark horse" candidate for the presidency, the new president after election chose to interpret his mandate as requiring annexation of Texas, and his eager predecessor Tyler, still in office, arranged for and signed the joint resolution on March 1, 1845.

Southern statesmen in the mid-nineteenth century, speaking for annexation of Texas, adduced some ingenious proslavery claims. Henry Wise of Virginia asserted, perhaps with tongue in cheek, that annexation would benefit northern abolitionists: so long as Texas remained a foreign country the abolitionists could do nothing about freeing the slaves there, but when it became part of the union they could work on slavery there to their hearts' content. Secretary of State John C. Calhoun, in 1844 during the debate over ratification of the Tyler annexation treaty, took advantage of a diplomatic note received from the British minister in Washington, Richard Pakenham, to write a reply giving in large detail the proslavery reasons for annexation of Texas. The argument was, in sum, a statement that slavery benefitted both the master and the slave, that it was an institution of piety and love rather than force and brutality, that its defense was the duty of the government of the United States. That government, Calhoun argued, intended to annex Texas to prevent antislavery-ites in England from undertaking, via British diplomacy, to free the slaves in Texas.

Just why Calhoun wrote this saucy diplomatic note in 1844 is not quite clear. One biographer has asserted that he did not mean to raise a row in England or in the American North but was only stating reasons for annexation as he understood them. He may have hoped to end the abolition propaganda, then beginning to pour in large quantities from the printing presses of the North. He may have hoped to rally antiabolition opinion to his side. He may have hoped to hasten the impending split of the nation into North and South, and to precipitate then and there, in 1844, a war for southern independence.

Antislavery men, opposing the slavery advocates, counseled that admission of Texas to the union as a slave state would be contrary to the constitution, and that the free states of the North had the right to nullify —that is, to deny the legality of—any federal statute passed to this effect. There was even some feeling that admission of Texas was sufficient reason for the North to dissolve the union. John Quincy Adams, old in years but young in heart, told the young men of Boston that "Your trial is approaching. The spirit of freedom and the spirit of slavery are drawing together for the deadly conflict of arms. The annexation of Texas to this union is the blast of the trumpet for a foreign, civil, servile, and Indian war, of which the government of your country, fallen into faithless hands, have already twice given the signal—first by a shameless treaty, rejected by a virtuous senate; and again by the glove of defiance, hurled by the apostle of nullification, at the avowed policy of the British empire peacefully to promote the extinction of slavery throughout the world. Young men of Boston: burnish your armor, prepare for the conflict, and I say to you, in the language of Calgacus to the ancient Britons, think of your forefathers! Think of your posterity!"

To no avail were the antislavery arguments against annexation. The feeling of manifest destiny was too strong and too popular in 1845, antislavery sentiment not yet strong enough. Tyler's joint resolution passed Congress with a whoop. "You might as well attempt to turn the current of the Mississippi," Old Hickory declared in a letter given to the press at the crucial political moment, "as to turn the democracy from the annexation of Texas to the United States . . . obtain it the U. States must—peaceably if we can, but forcibly if we must."

All but forgotten in the uproar were the pretensions of the Mexican government. Texas, Mexican diplomats had been claiming, was still part of Mexico, and annexation by the United States would be tantamount to a declaration of war. Upon passage of the joint resolution of March 1, 1845, the Mexican minister in Washington asked for and received his passports.

3. *The Mexican War*

A year elapsed after the annexation of Texas before the war with Mexico began. There followed after Tyler's resolution of March 1845 a period of maneuvering and uncertainty during which President Polk waited to see what the Mexicans would do. The president was not averse to war. Still, he did not wish war if he could get its fruits without any fighting. He therefore sent a representative to Mexico City, John Slidell, in the hope of obtaining Mexican recognition of a Texas boundary at the Rio Grande, in exchange for which the United States would assume payment of claims of its nationals against the Mexican government. (Because Mexico had been in turmoil for thirty years and more, many Americans had found their properties confiscated and sometimes their lives endangered by the various revolutionary troubles; these claims had been settled by a mixed claims commission for approximately two million dollars, but the Mexicans had refused to pay the claims.) This was Slidell's minimum proposal: recognition of the Rio Grande boundary in return for American assumption of the claims payments. In addition the emissary was empowered to purchase New Mexico and California for $25,000,000. Polk would have gone as high as $40,000,000. He especially desired California with its fine harbor of San Francisco.

The president's representative, Slidell, unfortunately for Mexico, met with rebuff. Before Slidell's journey to Mexico City, Polk had received a statement in writing from the Mexican foreign minister to the effect that an American commissioner would find a friendly reception. The Mexican government upon Slidell's arrival refused to treat with him, on the technicality that his credentials were those of a minister plenipotentiary rather than a special *ad hoc* representative. What happened was that the Mexican government of the moment, led by General Mariano Paredes, was in imminent peril of being thrown from office and could not face the hostility of popular opinion in the capital city should it undertake to negotiate with the Americans. The Mexican people—when one spoke of a "people" of Mexico in the nineteenth century he meant little more than the literate inhabitants of the capital—were determined that annexation of Texas would be tantamount to war.

Whatever sort of government was in control, it was a fatuous act in 1846 to turn down an overture from the government of the United States. The Mexicans were in the position of refusing to sell territories that they could not keep anyway. Napoleon in 1803, seeing that he could not hold Louisiana, had sold it. There were no Napoleons in Mexico in 1846 but only factional politicians who found momentary power too sweet to relinquish, be the responsibilities of their decisions ever so serious for the future of their country.

And so John Slidell went away, and President Polk, tired of the irresolution of his adversary, disposed American troops under Brigadier General Zachary ("Old Zack") Taylor in the disputed border area of Texas between the Nueces River and the Rio Grande. The local Mexican commander on April 25, 1846, surprised a company of American soldiers, killing or wounding sixteen and capturing the remainder, and the war was on—this even before news had reached the Mexican commander that the government in Mexico City had declared a "defensive war" against the United States. In Washington, Polk was preparing a war message to Congress when the welcome news arrived of the Mexican attack. War, Polk then could assert, had been forced upon the United States by act of Mexico. Congress declared on May 13, 1846, that "by the act of the Republic of Mexico, a state of war exists between that Government and the United States."

That this war with Mexico in the mid-nineteenth century was not a popular conflict soon became obvious to everyone. The war with Mexico of 1846–1848 never evoked the popularity that surrounded the first or second World Wars or the war with Spain in 1898. Not merely was there grumbling and disgruntledness in New England, but there were outright speeches against the war by such western opponents as Congressman Abraham Lincoln of Illinois. The issue on which opposition arose was, of course, the extension of slavery. Northern opposition to the war found expression everywhere from pulpits, rostrums, and "stump" platforms. No sooner had the war begun than it received a name indicating its alleged origin—President Polk's War. It was the dishonored successor of President Madison's War, unhonored predecessor to Mr. Lincoln's War, forerunner of the wars of Mr. McKinley, Mr Wilson, Mr. Roosevelt, Mr. Truman, and Mr. Johnson. The Mexican War, according to the critics of James K. Polk, was an "unhappy war, in which, by his own deliberate, unauthorized and criminal act, he has involved the country." On the floor of the House of Representatives the cantankerous abolitionist Joshua R. Giddings declared the conflict "a war against an unoffending people without adequate or just cause, for the purpose of conquest; with the design of extending slavery; in violation of the Constitution, against the dictates of justice, humanity, the sentiments of the age in which we live, and the precepts of the religion which we profess. I will lend it no aid," Giddings said during debate over an appropriation bill, "no support whatever. I will not bathe my hands in the blood of the people of Mexico, nor will I participate in the guilt of those murders which have been and will hereafter be committed by our army there. For these reasons I shall vote against the bill under consideration and all others calculated to support the war."

President Polk in taking the country to war against Mexico did not, incidentally, act from proslavery motives. Polk was dismayed at the debates over the slavery issue and became embittered after the war began by the reintroduction into Congress in January 1847 of the Wilmot Proviso to prevent the expansion of slavery into new territory. Slavery as an institution, the president always maintained, had no connection with the war or the peace. "Its introduction in connection with the Mexican War," he recorded in his diary, "is not only mischievous but wicked." Although a citizen of Tennessee and a slaveholder, like his predecessor Andrew Jackson, he had in mind first and foremost the territory and Pacific ports of California, and only after this goal was achieved would he concern himself over the slavery question. Economic interests, but of a territorial sort, moved Polk in his actions, peaceful and otherwise, toward Mexico.

The actual fighting of the Mexican War is not of immediate concern to the student of American diplomatic history but is of some interest. After Mexico's attack on General Taylor's forces along the Rio Grande, there followed some of the best campaigning in American military annals. Taylor led his troops into Mexico from their positions at the border, and on February 23, 1847, won the Battle of Buena Vista. Meanwhile, after a period of indecision in Washington, General Winfield Scott received permission to land a force at Veracruz, which he did on March 9, 1847, and marched overland to Mexico City itself. Scott advanced in record time and reached the capital in September 1847. There is no better story of the valor of American arms than the expedition of Scott's troops to the Halls of Montezuma, much of it across difficult and ruggedly mountainous terrain, ending with the storming of the causeways and gates of the imperial city of the Aztecs. Winning a brilliant victory with fewer than 6,000 troops, Scott consented to a peace arranged by an accompanying representative of the state department, its erstwhile chief clerk Nicholas P. Trist.

The Treaty of Guadalupe Hidalgo was concluded on February 2, 1848, and had a most interesting background. It was signed by Trist after his commission had expired. President Polk through Secretary of State James Buchanan had annulled Trist's commission, fearing that to have a negotiator accompanying Scott's army would seem to the Mexicans like a sign of American weakness. But Trist at this point began to fear that without an immediate peace there might develop a sentiment in the United States for taking all of Mexico. The Mexican government had been reconstituted through the efforts of General Scott, whose troops were billeted comfortably in the Mexican capital. The abject defeat of the Mexicans was so obvious that, as Trist knew, it might well encourage the more ambitious apostles of manifest destiny to stretch the American eagle's wings all the way to Guatemala. Even as Trist was deliberating his course of action, Senator Hannegan of Indiana introduced a resolution in the Senate, "That it may become necessary and proper, as it is within the constitutional capacity of this government, for the United States to hold Mexico as a territorial appendage." Two months later Senator Dickinson at a Jackson Day dinner offered the toast, "A More Perfect Union embracing the entire North American Continent." It was a serious situation. Trist from his point of view made the most of it. With Scott's consent, for the general was agreeable to finishing off the war, Trist negotiated his treaty at the little village of Guadalupe Hidalgo just outside Mexico City and sent the treaty off to Washington to see what Polk would do with it.

Polk was furious. The president, an able, conscientious, sincere man, was intensely suspicious of political plots during his administration—and he saw a plot in Trist's treaty.

Polk, it seems altogether fair to say, had begun the Mexican War not out of partisan but for national reasons. The president believed that his country's future demanded a border of Texas at the Rio Grande, and in addition he wanted to acquire New Mexico and especially California. This was a broadly national purpose, but as Whig opposition to the war became more vehement Polk found that matters of politics plagued his every move, that he had to be circumspect in his every act to fend off the Whigs and keep the war going to a victorious conclusion. He managed to do this, but only with difficulty, and one of his worst problems in the conduct of the war was that the two leading military commanders, Generals Taylor and Scott, were both Whigs and likely to profit personally from the war by being nominated on the Whig ticket for the presidency. Taylor, old "Rough and Ready," quickly became a popular figure, and as Taylor's political prospects rose Polk's opinion of his generalship went lower and lower. The president decided that Taylor was lacking in initiative and complained that he "simply obeys orders and gives no information to aid the administration in directing his movement." Still, there was no question but that Taylor was an effective field commander, and after the general's triumphs Polk finally had to admit, "After the late battles, which were well fought, the public opinion seems to point to him as entitled to the command." As for Scott, the political prospects were just as disquieting. The president wanted Scott out of Washington, where his presence was embarrassing to the secretary of war, but it was equally annoying to have to send Scott to command the

Veracruz expedition, for there was no telling what laurels this duty might bring. Polk had to circumscribe the reputations of Taylor and Scott, if possible, and conclude somehow an acceptable peace with Mexico. It was a difficult program.

The president believed that he had chosen the right man for the job of peacemaking when he picked out Nicholas P. Trist. Trist's background was irreproachable. The chief clerk of the state department was a long-time Democrat and had served for a while as General Jackson's private secretary. There could be, so Polk must have thought, no political difficulty in sending Trist to Mexico. Moreover, the chief clerk was not a person of stature in the Democratic Party, and hence there could be no chance of offending any faction of the party by appointing Trist. Too, by commissioning Trist as an executive agent, the president left the way open for a regular diplomatic mission under Secretary Buchanan, should such later seem feasible. And if Trist were a success, the credit for the enterprise would fall to his superiors, while if he were a failure he might conveniently be disowned. It seemed a perfect situation.

As luck would have it, Trist proved in no sense as useful as Polk had imagined. The chief clerk had a mind of his own, as evidenced in his singular decision to sign a treaty with the Mexicans after his commission had expired. And to add to this difficulty of Trist was the fact that Polk's envoy became, before signature of the Treaty of Guadalupe Hidalgo, a fast friend and confidant of General Scott. At first Trist and Scott had been bitter enemies. Both men were adepts as letter writers, and there followed a vindictive correspondence in which each sought to insult the other in the grossest manner. Observing this verbal battle with some amusement, one of Polk's supporters in Washington remarked that Scott and Trist would produce "a most voluminous, if not a luminous correspondence." Trist complained bitterly to the state department about Scott. Scott could not stand to think of Trist and declared that the latter, armed with "an ambulatory guillotine," would be "the personification of Danton, Marat, and St. Just, all in one." Then the two men came together in friendship. Scott soon was reporting to Secretary of War William L. Marcy that he regarded Trist as "able, discreet, courteous, and amiable." The general added that "So far as I am concerned, I am perfectly willing that all I have heretofore written to the Department about Mr. Trist, should be suppressed." Similarly Trist praised Scott to the department of state. To his wife he wrote that Scott was "the soul of honour and probity, and full of the most sterling qualities of heart and head: affectionate, generous, forgiving, and a *lover of justice*." When Trist of a sudden became ill, Scott put him in the charge of their mutual friend, General Persifer F. Smith, sent him some guava marmalade from his personal stores, and to top it all made Trist his guest at headquarters.

It was not unnatural that the Polk administration, surveying these developments, saw political complications in this Trist-Scott *rapprochement*, and Polk became obsessed by what he considered Trist's perfidy, disowning his peace commissioner and even refusing to pay him, making it necessary for Trist to petition the government to obtain recompense, twenty-two years later, for his personal expenses in Mexico. Polk felt that "Mr. Trist, from all I can learn, has lent himself to Gen'l Scott and is his mere tool, and seems to be employed in ministering to his malignant passions." The president in his diary for January 15, 1848, recorded having received "a very long despatch from Mr. Trist. It was dated on the 6th of Decr. last, and is the most extraordinary document I have ever heard from a Diplomatic Representative. . . . His despatch is arrogant, impudent, and very insulting to his Government, and even personally offensive to the President. He admits he is acting without authority and in violation of the positive order recalling him. It is manifest to me that he has become the tool of Gen'l Scott and his menial instrument, and that the paper was written at Scott's instance and dictation. I have never in my life felt so indignant, and the whole Cabinet expressed themselves as I felt. I told Mr. Buchanan that the paper was so insulting and contemptably [sic] base, that it require[d] no lengthy answer, but that it did require a short, but stern and decided rebuke, and directed him to prepare such a reply. . . . If there was any legal provision for his punishment he ought to be severely handled. He has acted worse than any man in the public employ whom I have ever known. His despatch proves that he is destitute of honour or principle, and that he has proved himself to be a very base man. I was deceived in him. I had but little personal knowledge of him, but could not have believed [it] possible that any man would have acted so basely . . . ."

Even so, the president had little choice but to submit Trist's treaty. As he wrote in his diary for February 21, 1848, "I looked, too, to the consequences of its [the treaty's] rejection. A majority of one branch of Congress is opposed to my administration; they have falsely charged that the war was brought on and is continued by me with a view to the conquest of Mexico; and if I were now to reject a Treaty made upon my own terms, as authorized in April last, with the unanimous approbation of the Cabinet, the probability is that Congress would not grant either men or money to prosecute the war. Should this be the result, the army now in Mexico would be constantly wasting and diminishing in numbers, and I might at last be compelled to withdraw them, and thus loose [sic] the two Provinces of New Mexico & Upper California, which were ceded to the U.S. by this Treaty. Should the opponents of my administration succeed in carrying the next Presidential election, the great probability is that the country would loose [sic] all the advantages secured by this Treaty. I adverted to the immense value of Upper California; and concluded by saying that if I were now to reject my own terms, as offered in April last, I did not see how it was possible for my administration to be sustained."

Trist's treaty, despite the improprieties of its conclusion, was not unwelcome, for Polk's agent had secured New Mexico and California plus Mexican acceptance of the Texan boundary at the Rio Grande, and the United States was to pay $15,000,000 and assume the adjusted claims of its citizens against the Mexican government. These terms, Polk realized, were virtually the maximum that Slidell had been empowered to negotiate in the abortive mission of 1846, and despite his intense disgust with Trist for acting without commission, the president sent the treaty to the Senate, which gave its advice and consent on March 10, 1848. After ratification by Mexico, Polk proclaimed the treaty in effect on the anniversary of American independence, July 4, 1848. By this stroke of war, following upon the stroke of diplomacy which had gained Texas in 1845, the United States had added altogether (including Texas) 1,200,000 square miles to its domain, an increase of more than sixty-six per cent.

What could one say about manifest destiny, as it had found fulfillment in the events of 1845–1848? The peaceful process by which the United States of America had been expanding across the enormously valuable North American continent had been punctuated by a short and sharp and altogether victorious war. At the time, people were asking whether political leaders from the southern portion of the United States had not forced the war with Mexico for the enlargement of their slave domains, for the miserable purpose of obtaining "more pens to cram slaves in." This fear, so far as concerned the reasoning of President Polk himself and probably many of his supporters, was unfounded. Even so, in the twentieth century when war would lead to the near-destruction of Western civilization, many people were again going to ask if the Mexican War were not an unjust war of aggression. Was, then, the Mexican War a conflict that for this latter reason should have been avoided? Should not the United States in 1846–1848 have trusted to its diplomacy and restrained its pursuit of manifest destiny, if that were possible?

The answer to this question is not easy. No American today would like to give up the territories secured from Mexico. Those expanses so varied in their riches gave us first gold, then oil, now uranium, and have increased enormously the power of the United States. If one may be permitted the luxury of reading the present into the past—assuredly a most unhistorical operation—he can easily see that at a time in the latter twentieth century when the power of the United States and the Union of Soviet Socialist Republics is so neatly balanced, any large subtraction from American power might have changed the course of history. This is no fanciful notion, pleasantly speculated upon in these pages, but an idea that bears some considerable possibilities for thought. What might have happened if the United States during the Second World War had not had enough economic and military strength to throw the victory to the Allies? Or for that matter, what might have happened in the gray spring of 1918, when the German offensive came within an ace of success, if the morale of Allied troops had not been bucked up by the prospect, soon to be realized, of two million American soldiers in France? If the nation had stopped at the Sabine River, if such statesmen as John Tyler and James K. Polk had taken Mexican complaints and protests as insuperable obstacles to realization of manifest destiny, the American people might today find their personal and public circumstances altogether unenviable.

If Texas had been allowed to go her own way in 1845, if the American government had continued timid and unresponsive to Texan requests for annexation there might have developed another large North American republic between the United States and Mexico. If the manifest destiny of the American people had received this blow there might have followed an independent California on the Pacific coast, perhaps an independent Oregon. The North American continent, already split south of the Rio Grande into half a dozen or more weak governments, would have gone the way of South America.

But the above comments are admittedly retrospective. The question remains as to whether the Mexican War was a just conflict—whether Americans should in good conscience have avoided the war by which their country took New Mexico and California from a weak Latin government, whether manifest destiny offered only an excuse for a land-hungry nation.

Americans may as well admit that in 1846–1848 they fought a war of aggression against Mexico. Such a confession is discomforting to make in the aggression-ridden twentieth century, but the facts of the case substantiate it. President Polk touched off the war when he ordered General Taylor to the line of the Rio Grande. He hoped to provoke the Mexicans and managed to do it. The war was an act of aggression by the United States for the purpose of conquering territory from a helpless neighbor. Mexico had little chance of defending itself. Although the American people were divided in their support of the war, the outcome was hardly ever in doubt, and the United States triumphed so completely that if there had been more unanimity at home the American flag might well have waved permanently over all of Mexico. Americans, surveying the Mexican War, can argue that their country brought order and prosperity to the regions it conquered, and especially that for the preservation of democracy in the twentieth century this nineteenth-century war was a fortunate affair. Such argument does not alter the fact that the method employed in 1846–1848 to extend American sovereignty westward to the Pacific was aggression and that the war against Mexico was not a just war.

This statement of fact, however, does not dispose of the justification for the war, manifest destiny, the mystic notion that the North American continent was destined to belong to the people of the United States. As one examines the course of Mexican-American relations in the early nineteenth century it does seem that, apart from the rightness or wrongness of the Mexican War, there was an undeniable logic in United States possession of Texas, New Mexico, and California. One has therefore the uneasy feeling that the result of the war was good but the means were bad, and that perhaps if the American people in 1846–1848 had been possessed of more wisdom they would have found another method, besides war—presumably a correct diplomatic method—by which to realize their good end, their manifest destiny.

A CONTEMPORARY DOCUMENT

[As mentioned, the New York editor John L. O'Sullivan invented the phrase "manifest destiny." If the population of the United States in the centennial year 1945 did not quite get up to O'Sullivan's prediction, it was not far from the mark. Source: *The United States Magazine and Democratic Review*, XVII (July–August 1845), 5, 9–10.]

. . . Texas is now ours. Already, before these words are written, her Convention has undoubtedly ratified the acceptance, by her Congress, of our proffered invitation into the Union; and made the requisite changes in her already republican form of constitution to adopt it to its future federal relations. Her star and her stripe may already be said to have taken their place in the glorious blazon of our common nationality; and the sweep of our eagle's wing already includes within its circuit the wide extent of her fair and fertile land. . . .

Why, were other reasoning wanting, in favor of now elevating this question of the reception of Texas into the Union, out of the lower region of our past party dissensions, up to its proper level of a high and broad nationality, it surely is to be found, found abundantly, in the manner in which other nations have undertaken to intrude themselves into it, between us and the proper parties to the case, in a spirit of hostile interference against us, for the avowed object of thwarting our policy and hampering our power, limiting our greatness and checking the fulfillment of our manifest destiny to overspread the continent allotted by Providence for the free development of our yearly multiplying millions. . . .

California will, probably, next fall away from the loose adhesion which, in such a country as Mexico, holds a remote province in a slight equivocal kind of dependence on the metropolis. Imbecile and distracted, Mexico never can exert any real governmental authority over such a country. The impotence of the one and the distance of the other, must make the relation one of virtual independence; unless, by stunting the province of all natural growth, and forbidding that immigration which can alone develope its capabilities and fulfil the purposes of its creation, tyranny may retain a military dominion which is no government in the legitimate sense of the term. In the case of California this is now impossible. The Anglo-Saxon foot is already on its borders. Already the advance guard of the irresistible army of Anglo-Saxon emigration has begun to pour down upon it, armed with the plough and the rifle, and marking its trail with schools and colleges, courts and representative halls, mills and meeting-houses. A population will soon be in actual occupation of California, over which it will be idle for Mexico to dream of dominion. . . . Whether they will then attach themselves to our Union or not, is not to be predicted with any certainty. Unless the projected rail-road across the continent to the Pacific be carried into effect, perhaps they may not; though even in that case, the day is not distant when the Empires of the Atlantic and Pacific would again flow together into one, as soon as their inland border should approach each other. But that great work, collosal as appears the plan on its first suggestion, cannot remain long unbuilt. Its necessity for this very purpose of binding and holding together in its iron clasp our fast settling Pacific region with that of the Mississippi valley—the natural facility of the route—the ease with which any amount of labor for the construction can be drawn from the overcrowded populations of Europe, to be paid in the lands made valuable by the progress of the work itself— and its immense utility to the commerce of the world with the whole eastern coast of Asia, alone almost sufficient for the support of such a road—these considerations give assurance that the day cannot be distant which shall witness the conveyance of the representatives from Oregon and California to Washington within less time than a few years ago was devoted to a similar journey by those from Ohio; while the magnetic telegraph will enable the editors of the "San Francisco Union," the "Astoria Evening Post," or the "Nootka Morning News" to set up in type the first half of the President's Inaugural, before the echoes of the latter half shall have died away beneath the lofty porch of the Capitol, as spoken from his lips.

Away, then, with all idle French talk of *balances of power* on the American Continent. There is no growth in Spanish America! Whatever progress of population there may be in the British Canadas, is only for their own early severance of their present colonial relation to the little island three thousand miles across the Atlantic; soon to be followed by Annexation, and destined to swell the still accumulating momentum of our progress. And whosoever may hold the balance, though they should cast into the opposite scale all the bayonets and cannon, not only of France and England, but of Europe entire, how would it kick the beam against the simple solid weight of the two hundred and fifty, or three hundred millions—and American millions—destined to gather beneath the flutter of the stripes and stars, in the fast hastening year of the Lord 1945!

ADDITIONAL READING

Edward Channing's *History of the United States*, despite the years that have elapsed since its writing, remains one of the best introductions to American history prior to the end of the Civil War, and his fifth volume, *The Period of Transition: 1815–1848* (New York, 1921), offers shrewd insight to the manifest-destiny viewpoint of that era. A colorful if controversial account of the times is *Arthur M. Schlesinger, Jr., *The Age of Jackson* (Boston, 1945). The author of this latter work is one of the most talented historical writers in the United States whose views are always interesting even if inspired by a large-D Democratic enthusiasm. See also two general volumes in the New American Nation series, *Glyndon G. Van Deusen, *The Jacksonian Era: 1828–1848* (New York, 1959) and *Ray A. Billington, *The Far Western Frontier: 1830–1860* (New York, 1956). A glancing account of diplomacy and military events is Nathaniel W. Stephenson, *Texas and the Mexican War* (New Haven, 1921), one of the Cronicles of America series edited by Allen Johnson and Allan Nevins, fifty-odd volumes allegedly written for the tired businessman, the student, and the professor who needs a quick prelecture briefing. *William A. Goetzmann, *When the Eagle Screamed: The Romantic Horizon in American Diplomacy, 1800–1860* (New York, 1966) treats American expansion with emphasis on Texas and the Mexican War. Two older but useful works are Jesse S. Reeves, *American Diplomacy under Tyler and Polk* (Baltimore, 1907) and G. L. Rives, *The United States and Mexico: 1821–1848* (2 vols., New York, 1913).

The Texas revolt and annexation appears in several books: William C. Binkley, *The Texas Revolution* (Baton Rouge, La., 1952), a series of four lectures; E. C. Barker, *Mexico and Texas: 1821–1835* (Dallas, 1928); Joseph W.

Schmitz, *Texan Statecraft: 1836–1845* (San Antonio, 1941); and Stanley Siegel, *A Political History of the Texas Republic: 1836–1845* (Austin, 1956). Justin H. Smith's *The Annexation of Texas* (New York, 1911) is a thorough monograph.

For the Mexican War see—for Mexican internal events—José Fernando Ramírez, *Mexico during the War with the United States*, Walter B. Scholes, ed., and Elliott B. Scherr, trans. (Columbia, Mo., 1950); Justin H. Smith, *The War with Mexico* (2 vols., New York, 1919); and Alfred Hoyt Bill, *Rehearsal for Conflict* (New York, 1947). The latter author believes that the war was a proving ground for the American army and gave to many American officers the experience necessary to wage the Civil War. See also Otis A. Singletary, *The Mexican War* (Chicago, 1960), a volume in the Chicago History of American Civilization series.

The war had a tendency to enlarge itself, as see J. D. F. Fuller, *The Movement for the Acquisition of All Mexico: 1846–1848* (Baltimore, 1936).

As for the idea or ideas behind annexation of Texas, and the Mexican War, and the movement for all Mexico, *Albert K. Weinberg, *Manifest Destiny* (Baltimore, 1935) shows the logical inadequacies of its subject without recognizing its virtues. Frederick Merk has stressed the idea of mission in *Manifest Destiny and Mission in American History* (New York, 1963) and *The Monroe Doctrine and American Expansionism: 1843–1849* (New York, 1965). Another interpretation—that it was not so much manifest destiny as desire for Juan de Fuca Strait, San Francisco, and San Diego that took Americans to California and Oregon—appears in Norman A. Graebner, *Empire on the Pacific: A Study in American Continental Expansion* (New York, 1955), a lively book written from manuscript materials. Graebner believes that the large movements of American diplomacy must be understood in terms of concrete objectives rather than philosophical notions.

Biographies include E. C. Barker, *The Life of Stephen F. Austin* (Nashville, 1925); Allan Nevins, *Frémont* (2 vols., New York, 1928); Marquis James, *The Raven: A Biography of Sam Houston* (Indianapolis, 1929); J. Fred Rippy, *Joel R. Poinsett: Volatile American* (Durham, N.C., 1935); W. H. Callcott, *Santa Anna* (Norman, Okla., 1936); *Marquis James, *Andrew Jackson: Portrait of a President* (Indianapolis, 1937); Oliver P. Chitwood, *John Tyler: Champion of the Old South* (New York, 1939); Holman Hamilton, *Zachary Taylor* (2 vols., Indianapolis, 1941–1951); Herbert P. Gambrell, *Anson Jones* (Garden City, N.Y., 1948); Charles H. Wiltse, *John C. Calhoun, Sectionalist: 1840–1850* (Indianapolis, 1951); Llerena Friend, *Sam Houston: The Great Designer* (Austin, 1954); Philip S. Klein, *President James Buchanan: A Biography* (University Park, Penn., 1962). Samuel Flagg Bemis's second volume on the indefatigable "JQA," *John Quincy Adams and the Union* (New York, 1956), a work which may well be the best of all Bemis's volumes on the history of American diplomacy, contains within a biographical framework the recent scholarship on Texas and the Mexican War. For Polk see Eugene I. McCormac, *James K. Polk* (Berkeley, Calif., 1922), now being superseded by the multivolume biography by Charles G. Sellers: *Polk: Jacksonian, 1795–*

1843 (Princeton, 1957), and *Continentalist, 1843–1846* (Princeton, 1966). Worth careful examination is Milo M. Quaife, ed., *The Diary of James K. Polk: During His Presidency, 1845 to 1849* (4 vols., Chicago, 1910), which has been boiled down in Allan Nevins, ed., *Polk, The Diary of a President: 1845–1849* (New York, 1929). No one can read the pages of this somber diary with its account of weekly church services, receptions at the White House for Sunday School children, long cabinet discussions over Texas and Mexico, the general agonizing over the right course in politics, diplomacy, and war, and still believe that this great American president was, as a critical historian of many years ago described him, "Polk the mendacious."

☆ *9* ☆

The Northeast and Northwest Boundaries

I remarked to him that the only way to treat John Bull was to look him straight in the eye; that I considered a bold and firm course on our part the pacific one; that if Congress faltered or hesitated in their course, John Bull would immediately become arrogant and more grasping in his demands; and that such had been the history of the British nation in all their contests with other powers for the last two hundred years.
—President James K. Polk to a congressman, 1846

The decade of the 1840's was an era in which the government of the United States established its continental boundaries as we know them today, with exception of the Gadsden Purchase of 1853 and the Alaska Purchase of 1867. It is important to note that while the major territorial changes of the era came through annexation (Texas) and conquest (the territory gained in the Mexican War), the boundaries in the northeast and and northwest were also at this time set out in their present-day form. The latter boundaries had been in dispute with Great Britain for many years. Their solution seemed hardly in prospect. Their relatively easy arrangement in 1842 and 1846 served as another proof, if such were needed, of the New World republic's manifest destiny, the triumph of virtue and vigor over the pretensions and decadence of the Old World, the irrepressible movement of the republic into its foreordained properties from sea to sea.

Boundary controversies may seem dull subjects for study, and perhaps they are. The fixing of the Canadian border with the present states of Maine and Washington was far less exuberant a task than the annexation of Texas, much less exciting than the Mexican War. What a humdrum business is the comparison of maps, the Levantine disputes of bargainers. At one juncture, and far from the moment of settlement, the Maine boundary argument had produced some thirty volumes of official analysis pro and con. But the solution of both boundary disputes was a major step in the nineteenth-century diplomatic accommodation of the British and American governments and peoples. And so far as concerned the territorial results of these abstruse controversies, the total of square miles gained or lost, the United States lost a considerable mileage in the northeast boundary settlement but gained an empire in the Pacific northwest.

1. *The northeast boundary dispute*

The Webster-Ashburton Treaty of 1842, concluded at Washington between the American secretary of state Daniel Webster, and the British plenipotentiary, Lord Ashburton, ended an argument over the northeast boundary between the United States and Canada which had continued since the Treaty of Paris of 1783.

In its origins the northeast boundary controversy was easily understandable. To determine the boundary between Maine and Canada was one of the lesser problems of Benjamin Franklin and his fellow peace commissioners at the end of the revolution. When Franklin, Jay, and Adams were negotiating with Richard Oswald in 1782, they did not, of course, act from carelessness, even in small matters. They did their best to avoid controversial articles in the treaty of peace. The maps of the day unfortunately were inaccurate, and the map used in 1782, a 1775 edition of Mitchell's Map of North America, was rather imaginative in its descriptions of the terrain along the northeast boundary of the former British colonies. In the preliminary articles of peace signed in 1782 the Americans, using Mitchell's Map, agreed unwittingly to a boundary that did not exist. The boundary was to begin on the Atlantic coast with the St. Croix River. There was no St. Croix River. Moreover, the negotiators of 1782 failed to append to their accord a copy of Mitchell's Map, nor did they even mention in the text of the treaty that they had used Mitchell's Map. The result of this confusion was to place in dispute an area over one hundred miles in length. The north-south gap between British and American claims spread out over 7,697,280 acres.

There followed efforts by mixed commissions, one created by Jay's Treaty and another twenty years later by the Treaty of Ghent, to patch up this boundary. The commission created by Jay's Treaty decided in 1798 that a river then called the Schoodiac was in truth the St. Croix, but

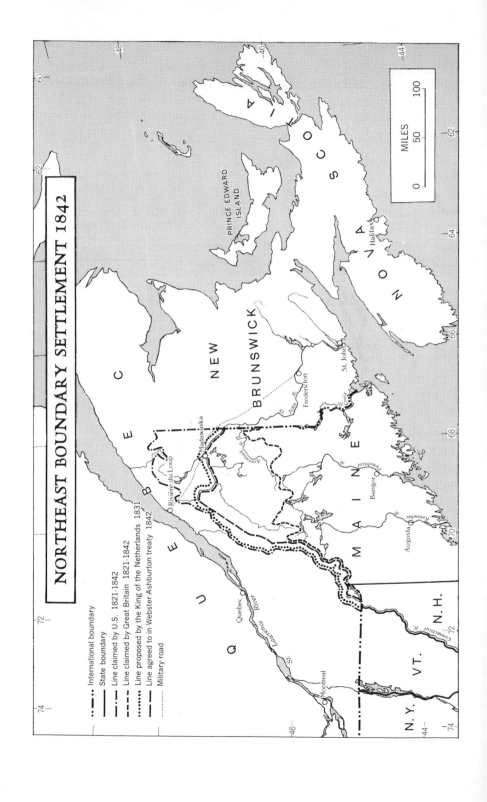

NORTHEAST BOUNDARY SETTLEMENT 1842

International boundary
State boundary
Line claimed by U.S. 1821-1842
Line claimed by Great Britain 1821-1842
Line proposed by the King of the Netherlands 1831
Line agreed to in Webster-Ashburton treaty 1842
Military road

MILES
0   50   100

QUEBEC

Montreal

Quebec

St. Lawrence River

Rivière du Loup

Madawaska

NEW BRUNSWICK

Fredericton

St. John

St. John R.

St. Croix

PRINCE EDWARD ISLAND

NOVA SCOTIA

Halifax

MAINE

Bangor

Penobscot R.

Kennebec R.

Augusta

Aroostook R.

N.H.

VT.

N.Y.

Connecticut R.

beyond running the boundary up that river to its source the commission failed, and the remainder of the northeast boundary, up around the hump of present-day Maine and New Hampshire and almost straight westward across the top of Vermont and New York to the St. Lawrence River, remained in dispute. With the clause in the Treaty of Ghent appointing a second mixed commission, there was another in anticipation of what might happen should the new commission disagree: in such case the two nations would refer their differences to a friendly sovereign or state and would consider his decision as "final and conclusive on all the matters so referred." The second commission disagreed, and after some considerable further negotiation during the 1820's the dispute was given to the king of the Netherlands.

That monarch probably took the only sensible course under the circumstances, though it quickly turned out to be the wrong course. The two sides in the dispute had not presented all their massive evidence, the voluminous and complicated documents relating to the controversy, but set only their two opposing maps before the arbitrator. Each disputant also was allowed to present a supporting statement. But neither side had conclusive support for its arguments, and so the king of the Netherlands split the difference between the two nations, running a line roughly through the middle of the disputed area. The British government was willing to accept this award, though it admitted that the Dutch king had erred technically, for his duty as an abitrator was to decide between the opposing claims and not to set out a compromise boundary. The American government under President Andrew Jackson—the year was 1831— was not unwilling to accept the royal error, to take the king's award, but Jackson was unwilling to accept responsibility for giving away what, to the citizens of Maine, was the territory of their state. He was in the process of building a Democratic Party machine in the East as well as in the West and South and did not wish to lose support in the state of Maine. He judiciously asked the advice of the Senate, which voted against the proposed compromise boundary. There matters rested through most of the 1830's.

In the later thirties some new factors entered, which urged a settlement of the northeast boundary. Of first importance was the large-scale insurrection by the Canadians against British rule which broke out in 1837 and received encouragement and supplies from the American side of the border. A band of pro-British Canadians crossed the river above Niagara Falls on December 29, 1837, seized the American ship *Caroline* (a notorious munitions-runner) as she was tied up on the American side of the river, cut her loose and sent her to destruction. This incident raised tempers mightily in America. According to a poem published at the time,

As over the shelving rocks she broke,
And plunged in her turbulent grave,
The slumbering genius of freedom woke,
Baptized in Niagara's wave,
And sounded her warning Tocsin far,
From Atlantic's shore to the polar star.

When a Canadian named Alexander McLeod boasted in 1840 that he had taken part in the *Caroline* fracas and had killed an American during the affair, there was an enormous hullabaloo. McLeod was tried in New York State and acquitted. But the McLeod affair, following the *Caroline* affair, both so exasperating to American public opinion, stirred British fears for retention of Canada in case of a war with the United States. From these fears came a British conviction that when the northeastern boundary should be settled there should be enough territory ceded to the Crown so that during winters when the St. Lawrence was frozen it would be possible to run military supplies overland from Halifax and St. John to Quebec and Montreal. In summer the land passage was a painful route, impassable to all save single travelers, but in winter, ice and snow supported sledges and permitted movement of larger groups and of bulk goods and artillery.

Then during the 1830's the citizens of Maine realized that the Aroostook Valley, part of the disputed area, was worth a diplomatic fight with Great Britain. The valley was a pocket of unusually rich limestone soils in the northern part of Maine, isolated from the rest of the state by a stretch of wilderness even in the twentieth century unpeopled. It lay undiscovered until the 1830's. Citizens of Maine had supposed that it was simply another forested area, with unyielding acid soil, a wilderness of conifers and ponded streams. Partly through exploration for proposed railroads, partly as a result of an expanding frontier movement, the "Roostook" Valley now took on importance. As one of the surveyors wrote upon return from this attractive area, "Are you a young man just starting in life, but with no capital save a strong arm—good courage, and a *narrow axe?* Go to the Aroostook; attend assiduously and carefully to your business; select a lot suitable for your purpose, and with the common blessings of providence, you will, in a very few years, find yourself an independent freeholder, with a farm of your own subduing, and with a capital of your own creating." To the able-bodied young men in the stony hill country of central and southern Maine, this was good news. When the British province of New Brunswick began granting land titles and claiming jurisdiction within this land that the residents of Maine deemed their own territory, there began in 1838 a small border strife known as the Roostook War. A fragile peace was arranged in March 1839 by intercession of the American general, Winfield Scott, but who knew when another Roostook War would erupt, perhaps bringing full-scale hostilities between the British and American peoples? This trouble incident to the discovery of the Aroostook Valley—like the trouble incident to the Canadian rebellion of 1837–1838—pointed up the need for a settlement of the northeast boundary controversy.

Such was the situation when Lord Ashburton came to Washington as a special British plenipotentiary in 1842, to reopen negotiations on the northeast boundary with President John Tyler's secretary of state, Webster. The Americans desired the Aroostook Valley. The British wished a military road. The boundary by this time had been in dispute for sixty years.

Ashburton arrived in April 1842, an admirable envoy for the task of Anglo-American pacification. He was sixty-seven years old, six feet tall, and after a long career had retired from the great financial house of Baring Brothers, of which family he was an illustrious member. The Barings had been notably friendly to Americans and, among other marks of their friendship, had assisted in the financing of the Louisiana Purchase—an acquisition, some people might have argued, that was an anti-British move by Napoleon. Ashburton had married the former Miss Maria Bingham of Philadelphia, whom he had met in the days when that city had been the capital of the United States. He was well acquainted with the lands of Maine, for the Bingham connection included estates there. His inclinations, then, were clearly American. During the disputation between the British and Americans that led to the War of 1812, he openly had taken the side of the Americans. And this wonderfully suited envoy had an unassailable political position in England. Had he so desired in 1842, he could have been a member of the Peel cabinet, but he preferred to lead a mission of conciliation with the Americans.

Popular interest was much aroused. Ashburton arrived aboard a frigate, he and his retinue of three secretaries and five servants, together with a mountain of luggage. He rented a house on the President's Square at $10,000 a year, with $1,000 more to cover any damage caused by his occupancy.

It was Ashburton's good fortune to find his American opposite, Webster, anxious—really too anxious—to conclude a treaty. The godlike Daniel was now in the latter years of his long public career, which had begun with his first appearance in Washington as a congressman in 1813. Webster seems to have coveted an appointment as American minister to Great Britain and believed that if he accommodated Lord Ashburton in 1842 he might facilitate his welcome in the British capital. He had known Ashburton for a long time. Despite service in Congress, he had been the legal agent of the Baring firm, as indeed he had acted as lawyer for numerous individuals and corporations, making three or four times his congressional salary through such employments. It may even have seemed natural in 1842 that, though secretary of state, he might well serve Ashburton again, and also of course himself.

Webster, however, needed some sort of argument to present to the people of Maine and the people of Massachusetts (which had retained half ownership in Maine's public lands after Maine detached itself from Massachusetts in 1820 and became a state) and also to the Senate of the United States, which had to advise and consent to any treaty that Webster obtained. If, say, he could obtain a map or two seeming to prove the rightness of the British claim in Maine, he could show this evidence to his countrymen and sign with Ashburton.

To Webster, who was fond of invoking the deity, it must have seemed almost providential that even before Ashburton's arrival he had received in February 1842 a letter from an acquaintance and professor at Harvard College, Jared Sparks. Later president of Harvard, author and editor of many volumes, a biographer of Washington, Sparks would become notorious among scholars of American history as the bowdlerizer of Washington's letters, which he "edited"—Sparks disliked the prose style of the Father of His Country, which at times bordered on the crude, and he improved it. Sparks also was the editor of a multivolume edition of the diplomatic correspondence of the American revolution, which he amended to such an extent that a later scholar, Francis Wharton, had to issue a complete new edition. Words meant little to Sparks.

Nor did lines on maps. During a residence in France, he had once worked among the 60,000 maps in the French diplomatic archives and had come on a map which, as he now recalled to his friend, supported the British claim in Maine. He assumed that he had seen the map on which Franklin in 1782 had marked "with a strong red line" the boundary between Maine and Canada. In his letter Sparks enclosed a nineteenth-century map of Maine on which, from his notes and memory of the map in the French archives, he had drawn the Maine boundary.

Webster's problem was evidence for the sly purpose of persuading Maine, Massachusetts, and the Senate. Sparks had given it to him. The secretary of state meanwhile picked up another worthless map from a secondhand dealer, a Mitchell Map formerly belonging to Baron von Steuben, on which someone (Franklin, so Webster assumed) had also marked a boundary coinciding with the British claim in Maine.

The secretary of state was delighted and at once gave Sparks an important task. He sent him up to Boston and to Augusta, the capital of Maine, to show the two maps to the people there as an argument that it was best to give in to the British.

It is of some interest to ask who paid Sparks's expenses, and the precise amount involved. The British foreign secretary, Lord Aberdeen, wrote Ashburton on July 2, 1842: "In order to insure success, you need not be afraid of employing the same means to a greater extent in any quarter where it may be necessary. In what you have done you have been perfectly right . . . ." As for what Aberdeen was talking about, Ashburton set it out in a letter of August 9 marked "private and confidential":

The money I wrote about went to compensate Sparkes & to send him, on my first arrival, to the Governors of Maine & Massachusetts. My informant thinks that without this stimulant Maine would never have yielded, and here it has removed many objections in other quarters. . . . I have drawn on you a bill for £ 2998 – 1 — 30 days sight for the purpose mentioned in my former private letter . . . . I am not likely to want anything more.

Ashburton's informant probably was Webster. The money involved was equivalent to about $14,500. Presumably this was not "travel money," for even in the nineteenth century it was possible for an individual to travel from Washington, D.C., to New England for less than $14,500. Some of the money seems to have been distributed "here," that is, in Washington, and most of the rest must have gone to Boston or Augusta. It is perhaps worth pointing out that when the entire disbursement had finished, the pockets of the two American distributors may not have been empty; for Sparks was a scholarly scamp, and Webster's needs for money were well known to be inexhaustible—Webster always lived to the far edge of his means.

Webster and Ashburton signed their treaty on August 9, 1842. At the time of passage of the Webster-Ashburton Treaty through the Senate, it was thought that Webster had followed the path of statesmanship in concluding a treaty that accepted roughly the line proposed by the king of the Netherlands in 1831. Webster in fact had accepted a line giving up 893 square miles more than the United States would have lost under the award of 1831, but compromise seemed proper in view of Webster's cartographical discoveries. When the secretary told Ashburton about the two maps, just prior to signature of the treaty, the Britisher felt that it was a shame he could not reopen the negotiation and push the American boundary farther southward. He believed, however, that Webster could not be blamed for withholding the maps justifying the British claims.

Alas for Daniel Webster's reputation as a diplomat. It soon developed that there were at least four maps in existence—two of which Webster with a little exertion might have procured—which justified the full American claim. One had belonged to John Jay, and was turned up among the Jay family papers in 1843. Another had been found in the British Museum in 1839 and sequestered at once by the foreign secretary at that time, Lord Palmerston. This was the map that had belonged to Richard Oswald, and which Oswald had sent to George III. When the latter monarch's papers went to the British Museum after his death in 1820, the important map went along. It had reposed in the Museum throughout the 1830's, until its existence became known during some remarks in the House of Commons in 1839. A few days afterward Palmerston took charge of the map, and when he went out of office in 1841 he presumably failed to inform his successor Lord Aberdeen. Palmerston that year had written on one occasion, with undue unction, to Lord John Russell: "With such cunning fellows as these Yankees it never answers to give way, because they always keep pushing on their encroachments . . . their system of encroachment is founded very much upon bully, they will give way when in the wrong, if they are firmly and perseveringly pressed." Palmerston himself, of course, was the bully, rather than "these Yankees." But he received assistance from the American secretary of state. If Webster had wished to establish the American claim in 1842, it could easily have been done, if not through forcing the former foreign secretary to acknowledge the existence of the Oswald-George III map, then through obtaining the Jay map. There also was a map in the Spanish archives (not discovered until 1933), sent there in 1782 by the Spanish ambassador in Paris, Count Aranda. More evidence was in the Lansdowne papers, from the correspondence of Lord Shelburne, prime minister in 1782, although, like the Oswald-George III map, this material doubtless was inaccessible to citizens of the United States.

Jared Sparks had worked on the Lansdowne papers a few years before and had shown his notes to Edward Everett, minister of the United States to London and a former governor of Massachusetts. Sparks and Everett considered themselves bound not to use the information against Britain in the current boundary dispute. Everett carefully urged Webster to search for maps in England. Webster told Everett not to make any search.

Daniel Webster thus took part in what personally was a discreditable episode, by which Great Britain gained 3,207,680 acres of American soil. The acreage turned out to be only poor spruceland, altogether unlike the limestone soils of the Aroostook Valley, but it was land which he should not have given up. Still, he and Ashburton had settled a long dispute and thereby improved the relations between their two governments—and better relations were to be advantageous indeed in later years.

2. The northwest boundary dispute

Settlement of the northwest boundary dispute came four years after the Webster-Ashburton Treaty, when in 1846 President Polk sent to the Senate a British-proposed treaty that ended several decades of argument.

"Oregon"—so the disputed territory in the northwest was called. The young poet William Cullen Bryant had seen the name in Jonathan's Carver's *Travels in the Interior of North America* (London, 1778) and applied it to the Columbia River in his "Thanatopsis":

> . . . the continuous woods
> Where rolls the Oregon, and hears no sound
> Save his own dashings . . . .

Bryant's source, Carver, had picked up the word from Major John Rogers, who had written of the "Ouragon" River beyond the Rocky Mountains. To Americans the word seemed almost mystical. The nation needed the territory through which the fabled river flowed to the sea.

One perhaps should explain that this sentiment for Oregon increased markedly with the passage of the years. In the nation's early era, Jefferson believed that it was not good for a republic to acquire far-off territories, perhaps taking his reasons out of ancient Greek history where republics had turned into empires and collapsed by overextension. Many of the early national leaders believed that Oregon, however attractive, was too far from the rest of the then United States and would itself become another American republic. As late as the 1820's, some of the old Jeffersonians such as Albert Gallatin believed that the whole trans-mountain region was beyond the national reach. In the Senate in 1825, Thomas Hart Benton of Missouri made one of his best classical speeches:

Westward, we can speak without reserve, and the ridge of the Rocky Mountains may be named without offence, as presenting a convenient, natural and everlasting boundary. Along the back of this ridge, the Western limit of the republic should be drawn, and the statue of the fabled god, Terminus, should be raised upon its highest peak, never to be thrown down.

Times were to change, and the feelings about Oregon changed, as did the feelings about Texas. Gallatin was to live to a great old age and in the 1840's would sound a trumpet blast for Oregon. Benton ardently supported him.

At stake in the Oregon dispute was a large wilderness, an area forty times the square mileage involved in the Maine controversy: all the land between the parallels 42° and 54° 40′, bounded on the west by the Pacific and the east by the continental divide. It was an area equal in extent to Great Britain and Ireland, France, Germany and Austria, Holland, and Belgium combined. This territory was in dispute first between Great Britain and Spain, then between Britain, Russia, and the United States, finally between the two English-speaking nations.

The British claim had a sound basis in discovery. After the sixteenth-century voyage of Sir Francis Drake and the touching along the Pacific coast, including the northwest, of the expedition of Captain Cook in the 1770's, there occurred the Nootka Sound affair of 1789–1790. As mentioned in a previous chapter, English fur traders in 1789 had built a post at Nootka Sound on Vancouver Island, and the Spanish captured it. The younger Pitt faced down the Spanish government in a diplomatic crisis which forced a recognition of British rights on the Oregon coast (although it was not then called that). The naval captain sent out by the British government to accept the Spanish restitution on Nootka proved to be none other than the redoubtable George Vancouver, whose appearance in those waters with the sloop of war *Discovery* and the armed tender *Chatham* was to give Britain a still larger claim to the Oregon country.

It was Vancouver's ill luck not to discover the Columbia River, his country's ill luck that this honor fell to an American. In the spring of 1792 the Britisher's ships were passing northward, and six miles out to sea the captain noticed river-colored water and beheld landward a line of breakers. Vancouver believed the bar inaccessible. At that moment he had a favorable wind. "Not considering this opening worthy of more attention," he sailed on to the northwest, leaving behind the Columbia River. Two days later he sighted a sail just ahead, the American ship *Columbia*, captained by Robert Gray. After an exchange of information Vancouver went on, and Gray proceeded south and sighted the bar passed up by Vancouver. In what one of his officers considered an act of madness Gray turned the prow of his vessel into the breakers and rode through them. On the other side he found the mouth of the mighty river, the mightiest in North America next to the Mississippi, which still bears his ship's name.

In the years just prior to the War of 1812, American and British explorers and traders moved into Oregon, confirming the claims of both nations. The Lewis and Clark expedition of 1804–1806 had wintered in 1805–1806 on the bleak Oregon coast, and in 1811 the fur trader Astor established his post at Astoria. Meanwhile the British North West Company, an aggressive organization, was sending trapping parties into the country north of the Columbia—and Astoria was sold to the North West Company in 1813, just before its formal capture by H.M.S. *Racoon*.

There followed a short interlude, as it proved, in the diplomacy of the Oregon question. The Ghent discussions said nothing about Oregon, for the British government was not keen on getting any expression of American opinion about that area which, set down in a diplomatic document, would seem to give the Americans an increased basis to dispute with the British. The colonial secretary, Lord Bathurst, afterward explained the case in this way to representatives of the North West Company, who were

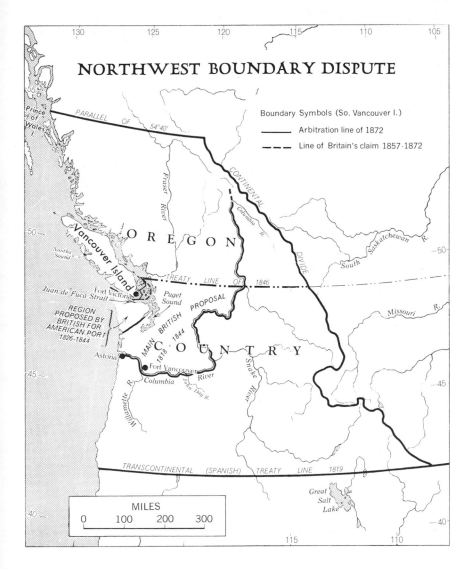

NORTHWEST BOUNDARY DISPUTE

Boundary Symbols (So. Vancouver I.)

———— Arbitration line of 1872

– – – – Line of Britain's claim 1857-1872

of course concerned for their trade. Because of the silence of the discussions at Ghent, the Americans on their part construed the peace treaty's general restoration of territories to include the post at Astoria.

During the lull in Anglo-American negotiations over Oregon, John Quincy Adams made several diplomatic moves that effectively excluded the Spanish and Russians from Oregon. In the summer of 1818, Adams in a stroke of genius proposed to the Spanish minister Onís the extension of the Spanish-American boundary line to the Pacific, and chose for this extension the line of 42°, the present-day northern boundary of the state of California. By so doing he strengthened the American claim to the Oregon country. A few years later an occasion arose for putting a limit on Russian expansion southward into Oregon. When the tsar in 1821 announced in a ukase that trade along the Pacific coast would be closed, out as far into the ocean as a hundred leagues, he commenced a train of events which limited rather than extended his North American domain. John Quincy Adams in the summer of 1823 spoke sharply with the Russian minister in Washington, and out of that conversation came the noncolonization principle of the Monroe Doctrine. The Russians hastily retreated and invited representatives of both the United States and Britain in St. Petersburg to negotiate a southern boundary to Russia's New World possessions. The line agreed upon, in separate Russian treaties with the Americans in 1824 and the British the next year, was that later well-known parallel of 54° 40'. The Russians would have retreated to 55° but wished to keep Prince of Wales Island entirely within their jurisdiction rather than have the line run across it.

With elimination of the Spanish and Russians, everything came down to a series of Anglo-American diplomatic discussions. The first of these occurred even before the Spanish-Russian exit from Oregon, in 1818, and there were subsequent negotiations in 1824, 1826–1827, and 1844–1846.

It would be easily possible to go into minute detail about these almost interminable conferences, held both in London and in Washington. Suffice it to say that in 1818 a treaty between the United States and Great Britain agreed upon a North American boundary of the forty-ninth parallel from the Lake of the Woods westward to the crest of the Rocky Mountains. The area from thence to the Pacific Ocean, Oregon, was to be "free and open" for a period of ten years. In 1827 another treaty extended the free-and-open arrangement indefinitely, subject to change if either signatory should give a year's notice. Meanwhile the area in dispute, between 42° and 54° 40', narrowed through a natural process to the land north and west of the Columbia River and south of the forty-ninth parallel, the central and western thirds of the present-day state of Washington. South of the Columbia lay the Willamette Valley, one of the finest pieces of rolling plain and lightly wooded farmland ever to be found in the United States. Settlers moved into that area in the 1830's, and the American settlements were so well rooted by the early 1840's that when the Oregon question came up for final solution there was no doubt about American possession of the Williamette. What the Americans wished, however, was to obtain a good port on the Pacific coast. The mouth of the Columbia, the site of Astoria, was not at all adaptable as a location for a second New Orleans—it was crossed by a bar, and the river anyway was navigable only for a hundred miles up to its falls. Because the Mexican War was not at this time in prospect, with its award to the United States of San Francisco and San Diego, it appeared as if the only way in which Americans might obtain a port would be to lay claim to some of the lands around Puget Sound and Juan de Fuca Strait, which meant persuading the British to extend to the Pacific the line of the Treaty of 1818—that is, the forty-ninth parallel. The American government offered to settle the boundary at the forty-ninth parallel in 1818, 1824, 1826, and 1845.

The British unfortunately would not go along with such a proposal. Great Britain during the course of the Oregon dispute always intimated willingness to divide the Oregon country at the line of the Columbia River, running the boundary up the Columbia until the river crossed the forty-ninth parallel. It offered such a boundary in 1818, 1824, 1826, and 1844. It further offered in 1826 and 1844 to yield to the United States a fragment of the Olympic peninsula fronting both on the Pacific and Juan de Fuca Strait, on which the Americans might construct a port. But this was as far as the British would go, for the London government insisted upon retaining control of the Columbia.

Behind the British stand was the fur trade, and the undisputed hold over that trade by the Hudson's Bay Company. After the War of 1812, Astoria, on the south side of the Columbia River, had passed back under

An 1846 cartoon on the Oregon boundary dispute.

"WHAT? YOU YOUNG YANKEE-NOODLE, STRIKE YOUR OWN FATHER!"

the stars and stripes, but John Jacob Astor in the meantime had given up the fur trade as unprofitable. In 1821 the Hudson's Bay Company merged with the previous British company in the area, the North West Company, and Parliament gave Hudson's Bay a monopoly of the fur trade, closing it to individual British subjects. The Hudson's Bay Company under its chief factor, Dr. John McLoughlin, gained a pre-eminent position in the Oregon country north of the Columbia. Farther up the river from Astoria, on the north side, opposite the present-day city of Portland, the British erected their Fort Vancouver, headquarters for the company, nucleus of British interests in the Oregon country. Dr. McLoughlin ruled the north-of-the-Columbia country with an iron hand, dispensing justice according to the customs of British law. He did not openly discourage American settlers in this part of Oregon, but it was clear that they were not entirely welcome. In any event, the settlers could find no lands in McLoughlin's satrapy that compared with the lush Willamette, and the Hudson's Bay Company region remained a country of trappers and Indians. In the year 1845 there were exactly eight Americans north of the Columbia. Seven of these had come in October of that year and established themselves in a little settlement at the head of Puget Sound. The eighth was an Americanized Englishman. There seemed only the most remote possibility in 1845 that the United States in any final settlement with Great Britain would be able to obtain the country north of the Columbia.

History sometimes works in strange and wondrous ways, and no one could have thought in the early 1840's that in 1846 Great Britain would solve the Oregon problem in a treaty with the Americans. A number of novel factors entered in the period between the Webster–Ashburton Treaty and the Oregon settlement of 1846. For one, there was a large wave of emigrants to the Willamette Valley, and these newcomers, many of them lawless individuals from Missouri and neighboring states, ready for any eventuality, best of all a fight against British possessions in the Oregon country, threatened in a not-too-subtle way the Hudson's Bay Company post at Fort Vancouver. Some of the new American Oregonians announced that at the first opportunity they would set fire to the fort. At Fort Vancouver the British maintained a large stock of merchandise for the fur trade, a year's extra stock in event the annual supply ship were wrecked during the course around Cape Horn. When American settlers began appearing in large numbers south of the Columbia, and some of them talked about moving northward, Dr. McLoughlin became so alarmed that in 1843 and 1844 he gave aid to some of the newcomers to prevent the latter in their penniless condition from taking sustenance, without payment or permission, from the stores at the company fort. Partly because of pressure from the new Willamette settlers, the Hudson's

Bay Company in 1844–1845 decided to move its base of supply from Fort Vancouver to Fort Victoria on the southern tip of Vancouver Island. The area south of the forty-ninth parallel also had been trapped out in the past few years, and no longer could support a large trading post. For a decade there had been talk about moving northward. By chance the move occurred at the moment when the Oregon question entered into a period of crisis and then settlement.

But the peculiar turns of British politics in the period 1841–1846 provide the key to understanding the settlement of the Oregon question. In 1841 the Tory government of Sir Robert Peel had come into office in Britain, with the capable and peaceful Lord Aberdeen as foreign secretary. Palmerston had left the foreign office, to the relief of all the chancelleries of Europe. One of the first fruits of this change had been the decision of the new government to send Ashburton to America to arrange a settlement of outstanding issues. Peel and Aberdeen hoped that Ashburton could settle everything, including the Oregon dispute. As it turned out, the summer heat and the fragile health of both Ashburton and Webster, plus some bad advice to Ashburton by an underling in the British foreign office, prevented settlement of Oregon in 1842. What Ashburton managed was good enough, though, and too good in terms of the rights of the United States. Both Ashburton and Webster were happy. The commissioners of Maine and Massachusetts, and the members of the United States Senate, seemed satisfied. All went well until Ashburton's treaty arrived in England, whereupon—although the vast generality of Britishers favored the treaty—Palmerston launched a campaign against what, for partisan reasons, he described as the Ashburton Capitulation. Ashburton had obtained more territory than the award of the king of the Netherlands in 1831 had granted. Palmerston in 1831 would have accepted that award; but in 1842 the disappointment of being out of office plagued him into extreme behavior. He wrote to his party chieftain, Lord John Russell, that the Webster–Ashburton Treaty was "one of the worst and most disgraceful treaties that England ever concluded."

The problem of Peel and Aberdeen was to contain the wrath of the terrible Palmerston. If the Conservatives could get the ear of Palmerston's chief in the Whig leadership, Russell, and persuade Russell that peace with the Americans was the best procedure, then Palmerston could rage as much as he wished, both in Parliament and in his newspaper, the London *Morning Chronicle* (known as the "Viscount Chronicle").

"Half hornet, half butterfly," was a description once awarded Palmerston. In a crisis of 1840 with the Turks over the actions of the pasha of Egypt, a crisis of serious proportion involving several great powers, Palmerston, who then was foreign secretary, had "steered the ship with astonishing self possession and admirable dexterity, and he brought her safely through the storm." But he had created the storm. He now seemed out of his mind on the subject of Oregon, which he coupled with that principal bugaboo of British mid-century politics, France. The famous chronicler of British political life in this era, Charles Greville, visited Palmerston at Broadlands in January 1845 and found him

full of vigour and hilarity, and overflowing with diplomatic swagger. He said we might hold any language we pleased to France and America, and insist on what we thought necessary, without any apprehension that either of them would go to war, as both knew how vulnerable they were, France with her colonies, and America with her slaves . . . .

What solved the Oregon dispute was the containment of Lord Palmerston. The Whigs under Russell sought to form a government in December 1845 and failed, because some Whigs refused to serve in the cabinet if Palmerston were in the foreign office. Meanwhile the shaky Peel cabinet learned that the Hudson's Bay Company was moving north to Vancouver Island, abandoning Fort Vancouver along the Columbia River. The great company at last was admitting that the river was not necessary to its economic position. Peel saw that it would be possible to go ahead on an Oregon treaty at the line of 49°. Aberdeen had been convinced of this possibility since December 1843 when he had so instructed the new British minister to Washington, Richard Pakenham, although he had then told Pakenham that he did not have cabinet support for 49° all the way to the sea. But Peel now was convinced, and he easily convinced Russell. The latter made a public speech at Glasgow in January 1846, in which he said it would be disgraceful for the United States and Britain to go to war over territory in Oregon. After this speech he assured Peel that the Whigs would support the Conservatives on the issue.

The essential surrender, the giving in by the British to the line of the forty-ninth parallel, had been made. Palmerston was gloriously contained and even came to behave himself so well—scenting an imminent return to office after good behavior, which came with the fall of the Peel ministry in June 1846—that he made an Easter excursion to Paris, his first visit in sixteen years. He was received and fêted.

The British arrangements had to await a formal invitation from the United States to reopen the Oregon negotiation, for in 1845 President Polk had closed it with a bang. A few months after coming into office Polk through his secretary of state, Buchanan, had made an offer of 49° to the British minister, Pakenham, but had refused to grant what his predecessors had included, a British right to share in the navigation of the Columbia below the forty-ninth parallel. Pakenham incautiously turned down this offer, not even venturing to take it for reference to the London government. Thereupon Polk instructed Buchanan to withdraw it. A confusion followed, in which Lord Aberdeen instructed Pakenham to re-open the negotiation. He was to try even for arbitration. The luckless minister could get nowhere, for the suggestion of arbitration led only into a jocular remark by Buchanan as to who should arbitrate. The secretary of state referred to a Pakenham proposal to nominate the governments of Hamburg or Bremen or the republic of Switzerland as arbitrator, in concession to the American feeling that no crowned head of Europe could be impartial if a republic were a party. Buchanan said he personally opposed arbitration but that if he were compelled to choose an arbitrator he would select the Pope, that "Both nations were heretics and the Pope would be impartial." Pakenham at this moment was so serious, perhaps in anticipation of a job about to be lost, that he did not catch the joke, and Buchanan had to label it for him.

It was at this time, just while the British were organizing their nonpartisan coalition in favor of 49°, that President Polk, having withdrawn his offer of 49° and refused arbitration, began to give serious evidence of desiring the old Russian line, 54° 40′. He had made statements in favor of the whole Oregon country before his election. The Democratic Party's platform had been "the reannexation of Texas and the reoccupation of Oregon." The Democrats in Congress had voted as a block for Texas, and seemingly Oregon ought to be the other part of the bargain. Former President Jackson, a little more than a month before he died on June 8, 1845, had written to Polk that "the rattling of British drums" was only to alarm the United States. He thought that "This bold avowal by peel & Russell of perfect claim to oragon must be met as boldly, by our denial of their right and confidence in our own. . . . I gave a thousand pledges for your cour[a]ge & firmness both in *war* & in *peace* . . . ." Polk early in 1846 was saying that the only way to handle John Bull was to look him straight in the eye. In a move which his supporters were not certain was a bluff or an expression of his real opinion, he asked Congress late in 1845 to authorize him to give "notice" to the British government of the expiration, after one year, of the "free and open" arrangement between the two countries governing Oregon (this in accord with the agreement arrived at in 1827 to extend the joint arrangement of 1818 in Oregon on a year-by-year basis, subject to notice).

By asking Congress for authority to give notice, Polk produced a congressional dispute the like of which has seldom been heard in American politics. Debate ran on week after week, consuming nearly five months before its end on April 23, 1846. The Mexican War was to break out early in May, but the imminence of that struggle could not stop the flow of Oregon oratory. According to one participant in the House of Representatives who at last got the floor after waiting for a whole month, by the time he rose to speak there had been so much talk on the notice, the British lion and the American eagle had been so often invoked, that "the roar of the one and the scream of the other now fall powerless upon the ears." No one seemed to mind, and there is every evidence that both the congressmen and the American public enjoyed the spectacle.

The argument kept coming that "All Oregon" was necessary for the future of the United States. Representative Andrew Kennedy of Indiana invited his auditors

to go to the West, and visit one of our log cabins, and number its inmates. There you will see a strong, stout youth of eighteen, with his better half, just commencing the first struggles of independent life. Thirty years from that time, visit them again; and instead of two, you will find in that same family twenty-two. This is what I call the American multiplication table. . . . Where, I repeat, without Oregon, are we to find room for our people? What are we to do with the little whiteheaded girls and boys—God bless them!—who throng our western valleys bright and blooming as the flowers that deck our illimitable prairies?

John S. Pendleton of Virginia agreed that Oregon had to be won by the American multiplication table but feared that if the country had to depend on the childless Polk and Buchanan, "Queen Victoria and Mr. Peel will beat us at that."

The congressional issue was over the form of the notice, whether or not notice should be just bald and plain—"naked" was the word of the moment—or whether it would be possible in a preamble to invite the British to negotiate (as the British by this time were wishing to do, though the American lawmakers did not altogether sense this). At one point Senator Lewis Cass of Michigan said incautiously that he, speaking for himself, was going to stay at 54° 40′, but that if any member of the Senate could convince him that the foundations of his position were wrong he would retreat to 49°. This was just the excuse needed for Benton of Missouri, who now had thrown down the god Terminus and wanted everything out to the Pacific coast. Benton demolished Cass's foundations, to his own satisfaction, and then twitted the Michigan senator in a stream of classical oratory. Cass, said Benton, was now a prisoner

in the hands of the Forty-Nines. He is now their prisoner, doomed to dwell at 49. He is not killed but taken. We may say of him as the consoling messenger said to Penelope:

> The great Ulysses is not dead,
> But far from wife and son,
> *He lives a prisoner, on a desert isle.*

I will not follow and say—"Detained by savage men!" For the Forty-Nines are not savage, but peaceful and merciful, and will allow the captive the full liberty of his person, on his parole of honor yesterday given, on a condition now become absolute, never to pass 49, never to use again that name of omen, the Russian line. . . . Henceforth the Senator's occupation is gone. War, inevitable war, can no longer be the burden of his song. War is now evitable. . . . It is peace that is now inevitable; and henceforth we must hear that dulcet sound. The effect of this change in the Senator's position must be great. On the Grecian band, of whom he is the Agamemnon, it must have a most diminishing effect, for the Ajaxes of this expedition, both big and little [here Benton looked significantly at two 54° 40' senators, William Allen of Ohio and Edward A. Hannegan of Indiana], must renounce it when their great chief has imposed the penalty of silence and inaction on himself.

It remained for Senator Hannegan, one of the little Ajaxes of 54° 40', to make the morality of his position, the immorality of the Forty-Niners', so clear that no one could mistake them. In the days of sailing ships this oratorical tactic was known as nailing one's colors to the mast. The Hannegan remarks came during the debate over notice, in which Polk's view of the merits of 54° 40' at no time was clear. A close friend of the president and Polk's former roommate in college, Senator William H. Haywood, Jr., of North Carolina, had come out for 49°, and his explanations sounded suspiciously inspired. Hannegan was enraged. Haywood had charged that 54° 40' was being agitated in order to put small men into large offices. This comment referred to the fact that Polk had forsworn a second term, and the Democratic presidential nomination for 1848 stood available, perhaps to some patriot of 54° 40'. Hannegan retorted, "I would much sooner be found a small man seeking a high place, than the subservient, pliant, supple tool—the cringing flatterer, the fawning sycophant, who crouches before power, and hurries from its back stairs to bring before the Senate its becks, and nods, and wreathed smiles." Hannegan reminded the Senate that Polk during the convention of the Democratic Party at Baltimore in 1844 (held, the Whigs maliciously liked to point out, in the Odd Fellows Hall) had been nominated on a platform of All Oregon. The intentions Haywood ascribed to Polk would betray the Baltimore platform and "make him an infamous man—ay, an infamous man." "Now, when you have got Texas, it means just so much of Oregon as you in your kindness and condescension think proper to give us. You little know us, if you think the mighty West will be trodden on in this way." Angrier and angrier, he said that if Haywood was correct in inferring that the president favored 49°, then it was too bad for Polk: "so long as one human eye remains to linger on the page of history, the story of his abasement will be read, sending him and his name together to an infamy so profound, a damnation so deep, that the hand of resurrection will never be able to drag him forth."

As if he had not said enough, the Indiana statesman concluded by warning that "so far as the whole tone, spirit, and meaning of the remarks of the Senator from North Carolina are concerned, if they speak the language of James K. Polk, James K. Polk has spoken words of falsehood, and with the tongue of a serpent."

A problem was developing within the Democratic Party. The eastern Democrats were bound by commerce to England, the southern Democrats by cotton; it was the West which had no ties and lusted after All Oregon. "These new States, full of enterprise, and fast becoming full of people, and being so circumstanced as to have nothing which could be put to hazard by war, seem to look upon war as a pleasant excitement or recreation," observed a horrified easterner. "They have no cotton crops, and no ships; while war would create much employment among them, raise the price (as they think) of their provisions, and scatter money." For Polk and the Democratic Party there was danger in this western mood. Polk had before him the recent history of the Tyler administration, when after the death of President William Henry Harrison the Whig Party split into a chaos of factions. The president deemed party regularity the very foundation of morality, public and private. As the historian of the Oregon question, Frederick Merk, has written, Polk

was, if anything, more narrowly partisan than his period. Any Whig seemed to him probably depraved, personally as well as politically. In his *Diary* he noted two exceptions to this rule—Senator Willie P. Mangum of North Carolina and the urbane Senator John J. Crittenden of Kentucky. These two he included, even if Whigs, in the ranks of honorable men. But to do this was an extraordinary feat of tolerance on his part and it occurred only in the latter years of his presidency.

The prospect of a party split, therefore, was horrible, worth avoiding at all cost.

The result was predictable. The president, who had said that the best procedure was to look John Bull straight in the eye, shifted his vision during the notice debate, looked into the political future rather than at his British adversary, and quietly joined Cass as a prisoner in the hands of the Forty-Nines. He acted with care. He allowed the Senate to compose a pacific preamble to the notice. The latter, preamble and all, arrived in London in May 1846 and led to an immediate offer by the British government of 49°, all the way out to the sea, the right of navigation of the Columbia River below 49° by the Hudson's Bay Company, and protection of the property of the company and of British subjects in the territory thus made American. Polk submitted this proposal to the Senate, which replied resoundingly in favor. He thereupon converted the proposal into a treaty which Buchanan signed with the perhaps astonished Pakenham, and to which the Senate consented on June 18, 1846, by the easy vote of 48 to 14. All fourteen nays were Democrats. Polk ratified the treaty on June 19, 1846. When the Oregon instrument arrived back in England, the Peel government had already fallen but had not yet left office, and the prime minister was able to announce the final ratification during his farewell speech in Parliament.

If there was sadness in the American West, the East and South were hardly unhappy. The Washington correspondent of the New York *Tribune* asked in truth what had happened to the alliterative slogan about Fifty-Four Forty or Fight, sometimes known as the four P's, Phifty-Phour Phorty or Phight. As if in reply, a Southern newspaper asserted that Phifty-Phour Phorty or Phight had now "phortunately phallen to phinal phlat phooted phixing at 'Phorty nine' without the 'Phight' against a phoreign phoe." Polk, despite the Hannegans, had given in to Great Britain, at least so far as attempting to get such an impossible boundary on the Pacific coast as 54° 40'. It was one thing to press territorial claims against a nation such as Mexico, and quite another to stand up to the most powerful nation in the world, as Britain was during the nineteenth century.

A CONTEMPORARY DOCUMENT

[Representative Kennedy of Indiana has not gone down in the pages of history as a great man, and indeed seems to have been something of a nonentity; but his speech in the House of January 10, 1846, in favor of the resolution for terminating the joint occupation of Oregon, captured the spirit of his section. Source: 29th Cong., 1st Sess., *Congressional Globe*, appendix, pp. 209–212. Kennedy, incidentally, was a Quaker, as he was careful to point out in a part of the speech not printed below.]

From the course this debate has taken, should a spectator enter this Hall, unacquainted with the subject that gave rise to it, he would be led to believe that the question pending was a declaration of war against Great Britain. All who have argued against the resolutions under consideration have declared that to pass them would inevitably lead to war. Now, I submit that this is not a question of peace or war. The very treaty which these resolutions propose to annul provides that said treaty may *at any time* be annulled by either party giving twelve months' notice of their intention to abrogate it. And has it come to this, that we cannot do what the treaty stipulates *may* be done by either party, without incurring the charge of wickedly rushing our country, unprepared, into a needless and desolating war? Sir, I hurl back this charge of seeking a war upon those who make it, for I will not believe that war must necessarily grow out of this question.

But be this as it may, so far as I am concerned, and so far as I understand the feelings and opinions of those whom I represent, this is not a question of peace or war, but a question of right, and I am determined it shall be so treated. Does the territory of Oregon belong to the United States? If it does, that fact precludes the question whether peace or war may result from our action or from the occupation of the territory. But it has been said that we have too long slept upon our rights to assert them now in peace. That does not result from our having suffered England jointly to occupy this magnificent territory in common with us, for commercial purposes, for a quarter of a century. This long and peaceable joint tenancy has resulted from the fact that our people were not made acquainted with the strength and clearness of our title. Thousands of the masses—the bone and sinew of our country—have not conned over all the old records and musty treaties in which our record of title is to be found, and learned therefrom its nature or extent; but while they were in doubt or ignorance as to our title, they were willing to see what could be done by diplomacy.

Now the case is altered, and we have, by proofs and arguments that have been laid before us, become satisfied that our title to the whole of Oregon, from 42° to 54° 40′ north latitude, is "clear and unquestionable." . . .

We, of the West, are not "bookish" men. What little education we have, we received after the labor of the day had been done, in the school of adversity, in the Far West, and almost on the verge of civilization, where our struggles have been with the Indian, and our wrestling with the bear—now no common occurrence. We have, therefore, left it to our agents to settle the question to whom, by the record, Oregon belongs. This they have done, and done well. Our part of the task, which is to maintain and defend our rights, is now to commence; and by the remembrance of the deeds of our fathers, and the strong affection we cherish for our wilderness-homes, we will defend them or perish in the attempt. We do not want war, and you slander us when you say that our hands are itching to grasp the steel of strife, and our hearts panting for the deadly conflict. No people more highly appreciate or value peace and brotherly love, that should bind in one unbroken chain all the families of man, than the people of the West. We know that our free institutions flourish best in the mild and genial atmosphere of peace; but, when it comes to the surrender of the patrimony of our fathers—to receding from, or yielding up our just rights upon our own soil, then, we say, peace can no longer be honorable; and *we* shall not hesitate when it comes to the question of *dishonorable peace, or honorable war.* . . .

I have been pained to hear, during this debate, allusion made to the western people as a war-loving and peace-hating people, who delight in blood and carnage, and who were anxious by their course to embroil this country in a war. Who are those men thus unkindly alluded to and unjustly assailed? They are sons of revolutionary sires, and spirits of noble daring, who have cleared the way for you into the heart of this magnificent empire. They have gone before you like the pillar of cloud by day and of fire by night, rolling back the Indian of the forest to give passage to civilization, as the waters of the Red sea were rolled back by the Great Jehovah to give passage to the children of Israel; and however scornfully you may treat them, or whatever estimate you may place upon them, I verily believe they are as pure and patriotic as the citizens of any other portion of this Union. While they are on the frontiers, where their instincts and duty lead them, upon the very soil designed by Providence as their inheritance, they will remain in peace and quiet, giving you no trouble, and making no unnecessary demands upon your Government. But I warn you from the consequences of an effort to stop their onward progress. Do not let the British get possession of Oregon, and block up the passes of the Rocky mountains against their western flight. Should you do it, and thereby turn back into the valley of the great West those whose disposition and choice it is to mingle in border scenes of hardship and suffering, you may introduce into our society an element that may tumble it into ruins, as did Samson the temple of Dagon when he seized its pillars at the city of Gaza. . . .

We have again and again, in the course of this debate, been reminded of the power and greatness of the government with which we are likely to come in conflict. I do not desire to speak harshly of the British Government; but I despise this constant vaunting of the greatness of England. Who, and what is she? The seat of her power is situated on a little island stuck down in the North sea. True, she has spread her arms like seas, to grasp in all the shores; but still she is not so terrible as to make the nation tremble. All of her greatness now depends upon her commerce. Clip her wings of that, and like the bird of Jove, she falls to the earth a lifeless carcass. I seek no conflict between my country and Great Britain. Let each pursue her path alone, and unmolested by the other. We will not go out of our way to attack the British lion; but if he chooses to lay himself across our path, and refuses to remove at a peaceful summons, then there will be no alternative—the American eagle will strike his talons into his nostrils, and you will see his blood spout as though a whale had been harpooned.

There is, I repeat, no occasion for war; and there will be none, unless the Government of Great Britain desire war with this country. If she does, she may make this question the pretext. Whether she wants war, remains to be seen. If it is the design of Providence that she shall decline, as she arose, by degrees, no conflict will come. If, on the other hand, it is her destiny to pay in blood the debt of blood she owes the world, then I have no objection to belong to the nation and to live in the age that shall chastise her for the evils she has inflicted on the human race. She is old and worn within; the blood of ages stains her skirts. If she is mad enough to attack the young giant of the Western World, whose tall shadow is already beginning to eclipse her glory, on her head be the consequences; and let those who are not engaged in the conflict stand from under, and prepare to hear a crash "as if the ribs of nature broke."

Some gentlemen scoff at what has been called the destiny of nations —or what is the same thing, the providence of God in the affairs of men. Sir, where were we two centuries ago? We were a handful of pilgrims landing upon Plymouth rock, and a small band of cavaliers planted on the sunny sands of the South. From this small beginning, and in this short time, what have we become? We have advanced by steady and peaceful strides, covering the continent with independent and industrious citizens, following up the red man foot by foot, driving him from haunt to haunt, until, like a small and broken cloud that skirts the far-off horizon, he now rests along the shores of the western ocean, ready to take his last plunge, and leave the graves of his fathers, to be visited no more forever. Is there no destiny in this? Is not the finger of God as plainly seen as when he first set in the heavens the star of Bethlehem? The man who sees it not must be either blind or infidel.

It is said by some that we do not need the Oregon territory for purposes of settlement. This is a great mistake; and that you may clearly see the error into which some have fallen, I invite you to go to the West, and visit one of our log cabins, and number its inmates. There you will see a strong, stout youth of eighteen, with his better half, just commencing the first struggles of independent life. Thirty years from that time, visit them again; and instead of two, you will find in that same family twenty-two. This is what I call the American multiplication table. Multiply this and the next generation by this table, and where, without Oregon, will you find room for our people? The greater portion of this multiplying mass of humanity have their faces turned towards the setting sun. "Westward ho!" is the cry; and you can no more stop them this side the shores of the Pacific than you can dam up the mighty waters of the Missouri, whilst the snows are melting on the Stony mountain in which it takes its rise. Where, I repeat, without Oregon, are we to find room for our people? What are we to do with the little white-headed girls and boys—God bless them!—who throng our western valleys, bright and blooming as the flowers that deck our illimitable prairies? . . .

Let us take a short retrospect of the past, in order to judge correctly of the future. Liberty, failing to find a foothold upon the old continent, took her flight to the New World. The causes which produced, and the consequences which followed, the American Revolution, planted deep in our soil the tree of liberty.

The formation of our Constitution linked closely together a chain of free republican States, as a rampart around that tree, to protect it from the outward pressure occasioned by the hostility of European Governments to the liberal principles which lay at the foundation of our system of Government. For half a century the representatives of legitimacy looked upon this experiment with great concern, and not a little fear of its consequences upon their own ill-gotten power, which must melt under the glowing light and scorching rays of the sun of liberty, casting back his bright effulgence upon the Old World, teaching man everywhere that God has given him rights, and demands that he should maintain them. At first it was hoped that this experiment would prove a failure; that rivalry and heartburnings would grow up between the North and the South, the East and the West, which would finally burst the bands of union, throwing the country into anarchy and confusion. Thank God, time has dissipated this hope; the last twenty years has convinced the world that our institutions are as stable as time, and as firm as the decrees of destiny. No sooner are the Governments of Europe convinced of the stability of our institutions, than they are startled by the exhibition of our principle of expansion, by the admission of a free Republic into the American Union. This to them was the passage of the Rubicon; it was the beginning of what will end in placing under the protection of the broad pinions of the American eagle the entire continent, stretching from Cape Horn to Bhering's Straits, and from the shores of the Atlantic to the waves of the Pacific.

This is what my friend from Illinois, [Mr. Baker,] whom I hail as a worthy Representative of Western Whigs, calls our "manifest destiny." . . .

There is in this discussion, to me, a new and very agreeable feature. The discussion indicates, and the vote will prove, that this is no "party question." There sits an aged and venerable man [pointing to John Quincy Adams] of the Whig party who has spoken and will vote with us, because he feels it his duty so to do. Whatever may be said of the hot haste of my youthful blood, I feel confident that whilst I follow the lead of one whose locks are whitened by the snows of eighty winters, I can do nothing rashly. . . .

ADDITIONAL READING

An excellent account of the northeast boundary dispute is in Samuel Flagg Bemis's *John Quincy Adams and the Foundations of American Foreign Policy* (New York, 1949); Adams's father began the settlement of the boundary at Paris in 1782, and JQA considered the boundary problem at Ghent in 1814. See also Claude M. Fuess, *Daniel Webster* (2 vols., Boston, 1930); A. B. Corey, *The Crisis of 1830–1842 in Canadian–American Relations* (New Haven, 1941); Thomas E. LeDuc, "The Maine Frontier and the Northeastern Boundary Controversy," *American Historical Review*, LIII (1947–1948), 30–41; Richard N. Current, "Webster's Propaganda and the Ashburton Treaty," *Mississippi Valley Historical Review*, XXXIV (1947–1948), 187–200; W. D. Jones, "Lord Ashburton and the Maine Boundary Negotiations," *MVHR*, XL (1953–1954), 477–490; and the same author's *Lord Aberdeen and the Americas* (Athens, Ga., 1958).

In *The Oregon Question* (Cambridge, Mass., 1967) the historian of the northwest boundary dispute, Frederick Merk, has brought together his articles published over many years, reprinting also a monograph entitled *Albert Gallatin and the Oregon Problem* (Cambridge, Mass., 1950). See the biography of Gallatin by Raymond Walters, Jr., *Albert Gallatin* (New York, 1957). John S. Galbraith, *The Hudson's Bay Company as an Imperial Factor: 1821–1869* (Berkeley, Calif., 1957) has a section on Oregon. For a detailed account of the same subject see Edwin E. Rich, *Hudson's Bay Company: 1670–1870* (3 vols., New York, 1961). Consult the standard biographies and monographs on Tyler, Polk, and manifest destiny, listed at the end of chapter eight. A clever article showing that the slogan "fifty-four forty or fight" became current in 1845 and that Oregon had minor importance in the election of 1844 is Edwin A. Miles, " 'Fifty-four Forty or Fight'—an American Political Legend," *Mississippi Valley Historical Review*, XLIV (1957–1958), 291–309.

Expansive Projects

Our people are like a young man of 18, full of health and vigor and disposed for adventure of any description.

—John C. Calhoun, 1846

For a number of years after the Mexican War and the settlement of the Oregon question, Americans continued to think in terms of manifest destiny, of boundaries and expansion, and in the 1850's the sense of manifest destiny took new form in the idea that there was something youthful about the American nation, that "young America" stood erect in the strength of early manhood, shoulder to shoulder with such new nations of Europe as young Hungary, young Italy, and young Ireland, facing the worn-out older nations of Great Britain, France, and Spain. When the Habsburgs suppressed the Hungarian revolution in 1849, young America in the pride of manifest destiny sent a thunderous warning to the Austrian government. A few years later it apprised Spain in no uncertain terms of the need for American annexation of Cuba. In the 1850's there was filibustering—*i.e.*, freebooting adventures, organized from the United States, against governments with which the American government was at peace—in Cuba and Nicaragua. There was speechmaking in Congress about Mexican annexation. In this era the United States also established diplomatic representation in the Far East, concluding several treaties with China and Japan which set up extraterritorial privileges and opened ports to trade. Where the American eagle would range appeared to be limited only by the youthful American imagination.

1. *Young America*

Young America was the form taken by manifest destiny after the Mexican War. By chance, the European revolutions of 1848 occurred in the same year that the United States concluded the Treaty of Guadalupe Hidalgo, and this coincidence gave support to the idea of young America, to the belief that America was young and that the powers of Europe were old. Edwin de Leon, in an 1845 address at South Carolina College, had observed, perhaps for the first time, that as there was a young Germany, a young Italy, and a young Ireland, so there might well be a young America. For "nations, like men, have their seasons of infancy, manly vigor, and decrepitude." The young giant of the West, America, stood at the full flush of "exulting manhood." The worn-out powers of the Old World could not hope to restrain or impede the giant's progress. Senator Lewis Cass of Michigan hence could remark in 1852 that American power should make itself felt in Europe. The nation, Cass urged, must not remain a "political cipher." The world must know that there are "twenty-five millions of people looking across the ocean at Europe, strong in power, acquainted with their rights, and determined to enforce them."

Americans, filled with such feelings of national importance, could not have been expected to look with indifference upon the suppression of youthful nations in Europe. Thus when the emperor of Austria, with the help of his fellow monarch the tsar of Russia, suppressed young Hungary in 1849, there was an almost national urge in the United States to do something. Daniel Webster, then secretary of state, found occasion in 1850 to insult Austria through the Austrian chargé in the United States, an unfortunate man named Huelsemann. The Huelsemann Note, as it thereafter was known, informed the Austrians that the events in Hungary "appeared to have their origin in those great ideas of responsible and popular governments on which the American constitutions themselves are founded. . . . The power of this republic, at the present moment, is spread over a region, one of the richest and most fertile on the globe, and of an extent in comparison with which the possessions of the House of Habsburg are but as a patch on the earth's surface." As to possible retaliation, "the government and people of the United States are quite willing to take their chances and abide their destiny." This, of course, was a preposterous note from a fresh young republic such as the United States to one of the most ancient monarchies of Europe. It was all the more extraordinary because the Hungarian revolution was, in a very real sense, none of the United States's business. The Imperial Austrian Government must have been incensed at Webster's brash and gratuitous lecture.

The most impressive demonstration of American solidarity with the cause of the defeated Hungarians came when the Hungarian leader Lajos Kossuth visited the United States in 1851–1852. The entire country feted this European revolutionary. Memorable were the demonstrations of affection in the American West. The Middle West—the West, as it was then—received Kossuth with open arms. His progress through Ohio in 1852, between Columbus and Cincinnati, marked the largest popular demonstration ever seen in that region. Perhaps 100,000 people lined the railroad tracks, and when Kossuth arrived in Cincinnati the shouts that went up from the mighty throng may have reached the throne of Francis Joseph himself. The exiled Hungarian leader, engaged in collecting donations, told the Ohio legislature in a special session that he and the state of Ohio were the same age, that Ohio had been admitted into the union in 1803, the year of his birth. Thus, he said, his heart had always throbbed with excitement at the name "Ohio." "It was like as if something of supreme importance lay hidden in that name for me to which my future was bounded by the very year of my nativity. This day my anticipations are realized."

Kossuth gradually discovered that American sympathies did not extend to the point of large cash donations, nor farther than verbal diplomatic support, and he returned crestfallen to Europe. Still, he had found a warm welcome in the United States. The defeated European revolutionaries of 1848 found that the United States was friendly and sympathetic to their national aspirations. In England in 1854 the American minister, James Buchanan, played host at the legation one night to a gala dinner party of a dozen or so expatriate revolutionaries, including Kossuth, Herzen, and Mazzini. To an American friend Buchanan afterward asked, "Weren't you afraid they would blow you up?" The friend was not afraid. It seemed natural that youthful America should sponsor the revolutionaries of other young nations.

So much for young America versus old Europe in the decade of the 1850's. How did this boisterous era in American history affect the Western Hemisphere? The idea of young America brought a burst of diplomatic activity in Central America and the Caribbean. Interest of the United States in Central America had appeared before the mid-nineteenth century, but with the annexation of California, the gold rush of 1849, and the popularity of the idea of manifest destiny, Central America and the Caribbean became highly important in the diplomacy of the United States.

The first move, the Clayton–Bulwer Treaty, concerned the isthmus of Panama. The then secretary of state of the United States, John M. Clayton, concluded it on April 19, 1850, with the British minister in Washington, Henry Lytton Bulwer—brother of the author of *The Last Days of Pompeii*. The treaty stipulated that neither Britain nor the United States would ever "obtain or maintain for itself any exclusive control" over a canal across the isthmus, and that "neither will ever erect or maintain any fortifications commanding the same, or in the vicinity thereof, or occupy, or fortify, or colonize, or assume, or exercise any dominion over Nicaragua, Costa Rica, the Mosquito Coast [the coast of present-day Nicaragua and Honduras], or any part of Central America." In an accompanying statement the British plenipotentiary announced that Her Majesty, Queen Victoria, "does not understand the engagements . . . to apply to Her Majesty's settlement at Honduras or to its Dependencies." This was to reserve British rights to an area which at about this time had become a crown colony. The Clayton-Bulwer Treaty had no immediate effect upon American history, and did not become important until fifty years later. It is worth mention at this point because it reflected the new continental interests of the United States and because it gave the appearance, no matter how insecure legally, of a national interest in the area of the Caribbean and Central America.

The American government meanwhile was making a strenuous diplomatic effort to purchase Cuba. American government leaders had long shown interest in Cuba, and the Cuban historian Herminio Portell-Vilá has compiled a list showing that every president from Jefferson to McKinley, excepting only Lincoln, who was too busy with the Civil War, coveted the Pearl of the Antilles. Jefferson had shown interest in Cuba, and John Quincy Adams, that soul of rectitude, had remarked in a memorable instruction to the United States minister in Spain that "the annexation of Cuba to our federal republic will be indispensable to the continuance and integrity of the Union itself." Polk in 1848 tried to open negotiations for purchase of Cuba, and instructed the American minister to Spain to offer as much as $100,000,000. This was a considerable price, for Polk in 1845 had been willing to give Mexico only between $25,000,000 and $40,000,000 for the boundary of the Rio Grande, together with New Mexico and California.

In 1854, during the administration of President Franklin Pierce, Secretary of State Marcy directed the American minister in Madrid, Pierre Soulé, to try to get Cuba for $130,000,000. This diplomatic effort is worth examination in some detail. The secretary had informed Soulé that if the American overture met refusal, Soulé should bend his efforts to make Cuba independent. By this he meant that the minister should use good offices and the arts of gentle persuasion to make the Spanish see that Cuba should be independent. The secretary forgot what sort of minister

When the Spanish rebuffed American efforts to annex Cuba, *Punch* was delighted. The caption reads, "Master Jonathan tries to smoke a Cuba, but it doesn't agree with him."

he was addressing in Madrid. Pierre Soulé was a typical American shirt-sleeves diplomat of the sort that so often obtained foreign posts of importance in the nineteenth century. A politician who had antagonized some of his fellow politicos in his native Louisiana, he was packed off to Spain in the hope that there he would be safely out of the way. Soulé at once embroiled himself with the Spanish. First he fought a duel with the French ambassador at Madrid. Next he presented the Madrid government an unauthorized ultimatum in the affair of the *Black Warrior,* an American ship that the Spanish authorities had detained in Cuba. Soulé gave the Spanish foreign office forty-eight hours to make amends for the seizure, without which he would demand his passports and leave. The Spaniards took him at his word and he left. Not content with this melodrama, he repaired to Belgium—he could not stay in France—and there on October 18, 1854, with his colleagues from London and Paris, James Buchanan and John Y. Mason, drew up a report on the Cuban question which became known, although it was signed in Aix-la-Chapelle, as the Ostend Manifesto.

Sent to Marcy as a private document, the manifesto's contents leaked out, and Congress in March 1855 published the dispatch. The administration had to repudiate the pronouncement of its three principal European diplomats, although it added luster to Buchanan's personal reputation and helped him win election to the presidency in 1856. The American diplomats had bluntly said in their Ostend Manifesto that "self-preservation is the first law of nature, with states as well as with individuals." This was no original idea. From there, however, they proceeded to a question: "does Cuba, in the possession of Spain, seriously endanger our internal peace and the existence of our cherished Union?" Should this question be "answered in the affirmative," said Messrs. Buchanan, Soulé, and Mason, "then, by every law, human and divine, we shall be justified in wresting it from Spain . . . upon the very same principle that would justify an individual in tearing down the burning house of his neighbor if there were no other means of preventing the flames from destroying his own home." The flames—and here was the rather shocking reasoning behind the Manifesto—were the possibility that the revolt going on in Cuba would come under the control of Cuban Negroes, that Cuba would be "Africanized and become a second St. Domingo, with all its attendant horrors to the white race, and suffer the flames to extend to our own neighboring shores, seriously to endanger or actually to consume the fair fabric of our Union." The diplomats in Europe, whether through conviction or a sense of political expediency or both, were appealing to the pro-slavery American South, which had just taken alarm over the Kansas-Nebraska Act of 1854 and was beginning to pursue tactics that were to lead to the Civil War. As had happened before, and would again, American diplomacy had become the plaything of domestic politics.

The Ostend Manifesto was, to be sure, a sensational expression of manifest destiny, but other such evidences of America's bumptiousness and territorial cupidity were not lacking in the mid-nineteenth-century. There were notably the filibustering exploits of Narciso López in Cuba and William Walker in Nicaragua and the filibustering plans (they never reached the stage of exploits) of George W. L. Bickley for Mexico. The decade of the 1850's, especially the early 1850's, was the heyday of filibustering in the Caribbean and Central America, and such exploits were intrinsic to the idea of young America. Contrary to belief then and later, this mid-century filibustering was not in its beginnings the scheming of slavery supporters in the southern United States, though it became more so by the end of the decade. The two principal freebooters of the era, López in Cuba and Walker in Nicaragua, were moved by desire for adventure and personal power rather than by missionary zeal to propagate slavery. Bickley was interested as much in adventure and the promotion of a secret fraternal order as in the spread of slavery. In the American North it was usually believed that filibustering was part of a southern slave plot, that the expansion of slavery, having failed with Trist's treaty in 1848, was being secretly furthered through encouragement of expeditions into the weakly governed states of Central America and the Caribbean. The fact that many of the men who gathered around López and Walker were southerners was largely the result of geography, for it was convenient to recruit men from the nearby American South. The filibustering of the 1850's was a personal matter, and such support as it received in the United States came from feelings of manifest destiny rather than desire to expand the institution of Negro slavery.

Narciso López, a native of Venezuela, counting on support from American citizens, attempted three expeditions to Cuba (1849, 1850, 1851) to free Cuba from Spanish rule. If successful, he might have arranged the subsequent annexation of Cuba by the United States. López acted with the support of southern slaveholders, and the institution of slavery beyond question would have continued had he been able to expel the Spanish. Still, as was mentioned, it was love of adventure rather than proslavery notions that moved him in his attempts to revolutionize Cuba. On the first attempt in 1849 he failed to get away from New York, where federal authorities detained him. The following year he did make it to Cuba but found the natives uninterested in liberation, and he barely got back to Key West ahead of a pursuing Spanish warship. The 1851 effort was disastrous, for the Spanish caught López and his men, executed the Venezuelan general and fifty of his followers, and gave the others long penal terms. In retaliation a mob sacked the Spanish consulate in New Orleans, and in further retaliation a mob in Madrid attempted to sack the American legation. Eventually the affair died down with President Millard Fillmore's secretary of state, Webster, acknowledging his country's error in permitting the filibustering expeditions. The Spanish pardoned the American survivors of the third López foray, and Congress voted $25,000 compensation to Spain for damage done the Spanish consulate by the New Orleans mob. Parenthetically one might note that during this episode of filibustering by López the five-barred flag with a single star which two generations later became the flag of the republic of Cuba first appeared, hanging in New York City from a staff above the offices of the New York *Sun*.

William Walker was a more interesting character than López, and in his activities he was for a while more successful. Short, slight of build, and shy, he had gone to California to work on a newspaper, only to desert that prosaic calling for adventure in Nicaragua in the late 1850's. His efforts there would have come to naught had it not been for the existence of the Accessory Transit Company, an American-owned organization whose business it was to convey across Nicaragua travelers to and from California. The Transit Company had facilitated the travel of tens of thousands of Americans. Passengers from New York and New Orleans landed at Greytown, proceeded in boats of light draft up the San Juan River to Lake Nicaragua, crossed the lake in steamers to a point on the west shore called Virgin Bay, and from there were conveyed in carriages over a macadamized road to San Juan del Sur and the steamer for San Francisco. It was like a picnic excursion, and a far cry from the disease-ridden and longer route across the Isthmus of Panama.

As the income from this route became lucrative in the 1850's, the Transit Company sought to protect itself from the volcanic animosities of Nicaraguan politics and employed Walker to keep the tiny republic in order. This was no difficult job, and Walker inaugurated himself president of Nicaragua. A faction of the Transit Company conspired with El Presidente Walker to cancel the company's charter and issue a new charter to themselves. Commodore Cornelius Vanderbilt, part owner of the company, found himself tricked and outwitted by Walker and the conniving faction. He therefore sent his own agent to the scene, who started a liberation movement of the Nicaraguans via neighboring Costa Rica. After a sanguinary campaign, directed by opposing groups of American capitalists, Walker was deposed, although in the general confusion of this so-called revolution of 1857 Nicaragua really lost out, for American interest in isthmian transit thereafter focused on Panama rather than Nicaragua and the latter country was obliged to turn to the cultivation of cotton, coffee, and bananas. Walker made two attempts to regain power in Nicaragua. On the first occasion in November 1857 he failed. On the second, in 1860, a British captain arrested him on the coast of Honduras and handed him over to the Hondurans, who shot him.

Last of the American filibusters was General George W. L. Bickley, President General of the American Legion, KGC. The "KGC" stood for Knights of the Golden Circle. A doctor of medicine in Cincinnati, Bickley in the late 1850's conceived the idea of a grand secret lodge that would advance American manifest destiny into the regions south of the Texas border. He organized his lodges throughout the South and began to prepare for possible military expeditions to Mexico. The president general was a suitable man for the task, being "a tall, fine looking, middle-aged gentleman, having an uncommonly fine expression of countenance, and a high intellectual forehead." He was disturbed by that "crookedest of all boundary lines, the Rio Grande," and decided that he could do something about it. His purposes he smoothed over with a frosting of morality, although it was common knowledge that Mexico was his goal. No matter that, as a Richmond newspaper remarked in 1860, it was difficult to elevate the morals of our neighbors by stealing their country. Bickley's imagination foresaw "energetic Anglo-Saxons" settled in Mexico, who would proceed with the "Texasizing" of that country, that is, annexing it to the United States as slave territory. To proslavery Americans of the late 1850's Bickley held out the prospect of dividing Mexico into twenty-five slave states. Fifty new slavery senators in Washington! The prospect was as impossible as it was alluring, for slavery could not easily flourish in the arid reaches of Mexico, a country devoid of both cotton lands and adequate facilities for transportation. Eventually "that arrant knave and unmitigated humbug, 'General' Bickley" met with failure, for his movement suddenly found itself overshadowed in 1860–1861 by the North–South slavery controversy which led to the Civil War. Perhaps, if this larger issue had not intervened, General Bickley would have become as famous as General Sam Houston twenty-five years before.

2. Expansive relations in the Far East

The 1840's and 1850's, the heyday of manifest destiny and young America, saw also a considerable diplomacy with the Far East, which deserves accounting in the present chapter. American diplomacy with the orient has acquired large importance in the twentieth century, especially since the Second World War, and it is hard to realize that throughout the nineteenth century Far Eastern affairs were of less concern to the United States than relations with Latin America. In the first decades of American diplomacy the interests of the United States in the Far East were chiefly the opening of markets to traders, Christianization of the heathen orientals, and introduction of Western ideas and industrial techniques. The problem of aggression in the Far East, by Japan or China, had no immediacy in the nineteenth century.

Trading, Christianizing, civilizing—these were the purposes of Americans. Trading inaugurated the relations of the United States with this distant area, and was the strongest single interest of American diplomacy until the year 1900 and even later. Christianization of the orient began early in the nineteenth century and grew large in fervor in the 1890's when Protestant Americans undertook "the evangelization of the world in this generation." Westernization, the third concern of Americans, always characterized contacts between the United States and the East. At first westernization was thought of in terms of bringing republican government to Asia, rather than technical knowledge, but by the late nineteenth century there was also interest in introducing American mechanical achievements.

American commerce with the orient began in 1784 when the *Empress of China* sailed out to Canton with a cargo of furs, raw cotton, lead, and thirty tons of a curious and utterly useless New England root which the Chinese called ginseng, and which they hoped would restore virility. This cargo the Americans exchanged for tea, cotton goods, silks, and chinaware. The profits were about thirty per cent. In the following years there were many more American trading voyages to Canton, and prior to the War of 1812 these voyages were highly profitable. Sometimes the owner of a vessel recovered the total cost of his investment in a single venture. Occasionally owners did better than that, for during a voyage in 1797–1798 the 93-ton vessel *Betsy* on an investment of $7,867 earned $120,000. It was, incidentally, in search of goods that would interest the Chinese that Yankee merchants developed a fur trade in the Pacific Northwest. In the course of pursuing the trade in furs the ship *Columbia* gave its name to the largest river of the northwest, and John Jacob Astor founded his trading post at Astoria. Sea-otter skins also proved valuable in the Canton market, and American traders ranged through the South Atlantic and the Pacific, collecting skins in the Falkland Islands, South Georgia, and the Aucklands. In the Falkland Islands one ship obtained some 80,000 skins worth three dollars apiece at Canton, and the cargo of Chinese tea with which this ship returned to America netted $280,000. In their search for products appealing to the Chinese taste, Yankee traders collected many items other than skins and furs, such as sandalwood, tortois shell, mother of pearl, snails, and—of course—birds' nests.

Then there was the opium trade, and it was through this that Westerners, including the Americans, made their first large gain in the markets of China. During the years prior to the Opium War of 1839–1842, all foreigners traded through the single port of Canton under the close supervision of designated Chinese intermediaries, the so-called hong merchants. Conditions of life and trade in Canton were bearable, but British merchants in the Far East were eager to obtain more privileges of trade and residence. The Opium War was their pretext. The trade in opium, one should explain, was only in small measure an American affair, and when the Chinese in 1839 sought to end the supplying of opium by Westerners the Americans in China were not greatly alarmed. As one congressman put it, if the Chinese ceased to smoke opium they might take up tobacco chewing. But when the English forces obtained a Chinese treaty opening four new ports in addition to Canton, the Americans grasped the chance to profit from Britain's use of military force. The result was the Treaty of Wanghsia, signed in a suburb of Macao on July 3, 1844, by the special American plenipotentiary, Caleb Cushing.

In this treaty, sometimes called the Cushing Treaty, the United States received rights of trade in the five treaty ports which China had opened to the British. The treaty also set down clearly, for the first time in any

Western convention with China, detailed definitions of extraterritoriality —special privileges on foreign soil—including the right to try both criminal and civil cases, to rent land, to build hospitals and churches and cemeteries, and to engage Chinese teachers, interpreters, and servants. There was a "most favored nation" clause to the treaty, according to which the United States would receive automatically any concessions granted by China to other nations in future treaties.

The Cushing Treaty was an epochal chapter in Sino-American relations, and in time it was supplemented by the Treaty of Tientsin of 1858, which opened eleven more treaty ports including Taiwan and stipulated the right of Americans to travel and trade throughout all China. This second treaty was another result of the military intervention of European powers in China, this time by the British and French. There were four separate treaties of Tientsin, by France, Britain, Russia, and the United States.

American missionary influence meanwhile was becoming an important factor in Chinese life. Of approximately 90 Protestant missionaries who had come to China by 1855, over half were from the United States. The effect of American missionary enterprise is not easily measured, but its influence upon China was at least equal to that of American trade. The leader of the Taiping rebellion of 1850–1864 was a Christian convert named Hung Hsiu-ch'üan, who confused his epileptic fits with visions of himself as a second Son of God, a divine younger brother of Jesus Christ. Hung in 1846 had come under the influence of an American Baptist missionary at Canton, the Reverend Issachar J. Roberts.

The spreading of Christianity, the fostering of trade, and the persistent hope of "civilizing" the Chinese: these were the principal strands of American interest in China during the nineteenth century. In the mid-century and after, some difficulties did appear in regard to Chinese immigration to the United States. Trouble came with the Burlingame Treaty between the United States and China, signed in 1868 on behalf of China by the former American minister to Peking, Anson W. Burlingame. The treaty had as its nominal purpose an elaboration of the previous Treaty of Tientsin, but the Burlingame Treaty was really a cheap-labor treaty, an effort to provide labor for the building of the transcontinental railroad across the American West. It was estimated that nine-tenths of the construction workers of the Central Pacific were Chinese. Without this source of cheap labor the line would never have been finished in time to receive the promised federal subsidies. As events turned out, the need for cheap labor came to an end just one year after the treaty was signed, for the railroad was completed in 1869. Thereafter the Chinese who had come to America to labor on the road, and whose predecessors had worked in the California gold mines, found themselves forced to turn to occupations competing directly with the labor of native Americans, and the slogan of the American West became "the Chinese must go." Congress in the Chinese Exclusion Act of 1882 forbade further immigration of Chinese laborers, and also stipulated that "hereafter no state court or court of the United States shall admit Chinese to citizenship." Subsequently renewed, the act lasted until 1943 when, under pressure of the enthusiasm for wartime collaboration with Nationalist China, the Chinese were granted an annual quota of 105 immigrants. This applied to all Chinese, rather than just those coming directly from China. This Act of 1943 at last ended a touchy problem of Sino–American relations; for years American missionaries in China had been hearing a great deal about the fact that Christian converts could go to the white man's heaven but not to the white man's country.

In the nineteenth-century history of American relations with the Far

Commodore Perry.

East there remains the saga of Commodore Perry and the opening of Japan, a product of the manifest destiny of the 1840's and early 1850's.

Who, first of all, was this Matthew C. Perry, the diplomat and sailor whose dignified and sensible bearing during his expedition to Japan was one of the reasons for the success of his mission? He was one of the outstanding officers in the American navy of his day and the younger brother of Oliver Hazard Perry, of Lake Erie fame, and had served in the War of 1812. Ever a forward-looking officer, the younger Perry had helped select the original location for the American Negro settlement in Liberia. He had first demonstrated the efficiency of the naval ram. He commanded one of the navy's first steam vessels, the *Fulton*—an awkward floating battery equipped with paddle wheels and four huge stacks which made a record run down Long Island Sound of twenty-eight miles in an hour and fifty-seven minutes. He was largely responsible for building the steam-propelled frigates *Mississippi* and *Missouri*, notable vessels in the slow progress of the American navy from sail to steam.

Why did manifest destiny result in Perry's opening Japan to Western trade and civilization in the early 1850's? There had been a large growth of the Shanghai trade after the Chinese opened that port to the United States in the Treaty of Wanghsia, and this trade made convenient a port of call in Japan. The increase of steam navigation produced the need for a coaling station in the vicinity of the Japanese Islands. The development of whale fisheries in the north Pacific had resulted in a number of wrecks of American vessels off Japanese shores. The sudden acquisition of California in the Mexican War had made Americans far more sensitive to Eastern matters. Upon Perry's departure for the orient his instructions stressed the extent to which the Far East had been brought closer to the United States by "the acquisition and rapid settlement by this country of a vast territory on the Pacific" and "the discovery of gold in that region."

The inspiration of Perry's trip to Japan is thus of record, and likewise it is not difficult to trace out the several steps by which his mission got under way. Some years before his voyage there had been an expedition of three American ships to Siam, where an American envoy accompanying the vessels, Edmund Roberts, on March 20, 1833, signed a treaty of commerce and amity, the first American treaty with a Far Eastern nation. Roberts on return to the orient in 1835 was commissioned to conclude a treaty with Japan but died before reaching the island kingdom. After this effort, and after Cushing's successful conclusion of a treaty with China in 1844, another attempt to obtain the friendship and trade of Japan for the United States was undertaken by Alexander H. Everett, who was the first American commissioner to China under the Cushing Treaty. Everett because of illness was unable to reach Japan, and Commodore

James Biddle, to whom the commissioner delegated his duties, arrived there in July 1846 but achieved nothing. After the Mexican War and some further unsuccessful contacts by Americans with the Japanese, President Millard Fillmore in March 1852 appointed Perry commander in chief of the East India Squadron and special envoy to Japan.

Perry, in accord with the spirit of his times, had a large vision of his mission. In addition to opening Japan he believed it desirable for the United States to acquire territory in the Far East, and recommended taking the Ryukyu Islands. "Now it strikes me," the commodore wrote from Madeira en route to Japan, "that the occupation of the principal ports of those islands for the accommodation of our ships of war, and for the safe resort of merchant vessels of whatever other nation, would be a measure not only justified by the strictest rules of moral law, but, what is also to be considered, by the laws of stern necessity; and the argument may be further strengthened by the certain consequences of the ameliorization of the conditions of the natives, although the vices attendant upon civilization may be entailed upon them." Happily, Perry's recommendation of the Ryukyus was passed over. For the United States, the Ryukyu Islands would have proved another charge on American funds and patience similar to the Philippines. In American possession they would have served during the twentieth century as another hostage to Japan for American good behavior and pliability in the event of Japanese aggression. Yet strange is the course of history, for the time would come when military necessity required the capture of the principal island of the Ryukyu group, Okinawa, at a cost of 45,029 American casualties—11,260 killed, 33,769 wounded—and at least several hundred millions of dollars.

Perry, reaching Japan in 1853, had some difficulty in treating with the Japanese before he eventually met with success. Until he could confer with officials of suitable rank and dignity, the commodore refused to discuss his mission with anyone. The Japanese in turn were not altogether happy to see Perry and would have been glad if he had sailed away. At last a Japanese potentate put his head into an eight-inch gun. He also tried to lift a sixty-four-pound iron cannon ball. After these exercises it was arranged that suitable individuals would receive Perry on shore and take from him, for delivery to the emperor, the letter encased in a gold box which the president or emperor of the United States had commissioned him to present. When Perry returned the following year he found the Japanese willing to conclude a treaty. The ruler of Japan at this time, the emperor's powerful viceroy the Tokugawa shogun, may have realized that it was futile for Japan to continue the isolationist policies of the past. The world had so shrunk, in terms of communication and trade, that an isolated Japan was an anachronism. The feudal society which had flour-

Perry lands in Japan, 1853.

Perry as seen by a Japanese artist.

ished for centuries in Japan was breaking down. A distinct merchant class had developed, possessing all the novel ideas of men of enterprise. This group was eager for foreign contacts, and the shogun in opening Japan followed the desires of these native merchants. As Finley Peter Dunne put it, in the words of Mr. Dooley, "Whin we rapped on the dure, we didn't go in, they come out."

Actually, Perry's treaty of 1854 was little more than a shipwreck convention and was in no sense a broad commercial treaty such as Cushing had secured at Wanghsia in 1844. It remained for the first American diplomatic envoy to Japan, Townsend Harris, to negotiate a full-blown treaty of commerce and amity. The Harris Convention of 1858 set the pattern of American relations with Japan until the end of the century. It stipulated an exchange of diplomatic representatives, the opening of five ports for purposes of trade, provisions of extraterritoriality, and a schedule of tariff duties. Other nations concluded treaties on the pattern of the Harris Treaty, and they lasted until, from 1871 to 1911, Japan negotiated to end the extraterritorial concessions and other servitudes on Japanese sovereignty.

After conclusion of the Harris Convention, the United States had the honor of being not merely the country which opened Japan to Western trade but the nation which received the first Japanese embassy. Japan sent a mission to America in 1860, and during its stay of three months it was feted, wined, dined, and received with enthusiasm and interest, despite the fact that the American nation stood on the brink of the Civil War. When the Japanese arrived in the national capital, they visited Congress and found the Senate's proceedings of much interest. This was the first time that a Japanese mission had witnessed a national legislature at work. Second Ambassador Muragaki and some of his confreres remarked afterward that it looked like the fish market in Tokyo.

Perhaps more important than Japanese visits to Congress were the visits of the mission to the Washington navy yard, and acquisition of a wide selection of American ordnance which was sent back to Japan on the *Niagara* along with army and navy men to teach its use. The services of these men were declined by the shogunate, which was reluctant to reveal the state of Japan's defenses. The Japanese, one should add, already had learned how to use the Western-style guns.

CONTEMPORARY DOCUMENTS

[The theme of young America versus old Europe offered endless possibilities for oratory, and the aging Daniel Webster, secretary of state under President Millard Fillmore, could not resist the opportunity. In 1850 he managed adroitly to insult the Austrian government in the Huelsemann Note. Perhaps the secretary of state felt that with this remarkable missive he had done enough for young America and as an old man he might therefore be able to forget the whole thing. Webster the politician soon sensed, however, that the American people were in an exuberant mood. Early in 1852, Kossuth turned up in Washington, and a great meeting was organized in behalf of the Hungarian patriot. In a letter of January 7, 1852, to President Fillmore, Webster cagily explained why he, the secretary of state, was going to attend the Kossuth meeting, which was to be held that very night. Source: *Writings and Speeches of Daniel Webster* (18 vols., Boston, 1903), XIII, 503.]

I have come to the conclusion that it is well for some of us to go to the dinner this evening. The President of the Senate is to preside, and the Speaker of the House is to act as Vice-President. It has been said that assurances have been given that nothing shall be said that shall justly be offensive to these gentlemen as anti-intervention men.

But what chiefly influences me, is, that I learned yesterday that preparations were making for a good deal of an attack upon us, if no member of the administration should pay Kossuth the respect of attending the dinner given to him by members of Congress, of all parties, as the nation's guest. I wish the Heads of Department could see their way clear to go, as I think I shall go myself. In the present state of the country, especially in the interior, where Kossuth is going, I should not like unnecessarily to provoke popular attack.

[At the Kossuth banquet that evening Secretary Webster outdid himself in praise of the guest of honor. Source: *ibid.*, 452–453, 461–462.]

I have great pleasure in participating in this festival. It is a remarkable occasion. He who is your honored guest tonight has led thus far a life of events that are viewed as highly important here, and still more important to his own country. Educated, spirited, full of a feeling of liberty and independence, he entered early into the public councils of his native country, and he is here to-day fresh from acting his part in the great struggle for Hungarian national independence. That is not all his distinction. He was brought to these shores by the authorities of Congress. He has been welcomed to the capital of the United States by the votes of the two Houses of Congress. I agree, as I am not connected with either branch of the Legislature, in joining, and I do join, in my loudest tone, in the welcome pronounced by them to him. The House of Representatives,—the immediate representatives of the people,—full themselves of an ardent love of liberty, have joined in that welcome; the wisdom and sobriety of the Senate have joined in it; and the head of the Republic, with the utmost cordiality, has approved of whatsoever official act was necessary to bid him welcome to these shores. And he stands here to-night, in the midst of an assembly of both Houses of Congress, and others of us met here in our individual capacity, to join the general acclaim, and to signify to him with what pleasure we welcome him to the shores of this free land—this asylum of oppressed humanity. Gentlemen, the effect of the reception thus given him cannot but be felt. It cannot but have its influence beyond the ocean, and among countries where our principles and our sentiments are either generally unknown or generally disliked. Let them go forth—let it be borne on all the winds of heaven—that the sympathies of the Government of the United States, and all the people of the United States, have been attracted toward those of her sons who have most distinguished themselves in that struggle. . . .

Gentlemen, I have said that a national government, where there is a distinct nationality, is essential to human happiness. I have said that, in my opinion, Hungary is thus capable of human happiness. I have said that she possesses that distinct nationality, that power of population and that wealth which entitle her to have a government of her own, and I have now to add, what I am sure will not sound well upon the Upper Danube, and that is that, in my humble judgment, the imposition of a foreign yoke upon a people capable of self-government, while it oppresses and depresses that people, adds nothing to the strength of those who impose that yoke. In my opinion, Austria would be a better and a stronger government to-morrow if she confined the limits of her power to her hereditary and German domains, especially if she saw in Hungary a strong, sensible, independent neighboring nation; because I think that the cost of keeping Hungary quiet is not repaid by any benefit derived from Hungarian levies or tributes. And then again, good neighborhood, and the good-will and generous sympathies of mankind, and the generosity of character that ought to pervade the minds of governments, as well as those of individuals, is vastly more promoted by living in a state of friendship and amity with those who differ from us in modes of government, than by any attempt to consolidate power in the hands of one over the rest.

Gentlemen, the progress of things is unquestionably onward. It is onward with respect to Hungary; it is onward everywhere. Public opinion, in my estimation at least, is making great progress. It will penetrate all resources; it will come more or less to animate all minds; and in respect to that country for which our sympathies to-night have been so strongly invoked, I cannot but say that I think the people of Hungary are an enlightened, industrious, sober, well-inclined community; and I wish only to add, that I do not now enter into any discussion of the form of government that may be proper for Hungary. Of course, all of you, like myself, would be glad to see her, when she becomes independent, embrace that system of government which is most acceptable to ourselves. We shall rejoice to see our American model upon the Lower Danube and on the mountains of Hungary. But this is not the first step. It is not that which will be our first prayer for Hungary. That first prayer shall be that Hungary may become independent of all foreign power—that her destinies may be intrusted to her own hands, and to her own discretion. I do not profess to understand the social relations and connections of races, and of twenty other things that may affect the public institutions of Hungary. All I say is, that Hungary can regulate these matters for herself infinitely better than they can be regulated for her by Austria; and, therefore, I limit my aspirations for Hungary, for the present, to that single and simple point,—Hungarian independence, Hungarian self-government, Hungarian control of Hungarian destinies. These are the aspirations which I entertain, and I give them to you, therefore, gentlemen, as a toast: *"Hungarian Independence*—Hungarian control of her own destinies; and Hungary as a distinct nationality among the nations of Europe."

ADDITIONAL READING

For the spirit of the 1850's the best introduction is Merle E. Curti, "Young America," *American Historical Review*, XXXII (1926–1927), 34–55. The Kossuth craze appears in J. W. Oliver, "Louis Kossuth's Appeal to the Middle West—1852," *Mississippi Valley Historical Review*, XIV (1927–1928), 481–495. See also M. E. Curti, "Austria and the United States, 1848–1852," *Smith College Studies in History*, XI (1926), No. 3; A. J. May, *Contemporary American Opinion of the Mid-Century Revolutions in Central Europe* (Philadelphia, 1927); A. A. Ettinger, *The Mission to Spain of Pierre Soulé: 1853–1855* (New Haven, 1932); and Andor Klay, *Daring Diplomacy: The Case of the First American Ultimatum* (Minneapolis, 1957).

The filibusters in Latin America have inspired a few books and articles: R. G. Caldwell, *The López Expeditions to Cuba: 1848–1851* (Princeton, 1915); W. O. Scroggs, *Filibusters and Financiers* (New York, 1916), dealing with William Walker; Lawrence Greene, *The Filibuster: The Career of William Walker* (Indianapolis, 1937); Ollinger Crenshaw, "The Knights of the Golden Circle: The Career of George Bickley," *American Historical Review*, XLVII (1941–1942), 23–50; Basil Rauch, *American Interest in Cuba: 1848–1855* (New York, 1948). Also consult Dexter Perkins, *The Monroe Doctrine: 1826–1867* (Baltimore, 1933); Irving Katz, "August Belmont's Cuban Acquisition

Scheme," *Mid-America*, L (1968), 52–63; *William H. Goetzmann, *When the Eagle Screamed* (New York, 1966); John A. Logan, Jr., *No Transfer* (New Haven, 1961).

A discussion of the sole territorial acquisition, despite all the hullaballoo of the time, appears in Paul N. Garber, *The Gadsden Treaty* (Philadelphia, 1923).

In part because of their frequently exotic details, American relations with the Far East during the nineteenth century have interested many writers. A general account is Tyler Dennett, *Americans in Eastern Asia* (New York, 1922). Among the many books of merit on China are Kenneth Scott Latourette, *The History of Early Relations between the United States and China: 1784–1844* (New Haven, 1917); Eldon Griffin, *Clippers and Consuls: American Consular and Commercial Relations with Eastern Asia, 1845–1860* (Ann Arbor, Mich., 1938); Ssu-yu Teng, *Chang Hsi and the Treaty of Nanking: 1842* (Chicago, 1944); *Maurice Collis, *Foreign Mud* (New York, 1947); *John King Fairbank, *Trade and Diplomacy on the China Coast: The Opening of the Treaty Ports, 1842–1854* (Cambridge, Mass., 1953); Earl Swisher, *China's Management of the American Barbarians: A Study of Sino-American Relations, 1841–1861, with Documents* (New Haven, 1953); F. Wells Williams, *Anson Burlingame and the First Chinese Mission to Foreign Powers* (New York, 1912); and, partly on China, Claude M. Fuess, *The Life of Caleb Cushing* (2 vols., New York, 1923). A general account is Foster Rhea Dulles, *China and America: The Story of Their Relations since 1784* (Princeton, 1946). For Japan there is Arthur Walworth, *Black Ships Off Japan* (New York, 1946), concerning the Perry expedition; Henry F. Graff, *Bluejackets with Perry in Japan* (New York, 1952); William L. Neumann, "Religion, Morality, and Freedom: The Ideological Background of the Perry Expedition," *Pacific Historical Review*, XXIII (1954), 247–257; Foster Rhea Dulles, *Yankees and Samurai: America's Role in the Emergence of Modern Japan* (New York, 1965); Samuel Eliot Morison, *"Old Bruin": Commodore Matthew Calbraith Perry* (Boston, 1967); Carl Crow, *He Opened the Door of Japan* (New York, 1939), on Townsend Harris; and Chitoshi Yanaga, "The First Japanese Embassy to the United States," *Pacific Historical Review*, IX (1940), 113–138. A general account is Payson J. Treat, *Diplomatic Relations between the United States and Japan: 1853–1895* (2 vols., Stanford, Calif., 1932). *William L. Neumann, *America Encounters Japan: From Perry to MacArthur* (Baltimore, 1963) is a new volume of large merit because it is both highly readable and highly reliable. A biography of Horace Allen, the American missionary doctor and diplomat to Korea, is by Fred H. Harrington, *God, Mammon and the Japanese* (Madison, Wis., 1944).

American political leaders of the era appear in Holman Hamilton, *Zachary Taylor* (2 vols., Indianapolis, 1941–1951); Roy F. Nichols, *Franklin Pierce* (Philadelphia, 1931); Ivor D. Spencer, *The Victor and the Spoils: A Life of William L. Marcy* (Providence, R.I., 1959); Philip S. Klein, *President James Buchanan* (University Park, Penn., 1962).

☆ **11** ☆

Civil War

We are not enemies but friends. . . . The mystic chords of memory, stretching from every battlefield and every patriot grave to every living heart and hearthstone in the broad land, will yet swell the chorus of the Union. . . .
—President Abraham Lincoln, first inaugural, 1861

Manifest destiny, variously interpreted, was the presiding idea of the American Civil War. It may appear odd that no sooner had the sentiments of young America filled the halls of Congress than the oratory of secession arose, seemingly the negation of manifest destiny. In fact, the new government of the Confederate States of America considered itself the fulfillment of manifest destiny. And not a few southerners in 1861 envisioned their own special continuance of manifest destiny through taking lands in Mexico and Central America and the Caribbean, territories that the United States had neglected during the 1840's and 1850's. As for the men of the Union, they also acted in accord with manifest destiny, believing that on the continent of North America the will of God required one great republic instead of two. God had ordained it. The long blue columns and the thousands of creaking wagons moved slowly over the dusty roads toward the South under the impulse of verses impossible to forget. "Mine eyes have seen the glory of the coming of the Lord . . . ."

It was not at first evident which version of manifest destiny would win, and foreign observers looking at the Civil War during its initial months and well into the year 1863 were inclined to bet on the South, to doubt the North's ability to reconquer the rebellious states. The bulk of the population, the twenty-two million people in the northern states and territories, stood loyal to the government in Washington. But the southern side, though only nine million in population (including four million slaves), gave evidence of being able to put better armies into the field. The South's populace was accustomed to outdoor life, even frontier life. Large sections of the Deep South, the cotton South, were virtually parts of the frontier, barely thirty or forty years into civilization, representing in no sense the settled and porticoed existence so many present-day Americans remember from the movie of Margaret Mitchell's *Gone with the Wind*. The southerners were also trained fighters. Many of the best officers of the prewar American army had been southerners. The northern officers and men had to come from the farms and teeming cities where life was rough enough but no approximation to life in the army. At the outset of the fighting the North showed up badly. In the Battle of Bull Run, fought outside Washington on July 21, 1861, the northern formations broke into a chaotic rout, 30,000 raw Union soldiers running for miles to get away from the avenging Confederates, littering the road back to Washington with their new equipment. In subsequent confrontations the southerners appeared easily to hold their own, often despite northern superiority in manpower and arms.

Fortunately for the northern apostles of manifest destiny, a marked difference in the political leadership of the two sections slowly became evident, and this difference proved decisive. In his *The Statesmanship of the Civil War*, Allan Nevins has written that the principal Confederate, Jefferson Davis, was little more than a politician. Davis lacked flexibility and imagination. The tall, aristocratic, reserved individual who led the Confederacy was implacable. One could say of Davis as of the younger Pitt: "He never grew—he was cast." The Union leaders, however, proved themselves statesmen. Abraham Lincoln, perhaps the most talented individual in American history, had won the presidential election of 1860: his qualities hardly need description. He brought common sense and vision to whatever he dealt with, and one of his lesser known activities during the war was to control and guide the country's foreign policy until his generals at last had fought the huge rebellion to a standstill. This he did despite the manifold military and domestic political problems which crowded his attention. To American Civil War diplomacy Lincoln added wisdom and patience; he brought to it the sure touch of the born leader of men.

The president masterfully controlled and ordered the actions of his secretary of state, William H. Seward, a person of large abilities if impulsive behavior. Henry Adams remembered Seward as a "slouching, slender figure" with "a head like a wise macaw; a beaked nose; shaggy eyebrows; unorderly hair and clothes; hoarse voice; offhand manner; free talk, and perpetual cigar." The secretary's so-called April Fool's Day proposition of 1861 to Lincoln urged the president to give him the reins of office so that he could then save the Union by starting a foreign war with France or Spain! ". . . whatever policy we adopt," Seward had written the president, "there must be an energetic prosecution of it."

For this purpose it must be somebody's business to pursue and direct it incessantly.

Either the President must do it himself, and be all the while active in it; or

Devolve it on some member of his Cabinet. Once adopted, debates on it must end, and all agree and abide.

It is not in my especial province.

But I neither seek to evade nor assume responsibility.

At such points in the conduct of Civil War diplomacy Lincoln intervened and kept affairs in balance. The president cut off the imprudent projects and activities of his secretary of state. He enabled the brilliant but effervescent Seward to conduct diplomacy with such deftness that Seward would go down in history as one of the greatest of American secretaries of state.

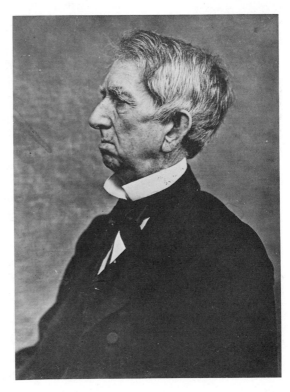

Henry Adams said William H. Seward had a head like a wise macaw.

1. *The chief object*

Of the diplomatic problems confronting the Union, by far the most important was the preservation of good relations with Great Britain—the ensuring of British neutrality, prevention of any interference with the North's blockade of southern ports which, if maintained long enough, was certain to destroy southern military resistance by cutting off supplies to the Confederate troops. The South lacked the industrial capacity to supply its armies and needed arms and munitions from abroad. The government of Great Britain, most powerful in the world, could have insisted that the North open southern ports, and could have forced the North to do so, either by sending in the royal navy or by permitting the South to construct a navy in British shipyards.

To the wondering Union diplomats the position of Great Britain was at first a huge question mark. Upper-class members of English society had always disliked the American experiment in democracy and predicted that it would degenerate into anarchy and chaos, as democracies had done before. All the doctrines of political economy and public philosophy taught that republics could exist only in a limited territory, and that the larger a republic's expanse the weaker became its hold over its citizens. The Mexican War offered the spectacle of the American glutton eating itself to death. The denouement of 1861 proved the wisdom of history. A distinguished English historian, Edward A. Freeman, published in 1863 the first volume of a work entitled *History of Federal Government, from the Foundation of the Achaian League to the Disruption of the United States.* That Freeman would never conclude his second volume was not apparent at the time the initial tome appeared.

Apart from the teachings of political economy, public philosophy, and Freeman's history, the leaders of the British government had their own reason for finding the division of the American republic attractive. The prime minister in 1861, Lord Palmerston, according to the recollection of William E. Gladstone, "desired the severance as a diminution of a dangerous power." In South America in 1828 Britain had sponsored the dissolution of Brazil into Brazil and Uruguay under a policy of *divide et impera.* Why not do the same in North America?

What would happen—that was the question. When the new American minister to London, Charles Francis Adams, set foot on British shores in May 1861, it was to learn that the London government had just recognized the belligerency of the South. Adams's young son Henry thought his father's mission hopeless. He saw no friendship for the North in Great Britain and believed that the Adamses, venturing to London, were like "a family of early Christian martyrs about to be flung into an arena of lions, under the glad eyes of Tiberius Palmerston."

It seemed an ill piece of luck that Palmerston should have been in office as prime minister at the time of the American Civil War. There was not much reason to expect good treatment from the man who had been so hostile during the northeast boundary dispute of a generation before. Young Henry Adams considered Palmerston an impossible individual, a deplorable anachronism, a throwback in ideas and action to a half-century before the Civil War, to the era of Napoleon. Once Adams attended a reception at the prime minister's house and encountered trouble with a functionary of the household. Adams

gave his name as usual at the foot of the staircase and was rather disturbed to hear it shouted up as "Mr. Handrew Haddams!" He tried to correct it, and the footman shouted more loudly: "Mr. Hanthony Hadams." With some temper he repeated the correction and was finally announced as "Mr. Halexander Hadams," and under this name made his bow . . . to Lord Palmerston who certainly knew no better.

If the introduction annoyed Henry, he had formed his opinions well before. Years later he recalled the prime minister's laugh as Palmerston stood at the door that evening receiving the guests. "The laugh was singular, mechanical, wooden, and did not seem to disturb his features. 'Ha! . . . Ha! . . . Ha!' Each was a slow, deliberate ejaculation, and all were in the same tone, as though he meant to say: 'Yes! Yes! Yes!' by way of assurance. It was a laugh of 1810 and the Congress of Vienna."

The news of Bull Run delighted Palmerston. The Yankees were losing. Privately he wrote that

The defeat at Bull's Run—or rather at Yankee's Run—proves two things. First, that to bring together many thousand men and put uniforms upon their backs and muskets in their hands is not to make an army: discipline, experienced officers and confidence in the steadiness of their comrades are necessary to make an army fight and stand: secondly, that the Unionist cause is not in the hearts of the mass of the population of the North. The Americans are not cowards: individually they are as reckless of their own lives as of the lives of others . . . and it is not easy to believe that if they had felt they were fighting for a great national interest they would have run away as they did from the battle . . . . The truth is the North are fighting for an idea chiefly entertained by professional politicians, while the South are fighting for what they consider, rightly or wrongly, vital interests.

Gradually, slowly, sometimes imperceptibly, the advantages of Union leadership, northern military victories, recognition by the government of Great Britain that its own self-interest lay in a victory of the Union over southern separatism, the chapter of accidents, whatever it was—perhaps the inscrutable processes of manifest destiny—all combined to force a change in the British attitude. It was slow business, but the first quiet turns for the better eventually increased and multiplied until no one in his right mind, not even Jefferson Davis, could look any longer to the British to assist the South's cause. The Civil War was half over before the change in the British attitude was discernible, and until the end of the war some individuals watched with trepidation every twist of British policy, remaining to the very last uncertain what the London government would do to the United States. The change occurred, and with it the southerners lost the war.

Many factors and forces contributed to this outcome. Not least had been Seward's appointment of C. F. Adams to the London legation. There could have been no better choice. Son of John Quincy Adams, grandson of John Adams, third Adams to hold appointment by his country to the Court of St. James's, C. F. Adams had attended an English public school and thoroughly understood the proprieties of English society. Unlike the Confederate commissioner to England, James M. Mason (not to be confused with the John Y. Mason of Ostend Manifesto fame), who while listening to the House of Commons debates would spit tobacco juice over the carpet in front of him, Adams knew perfectly how to behave. When he faced the British foreign secretary of the day, Earl Russell, it was as one noble lord speaking to another. Russell resembled no one so much as Adams's own father, John Quincy Adams. Adams and Russell were both small, funereal men, and their meetings and epistolary exchanges were conducted with such icy propriety that there soon emerged something close to mutual understanding if not appreciation.

The North had an apparently inexhaustible reservoir of good men to send to England, persons who could talk to influential Britishers and persuade them that if they backed the South they would be backing the wrong side. Some of these individuals went to England on their own, such as the great northern preacher, once the pride of Indianapolis but by the time of the Civil War the leading cleric of Brooklyn, Henry Ward Beecher. When this masterful man of God spoke to Britishers, they were likely not merely to feel northern sentiments but to weep them; Beecher was a marvelous tear-jerker. Lincoln sent the able New York politico, Thurlow Weed, who performed prodigies for the North, according to Weed's reminiscences; at one crucial juncture in northern fortunes Weed spoke with the wife of Foreign Secretary Russell who, Weed recalled, carefully gave the visiting New Yorker an indication of Russell's true pro-northern sentiments. Other individuals, including an Episcopal bishop and a Roman Catholic archbishop, argued the northern cause.

The southern cause encountered numerous ill turns of fortune, chief of which was British reaction to the slavery issue. The existence of Negro slavery in the South made the work of Confederate supporters in England immensely difficult. In the early nineteenth century the British people had led a world campaign to abolish slavery, to which their diplomats had sought to commit all the powers of Europe. The southern views on slavery were well known in England. Vice President Alexander H. Stephens in a speech at Savannah on March 21, 1861, had said that "the new Constitution has put at rest forever all the agitating questions relating to our peculiar institutions—African slavery as it exists among us—the proper status of the Negro in our form of civilization. This was the immediate cause of the late rupture and present revolution." He added that Thomas Jefferson and his contemporaries of the revolutionary era had believed that slavery "was wrong in principle, socially, morally, and politically." But, Stephens said, "these ideas were fundamentally wrong. They rest upon the assumption of the equality of races. This was an error." It was in this speech, and at this point in it, that Stephens blurted out the stupidity that was to circulate ever after: "Our new government is founded upon exactly the opposite ideas; its foundations are laid, its cornerstone rests, upon the great truth that the Negro is not equal to the white man; that slavery, subordination to the superior race, is his natural and moral condition."

Many of the eminent Victorians—Acton, Bulwer-Lytton, Charles Dickens, Matthew Arnold, Herbert Spencer—had ranged themselves on the side of the South at the beginning of the war. They liked the aristocratic traditions of the South and saw a reflection of their own upper-class English way of living. But it was difficult to keep them in support of slavery. The North had the advantage of a moral cause. Alfred Lord Tennyson, certainly one of the leaders of mid-Victorian society, admitted his sympathy for southern culture and traditions but found that the "Battle Hymn of the Republic" haunted him. He discovered himself unwittingly humming the republican melody and wondered why the South had failed to produce such a glorious call to arms.

As for the middle classes and the workingmen of England, in the Union's fight for life they saw nothing less than the cause of liberty. Southern attempts to convert them proved to no avail, even though the shortage of raw cotton from the South shut down mills and cost thousands of workers their jobs. People suffered in the Lancashire mill district, where the rolls of those on poor relief reached a high of 284,418 in December

1862; private relief, organized on a national scale, extended to 236,000 people. This meant that in Britain the grand total of distress, caused in large part by the cotton famine, extended to more than half a million persons. These poor people were not willing to champion slavery in America to relieve their own condition.

With the emancipation proclamation in effect after January 1, 1863, and supported by the blunders of his opponent in Richmond, Lincoln found that diplomacy toward antislavery England was growing markedly easier. Britishers noticed that the Confederate representative in England, James M. Mason, had been the author—when a decade before he had been senator from Virginia—of the Fugitive Slave Law. Escaped slaves, such as the former coachman of Jefferson Davis, were introduced at emancipation meetings. George Francis Train, a private American citizen living in Britain, did valiant work for the cause—resorting to such tricks as advertising a debate and "for want of speakers on the Southern side" appointing himself to defend the Confederacy. He would begin the South's defense by stating, "We in Secessia have based our Constitution and reared our Temple of Despotism on one acknowledged cornerstone—NEGRO SLAVERY." John Bright and Richard Cobden, the two prominent English reformers, sided with the North. Bright spoke typically at Birmingham on December 18, 1862, when he said:

I blame men who are eager to admit into the family of nations a State which offers itself to us, based on a principle . . . more odious and more blasphemous than was ever heretofore dreamed of . . . . The leaders of this revolt propose this monstrous thing—that, over a territory forty times as large as England, the blight and curse of slavery shall be forever perpetuated.

The only real cause of the Civil War, Bright contended at emancipation gatherings, was slavery, slavery, slavery.

The South still hoped that the cotton famine would force British intervention. Some years before the war, in 1855, a book had appeared in the United States entitled *Cotton is King*, written by a northerner from Cincinnati named David Christy. Southerners had seized upon this phrase which resounded in speeches and journals and newspapers. People began to believe it true. When the Civil War commenced, southern diplomacy in Great Britain seemingly needed to be only a kind of cotton diplomacy— *King Cotton Diplomacy*—as the twentieth-century historian Frank L. Owsley entitled his history of Southern diplomacy during the Civil War. One-fifth of the population of England in 1861 lived, directly or indirectly, from the production of cotton cloth. The overwhelming bulk of British supplies of cotton came from the American South. Beginning with the year 1850, cotton production in the southern states had increased tremendously. In the years 1849–1851 something over a million bales of American cotton had been exported annually to Great Britain. By the years 1858–1860 nearly two million bales went to Britain each year. This quantity was only four hundred thousand bales short of all British cotton imports in the same years. King Cotton Diplomacy, so it appeared in 1861, would almost without effort ensure southern independence, especially when the British ruling classes were prejudiced in favor of the aristocratic South.

By a quirk of fate, cotton proved a poor diplomat. What happened, curiously, was that the opening of the Civil War found the cotton crop of 1860 almost entirely exported. And it had been the largest crop on record, nearly four million bales, of which 3.5 million were sent abroad, Liverpool receiving most of them. A surplus both of raw cotton and of manufactured cotton goods accumulated in Britain. Mill owners raised their prices, anticipating a shortage. Consumers of cotton goods withheld purchases, partly because they had bought heavily, partly because of rising prices. A renewed demand for cotton goods even at high prices came only in the winter of 1862–1863. By that time, of course, no raw cotton was available. Before southern diplomacy was able to exploit this situation, the North won the battles of Vicksburg and Gettysburg and sealed the South's fate.

It was widely believed in the North during the war that by wheat, rather than arms, northern diplomacy would triumph—that northern exports of wheat to England during the years 1860–1863, years of poor European crops, would tie Britain to the northern cause as effectively as southerners had dreamed would be the case with cotton. According to a contemporary jingle,

> Old King Cotton is dead and buried,
> Brave young Corn is King.

Exports of wheat to Britain increased greatly during these years. The grain crisis was general in Europe, and the usual sources of British supply during lean harvests, the Baltic and Black Sea countries, were exporting their surpluses to Western Europe, leaving Britain no recourse but to turn to America. Whether the need of Britain for grain was so great as to attach that nation to the northern cause must be a matter of doubt. Surely it helped relations between the two countries. Perhaps Britishers thought that they were more dependent on northern grain than they were, and in such case the thought would have been equivalent, in diplomatic effect, to actuality.

But to turn now to the specific diplomatic events of the war. In the early years of the Civil War came two crises with Great Britain, the *Trent* affair and the dispute over the Laird rams.

2. *The* Trent *affair and the case of the Laird rams*

The affair of the steamer *Trent* was the more serious. The British government had recognized southern belligerency in May 1861, a move that followed naturally from Lincoln's proclamation of a blockade of southern ports, and the danger was that (1) recognition of belligerency might change into (2) recognition of southern independence and (3) destruction of the blockade. The *Trent* affair raised British tempers near to a point of explosion in the winter of 1861–1862 and threatened to force the London government to take the second and third steps mentioned above. Henry Adams in London telegraphed his father frantically—Charles Francis Adams was visiting in the country—when the legation learned that Captain Charles Wilkes of the United States navy on November 8, 1861, had forcibly removed two Confederate commissioners from the British mail steamer *Trent*, then passing through the Caribbean, and taken the commissioners to Boston where federal authorities imprisoned them. Kidnaping of nationals from the vessels of a neutral had been a favorite practice of Great Britain for decades, and had helped bring on the War of 1812. But by 1861–1862 the views of the British had changed as a result of the nearly fifty years of relative peace. Humanitarian sympathies enlisted during the Crimean War of 1854–1856 had brought the Declaration of Paris of 1856, wherein Britain accepted some small-navy principles of naval warfare and neutrality. By the time of Captain Wilkes's action with the *Trent* the British government had turned turtle its ideas about impressment and was willing to challenge anything resembling impressment.

Captain Wilkes, it is true, had not taken off the two Confederate commissioners as an act of impressment. After consulting hastily some law books in his cabin he had reasoned to himself that the two Confederates, James M. Mason and John Slidell—the latter the same man who had gone to Mexico for President Polk in 1846—were embodied dispatches from a belligerent power, or else rebellious citizens of the United States, and in either case removable from the *Trent*. Wilkes should have taken the steamer into port, for it was carrying southern diplomatic dispatches to Europe, but such a course, although technically correct, would have wrought even stronger feeling in Britain than Wilkes's removal of only the southern commissioners.

The impressment of Mason and Slidell, or the seizure of these two re-

The USS *San Jacinto* stopping the British steamer *Trent*.

bellious citizens or embodied dispatches, was in its details a comic-opera affair, and anyone who recalls the manner in which this Caribbean contretemps occurred must wonder what had happened to the American and British senses of humor. People in 1861 should have laughed at the *Trent* affair rather than become angry. Prior to the capture Wilkes had fired two shots across the bow of the British steamer, and this began the comic tragedy. He then sent on board the *Trent* his representative, Lieutenant

D. M. Fairfax, who asked for Mason and Slidell. A British naval commander, at the moment a passenger on the ship, thereupon appeared in full uniform and made a long speech to the effect that "In this ship I am the representative of her majesty's government, and I call upon the officers of the ship and passengers generally to mark my words, when, in the name of the British government, and in distinct language, I denounce this as an illegal act . . . ." Fairfax ignored the speech and asked once more for the two southern envoys. Mrs. Slidell expressed surprise that Captain Wilkes would wish to take off the two eminent passengers, thus arousing England. Mr. Mason suggested to Mrs. Slidell that she keep quiet. The two southern diplomats refused to go peaceably, and a boatload of marines was summoned from the American ship, the *San Jacinto*. Messrs. Mason and Slidell repaired to their respective cabins and arranged their luggage but still insisted that force would be necessary to move them. Lieutenant Fairfax said to his men, "Gentlemen, lay your hands upon Mr. Mason." They did so, seizing him by the shoulders and the coat-collar. The problem then became Mr. Slidell, who insisted that considerable force would be necessary to remove him. He attempted to jump out of a porthole, perhaps to escape, but two officers seized him and conveyed him to the boat with Mason. Meanwhile had occurred an incident with Miss Slidell, the Confederate diplomat's fair young daughter, aged perhaps seventeen. Some accounts have it that she screamed and slapped Lieutenant Fairfax, but apparently nothing more happened than that, as she was confronting Fairfax, the ship rolled slightly and she involuntarily touched the lieutenant's shoulder. The entire party soon was transferred to the *San*

James M. Mason (L.) and John Slidell (R.), photographs by Matthew B. Brady.

Jacinto, and taken north to Fort Warren in Boston harbor. During the voyage the prisoners were treated to every courtesy. Captain Wilkes gave up his cabin to his guests and they dined at his table.

Upon Wilkes's arrival in the United States the real trouble began. The captain was treated to an enthusiastic public demonstration by his fellow countrymen. The tumultuous nature of his welcome, the laurels which came his way for his exploit, were so many and sincere and heartfelt that the Lincoln administration in Washington faced a grave situation, in terms of coming to agreement with Great Britain over the capture. The American public, having heard for months about northern military defeats, became almost hysterical at the capture of Mason and Slidell, and in the height of this enthusiasm it was extremely difficult for Seward and Lincoln to back down in any diplomatic dealings over the matter. Congress congratulated Wilkes, Secretary of the Navy Gideon Welles commended him, Governor Andrews of Massachusetts at a banquet tendered Wilkes in Boston on November 26 called Wilkes's action "one of the most illustrious services that had made the war memorable," and added, in a phrase that infuriated the English press, "that there might be nothing left to crown the exultation of the American heart, Commodore Wilkes fired his shot across the bows of the ship that bore the British lion at its head." *The New York Times* was certain that Great Britain "will applaud the gallant act of Lieut. Wilkes, so full of spirit and good sense, and such an exact imitation of the policy she has always stoutly defended and invariably pursued . . . as for Commodore Wilkes and his command, let the handsome thing be done, consecrate another *Fourth* of July to him. Load him down with services of plate and swords of the cunningest and costliest art. Let us encourage the happy inspiration that achieved such a victory."

When the British heard the news of Wilkes's "victory," they were as incensed as Americans were pleased. Immediately a crisis was at hand. A long-time American resident in London wrote to Seward on November 29, 1861, that "There never was within memory such a burst of feeling as has been created by the news of the boarding of [the *Trent*]. The people are frantic with rage, and were the country polled, I fear 999 men out of a thousand would declare for immediate war. Lord Palmerston cannot resist the impulse if he would."

The first impulse of the British government was to prepare for war, and on November 30 orders went out to hold the British fleet in readiness, to begin preparations for sending troops to Canada, and to initiate munitions and supply activities. But the more the British government considered the matter, the less certain it became that war was the proper course. For one thing there was the embarrassment of Canada. The British minister in Washington, Lord Lyons, wrote to Russell on December 3,

1861, that "Mr. Galt, Canadian Minister, is here. He has frightened me by his account of the defencelessness of the Province at this moment." Russell himself perused Alison's book on the War of 1812 and came to a startling conclusion: he wrote to Palmerston on December 11 that although the American army for invasion of Canada in 1812 had numbered but 2,500 men, "We may now expect 40 or 50,000." A few days later he informed the prime minister that "Lyons gives a sad account of Canada."

A second reason for hesitation in London was uncertainty about what was going on in Washington. Steamers in 1861 took from ten days to two weeks to carry instructions and dispatches back and forth. During the crisis the London government often had the feeling that perhaps the Washington government had surrendered over the issue, or was about to, and for that reason it would not do to boil the crisis up into a war when in fact a war might not be necessary. How fortunate that at this time no instantaneous transatlantic communication existed. Cyrus Field had put an Atlantic cable into operation on August 4, 1858, and the contraption had gone dead a few days later, presumably because he had failed to insulate the cable sufficiently and salt water had corroded it. There would be no working cable until 1866. The Lincoln administration, perhaps even the Palmerston cabinet, must have thanked God for Field's mistake, which slowed down communication during the affair, giving diplomacy time to work.

A third factor in effecting a peaceful solution was the pacific feeling of Queen Victoria's consort, Prince Albert, who as the queen's private secretary and confidential adviser softened a note that Russell had been ready to send to Washington. The foreign secretary apparently had been ready to send an ultimatum, but Prince Albert toned down the note so that it only empowered the British minister in Washington, Lyons, to make an inquiry and ask for reparation. In the *Trent* affair the prince regent engaged in the last official act of his career. When he was reading the papers of the case he was already without appetite, "very wretched." When he brought the redraft of the American note in to the queen he said to her, as she afterward recalled, "I could hardly hold my pen." He soon died, on December 14, 1861. His death plunged the nation into mourning, and the enforced period of devotion was not without its soothing effect on Anglo-American relations. The misfortune of the royal house became the fortune of the American government. Queen Victoria ever afterward harbored friendly feelings for the United States, for had not the beloved prince recommended moderation toward the Americans as his last official act in this world?

After public opinion had had its day and the incident of the *Trent* began to lose its immediacy, the diplomats on both sides of the Atlantic set to work and settled the affair amicably. The Lincoln cabinet met on Christmas day 1861 and was unable to arrive at a solution, but a further meeting the next day made possible the release of the Confederate commissioners, who went unharmed off to Europe. The crisis was over, and the astonished son of Minister Adams found that "the *Trent* Affair passed like a snowstorm, leaving the Legation, to its surprise, still in place."

As a kind of aftermath to the case of the *Trent*, 11,000 British troops were sent to Canada after the *Trent* affair had blown over. Their arrival served to accentuate rather than relieve the hostage-like geographical position of Canada next to the United States. Arrival of the troops gave Seward a chance to play on the English what Lord Lyons described disgustedly as a trick. A private company in Montreal asked the secretary of state's permission to land some officers' baggage at Portland and transport it across Maine—the St. Lawrence River was then full of ice—and this gave Seward his chance to offer to the British all facilities for landing and transporting to Canada or elsewhere their troops, stores, and munitions of war.

It thus appeared that the Americans had the last word in the famous *Trent* affair.

As for the second crisis in British-American relations—the affair of the Laird rams—this controversy arose in the summer of 1863 over construction by the British shipbuilding firm of William Laird and Sons of some new-style ironclad rams for the Confederate government. The destination of these vessels was thinly disguised by consigning them to the private Paris firm of Bravay and Company. The rams were being built for M. Bravay, who supposedly had bought them for His Serene Highness the Pasha of Egypt. To deceive the unwary the vessels received fine-sounding Eastern names, *El Tousson* and *El Monassir*. Still, what M. Bravay would do with two such vessels was cynically plain: he would sell them to the Confederacy. The task of Minister Adams in London was to stop the sailing of these vessels. Adams had been unable to halt the *Alabama* in 1862, and several other Confederate vessels had gotten to sea despite the vigilance of American consuls in British shipbuilding ports. He determined to stop the rams, for if they escaped they might break the northern blockade.

What were these so-called naval rams that dominated Anglo–American diplomacy in the year 1863? The design of these vessels was interesting, for it gave evidence of the revolution in naval warfare which had begun some few years before the Civil War and already had made obsolete all the wooden navies of the world. Of this revolution, more in another chapter. The Laird rams were revolutionary enough in design to have given promise of destroying the Union blockade of the South, had they gotten to sea and arrived off the American coast. By present-day standards they were tiny ships, perhaps the size of a destroyer, about 1,500 tons displacement, 230 feet long with a beam of 40 feet. But they were armored with four and one-half inches of iron plate, and each was equipped with a formidable wrought-iron "piercer" at the prow, about seven feet in length. This piercer gave to the ships the name of rams, and the idea was that the piercer, three feet under the surface of the water, could be rammed into the wooden blockade ships of the northern navy and sink them. The Laird vessels, being ironclad, would be impervious to shot and shell while they made the run into a northern sailing vessel.

The rams' design was ingenious and had some short-term value, though the continuing revolution in ship construction soon made them obsolete. It turned out that any vessel in motion was likely to provide a poor target for a ram. In Hampton Roads in March 1862, the C.S.S. *Virginia* (formerly U.S.S. *Merrimack*) had rammed and sunk the wooden sloop *Cumberland* on the day before the classic encounter with the *Monitor*, but the *Cumberland* had been dead in the water when pierced by the *Virginia*'s two-foot-long, 1,500-pound cast-iron ram. Indeed, the Confederate vessel, although it managed to sink the Union sloop, had so embedded its piercer in the *Cumberland* that when it reversed engines to pull out the piercer, the great iron beak came off. And if the *Cumberland*—and the other sailing ship sunk by the *Virginia* that day, the frigate *Congress*—had possessed steam, it might have gotten away. After the Civil War, Charles Francis Adams in 1867 watched the great naval review at Portsmouth, where one of the two Laird rams (by this time the British navy had bought them) was pointed out to him. He afterward wrote, "as I looked on the little mean thing, I could not help a doubt whether she was really worthy of all the anxiety she had cost us."

At the time, however, in 1863, Adams and other individuals believed the rams' escape from England might well decide the course of the war. The chief Confederate naval agent in England, James D. Bulloch, wrote on July 9, 1863, to the South's secretary of the navy, Stephen R. Mallory, "our vessels might sail southward, sweep the blockading fleet from the sea front of every harbor . . . , and cruising up and down the coast could prevent anything like permanent, systematic interruption of our foreign trade in the future." And if the rams had opened the South's trade, if cotton again had entered English ports in quantity, the South would have gained foreign exchange with which to buy military supplies in Europe. Equipped from abroad, the Confederate armies in Virginia and elsewhere could take the offensive in earnest, whip the northerners, and, perhaps, end the Civil War.

What to do about the Laird rams was Minister Adams's most pressing diplomatic problem in 1863. The British government through Earl Russell announced to the American government in April of that year that it would allow no more vessels to be constructed in British ports for sale to the Confederates. Adams was uncertain how far British intentions would be accompanied by actions, for the famous *Alabama* had escaped when the queen's advocate, through an understandable but unfortunate coincidence, had suffered a stroke and become insensible at the time the *Alabama* papers were on his desk. Adams feared that the rams somehow would escape. An altogether unnecessary crisis followed. Earl Russell had informed Minister Adams in a letter of September 1, 1863, that the govern-

The *Virginia* (*Merrimack*) rams the *Cumberland*.

ment had no legal basis for action against the rams. On September 3, Russell wrote, however, to Palmerston that he was seizing the rams as a matter of public policy, if not of law. On September 4 he wrote to Adams that the question was under "serious and anxious consideration." Having not yet received Russell's second note (it arrived in the afternoon of September 5), being only in possession of the note of September 1, Adams on the morning of September 5 sent off a note to Russell containing the blunt phrase, "It would be superfluous in me to point out to your lordship that this [the escape of the rams] is war." On September 8 a note from Russell reached Adams that the government had detained the rams, which the royal navy then bought.

As we now see, this note-writing over the rams might well have been avoided. In the confusion over decisions, notes, and—on Adams's part—some very tart language indeed, the larger proportions of the controversy tended to get lost from view. On Russell's side, the foreign secretary early in the Laird rams affair should have realized that the Foreign Enlistment Act of 1819 under which the British government sought to maintain its neutrality during the American Civil War was utterly inadequate for the situation of 1861–1865. The act had a loophole which permitted construction of vessels so long as shipbuilders did not arm them. It made no provision for seizing vessels on suspicion of unneutral destination. Having realized these inadequacies of the act, Russell might have persuaded his chief Lord Palmerston to obtain from Parliament an adequate neutrality act, or else announced clearly, unequivocally, and often to the worried American minister that as a matter of policy the government would not allow the Laird rams to put to sea and obtain armament in some remote West India island as had other Confederate raiders constructed in England. Having allowed the *Alabama* to put to sea—which resulted later in a most expensive arbitration with the American government—Russell's diplomacy, fumbling the Laird case, was less than successful. Worse yet, so Henry Adams concluded, the foreign secretary "had put himself in the position of appearing to yield only to a threat of war."

But on the side of Adams there was an equal culpability. The American minister did not, it is true, really threaten war with Great Britain. He had embedded his "superfluous" statement in a note which, if read in full, said a good deal less. As the historian Frank J. Merli has written,

It is well to note that, contrary to popular opinion, while this note came close to threatening a breach of diplomatic relations, it did not threaten war. When read in entirety, "by its four corners," as the lawyers say, the note indicates that Adams did not intend his remarks as a threat. Had he substituted "unneutral act" in place of "war" the note would have attracted much less attention from historians. As his diary makes abundantly clear, he was playing for time, though genuinely frightened by the prospect of war.

Adams's fault was that, as Merli relates, he "allowed frayed nerves to overcome courtesy and tact. . . . The note [of September 5] displayed, understandably but regrettably, all the attributes of American pressure that the British found obnoxious."

The crisis passed, as had the *Trent* affair before, and this was all that mattered. The South did not gain recognition from the British government. The blockade of southern ports tightened each year that the war continued, without the slightest effort by Great Britain to intervene. The shadow of defeat fell over the Confederacy as the South both at home and abroad failed to ensure its manifest destiny.

3. British hindsight

Thus went diplomacy toward Great Britain during the Civil War. By the year 1865 and the end of the great war in the Western Hemisphere, American diplomacy had proved in every way successful. The government of the United States, having triumphed over an unprecedentedly large revolt by almost an entire section of the nation, found its prestige restored in Europe.

When the Union survived with its territory undiminished, there was extreme embarrassment among many British men of prominence. William E. Gladstone, chancellor of the exchequer in 1862, had proclaimed—and perhaps not without thought, for he was sending up a trial balloon for Russell, who at the moment wished to recognize the Confederacy—that "Jefferson Davis and other leaders of the South have made an army; they are making, it appears, a navy; and they have made what is more than either,—they have made a nation. . . . We may anticipate with certainty the success of the Southern States so far as regards their separation from the North." This was the same Gladstone who later said that the American constitution was "the most remarkable work . . . to have been produced by the human intellect, at a single stroke, in its application to political affairs." In 1896, when the American nation had become a world power potentially far greater than England, Gladstone confessed his sin of 1862,

An undoubted error, the most singular and palpable, I may add the least excusable of them all, especially since it was committed . . . when I had outlived half a century . . . . That my opinion was founded upon a false estimation of the facts was the very least part of my fault. I did not perceive the gross impropriety of such an utterance from a Cabinet Minister of a power allied in blood and language and bound to loyal neutrality . . . . My offence was indeed only a mistake, but one of incredible grossness, and with such consequences of offence and alarm attached to it that my failing to perceive them exposed me to very severe blame. It illustrates vividly that incapacity which my mind so long retained, and perhaps still exhibits, an incapacity of viewing subjects all round . . . and thereby knowing when to be silent and when to speak.

With the successful end of the war, Britishers came not merely to appreciate the Union cause but to understand the high abilities of the principal Union statesman, President Lincoln. The British minister to Washington, Lyons, had offered the typical remarks about Lincoln a few years before, just prior to the president's first inauguration: "Mr. Lincoln," Lyons had written privately, "has not hitherto given proof of his possessing any natural talents to compensate for his ignorance of everything but Illinois village politics. He seems to be well meaning and conscientious, in the measure of his understanding, but not much more." During the early part of the war, the future Field Marshal Viscount Wolseley visited the South and wrote that the Union cause had degenerated to "merely the military despotism of a portion of the States striving under the dictatorship of an insignificant lawyer to crush out the freedom of the rest." Now all this had changed. By the end of the war the "insignificant lawyer" had become the "far-seeing statesman of iron will." When news of the president's assassination reached England in the spring of 1865, there was a near panic. One newspaper reported that not since Henry IV of France had been slain by Ravaillac had "the whole of Europe rung with excitement of so intense a character." The House of Commons adjourned. The House of Lords adjourned, an act which some individuals said was unprecedented. Queen Victoria wrote a personal letter to Mrs. Lincoln comparing the president's untimely demise to that of her own lamented husband. The magazine of British humor, *Punch*, made one of the most famous apologies in British literary annals. *Punch*, like the *Times* of London, had filled hundreds of columns with sneeringly sarcastic comments about the Lincoln government, and many of its sallies had been at the expense of the dead president. *Punch* apologized in the well-known lines,

> Between the mourners at his head and feet,
> Say, scurril-jester, is there room for you?
>
> Yes, he had lived to shame me for my sneer,
> To lame my pencil, and confute my pen—
> To make me own this hind of princes peer,
> This rail-splitter a true-born king of men.

4. *Relations with France, Mexico, and Russia*

Anglo-American relations were of prime importance in the diplomacy of the Civil War, but they were not the only diplomatic relations of the time, nor always the most important, for Lincoln and Seward planned carefully their diplomacy in respect to several other nations: France, Mexico, Russia. To Britain had gone the best of the American diplomats in the 1860's, C. F. Adams. To France went a deserving political leader, William

L. Dayton. But Dayton's consul general was John Bigelow, second only to Adams in ability. To Mexico in 1861 went a friend of Mexico and former senator from Ohio, Thomas Corwin. To Russia the president sent two politicos, Cassius Marcellus Clay and Simon Cameron.

The Union men in France had two difficult persons to watch. One was the emperor of the French, Napoleon III, who while ever willing to fish in the troubled American waters took care to keep his feet dry. In the retrospect of the quick defeat of the French forces in the Franco-Prussian War of 1870–1871, the emperor would appear a tragic figure incapable of standing up to a major enemy. Such a saddening future for France would have seemed impossible to Americans in the 1860's—nor, for that matter, would the British government have been willing to count on such an outcome, and British policy for years cycled around the supposed threat of Bonapartism. Throughout the 1860's Napoleon III, displaying his enormous double mustache with its marvelously waxed sword-like upperworks, appeared always on the verge of some devilish activity. It was said that he was the greatest diplomat of the Continent because no one knew what he was going to do next. That was true enough, because Napoleon himself did not know. To the Americans he seemed capable of allowing the Confederates to construct a navy in his ports, and there was some minor construction of vessels in France. Only one

Napoleon III.

got to sea. Napoleon also sent troops to the New World for an expedition into Mexico, a much more serious project, and in 1864 persuaded the Archduke Maximilian (Napoleon's "Arch Dupe," according to Americans) to take a Mexican throne. More about that subject in the following chapter.

The other person whom Union men watched in France, a person more devious even than Napoleon III, was the Confederate commissioner Slidell, the same who had sought to crawl out of a porthole of the *Trent* in 1861, only to be seized by two Union officers. The Cincinnati newspaperman Murat Halstead once described Slidell as "a gentleman with long, thin white hair, through which the top of his head blushes like the shell of a boiled lobster. The gentleman has also a cherry-red face, the color being that produced by good health and good living joined to a florid temperament." Slidell devoted much of his diplomacy in Paris to getting close to Napoleon III. This attempt unfortunately was a waste of time, for Napoleon paid little attention to his importunities. What energies Slidell had left he put into an effort to arrange a Confederate loan based on cotton futures, a promise of future delivery of cotton being the basis for the loan. The loan project was an equal waste of time. News of Vicksburg and Gettysburg sent the price of Confederate bonds tumbling. Some interesting monkey business occurred with the loan, apart from the turn in Confederate military fortunes, but it is probably impossible to know precisely what happened. One story has it that a Union man, Robert L. Walker, formerly a United States senator from Mississippi, ruined the futures scheme, as at crucial moments it appeared as if a mysterious "bear party" was operating against the bonds. It is likely that part of the loan's trouble was the maneuvering of the Confederate bond house, Erlanger and Company, under control of a friend of Slidell, Baron Emile Erlanger. The loan at first had gone well, the issue greatly oversubscribed. The price of the bonds rose above par. When the price trembled, preceding its fall toward zero, Erlanger perhaps sold his personal holdings at the same time he was using Confederate funds to bull the market. Altogether, after deductions for commissions and market support, the Richmond government seems to have obtained $6,419,650, from the $15,000,000 loan, a sum hardly commensurate with the trouble of getting the project in motion. It was said that Erlanger personally netted $2,700,000. Confederate diplomacy in France came to no larger result than this. There was, though, a marital result: Erlanger's son married Slidell's daughter Matilda, who became a baroness.

As for Union diplomacy toward Mexico, it was largely a holding operation. When the French commenced their intervention late in 1861, the weak Mexican native regime had fled to the northern provinces. Secretary Seward produced a scheme to lend money to this government, by which he proposed to take a sort of first mortgage on a large piece of Mexican territory. If his intentions were entirely honorable, many Europeans frowned upon this proposition from a country which fifteen years before had not acted with restraint in Mexico, and they claimed that Seward's idea looked toward foreclosure. The secretary took back this proposal and thereafter contented himself with moral support to the Mexicans and with dire warnings to European powers thinking of intervention south of the Rio Grande.

The American minister to the legitimate government of Mexico, Corwin, was every bit as agile and discreet as the Lincoln administration's other leading diplomatic representatives, and American diplomacy maintained itself handsomely in Mexico. Corwin had been adamantly against the Mexican War, and after the Treaty of Guadalupe Hidalgo had written sarcastically to a friend that the treaty gave to the United States a third of Mexico immediately "with the implied understanding that the ballance [sic] is to be swallowed when our anglo-saxon gastric juices shall clamor for another Cannibal breakfast." By the time of the Civil War he could ably represent his country in the sovereign state of Mexico. He got along famously with the Mexicans after he persuaded Mexican espionage agents to open the mail of his Confederate rival, Colonel John Pickett. To Corwin's delight the Mexicans discovered that Pickett had been calling them "a race of degenerate monkeys . . . robbers, assassins, blackguards and lepers," and had been urging the South to conquer Mexico. Minister Corwin had no difficulty ingratiating himself with the government of Mexico, then headed by the full-blooded Indian Benito Juárez.

As for Russia, perhaps the first minister whom Lincoln sent to St. Petersburg, the Kentucky statesman Cassius Marcellus Clay, so scared the Russians that he made them friendly to the northern cause. They could hardly have been otherwise, with Clay in the vicinity. Lincoln later translated to Russia his discredited secretary of war, the Pennsylvania spoilsman Simon Cameron, but by the time Cameron arrived everything was under control.

Clay was nothing if not colorful. He was one of the "fightingest" men in a fighting state. His political rivals once imported into Kentucky for the special purpose of ending Clay's career a man from New Orleans named Sam M. Brown, "hero of forty fights and never lost a battle." The fight began when Clay heckled Brown at a political meeting. Brown knocked Clay down with a club. Clay rose with bowie knife in hand. Brown shot Clay with a pistol at point-blank range. The shot struck the scabbard of Clay's knife which hung around his neck. Clay then worked Brown over with the bowie knife, cutting off an ear, skewering out an eye, and threw the hero of New Orleans over a wall into a pond of water.

Shortly after Lincoln's inauguration the Kentucky statesman had appeared in Washington carrying an arsenal—Lincoln's private secretary, John Hay, saw him at a White House reception wearing "with a sublimely unconscious air, three pistols and an Arkansas toothpick." En route to Russia he passed through London, where the secretary of the American legation, Benjamin Moran, saw him one evening in a hotel, waiting for lodgings. Clay

was walking up and down the magnificent hall like a chafed lion and looked a man to be avoided in the gas light, surrounded as he was by his suite of three tall, sharp-faced Kentuckians. I . . . was surprised to find him a man of some 50 years, 6 feet high, well proportioned, with a fine manly face, and the form of a hero. Oddly enough, he wore a blue dress coat with gilt buttons, and I could not but smile to see an Envoy to Russia in such a costume.

Clay was no person to smile at. In Russia, naturally, he made a considerable impression. He carried a bowie knife on all occasions. For formal dress he wore an eighteen-inch blade with a pearl handle and an eagle on the haft. For street wear he preferred bone-handled knives. He was the despair of Russian gentlemen seeking duels. Never the challenger, Clay always had a choice of weapons, and out of a wide variety of lethal instruments, including all manner of guns, daggers, and pistols, the American minister unfailingly chose the bowie knife.

By the mid-point of the American Civil War, 1863, the Russians were unquestionably friendly toward the United States, perhaps because of Clay. That year a rebellion broke out in Poland, and for a short time it seemed to the St. Petersburg government that the European powers might intervene. The Russians sent their Baltic fleet to New York and their Far Eastern squadron to San Francisco, supposedly for goodwill visits, actually for protection and replenishment in event of hostilities. The citizens of the United States treated the Russian sailors to an unremitting round of dances and fetes and banquets. For one feast in New York City, Delmonico's prepared 12,000 oysters, 1,200 game birds, 250 turkeys, 400 chickens, 1,000 pounds of tenderloin, all to be washed down with 3,500 bottles of wine. According to a reporter present at this banquet, the Russian guests were worn out by the expressions of friendship and affection extended to them.

And so the diplomacy of the United States, of the Union cause, survived the tragic ordeal of the worst war in the Western world during the near-hundred years between the defeat of Napoleon at Waterloo and the

Battle of the Marne in 1914. It was a terrible war, the largest catastrophe to befall the United States in all its history, in which over 600,000 Union and Confederate men died, albeit only a third of these deaths were battlefield casualties. The size of the Civil War becomes evident when one considers that American losses during the Second World War were about 250,000. Losses in the American revolution were about 4,500.

It is interesting to speculate what might have happened if all the British predictions about the Civil War had been fulfilled and the United States had divided into two nations, North and South. Slavery would not have survived the increasing industrialization which occurred so quickly in North America after the Civil War and had begun well before. But if the South otherwise had achieved its manifest destiny the world of the twentieth century would have been vastly different.

A CONTEMPORARY DOCUMENT

[The secretary of the American legation in London, Benjamin Moran, was a sour, introverted individual, a frustrated writer, and intensely loyal to the Union. His diary of events in London at the time of Lincoln's assassination shows the depth of English sentiment at that saddening time. Source: Sarah Agnes Wallace and Frances Elma Gillespie, eds., *The Journal of Benjamin Moran: 1857–1865* (2 vols., University of Chicago Press, 1948–1949), II, 1415–1417, 1419–1421.]

Wednesday, 26 Ap'l. 1865. At about half past twelve to-day when the Rev. Dr. Bliss and others were here, Mr. Horatio Ward came in with the news that telegrams had been received in London announcing the assassination of President Lincoln and the attempt to take the life of Mr. Seward. I was horror struck and at once went up with Mr. Ward to announce the intelligence to Mr. Adams. He turned as pale as death . . . . About one o'clock we received an official telegram from Mr. Secretary Stanton, giving full particulars, and saying that Mr. Seward had at the same time, about 10½ o'clock on 14 April, been attacked by an assassin in his bed, that his sons Fred'k and Major Seward had been dangerously stabbed, & a male servant killed but, Mr. Seward himself was living. It was announced that Mr. Lincoln had been shot from behind in his private box in the Theatre at Washington, and had died on the 15th, or the next morning at 7.30, or thereabouts. Mr. Adams was directed to communicate this at once to the other American Ministers in Europe. . . .

Thursday, 27 April, 1865. I dined yesterday at McHenry's and met with many expressions of sympathy on the death of Mr. Lincoln. I got here at 8.30 this morning and have been crowded to death almost with visitors. . . . Lord Russell called and expressed to Mr. Adams as much sympathy as he was capable of. He said no such excitement had ever before prevailed in England. Mr. Potter was here with the Address. It was gotten up by him and commits the House of Commons to sympathy with the U.S. All the Englishmen who have called here have been deeply affected, and many wept. . . . It is twelve years to-day since I left home. . . .

Sunday, 30 April, '65. Last evening I went to the great meeting of the London Emancipation Society at St. James' Hall on the assassination of President Lincoln. In all my London experience I never saw so much enthusiasm or heard so many good speeches. The feeling of profound and heartfelt sympathy was deep and unmistakeable. Mr. Wm Evans presided well. Mr. W. E. Forster made a calm, statesman-like speech, and so did young Lyulph Stanley. The room was draped in black and three United States flags were graceful entwined in crape at the east end of the room. The floor, the balcony, the galleries, and the platform of the great hall were literally packed with ladies and gentlemen and the sea of up-turned faces showed a greater number of fine heads than I ever before saw in any assembly of the same size. It was an intelligent audience. And the warmth of the applause, the earnest detestation of the murder, and the condemnation of slavery made me inwardly vow that hereafter I would think better of the feelings entertained towards us by Englishmen than ever before. And that if ever any chance of quarrel should occur between the two Countries, and I should hear an uninformed countryman of mine denouncing honestly and mistakenly, the spirit of England towards us, the recollection of what I saw then would nerve me to declare that we had friends in England in our day of sorrow, whose noble sympathy should make us pause, and the remembrance of whose kindly words and manly grief at the assassination of our great and good President, should never be forgotten, but should prompt us to stifle the voice of discord and forgive injuries. In this I am sure I am right. The loud bursts of applause at the mention of Mr. Lincoln's greatness—and indignation at his murder, were intense and without a parallel in my experience. There were some thoroughly democratic speeches made, and expression given to many injudicious sentiments against the British aristocracy, which I fear may be turned against us. But I hope not. It is such follies that damage the best cause—and I have always observed that British democrats instead of relying on the merit of their cause, run away with themselves by abusing the nobility. . . .

Monday, 1 May, 1865. . . . I drove to the House of Commons and heard Mr. Disraeli second the Address of Condolence to the Crown on the Assassination of Mr. Lincoln. I regretted not being there earlier to hear Sir George Grey. But Mr. D'Israeli spoke with great sincerety, condemned in unmeasured terms the great crime, and expressed deep sympathy with the President and people of the United States. There was a large attendance of Members, and crowds of people waiting outside to get in. I never saw so many people waiting outside on any previous occasion. And every word I heard spoken in the Commons was in favor and in praise of the self-made American —whose honesty raised him so high—and who was so much abused in that very house a few years ago. The resolution was passed unanimously and every body seemed honestly impressed with the enormity of the murder, and with the worth of Mr. Lincoln. As the matter was ended there I went to the House of Lords. Earl Russell was speaking. The House was very much crowded, the Duke of Cambridge being among the Peers, and there were twelve or fourteen bishops. Every word about Mr. Lincoln was kindly. And as an American I felt proud of the self-made Illinois lawyer, who by his honesty, his singlemindedness, and his love of freedom, had extorted words of admiration from the two greatest deliberative assemblies in the world. Yes, that crowded House of English Lords—the proudest nobles in the world—pressed forward to hear the respective chiefs of their parties speak words of praise of Abraham Lincoln, and like the commons, passed unanimously an Address to the Throne on his assassination. . . .

ADDITIONAL READING

The best one-volume general treatments of the diplomacy of the Civil War are *Jay Monaghan's *Diplomat in Carpet Slippers: Abraham Lincoln Deals with Foreign Affairs* (Indianapolis, 1945), beautifully written and filled with colorful detail, and Philip Van Doren Stern, *When the Guns Roared: World Aspects of the American Civil War* (Garden City, N.Y., 1965), also an engaging account. See the scattered chapters in Edward Channing's sixth volume in *A History of the United States,* entitled *The War for Southern Independence: 1849–1865* (New York, 1925); James G. Randall, *Lincoln the President* (4 vols., New York, 1945–1955), the last volume written in large part by Richard N. Current; *Clement Eaton, *A History of the Southern Confederacy* (New York, 1954), containing a chapter on "Confederate Diplomacy"; and *David Donald, ed., *Why the North Won the Civil War* (Baton Rouge, La., 1960), which includes essays by Norman A. Graebner, "Northern Diplomacy and European Neutrality," and David M. Potter, "Jefferson Davis and the Political Factors in Confederate Defeat." A masterful analysis is E. D. Adams, *Great Britain and the American Civil War* (2 vols., London, 1925), composed after meticulous and skeptical examination of available material, manuscript and printed. A view of southern diplomacy during the war is Frank L. Owsley, *King Cotton Diplomacy* (rev. ed. by Harriet C. Owsley, Chicago, 1959).

The *Trent* affair, surprisingly neglected by historians, appears in two old and inadequate accounts, Thomas Harris's *The Trent Affair* (Indianapolis, 1896); and Charles Francis Adams, "The *Trent* Affair," *American Historical Review*, XVII (1911–1912), 540–562; together with a popular volume, Evan John [E. J. Simpson], *Atlantic Impact: 1861* (London, 1952). Gordon H. Warren is preparing a new book on this subject. For British neutrality during the war, there is the reflective article by James P. Baxter III, "The British Government and Neutral Rights, 1861–1865," *American Historical Review*, XXXIV (1928–1929), 9–29; and the more recent analysis by Wilbur D. Jones, "British Conservatives and the American Civil War," *American Historical Review*, LVIII (1952–1953), 527–543. One of the major irritants in Anglo-American affairs is considered in W. D. Jones, *The Confederate Rams at Birkenhead* (Tuscaloosa, Ala., 1961). Frank J. Merli has restudied definitively the Confederate attempt to build a navy in England in his forthcoming book to be published by the Indiana University Press. See also his article, written with Thomas W. Green, "Great Britain and the Confederate Navy," *History Today*, XIV (1964), 687–695. For their special subjects consult M. P. Claussen, "Peace Factors in Anglo-American Relations, 1861–1863," *Mississippi Valley Historical Review*, XXVI (1939–1940), 511–522; Donaldson Jordan and E. J. Pratt, *Europe and the American Civil War* (Boston, 1931); and Robin W. Winks, *Canada and the United States: The Civil War Years* (Baltimore, 1960).

Biography, diary, and autobiography appear in such works as Robert D. Meade, *Judah P. Benjamin: Confederate Statesman* (New York, 1943); Margaret Clapp, *Forgotten First Citizen: John Bigelow* (Boston, 1947); *Martin Duberman, *Charles Francis Adams: 1807–1886* (Boston, 1961); David L. Smiley, *Lion of Whitehall: The Life of Cassius M. Clay* (Madison, Wis., 1962); Glyndon G. Van Deusen, *William Henry Seward* (New York, 1967); S. A. Wallace and F. E. Gillespie, eds., *The Journal of Benjamin Moran: 1857–1865* (2 vols., Chicago, 1948–1949), by the secretary of the American legation in London from 1857 to 1875; *Henry Adams, *The Education of Henry Adams* (Boston, 1918), a classic memoir by the son of the American minister, dealing not merely with the Civil War but with politics, society, and life in the latter nineteenth century.

For France see Henry Blumenthal, *A Reappraisal of Franco-American Relations: 1830–1871* (Chapel Hill, N.C., 1959).

On relations with Russia there are several articles by Frank A. Golder, who prior to the Bolshevik revolution was able to exploit the Russian archives: "Russian–American Relations during the Crimean War," *American Historical Review*, XXXI (1925–1926), 462–476; "The American Civil War through the Eyes of a Russian Diplomat," *American Historical Review*, XXVI (1920–

1921), 454–463, an analysis of the dispatches of Baron de Stoeckl; "The Russian Fleet and the Civil War," *AHR*, XX (1914–1915), 801–812. On the latter subject see also Thomas A. Bailey, "The Russian Fleet Myth Reexamined," *Mississippi Valley Historical Review*, XXXVIII (1951), 81–90. More general treatments appear in Foster Rhea Dulles, *The Road to Teheran* (Princeton, 1944); and Thomas A. Bailey, *America Faces Russia* (Ithaca, N.Y., 1950).

An instructive view of the requisites of statesmanship—far beyond the usual quips that a statesman is a dead politician, or that a politician as compared to a statesman has the disadvantage of being alive—is *Allan Nevins, *The Statesmanship of the Civil War* (New York, 1953).

The Republic at Peace

It is sufficient to say that, in the President's opinion, the emancipation of this continent from European control has been the principal feature in its history during the last century.

—Secretary of State William H. Seward, 1862

It is not too much to say that the years before, during, and after the Civil War—the two decades and more that followed the Treaty of Guadalupe Hidalgo—were filled by the notion of manifest destiny. In the period from 1848 to 1872 the diplomacy of the United States was not, as historians sometimes have drawn it, a series of unconnected episodes tenuously ordered by the rise and fall of presidential administrations. It showed clear evidences of the same motive force that had demonstrated itself in previous decades of American diplomatic history.

After the end of the war came the expulsion of the French from Mexico, where they had ensconced themselves behind their imported emperor, Maximilian. The diplomatic actions of Secretary of State Seward toward this French intervention were taken under the Monroe Doctrine, and the doctrine of 1823 assuredly was a statement of manifest destiny. In the same year in which the French departed, 1867, Seward bought Alaska from the Russians, again a sign of the spirit of the times. He and his successor at the department, Hamilton Fish, participated in two unsuccessful island projects. Seward tried to buy the Danish West Indies (the present-day Virgin Islands). He and Fish took interest, if with varying enthusiasm, in the Dominican Republic. Here, even with failure, was an appearance of manifest destiny. And Fish presided over the negotiation leading to the Treaty of Washington of 1871 and the Geneva arbitration of the next year, the latter a piece of diplomacy which marked a veritable triumph of American expansive feelings.

1. *Maximilian*

A major act of diplomacy during the 1860's was the negotiation leading to the departure of the French from Mexico. Usually known in American history as "the Maximilian affair," the French intervention and eventual retreat, accompanied by increasingly pointed notes by Secretary of State Seward, brought to an end the most serious threat to the Monroe Doctrine in the entire history of that great pronouncement from its enunciation in 1823 to the present time.

The trouble in Mexico went back to the establishment of Western civilization upon the ruins of the native Mexican culture, the subjugation of Mexico along with all Spanish America by the conquistadores of the sixteenth century. Although the Spanish government enjoyed its great era of international importance during the first century after Columbus, the basis of Spain's wealth and influence in the American colonies was too fragile to last. It was exploitation, enslavement of the Indians. With due passage of time the Indians were certain to demand their freedom.

The Indians of Mexico never had a chance against the Spanish until after Mexican independence in 1821. At first the Spanish-descended populace in the neighborhood of the City of Mexico chose to denominate itself the government of Mexico and showed little interest in the native Mexicans, that is, the Indians. Then the submerged people of Mexico managed slowly to assert themselves. The more they did so the more the Spanish-descended Mexicans sought to fasten the lid upon their discontent. By the time of the American Civil War the republic of Mexico was in a state of political chaos which almost defies description. It was this chaos which provided the excuse for European intervention commencing in 1861, and the background for American diplomatic intervention after the Civil War on the side of Mexican independence.

Consider the condition of Mexican politics by 1861. Mexico had been free of Spanish rule for forty years, and experienced thirty-six changes of government and seventy-three presidents. President James Buchanan of the United States aptly described the Mexican government of his time as "a wreck upon the ocean, drifting about as she is impelled by the different factions." The Mexican War probably had not helped matters, although one can argue that Mexico's defeat probably made no difference in what had become a perennial contest for possession of Mexico City. At the end of the conflict, when American troops evacuated the city, a liberal president, José Joaquin Herrera, was in power. The Mexican appetite for revolution soon prevailed, and that disgraceful prince of adventurers, Santa

Anna, was back in power in 1853. The monarchists were behind Santa Anna, and the general appointed as his minister of foreign affairs an able member of the monarchist group in Mexico City, Lucas Alaman—who promptly appealed to the European powers to save his country from American imperialism. The moment was inopportune, as the European nations were about to begin the Crimean War. After that conflict ended in 1856, the adventurous foreign policy of the French emperor, Napoleon III, kept Europe in turmoil; leading in 1859 to a war against Austria, in support of Italian unification. For the arrangement of a monarchy in Mexico the 1850's proved too hectic a time, too competitive for European attention. In the last years of the decade Mexico then plunged into a bitter civil war, far worse than the conflicts which previously had accompanied the game of musical chairs in the capital. This time it was a racial as well as political conflict, or so it seemed, as the full-blooded Indian, Benito Juárez, contested for the presidency of the republic and secured it in January 1861.

Juárez's fight for power was marked by some interesting American diplomacy—interesting in its propositions and in the expansionist ideas which underlay them. For a decade or so the Americans had been showing interest in adding to the acquisitions of the Mexican War. In 1850 the United States government concluded the Clayton–Bulwer Treaty, looking forward to an isthmian canal. The treaty provided for sharing of political influence in Central America with the government of Great Britain. (A previous chapter has remarked upon this feat in the same year the Compromise of 1850 to allay the slavery controversy was concluded.) Even after the slavery controversy reopened in 1854 with the Kansas-Nebraska Act, and domestic events were proceeding toward the denouement of 1861–1865, the American government continued to covet the lands south of the Rio Grande. Dexter Perkins has written of "the yearning for Mexican territory" which characterized American politics during the latter 1850's. Some highly placed Americans took interest in the Isthmus of Tehuantepec, hoping for transit rights from Mexico, and perhaps even canal rights. If it was necessary to divide influence over Central America, the United States might dominate the Mexican isthmus. Americans also were willing to establish their influence in the Mexican provinces of Sonora and Chihuahua.

As for the territorial propositions, they were not long in coming. The American minister to Mexico City during Santa Anna's rule in the 1850's, James Gadsden of South Carolina, was a strong Monroe Doctrine man, but he failed to get along with Secretary of State William L. Marcy, who perhaps had become wary after the publication of the Ostend Manifesto. In the quarrels of the Mexican political parties Marcy pursued a correct policy of nonintervention. Not so his successors. During the bitter strife between Juárez and the Mexican conservatives in 1858–1861, the administration of President Buchanan (the president, when minister to Great Britain a few years earlier, had himself written the Ostend Manifesto) sought to aid Juárez and also gain something from the effort to support Mexican republican institutions. Pressed by opponents, Juárez was willing to deal. The result was a series of projects, one of which was the McLane–Ocampo Treaty of 1859, signed by the American minister to Mexico and the foreign minister of the Juárez government. The treaty gave the United States the right of transit across Tehuantepec and, under certain conditions, the right of direct intervention in Mexico. The United States government in exchange would offer a loan of $4,000,000. The Senate in May 1860 defeated the McLane–Ocampo agreement decisively, by vote of 27 to 18. What with the presidential election and the secession crisis which soon followed, Buchanan's work was at an end. The ensuing Lincoln administration did not hesitate to survey the Mexican prospects, and Secretary Seward for a while had in mind a sort of mortgage of Mexican territory, on the basis of which the Washington government would lend Juárez funds.

Affairs in Mexico meanwhile were veering toward foreign intervention. Juárez made a triumphant entry into Mexico City in January 1861. Not so triumphantly—or perhaps with a hope that the European troubles of the 1850's would continue into the 1860's and prevent intervention—Juárez on July 17, 1861, suspended the international obligations of the Mexican government. Europe now was peaceful, and the French government moved to collect 40,000,000 francs. In October 1861, Napoleon III concluded the Convention of London, which provided for a joint French–British–Spanish expedition to Mexico to collect the defaulted debts.

The purpose of the French, and to a far lesser extent of the British and Spanish, was to restore monarchy in Mexico, not really to collect debts. After all, the expedition to collect 40,000,000 francs cost 274,698,000 francs. The British went along with the expedition because leaders of the government of the day were glad to spread conservatism into the New World. The Spanish government believed the time right for action, that the American Civil War had made monarchy practical:

Those men [exclaimed Señor Rio y Roas] who said America for the Americans that is, America for the Anglo-Americans, for the Yankees, for the United States, America surrounded by an idea wall, like the great wall of China, America cut off from the world, divorced from Human civilization, those men who professed that insolent, absurd, and inhuman doctrine, have begun to see what they called the manifest destiny of America was not a decree of God, and that the order of his Providence was a very different one.

Most of all three nations, the French considered a Mexican monarchy a great coup in the proper organization of the world, not merely in the New World. Napoleon III had in mind to change the balance of the New World in favor of his own balance (in part adjusted during the Italian campaign) in Europe. If George Canning had once claimed to have called the New World into existence to redress the balance of the Old, Napoleon might do the same. He could hem in the ambitious Yankees, involved in their Civil War; and he could arrange for the emergence of a strong Mexican state which, in event of trouble in Europe, might send troops to help settle problems there.

The British contingent in Mexico never was large, comprising only 700 marines, and they together with the supporting Spanish troops withdrew in May 1862, leaving all Mexico to Napoleon's conquest, if he could accomplish it. Taking Mexico proved difficult, for at one juncture Napoleon's forces met defeat at Puebla, requiring reinforcements and a new commander. They entered Mexico City on June 7, 1863. The French general in charge summoned a Council of Notables, which elected as emperor the brother of the emperor of Austria, the Archduke Maximilian. Napoleon III had chosen him even before arranging the joint intervention in October 1861. Maximilian and his consort Carlotta (the Belgian princess Charlotte) landed at Veracruz on May 28, 1864.

By this time American policy toward this gross violation of the Monroe Doctrine was crystal clear, and its success—as Napoleon should have realized—awaited only the end of the Civil War. Earlier, on April Fool's Day 1861, Seward had proposed a war against Europe, but he quickly recovered from this aberration and began to counsel the tactic of delay in regard to the Mexican intervention, all the while insisting on American rights. After the secretary of state sent the French government one especially careful representation, Seward's friend Thurlow Weed, then in Paris, wrote approvingly, "Your despatch on Mexican matters breaks no eggs. It makes a record, and there, I hope you are at rest." Juárez's able minister in Washington, Matias Romero, pressed the secretary. Between October 1, 1861, and June 30, 1862, Romero held fifty-three personal interviews with Seward. The latter would not budge beyond affirming the position of the American government under the Monroe Doctrine (incidentally, throughout the entire Mexican negotiation Seward was never to mention the doctrine by name). John Bigelow in Paris in the spring of 1864 urged the secretary to take a more outspoken attitude. Seward answered:

With our land and naval forces in Louisiana retreating before the rebels instead of marching toward Mexico, this is not the most suitable time for offering idle menaces to the Emperor of France. We have compromised nothing, surrendered nothing and I do not propose to surrender anything. But why should we gasconade about Mexico when we are in a struggle for our own life?

When the war ended, though, it was evident that Seward would become explicit with the French.

In retrospect it is a pity that after the French government made a mistake it could not acknowledge it. With the brooding introspection which no man of affairs can afford, Napoleon III had hardly entered the Mexican campaign before he wished to get out. His position was awkward, once expenses of the intervention began to mount, once the feelings against the

Maximilian and Carlotta of Mexico.

expedition held by the bulk of the French people began to become manifest despite the discreet arrangements of Napoleon's censorship. Maximilian's incapacity—his inability to organize Mexico—also became evident. "Maxl," as the Mexican emperor was known intimately, meditated on the possible marriage of his brother, Ludwig Viktor, to a daughter of the emperor of Brazil, and on the gradual absorption of Central America by his regime in Mexico City. It was a foolish calculation. The Austrian minister in Paris, Prince Metternich, had declared: "What a lot of cannonshots it will take to set up an emperor in Mexico, and what a lot to maintain him there." Napoleon knew this, and in an interview in November 1863 with the former British minister to Mexico, Sir Charles Wyke, unburdened himself. "I realize that I have got myself into a tight place," he told Wyke, "but the affair has got to be liquidated." Wyke urged exactly such a course. "That," the emperor said, "would amount to admitting a mistake, and in France it is no longer permissible to make mistakes."

At last came the end of the American Civil War, and the beginning of the end of the Maximilian affair. Matters never had worked out as intended. There was something incredibly foreign about the audiences and pomp with which in the latter nineteenth century a European archduke sought to fasten the customs of royalty upon a primitive government and people. The assorted Mexican dignitaries in their stiff black suits, their wives in crinolines and laces, could not reproduce Vienna or Madrid or even the pomp of the small Italian courts, which had passed into history.

The Mexican intervention was too improbable a venture. It was all a sad dream which occurred in the shadow of France's disaster at Sedan in 1870. It may be true that the French contingent in Mexico, which eventually numbered 28,000 men, was not so large as to embarrass Napoleon's position in Europe. The French regular army consisted of 400,000 troops, and if the best troops went to Mexico there were many left. The expense of the Mexican venture, high enough, was not impossible. The tragedy of the Mexican business for Napoleon was that it preoccupied him, that he spent his time dreaming rather than watching the diplomacy of Bismarck toward Denmark (war broke out in 1866) and Austria (war in 1867), after which would come the fateful Franco-Prussian War.

Seward carefully put pressure on Napoleon's government, and indeed it was all he could do to restrain his fellow countrymen, some of whom were ready for another war. Seward's way was not bluster, but quiet statements of fact followed by questions about the time at which it would be convenient for Napoleon to remove his troops. As the year 1865 moved on, Seward's tone heightened. In Paris at the palace of the Tuileries where Napoleon lived—the palace itself would go up in flames during the siege of Paris in 1870–1871—there was marked nervousness. It was coupled with embarrassment that the Americans, not long before so occupied, now so unoccupied, were balancing their power all over their hemisphere. A military solution was possible. General Grant after Appomattox entered into relations with Romero, and the minister declared to Grant that he would like to invite Sherman or Sheridan to lead an expedition. "My wife would like to have me go to Mexico, myself," said the general, after a pause. About 40,000 American troops were along the Rio Grande, and in the cabinet Grant argued for an expedition. General Schofield wished to go to the Rio Grande and take volunteers across into Mexico. Seward spiked that proposition by offering the egotistical Schofield a special mission to Paris. The secretary said to Schofield (according to Schofield): "I want you to get your legs under Napoleon's mahogany and tell him he must get out of Mexico." Once Schofield got to France, Bigelow kept him from seeing people of importance, perhaps under an arrangement with Seward. It nonetheless was fairly anxious work, holding back those Americans who wished to give manifest destiny some manifest support.

Napoleon gave in to Seward's careful diplomacy. He instructed Marshal Bazaine on January 31, 1866:

Circumstances stronger than my will oblige me to evacuate Mexico; but I wish to do so leaving behind me for the Emperor Maximilian every chance of maintaining himself with his own forces. You must put all your zeal and intelligence into the task of organizing something durable in the country, in order that our efforts may not be a dead loss. To accomplish this difficult task, you have a year or eighteen months.

Napoleon set up dates for evacuation, with the first contingent to leave in November 1866. He changed his mind, deciding to bring out all the troops in the spring of 1867. Seward sent a long cable of protest to Paris, at a cost of some $13,000, and before Bigelow could present it he gave it to the American press. Bigelow thoughtfully toned it down. But Napoleon could have obtained the text through the American press and presumably did so. The troops left as quickly as he decently could bring them home.

At that moment Napoleon's puppet emperor should have retired to Europe, leaving Mexico for the Mexicans. Maximilian possessed too much pride for this maneuver, and declared that he would stand by his own country, meaning Mexico, that he had become a Mexican and could not return to Europe. For this statesmanship Maximilian's subjects captured and executed him at Queretaro in 1867. To no avail had the Spanish ambassador pleaded personally with Secretary Seward for assistance in saving the young monarch's life. Seward had replied (crunching a radish), "His life is quite as safe as yours and mine." To no avail had Maximilian's wife, the beautiful Empress Carlotta, taken her husband's case to Napoleon III, who would do nothing, and to the Pope, who could do nothing. Her reason departed, and she lived on in almost complete insanity, a pathetic relic of Napoleon III's expedition to found a monarchy in the New World. When she died in 1927 in the era of Calvin Coolidge, the Habsburgs and Napoleons had long since retired from the stage of public affairs.

2. *Alaska*

The second achievement of Seward's post-Civil War diplomacy, and a positive achievement as compared to the negative victory of getting the French out of Mexico, was the purchase of the huge territory of Alaska from tsarist Russia in 1867. Alaska totaled some 591,000 square miles, over twice the size of Texas, equal nearly to a fifth of the continental United States. The purchase price, $7,200,000, meant that Seward bought this imperial domain for two cents an acre, which may well be cheap even for ice—if one took at face value the claims of the critics of the purchase that Alaska was one great sheet of ice.

Russian America: so Alaska was called in the prepurchase era. It only took the name of Alaska after Senator Charles Sumner of Massachusetts so denominated it during his great Senate speech in support of the treaty. Sumner borrowed the name from the Aleut word for "continent," meaning the land east of the Aleutians.

The long years of Russian attempts to colonize Alaska or at least make it productive had turned toward failure by the 1860's. As much as anything, it was the near failure of the Russian American Company (caused by the gradual extermination of the sea otter) that induced the Russian government to sell. After the death of the company's organizer, Alexander Baranov, in 1819, company fortunes had declined until by the end of the American Civil War it was evident that the Russian government would have to take over the company or subsidize it heavily. The authorities in St. Petersburg were unwilling to follow either course. They also were concerned that the state of affairs prevailing during the Crimean War, a neutralization of Alaska which prevented its capture by the British, might not obtain in a future conflict. The cost of taking over or subsidizing the company, plus the cost of making this extremity of Russia's Asiatic possessions defensible, seemed a double charge upon Russia's already too modest treasury, and common sense urged a sale to the Americans. It might even be possible to capitalize on the good will of the Americans, so much in evidence during the Civil War, to persuade them to buy what the Russian government wished to sell.

The decision to sell had come gradually, and there had been signs that the Americans might be interested. The senior senator from California, John Gwin, together with Assistant Secretary of State John Appleton, had talked with the Russian minister, Baron Edouard de Stoeckl, in 1860, and Gwin had said how anxious he and his fellow Californians were to arrange the purchase of Alaska. The senator admitted that the rest of the country might not feel the same way about Russian America and said it would be necessary to await the coming into office of the new administration and Congress. The election of Lincoln, of course, led to the Civil War, which ended most of the talk of Alaska. During the war there was some indication of interest. The private American promoter, P. McD. Collins, conceived the project of a telegraph line across Russian America and Siberia to Europe, to replace the Atlantic cable, which had gone dead before the Civil War. Perhaps this project caught the imagination of the Russians, for it gave evidence that Alaska might have value if only as a base for communication. Collins secured a right of way from the St. Petersburg government in 1863. Construction ceased in 1866 when Cyrus Field successfully spanned the Atlantic with a cable.

Meanwhile Secretary of State Seward had begun to envision the purchase of Alaska. The destruction of whaling vessels in the far north by the Confederate raider *Shenandoah* in 1865 bothered Seward. In the course of the last months of the war and for a while after the end of the fighting on the North American continent, the *Shenandoah* was capturing whalers and burning them. Frederick W. Seward, the son of the secretary, who acted as his father's assistant secretary of state, wrote years later that his father during the war "had found the Government laboring under great disadvantages from the lack of advanced naval outposts in the West Indies and the North Pacific; so at the close of hostilities he commenced his endeavors to obtain such a foothold in each quarter." Seward wished to annex the Dominican Republic and buy the Danish West Indies, and he hoped to negotiate a treaty of annexation or reciprocity with the Hawaiian Islands, then under a native dynasty. He appropriated Midway Island during 1867, the same year as the Alaska Purchase. The experience of the war moved him in this direction, probably together with his own instinct of manifest destiny. And so far as concerned Pacific possessions it was not merely a belief in the needs of defense and manifest destiny but a continuation of the fascination shown by several generations of Americans before him in developing a trade with the hundreds of millions of people in China, for which trade Hawaii and Midway and Alaska would serve as territorial vestibules.

One point fairly evident is that if Seward displayed all the feeling of the generations before him and desired Alaska for reasons of defense, manifest destiny, and the China trade, he understood that as late as 1867 it still was possible to obtain a considerable popular support for acquiring Alaska. Historians have sometimes drawn Seward as almost singlehandedly arranging and pushing through Congress the Alaskan treaty. He could not have done this without popular support. John Bigelow once wrote of Seward, whom he knew well, "One thing in which he excelled all the men of his time that I knew, was his sagacity in discerning the trend of public opinion. When he discerned it, he reverently bowed to it. In that sense he was pre-eminently a representative man." Seward sensed that he could get the consent of Congress for this huge accretion of national territory. He managed to do it, because the purchase of Alaska had a public consensus behind it.

The secretary's collaborator in the purchase, the Russian minister Stoeckl, was every bit as eager for the purchase, if for different reasons, problems of the province's finances and defense set out above. Stoeckl arranged the sale as his last work of Russian diplomacy, prior to what he hoped would be appointment to the Russian legation at The Hague. The minister had been in the United States since 1841, when he had arrived as an elegant bachelor of thirty-three years possessing a dubious title of "baron." He had become accustomed to America, marrying Miss Eliza Howard of Springfield, Massachusetts, but he always distrusted the Americans en masse, if not in particular, and he detested democracy. He had been ready for The Hague when he returned to Russia in 1866, only to be summoned to the Winter Palace in St. Petersburg on December 16, for a private meeting during which the decision was taken to unload the costly northern colony on the United States. The finance minister, present at this historic session, told Stoeckl—who was to return to America to consummate the sale—not to take less than $5,000,000. The tsar specially asked Stoeckl to return for this task and eventually was to reward him with a purse of $17,000. (Following the sale of Alaska, Stoeckl failed to get the legation at The Hague and would spend his last years in bitter retirement in Paris, angered by this personal result of his long American mission.)

The minister, now on special mission, returned to the United States early in 1867 and soon obtained an indication from the American secretary of state that the United States would buy Alaska if the opportunity presented itself. According to a well-known account, one evening Stoeckl stopped by the house of the secretary while Seward was playing whist, said that he, Stoeckl, now had authority to sell, and proposed a meeting the next day to arrange the terms. "Why wait until tomorrow?" said the anxious Seward, who offered to open the department of state immediately. Seward said he would be ready for business in a very short time, and that he could locate his secretaries and Senator Sumner if Stoeckl could find the members of his own staff. Frederick Seward later was to describe in graphic terms the scene in which Stoeckl and the American secretary of state drew up the terms that night, signing the treaty in a gleam of gaslight at 4:00 A.M. on March 30, 1867. The next morning President Johnson sent in to a startled Senate a treaty for the cession of Russian America.

It was wisdom if not statesmanship that led Seward to invite the senator from Massachusetts, chairman of the committee on foreign relations, to this midnight affair of March 29–30. Sumner was becoming hostile toward the Johnson administration and was not personally fond of Seward's well-known territorial projects. As it turned out, Sumner did not make it to the signing of the treaty at the state department; he went to Seward's house that evening and conversed with the Russian minister who was there, but perhaps feeling himself too old for nocturnal events, he went home to bed. Seward's care in informing Sumner nonetheless helped persuade the latter to champion the Alaska treaty in the Senate.

In his Senate speech of April 9, 1867, Sumner not only gave Alaska its name; he spoke with what his contemporaries considered enormous eloquence. It was a short speech for his day, lasting a mere three hours, but it was enough to win consent for the treaty, by vote of 37 to 2. A motion had been introduced to make the vote unanimous as a gesture of cordiality toward Russia, "the old and faithful friend of the United States," and with that imperative the treaty had passed with only the two negatives. Sumner afterward wrote out the address—he had used notes when he spoke—for publication in the *Congressional Globe* (the predecessor of the *Congressional Record*); he spent six weeks amplifying the speech, and when printed it was equivalent to a small book containing the diplomatic, military, political, social and intellectual history of Alaska to A.D. 1867.

Everything had moved so rapidly from engrossing the treaty to consent and ratification that Seward could feel that with the help of Sumner he had "pulled it off," but there was still the problem of getting the appropriation through the House of Representatives. Here the treaty ran into an unexpected delay which indeed went on for so long that it was only the next year, July 14, 1868, and by vote of 113 to 43, that the appropriation passed. In the course of this delay the gathering anti-Johnson forces— the president came within one vote of impeachment on May 16, 1868— used every stratagem to embarrass the administration and even the secretary of state who had signed the treaty in the middle of the night. In the rancors of post-Civil War America, the high political antagonisms engendered partly by the problems of reconstruction of the South and partly by the personal edginess of Andrew Johnson, the appropriation for Alaska encountered deep trouble, so much so that at one point the Russian minister thought it might be a good idea to offer the territory to the United States as a gift, if only to shame the House of Representatives into action. He allegedly held back from this tactic only because he feared that the shameless House might accept.

Seward had support during the grand Alaskan debate of 1867–1868. If Eastern newspapers were against the purchase, papers of the Pacific coast generally were favorable. The chairman of the House committee on ways and means, N. P. Banks, had visions of the Pacific Ocean:

That ocean will be the theatre of the triumphs of civilization in the future. It is on that line that are to be fought the great battles of the hereafter. It is there that the institutions of the world will be fashioned and its destinies decided. If this transfer is successful, it will no longer be an European civilization or an European destiny that controls us. It will be a higher civilization and a nobler destiny. It may be an American civilization, an American destiny of six hundred million souls.

Banks considered Alaska a key to the China trade, as did such individuals as Representative G. S. Orth of Indiana, who also saw a patriotic problem. Orth asked what he considered a pregnant question:

Shall the flag which waves so proudly there now be taken down? Palsied be the hand that would dare to remove it! Our flag is there, and there it will remain. Our laws and our institutions are there, guaranteeing protection to its present inhabitants, and to the thousands who shall inhabit it hereafter.

Many individuals showed a prescience of what would happen to Alaska, that both economically and militarily the purchase would turn out all right. Revenues from taxes within a few decades were greater than the purchase price, and even before the Klondike rush in 1896 gold production far surpassed the figure of $7,200,000. Possession of Alaska proved almost as helpful in a military sense as was the later acquisition of the Hawaiian Islands. Brigadier General William Mitchell in 1935 could claim with some truth that "Alaska is the most central place in the world for aircraft. And that is true either of Europe, Asia or North America, for in the future I think whoever holds Alaska will hold the world, and I think it is the most important strategic place in the world." And if twentieth-century arguments or arguments supportable only by the year, say, 1900, were not believable in 1867, there was the contemporary opinion of the Victoria (British Columbia) *Colonist*, of May 16, 1867:

By it the United States virtually secures control of the Coast, opens a new field for American enterprise and capital, and places the whole of Her Majesty's possessions on this coast in the position of a piece of meat between two slices of bread, where they may be devoured at a single bite.

The critics of the purchase nonetheless had a field day. Much of the criticism in Congress centered around the lack of consultation with the House of Representatives in the making of treaties—members were annoyed that Seward had concluded the treaty before securing an appropriation for the purchase. Few members of the House seemed convinced that the territory was as valuable as Seward's spokesmen claimed. And criti-

OUR NEW SENATORS.

SECRETARY SEWARD—" *My dear Mr. Kamskatca, you really must dine with me. I have some of the very finest tallow candles and the lovliest train oil you ever tasted, and my whale's blubber is exquisite—and pray bring your friend Mr. Seal along with you. The President will be one of the party.*"

An American newspaper cartoon of 1867 shows Secretary of State Seward and President Andrew Johnson welcoming the representatives of the new Alaska territory to Washington.

cism in and out of Congress had the advantage of humor or grotesque exaggeration, which the supporters of the purchase were hard put to answer. These amusing barbs and shafts were difficult to refute by solemn arguments about the China trade or military advantage or even manifest destiny. "Seward's icebox," said some of the critics. "Seward's folly," said others. The purchase was a "dark deed done in the night," they contended, with truth except for the initial adjective. The New York diarist, George Templeton Strong, thought of applying to President Johnson "for some little place in the new Territory of Sitka. I would make a good superintendent of walruses—a very efficient and disinterested head of a Polar Bears' Bureau." The New York *Herald* eventually supported cession, but at the outset criticized Seward by advising him to buy Patagonia at the tip of South America, "to make both ends meet." It also published the following advertisement:

CASH! CASH! CASH!—Cash paid for cast-off territory. Best price given for old colonies, North or South. Any impoverished monarchs retiring from the colonization business may find a good purchaser by addressing W. H. S., Post Office, Washington, D.C.

Congressman Washburn of Wisconsin said that if the country wanted a white elephant it could obtain a vastly better one "in Siam or Bombay for one-hundredth part of the money, with not one ten-thousandth part of the expense in keeping the animal in proper condition." Representative Price of Iowa said that the place cost too much: "Seven million dollars in gold! How many hearts would this lift from the verge of despondency? How many orphans' tears would it wipe away! How many widows' hearts would it make sing for joy!" *Harper's Weekly* for April 27, 1867, remarked that the climate was bracing; that as far as the eye could reach the fields were white with the harvest, the ice crop most promising; the cattle sat all day cross-legged on cakes of ice, and gave ice cream rather than milk; that all important points along the coast were covered with ice, very slippery indeed, impossible for an enemy to get a foothold on; that never was a place so much in need of buying.

Seward bought, and so did the Senate and President Johnson. The flag was raised at Sitka on October 18, 1867, and in the following summer the House of Representatives appropriated the funds.

The appropriation was surrounded with an aura of corruption which has never been dispelled, and perhaps never can be. More than half a century ago the historian Frank A. Golder investigated the Russian archives and concluded that congressmen were bought, although the archives held no direct evidence about individuals. Even at the time it was known that

Stoeckl disbursed $165,000 which he received from his account in the Riggs Bank in Washington. To recompense the Russian American Company, Stoeckl had persuaded Seward to add $200,000 to the purchase price of $7,000,000, making the somewhat odd total price of $7,200,000. The minister reported to his superiors in St. Petersburg that he had used the greater part of the $200,000 for "secret expenses," as well he might have when, after all, Seward could have beaten him down to $5,000,000. Seward passed along to President Johnson the gossip that $30,000 had gone to the newspaperman John Forney, $8,000 to N.P. Banks, $20,000 to former Secretary of the Treasury Robert J. Walker (the same who perhaps was active against the Erlanger loan during the Civil War), and $20,000 to F. P. Stanton. Seward's gossip had it that Thaddeus Stevens took $10,000. The latter disbursement may not have occurred. According to John Bigelow's memoirs published many years later, Bigelow spoke to Seward during an after-dinner whist game and the secretary of state then said that Stevens was to get only $1,000: "One thousand more were to have been given to poor Thad. Stevens, but no one would undertake to give that to him, so I undertook it myself. The poor fellow died, and I have it now." But when questioned under oath at a congressional hearing, Seward said that "I know nothing whatever of the use the Russian minister made of the fund, I know of no payment to anybody, by him or of any application of the funds which he received."

Perhaps it would be best to let this mystery disappear into history, unresolved. The point of importance is that Alaska in 1867 entered the American national domain, at a low place in Russian imperial ambitions, at a time generally when empire seemed a passing phase of European history, before the hectic imperialism of Africa and Asia was to begin moving the nations of Europe toward a world war and into the appalling politiques of the twentieth century. In the case of Alaska the United States did not profit from Europe's distress but from Europe's indifference. A profit, though, it was, another piece of republican good luck.

3. *The Danish West Indies and the Dominican Republic*

The first two arrangements of the government of the United States in the years after the Civil War, getting the French troops out of Mexico and then acquiring Alaska by purchase, turned out exceedingly well—and upon his retirement in March 1869, Secretary Seward could congratulate himself, as he assuredly did, that his eight years of diplomacy had redounded to the success of the republic. But perhaps Seward had been successful because he first had worked under President Lincoln, and then in the postwar period under Johnson, who had been too busy with domestic affairs to force Seward to deviate from the policies the secretary pursued after his great mentor's death. It was the singular ill fortune of Seward's successor, Hamilton Fish, to have to conduct diplomacy under the direction and occasional interference of Ulysses S. Grant, a president who was no more learned in diplomatic matters than Andrew Johnson but assuredly was more assertive. Grant's political position was as secure in 1869 as that of any president throughout the nineteenth century: he was a war hero. And when he became president he believed he was just as learned at politics as he had been at military tactics and strategy.

Secretary Fish fortunately was the best man in Grant's cabinet, and was a strong enough personality to be able to stand up to the president and, on several occasions, to offer his resignation if policy went contrary to his own desires. Fish often saved Grant from error in foreign relations, and the only pity was that there was no one in the cabinet who could have done the same for domestic affairs.

Hamilton Fish was an unlikely secretary of state. He had no experience in diplomacy prior to the day when he became secretary and began to preside over the menage of clerks and functionaries who, during most of his secretaryship, carried on their duties in the former orphan asylum which served as the state department's headquarters. Fish had been born in New York State in 1808, the year of the embargo, and had grown to manhood in the postwar era of good feelings. He served a term in Congress in the early 1840's, was governor of New York in 1849–1851, and was elected to the Senate as a Whig in 1851. Then the Whig Party went to pieces, and apparently Fish's political career went likewise. Even though he joined the Republican Party, he retired in 1857 instead of running for re-election. For twelve years thereafter Fish held no elective office, although he was active in politics during the war. Then in 1869 Grant nominated a man named Wilson as secretary of state, and Wilson declined. Grant nominated Fish, who recently had served as a host when the then presidential candidate was in New York State. Fish declined. Grant sent his name to the Senate anyway, and Fish came to Washington, as he wrote his friend Senator Sumner, "with a heavy heart and with unnumbered misgivings." His coming into office recalled the patrician hesitations of some of the earlier statesmen of the republic, the sort of Adams-like reluctance, apparently real, to take office.

Fish's friend Sumner, to whom he had written about the heavy heart, proved the worst trial of his secretaryship, save only the projects and activities of President Grant. According to Allan Nevins, the senator from

Thaddeus Stevens, photographed by Matthew B. Brady.

Massachusetts was "probably the most intolerant man that American history has ever known." Thaddeus Stevens of Reconstruction fame, he whose photographed scowl has gone into history as the very symbol of bitterness and intolerance, was full of the milk of human kindness if compared to Sumner. The senator once stigmatized President Grant as "a colossus of ignorance," and described his friend Secretary Fish as "a gentleman in aspect with the heart of a lackey." Sumner's difficulty perhaps was his vanity; after meeting him President Lincoln had once remarked to an acquaintance: "I have never had much to do with bishops down where we live; but, do you know, Sumner is just my idea of a bishop." He was not a bishop—perhaps that was the trouble. He was chairman of the Senate foreign relations committee, and in this post of importance Secretary Fish and even President Grant had to deal with him or, as Grant eventually did, undo his dignity and thereby unleash his wrath.

Hamilton Fish and his predecessor Seward both were great secretaries of state, and it is interesting that despite their high qualities, their similar devotion to the long future of the republic, they each came a cropper over islands in the Caribbean. Seward decided to buy the Danish West Indies

—the Virgin Islands. Fish, if with far less ardor, supported the project of President Grant to annex the Dominican Republic to the United States.

Seward at the end of the Civil War elaborated a grand scheme to expand American territory in the areas near the United States, and Alaska as well as the Danish West Indies fitted this plan. Indeed the secretary had a vision of the departure of all foreign nations from their territorial holdings in North America, with all the islands becoming republics—forming in part a black confederacy of the Caribbean—or attaching themselves to the United States by purchase. The Danish government possessed an island group some forty miles east of Puerto Rico, consisting chiefly of three islands: St. Thomas, St. Croix, and St. John. Seward set out to buy these islands.

The Danes were willing, if for a price, and it was the price which eventually proved Seward's undoing. True, as the negotiation wore on the secretary began to observe that the Congress and the American public were becoming ever less interested in manifest destiny, and after election to the presidency in November 1868, Ulysses S. Grant was not interested at all. Seward might have put through the sale if the Danes had not begun to haggle as if they were selling carpets rather than islands. The palaver began at $5,000,000 gold, and from there the talk moved toward $15,000,-000. Seward and the Danish minister, Raasloff, began to dicker for specific islands or combinations and exclusions. Seward talked the cabinet into $7,500,000 for all three. The Danes then wished to hold back one.

The problem was essentially time, and during the dickering the sands of manifest destiny ran out. Humorists (that was hardly the word for them, since when the United States finally bought the Danish West Indies in 1917 the price was $25,000,000, not $15,000,000) also entered the debate. Mark Twain pointed out how earthquakes and hurricanes had reduced the value of West Indian real estate; he was referring to the fact that a hurricane had produced a tidal wave which caught the U.S.S. *Monongahela* off St. Thomas and tossed the valiant warship into the island's principal town. Grant at last ended the negotiation, which resumed many years later during the First World War.

The other negotiation related to the Dominican Republic, where the state department under Secretary Fish, urged on by President Grant, found itself receiving offers of annexation from none other than the president of that Caribbean island.

The background of the Dominican negotiation was complicated, in a small sort of way. The republic had enjoyed a checkered history as an independent nation and actually had hardly established its independence before the United States received the offers of annexation. The republic constituted the eastern two-thirds of Santo Domingo or Española, which after a successful revolt against Spain in 1821 had been almost immediately annexed by Haiti and ruled until 1844. Thereafter it did not maintain its independence well. The Spanish sought to reannex it beginning in 1861, during the American Civil War. By 1865 they gave up. Secretary of State Seward meanwhile had interested himself in Samaná Bay in 1864, and in December 1866 sent his son Frederick to purchase the bay for $2,000,000. The Dominican government, like the Danes, began to haggle. The political situation on the island at that time was volatile anyway, and the discussion came to an end. Serious negotiation for annexation of the island republic awaited the era of Secretary Fish.

It was President Grant who, as mentioned, found the Dominican Republic so attractive a place for American expansion, and his reason for desiring the little country, however simplistic it may now seem, deserves some explanation. Grant ardently desired the Dominican Republic as a place to which American Negroes might go. The account of his purpose in the Dominican Republic as it appears in his memoirs relates a hope to give the Negroes of America, newly freed, a land where they might govern themselves.

The island is upon our shores, is very fertile, and is capable of supporting fifteen millions of our people. The products of the soil are so valuable that labor in her fields would be so compensated as to enable those who wished to go there to quickly repay the cost of their passage. I took it that the colored people would go there in great numbers, so as to have independent states governed by their own race. They would still be States of the Union, and under the protection of the General Government; but the citizens would be almost wholly colored.

A simple scheme, one might say. And perhaps more than that? Was President Grant seeking to get rid of the newly enfranchised American Negroes by putting them outside the continental United States, on Española, thereby solving what he undoubtedly believed was a very difficult domestic problem? This is a possible interpretation of Grant's proposition as set out in his memoirs. And yet the post-Civil War president ought to be taken at face value; in politics he was a simple man, and the simplicity of his scheme for the Dominican Republic should not be translated into skulduggery.

The fact that Fish went along with Grant's chimerical desire to annex the Dominican Republic has often bothered students of Fish's career, and it is of note that the secretary's biographer, Nevins, has asserted without qualification that the decision to support Grant was extremely well-taken. By acceding to Grant's desire, supporting his efforts to buy, Fish maintained himself in office—instead of allowing what otherwise surely would have been so strong a difference to arise between himself and the president that it would have forced his resignation. The secretary of state was able to prevent the president from recognizing the insurgents in Cuba who in 1868 began a decade-long and unsuccessful war against their Spanish governors, and also was able to negotiate eventually a settlement of the *Alabama* claims with Great Britain, a negotiation which became Fish's claim, a rightful one, to historic greatness. Indeed, if Grant had recognized the belligerency of the Cuban insurgents, the president would have ruined an important part of the American case against Great Britain in the *Alabama* negotiation—which rested on a claim that the British government in 1861 had been hasty in recognizing the belligerency of the Confederates. Fish was discreet about his true feelings over the Dominican Republic and afterward said only that if he had acted by himself his ardor might have been less than in fact he displayed. He went along, to preserve his authority for better occasions.

The failure of Grant's and Fish's efforts to annex the Dominican Republic occurred less because of money, as in the case of the Virgin Islands, than because of the unsavory individuals to whom Grant entrusted the more intimate details of the negotiation. Money was surely a consideration for the desperate President Buenaventura Baez, who would need an establishment in Paris, or Madrid, or somewhere, to which to repair after he had given his country away. He may also have contemplated a distribution of cash to his several friends and relatives who had supported his negotiation with Grant's representatives. The Dominicans were somewhat in favor of annexation, if one may make a statement about the condition of public opinion in a largely illiterate country in the latter nineteenth century. The essential trouble, though, was that American public opinion, observing the secrecy with which Grant began to negotiate for the Dominican Republic, observing also the fact that the principal negotiator on the American side was Grant's old wartime chief of staff, General Orville H. Babcock, began to suspect another negotiation in the night. Babcock did not help matters by enrolling some of his friends whose reputations were not good enough for daytime negotiation. The project's initial appearance was as a sort of unofficial sale, which Grant rejected in favor of a regular treaty. By the time it got to the Senate, it was too much for Senator Sumner, who then was in full flight against the president. Sumner raised all his best oratory against the Dominican treaty and garnished his address with a Biblical comparison, describing the island republic as Naboth's Vineyard—the presumption being that Grant was King Ahab. The treaty went down to defeat.

The secretary's part in all this was as close to negative as he, Fish, could come and still maintain due loyalty to the president, who regarded the Dominican issue, and opposition to Sumner, as a test of loyalty to the administration. As noted, Fish could only stand behind the president and show signs of support. Fortunately, Sumner defeated the treaty, and the secretary could then take his own attention from Dominican real estate and all the unnumbered problems such an acquisition could have presented to a country still sharply divided over the issue of how to reconstruct the states of the American South. The secretary could concentrate on the issue of the *Alabama* claims.

4. *Hamilton Fish and the* Alabama *claims*

A major accommodation with Great Britain was settlement of the *Alabama* claims controversy, arranged after the Civil War in the Treaty of Washington of 1871 and the subsequent Geneva arbitration of 1872. The problem here was largely the depredations of the Confederate cruiser *Alabama* during the recent war, together with the activities of sister ships such as the *Oreto* (alias the *Florida*). At the time of the Civil War the British government had on its statute books a set of regulations for preserving the neutrality of its citizens, known as the Foreign Enlistment Act. It proved no better a statute than the neutrality act which the American government had amended in 1838 at the time of the Canadian insurrection against British rule. Had tempers during the war been cooler, the Americans might have recognized the embarrassment of the British with their own laws, but tempers were not cool then or later, and, moreover, it was no sheerly legal matter when vessels, after being constructed in British shipyards, were then able by a subterfuge or two to sail the high seas and decimate Union shipping or drive it to the protection of other flags. The procedure under which Confederate agents operated in Great Britain was that they must not arm their new vessels within British jurisdiction, and the result was carefully planned meetings of the vessels with supply ships outside of British control, perhaps at some lonely island where the guns could easily be taken on board.

The Confederate cruisers were a scourge upon the seas and a deep embarrassment to the Union cause. It was necessary for the Union navy to send many more vessels in pursuit of the Confederates than the numbers of Confederate cruisers warranted. It seemed as if the *Alabama*, the most notorious of the raiders, was always in some place other than the Union navy expected. The crew of the *Alabama* and their doughty captain, Raphael Semmes, also showed an insouciance which, even after passage of a century and more, seems at the least outrageous. At one juncture, spending Christmas on the Arcas Islands, some of the ship's officers prepared a souvenir of their visit. According to the log of the master's mate,

In anticipation of news being received of Lincoln's proclamation [of emancipation] a tombstone, consisting of a board about four feet in length and two in breadth, was sent on shore and placed in the most prominent position the largest island afforded. In black letters on a white ground was the following: "In memory of Abraham Lincoln, President of the late United States, who died of nigger on the brain, 1st January, 1863."—"290." Upon a piece of paper, protected from the weather, was written in Spanish the following: "Will the finder kindly favour me by forwarding this tablet to the United States' Consul at the first port he touches at."

Little wonder that the government of the United States, emerging victorious from the war, proceeded to bring the British to account for allowing construction of these raiders.

The resultant Treaty of Washington, wrote the dean of American international lawyers after the turn of the twentieth century, John Bassett Moore, was "the greatest treaty of actual and immediate arbitration" the world has ever seen. This treaty, Moore wrote, occupies a place in the annals of American diplomatic history second only to the Treaty of Paris of 1783.

It would be incorrect to contend that the Treaty of Washington in its negotiation or outcome elicited great attention at the time, from Americans or Europeans. In the United States people were much more interested in Tammany scandals, amnesty for some of the former southern leaders, an Indian warrior named Red Cloud who had threatened disaster in the American West, Mrs. Lincoln's request for a pension, and assorted murder trials. In Great Britain there was concern over troubles in Ireland, reform of the English school system, the death of Charles Dickens, reorganization of the British army. The Treaty of Washington was concluded in the summer of 1871 in an atmosphere of quiet indifference, which suited exactly the pacific purposes of the British and American commissioners meeting in the American capital. They might have faced an impossible task, had public opinion in the two countries been aroused and every turn of the negotiation seized upon by newspapers as a subject for emotional outburst.

Both sides in 1871 were eager to come to a conclusion over the vexatious issues separating the two countries—*Alabama* claims, fisheries, joint use of Canadian waterways such as the St. Lawrence. During a crisis with Russia in 1870 the British found themselves without allies in Europe and were anxious to strengthen ties with the United States. In the midst of the

Franco–Prussian War of 1870–1871, the Russian government had denounced the decision arrived at during the Crimean War of 1854–1856, namely that Russia should not maintain a fleet in the Black Sea, and when the Russian foreign minister unilaterally repudiated this engagement the British found themselves facing Russia alone: the Austrian government was weak, the German government friendly to the Russians, the French government being overthrown in war by the Germans. During the war scare that accompanied the Russian denunciation, there was fear that in event of hostilities there might be a repetition, to Britain's disadvantage, of what had happened during the American Civil War. The Americans might permit the Russians to build a large number of *Alabamas* to venture forth to prey on British commerce all over the world. It was understandable why in 1871 the British were eager to come to an agreement with the United States.

The Americans had their own reasons for pressing a settlement of issues with Great Britain. In the years after the Civil War the American economy enjoyed a tremendous development, evident in construction of railways across the West. Railways and other enterprises required capital from abroad, in particular from the center of world finance, Great Britain. So long as relations between the two countries were strained, every small crisis between London and Washington had a marked effect on the value of American bonds and the availability of British capital. It was, therefore, much to American interest to ensure peace with the British. Moreover, it was peculiarly advantageous for the Grant administration to undertake a grand treaty and arbitration, for in domestic politics a succession of troubles was leading to a split in the Republican Party in the election of 1872. The Liberal Republicans, as they called themselves, were crying for reform. Grant was unwilling to give it to them, but he was willing to seek a diplomatic triumph that would serve his administration in 1872.

The diplomatic antecedents of the Treaty of Washington reached back before the Grant administration to the time of Secretary of State Seward, for it was he who at the end of the war had undertaken to clear away the diplomatic issues that had been postponed until the victory. Seward had announced that Great Britain must pay for the depredations of Confederate cruisers built in British ports, and early in the postwar years he had raised the claim for indirect as well as direct damages. By this claim he meant that the Confederate cruisers had made so much difficulty that they had postponed Union victory. Britain should pay for the cost of additional war imposed by the cruisers. Senator Sumner took up this contention and demanded that in return for American cancellation of the indirect claims Britain undertake a "hemispheric withdrawal"—from

Canada, Jamaica, Bermuda, the Bahamas, Trinidad and other West Indies islands, and British Honduras, British Guiana, the Falklands, and South Georgia. In Sumner's opinion Canada might gravitate to the United States, and perhaps the other formerly British territories would follow. Through the American minister in Great Britain, Reverdy Johnson, and the British foreign secretary, Lord Clarendon, Seward in his last months in office negotiated the Johnson–Clarendon Convention, signed January 14, 1869, providing for general adjudication of American claims against Great Britain, with no specific mention of the *Alabama* claims. Led by Sumner, the Senate rejected this convention on April 13, 1869, by a vote of 54 to 1. The Grant administration under direction of Secretary Fish reopened negotiations.

On New Year's Day 1871, Sir John Rose, a private British gentleman who was in the complete confidence of the foreign office, was on the high seas en route from London to the United States to converse with Secretary Fish. Upon Rose's arrival the two men in their first conversation talked for six hours and at once set on foot a new negotiation. A British commission came to Washington that spring. It met in many sessions with an American commission, and these discussions accompanied conferences between Fish and the leader of the British commission, Earl de Grey. A spring fox-hunt was arranged in Virginia. De Grey took a house for the commission in Washington, and champagne flowed freely. Reporters had a busy time following the festivities of the occasion. Secretary Fish gave many return dinners, and it was at one of these that a reporter bribed a waiter to conceal him under the table, where he took notes on the conversation. Finally, at the signing of the Treaty of Washington on May 8, 1871, the American and British negotiators took leave of each other, concluding their labors with a repast of strawberries and ice cream.

The negotiations, although tortuous, had not been difficult. The fisheries question, which concerned allowing Americans inshore fishing privileges in British North America, outlasted all the others. Seventeen sessions of the commission were devoted to Canadian questions, chiefly the fisheries, also including American navigation of the St. Lawrence, Canadian navigation of Lake Michigan, Canadian use of certain Alaskan rivers, and reciprocal use of local canals connecting with the Great Lakes–St. Lawrence system along the international boundary. Ten additional sessions went to the claims against England. Four sought to draw the proper boundary in San Juan de Fuca Strait, an issue left unsolved from the Oregon Treaty of 1846. The San Juan channel dispute was submitted for arbitration by the German emperor, who in an award of 1872 gave San Juan Island to the United States. The Treaty of Washington allowed citizens of the United States to use the St. Lawrence. Canadians received navigation rights on rivers flowing out of British territory to the sea through Alaska. The Canadians received a temporary, later (in a treaty of 1909) permanent, right to navigation of Lake Michigan. Reciprocal use of the local canals connecting with the Great Lakes–St. Lawrence system was to be arranged, and was so arranged, with local authorities, state and Dominion.

As for the troublesome fisheries question, this was decided for a minimum of ten years, during which citizens of the United States enjoyed Canadian inshore fishing privileges. A commission met in Halifax to determine a cash equivalent for this Canadian concession (it awarded Canada the sum of $5,500,000). The United States also was to admit without duty Canadian fish and fish oil and to open coastal fisheries of the United States north of the thirty-ninth parallel. The fisheries articles of the Treaty of Washington expired in 1885, and the fisheries dispute thus reopened continued until it was arbitrated in 1910. At the time, in 1871 at Washington, it was considered virtually solved. The Canadian prime minister, Sir John Macdonald, one of the British commissioners, felt regretful about the fisheries, and his final surrender was humorously set down in Secretary Fish's diary: "When Sir John Macdonald was about to sign, while having the pen in his hand, he said to me (in a half-whisper) 'Well, here go the fisheries.' To my reply, 'you get a good equivalent for them,' he said, 'No, we give them away—here goes the signature.'; and thereupon signed his name, and rising from the table, said. 'They are gone.' "

In regard to the *Alabama* claims, the treaty established an arbitral tribunal of five men, to be named by President Grant, Queen Victoria, the king of Italy, the president of the Swiss Confederation, and the emperor of Brazil. The tribunal was to meet in Geneva at the earliest possible date. It was to act on the American claims in accord with three famous principles laid down in the Treaty of Washington, which are worthy of special notice because they since have passed into international law. First, a neutral government was bound to use "due diligence" to prevent the outfitting or arming of any vessel which it had "reasonable ground" to believe was intended to make war against another nation, and to prevent departure of any such vessel. Second, a neutral government should prevent a belligerent from making use of its ports or waters as a base of naval operations, or for procuring military supplies, arms, or recruits. Third, it must exercise due diligence in its ports and waters and over all persons within its jurisdiction to prevent violation of these obligations. At the demand of the American commissioners the Treaty of Washington contained an express British statement of regret "for the escape, under whatever circumstances, of the *Alabama* and other vessels from British ports, and for the depredations committed by those vessels."

The treaty was a triumph for Hamilton Fish, its negotiator. By writing into the treaty the principles of the arbitration, Fish bound the arbitrators to accept in advance a large part of the American case, and only the amount of damages remained in question.

The Senate at once gave approval to the treaty on May 24, 1871, which was Queen Victoria's birthday. Ratifications were formally exchanged in London on Bunker Hill Day, June 17. President Grant proclaimed the treaty in full effect on July 4. There remained only the arbitration itself.

To Geneva the United States sent Charles Francis Adams as one of the five arbitrators. To present the American case Fish and Grant chose William M. Evarts, leader of the American bar, together with Caleb Cushing, the negotiator of the Cushing Treaty with China in 1844 and one of New England's most eminent citizens, and Morrison R. Waite, soon to be chief justice of the United States.

At Geneva the arbitrators—American, British, Brazilian, Swiss, and Italian—heard presentations of the American claims, presentations almost wrecked by the ill-advised revival of the indirect claims. The British during the Washington negotiations had thought the indirect claims had been put to rest. Secretary Fish and his principal assistant in preparation of the American case at Geneva, J. C. Bancroft Davis, resurrected the claims without advising the British of their peculiar purpose for so doing: they advanced the indirect claims at Geneva only to satisfy American public opinion, and not for the serious attention of the Geneva tribunal. The British government was incensed by the American demands for an award equivalent to the cost of the Civil War after the battle of Gettysburg. Lord Granville, the foreign secretary, estimated these claims with seven per cent interest at $4,500,000,000, "an incredible demand." Prussia's recent exaction of a billion-dollar indemnity from France had made a painful impression upon all Europe, and here were the Americans at Geneva demanding several times that much. The British prime minister, William E. Gladstone, almost lost his temper, for Gladstone estimated that the "war prolongation claim" might come to $8,000,000,000. In a letter to Queen Victoria he compared the American indirect claims to Russia's abrogation of the Black Sea clauses: "Even bearing in mind the proceeding of Prince Gortschakoff in the autumn of 1870, Mr. Gladstone is constrained to say that the conduct of the American Government in this affair is the most disreputable he has ever known in his recollection of diplomacy." Confronted with this sort of accusation, Secretary Fish ruffled momentarily and foresaw the end of his cherished arrangement of issues with Great Britain, but he recovered his poise, issued suitable disclaimers on the indirect claims, allowed an arrangement at Geneva whereby the arbitrators unanimously threw out these American pretensions, and the arbitration moved forward to its conclusion, an award of $15,500,000 to the American government. Fish realized in regard to the indirect claims that it would be poor business for the United States to establish a precedent for them in international law. As he wrote privately to a friend, "I may say to *you*, that I never believed that the Tribunal would award a cent for the 'indirect claims'; it is not the interest of the United States, who are habitually neutrals, to have it decided that a neutral is liable for the indirect injuries consequent upon an act of negligence. We have too large an extent of coast and too small a police, and too much of the spirit of bold speculation and adventure, to make the doctrine a safe one for our future."

The Geneva tribunal labored from the end of June 1872 to mid-September, in the small Salle des Conférences in the Hôtel de Ville—now known as the Salle de l'Alabama. The neutral arbitrators, Swiss, Brazilian, and Italian, were the deciding factors in the arbitration, and the Americans at Geneva left nothing undone which would sway the neutrals toward the American side. Bancroft Davis, present during the deliberations, flattered the neutral arbitrators to a point where they were altogether willing to decide in favor of the United States. He took the additional precaution to bribe the French newspaper press, read by the neutral arbitrators. In this regard he did a thorough job, for as he wrote to Fish, his list included "all the important political papers except the *Debats* and the *France*, and the *Journal de Paris*. The first two are bought by England; the latter I don't know about." One must suspect that in other ways the arbiration was not altogether judicial, for the Brazilian arbitrator at one point seems to have decided against the British on the basis of ability to pay; he told the British counsel that "You are rich—very rich." By such assumptions, together with the American precautionary measures, together with the preliminary surrender of the British position contained in the stipulations of the Treaty of Washington, the United States obtained its diplomatic victory at Geneva.

The financial settlement, as mentioned, was $15,500,000 to the United States. Simultaneously, the private claims of British citizens against the United States were established at $1,929,819 and an award of this amount was made to Britain. American private claims against Britain were dismissed. If one considers, then, the award in Halifax of $5,500,000 to Canada for inshore fishing privileges, the net American financial gain from the Washington Treaty of 1871 was $8,070,181, a tidy sum—not to mention the precedent established in favor of American principles of neutrality.

Perhaps, one should say in conclusion, John Bassett Moore overesti-

This receipt from the American treasury was framed and hung next to the desk of the British foreign secretary during the First World War, Sir Edward Grey, where the American ambassador and other visiting diplomats could see it and take notice.

mated the importance of the Treaty of Washington and the Geneva arbitration when he described it as the largest triumph of American diplomacy after the Treaty of Paris ending the American revolution. This praise seems a little overdone, for the Treaty of Washington was not itself difficult to conclude, and the arbitration at Geneva, after trouble with the indirect claims, proceeded easily to its foreordained end. Even so, the Geneva award marked the greatest arbitration in American diplomatic history, perhaps in world history. The achievement of Hamilton Fish in 1871–1872 in arranging all the issues outstanding between the United States and Great Britain must go down as a major act of statesmanship, comparable to John Quincy Adams's negotiation of the Transcontinental Treaty with Spain more than fifty years before.

Such was the diplomacy of the United States in the few years after the Civil War. The retreat of the French from Mexico in 1867, the purchase of Alaska, the schemes for purchase of the Danish West Indies and annexation of the Dominican Republic, the Treaty of Washington and the Geneva arbitration: these developments (or attempted developments) were caused, in one way or other, by the Americans' belief in manifest destiny, that the most valuable portions of the North American continent were destined to fall under the sovereignty of the government of the United States. What at first might appear as a series of unrelated episodes becomes intelligible when one considers the factor of manifest destiny. In the perspective of the twentieth century this idea may seem a peculiarly nineteenth-century proposition, a confusion of national ambitions with historical inevitability and divine guidance. Still, if one surveys the territorial expanse of the American nation as it stood in the golden year 1872, there does seem to have been something mystical, something defiant of ordinary logic, in this growth of an infant nation to proportions of world power during not quite a century of independence.

"The British Lion Disarmed," by Thomas Nast. In spite of the *Alabama* claims, America and the British lion were not enemies.

A CONTEMPORARY DOCUMENT

[Senator Sumner lived in an age of oratory, and he enjoyed smothering his points with facts and analogies. His speeches, if long, had the virtue of an obvious clarity. When he moved against the Johnson-Clarendon Convention in a Senate speech of April 13, 1869, it was not difficult to grasp the burden of his remarks. Source: *The Works of Charles Sumner* (15 vols., Boston, 1875–1883), XIII, 73–74, 84–86.]

At last the Rebellion succumbed. British ships and British supplies had done their work, but they failed. And now the day of reckoning has come,—but with little apparent sense of what is due on the part of England. Without one soothing word for a friendly power deeply aggrieved, without a single regret for what Mr. Cobden, in the House of Commons, called "the cruel losses" inflicted upon us, or for what Mr. Bright called "aid and comfort to the foulest of all crimes," or for what a generous voice from Oxford University denounced as a "flagrant and maddening wrong," England simply proposes to submit the question of liability for individual losses to an anomalous tribunal where chance plays its part. This is all. Nothing is admitted, even on this question; no rule for the future is established; while nothing is said of the indignity to the nation, nor of the damages to the nation. . . .

This is what I have to say for the present on *national losses* through the destruction of commerce. These are large enough; but there is another chapter, where they are larger far: I refer, of course, to the national losses caused by the prolongation of the war, and traceable directly to England. Pardon me, if I confess the regret with which I touch this prodigious item; for I know well the depth of feeling which it is calculated to stir. But I cannot hesitate. It belongs to the case. No candid person, who studies this eventful period, can doubt that the Rebellion was originally encouraged by hope of support from England,—that it was strengthened at once by the concession of belligerent rights on the ocean,—that it was fed to the end by British supplies,—that it was encouraged by every well-stored British ship that was able to defy our blockade,—that it was quickened into frantic life with every report from the British pirates, flaming anew with every burning ship; nor can it be doubted that without British intervention the Rebellion would have soon succumbed under the well-directed efforts of the National Government. Not weeks or months, but years, were added in this way to our war, so full of costly sacrifice. The subsidies which in other times England contributed to Continental wars were less effective than the aid and comfort which she contributed to the Rebellion. It cannot be said too often that the *naval base* of the Rebellion was not in America, but in England. The blockade-runners and the pirate ships were all English. England was the fruitful parent, and these were the "hell-hounds," pictured by Milton in his description of Sin, which, "when they list, would creep into her womb and kennel there." Mr. Cobden boldly said in the House of Commons that England made war from her shores on the United States, with "an amount of damage to that country greater than would be produced by many ordinary wars." According to this testimony, the conduct of England was war; but it must not be forgotten that this war was carried on at our sole cost. The United States paid for a war waged by England upon the National Unity.

There was one form that this war assumed which was incessant, most vexatious, and costly, besides being in itself a positive alliance with the Rebellion. It was that of blockade-runners, openly equipped and supplied by England under the shelter of that baleful Proclamation. Constantly leaving English ports, they stole across the ocean, and then broke the blockade. These active agents of the Rebellion could be counteracted only by a network of vessels stretching along the coast, at great cost to the country. Here is another distinct item, the amount of which may be determined at the Navy Department.

The sacrifice of precious life is beyond human compensation; but there may be an approximate estimate of the national loss in treasure. Everybody can make the calculation. I content myself with calling attention to the elements which enter into it. Besides the blockade, there was the prolongation of the war. The Rebellion was suppressed at a cost of more than four thousand million dollars, a considerable portion of which has been already paid, leaving twenty-five hundred millions as a national debt to burden the people. If, through British intervention, the war was doubled in duration, or in any way extended, as cannot be doubted, then is England justly responsible for the additional expenditure to which our country was doomed; and whatever may be the final settlement of these great accounts, such must be the judgment in any chancery which consults the simple equity of the case.

This plain statement, without one word of exaggeration or aggravation, is enough to exhibit the magnitude of the national losses, whether from the destruction of our commerce, the prolongation of the war, or the expense of the blockade. They stand before us mountain-high, with a base broad as the Nation, and a mass stupendous as the Rebellion itself. It will be for a wise statesmanship to determine how this fearful accumulation, like Ossa upon Pelion, shall be removed out of sight, so that it shall no longer overshadow the two countries. . . .

Again I say, this debate is not of my seeking. It is not tempting; for it compels criticism of a foreign power with which I would have more than peace, more even than concord. But it cannot be avoided. The truth must be told,—not in anger, but in sadness. England has done to the United States an injury most difficult to measure. Considering when it was done and in what complicity, it is truly unaccountable. At a great epoch of history, not less momentous than that of the French Revolution or that of the Reformation, when Civilization was fighting a last battle with Slavery, England gave her name, her influence, her material resources to the wicked cause, and flung a sword into the scale with Slavery. Here was a portentous mistake.

Strange that the land of Wilberforce, after spending millions for Emancipation, after proclaiming everywhere the truths of Liberty, and ascending to glorious primacy in the sublime movement for the Universal Abolition of Slavery, could do this thing! Like every departure from the rule of justice and good neighborhood, her conduct was pernicious in proportion to the scale of operations, affecting individuals, corporations, communities, and the nation itself. And yet down to this day there is no acknowledgment of this wrong,—not a single word. Such a generous expression would be the beginning of a just settlement, and the best assurance of that harmony between two great and kindred nations which all must desire.

ADDITIONAL READING

Expansion was in the air by the end of the American Civil War. For the general subject see Joe Patterson Smith, *The Republican Expansionists of the Early Reconstruction Era* (Chicago, 1933); and Roy F. Nichols, *Advance Agents of American Destiny* (Philadelphia, 1956). Many soldiers, North and South, hardly knew what to do with themselves after Appomattox, and some of them went off to strange lands. William B. Hesseltine and Hazel C. Wolf, *The Blue and the Gray on the Nile* (Chicago, 1961) sets out the work of the ex-soldiers who went to Egypt to organize the troops of the khedive. *Walter La-Feber, *The New Empire: An Interpretation of American Expansion, 1860–1898* (Ithaca, N.Y., 1963) is an interpretation, primarily economic, of expansion down to the Spanish–American War. See also the new book by Foster Rhea Dulles, *Prelude to World Power: 1860–1900* (New York, 1968), a volume in the American Diplomatic History series.

For the demise of Maximilian the best source remains Egon Caesar Count Corti, *Maximilian and Charlotte of Mexico* (2 vols., New York, 1928), a work translated from the German. Present-day readers may find Corti tedious. "Of all the tragedies in history," he writes, "there is scarce one which has so deeply excited the sympathy of the world as that of the ill-fated Emperor and Empress of Mexico. Their experiences, their efforts and their hopes, their battles and their sufferings, transcend the fate of any other pair of human beings." Admittedly, the fate of the emperor and empress was dire. Charlotte passed into insanity, believing that Napoleon III was seeking to have her poisoned. She made a pathetic visit to the Pope in Rome in the course of which she refused to leave the papal chambers for fear that Napoleon's agents would trap her. She died in her Belgian castle in 1927. In addition to reading Corti, keeping in mind a few other tragedies since the deaths of Maximilian and Charlotte, the reader should consult Harford M. Hyde, *Mexican Empire: The History of Maximilian and Carlota of Mexico* (London, 1946), together with such accounts as Henry Blumenthal, *A Reappraisal of Franco–American*

Relations: 1830–1871 (Chapel Hill, N.C., 1959), and Dexter Perkins, *The Monroe Doctrine: 1826–1867* (Baltimore, 1933). See also Glyndon G. Van Deusen, *William Henry Seward* (New York, 1967).

The literature on the Alaska Purchase, like that concerning the Barbary pirates, hardly does justice to its subject. Interesting background appears in Thomas A. Bailey, *America Faces Russia* (Ithaca, N.Y., 1950); Foster Rhea Dulles, *The Road to Teheran: The Story of Russia and America, 1781–1943* (Princeton, 1944); Benjamin P. Thomas, *Russo–American Relations: 1815–1867* (Baltimore, 1930); and Hector Chevigny, *Russian America: The Great Alaskan Venture, 1741–1867* (New York, 1965). F. A. Golder used the tsarist archives for "The Purchase of Alaska," *American Historical Review*, XXV (1919–1920), 411–425. Some years later Thomas A. Bailey re-examined the problem in his "Why the United States Purchased Alaska," *Pacific Historical Review*, III (1934), 39–50. But the book-length accounts of the purchase are hardly satisfactory. Victor J. Farrar, *The Annexation of Russian America to the United States* (Washington, 1937) is a patchy narrative dominated by a recital of documents and dates. The centennial of the purchase, 1967, came and passed without a scholarly offering on the subject. The University of Alaska published a set of documents with commentary: Archie W. Shiels, *The Purchase of Alaska* (College, Alaska, 1967). Ronald J. Jensen of Indiana University is restudying the entire subject, in hope of a book which will set out the purchase in all its color, its propriety and impropriety.

For the Danish West Indies and the Dominican Republic it is helpful to consult W. B. Hesseltine, *Ulysses S. Grant: Politician* (New York, 1935), and then resort to the two monographs by Charles C. Tansill, *The Purchase of the Danish West Indies* (Baltimore, 1932) and *The United States and Santo Domingo: 1798–1873*.

The Geneva arbitration has been treated in detail in print, with use of manuscript sources, only by Allan Nevins's *Hamilton Fish: The Inner History of the Grant Administration* (New York, 1936). Canada, the hostage in the negotiation of the claims, appears in such volumes as Charles C. Tansill, *The Canadian Reciprocity Treaty of 1854* (Baltimore, 1922); Lester B. Shippee, *Canadian–American Relations: 1849–1874* (New Haven, 1939); Charles P. Stacey, "The Myth of the Unguarded Frontier, 1815–1871," *American Historical Review*, LVI (1950–1951), 1–18; and Donald F. Warner, *The Idea of Continental Union: Agitation for the Annexation of Canada to the United States, 1849–1893* (Lexington, Ky., 1960).

☆ **13** ☆

The New Manifest Destiny

God has not been preparing the English-speaking and Teutonic peoples for a thousand years for nothing but vain and idle self-admiration. No! He has made us the master organizers of the world to establish system where chaos reigns. . . . He has made us adepts in government that we may administer government among savages and senile peoples.
—Senator Albert J. Beveridge of Indiana, 1899

A new feeling of manifest destiny appeared in the United States at the end of the nineteenth century, and it opened an exciting epoch in the history of American foreign relations. This notion differed drastically from its mid-century predecessor, the belief that the United States was destined to extend territorially across the North American continent; according to the newly manifest destiny, America should take its jurisdiction overseas to noncontinental possessions in the Caribbean, Pacific, and Far East. With the purchase of Alaska and expulsion of the French from Mexico in the year 1867, the old spirit of manifest destiny had run out. The old interest in territorial expansion had spent itself by the end of the Civil War, and for thirty years afterward there were few moves of importance in American diplomacy. From the inauguration of President Grant in 1869 to the end of the second administration of Grover Cleveland in 1897, Americans were busy with many other things—this was the period of the emergence of modern America, of change from an agricultural to industrial economy, from rural life to city life. It marked the settlement of the West, the closing of the frontier. Issues of foreign affairs fell from sight. They were occasionally raised by officials in Washington, but only for purposes which smacked of domestic politics. "I have sometimes been inclined to think," Senator George F. Hoar of Massachusetts once remarked about this quiescent era, "that when you saw uncommon activity in our grave, reverend, and somewhat sleepy Committee on Foreign Relations . . . it was circumstantial evidence, not that there was any great trouble as to our foreign relations, but that a Presidential election was at hand." Even so, by the mid-1880's and early 1890's a change began to appear in popular and official sentiment. The period of economic growth was slacking off, the dire memories of 1861–1865 were disappearing, the sectional wounds were closing. There arose talk of overseas possessions, of a novel kind of manifest destiny. The Republican Party in 1892 pledged its belief in "the achievement of the manifest destiny of the republic in its broadest sense." The action to achieve this destiny, so solemnly avowed, in the late 1890's commenced a new chapter in the diplomacy of the United States.

The new manifest destiny differed in several ways from its predecessor. For one thing, it was virtually a carbon copy of the contemporary imperialism of European powers in Africa and Asia. There was, undeniably, an American imperialism at the end of the nineteenth century. The latter years of the nineteenth century were the heyday of European imperialism —Cecil Rhodes was consolidating large territories in Africa, Germany was sending colonists to the Cameroons and other places in Africa, and France in Africa and Asia was bringing millions of strange peoples under its rule. The territories that came to the United States as a result of the new manifest destiny brought several millions of alien peoples under American rule. Some of these peoples eventually became American citizens, but many never did.

Then too, in its peculiar philosophical roots the new manifest destiny stood apart from the old. The views of American destiny current at the time of the Mexican War derived from no philosophy in particular, but had come out of American experience, out of the long-dreamed-about destiny of the settlers of the New World, out of the ambitions of revolutionary patriots who thought that their republican experiment might well be destined to rule a continent. But the new manifest destiny could trace its origin to a distinct body of philosophical ideas, to the views of the so-called Darwinists. Darwinism was highly popular in America in the later nineteenth century. According to Darwinist beliefs the United States was a strong nation bound to extend its power over weaker nations, a national instance of what the biologists had found in the plant and animal kingdoms, natural selection, survival of the fittest.

Perhaps most noteworthy about this viewpoint was the essential intolerance of its advocates, their notion of American superiority argued from the biology of Darwin, which made the period of the new manifest destiny a saddening episode in American history. Ever since the foundation of the republic, and for a century and a half before that, the feeling had existed in America that in the New World all men were equal in rights if not in ability. The Western Hemisphere had a view of humanity different from that of Europe and Asia. Americans, so it was believed, had banded together to fight intolerance and superiority, so that everyone who wished could pursue his future in his own way. The apotheosis of this belief came during the Jacksonian era in the United States. Democracy thereafter seemed to rule supreme. To be sure, in the institution of Negro slavery Jackson's view of humanity carried within itself the seeds of its destruction, but the slavery incubus was destroyed in the Civil War. After 1865 Europeans and Asians alike began to become accustomed, as Americans long had been, to describing the United States as a model for governments everywhere. Then, at this very moment, the United States succumbed to the idea of American superiority, interpreted in Darwinian terms of natural selection. With this false view of themselves, preening themselves on their destiny, Americans in the last years of the nineteenth century began to look for overseas territory to conquer.

There were some similarities between the new manifest destiny and the old, especially the idea of expansion southward and northward, to Central and South America and to Canada. The mid-century expansionist enthusiasm had serious projects for Central America and the Caribbean and even sought to extend American influence as far into the Pacific as Japan. The drive, the zeal and missionary spirit, the feeling of necessity and inevitability, was present at the end of the nineteenth century as before. In this latter era John Hay found in the impulse to expand an indication of an irresistible cosmic tendency: "No man, no party, can fight with any chance of final success against a cosmic tendency; no cleverness, no popularity avails against the spirit of the age." There was little difference between this outlook of inevitability and the dogmatic assurance about the American future that marked the mid-century. Still, there were drastic differences between the old and new versions of manifest destiny which in sum were far more important than any similarities.

1. *The philosophy of the new manifest destiny*

The intellectual justification for the new manifest destiny began in the year 1859, just before the American Civil War, when Charles Darwin published his *On the Origin of Species,* which referred in its subtitle to *The Preservation of Favored Races in the Struggle for Life.* Its vocabulary included "natural selection," "survival of the fittest," and "struggle for existence." Darwin had been talking about pigeons, but there seemed no reason why his theories should not apply to human beings. Whatever the gap between Darwinian theories and their application by eager publicists who never read the scientist's words except at fourth- or fifth-hand, politics and diplomacy thenceforth had to live with the notion that life was a struggle in which the fittest survived. From this notion was derived a corollary, that success is an indication of fitness—that survival is, of necessity, fitness—and the secondary corollary that a nation which achieved the ordinary measurements of a great power (large military establishment, economic strength, population) was by this fact a fit nation, a chosen nation, qualified to instruct other and less successful nations in the facts of life. This, to be sure, was an erroneous doctrine. Survival, as anyone who observes the results of war can attest, does not always mean survival of the fittest: the fittest young men are those who go to war and are killed or wounded fighting the fittest young men of the other side. The political Darwinists also forgot or overlooked the phenomenon of mutual aid, to which man owes much of his survival and achievement: by helping each other the members of the human race have risen to wealth and to such security as they have. And the survival-of-the-fittest enthusiasts forgot that the cause of progress was not the struggle of man against man but the struggle of man against his environment. In the heat of the Darwinian dialectic these subtleties were lost from view. In the United States of the late nineteenth century, even those persons who rejected biological evolution often accepted without demur the necessity of the struggle of man against man, nation against nation; many individuals cheerfully confused the Christian religion with such beliefs and concluded that the American people, a successful people (and therefore a fit people), were a chosen people, God's anointed.

There thus seemed no reason to doubt the destiny of the United States. Americans basked in their own excellence. Even Darwin seems to have fallen under the spell of American success and in his 1871 work *The Descent of Man* wrote, "There is apparently much truth in the belief that the wonderful progress of the United States, as well as the character of the people, are the results of natural selection; the more energetic, restless, and courageous men from all parts of Europe having emigrated during the last ten or twelve generations to that great country . . . ."

From this feeling of American superiority came many vices, which cannot be recited here. One can only guess at how boorish and rude some Americans must have appeared to their contemporaries in other countries at the turn of the century. From available testimony it would seem that they possessed an obnoxious sense of mission, a misplaced zeal that to less successful peoples, peoples perhaps slated for imperial tutelage, made them appear patronizing, greedy, and vain. The traditional American idea that the United States had a mission in the world, a mission to spread to the corners of the earth the values of democracy, began to change into something markedly different: before the Civil War the usual statement of the doctrine of mission had been that the United States should be a witness, in confident but quiet modesty, for democratic principles; after the war the doctrine of mission changed from witnessing to proselytizing. The idea was that if backward peoples did not desire to learn about democratic principles, those principles would be thrust upon them.

The new manifest destiny—taking for its philosophy the Darwinian beliefs, giving a novel and unfortunate interpretation to the American idea of the mission of democracy—also encumbered itself with racism, with the idea of Anglo-Saxon or Aryan superiority. Like the American doctrine of mission, racism in the United States antedated Darwinism. Gobineau's *Essai sur l'Inégalité des Races Humaines* had appeared in 1853–1855 without using any of the Darwinian discoveries. Many Americans long had been convinced of the inferiority of the Indian and the Negro. Racist arguments had been heard at the time of the Mexican War. But racism became a respectable intellectual position after the Civil War when Americans learned the tenets of Darwinism. American scholars in the 1880's and 1890's, many of them fresh from German university seminars where they had imbibed German nationalism as taught by Heinrich von Treitschke and Leopold von Ranke, put forward ideas of racial superiority. When the first important American graduate school was established in Baltimore at Johns Hopkins University, Herbert Baxter Adams, the instructor of a group of brilliant graduate students which included the youthful Woodrow Wilson, advanced the thesis that all that was worthwhile in American and English government could be traced back in "germ" form to the tribal inhabitants of the Teutonic forests. The young Henry Adams, trained as a historian in this period, later wrote that "I flung myself obediently into the arms of the Anglo-Saxons in history." Such outstanding teachers as John W. Burgess of Columbia taught the primacy of the Anglo-Saxon race, the struggle for existence, the survival of the fittest. "Indifference on the part of Teutonic states to the political civilization of the rest of the world," Burgess announced, "is . . . not only mistaken policy, but disregard of duty." John Fiske, a Harvard-trained historian and philosopher, as early as 1880 gave a series of lectures in England to the effect that the dispersion over the world of the magnificent Aryan political system would eliminate war, and was the next step in world history.

Consider the effect of the writings and lectures of such an individual as Fiske, whose very name almost has been forgotten but whose ideas bore an enormous authority in the last years of the nineteenth century. For a short while Fiske was librarian of Harvard. He was not a regular member of the faculty of history, but he had the stamp of Harvard. He was an energetic and clever writer and speaker in an age of oratory and popular history. He believed in the Darwinian arrangements as if they were Holy Writ and spread the biologist's ideas all over the United States. A testimony to his popularity is that *The Works of John Fiske*, together or in single volumes, still crowd secondhand bookstores throughout the country. Any bibliophile examining a turn-of-the-century American personal library of any size, even a small library, will find at least one of Fiske's books. Their message was clear. In *The Destiny of Man Viewed in the Light of His Origin* (1884), which went through at least nineteen printings, Fiske wrote typically that the old, easy world of Biblical Creation was no more:

With the advent of the Copernican astronomy the funnel-shaped Inferno, the steep mountain of Purgatory crowned with its terrestrial paradise, and those concentric spheres of Heaven wherein beatified saints held weird and subtle converse, all went their way to the limbo prepared for the childlike fancies of untaught minds, whither Hades and Valhalla had gone before them. In our day it is hard to realize the startling effect of the discovery that Man does not dwell at the centre of things, but is the denizen of an obscure and tiny speck of cosmical matter quite invisible amid the innumerable throng of flaming suns that make up our galaxy.

What hope, then, for man? Was he only an infinitesimal speck living on an obscure, tiny, invisible speck? No, said Fiske! The individual who has

mastered the Darwinian theory, he who recognizes the slow and subtle process of evolution as the way in which God makes things come to pass, must take a far higher view. He sees that in the deadly struggle for existence which has raged throughout countless aeons of time, the whole creation has been groaning and travailing together in order to bring forth that last consummate specimen of God's handiwork, the Human Soul.

Fiske was a convincing philosopher—if his auditors and readers allowed themselves to be pulled along by his logic. He did not stop his intellectual discourses with the mere placing of man in infinity and the announcement of man's Human Soul. He disarmed his followers with side commentary about how it was possible for man to throw off the brute inheritance and to learn to live in accord with the dictates of Christianity. It would be possible, he believed, for the spark of divinity in men to ensure their immortality onward into the aeons of time. But the sublime thoughts with which he encased his theory were disguises for his essential racism. He catered to European and particularly Anglo-Saxon audiences. Fiske never would have proved a popular lecturer in the aboriginal Chautauqua circuits of, say, Australia. Consider the following passage about brain capacities which he inserted into his *Destiny of Man:*

As we pass to higher mammalian forms, the growth of the cerebrum becomes most conspicuous, until it extends backwards so far as to cover up the cerebellum, whose functions are limited to the conscious adjustment of muscular movements. In the higher apes the cerebrum begins to extend itself forwards, and this goes on in the human race. The cranial capacity of the European exceeds that of the Australian by forty cubic inches, or nearly four times as much as that by which the Australian exceeds the gorilla . . . .

Nor could Fiske have hoped for the plaudits of any such individuals as the present-day readers of the well-known book on child care and development by Dr. Benjamin Spock ("The cerebral surface of a human infant," Fiske wrote, "is like that of an ape"). Fiske was convinced that scholars, especially old scholars, were the best specimens of God's supreme handiwork, the Human Soul:

In an adult savage, or in a European peasant, the furrowing is somewhat marked and complicated. In the brain of a great scholar, the furrows are very deep and crooked, and hundreds of creases appear which are not found at all in the brains of ordinary men. In other words, the cerebral surface of such a man, the seat of conscious mental life, has become enormously enlarged in area; and we must further observe that it goes on enlarging in some cases into extreme old age.

That greatest exponent of the new manifest American destiny, Theodore Roosevelt, the individual who more than any other was the leader of American territorial expansion at the turn of the century, was as certain of the Darwinian truths as if he had discovered them himself. "TR" was verily a mirror to the Darwinian prejudices of his age. "I preach to you . . . my countrymen," he was saying in 1899, "that our country calls not for the life of ease but for the life of strenuous endeavor." Here was an activist manifestation of the idea of survival of the fittest. And again:

The timid man, the lazy man, the man who distrusts his country, the over-civilized man, who has lost the great fighting, masterful virtues, the ignorant man, and the man of dull mind, whose soul is incapable of feeling the mighty lift that thrills "stern men with empire in their brains"—all these, of course, shrink from seeing the nation undertake its new duties.

The typical Rooseveltian preachments against race suicide were the normal notions of a Darwinian enthusiast. Roosevelt believed that every

American family should have at least four children, and at Sagamore Hill he raised five. One could not have expected an individual like him to have had patience with such persons as Henry James who, wearied of the grosser tendencies of American life, sought refuge from the struggle for existence by emigrating to England. James once confessed to William Dean Howells that he had abandoned the "uniform, monotonous American scene" in order to "feast his eyes upon the more grateful arrangements of Europe." Roosevelt could not abide such ideas. James, he believed, was a "miserable little snob" whose "polished, pointless, uninteresting stories about the upper social classes in England" made "one blush to think he was once an American." Love of country was essential to the struggle for existence, Roosevelt maintained. Without it a nation sank into degeneracy and weakness, exposing itself to conquest by some virile enemy. Eventually TR thanked heaven that Henry James was "now an avowedly British novelist," for he was a "man in whom intense love of

Theodore Roosevelt was no man to agonize over decisions.

country is wanting . . . a very despicable creature, no matter how well equipped with all the minor virtues and graces, literary, artistic, and moral."

Many of the religious leaders of America were as enthusiastic about social Darwinism and its international corollary, the White Man's Burden, as were the political leaders and college teachers. A notable example was the Reverend Josiah Strong, who in 1885 published a small volume entitled *Our Country: Its Possible Future and Its Present Crisis*. This book sold 170,000 copies and was translated into many foreign languages. Something of an individualist and a believer in the social gospel, Strong was nevertheless against immigrants, Catholics, Mormons, saloons, tobacco, large cities, socialists, and concentrated wealth. In his writings he managed to combine these prejudices of rural Protestant America with a strong feeling of manifest destiny. *Our Country* was a diatribe for Anglo-Saxon and American supremacy in the world. The Anglo-Saxon people, he wrote, "is multiplying more rapidly than any other European race. It already owns one-third of the earth, and will get more as it grows. By 1980 the world Anglo-Saxon race should number at least 713,000,000. Since North America is much bigger than the little English isle, it will be the seat of Anglo-Saxondom." Was there room for doubt, he asked, that this wonderful Anglo-Saxon race, "unless devitalized by alcohol and tobacco, is destined to dispossess many weaker races, assimilate others, and mold the remainder, until, in a very true and important sense, it has Anglo-Saxonized mankind?" Strong saw the future expansion of America as not merely destiny already in part made manifest, but the desire of Almighty Providence, whose commandment was "Prepare ye the way of the Lord!" His was a powerful and typical voice in an era when in American colleges thousands of student volunteers for missionary service abroad were striving to realize the vision of the YMCA leader John R. Mott, "the evangelization of the world in this generation."

Some Americans, many in aggregate, unfortunately few in influence, opposed Darwinism and the new idea of manifest destiny, but their efforts were unsuccessful. And many of the Darwinists themselves, when faced with the results of their teaching, drew back and became anti-imperialists, opposing the war with Spain in 1898. John W. Burgess of Columbia, stout defender of Darwinism, took himself into the anti-imperialist camp in 1898, arguing that it would be "disastrous to American political civilization" to extend American authority over subject peoples. David Starr Jordan, president of Stanford University, a biologist and Darwinist, opposed imperialism as the wrong means to the right end. Jordan believed that the white race was superior to other races; he contended that the inequality of progress which could be seen among the many races of the world argued biological inequality; but he thought that to use force to advance American manifest destiny—as the United States did at the turn of the century—was degrading and would pull the race down toward the level of the conquered, inferior races.

Many Americans held variants of these views, and it would be inaccurate to argue that the new manifest destiny, with its intellectual justification of Darwinism, found acceptance everywhere. But it was difficult to stand against the supporters of the new manifest destiny, given the popularity of the Darwinian ideas. Some anti-imperialists tried to use the arguments of Darwinism to combat the new American foreign policy. Members of the Democratic Party (expansionism was strongest in the Republican Party) could not challenge openly the idea on which imperialism rested, Anglo-Saxon racial superiority, because this would be an uneasy topic in the American South. Southern Democrats, if anti-imperialist, chose to contend that annexation of overseas territories diluted American nationality by adding inferior island breeds.

It is a curious fact that Darwinism, the philosophy of the new manifest destiny, met its demise during the First World War, when the Germans advanced the idea of Teutonic superiority in support of their hegemony of Europe. It was ironical that American participation in the World War occurred just at the time when it proved necessary to discredit Darwinism, for the Darwinian ideas had extolled the virtues of such a military conflict as the United States entered in 1917.

2. The new American navy

It was under the impulse of the new sense of manifest destiny that there came an important development for American diplomacy in the 1880's and 1890's: the rejuvenation of the American navy. The appearance of the new navy at the end of the nineteenth century had a notable effect on diplomacy. It increased American stature abroad, making easier the tasks of the republic's diplomats. It also increased the belligerence of public opinion; Americans were proud of their navy, and it was no small factor in the outbreak of the war with Spain in 1898.

At the end of the Civil War, it is worth pointing out, the American navy was a powerful fleet, perhaps the most powerful in the world. It was certainly the largest. Secretary of the Navy Gideon Welles had bought up almost any ship that would float, and some that would not. The wartime navy comprised an odd assortment of a few regular navy ships, hasty new construction, together with merchant vessels and yachts. Occasionally there was a ship of quality, such as the *Monitor* so fortuitously on hand at Hampton Roads in 1862. Lesser ships did well enough if their commanders used some ingenuity. The quality of ships usually did not matter so long as there were enough vessels to blockade the major southern ports, and a few ships such as the *Monitor* for special missions. In terms of seamen afloat, and numbers of ships, the Union navy was enormously impressive in size, and if one counted the number of guns—that usual indicator of naval importance—it was similarly impressive.

Then came the end of the Civil War, and the end of the large Union navy. Within nine months of Appomattox, the auctioneer and the axe took care of this fleet, reducing the Civil War navy from 971 ships to 29.

In design these remaining ships were quickly outmoded by construction of new and far more formidable vessels by the navies of foreign powers. There had been a time in history, not far removed from 1865, when after a great war it was wise policy to do nothing with one's ships except lay up some of the vessels and keep the better ones seaworthy. Ship design changed slowly prior to the mid-nineteenth century. Nelson's flagship *Victory* had been laid down in 1759 and was as powerful in 1805 as at the time of her launching nearly half a century before. The year 1865, unfortunately, was a far different moment in the annals of naval construction, for there was in process a revolution in ship design. In truth, several revolutions were under way: introduction of the steam-driven warship; of the screw propellor; of rifled shell guns instead of smooth-bores and round shot; of armor plate; and of iron ships. The years from roughly 1855 to 1885 introduced the modern warship as we now know it; more changes occurred in this era than all the years before or since, in the entire span of centuries during which men have used the sea as a place of battle.

Take first of all the introduction of the steam warship. It is easy to see what steam meant for vessels which formerly had to depend upon the prevailing winds. A twentieth-century American usually believes that in the days of sailing ships it was possible to go easily almost everywhere. This belief was not true, for ships crossing large bodies of water such as the Atlantic Ocean had to follow the so-called trade routes where the winds were likely to be hospitable. Broad expanses of ocean were virtually unnavigable unless captains resorted to the slow and laborious device of tacking. Steam therefore opened huge ocean areas to practical navigation. And this was only one of its results. The historian Bernard Brodie has asked rhetorically what steam did to naval power. His answer was that it

completely revised the conditions governing naval tactics; it modified the whole geography of position and distance, thus profoundly affecting strategy; it enhanced the potential military power of industrialized states; and it injected the all-important factor of fuel into the problem of naval supplies, thus affecting the range of fleets and the strategic importance of stations abroad. In short, the steam warship was the most important development since the fifteenth century, when the discovery of the art of tacking inaugurated the era of the sailing ship.

For nearly forty years after steam propulsion became feasible for ships, the navies of the world were wary of it, because of the vulnerability of paddle wheels to gunfire. The inventor of the *Clermont*, Robert Fulton, had used steam for a strange vessel he designed during the War of 1812, the *Demologos*, or "Voice of the People," a remarkable ship, since among its virtues were hull walls almost five feet thick that made the vessel virtually impregnable to the ordnance of its day. A channel-way down the middle of the ship contained the paddle wheel, protected on all sides. The boiler was on one side and the engine on the other, both low in the hull. Most of the other working parts were below the main gun deck. Even so, the *Demologos* did not encourage construction of other steam warships, despite the increasingly rapid adoption of steam for commercial vessels. A ship like the *Demologos* had its awkwardnesses, and any ship built on the usual lines had the usual vulnerability: an opposing warship needed only to lob a shot into the wheels. The *Demologos* was the only steam warship in the American navy (not counting a little 100-ton steamer purchased in 1822) until it blew up in 1829. During the 1830's the French and British navies used some steamships, but naval men generally did not like "tea kettles" because of their vulnerability, preferring their old-time sloops, frigates, and ships of the line.

It must always seem odd that the obvious solution to the paddle-wheel problem, the screw propellor, did not make its appearance in a warship until 1843, when the United States navy, upon the persuasion of Captain Robert Stockton, launched the *Princeton* with a screw designed by the Swedish inventor John Ericsson, the later inventor of the *Monitor*. The American steam genius, Fulton, had put no trust in propellors, deeming the paddle wheel more worthy of experiment, despite the fact that the wheel's depth varied with the loading of a vessel and also worked against itself. Steam authorities even in England believed that it would be impossible to steer a ship with a screw propellor. Ericsson in 1836 installed a screw propellor on a barge and demonstrated it to four members of the British admiralty, but they deemed the idea impractical. The *Princeton*, that ill-fated ship on which Secretary of State Abel P. Upshur was killed during the accidental explosion of a cannon, and on which President Tyler escaped death narrowly, had the honor of being the first warship to use the device.

All the major navies of the world meanwhile had begun to experiment with new ordnance. A French artillery officer, Henri Joseph Paixhans, had published a treatise in 1822 recommending the use of shell guns on ships. They were employed in action in 1827 during the Greek war for independence. The shell gun was a naval commonplace by the time of the Civil War. Although an argument continued for some years as to whether solid shot might have better armor-piercing qualities, shells for that special purpose eventually appeared. The navies also developed the wrought-iron gun, rifling, the breech loader, slow-burning powders. Perhaps most important of all inventions in ordnance was the hooped or built-up gun, not an invention so much as rediscovery of a device abandoned three centuries earlier. In the built-up gun, the inner barrel was fortified by coils or cylinders which were shrunk on, giving the barrel a considerable compressive tension; it had much more resistance at the moment of explosion—that is, the explosion was less likely to expand the inner barrel beyond its elastic limits. Contrary to the behavior of so much of the ordnance of the nineteenth century, built-up guns seldom blew up in the faces of the men who served them. Without the built-up gun, armor quickly would have attained a complete impenetrability to gunfire.

Improved guns produced a contest with armor, which was in furious progress well before the fight between the *Merrimack* and the *Monitor*. The European powers by March 1862 had nearly a hundred ironclad vessels built or building.

Construction of iron ships assisted the solution of many problems of naval design, for the vessels of the middle and latter nineteenth century simply were beginning to be too full of complexities to fit into the relatively limited sizes possible for wooden vessels. The length of the great timbers, the natural growth of large trees, dictated the size of a wooden ship. It was possible to stretch out the timber size through such methods as "scarfing" (fitting timbers together) which produced a weaker frame. A ship launched by the British in 1859, the *Victoria*, of about 6,000 tons displacement, represented almost the maximum size possible for a wooden vessel. The building of the enormous iron-hulled merchant vessel *Great Eastern* between 1854 and 1858 demonstrated the feasibility of iron ships of huge dimensions. Architects thereby received much more room for their machinery, ordnance, and armor. The history of naval vessels for the next century would be the progress of ships toward ever greater size.

Steam, the screw propellor, new ordnance, armor plate, iron ships: these inventions created revolutions in warship design. In the twentieth century would come the submarine, the airplane, and the novel bombs and missiles of the present day.

What did all this, or at least the first five of the naval revolutions mentioned above, mean for the American navy after 1865? For almost twenty years it meant nothing. In the years immediately after the Civil War, American officers on countless occasions were embarrassed when foreign officers, boarding an American warship and observing the collection of marine antiquities and curios which made up the ship's armament and gear, acted as if they were visiting a museum and spoke sadly about the past. While other navies went from new vessel to new vessel there was even a retrograde movement in the American fleet, from steam to canvas. Some American sailing vessels during the Civil War had been equipped with auxiliary steam engines, but policy in the navy department afterward became so archaic that according to the navy regulations of 1870 no steam was to be used except when absolutely necessary. As a naval officer of that unhappy period reminisced many years later, "To burn coal was so grievous an offense in the eyes of the authorities that for years the coal-burning captain was obliged to enter in the logbook in *red ink* his reasons for getting up steam and starting the engines." The department also cautioned commanding officers using steam that if the department did not agree with the justification in any instance, they themselves might have to pay for the coal. Coal seemed so uncouth, so unseamanlike. After a day of coaling, the black dust was all over the ship. When a ship was steaming, smoke and soot covered the superstructure. And after everything was finished, and the sails up again, some poor devil or devils would have to clean out and empty the cinders from the firebox. Steam propulsion also created an esthetic problem, quite unassociated with dust and cinders. A smokestack did not look shipshape. It cluttered up the silhouette. The stacks of some ships had hinges at the deck, so they could be folded out of sight when the ships were in port. After 1865 the navy went doggedly downhill under the direction of such unimaginative officers as Admiral David D. Porter, who seems to have thought that steam had been invented in hell. The reactionary line officers determined to put the engineer officers in their places and managed to do so, virtually eliminating them. The technicians could not, so the old salts maintained, take over the navy.

When the line officers thought of any advanced type of ship at all, it was the Civil War monitor. Beyond this their horizons of design did not extend. As late as 1887 Admiral Porter was urging the repair of the aged and rotting single-turreted monitors of the war of 1861–1865, and he recommended construction of as many new monitors as cruisers, contending that vessels of the monitor type, properly equipped and handled, "would be a match for the heaviest European ironclad that could reach our shores." Admittedly the monitors had some political advantage, because they looked ferocious and lent assurance to the inhabitants of whatever port they happened to be in; their local presence could also reflect glory upon the local congressman who had arranged their stationing. As port defenders they were a joke, for their guns were not large enough to range out to the ships of any respectable attacking fleet, and those ships in turn would be able to bombard the port and the monitor from outside the American vessel's range.

It was thoughtful of Admiral Porter to recommend the stationing of his monitors in harbor, for they were notorious sailors on the high seas. Their freeboard was so low that in any kind of seaway their gun ports and the bases of their revolving turrets had to be caulked so tightly that if a monitor had met an opposing warship on the high seas it would have had, so to speak, to keep its mouth shut. Then the roll of the vessels was so quick, under three seconds, that it was impossible to sight a gun during the short interval. Worst of all, they had only about twenty percent reserve buoyancy, so that if they took on as little as one-fifth of their weight in water, they would turn turtle—just as the first *Monitor* had done after it left Hampden Roads. Any respectable war vessel had a reserve buoyancy of eighty per cent.

In the postwar days of the navy the *raison d'être* of naval appropriations was the maintenance of employment in the many local navy yards, in which individual congressmen always took keen interest. It did not matter what the yards did, so long as they did something and met the payrolls. The usual procedure was to tear down vessels after a few years and rebuild them from stem to stern, whether they needed it or not, whether the resulting reconstruction would improve their fighting qualities or leave them the same. The yards frequently rebuilt obsolescent vessels and downright impossible vessels (for war purposes). About the year 1880 someone decided that it was time to rebuild the *Omaha*, a wooden ship not worth keeping in the fleet. A half million dollars went into its overhaul, more than a new and modern ship of comparable type would have cost.

In rebuilding the poor *Omaha*, the navy carefully showed its deplorable lack of architectural judgment. Each of the various navy bureaus worked out solutions to its own problems aboard the *Omaha*, without concern for the ship's general welfare. When the *Omaha* at last put to sea in 1884 it had only room enough for coal for four days' steaming. Frightful mistakes were made in the yards, with the presumably full guidance of the navy department. When the *Maine*, that ill-fated ship, was built in the 1880's, no one thought to consider how it might lie in the water when fully loaded. The stores at last were put aboard, and it was discovered that the loading plans were rather in error, because the ship drew three feet more water forward than aft. Forty-eight tons of ballast installed near the stern straightened it up.

The American navy had too many officers, and some wag said it was easier to lay up a ship than an admiral. The Americans could boast 1,473 officers, whereas the British navy with a fleet of 341 ships had 2,571 officers. The navy was laughed at because ships were crowded with officers so that they might get their sea pay. Promotion also depended strictly upon length of service (much like the salary schedules of American high school teachers). Any officer apparently could become an admiral if his state of health permitted him to live long enough. One commanding officer who managed to run his ship aground three times in a brief passage from Annapolis to the sea attained the rank of rear admiral.

Congressman (later President) James A. Garfield remarked in a celebrated speech of 1878 in the House of Representatives: "Our fathers said: 'Though we will use the taxing power to maintain a small Army and Navy sufficient to keep alive the knowledge of war, yet the main reliance for our defense shall be the intelligence, culture, and skill of our people.'"

The navy's officers of the line unfortunately were subject to no instruction from the secretaries of the navy, who might have interrupted the peace of the navy department in Washington and made some changes for the good of the service. This the succession of political secretaries did not do, either from indifference or gross incompetence or ignorance, perhaps the latter more than anything else. It was alleged of Rutherford B. Hayes's secretary of the Navy, Richard W. Thompson of Indiana, that he was so densely ignorant of naval affairs as to express surprise upon learning that ships were hollow.

Some realization of the antiquity of the post-Civil War fleet occurred when, during a minor crisis with Spain over capture of a filibuster ship off Cuba, the navy engaged in fleet maneuvers in the Gulf early in 1874. The appearance there of the American navy—the "heterogeneous collection of naval trash," of "antiquated and rotting ships"—shook the morale of the entire service. But the turning point in the navy came with the short-lived administration of President Garfield in 1881, when it was suddenly realized in connection with a minor Latin American war that the republic of Chile had a better navy than the United States. The assertion was made, with some justification, that a ship of the Chilean navy could have destroyed the entire United States fleet. Apropos this petty Latin American conflict it was rumored that "when Admiral Balch undertook to make some kindly suggestions . . . the Chileans simply told the American admiral, and the American government through him, that if he did not mind his own business, they would send him and his fleet to the bottom of the ocean."

This sort of provocation, if it never happened, was a possibility, and

American pride simply could not stand the thought of a Chilean ship sinking an entire fleet and its admiral with it. There also was fear of blockade of American ports, in event of some unforeseen war, and in such a case millions of dollars would have been lost if the blockade had lasted as long as a week. It seemed good business to pay a little money in advance and have a navy. There was fear, too, of a large indemnity that might be enforced by a victorious enemy nation, such as France after 1871 had to pay to Germany. Worries such as these were intensified with the British bombardment of Alexandria in 1882, when the 80-ton British naval guns pounded the Egyptian fortifications to pieces. An American vessel, the *Lancaster*, stood on the sidelines, carrying sail and armed with smoothbore guns. If British warships, so Americans began to say, could operate from Malta, then they could operate from Halifax or Jamaica; and if the continental United States were not in danger, how about Panama, considering that the British had taken Suez? Canada was deepening and widening the Welland canal, ostensibly to enable larger merchant vessels to reach the Great Lakes, but perhaps to let in the British fleet? Only a forty-year-old sidewheeler, the *Michigan*, stood guard along the lake frontier—in accord with the Rush-Bagot Agreement (1817) which had limited naval armaments by both parties on the Great Lakes to a number and size of ships barely adequate for customs regulation. About this time the U.S.S. *Tallapoosa*, a warship in the American fleet, was run down by a coal barge. It seemed as if something had to be done about the condition of the United States navy. The combination of events and fears and humiliation led in 1883 during the administration of President Chester A. Arthur to an act of Congress providing for three small "protected" cruisers and a dispatch boat, the first step toward a new American navy.

The act of 1883 was a beginning, and more new construction swiftly followed. The vessels appropriated in 1883, completed in 1885 and 1887 and known as the White Squadron, much admired by the American public, proved rather unsatisfactory. In addition to their engines all of them carried full sail rigs. They had no side armor (in the terminology of the day they were not armored; their deck armor categorized them merely as protected), and they were vulnerable to any armored ship able to catch up with them. In speed they were soon outdistanced by foreign construction. And it was belatedly recognized that commerce destroyers, in the old American tradition, were no longer feasible for the United States in an age when steam vessels required numerous coaling stations to operate outside coastal waters. During the first Cleveland administration of 1885–1889, the White Squadron gave way, on the designing boards and in appropriation for construction, to new vessels aggregating nearly 100,000 tons. The ships authorized under Cleveland included the famous

Maine, a typical battleship of its day, displacing less than 7,000 tons, with maximum speed of less than 18 knots, carrying four ten-inch guns. Still, the very year it was launched, 1890, marked its assignment to a second rank in the new American navy, for in the naval act of 1890 Congress made appropriation for first-class—that is, high seas—battleships. This program resulted in some famous vessels including the battleships *Indiana*, *Massachusetts*, and *Oregon*. The *Oregon* class displaced about 10,000 tons, had a speed of 15.5 to 17 knots, was armed with four 13-inch and eight 8-inch pieces, and cost between $5,500,000 and $6,500,000. The *Oregon*, incidentally, became one of the best known ships ever to serve in the American navy and had a long and gallant career of over sixty years—the ship rounded the Horn in 1898 from Pacific to Atlantic to help blockade the Spanish fleet at Santiago, served in the First and Second World Wars, and finally was sold to a Japanese firm and broken up for junk in the year 1957.

With the battleship appropriation of 1890 the United States at last gave up its ideas of a navy of commerce raiders. It set out to construct a battle fleet capable of opposing the greatest ships of the world. The American public at first did not realize this, and until the end of the decade—the naval act of 1900 was the first exception to this rule—it proved wise policy to designate the new battleships as "seagoing coast-line battleships."

USS *Oregon*.

The navy was building, and the appropriation of 1890 was passing through Congress, when a book appeared by Captain Alfred Thayer Mahan, *The Influence of Sea Power upon History*, which in its effect upon history was as important as that other fateful nineteenth-century opus, *On the Origin of Species*.

The author of this seminal volume on the importance of sea power was by the time of its publication a middle-aged career naval officer, an unlikely candidate for what he soon became—the oracle of naval strategy throughout the world. The parallel between his career and that of the present-day diplomatic historian George F. Kennan is remarkable. Like Mahan, Kennan spent a quarter century of his life as a fairly subordinate official before he too began to publish best-selling books about history. Mahan's forebears had included the Colonel Sylvanus Thayer who was one of the founders of the Military Academy at West Point. The future naval strategist graduated from Annapolis in time to take part in the Civil War, and his first book was a little-known work published in 1883 entitled *The Gulf and Inland Waters*, the third volume of a history of the navy during the war of 1861–1865. In the dull postwar years Mahan spent much time afloat. In no sense was he the "swivel-chair admiral" which the late

Captain Alfred Thayer Mahan.

historian Charles A. Beard once described in a notable book about American history. He served in the Far East for a while. Indeed his duties took him all over the world, to South America and Africa and Europe. He had the good luck to be in Paris during the last days of the Second Empire and was in Rome when the temporal power of the papacy came to an end. The distinguished historian of American intellectual history, Ralph H. Gabriel, has written that "He had, as a result of professional duty and of good fortune, such a world view as was to be found in post-Appomattox America only among the students who had returned from graduate study abroad." This was the man who commenced his academic studies in earnest in 1884 when Rear Admiral Stephen B. Luce obtained his appointment to the new Naval War College at Newport. At that time Mahan was an avowed anti-imperialist. His studies converted him to imperialism. He had finished the book by September 1886, except for its summary pages, and was giving it in the form of lectures at the college.

The Influence of Sea Power upon History contained a message of extreme clarity, easily understandable to hasty readers who needed only to peruse the first and final chapters and not wade through the book's technical middle sections. Mahan taught that naval power was the key to national greatness. He said that nations may rise or decline but never stand still, that expansion was essential, that to support expansion a government must have access to accumulated wealth, that a large and flourishing foreign commerce was the best means of accumulating wealth, that a navy was necessary to secure and ensure foreign commerce, and that a navy required colonies for coaling stations. Mahan had generalized his theories from the rise of England and the British navy, and *The Influence of Sea Power upon History* dealt with the history of English sea power from 1660 to 1783. He put into a coherent philosophy the strategic principles which the British admiralty had been pursuing almost blindly for over two hundred years. In the year 1890 the world power of Great Britain had not yet been challenged and stood at its zenith; Mahan's message about its origins and progress was the more convincing because of this fact. Without command of the seas, Mahan argued, no nation could attain the fullest measure of internal well-being, or the greatest influence in world affairs.

What might prevent a naval power from overexerting its authority, taking advantage of weaker nations? Mahan believed that Providence somehow would teach the great naval powers to use their power for righteous ends. The balance of power he deemed equivalent to the necessary moral freedom of individuals. He believed in the natural balance of forces among competing nations, an international counterpart of the doctrine of laissez faire for domestic economies—free competition in the open market.

In retrospect it is easy to see that Mahan's sea-power doctrines did not explain many historical facts and caricatured others. Mahan failed to recognize the uniqueness of Britain's historical position athwart the chief western entrances to the continent of Europe, the island empire possessing as well such strategic places as Gibraltar, Malta, Alexandria, Singapore, the Falklands, and (after the Boer War of 1899–1902) the Cape of Good Hope. Mahan underestimated the importance of non-naval factors in Britain's rise to world power, such as the coming of the industrial revolution to England a half-century before it spread to other countries. His teachings largely ignored the circumstances of the late nineteenth century, when a great power required many more accoutrements than a large and powerful navy.

And his vision of free competition in the international power market did not extend into the power-mad twentieth century. Mahan died in December 1914. In the two world wars of the first half of the twentieth century the American navy fortunately would find itself allied with the navy of Great Britain, but the Germans and Japanese, following only too well the dogmas of Mahan, gave serious international trouble. German determination to best the British navy was one of the several leading causes of the First World War. Admiral Alfred von Tirpitz cited Mahan to the effect that a great power needed a large navy but overlooked the fact that a navy for Germany was a luxury, whereas for the inhabitants of the British Isles it was a necessity. When after the German defeat a young lieutenant in 1919 was browsing through the former Kaiser's books in the library at Potsdam, he came on a fully marked-up copy of Mahan's *Influence of Sea Power upon History*, annotated in the hand of William II. The futile Battle of Jutland, when the Germans in 1916 bested the British Home Fleet but failed to alter the strategic naval balance, was one of the results of Mahan's teachings. When the British commanders on that fog-bound afternoon espied the low and faraway silhouettes of the German ships and soon saw the rippling flashes of great guns followed seconds later with the deathly, thunderous booming, it was Mahan come to judgment. The sudden conversion of great British battle cruisers into orange sheets of flame, and miles-high pillars of smoke, marked the deaths of thousands of seamen in a futile naval contest. Mahan had foretold that the contest for world supremacy would be fought out at sea. In the actual event, the contest was fought out in northern France.

As for the Japanese navy, it too learned the supposed lessons of Mahan, and at enormous cost unlearned them.

Mahan was not an original thinker but gathered together in brilliant scholarly form the leading ideas of his time. The later Italian theorist of air power, General Emilio Douhet, was an original thinker. It did not seem to matter, for the theory of population bombing advanced by Douhet proved even more humanly devastating and more strategically erroneous than the theory of sea power.

Mahan's major impulse probably was to produce an argument for more naval construction. He did so at the propitious moment. "It was not that what he said was profound," Walter Millis has written,

but that he had the luck to say it at a moment in history when countless prosperous and influential persons were looking for precisely this justification for courses which they wished for their own reasons to pursue. Mahan taught that sea power, in and of itself, was a good in peace or war; and in so doing he tossed an apple of discord into the affairs of nations for which there was to be no lack of ambitious contenders.

Navalism, one also should emphasize, was not so much the result of Mahan's writings, however convincing they were, or of the naval or commercial or political tendencies of his era. It came from something deeper, for it grew out of the fateful philosophy of the time, Darwinism, the feeling that life was a race and that the rewards fell to the fittest. In America Mahan's book was one of the major works in support of the new manifest destiny.

A CONTEMPORARY DOCUMENT

[The humorist Finley Peter Dunne invented an Irishman, Martin Dooley, whose place of business was a saloon on Archey Road in the city of Chicago. A doctor of philosophy, and also "traveller, archaeologist, historian, social observer, . . . economist," Dooley was accustomed to converse with his friend Mr. Hennessy. As Dunne put it, Dooley "observes the passing show, and meditates thereon. His impressions are transferred to the desensitized plate of Mr. Hennessy's mind, where they can do no harm." "There's no betther place to see what's goin' on thin the Ar-rchey Road," said Mr. Dooley. "Whin th' ilicthric cars is hummin' down th' sthreet an' th' blast goin' sthrong at th' mills, th' noise is that gr-reat ye can't think." Dooley, according to his inventor, Dunne, refused to go into politics—he "resolutely declined to leave the bar for the forum." That did not prevent him from commenting on political questions. Shortly after the end of the Spanish-American War, Dooley turned his inquiring mind to the problem of the Anglo-Saxons, an issue which apparently bothered him. Source: Finley Peter Dunne, *Mr. Dooley: In Peace and in War*

(Boston, 1899), pp. 53–56.]

"Well," said Mr. Dooley, "I see be th' pa-apers that th' snow-white pigeon iv peace have tied up th' dogs iv war. It's all over now. All we've got to do is to arrest th' pathrites an' make th' reconcentradios pay th' stamp tax, an' be r-ready f'r to take a punch at Germany or France or Rooshia or anny counthry on th' face iv th' globe.

"An' I'm glad iv it. This war, Hinnissy, has been a gr-reat sthrain on me. To think iv th' suffrin' I've endured! F'r weeks I lay awake at nights fearin' that th' Spanish ar-rmadillo'd lave the Cape Verde Islands, where it wasn't, an' take th' thrain out here, an' hur-rl death an' desthruction into me little store. Day be day th' pitiless exthries come out an' beat down on me. Ye hear iv Teddy Rosenfelt plungin' into ambus-cades an' Sicrity iv Wars; but d'ye hear iv Martin Dooley, th' man behind th' guns, four thousan' miles behind thim, an' willin' to be further? They ar-re no bokays f'r me. I'm what Hogan calls wan iv th' mute, ingloryous heroes iv th' war; an' not so dam mute, ayther. Some day, Hinnissy, justice'll be done me, an' th' likes iv me; an', whin th' story iv a gr-reat battle is written, they'll print th' kilt, th' wounded, th' missin', an' th' seryously disturbed. An' thim that have bore thimsilves well an' bravely an' paid th' taxes an' faced th' deadly newspa-apers without flinchin' 'll be advanced six pints an 'given a chanst to tur-rn jack f'r th' game.

"But me wurruk ain't over jus' because Mack [President Mc-Kinley] has inded th' war an' Teddy Rosenfelt is comin' home to bite th' Sicrety iv War. You an' me, Hinnissy, has got to bring on this here Anglo-Saxon 'lieance. An Anglo-Saxon, Hinnissy, is a German that's forgot who was his parents. They're a lot iv thim in this counthry. There must be as manny as two in Boston: they'se wan up in Maine, an' another lives at Bogg's Ferry in New York State, an' dhrives a milk wagon. Mack is an Anglo-Saxon. His folks come fr'm th' County Armagh, an' their naytional Anglo-Saxon hymn is 'O'Donnell Aboo.' Teddy Rosenfelt is another Anglo-Saxon. An' I'm an Anglo-Saxon. I'm wan iv th' hottest Anglo-Saxons that 'iver come out iv Anglo-Saxony. Th' name iv Dooley has been th' proudest Anglo-Saxon name in th' County Roscommon f'r many years.

"Schwartzmeister is an Anglo-Saxon, but he doesn't know it, an' won't till some wan tells him. Pether Bowbeen down be th' Frinch church is formin' th' Circle Francaize Anglo-Saxon club, an' me ol' frind Dominigo that used to boss th' Ar-rchey R-road wagon whin Callaghan had th' sthreet conthract will march at th' head iv th' Dago Anglo-Saxons whin th' time comes. There ar-re twinty thousan' Rooshian Jews at a quarther a vote in th' Sivinth Ward; an', ar-rmed with rag hooks, they'd be a tur-r-ble thing f'r anny inimy iv th' Anglo-Saxon 'lieance to face. Th' Bohemians an' Pole Anglo-Saxons may be a little slow in wakin' up to what th' pa-apers calls our common hurtage, but ye may be sure they'll be all r-right whin they're called on. We've got together an Anglo-Saxon 'lieance in this wa-ard, an' we're goin' to ilict Sarsfield O'Brien presidint, Hugh O'Neill Darsey vice-prisidint, Robert Immitt Clancy sicrety, an' Wolfe Tone Malone three-asurer. O'Brien'll be a good wan to have. He was in the Fenian r-raid, an' his father carrid a pike in forty-eight. An' he's in th' Clan. Besides, he has a sthrong pull with th' Ancient Ordher iv Anglo-Saxon Hibernyans.

"I tell ye, whin th' Clan an' th' Sons iv Sweden an' th' Banana Club an' th' Circle Francaize an' th' Pollacky Benivolent Society an' th' Rooshian Sons of Dinnymite an' the' Benny Brith an' th' Coffee Clutch that Schwartzmeister r-runs an' th' Tur-rnd'ye-mind an' th' Holland society an' th' Afro-Americans an' th' other Anglo-Saxons begin f'r to raise their Anglo-Saxon battlecry, it'll be all day with th' eight or nine people in th' wurruld that has th' misfortune iv not bein' brought up Anglo-Saxons." . . .

ADDITIONAL READING

The best introductions to the new manifest destiny appear in chapters in Ralph H. Gabriel, *The Course of American Democratic Thought* (rev. ed., New York, 1961); *Richard Hofstadter, *Social Darwinism in American Thought: 1860–1915* (Philadelphia, 1944); the first chapter of *Julius W. Pratt's *Expansionists of 1898* (Baltimore, 1936); and especially Ernest R. May, *American Imperialism: A Speculative Essay* (New York, 1968). See also Bert J. Loewenberg, "Darwinism Comes to America," *Mississippi Valley Historical Review*, XXVIII (1941), 339–369. There are pertinent sections in *Henry Steele Commager, *The American Mind: An Interpretation of American Thought and Character since the 1880's* (New Haven, 1950); Edward McNall Burns, *The American Idea of Mission: Concepts of National Purpose and Destiny* (New Brunswick, N.J., 1957); and Russel B. Nye, *This Almost Chosen People: Essays in the History of American Ideas* (East Lansing, Mich., 1966). Examples of the literature of the time are Josiah Strong, *Our Country* (New York, 1885) and John W. Burgess, *Political Science and Comparative Constitutional Law* (2 vols., Boston, 1890). A challenge to the new ideas of manifest destiny is Ralph Barton Perry, *The Present Conflict of Ideals* (New York, 1918), a volume inspired by the World War and Germany's bid for leadership. Robert L. Beisner, *Twelve Against Empire: The Anti-Imperialists, 1898–1900* (New York, 1968) sets out the view of selected protesters. For the new navy see first of all the general account in Harold and Margaret Sprout, *The Rise of American Naval Power: 1776–1918* (Princeton, 1939). Historical and technical background can be found in Samuel Eliot Morison, *"Old Bruin"* (Boston, 1967) for Commodore Perry's contribution to the new navy; James Phinney Baxter III, *The Introduction of the Ironclad Warship* (Cambridge, Mass., 1933); John A. S. Grenville and George B. Young, *Politics, Strategy, and American Diplomacy: Studies in Foreign Policy, 1873–1917* (New Haven, 1966), which has an opening chapter on Admiral Stephen B. Luce; David M. Pletcher, *The Awkward Years: American Foreign Relations under Garfield and Arthur* (Columbia, Mo., 1961); Daniel J. Garrison, *The Navy from Wood to Steel: 1860–1890* (New York, 1962), a volume in the Watts Histories of the U.S. Navy; Brayton Harris, *The Age of the Battleship: 1890–1922* (New York, 1965), a very able volume, one of the Watts Histories; Walter R. Herrick, *The American Naval Revolution* (Baton Rouge, La., 1966); Gordon C. O'Gara, *Theodore Roosevelt and the Rise of the Modern American Navy* (Princeton, 1943). See also William E. Livezey, *Mahan on Sea Power* (Norman, Okla., 1947). A thoughtful view of Mahan is Julius W. Pratt, "Alfred Thayer Mahan," in William T. Hutchinson, ed., *The Marcus W. Jernegan Essays in American Historiography* (Chicago, 1937). Consult Mahan's **The Influence of Sea Power upon History: 1660–1783* (Boston, 1890), and also his magazine articles written in the 1890's and after, which were collected and published every two or three years under various titles. W. D. Puleston, *Mahan* (New Haven, 1939) is the best biography. See also such accounts as Robley D. Evans, *A Sailor's Log* (New York, 1901) and Edwin A. Falk, *Fighting Bob Evans* (New York, 1931).

☆ 14 ☆

New Opportunities

Today the United States is practically sovereign on this continent, and its fiat is law upon the subjects to which it confines its interposition.
—Secretary of State Richard Olney, 1895

Americans in the last years of the nineteenth century began looking outside the continental United States for coaling stations and colonies. Alfred Thayer Mahan in his book published in 1890 said that such territorial holdings were necessary for a great nation. During the successive administrations of Presidents Grover Cleveland (first term, 1885–1889), Benjamin Harrison (1889–1893), Cleveland again (second term, 1893–1897), and William McKinley, the proponents of the new manifest destiny moved out of the realm of theory and into that of action, first pressing their program in diplomatic crises over Samoa and Hawaii, Chile and Venezuela, and ultimately in 1898 in the Spanish-American War.

1. *Samoa and Hawaii*

It is of interest that the American involvement in the first of these outlandish places, Samoa, had commenced long before the era of the new manifest destiny, indeed during the sunset era of the old manifest destiny. An American naval officer had negotiated a treaty with Samoan native chieftains in 1872. The treaty failed in the Senate, but President Grant next year dispatched a special agent, Colonel A. B. Steinberger, who set himself up as premier of the islands. This American adventurer might have succeeded but for the quick action of a British naval officer, supported by English missionaries. The American government arranged in 1878 for rights to a naval station at Pago Pago. All this at the time when

357

expansionism apparently was over—when the purchase of Alaska and the expulsion of the French forces from Mexico marked a closing of the old chapter of manifest destiny. Perhaps the American people as a whole were not aware of what agents of their government were doing in the South Seas, adjusting the politics of the little group of islands named the Samoas which aggregated scarcely a thousand square miles set down in a vast waste of the Pacific Ocean.

Apart from these Samoan contacts by the government in Washington, not much happened until the mid-1880's, when a new sense of manifest destiny, keyed by its strident philosophy of Darwinism, began once more to rouse American territorial instincts. For fifteen years and more after the events of 1867, hardly a territorial project (save President Grant's abortive scheme for the Dominican Republic) disturbed the surface of foreign affairs. The Treaty of Washington of 1871 and the Geneva arbitration of the next year were important diplomatic events and, in a real sense, exhibitions of manifest destiny; but both were mainly results of the Civil War rather than novel moves of American policy. It was not until the first administration of Cleveland that the Samoas began to be talked about by the American public and entered into the larger arrangements of policy.

Cleveland's secretary of state, Thomas F. Bayard, took great interest in diplomacy concerning Samoa. He got himself into an involved politique with the governments of Great Britain and Germany, in which he unfortunately failed to understand how events in Samoa bore an intimate relation to events in Europe. He failed to understand the nature of German interest in colonial projects, a late interest which was becoming pressing by the mid-1880's. Under the guidance of the "iron chancellor," Prince Otto von Bismarck, the Germans at first had shown no interest in colonies. Bismarck had encouraged the French government, after its defeat in the Franco-Prussian War of 1870–1871, to pursue colonial projects, in the hope that the French would take their energies outside Europe and not bother his own projects for the Continent. The French were vastly unhappy about their defeat in the war, and Bismarck wanted them out of the European political front yard; better, he thought, to get them into the colonial back yard. But the mere sight of the French republic adding territories in Africa and Asia, coloring the map of the world with green, the French imperial color, at last began to make colonies attractive to the German government and people. By the mid-1880's Bismarck's Germany began to seek out colonial territories. It was almost too late. The search became frantic, because the French and the British (the British map color was red) had colored almost all the best pieces of territory in Africa and Asia. In the 1860's a private firm, J. C. Godeffroy of Hamburg, had gained valuable land and shipping interests in Samoa. Hence the German political interest in the mid-1880's in an otherwise inconsequential island group which a decade earlier would have attracted no attention from anyone except a few ambitious American agents.

Bayard's diplomacy toward Samoa suffered from the secretary's inability to understand the German colonial frustration, and also from the diplomatic deal which the British and Germans had worked out between themselves about this time, to the disadvantage of American interests in Samoa. The British had gone into Egypt in 1882 in the so-called "temporary" occupation which was to last until 1956, and they were embarrassed in their Egyptian enterprise because of lack of sanction by what they themselves considered throughout the nineteenth century to be the major political authority of Europe, the concert of Europe, as it was known after the Congress of Vienna of 1814–1815. The act of Prince Gorchakov in 1870, in unilaterally abrogating the Black Sea clauses of the Treaty of Paris of 1856 following the Crimean War, had greatly affronted Prime Minister Gladstone, who felt that such an act was the business of the concert of Europe, and that Gorchakov had indulged in an illegality. Although not too much later the British themselves found their interest in the Suez canal so important that they occupied Egypt, they believed that they needed the sanction of the other great European powers for this act. In 1884 the concert of Europe met at Berlin in a conference over the governance of the Congo. At this conference the British and German representatives made a quiet agreement between themselves that in return for German recognition of British rule in Egypt the British government would show a benevolent passivity toward German projects in equatorial Africa and the South Seas. Bismarck then sought a protectorate in Samoa.

After the British-German agreement, the Samoan kettle began to boil. The Samoans knew they were in trouble, and began to appeal to the New Zealanders against what they considered the cupidity of the Germans and the disinterest of both the British and the Americans. The New Zealanders were willing to take the islands but needed the sanction of the London government which, of course, they could not get. The Germans thereupon set to work and harried the Samoan king, Malietoa, for showing too much sympathy toward New Zealand. Word was received in Washington in January 1886 that the German consul at Apia had hauled down the Samoan flag and raised the German flag. The Germans meanwhile had set up their own man, Tamasese, as potentate.

Matters arrived at a state of some complexity when the local representative of the United States, Consul Greenebaum, interpreted his instructions with extreme liberality, and on appeal from the ex-king, Malietoa, Greenebaum raised the American flag.

By this time Samoan politics were too complicated for the local people to handle. After Britain and Germany decided to send a two-power commission to investigate matters, Bayard insisted on American participation. The secretary convened a conference in Washington in 1887 to settle affairs on the basis of the commissioners' reports (the Germans had refused to allow a joint report) and discovered he could get nowhere. The Germans and British previously had agreed on German preponderance in Samoa.

Unable to budge Bayard, who insisted on keeping Samoa neutral and independent, the Germans set out to arrange the situation unilaterally. They deported Malietoa for his "crimes" against Germany and gave their king, Tamasese, a German military adviser named Brandeis. After a few months the Samoans flocked to a new champion, Mataafa, who led them against Germany's puppet. By late 1888 the German consul at Apia had so far mismanaged the affair that he tried to impose martial law to halt arms sales to Mataafa, an effort which affected the British and Americans. Although American nationals had less than $100,000 invested in Samoa, and only two or three businesses there, Bayard decided to take a stand. He dispatched three warships and an admiral to Samoa. Coming too late in the Cleveland administration, the move brought neither political nor diplomatic benefit. Disaster came in the form of a hurricane which in March 1889 wiped out the German and American naval forces.

Seeing the trend of his efforts in Samoa, Bismarck meanwhile had resigned himself to a tripartite settlement, and a new three-power conference was arranged to meet in Berlin early in 1889. The Cleveland administration was about to give way to that of Benjamin Harrison, and Bayard's designated successor, James G. Blaine, the "plumed knight," as his followers in American politics described him, studied up on Samoa. Mrs. Blaine, who invariably reflected her husband's interests, wrote on February 10, 1889, to one of her children: "Now your father is reading aloud Samoa to Walker [Blaine's son, who was to become assistant secretary of state], and my thoughts diverge to Malietoa." And a day later: "Your father is now looking up Samoa on the map. It would be worth your while, if you have not already done so, to read up Samoa." Blaine took the matter seriously, and by the time he was ready to write the instructions to the American commissioners to the Berlin Conference he had a grasp of the question, at least the ins and outs of the local politics, if not of the high politics of Europe. The conference met late in April 1889, and after sessions of six weeks—a considerable conversation on Samoa, one must say—reached an agreement in the form of a general act, declaratory of the views and purposes of the three powers. The signatories ratified this agreement, and it received the assent of the native regime in Samoa.

The arrangement of 1889 eventually proved unsatisfactory, and a decade later the three powers signed a treaty in Berlin on December 2, 1899, which partitioned the Samoas. The reasons for partition were complicated. The three-power protectorate established in 1889 had restored Malietoa. But it had virtually taken political power away from the Samoans, leaving the natives with the shadow of self-government. The two newcomers to world power, Germany and the United States, wished sole ownership of territory in the Samoas. It seemed better to tidy up affairs in the Samoas by dividing the islands rather than by a condominium. Britain apparently was indifferent to the political fate of the islands and began to think of the Boer War, which commenced in South Africa on October 12, 1899—although pressure from New Zealand, where the Samoan question seemed more important, may have moved the British also in the direction of a partition. By the treaty of 1899 Germany received the two largest islands, and the United States obtained several islands, including Tutuila with its harbor of Pago Pago. Britain received from Germany a compensation in the form of the Tonga Islands, located just south of the Samoas, together with part of the Solomon Islands and some adjustments in West Africa. All this complication over the Samoas serves to indicate the nature of international dealing in the age of imperialism. The German gains from this bargaining disappeared in 1914 at the beginning of the First World War when New Zealand forces occupied the German Samoas.

In the Pacific area the territorial cupidity of Americans during this era extended to another island group, the Hawaiians, and in the 1890's a crisis over the government and territory of Hawaii led by the end of the decade to annexation.

It was largely Hawaiian sugar which produced the series of events leading to the final planting of the American flag upon the islands—to inclusion of the islands in the maps of the day, their ownership identifiable from the American map color which, inappropriately, was yellow. American interest in Hawaii had appeared early in the nineteenth century, after a group of missionaries journeyed to Oahu and undertook to convert the natives to Christianity. The sons and grandsons of this missionary group gained economic control of the islands, and their development of sugar plantations linked the Hawaiian economy to that of the United States. The raising of sugar was no large industry in the islands until arrangements were made to offer this sugar in the American market. Secretary of State Seward negotiated a treaty with the Hawaiian monarchy in 1867 which he hoped would be a preliminary to annexation, but the Senate finally got around to the treaty in 1870 and rejected it. Another treaty in 1875 admitted Hawaiian sugar into the United States duty-free, giving the islanders an advantage of nearly two cents a pound over other foreign producers. It was this treaty which so encouraged sugar growing. Before 1875 sugar had been mainly a home industry. After 1875, American speculators formed corporations and imported thousands of Chinese and Japanese laborers, radically changing the economy of the islands. By the turn of the century Hawaii had a polyglot population of approximately 40,000 Hawaiians and half-castes, nearly 30,000 Chinese and Japanese, 9,000 Portuguese, and almost 2,000 Americans. All for two cents a pound.

The treaty of 1875 pledged the Hawaiian government not to alienate any port or territory in the kingdom to any other power and made the islands a political as well as economic colony of the United States. The treaty inasmuch as told the European powers and Japan to keep their hands off Hawaii. The presumption was that the United States sometime in the future would annex the islands.

A treaty in 1884 between the two nations, Hawaii and the United States, set aside Pearl Harbor for the exclusive use of the American navy —a fateful document, so little noticed or appreciated at the time. When Cleveland came into office in 1885 he found the convention over Pearl Harbor still pending. Cleveland was the least imperialistic of American presidents, a "little American" if one may speak of Americans in the way that counterparts in Britain were known as "little Englanders." He saw that the Hawaiian Islands held importance for the United States. After careful study he declared in his second annual message on the state of the union that he held an "unhesitating conviction that the intimacy of our relations with Hawaii should be emphasized. . . . The paramount influence we have there acquired, once relinquished, could only with difficulty be regained, and a valuable ground of vantage for ourselves might be converted into a stronghold for our commercial competitors." The Pearl Harbor treaty was ratified and proclaimed on November 9, 1887.

Shortly thereafter—with the McKinley Tariff Act of 1890—the islanders found themselves in economic trouble. As mentioned, prior to that year Hawaiian sugar producers had sold their product in the United States without paying a tariff, unlike other foreign sugar vendors. With the McKinley Act this situation changed: the act took off the tariff, so that the Hawaiians had to compete with everyone else in the American market; to protect the higher-cost American domestic sugar producers, the act awarded domestic sugar a bounty of two cents a pound. Within the American market, prices fell to the world level. The two-cent bounty and elimination of the tariff broke Hawaiian sugar prices, which plummeted from $100 to $60 a ton, with an estimated loss to Hawaiian producers of $12,000,000, according to the American minister in Honolulu, John L. Stevens. Prior to Congressman McKinley's tariff, American absentee sugar owners had been rejoicing in dividends of from twenty to eighty percent. In 1890, the year of the dismal tariff, the United States had taken more than 99 percent of the exports of the Hawaiian Islands, a figure which in the world of economic analysis is as close to totality as any figure on exports can be. The tariff was a body blow to the Hawaiian sugar economy.

One might have thought that the obvious Hawaiian answer to the sugar problem was annexation to the United States, by which the producers would gain the bounty. Actually the sugar barons opposed annexation, despite the bounty's attraction; if their plantations came under the American flag, there would be no more contract labor from the orient, because American law would forbid this practice that amounted at times to virtual slavery.

In the midst of the economic crisis came a political crisis. The government of the islands in 1891 changed—much for the worse, the white Hawaiians believed. The native dynasty brought to the Hawaiian throne Queen Liliuokalani, an exponent of a firm anti-American policy. Her arrival on the scene threatened to undo the islands' delicate political balance. It was not merely that she had not favored the American naval

Queen Liliuokalani, the last monarch of Hawaii, and a lady of determination.

base at Pearl Harbor and opposed annexation (which would have taken away her throne). She was pro-native to the extent that she wished to wrest political power from the white-dominated Hawaiian legislature, the institution which the whites believed was the balance wheel of the monarchy. As Allan Nevins has put the situation in his notable biography of Cleveland, in the struggle for political supremacy between the whites and the Polynesian and Asian peoples, Liliuokalani decided not for a working compromise but for Polynesian and Asian supremacy. She precipitated the end of the monarchy when on Saturday, January 14, 1893, the day set for proroguing the legislature, she proclaimed a new constitution by royal edict. Three days later the white group in the islands overthrew her rule.

The revolution of January 17 received the enthusiastic support of the American minister to the islands, Stevens, who co-operated with the plotters against the government to which he was accredited. Stevens's act was hardly unprecedented in the annals of American or any other large nation's diplomacy, but an aura of skulduggery always surrounds such activity and it is best for a co-operating minister to be careful. Discretion was not one of Minister Stevens's qualities. On the evening before the revolution he arranged with Captain G. C. Wiltse of the cruiser *Boston*, then in harbor at Honolulu, to have a party of bluejackets and marines sent ashore, equipped with two light cannon. Detachments stationed themselves at the legation and consulate. The remainder, after some marching around the city, quartered themselves in an empty building known as Arion Hall, conveniently across the street from Government Building, little more than a stone's throw, not to mention a shot from a light cannon, from the Royal Palace. The marines and sailors remained ensconced in this strategic location during the revolutionary events of the next day, and their presence did not harm the revolutionists' cause. Everyone knew the sentiments of Minister Stevens and presumed he was supporting the revolution. He had given a Fourth of July oration in 1892 in which he referred to Hawaii, his place of diplomatic residence, as "a monarch-cursed country."

The revolution went off without a hitch, at least not much of a hitch. Only one shot was fired and one person wounded, despite the marching of marines and sailors and the rifle-carrying activities of the revolutionaries. Stevens allowed the revolutionists to raise the American flag over Government Building on February 1, 1893, and proclaimed Hawaii a United States protectorate. He informed his superiors in Washington that "the Hawaiian pear is now fully ripe, and this is the golden hour for the United States to pluck it."

A delegation of successful revolutionists hurried to Washington and on February 14, 1893, signed a treaty of annexation with the American secretary of state, by this time John W. Foster (who had replaced the ailing Blaine in 1892). President Harrison sent the treaty to the Senate the next day.

Then the trouble occurred, and it may have been entirely an issue of Indiana politics. How often have purely domestic concerns affected American foreign policy! The Senate duly avoided action on the Hawaiian treaty until Cleveland came into office in March 1893. Cleveland meanwhile had chosen Walter Q. Gresham of Indiana as secretary of state-designate. Gresham was a Republican, though a supporter of Cleveland. It is entirely possible that the acute dislike by Gresham for his fellow citizen of Indiana, Benjamin Harrison, produced the ensuing difficulty over the Hawaiian treaty. Back in the year 1888, Gresham had been a leading contender for the presidential nomination of the Republican Party and had been running ahead of Harrison on the ballot in the Chicago convention until Harrison apparently succumbed to "Boss" Thomas Platt of New York, who had put a price on New York's uncommitted convention votes: Platt wished to be secretary of the treasury in any forthcoming Republican administration. Gresham had refused Platt's overtures. It is understandable that Gresham thereafter hated Harrison with a passion (although Benjamin Harrison was hardly an attractive individual anyway —it was said that he was such a cold man that when he entered any room the temperature immediately went down ten degrees). Could it not be, then, that at the time Secretary-designate Gresham visited the president-elect and discussed foreign affairs, including the Hawaiian treaty, he advised Cleveland to investigate the treaty, so obviously a Republican measure championed by Secretary Foster (also from Indiana) and by President Harrison?

Gresham and Cleveland had other reasons for believing that Hawaii should not become an American territorial appendage, but it must have made Gresham feel good to destroy one of the final acts of his political enemy Harrison. Five days after taking the oath of office, President Cleveland withdrew the Hawaiian treaty from the Senate for "the purpose of reexamination."

The president sent out a special commissioner to investigate the situation in Hawaii, a former chairman of the House committee on foreign affairs, ex-Congressman James H. Blount, and to the chagrin of the Hawaiian whites Blount proved a partisan investigator. His appointment by the president at first did not bother them, for they noted that the ex-congressman might have some prejudices favorable to their side. Blount was from Georgia, and they presumed he would understand their problems both with the native Hawaiians and with the Chinese and Japanese. One of the white Hawaiian commissioners in Washington wrote that "As a southerner he is thoroughly familiar with the difficulties attendant upon government with an ignorant majority in the electorate and will thoroughly appreciate the situation upon this point." But Blount ignored the revolutionists and consorted with friends of the deposed queen. He had gone to the islands bearing full authority over all American diplomatic and naval officers there, as "commissioner paramount" (this designation soon brought him the sobriquet of "Paramount Blount"). He submitted his report to the president in the summer of 1893, and it was harshly critical of the actions of Minister Stevens and mentioned specifically the minister's dispatch about the pear being ripe.

Secretary of State Gresham was hardly saddened by this report. In addition to other feelings the secretary had sympathized with the queen, whose cause had aroused some favorable sentiment in the United States. Gresham's wife was certain that her husband had the proper thoughts about the deposed island female potentate, and in her book about her husband, published after his untimely death in 1895, she noted with obvious satisfaction: "A woman in trouble, my husband would certainly side with her against the power, greed and lust of man."

For a mixture of motives the case was decided, and Cleveland refused to send the treaty back to the Senate, instead sending a new minister to the Hawaiians. The result was not happy. Minister Willis called upon President Sanford B. Dole (whose pineapple corporation would become well known to Americans of later years) and suggested that the president resign. In an emphatic reply four days later Dole invited Willis to go to hell. He said that the United States had recognized the provisional government, that President Cleveland had no right to interfere in Hawaii's internal affairs, and he reiterated his hope for annexation.

"Queen Lil," with her unerring instinct for political disaster, did not help this impasse by refusing, in event of her restoration, to promise a full amnesty for all persons concerned with the uprising. In a secret interview at the American legation on November 13, 1893, this doughty lady said, "There are certain laws of my Government by which I shall abide. My decision would be, as the law directs, that such persons should be beheaded . . . ."

Clearly, the white Hawaiians could never allow Queen Lil to sit on the throne again, even if the United States government was not willing to go ahead with annexation. The revolutionists arranged a constitution which perpetuated the "missionary group" in power. Appropriately the new republic was proclaimed on July 4, 1894.

In the United States the many supporters of annexation now fumed. According to the New York *Commercial Advertiser*, which set out its sentiments in a major piece of editorial prose,

In ordering Old Glory pulled down at Honolulu, President Cleveland turned back the hands on the dial of civilization. Native rule, ignorant, naked, heathen, is reestablished; and the dream of an American republic at the crossroads of the Pacific—a dream which Seward and Marcy and Blaine indulged, and the fulfillment of which the more enlightened of our 65,000,000 people awaited with glad anticipation—has been shattered by Grover Cleveland, the Buffalo lilliputian! [Cleveland's home was in Buffalo.] He has ordered his man Blount, a Southern reactionary, to allow the gathering fabric of a stable government at Honolulu and of nobler things to fall to pieces. He has declared that the superstitious orgies of the heathen queen and her wild-eyed Kanakas may be resumed; that American property interests may no longer have the abiding protection that such men as Dole and Armstrong and Bishop declare is essential; that the Hawaiian islands shall be tossed a prize into the arena of international strife, for which the Japanese, the English, and heaven knows who else may scramble and quarrel.

These horrible prospects were not to materialize. The Hawaiian republic maintained a tranquil existence until 1898 when the United States annexed it during the Spanish-American War.

What can one conclude about the history of these events in Hawaii, from the dethronement of Liliuokalani to Cleveland's refusal to annexation? They have often been decried as a sorry and shabby episode in American diplomacy, an affair in which a majority of the Hawaiian people was thwarted by a planter clique of white Hawaiians and the American minister. Perhaps this description applies, but one must realize that the Hawaiian situation was complicated. The planters and middle-class whites represented the only substantial economic group in the islands, and their plans for developing Hawaii could not continue under the rule of a backward dynasty. Nor could they easily heed the desires of the Hawaiian people or the contract workers. Moreover, it was strategically advantageous for the United States to do as it later did, annex the Hawaiian Islands. The Hawaiian archipelago offered a well-situated base from which to control the Pacific approaches to the American west coast. If America had not annexed Hawaii in 1898, some other great power, perhaps Germany or Japan, would have done so. The action of Minister Stevens in 1893 must be considered in the light of these circumstances, and in retrospect the effort to obtain annexation does not appear unreasonable.

2. Chile and Venezuela

In the 1880's and 1890's there were also troubles in Latin America—albeit not over possible annexation—with Chile and Venezuela. The difficulty with Chile can be dismissed rather briefly. It is of interest to the student of American diplomacy only because it illustrates the growing sensitivity of American public opinion to all international difficulties, and because it shows a considerable change in American naval attitudes since the fabled occasion in 1881 when the Chileans threatened to send Admiral Balch and his fleet to the bottom of the ocean. Presumably poor Balch then had done nothing because he could do nothing; the Chileans had him cornered. Ten years later the American navy may not have drastically improved—that would require several more years of construction—but at least commanders were ready for trouble. Indeed, they were anxious for it.

The new Chilean difficulty came after the United States in the summer of 1891 had sought to prevent shipment of arms to some Chilean revolutionists. As the luck of the United States frequently has it in Latin America, the revolutionists took over the government and were unfriendly toward the nation which had denied them arms. When an American cruiser, the *Baltimore*, sent about a hundred members of its crew ashore on leave at Valparaiso on October 16, 1891, and crew members visited the True Blue Saloon, a mob attacked the unarmed sailors during the return through the streets to their vessels, killing two Americans and injuring sixteen. Some of the sailors were thrown into the local jail. President Harrison was incensed, and when his pacific-minded secretary of state, Blaine, sought to defend the Chileans in a cabinet meeting, the president leaned forward and with an emphatic gesture declared: "Mr. Secretary, that insult was to the uniform of the United States sailors." Harrison sent a special fourteen-page message to Congress on January 25, 1892, virtually asking for war. The country was enormously stirred by the Chilean insult. The commander of a naval vessel which replaced the *Baltimore* in Chilean waters, Robley D. Evans, found himself known to the American public as Fighting Bob.

Commander Evans had not been involved in the original trouble at Valparaiso; but when his ship, the *Yorktown*, arrived in harbor, there appeared the makings of a further fracas, which Fighting Bob duly solved. The Chileans in torpedo boats made a number of close passes at the *Yorktown*, on one occasion missing her by less than six feet. Evans's ship was not a vessel with many fighting qualities, hardly more powerful than a converted yacht, so in case of hostilities his position was none too good. Fighting Bob did not hesitate, however, and "gave orders, if one of them even scratched the paint on the *Yorktown*, to blow the boat out of the water and kill every man in her, so that there could be no question of an accidental collision. I then saw the officer in charge of the drills, and told him that he certainly had great confidence in the steering gear of his torpedo boats; that if anything should jam so that one of them struck me I would blow her bottom out. He replied that the water in the harbor belonged to his Government, and that he proposed to use it for the purpose of drilling his boats. I answered that I was fully aware of the ownership he had stated, but that the *Yorktown* and the paint on her belonged to the United States . . . ." Happily, tempers cooled at Valparaiso, and the Chilean government apologized for the attack on the crew of the *Baltimore* and paid an indemnity of $75,000. That was that. Harrison referred to the settlement in his annual message of December 1892 and said he accepted the reparation not only as an indemnity for a wrong done, but as most gratifying evidence that the government of Chile rightly appreciated the willingness of the American government to act in a spirit of fairness and friendliness in its intercourse with that brave people.

But the memory of the *Baltimore* affair was not easy to remove with kind words, spoken even by the president of the United States, and the Chileans had, one might say, the last word on this absurd affair through the legend of Carlos Peña. Down through the years this legend has testified to Chilean bravery. According to Chilean recollection, a final settlement of the *Baltimore* episode necessitated the sending of a Chilean warship either to Valparaiso or to San Francisco, California (the legend varies on this point), to strike its colors before the haughty Americans. *Teniente* Peña volunteered to perform this hateful task of lowering his country's flag. As the flag touched the deck, he turned to the band and asked it to play the Chilean national anthem. Then, holding the flag close to his breast, he shot himself through the heart.

A few years later, in 1895, came the much more serious Venezuelan incident, arising out of a controversy between Venezuela and Great

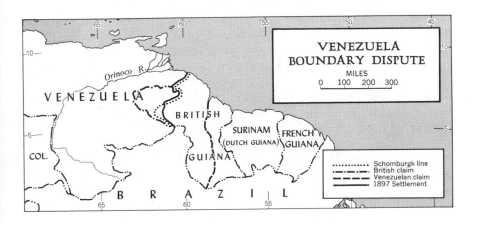

Britain over the boundary line of British Guiana. The dispute between the two nations went back to 1814 when the British had taken their part of Guiana from the Dutch. A British engineer, Sir Robert Schomburgk, made a survey of the boundary in 1840 and proposed a line which Venezuela rejected. Thereupon the dispute lapsed because of its essential unimportance, until in the 1880's gold was discovered in the contested region. The British in 1887 refused the good offices of the United States in settling the dispute; Cleveland in his annual message to Congress of 1894 offered to renew his attempt of 1887 to bring about an arbitration; Britain refused to arbitrate.

Here, assuredly, the British government under Lord Salisbury made a grievous miscalculation, for the new confidence in manifest destiny was waxing strong in America in the early 1890's. On every hand the imperialists were making themselves known. The anti-imperialists were losing all influence. Theodore Roosevelt could describe the anti-imperialists in 1895 as "solemn prattlers" who

strive after an ideal in which they shall happily unite the imagination of a green grocer with the heart of a Bengalese baboo. They are utterly incapable of feeling one thrill of generous emotion, or the slightest throb of that pulse which gives to the world statesmen, patriots, warriors, and poets, and which makes a nation other than a cumberer of the world's surface.

The British just before the crisis over the Venezuelan boundary allowed one of their naval commanders to get into a confrontation with the government of Nicaragua. A man-of-war of the royal navy landed troops at the port of Corinto to obtain redress for the expulsion of a British consul from the little Central American republic. In May 1895 the Nicaraguans gave in and paid the British government approximately $360,000. The Cleveland administration argued cautiously that the British occupation of Corinto, avowedly temporary, did not constitute a violation of the Monroe Doctrine. But popular protests in the United States rose to a deafening roar. Critics at once pointed out the temporary nature of the British occupation of Egypt in 1882. Then the British admiral at Corinto seems to have described the Monroe Doctrine, with a horrendous lack of diplomacy, as an obsolete doctrine and a myth. The patriots raged. Someone discovered—*horribile dictu*—that at a banquet in England the American ambassador, former Secretary of State Bayard (who, incidentally, in 1893 was the first American diplomat appointed to ambassadorial rank), had proposed a toast to Queen Victoria. Bayard, according to the New York *Tribune*, lacked "the superb and indispensable quality of making himself disagreeable at the proper time." He was, in a word, an Anglophile. The Cleveland administration, listening to such criticism from the Republican opposition, hearing it from many Democrats, yielded to popular clamor when after the Nicaraguan affair came Britain's refusal to arbitrate the Venezuelan boundary. The administration took a stand on Venezuela. The first hint of trouble came when a friend of the president made a speech in Detroit to the toast, "Our Veterans: Can They Hear the Bugle Call?"

The Monroe Doctrine was behind that bugle call, and almost any exaggeration seemed allowable. The New York *Tribune* on May 20, 1895, remarked that the principles of the doctrine were "coeval with the very existence of our government." The young Senator Henry Cabot Lodge, who possessed a Harvard Ph.D. in history and should have known the then modest record of achievement of the pristine doctrine of his country, wrote an abysmally unhistorical philippic for the *North American Review*, published in June 1895. His friend Roosevelt, who years later in 1912 would serve a year as president of the American Historical Association, found the article "admirable." TR in 1895 was police commissioner of New York City, but he found his duties apparently not pressing enough to keep him from surveying foreign policy. He sought out the American correspondent of the London *Times*, George W. Smalley, and spoke to him "as plainly as mortal can," telling him that "the general sentiment of the country was rather hostile to England and was very strong in support of the Monroe Doctrine."

It so happened that Secretary of State Gresham took sick and died late in May 1895, and President Cleveland passed the cabinet post to the then attorney general, Richard Olney of Massachusetts. It was a momentous succession. Olney had given evidence of strong ideas and actions when in the previous year he had persuaded the president to use troops to break the Pullman strike in Chicago. Now he would use a diplomatic note to break the pride of Great Britain over the Venezuelan boundary.

It is curious that almost the first action that Olney took as secretary of state was to compose his massive attack upon the British position concerning the boundary, which he laid before Cleveland for approval prior to cabling it to London. The president in July 1895 was at his summer house, Gray Gables, on Buzzards Bay, preoccupied for a few days, as he put it in a note to the anxious Olney, because "our family was augmented by the addition of a strong plump loud-voiced little girl." Nearby at his house in Falmouth, Olney waited for the presidential answer, and at last it came. Cleveland approved:

I read your deliverance on Venezuelan affairs the day you left it with me. It's the best thing of the kind I have ever read and it leads to a conclusion that one cannot escape if he tries—that is, if there's anything in the Monroe Doctrine at all. You show there is a great deal of that and place it I think on better and more defensible ground than any of your predecessors—*or mine*. Of course I have some suggestions to make. I always have. Some of them are not of much account and some of them propose a little more softened verbiage here and there.

Several cabinet members went over the message and presumably softened the note, which Olney then forwarded under date of July 20, 1895.

The note was a dilly. In refusing to allow the annexation of Hawaii, Cleveland had put the United States on a high moral plane, and he now insisted upon holding Britain to the same severe standard of international ethics. As for Secretary Olney, the secretary believed that what he was telling the British government was a series of truths. The secretary was a dyed-in-the-wool New Englander, and his note bore sure traces of Puritan conscience and Yankee businesslike brusqueness.

The note of July 20 offered the Olney Corollary to the Monroe Doctrine; it said that United States intervention in Latin America was permissible and even desirable to force a settlement of any dispute involving the Monroe Doctrine. But it was not so much what Olney and Cleveland said but the way the note expressed those thoughts. Olney read the British a lecture:

The civilized states of Christendom deal with each other on substantially the same principles that regulate the conduct of individuals. The greater its enlightenment, the more surely every state perceives that its permanent interests require it to be governed by the immutable principles of right and justice. Each, nevertheless, is only too liable to succumb to the temptations offered by seeming special opportunities for its aggrandizement, and each would rashly imperil its own safety were it not to remember that for the regard and respect of other states it must be largely dependent upon its own strength and power. Today the United States is practically sovereign on this continent, and its fiat is law upon the subjects to which it confines its interposition. Why? It is not because of the pure friendship or good will felt for it. It is not simply by reason of its high character as a civilized state, nor because wisdom and justice and equity are the invariable characteristics of the dealings of the United States. It is because, in addition to all other grounds, its infinite resources combined with its isolated position render it master of the situation and practically invulnerable as against any or all other powers.

Shades of the Huelsemann Note of 1850! The Ostend Manifesto of 1854! Not without reason, President Cleveland described it privately as a 20-inch gun.

Some of the detailed argument of the note was hardly worth defending on historical principles. Olney said that Great Britain had given the original enunciation of the Monroe Doctrine "an open and unqualified adhesion which has never been withdrawn." He said that the doctrine was a rule "openly and uniformly declared and acted upon by the executive branch of the [United States] government for seventy years." And he cavalierly ignored Canada and other British New World possessions when he argued that "distance and three thousand miles of intervening ocean make any permanent political union between a European and an American state unnatural and inexpedient" and asserted that this proposition "would hardly be denied."

Ambassador Bayard, undeniably unhappy, did not find an opportunity to deliver the note to Lord Salisbury (who was both prime minister and foreign secretary) until August 7. Upon listening to the note Salisbury was perplexed. According to Bayard,

At the conclusion of my reading and statement, his Lordship made courteous expression of his thanks, and expressed regret and surprise that it had been considered necessary to present so far-reaching and important a principle and such wide and profound policies of international action in relation to a subject so comparatively small.

As if there were not enough diplomatic trouble, more ensued when the British government took nearly four months to answer the American note of July 20. Olney and Cleveland had hoped that the reply would arrive before Congress convened in December 1895. It is possible that Bayard—who some people insisted gave too much satisfaction to Englishmen to be wholly satisfactory to Americans—failed to impress on Salisbury the urgency of the situation. British casualness, or ignorance, seems also to have mistaken the date for the meeting of Congress, and although the reply had been drawn up by November 26 it went to the United States through the mails instead of by cable. Salisbury, one should add, was busy. He was immersed in the Near Eastern problem. Moreover, his subordinates wished to make a good case in the reply. The principle of arbitration already had led to the Geneva arbitration of 1872, and the British feared that if they admitted the principle in boundary cases their interests would be whittled down all over the world by neighboring states concocting boundary claims.

The British ambassador, Sir Julian Pauncefote, read Salisbury's reply to Olney during a meeting at the embassy on December 6. The reply was another grievous miscalculation. As Dexter Perkins has written, "To the arrogance of Olney, Lord Salisbury opposed a superior dogmatism, a patronizing self-confidence . . . ." The year 1895, Perkins points out, was the last time for many years that the British would treat the American government with supercilious indifference. Salisbury's commentary on the Monroe Doctrine was a masterpiece of arrogance:

In the remarks which I have made I have argued on the theory that the Monroe Doctrine itself is sound. I must not, however, be understood as expressing any acceptance of it on the part of Her Majesty's Government. It must always be mentioned with respect, on account of the distinguished statesman to whom it is due, and the great nation who have generally adopted it. But international law is founded on the general consent of nations; and no statesman, however eminent, and no nation, however powerful, are competent to insert into the code of international law a novel principle which was never recognized before, and which has not been since accepted by the Government of any other country. The United States have a right, like any other nation, to interpose in any controversy by which their own interests are affected; and they are the judge whether those interests are touched, and in what measure they should be sustained. But their rights are in no way strengthened or extended by the fact that the controversy affects some territory which is called American.

He asserted that the union between Britain and Canada, or Jamaica, or Guiana, was expedient and natural, and that the whole empire was prepared to maintain the fact. As for Canada, he denied that the fiat of the United States extended north of the Great Lakes.

Salisbury refused to submit the Venezuela-British Guiana boundary to arbitration.

Receiving this piece of intemperance, Cleveland was "mad clean through," as he put it. He was annoyed to have had to wait for the British reply and angered to receive this kind of reply. He sent a special message to Congress on December 17, 1895, asking an appropriation of funds for a commission to determine the true Venezuelan boundary and declared that it would be the duty of the United States to maintain that boundary against any aggressors. He reiterated the importance of the Monroe Doctrine: "If the balance of power is justly a cause for jealous anxiety among the Governments of the Old World and a subject for our absolute noninterference, none the less is an observance of the Monroe Doctrine of vital concern to our people and their government." The president brought all of his best rhetoric to bear against the British government:

In making these recommendations I am fully alive to the responsibility incurred, and keenly realize all the consequences that may follow. I am, nevertheless, firm in my conviction that while it is a grievous thing to contemplate the two great English-speaking peoples of the world as being otherwise than friendly competitors in the onward march of civilization, and strenuous and worthy rivals in all the arts of peace, there is no calamity which a great nation can invite which equals that which follows a supine submission to wrong and injustice, and the consequent loss of national self-respect and honor, beneath which are shielded and defended a people's safety and greatness.

A wave of enthusiasm swept the country. Both Houses of Congress unanimously voted funds for the boundary commission, perhaps a record vote on an issue of foreign affairs.

The popularity of the United States in Latin America, not always at a remarkable level, rose up almost out of sight. Venezuelans received the Cleveland message with raptures. The American minister reported that a crowd of at least 20,000 people gathered in front of the legation, and in their excitement nearly wrecked his building. Venezuela's Academy of History held a special meeting on December 23, 1895, to express its "profound gratitude" to the noble United States. On Christmas Day a great procession passed through Caracas bearing the flags of Venezuela and the United States, a parade so impressive that an enthusiastic editor, attempting to describe it, declared that the pen fell helpless from his fingers.

There was no such sentiment in London, where Salisbury said he thought the excitement in America would "fizzle away."

Fortunately for Anglo-American amity, the British soon took a second measurement of what they had said to their American cousins. The emperor of Germany, William II, in a famous telegram of January 3, 1896, to President Kruger of the Transvaal, congratulated the Boers on defeating the British-led Jameson raid into their territory. The British government then was moving to the brink of war with the Boers, and the German telegram raised a storm. In a dispatch to Olney, Ambassador Bayard on January 15, 1896 noted: "There has been a welcome and unmistakable difference observable, in the manner in which the possibilities of conflict with the United States—and with Germany—were discussed and treated in this country." The prospect of a war with the United States appalled the British government and people. But the tide had turned even before the Kruger telegram, as leading Britishers and even Salisbury were seeing the need of protecting their American flank, of keeping on friendly terms. Salisbury once had described Britain's independent position in the world as "splendid isolation." It no longer seemed splendid.

Salisbury practically accepted the American position in March 1896 by allowing Pauncefote in Washington to discuss the boundary question either with the representative of Venezuela or with the government of the United States as the friend of Venezuela. Pauncefote and Olney arranged a treaty of arbitration, signed in Washington on February 2, 1897, by the Venezuelan representative and the British ambassador. It exempted no part of the boundary from arbitration, as the British for a time had sought to do. Cleveland was happy, since the United States government had negotiated the treaty but Venezuela and Britain had signed it. As he commented afterward: "This was a fortunate circumstance, inasmuch as the work accomplished was thus saved from the risk of customary disfigurement at the hands of the United States Senate." An arbitral tribunal of five judges handed down a decision in the autumn of 1899 upholding the principal British contentions but at two points giving Venezuela territory within the Schomburgk line.

For a short time, because of his unbending attitude toward the Venezuelan boundary dispute, Cleveland found himself a popular figure among his fellow Americans. There was applause over the way in which he had dealt with Great Britain. People felt that he at last had taken a strong stand for his country. The imperialists, of course, had failed to convert Cleveland—no special plaudits could have moved that massive conscience. Grover Cleveland was a stubborn man who would act on a matter when he was convinced of the rightness of his position. The Venezuelan affair, he seems to have believed, involved the dignity

British members of the Venezuela boundary tribunal.

of the United States. In regard to Hawaii he saw no reason for annexation, and generally was most unsympathetic toward American overseas expansion. By conviction he was an anti-imperialist, reflecting perhaps the views of the cautious New York business community with which he had associated during the interim between his two terms of office. A conservative man in ideas and actions, by the end of his second administration in March 1897 he found himself almost completely out of touch with American public opinion. It was primarily because of Cleveland's conservative views on national finance that the Democratic Party deserted his leadership in 1896 in favor of William Jennings Bryan, and the election of 1896 was fought over domestic issues rather than questions of foreign policy. Yet Cleveland had become old-fashioned not merely because of his ideas of domestic economics but because he was an anti-imperialist, an unbeliever in overseas expansion. When he retired to Princeton to live out the remaining few years of his life, his departure from the seat of national government in Washington signified—though this was not at first realized in the flush of McKinley's triumph over "Bryanism"—the passing of the post-Civil War era of inaction in American foreign policy.

A CONTEMPORARY DOCUMENT

[The Olney Corollary to the Monroe Doctrine, dated July 20, 1895, a communication from Secretary Olney to Ambassador Bayard which the latter then presented to Lord Salisbury, was hardly diplomatic in its claims and professions. Olney's deliverance, as President Cleveland privately described it, nonetheless showed the American national humor in the 1890's, the era of new opportunities. Source: *Foreign Relations of the United States: 1895* (2 vols., Washington, 1896), I, 545, 552, 554–555, 557–558.]

I am directed by the President to communicate to you his views upon a subject to which he has given much anxious thought and respecting which he has not reached a conclusion without a lively sense of its great importance as well as of the serious responsibility involved in any action now to be taken.

It is not proposed, and for present purposes is not necessary, to enter into any detailed account of the controversy between Great Britain and Venezuela respecting the western frontier of the colony of British Guiana. The dispute is of ancient date . . . .

By the frequent interposition of its good offices at the instance of Venezuela, by constantly urging and promoting the restoration of diplomatic relations between the two countries, by pressing for arbitration of the disputed boundary, by offering to act as arbitrator, by expressing its grave concern whenever new alleged instances of British aggression upon Venezuelan territory have been brought to its notice, the Government of the United States has made it clear to Great Britain and to the world that the controversy is one in which both its honor and its interests are involved and the continuance of which it can not regard with indifference. . . .

That America is in no part open to colonization, though the proposition was not universally admitted at the time of its first enunciation, has long been universally conceded. We are now concerned, therefore, only with that other practical application of the Monroe doctrine the disregard of which by an European power is to be deemed an act of unfriendliness towards the United States. The precise scope and limitations of this rule cannot be too clearly apprehended. It does not establish any general protectorate by the United States over other American states. It does not relieve any American state from its obligations as fixed by international law nor prevent any European power directly interested from enforcing such obligations or from inflicting merited punishment for the breach of them. It does not contemplate any interference in the internal affairs of any American state or in the relations between it and other American states. It does not justify any attempt on our part to change the established form of government of any American state or to prevent the people of such state from altering that form according to their own will and pleasure. The rule in question has but a single purpose and object. It is that no European power or combination of European powers shall forcibly deprive an American state of the right and power of self-government and of shaping for itself its own political fortunes and destinies. . . .

Is it true, then, that the safety and welfare of the United States are so concerned with the maintenance of the independence of every American state as against any European power as to justify and require the interposition of the United States whenever that independence is endangered? The question can be candidly answered in but one way. The states of America, South as well as North, by geographical proximity, by natural sympathy, by similarity of governmental constitutions, are friends and allies, commercially and politically, of the United States. To allow the subjugation of any of them by an European power is, of course, to completely reverse that situation and signifies the loss of all the advantages incident to their natural relations to us. But that is not all. The people of the United States have a vital interest in the cause of popular self-government.

They have secured the right for themselves and their posterity at the cost of infinite blood and treasure. They have realized and exemplified its beneficent operation by a career unexampled in point of national greatness or individual felicity. They believe it to be for the healing of all nations, and that civilization must either advance or retrograde accordingly as its supremacy is extended or curtailed. Imbued with these sentiments, the people of the United States might not impossibly be wrought up to an active propaganda in favor of a cause so highly valued both for themselves and for mankind. But the age of the Crusades has passed, and they are content with such assertion and defense of the right of popular self-government as their own security and welfare demand. It is in that view more than in any other that they believe it not to be tolerated that the political control of an American state shall be forcibly assumed by an European power.

The mischiefs apprehended from such a source are none the less real because not immediately imminent in any specific case, and are none the less to be guarded against because the combination of circumstances that will bring them upon us cannot be predicted. . . .

[There followed immediately the strictures quoted above, p. 372.]

ADDITIONAL READING

For the period of new opportunities, the 1880's and the early 1890's, there are several general accounts with which to begin: European diplomacy appears in William L. Langer, *European Alliances and Alignments: 1871–1890* (New York, 1931) and *The Diplomacy of Imperialism: 1890–1902* (2nd ed., New York, 1951); and on the American side there is Dexter Perkins, *The Monroe Doctrine: 1867–1907* (Baltimore, 1937); *Foster Rhea Dulles, *The Imperial Years* (New York, 1956); two volumes in the New American Nation series, *Harold U. Faulkner's *Politics, Reform and Expansion: 1890–1900* (New York, 1959) and *John A. Garraty's *The New Commonwealth: 1877–1890* (New York, 1968); *Ernest R. May, *Imperial Democracy: The Emergence of America as a Great Power* (New York, 1961), a careful examination of the American and European archival collections; *Julius W. Pratt, *Expansionists of 1898* (Baltimore, 1936); *Walter La Feber, *The New Empire* (Ithaca, N.Y., 1963); and Foster Rhea Dulles, *Prelude to World Power: 1860–1900* (New York, 1968).

Scholarship on Samoa is surprisingly large, considering the smallness of the territory in question. The reason for the extent of this literature, of course, may well be the color, the drama, of the Samoan question in world politics, and not least in American politics. A good beginning point is the American trade with the area, which appears in part in Ernest S. Dodge's charming *New*

England and the South Seas (Cambridge, Mass., 1965), by the director of the Peabody Museum. The leading monograph on Samoa is by George H. Ryden, *The Foreign Policy of the United States in Relation to Samoa* (New Haven, 1933). See also Sylvia Masterman, *The Origins of International Rivalry in Samoa: 1845–1884* (Stanford, Calif., 1934). The famous episode involving the ships of the three powers—British, American, German—appears in Robert Louis Stevenson's contemporary *A Footnote to History* (New York, 1895). The distinguished author was spending his last days on the islands and found the local scene surprisingly active. A recent and racy account is by Edwin P. Hoyt, *The Typhoon that Stopped a War* (New York, 1967). Statesmen and diplomats receive consideration in Alice F. Tyler, *The Foreign Policy of James G. Blaine* (Minneapolis, 1927); Charles C. Tansill, *The Foreign Policy of Thomas F. Bayard: 1885–1897* (New York, 1940); and Edward Younger, *John A. Kasson: Politics and Diplomacy from Lincoln to McKinley* (Iowa City, 1955), concerning one of the American negotiators at the Berlin Conference of 1889. Jon Holstine presently is putting these disparate literary pieces of Samoa scholarship together into a narrative of the entire involvement of the United States in obtaining territory in the Samoan Islands in the latter nineteenth century.

Hawaii also has occupied writers, and the most recent general account of diplomatic relations is by Merze Tate, *The United States and the Hawaiian Kingdom: A Political History* (New Haven, 1965). See also Sylvester K. Stevens, *American Expansion in Hawaii: 1842–1898* (Harrisburg, Pa., 1945); W. A. Russ, Jr., *The Hawaiian Revolution: 1893–1894* (Selinsgrove, Pa., 1959) and *The Hawaiian Republic: 1894–1898* (Selinsgrove, Pa., 1961); Richard D. Weigle, "Sugar and the Hawaiian Revolution," *Pacific Historical Review,* XVI (1947), 41–58; and Thomas A. Bailey, "The United States and Hawaii during the Spanish–American War," *American Historical Review,* XXXVI (1930–1931), 552–560. Presidential judgment had something to do with the annexation of Hawaii, for which see Harry Barnard, *Rutherford B. Hayes and His America* (Indianapolis, 1954); and Allan Nevins, *Grover Cleveland: A Study in Courage* (New York, 1932).

The Chilean episode appears in detail in Herbert Millington, *American Diplomacy and the War of the Pacific* (New York, 1948); Albert T. Volwiler, "Harrison, Blaine, and American Foreign Policy, 1889–1893," *American Philosophical Society Proceedings,* IX (1938), 637–648; Robley D. Evans, *A Sailor's Log* (New York, 1901); and Edwin A. Falk, *Fighting Bob Evans* (New York, 1931). Frederick B. Pike, *Chile and the United States: 1880–1962* (Notre Dame, Ind., 1963) is an excellent general account.

Cleveland's policy toward Venezuela and Great Britain appears generally in Nevins's *Grover Cleveland* and in G. R. Dulebohn, *Principles of Foreign Policy under the Cleveland Administrations* (Philadelphia, 1941). See also the biography of Cleveland's righthand man, Henry James's *Richard Olney and His Public Service* (Boston, 1923). The best scholarly account is Nelson M. Blake, "Background of Cleveland's Venezuelan Policy," *American Historical Review,* XLVII (1941–1942), 259–277. For the British side see Alexander E.

Campbell, *Great Britain and the United States: 1895–1903* (Glasgow, 1960); John A. S. Grenville, *Lord Salisbury and Foreign Policy: The Close of the Nineteenth Century* (London, 1964); and especially Bradford Perkins's new work, properly entitled *The Great Rapprochement: England and the United States, 1895–1914* (New York, 1968).

The War with Spain

There may be an explosion any day in Cuba which would settle a great many things.

—Senator Henry Cabot Lodge to Henry White, January 1898

In a military sense the Spanish-American War was one of the least impressive conflicts of the nineteenth century. The war boiled up suddenly in the springtime of 1898. It was an exhilarating experience, sensational, not dangerous. The outcome was never in doubt. The antagonist, Spain, had a population of eighteen million compared with the seventy-five million people in the United States. Captain Alfred Thayer Mahan, in Europe when the war started, was asked how long it would last, and he answered, "About three months." By the end of the summer the fighting was over, won by the small but new and efficient American navy against the antiquated seagoing contraptions that passed for the navy of Spain. In the peace that followed the Spanish relinquished the remnants of a once grand empire: Cuba, Puerto Rico, Guam, the Philippine Islands. The war had no visible effect upon the large questions of international politics, especially the European balance of power which at the moment was gaining the attention of the world's statesmen. The Spanish-American War was a ripple on the surface of world affairs, and by the time the peace conference assembled in Paris in October 1898, relations between the United States and Spain were again almost cordial. Perhaps the Spanish realized, although they could not admit it, that if the United States had not taken their colonies, some other power would have.

Behind this summer turmoil of 1898, however, there was a deeper than military meaning, which makes the war of interest to the student of diplomatic history. The war suddenly brought into focus the ideas which had been generating in the minds of Americans in the 1880's and 1890's—

ideas which, once the weariness and near-exhaustion of the Civil War disappeared, had fired the imagination of the American people. Several years before the war of 1898, the American nation had begun to look outward and exert its influence abroad. This new attitude was not merely a matter of interest in Latin America, interest in a revival of the Monroe Doctrine, for, as we have seen, there was interest also in Samoa, an island group far beyond the bounds of the Western Hemisphere as imagined by Colonel Monroe in 1823. Americans perhaps had blundered into Samoa and failed to realize the difficulties of holding territory deep in the South Seas. Samoa nonetheless indicated that the United States was a world power, and when during the war with Spain an opportunity was presented to take more territory outside the Western Hemisphere, it was hardly to be expected that the United States would hesitate. The meaning of the Spanish-American War lay in its appeal to the emotions of the new manifest destiny. The war focused these emotions and attached them to new and widely dispersed territories.

1. Cuba

Cuba was the precipitating cause of the war. The Ever-Faithful Isle, as it was known because of its loyalty to Spain during the Latin-American revolutionary period, had in the mid-nineteenth century begun to acquire feelings of nationalism. Cuban nationalism produced open warfare for a decade beginning in 1868, a long and savage guerrilla conflict between Spanish military forces and the revolutionaries which was confined chiefly to the wild and unsettled eastern end of the island and did not afflict the rich and populous western half which includes Havana. The war of 1868–1878 was led by the revolutionary general Máximo Gómez, a Santo Domingan who seems to have acted under the revolutionary ardor which possessed so many Latin Americans during the period of liberation; for while the era of Bolívar and San Martín had long since passed, in Gómez there still burned the revolutionary fire. It is possible that during the insurrection of 1868–1878 most Cubans did not desire liberation. Perhaps Gómez did not secure enough assistance from Cuban expatriates in the United States. The American government and people in the years after their own Civil War were too weary of warfare and too busy with their own concerns to assist the Cuban revolutionists. The revolt spent itself and on February 10, 1878, there was signed the Pact of Zanjón, by which the insurgent Cubans received amnesty and the island was granted the same system of government enjoyed by Puerto Rico. It developed later that in the weariness and confusion which attended the end of the war neither side had known, when the pact was signed, the nature of the government enjoyed by Puerto Rico.

Had the United States desired to intervene in Cuba during this insurrection, there had been at least one opportunity, the famous *Virginius* episode of 1873, when Spanish authorities seized the ship *Virginius* and took it into Santiago. Captured on the high seas far beyond Cuban territorial waters, the ship, although flying the American flag, was obviously on a filibustering expedition. The crew and passengers, despite their American-sounding names, were of a strongly Cuban countenance. They were all able-bodied males and had no legitimate business which they could claim to be pursuing so close to the insurrectionary island of Cuba. After a short trial the Spanish decided to shoot these men as pirates, and fifty-three were killed before a British captain sailed in with a warship and stopped the executions. The *Virginius* affair would have offered an excuse for American action, had the United States in 1873 wished to start a quarrel with Spain. Instead the state department under Hamilton Fish bided its time, inquired into the circumstances of the case, and ascertained that the ship was falsely flying the American flag. The secretary of state obtained a Spanish apology and indemnity for the dubiously American citizens killed. If the United States had been spoiling for a fight, here was an incident which could easily have been used. Spain at the time was undergoing a civil war, and there could have been no Spanish defense of Cuba against American invasion. But there was no American willingness to invade and take Cuba. Perhaps the coincidence of the *Virginius* incident with a domestic economic crisis, the panic of 1873, had some part in the general American desire to avoid war.

The revolution of 1868–1878 came to an end with the Pact of Zanjón, and there followed a period until 1895—when a new revolt broke out—during which there was peace and something approaching prosperity in Cuba. One of the most important causes of American concern over the island, the continuing existence there of the institution of human slavery, was eliminated when Spain abolished slavery in the colony in 1886 after a gradual emancipation. Meanwhile the sugar plantations expanded and began to flourish under the beneficent terms of the McKinley Tariff of 1890, which provided for reciprocity agreements. Spain and the United States arranged in 1891, in return for Spanish concessions, for free entrance of Cuban sugar into the United States. Unfortunately, a new American tariff act of 1894 ended the reciprocity. This act followed the business panic of 1893, and the general business stagnation of the mid-1890's together with the new and unfavorable American tariff almost ruined the Cuban economy. The island again was ready for revolt.

At the beginning of the second Cuban revolution in 1895, few individuals in the United States were willing to go to war to liberate Cuba from Spain. American economic interests, about $50,000,000 in Cuban property and $100,000,000 annually in trade, were not large enough to generate enthusiasm for the revolution. There also occurred in 1895 the far more interesting Venezuelan crisis, precipitated by President Cleveland and Secretary Olney against a first-class world power, Great Britain. Then came the election of 1896, when the United States, for one of the few times in its history, seemed to be dividing politically along economic lines, the poor against the rich. Once that vision had dissolved, the nation concentrated its energies on bettering business conditions, which had stagnated after the panic of 1893. Only after the presidential election did the business cycle at last begin to move upward, after four long and grinding years of depression, and in the United States there was little eagerness to risk this gain in the uncertainties of a foreign war.

The Cubans by this time had turned their revolution against Spain into a ferocious contest, and to Americans it seemed evident that the rebels because of their wanton acts deserved no sympathy, though they constantly sought it. They were pursuing a scorched-earth policy, burning crops and destroying food in the hope of either forcing the Spanish government to grant independence or forcing the United States to intervene for independence. These tactics infuriated President Cleveland, who privately referred to the revolutionaries as "rascally Cubans." From his successor after March 1897, President William McKinley, there was more sympathy, but McKinley was determined not to be involved: the Republican administration was a business-oriented administration, devoted to the welfare of the American industrialist, and businessmen in 1897 and early 1898 shunned war. The Cuban tactics of destruction had no effect on the policy of the United States and little effect upon the Spanish government, which in 1896 had sent over a new captain-general, Valeriano Weyler.

General Weyler undertook a rigorous policy of forcing the population in the disaffected Cuban provinces into concentration camps, separating the people from the revolutionaries, and thereby identifying the latter. His arrival in Cuba marked a turning point in American sentiment toward the Cuban revolution. Before Weyler adopted his policy of herding the Cubans to concentration camps, the government of the United States had stood against intervention. American hesitation over Cuba stemmed, as was mentioned, from dislike of the destructive tactics of the rascally Cuban revolutionaries. It came also, one should add, from the problem of disposing of the island once Americans should intervene and expel the Spanish. The Cubans, most informed Americans believed, could not govern themselves. Nor could the island be annexed and brought into the American union. Annexation would have precipitated grave difficulties because of the mixed racial composition of the Cuban population. Moreover, many Cubans were illiterate. Regarding annexation, William Graham Sumner of Yale had spoken much to the point: "The prospect," Sumner said, "of adding to the present Senate a number of Cuban Senators, either native or carpetbag, is one whose terrors it is not necessary to unfold." But Americans could not overlook the miseries of General Weyler's camps. Weyler appears to have been a man of decent intentions who was a victim of the inefficiency of Spanish colonial administration. It was easy to bring the people into the camps, but the subsequent duty of feeding them and watching over sanitation was too much for Spanish bureaucracy. Cuba by late 1897 was in a tragic plight. Perhaps as many as 200,000 Cubans died in the camps. And errors of Spanish administration had been compounded by the actions of the Cuban revolutionaries, who in hope of increasing the general misery of the island took measures to prevent the feeding of the *reconcentrados*.

Americans were shocked by what was going on so close to their shores and there began to be talk of intervention. This was at once encouraged by the famous newspaper circulation war in New York City between the New York *Journal*, owned by William Randolph Hearst, and the *World*, owned by Joseph Pulitzer. These two newspapers took advantage of every little change in American-Spanish relations to increase their circulation. They stopped at nothing to blow up the trouble in Cuba into a crisis of major proportions. As E. L. Godkin, a more staid and gentlemanly contemporary of Hearst and Pulitzer, said at the time, and without much exaggeration, "Nothing so disgraceful as the behavior of these two newspapers . . . has ever been known in the history of journalism."

One may ascribe the outbreak of the Spanish-American War to several circumstances: the trouble in Cuba following 1895; the yellow journalism of Hearst, Pulitzer, and similar editors; the famous episode of the Dupuy de Lôme letter (February 9, 1898); and the sinking of the battleship *Maine* in Havana harbor on February 15, 1898.

The letter was written to a friend in Cuba by the Spanish minister in the United States, Dupuy de Lôme. The circumstances surrounding its composition were altogether understandable. All diplomats are by the nature of their work repressed individuals—they know and feel so much more than they dare say officially that there is a temptation to confide intimate thoughts to friends. The Spanish minister by the autumn of 1897 was receiving increasing advices about Cuba from American government officials, and he may be excused for finding some of them impertinent. The result was an undiplomatic private letter. Señor Dupuy de Lôme did not like the tone of President McKinley's state-of-the-union address in December 1897 and wrote to his friend in Cuba, "Besides the ingrained and inevitable coarseness with which it repeated all that the press and public opinion in Spain have said about Weyler, it once more shows what McKinley is, weak and a bidder for the admiration of the crowd, besides being a common politician who tries to leave a door open behind himself while keeping on good terms with the jingoes of his party." One can only imagine Dupuy de Lôme's embarrassment when he learned that this letter had been stolen from the desk of his correspondent and was in the hands of Hearst and the New York *Journal*. He hastily resigned his post.

The minister had said of McKinley what many Americans believed and published daily in their own newspapers, but a foreign diplomat must be discreet. McKinley had in truth seemed to many of his countrymen pre-eminently a politician, the more so when compared to the courageous Grover Cleveland. As McKinley talked in meaningless generalities while desire for intervention in Cuba mounted, Theodore Roosevelt found him as "spineless as a chocolate eclair." A current joke went, "Why is McKinley's mind like a bed?" (Answer: "Because it has to be made up for him every time he wants to use it.") But the truth or falsity of Dupuy de Lôme's opinions was no issue in 1898, and the Spanish minister inflamed the American people against Spain when he repeated the popular wisdom.

Almost immediately following this *faux pas* occurred the *Maine* disaster. The battleship was in Havana harbor on the not very convincing pretext of a courtesy visit. Probably the reason for the *Maine's* visit was that the McKinley administration feared not to have a ship in Havana should trouble break out and American citizens ask for protection. It was risky to send a ship to Havana during the revolutionary chaos, but McKinley was almost forced to protect his countrymen when Americans by the latter 1890's were becoming so sensitive to their rights and position in the world. He did not reckon how desperate the Cuban situation was. The Cuban revolutionaries—perhaps—made their supreme effort to secure American intervention.

The *Maine* on the evening of February 15, 1898, sank at its moorings after a terrific explosion, the detonation of the magazines. Of 350 officers and men aboard, 252 were dead or missing and 14 died afterward. A naval court of inquiry in 1898 found in favor of an external explosion touching off the magazines. When the vessel was raised in 1911 an inward buckling of its plates was evident, and a second court of inquiry then reported, as had the first court, that "the injuries to the bottom of the *Maine* . . . were caused by the explosion of a low form of explosive

The battleship *Maine*, entering Havana harbor, and after the explosion.

exterior to the ship." The hulk was towed out to sea in 1912 and sunk in 600 fathoms of water. No one to this day has discovered who or what in 1898 blew up the *Maine*. One can say only that the vessel's destruction greatly benefited the Cuban revolutionaries, already distinguished by the abandon with which they conducted their guerrilla actions against the Spanish. The sinking of the *Maine*, as few other events could have done, precipitated the United States entry into the revolutionary struggle against Spain.

The American people and Washington officials were at first incredulous and then deeply angered. Years afterward the watchman in the White House remembered McKinley pacing the floor in the first shock of the news, murmuring "The *Maine* blown up! The *Maine* blown up!" Hearst's New York *Journal* emblazoned for its readers, THE WARSHIP MAINE WAS SPLIT IN TWO BY AN ENEMY'S SECRET INFERNAL MACHINE. "Remember the *Maine*," became a national watchword:

> Ye who made war that your ships
> > Should lay to at the beck of no nation,
> Make war now on murder, that slips
> > The leash of her hounds of damnation;
> Ye who remembered the Alamo,
> Remember the *Maine!*

In a Broadway bar a man raised his glass and said solemnly, "Gentlemen, remember the *Maine!*" Through the streets of American cities went the cry, "Remember the *Maine!* To hell with Spain!"

After this disaster at Havana, it is doubtful if McKinley or anyone could have checked the course of events. The argument frequently advanced, that McKinley could have defied the war hawks of 1898 in Congress, does not seem plausible, for Congress in such a case would likely have voted a declaration of war and overridden him. If the Spanish government had granted Cuba immediate independence, this alone might have prevented hostilities with the United States. Such an action was impossible for a sovereign nation, especially after the belligerent tone of American public statements about the sinking of the *Maine*. The Spanish did almost everything except grant immediate independence, but to no avail. The American minister to Spain was instructed on March 27 to notify the Madrid government that the United States had no territorial ambitions in Cuba but that there should be a Cuban armistice until October 1, as well as revocation of the concentration-camp policy. The Spanish agreed to the second demand on April 5 and granted the armistice on April 9. President McKinley had this information on April 10. The presi-

Hearst's New York *Journal* blames the Spanish.

dent hesitated, for the Spanish had met the American terms. The armistice declaration contained a qualifying phrase (the captain-general in Cuba was ordered by Madrid "to grant a suspension of hostilities for such time as he might think prudent to prepare and facilitate peace negotiations") and this might be construed as an attempt to stall matters until the Spanish military forces could consolidate their positions and prepare to reopen the war. Such was the construction put upon the Spanish offer by Henry Cabot Lodge, who described it casually in his diary as a "humbug armistice."

Yet Spain by this time was in no position to procrastinate with the United States, and the unfortunate wording of the instruction to the captain-general was probably inadvertent. McKinley may have realized this. He may also have realized that he could not control Congress. At this time, while talking about the Cuban crisis to a friend, the president broke down and cried, so his friend later wrote, like a boy of thirteen. The president said he hadn't slept more than three hours a night, he thought, during the past two weeks. This was the period when the belligerent Theodore Roosevelt, coming away from a visit to the White House, angrily asked: "Do you know what that white-livered cur up there has done? He has prepared *two* messages, one for war and one for peace, and doesn't know which one to send in!" McKinley resolved his doubts on April 11 by submitting the matter to Congress.

There could be no question of the outcome. The congressional joint resolution of April 20 demanded the independence of Cuba, withdrawal of Spanish forces, empowered the president to force Spain's withdrawal, and disclaimed any intention by the United States of exercising "sovereignty, jurisdiction or control" over Cuba. This latter clause, the Teller Amendment, passed Congress without a dissenting vote. McKinley signed the war resolution on April 20, dispatched an ultimatum to Spain, and received in return a Spanish declaration of war.

2. *The course of the war*

During the Spanish-American War there was scarcely a military campaign worthy of the name. The war began in late April and ended with an armistice on August 12. During this time Commodore George B. Dewey blew up ten old Spanish ships in Manila bay (May 1), and a minuscule Spanish squadron was sunk near the harbor of Santiago de Cuba (July 3). American land forces under General William R. Shafter accepted the surrender of Santiago after skirmishes and some sharp fighting, and in the Far East General Wesley Merritt on August 14, unaware of the armistice signed in Washington two days earlier, took Manila after a token resistance by the Spanish forces to keep out the insurgent Filipinos. With this, and including the virtually unopposed campaign by General Nelson A. Miles in Puerto Rico, the war came to an abrupt end. The result had never been in doubt. The military operations on some occasions became so ludicrous that Mr. Dooley, the mythical Chicago Irishman created by Finley Peter Dunne, could remark, apropos General Miles's Puerto Rican expedition, that it was "Gin'ral Miles' gran' picnic an' moonlight excursion . . . 'Tis no comfort in bein' a cow'rd," he added, "whin ye think iv them br-rave la-ads facin' death be suffication in bokays an' dyin' iv waltzin' with th' pretty girls iv Porther Ricky."

Annexation of the Hawaiian Islands came at last during the Spanish-American War. Acquisition of these islands had been urged in the United States for several reasons. There was a moral argument: the islands had been begging for annexation and had placed themselves in danger, for Spain might attack them. There was another argument to the effect that Hawaii should be annexed as a war measure—the islands were necessary for prosecution of the war. This contention broke down on at least two counts, namely that the war was practically over after sinking of the Spanish squadron at Santiago on July 3 (Hawaii was annexed on July 7), and that Hawaii was a less advantageous stopping place for ships en route to the Far East to support Dewey in the Philippines than was another harbor which the United States already owned, Kiska in the Aleutian Islands. Kiska was a far more commodious harbor than Honolulu, and the Kiska route was several hundred miles shorter than that via Hawaii. Moreover, Kiska was closer to being a halfway point to the Philippines than was Honolulu. A number of ships in the American navy could not carry sufficient coal for the Honolulu-to-Manila run. The northern route also was more healthful for transporting soldiers. But there was real point in a third contention for annexing Hawaii—that the Hawaiians should be annexed to facilitate the future defense of the United States. The defense argument, unlike the war-measure argument and the moral argument, was sound in 1898, before the era of air power made American possession of the Hawaiian chain even more important. The war lent urgency to the defense argument, and the McKinley administration, to play safe with a still doubtful Congress, submitted the proposal for annexation of Hawaii in the form of a joint resolution requiring only a majority vote.

Grover Cleveland, retired in Princeton, remained adamant to the end, and inquired of his friend Olney, "Did you ever see such a preposterous thing as this Hawaiian business?" Cleveland in January 1898 had said that annexation of islands in the Pacific was "a perversion of our national mission. The mission of our nation is to build up and make a greater country out of what we have, instead of annexing islands." His anti-imperialism certainly suggested one way of resolving doubts over annexation. Perhaps, however, there could have been a middle position between that of Cleveland—taking no islands at all—and the decision of the McKinley administration to annex both the Hawaiian Islands and the Philippine Islands. Perhaps Hawaii would have been enough new territory.

The most fateful territorial acquisition of the Spanish-American War was the taking of the Philippines, after Dewey had sunk the Spanish squadron. Annexation of the Philippines was of large importance to the future of American diplomacy. It projected the United States far into the Western Pacific, and so close to Japan and China—two future trouble spots of the world—that American interests, once established in the Philippines, were almost bound to become involved and probably hurt in Far Eastern rivalries quite as remote from the American national interest as had been the European rivalries against which President Washington once had counseled. The British admiral P. H. Colomb, writing in the *North American Review* for October 1898, showed with remarkably prescience what might happen to the United States because of annexation of the Philippines. Taking the islands, the admiral stated, meant that America was "for the first time giving hostages to fortune, and taking a place in the world that will entail on her sacrifices and difficulties of which she has not yet dreamed. . . . with outlying territories, especially islands, a comparatively weak power has facilities for wounding her without being wounded in return." This move into the Far East has seemed in retrospect very unwise. Perhaps, on the other hand, it was only the working out of American destiny, and could not have been humanly avoided. The victor of Manila bay, surveying his triumph over the Spanish fleet, declared that "If I were a religious man, and I hope I am, I should say that the hand of God was in it." Of this, more later; here is the place and time to recount the administrative intrigue by which the United States became prepared in 1898 to take the Philippines, once war had started over Cuba.

The intrigue was such a natural expression of Theodore Roosevelt's exuberance that perhaps there was no intrigue at all. Roosevelt was assistant secretary of the navy, having been placed in that post (according to "Boss" Platt of New York, who put him there) because "Theodore" could "probably do less harm to the [Republican Party] organization as Assistant Secretary of the Navy than in any other office that can be named." Roosevelt bent his energies to developing the fighting readiness of the new American navy, the readiness of the new battleships and cruisers which in the last decade or so had been coming off the ways of American shipyards. In the spring of 1898 it was obvious to him that a war with Spain was imminent, and he took it upon himself to prepare the

American Asiatic squadron. By some string-pulling he arranged the appointment of his friend, Commodore Dewey, to command it. Roosevelt told Dewey, who was a far better sailor than politician, that political influence was being exerted by other candidates for the squadron and that Dewey should seek out a senator. Dewey obtained the assistance of Senator Redfield Proctor of Vermont. After he received the appointment he discovered that no influence had been exerted by the other candidates. Roosevelt's left-handed manner of securing Dewey's appointment so annoyed Roosevelt's superior, Secretary of the Navy John D. Long, that Long refused Dewey the temporary rank of rear admiral which went with the Asian command, and Dewey was a commodore at the time of Manila bay.

Nor was this the only Rooseveltian maneuver, for there was the famous occasion on February 25, 1898, when Secretary Long went home for an afternoon rest and left Roosevelt as acting secretary of the navy. TR broke loose in the department that afternoon, moved ships around as if they were yachts, and among other things ordered Dewey, at last in the Far East at Hong Kong, to coal his ships and prepare for offensive operations in the Philippines in the event of war. Dewey was not to allow the Spanish squadron to leave the islands, for fear it might somehow find its way to the American west coast and ravage Seattle and San Francisco.

It is difficult to take seriously the fear that the Spanish ships in Manila could endanger the American Pacific coast. One might have thought, too, that when Secretary Long returned from his afternoon rest he could have countermanded his assistant secretary's orders and perhaps demanded Roosevelt's resignation. Nothing happened; Roosevelt stayed at the department, and when war came, Dewey was ready. After the Spanish squadron had been destroyed the commodore requested army troops to the number of 5,000 to invest Manila. The war department sent 11,000 and Manila was taken.

The investiture of Manila went off without a hitch, except for some friction that developed between Dewey and the commander of a German naval squadron then in Manila harbor. This friction was later interpreted as endangering peace between the United States and Germany. The Germans had originally blundered by sending to Manila a vice admiral in charge of a squadron slightly stronger than Dewey's, and during the summer there had been trouble over the blockade regulations which, Dewey claimed, the Germans violated. Dewey at Manila told Admiral Otto von Diederichs's flag lieutenant that if Germany wished war she could have it. He also told some newspapermen that he had a plan to engage, if necessary, the German fleet. When Dewey on August 13 was preparing to bombard Manila in support of General Merritt's troops, the

BE CAREFUL.

Emperor William of Germany seemed too interested in Far Eastern real estate.

squadrons of France, Germany, and England, then in harbor, eagerly jockeyed for position to observe the firing. In the course of the position-taking, the Germans managed to get to the left of Dewey's ships, the French were behind the Germans, and the British in an ungentlemanly maneuver sailed into position immediately in front of the Germans. The German admiral had to move his flagship from its moorings to get a better view of the hostilities. Later the story arose that the German squadron had threatened Dewey's operations, and that the British moved in between the Germans and Dewey to protect the American commodore. But there was never any danger of war with Germany. Dewey later asked Frederick

Palmer, who ghosted his *Autobiography*, to omit these contretemps from the record.

The Spanish-American War had no serious repercussions upon the European balance of power, for none of the European powers other than Spain became involved in it. Likewise, so far as concerned the two combatants, the war did not permanently impair their good relations—at the peace conference there appeared little enmity between American and Spanish negotiators. The summer of hostilities in 1898 did mark a notable consolidation of American nationalism. The war gave to the entire American people a vague feeling of danger, of risky adventure, and all but remnants of those political passions between North and South which had grown out of the Civil War and reconstruction disappeared in the comradeship of a national war. The events of the Civil War era had by this time slipped far into history. "The youngest boy who could have carried arms at Gettysburg," Paul H. Buck has written, "was a man of fifty when the century closed . . . . By far the greater portion of the generation which had listened with awe while the guns boomed in Virginia and the ships of war steamed on the Mississippi slept in silent graves in which the issues for which they had contended were buried with them. The old had given way to the new." McKinley during a speech at Atlanta in 1898 affirmed the care of Confederate graves to be a national duty. When the president appointed four temporary major generals, he diplomatically chose two ex-Confederate generals, Joseph ("Fighting Joe") Wheeler and Fitzhugh Lee. Fitzhugh Lee, nephew of Robert E. Lee, already had come to public attention in performing his duties as consul general at Havana at the time the *Maine* was sunk. Fighting Joe Wheeler went to Cuba and took part in the surrender of the island. During the campaign before Santiago there occurred the rather humorous incident when General Wheeler at one point in a battle cried, "The Yankees are running! Dammit! I mean the Spaniards!" The nation, both North and South, fought together in the Spanish-American War, and this to all American patriots was a heartwarming scene.

There were many touching evidences of this new national unity, but perhaps no event was more poignant than the demonstration that occurred when on May 20, 1898, the Sixth Massachusetts Regiment marched through Baltimore on its way to camp. In 1861 the regiment had been stoned by hostile mobs as it marched to defend Washington. The Massachusetts men in their uniforms of blue with the gallant new leggings, broad-brimmed campaign hats slouched over their faces, pennants flying, marched through the streets in 1898 with the regimental band playing "Dixie." Senator Lodge, having journeyed up from the capital to see the parade, wept unashamedly. "It was 'roses, roses all the way'," he afterward remembered, "—flags, cheers, excited crowds. Tears were in my eyes. I never felt so moved in my life. The war of 1861 was over at last and the great country for which so many men died was one again."

3. *The Paris peace conference of 1898*

The Spanish ambassador at Paris on July 19, 1898, requested the French foreign minister, Théophile Delcassé, to mediate between Spain and the United States. This the foreign minister did through his ambassador in Washington, Jules Cambon, and Cambon on August 12 signed an armistice on behalf of the Spanish. According to its terms a peace conference was to assemble in Paris not later than October 1. President McKinley appointed five peace commissioners: the chairman of the Senate committee on foreign relations, Senator Cushman K. Davis; the next ranking Republican member, Senator William P. Frye; the leading minority member of the foreign relations committee, Senator George Gray; Secretary of State William R. Day (who on September 30 yielded his secretaryship to John Hay); and Whitelaw Reid, publisher of the New York *Tribune*. Curiously there was some question over the propriety of McKinley's appointments, because the three senators, so the contemporary argument ran, would have to vote on their own handiwork after returning from Paris. The politically astute McKinley ignored such pleas and set a precedent which Woodrow Wilson twenty years later might well have followed at the peace conference of 1919.

Upon arrival in Paris the commission was treated to an elaborate luncheon of twenty-six covers given by Delcassé at the Quai d'Orsay Palace, September 29, 1898: oysters, lake trout, beef, cutlets Sévigné d'ivoire, duck, partridges, ham, salads, artichokes au champagne, ices (Russian style), fruits, French wines. During the deliberations which followed— the conference lasted two months and two days—the peace commissioners meeting in a large room of the French foreign office had constant access to an anteroom containing a well-stocked larder. In view of the paucity of diplomatic business before the conference, this may explain why its sessions took so long. There were only two unsettled questions, namely the Cuban debt (should the United States assume it?), and the Philippines (should the islands be annexed?). The American commissioners refused to assume the $400,000,000 Cuban debt. As for the Philippines, there was little to discuss, because the question would have to be settled in Washington.

Until Dewey encountered the Spanish squadron the Philippines meant little to the American people. McKinley himself said afterward, "When we received the cable from Admiral Dewey telling of the taking of the Philippines I looked up their location on the globe. I could not have told where those darned islands were within 2,000 miles!" As debate grew in volume over disposition of the Philippines, Mr. Dooley remarked to his good friend Mr. Hennessy that " 'tis not more thin two months since ye larned whether they were islands or canned goods. . . . Suppose ye was standin' at th' corner iv State Sthreet an' Archey R-road, wud ye know what car to take to get to th' Ph'lippeens? If yer son Packy was to ask ye where th' Ph'lippeens is, cud ye give him anny good idea whether they was in Rooshia or jus' west iv th' thracks?" But the governing fact of the Philippine question was that the United States had taken possession of Manila. Hennessy had begun the above colloquy by remarking that "I know what I'd do if I was Mack. I'd hist a flag over th' Ph'lippeens, an' I'd take in th' whole lot iv thim." After protests from Dooley he still was saying "Hang on to thim. What we've got we must hold." Hennessy captured the essence of the Philippine argument, for possession was nine-tenths of the decision.

Taking the islands was easier for the McKinley administration when American businessmen began to see in the Philippines a stepping-stone —vestibule, anteroom, or general entrance—to the China trade. Markets in China, as we shall see in the next chapter, had long intrigued American businessmen. The new sense of manifest destiny had stemmed in part from the feelings of the American business community that the domestic market of the United States was saturated, and that expansion of foreign trade was the only hope of further developing the American economy. Businessmen, down to the beginning of hostilities with Spain, had opposed war, believing that a war could only harm the economy. A war's effects, business leaders maintained, would perhaps include derangement of the currency and a revival of the free-silver agitation. They suspected that most of the jingoes were free-silverites. "Free Silver and Free Cuba," so Senator Lodge believed, would be the Democratic Party's campaign slogan in the election of 1900. With the taking of Manila, business fears began to evaporate. Business pressures to keep the Philippines in anticipation of the China trade converged upon Washington at the same time that retention of the islands was attracting popular support throughout the country. The railway magnate, James J. Hill, declared that whoever controlled the trade of the orient held the world's purse strings. The Philippines, according to another business figure, were the key to the orient. Senator Lodge argued that Manila was the great prize and "the thing which will give us the eastern trade."

The China trade was, one should add parenthetically, a mirage. It has never amounted to anything. In 1898 the mirage was more important than reality, especially after the nation had just emerged from the difficult economic era of the mid-1890's.

There was no chance of the United States taking part of the Philippine Islands—say Luzon with Manila. It was a case of all the islands or none. General Merritt went to Paris from Manila to give his views to the peace commissioners, and while he at first indicated that Luzon might be held alone, under further questioning he admitted that Manila was prosperous only because it was the capital of the archipelago. Militarily, too, there could be little advantage, and positive disadvantage, in allowing the other islands to pass under control of some power other than the United States.

If the United States refused to take the islands, they would probably have passed to one of the European powers, perhaps Germany (Japan and England were also interested). Germany made an agreement with Spain, after Spain's armistice with the United States and before the assembling of the Paris peace conference, in which it was stipulated that Spain would resist any demands of the Americans for the Caroline Islands, if such demands were made, and that after the peace settlement these islands would be sold to Germany.

President McKinley is reported by many people who saw him at the time to have been much worried about the fate of the Philippines. What, he asked casual visitors to the White House, could he do with the islands? At one juncture he said that "If old Dewey had just sailed away when he smashed that Spanish fleet, what a lot of trouble he would have saved us." Old Dewey had not sailed away, and popular opinion in the United States had risen to such heights of adulation over the hero of Manila bay (Dewey had still to disappoint his admirers by displaying his political vanity) that the commodore could not have departed from the scene of his triumph even if the national interest dictated it.

A religious factor, albeit one based on something of a misunderstanding, exerted a considerable influence in the American decision to take the Philippines. American Protestants looked to the islands as an area to be Christianized. President McKinley, a devout Methodist who instituted hymn singing in the White House each Sunday evening during his years of office, was much concerned over the religious needs of the Filipinos. Mrs. McKinley, according to one White House visitor, "talked ten to the minute about converting the Igorrotes. . . . Anyhow she wants you and Alice to pray for the Igorrotes." Actually, of course, the Philippine Islands were the single flourishing outpost of Christianity in the Far East, for most of the Filipinos were Catholics, having been converted by the Spanish some centuries before the Spanish-American War. American Catholics found the religious argument for retention of the islands difficult to follow. Nonetheless it was of importance.

Having made up his mind, somehow or other, and reinforced his opinions by a speaking trip through large areas of the Middle West where he received ovations after such words and phrases as *destiny, duty, humanity,* and *the hand of the Almighty God,* McKinley sent word to the American peace commissioners in Paris. The Spanish commissioners had no recourse except, after a month and more of stalling, to acquiesce.

The terms of the Treaty of Paris, signed on December 10, 1898, were cession of the Philippine Islands, Puerto Rico, and Guam. The latter island, 3,300 miles west of Honolulu, was well situated as a naval station en route to the Philippine Islands, and the decision to retain the Philippines led logically to inclusion of Guam in the peace settlement of 1898. The United States paid $20,000,000 for the Philippines. Spain surrendered all claim to Cuba and agreed to assume the Cuban debt.

Secretary Hay gives four drafts for $5,000,000 each to the French Ambassador, M. Jules Cambon, to be paid to Spain for the Philippine Islands.

There was a small crisis in getting the treaty through the Senate, for until the end of debate the issue lay in doubt and the vote on February 6, 1899, was close, 57 to 27, one vote above the necessary two-thirds majority. William Jennings Bryan, who had felt some of the martial spirit during the war and volunteered as a colonel of cavalry, greatly assisted the McKinley administration in urging the treaty upon some of the reluctant Democratic senators. It was said that the non-Republican senators (Democrats, Populists, and some independents) who voted for the treaty were partly converted by the counsel of Bryan, personally given during a

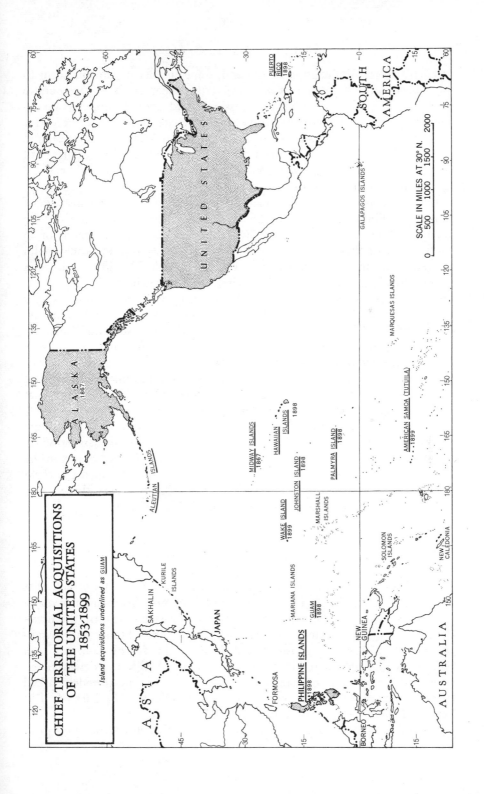

CHIEF TERRITORIAL ACQUISITIONS
OF THE UNITED STATES
1853-1899

Island acquisitions underlined as GUAM

SCALE IN MILES AT 30° N.

ASIA

SOUTH
AMERICA

UNITED STATES

ALASKA
1867

ALEUTIAN ISLANDS

MIDWAY ISLANDS
1867

HAWAIIAN
ISLANDS
1898

JOHNSTON ISLAND
1898

PALMYRA ISLAND
1898

AMERICAN SAMOA (TUTUILA)
1899

PUERTO
RICO
1898

GALAPAGOS ISLANDS

MARQUESAS ISLANDS

WAKE ISLAND
1899

MARSHALL
ISLANDS

MARIANA ISLANDS

GUAM
1898

SOLOMON
ISLANDS

NEW
CALEDONIA

NEW
GUINEA

SAKHALIN

KURILE
ISLANDS

JAPAN

FORMOSA

PHILIPPINE ISLANDS
1898

BORNEO

AUSTRALIA

hurried trip to Washington. In the end, some further arguments seem to have been offered to one or two wavering senators. The Democratic Senator Gray, who as a peace commissioner had strongly opposed taking the Philippines, voted for the treaty in the Senate and shortly thereafter received a federal judgeship from the Republican McKinley. One should add that the McKinley administration could have waited if necessary until March 4, 1899, and the admission of a sufficient number of recently elected Republican senators to approve the treaty.

But the importance of the Spanish-American War in the history of American diplomacy does not lie in the closeness of the vote on the treaty, for that could have been favorably changed a month later, or in the relation of the war to the diplomacies of the European powers who by 1898 were pursuing the rivalries which led to the World War in 1914 —the powers did not believe their vital interests challenged by the war, and Germany, while wistful about the disposition of the Philippines, was content with receiving the Caroline and Palau Islands and the Mariana Islands with the exception of Guam. Nor did the new status of Cuba, an American protectorate, affect greatly the cause of American history. The importance of the Spanish-American War for the diplomatic history of the United States lies in its appeal to the new sentiment of manifest destiny, its lending of substance and a feeling of achievement to what hitherto had been largely dreams and hopes. America in 1898 "emerged" as a world power, to use the verb of the day. The experience was thrilling to the national psyche. At the moment few individuals foresaw how acquisition of the Philippine Islands had committed the United States in the far Pacific, and that in subsequent years with the rise of Japan to world power there would come difficulties that eventually, forty-three years after 1898, would lead the country into a first-class Asian war.

CONTEMPORARY DOCUMENTS

[In explaining why the McKinley administration decided in 1898 that the United States should take the Philippine Islands, historians for many years have remarked the piquant details of an interview held by the president with a group of Methodists visiting at the White House on November 21, 1899. McKinley's visitors had thanked him for his courtesy to a church assemblage currently being held in Washington, listened to an appropriate response, and had turned to leave, when the president asked them to remain a moment. Source: Charles S. Olcott, *The Life of William McKinley* (2 vols., Boston, 1916), II, 109–111.]

Hold a moment longer! Not quite yet, gentlemen! Before you go

I would like to say just a word about the Philippine business. I have been criticized a good deal about the Philippines, but don't deserve it. The truth is I didn't want the Philippines, and when they came to us, as a gift from the gods, I did not know what to do with them. When the Spanish War broke out, Dewey was at Hongkong, and I ordered him to go to Manila and to capture or destroy the Spanish fleet, and he had to; because, if defeated, he had no place to refit on that side of the globe, and if the Dons were victorious, they would likely cross the Pacific and ravage our Oregon and California coasts. And so he had to destroy the Spanish fleet, and did it! But that was as far as I thought then.

When next I realized that the Philippines had dropped into our laps I confess I did not know what to do with them. I sought counsel from all sides—Democrats as well as Republicans—but got little help. I thought first we would take only Manila; then Luzon; then other islands, perhaps, also. I walked the floor of the White House night after night until midnight; and I am not ashamed to tell you, gentlemen, that I went down on my knees and prayed Almighty God for light and guidance more than one night. And one night late it came to me this way—I don't know how it was, but it came: (1) That we could not give them back to Spain—that would be cowardly and dishonorable; (2) that we could not turn them over to France or Germany—our commercial rivals in the Orient—that would be bad business and discreditable; (3) that we could not leave them to themselves—they were unfit for self-government—and they would soon have anarchy and misrule over there worse than Spain's was; and (4) that there was nothing left for us to do but to take them all, and to educate the Filipinos, and uplift and civilize and Christianize them, and by God's grace do the very best we could by them, as our fellow-men for whom Christ also died. And then I went to bed, and went to sleep, and slept soundly, and the next morning I sent for the chief engineer of the War Department (our map-maker), and I told him to put the Philippines on the map of the United States, and there they are, and there they will stay while I am President!

[An interesting aspect of this account is that the president's words, quoted by the biographer Olcott, came from a recollection of the interview by one of the members of the delegation in 1899, printed in the *Christian Advocate* for January 22, 1903. By this time McKinley had been dead for well over a year. The author of the recollection in the *Advocate*, Brigadier General James F. Rusling, was an author of sorts, and in one of his books, *Men and Things I Saw in Civil War Days* (New

York, 1899, pp. 14–15), he described an interview, at which he was present, between Major General Daniel E. Sickles and President Lincoln on Sunday, July 5, 1863, just after the Battle of Gettysburg. At that time Rusling was a member of Sickles's staff. Sickles had lost a leg at Gettysburg and was lying in a hospital bed in Washington.]

When Mr. Lincoln's inquiries seemed ended General Sickles, after a puff or two of his cigar in silence, resumed the conversation substantially as follows:

"Well, Mr. President, I beg pardon, but what did you think about Gettysburg? What was your opinion of things while we were campaigning and fighting up there?"

"O," replied Mr. Lincoln, "I didn't think much about it. I was not much concerned about you!"

"You were not?" rejoined Sickles, as if amazed. "Why, we heard that you Washington folks were a good deal excited, and you certainly had good cause to be. For it was 'nip and tuck' with us a good deal of the time!"

"Yes, I know that. And I suppose some of us were a little 'rattled.' Indeed, some of the Cabinet talked of Washington's being captured, and ordered a gunboat or two here, and even went so far as to send some government archives abroad, and wanted me to go, too, but I refused. Stanton and Welles, I believe, were both 'stampeded' somewhat, and Seward, I reckon, too. But I said: 'No, gentlemen, we are all right and we are going to win at Gettysburg;' and we did, right handsomely. No, General Sickles, I had no fears of Gettysburg!"

"Why not, Mr. President? How was that? Pretty much everybody down here, we heard, was more or less panicky."

"Yes, I expect, and a good many more than will own up now. But actually General Sickles, I had no fears of Gettysburg, and if you really want to know I will tell you why. Of course, I don't want you and Colonel Rusling here to say anything about this—at least not now. People might laugh if it got out, you know. But the fact is, in the very pinch of the campaign there, I went to my room one day and got down on my knees, and prayed Almighty God for victory at Gettysburg. I told Him that this was His country, and the war was His war, but that we really couldn't stand another Fredericksburg or Chancellorsville. And then and there I made a solemn vow with my Maker, that if He would stand by you boys at Gettysburg, I would stand by Him.

"And after thus wrestling with the Almighty in prayer, I don't know how it was, and it is not for me to explain, but, somehow or other, a sweet comfort crept into my soul, that God Almighty had taken the whole business there into His own hands, and we were bound to win at Gettysburg! And He *did* stand by you boys at Gettysburg, and now I will *stand by Him*. No, General Sickles, I had no fears of Gettysburg, and that is the *why!*"

ADDITIONAL READING

There are several books concerning the origins and course of the Spanish-American War, and among them are *Walter Millis, *The Martial Spirit: A Study of Our War with Spain* (Boston, 1931), written with a view to the humor and occasional ridiculousness of the conflict; Orestes Ferrera, *The Last Spanish War* (New York, 1937), a Spanish interpretation; *Ernest R. May, *Imperial Democracy* (New York, 1961), the latest scholarship; *H. Wayne Morgan, *America's Road to Empire: The War with Spain and Overseas Expansion* (New York, 1965), a volume in the America in Crisis series; *Walter La Feber, *The New Empire* (Ithaca, N.Y., 1963). A fascinating volume of pictures and text is Frank Freidel, *The Splendid Little War* (Boston, 1958). A little frothy and impressionistic, Gregory Mason's *Remember the Maine* (New York, 1939) is nonetheless worth attention. *Julius W. Pratt's *Expansionists of 1898* (Baltimore, 1936) deals with Hawaii and the Philippines. See also *Foster Rhea Dulles, *The Imperial Years* (New York, 1956) and Wilfrid Hardy Callcott, *The Caribbean Policy of the United States: 1890–1920* (Baltimore, 1942). Two monographs are Joseph E. Wisan, *The Cuban Crisis as Reflected in the New York Press: 1895–1898* (New York, 1934) and John Edward Weems, *The Fate of the Maine* (New York, 1958). Thomas A. Bailey treats an important aspect of the war, "Dewey and the Germans at Manila Bay," *American Historical Review*, XIV (1939–1940), 59–81. See also W. R. Braisted, *The United States Navy in the Pacific: 1897–1909* (Austin, Tex., 1958).

For the statesmen of the period see *Howard K. Beale's excellent *Theodore Roosevelt and the Rise of America to World Power* (Baltimore, 1956), together with the somewhat dated but eminently readable *Henry F. Pringle, *Theodore Roosevelt* (New York, 1931). A much better account of TR is *William Henry Harbaugh, *Power and Responsibility: The Life and Times of Theodore Roosevelt* (New York, 1961). TR's reminiscences in his *Autobiography* (New York, 1913) are always interesting if at times inaccurate. H. H. Kohlsaat, *From McKinley to Harding: Personal Recollections of Our Presidents* (New York, 1923) is a mine of quotation on McKinley. See also Margaret Leech's marvelous *In the Days of McKinley* (New York, 1959), a "life and times" in colorful detail. Other biographies are Tyler Dennett, *John Hay: From Poetry to Politics* (New York, 1933), a brilliant book about that *fin de siècle* statesman, relating Hay's continuing luck with appointments and perquisites down to the time of appointment as secretary of state and even through the secretaryship; Claude G. Bowers, *Beveridge and the Progressive*

Era (New York, 1932), best for that Indiana statesman and "jingo"; Joseph E. McLean, *William Rufus Day* (Baltimore, 1946), on McKinley's second secretary of state; *Richard W. Leopold, *Elihu Root and the Conservative Tradition* (Boston, 1954), an extremely able account by a close student of American diplomacy, a volume in the Library of American Biography series; the longer account by Philip C. Jessup, *Elihu Root* (2 vols., New York, 1938); W. A. Swanberg, *Citizen Hearst* (New York, 1961), a hostile book which was denied the Pulitzer Prize because of a committee opinion that the prize should be only for biographies on individuals worthy of emulation. For titles concerning William Jennings Bryan, who was just beginning to touch issues of foreign affairs, see suggestions for additional reading at the end of chapter eighteen.

The territorial results of the war appear in parts of Julius W. Pratt's *America's Colonial Experiment: How the United States Gained, Governed, and In Part Gave Away a Colonial Empire* (New York, 1950). Consult also Earl S. Pomeroy's attractive volume, *Pacific Outpost: American Strategy in Guam and Micronesia* (Stanford, Calif., 1951). For Britain's acquiescence in America's new world position see Charles S. Campbell, Jr., *Anglo-American Understanding: 1898–1903* (Baltimore, 1957); Alexander E. Campbell, *Great Britain and the United States* (Glasgow, 1960); R. G. Neale, *Great Britain and United States Expansion: 1898–1900* (East Lansing, Mich., 1966); and Bradford Perkins, *The Great Rapprochement* (New York, 1968).

Mr. Dooley's witty disgust with American imperialism is in Finley Peter Dunne's *Mr. Dooley: In Peace and in War* (Boston, 1898) and Elmer Ellis, ed., *Mr. Dooley at His Best* (New York, 1938).

*Paul H. Buck, *The Road to Reunion: 1865–1900* (Boston, 1937) shows a signal result of the war, the consolidation of American nationalism.

☆ 16 ☆

The Far East, 1899-1921

>Wherever man oppresses man
> Beneath Thy liberal sun,
>O Lord be there, Thine arm laid bare,
> Thy righteous will be done.
>   —Protestant hymn, verse by John Hay

1. *The open door notes*

By the end of the nineteenth century the westernization of the orient, despite some initial resistance, had proceeded rather far. The Japanese took over Western culture wholesale, in many cases jettisoning their heritage of centuries in favor of the latest Western nicknack. One westernized Japanese destroyed a precious collection of Japanese prints to fill his house with cheap Western art. As for the Chinese, they at first proved more resistant to Western ways, but by the end of the century there was scarcely a locality in China, hinterland or coast, where the influence of the Western world had not reached.

It was perhaps coincidental that the disruptive effect of westernization in China was accompanied by a decline in vigor of the Manchu dynasty. The Manchus had begun their reign with considerable prestige and power in the mid-seventeenth century, but after two hundred years the Taiping rebellion, together with disorders by the so-called Nien Fei bandits, who ravaged large parts of the country, had shaken the Dragon Throne to its foundations. The authority of Peking was tenuous in the extreme by the end of the nineteenth century, and it was obvious to all intelligent observers that the Manchu empire was breaking up, that a chaotic situation was arising not unlike that of India at the beginning of the eighteenth century. As in India, an opportunity presented itself to

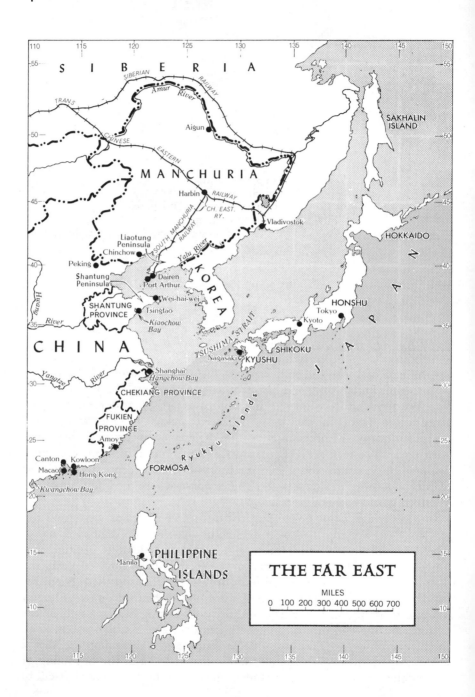

THE FAR EAST

MILES
0 100 200 300 400 500 600 700

Western powers. But whereas in India only British power was able to take great advantage of the weakness of the native dynasty, in China in the 1890's all the major powers of Europe sought to take part of the spoils.

The first move was by the Russians, and their greed was quickly matched by that of the other nations. After the Japanese had defeated the Chinese in a war in 1894–1895, demonstrating to the world the weakness of the Manchu regime, the tsarist government concluded in June 1896 the Li-Lobanov Treaty providing the right to construct a railway across Manchuria—the Chinese Eastern Railway—as a short-cut for the Trans-Siberian route to Vladivostok. Moves by the other powers followed at once. When two German missionaries were murdered by Chinese bandits in the Shantung peninsula in November 1897, the Germans in early March 1898 extracted a convention giving them a 99-year lease on Kiao-chow bay and its port of Tsingtao, together with economic rights in Shantung. Three weeks later the Russians undertook to procure a 25-year lease of the southern part of the Liaotung peninsula including Talien-wan (Dairen) and Port Arthur, with the right to construct a railroad from Harbin in the north to the newly leased ports (this railroad, at first a feeder of the Chinese Eastern, became known after the Japanese acquired it in 1905 as the South Manchuria Railway). The British in a strategic counter took a 99-year lease of Kowloon opposite Hongking and a lease on Wei-hai-wei on the Shantung peninsula "for so long a period as Port Arthur shall remain in the occupation of Russia." Meanwhile they had obtained other privileges from China, along with a pledge not to alienate to a foreign power any of the Yangtze Valley. The French obtained Kwang-chow bay in South China. Japan obtained rights in Fukien province opposite Formosa. Only the Italians, seeking in 1899 a naval station in Chekiang province, were successfully rebuffed.

The United States was at first oblivious to the impending chaos in China and to the probability that the Western nations would cut up the decrepit Manchu empire, although the turn of events in China coincided with the Spanish-American War and the somewhat fortuitous acquisition of the Philippine Islands, by which the United States became a Far Eastern power. The British government in March 1898 had suggested a joint Anglo-American approach to the other Western powers interested in China, calculated to avoid a partition of the Chinese empire and a parcel-ing-out of its trade among the partitioners. Because of the imminent war with Spain, President McKinley failed to heed the British request. Again, in January 1899, the British ambassador in Washington made an inquiry of the state department, suggesting co-operation of London and Washington in the Far East. Once more the American government evinced no interest.

At this point came a personal intervention which always has intrigued students of American diplomacy. The Far Eastern adviser of Secretary of State Hay was William W. Rockhill, an "old China hand" intensely devoted to the welfare of the Chinese people. He feared that a partition of the Manchu empire would only mean further exploitation for the already downtrodden Chinese population. Rockhill was visited in the summer of 1899 by a friend from China, another old China hand, a Britisher named Alfred E. Hippisley. The latter suggested that in view of the concession-hunting in China the time was ripe for an American diplomatic move in favor of China, an attempt to obtain adherence by the powers of Europe to a commercial policy of the "open door" in China. The extraordinary nature of Hippisley's proposal becomes manifest when one realizes that Great Britain already had attempted twice to obtain the co-operation of the United States in promoting the open-door policy in China. Could it be that the British foreign office, wise in the ways of diplomacy, had undertaken to influence American policy through an intermediary?

Actually there appears to have been nothing untoward or devious about the connection of this policy with the Britisher, Hippisley, for the latter was a genuine friend of the Chinese people, as was his American confidant Rockhill. Hippisley had long been an official of the Imperial Chinese Maritime Customs Service, a British-administered organization but one distinct in interests, responsibility, and outlook from the foreign office. Hippisley by 1899 was second in charge of the customs service, was doubtless concerned over the service's control of tariffs in the new spheres of interest of the Western powers, and for this reason alone had justification for seeking through Rockhill an American move to protect the open door and generally China's control over trade throughout the empire. Moreover, both he and Rockhill were students of Chinese history and culture, and they for this reason too were interested in a pro-Chinese diplomatic move by the United States. Hippisley had long been a Sinologue, and Rockhill was one of the world's authorities on Tibet. There was thus an easy explanation of why Hippisley proposed the open door to Rockhill and why the latter responded by forwarding Hippisley's proposition to Secretary of State Hay. The two men naturally would talk in terms of the threatened closing of the China market, which would attract the American people, rather than presenting an argument purely in terms of China's welfare or of China's control over customs.

Hippisley, as is well known, drew up a memorandum on the open door. His friend Rockhill revised this analysis for presentation to President McKinley and afterward put the substance of the revised memorandum in the form of diplomatic notes which, with minor changes, were adopted by Secretary Hay and sent out to Berlin, St. Petersburg, London, Paris, Rome, and Tokyo on September 6 and November 17, 1899. This was the first open door note, containing the following three points:

First. The recognition that no power will in any way interfere with any treaty port or any vested interest within any leased territory or within any so-called "sphere of interest" it may have in China.

Second. That the Chinese treaty tariff of the time being shall apply to all merchandise landed or shipped to all such ports as are within said "sphere of interest" (unless they be "free ports"), no matter to what nationality it may belong, and that duties so leviable shall be collected by the Chinese Government.

Third. That it [each power] will levy no higher harbor dues on vessels of another nationality frequenting any port in such "sphere" than shall be levied on vessels of its own nationality, and no higher railroad charges over lines built, controlled, or operated within its "sphere" on merchandise belonging to citizens or subjects of other nationalities transported through such "sphere" than shall be levied on similar merchandise belonging to its own nationals transported over equal distances.

The note could by no stretch of the imagination be described as epoch-making. The traditional American commercial policy toward China during the nineteenth century had been a policy of free competition among the powers for trade—in other words, a policy of the open door in regard to China. There had not hitherto, it is true, been an effort to line up the other powers to favor this policy. The open door, as traditionally interpreted, had been a unilateral policy of the United States, contained only in treaties with China. But sooner or later it would have been elaborated in diplomatic intercourse with the nations interested in Chinese trade. To make multilateral this doctrine of fair trade in China was perhaps no more than a logical development of a traditional American policy. The first open door note contemplated free commercial intercourse under the Chinese treaty tariff of five per cent—within the spheres of interest of the various powers. It did not contemplate abolition of the spheres of interest, although Hay's adviser Rockhill, to be sure, thought that by providing for collection of duties by the Chinese he had taken a stand in favor of protecting Chinese sovereignty within the spheres.

It was in the year 1900 that Hay made a second open door effort, one far more important than the initiative of the previous year, and much different. An outbreak of antiforeign agitation in China, the Boxer rebellion, had required an expedition by an international force of 19,000 troops —including an American contingent—to rescue the besieged legations in Peking. On July 3, 1900, when it was uncertain whether the besieged legations in Peking would be saved, and when it seemed likely that after taking Peking the troops of the powers would engage in a grand division of Chinese territory, Hay made the bold and—in view of the conditions under which he made it—imaginative move of sending a circular note to the powers favoring the territorial integrity of China. This second open door note, unlike its predecessor, was a novel statement of American policy. In the note of 1900 the secretary of state advanced to ground quite different from that covered by his note of the year before. In some ways the two open door notes should not be coupled, for the second note in its stipulations regarding Chinese territorial integrity contradicted the note of September–November 1899. The first note had stipulated commercial freedom for all nations within any of the spheres of interest. In his second open door note Hay announced that American policy sought to "preserve Chinese territorial and administrative entity," that is, that the United States was taking a stand against the further partitioning of China.

The second note, like the first, expressed the views of Hay's adviser Rockhill (and of his adviser, Hippisley), but neither Hippisley nor Rockhill nor Hay dreamed that the open door policy would be more than a temporary buttress to Far Eastern peace. They did not envision that their diplomacy of the moment, "a kind of *modus vivendi*" as Rockhill described the first open door notes, would become a cardinal doctrine of twentieth-century American policy in the orient. As the twentieth century advanced and Japan became ever more powerful in the Far East, threatening the integrity of China in numerous ways and on various occasions, American diplomacy tended to distort the sense of the second Hay open door note. The idea of preserving Chinese territorial and administrative entity, in itself a somewhat ambitious policy, gave way almost unconsciously to the idea of downright guarantee of Chinese territory. There had never been a contractual guarantee of Chinese territory by the United States. But by 1941 the American public was virtually convinced that this was traditional American policy.

2. *Rooseveltian diplomacy, 1900–1909*

The year 1900 was certainly a signal year in modern Chinese history, what with the suppression of the Boxer rebellion by the troops of the powers, and their forceful occupation of Peking. The nations imposed upon China a large claim for damages in the form of an indemnity of $738,820,707, distributed among Britain, France, Germany, Italy, Austria-Hungary, the United States, and Japan. The United States after accepting $4,000,000 to satisfy private claims, eventually remitted the remaining payments for the purpose of training Chinese students in America. The other nations kept the indemnities due them. In such wise the new century opened, but in 1900, it seems safe to say, the shape of the future was still uncertain. Settlement of the Boxer rebellion seemed to quiet affairs in the orient—for good, so many Americans and Europeans hoped.

In the year 1900 it was Russia, not Japan, which appeared to be the problem of the orient. Although Japan had defeated China in 1894–1895 in an exhibition of military prowess that boded ill for the future, when the powers had reached Peking and there was looting by some of the troops of the European nations the Japanese soldiers were well-behaved. In 1900 the Russians, far more than the Japanese, seemed the nation to watch. Russia had participated in a triple intervention along with Germany and France to thwart Japan in 1895, after the Japanese had won the war against China. At that time the tsarist government had insisted that Japan not take the southernmost part of Manchuria, the Liaotung peninsula, including a port on its tip which controlled the approaches to Peking. Faced with the intervention of three European powers, the Japanese in 1895 diplomatically withdrew their claims to Liaotung. The next year the Russians began moving into northern Manchuria under an agreement with the Chinese. By the time of the Boxer rebellion Russia was ready to occupy Manchuria, including all of the Liaotung peninsula, the territory denied to Japan in 1895. Russia also was showing considerable interest in Korea.

Russia was the power to watch—so the observers were writing at the turn of the century. Because of the clear record of Russian imperialism in the Far East, the powers, including the United States, were highly suspicious of the tsar's government. Theodore Roosevelt, upon succeeding the assassinated McKinley in the presidency, was thoroughly distrustful of the activities of tsarist Russia in the orient. After the Boxer rebellion, when trouble began to increase between Russia and Japan and war loomed, TR was happy to say that in case of a Russo-Japanese war he hoped Japan would win. The Russians were attempting to close Manchuria to foreign trade, on the theory that Manchuria was no longer a part of China. This was contrary to the idea of the open door, and other Americans than Roosevelt hoped that if Russia and Japan went to war, Japan would win and open Manchuria to trade. Japan would serve as houseboy for the open door.

The war between Japan and Russia began and ended with Russian naval defeats. After pressing the Russians to agree over a partition of Korea, and discouraged at the delay and evasion and the continuing expansion of Russian power in the Far East, Japan had severed diplomatic relations with Russia on February 6, 1904, and two days later suddenly attacked the tsarist fleet at Port Arthur, declaring war two days after hostilities began.

Japanese troops invested Russian positions in Manchuria, giving no heed to the neutrality of Chinese soil, and in a matter of a few months, albeit with expenditure of over 100,000 Japanese lives, the island empire had bested one of the most ancient of European nations. The last hope of the Russians was the thirty-two ships of the Baltic fleet, sent on a long voyage through the Mediterranean and the Indian Ocean to the Far East, only to be annihilated by Japan's Admiral Togo in Tsushima strait.

What happened during the Russo-Japanese War of 1904–1905 was one of the surprises of the twentieth century—the abject defeat of Russia, the emergence of Japan as one of the first-class military powers of the world. Although they had disliked the Russians, the Americans had not bargained for this development. Japan, by defeating Russia, unsettled the entire Far East in a way that no event had done before, and the vulnerability of the Philippines began to appear as a major security problem for the United States. The Americans, perhaps, had only themselves to blame for this turn of affairs. They had for decades been doing their best to avoid any breakup of Japan similar to that of China, and in pursuing this purpose had done much to bolster Japan's military capabilities. American military assistance had begun with Perry's gift of one cannon from the *Saratoga*. The commodore had recommended to the navy department that two more be sent, for such gifts, he said, would on some future occasion be "returned a hundred-fold." The Japanese mission to the United States in 1860 had received a hundred muskets, four howitzers, shells and shell-filling machines. The United States sold three war vessels to Japan in 1863 and delivered them in 1865. Annapolis was opened to Japanese students in 1868. By contributing a number of political advisers to the Japanese government in the latter nineteenth century, the United States further helped to make Japan a strong naval power. Mahan himself said that his writings had been more fully translated into Japanese than into any other language. But in the war of 1904–1905 the Japanese had suddenly exhibited the results of this American tuition in a new and startling and not altogether pleasant manner.

After initial requests from the belligerents, President Roosevelt undertook to mediate the war in the summer of 1905, and this task he performed with his usual aplomb, bringing his work of peace to a suitable end in the Treaty of Portsmouth, signed by Japan and Russia at Portsmouth, New Hampshire, on September 5, 1905. By this treaty Japan acquired the South Manchuria Railway, the Liaotung peninsula under guise of a leasehold, and the southern half of Sakhalin Island. Russia acknowledged Japan's paramount interest in Korea.

The Portsmouth Treaty, narrowly considered, was a diplomatic accomplishment of the first order, and the American president eventually re-

Theodore Roosevelt at Portsmouth, with (L. to R.) Witte, Rosen, Komura, and Takahira.

ceived the Nobel Peace Prize for his work in 1905. Unfortunately, in its long-term effects on American policy the treaty was hardly a triumph—indeed it was a disaster—for in reality it inaugurated the American-Japanese political antagonism that would plague American relations with the Far East during the first half of the twentieth century. Policy could no longer placidly continue in the nineteenth-century pattern of trade-Christianity-civilization. The Portsmouth Treaty, it is true, was probably the best treaty that either Russia or Japan could have obtained in the summer of 1905. The Russians were exhausted and the tsarist regime faced the first stirrings of the revolution that would engulf it in 1917. The Japanese were in equally bad straits, for their credit abroad was such as to dictate a speedy end to the war. Japanese finances had long been precarious, and the burden of further war in 1905 was almost too much to endure. The Japanese representatives at Portsmouth should have been satisfied with the peace treaty, and they were pleased, but they had failed to get an indemnity from Russia and obtained only half of Sakhalin. The government in Tokyo diplomatically allowed popular disappointment to focus on the American president who had mediated the peace, rather than the Japanese envoys who had signed it. Anti-American riots broke out in Tokyo, mobs burned four American churches, the United States embassy was placed under guard, and in subsequent years—as the Japanese spread further into Manchuria, taking advantage of Western weakness or preoccupation elsewhere—the rift in American-Japanese relations widened into a chasm.

In the uneasy years after the outbreak of the Russo-Japanese War there followed three special agreements by which Japan and the United States sought to allay their mutual suspicions and somehow recreate the friendly atmosphere that had prevailed in an earlier era: the Taft-Katsura Agreement (1905), the Root-Takahira Agreement (1908), and the Lansing-Ishii Agreement (1917). Unfortunately each agreement produced disagreement and became a milestone in the antagonism developing between the United States and Japan. Each was accompanied by other untoward happenings and occurrences: the so-called Gentlemen's Agreement concerning immigration, the Knox neutralization scheme, the China consortium, the Twenty-One Demands.

The Taft-Katsura Agreement, an "agreed memorandum" between Secretary of War William Howard Taft and the Japanese premier, Taro Katsura, dated July 29, 1905, marked the initial effort of President Roosevelt to reach a harmonious arrangement with the Japanese government. It was obvious to Roosevelt that Japan was the coming power in the orient, and since the United States had acquired the Philippines, islands which lay at Japan's doorstep, it was prudent to placate the owners of the house. Placation meant giving away, in effect, an old edifice which lay close to the house, the kingdom of Korea. According to the Taft-Katsura Agreement, which supposedly bound only the administration then in power at Washington (though it is difficult to imagine how such an agreement could bind merely a single administration), the United States recognized Japan's dominant position in Korea, and the Japanese disavowed "any aggressive designs whatever" on the Philippines.

No sooner was this memorandum drawn and the Portsmouth Treaty signed than trouble appeared with Japan, in an unexpected quarter—the segregating of Japanese school children together with Chinese and Koreans in the San Francisco schools. We have seen how the immigration of the Chinese to California in the years after the discovery of gold and during construction of the transcontinental railroad became in time an exceedingly sore point in California and eventually forced an exclusion act through Congress in 1882. It was easy to exclude the Chinese, for the Chinese government was unable to do much more than protest such an act by the Americans. In the case of the Japanese, in the years after the Russo-Japanese War when the Japanese government was feeling its power and able to protest with vigor and effect, to take discriminating measures was far more dangerous. Yet in 1906, just a year after signature of the Portsmouth Treaty, the issue of Japanese immigration to California arose in this singularly ugly form. It is true that some adult Japanese had been attending grade schools—not a desirable situation, although these Japanese grownups were only trying to learn the English language. The action of the San Francisco school board was in any event precipitous and undiplomatic in the extreme and raised a storm in Japan. The whole issue of Japanese immigration to California suddenly came into the open, and the utmost diplomacy had to be exercised with the Californians, and with the Japanese, before the matter was settled by the Gentlemen's Agreement in 1907–1908. According to this agreement, a series of diplomatic notes, Japan would not allow laborers to obtain visas to the mainland of the United States, and thus halted the immigration which was causing so much trouble in California. The San Francisco school board, under its president—an erstwhile bassoon player under indictment for fraud—rescinded its rule.

Trouble again arose in California in 1913 when the legislature took under consideration a bill making it impossible for Japanese to own or lease land for agricultural purposes. President Woodrow Wilson was reduced to sending Secretary of State William Jennings Bryan to California in April 1913 to plead with the governor and the legislature. The discriminatory legislation as finally passed was so ingeniously worded as to sound less offensive than it was. Without directly affronting Japan or violating the letter of America's treaty obligations, it barred Japanese from owning agricultural land. The Californians later in 1920 passed an act refusing to Japanese the right to lease agricultural land. Over a dozen states during the early 1920's followed California's example.

What with the increase of Japanese power in the orient signalized by the Russo-Japanese War, and the necessity of concluding an agreement for protection of the Philippines, the Roosevelt administration's original friendliness for Japan had dissipated. Relations between the two nations had not been improved by the San Francisco school controversy. Roosevelt in 1907 conceived the idea of sending the American battleship fleet around the world, stopping at oriental ports en route, in the hope that a display of American power would impress the Japanese. This was a typical Rooseveltian move, in its feeling for display and show of force, and TR later boasted in his *Autobiography* that it was "the most important service that I rendered to peace." This boast may have been true. Probably the battleship fleet did impress the Japanese people with the growing strength of America.

Meanwhile the Root-Takahira Agreement had been concluded on November 30, 1908, an agreement over which there has always been a controversy, for no one has ever established the precise meaning of this accord concluded by Secretary of State Elihu Root and the Japanese ambassador in Washington, Kogoro Takahira. In the exchange of notes between the two statesmen it was declared that the two governments wished to maintain the *status quo* in the region of the Pacific Ocean, together with the open door in China, and that each would respect the territories of the other and support "by all pacific means at their disposal the independence and integrity of China and the principle of equal opportunity." This seemed to indicate that the United States would not challenge Japan's newly created position in Manchuria; the peaceful promises by Japan in turn pointed to another guarantee of the Philippines, together with Hawaii and Alaska. The Japanese doubtless considered the Root-Takahira Agreement a complement to their new position evidenced in the Anglo-Japanese Alliance of 1902, the Portsmouth Treaty, and agreements of 1907 with France and Russia. Secretary Root hoped and later affirmed that the agreement would ensure the open door in Manchuria rather than any special Japanese-fashion "status quo." There was no meeting of minds in the curious Root-Takahira Agreement, stemming as it did from the multiplying uncertainties and frictions of American-Japanese relations. It was one more attempt to find some formula that might make for better feeling between Washington and Tokyo.

3. *The Far East and the First World War*

The Far East, as we have seen, was in ferment in the years after the turn of the century, the decline of Manchu strength in China coinciding with the rising power of Japan. And these disturbing factors—Japanese power, the decline of China—were joined by a third complication, the embroilments of Russia in the Far East. The Russo-Japanese War had been an illustration of the novel difficulties in Asia.

The entire Far Eastern situation was enormously complicated by the developing antagonisms of Europe. Russia's diplomacy in the East, to name but one example, was closely linked to the deepening international crisis on the Continent. The alignments of the First World War were forming. The Triple Alliance of Germany, Austria-Hungary, and Italy soon would face the Triple Entente of Great Britain, France, and Russia. Far Eastern politics became the back yard of European politics. The German kaiser had striven for some time to interest his cousin, the tsar, in Far Eastern territory, to turn the attention of Nicholas II from Europe. William II and Nicholas II—"Willy" and "Nicky," as they signed their personal correspondence—had encouraged each other with the titles of Admiral of the Atlantic (Willy) and Admiral of the Pacific (Nicky). Insofar as Nicky took Willy seriously, and there is some evidence that he did, the ultimate result of these imperial pleasantries was the defeat of Russia by Japan and a weakening of the Franco-Russian alliance in Europe. It was, one should add, a somewhat mixed victory, for it meant too the weakening of the monarchical principle in Russia, which in due time had repercussions for European monarchs, as the kaiser would learn.

The quest of Great Britain for alliances and friendships in the years before the First World War—conclusion of the Anglo-Japanese Alliance of 1902, and after it the *rapprochement* with France signalized by the entente with Britain of 1904 and the Anglo-Russian Entente of 1907—also had its effects in the Far East. The Anglo-Japanese Alliance enlisted Japanese support of British interests in Asia and gave Britain a freer hand in Europe. The alliance was directed also, and this was Japan's *quid pro quo*, against Russia, for it promised that should Japan engage in a war with another power (that is, Russia) and that power be joined by a third power (that is, France, in accord with the Franco-Russian Alliance of 1894), then Britain would enter the war on the side of Japan. In effect this arrangement gave Japan assurance that in a war with Russia there would be no intervention by France.

This is not the place to set down in detail the Far Eastern ramifications of European politics; what mattered for American diplomacy was that after the Treaty of Portsmouth a new international arrangement took effect in the Far East, in large part a result of European political developments: Russia in 1907 concluded the entente with Britain, France had done so in 1904, and because of the already existing Franco-Russian and Anglo-Japanese alliances Japan therefore came to an agreement with Russia (Japan, Russia, France, and Britain would side against Germany in 1914). The Russo-Japanese *rapprochement* that took place during the years 1907–1910 was, of course, at the expense of China. Russia and Japan formally divided Manchuria into two spheres of interest, its southern part to Japan, its northern to Russia.

In view of this new alliance structure, any intervention by the United States in Far Eastern politics was likely to affect directly the European balance of power. Here was a new problem for American diplomacy in the Far East. But one must doubt whether the individuals who directed American policy after the era of Theodore Roosevelt really appreciated it. They knew that there had been a traditional American policy in the Far East, and that the rise of Japanese power had made that policy difficult. They saw the troubles in China, the crumbling of the Manchu empire which in 1911–1912 brought disintegration of the dynasty and proclamation of a republic. They had no sense of the connection of Far Eastern and European diplomacy. In the years between 1900 and 1914, and especially in the era 1905–1914, any sort of American diplomacy in the orient without knowledge of the factors and forces governing European international relations would have been foolish, or dangerous, or both.

Theodore Roosevelt had sensed the problems of American policy and he sought to placate Japan in the agreements of 1905 and 1908, but his successor President Taft unfortunately forgot the power equation in the Far East. Taft was a constitutional lawyer, and together with his secretary of state, Philander C. Knox, also a lawyer, he endeavored to promote American trade with China through legalistic maneuvering of a sort which would not have brought results in the nineteenth century, to say nothing of the twentieth. The two blunders of the Taft administration, and they were blunders, were the attempted neutralization of the existing Manchurian railways, sponsored by Secretary Knox, and the effort of the administration to promote a China consortium for developing Manchuria.

The Knox neutralization scheme was one of the most foolish proposals ever made by an American diplomat. The secretary of state was secure in his ignorance of Manchurian realities, that is, of the new friendship of Japan and Russia in Manchuria. He attempted through Britain, France, Germany, Japan, and Russia to obtain for China an international loan of sufficient size to enable that government to buy up all the foreign railways in China, including Manchuria, and thereby "neutralize" the roads by retiring foreign capital. As an alternative he suggested construction under neutral administration of a north-south railway through Manchuria from Aigun to Chinchow. He overlooked the fact that the railroads of China, particularly Manchuria, had always been a prime means of foreign intervention, and that Russia's Chinese Eastern Railway in northern Manchuria and Japan's South Manchuria Railway were the thread on which these two nations had strung their interests in Manchuria. To ask those countries to neutralize their railway concessions was to ask retirement from an area over which wars had been fought in 1894–1895 and 1904–1905. The American secretary of state had made a preposterous suggestion. The European powers accepted the Knox proposal in principle, but would do nothing more. Japan argued in reply to Knox that his suggestion was at variance with the Peace of Portsmouth and arrangements for concessions in Manchuria made with China at the end of that conflict. The Russians, after perfunctorily expressing enthusiasm for the open door and equal opportunity in Manchuria—as the Japanese had also done—contended that Knox's proposal was against their interests and refused to accept it. As a result of the neutralization scheme, Japan and Russia concluded a new agreement in July 1910 strengthening their agreement of 1907.

Undaunted, Knox set out to force American capital into a new international consortium which was organizing to finance currency reform and industrial development in Manchuria. The United States went to the length of sending a special message from President Taft to the prince regent of China, begging the latter to look with favor upon American entrance into the consortium. The matter dragged on, and China was plunged into the revolution of 1911–1912, precipitated by foreign demands for concessions. The Americans finally were admitted to the consortium, but Wall Street financiers were reluctant to take part and demanded explicit government support. When Wilson became president in March 1913, he refused to support the consortium and allowed American bankers to leave what they had never wished to enter in the first place.

By the time of the Wilson administration, the American diplomatic position in the Far East had deteriorated to a grievous state, and with outbreak of the World War in 1914 the American government was beset with problems of neutrality. Little energy remained for Far Eastern matters. Neither the United States nor the European nations could do anything against the shameless demands made by Japan upon China in 1915. The Twenty-One Demands, as they were called, contained several conditions which if accepted by the Chinese would have brought that hapless nation directly under the control of Tokyo. The United States protested on May 11, 1915, that it would not recognize any situation forced upon China by Japan. Luckily the crisis passed when the Japanese decided not to force their most rigorous demands upon the Chinese.

But in 1917, when the United States entered the war, there came another opportunity for the Japanese, this time to obtain a concession directly from the Americans. France and Britain were sending missions to the United States in the spring of 1917, to arrange the policy and details of American participation in the European conflict, and the Japanese sent a special envoy, Viscount Kikujiro Ishii, but not on the same sort of mission the European governments were undertaking. Ishii was instructed to secure from the American government a recognition of Japan's position in Asia. Unblushingly performing his embassy, he threatened that Japan might go over to the side of Germany and abandon the Allies. He told Secretary of State Robert Lansing that Germany three times had sought to persuade Japan to forsake the Allied cause, and the hint was altogether obvious. The Lansing-Ishii Agreement was concluded on November 2, 1917, in this difficult atmosphere.

The agreement between Secretary of State Lansing and the special Japanese ambassador was if anything more ambiguous than the Root-Takahira Agreement of nine years before. "The governments of the United States and Japan," it stipulated, "recognize that territorial propinquity creates special relations between countries, and, consequently the government of the United States recognizes that Japan has special interests in China, particularly in the part to which her possessions are contiguous. The territorial sovereignty of China, nevertheless, remains unimpaired . . . ." Lansing always maintained that he had only recognized the "special interests" of Japan in China, interests of an economic nature created by geographical propinquity and contiguity. The Japanese translated the phrase "special interests" as "paramount interests," and refused to consider them as limited to economic concerns. Later Ishii wrote in his *Diplomatic Commentaries* that he and Secretary Lansing were only "performing the role of photographers, as it were, of a condition," namely, Japan's paramount situation in the Far East. "Even though Americans may destroy the print because it is not to their liking," Ishii added, "the negative will remain. And even if the negative also be destroyed, does not the substance of the picture remain?"

What could one conclude about all these perplexities of American-Japanese relations? Certainly there could be no doubt about Japanese intentions in Eastern Asia when in the year 1919 the peace conference for the First World War met in Paris. The Japanese by this time, not content with a sphere of interest in Manchuria and virtual hegemony over China, had made an effort to separate Siberia from Russia. Japan had sent over seventy thousand troops into Siberia, nominally to assist in the protection of Allied war materials stored at Vladivostok. The supposed purpose of sending these Japanese troops, together with contingents from other nations including the United States (the United States contingent in Siberia never numbered more than nine thousand), Britain, Serbia, Italy, and Rumania, had been to hold these stores against the Bolsheviks, who had taken over the Russian government in November 1917 and soon thereafter made a separate peace with the Germans. There was also, one should add, another purpose of the Allied troops in Siberia, namely to facilitate the exit from Russia of thousands of Czechs, former enemy prisoners freed by withdrawal of Russia from the war, who wished to pass over the Trans-Siberian Railway and take ship from Vladivostok to Europe, there to fight on the Allied side against Austria-Hungary to achieve an independent Czechoslovakia. A third purpose for Allied intervention in Siberia, set forth by the United States, was to assist the Russians with self-government or self-defense. But it was the hope of the Japanese to intrigue with Russian factional leaders and assist to power a pro-Japanese regime which some day might place Siberia under Japanese sovereignty. The Japanese war ministry defied the foreign office and forced Japan's diplomats at home or abroad to defend the actions of the military. Eventually the Japanese government went back under civil control. Meanwhile the United States and the other allies withdrew their troops. Japanese troops left Siberia in October 1922.

At the Paris Peace Conference of 1919 there was, in addition to such difficulties with the Japanese, the problem of Shantung, the formerly German sphere of interest in China. If the Allied leaders at Paris had not recognized Japan's right to economic and other concessions in Shantung, the Japanese delegation would have retired from Paris. "They are not bluffers," Wilson told one of his assistants in 1919, "and they will go home unless we give them what they should not have." When a recognition of Japanese interests in Shantung was written into the Versailles Treaty, the president accepted it, realizing sadly that it "was the best that could be had out of a dirty past."

Other advantages accrued to Japan at the Paris Peace Conference, for in addition to Shantung the Japanese were confirmed in their control over the former German Pacific islands north of the equator. Japan had taken the islands at the outset of the war, under a secret arrangement with Great Britain whereby the British took the German islands south of the equator. By the peace settlement of 1919 the islands went to Japan as a mandate, a special colonial trust, of the new League of Nations. The Japanese were supposed to administer these former German possessions for the benefit of the inhabitants thereof, but in fact the islands became Japan's private property and were fortified contrary to League rules for mandated territories.

The peace conference of 1919 marked generally a triumph for Japan. The island empire was included as one of the five great powers represented on the Council of Ten (to which each of the powers sent two delegates). This marked a large addition to Japanese prestige, for the council was designed to serve as a sort of executive body for the peace conference. Later, when the council gave way to the Big Four—private meetings of the leaders of Britain, France, the United States, and Italy—and the Big Three (Italy withdrawing), the Japanese received a careful explanation from President Wilson's adviser, Colonel Edward M. House, who assured one of the chief delegates from Tokyo, Baron Makino, "that the work of the Four will be submitted to him before its final adoption and that then the Big Four will be expanded into the Big Five."

Japan, it is true, did lose face at the conference when Makino in the last session of the League of Nations Commission, the committee for drafting the League Covenant, raised the issue of racial equality and asked for a statement in the preamble of the Covenant, then in final draft, of "the principle of equality of nations and the just treatment of their nationals . . . as a fundamental basis of future international relations in the new world organization." Under unbearable pressure from Prime Minister William M. Hughes of Australia, the British delegate at the commission meeting, Lord Robert Cecil, refused to admit the principle of racial equality. In the voting that followed the British and American delegations abstained, which was equivalent to voting against the Japanese proposal. This was an unpleasant pill for the Japanese representatives at Paris, but the gains to Japan at the conference were otherwise so impressive and gratifying that the Japanese in 1919 could well feel that, racially equal or not, they had achieved a large and important place in the world family of nations, including perhaps an unassailable position in the affairs of the Far East.

This latter notion was not the view of the great powers of the West, in particular Britain and the United States, who at length reorganized the affairs of the orient according to their desires, for a time, at the Washington Naval Conference of 1921–1922—which must be dealt with in another chapter.

Suffice to close this present chapter by remarking the transfer at the end of the First World War of the bulk of the American fleet from Atlantic to Pacific. There it remained as a counterpoise to the Japanese navy during the increasingly critical relations between the United States and Japan in the 1920's and 1930's. This transfer symbolized the end of an era in American relations with Europe, the period during which Americans feared Europe more than Asia, and the beginning of a new outlook on world affairs in which the security of the United States vis-à-vis Japan began to occupy the calculations of American strategists, military and diplomatic.

During the nineteenth century, as we have seen, three broad interests came to dominate American relations with the Far East. American Far Eastern diplomacy in the nineteenth century resulted in several treaties envisioning an open door for American commercial enterprise. The open door notes of 1899 and 1900 were further and, at least in the case of the note of 1899, logical elaborations of this policy.

At the beginning of the twentieth century new political complications appeared—the crumbling of the Manchu empire, the rise of Japan to the position of a great power, the close connection of Asian diplomacy with the diplomacy of Europe. These novel factors began to plague the state department and produced several agreements with Japan, together with such policy efforts as Secretary Knox's neutralization scheme and his equally ill-advised support of the China consortium. All such measures looked directly or indirectly to the soothing of Japan and the adjustment of American interests to the new and much more dangerous turn of Far Eastern affairs. American relations with Japan nonetheless deteriorated, and by 1921 the specter of war was fully visible, twenty years before the event.

CONTEMPORARY DOCUMENTS

[To the people of the United States the Boxer rebellion of 1900 was a shocking affair, a reversion to barbarism by the Chinese. Americans had thought that the Chinese people and government appreciated Western ways and assistance. Minister E. H. Conger's description of what happened in Peking was dated August 17. Source: *Foreign Relations of the United States: 1900* (Washington, 1902), 162–166.]

. . . The Chinese Government had, since June 19, been continually insisting upon our leaving Pekin under Chinese escort, to which we were determined never to consent, because it was undoubtedly a plan to ambush us. This may be more easily believed, since the identical officers and soldiers who were, by imperial orders, daily shooting us down had been selected as our escort. So by one excuse and another we put off a final decision or definite refusal, as may be seen by the copies of correspondence inclosed. . . .

Resolving among ourselves that we would never go under a Chinese escort, but deeming it wise not to refuse point-blank, and thus give them ground for attack, we replied courteously, declaring it impossible to leave within the time, and requesting an interview at 9 o'clock the next morning with the prince and ministers at the yamen, opening the way for further discussion. The reply accomplished its purpose. The time was postponed temporarily . . . .

The morning of the 20th, at 8:30, the ministers met at the French legation ready to proceed in a body to the Tsungli Yamen as soon as notified that the prince would be there. Not receiving any word by 9 o'clock, the German minister, Baron von Ketteler, who had personally notified the yamen that he was coming there on business, started with his interpreter, commissioned to tell the prince and ministers that the corps was patiently waiting to hear from them.

Upon arriving almost to the yamen he was brutally murdered, shot through the head by a man (so says his interpreter, whose chair immediately followed) wearing the insignia of a Chinese official. The interpreter, Mr. Cordes, was at the same time seriously wounded, but succeeded in escaping to the American Methodist Mission compound, which was guarded by American marines. Two mafoos accompanied the baron, one of whom immediately ran to the Tsungli Yamen and returned with some of the secretaries to the place, to find the official chairs demolished, but the minister's body already taken away. The other returned quickly to the legation, and an officer and 20 men started for the spot, but before they reached it were met by a strong cordon of Chinese soldiers, through which they were not strong enough to pass. The body was found yesterday, buried in a rough coffin near where he fell, and to-day was decently interred in the German legation. This was the last attempt of any of the ministers to visit the Tsungli Yamen.

The Chinese army had turned out against us; the whole quarter of the city in which the legations are situated was surrounded by its soldiers, firing began on all sides and the battle against the representatives of all foreign governments in China was begun.

The Methodist compound where all our missionaries had gathered was abandoned; all coming to the legation at 12 noon. By 4 o'clock the situation had become so acute that all foreigners, except the guards and a few men in each legation, repaired to the British legation, and the refugee native Christians, about 2,000, were placed in the grounds of Prince Su, near by.

Our lines of defense were quickly shortened and strengthened, trenches and barricades built, and the siege was on.

Four hundred foreigners, 200 of them women and children, with over 100 soldiers, were crowded into the British legation. In the house given to our legation 30 people were for two months crowded into six small rooms; but all were thankful that there existed so convenient and safe a place to go.

The first attempts of the enemy were to burn us out by firing buildings adjoining us, but by means of heroically fighting those inflamed by the enemy, burning and tearing down others ourselves, we soon had the British legation pretty safe from this danger. However, from this date until July 17 there was scarcely an hour during which there was not firing upon some part of our lines and into some of the legations, varying from a single shot to a general and continuous attack along the whole line.

Artillery was planted on all sides of us, two large guns mounted on the walls surrounding the palace, and thousands of 3-inch shells and solid shot hurled at us. There is scarcely a building in any of the legations that was not struck, and some of them practically destroyed. Four shells struck our gatehouse, tearing away our flagstaff; four exploded in the servants' quarters; three struck my residence, two of them exploding inside; two struck the office building, and two the house of Mr. Cheshire, while the roofs of nearly all the buildings in the compound were sadly damaged by innumerable bullets. To show in what storms they came, five quarts of them were picked up to be remolded into new ammunition in one hour in our small compound.

Our lines were at first made as short as possible and inclosed all the legations except the Belgian, and were still further shortened after the burning of the Austrian, Italian, and Dutch legations and the imperial customs. Trenches were dug, streets barricaded along these lines as fast as possible, but nearly all the work on these had to be done under cover of darkness.

A veritable fortress was made of the British legation, walls were strengthened and raised, openings filled, bombproof cellars constructed, counter tunnels to prevent mining made, and everything possible with our poor tools and materials was effectively done. In our first barricades carts and furniture were employed and thousands upon thousands of sand bags made in which every obtainable material was used—satin portières, silk curtains, carpets, oriental rugs, table linen, towels, bedding, embroideries, cloths, silks, etc.

Fortunately for us we had the missionaries and their converts with us. The former, being familiar with the Chinese language and character, ably organized, superintended, and directed the Chinese, who were invaluable help in constructing fortifications, and without which it could not have been done. . . .

Sir Claude MacDonald, the British minister, was chosen for the general command, and gave every satisfaction. He selected Mr. H. G. Squiers, first secretary of this legation, as his chief of staff, whose military training and experience had not been forgotten, but which, thrown with energy and determination into the work, were invaluable to the end.

Necessary committees were created, and the camp was thoroughly organized. Stores of wheat, rice, and coal found within our lines were quickly gathered into a general commissariat, which, with such canned goods as we had in store, together with all our riding horses and cart mules, have furnished us a substantial if not a very palatable subsistence since.

The Chinese seem to have an innumerable soldiery and an inexhaustible supply of ammunition. We began with only 400 marines, sailors, and soldiers altogether, and some 50 miscellaneously armed civilians. For the most part, therefore, we simply sat and watched, firing only when necessary; but occasionally a severe attack had to be resisted or a sortie made, which invariably, on our side, was successful. But these frequently cost lives of brave men. Altogether we have lost—killed, 65; wounded, 135; died of disease, all children, 7. Of the United State, marines, Sergeant Fanning and Privates King, Kennedy, Turner, Tutcher, Fisher, and Thomas were killed; Captain Myers, Dr. Lippett, and 14 others wounded. The loss of the Chinese is known to be ten times as great as ours.

To our marines fell the most difficult and dangerous portion of the defense, by reason of our proximity to the great city wall and the main city gates, over which large guns were planted.

Our legation, with the position which we held on the wall, was the key to the whole situation. This given up, all, including many Chinese Christians, would at once be drawn into the British legation and the congestion there increased by several hundred. The United States marines acquitted themselves nobly. Twice were they driven from the wall and once forced to abandon the legation, but each time, reenforced, immediately retook it, and with only a handful of men, aided by 10 Russian sailors and for a few days a few British marines, held it to the last against several hundred Chinese with at least three pieces of artillery.

The bravest and most successful event of the whole siege was an attack led by Captain Myers, of our marines, and 55 men—Americans, British, and Russians—which resulted in the capture of a formidable barricade on the wall defended by several hundred Chinese soldiers, over 50 of whom were killed. Two United States marines were killed and Captain Myers and 1 British marine wounded. This made our position on the wall secure, and it was held to the last with the loss of only one other man.

This position gave us command of a water gate under the wall, through which the entrance of the relief column was made into this, the Tartar city. The English arrived first, and General Chaffee, with the Fourteenth Infantry and Captain Riley's battery, a few moments thereafter. . . .

The Chinese Government was pretending to us and proclaiming to the world that they were "protecting" us, when in fact if a thousandth part of the shots fired at us by their soldiers had taken effect we would all have been killed long ago. It is understood, also, that they represented abroad that they were "provisioning" us. They did send us on two occasions a few small watermelons, cucumbers, and egg plant, and on another three sacks of flour, but nothing more. We tried to establish a market where under a flag of truce, we might purchase a few eggs and some fruit or fresh meat. They consented, but the firing of their soldiers prevented it.

On July 14 a note signed "Prince Ching and others" came to us by a messenger again inviting us to ambush, this time at the Tsungli Yamen, but we didn't go. However, a correspondence was started, which for a time caused a cessation of artillery firing and lessened greatly the rifle firing, showing that the Government could control it if desired. . . .

So the movement began, first upon the native Christians, thousands of whom have been most brutally butchered, then against the missionaries, many of whom have been murdered and their property destroyed. The most harrowing details are coming in of horrible atrocities perpetrated in the country districts while we have been besieged; then against the foreign merchants and all foreign business interests, and finally against all the official representatives of foreign powers in Pekin. . . .

[Considering what almost became the fate of the American minister in

Peking and his charges, the second open door note of July 3, 1900, was an extraordinarily mild statement of American policy. Designed for the circumstances of the moment, of course, the note committed the United States only to "preserve Chinese territorial and administrative entity," but it came to mean something considerably more than that. Source: *Foreign Relations of the United States: 1901* (Washington, 1902), appendix, p. 12.]

In this critical posture of affairs in China it is deemed appropriate to define the attitude of the United States as far as present circumstances permit this to be done. We adhere to the policy initiated by us in 1857 of peace with the Chinese nation, of furtherance of lawful commerce, and of protection of lives and property of our citizens by all means guaranteed under extra-territorial treaty rights and by the law of nations. If wrong be done to our citizens we propose to hold the responsible authors to the uttermost accountability. We regard the condition at Pekin as one of virtual anarchy, whereby power and responsibility are practically devolved upon the local provincial authorities. So long as they are not in overt collusion with rebellion and use their power to protect foreign life and property, we regard them as representing the Chinese people, with whom we seek to remain in peace and friendship. The purpose of the President is, as it has been heretofore, to act concurrently with the other powers; first, in opening up communication with Pekin and rescuing the American officials, missionaries, and other Americans who are in danger; secondly, in affording all possible protection everywhere in China to American life and property; thirdly, in guarding and protecting all legitimate American interests; and fourthly, in aiding to prevent a spread of the disorders to the other provinces of the Empire and a recurrence of such disasters. It is of course too early to forecast the means of attaining this last result; but the policy of the Government of the United States is to seek a solution which may bring about permanent safety and peace to China, preserve Chinese territorial and administrative entity, protect all rights guaranteed to friendly powers by treaty and international law, and safeguard for the world the principle of equal and impartial trade with all parts of the Chinese Empire. . . .

ADDITIONAL READING

*A. Whitney Griswold's *The Far Eastern Policy of the United States* (New York, 1938) is excellent for American relations from the turn of the century until the First World War, after which its sources thin out. Griswold's beautifully written book has influenced a generation and more of students and teachers and is still much worth reading, although its author was "sour" on the Far East because of disappointments to American relations, diplomatic and economic, stemming from the Great Depression. This book was the first volume to exploit the Rockhill papers. Beginning with the war of 1914–1918 its sources are altogether unsatisfactory for present-day readers; the last part of the volume, which takes American relations with the Far East down to the mid-1930's, is based on only three or four published accounts or documentary collections. See also three other general volumes: Alfred L. P. Dennis, *Adventures in American Diplomacy: 1896–1906* (New York, 1928); *Foster Rhea Dulles, *The Imperial Years* (New York, 1956); and Julius W. Pratt's excellent new survey, *Challenge and Rejection: 1900–1921* (New York, 1967), a volume in the American Diplomatic History series.

For China a brief introduction is in F. R. Dulles's *China and America* (Princeton, 1946). Among the many special works are Tyler Dennett, "The Open Door," in Joseph Barnes, ed., *Empire in the East* (Garden City, N.Y., 1934), a thoughtful, reflective account; Charles S. Campbell, Jr., *Special Business Interests and the Open Door Policy* (New Haven, 1951); and a new study written under the present-day concern about China, Paul A. Varg's *The Making of a Myth: The United States and China, 1897–1912* (East Lansing, Mich., 1968). See also Charles Vevier, *The United States and China: 1906–1913* (New Brunswick, N.J., 1955). Studies of the Wilson administration and China are Tien-yi Li, *Woodrow Wilson's China Policy: 1913–1917* (New York, 1952); Roy Watson Curry, *Woodrow Wilson and Far Eastern Policy: 1913–1921* (New York, 1957); and Russell H. Fifield, *Woodrow Wilson and the Far East: The Diplomacy of the Shantung Question* (New York, 1952). The missionary influence upon American relations with China was one of the major strands of sentiment between the peoples of the two nations, and for this subject see the massive studies in the history of missions by Kenneth Scott Latourette. Edmund S. Wehrle, *Britain, China, and the Antimissionary Riots: 1891–1900* (Minneapolis, 1966) shows how missionaries began to embroil the Western powers in the politics of China. Paul A. Varg, *Missionaries, Chinese, and Diplomats: The American Protestant Missionary Movement in China, 1890–1952* (Princeton, 1958) is an essential book for this era.

For Japan see Payson J. Treat, *Diplomatic Relations between the United States and Japan: 1895–1905* (Stanford, Calif., 1938) and the recently published book by *William L. Neumann, *America Encounters Japan* (Baltimore, 1963). More specifically there is Tyler Dennett's *Roosevelt and the Russo-Japanese War* (Magnolia, Mass., 1958), and Thomas A. Bailey's *Theodore Roosevelt and the Japanese-American Crises* (Stanford, Calif., 1934) and "The Root-Takahira Agreement of 1908," *Pacific Historical Review*, IX (1940), 19–35; Raymond A. Esthus, *Theodore Roosevelt and Japan* (Seattle, 1966); Charles E. Neu, *An Uncertain Friendship: Theodore Roosevelt and Japan* (Cambridge, Mass., 1967); and Eugene P. Trani's forthcoming book, from the University of Kentucky Press, on Theodore Roosevelt and the Treaty of Portsmouth.

Naval rivalry was of considerable importance, for which see O. J. Clinard, *Japan's Influence on American Naval Power: 1897–1914* (Berkeley, Calif., 1947); W. R. Braisted, *The United States Navy in the Pacific: 1897–1909* (Austin, Tex., 1958); and especially the colorful book by Robert A. Hart, *The Great White Fleet* (Boston, 1965), a stirring account of the fleet's trip around the world, written from hitherto unused naval manuscript sources. Hart discovered that among other items taken around the world were about five dozen pianos. The ships carried so much gear that they were low in the water, and before any action it might have been necessary to throw the pianos overboard. Roger Daniels, *The Politics of Prejudice: The Anti-Japanese Movement in California and the Struggle for Japanese Exclusion* (Berkeley, Calif., 1962) is an interesting account of that subject; see also the study by Bryan's scholarly biographer Paolo E. Coletta, " 'The Most Thankless Task': Bryan and the California Alien Land Legislation," *Pacific Historical Review*, XXXVI (1967), 163–184. Burton F. Beers has set out *Vain Endeavor: Robert Lansing's Attempt to End the American-Japanese Rivalry* (Durham, N.C., 1962); the intervention in Siberia has inspired a large literature, notably William S. Graves, *America's Siberian Adventure: 1918–1920* (New York, 1931), by the commander of the American troops; Betty Miller Unterberger, *America's Siberian Expedition: 1918–1920* (Durham, N.C., 1956); James W. Morley, *The Japanese Thrust into Siberia: 1918* (New York, 1957); and George F. Kennan's prize-winning volumes, *Russia Leaves the War* (Princeton, 1956) and *The Decision to Intervene* (Princeton, 1958). See also Richard H. Ullman, *Intervention and the War* (Princeton, 1961). The Japanese view of the world in the early twentieth century, not least the United States, appears in W. R. Langdon, trans., Kikujiro Ishii, *Diplomatic Commentaries* (Baltimore, 1936). Ishii was perhaps Japan's most distinguished diplomat of his time. In the 1930's he supported the expansionists, and he was killed during the Second World War in one of the fire-bombings of Tokyo by the United States Air Force.

Standard biographies and diplomatic biographies are *Howard K. Beale, *Theodore Roosevelt and the Rise of America to World Power* (Baltimore, 1956); *Henry F. Pringle, *Theodore Roosevelt* (New York, 1931); *William Henry Harbaugh, *Power and Responsibility* (New York, 1961); Fred H. Harrington, *God, Mammon, and the Japanese: Dr. Horace N. Allen and Korean-American Relations, 1884–1905* (Madison, Wis., 1944); Tyler Dennett's *John Hay* (New York, 1933); Paul A. Varg, *Open Door Diplomat: The Life of W. W. Rockhill* (Urbana, Ill., 1952), a fascinating account of the high-strung, strange, yet likable scholar-diplomat; Herbert D. Croly, *Willard Straight* (New York, 1924); Henry F. Pringle, *The Life and Times of William Howard Taft* (2 vols., New York, 1939). For biographies of President Wilson see suggestions for additional reading at the end of chapter 20.

☆   *17*   ☆

Colossus of the North

There is a homely adage which runs, "Speak softly and carry a big stick; you will go far."

—Vice President Theodore Roosevelt, September 2, 1901

The relations of the United States with Latin America compare in one respect to relations with the Far East, namely that—as in Asia—there have been two major periods of policy. The first of these, which might well be described as the era of intervention, ran roughly from the time of the Spanish-American War down to entrance of the United States into the World War in 1917. In the initial period the United States wrested Cuba from Spain, then in 1903 allowed the Panamanians to revolt from Colombia and cede a canal zone. Afterward came the series of interventions—Dominican Republic in 1905, Nicaragua in 1911, Haiti in 1915, Mexico in 1913–1917. When a crisis occurred with Germany, it seemed wise policy to abandon intervention in Mexican politics, and the American army pulled out of northern Mexico in February 1917. Victory in the First World War removed the need for protection of the canal approaches in the Caribbean, and after the decade of the 1920's had passed mostly in inaction, the United States in the 1930's recognized the need for a new policy toward the Latin republics and put it into effect, beginning with the Montevideo Conference of 1933, the policy of the good neighbor, which was the liquidation of protective imperialism.

1. *Cuba*

The deplorable situation in Cuba led in the early spring of 1898 to American intervention in that island, and it is a testimony to American

432

good will and early interest in the twentieth-century notion of national self-determination, Cuba for the Cubans, that even before intervention, the Congress of the United States opted against taking Cuba as a territorial appendage (to use a nineteenth-century imperialist phrase). The nations of Europe, observing the passage through Congress of the resolutions favoring intervention in Cuba, must have wondered if the Teller Amendment to these resolutions meant what it said. How unbelievable for Europeans to read at the *fin de siècle*, an era in balancing of power equal only to the hectic alliance-making of the latter eighteenth century in the era of American independence. And how strange that the Americans carried out their resolve in the following few years.

The resolutions favoring intervention, approved by the president on April 20, 1898, sounded familiar enough to Americans who liked the phrases of liberty, and to Europeans who saw only the phrases of double-dealing. The resolves declared, "the people of Cuba are, and of right ought to be, free and independent," demanded that Spain "at once relinquish its authority and government in the Island of Cuba and withdraw its land and naval forces from Cuba and Cuban waters," and—much like a latter-day resolution concerning Vietnam—empowered the president to use the forces of the United States to back up this demand. Senator Henry M. Teller of Colorado thereupon had added the famous declaration: "That the United States hereby disclaims any disposition or intention to exercise sovereignty, jurisdiction, or control over said Island except for the pacification thereof, and asserts its determination, when that is accomplished, to leave the government and control of the Island to its people."

President William McKinley, he who had said that he would have no jingo nonsense during his administration, was a bit slow to put the Teller Amendment into effect, and in his annual message of 1899, a portion of which he devoted to Cuban matters, he may even have sought to put the Cuban case in such a way that his countrymen would contemplate going back on their promise of Cuban independence. Or it may have been just his way of stating facts in a resounding manner. The president remarked that the United States had "assumed before the world a grave responsibility for the future good government of Cuba." Good enough. The new Cuba, he added, "must needs be bound to us by ties of singular intimacy and strength if its enduring welfare is to be assured." Perhaps not so good. But it was not long before McKinley was taking measures to patch up the machinery of government in the once Ever-Faithful Isle. In 1899 he appointed General Leonard Wood as military governor, and Wood began a series of political, social, and medical reforms which bade fair to transform Cuba from the sinkhole

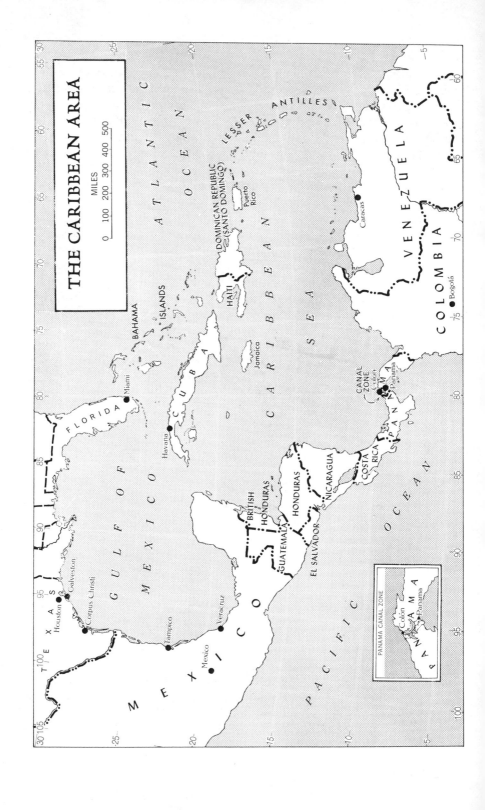

THE CARIBBEAN AREA

MILES

0 100 200 300 400 500

ATLANTIC

OCEAN

LESSER ANTILLES

BAHAMA ISLANDS

DOMINICAN REPUBLIC (SANTO DOMINGO)

Puerto Rico

HAITI

CARIBBEAN SEA

Jamaica

CUBA

Havana

Miami

FLORIDA

GULF OF MEXICO

T E X A S
Houston
Corpus Christi
Galveston

Tampico

Veracruz

Mexico

M E X I C O

BRITISH HONDURAS

HONDURAS

GUATEMALA

EL SALVADOR

NICARAGUA

COSTA RICA

PANAMA
Colón
Panamá

CANAL ZONE

PACIFIC OCEAN

VENEZUELA

Caracas

COLOMBIA

Bogotá

PANAMA CANAL ZONE

P A N A M A

Colón

Panamá

it had become under Spanish rule. Wood remained in office only until 1902, when he moved on to other imperialist tasks under guidance of his new commander in chief in the White House, his onetime lieutenant colonel of the Rough Riders. Under Wood's agency and that of his successors, the Americans cleaned up Cuba, as they long had wished to do. In the course of the cleaning they made sure that their measures would have a modest permanency—who in his right mind would not? A correspondence between Wood and Secretary of War Elihu Root explored the possibility of provisos in the Cuban constitution which was taking shape in 1901–1902. At administration behest Senator Orville H. Platt of Connecticut wrote out these provisos in the army appropriation bill of 1901. Root wanted these timely points in the Cuban constitution. The Cubans were not happy about this improvement upon their constitutional labors. Wood wrote to Root, with considerable acumen, that it might be best to force the Platt Amendment upon them, so that the politicos could report to their constituents that they had signed under duress. This stratagem produced an appendix to the Cuban constitution containing the Platt Amendment. The amendment also was embodied in a treaty of May 22, 1903, between Cuba and the United States, which remained in force until replaced by another treaty in 1934.

According to the Platt Amendment, the Cuban government could not enter any treaty impairing Cuban independence; it could not contract a public debt in excess of ordinary revenues; the United States might intervene to preserve independence and maintain law and order; and Cuba agreed to allow the United States navy to develop coaling stations such as Guantánamo bay (still held).

Cuba under American tutelage was not a perfect example of a wayward colony brought to salvation. The Cuban sugar crop enjoyed special arrangements in the American market. Investment in the island by citizens of the United States went up from an estimated $50,000,000 at the time of the Spanish-American War to more than $200,000,000 by 1911, and more than $500,000,000 by 1920. Americans such as the young Norman Davis—later to serve as undersecretary of state during the Harding administration and as ambassador-at-large during the administrations of the Democrat Roosevelt—went down to Cuba and learned Spanish and flourished in such pursuits as banking and insurance. Havana changed from seedy elegance to the hustle-bustle of a big town turning into a city. The Morro Castle became a tourist attraction and symbol of a political system gone forever. The Cubans nonetheless chafed at their instruction in democracy and the American proscription of the practice of revolution. The United States government intervened frequently, taking over the Cuban government in 1906–1909, until in the late 1920's when the temper of nationalism became too high. Then the *norteameri-canos* backed away from such policies, turning to the civilities of the good neighbor, whatever that phrase meant in future years when the Cubans found themselves under regimes so difficult that they may have wished for the reappearance of American marines.

Perhaps the trouble was that Americans felt themselves superior to Cubans, and despite the many well-intentioned efforts at reform they failed to win the hearts and minds of the people of Cuba. One does not have to look far to find corroboration of this theory. American diplomats, spending a few years in Cuba prior to passing on to some more prestigious assignment, looked upon the Cubans as children capable of a behavior not in vogue on the mainland north of the Rio Grande. Riffling through the yellowing diplomatic memoirs of the era, the inquiring student can find descriptions of Cubans such as the following, of a Cuban young lady whom Second Secretary Norval Richardson of Mississippi happened to meet on shipboard en route to Havana:

She was pretty, in a dark undistinguished way, dressed badly—at least indifferently—and had a sort of good fellowship that almost amounted to familiarity; and her use of English was amazing. It was a bewildering combination of slang and bad grammar.

When she found out—by asking a series of personal questions—that I was to be in the Legation, she informed me that she had known all the American diplomats very well and that the present Minister was a great friend of her family.

This led me on to asking where she had learned to speak English so fluently—I put it that way—and she confessed that she hadn't known a word until she began to meet Americans; as a matter of fact, she had learned it entirely from talking to the secretaries of the Legation. I found out after arriving in Habana that she was of one of the oldest and most distinguished Cuban families and was considered one of their most cosmopolitan products—this latter quality having been achieved at some place in the Catskills, where she spent each summer. Her appetite and choice of food also appeared to me to throw some light on Cuban habits. She devoured quantities of Bologna sausages, raw onions and beer—even at breakfast; and in her attempts to teach me the proper pronunciation of such simple Spanish phrases as "I want two poached eggs and a slice of toast" she would grow violently angry at my stupidity and often throw the book across the deck. I am not picturing her as the most distinguished representative of the Cubans I was to know later—she was not that by any means; she was just the first Cuban I met.

Young Richardson entitled his memoir *My Diplomatic Education* (1923) and dedicated it to his wife. He closed his book with some explanation of how ladies should make good diplomats although, he added with haste, diplomacy was very dangerous for ladies, who represent a refinement in civilization—unfamiliarity with accepted forms was not forgiven them as it might be in a man. Perhaps the diplomatic service had concentrated Richardson's mind on a few topics, even one. Still, in his description of the Cuban young lady he was revealing the prejudices of his fellow countrymen, and so long as Americans went out to live and work in Spanish-speaking lands with such ideas they were bound to get into diplomatic if not other trouble. It may be that America's attempted serious reforms in Cuba could not stick because the spirit behind them was not right.

2. "I took the Canal Zone"

In setting out the interventions of the United States government in Latin America, interventions which for the most part made sense at the time, even if they do not seem noble to a later generation, it is embarrassing to relate one major mistake in the actions of Washington officials, the intervention in Panama in 1903 to obtain the Panama canal zone. Here was a highly undiplomatic and totally unnecessary act which has been a blot on the national escutcheon ever since and will require many years, perhaps to the year 2000, before Latin Americans will forget it. President Theodore Roosevelt had tired of the slowness of the Colombian senate in consenting to a canal zone for the United States in the Colombian province of Panama. He protected a revolution which broke out in Panama by recognizing within three days the new Panamanian regime, with which he soon signed a treaty giving rights to the United States for constructing a canal. This was a totally unnecessary affair, because Roosevelt could either have paid the price desired by the Colombians or could have obtained a canal site across Central America through Nicaragua. TR was in too much of a hurry to build a canal. He was too much moved by the obvious need of the United States after 1898 for a canal—the increasing demand for cheap ocean transportation between the United States's east and west coasts, the hurried voyage of the *Oregon* around Cape Horn in 1898 to join the fleet off Santiago de Cuba, the existence after the Spanish-American War of the new Pacific possessions of the United States. One might charitably say that Roosevelt moved before he thought things out, although more probably he never thought things out but simply moved. The intervention at Panama thereupon became the greatest blunder made by the American government among its Latin neighbors from the beginning of relations down to the present day.

The setting of the stage for the Panama drama began with some moves of American diplomacy prior to the coup of November 1903. Initially the United States had to arrange with Great Britain for abrogation of the Clayton-Bulwer Treaty of 1850, which had debarred either nation from exclusive rights in any canal built across the isthmus of Panama and required neutralization of such a canal under international auspices. Abrogation was duly secured in the so-called second Hay-Pauncefote Treaty, concluded on November 18, 1901, by Secretary of State John Hay and the British ambassador in Washington, Sir Julian Pauncefote. The first Hay-Pauncefote Treaty, signed on February 5, 1900, had come to grief because it did not provide for American fortification of the proposed canal; the second treaty, by saying nothing about fortification, provided for it implicitly.

There then was the question of routes: Nicaragua or Panama. Much sentiment favored cutting the canal through Nicaragua instead of Panama, but in 1902 the Panama route became practically certain. For one thing, important individuals in Washington, including President Roosevelt, became convinced that the Panama route was easier and better. For another, the Panama route was financially the more attractive. The New Panama Canal Company, a French company which owned the rights to the route, reduced its price for selling out to the United States to a competitive figure. This company was the successor of the concern which, under direction of the builder of the Suez Canal, Ferdinand de Lesseps, had gone bankrupt in 1888 after squandering $400,000,000 on a Panama canal, which the old company had left only about two-fifths finished. The New Panama Canal Company had been asking $109,141,-500 for its rights (the United States then having to pay for the remaining construction), until an American commission estimated that the construction cost of the Nicaragua route was $189,864,062, only $45,630,704 more than remaining construction cost of the Panama route. The New Company was pricing its route out of the competition. Thereupon the New Company came down to $40,000,000 for its rights, which gave the Panama route an anticipated total cost (rights plus remaining construction) cheaper by $5,630,704 than the cost of the route through Nicaragua. After this financial de-escalation, Congress passed the Spooner Act, which became law on June 28, 1902, stipulating that the canal should be constructed in Panama and the New Company receive its $40,000,000, provided an agreement could be made with Colombia. But if such an agreement could not be made, the United States, the act stated, should come to an arrangement with Nicaragua and construct the canal there. Secretary of State Hay on January 22, 1903, concluded a treaty with the Colombian chargé in Washington, Dr. Tomás Herrán, providing for

$10,000,000 to Colombia and $250,000 annually as rental, the rental to begin in nine years. The United States was to receive a 99-year lease of the canal zone, subject to renewal.

At this point the Colombian senate refused to ratify the treaty, because of the indefinite nature of the lease and a stipulation for mixed American-Colombian courts in the canal zone. The senators also knew that President Sanclementi's government in 1900 had used a legislative decree to extend the franchise of the New Panama Canal Company, due to run out in 1904, by six more years—this in consideration of the payment of $1,000,000. After passage in the United States of the Spooner Act, authorizing $40,000,000 to the New Company, it seemed a false economy to have extended the franchise. The idea occurred to the Colombian senate that if a court of Colombian law were to find the extension by legislative decree unconstitutional, it would be possible to take all the money by waiting an extra year to 1904. In Washington, Secretary Hay was incensed. He described the Colombian senators as "greedy little anthropoids." Someone in the Roosevelt cabinet suggested a limerick with the inscription, "Lines for the Inspiration of the State Department in dealing with Dago Nations:"

> There was a young lady named Tucker,
> Who went up to her mother and struck her.
> Her mother said "Damn! Do you know who I am?
> You act like you was a mucker!"

President Roosevelt was deeply angered at what he considered highway robbery. "Make it as strong as you can to Beaupré [A. M. Beaupré, the American minister to Colombia]," TR wrote Secretary Hay. "Those contemptible little creatures in Bogota ought to understand how much they are jeopardizing things and imperiling their own future." On August 17, 1903, he said that "we may have to give a lesson to those jack rabbits." On September 15 he referred to the Colombians as "foolish and homicidal corruptionists." On October 5 he said it might be well "to warn these cat-rabbits that great though our patience has been, it can be exhausted." The president was ready to welcome any turn of events in Panama that would take matters out of the hands of the Colombians. Because the New Panama Canal Company was as interested as the president in this matter, albeit for different reasons (the $40,000,000), it is understandable how word of the president's humor reached the ears of officers of the canal company, and the latter gentlemen wasted no time in seizing their opportunity. They were seconded in their enthusiasm, quite understandably, by the inhabitants of Panama, who feared that the delay of the Colombian senate might lead the United States to choose the alternate waterway in Nicaragua and destroy the prospect, which otherwise would be excellent, for a boom in the Panamanian economy.

The company's initiative was prosecuted by two important agents. One was a French soldier of fortune who had formerly been de Lesseps' chief engineer, Philippe Bunau-Varilla. The other was the lawyer for the New Panama Canal Company, William Nelson Cromwell of the New York firm of Sullivan and Cromwell. Working together, they managed to engineer a revolution in Panama and ease the way in Washington, if such easing were needed, for American recognition of the revolutionaries. Bunau-Varilla had come from France in 1901 to launch his campaign for the Panama route. As he later described his activities, which met with such great success, "fortune smiled" upon him for the next years, and "At every turn of my steps it seemed as if I were accompanied by a protecting divinity. Every time I was in need of a man he appeared, of an event it took place." At the crucial point in the whole affair, he operated from Room 1162 in the old Waldorf-Astoria in New York, which, he later wrote, "deserves to be considered as the cradle of the Panama Republic." There he put together the constitution of the state and readied a declaration of independence; his wife stitched the new national flag. The flag looked very much like that of the United States, but with yellow instead of white for the background and two suns instead of stars. Preparatory to events, he readied for himself a commission as Panama's first minister to the United States. Meanwhile the lawyer Cromwell was busy in Washington instructing members of the Senate about the plight of the suffering Panamanians.

When the revolution came off in Panama on November 3, 1903, it was hardly unexpected, and everything occurred with complete success, thanks in part to arrival the day before of the U.S.S. *Nashville* at Colón on the Caribbean side of the isthmus. The presence of the American vessel lent substance to the hope of the revolutionists on the Pacific side, in Panama City, for American support. The *Nashville* did not prevent the Colombians from landing 474 troops at Colón to suppress the uprising. Happily, railroad officials on the spot (the railroad was owned by the New Panama Canal Company) failed to make any transportation available so that the troops could cross the isthmus to Panama City. The revolution duly broke out in Panama City at about six o'clock on the evening of November 3, and it was over almost as soon as it began. Except for a brief shelling by a Colombian gunboat, which killed a Chinese who was in bed and mortally wounded a donkey in the slaughterhouse, there was no violence. Bunau-Varilla's henchman Dr. Manuel Amador Guerrero, the new president of the republic, paid off the soldiers who supported the revolution at a rate allegedly of $35,000 and $30,000 for two generals, from $6,000 to $10,000 each for the lesser officers, and $50 apiece for the men. Amador made a speech and complimented his countrymen: "The world is astounded at our heroism! Yesterday we were but the slaves of Colombia; today we are free. . . . President Roosevelt has made good. . . . Free sons of Panama, I salute you! Long live the Republic of Panama! Long live President Roosevelt! Long live the American Government!"

The United States recognized the new regime on November 6, an interval between revolution and recognition which was then considered appallingly short. Fifteen days after the revolution, on November 18, 1903, Secretary Hay and Minister Bunau-Varilla made a treaty granting to the United States in perpetuity the use and control of a canal zone ten miles wide across the isthmus of Panama. The treaty gave the United States "all the rights, power and authority within the zone . . . which the United States would possess and exercise if it were the sovereign of the territory." The American government agreed to pay $10,-000,000 and an annual fee of $250,000, the same arrangement offered in the Hay-Herrán Treaty with Colombia, beginning nine years after exchange of ratifications which occurred in 1904. "The United States," according to the first article of this treaty, "guarantees and will maintain the independence of the Republic of Panama." This article made Panama a protectorate, which ended only with a treaty between Panama and the United States signed March 2, 1936, ratified in 1939.

A question never answered about the Panama affair is "Who received the $40,000,000?" According to his own statement, Bunau-Varilla held $115,000 worth of stock in the New Panama Canal Company. Cromwell presumably had holdings, or at the least was working for someone for his legal fee, which turned out to be $832,449.00. To this day it has not been revealed how the $40,000,000 was distributed. The United States government paid the money to J.P. Morgan and Company, which disbursed it.

American policy, as stated at the outset of this discussion, blundered in the business at Panama in 1903, producing an obvious farce of a revolution, a black mark on the record of the United States in Latin America. The United States easily could have constructed a canal through Nicaragua, where the canal would have been much closer to the United States and saved time and trouble on coast-to-coast shipping. Or if President Roosevelt had been firm with the senators of Colombia, threatening to take his canal business to Nicaragua, they perhaps would have accepted his offer of $10,000,000. If Roosevelt had to have the Panama route, it would have been better if he had paid whatever price

Building the Panama Canal. This photo shows progress being made at Bas Obispo, August 1907.

was desired in Colombia.

TR received a large volume of public criticism over the Panama affair, and his sensitivity to it led to a semihumorous situation one day during a cabinet meeting. The president had turned to his attorney general, Philander C. Knox, and said: "I think, Mr. Attorney-General, that it will be just as well for you to give us a formal legal opinion sustaining my action in this whole matter." The attorney general looked quizzically at the president and said, with a smile: "No, Mr. President, if I were you I would not have any taint of legality about it."

After leaving office Roosevelt compounded the Panamanian imbroglio in a speech in 1911 at the University of California by asserting:

I am interested in the Panama Canal because I started it. If I had followed traditional conservative methods, I should have submitted a dignified State paper of probably ten hundred pages to the Congress and debate would have been going on yet. But I took the Canal Zone, and let Congress debate, and while the debate goes on the canal does also.

This was all Colombia needed. Bogotá turned in a bill for indemnity. The Democratic Wilson administration in 1914, the year the canal opened, came close to paying it—so close that Roosevelt had to enlist his friend Cabot Lodge to block the appropriation in the Senate. After TR's death, and apparently inspired by prospects of oil concessions in Colombia, the United States in 1921 paid $25,000,000 in what might be described as hush money.

Nor was paying off the Colombians the end of the Panama trouble— the United States later had to pay off the Panamanians. At the outset the relations between the government of the United States and the sovereign new nation of Panama were uncomplicated and, one might say, direct. When the first American minister to Panama wished to tell President Amador what to do he summoned the president to the legation. Over the years this arrangement changed. The basic agreement of 1903 over the canal had to be changed, too. Renegotiation of the treaty in 1936 raised the annual rental from $250,000 to $430,000. The rent went up to $1,930,-000 in 1955. The Panamanians that year had asked for $5,000,000. Forgotten were the huzzas for President Roosevelt. Panamanian students commemorated the anniversary of the signing of the Hay–Bunau-Varilla Treaty as a day of mourning, and not least of the ceremonies was the burning in effigy of the French author, whose memory was not cherished in the land of which he had been so fond. Serious trouble occurred in 1964 when American high school students at the Balboa High School within the canal zone raised an American flag, in defiance of an agreement that within the zone both the United States and Panamanian flags should appear side by side. In the ensuing riots twenty-one Panamanians and four American soldiers were killed and some 350 persons injured. Once tempers cooled, the result was another move by the Panamanians to renegotiate the canal treaty.

3. *The corollary*

The third interference of the United States in the Caribbean-Central American area was in the Dominican Republic in 1905, and it gave rise to the famous Roosevelt Corollary to the Monroe Doctrine. But before setting out the manner in which President Roosevelt chose to solve the woes of the Dominican government, one must relate the so-called Venezuelan affair of the winter of 1902–1903, for this attempted European intervention in the New World led through a tortuous process to Roosevelt's corollary.

It may be that good behavior by a great country toward a small one breeds contempt, that the altruism which moved President Grover Cleveland and Secretary of State Richard Olney to protect Venezuela in 1895 was in the longer view of things a mistake; the government of Venezuela, so suddenly protected, may have come to believe that it could play fast and loose with European nations and then hide behind the Monroe Doctrine. At the turn of the twentieth century, the dictator of Venezuela was a rascal named Cipriano Castro, who without much effort had managed to create for his country a large bonded debt. In the name of his country he also refused to pay. The problem of the foreign bondholders was to get their money, and in sheer desperation the British and German and Italian governments sent gunboats to Venezuela in December 1902, sank three of Castro's gunboats, blockaded five ports and the mouths of the Orinoco River, and threatened to put troops ashore.

What would the United States do for its erstwhile ward, the government of Venezuela, now so cruelly attacked? Theodore Roosevelt a year or so before, while still vice president, had remarked in a letter to his German friend and tennis companion, Baron Speck von Sternburg, that if one of the little Latin American nations misbehaved the best procedure would be to spank it. Obviously, no notion of a Roosevelt Corollary had crossed his mind. When the bond crisis occurred in Venezuela, Roosevelt, now president, seems to have changed his mind. Years later, during the First World War, Roosevelt testified that he indeed had sent Admiral Dewey and the United States fleet into the vicinity of Puerto Rico and had been willing to use force to throw the Germans out of Venezuela in case they went into it. The first hint of the historical proportions of Roosevelt's actions in the Venezuelan crisis appeared in 1915 when William R. Thayer published a two-volume life of John Hay, for which Roosevelt had corrected the proofs. A year later, and apparently with some reluctance, TR set down his recollection in a letter which Thayer published as an appendix to a new printing of the Hay biography:

I speedily became convinced that Germany was the . . . really formidable party, in the transaction. . . . I became convinced that England would not back Germany in the event of a clash over the matter between Germany and the United States, but would remain neutral. . . . I also became convinced that Germany intended to seize some Venezuelan harbor and turn it into a strongly fortified place of arms, on the model of Kiaochow, with a view to exercising some measure of control over the future Isthmian Canal, and over South American affairs generally. . . . Germany declined to agree to arbitrate . . . and declined to say that she would not take possession of Venezuelan territory, merely saying that such possession would be "temporary"— which might mean anything. I finally decided that no useful purpose would be served by further delay, and I took action accordingly. I assembled our battle fleet, under Admiral Dewey, near Porto Rico, for "maneuvres," with instructions that the fleet should be kept in hand and in fighting trim, and should be ready to sail at an hour's notice. . . . I saw the [German] Ambassador, and explained that in view of the presence of the German squadron on the Venezuelan coast I could not permit longer delay in answering my request for an arbitration, and that I could not acquiesce in any seizure of Venezuelan territory. The Ambassador responded that his Government could not agree to arbitrate, and that there was no intention to take "permanent" possession of Venezuelan territory. I answered that Kiaochow was not a "permanent" possession of Germany's—that . . . I did not intend to have another Kiaochow, held by similar tenure, on the approach to the Isthmian Canal. The Ambassador repeated that his Government would not agree to arbitrate. I then asked him to inform his Government that if no notification for arbitration came during the next ten days I would be obliged to order Dewey to take his fleet to the Venezuelan coast and see that the German forces did not take possession of any territory. He expressed very grave concern and asked me if I realized the serious consequences that would follow such action; consequences so serious to both countries that he dreaded to give them a name. I answered that I had thoroughly counted the cost before I decided on the step, and asked him to look at the map, as a glance would show him that there was no spot in the world where Germany in the event of conflict with the United States would be at a greater disadvantage than in the Caribbean sea. A week later the Ambassador came to see me, talked pleasantly on several subjects, and rose to go. I asked him if he had any answer to make from his Government to my request, and when he said no, I informed him that in such event it was useless to wait as long as I had intended, and that Dewey would be ordered to sail twenty four hours in advance of the time I had set. He expressed deep apprehension, and said that his Government would not arbitrate. However, less than twenty four hours before the time I had appointed for calling the order to Dewey, the Ambassador notified me that His Imperial Majesty the German Emperor had directed him to request me to undertake arbitration myself.

How correct was this account? Recalling his anger against the Germans, Roosevelt may have been thinking more about his current— 1915–1916—feelings about the Germans. Controversy at once arose over his version of the affair, and some well-known scholars such as Dexter Perkins, the historian of the Monroe Doctrine, have believed that Roosevelt made up the crisis out of whole cloth. A more recent writer, the late Howard K. Beale, in a volume entitled *Theodore Roosevelt and the Rise of America to World Power* (1956) devoted forty exhaustive pages to the problem, with explanatory notes, and concluded that Roosevelt's memory in 1915–1916 was essentially correct: that there had been a crisis thirteen years earlier with Germany over Venezuela, and that the president had forced the Germans into line. Beale concluded, "it seems certain that the substance of the story was not an invention of war years and that only the color and tones were heightened in the account recorded in 1916."

Whatever the proportions of the crisis in showing what an American president did, or an ex-president thought he had done, to preserve his country's hegemony in the Caribbean, the Venezuelan affair has interest for the historian because it led into an important diplomacy with the Dominican Republic and resulted in the Roosevelt Corollary to the Monroe Doctrine. After the European intervention in Venezuela, and Roosevelt's intervention of whatever sort, the president had arranged with Castro and the intervening governments to send the bond dispute to arbitration. The disputants appealed to a three-man tribunal chosen by the tsar of Russia from the panel established by the First Hague Peace Conference of 1899 (the latter conference had met in the Dutch capital to consider ways to world peace and included twenty-six nations, among them the United States; for the conference, see below, ch. 18, pp. 485–486). The tribunal decided on February 22, 1904, that Venezuela should pay its debtors and that—this was the rub of the judgment —payment should be first to the nations which had engaged in the naval demonstration. The tribunal's decision put a premium on force in the collection of debts. Several of the Latin American governments, especially in Central America and the Caribbean, were now wide open, so to speak, to foreign naval demonstrations and perhaps even foreign occupations. No American president at the turn of the twentieth century, observing the fiscal chaos south of the United States, could have ignored the danger. TR thereupon produced a policy, applied first to the Dominican Republic, which became known perhaps inappropriately as the Roosevelt Corollary to the Monroe Doctrine.

The corollary was no sudden announcement. Roosevelt allowed an official of the state department to remark in February 1904, at the time of the Hague decision, that the ruling put a premium on violence. In May 1904 he arranged for Secretary of War Root to read to a public assemblage a presidential letter in which Roosevelt made a statement almost identical to his later message to Congress in December 1904, the message which became known as the Roosevelt Corollary. He was not willing to make his letter to Root a formal pronouncement, to the extent of communicating it to Congress, until he won the presidential election in November. Then came the formal statement of December 6:

Chronic wrongdoing, or an impotence which results in a general loosening of the ties of civilized society, may in America, as elsewhere, ultimately require intervention by some civilized nation, and in the Western Hemisphere the adherence of the United States to the Monroe Doctrine may force the United

States, however reluctantly, in flagrant cases of such wrongdoing or impotence, to the exercise of an international police power.

The president explained himself further in a message to the Senate on February 15, 1905:

The United States . . . under the Monroe doctrine . . . can not see any European power seize and permanently occupy the territory of one of these republics; and yet such seizure of territory, disguised or undisguised, may eventually offer the only way in which the power in question can collect any debts, unless there is interference on the part of the United States.

As for the little country to which he then applied the corollary, the Dominican Republic, that nation was in a saddening state. As set out in an earlier chapter (pp. 316–319), at the end of the 1860's President Grant had wished to annex the country, and President Baez had been willing. Fortunately for the United States, Senator Sumner in the speech about King Ahab and Naboth's vineyard had made annexation impossible, and revolution overtook President Baez. But that was not the end of things, for Baez was a patriot if compared to one of his successors, President Ulises Heureaux (the latter-day individual who remarked on

Theodore Roosevelt, "The World's Constable," protecting the Latin American nations from Europe.

one occasion that he did not care what history might say about his presidency, because he would not be there to read it). Heureaux's presidency was a national disaster, and his assassination in 1899 left the country in dire straits. The Dominican Republic went from bad to worse —"to hell in a hack," to use a contemporary expression—until President Roosevelt invoked the corollary in 1904.

The president of the United States intervened to prevent intervention by foreign governments seeking to protect their bondholders. Roosevelt wished to insure the rights of all bondholders. But there were interesting sides to the question. The Dominicans had gotten deeply into debt with the citizens of quite a few nations: France, Belgium, Italy, Great Britain, Germany, the United States, the Netherlands, Mexico, Spain, Sweden, and Norway. It was hard to say how much information the purchasers of Dominican bonds possessed when they acquired their paper pledges. Presumably some individuals knew very well what they were getting, or might get, and were out to profit by whatever international crisis might arise. Other investors were what Americans would have described as suckers. French peasants apparently bought the bonds in belief that they were buying securities of the Dominican religious order. Whatever the deception, the holders of the New World's Dominican bonds soon were willing to have their governments intervene. After February 1904, the European bondholders were especially anxious for forcible intervention, since such a course in Venezuela had produced preferential treatment through the ruling of the Hague tribunal. The French, Belgian, and Italian bondholders managed to arrange for payments on their bonds beginning November 1, 1904. Not to be outmaneuvered, an organization representing American and British capital, known piquantly as the San Domingo Improvement Company, in an ungentlemanly maneuver got hold of the Dominican customs house at Puerto Plata. It was, then, an impossible situation.

Presidential action from Washington was accompanied by some confusion, but eventually everything worked out. Roosevelt took over all the Dominican customs houses. He sought first to do this by executive agreement, perhaps feeling that if he tried a treaty the delay for debate in the Senate would create only more confusion in a situation already filled with it. He may also have believed that his election in 1904 allowed him a certain freedom in foreign affairs. When the text of the proposed executive agreement reached Washington, there was an obvious resentment in the Senate, and Roosevelt changed the form of agreement to a treaty. When sentiment in the Senate then turned clearly against the treaty, he reluctantly arranged that the treaty not come up for a vote. The president managed a financial *modus vivendi* in the Dominican Republic for two years, 1905–1907, a retired American colonel acting as collector of customs, at the end of which time the Senate consented to the treaty.

The results in the Dominican Republic meanwhile were heartening to everyone but revolutionists. Roosevelt in September 1905 penned what Dexter Perkins has described as "an engaging note" to the secretary of the navy:

As for the Santo Domingo matter, tell Admiral Bradford to stop any revolution. I intend to keep the island in the *statu quo* until the Senate has had time to act on the treaty, and I shall treat any revolutionary movement as an effort to upset the *modus vivendi*. That this is ethically right, I am dead sure, even though there may be some technical or red tape difficulty.

Under the *modus vivendi* and subsequent treaty the Dominican Republic received more money from customs, after service on the debt, than had come in altogether under Dominican collection prior to 1905.

Money, the student of history might conclude, was the root of more evil in the Dominican Republic than met Roosevelt's eye. He disposed of one evil, financial insolvency, only to create a situation far worse than a few slow-paying bonds. The financial intervention of 1905 led to an American military occupation in 1916 under auspices of the navy, which continued until 1924, with a provisional republic established two years before the navy departed. A member of the marine-trained Dominican constabulary, Rafael Leonidas Trujillo y Molina, thereupon took charge of the republic, and turned it into a satrapy which any of Alexander the Great's generals of ancient times would have appreciated.

4. *Nicaragua*

President Theodore Roosevelt must have hoped that his contribution to the Monroe Doctrine would settle things in Latin America. It did settle them, for a few years, but even in the Dominican Republic the arrangement eventually came apart. Roosevelt's successor President William Howard Taft had to confront trouble in Nicaragua where the dictator-president, General José Santos Zelaya, tried to cancel the United States-Nicaragua Concession, a mining property owned by a Pittsburgh corporation, the principal American property in Nicaragua, so that he could sell it again for better terms. Reportedly Zelaya planned secret advances to Japan for a canal treaty. The dictator was also trying to pull apart a treaty settlement which Presidents Porfirio Díaz of Mexico and Roosevelt of the United States had persuaded the republics of Central America to conclude among themselves at Washington in 1907, according to which they promised to submit all their disputes to arbitration and, generally, not go to war with each other or foment revolutions in each other's territories. Understandably, the United States had little love for the Nicaraguan dictator. When a revolution against him broke out in 1909, Zelaya executed two American citizens, professional dynamiters, for laying mines in the San Juan River in support of the revolutionists (the Americans held commissions in the revolutionary army and considered themselves prisoners of war). President Taft broke diplomatic relations, and the dictator was overthrown.

Nicaragua thereupon became a ward of the United States. The individual who had been secretary of the American concession in Nicaragua, Adolfo Díaz, rose to power, and his administration on June 6, 1911, signed a treaty, the Knox-Castrillo Convention, with Secretary of State Knox, TR's erstwhile attorney general. The treaty was identical with another treaty signed by the United States in 1911 with Honduras. Knox would have liked to deal the same way with Guatemala. The Senate rejected the Nicaraguan and Honduran treaties, but in Nicaragua the New York bankers whom Secretary Knox had enlisted to set aright the finances of that country went ahead anyway and with the help of the state department set up a financial regulation which lasted until 1914. A substitute then was arranged for the Knox-Castrillo Convention which had failed in the Senate. This Bryan-Chamorro Treaty, signed by Secretary of State William Jennings Bryan and the Nicaraguan minister in Washington, Emiliano Chamorro, in 1914 (ratified in 1916), provided that the United States should have perpetual and exclusive right to construct a canal through Nicaragua, together with a 99-year lease on Great and Little Corn Islands in the Caribbean and a 99-year right to establish a naval base on the Gulf of Fonseca, both the lease and right subject to renewal for another 99-year period. Which is to say that the lease and right if renewed could run to the year 2114. In return the United States gave Nicaragua $3,000,000.

An instance of imperialism? Students of American diplomacy should notice the name of the American negotiator, Secretary Bryan, an anti-imperialist. All of which brings to mind the story about Bryan's theory, at one time put forth, that no man in the United States ought to possess a sum of more than $100,000. The story has it that Bryan in later years made a killing in Florida real estate, and became a millionaire, and that when asked about his theory of the $100,000 limit he replied with a twinkle in his eye that times had changed.

In Nicaragua during the Taft era the government of President Díaz sorely needed support, and Taft in 1912 brought in at Díaz's request a "legation guard" of 2,700 marines, and except for a brief trial withdrawal in 1925, which did not work, the marines stayed until 1933.

In the latter 1920's, beginning in 1925, a Nicaraguan revolution threatened serious trouble for the United States, and critics of American policy in Latin America still frequently cite the actions of the American government at that time as a horrible example of imperialism. In point of fact the politics of Nicaragua in 1925–1928 were rather confusing, even to Nicaraguans, and the behavior of the Colossus of the North proved remarkably impartial if slightly imperial.

The trouble came in 1925 when President Coolidge determined to pull out the marines. A Nicaraguan election had brought to power President Carlos Solórzano, who was a coalition candidate—a promising innovation in Nicaraguan politics, meaning that Solórzano represented both the Liberals and the Conservatives, the country's two traditional factions. The new president pleaded with Coolidge to keep the marines in Nicaragua long enough for his regime to train a constabulary to replace them, and Coolidge went along with this proposition, agreeing to withdraw the marines—by this time there were only about a hundred of them—on August 1, 1925. The American president kept his word. Three weeks after the marines left, the revolution broke out: the Second Nicaraguan Revolution, one might describe it in terms of American involvement, the First having occurred during the expulsion of Zelaya and installation of Zelaya's successor Díaz.

The trouble with the Second Revolution, to be brief, was that Solórzano apparently received $30,000 from the strong man of Nicaraguan politics, General Chamorro (of the Bryan-Chamorro Treaty). Chamorro then sent Solórzano to California and expelled Vice President Juan Sacasa, who went to Washington. Chamorro took over the country through a series of fast constitutional shuffles. In the course of these shuffles he violated the spirit of a Central American treaty of 1923, concluded in Washington, which forbade dubious successions to presidencies. Chamorro soon was president, by hook and crook. He was fortunate enough to take office at a time when the Nicaraguan treasury was full—hence the ease with which he could dispense $30,000 to Solórzano.

The grand question became what the United States would do. Apart from the embarrassment of Chamorro's violation of the United States-sponsored treaty of 1923, the question was the more embarrassing because Chamorro was saying publicly that the American government could not do a thing to get him out of office. The American minister in Managua received the intelligence that Chamorro in conversation had said, "To Hell with the United States, with the State Department, and with its diplomatic representative here!"

The American government began to put pressure on General Chamorro, and the result was a long involvement which went far beyond what anyone in Washington had intended when Chamorro first took possession of his tiny little country of approximately 700,000 people, 72 per cent of whom were illiterate, and with whom the United States's nationals had invested only a few millions of dollars, nothing at all compared with investment in Cuba and Mexico, less than in any other Latin American country except Paraguay. The American minister went home on leave in 1926 and his chargé d'affaires, Lawrence Dennis, a young man with an authoritarian disposition, pressed Chamorro unmercifully to resign, which Chamorro eventually did after emptying the Nicaraguan treasury. The United States's old friend Díaz became president. Solórzano's vice president, Sacasa, thereupon appeared back on the scene, having come from Washington via Mexico City, where he seems to have received certain promises of support. Sacasa appointed José Moncada as his chief general, and Moncada proved a better chieftain than Díaz's generals. President Coolidge and Secretary of State Frank B. Kellogg began to find themselves in the middle of a tornado of public opinion, with Senator William E. Borah of Idaho, the chairman of the foreign relations committee, trumpeting his criticisms up and down the land. Coolidge in the spring of 1927 appointed Henry L. Stimson to go down to Nicaragua and clean up the situation, bringing peace so that the United States could get its marines out (once Sacasa raised the flag of revolution the marines had returned and, after trying to declare areas of the country off limits to revolutionists, were in danger of getting shot at from both sides). Stimson arranged the Peace of Tipitapa, at a locality of that name, and the resultant marine-supervised elections in 1928 gave the presidency to Moncada, who soon was appreciating United States help almost as fervently as had his predecessor Díaz.

For a while under Moncada's presidency the marines sought to eliminate a dissident of the new regime, General Augusto César Sandino, a Nicaraguan Robin Hood who considered President Coolidge the sheriff of Nottingham. Sandino was accustomed to leave chits with fellow Nicaraguans from whom he had requisitioned supplies, which stated that "The Honorable Calvin Coolidge, President of the United States of North America, will pay the bearer $———," inserting the amount of the levied goods. A force of 5,480 marines and the marine-trained *Guardia Nacional* sought to catch Sandino, without result. Finally the Nicaraguan army betrayed him during a truce in 1934 and shot him.

When the marines left Nicaragua in 1933, the general in charge of the *Guardia*, by name of Anastasio Somoza, took over the country, and he and his descendants have ruled Nicaragua down to the present writing.

As we see it now, the Nicaraguan intervention from 1912 to 1933 was a mismanaged affair, not because it did too much in Nicaragua but because it did not do enough. The United States interfered barely enough to keep the elected government in power and the finances in order, but not enough to regenerate Nicaragua. The intervention aroused the animosity of some Nicaraguans, of other Latin American governments such as Mexico, and of many well-intentioned American citizens, such as Senator Borah, who thought that what looked like imperialism was imperialism. At this point, having lost support of these bodies of public opinion anyway, the United States government might well have become more drastic with its measures in Nicaragua and done a thorough job.

5. Haiti

Another intervention in the Caribbean region—following upon the Cuban, Panamanian, and Dominican affairs, and the occupation of Nicaragua—occurred in Haiti in 1915.

The problem of Haiti was in part that of too many revolutions. Haitians by 1915 had endured a long history of revolts. In the late eighteenth century a revolution had broken out against the French, led by Toussaint l'Ouverture. An ever more saddening series of forcible changes of regime followed, until by the early twentieth century Haiti was sunk in political ineptitude. Between 1911 and 1915 the presidency of Haiti was occupied by a bewildering series of statesmen, several of whom met personal misfortune in office: Antoine Simon, Cincinnatus Leconte (blown up with the presidential palace), Tancrède Auguste (died presumably by poison), Michel Oreste, Oreste Zamor, Davilmar Théodore.

The Haitian problem was partly the government's defaulting on foreign-held bonds. The French and German governments in March 1914 proposed a joint customs receivership with the United States. President Vilbrun Guillaume Sam, coming to power in March 1915, faced a huge (for Haiti) debt of about $24,000,000, part of which was owed to American financial interests and much of the remainder to Europeans.

There also was a danger that foreign nations might use Haiti as a place for establishing a naval base, perhaps to threaten the Panama canal. Years later, after the United States had taken care of Haiti, former Secretary of State Robert Lansing was to tell darkly of German sailors having landed in secret at Port-au-Prince, only to withdraw suddenly on the eve of the outbreak of war in Europe.

The United States bided its time. In 1908 Albert Shaw, editor of the *Review of Reviews,* inquired of Secretary of State Elihu Root whether, since the American government had established control over Cuba, Panama, and the Dominican Republic, Root could not "invent a way to put Haiti under bonds." Root answered, "for any positive step . . . we must wait for the 'psychological moment.' "

The moment did not occur until President Sam created a crisis and expired therefrom.

Sam's end was nothing if not violent. His predecessor in the presidential chair, Théodore, had a friend named Dr. Rosalvo Bobo, who as soon as Sam became president traveled into the Haitian wilds, there to raise a revolt. Thereupon Sam seized 170 alleged partisans of Bobo, in and around Port-au-Prince. An attack on the palace on the night of July 26, 1915, persuaded President Sam to massacre almost all of his prisoners, 167 of them. Two days later, on July 28, the enraged populace of Port-au-Prince rose up. Sam sought asylum in the French legation. The mob invaded the legation, found the president hiding behind a bureau, and threw him out into the street. The mob then cut him into small pieces and paraded these trophies around the capital city. At this juncture President Wilson instructed the marines to land, and the U.S.S. *Washington,* flagship of Rear Admiral Caperton, dropped anchor in Port-au-Prince that very afternoon. Before nightfall the marines had occupied the town.

The marines governed the republic for several years. The United States government simply took over the country. Marine control was so obvious that former Assistant Secretary of the Navy Franklin D. Roosevelt, running for the vice presidency in 1920, and alluding to the Dominican Republic as well as Haiti, could remark concerning his government experience that "One of my jobs was to look after a couple little republics that our navy is running." Young FDR also took credit in 1920 for writing the Haitian constitution, put into force in 1918; he described it as "a pretty good constitution, too." Secretary of the Interior Franklin K. Lane, knowing that his colleague Secretary of the Navy Josephus Daniels was queasy about the marines' work, was accustomed to rise at cabinet meetings of the Wilson administration and with mock seriousness proclaim to Daniels: "Hail the King of Haiti." The marines arranged for ratification of the 1918 constitution with a considerable artistry, and the vote came out 69,377 Haitians in favor, 355 against. Major General Smedley D. (Old Gimlet Eye) Butler liked to brag about his road-building program which had resulted in many miles of highway in a very short time and at remarkably little cost. He usually did not add that the Haitian government under his supervision had forced the natives into working for nothing, rather like the ancient French custom of the *corvée.* When the Haitians rose in revolt, Butler put them down. No wonder it was with difficulty that the marines found a Haitian willing to be president, in succession to President Sam. President Philippe Sudre Dartiguenave, elected in August 1915, signed a treaty on September 16 under which the Haitian republic became a protectorate of the United States. The treaty contained articles similar to those of the Platt Amendment for Cuba and was not terminated until 1934 when the marines left. Customs control continued in modified form until 1941.

Marine control, as mentioned, was roughly efficient. In 1917, Assistant Secretary Roosevelt paid a ceremonial visit to President Dartiguenave, and a symbolic incident occurred when the president of Haiti started to climb into his official limousine ahead of the United States assistant secretary. General Butler seized President Dartiguenave's coat collar and commenced to pull him back, but Roosevelt stepped aside and insisted that the Haitian should take precedence.

The constitution along with the marines helped make Haiti a more orderly place for a short time. The American government under President Franklin D. Roosevelt concluded an executive agreement with the Haitian government in 1933, under which the marines withdrew in the following year, and fiscal supervision ended in 1941. Since the American withdrawal, the Haitian government unfortunately has deteriorated, the rapacity and rascality of officials matching and outdoing the record of the early twentieth century. The current regime—that of President Dr. François Duvalier—is as bad as and perhaps worse than any government east or west of the iron curtain or any other curtain.

6. The Mexican intervention

The greatest of all the American interventions was the effort of President Woodrow Wilson in 1913–1917 to move Mexican politics in the direction he deemed proper—so the Mexicans would "elect good men" and protect American lives and property. The latter was no idle concern, for American holdings in Mexico, large and small, amounted to approximately one billion dollars.

For the United States the troubles with Mexico began shortly after the collapse of the regime of President Porfirio Díaz, who was ruler of the country from 1876 until 1911. Under General Díaz the nation had settled down and become prosperous, with many of its economic resources being exploited by foreign companies, particularly American. What with all the turmoil elsewhere in Latin America at the turn of the century, Díaz seemed a man whom Americans could trust. His regime appeared so wonderfully solid, its achievements so remarkable. One may therefore excuse Secretary of State Root when upon visiting in Mexico City in 1907 he offered a fulsome tribute to the Mexican president:

No one lives to-day who I would rather see than President Diaz. If I were a poet I would write sophistry; if I were a musician I would compose triumphal marches; if I were a Mexican I should feel that the steadfast loyalty of a life-time could not be too much in return for the blessings that he had brought to my country. As I am neither poet, musician, nor Mexican, but only an American who loves justice and liberty and hopes to see their reign among mankind progress and strengthen and become perpetual, I look to Porfirio Diaz, the President of Mexico, as one of the great men to be held up for the hero worship of mankind.

Unfortunately for Root's enthusiasm, Díaz was growing old, his control over the government slipping, at the very moment when Root was singing these singular praises. An increasing Mexican nationalism, popular unwillingness to tolerate all the favors bestowed upon foreign capitalists, led at last to the president's retirement to Europe, where he died a poor man—he had not governed Mexico for his personal gain but for the good, as he saw it, of his country.

During the few years of his exile in Paris, Díaz liked to relate to admirers that at a crucial moment when rioters were in front of the presidential palace he had suffered from an infernal toothache, which prevented him from exercising a clarity of judgment sufficient to put the rioters down by force.

Whatever the reason for Díaz's departure, it was certainly true that when he left for Europe a grand political confusion settled upon Mexico. At first the government passed into the hands of Francisco I. Madero, who was no match for the animosities and intrigues which swirled down on the City of Mexico. Madero usually has been described as a dreamer. Perhaps also he was crazy. A small man, only five feet four inches in height, Madero had begun his adult life as a gentleman farmer but soon turned his attention to other pursuits, including spiritualism and homeopathic medicine as well as politics. One evening while waiting upon a patient, sitting in a darkened room, he had found himself doodling on a pad of paper, and psychic forces began to move the pencil which inscribed in firm letters, "Love God above all things and thy neighbor as thyself." Madero experimented with spirit writing under more controlled conditions, and the same message recurred, together with other messages. Gradually he got in touch with the great minds of the past who helped him overcome his indifferent literary talents and he began to write excellent essays. He began also to believe that he was a chosen instrument to regenerate Mexico, Latin America, perhaps the world. This was the man who at first took over the presidency from Díaz. At one meeting with the American ambassador, Henry Lane Wilson, the president of Mexico placed a third chair in the circle and announced to the ambassador that a friend was sitting there. The friend was invisible, Madero explained, but there nonetheless.

It was not unexpected that this visionary would run into trouble, and so Madero did, in the person of his principal military commander, General Victoriano Huerta. The latter was a full-blooded Indian whose two hallmarks were an incongruous pair of spectacles and a brandy bottle near at hand. Huerta's drunkenness, incidentally, public knowledge in the Mexican capital, soon was to bring his demise while in exile in the United States, where in 1916 he succumbed to cirrhosis of the liver. But Huerta in early February 1913 evicted Madero from the presidential palace and after a quick constitutional arrangement assumed the presidency.

The general then murdered Madero, together with Vice President Jase Pino Suarez. Huerta had sworn on a scapulary of the Virgin of Guadalupe, likewise on a medal of the Sacred Heart of Jesus, also by the memory

General Victoriano
Huerta, 1915.

of his mother who once had worn these holy images, that he would permit no harm to come to Señor Madero. Having made these commitments, he then visited the American ambassador, H. L. Wilson, and asked what he should do with Madero. Huerta suggested either exiling him or putting him in a lunatic asylum. Wilson replied that Huerta "ought to do that which was best for the peace of the country." This was, to use a later expression, open-ended advice. And so it happened that when an armed guard was transferring the ex-president and ex-vice president to a penitentiary at 2:00 A.M. the two men were shot, on the trivial claim that they were trying to escape. In actual fact this was a favorite Latin American way of execution.

The crisis in Mexico City occurred on February 9–18, 1913, the "tragic ten days" of Mexican history, and it caught the government of the United States in an uneasy position, for the Democrats and Woodrow Wilson were coming into Washington, Taft and the Republicans leaving the government. There was no American policy toward the events in Mexico until Wilson took office on March 4.

The new president had pronounced views on the Mexican situation. "I will not," he said privately, "recognize a government of butchers." He recalled Henry Lane Wilson and refused to appoint a successor. He laid down a policy on March 11, 1913, in regard to recognition of regimes in Latin America, declaring that recognition was "possible only when supported at every turn by the orderly processes of just government based upon law, not upon arbitrary or irregular force. We hold, as I am sure all thoughtful leaders of republican government everywhere hold, that just government rests always upon the consent of the governed, and that there can be no freedom without order based upon law and upon the public conscience and approval. We shall look to make these principles the basis of mutual intercourse, respect, and helpfulness between our sister republics and ourselves."

This new Wilsonian pronouncement, one should explain, stood in opposition to the recognition policy of the United States since the time when Thomas Jefferson was secretary of state. Jefferson had established the practice that any government in control of its territory and people—a government de facto—was a government de jure so far as concerned the United States, to be recognized as soon as decently possible. Wilson was undertaking to pass upon the legality of governments in Latin America, and presumably an illegal government would be for him, and his successors in office he doubtless hoped, an immoral government which it would be impossible to recognize. The Wilsonian theory for Latin America lasted until Secretary of State Henry L. Stimson revoked it on September 17, 1930, and went back to the practice of Jefferson. An exception to this rule of recognition was the Central American republics, which in the peace settlement of 1907 had sought, among other measures, to invoke a special recognition policy among themselves. These states, ridden by revolts and interventions across their several borders, had written out a code of proper revolutionary behavior, which even went to the length of stipulating what officials in a given government could and could not, by revolution, take office in a new regime. The treaty of 1907 was redrawn in 1923, and the United States, although not a signatory of the treaty of 1923, adhered to its specified recognition policy and followed the dictates of the treaty during revolts in Nicaragua in 1925, in Guatemala in 1930, and in El Salvador in 1931. The Central American states themselves abandoned their agreement in 1934, at which time the United States reverted, for this area of the Western Hemisphere, to its general recognition policy in Latin America as laid down in 1930—which, as mentioned, superseded Wilson's policy of 1913, returning American practice to that of Jefferson's time.

The president in 1913 refused to recognize Huerta the murderer, and he made his policy toward Mexico into a general policy toward all of Latin America, nonrecognition of any government which subverted the liberties of its people. This policy he hoped would freeze out the new dictator in Mexico City. It certainly would have done so in any of the smaller Central American states, but Mexico, as events turned out, was too large a state to handle in this way.

Huerta on October 10, 1913, threw 110 members of the Mexican chamber of deputies into prison and inaugurated a full-fledged military dictatorship. At this point President Wilson was still unwilling to interfere with open force in Mexico, though he was willing to use all diplomatic pressures. In a famous speech at Mobile, Alabama, on October 27, 1913, he declared that the United States "will never again seek one additional foot of territory by conquest." Having set out his position he employed diplomacy for the next months to oust the Mexican general from power. He obtained the support of the British in this venture, promising to Sir William Tyrrell, the representative of the British foreign secretary Sir Edward Grey, "I am going to teach the South American republics to elect good men" and that the United States would work to establish a government in Mexico under which foreign contracts and concessions would be safe. The British had been friendly to Huerta because they thought he would protect foreign investment, rather than undertake a series of social reforms as Madero had been threatening to do. But the British, when Wilson duly approached them, withdrew recognition from Huerta.

Then came the Tampico incident, on April 9, 1914, when a boatload of American sailors landed at that port from an American ship and by error entered a restricted area without permission from the local authorities. The sailors were arrested, and afterward the local commander, a Huertista, upon learning of the incident, released the Americans and sent off an apology to Rear Admiral Henry T. Mayo, commanding the American squadron in the vicinity. The affair might have ended there, but perhaps in memory of the *Baltimore* incident of over twenty years before, the admiral demanded a 21-gun salute to the American flag. President Wilson, upon learning of the affair, and willing to make trouble for Huerta, backed him up. Wilson on April 18, 1914, issued an ultimatum to Huerta to salute the American flag or take the consequences. Then, when the American government learned that a German steamer was scheduled to arrive at Veracruz with a load of ammunition for Huerta, Rear Admiral Frank F. Fletcher was ordered to occupy that port forcibly. Marines and sailors went ashore on April 21 and soon occupied the town, at a cost of 19 American dead and 47 wounded, the Mexicans losing at least two hundred killed and another three hundred wounded. A difficult situation had arisen, because Wilson had not prepared the American public for this eventuality, and indeed the entire decline of American-Mexican relations had not been understood by the American people. To make matters worse, the followers of Huerta's enemy and rival in Mexico, the revolutionary commander Venustiano (Don Venus) Carranza, who was in the field against Huerta, condemned the occupation of Veracruz as wholeheartedly as did the Huertistas who controlled the town. The Americans left on November 23, 1914. The adjournment of the incident was obscured by the fall from power of Huerta and the occupation of Mexico City by Carranza in August, and by the beginning of the World War in Europe that same month.

Huerta had caused plenty of trouble, and Wilson was glad to be rid of him. Publicly he had condemned the wily Mexican and now had forced the general's retirement from the president's palace in Mexico City. Privately Wilson had a "sneaking admiration" for his opponent and confessed to finding Huerta "a diverting brute . . . so false, so sly, so full of bravado, yet so courageous . . . seldom sober and always impossible yet what an indomitable fighter for his country." Huerta on his part never seems to have viewed President Wilson as anything more than the Puritan of the North.

The new government in Mexico City, headed by Carranza, soon showed a singular incompetence, in fair part because of the personality of its president. Don Venus was a dull, uninspiring man, of slender intellectual ability, every bit as rigid as the Puritan of the North. His countenance, peering from behind an impressive gray beard, commanded neither the love nor hate of fellow Mexicans. He was a conservative, middle-class

liberal, hardly fitted to cope with the almost exploding revolutionary sentiment within his country which rapidly was moving from political to
economic and social goals. Nor could Carranza understand the purposes of
the United States, any more than those of his countrymen. The United
States had helped his regime into power by weakening the government
of Huerta. But he easily convinced himself that the United States was trying to do him in, evidently believing the quip of one of his predecessors,
Díaz, who once had lamented about "Poor Mexico, so far from God and
so near the United States."

What was President Wilson to do? The president of the United States,
who had tried so hard to teach Mexico to elect good men, had received

Pancho Villa and his generals. Left to Right: Fierro, Villa, Ortega, Medina.

Carranza for his trouble. And unfortunately, a split now occurred in the forces of President Carranza—the succession, one recalls, had been Díaz, Madero, Huerta, Carranza—and there appeared the formidable figure of Doroteo Arango, or Pancho Villa, a wild and woolly character who could submit to control by no one, least of all a staid individual like Carranza, whose government he set out to pull down. In the year 1915 fighting between the troops of Carranza and Villa swayed back and forth inconclusively, while the United States was busy worrying about conditions on the high seas because of the European war. The *Lusitania* was torpedoed in May 1915, and the crisis with Germany over its sinking lasted through much of the summer. But in 1916 American attention came back to Mexico, and for a while the major problem of American foreign policy appeared not to be the fighting in Europe but the troubles south of the border.

Villa, to arouse an American intervention in Mexico and (so he hoped) discredit Carranza, met a Mexican Northwestern train at Santa Ysabel on January 11, 1916, carrying 17 young American college graduates who had just come into Mexico from California under a safe conduct from Carranza to open a mine. Villa killed 16 of them on the spot. When this gesture failed to bring results, he made a desperate raid into American territory at Columbus, New Mexico, on March 9, 1916, burning the town and killing 17 Americans. The United States government rose in wrath and President Wilson sent Brigadier General John J. Pershing across the border six days later, with 6,600 troops. The expedition penetrated more than 300 miles into Mexico in search of the errant Villa. On June 18, 1916, when the situation had worsened—that is, when Villa was nowhere to be found—Wilson called out for protection of the border virtually the entire National Guard, some 150,000 men.

For the remainder of the year tension was considerable, although the meeting of a commission of Mexicans and Americans managed to neutralize the affair during the touchy period preceding Wilson's re-election in the autumn of 1916. Then the imminence of American involvement in the European war made advisable a withdrawal of the punitive expedition. The withdrawal was completed on February 5, 1917, and a chapter of American-Mexican relations was finished. The United States extended *de jure* recognition by sending Ambassador Henry P. Fletcher to Mexico City on March 3, a month before the declaration of war against Germany.

It was probably unwise of Wilson to interfere in Mexico, even to the extent of withdrawing the American ambassador as he did in March 1913. In the case of smaller Latin republics such policy held hope of success, and perhaps in the nineteenth century it was not so difficult to coerce larger nations such as Mexico. But by the early twentieth century the time had passed for such action, for the nationalism of peoples everywhere in Latin America had risen to a point where the United States could not undertake drastic measures without raising local hatred and ill-feeling to a point where they not merely made the immediate measures useless but continued for years thereafter. After the Wilson intervention, it took nearly a generation before American relations with Mexico were placed on a solid foundation.

What may one conclude about the era of American intervention in Latin America? Was it a period when the Colossus of the North loosed its power without stint or limit, and drastically—and erroneously—infringed on the sovereignty of many of the states south of the border? In Central America and the Caribbean, only El Salvador together with Guatemala, Costa Rica, and Honduras (the latter three nations controlled, some people said, by the United Fruit Company) remained without benefit of direct American guidance. President William Howard Taft in a well-intentioned phrase had said that his administration's policy was one of "substituting dollars for bullets," and gave credibility to the accusation of "dollar diplomacy," unfortunately alliterative in all the major Western languages. Critics of American foreign policy usually have had a double tactic: they first have rung the changes on dollar diplomacy, and then have turned to the accusation that the United States practiced imperialism in Latin America just like the imperialism of France, Britain, and Germany in Africa and Asia.

This argument, that in this era after the turn of the century the United States simply stepped on the Latin American governments closest to its borders, overlooks the perhaps naive but nonetheless sincere belief of many citizens of the republic of North America that their government was helping its smaller sister republics. More important, it overlooks the strategic reason for most of the interventions: the closeness of the Central American and Caribbean countries to the Panama canal. It may be that the Mexican intervention could not properly be considered under this latter justification, but one could say that Mexico geographically, right next to the United States, was all the more a concern of the government in Washington. Humanitarian impulse and military strategy should have answered the critics of American policy in Latin America after the Spanish War of 1898. And if the critics did not find such contentions convincing, they might have observed that when the security of the canal approaches was assured, after the World War of 1914–1918, the United States gave up its interventions and became a good neighbor.

A CONTEMPORARY DOCUMENT

[President Theodore Roosevelt never for a minute considered that the United States government under his direction had done anything wrong in regard to obtaining a zone for a canal in Panama. He summed up his thinking on this subject in *An Autobiography* (New York, 1913; reprinted 1920), chapter fourteen, "The Monroe Doctrine and the Panama Canal," pp. 512, 514, 516, 521–524.]

By far the most important action I took in foreign affairs during the time I was President related to the Panama Canal. Here again there was much accusation about my having acted in an "unconstitutional" manner—a position which can be upheld only if Jefferson's action in acquiring Louisiana be also treated as unconstitutional; and at different stages of the affair believers in a do-nothing policy denounced me as having "usurped authority"—which meant, that when nobody else could or would exercise efficient authority, I exercised it. . . .

I took final action in 1903. During the preceding fifty-three years the Governments of New Granada and of its successor, Colombia, had been in a constant state of flux; and the State of Panama had sometimes been treated as almost independent, in a loose Federal league, and sometimes as the mere property of the Government at Bogota; and there had been innumerable appeals to arms, sometimes for adequate, sometimes for inadequate, reasons. The following is a partial list of the disturbances on the Isthmus of Panama during the period in question, as reported to us by our consuls. . . .

The above is only a partial list of the revolutions, rebellions, insurrections, riots, and other outbreaks that occurred during the period in question; yet they number fifty-three for the fifty-three years [from 1850 to 1902], and they showed a tendency to increase, rather than decrease, in numbers and intensity. . . .

When, in August, 1903, I became convinced that Colombia intended to repudiate the treaty made the preceding January, under cover of securing its rejection by the Colombian Legislature, I began carefully to consider what should be done. By my direction, Secretary Hay, personally and through the Minister at Bogota, repeatedly warned Colombia that grave consequences might follow her rejection of the treaty. The possibility of ratification did not wholly pass away until the close of the session of the Colombian Congress on the last day of October. There would then be two possibilities. One was that

Panama would remain quiet. In that case I was prepared to recommend to Congress that we should at once occupy the Isthmus anyhow, and proceed to dig the canal; and I had drawn out a draft of my message to this effect. But from the information I received, I deemed it likely that there would be a revolution in Panama as soon as the Colombian Congress adjourned without ratifying the treaty, for the entire population of Panama felt that the immediate building of the canal was of vital concern to their well-being. Correspondents of the different newspapers on the Isthmus had sent to their respective papers widely published forecasts indicating that there would be a revolution in such event. . . .

No one connected with the American Government had any part in preparing, inciting, or encouraging the revolution, and except for the reports of our military and naval officers, which I forwarded to Congress, no one connected with the Government had any previous knowledge concerning the proposed revolution, except such as was accessible to any person who read the newspapers and kept abreast of current questions and current affairs. By the unanimous action of its people, and without the firing of a shot, the state of Panama declared themselves an independent republic. The time for hesitation on our part had passed. . . .

From the beginning to the end our course was straightforward and in absolute accord with the highest of standards of international morality. Criticism of it can come only from misinformation, or else from a sentimentality which represents both mental weakness and a moral twist.

ADDITIONAL READING

For early twentieth-century Latin American policy, excluding Mexico, the leading account now is Dana C. Munro's *Intervention and Dollar Diplomacy in the Caribbean: 1900–1921* (Princeton, 1964), by an author who has had a long state department experience and joins that knowledge with a rich scholarly background. See also the last volume of Dexter Perkins's able trilogy on the Monroe Doctrine which considers the years 1867–1907 and Perkins's general account, his one-volume synthesis, which in its revised edition goes to the mid-1950's. There are pertinent chapters in Julius W. Pratt, *America's Colonial Experiment* (New York, 1950); the same author's *Challenge and Rejection: 1900–1921* (New York, 1967); *Foster Rhea Dulles, *The Imperial Years* (New York, 1956); together with the following volumes in the American Foreign Policy Library series edited by Crane Brinton: Dexter Perkins, *The United States and the Caribbean* (Cambridge, Mass., 1947); Arthur P. Whitaker, *The

United States and South America: The Northern Republics (Cambridge, 1948), and *The United States and Argentina* (Cambridge, 1954); *Howard F. Cline, The United States and Mexico* (rev. ed., Cambridge, 1963). A book which set the tone of criticism in the United States after the First World War is Scott Nearing and Joseph Freeman, *Dollar Diplomacy: A Study in American Imperialism* (New York, 1926). Latin Americans have gone so far as to assert an imperialism of words—that citizens of the United States have misappropriated the words "America" and "Americans" to describe themselves. Samuel Flagg Bemis wittily and handily disproves this assertion in " 'America' and 'Americans,' " *Yale Review*, LVII (1967–1968), 321–336. As Bemis points out, the first words of Pope Paul VI as he descended at Kennedy International Airport in October 1965 were: "Greetings to you, America!" Such usage had become fixed centuries ago, long before the department of state fussily changed the legend on the escutcheons and name plates of its missions abroad to read "United States of America" rather than, simply, "American Embassy" etc.

American (*sic*) policy in Cuba appears in David F. Healy, *The United States in Cuba: 1898–1902* (Madison, Wis., 1963); D. A. Lockmiller, *Magoon in Cuba* (Chapel Hill, N.C., 1938), concerning the governor with the unlikely name. See also the account in Hermann Hagedorn, *Leonard Wood: A Biography* (2 vols., New York, 1931).

Sheldon Liss, *The United States and the Panama Canal* (Notre Dame, Ind., 1967) offers the diplomacy of the canal down to the near present; and other general accounts of the taking of the canal zone are in Charles S. Campbell, Jr., *Anglo-American Understanding* (Baltimore, 1957); Alexander E. Campbell, *Great Britain and the United States* (Glasgow, 1960); Bradford Perkins, *The Great Rapprochement* (New York, 1968); E. Taylor Parks, *Colombia and the United States: 1765–1934* (Durham, N.C., 1935); J. Fred Rippy, *The Capitalists and Colombia* (New York, 1931); Arthur H. Dean, *William Nelson Cromwell* (New York, 1957); together with the special studies by Dwight C. Miner, *The Fight for the Panama Route* (New York, 1940); Gerstle Mack, *The Land Divided* (New York, 1944); Miles P. Du Val, Jr., *Cadiz to Cathay: The Story of the Long Diplomatic Struggle for the Panama Canal* (2d ed., Stanford, Calif., 1947) and the same author's *And the Mountains Will Move* (Stanford, 1947). A curious autobiographical account, by the curious Frenchman who was one of the prime movers behind the Panama revolution, is Philippe Bunau-Varilla's *Panama: The Creation, Destruction, and Resurrection* (New York, 1914).

The Dominican Republic's checkered relations with the United States at the turn of the twentieth century, including an account of the second Venezuelan crisis of 1902–1903 and the Roosevelt Corollary, appear in M. M. Knight, *The Americans in Santo Domingo* (New York, 1928); Seward W. Livermore, "Theodore Roosevelt, the American Navy, and the Venezuelan Crisis of 1902–1903," *American Historical Review*, LI (1945–1946), 452–471; *Howard K. Beale, *Theodore Roosevelt and the Rise of America to World Power* (Baltimore, 1956); John Garry Clifford, "Admiral Dewey and the Germans, 1903: A New Perspective," *Mid-America*, XLIX (1967), 214–220, more proof of Roosevelt's threatening "the Dutch," from the diary of Mrs. Dewey, who relates a tale about her husband damning the Dutch; John A. Logan, Jr., *No Transfer* (New Haven, 1961), the worry of the president; W. Stull Holt, *Treaties Defeated by the Senate* (Baltimore, 1933), concerning Roosevelt's troubles with a Dominican treaty.

The first Nicaraguan occupation is in Munro's *Intervention and Dollar Diplomacy in the Caribbean* (Princeton, 1964). The second now has consideration, in all its oddly colored detail, in William Kamman, *A Search for Stability: United States Diplomacy Toward Nicaragua, 1925–1931* (Notre Dame, Ind., 1968), a model of research and writing.

Haiti's background of chaos is in Rayford W. Logan, *The Diplomatic Relations of the United States with Haiti: 1776–1891* (Chapel Hill, N.C., 1941). Some account of the American marine occupation appears in Josephus Daniels, *The Wilson Era: Years of Peace—1910–1917* (Chapel Hill, N.C., 1944); see also E. David Cronon, ed., *The Cabinet Diaries of Josephus Daniels: 1913–1921* (Lincoln, Nebr., 1963). Assistant Secretary Roosevelt's concerns are in Frank Freidel's first volume, *Franklin D. Roosevelt: The Apprenticeship* (Boston, 1952).

Mexican-American relations have produced a large literature. There is a general treatment in *Arthur S. Link, *Woodrow Wilson and the Progressive Era: 1910–1917* (New York, 1954), a volume in the New American Nation series, and in Link's multivolume *Wilson* (Princeton, 1947–   ); in Frank Tannenbaum, *Mexico: The Struggle for Peace and Bread* (New York, 1950); *Barbara W. Tuchman, *The Zimmermann Telegram* (New York, 1958); and *Lesley B. Simpson, *Many Mexicos* (Berkeley, Calif., 1947). Studies of merit are John Gaddis, "Porfirio Díaz and His Image in the United States," *Paisano: The Historian of the University of Texas*, V (1966–1967), 1–14, relating how Díaz enlarged an "image" for himself; Charles C. Cumberland, *Mexican Revolution: Genesis under Madero* (Austin, Texas, 1952); Stanley R. Ross, *Francisco I. Madero: Apostle of Mexican Democracy* (New York, 1955); *Robert E. Quirk, *An Affair of Honor: Woodrow Wilson and the Occupation of Veracruz* (Lexington, Ky., 1962), an account of large literary and scholarly value, critical of Wilson's intervention; the same author's *The Mexican Revolution* (Bloomington, Ind., 1960), definitive description of campaigning and diplomacy in the first era of the revolution; Clarence C. Clendenen, *The United States and Pancho Villa* (Ithaca, N.Y., 1961), a military historian's sprightly analysis, by a participant in the punitive expedition.

Pertinent biographical references appear in the suggestions for additional reading at the ends of chapters sixteen, eighteen, and twenty.

☆ **18** ☆

World Power

We're a gr-reat people. We are-re that. An' th' best iv it is, we know we are-re.
——Finley Peter Dunne, as "Mr. Dooley"

There is no more instructive chapter in the history of American foreign policy than the era from the Spanish War down to the beginning, in Europe, of the First World War, for this was the time when the United States came at last to full appreciation of its power in the world but not, alas, to understanding of what its power should mean in terms of responsibility for the peace of Europe. The tragedy of American foreign policy in the crucial decade and a half before the outbreak of the war of 1914–1918 was that when American power had become evident to the nations of the world, and to the American people, the nearly one hundred million individuals—the population reached that figure during the Wilson administration—composing the people of the United States proved unwilling to use that power in the place where it most needed application: Europe. Alfred Thayer Mahan has been credited with a dictum regarding American policy for that heady era—in the Far East co-operation, in Europe abstention, in Latin America dominance. The ringing nouns misled readers into believing that they were hearing something novel, and the last word, dominance, seemed to prove that they were. The difficulty with this logic was that it offered nothing more for the most important of the three areas of the world, Europe, than countless American commentators and officials had been offering since the beginning of the republic. At the turn of the twentieth century the Far East was in a state of confusion which would last for decades, down to the present writing. Latin America, for all of its future importance and its then pressing importance as the location of the Panama canal, was not to be an amphitheater of world politics during the lifetimes of

468

Americans living in the years before the First World War, nor indeed during at least the first half of the twentieth century. The Cuban missile crisis of 1962 was properly a world crisis rather than an affair of Latin America. But Europe was to explode in 1914, and the four subsequent years of savage warfare tore apart European civilization as people hitherto had known it. Neither Europe nor the world could ever be the same again. Perhaps an American intervention in 1914, on the side of peace, against the automatic workings of the alliance system which so speedily threw Europe into chaos, would not have preserved the world from the many changes which were to come. But surely the world could have gotten along without some of those changes—such as the First World War, the Great Depression, Adolf Hitler's achievement of power in Germany, the resultant Second World War, and the terrible loss of life during that war, including the near eradication of European Jewry. An active and responsible American policy for peace, a policy willing to use force to preserve peace, might have forestalled such events. The world would have been a far better place—the result worth whatever cost had come to the republic of the New World.

And so the Old World continued its blundering way toward war, and as diplomats of the chancelleries of the old capitals made their arrangements, their alliances and ententes and secret military understandings, the people of the New World went pretty much their own ways. One cannot say that the American failure of policy was responsible for what Europe did in 1914, for Europeans were responsible for that, but, again, it might have been possible for the United States to have prevented what happened. Nor can one say that Americans consciously, with clear understanding of the alternatives, made a decision in 1898–1914 to do what they did. Many Americans never thought about foreign policy, and many thought very little, and even among the leaders of the American government there was much more thought about the domestic problems of the United States, which then seemed to almost everyone the serious problems. Sometimes the important decisions are not decisions at all, and this was the way that the United States in the main stayed out of the affairs of Europe when, as we now see, the nation should have entered on the side of democracy and peace, with all the force, diplomatic and military, it could bring to bear.

1. *Imperial years*

Theodore Roosevelt has already appeared in these pages, and it may seem repetitious to raise up issues and questions about his policy again

—but short of looking at Theodore (at the man whom Mark Hanna derisively referred to as "Teddy") one cannot understand American policy in the prewar years. For Theodore, "TR," he of the right fist pounding into the cupped left hand, the quivering eyeglasses, the shaking mustache, and the flashing teeth, this caricature of action incarnate, "pure act" as Henry Adams once said in recalling that quality which medieval theologians attributed to God: without this grand personality it would be impossible to describe American policy concerning Europe prior to 1914. Roosevelt pranced across the world stage during these formative years of the world's trouble. His personality was stamped so indelibly upon the minds and attention of European peoples as well as rulers that when, out of office and back from his big game hunt in Africa, Roosevelt turned up in London at the time of King Edward VII's funeral, no one in the solemn cortege, not excepting the royal corpse, received so much attention.

The American president of 1901–1909 moved into world politics, not least the politics of Europe, with the same dash and authority as he took into domestic politics and every other aspect of life, human and animal, to which he could attach his mind. He enjoyed his diplomatic duties. He found it amusing that whenever someone of importance in Europe did something inconsequential he was supposed to take notice, that (for example) whenever a new member of royalty was born—presumably with all the pain and commonness of that act as experienced by all individuals who give birth and are born—he was supposed to send congratulations. He was glad to relegate the chores of formality to old Alvey Adee, whose literary productions fascinated him. Adee thereby inspired one of his best pieces of description:

I write four or five letters or telegrams every day and old Adee does that for me. I never see them unless there is something of special importance. But I am always sending a congratulation, or a felicitation, or a message of condolence or sympathy to somebody in a palace somewhere or other, and old Adee does that for me. Why, there isn't a kitten born in a palace anywhere on earth that I don't have to write a letter of congratulation to the peripatetic Tomcat that might have been its sire, and old Adee does that for me!

Adee slipped one time and in answering the florid telegram of President Pardo of Peru, intending to give Pardo a telegram of equal felicitation from Roosevelt and his countrymen, incautiously used the phrase "me and my people." This royal remark got into American newspapers. Roosevelt was annoyed, if also amused, but could not say anything because then it would be apparent that he had never seen President Pardo's initial effusion.

Theodore Roosevelt, the man whom Mark Hanna derisively referred to as "Teddy."

It was during the Roosevelt years that the American president, perhaps out of a desire to avoid using un-American terms such as "Your Majesty," began to address the crowned heads of Europe as William, Edward, etc., and the royalties wrote back to him in similar Rotarian vein. The correspondence of the Roosevelt years, president to emperor and the like, had a personal touch which did sometimes sound as if on the American side it came from "me and my people." The president was willing to use informality and friendliness to advance peace in Europe and the world—all this apart from his perhaps initial desire to avoid titles improper for Americans to use.

The president, one must add, could never have cut such a swath through the politics of Europe and elsewhere if he had not enjoyed some considerable support. Roosevelt operated, so to speak, through a group of highly placed friends, both Americans and foreigners. Support from these individuals allowed him to pursue policies in a way which seemed incredible when Roosevelt's private papers were opened in the late 1920's, after the experience of the First World War and its aftermath when Americans helped Europe with enthusiasm and then came to distrust all things European. The opening of TR's papers in the Library of Congress produced a spate of excited scholarly and even public comments about how removed from traditional ways was the Republican Roosevelt. His correspondence showed, however, that he had managed to weave a web of letters around his highly placed friends. With them, Roosevelt and company had been able to exert an American influence on Europe which, however insufficient it had proved, was far larger than it would have been without the Roosevelt group. Meanwhile, in the years before the First World War, in the era of sailor suits and straw hats and long skirts and "Alice blue" gowns, the average American had enjoyed himself at home, content to leave foreign affairs in the hands of Roosevelt and friends.

The president's official supporters, his secretaries of state, John Hay and Elihu Root (Secretary Robert Bacon was an appointee for a few days at the end of Roosevelt's second term), were quite different individuals, but each in his way helped ably to advance the policies of the president. Hay was given to caution and inferential statements, and when he opposed the president he did so with a deftness which Roosevelt sometimes missed and which on other occasions seemed to the president a sign of weakness, so that when Hay died in 1905, and a nation mourned, Roosevelt was annoyed at the adulation and some years later explained privately that Hay had not been a great secretary of state. In a letter to Senator Lodge of January 28, 1909, he said,

I think he was the most delightful man to talk to I ever met, for . . . he continually made out of hand those delightful epigrammatic remarks which we would all like to make . . . . But he was not a great Secretary of State. . . . He had a very ease-loving nature and a moral timidity which made him shrink from all that was rough in life. . . . His close intimacy with Henry James and Henry Adams—charming men, but exceedingly undesirable companions for any man not of strong nature—and the tone of satirical cynicism which they admired . . . marked that phase of his character which so impaired his usefulness as a public man.

As for Secretary Root, he and Roosevelt had worked well when Root was secretary of war, a holdover from the McKinley cabinet, but by the time Root came to the secretaryship of state after the death of Hay, Roosevelt had won the election of 1904 and become president in his own right, and he and Root did not always hit it off. Withal Roosevelt admired the cautiously conservative judgment of Root, for he knew that by taking Root's opinions he could seldom make mistakes. It was comforting to try out ideas on Root for size. When the secretary of state howled with pain, Roosevelt was warned. He later wrote, with affection for the man who had helped him, "He fought me every inch of the way. And, together, we got somewhere."

Each of the two secretaries of state was a tower of strength in his own way, if the one was not as much appreciated as the other. In addition there were the senatorial friends and the cabinet colleagues. Lodge stood out among the friends in the Senate. By the time of Roosevelt's presidency, this representative of Massachusetts had become a power in the land, and he proved a power to Roosevelt. There were other friendly senators, whom Roosevelt usually could use to exert influence on that jealously emotional body. The cabinet contained fervent and effective supporters such as Philander Knox, later secretary of state and senator, who could quip affectionately with the president about the taking of Panama. There also were supporters among the men of military affairs, like William E. Sims, whom Roosevelt saved from a near-total obscurity. Sims could help him get rid of naval dead wood. And Roosevelt and Mahan were on the best of terms. Mahan acted as a presidential prophet through the influential journals of opinion in which his political articles constantly appeared. The president also was friendly with what a later generation, copying a word out of the lexicon of communism, would describe as the intelligentsia of his day, the intellectuals, such men as Henry and Brooks Adams, President Charles W. Eliot of Harvard, and countless others. The literati, the intellectuals, were not always privy to Rooseveltian secrets, and the president used them as they hoped to use him, but there was an easy commerce between Roosevelt and these men, and they helped advance his policies for Europe and elsewhere.

Not less important were the special friends of the tennis cabinet, as Roosevelt's athletically-inclined close associates were known collectively. When Cecil Spring (Springy) Rice and Hermann Speck (Specky) von Sternburg were in attendance, the president glowed with enthusiasm. An influential Britisher, Arthur Lee, had shared a tent during the campaign in Cuba, and in later years Lee and Roosevelt exchanged confidences. The French ambassador, Jusserand, became such a friend that on the occasion of Roosevelt's retirement from the White House in 1909, a ceremonial affair when Jusserand was to make a speech of presentation to the president, the ambassador was so overcome with emotion that he could not speak, and the presentation had to be made by someone else. Henry White, in the Roosevelt years an active member of the foreign service, often communicated directly with the president, and TR wrote White, ignoring the various gentlemen such as Ambassador Choate to whom White was, by the diplomatic table of organization, a subordinate. The tennis cabinet never met in full session, and the name may have had more newspaper appeal than it deserved, but the individuals to whom Roosevelt gave confidences during his presidency never forgot "the Roosevelt years" and were able, even if foreign nationals, to serve the president for the good of the United States as well as that of their own countries. Off the tennis cabinet would go into Rock Creek Park, not to play with rackets but to scramble down gorges and across streams, and up the boulders again toward daylight, puffing and panting, a line of willing and sometimes not-so-willing explorers, following the burly figure in the lead—reducing their diplomatic feelings to common thoughts and making it easier for the president to speak directly with them when the situation somewhere demanded.

2. *A symbol for Europe, and a meeting that succeeded*

If there was one single symbol of America's new place in the world, or the world's new place in the calculations of America, it was possession of the Philippine Islands. What might seem otherwise as an episode in American foreign relations, the chance stumbling into ownership of a piece of real estate, which for the better interests of the United States the nation should not have acquired, became understandable to Europeans (if not to some doubting Americans) when looked at this way. It was one thing to acquire territory in the area of the Caribbean, such as the Panama canal or Puerto Rico, and many effervescent speeches were made about these acquisitions, about how they raised the United States to the situation of primary power in the Western Hemisphere, indeed the whole world. It was another thing to remark, and the speakers did not say it, that the Caribbean was a long way from Europe and the seat of the world's important diplomacy. It was similarly almost irrelevant to the politics of Europe when the United States during the Spanish-American War had picked up the Hawaiian Islands, natural appendages to a North American power with an exposed Pacific coast. The same could be said about the acquisition, earlier, of the Samoas, not to mention Guam and Midway. The same could not be said about the Philippine Islands, which lay in Japan's sphere, not that of the United States, and which could produce no logic of territorial proximity or military safety. Moreover, the Philippines were too large an island group, too populated with rebellious subjects, their acquisition too recent, for Americans to claim that they were altogether the products of chance—well, if they were the products of chance, their acquisition had careful confirmation at the long peace conference in Paris in the autumn of 1898. The Philippines therefore were a symbol of American empire, evidence that the United States was planting its flag in ways well known and understood to European powers, in what was called in that simple day imperialism without anyone smiling or making bright remarks.

Possession of the Philippines put a stamp on American policy which for a generation or two proved ineradicable, and Roosevelt—who did not mind the appearance of empire anyway—had to face up to the fact of possession, as did his countrymen. His era for the first time in American history was seriously imperial.

The president did not try to weasel out of his country's responsibilities to educate, uplift, civilize, and Christianize, as McKinley may have put the case to the Methodist clergymen in 1899. Roosevelt took up the burden of imperialism in what he described countless times as a manly way and did not shirk or compromise his country's responsibilities. He did this more easily, to be sure, because from the start of American intervention in the islands he had opposed Philippine independence. The local patriots had risen against the Spanish in 1896 and were ready to take over the government of the islands at the very minute that the Americans were expelling the Spaniards. Roosevelt, a lieutenant colonel in 1898, did not hesitate to defend the army's role in keeping the insurgents out of Manila, and he ardently supported the army in the years down to 1902 and the end of the Filipino War. In the campaign of 1900 when he was running for vice president, with McKinley sitting on the front porch in Canton, Ohio, Roosevelt traveled thousands of miles and dealt with every issue he could think of, and some he should not have thought of. In regard to the Filipino rebellion he described Aguinaldo's patriots as "Chinese halfbreeds" and worse. He considered it preposterous to compare Aguinaldo to George Washington. He compared the Filipino leader to Benedict Arnold. He refused to concede the legitimacy of the native independence movement. Such a view he considered akin to shirking of American responsibility, handing the Philippine Islands back to barbarism or savagery.

His policies in the islands, and those of his successor Taft, were to make the islanders fit for self-government sometime in the long future. First they had to learn about good government, with the help of American assistants everywhere in the island regime. Schools likewise had to be established. Roosevelt insisted that no religious creed should appear in island education, but there should be education on the American secular model. He also moved to get the Catholic Church out of the Philippine land problem, in the case of the so-called friar lands—lands which had belonged to the friars before the revolution beginning in 1896, and which peasants had appropriated. The president settled the question by agreeing to pay the Church about fifty per cent more than the lands' appraised value and to give up the demand he had made at the outset that the Vatican withdraw the friars. By 1912, 50,000 Filipinos worked small farms purchased on generous terms from the American government.

Politically and militarily the Philippine empire proved an embarrassment, as Roosevelt realized before the end of his presidency. The president told a churchman in 1907 that the best thing for the Philippines would be a succession of administrators like the islands' first civil governor, "Will" Taft, to administer them for the next century, but that changing administrations in the United States probably would prevent this, and he was not sure anyway that the American people would be willing to support the Philippine burden. It was that same year, the year the fleet started round the world, that he sent Leonard Wood, in command of the islands, coded instructions in case of attack.

In the conversation with the church leader, related above, he had commented, concerning military affairs, that "from a military standpoint the Philippines form our heel of Achilles." Here was a prescient remark. The future importance of the Philippines was not altogether in evidence in 1907, and for that era their importance was as a symbol, serving to remind Americans that their nation was not unlike the imperial powers of Europe.

Being an imperial power, like the great powers of the Old World, the United States under Roosevelt's leadership had to do something for European affairs, it seemed. It could not "just stand there," speechless, motionless. It was of course to be expected that Americans seeking a safe involvement would look for something on the fringes of large events.

Roosevelt therefore chose Morocco, on the geographical fringe of Europe—a territory that nonetheless, as it turned out, carried more European destinies than he had anticipated. The single major Rooseveltian intervention in Europe (apart from mediation of the peace of Portsmouth, which was more an Asian affair, though involving Russia) was over Morocco.

There were actually two Moroccan interventions, and the first was far less important than the second, though far more flamboyant. The initial intervention arose out of the exigencies of the Republican national convention in 1904. The Republicans had assembled in Chicago to nominate Roosevelt, and there was not much chance that they could do otherwise, because the president controlled the "steamroller," that is, the Republican delegations from the South who were all in the president's pocket, beholden for federal appointments if not for local support. Roosevelt was going to get the nomination, and probably the election. The country agreed with Viscount Bryce, who said Roosevelt was the greatest president since Washington (prompting a Roosevelt friend to remember Whistler's remark when told he was the greatest painter since Velazquez: "Why drag in Velazquez?"). The president simply needed some enthusiasm from the professional politicians in attendance. At the convention there were no bands, no parades, hundreds of empty seats. The northern Republicans were so disaffected, so listless, so unconcerned and uncaring, that they were embarrassing the party managers who had to give some impression of joy. The delegation from Roosevelt's home state, New York, was so ostentatiously cold that one reporter predicted they would all go home with pneumonia. So Roosevelt, or Secretary of State Hay, probably the latter at the direction of the former, turned to Morocco.

In the land where the umbrella was the mark of sovereignty, the problem for the United States was that an American citizen of Greek extraction named Ion Perdicaris had been seized by a dreadful bandit named Raisuli. Perdicaris's problem in turn was really Raisuli's problem —the Moroccan sultan, Abdul-Aziz. It was, indeed, a complicated story. The sultan had gone crazy in a minor way. Not content with innumerable bicycles, 600 cameras, 25 grand pianos, and a gold automobile (there were no roads), he desired western reforms. Nothing if not thoroughly western, he also had applied to French bankers and thereby obtained a western-style debt. All this westernization roused the tribes. He had harshly treated and aroused Raisuli some years before. What with the disaffection, the bandit chieftain decided that if he could kidnap a prominent foreigner he could get the sultan into more trouble and extract something for himself. Raisuli did not care about what the foreigners might threaten to do; that would be the sultan's problem. Consul Samuel Gummeré walked blindly into this trap, became duly incensed at the treatment of Perdicaris, an American citizen, and asked Secretary Hay for an ultimatum.

Raisuli and Perdicaris nonetheless had created a convenient situation. Mindful of the Republican convention, in such doldrums, Hay sent to Chicago the following ringing cable:

THIS GOVERNMENT WANTS PERDICARIS
ALIVE OR RAISULI DEAD.

Simultaneously, that June 22, 1904, Hay gave out the cable to the press. He also had told Gummeré, contrary to the latter's request for an ultimatum, "Do not land marines or seize customs without Department's specific instructions." This sentence he left out of the message given to the press.

There was an uproar, Perdicaris was released, Raisuli extracted so many concessions from the sultan that the poor man must have had to sell his pianos, and Roosevelt was nominated by acclamation at Chicago; but before it was over there were seven American warships in harbor at Tangier, and the Moroccan native government was so weakened that it was hardly able to stand when, less than a year later, the German government for a very different reason produced another crisis over Morocco.

For the American government the Perdicaris affair had a quiet but bitter end when the state department discovered that the individual it had protected in Morocco might not have been a citizen of the United States. In 1862, during the American Civil War, Perdicaris had turned up in Greece and taken Greek citizenship, apparently as a precaution to prevent some property in the South from being confiscated by the Confederates. Hay found out about this, and so did Roosevelt. Hay clamped the lid of secrecy on the whole business, at least until after the election of November. "As to Paregoric or is it Pericarditis," the secretary of state wrote to Assistant Secretary Adee on September 3, "it is a bad business. We must keep it excessively confidential for the present." There were no leaks. Perdicaris was happy over his rescue and was not going to say anything. The truth remained unknown until 1933 when the historian Tyler Dennett published a biography of John Hay and related the affair's inner workings.

The second American involvement in Morocco, much less flamboyant but far more important, occurred when the German emperor William II at the urgent request of his foreign office, stepped ashore at Tangier on March 31, 1905, rode into the city on a horse which was much too spirited for the emperor to handle easily with his withered arm, and made a speech affirming the fine qualities and independence of the sultan. The speech was a careful counter to the increasing French influence in Morocco after the Franco-British entente of 1904, an agreement which had stipulated a dominant French influence in exchange for France's recognition of British dominance in Egypt. The German government, of course, wished to nullify the Franco-British entente, to discourage co-operation between the two nations, which if exercised in colonial matters might carry over into a co-operation upon the continent of Europe against the interests of Germany.

The Germans pushed hard after the speech at Tangier, and managed so to alarm the French government that the premier, Pierre-Maurice Rouvier, dismissed Foreign Minister Delcassé, the well-known destroyer of the work of Bismarck. They told the United States, more simply, that they were seeking the open door in Morocco.

A full crisis was upon Europe, over the same insignificant locality where John Hay had produced a fuss the year before. This time Roosevelt believed that the United States had to show statesmanship, and, acting with his full powers and some that perhaps were not his, he did so. If there was a single occasion when Roosevelt did something seriously important for European peace, it was his activity in allaying the Moroccan crisis of 1905. He talked the European powers into a conference, which was held at Algeciras in southern Spain beginning in January 1906. He then so maneuvered the German emperor that William's minister, Chancellor Bernhard von Buelow, made a concession in a cable to Ambassador von Sternburg which the latter interpreted as an agreement by the emperor to follow Roosevelt's lead at the conference. At a crucial point in the conference Roosevelt reminded the German government of this outstanding blank check and forced the Germans to fill it in the way he wished. His wish turned out to be an agreement to give the French the dominance in Morocco they had been seeking to assert when the emperor, the year before, had intervened. After exerting this pressure, Roosevelt buttered up the emperor by cabling "sincerest felicitations on this epochmaking political success at Algeciras." His majesty's policy, the president said, "has been masterly from beginning to end."

Europe might have gone to war in 1905–1906, for it was not easy for the French to jettison such a foreign minister as Delcassé. The Germans on their part had laid their national prestige on the line. Roosevelt well deserved the Nobel peace prize, which he received for this work and the mediation at Portsmouth the preceding year.

There was some hostile talk among his countrymen about this participation in one of the major crises of European politics, but the president managed to carry through his Moroccan policy without interference by Congress or public opinion. This occurred partly because the American people did not understand how closely Europe was moving toward war and how close their president was to the fire. Roosevelt was able to point out that the United States had taken part in the Madrid Conference of 1880 which had regulated affairs in Morocco, declaring the sultan independent; the Algeciras Conference, he said, was only a successor of that meeting. Then, too, the Perdicaris affair was not long past, and it made easier the serious diplomacy toward Europe of 1905–1906.

3. *TR and Alaska*

The manner in which the United States government took part in the affairs of Europe, contrary to the supposed dictum of Mahan, was usually fairly subtle and indirect. In one respect it consisted of the personal impression made by Theodore Roosevelt, supported by his influential friends, upon the crowned heads, the elected leaders, and the peoples of Europe. In another it involved the Philippine symbol, which gave evidence that the United States was an imperial power among the other imperial powers which, with exception of Japan, were all nations of Europe: in this sense the United States joined a European club. Another part of America's relations with Europe during these prewar years had to do with, of all places, Alaska, where a quarrel over the boundaries of the panhandle threatened serious disagreement, if not an armed conflict, between the United States and Canada, and thereby Britain, at a time when the British were becoming extremely sensitive to their need of American support in Europe. The solution of the Alaskan boundary in 1903 was one more, perhaps the last, instance of America's advantage from Europe's distress.

The origin of the panhandle argument with Britain lay in the uncertainties of the Anglo-Russian treaty of 1825, wherein the two nations had sought to establish the boundary between Russian Alaska and British Canada. According to this treaty the line started at the southern end of the panhandle, at 54° 40'—but the next point chosen turned out after subsequent surveys to be nonexistent. The treaty then compounded this confusion by taking the boundary northward from crest to crest along a mythical mountain range. A third confusion appeared in the section of the treaty that stated that where a line from crest to crest would be more than ten marine leagues (a marine league equals 3.45 miles) from the ocean, the boundary should run parallel to indentations of the coastline and not more than ten leagues from it. Because the Alaskan coast was split by numerous islands, large and small, and by long

Line claimed by Great Britain until 1903

Award line 1903 (further clarified by exchange of notes 1905)

ALASKA
BOUNDARY DISPUTE
1898-1903

MILES
0   50   100   150   200

narrow bays (or canals, as they are called), such a line was geometrically impossible. The only saving feature of the Anglo-Russian treaty of 1825 was its intent, which was reasonably clear: Russia was seeking, and to this the British had agreed, to retain control of the coast down to 54° 40'.

No one cared about the panhandle lands until gold was discovered in the Canadian Klondike in August 1896, whereupon it was suddenly realized that the easiest access to the gold fields was across the panhandle. The Canadians in June 1898 laid claim to a boundary which would have given them the narrow bays and hence a free passage to the

Klondike fields. Their claim to one of the largest bays, the Lynn canal, threatened to bisect southeastern Alaska. On the Lynn canal were the three important settlements of Pyramid Harbor, Dyea, and Skagway, each harbor leading to a pass over the mountains to the gold fields. The Canadians offered to negotiate, provided the United States would agree in advance to give them Pyramid Harbor. The Canadian claim was a barefaced fraud, a diplomatic holdup. Secretary of State Hay wrote on June 15, 1899, to the American ambassador in London, Choate, that "It is as if a kidnapper, stealing one of your children, should say that his conduct was more than fair, it was even generous, because he left you two."

From the outset the American government refused to give in to this chicanery, and Secretary Hay in 1899 proposed a commission of six men, three Americans and three chosen by Great Britain, decision to be by majority vote—which meant that the Americans could not lose and, if one Britisher budged, would win. Nothing came of this proposition in 1899. The Canadians would not consent to it. The British were occupied by trouble with the Boers in South Africa (the Boer War began in October 1899 and lasted to June 1902). Hay had other irons in the fire, such as announcement of the open-door policy for the Far East. In Central America he was attempting to amend the Clayton-Bulwer Treaty so as to enable the United States to begin construction of an isthmian canal. He half expected the British government to attempt to trade concessions in the isthmus for concessions in Alaska, but the government of Lord Salisbury fortunately played fair with the Americans, perhaps because of the Boer War. Salisbury apparently realized also that the Canadian claims in the panhandle were outrageous.

The issue lapsed until the year 1902 when the Canadian government through Prime Minister Sir Wilfrid Laurier intimated to the first secretary of the American embassy in London, Henry White, that the Hay formula of 1899 would be the best way out of the situation. Laurier had publicly advocated the Canadian position and could not back down before his countrymen, but he wanted to get out of his pledge and wished to do it through the Hay proposal of a six-man commission. Hay in a letter of July 14, 1902, proposed this course to his chief in the White House, Roosevelt. The commission would not be an arbitral tribunal, he assured TR. "I do not think they [the Canadians] have a leg to stand on, and I think any impartial court of jurists would so decide. At the same time I recognize the danger of submitting such a matter to an ordinary arbitration, the besetting sin of which is to split the difference. My suggestion was a submission of the question of the interpretation of the treaty of 1825 to a tribunal of six, three on a side, a majority to decide. In this case it is impossible that we should lose, and not at all impossible that a majority should give a verdict in our favor." This seemed, certainly, a safe course.

Roosevelt at this point, however, began to get difficult, and Hay's biographer, Dennett, has concluded that the president was trying to drum up a campaign issue for 1904. TR did allow Secretary Hay on January 23, 1903, to sign a treaty with the British ambassador in Washington, Sir Michael Herbert, giving the controversy to a six-man commission. But then he began to make difficulties, small and large. Five days after the treaty went to the Senate for advice and consent, the president withdrew it for a significant "correction." He had discovered that the commission of six was referred to in the body of the treaty as a "tribunal" but in the preamble was described as an "arbitral tribunal." The adjective had to come out. Hay's assistant, Adee, reported to the secretary on January 31, 1903, that the first sheet of the treaty had to be "re-engrossed, with the necessary changes. It will be ready on Monday, when the seals can be broken, the treaty untied, the new sheet substituted, and the blame thing retied ready for re-apposition of the seals, which can be done without re-signing." The British accepted the treaty with the excised adjective.

There followed two typical Roosevelt maneuvers. First the president appointed, under the terms of the treaty of 1903, the American members of the commission. The treaty stipulated "impartial jurists of repute who shall consider judicially the question submitted to them," and TR chose ex-Senator George Turner of Washington, Senator Lodge, and Secretary of War Root. Root was a member of the administration, presumably no impartial individual. Lodge was the president's bosom friend. Turner represented a state which was highly interested in the fate of the panhandle. The Canadian prime minister, Laurier, at this precise moment engaged in getting the treaty through the Canadian parliament, protested bitterly to Hay. The secretary of state was appalled at Lodge's appointment, though he could not intimate this to Sir Wilfrid. He wrote to his good friend Henry White how the Massachusetts senator "as if the devil were inspiring him . . . took occasion last week to make a speech in Boston, one half of it filled with abuse of the Canadians, and the other half with attacks on the State Department. He is a clever man and a man of a great deal of force in the Senate, but the infirmity of his mind and character is that he never sees but one subject at a time . . . . Of course, you know his very intimate relations with the President . . . ."

Not content with this sabotage of Hay's negotiation, Roosevelt sent his views on the Alaska boundary to White and to Justice Oliver Wendell Holmes of the supreme court, visiting in England, and suggested that

White and Holmes speak to the British prime minister, Arthur Balfour, and to Joseph Chamberlain, the colonial secretary: the president contended, via his two intermediaries, that if the commission did not decide the way it should, then he, Roosevelt, would run the boundary line and the Canadians and British could make the most of it. Hay gently protested to Roosevelt on September 25, 1903, that "Of course the matter is now *sub judice*. You can say nothing about it . . . ."

Finally on October 20, 1903, the commission, meeting in London, voted in favor of the American claim. The two Canadian members championed their side to the end, but to no avail, for the British member, the lord chief justice, Lord Alverstone, vóted with the United States. Hay was elated. As he informed his wife in a letter of October 24, the president "loaded me with compliments today in the Cabinet meeting. 'Nobody living could have done the work as I did,' etc. etc. 'It was the biggest success of my life.' Etc." The completeness of the victory, the secretary concluded, was "something amazing. We have got everything we claimed . . . ." "I think myself," he wrote, "that Lord Alverstone is the hero of the hour. No American statesman would have dared to give a decision on his honor and conscience against the claim of his own country."

Whether Alverstone gave his decision on the basis of the evidence or because of the president's carefully communicated views is difficult to say. He doubtless learned of TR's threat to run the boundary in case the commission did not do its duty. He may have concluded that the advices of law and politics in this case nicely coincided. In a public speech after the decision Alverstone said that "If when any kind of arbitration is set up they don't want a decision based on the law and the evidence, they must not put a British judge on the commission." Perhaps this was the sole basis of the lord chief justice's stand. One should probably be content with this explanation, publicly offered, and with it draw the veil over the Alaska boundary decision of 1903.

4. *Pacts of peace*

With the exception of Theodore Roosevelt's diplomacy during the Algeciras Conference, the acts of the government of the United States toward the governments of Europe were indirect in the years before the First World War. A careful American approach to Europe during this era was support for creation of a network of pacts for peaceful settlement of international disputes. Americans always had been interested in international law, strengthening the laws of war and especially the rights of neutrals, and once the last great war for neutral rights, so people thought, had ended in 1814 it was easy to transfer this interest into, for example, support for treaties of arbitration. To many citizens of the United States, arbitration treaties were an American policy first explored in the mixed commissions of Jay's Treaty of 1794, and of course the policy had its most notable expression in the Geneva arbitration of 1872. Theodore Roosevelt probably saw a slightly different usefulness for arbitration treaties and general pacts of pacific intention than did many supporters of these treaties, for he envisioned them as helping the European powers through their smaller problems—it was a way in which he could contribute modestly to European peace. In this regard Roosevelt had the best of good will. He once told his friend Spring Rice that he did not wish to be an international Meddlesome Mattie, but that he would try to help where he could.

At the end of the nineteenth century, in 1899, the century's last year by some definitions (there was a large argument, in which even the Pope intervened, over what year constituted the end of the century), a peace conference assembled at The Hague, sponsored by the tsar of Russia, with the avowed purpose of establishing international conventions of peace. The Russian government had taken interest in this First Hague Peace Conference because of concern for its own armaments, a desire to halt the equipping of its rivals with new and improved field artillery (the so-called French 75's). This Russian purpose, a limit to the new artillery, did not find much favor at the peace conference, but there were some other achievements. There were declarations against asphyxiating gas, expanding (dum-dum) bullets, and the throwing of projectiles from balloons. These declarations were useless, it turned out, as the powers should have devoted their attention to the machine gun and the submarine, given the importance of those weapons in the forthcoming World War. The conference did arrange for the establishment of a panel of jurists to which any quarreling nations might resort for arbiters of their disputes, the Permanent Court of Arbitration. In subsequent years this court dealt with some minor problems, and at the behest of President Roosevelt during the Venezuelan affair of 1902–1903 dealt with a major one, the question, as mentioned in chapter seventeen, of what nations in the debt controversy with the Venezuelan government should have first claim on payment.

The historian Calvin D. Davis has set out carefully the preliminaries, discussions, and results of the First Hague Peace Conference, showing that the United States government sent a delegation largely because of the public sentiment for disarmament and a peace program, particularly arbitration. McKinley did not expect large results, and there was none. In view of the rivalries of the powers which were becoming so marked at this time, and the important ententes and alliances which were made or tightened in the years immediately after, it was a pity that the conference could not address itself to major problems of Europe instead of patching a few weak places in the laws of war and setting up a panel for a world court. Davis concluded that the agreements of 1899 were "masks concealing failure." One of the American delegates, Mahan, was almost the last person in the United States who would have favored arbitration or any other serious abridgement of the warmaking power of any nation.

The First Hague Conference nonetheless was followed by the Second. Roosevelt issued a call for a new conference in October 1904, but then delayed further action because of the Russo-Japanese War. When in the next year, 1905, the tsar indicated he would like to call the conference, Roosevelt easily consented, but he failed to exert the influence upon the Second Hague Peace Conference that he had exercised at Portsmouth and at Algeciras. The reason may have been that the year 1907 was less exigent personally to Roosevelt than the year in which he had issued his call, a presidential election year. More probably it was because he did not see any possibility of large results from the Second Hague Peace Conference and cautiously abstracted himself from what was likely to be an unsuccessful meeting.

After what was considered the success of the first meeting at The Hague, many people in the United States and elsewhere looked forward to the second, and Roosevelt did seek to disabuse them of their hopes. Andrew Carnegie, a self-appointed apostle of peace, was writing fervent letters to his highly placed friends, talking to the British, conferring with the Germans, bringing the British peace advocate, William T. Stead, over to converse with Roosevelt. The president stood aside. To President Eliot of Harvard, whom he suspected of being a visionary, he wrote that

In The Hague my chief trouble will come from the fantastic visionaries who are crazy to do the impossible. . . . the United States Navy is an infinitely more potent factor for peace than all the peace societies of every kind and sort . . . . At The Hague I think we can make some real progress, but only on condition of our not trying to go too far.

The preliminary negotiations for the meeting were not hopeful. Roosevelt at first believed that without great self-sacrifice the United States might favor limitation of armaments, though not reduction and certainly not disarmament. He wrote privately in 1905 that, if the American government could replace worn-out units in the navy with "thoroughly efficient ones," it might not be necessary to have any increase in naval tonnage. Mahan in December 1904 meanwhile suggested a tonnage limit for single ships, and Roosevelt favored 15,000 tons and sought to influence the great naval powers to subscribe to this limit. But both men later came to see that this single-ship tonnage limit was impractical; the British navy was just finishing the *Dreadnought*, an all-big-gun battleship which required a larger tonnage. It was at this difficult time that the German emperor said undiplomatically that Edward VII had pronounced the forthcoming conference a "humbug." Edward said virtually the same to Ambassador Whitelaw Reid one morning on the esplanade at Biarritz. Ambassador George von Lengerke Meyer, visiting in England, reported similarly. The king seemed to be worrying that the change of cabinet in the British government in 1905 which had ousted the Conservatives and brought in the Liberals might have brought in some weak thinkers. He need not have feared. Foreign Secretary Sir Edward Grey had an instinctive appreciation of efforts for peace, but was a practical man and soon discovered that the forces working against the Second Hague Peace Conference were too strong. "The difficulty in regard to one nation stepping out in advance of the others is this," Grey explained to Parliament, "that while there is a chance that their courageous action may lead to reform, there is also a chance that it may lead to martyrdom." As for the German government, it openly refused to discuss disarmament at the peace conference. The German ambassador in Paris said that William was in a difficult position because of having yielded at Algeciras and could not give in on armament.

When the Second Hague Peace Conference at last assembled, there was not much in the way of results. One may agree with the judgment of "Mr. Dooley" that the "larger question" at the Second Hague Peace Conference was how future wars should be conducted in the best interests of peace. The chief American delegate at the conference, Ambassador Choate, said in one of his reports, "There is very great reluctance on the part of these fighting nations to bind themselves to anything." Roosevelt hoped to obtain a rule preserving private property at sea from capture in wartime, but the British government refused. He was willing to negotiate a general arbitration treaty, but the German government and seven other European states voted against compulsory arbitration even of legal disputes. He thought that the collection of debts à la Venezuela was one matter that nations should agree to arbitrate. The result was the Porter Resolution, a definition of when nations after offering to arbitrate might go to war.

A third conference, scheduled for 1915, had to be postponed, and at the end of the First World War the conference idea disappeared into the grander proposition of the League of Nations.

In addition to the Hague Peace Conferences the American government pursued several projects for groups of bilateral arbitration treaties, capped by a group of bilateral conciliation treaties sponsored by Secretary of State William Jennings Bryan just prior to the World War. These treaties are best described by the names of the secretaries of state or presidents who sponsored them: Olney, Roosevelt, Root, Taft, Bryan.

Secretary Olney in 1897 had proposed a model arbitration treaty with Great Britain to prevent such occurrences as the Venezuelan affair of 1895, and it may well be that the failure of Olney's treaty in the Senate, the failure of the very first in the series of projects for bilateral treaties for peaceful settlement of disputes, showed how futile such a course would be. It was during the defeat of the Olney treaty that the Senate asserted its right to supervise each and every arbitration arrangement concluded by the United States government even under an arbitration treaty. That is, there had to be two treaties, the one setting out an intention to arbitrate and the second defining, for a specific occasion, the terms. No administration, it seemed, could arrogate the treatymaking power of the Senate. An American arbitration treaty hence meant little or nothing, until the Senate decided what it meant in each specific case. There was no pledge to do anything. The Olney treaty failed after sixteen amendments. Its failure was a bipartisan proposition, if one may use the late Senator Arthur H. Vandenberg's unlovely adjective to apply to an era long before his own. By trying to by-pass the Senate in any particular arbitration, so the disgusted Olney wrote Henry White, the treaty had "committed the unpardonable sin." It thus is possible to say with the historian W. Stull Holt, that with the demise of the Olney-Pauncefote Treaty in 1897 went down all future hopes for arbitration as a practical policy advanced by the government of the United States. Before 1897 the claim of Americans to be leading the arbitration movement was largely justified. In his volume, *Treaties Defeated by the Senate* (1933), which is still the best work on the subject, Holt said, "Since 1897, despite many and vehement assertions of devotion to that ideal, the record reveals that in action the United States has not only lagged behind the advancing practices of the rest of the civilized world but has even retrograded."

Roosevelt nearly a decade later allowed negotiation of ten general arbitration treaties, signed between November 1904 and January 1905, including treaties with the governments of France, Germany, and Great Britain. Negotiations were in progress with other countries. The treaties contained involved stipulations, but one of them set out that the parties in dispute before appealing to the Hague Court were to conclude a "special agreement" defining the issue in dispute, the scope of the arbitrator's powers, and the procedure to be followed. This proviso was the kiss of death, and by vote of 50 to 9 the Senate amended the treaty with France so as to substitute the word "treaty" for the word "agreement." Roosevelt seems to have been only moderately annoyed, and whether his feeling was more over the Senate's pretensions than over the failure of his arbitration effort is difficult to say. He had advocated the arbitration treaties well before the presidential election of 1904, and this advocacy did not harm his campaign. Perhaps he afterward had no need for the treaties. In any event he seems to have felt that he had done his duty, and he turned his attention elsewhere until his second secretary of state, Root, championed and concluded, with Senate approval, a new set of treaties beginning in 1908.

The point noticeable about the Root treaties, which Roosevelt supported with some show of enthusiasm, was that they provided for a second treaty in each case of arbitration—the very proviso to which the president in 1904–1905 had objected; he had said openly at that time that this provision made arbitration treaties useless. Could it be that every electoral year, 1904 and 1908 at least, was a good year for arbitration treaties? Twenty-five treaties on the useless Root model of 1908 were signed and ratified, duly excepting from arbitration all questions of vital interests, independence, and national honor, or disputes involving third parties, and also containing, as mentioned, the provision for a second treaty allowing the consent of the Senate. Not a single dispute was ever arbitrated under these treaties. "I only went into them," Roosevelt explained some years afterward to his friend Spring Rice, "because the general feeling of the country demanded it."

President Taft tried to advance a new set of treaties in 1911, and began by proposing arbitration treaties with Great Britain and France. According to Taft's proposed plan there was to be arbitration of all differences "justiciable in their nature by reason of being susceptible of decision by the application of the principles of law or equity." The British and French treaties provided for a Joint High Commission of Inquiry to make advisory reports on nonjusticiable disputes and to decide whether disputes were justiciable. A special treaty in each case, setting out the powers of the arbitrators, the questions at issue, and other matters, would precede the arbitration. Each treaty was an agreement to make a second treaty. Taft pressed the issue, and the French and British signed on August 3, 1911. In the complicated terms of these treaties the Senate at once espied a flaw, the Joint High Commission of Inquiry. This harmless proviso infringed on the treatymaking power. The Senate cut the two treaties into shreds and voted overwhelmingly for the pieces, 76 to 3. A hurt President Taft withdrew the treaties, or what was left of them. Soon he lost his bid for re-election. Ruefully, but with humor, Taft later described what had happened. When the treaties reached the Senate, he wrote,

that august body truncated them and amended them and qualified them in such a way that their own father could not recognize them. . . . And since the treaties had really been framed as models, when they came back thus crippled and maimed, they were not very useful. So I put them on the shelf and let the dust accumulate on them in the hope that the Senators might change their minds, or that the people might change the Senate; instead of which they changed me.

The last set of treaties proved to be treaties of conciliation, rather than arbitration, sponsored by Secretary Bryan in the Wilson administration. Bryan long had been contemplating such instruments and, in 1912 in a letter to Taft, noted that the Peace Parliament at London had endorsed them in 1906. He diplomatically told Taft in 1912 that the latter's treaties did not offer so much for world peace as did conciliation instruments of the sort he had in mind. The secretary of state of 1913 lost no time submitting a proposition to Wilson's cabinet. He proposed for each treaty a commission of five persons—one member from each nation; two other members, one chosen by each nation; and a fifth member chosen by the four. He proposed a time limit during which the commission would deliberate on a dispute brought before it, six months or one year, during which the disputing nations could not go to war. Thursday, April 24, 1913, at noon, the secretary presented his peace plan to some thirty-six members of the diplomatic corps in Washington.

What the hardened members of the corps thought of this proposition is difficult to say. At diplomatic receptions Bryan, a teetotaler, already had mortgaged his credit with Washington diplomats by serving grape juice, and there was talk of milk.

In the subsequent negotiations Wilson's secretary of state showed the same attractive idealism and the same bewildering simplicity of mind which had taken him so far in American politics but denied him its principal prize, the presidency. If it was true that as secretary of state Bryan often spent his time in the department talking to visiting politicos, or found plenty of time to lecture on the Chautauqua circuit for a fee, no one could accuse him of failing to pursue his peace proposal of 1913. He hounded laggard nations, pushing them along the road toward peace. When he signed one treaty, he would try to use the occasion to produce another. When his entreaties to Brazil, Argentina, and Chile led at last to an arrangement for ceremonies in Washington, he cabled his envoy in Madrid, March 14, 1914:

I am expecting to sign treaty with Brazil, Argentina, and Chile within a few days. The three treaties will be signed on the same day. As the South American countries were formerly colonies of Spain and speak the Spanish language, it occurs to me that Spain might be pleased to arrange her treaty so as to have it signed at the same time. Please bring the matter to the attention of the Foreign Office.

No ignorance of Brazilian linguistic and political history could divert him from his course. He allowed, apparently, some of his ministers a fairly free rein for the purposes of peace. His minister in Teheran wrote on October 29, 1913, "In view of his delays in the matter of the peace proposition, I told the Foreign Minister I suspected him of being engaged in preparing a declaration of war against my country, and that I should be pleased if he would let me have either that or the other thing." There were disappointments. The chargé in Stockholm, Jefferson Caffery, later to have a long and well-known ambassadorial career, cabled on July 31, 1914, "Present minority conservative government now devoting entire energy to obtain high grade army and navy." Notwithstanding the outbreak of the World War, Bryan pursued any and all nonsignatory nations. He sent a telegram to the German ambassador at the Ritz Carlton in New York on September 29, relating that he had signed with twenty-six nations including Britain and France. "Your country and Austria have already approved of the principle. It would make our joy complete if your Government and Austria would enter into treaties . . . ." As for the Belgian government, for which conciliation at the moment held few attractions, Minister Brand Whitlock wrote Bryan on November 16, that before the outbreak of war Belgium had been interested, but that after the commencement of hostilities and during its subsequent movements from place to place the government was "so overtaxed and harried" that it could not consider the matter; Whitlock had not insisted further, and would not, unless Bryan insisted.

Bryan negotiated thirty treaties for the advancement of peace, and the Senate accepted all but two, those with Panama and the Dominican Republic, seeming to believe that conciliation was unnecessary with these wards of the United States, that a one-year delay before hostilities would open a door to chaos. Six others—with Argentina, Greece, Nicaragua, Persia, El Salvador, and Switzerland—never went into effect because the other country failed to ratify. Bryan in November 1914 presented a paperweight plowshare to each of the diplomats with whom he had signed treaties. The paperweights were made of steel and nickel-plated. The steel was composed of melted swords, with the inscription on the plowshares from Isaiah: "They shall beat their swords into plowshares." The sentences on the beam of the plow set out the contributions Bryan had made to diplomatic phraseology. The war department had produced the condemned swords. The navy department rendered them into paperweights.

Like the Root arbitration treaties, these Bryan conciliation treaties were never invoked.

5. *A gathering of sentiment*

The first years of the twentieth century had advanced the nations of Europe inexorably toward the First World War, and when the war came it found the secretary of state of the United States negotiating a set of useless treaties, which Bryan, unperturbed, continued to do until his retirement from office in 1915. The American people seemed equally removed from the holocaust. The prewar years had passed with a rapid increase in national productivity and a continuing increase in patriotic sentiment, accompanied by—as the political crises in Europe accumulated ever more intensity—a growing belief that Americans were not like other peoples and lived in a land insulated even from the extraordinary combinations and collisions of the old continent. The one president who had sensed the movement toward disaster in Europe, Roosevelt, and had done something about it at a great international conference, had not managed, despite his extraordinary qualities of leadership, to take the American people along with him, and when he went out of office the hope of any major assistance to Europe went with him.

The affairs of Europe may not have aroused more than surface curiosity after Algeciras, and one could write that the American people were innocent, which was true, and that there would be an end to innocence, also true. The major movement of American sentiment in the years before 1914 was perhaps at the time unnoticeable and was to become apparent only in retrospect. Bradford Perkins, in a volume published a half century and more after the events it described, has recently pointed out that a "great *rapprochement*" occurred between Americans and Britishers in the two decades before 1914. This *rapprochement*, Perkins rightly remarks, was the signal event of the time, even if it produced few immediate results in American foreign relations. It was, of course, a change in sentiment somewhat visible in the years immediately after the Venezuelan dispute of 1895, when the British, with both the second Hay-Pauncefote Treaty and the resort to arbitration after the second Venezuelan affair of 1902–1903, showed that they were surrendering their position in the Caribbean, withdrawing in favor of the United States. The American government in turn was carefully neutral during the Boer War of 1899–1902, and Roosevelt spoke of a British Monroe Doctrine for South Africa which would warn off others, like the German emperor, as the United States had done in its own hemisphere. After 1901–1903 the ties became ever stronger between Americans and Britishers, and eventually—in 1917–1918—were to determine the outcome of the World War. But the gathering of sentiment in the United States in favor of the British people, and against their enemies, was a slow proposition and often was hidden from view. If the average American had been queried by some precursor of the Gallup pollsters, he would have denied the fact of a great *rapprochement*.

In this respect as in others, Theodore Roosevelt's changes of mind are interesting as reflecting changes in his countrymen, and it is helpful to set them out because Roosevelt was loquacious, eloquent, and almost instinctively right, if often prematurely so, in sensing where his countrymen should and would go in foreign affairs. Consider his attitude toward the distinguished British writer Rudyard Kipling, whose pronouncements and ideas he at first acquaintance heartily disliked. Following the practices of many other Britishers, Kipling had said unpleasant things about America, and Roosevelt bridled. TR could not abide British condescension. He hoped it was true that Kipling had been barred from the Players Club of New York. "There is no earthly reason he should not call New York a pig trough, but there is also no reason why he should be allowed to associate with the pigs." He feared that Kipling was a cad. Later he changed his mind and came to appreciate him—"a pleasant little man, bright, nervous, voluble," if "rather underbred." By 1914, Roosevelt's dislike of condescension was not enough to prevent his seeing the importance of Britain's entering the World War against German power and ruthlessness. On the day that Britain entered the war, he spoke excitedly to a small group of young men—including Felix Frankfurter, Herbert Croly, and the English reformer Charles Booth—who called upon him at Sagamore Hill. "You've got to go in! You've got to go in!' he exclaimed to Booth. For a few months thereafter he controlled his pro-British instincts, but then he turned to the grand project of Anglo-American cooperation to which he devoted himself until his death in 1919.

The whole nation changed its views in the prewar years. If in 1896 the Republicans had found it necessary to put out a precautionary pamphlet entitled *How McKinley is Hated in England*, there was less and less of this as the years advanced. As Bradford Perkins has written of the great *rapprochement*, it was a combination of Anglo-Saxonism, that is, corrupted Darwinian ideology and faith in limited government; imperialism, and America with the feeling of an *arriviste*, a late arrival, happy to be a member of the British club; and finally the German shadow. A movement to celebrate the centennial of Anglo-American peace in the summer and autumn of 1914 was disrupted only by the beginning of the war. A German sympathizer in the United States pointed out that never had there been a war with Germany, and why should Americans celebrate peace with England, but this logic did not seem to matter.

An evidence of renewed American appreciation of the former mother country appeared in the ending, in June 1914, of a two-year dispute between the United States and British governments over the exemption of American coastwise shipping from Panama canal tolls. This complex argument took its origin from the bill which President Taft signed into law in 1912, in anticipation of the opening of the canal in 1914. The British explained that the exemption was contrary to the second Hay-Pauncefote Treaty. They said that the exemption shifted to other users the share of maintenance costs escaped by coastwise shippers. It also raised a question of what ships, strictly speaking, were engaged in coastwise trade, for almost all American vessels carried mixed cargoes, part going from coast to coast, part in transit from or to foreign ports. The Americans replied that many nations subsidized their national shipping, and what was the difference between granting an exemption and returning the same amount as a subsidy? All three presidential platforms and all three candidates in the election of 1912—Taft, Roosevelt, and Wilson—favored exemption. Wilson then changed his mind and pushed for removal. To uncertain congressmen he contended that the British government at American behest had removed an objectionable pro-Huerta minister in Mexico, and this other removal would be a *quid pro quo*. Both houses of Congress agreed, just before the opening of the World War, and there followed almost an outburst of pro-American sentiment in England, which kindled a complimentary and altogether timely enthusiasm in the United States.

The American president in 1914, Wilson, was probably not the most promising choice as chief executive for the dreadful problems that soon would lie before the country, submarine warfare and the trenches in France. The outbreak of war produced a notable if private outburst from former President Roosevelt, who unburdened himself to his old tentmate Lee on August 1, 1914:

As I am writing, the whole question of peace and war trembles in the balance; and at the very moment . . . our own special prize idiot, Mr. Bryan, and his ridiculous and insincere chief, Mr. Wilson are prattling pleasantly about the steps they are taking to procure universal peace by little arbitration treaties which promise impossibilities, and which would not be worth the paper on which they are written in any serious crisis. It is not a good thing for a country to have a professional yodeler, a human trombone like Mr. Bryan as Secretary of State, nor a college president with an astute and shifty mind, a hypocritical ability to deceive plain people, . . . and no real knowledge or wisdom concerning internal and international affairs as head of the nation.

These opinions were trenchant, and not altogether inaccurate. But before long Wilson and the nation looked ahead to what they had to face.

A CONTEMPORARY DOCUMENT

[Beginning in the 1890's, Theodore Roosevelt made the same speech year after year, in which he pointed out the importance of war, the need to defend high ideals to the death if necessary. His logic contained crudities, especially his assumption that his opponents were absolutely, utterly wrong; but in sensing the national interest of the United States the president of 1901–1909 was almost instinctively right. Source: *An Autobiography* (New York, 1913; reprinted 1920), chapter fifteen, "The Peace of Righteousness," pp. 532, 534–536.]

There can be no nobler cause for which to work than the peace of righteousness; and high honor is due those serene and lofty souls who with wisdom and courage, with high idealism tempered by sane facing of the actual facts of life, have striven to bring nearer the day when armed strife between nation and nation, between class and class, between man and man shall end throughout the world. Because all this is true, it is also true that there are no men more ignoble or more foolish, no men whose actions are fraught with greater possibility of mischief to their country and to mankind, than those who exalt unrighteous peace as better than righteous war. . . .

Yet amiable but fatuous persons, with all these facts before their eyes, pass resolutions demanding universal arbitration for everything, and the disarmament of the free civilized powers and their abandonment of their armed forces; or else they write well-meaning, solemn little books, or pamphlets or editorials, and articles in magazines or newspapers, to show that it is "an illusion" [reference to a then popular book by Norman Angell, *The Great Illusion*] to believe that war ever pays, because it is expensive. This is precisely like arguing that we should disband the police and devote our sole attention to persuading criminals that it is "an illusion" to suppose that burglarly, highway robbery and white slavery are profitable. It is almost useless to attempt to argue with these well-intentioned persons, because they are suffering under an obsession and are not open to reason. They go wrong at the outset, for they lay all the emphasis on peace and none at all on righteousness. They are not all of them physically timid men; but they are usually men of soft life; and they rarely possess a high sense of honor or a keen patriotism. They rarely try to prevent their fellow countrymen from insulting or wronging the people of other nations; but they always ardently advocate that we, in our turn, shall tamely submit to wrong and insult from other nations. As Americans their folly is peculiarly scandalous, because if the principles they now uphold are right, it means that it would have been better that Americans should never have achieved their independence, and better that, in 1861, they should have peacefully submitted to seeing their country split into half a dozen jangling confederates and slavery made perpetual. . . .

I remember one representative of their number, who used to write little sonnets on behalf of the Mahdi and the Sudanese, these sonnets setting forth the need that the Sudan should be both independent and peaceful. As a matter of fact, the Sudan valued independence only because it desired to war against all Christians and to carry on an unlimited slave trade. It was "independent" under the Mahdi for a dozen years, and during those dozen years the bigotry, tyranny, and cruel religious intolerance were such as flourished in the seventh century, and in spite of systematic slave raids the population decreased by nearly two-thirds, and practically all the children died. . . . Yet this well-meaning little sonneteer sincerely felt that his verses were issued in the cause of humanity. Looking back from the vantage point of a score of years, probably every one will agree that he was an absurd person. But he was not one whit more absurd than most of the more prominent persons who advocate disarmament by the United States, the cessation of up-building the navy, and the promise to agree to arbitrate all matters, including those affecting our national interests and honor, with all foreign nations.

ADDITIONAL READING

The heady imperial qualities of the years at the turn of the century appear in many volumes, including the Roosevelt autobiography and other biographies and general diplomatic accounts mentioned at the ends of preceding chapters. See especially Ernest R. May, *American Imperialism* (New York, 1968); Robert A. Hart, *The Great White Fleet* (Boston, 1965), for a typical display of the era; the commentaries of Mr. Dooley by Finley Peter Dunne, collected and published under varying titles, including the collection edited by Elmer Ellis; Elting E. Morison's reprinting of three long Roosevelt letters in *Cowboys and Kings* (Cambridge, Mass., 1954); Nelson Manfred Blake, "Ambassadors at the Court of Theodore Roosevelt," *Mississippi Valley Historical Review*, XLII (1955–1956), 179–206, an article of lasting value; and John Garry Clifford, "Admiral Dewey Visits Chicago," *Journal of the Illinois State*

Historical Society, XL (1967), 245–266, a tale of contemporary patriotism and political ambition.

The Philippine occupation has an accounting in Hermann Hagedorn, *Leonard Wood* (2 vols., New York, 1931); Garel A. Grunder, *The Philippines and the United States* (Norman, Okla., 1951); Rowland T. Berthoff, "Taft and MacArthur, 1900–1901: A Study in Civil-Military Relations," *World Politics*, V (1952–1953), 196–213, about the friction between William Howard Taft and General Arthur MacArthur, the father of the later well-known general; and *Leon Wolff, *Little Brown Brother* (New York, 1961), a hostile account of water cures and other inhuman acts by American soldiery. A fascinating book of readings taken from testimony before the Senate Committee on the Philippines in 1902 is *Henry F. Graff, ed., *American Imperialism and the Philippine Insurrection* (Boston, 1969), a volume in the series Testimony of the Times: Selections from Congressional Hearings, under the general editorship of John A. Garraty. Forrest C. Pogue's *George C. Marshall: Education of a General* (New York, 1963) has a section on a young lieutenant's education in the occupation. The Moroccan affair and conference appears in Barbara W. Tuchman, "Perdicaris Alive or Raisuli Dead," *American Heritage*, X (1959), 18–21, 98–101, a clever article about two scamps, Perdicaris and Raisuli, and two statesmen-scamps, John Hay and Theodore Roosevelt; Alfred Vagts, *Deutschland und die Vereinigten Staaten in der Weltpolitik* (2 vols., New York, 1935), which treats the crisis in long detail; and Eugene N. Anderson, *The First Moroccan Crisis: 1904–1906* (Chicago, 1930), for European aspects. Allan Nevins's *Henry White* (New York, 1930) considers the work of the American negotiator.

On the Alaska boundary arbitration see Charles C. Tansill, *Canadian-American Relations: 1875–1911* (New Haven, 1943); Charles S. Campbell, Jr., *Anglo-American Understanding* (Baltimore, 1957); Alexander E. Campbell, *Great Britain and the United States* (Glasgow, 1960); Bradford Perkins, *The Great Rapprochement* (New York, 1968). Thomas A. Bailey's "Theodore Roosevelt and the Alaska Boundary Settlement," *Canadian Historical Review*, XVIII (1937), 123–130 cuts to size TR's role in the success of the negotiation and corrects the statements in *Henry F. Pringle, *Theodore Roosevelt* (New York, 1931). A few years later, when the trauma of arbitration had passed, American-Canadian relations looked toward friendship with an American offer in 1911 of a treaty of commercial reciprocity, not discussed in the present narrative; but Taft's nemesis, the Senate, turned it down; for which see L. Ethan Ellis, *Reciprocity: 1911* (New Haven, 1939). Biographies of statesmen involved in the Alaska arbitration are Tyler Dennett, *John Hay* (New York, 1933); Allan Nevins, *Henry White* (New York, 1930); P. C. Jessup, *Elihu Root* (2 vols., New York, 1938); *Richard W. Leopold, *Elihu Root and the Conservative Tradition* (Boston, 1954); John A. Garraty, *Henry Cabot Lodge* (New York, 1953).

For the movement to strengthen international law there is a large literature. The best place to begin is John Bassett Moore's "International Arbitration: Historical Notes and Projects," in *The Collected Papers of John Bassett Moore*

(7 vols., New Haven, 1944), II. Although published originally in 1896, this long article—actually a short book—remains the best history of international arbitration in English. For its special subject see Calvin D. Davis, *The United States and the First Hague Peace Conference* (Ithaca, N.Y., 1962), a definitive account. Its author is completing a book on the Second Hague Peace Conference. Accounts of the Olney arbitration treaty and the Roosevelt and Root treaties appear in W. Stull Holt, *Treaties Defeated by the Senate* (Baltimore, 1933). Bryan and his times is in the subject's own *The Old World and Its Ways* (St. Louis, 1907), an account of his trip; William Jennings and Mary Baird Bryan, *The Memoirs of William Jennings Bryan* (Philadelphia, 1925), published the year of his death; Merle E. Curti, "Bryan and World Peace," *Smith College Studies in History*, XVI (1931), Nos. 3–4. Bryan's early years have been reviewed with great care in Paolo E. Coletta, *William Jennings Bryan: Political Evangelist, 1860–1908* (Lincoln, Nebr., 1964). Coletta has a second volume in press on Bryan as secretary of state; a third volume will cover Bryan's remaining years after 1915.

The gathering of pro-British sentiment appears in the books by R. G. Neale, *Great Britain and United States Expansion* (East Lansing, Mich., 1966); and by Charles C. Campbell, Jr., Alexander E. Campbell, and Bradford Perkins, mentioned above. See also *Henry F. May, *The End of American Innocence: A Study in the First Years of Our Own Time, 1912–1917* (New York, 1959); Alan Valentine, *1913: America Between Two Worlds* (New York, 1962); Cushing Strout, *The American Image of the Old World* (New York, 1963); and D. C. Watt, *Personalities and Policies: Studies in the Formulation of British Foreign Policy in the Twentieth Century* (Notre Dame, Ind., 1965), which has a chapter on "America and the British Foreign-Policy-Making Elite, from Joseph Chamberlain to Anthony Eden, 1895–1956."

19

Neutrality, 1914-1917

Force will not accomplish anything that is permanent, I venture to say, in the great struggle which is now going on on the other side of the sea.

—Woodrow Wilson, speech in New York, 1916

Although people in Europe and America had been talking about a war for years, few had really expected it when it came at last in the first days of August 1914. Signs of trouble had appeared in Europe toward the end of the nineteenth century. France in 1894 had secured an alliance with Russia, and the people and government of the United States had watched the development of the dangerous competitive system of alliances of Europe—the Franco-Russian Alliance was designed to balance the alliance concluded in 1879 between Germany and Austria-Hungary. Ten years after their alliance with Russia, the French obtained an entente with the British, and the lines were drawn for the war of 1914–1918. The nations, meanwhile, were arming to the teeth. Even so, Americans and Europeans alike thought that a general European war, often predicted, could not occur, for they felt that civilization had advanced too far to permit a war on the order of the Napoleonic wars of a century before. New designs in ordnance—naval and land—and other inventions in weaponry seemed to point to so horrible a toll in any new war that such a conflict was humanely unthinkable.

A series of untoward diplomatic and military events nonetheless shook the peace of Europe until at last the First World War began. Germany and France vied for influence over Morocco in 1905–1906, and again in 1911. In 1911 Italy declared war on Turkey, to despoil the latter of the African territory of Tripoli. In 1912 there occurred a Balkan War of Turkey versus Bulgaria, Montenegro, Serbia, and Greece. This conflict ended in 1913, followed almost without pause by another: Bulgaria against Montenegro, Serbia, Greece, and Rumania. Western Europe seemed secure from war until, on June 28, 1914, a fanatical Bosnian revolutionary named Gavrilo Princip assassinated the heir to the Austro-Hungarian throne, the Archduke Francis Ferdinand, whom Princip shot down in cold blood together with his wife in Bosnia's capital city, Sarajevo. A month later the Austro-Hungarian government, suspecting with good reason the complicity of the Serbian government, declared war on Serbia. This declaration brought into play the alliance system of Europe; when Serbia's ally Russia entered the fray, the other nations quickly followed, each fearful that an adversary might obtain an advantage in mobilization of its armies. And so, after the shots rang out in Bosnia, the peace among the major powers of the Continent, preserved since 1871, came to a flaming end.

1. *The problem of American neutrality*

The eruption of a great European war in the first four days of August 1914 caught the government of the United States almost completely unprepared. The state department in Washington had no appreciation of the imminence of hostilities, having heard little from American diplomatic representatives abroad. The latter, although they were on the ground—residing in the dozen or so capitals of the European nations—failed to sense the coming of the catastrophe. The very existence of Sarajevo was unknown to the American minister to Belgium, Whitlock, who during the crisis was at his country place outside Brussels writing a novel about rural life in Ohio. "I had never heard of Sarajevo," he later wrote. "I had not the least idea where it was in this world, if it was in this world." The American vice consul in Budapest, Frank E. Mallett, did send a warning of probable war to Washington, in a report dated July 13, more than two weeks after the assassination of the archduke on June 28. Mallett, being only a vice consul, hesitated to dispatch his report by the expensive cables, so he sent it by mail and it arrived in Washington on July 27.

After the shock of the first days of August 1914, the American government through President Wilson proclaimed on August 4 its neutrality toward the European conflict. The vast majority of the American people expected to remain neutral during the fighting that followed. The war seemed another of those ordinary foreign combinations and collisions against which Washington had warned in 1796. Wilson on August 19 urged Americans to be "neutral in thought as well as in action." For the president the war was, to use the phrase of Ambassador Walter Hines Page in London, "this huge quarrel." At the outset Wilson could find no idealistic purpose in the war. He would have agreed with the British leader David Lloyd George, who later remarked that in 1914 Europe slithered into war. "America," Wilson said on July 4, 1919, "did not at first see the full meaning of the war. It looked like a natural raking out of the pent-up jealousies and rivalries of the complicated politics of Europe." As late as 1916 the president could say sincerely that with the objects and causes of the war "we are not concerned. The obscure foundations from which its stupendous flood has burst forth we are not interested to search for or explore." When in December 1916 he sought to mediate between the angry belligerents, he said that the objectives for which the Allies and the Central Powers claimed they were fighting were "virtually the same." A fond hope for neutrality characterized the entire American diplomatic stand in the years from 1914 to 1917.

The United States viewed the war in terms of international law and protection of neutral rights. The neutral rights of Americans, as laid down by the congressional plans for commercial treaties of 1776 and 1784, had stipulated a wide latitude for American trade during European wars: neutral ships would ensure the neutrality of goods carried, except for contraband ("free ships make free goods"); there would be a narrow definition of contraband; neutrals had the right to trade between ports of a belligerent, that is, to take over a belligerent's carrying trade; blockades had to be conducted close to ports, with no paper blockades, so that any neutral carrier attempting to enter a blockaded port would be subject to "imminent danger." These principles had been codified in the Declaration of Paris of 1856, following the Crimean War of 1854–1856, and generally accepted by the major powers of Europe. A Declaration of London in 1909 further defined neutral rights, and although in the years between 1909 and 1914 the declaration was never ratified by enough nations to carry it into effect, Americans at the outset of the war believed that the belligerents would accept it. For everyone, Americans and Europeans alike, thought in 1914 that the new war would be along the lines of the Franco-Prussian War of 1870–1871, with fighting lasting little more than a few weeks or months. It seemed entirely feasible that in such a war the American view of neutral rights could prevail.

This hope, as events turned out, was vain. After the German rush through Belgium and down toward Paris ground to a bloody halt at the Marne in the autumn of 1914, the war turned into a trench conflict that lasted for four years, until November 11, 1918. The war on the high seas thereupon acquired the old familiar meaning. Both the Allies and the Central Powers found themselves short of almost all the materials requisite for a prolonged war. The Allies turned to the United States as a source of supply; they had no intention of permitting similar succor to reach the

Germans. The Central Powers accepted the Declaration of London of 1909, on condition that the Allies would do so; any definition of neutral rights was likely to assist a weak naval power. The British before the war had rejected the declaration, and the United States therefore had held up final ratification. After the war began the British continued to hesitate over the declaration and then accepted it with reservations which amounted to rejection. The American government made some attempts to persuade the British to reconsider and then settled down to seeking recognition by the belligerents of as many neutral rights as possible.

Two complicating factors, in addition to a rapidly developing British tendency to violate all inconvenient rules of neutrality, forced their way into American calculations at this point. These factors, both innovations in sea war, were Britain's employment of mines in quantity and Germany's use of the submarine.

Extensive use of mines first engaged the lawyers of the state department when the British government on November 3, 1914, announced that the "whole of the North Sea must be considered a military area," and that henceforth all neutral ships should enter that sea by way of the straits of Dover and stop at a British port for sailing directions through the mine fields. Extensive possibilities of cutting neutral trade with Germany arose when the British mined the North Sea, which according to international law was not territorial waters. The law of nations notwithstanding, the British in their North Sea proclamation took over as their own a huge part of the high seas. Thereafter the British checked on all North Sea traffic at the straits of Dover. They delayed for weeks or months on some flimsy pretext any vessel carrying goods which although admittedly noncontraband were in some way useful to the Central Powers. The British meanwhile began to extend the contraband lists to include anything of remote value to their enemies. From the moment that the European war after the Marne changed from a war of movement to a war of position, the admiralty commenced the infringement of neutral rights, all the while attempting to enlarge neutral duties to a degree that would stop all trade with Germany. Mining the North Sea was the first major step in the elaboration of this policy.

Extensive employment of mines had not been part of nineteenth-century warfare. Nor had nineteenth-century war anticipated extensive use of the submarine. The submarine raised many difficult military, moral, and legal issues. The trouble began when the British mined the North Sea and the Germans retaliated by announcing in February 1915 that the waters surrounding Great Britain were henceforth to be considered a war zone in which vessels, presumably neutrals included, would be sunk by submarines without warning. There was no legal precedent for this

German action other than the rule of international law permitting retaliation. The rule limited retaliation to actions in kind—but it was possible to argue that a British blockade by large mine fields sown far out on the high seas justified a loose German counterblockade by submarine.

The British government at once set out to negative the German tactic of unrestricted submarine warfare. The British demanded that undersea vessels should act in accord with the accepted rules of war for cruisers, then the only rules of international law concerning ships at sea. The Germans disputed this British contention: the submarine could not behave like a surface cruiser; it is one of the axioms of war that the nature of a weapon determines its tactics, and the submarine, then a weak and fragile vessel, could not afford to fire its torpedoes from the surface if there were any chance either of enemy gunfire or ramming, both of which defenses could be used by any ordinary merchant vessel.

Here lay the difficulty: the submarine, by nature an instrument of ambush, could not effectively follow the rules of cruiser warfare; a submarine had to act like a submarine. This necessity involved sinking merchant ships without warning. But the British, to give point to their contention that the submarine must act like a cruiser, armed their merchantmen early in 1915 and on February 10, 1915, secretly instructed them to ram submarines wherever possible. What could the Germans do? An armed merchantman firing on a submarine, or a merchantman attempting to ram a submarine, becomes *ipso facto* a vessel of war and is automatically subject to attack by the submarine, the latter using any means within its power to sink the merchantman. Yet the submarine captain, observing the rules of cruiser warfare, could legally go over to unrestricted warfare only after a merchant vessel had acted in a belligerent manner, and by that time it might well be too late for the submarine captain and his crew. Nor could the submarine, a cramped vessel, take on board the passengers and crew of a victim. To expect the submarine to behave militarily, morally, and legally like a cruiser was to demand the impossible. This is what the British government did demand, for understandable military reasons—the British wanted to prevent Germany from using submarines in an effective way.

When the Germans on February 4, 1915, announced unrestricted submarine warfare to begin two weeks from that date, February 18, the United States likewise protested Germany's submarine tactics, but from reasons moral and legal rather than military. The United States, in opposing Germany's use of the submarine in the First World War, argued largely from the sense of humanity and neutral rights. The inhumane aspects of submarine warfare were patent to everyone. The Germans themselves were uneasy about the inhumanity of submarine warfare and felt able to justify it only as a necessary measure of war. As for neutral rights, American foreign policy had sought for almost a century and a half to make them prevail. Neutral rights had been codified in the nineteenth and early twentieth centuries after a persistent American effort. The United States, now a great power and recognized as such by the nations of the world, was not going to stand by meekly while the rules of neutrality, so painfully written into international law, were flouted. When the Germans in retaliation against Britain's mining of the North Sea declared unlimited submarine war, the president clearly made known the American position. Wilson edited the note which Secretary of State Bryan dispatched to Berlin on February 10, 1915, and which set down in explicit terms that Germany would be held to a "strict accountability" for any American lives or property injured because of such a deviation from the accepted rules of warfare on the high seas.

Wilson in addition held out for the right of American citizens to travel, if they chose, on passenger ships of the belligerent powers, in practical effect those of Britain and France. This latter was a fateful request. It was something that Americans had not previously insisted upon—though in former wars the right to travel on belligerent ships had never been much of an issue, few Americans having business in Europe in those days. Travel on belligerent ships was to lead to so much difficulty during the First World War that some later writers on international law have argued that the United States should have forgone the right—which, so these writers have contended, was not a right in law anyway, but only a privilege. They have even argued that Wilson chose to interpret neutral rights in this way because he was partial to the British cause, wittingly or unwittingly, and demanded the utmost in neutral rights from the Germans. But even later, when the Gore-McLemore resolutions were presented to Congress in 1916 to the effect that no American could travel on a belligerent vessel headed for the danger zone in Europe, Wilson in acting to prevent passage of the resolutions certainly showed not the slightest favoritism for the British cause. He refused to surrender his position in this matter, and simply chose to construe neutral rights liberally to include the right of Americans to travel on belligerent ships.

The preceding pages have sketched in briefest terms the first belligerent actions against neutral rights, and the American response: (1) British mining of the North Sea in November 1914; (2) the German response of February 1915, unrestricted submarine warfare around the British Isles; (3) the American warning to Germany in February 1915 of strict accountability. These three initial steps in the breakdown of American neutrality were followed by (4) the sinking of the *Lusitania* in May 1915 and a consequent German promise to spare liners; (5) a new German campaign of submarine warfare beginning March 1, 1916, under the claim that all armed merchantmen were warships; (6) an American note to Berlin after the torpedoing of the unarmed French channel packet *Sussex* (March 24, 1916), announcing that further attacks on unarmed ships would result in a breaking of diplomatic relations; (7) the final German announcement, after a temporary backdown over the *Sussex* "ultimatum," that effective February 1, 1917, all ships around the British Isles would be sunk without warning. This last German act brought a break in diplomatic relations between Washington and Berlin and was followed two months later by war.

It is interesting to notice that at the beginning of each year—1915, 1916, 1917—the Germans made an attempt to increase the rigor of their submarine warfare. Twice they gave in to American demands—after the sinking of the *Lusitania* in May 1915 and of the *Sussex* in March 1916. On the third occasion they did not give in, and the United States went to war.

Germany's use of submarines, which eventually led to the entry of the United States into the First World War, had not been planned in advance of the war. The prewar head of the German navy, Admiral Tirpitz, did not believe in submarines, and 1914 found Germany with fewer submarines than England or France. Germany had 27, England 55, France 77. About half the German submarines were seaworthy. Two years were required to build a U-boat. By the beginning of 1915, when Germany first sought to carry on unrestricted submarine warfare, there were only twenty usable vessels. At any one time a third of these were in drydock, another third sailing to or from an assignment, and only a third—that is, seven—could be in striking position. It was actually with four submarines that Germany in February 1915 declared unrestricted submarine warfare. When this move was re-enacted in 1916 the number of seaworthy U-boats had risen to a bare fifty, of which some were needed in the Mediterranean. At any given time in 1916 the Germans could only send eleven or twelve submarines into the Atlantic sea lanes. In the spring of 1917 Germany could send between twenty-five and thirty U-boats into western waters. It is curious how much havoc, diplomatically and militarily, a few submarines produced during the First World War.

2. *The American case against Germany*

In retrospect there is no doubt that Germany's submarine measures, above anything else, brought the United States into the First World War in 1917. If the German government had used some other means of warfare against the Allies, it seems certain that the United States would not have entered the war. This is not to say that the submarine issue alone antagonized the Americans, that there were no other issues on which the American people took issue with the Germans, but that the submarine issue was crucial in the American decision for war.

At the beginning of the war in 1914 the German government had blundered badly, so far as American opinion was concerned, by invading Belgium contrary to a solemn treaty of guarantee which Germany had signed. Americans were incensed by this act. Emotional and moralistic, they saw this attack by Germany on a weak neighbor, contrary to treaty, as a moral atrocity. The treaty of guarantee was admittedly old, almost a dead letter, negotiated in 1839, but it was a treaty and not a "scrap of paper'" as the German chancellor, Theobald von Bethmann Hollweg, described it to the British ambassador when the latter asked for his passports. Germany violated the treaty over the protests of the Belgians, whose King Albert is credited with an epigram when asked if the German troops could march through his country: "Belgium is a nation, not a thoroughfare." The Germans had marched, Belgium had futilely declared war, and the Belgian army after a stout defense had fallen back into northern France.

A German occupation followed in Belgium, and during its four years the Germans used the harshest measures to keep the restive Belgian population in order. When the British government on May 12, 1915, published the Bryce Report giving details of German atrocities in Belgium, the American public was revolted. Here, as in the invasion of Belgium in 1914, was a second black mark against Germany. It is true that in the light of postwar investigation the veracity of some of the deeds instanced in the Bryce Report has come into question. There are no proofs of many of the wanton cruelties set down in it. But Bryce had long been a student of the United States, had made a wide reputation in America by publishing in 1888 a two-volume study entitled *The American Commonwealth*, and had been British ambassador to Washington during the Taft administration. His name, in American eyes, lent support to the official British report on German atrocities. Bryce, as we now see, should have made some effort to investigate the volume with which he associated his name, but he did not. Yet despite the falsity of many of the British charges in regard to Belgium, there was a considerable case against German occupation policy there. The Germans in their conduct toward Belgium did not behave well. They executed some 5,000 Belgian civilians, some in large groups, chosen indiscriminately as hostages for Belgian good behavior. Whenever some German soldier was shot down by Belgian patriots, the Germans retaliated by shooting hostages. If the more lurid atrocity stories of violated women

German ambassador, Count von Bernstorff, shown next to the embassy's warning and the Cunard Line's notice of the *Lusitania*'s sailing. According to the American view of neutral rights, the German government could not legally endanger the lives of American citizens traveling aboard belligerent vessels, and it seemed doubly insulting to have the embassy print such an advertisement in American newspapers. The drawing is by W. A. Rogers.

and bayoneted babies contained little truth, there remained this execution of hostages which, although perhaps militarily justifiable, was humanely outrageous. To the sensitive public opinion in America, an opinion highly idealistic, German occupation policy in Belgium was unspeakably reprehensible.

Publication of the Bryce Report had come at a time to heighten its effect. A few days earlier, May 7, 1915, was the date of the most shocking episode of the entire period 1914–1917, the sinking by a German submarine of the *Lusitania*, pride of the British merchant marine, largest and swiftest vessel on the transatlantic run. The Germans early in 1915 had announced their war zone around the British Isles, and this entailed sinking not merely warships and cargo ships but also liners. The Allies refused to believe that German submarines would attack the largest liners. There was a technical basis for such reasoning: until the *Lusitania* went down, the Germans had not been able to sink any vessel traveling faster than fourteen knots; because the liners were swift vessels it was deemed im-

The *Lusitania* leaving New York, May 1, 1915, on her last voyage.

probable that they could be attacked. And they possessed watertight bulk-heads which presumably would minimize loss of life if they were attacked. Unfortunately, and contrary to such reasoning, Captain Turner of the *Lusitania* disobeyed his instructions as his ship came within sight of the Irish coast (he slowed down his vessel and refrained from zigzagging). Thus Commander Schwieger of the *U-20* managed (the following is from his ship's log) to get a sight on "four funnels and two masts of a steamer . . . . Ship is made out to be large passenger steamer. . . . Clean bow shot at a distance of 700 meters . . . . Torpedo hits starboard side right behind the bridge. An unusually heavy explosion takes place with a very strong explosion cloud (cloud reaches far beyond front funnel). The explosion of the torpedo must have been followed by a second one (boiler or coal or powder?). . . . The ship stops immediately and heels over to starboard very quickly, immersing simultaneously at the bow . . . the name *Lusitania* becomes visible in golden letters." With this act of inhu-manity—1,198 people drowned, including 128 Americans—Germany committed one of the cardinal errors of the war.

No one remembered that the German authorities, in newspaper adver-tisements, had warned prospective passengers that the *Lusitania* was deemed subject to attack. No matter that the German emperor on June 6, after the *Lusitania* sinking, issued secret orders to his submarine com-manders not to attack liners without warning, and that after an accidental attack on the British liner *Arabic* the German ambassador in the United States, although without authorization, made the imperial orders public. The American people were horrified at the sinking of the largest Atlantic liner. "Damnable! Damnable! Absolutely hellish!" cried the evangelist Billy Sunday.

More than any other single factor, Commander Schwieger's chance torpedo shot (he had, incidentally, almost finished his cruise; it was his last torpedo) hurt the German cause in America. The American people were incensed at Germany and with almost one voice supported the Wil-son administration's diplomatic protests. When Secretary Bryan refused to sign a stiff note to Berlin and resigned his office on June 7, his devotion to his conception of moral law received little public sympathy. "I must act according to my conscience," the idealist remarked sadly at a luncheon after his last cabinet meeting. "I go out into the dark. The President has the prestige and the power on his side . . . ." This final sacrifice of Bryan's political career was to no avail, for anti-German feeling was far too widespread. There was never, to be sure, any serious possibility of America going to war over the *Lusitania* outrage. The country was un-ready for such action, but it was ready for the strongest diplomatic pro-tests.

The German case thus suffered in the United States because of the Belgian invasion and occupation and the sinking of the *Lusitania*. These acts were monumental instances of the German policy of *Schrecklichkeit* (frightfulness). There were other irritations, such as the crude attempts to sabotage American war industry which in December 1915 resulted in expulsion from the country of the German military and naval attachés, Captains Franz von Papen and Karl Boy-Ed. The Austrian ambassador in the United States, who bore the unfortunate name of Dumba, was also expelled after the British secret service intercepted and published some compromising correspondence, showing that he had been privy to schemes for fomenting strikes in munitions factories. Then there were the continuing incidents over German submarine warfare. After sinking of the *Lusitania* there was a lull as the Germans abandoned for the moment their unrestricted submarine tactics, but early in 1916 they again undertook to expand submarine warfare and a new crisis arose when a submarine sank the *Sussex* on March 24, 1916. President Wilson gave the German government a virtual ultimatum in the matter of unrestricted submarine warfare—that if the Germans used it again, a third time, the United States would break diplomatic relations. The German government backed down again—the Germans promised this time to exempt merchantmen as well as liners from sudden attack—and relations between Washington and Berlin became relatively placid for the rest of the year 1916, until the crisis of January 1917.

Meanwhile relations with Britain reached what was probably an all-time low during the entire war period. The British, having observed how successfully they had impressed the American people as compared with the clumsiness of the Germans, may have overplayed their hand and become too confident that no matter what they did their cause in America was safe. It was, of course, not so safe. The London government did not understand how neutral President Woodrow Wilson was trying to be. Even in 1915 the state department had sent the British a note of such coldness that Ambassador Page characterized it as containing "nothing in its tone to show that it came from an American to an Englishman: it might have been from a Hottentot to a Fiji-islander." The British blacklist of American firms suspected of trading with the Central Powers raised particular difficulty in 1916. The British government had compiled a list of all firms, American or those of other neutral nations, suspected of trading with Germany or Germany's allies, and goods consigned to such firms were declared subject to capture and confiscation by the royal navy. Although the blacklist was generally accurate, it did mark a gross violation of neutral rights as historically interpreted by the United States. "This blacklist business is the last straw," Wilson wrote to his chief adviser on foreign affairs, Colonel Edward M. House. An order in council about this time had set aside all that remained in British maritime practice of the Declaration of London. The British army in 1916 ruthlessly suppressed the Irish rebellion, stirring up the hatred of Irish sympathizers in America. American relations with Britain in 1916 became almost as taut as those with Germany.

It was in this situation, facing a serious crisis with both the British and the Germans, that President Wilson undertook a mediation of the war, an effort to bring to an end in Europe what had become a terrible slaughter, and to end it with, as Wilson described his purposes, a peace without victory.

The initial proposal of mediation, which proved unsuccessful, was the House-Grey Memorandum. The President's trusted adviser, Colonel House, had been in Europe in the spring of 1915 and again a year later, in the spring of 1916. On the latter occasion the colonel had become definite in discussions with the British foreign secretary, Grey, and the two men together had sketched out a way to end the war: "on hearing from France and England that the moment was opportune," the United States would invite the belligerents to a peace conference; should Allied acceptance be followed by German refusal, the United States would probably enter the war against Germany; or if the conference met and failed to secure peace, "the United States would [probably] leave the Conference as a belligerent on the side of the Allies, if Germany was unreasonable." The cautious Wilson had inserted the second "probably" (bracketed above) when the House-Grey Memorandum came to him for approval.

Nothing resulted from this pacific effort. Sir Edward, like Wilson, became cautious and told House that the time to put the plan into effect would perhaps arrive with autumn. In the summer of 1916 the British expected to mount a great offensive on the western front. The French, moreover, were fighting a gigantic battle at Verdun, and for them the time for mediation was later, not at the moment. But after the French held the Germans at Verdun they were less interested in mediation than before. As for the British, when they were defeated on the Somme they wished to wait until the military situation was more favorable. The Lloyd George ministry, replacing that of Herbert Asquith in December 1916, favored a policy toward Germany of a knock-out blow, and was more firmly against Wilson's "interference" than was the cabinet of Asquith. By this time the American president was highly irritated, for he and House had placed their hopes on the proposed plan of peace. The nonpursuit of the House-Grey Memorandum seemed to be one more of the difficulties which Great Britain was making in the latter months of 1916.

After the presidential elections in the United States, Wilson made a final mediation effort. The president at the outset was placed in a position of seeming to follow a German initiative, for the Germans on December 12, 1916, called for peace negotiations, hoping to gain the initiative by anticipating Wilson's move and catching him and the Allies off balance. He went ahead and on December 18 requested both parties to the war to state their war aims. The Allies obliged by asking for a settlement that the German government would not accept: "restoration of Belgium, of Serbia, and of Montenegro [the latter two nations, like Belgium, had been occupied] and the indemnities which are due them." After much prodding the Germans confidentially communicated terms to Wilson, but these were as impossible as those of the Allies: hegemony over Belgium, and a slice of France; only a small part of Serbia would be returned; much of Rumania was probably to pass to Bulgaria; there would have to be indemnities for Germany, and colonies. At the same time that it revealed peace terms, the German government on January 31, 1917, sent word through Ambassador Johann von Bernstorff of a new unrestricted submarine campaign.

The German admiralty had concluded that there was an excellent chance of knocking Britain out of the war by a blockade of the British Isles, the blockade including not merely munitions but everything, particularly food coming to Britain from the United States, India, and Argentina (especially the latter two countries, for harvests in the United States had been poor in 1916). The admiralty and the leaders of the German general staff knew that unrestricted submarine warfare would bring the United States into the conflict on the side of the Allies, but they were prepared to take this chance. They knew that American armaments were almost entirely naval. Great Britain controlled the seas anyway, and if the American fleet were added to the British it would make little difference in the outcome of the war. The American peacetime army was of no military importance, and the Germans calculated that before the United States could raise, equip, and train a great army, let alone transport it across the Atlantic, the war would be over. If the United States in 1917 had possessed a dozen ready army divisions the German government might well have hesitated. The United States did not have the ready army divisions, and Admiral Eduard von Capelle, Tirpitz's successor as minister of marine, declared that the military significance of American intervention would be "zero, zero, zero!" The unrestricted submarine campaign began on February 1, and on February 3 Wilson severed diplomatic relations.

Between the breaking of relations and the declaration of war there was a lapse of two months during which Wilson and the country determined on a course of action. War was not inevitable even after Bernstorff received his passports, for the nation could have followed a course of armed neutrality. Wilson seems to have wavered during this crucial period, waiting until Germany had given unmistakable indication of how seriously it would take the protests of the United States over its violations of neutral rights and, generally, its conduct of the war.

Wilson conceivably had armed neutrality in view when during February he asked Congress for authority to arm American merchant ships. He was not given it; in the Senate a "little group of willful men" by filibuster kept the bill from coming to a vote before the Sixty-fourth Congress ended on March 4 under the then law.

Meantime, the course for the American government became clear. A German submarine on February 25 sank the Cunard liner *Laconia;* it was the *Lusitania* all over again. This news came to the White House almost simultaneously with intelligence of the Zimmermann Telegram, in which the German foreign secretary, Alfred Zimmermann, sought to entice the Mexican government into war, not yet declared, with the United States, promising that Mexico might "reconquer the lost territory in New Mexico, Texas, and Arizona." This incredible missive incensed President Wilson because it had been transmitted to Mexico from Berlin via the American embassy in Berlin and the state department in Washington. Because of British control of the cables, Wilson had allowed the Germans to use American channels; the Germans had used them to transmit a hostile message. American newspapers published the Zimmermann Telegram on March 1. On March 12 a German torpedo sank the American steamer *Algonquin;* all of the crew were saved. Then word arrived on March 18 that the Germans had sunk three American freighters; on the *Vigilancia* fifteen crew members lost their lives, six of them Americans. Two days later the cabinet unanimously advised the president to call Congress as soon as possible and ask for a declaration of war.

Wilson called Congress into special session. The Senate arranged to limit debate, but now it was asked to declare war rather than mere armed neutrality. President Wilson delivered his war message to Congress in person on April 2; the joint resolution declaring war was passed on April 6, with overwhelming majorities.

3. *Decision for war*

To report these events does not altogether explain the official and popular decision for war. The reasons which took the United States to war in 1917 have been and will continue to be examined, questioned, and debated.

There had been the major issue of neutral rights between the United

Stop!

Wilson halts U-boat destruction.

States and Germany, and this had brought the break in relations in February 1917.

There was the case against Germany which consisted partly of *Schrecklichkeit*—the invasion of Belgium, occupation policy in Belgium, the sinking of the *Lusitania* (connected, of course, with neutral rights)—and partly of such lapses as attempted sabotage of American industry, virtual sabotage (through harsh terms) of the president's mediation effort, and the proposal to Mexico in the Zimmermann Telegram.

There were historical traditions and attitudes. It was easy for the people of the United States to recognize at this crucial time the tie of common language and kinship between America and Great Britain. The slow but sure change of sentiment between 1898 and 1914, related in the previous chapter, now appeared to Britain's advantage.

Also, while the decision was making, the issue of good versus bad was somewhat clarified by the first Russian revolution of March 12, 1917. The tsarist power was overthrown and a republic set up (this lasted until November 1917, when the Bolsheviks overthrew it). The Russian republic of March was substituted in the Allied coalition for an embarrassingly autocratic member, and the change strengthened the feeling of Americans that the Allies were fighting the despotisms of Central Europe.

There was the trade in munitions and foodstuffs, the economic ties between the United States tnd the Allies. Despite the increased stringency of Allied measures and German countermeasures in 1914–1917, American foreign trade had by no means been eliminated. Trade with the Allies increased dramatically and took on the characteristics of a boom. Prosperity came to American industry, which had been in the doldrums at the beginning of the war. The American merchant made his profits, and likewise the American farmer received a share of the new commerce, since Britain stood in need of foodstuffs as well as of war material. The American economy by 1916 thus had become attuned to the requirements of the Allies. This is not to say, however, that economic bonds had a large part in bringing the United States into the First World War. As a result of the investigation of the American munitions industry by a Senate committee under the chairmanship of Gerald P. Nye of North Dakota in the mid-1930's, many Americans came to believe that in 1914–1917 the bankers and the munitions makers—the "merchants of death"—had driven the United States to war. This belief was partly responsible for the series of neutrality acts which Congress passed in the middle and later 1930's. In actual fact there was not much truth to the merchants-of-death argument. One cannot doubt that many individuals, bankers and armament manufacturers, made fortunes from the wartime munitions trade. The United States Steel Corporation, to mention one example, flourished during the period and sweated out much of the "water" with which it had been capitalized at the turn of the century—the virtually paper issues of stocks and bonds, unsupported by physical assets of the corporation. Likewise such great banking houses as J. P. Morgan and Company floated the Allied bond issues in the United States and took profits from such transactions. The Morgan firm acted as Allied agent in this country in 1914–1917, and the Morgan partners put some considerable pressure on the Wilson administration to permit floating of bonds and loans under the neutrality proclamation of 1914. This pressure, the profits of financiers, and the profits of the munitions firms were uncovered, so to speak, in the Nye investigation of the 1930's, and many people at that time, anticipating uneasily another World War, were quick to conclude that profiteers had taken the United States into the war of 1914–1918. Still, there seems clearly to have been little if any skulduggery involved in the financing and munitions-trading of the First World War, and one should conclude that forces other than these moved the country to belligerency in 1917.

There were persuasive and, judged by the result, successful efforts to get United States support for the Allies. These efforts supported another argument much bruited about in the 1930's, again in anticipation of a Second World War, to the effect that crafty British propaganda in the years of American neutrality in 1914–1917 had hoodwinked the American people and finally brought them into the conflict on the side of the British. The British government, according to the "disclosures" of the 1920's and 1930's, had carefully set on foot a propaganda campaign to convert the United States to its side, and this campaign had met with success. What should one conclude about this? Again, there seems to have been an over-statement of a case. There is no question that the British government set up a special propaganda effort, cleverly kept secret and unofficial, to enlist American sympathies with the Allied cause. British books were sent over to the United States, and speakers came to talk about the general similarity of English culture to that of Americans. Influential Britishers wrote letters to their American friends, asking for sympathy with the cause in Europe. All in all, a large effort went into bringing the United States into the First World War. Since the United States entered the war, perhaps one should say that the effort was successful—though this reasoning really begs the question. There were many reasons, other than British propaganda, that brought the United States to declare war on Germany. And one might say, in conclusion, that there is nothing wrong with one country representing its cause to another country—that the United States does this publicly and openly today, in its official information services, all over the world. The accusations about British propaganda current in the interwar years stemmed partly from fear of more propaganda and a Second World War, and partly from sheer unacquaintance with the arts of peaceful persuasion. "Public relations" was a new industry in the United States as elsewhere in the 1920's and for some time thereafter, and there was fear of what might happen should the supposed wizards of press agentry set to work on national populations and deal in questions of foreign policy rather than tooth paste and cigarettes. This fear, as we now see, was unfounded, though the effects of propaganda of various sorts and sources upon American life have admittedly been of importance.

There was some consideration of balance of power in the traditional sense of that phrase, although nothing seems to have come of it. A few writers, notably Walter Lippmann, contemporaneously and later have sought to show that in 1917 the United States entered the war to redress the balance of power in Europe. Lippmann would argue that despite the many other factors mentioned above which moved the American government toward war, the final decision was taken in the highest circles in Washington on the basis of the world balance of power—the need to offset the military power of Germany, which was threatening to engulf the Continent, with the power of the colossus of the New World. According to the Lippmann contention, here was another time when the New World redressed the balance of the Old. The argument comes to rest uncertainly on the understanding of European politics by the president and his advisers. The president is deemed to have acted implicitly on a balance-of-power basis, and also at the behest of some of his advisers, especially Bryan's able successor, Secretary of State Robert Lansing. Yet, while it is not difficult to show that Lansing had a strongly developed sense of balance of power, it is much more difficult to show such reasoning on the part of Wilson. It was certainly in the interest of national security to go to war, and it might be comforting to believe that, since logic demanded entrance, logic was the source of action. From available evidence there is no proof that the American president in 1917 acted out of reasoning different from that which moved most of his fellow citizens, and there is no evidence that his fellow citizens were moved by concern for the balance of power.

Perhaps one should conclude that the reasoning which took Wilson and the American people away from the feelings of August 1914 to the remarkable singleness of purpose on April 6, 1917 (the congressional vote in favor of war was overwhelming, 82–6 in the Senate, 373–50 in the House), was a view of balance of power, but not the traditional view. The decision in 1917 was emotional, grounded in the belief, indeed conviction, that right, in the person of the Allies, was battling wrong, personified by the Central Powers. There was abroad, so Wilson and his fellow Americans believed, a highly organized, savage campaign against decency and morality, and in the early spring of 1917 evil was weighing heavily in the balance against good. The American people, having enjoyed throughout their history an abundant life in a material sense, having from their own successes come to believe that their principles were correct principles, lacking bitterness and cynicism about the motives and behavior of foreign peoples, were willing to take a stand against what most students even today would grant was a ruthless German military ambition. The American people, to the entire disbelief of contemporary foreign observers and to the disbelief of their own children of the next generation, were willing to take a stand in the world for principle. Americans in the long months of neutrality, from 1914 to 1917, had come to feel that their principles were being challenged. "The world," Wilson said in his war message, "must be made safe for democracy."

A CONTEMPORARY DOCUMENT

[The long months of American neutrality, from August 1914 to April 1917, produced conflicting opinions of what the United States should do in the crisis of the European war, and President Wilson was much concerned about the idea of Americanism, namely, whether the nation would continue to advance its mission of democracy and peace or fall prey to the passions of Europe. He went out of his way to address several thousand foreign-born citizens, after ceremonies of naturalization, at Philadelphia, May 10, 1915. By chance when he gave the address the *Lusitania* had been sunk three days before. Source: Albert Shaw, ed., *The Messages and Papers of Woodrow Wilson* (2 vols., New York, 1924), pp. 114–118.]

Mr. Mayor, Fellow-Citizens:

It warms my heart that you should give me such a reception; but it is not of myself that I wish to think tonight, but of those who have just become citizens of the United States.

This is the only country in the world which experiences this constant and repeated rebirth. Other countries depend upon the multiplication of their own native people. This country is constantly drinking strength out of new sources by the voluntary association with it of great bodies of strong men and forward-looking women out of other lands. And so by the gift of the free will of independent people it is being constantly renewed from generation to generation by the same process by which it was originally created. It is as if humanity had determined to see to it that this great Nation, founded for the benefit of humanity, should not lack for the allegiance of the people of the world.

You have just taken an oath of allegiance to the United States. Of allegiance to whom? Of allegiance to no one, unless it be God—certainly not of allegiance to those who temporarily represent this great Government. You have taken an oath of allegiance to a great ideal, to a great body of principles, to a great hope of the human race. You have said, "We are going to America not only to earn a living, not only to seek the things which it was more difficult to obtain where we were born, but to help forward the great enterprises of the human spirit—to let men know that everywhere in the world there are men who will cross strange oceans and go where a speech is spoken which is alien to them if they can but satisfy their quest for what their spirits crave; knowing that whatever the speech there is but one longing and utterance of the human heart, and that is for liberty and justice." And while you bring all other countries with you, you come with a purpose of leaving all other countries behind you—bringing what is best of their spirit, but not looking over your shoulders and seeking to perpetuate what you intended to leave behind in them. I certainly would not be one even to suggest that a man cease to love the home of his birth and the nation of his origin—these things are very sacred and ought not to be put out of our hearts—but it is one thing to love the place where you were born and it is another thing to dedicate yourself to the place to which you go. You cannot dedicate yourself to America unless you become in every respect and with every purpose of your will thorough Americans. You cannot become thorough Americans if you think of yourselves in groups. America does not consist of groups. A man who thinks of himself as belonging to a particular national group in America has not yet become an American, and the man who goes among you to trade upon your nationality is no worthy son to live under the Stars and Stripes. . . .

See, my friends, what that means. It means that Americans must have a consciousness different from the consciousness of every other nation in the world. I am not saying this with even the slightest thought of criticism of other nations. You know how it is with a family. A family gets centered on itself if it is not careful and is less interested in the neighbors than it is in its own members. So a nation that is not constantly renewed out of new sources is apt to have the narrowness and prejudice of a family; whereas, America must have this consciousness, that on all sides it touches elbows and touches hearts with all the nations of mankind. The example of America must be a special example. The example of America must be the example not merely of peace because it will not fight, but of peace because peace is the healing and elevating influence of the world and strife is not. There is such a thing as a man being too proud to fight. There is such a thing as a nation being so right that it does not need to convince others by force that it is right. . . .

When I was asked, therefore, by the Mayor and the committee that accompanied him to come up from Washington to meet this great company of newly admitted citizens, I could not decline the invitation. I ought not to be away from Washington, and yet I feel that it has renewed my spirit as an American to be here. In Washington men tell you so many things every day that are not so, and I like to come and stand in the presence of a great body of my fellow-citizens, whether they have been my fellow-citizens a long time or a short time, and drink, as it were, out of the common fountains with them and go back feeling what you have so generously given me—the sense of your support and of the living vitality in your hearts of the great ideals which have made America the hope of the world.

ADDITIONAL READING

Books dealing with the outbreak of the First World War in Europe are innumerable. Heading the literature are the volumes by Sidney B. Fay, *Origins of the World War* (2 vols., New York, 1929) and Bernadotte Schmitt, *The Coming of the War* (2 vols., New York, 1930). Schmitt has brought his account closer to date in "July 1914: Thirty Years After," *Journal of Modern History*, XVI (1944), 169–204. A new study is Luigi Albertini, *The Origins of the War of 1914* (3 vols., London, 1952–1957). A popular account of the coming of the war is Ludwig Reiners, *The Lamps Went Out in Europe* (New York, 1955). Two biographies of prewar diplomats are Sir Harold Nicolson, *Portrait of a Diplomatist* (New York, 1930), a study of Nicolson's father, Sir Arthur Nicolson; and Charles W. Porter, *The Career of Théophile Delcassé* (Philadelphia, 1936). A recent and beautifully written account of how the nations blundered into war, and how the war stalemated in its first month, is *Barbara W. Tuchman, *The Guns of August* (New York, 1962).

American entrance into the war, the 1914–1917 era, has had much examination. Richard W. Leopold, "The Problem of American Intervention, 1917: An Historical Retrospect," *World Politics*, II (1950), 405–425 is a good introduction to the literature. Walter Millis, *Road to War: America, 1914–1917* (Boston, 1935) is a most interesting and able work, although it does not manage the humor of Millis's previous book on the Spanish-American War—after all, the First World War was not an amusing war. Charles C. Tansill, *America Goes to War* (Boston, 1938) is a more detailed anti-Wilson study. Charles Seymour's *American Neutrality: 1914–1917* (New Haven, 1935) stresses the importance of the submarine in the declaration of war against Germany. *Arthur S. Link, *Woodrow Wilson and the Progressive Era: 1910–1917* (New York, 1954) contains a careful view of its subject, in essential agreement with Seymour. The best book on American entrance is now *Ernest R. May, *The World War and American Isolation: 1914–1917* (Cambridge, Mass., 1959), which makes extensive use of unpublished German records.

As for the involved question of neutral rights, an able account is R. G. Albion and J. B. Pope, *Sea Lanes in Wartime* (2d ed., Hamden, Conn., 1968). W. E. Lingelbach, "England and Neutral Trade," *Military Historian and Economist*, II (1917), 153–178 is an excellent treatment, unfortunately published in a defunct periodical. For the most spectacular event of the neutrality era see Thomas A. Bailey, "The Sinking of the *Lusitania*," *American Historical Review*, XLI (1935–1936), 54–73, based on Commander Schwieger's diary and other materials; and more recently the popularization by A. A. and Mary

Hoehling, *The Last Voyage of the Lusitania* (New York, 1956). For the important activities of Wilson's second secretary of state see *War Memoirs of Robert Lansing* (Indianapolis, 1935); and Daniel M. Smith, *Robert Lansing and American Neutrality: 1914–1917* (Berkeley, Calif., 1958). After entrance into the war, the United States reversed its practice on neutral rights and duties, if not its position; this story appears in Thomas A. Bailey, *The Policy of the United States toward the Neutrals: 1917–1918* (Baltimore, 1942).

During the 1920's and 1930's, there was much concern in the United States over whether the nation was talked into war in 1914–1917 by propaganda from the Allies. As we now see, this concern overrated the effect of propaganda. Typical of the genre is James Duane Squires, *British Propaganda at Home and in the United States from 1914 to 1917* (Cambridge, Mass., 1935). More interesting and worthwhile are such studies as James M. Read, *Atrocity Propaganda: 1914–1919* (New Haven, 1941); Horace C. Peterson, *Propaganda for War: The Campaign against American Neutrality, 1914–1917* (Norman, Okla., 1939); and the sequel to the latter volume, *Horace C. Peterson and Gilbert C. Fite, *Opponents of War: 1917–1918* (Madison, Wis., 1957). For its special subject see Armin Rappaport, *The British Press and Wilsonian Neutrality* (Stanford, Calif., 1951).

The final decision for war, taken in the early months of 1917, is still an intriguing subject. An excellent little book which deserves close and careful reading is Samuel R. Spencer, Jr., *Decision for War: 1917* (Rindge, N.H., 1953). Spencer examines the importance of such events as the Zimmermann Telegram and Germany's sinking of the British liner *Laconia*. *Barbara W. Tuchman, *The Zimmermann Telegram* (New York, 1958), is a sparkling account, written with that author's flair. Edward H. Buehrig's thoughtful *Woodrow Wilson and the Balance of Power* (Bloomington, Ind., 1955) considers the possibility that Wilson came out for war because of Germany's threat to the balance of power in Europe and the world.

For other books bearing on the above subjects, see titles listed at end of chapter twenty.

20

War and Peace

Germany has once more said that force, and force alone, shall decide whether
Justice and peace shall reign in the affairs of men, whether Right as America
conceives it or Dominion as she conceives it shall determine the destinies of
mankind. There is, therefore, but one response possible from us: Force, Force
to the utmost, Force without stint or limit, the righteous and triumphant Force
which shall make Right the law of the world, and cast every selfish dominion
down in the dust.

— Woodrow Wilson, speech in Baltimore, 1918

1. *Wartime diplomacy, 1917–1918*

When the United States entered the First World War many questions at
last were resolved or adjourned, and it was with considerable relief that
the leaders of the American government could clear the decks, so to speak,
and face the major problem that confronted them: defeating the Central
Powers. Diplomacy during the war became of necessity a concern secondary to the military effort. Still, there was a place for diplomacy and a large
one, in any war such as the conflict in 1917–1918, fought by a coalition.
President Wilson—as would be true of President Franklin D. Roosevelt a
generation later, in 1941–1945—found himself deeply involved in what
might be described as "coalition diplomacy," the holding together and in
some important instances the direction of the Allied war effort. The diplomacy of interallied co-ordination was a major concern in 1917–1918,
and the president performed it brilliantly. There were, in addition, two
other diplomatic tasks which Wilson undertook. One was in regard to
Austria-Hungary—bringing pressure upon the Dual Monarchy to get out
of the war. The other consisted of a calculated and eventually successful
effort to persuade the German people to give up fighting and make peace
with the Allies.

The principal diplomatic effort of the war years came over the business of interallied co-ordination. In the same month that the United States entered the war, the British government sent a mission to America headed by the foreign secretary, Arthur Balfour, to discuss Allied requirements and seek to discover how the United States as a belligerent might best contribute to an Allied victory. Not to be outdone, the French simultaneously sent a mission consisting of René Viviani, a former premier, and also, to discuss military matters, Marshal Joseph Joffre. The Italians and Belgians likewise sent missions, and, as we have seen in a previous chapter, the Japanese sent Viscount Ishii to the United States to obtain some concessions for the island empire which were not connected with the Allied war effort. Little came of any of these initial missions, including the mission of Ishii, but they did serve to emphasize at the outset of American belligerency the need for Allied co-operation in the common effort against the Central Powers.

One result of Balfour's visit was the setting up of a special system of contact between the British foreign secretary, once he had returned to London, and the American government. In a private arrangement that completely by-passed the state department, Balfour set up a special British government code by which he could communicate directly with the chief of British military intelligence in the United States, Sir William Wiseman. Wiseman maintained a suite in a New York hotel which was directly above a suite occupied by Colonel House, Wilson's confidant. House, in turn, had a direct and private wire from his suite to the White House. It was a most effective arrangement. If exasperating to Secretary of State Lansing, who thus was left completely in the dark as to many Anglo-American arrangements on the highest level, it was probably for the best in many ways, for in this manner the British government could deal intimately with the American president instead of going through the rigmarole of sending formal notes between the respective foreign offices.

This arrangement was efficacious only between the two English-speaking allies, and it was an arrangement of channels rather than a solution to the many problems of concern that confronted Britain, the United States, France, Russia, and the other powers aligned against the Central Powers. After the United States entered the war, the special Franco-British purchasing arrangements through J. P. Morgan and Company were dropped, as the Morgan Company rightly believed that it could not continue to carry on what was now a proper function of the government of the United States. This change required a new American organization, and the Morgan procedures were, unfortunately, not at once assumed by the government in Washington. There was muddle in this regard until an arrangement was made in late August 1917 for a purchasing commission in Washington. A protocol to this effect was signed by the United States, Britain, France, and Russia.

Such a purchasing commission could not co-ordinate the requirements of the Allies with those of the Americans, which were increasing as an American army of enormous size and power began to come into being, and so pressure appeared for more co-ordination, perhaps an American mission to Europe. Colonel House was mentioned as a possible head for such a mission, and without hesitation President Wilson nominated House, who with a full complement of advisers arrived in London on November 7, 1917. The House mission performed yeoman service, conferring with the British until November 21, after which it went on to Paris and joined an Interallied Conference at which eighteen nations were represented, from Belgium to Siam.

The Interallied Conference of November 1917 was one of the most fruitful diplomatic events of the war, when one considers the many decisions that resulted, directly and indirectly. The first plenary session opened with a speech of welcome by the new French premier, Georges Clemenceau, who had just formed his ministry dedicated to victory, and who had promised that he would make a brief talk. He spoke five sentences, concluding: "The order of the day is work. Let us get to work." The conference thereupon adjourned for executive sessions of committees of technical experts. From this discussion at Paris came many important decisions. One was a plan that the Americans would place in France by the end of 1918 at least thirty divisions of troops, approximately a million men, available for the campaign envisioned for early 1919. As events turned out, the Americans had their million in France by June, 1918, and doubled the number by October. It was these fresh American troops which broke the back of the German army on the western front and enabled the Allies to win the war. There were other agreements at the Interallied Conference, such as the decision to send a battleship division to reinforce the British Grand Fleet. British naval authorities were extremely nervous over the accuracy of German naval gunfire as exhibited at the Battle of Jutland in 1916. Appearance of American warships in Europe, ensuring a preponderance of Allied naval power against a possible second German challenge, greatly reassured the British naval command. Another agreement at the conference in November 1917 in Paris was that the British and Americans together would close the North Sea to German submarines by construction of a mine barrage, which incidentally marked a reversal of the American stand against mining of the high seas. There was also agreement at the conference on blockade policy, and on methods of rationing trade with neutrals on the European continent so as to ensure that the neutrals would not transship goods to Germany or Germany's allies.

The Interallied Conference set up standing committees which met in London and Paris. There were the interallied council on war purchases and finance, the maritime transport council, the interallied naval council, the food council, the interallied petroleum conference, the interallied munitions council. The Europeans must have been aghast at the organizational mania of the Americans, but because they needed American goods, they complied with the desires of the New World republic. As one Frenchman, André Tardieu, put it (Tardieu was France's chief of a permanent commission of co-ordination in the United States): "When Americans fall in love with an idea, even if their enthusiasm does not last, it is always intense. In 1917 and 1918, they had a passion for the organization of interallied war machinery, the weight of which was not always borne gladly by Europe." Eventually, he concluded, the Europeans did come to see that only through united efforts, rather than independent measures, could the war be won.

The European Allies themselves on November 7, 1917, urged on by military disaster on the Italian front, took a step in the direction of unifying their efforts. The Italian army had cracked at Caporetto on October 27, 1917, and in a short time three quarters of a million Italian troops were killed, wounded, or made prisoner. This debacle brought the British, French, and Italians to a meeting at Rapallo early in November where they created an interallied Supreme War Council. The council was to act "as an agency for the adoption and maintenance of a general policy for the Allies in the prosecution of the war, consistent with the total resources available and the most effective distribution of those resources among the various theaters of operations." It was not a supreme command for the Allied forces—that would not come until later, in the spring of 1918, when the almost successful German general offensive in the west forced the Allies to designate Marshal Ferdinand Foch as supreme allied commander. But if it was not a supreme command, the Supreme War Council was a political organization of considerable importance. General Tasker H. Bliss, a former chief of staff of the American army, sat as one of the military advisers from the first meeting of the council. Colonel House represented the United States at the meeting in December 1917 and as Wilson's personal representative sat with the prime ministers of the other powers. After House's return to the United States, the president appointed no one in his place, although permitting the councilor of the Paris embassy, Arthur Frazier, to attend as a "listener." Wilson wished to emphasize that the United States, having not signed the formal instrument of alliance between the Allied powers and having thereby assumed only the role of "associate" in the war, was not taking part in the Allies' political discussions. This, to be sure, was a false position, and when in late 1918 the question of an armistice with Germany arose in the Supreme War Council, Colonel House entered its sessions and discussed the matter in fullest participation with representatives of the other nations.

One might conclude this discussion of the vitally important work of interallied co-ordination by again citing an opinion of André Tardieu. "Nations remember only the high spots of wars," he wrote in the 1920's. "What did they grasp of the tragic period of 1917–1918? The Rumanian disaster, Caporetto, the British Fourth Army, the Chemin des Dames. Were those the decisive events of the great struggle? No! The essential things were the problems of transportation, rotation of shipping and submarine sinkings, the financial problem, the problems of co-operation. Any shortcoming in the adjustment of effort, any breakdown in the machinery of supply, might have left our soldiers weaponless."

The United States, it can justly be said, was responsible for much of this work of interallied co-ordination.

Another of President Wilson's diplomatic tasks of the war period was his bringing of pressure upon the Central Powers with the hope of persuading them to give up fighting. Like the diplomacy of co-ordination, this was an informal sort of negotiation. It was much different from the usual note-sending and note-receiving that marks the normal peacetime dealing of nation with nation. There were no American diplomatic representatives in Berlin or—after the American declaration of war in December 1917—in Vienna, and American moves had to be made through special emissaries and through diplomatic posts in neutral countries.

The policy of the United States was generally well adapted to the situation of 1917–1918, for it focused on Austria-Hungary. The German government had become extremely bellicose after the appointment in autumn 1916 of General Erich Ludendorff as quartermaster general of the imperial army, and there could be little hope for a peace offensive directed at Berlin. Austria-Hungary, however, had incautiously gone to war in 1914 and almost from the start was anxious to get out. The Austrian declaration of war on Serbia had set off the European alliance system, almost like a string of fire-crackers, and the war had hardly begun before the old Emperor Francis Joseph was wishing for peace: if Austria-Hungary could get out with a black eye and no bones broken, the emperor said, he would be happy. Upon the death of Francis Joseph in late 1916, the young Emperor Charles came to the throne and was equally anxious for peace. Charles knew even better than his great uncle that the empire was torn by the dissension among its national minorities, which already had brought a high rate of desertion from the imperial army. If the monarchy did not soon have peace, it would fall apart. To this inviting situation the United States directed a considerable diplomatic effort.

President Wilson and the American government nourished the hope of getting Austria-Hungary out of the war and, at the same time, maintaining the territorial integrity of the empire—avoiding its breakup into several small national states. There were unofficial and inconclusive conversations in Switzerland between emissaries of the Emperor Charles and an American resident in that neutral country, George D. Herron. There was a short exchange between Wilson and Charles, through the king of Spain. But Austria had become almost a captive state of the Hohenzollern empire. Strong bodies of German troops had deployed close to Vienna, and while the young emperor pursued his somewhat naive negotiations, the Germans by indirect pressure kept him from going too far.

Meanwhile the nationalities subject to the Habsburg throne planned to capitalize the opportunity in a revolutionary sense, and by early summer of 1918 the situation was beyond repair. No longer satisfied with autonomy, the nationalities demanded freedom. The American government acquiesced in this change in the situation, assuming that the Austro-Hungarian empire could not survive the war. In the summer of 1918 the United States recognized the Czechoslovak National Council in Paris and also the national aspirations of the empire's Serbs, Croats, and Slovenes. The Emperor Charles in October 1918 tried vainly to federalize his empire, but the time had passed when such a move was possible. With jubilation the refugee Czechoslovak statesman, Thomas Masaryk, then in America, observed the collapse of his people's ancient Austrian enemy. This new political situation in Central Europe was, one should emphasize, created by the pressures of the war rather than any initiative on Wilson's part. The American president rather reluctantly used Central European nationalism to hasten the last stages of the war. He thereby obtained Austria-Hungary's capitulation seven days before that of Germany, in early November 1918.

Wartime diplomacy toward Germany had to move along different lines. The Second Reich, the empire of Bismarck, made by blood and iron in 1871 from the union of north and south Germany, offered no opportunity in 1917–1918—given the ardent Germanism which in the latter nineteenth century superseded German provincial feeling—to split the empire into its pre-1871 divisions. American tactics therefore were to separate the Berlin government from its people, under the somewhat meretricious but nonetheless useful argument that the government did not represent the people. With the German people, Wilson said in his war message, "we have no feeling . . . but one of sympathy and friendship." Similar statements appeared throughout his speeches in the period of American belligerency, 1917–1918.

The principal move by the American government to drive a wedge between government and people in Germany was the announcement, on January 8, 1918, of the Fourteen Points: (1) open covenants of peace, openly arrived at; (2) freedom of the seas; (3) removal, "so far as possible," of trade barriers; (4) reduction of armaments "to the lowest point consistent with domestic safety"; (5) equitable adjustment of colonial claims; (6) evacuation of Russia; (7) evacuation and restoration of Belgium; (8) assignment of Alsace-Lorraine to France; (9) readjustment of Italian frontiers "along clearly recognizable lines of nationality"; (10) "autonomous development" for the peoples of Austria-Hungary; (11) evacuation of Rumania, Serbia, and Montenegro, with access to the sea for Serbia; (12) reduction of Turkey to territory containing only peoples of Turkish descent; (13) independence of Poland, with access of Poland to the sea; (14) establishment of a league of nations. The chief motive of the Fourteen Points, one should explain, was to keep Russia in the war (the Bolsheviks had come to power on November 6–7, 1917) by a statement of more liberal war aims than Colonel House had been able to secure at the Interallied Conference at Paris in November 1917. There was also the need to reassure the Allied peoples that there was idealism in the Allied war aims. These were the immediate reasons, the impulse, behind Wilson's announcement of the Fourteen Points, but he directed his speech to the German people, hoping to persuade them to get out of the war. The Fourteen Points were a master stroke in what a later generation would describe as psychological warfare. Learning of the Fourteen Points, the German people could see that the Allies had a reasonable peace program, and they could ask themselves why they were continuing to fight in what had become a catastrophic world conflict.

Proof of the effectiveness of the Fourteen Points and other of Wilson's speeches explaining his peace program came when, prior to the armistice of November 11, 1918, the American president managed to obtain from both the Germans and Allies an express recognition—which in the case of the Allies became known as the "prearmistice agreement"—of the Fourteen Points as a basis of peace. This was one of Wilson's major triumphs as a diplomat. The prearmistice agreement became the foundation for the entire peace settlement at Paris in 1919. It was of the utmost historical importance, for without considering its pledges and exceptions no student can appreciate the Treaty of Versailles and the later German efforts to revise the treaty. The prearmistice agreement became possible when General Ludendorff, after a rupture of his lines in northern France, told the German civil government on September 29, 1918, that it must sue for peace and do so quickly. The government, which the German general staff had dominated for two years, displayed an unwonted initiative and at once asked for peace on the basis of the Fourteen Points, communicating directly with President Wlison and not the Allies. Wilson kept the negotiations in his own hands while he persuaded the Germans to democratize their government and drop the emperor. At the same time he persuaded the Allied statesmen—not without a broad hint from Colonel House, then sitting on the Supreme War Council in Paris, that the United States might make a separate peace—to accept the Fourteen Points. The British prime minister, Lloyd George, accepted the points with a reservation that there must be further discussion of Wilson's point 2, freedom of the seas. The British also desired a large financial reparation from Germany, and so they drafted a reservation on this matter—it was written mainly by Sir William Wiseman—which was accepted by the French premier, Clemenceau, and the Italian premier, Vittorio Orlando. With these reservations, communicated to and accepted by the German government, together with explanation by Wilson to the Allies (but not to the Germans) that certain of the points, such as point 10 pertaining to Austria-Hungary, had to be modified in view of recent events, the Germans on November 8 sent plenipotentiaries to Marshal Foch's railroad car, then in the forest of Compiègne in northern France, and there in the early morning of November 11, 1918, they signed the armistice.

2. The Paris Peace Conference

The war was over, and the making of peace could begin. American diplomacy had enunciated the Fourteen Points as a basis of peace, and in the prearmistice agreement gained Allied approval of them. The Germans had consented to them. The diplomats of the New World would now have an opportunity to see how much of the American peace program could be secured at the peace conference.

Wilson decided to go in person to Paris, and this decision at the time and later was written down as a major diplomatic error. His presence assuredly put him into the hurly-burly of what was bound to be a difficult conference. The president had much to lose in personal reputation and little to gain by going to Europe to assist in making the peace. He went; and he obtained at Paris much of his program, notably the League of Nations, which an individual with less prestige might never have secured.

But did President Wilson at Paris lose some vital issues for the United States, apart from his victory on the League of Nations? There has persisted a popular belief in his "blunders" at Paris—a belief that a gullible American president, journeying to Europe to make peace in 1919, encountered issues which he did not understand, and that cunning European diplomats at Paris persuaded Wilson to give away everything that the

Wall Street celebrates the Armistice, November 1918.

President Wilson, on
board the *George
Washington*, headed for
Paris.

United States won in the World War.

The simple process by which the Paris conference accomplished its tasks,
in meetings of three or four of the leading statesmen, seemed to show
personal decision at the peace table. Three or four men, it was easy to
believe, could make mistakes. Everyone watched with apprehension at
the time, an apprehension which deepened into suspicion, as the conference followed a normal process of shrinking to a manageable size. Although it began with a large body of delegates, it was dominated at once
by the Council of Ten (which was a reincarnation of the wartime Supreme War Council—foreign ministers and prime ministers or chief delegates of Japan, Italy, France, Britain, and the United States). It ended as
a private meeting of the Big Four (the prime ministers of Italy, France,
Britain; the president of the United States) and, frequently, the Big
Three (Clemenceau, Lloyd George, and Wilson): Lloyd George, the politically agile prime minister of England, "a Welsh witch" as John Maynard Keynes described him; Clemenceau, conservative, uncharitable,
realistic in the old-fashioned manner of diplomacy; Wilson, a great man
in many ways, but edgy and irritable at Paris, and tired.

A hero's welcome for Wilson in Europe.

Even so, one must doubt that Wilson made many mistakes at Paris. Certainly on technical matters he was on almost all occasions hedged about by solid information from his advisers. There was much professional advice available in Paris, and the president was seldom in the predicament of having to make a subjective decision. Wilson needed this help. His declarations during the war months had been general in nature. Despite his background as a student of history, the president was not well grounded in European history. Colonel House as early as autumn of 1917 had therefore taken steps to marshal for the peace conference a corps of American specialists, and the resulting Inquiry, a group of experts drawn mainly from university faculties, devoted itself to minute examination of the problems of Europe, especially possible boundary changes in Eastern Europe. The Inquiry was a serious group, established for a serious purpose, and its information was in the main highly accurate. At the conference the experts of the Inquiry stood available to the president and other members of the American delegation. As events turned out, the Inquiry and a somewhat similar group in the British delegation, together with experts from the other Allied nations, wrote the major portions of the Versailles Treaty with Germany and the treaties with the other Central Powers.

This is not to say that there were no large political questions at Paris

A sketch of the Big Four deliberating at Paris, by Edouard Réquin.

subject to decision by the statesmen of the great powers, for there were such questions, running far beyond the technical into the political on a grand scale. One need only mention reparations—how much should Germany pay, and to whom? What should be done about Germany's border along the Rhine—should the border territory pass to France, or should there be provisions for demilitarization and occupation, with eventual retirement of Allied forces upon German good behavior? What should happen to the Saar, the rich coal-bearing valley—should it go to France permanently because of Germany's dynamiting of many of France's mines? There were the Polish questions, of borders and access to the sea; the difficulty of rearranging the peoples and borders of the Adriatic area, where, as in Poland, there was centuries-old confusion which had been adjourned so long as the Austro-Hungarian empire existed; the problem of the former Turkish territories in the Middle East, which had to go, apparently, to one or several of the victorious Allied powers; the need for parceling out former German colonies in the Pacific, including Germany's sphere of influence in the Shantung peninsula of China. In such political questions no experts could be of much help. Here the leading statesmen of the conference—Wilson, Lloyd George, Orlando, and Clemenceau—had to make decisions. But one should point out that even at these points, in the nontechnical areas, Wilson and the other leaders of the Allies could act only within definite limits, for each of them lacked the power of independent decision because he was curbed by the politics of democracy: Wilson was subject to advice and consent of the Senate; Lloyd George was heckled by the press in England, especially that of the sensational press magnate, Lord Northcliffe; Orlando had little power of decision because of the popular hysteria over Adriatic possessions, whipped up by patriots such as Gabriele d'Annunzio; Clemenceau was the prisoner of the

French passion for revenge and security.

The idea is false that Wilson had a wide area of decision at Paris and blundered badly because of his personal foibles and incapacities, thereby losing the peace. Personal decision—blunders—could hardly characterize the peace conference of 1919. The idea of a personal conference flourished in the overimaginative brains of newspaper correspondents, and in the disappointments and disillusions of nations which after 1919 did not have what they wanted. It was easy to point to three or four elderly men sitting in a book-lined study in Paris, and to say, "*There* was the trouble," whether it was there or not.

The results of the conference gradually became evident in the months from its beginning on January 18, 1919, until signature of the treaty with Germany on June 28, 1919—the fifth anniversary of the assassination of the Archduke Francis Ferdinand at Sarajevo. The majority of the 440 articles of the Treaty of Versailles were technical and noncontroversial. A few of them stood out in importance or in seeming importance. The first twenty-six comprised the Covenant of the League of Nations. The Covenant became, incidentally, the first twenty-six articles of all of the Paris peace treaties (St. Germain with Austria, Trianon with Hungary, Neuilly with Bulgaria).

In the German treaty, article 231 was the famous war-guilt clause, which blamed Germany and its allies for beginning the war in 1914. Perhaps a special error of the German treaty, fraught with future difficulty, was the postponement of setting of the amount of reparations which Germany was to pay, and the fact that reparations were to include the cost of Allied pensions. The boundaries of Germany in the west underwent some changes. Alsace-Lorraine was given to France. Two small patches of land, Eupen and Malmédy, went to Belgium. The Saar Valley was placed for fifteen years under a temporary League administration, with its future status to be decided at the end of that time; the mines of the Saar went to France, and if the territory was returned to Germany by plebiscite in the year 1935 the Germans were to purchase the mines. There were to be no German fortifications west of a line fifty kilometers east of the Rhine, and certain German territory west of the Rhine was to be occupied by Allied troops for periods of five, ten, and fifteen years. In the east, Germany's province of East Prussia was separated from the remainder of German territory by a Polish corridor—a severe settlement excusable on the basis of self-determination and Poland's need for access to the sea, inexcusable to Germans, who for centuries had possessed the corridor lands. Danzig, the former German port now in the new corridor, was denominated a free city under control of the League of Nations. In Upper Silesia, in southeast Germany, there was a plebiscite to determine what

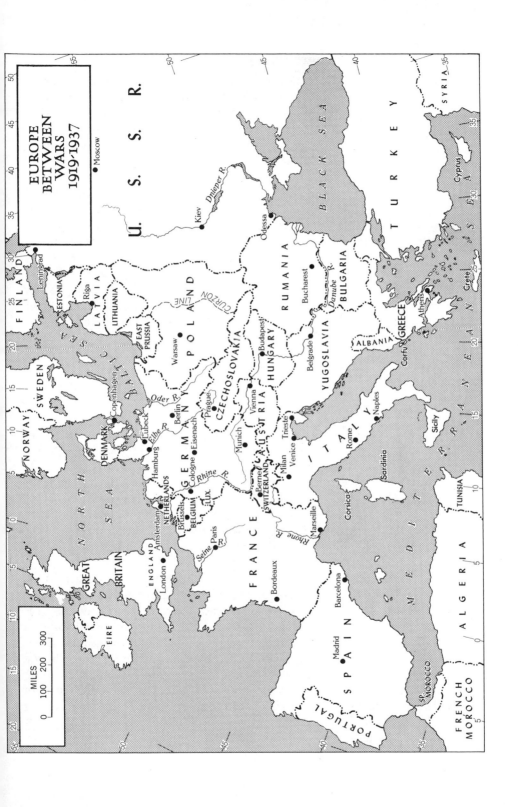

EUROPE
BETWEEN
WARS
1919-1937

MILES
0 100 200 300

U. S. S. R.

• Moscow

Kiev •   Dnieper R.

FINLAND

Leningrad

ESTONIA

LATVIA

LITHUANIA

EAST
PRUSSIA

Riga

BALTIC SEA

NORWAY

SWEDEN

NORTH
SEA

Copenhagen

DENMARK

Lübeck

Elbe R.

Hamburg

Berlin •

Oder R.

POLAND

CURZON LINE

Warsaw •

Odessa •

BLACK SEA

RUMANIA

Bucharest •

Danube R.

BULGARIA

Cologne • Eisenach

GERMANY

Prague •

CZECHOSLOVAKIA

Munich •

Vienna •

AUSTRIA   HUNGARY

Budapest •

Belgrade •

YUGOSLAVIA

ALBANIA

GREECE

Corfu

Athens •

TURKEY

SYRIA

Cyprus

Crete

GREAT
BRITAIN

EIRE

ENGLAND

London •

NETHERLANDS

Amsterdam •

Brussels •

BELGIUM   Lux.

Rhine R.

Berne •

SWITZERLAND

Milan •

Trieste •

Venice •

ITALY

Rome •

Naples •

Sardinia

Sicily

FRANCE

Seine R.

Paris •

Bordeaux •

Rhône R.

Marseille •

Corsica

MEDITERRANEAN SEA

SPAIN

Madrid •

Barcelona •

PORTUGAL

ALGERIA

TUNISIA

FRENCH
MOROCCO

SP. MOROCCO

lands would remain German and what would go to Poland. In the north of Germany two parts of Schleswig were to decide their nationality, Danish or German, by plebiscite. Germany under the Treaty of Versailles lost nearly four million people in the east, a third of whom were of German nationality. Altogether it lost by the treaty over six million people, or one-tenth of its population. It lost one-eighth of its territory.

The problems of the Paris conference were extraordinarily numerous, but the treaty with Germany was not a vindictive instrument in view of the more than four years of bitter fighting which had preceded it. It compared favorably indeed to Germany's Treaty of Brest-Litovsk with Bolshevik Russia, signed on March 3, 1918, by which Russia gave up all claims not merely to Poland, Finland, and the Baltic states, but to the Ukraine and the Caucasus. If Germany had won the war in the west, it would have demanded annexation of the Briey-Longwy iron district from France, Liège from Belgium, and in addition a close economic control over Belgium. One can say therefore that Allied ambition was considerably less than the German during the First World War. And under the Treaty of Versailles and the other treaties with defeated nations there was always the hope of the League of Nations. President Wilson hoped that such imperfections as would appear in the peace settlement could be taken to the new international tribunal where there could be discussion, compromise, and peaceful change.

It is saddening to reflect upon the manner in which this peace settlement of 1919 was lost, of how the divisions among the Allies which became evident at the Paris Peace Conference lasted for twenty years thereafter and enabled Germany, the defeated power at Paris, to begin another World War. It was tragic that at Paris the Italian delegates had to appease their own public at home and champion more territory for Italy than would have passed to it under the terms of the generous Treaty of London of 1915 (Fiume, seized after the war by Italian patriots led by d'Annunzio, had not been offered to Italy under the Treaty of London). The Japanese used the conference to enforce their claims on Shantung, the large Chinese province containing thirty million people, and in view of the small contribution of Japan to the defeat of Germany this was an excessive demand, embarrassing to the Allies and so humiliating to China that there was bound to be future trouble. The French representatives at the Paris conference were forced by their public opinion (if they did not already think this way themselves—certainly Clemenceau did) to be bitter and grasping; this course was mistaken, although entirely understandable for a nation which had lost 1,385,000 of its finest young men, with more than three million wounded. The British under the leadership of Lloyd George were not interested in territorial acquisition, even if the colonial premiers were determined to acquire control of the former German colonies. Despite the empire's grievous loss of 947,000 men killed, British leaders desired to promote Germany's economic welfare. But the British prime minister was an opportunist in his approach to politics, whether national or international, and he lent uncertainty and something of cheapness to a meeting which needed dignity and a convincing atmosphere.

President Wilson, in poor health towards the close of the conference after a serious attack of influenza in April 1919, did his best to. hold up American ideals to the peoples and statesmen of Europe. In this effort he was in fair measure successful, but he became so preoccupied with the task that he failed to keep in touch with the changing political situation in the United States and eventually lost at home everything that he gained abroad. He persisted in believing that domestic politics would be adjourned not merely for the period of the war, but for the period of peacemaking as well. He failed, and it was a foolish error, to appoint to the American peace delegation domestic political leaders of standing. Neither General Bliss, nor Colonel House, nor Secretary Lansing, nor the former diplomat Henry White, could keep him in touch with political developments in the United States. Wilson lost contact with American public opinion, despite a trip home in February and early March of 1919 to sign necessary legislation and plead the cause of the League of Nations to members of the United States Congress. If the Congress seemed slightly inattentive, it might have been because the Republican Party had gained control in both the House and Senate as a result of the November 1918 election. After return to Paris the president worked incessantly, and when the moment came in June 1919 to sign the German treaty he was close to exhaustion.

Apart from the understandable errors of peacemaking forced upon the statesmen of the great powers by public opinion in their home countries, one might mention at this point a special factor, namely Russia, which, while much talked about in the springtime and summer of 1919, was left undecided at the peace conference. If the Paris conferees made a cardinal error above and beyond any other mistakes, it was their sidestepping of the Russian question. Russia, to be sure, had been much in the minds of the Allies ever since the tsarist government had disappeared with the first Russian revolution of March 12, 1917. After the first revolution, people hoped that the new government would prove more efficient than the old and that the Russian front, from being something of a holding operation, would become a serious theater of operations against the Germans. Instead the weak republic gave way in November to the Bolsheviks, and at once the strange group of fanatics, so they seemed, led by

Vladimir Lenin and Leon Trotsky, threw in the sponge and made peace with the Germans at Brest-Litovsk on March 3. This was a large blow to Allied fortunes, for it enabled the German army to transfer many of its divisions from the Russian front to France. Luckily for the Allies, the Germans were not thorough enough in transferring troops—they could have sent across Germany many more than they did—and the western front held again in 1918 despite a great German offensive.

But at the peace conference at Brest-Litovsk the Bolsheviks led by Trotsky had talked long and loud about the rights of workers in Europe and their oppression by the capitalists, and this doctrine, though poked fun at in Allied newspapers, began toward the end of the year 1918 to worry Allied leaders. When after the German surrender the reds set up a communist regime in Bavaria, and when early in 1919 the radical premier of Hungary, Michael Károlyi, surrendered his government to the communist revolutionary Béla Kun, and when the Russians entered the Ukraine after the Germans left it—with all these happenings, people everywhere began to wonder about this movement known as communism. There was a "red scare" in the United States, and in other countries, in 1919. The statesmen at Paris worried about the durability of any peace they might conclude, finding themselves in the position of winning a war only to make the world safe for communism, hardly an attractive prospect.

What to do about the Bolsheviks in Europe was one of the major questions at the peace conference, but unhappily the problem was never resolved. Some individuals such as Winston Churchill and Marshal Foch were all for sending troops to Russia and putting the Bolsheviks down by force. Yet such an expedition ran counter to all the feelings among Allied peoples at the time—it was impossible to stir up enthusiasm for more fighting, after November 1918, and anyway it seemed that perhaps with the passage of some months the Russian confusion would right itself. Britain and France sponsored various "white" leaders in Russia in 1919 and 1920, and the occupations of Siberia and Murmansk, originally for military purposes, tended at times to become political interventions. But the attitude of President Wilson, which was to let the Russians find a new course according to their own preferences, gradually prevailed. This did not mean that Wilson was willing to recognize the Bolshevik regime, for he was not, and he so instructed his last secretary of state, Bainbridge Colby, in the summer of 1920. Colby announced the nonrecognition of communist Russia because the regime had subverted popular government, and this policy prevailed until another Democratic president changed it in 1933. Meanwhile the opportunity for intervention in Russia, if there had ever been one, had passed away as the regime of the Bolsheviks established itself during the 1920's and 1930's beyond any chance of destroying it.

The difficulty in regard to Bolshevik Russia, the reason why the problem was not solved, was in the main, as mentioned, the war weariness of all the Allied peoples. Public opinion by 1919 had turned to other concerns than the problems arising out of the World War. People were tired of war and wished to hear no more about it, not even about its settlement by the peace conference at Paris. By the autumn of 1919 when the Versailles Treaty was ready for approval by the nations of the world, the treaty encountered something close to indifference. "In this autumn of 1919," wrote Keynes, then in process of composing a polemic which bitterly criticized the treaty, people were "at the dead season" of their fortunes. "The reaction from the exertions, the fears, and the sufferings of the past five years is at its height. Our power of feeling or caring beyond the immediate questions of our own material well-being is temporarily eclipsed. The greatest events outside our own direct experience and the most dreadful anticipations cannot move us. . . . We have been moved already beyond endurance, and need rest. Never in the lifetime of men now living has the universal element in the soul of man burnt so dimly."

Keynes's words were intended to describe popular feeling in England and France, but his description was true of the United States as well. In America the exertions of the war, while great, had not been beyond endurance. They had been endurable, and the nation in a war in Vietnam some fifty years later would lose more than half as many young men as in the First World War (Vietnam: over 36,000 killed by mid-1969; First World War: 53,398 dead). The American exertion in 1917–1918, however, had been a great one in a spiritual sense. The American people had gone to war hoping for accomplishments not possible at the moment, such as making the world safe for democracy. To Europeans this latter phrase was a slogan but to Americans for a brief period it became a reality. When that reality faded and disappeared in the petty quarrels of the Paris Peace Conference, there came immense weariness with internationalism, and it could be said of Americans as of Europeans that "Never in the lifetime of men now living has the universal element in the soul of man burnt so dimly." Americans were ready to retreat from participation in the peace settlement, and they were ready for the general retreat into isolation which characterized the next twenty years of their diplomatic history.

3. Lodge versus Wilson

The withdrawal of the United States from Europe after the First World War became obvious when the Senate in 1919–1920 refused three times to consent to ratification of the Treaty of Versailles. Here was a public announcement to all the world that the American government would be strictly an onlooker while the nations of Europe attempted to repair the war's grave damage to their political, social, economic, and intellectual life. Yet an acute observer in the United States might have predicted this American withdrawal from "foreign entanglements" long before it became obvious in the Senate's refusal of the Treaty of Versailles. There had been premonitory rumbles from the retired sage at Oyster Bay, Theodore Roosevelt, who during the months of American participation in the war had been unable, despite initial resolves, to refrain from public jeers and sarcasm at what he described as Wilson's idealism. TR had thought that Wilson during the period of neutrality had been a pacifist, afraid to fight. In his private correspondence during the war Roosevelt vented his spleen without stint or limit (to borrow a Wilsonian phrase). "That skunk in the White House"—so he was heard to describe the president over the telephone to a friend. Roosevelt still had a hold of the affection of the American people, and his opposition boded ill for Wilson's program. When Wilson, upon the advice of party leaders, broke the wartime domestic political truce by asking for return of a Democratic Congress in the November 1918 elections, the lid was off, and the president's party was defeated at the polls.

Wilson contributed in other ways to the undoing of his international program. Upon American entrance into the war, he made a serious error in pitching his war speeches on too high an emotional level. His oratorical gifts ran away with him, and he made the fight too much of a struggle for justice and morality and right principle. These had been the values to which American politicians since the beginning of the republic had appealed. These were such slogans as could always stir the idealistic American electorate. But the American people by 1917 sadly needed tuition in the facts of international life, namely, that a great power must act affirmatively in the world, that to protect its interests it could not enter the world balance of power only when it felt like it but would have to keep military weight constantly in the balance, in time of peace as well as of world war. Wilson talked, instead, about moral responsibility and legal rectitude. He was so incautious as to announce on one famous occasion that the balance of power was forever discredited. Likewise he stressed during the war the importance of a parliament of man without inquiring carefully into mankind's willingness to depend on such an assemblage for settlement of international disputes.

Still, the most important factor militating against the continued participation of the United States in the work of world peace after 1918, a factor more important than any mistakes that Woodrow Wilson made, was the traditionally isolationist outlook of the American people toward foreign affairs. The American people, as mentioned, lacked international political training. Although the intellectual upbringing of Americans had been intensely political, politics always stopped at the water's edge. The generality of Americans did not know about the sort of politics that went on between nations. The century which separated Waterloo from the World War had allowed Americans to engage in a Civil War and develop half a continent without serious threat of foreign intervention. In 1919, having "paid their debt to Lafayette," the American soldiers returned home and divested themselves not merely of their uniforms but of all friendly remembrance of the cause for which they had fought. The World War to them became an unpleasant interlude, an interruption to the normal processes of life in the United States. The traditional American public attitude of isolation could easily reassert itself in 1919. There had been no intellectual preparation for what the wartime president's critics soon were describing as Wilsonian internationalism.

The role of Senator Henry Cabot Lodge in the Senate's rejection of the Versailles Treaty becomes intelligible when one realizes the forces which lay behind him and which he so well represented. To say that Lodge was the architect of America's post-Versailles isolation would be a gross misstatement. The senior senator from Massachusetts stood for traditional nineteenth-century ways of American international behavior. He represented the post-Waterloo belief that in foreign affairs America must have a free hand. Lodge loved England and visited many friends there on his summer trips abroad. He was happy to see the United States enter the war on the side of England against Germany in 1917. After the danger of German power disappeared, he wished to return the United States to the time-honored policy of the free hand. The leading element in Lodge's attitude toward the League and the Treaty of Versailles was traditionalism. The treaty's failure in the Senate was a result of this prevailing intellectual current. No single man or small group of men could change it. Political leaders, if they wished to stay snugly in office, had to act within it, and this is what Henry Cabot Lodge did.

At the outset of the anti-League battle, Lodge found considerable support in the Senate for his stand against the treaty. The president's war leadership had taken away much of Congress's usual power, and the senators were aching to display their importance. Wilson had failed to consult congressional leaders while drawing up the Covenant in Paris. He had gravely offended the Senate by refusing to appoint a member of that body, preferably a Republican member, to the peace commission. Lodge found animosity toward Wilson among his colleagues, and just before midnight on March 3, 1919, the day before the session of Congress was to end, he read to the Senate in a clever maneuver a round-robin statement signed by thirty-seven Republican senators and senators-elect (two other Republican senators added their names by telegraph the next day) which advised that "the constitution of the league of nations in the form now proposed . . . should not be accepted by the United States," and that the proposal for a league of nations should be taken up for discussion at Paris only after the conference had negotiated peace terms with Germany.

This was a clear ultimatum to Wilson from more than one-third of the Senate's membership. The president ignored it.

Meanwhile, and as a result of the November 1918 elections, the Republican Party organized Congress. By a majority of 49 to 47 (there would have been a tie if Henry Ford had won the close contest in Michigan) the Republicans organized the Senate in 1919, and Henry Cabot Lodge became chairman of the foreign relations committee. Of the committee's membership of seventeen, ten were Republicans, among them six irreconcilably anti-League senators. The irreconcilables would dominate the Republican majority and thus the committee itself. With Lodge as chairman the committee could determine the conditions under which the Senate received and considered the Covenant. Former President Taft and many others individuals accused Lodge of stacking the committee against the Covenant. To this accusation the senator neither at the time nor later made a reply. In his posthumous book, *The Senate and the League of Nations,* his comment was "It will be seen at once that this was a strong committee and such as the existing conditions demanded."

By the spring of 1919, with the situation in the Senate ominous, two moderate Republican leaders, former President Taft and President A. Lawrence Lowell of Harvard, cabled Wilson in Paris that it was essential to soothe the Senate's feelings. This soothing, they believed, might be done by a few small changes in the Covenant, including a Monroe Doctrine reservation. Wilson managed, though with some difficulty, to insert such a reservation in the Covenant's article 21. But no small changes would accommodate Lodge, who wished for a complete return to traditionalism in American foreign policy.

The tactics of the senator were to prolong the preliminaries and to delay the Senate's advice and consent to the treaty until American opinion came around to his side. Lodge in the summer of 1919 studiously procrastinated when the treaty in the course of senatorial procedure came first before the committee on foreign relations. He consumed two weeks reading the document aloud. Most of his colleagues absented themselves from the committee chamber, and on at least one occasion the committee clerk left the room, leaving Lodge reading to himself. He then arranged public hearings, an unprecedented step in consideration of a treaty, which required six additional weeks. The senator obtained for the foreign relations committee an invitation to the White House for a conference with the president, and there on August 19, 1919, Wilson answered senatorial questions for three hours. Lodge's tactics finally drove Wilson into a rash act, a speaking tour for the treaty—and this in turn had a most unexpected result.

In September of 1919, in twenty-two days, the president delivered thirty-six speeches averaging about an hour in length, traveled more than eight thousand miles, and stood up in a swaying automobile during a dozen parades. Sixty-two years old, worn by illness and the rigors of negotiation at Paris(not to speak of the requirements of twenty months of war leadership), Wilson was unable to stand the strain and collapsed at Pueblo, Colorado, on September 26, 1919. His assistants hurried him back to the White House, where he suffered a paralytic stroke.

Had Wilson died that glorious night in Pueblo, while cheer after cheer swept through the huge auditorium, he would have met a hero's end. Ex-Senator Beveridge, one of the president's most vicious critics, later remarked that if this had happened Wilson would have become a greater martyr than Lincoln. His beloved Covenant would have passed the Senate. Instead there came the collapse and the stroke, and for seven and one-half months the president lay almost helpless in the White House. The stroke thickened his speech, and withered the left side of his face and body. "My God, the President is paralyzed!" Dr. Grayson cried as he burst out of the sick man's room shortly after the attack. Mrs. Wilson later wrote that "for days life hung in the balance." For weeks and months, leaders of the administration could approach the ailing man only through his wife, who took it upon herself to decide what specific written communications she would pass in to her husband. The president did not meet the cabinet during this time, and in his sickness grew suspicious of everyone. He broke with Colonel House, and cavalierly dismissed Secretary Lansing. During his illness the Treaty of Versailles met defeat in the Senate.

4. *The defeat of the treaty*

The position on the treaty taken by the so-called irreconcilable senators, led by William E. Borah of Idaho, was of critical importance. The irreconcilables had pledged themselves to do everything in their power to achieve the treaty's rejection. They became known as bitter-enders and the Battalion of Death; according to a recent critic they possessed a state of mind compounded of "varying amounts of traditionalism, ignorance, bigotry, fear of the untried, prejudice, personal pique, partisanship, political ambition, and a natural bent for destructiveness." Their chief Borah had never been outside of the United States, but this had not prevented him from becoming a senatorial expert on foreign affairs. Indeed, the "lion of Idaho" succeeded to the chairmanship of the committee on foreign relations when Lodge died in 1924. Borah was enormously effective on a rostrum, and was considered one of the orators of his generation. His talents unfortunately seemed always on the side of obstruction and hypercriticism, and although an honest individual (he was the only irreconcilable for whom Wilson retained respect) he was much given to making debaters' points against whatever subject he was opposing. It was the Idahoan's propensity for contrariness which prompted Washington wits to comment, when they saw Borah taking his daily horseback ride in Rock Creek Park, that it was marvelous that horse and rider were both going in the same direction. In the fight over the Treaty of Versailles the Idaho senator was uncompromising. He declared that if he had his way the League of Nations would be "twenty thousand leagues under the sea." He wanted "this treacherous and treasonable scheme" "buried in hell" and insisted that he would not change his mind if Jesus Christ himself came to earth and pleaded for the Covenant. Borah's forensic gifts were ably seconded by the leather-lunged Senator Hiram Johnson of California, by the narrow legal erudition of Senator (formerly Secretary of State) Philander C. Knox of Pennsylvania, the wit of Senator George Moses of New Hampshire, and the active mentality of Senator Frank Brandegee of Connecticut. There was also the demagogy of Senator James A. (Jim) Reed of Missouri, a Democrat. Only a dozen or so in number, the irreconcilables were formidable in ability.

Their strength provided Senator Lodge with an excuse, if he needed one, for organizing the defeat of the Treaty of Versailles. Lodge maintained at the beginning of his senatorial maneuvering against the treaty that he was in reality in favor of the treaty and the League of Nations if these Siamese twins (the Covenant was part of the treaty) could be given suitable reservations during their passage through the Senate. Most of the Republican senators, except Porter J. McCumber of North Dakota, who sided with the Democrats, favored either mild or strong reservations. Lodge was ostensibly a strong reservationist. But as majority leader he had to keep all Republicans—mild, strong, and irreconcilable—under control, a difficult task because of the margin, two votes, by which the party had organized the Senate. The irreconcilables led by Borah were threatening to jump the party traces.

Borah had never been a reliable party man. The nightmare of 1912 when Theodore Roosevelt split the Republican Party and gave the election to Wilson was ever in Lodge's memory. Borah and the other irreconcilables in 1919 threatened the elderly majority leader with a secession from the party if they did not have their way in the Versailles Treaty. On one occasion Lodge complained that certain senators were browbeating him by addressing him in language which "no man of my age should be obliged to hear." According to Lodge's most recent biographer, the Massachusetts senator came to an agreement with Borah. If Borah and his fellow irreconcilables would support the party during the preliminary voting on reservations, they could vote against the treaty's final passage. If the treaty failed, they would achieve their objective, and if it passed, it would be less objectionable than the Wilsonian proposal of a treaty without reservations.

In retrospect the motives of the several Republican factions in the Senate appear rather clearly. The irreconcilables wished for the total defeat of the treaty, including, of course, the League of Nations. Theirs was the pure, unadulterated traditionalist stand in international affairs. As for those senators who were willing to vote for the treaty with reservations of varying severity—the strong reservationists and mild reservationists—they too were traditionalists, although the wartime Wilsonian infection had influenced their judgment. They feared for what they would have loosely described as American rights and wished distinct reservations of American sovereignty. Senator Warren G. Harding, a strong reservationist, was typical of this feeling when he asserted, "I could no more support mild reservations than I could support mild Americanism." The task of Lodge as Republican manager of the Senate was clear: it was to avoid at all costs a party split. Given Lodge's traditionalist views of American policy and a personal dislike he harbored for Wilson, it should have been obvious that he would almost welcome the chance to hold his party together at the expense of the Treaty of Versailles.

By the end of the summer, the foreign relations committee under Lodge's leadership had produced thirty-eight amendments and four reservations, later boiled down into fourteen reservations. The United States, according to these reservations, in case of its withdrawal from the League reserved to itself sole judgment as to whether it had fulfilled its obligations under the Covenant. The American government could not accept a territorial mandate under the League without vote of Congress. The Council and Assembly could not consider questions which pertained to the domestic jurisdiction of the United States. The Monroe Doctrine was "wholly outside the jurisdiction of the League of Nations" and entirely unaffected by any provision of the Treaty of Versailles. America withheld its assent to the Shantung settlement and reserved complete liberty of action. Congress might enact, if it wished, a law in regard to appointment of American representatives to the League. The reparations commission of the League would have no right to interfere with trade between the United States and Germany, without the consent of Congress. American expenses in the League would be subject to an act of appropriation by Congress. The committee asked for the right to increase armaments of the United States, under any League plan of disarmament, in case the United States were threatened with invasion or engaged in war. Nationals of covenant-breaking states, residing in the United States, might continue their normal relations. The American government must have the right to regulate private debts, property, rights, and interests of citizens of the United States. Assent was withheld to the section of the Versailles Treaty setting up an international labor organization, until Congress voted approval. The United States was to be protected against any unequal vote, in the League, of the British empire.

In particular Lodge's committee criticized article 10 of the Covenant, which the committee considered a dangerous departure from the vital principles of American foreign policy. Lodge chose to see foreshadowed in article 10 the end of a safe and wise tradition. The nation had never consented to commit itself in advance to international actions except in obvious cases such as intervention by foreign powers in the Western Hemisphere; but in article 10, according to Lodge, the nation would bind itself to decisions by an alien body sitting in Europe. Yet the perils of article 10 were largely imaginary. A close reading of the Covenant revealed the article as less than dangerous. League members undertook to "respect and preserve" (but not specifically to guarantee) "as against external aggression" (*aggression* was a difficult word to define) each other's "territorial integrity and existing political independence" (what this meant was not altogether clear). Nonetheless Lodge's committee balked at article 10. The senator's close friend, Elihu Root, pointed out that, so far as concerned the phrase "respect and preserve," he was willing to agree to "respect," but that "preserve" was tantamount to "guarantee." President Wilson, however, declared article 10 the "heart of the Covenant" and insisted that any reservation of the article was utterly unacceptable.

On November 19, 1919, the Senate voted twice on the treaty. The first roll call was with the fourteen Lodge reservations. The vote was 39 for, 55 against (the irreconcilables voting with the Democrats). A second roll call on the treaty without reservations resulted in 38 for, 53 against. Both with and without reservations the treaty failed to obtain a simple majority. In a third and final vote on the treaty on March 19, 1920, after there had been added to the Lodge reservations a fifteenth reservation favoring the independence of Ireland, the treaty failed again—49 for, 35 against—lacking seven votes of the necessary two-thirds majority.

It was Woodrow Wilson's misfortune, unlike his counterparts in American history, Lincoln and Franklin D. Roosevelt, to live on into the final act of his era, and when he died in 1924 he had seen his handiwork discredited. One of his last moves as president was to insist that the election of 1920 be a "great and solemn referendum" on the League and the treaty.

Three senators refuse to give the lady a seat. Cartoon by Rollin Kirby.

Two Ohio newspaper editors, Harding and James M. Cox, competed for the presidency in 1920, and the election was a travesty of Wilson's solemn referendum. Cox with courage came out in favor of the League, but Harding's managers played safe by taking the advice of the wily Senator Boies Penrose of Pennsylvania, who told them to "Keep Warren at home. Don't let him make any speeches. If he goes out on a tour, somebody's sure to ask him questions, and Warren's just the sort of damn fool that'll try to answer them." The amiable Harding confined himself to "bloviations" (as he liked to describe his campaign oratory and statement making) from his front porch in Marion, Ohio. It was said that during the campaign he took fourteen. different positions on the League. It was in one of his speeches that he accidentally made the famous declaration, "America's present need is not heroics but healing; not nostrums but normalcy; not revolution but restoration." In vain did thirty-one prominent Republicans, among them President Nicholas Murray Butler of Columbia University, Henry L. Stimson, President Lowell, and former President Taft, issue a manifesto near the end of the campaign advising that Harding favor the League of Nations. The only result of this belated effort to remind the candidate of the large pro-League faction within the Republican Party seems to have been an inclusion of a favorable reference to the League in the first draft of Harding's inaugural address; but, so the story goes, Mrs. Harding blue-penciled the reference during one of her revisions of the text.

Such was the fate of the great crusade which had begun for America in 1917. "We have torn up Wilsonism by the roots," Lodge rejoiced after learning of Harding's unprecedented majority of seven million votes. The hopes of humanitarians that the World War would inaugurate what Lord Robert Cecil called a "great experiment" in keeping the peace, that the war to end war would not have been fought in vain, disappeared when the traditionally isolationist views of the American people reasserted themselves after the war. The League of Nations, President-elect Harding told his fellow citizens in his victory speech, was deceased. "You just didn't want a surrender of the United States of America to go under American ideals. That's why you didn't care for the League, which is now deceased." Senator Lodge announced, more bluntly, that the League was dead. The United States under the Harding administration terminated the technical state of war with Germany by resolution of Congress, July 2, 1921, and signed a Treaty of Berlin on August 25 confirming to the American government all rights stipulated in the Treaty of Versailles. Similar treaties followed with Austria (August 24) and Hungary (August 29), and a series of later pacts established diplomatic relations with Turkey and with the seven new states which had emerged from the war in Eastern Europe.

CONTEMPORARY DOCUMENTS

[Feelings ran high over the making of the peace in 1919, and President Wilson was nothing if not partisan in his opinions of opponents. Only within the confines of his family may a president speak off the record, and it is almost certain that the following opinions got back to his opponents. The following excerpts are from a speech delivered to members of the Democratic National Committee at the White House on February 28, 1919. Source: Joseph P. Tumulty, *Woodrow Wilson As I Know Him* (Garden City, N.Y., 1921), pp. 377–379. One must bear in mind that the president had returned home briefly from the Paris Peace Conference to carry on the business of domestic government and was about to return to the conference to conclude the Treaty of Versailles.]

. . . I wish I could stay home and tackle this job with you. There is nothing I would like to do so much as really to say in parliamentary language what I think of the people that are opposing it. I would reserve the right in private to say in unparliamentary language what I think of them, but in public I would try to stick to parliamentary language. Because of all the blind and little, provincial people, they are the littlest and most contemptible. It is not their character so much that I have a contempt for, though that contempt is thoroughgoing, but their minds. They have not got even good working imitations of minds. They remind me of a man with a head that is not a head but is just a knot providentially put there to keep him from ravelling out, but why the Lord should not have been willing to let them ravel out I do not know, because they are of no use, and if I could really say what I think about them, it would be picturesque. But the beauty of it is that their ignorance and their provincialism can be made so perfectly visible. They have horizons that do not go beyond their parish; they do not even reach to the edges of the parish, because the other people know more than they do. The whole impulse of the modern time is against them. They are going to have the most conspicuously contemptible names in history. The gibbets that they are going to be executed on by future historians will scrape the heavens, they will be so high. They won't be turned in the direction of heaven at all, but they will be very tall, and I do not know any fate more terrible than to be exhibited in that future catalogue of the men who are utterly condemned by the whole spirit of humanity. If I did not despise them, I would be sorry for them.

Now I have sometimes a very cheering thought. On the fifth of March, 1921, I am going to begin to be an historian again instead of an active public man, and I am going to have the privilege of writing about these gentlemen without any restraints of propriety. The President, if my experience is a standard, is liable some day to burst by merely containing restrained gases. Anybody in the Senate or House can say any abusive thing he pleases about the President, but it shocks the sense of propriety of the whole country if the President says what he thinks about them. And that makes it very fortunate that the term of the President is limited, because no president could stand it for a number of years. But when the lid is off, I am going to resume my study of the dictionary to find adequate terms in which to describe the fatuity of these gentlemen with their poor little minds that never get anywhere but run around in a circle and think they are going somewhere. I cannot express my contempt for their intelligence, but because I think I know the people of the United States, I can predict their future with absolute certainty. I am not concerned as to the ultimate outcome of this thing at all, not for a moment, but I am concerned that the outcome should be brought about immediately, just as promptly as possible. So my hope is that we will all put on our war paint, not as Democrats but as Americans, get the true American pattern of war paint and a real hatchet and go out on the war path and get a collection of scalps that has never been excelled in the history of American warfare.

[Almost a month later Senator William E. Borah wrote a private letter to a constituent in which he set out the views of Wilson's opponents. Source: Borah to John W. Hart; Menan, Idaho; March 24, 1919, William E. Borah MSS deposited in the Library of Congress, Washington, D.C.]

I thank you cordially for your letter but it was no surprise to me. There is too much red blood in your system to subscribe to this treacherous, unAmerican scheme. Taft is doing the same thing now that he tried to do when he was President, surrender the government to certain sinister influences. There has not been an American administration since that of Buchanan more under the influence of the interests which are not in harmony with the welfare of the people generally. It is quite natural that he should come under the dominating influence of any scheme which intends to transfer the sovereign power of this government to aliens. This is plain talk but if it did not come from the heart I would not utter it. I simply utterly distrust them.

I hope, Hart, that you will write a letter to Hays. I am getting tired of this creeping, crawling, smelling attitude of the Republican party upon an issue which involves the independence of this Republic. If the Republican party cannot stand up in a fight of this kind then it is unfit for the confidence of the American people and the American people will say so the first opportunity they have. The doctrine of treachery and disloyalty ate at the moral fiber of the Democratic party for fifty years and when the people awaken to the fact that this is a studied and deliberate attempt to transfer the sovereignty of this government to a tribunal controlled by aliens they will damn forever the parties which connived at such a scheme or which cowardly sat by like Saul of old while the murder was being committed. This is a fight to the finish and those who are not for the Republic are against it. If the Republican party has no creed upon this matter there will be a party that has a creed. The white livered cowards who are standing around while the diplomats of Europe are undermining our whole system of independence and self control will have no hearing when the American people come to know the facts.

ADDITIONAL READING

General accounts of America during the First World War, useful despite the lapse of years since their publication, are Charles Seymour's *Woodrow Wilson and the World War* (New York, 1921), a volume in the Chronicles of America series, a remarkable appraisal considering that Seymour was writing of events so close to his time of publication; and the same author's *American Diplomacy during the World War* (Baltimore, 1934), which contains interviews and correspondence with leading participants. Preston W. Slosson, *The Great Crusade and After: 1914–1928* (New York, 1931), a volume in the History of American Life series edited by Arthur M. Schlesinger, Sr. and Dixon Ryan Fox, is still good reading. See also *Henry F. May, *The End of American Innocence* (New York, 1959). Recent general works of merit are Jean-Baptiste Duroselle's *From Wilson to Roosevelt: Foreign Policy of the United States, 1913–1945* (Cambridge, Mass., 1963), by a scholarly Frenchman; and *Daniel M. Smith, *The Great Departure: The United States and World War I, 1914–1920* (New York, 1965), a volume in the America in Crisis series; and Julius W. Pratt, *Challenge and Rejection: 1900–1921* (New York, 1967).

For their special subjects see Oscar O. Winther, trans., Hans P. Hanssen, *Diary of a Dying Empire* (Bloomington, Ind., 1955), good for the atmosphere of Germany in the midst of the war; Victor S. Mamatey, *The United States and East Central Europe, 1914–1918: A Study in Wilsonian Diplomacy and Propaganda* (Princeton, 1957), an expert analysis; David F. Trask, *The United*

States in the Supreme War Council: American War Aims and Inter-Allied Strategy, 1917–1918 (Middletown, Conn., 1961); Gaddis Smith, *Britain's Clandestine Submarines: 1914–1915* (New Haven, 1964), the arrangement prior to American entrance into the war whereby the American industrialist Charles M. Schwab managed the construction of British submarines in Canada; Burton F. Beers, *Vain Endeavor: Robert Lansing's Attempt to End the American-Japanese Rivalry* (Durham, N.C., 1962); Edward M. Coffman, *The War to End All Wars: The American Military Experience in World War I* (New York, 1968), the latest and best account of its subject; John Garry Clifford's forthcoming book on the civilian training camps and American military preparedness; Ross Gregory's forthcoming volume, to be published by the University of Kentucky Press, on the ambassadorship of Walter Hines Page; and the same author's "A New Look at the Case of the *Dacia*," *Journal of American History*, LX (1968), 292–296, concerning an American vessel captured by the Allies prior to entrance of the United States into the war.

Woodrow Wilson, the man and statesman, has continued to excite controversy. Wilson's career, marked by large successes and by final defeat, also has fascinated academic biographers, who like to recall that Wilson was the only college professor of history to become president. The best introduction to Wilson books is Richard L. Watson, Jr., "Woodrow Wilson and His Interpreters," *Mississippi Valley Historical Review*, XLIV (1957–1958), 207–236. Robert H. Ferrell, "Woodrow Wilson: Man and Statesman," *Review of Politics*, XVIII (1956), 131–145 contains an appraisal of Wilson not elaborated in this text. Biographically a fine study of Wilson is being done by Arthur S. Link, *Wilson* (Princeton, 1947–   ), of which five volumes have appeared, a masterful portrayal of Wilson and his times; the first volume, *Wilson: The Road to the White House*, is available in paperback. Arthur Walworth, *Woodrow Wilson* (2d ed., two vols. in one, Boston, 1965), is the best finished biography. See also the short biography by John A. Garraty, *Woodrow Wilson* (New York, 1956), a beautifully written essay. An early biography, still attractive, is William Allen White's *Woodrow Wilson* (Boston, 1924).

The centennial in 1956 of Wilson's birth inspired several notable books about Wilson, among them John Wells Davidson, *A Crossroads of Freedom: The 1912 Campaign Speeches* (New Haven, 1956); Em Bowles Alsop, ed., *The Greatness of Woodrow Wilson* (New York, 1956), a series of essays by authorities; Edward H. Buehrig, ed., *Wilson's Foreign Policy in Perspective* (Bloomington, 1957), a splendid set of five essays; Arthur P. Dudden, ed., *Woodrow Wilson and the World of Today* (Philadelphia, 1957), essays by Link, Eric F. Goldman, and William L. Langer; *Arthur S. Link, *Wilson the Diplomatist: A Look at His Major Foreign Policies* (Baltimore, 1957), Wilson and his times; and Alexander L. and Juliette L. George, *Woodrow Wilson and Colonel House: A Personality Study* (New York, 1956), a psychological analysis.

Other volumes are *Herbert Hoover's memoir, *The Ordeal of Woodrow Wilson* (New York, 1958). A curiosity, written in the latter 1930's and published many years later, is Sigmund Freud and William C. Bullitt, *Thomas Woodrow Wilson* (Boston, 1967); this book draws a fancy interpretation of Wilson's childhood, now refuted by discovery of a large group of papers relating to that era in Wilson's life which Arthur Link has published in the first volume of *The Papers of Woodrow Wilson*, for the years 1856–1880 (Princeton, 1966). See also Kurt Wimer's spendid articles on Wilson, perhaps a dozen all told, published in a variety of journals, which deserve collection in a book. Also *Gene Smith, *When the Cheering Stopped* (New York, 1964).

Volumes on the peace conference and the Senate's defeat of the Treaty of Versailles could fill libraries, and one can only list a few of the obvious titles. First in the order of events would come Harry R. Rudin's excellent *Armistice: 1918* (New Haven, 1944). A summary of peace-conference literature, up to its date of publication, is Paul Birdsall, *Versailles Twenty Years After* (New York, 1941). Thomas A. Bailey's *Woodrow Wilson and the Lost Peace* (New York, 1944) and *Woodrow Wilson and the Great Betrayal* (New York, 1945), combined in one volume in 1947 under the title *Wilson and the Peacemakers*, is an able synthesis. Stephen Bonsal's *Unfinished Business* (Garden City, N.Y., 1944) and *Suitors and Suppliants* (New York, 1946) sets out Colonel Bonsal's experiences from his diary. Another diary, with comment, is Sir Harold Nicolson, *Peacemaking* (Boston, 1933), an admirable account. John Maynard Keynes's *Economic Consequences of the Peace* (New York, 1920), has the famous characterizations of the Big Three and some acid comments on the peace. A refutation is Étienne Mantoux, *The Carthaginian Peace: Or the Economic Consequences of Mr. Keynes* (New York, 1952), by a gallant young Frenchman, the son of Paul Mantoux (for whom, see below), who died fighting with the forces of the Allies in the very last days of the Second World War. Louis L. Gerson, *Woodrow Wilson and the Rebirth of Poland: 1914–1920* (New Haven, 1953), explores this complex subject. G. Bernard Noble, *Policies and Opinions at Paris: 1919* (New York, 1935) is an important work. Details appear in Hunter Miller, *The Drafting of the Covenant* (2 vols., New York, 1928). See also the notes published by the official interpreter of the Big Four, Paul J. Mantoux, *Les déliberations des Conseil des Quatre (24 mars–28 juin 1919)* (2 vols., Paris, 1955). Recent books on the making of the peace include Laurence W. Martin, *Peace without Victory: Woodrow Wilson and the British Liberals* (New Haven, 1958); Seth P. Tillman, *Anglo-American Relations at the Paris Peace Conference of 1919* (Princeton, 1961); Roland N. Stromberg, *Collective Security and American Foreign Policy: From the League of Nations to Nato* (New York, 1963), a thoughtful book indeed; Lawrence E. Gelfand, *The Inquiry: American Preparations for Peace, 1917–1919* (New Haven, 1963), itself a masterly inquiry; Harold B. Whiteman, Jr., ed., Charles Seymour, *Letters from the Paris Peace Conference* (New Haven, 1965), a nostalgic memoir of letters by the young Seymour to his wife.

On the fate of the Treaty of Versailles in the United States, see Dexter Perkins, "Woodrow Wilson's Tour," in Daniel Aaron, ed., *America in Crisis* (New York, 1952); W. Stull Holt, *Treaties Defeated by the Senate* (Baltimore, 1933), chapter ten; Henry Cabot Lodge, *The Senate and the League of Nations* (New York, 1925), a long apology, buttressed by appendixes and extensive quotations, with personal comment on Wilson; *Selig Adler, *The Isolationist*

Impulse (New York, 1957); Ruhl J. Bartlett, *The League to Enforce Peace* (Chapel Hill, N.C., 1944), concerning the principal private American organization for a league of nations; F. P. Walters, *A History of the League of Nations* (2 vols., London, 1952); J. Chalmers Vinson, *Referendum for Isolation: Defeat of Article Ten of the League of Nations Covenant* (Athens, Ga., 1961); and Ralph A. Stone's forthcoming book on the irreconcilables in the Senate, to be published by the University of Kentucky Press. For the effect of immigrants—those individuals whom Theodore Roosevelt described as hyphenates—see Louis L. Gerson's superb study, *The Hyphenate in Recent American Politics and Diplomacy* (Lawrence, Kan., 1964); and Joseph P. O'Grady, ed., *The Immigrants' Influence on Wilson's Peace Policies* (Lexington, Ky., 1967).

In the perspective of our own time, American relations with Russia have appeared far larger in importance than they did in 1917–1919, and here the student may consult titles on the Siberian intervention set out at the end of chapter sixteen; *Arno Mayer, *Political Origins of the New Diplomacy: 1917–1918* (New Haven, 1959), and the same author's *Peacemaking: Containment and Counterrevolution at Versailles, 1918–1919* (New York, 1967); Christopher Lasch, *The American Liberals and the Russian Revolution* (New York, 1962); John M. Thompson, *Russia, Bolshevism, and the Versailles Peace* (Princeton, 1966); and Beatrice Farnsworth, *William C. Bullitt and the Soviet Union* (Bloomington, Ind., 1967), concerning the young man who engaged in a special mission to Russia during the Paris Peace Conference.

For statesmen and influential people of the time there are such volumes as André Tardieu, *France and America* (Boston, 1927); Allan Nevins, *Henry White* (New York, 1930); Claude G. Bowers, *Beveridge and the Progressive Era* (New York, 1932); Merle E. Curti, "Bryan and World Peace," *Smith College Studies in History*, XVI (1931), Nos. 3–4; *Lawrence W. Levine, *Defender of the Faith: William Jennings Bryan, the Last Decade, 1915–1925* (New York, 1965), the years when the former secretary of state went out into the dark; Paolo Coletta's forthcoming volume on the same subject; Philip C. Jessup, *Elihu Root* (2 vols., New York, 1938); *Richard W. Leopold, *Elihu Root and the Conservative Tradition* (Boston, 1954); John M. Blum, *Joe Tumulty and the Wilson Era* (Boston, 1951), on Wilson's private secretary; Claudius O. Johnson, *Borah of Idaho* (New York, 1936); Marian C. McKenna, *Borah* (Ann Arbor, Mich., 1961), an up-to-date account; Warren F. Kuehl, *Hamilton Holt* (Gainesville, Fla., 1960); John A. Garraty, *Henry Cabot Lodge* (New York, 1953); Henry F. Pringle, *Life and Times of William Howard Taft* (2 vols., New York, 1939); Charles Seymour, ed., *Intimate Papers of Colonel House* (4 vols., Boston, 1926–1928); *John M. Blum, *The Republican Roosevelt* (Cambridge, Mass., 1954). The valedictory of the League fight appears in *Samuel Hopkins Adams, *Incredible Era: The Life and Times of Warren Gamaliel Harding* (Boston, 1939). See also the newly published volume by Francis Russell, *The Shadow of Blooming Grove: Warren G. Harding in His Times* (New York, 1968).

☆ **21** ☆

The Twenties

Humanity is not helpless. This is God's world! We can outlaw this war system just as we outlawed slavery and the saloon.
—Raymond Robins, article in the *Annals of the American Academy*, 1925

1. *The United States and Geneva*

Joseph C. Grew as ambassador to Japan in the 1930's became one of America's most trusted diplomats, but earlier in his life when he was not so well known and was American minister to Switzerland in the 1920's, he had to be extremely careful not to be seen near, and of course not in, the League of Nations buildings at Geneva. Once a correspondent of the Chicago *Tribune* found Grew near the entrance to that den of internationalists, and the minister spent several uncomfortable days until arrival of the Paris papers showed that the meeting had passed unnoticed.

Charles Evans Hughes, President Harding's secretary of state, for a while allowed League of Nations communications to the American government to be received at the state department without acknowledgment.

The United States during the 1920's (and this was true also of most of the 1930's) was in the world but not of it. American foreign policy was devoted to the principle of peace, and the republic did not belong to the chief world organization dedicated to that ideal. As years passed and the heat of battle over the Covenant of the League of Nations subsided, there was an increasing interest in the nonpolitical activities of the Geneva institution. The first American flirtation with the League was over restricting the world-wide opium traffic, and a delegation from the United States, arriving in Geneva in 1924, gradually learned to take part in this cause, although not before it on one occasion temporarily walked out of a committee meeting, "acting on motives of delicacy," that is, fear lest its presence imply American recognition of the League. There followed a careful participation in such other League activities as regulation of the international traffic in arms (1925), a communications and transit conference (1927), a general economic conference (1927), abolition of import and export restrictions (1927), economic statistics (1928), counterfeiting of currency (1929), codification of international law (1930), and buoyage and lighting of coasts (1930). These activities, of course, were nonpolitical, unconnected with the large problems of international affairs.

One of the more notable American activities at Geneva was membership in the preparatory commission for the General Disarmament Conference, to the Geneva meetings of which the United States sent a delegation. The preparatory commission commenced its dreary life in 1926, incident to Germany's joining the League in that same year. The duty of the commission was to draw up a draft treaty on disarmament which the nations would debate in the future conference. The commission's meetings turned into technical controversies against some types of armament and in favor of other presumably less aggressive varieties. During five years of wrangling, a subcommittee alone used 3,750,000 sheets of typescript, enough to permit the commission's Polish or Swedish delegations to walk home on a path made of committee paper. (Speaking of paper, it is perhaps worthwhile observing, parenthetically, that in the year 1967 the United Nations Organization produced 600,000,000 pages of written matter, printed or mimeographed—enough paper, end to end, to stretch 100,000 miles.) Finally in 1930 the preparatory commission produced a draft convention which upon the meeting of the General Disarmament Conference at Geneva in 1932 was promptly scrapped.

But in the annals of United States co-operation with the League, the most important issue was whether the United States should join the World Court. The League's World Court, more properly known as the Permanent Court of International Justice, has often been confused with the Permanent Court of Arbitration established in 1901 after the First Hague Peace Conference. The Hague court was not permanent but comprised only a panel of international jurors from which disputing nations might draw for arbitration of controversies. The World Court consisted of a group of judges who sat during court sessions at The Hague and passed upon cases brought before them. Any state, whether a member of the League or not, could belong to the World Court by subscribing to its protocol. There was little danger to national sovereignty in joining because the jurisdiction of the court was always optional.

The idea of a world-wide international law presided over by a court has always found favor among legal-minded American diplomats, as well as among many private American citizens interested in world peace. President Harding made the first gesture toward American adherence to the World Court protocol when he commended it to the Senate in February 1923. Three years later, on January 27, 1926, the Senate approved, 76 to 17, but with five reservations of which the last was the most important: ". . . nor shall it [the Court], without the consent of the United States, entertain any request for an advisory opinion touching any dispute or question in which the United States has or claims an interest." This was a singularly foolish reservation, but it arose out of the Senate's concern about approaching the untouchable League of Nations. Why an American judge on the World Court could not have given a little advice to the League, once in a while, was difficult to understand. Of course a large political question might by some odd chance come before the court— and did, in fact, when the question of *Anschluss*, in the form of joining Austria to Germany in a customs union, was taken to the court in 1931. But if the United States had ventured an opinion in this matter, would it have made any difference in the broad course of European and world history?

The Senate in 1926 believed that for an American judge to give an advisory opinion would make a large difference. The court question continued wearily on. The elder statesman Elihu Root, who had taken part in 1920 in drawing up the World Court protocol, tried to draw up a compromise between the Senate and the forty-eight nations who were members of the court, and at the age of 84 he made a trip to Geneva in 1929 to revise the protocol. President Herbert Hoover in 1930—without much enthusiasm but, so one observer reported, to enable "old Elihu Root to die happy"—resubmitted the court proposal to the Senate with the Root compromise. There the matter languished until 1935, when Hoover was gone, Franklin Roosevelt was president, and the Senate was roused to action. But an eleventh-hour campaign of opposition led by William Randolph Hearst and the Detroit "radio priest," Father Charles E. Coughlin, deluged Washington with tens of thousands of protesting telegrams, and on January 29, 1935, the court failed to receive a two-thirds vote, 52 in favor, 36 opposed. A shift of seven votes would have saved the day.

The court issue had engendered a long debate during the fifteen years it was before the Senate, and in retrospect one must lament the energy expended on so minor a cause. Some individuals, such as Elihu Root, devoted almost all their time to the court; yet the issue was never as important as that. The American ideal of an international court could never in the 1920's and 1930's have been realized fully, given the weakness of international law. Perhaps the World Court approach to international order was logically right and thus should have had more hearing than it received. There is much to say for so rational an approach to foreign relations, and it may be a mistake to write it off completely as a waste of time. Still, in terms of the customs and habits of nations in the 1920's, the World Court was not a practical measure for bringing about world peace, and an effective court may well prove to be nothing but a noble dream in the power-dominated twentieth century. After establishment of the United Nations a second World Court appeared, this time known as the International Court of Justice instead of the Permanent Court of International Justice. All members of the United Nations are members of the new world court, which is entitled to give advisory opinions on legal questions to the General Assembly and Security Council. Little has been heard yet from the court or its activities.

One should not conclude this account of American co-operation with the League without mentioning the so-called war debts, a discordant factor in post-1918 United States relations with Europe. Though not directly connected with the League, the question served to raise a wall of antagonism between the United States and its debtor nations, which were virtually all League members.

During the war the Allies had stretched to the utmost their private credit in the United States; when in 1917 the limit of this was in sight, they turned to the American government, which freely lent money raised by the liberty- and victory-loan drives. Some $7,000,000,000 was advanced to the European powers in this way, and approximately $3,000,000,000 more was included in loans after the end of hostilities. After the war, the debtors halted their interest payments on these public loans pending readjustment downward of the interest rate, originally five per cent. Congress in 1922 created the World War Foreign Debt Commission, which between 1923 and 1930 renegotiated the debts to an average interest rate of 2.135 per cent and made the obligations payable over sixty-two years. The principal plus interest over that period would have totaled more than $22,000,000,000. Terms extended to the debtors varied somewhat according to ability to pay; the British government in 1923 was allowed a reduction of interest to 3.3 per cent, whereas France (1926) received a new rate of 1.6 per cent and Italy (1925) 0.4 per cent.

It was comparatively easy to speak of debts and interest rates, and everything appeared to be settled by the mid-1920's, but the American government gradually discovered that signature of renegotiated notes by the debtor nations did not mean intention to pay. Part of the difficulty of payment consisted in problems of exchange. To obtain dollar exchange it was necessary for debtor countries to sell goods or services directly or indirectly to the United States, and the alternative was to send gold shipments. The latter interfered with the "cover" for domestic currencies. As for the former course, it was impossible to send large supplies of goods over the American tariff, raised in 1922 and again in 1930. Postwar subsidies to American steamship companies deprived the European nations of one of their traditional ways of obtaining dollars. The nations might have paid the debts somehow if they really had wished to do so. They did not, and as is frequently the case, they united against their creditor. The French set the tone of this rebellion by rechristening Uncle Sam "*l'Oncle Shylock*," and Parisian editors instructed their cartoonists to change the stars on Sam's hat to dollar signs. There followed a series of diplomatic maneuvers by the debtors. The first move, taken before American renegotiation of the debts, linked debt payment to the payment of German reparations under the Treaty of Versailles.

According to article 231 of that treaty, Germany was responsible for beginning the war, and article 232 specified that Germany would have to pay the costs arising out of war damages, including both physical damages and pensions to Allied veterans. The German government in 1919 had no choice but to accept the Allied view of reparations. But collection from Germany soon began to grow difficult, partly because of the drastic postwar currency inflation which reached its peak in 1923 when the value of the German mark sank to $\frac{1}{4,000,000,000,000}$ of a dollar. The Germans made no effort to stop the inflation. They did not wish to pay reparations, were almost eager to appear as bankrupts. The French government, itself in financial difficulties, nonetheless hopefully maintained that *le Boche payera tout*, the Germans would pay for everything, including French obligations to the United States. The British government accepted the French idea of linking debts and reparations, and Foreign Secretary Balfour in a note of August 1, 1922, announced this formally as Britain's policy. "In no circumstances," he said, "do we propose to ask more from our debtors than is necessary to pay our creditors . . . ." He was stating a consensus not only of London and Paris but of all America's debtors. It was to no avail that American presidents from Wilson to Hoover refused to connect debts with reparations, for the linkage had already been accomplished by the statesmen of Europe.

During the 1920's the flimsy structure of international payments to debtors and creditors preserved an appearance of stability. As holes appeared they were filled—by the Dawes Plan of 1924, which put German reparations on a plan of payment, and by the Young Plan of 1929, which reduced the original estimate of reparations, set in 1921 at about $33,000,000,000 plus interest, to $9,000,000,000 plus interest, the latter sum payable over fifty-nine years—to the year 1988—at an interest rate of 5½ per cent (the total reparations bill under the Young Plan, including principal and interest, would have been about $26,000,000,000). Although the United States had no official part in these two plans, they bore the names of

American financiers serving privately, Charles G. Dawes and Owen D. Young. It was curious that the number of annual installments for reparations under the Young Plan approximated the then remaining number of European debt installments to the United States as determined by the renegotiations of the Foreign Debt Commission. And there was more coincidence in the provisions for payment of debts and reparations than simply the similarity in the number of annual installments. As mentioned, the principal and interest in each case was about the same—the sum of debts plus interest owed the United States after renegotiation of the interest rate amounted to more than $22,000,000,000, whereas the sum of reparations plus interest owed by Germany to the Allies amounted to about $26,000,000,000 as fixed in the Young Plan. The annuities under the Young Plan were of two sorts, unconditional and conditional, the latter depending upon German prosperity; the unconditional annuities for the year 1931 amounted to $153,000,000, and the conditional annuities for the same year were set at $257,000,000 (total, conditional and unconditional, of $410,000,000); the conditional annuities approximated the total of war debt schedules established by the United States with its debtors in the 1920's—debt payments for 1931 totaled $241,000,000.

The whole arrangement for debts and reparations finally broke under the weight of the Great Depression in the years after 1929. The United States in June–July 1931, under the leadership of President Hoover, negotiated a moratorium on both reparations and war debts. The purpose was to save American private loans in Germany, which would have become uncollectible had reparations payments continued. The American banking structure was so weakened by the depression that for the bankers to lose their German collateral would have invited wholesale bank closures. Hoover in his moratorium was forced to acknowledge tacitly the connection between reparations and war debts, because the European nations would not consider temporarily giving up reparations unless the United States postponed debt payments. Unfortunately, despite the moratorium of mid-1931, American credits in Germany were frozen solid by the end of the summer, and American investors lost the large amounts of money which they had pumped into Germany after 1924, several billions. This money had far more than enabled Germany to make annual reparations payments (part of which, of course, went circuitously to the United States as war debt installments). It is true that had American money not gone to Germany it would have passed into the New York stock market and been lost there, but American funds in the 1920's in Germany financed the re-equipment of large segments of German heavy industry, which a decade later as armament industries were turned against their benefactors by Hitler. Much American blood and treasure had to be expended during the Second World War on the destruction of these industrial complexes. In the post-1945 period the United States has helped rebuild them once more.

When the American government by 1931 had come around to the European interpretation of debts and reparations—that they were inseparable—Germany declared itself unable to continue reparations. The European Allies, as we have seen, refused to agree to a moratorium on reparations unless the United States agreed to postpone payment of the war debts. Shortly thereafter the Allies in effect canceled reparations at Lausanne in June 1932 when they lowered the reparations bill to $750,-000,000. This arrangement depended upon a renegotiation of the war debts by the United States, but the damage had been done. The Germans would pay no more; neither would the Allies. When for the first time after expiration of the Hoover Moratorium the semiannual debt installments fell due on December 15, 1932, Britain paid, as did Italy, Czechoslovakia, Finland, Latvia, and Lithuania. The rest of the nations defaulted or made useless gestures such as depositing part payments in blocked accounts. Finland was the only European country after 1933 which attempted to continue paying its debt.

In anger, Congress in 1934 passed the Johnson Debt Default Act, which prohibited defaulting governments from floating loans in this country. The neutrality laws of 1935-1939—about which more later—reiterated this prohibition of government loans to debtors. The Lend-Lease Act of 1941, however, allowed the president in a latitudinarian way to "lend, lease, or otherwise dispose of" government properties, and the neutrality laws were amended in 1942 so as not to apply when the United States was at war.

In surveying the sad history of the war debts, one must conclude that when a loan is likely to be considered a gift, statesmen should accept the inevitable and make a virtue of necessity. This was the course followed in the Second World War, but during the first war there was no precedent for such largesse, and time-honored custom dictated that nations should pay and not repudiate their debts. Under this then-prevailing practice the United States asked for payment, and no other single postwar international policy pursued by the state department met with such cordial approbation from American taxpayers. President Coolidge allegedly remarked of the European debtors that "They hired the money, didn't they?" To his generation he seemed uncommonly sensible. His countrymen failed to comprehend the manner in which the war debts estranged them from their friends in Europe, who were already distrustful because of the American attitude toward the League of Nations. Any advantages accruing from the minor nonpolitical co-operation of the United States with the League were wiped out by the bad feeling engendered over the war debt and reparations issues. The bond of sentiment between the United States and the democratic nations of Western Europe, a bond which in 1917–1918 had been so strong, was stretched in the postwar years almost to the breaking point. With the coming of a Second World War the strained friendship of Americans and Europeans would require extraordinarily careful attention.

2. *Alternatives to the League—treaties of peaceful settlement*

The United States during the 1920's, outside the League of Nations, felt that it had to do something for world peace. The department of state tried to discover alternatives to the League which would be acceptable to the American people, and from this search came two general lines of procedure in American diplomacy—treaties for avoidance of war, and treaties of disarmament. These alternatives to the League were compatible with the American tradition of isolation and neutrality in international affairs. Insofar as they were not an adequate international program in the 1920's, they indicated that the traditional principles, isolation and neutrality, were inadequate. But treaties for avoidance of war and treaties of disarmament were the American prescription for world peace in the 1920's. They were even announced as cure-alls, and in the early 1930's Secretary of State Cordell Hull supplemented them with his ideas of economic disarmament by lowering tariff barriers through reciprocal trade agreements. Such alternatives to the League of Nations, it is not unfair to add, had slight effect in promoting world peace.

What kind of treaties for the avoidance of war concerned the United States government after the refusal in 1919–1920 to adhere to the League of Nations? During the 1920's there flourished interest in a program of bilateral arbitration and conciliation treaties, and Secretary of State Frank B. Kellogg made some considerable effort to satisfy the popular demand for these pacts. He discarded in 1927 the arbitration formula used at the state department nineteen years earlier by Elihu Root—a formula excepting from arbitration questions affecting the United States's vital interests, independence, or national honor, or disputes involving third parties—in favor of a formula reserving from arbitration only cases involving domestic questions. This was a dubious improvement, for a reservation of domestic jurisdiction was large enough to permit evading almost any arbitration. Even so, the Kellogg arbitration treaties sounded, at least, as if they were broader than the Root treaties.

Kellogg in 1928 likewise undertook to revise and extend the United States's network of conciliation treaties as established before the First World War by Secretary William Jennings Bryan. When Bryan had concluded the treaties in 1913–1915, he had appointed the commissioners under the terms of each treaty, but with lapse of time the personnel in many cases died and nothing was done about new appointments. Kellogg filled out the commissions again.

Altogether, Kellogg and his successors concluded twenty-seven arbitration treaties on the Kellogg model. Six of the old Root treaties remained in force. Eventually, with additional negotiations by Kellogg and others, there was a total of forty-three Bryan treaties. The grand total of instruments thus reached seventy-six!

These moves had little effect upon the course of American diplomacy. No nation has ever resorted to the provisions of the Bryan conciliation treaties. Nor is there a single recorded instance of the employment in an international controversy of the Root or Kellogg arbitration treaties. Some Americans interested in the obvious merits of arbitration and conciliation have comforted themselves that the existence of the innumerable Bryan, Root, and Kellogg treaties has served somehow to allay international tensions.

Arbitration has faded away in international affairs, and little is heard about it in the latter twentieth century. It has no attraction to present-day statesmen or to popular opinion. At the turn of the century American public opinion regarded arbitration highly. Theodore Roosevelt could say of the Root treaties that he "went into them because the general feeling of the country demanded it." Perhaps people in our own time have come to realize that the nineteenth century was the most renowned legal century of modern history, a moment when it seemed as if world order might be brought into reality, when rules for peaceful intercourse among nations appeared not as dreams but possibilities. Perhaps Americans today know that after the turn of the twentieth century, with its great power conflicts, its two world wars and threat of a third, arbitration has receded into the realm of dreams, along with so many other noble projects such as binding international law and a truly powerful world court. Arbitration had passed out of the area of practicality at the turn of the century, some years before Elihu Root took it up. The idea was passé indeed by the time of the secretaryship of Frank B. Kellogg in the 1920's.

But it was not through bilateral treaties of arbitration or conciliation that the United States made its most significant effort for pacific settlement of international disputes after the World War, for this effort came at Paris in 1928 when Secretary Kellogg, together with representatives of the great powers, signed a treaty for renunciation of all war and for settle-

Kellogg signs the Pact of Paris.

ment of all disputes by peaceful means. Nearly every nation in the world eventually signed the Kellogg-Briand Pact, except a few such holdouts as Argentina, Bolivia, El Salvador, and Uruguay, together with five uninvited little countries—Andorra, Monaco, Morocco, Liechtenstein, and San Marino.

A dull topic for discussion, the Kellogg Pact: so it might seem if superficially considered. Actually it marked some of the shrewdest diplomacy one can discover in international relations in the twentieth century. Its roots went back to the First World War and France's position as a result of that war, when after the armistice of 1918 the French had what might be described as acute feelings of insecurity. France had triumphed over Germany during the war only by alliance with Britain, Russia, and the United States, and Frenchmen not without reason were worried about the future of their country, with a small birth rate and a population of about forty million as opposed to Germany's sixty-odd million and rapidly increasing population. France after 1918 suffered from "pactomania," a

Aristide Briand.

desire to sign promises with anyone in or out of Europe to protect *la patrie* on some untoward day when Germany might seek revenge for the First World War. In the quest for security the French foreign minister of the later 1920's, Aristide Briand, one of the cleverest diplomats of the past half century, offered to Secretary of State Kellogg a pact between France and the United States pledging both countries never to go to war against each other.

This offer by Briand was intensely embarrassing to Secretary Kellogg, who at first sought to stall it. Briand made the proposal of an antiwar treaty in 1927 because he was attempting to drag the United States into his security system in Europe. The proposal of perpetual peace between the United States and France was in truth a negative military alliance. If America were to sign such a promise, it meant that regardless of how hard the French pushed the United States in violation of neutral rights (as the

British had done in 1914–1917), in any future war when France was, say, fighting Germany, the Americans could not side in reprisal against France, for the antiwar treaty would prevent it. Kellogg, of course, wanted nothing to do with such a proposition.

The American secretary of state was furious with Briand. And not the least part of Kellogg's ill humor came because he discovered that the foreign minister had marshaled in support of this antiwar proposition the many American private organizations for world peace which had sprung up before and especially after the war. Many important private American citizens, who knew how to put pressure on the government in Washington, began to demand of Kellogg that he sign with France. Women's organizations, led by such personalities as Miss Jane Addams and Mrs. Carrie Chapman Catt, made Kellogg's life miserable with their visitations and expostulations. The secretary, who was known privately to possess a Ph.D. in profanity and invectives, swore at the "god-damned pacifists," but to no avail. He made it known through intermediaries that he wanted the peace organizations to leave him in peace. Finally he discovered a way to outwit the French foreign minister, and the resulting treaty became the Kellogg-Briand Pact, America's greatest contribution to peace in the interwar years.

There is a well-known and justly admired axiom of diplomacy to the effect that the more signatories to an agreement the less binding it becomes, and Kellogg invoked this hoary truism against his antagonist in December 1927, proposing to Briand a multinational treaty renouncing war. There was enormous glee in the state department. Kellogg's able assistant secretary of state, William R. Castle, who had been behind the widening of the original French proposal, wrote privately in his diary that the trick had been turned, that Briand was now out on a limb, that the foreign minister was caught with cold feet which were going to be positively frozen when the state department drove him out into the open. As for Briand, the foreign minister after Kellogg's counterproposal made one maneuver after another to drop the whole business of an antiwar pact. Every time he suggested that a committee of jurists or a conference of foreign ministers examine Kellogg's counterproposal, the secretary of state refused to be taken in, and Briand became ever more embarrassed as his American opponent invited other states to adhere to the antiwar pact. It was getting, indeed, to be a public humiliation of the foreign minister of France. It was all that Briand could do to stand up against the perverse zeal of the Americans. Himself a possessor of the Nobel Prize for peace, which he had won earlier in the 1920's for the Treaty of Locarno among France, Britain, Italy, and Germany, he could not resist indefinitely the public pressure, in Europe as well as America, that he take a position for peace.

Finally, Secretary Kellogg became enamored of the new multinational proposal, originally conceived only to counter Briand, and began to believe that such a pledge against war by the nations of the world would help prevent future wars. After he placed within the proposed antiwar treaty enough reservations of self-defense and other matters to make the pact agreeable to prospective signatories, Kellogg was able to persuade the French foreign minister to bring the powers together in Paris for a ceremony of signature, which was done by the great powers—other nations acceding thereafter—on August 27, 1928.

The treaty contained two substantive articles: first, "The High Contracting Parties solemnly declare in the names of their respective peoples that they condemn recourse to war for the solution of international controversies, and renounce it as an instrument of national policy in their relations with one another"; second, "The High Contracting Parties agree that the settlement or solution of all disputes or conflicts of whatever nature or of whatever origin they may be, which may arise among them, shall never be sought except by pacific means."

Statesmen signed the Pact of Paris, as the Kellogg-Briand Pact was alternately called, with tongue in cheek, and the only discernible influence of this grand treaty was to inaugurate a fashion whereby wars would be fought under justification of self-defense and without formal declaration of hostilities. An American senator, during debate over ratification of the treaty, said that it was an international kiss. Senator Carter Glass of Virginia announced to his colleagues that he intended to vote for the pact, "but I am not willing that anybody in Virginia shall think that I am simple enough to suppose that it is worth a postage stamp in the direction of accomplishing permanent peace." But the pact had large popular support and in the United States was politically irresistible. Many people believed that with it they had taken a large step in the direction of peaceful settlement of international disputes. Ever since the Senate and Woodrow Wilson had defeated the Treaty of Versailles, numerous Americans had felt sorry that their country had abandoned the world after the crusade of 1917–1918. To them it seemed that the heart of the world was broken when the United States stayed out of the League. They were willing to believe that a private American measure such as the Kellogg-Briand Pact, if coupled with arbitration and conciliation treaties and co-operation with the League in humanitarian tasks and the World Court, could indirectly redress the loss to the Geneva organization of American abstention from membership. In the year 1928 there was rejoicing that the United States, once more, had put its weight in the scales for righteousness. Few Americans understood the politique that lay behind the Kellogg-Briand Pact. If they had they would have been sorely disappointed.

3. *Another alternative to the League—disarmament*

The Kellogg-Briand Pact and the bilateral arbitration and conciliation treaties were the American substitutes for the League. In addition the state department relied on treaties of disarmament, or as the term came to mean, limitation of armament. The idea flourished after the First World War that large armaments had caused the war, and that if the nations of the world would limit their weapons, peace would follow. Disarmament gained support not merely from the American people but from their political leaders, most of whom after 1918 were sincerely anxious for the United States to set Europe an example of arms limitation. The United States's influence for disarmament lay chiefly, one should add, in naval arms, for the American postwar military establishment was weak in land armaments.

The immediate problem in naval disarmament at the end of the First World War was that of the three major naval powers, Great Britain, the United States, and Japan; the latter two were threatening a naval race. This postwar rivalry presented serious questions for all three powers, but especially for the Japanese. Japan, despite a strengthening of its economic position during the war, could not continue a naval competition over an indefinite period of time, for by 1921 one-third of the Japanese budget was going into naval construction and maintenance. Moreover, other factors did not favor Japan. To be sure, Japan during the World War had destroyed the balance of power in the Far East, but with the armistice of 1918 the balance in Europe had also been destroyed, to the disadvantage of Japan. France and Great Britain could redistribute their sea power to distant parts of the world and were better able to defend their territories and interests in the Far East than at any time since the rise of the German navy at the turn of the century. At the end of the war, the main American battle fleet was transferred to the Pacific, the base at Pearl Harbor was developed, and there was talk of bases in the Philippines and Guam to match Britain's base at Singapore. Should Britain and the United States achieve between themselves an entente, a working relationship of their navies, there was danger of Japanese isolation. For Japan, a conference on limitation of naval arms had its attractions. It was shrewd diplomacy for Japan to begin a retreat before compulsion changed it into a rout.

For the Americans and British it was equally obvious that a naval conference might be convenient. Although there was a considerable rivalry between the high commands of the American and British navies—a feeling on each side that the other navy was too large—and although there was talk at the end of the World War of an Anglo-American naval race, still neither Congress nor Parliament would have voted appropriations for such a contest. The British government was hard-pressed for money after the World War and could never have survived an expensive arms race with the United States. As for the American navy, it had emerged from the war almost as large as the British, and the high command of the American navy was all set to resume the postponed building stipulated in the naval act of 1916, but Congress by 1921 was in a balky mood and let it be known that no money for such a purpose would be forthcoming. Co-operation, not antagonism, was the obvious course for the two English-speaking nations. It was common sense that the British and American navies undertake a mutual limitation in a diplomatic conference. And by co-operating in naval policies, the two powers would be able to present a unified front to the Japanese.

In the United States, before the end of Wilson's second administration, Senator Borah was trumpeting for a conference. The Harding administration, wishing to head off the British, who were about to propose a meeting, offered on July 11, 1921, to organize a conference in Washington. The intention was to deal with both sea and land armaments, but the conference after coming together devoted itself to naval arms.

Representatives of nine invited nations met in Washington on November 11, 1921, to observe formally the third anniversary of the armistice. The following day they held their first plenary session. In addition to delegations from the United States, Britain, and Japan there were representatives of the lesser naval powers, France and Italy, and because it was impossible to deal with Japanese armaments without considering problems of the Far East, China obtained an invitation to the meeting, as did also Portugal (because of Macao), the Netherlands (the East Indies), and Belgium (interests in Chinese railways, and a concession at Tientsin). President Harding gave a stirring address, and then came the surprise of the occasion: the permanent chairman of the conference, Secretary of State Hughes, in what seemed an ordinary speech of greeting, declared suddenly that "the way to disarm is to disarm." In regard to the possibility of an armaments race Hughes said, "There is only one adequate way out and that is to end it now." He thereupon offered some devastatingly concrete suggestions.

Consternation reigned in the hall. According to the journalist Mark Sullivan, when the secretary made his enumeration of British ships to be sunk, Admiral Sir David Beatty "came forward in his chair with the manner of a bulldog, sleeping on a sunny doorstep, who has been poked in the stomach by the impudent foot of an itinerant soap-canvasser seriously lacking in any sense of the most ordinary proprieties or considerations of personal safety." All the official documents in the world, Sullivan later wrote, "can't convey as much essential fact to the distant and future reader as did the look on Lord Beatty's face to the historian who had the advantage of being in the room when Mr. Hughes, in that sensational opening speech of his, said that he would expect the British to scrap their four great *Hoods*, and made equally irreverent mention of the *King George the Fifth*."

During the following days some American naval officers went about saying, half humorously, in a paraphrase of an old Latin *morituri salutamus*, "We who are about to be abolished, salute you."

Hughes's proposals for limitation of naval armaments, considered revolutionary at the time, were in actual fact rough approximations of then existing naval strengths, although (as he made so plain in his speech) it would be necessary for the powers to scuttle some craft to achieve his proposed figures. What he had proposed amounted in tonnage to what a newspaperman happily described as a scale of 5-5-3-1.67-1.67. After adjustment to be completed in the year 1942, Britain and the United States would have parity at 5 (a battleship tonnage of 525,000, aircraft carriers 135,000), Japan a ratio of 3 (battleships 272,000; carriers 81,000), and Italy and France 1.67 (175,000; 60,000). Although for the three largest naval powers these figures were based roughly on existing naval strength, ships built and building, for France and Italy the ratio was an arbitrary figure. Neither of the latter nations had embarked upon a postwar battleship program, but it was essential to assign them a ratio because Britain was insisting upon a two-power standard against continental navies—the British fleet must equal the combined strength of the two largest continental navies—and would have refused otherwise to accept a ratio with Japan and the United States.

After the initial confusion and protests, the major conferees accepted these figures. French pique at a ratio equal only to Italy's made it impossible for Hughes to extend limitation beyond the categories of battleships and aircraft carriers (the latter were limited because the powers might otherwise have converted their excess battleships into carriers).

Limitation of armaments was the major but not the sole task of the Washington Conference, for in the work of persuading the Japanese to accept a battleship and carrier ratio inferior to Britain's and the United States's, the conference made several political arrangements in the Far East. Japan consented to refrain from further fortification and construction of naval bases in some of the island groups—the Kuriles, Bonins, Ryukyus, Pescadores, also Formosa and Amami-Oshima—and in return Britain and America agreed not to construct additional fortifications or bases in their possessions east and north of Singapore and west of Hawaii. The result was to expose Hong Kong and the Philippines in event of future war. One must add, however, that Japan's possession of the Marianas, Marshalls, and Carolines, taken from Germany during the World War, virtually precluded a successful defense of the Philippines, and Secretary Hughes at the Washington Conference was giving away only what had already been lost. Hong Kong, of course, was from the beginning indefensible. The agreement was binding until December 31, 1936, subject thereafter to termination upon two years' notice. It was believed that the Japanese, so long as they had an inferior naval ratio, could safely be allowed mastery of the far Pacific, and the peaceful behavior of Tokyo governments for the remainder of the 1920's seemed to confirm the wisdom of this decision. The Washington Conference in effect partitioned the world among the three naval powers: Japan dominated the Far Eastern seas, the United States the Western Hemisphere, and Britain from the North Sea eastward to Singapore. The naval treaty as concluded on February 6, 1922, became known as the Five-Power Treaty.

A Four-Power Treaty signed on December 13, 1921, had as its purpose the abrogation of the Anglo-Japanese Alliance of 1902, which had been periodically renewed until 1921. In the renewal of 1911 the Japanese government had suggested that the treaty be inapplicable against any nation with which either ally had a general treaty of arbitration. When the Senate loaded down with reservations the Anglo-American arbitration treaty negotiated in the administration of President Taft, the British government had a private understanding with the Japanese that under no circumstances could the alliance be invoked against the United States. After the World War, and in view of the possibility of a Japanese-American naval race, the British in 1920 announced publicly that the Anglo-Japanese Alliance would not apply in event of hostilities, but Prime Minister Arthur Meighen of Canada became worried and at an imperial conference in the summer of 1921 demanded—against opposition of his colleagues from Australia and New Zealand, who feared an ostracized, vengeful Japan—that the mother country abrogate the Japanese Alliance. The Four-Power Treaty proved the vehicle for this task.

Ostensibly the treaty extended responsibility for keeping peace in the Far East to the United States and France, in addition to Japan and Britain, but the pact contained only (1) a pledge to respect each other's "rights in relation to their insular possessions and insular dominions in the region of the Pacific Ocean"; (2) a promise that in any controversy (excluding matters of domestic jurisdiction) between the signatories pertaining to the Pacific Ocean, not settled by diplomacy, the disputants would invite the other members to a conference; (3) an agreement for consultation in event a nonsignatory should threaten the rights of the parties; (4) specific abrogation of the Anglo-Japanese Alliance. Shortly after the Washington Conference, Elihu Root stated the effect of the pact when he declared, "I doubt if any formal treaty ever accomplished so much by doing so little."

The United States during the conference was able to obtain a Nine-Power Treaty, a pledge by all the conferees at Washington to respect the principle of the open door in the Far East and to refrain from using the unsettled situation in China to advance their special interests at the expense of nationals of other countries. The former promise, reaffirming the open door, strengthened the individual pledges given to Secretary of State Hay in 1899. The promise to refrain from exploiting the unsettled situation in China restated the second open door note of 1900. This latter promise had been a secret protocol to the Lansing-Ishii Agreement of 1917, and its inclusion in the Nine-Power Treaty was followed a year later on April 14, 1923, by cancellation of the 1917 agreement.

There were three other Far Eastern arrangements at Washington. The attention which the Senate had given to Shantung during the debate over the Versailles Treaty indicated that this question would have to be solved before any treaty for naval limitation could be ratified, and the Japanese delegates at Washington in separate negotiation with representatives of China, with Secretary Hughes and Lord Balfour serving as impartial observers, agreed upon evacution of troops from the Shantung peninsula and return of Chinese sovereignty and customs control, subject to retention by Japan of important economic concessions. The second arrangement by Japan at Washington had to do with the Pacific island of Yap, where cable rights were granted the United States. Thirdly, the Japanese promised an early end to their occupancy of parts of Russian Siberia and the northern half of the island of Sakhalin. Siberia was evacuated in 1922, northern Sakhalin in 1925.

Japan thus was the principal loser at Washington. This humiliation, preceded by refusal of the Paris Peace Conference to grant the principle of racial equality, followed in 1924 by the United States's complete barring of Japanese immigration, badly hurt Japanese pride, serving to create a situation where not too many years later the Japanese would use mercilessly a deteriorating political situation in Europe to expand their power in Asia.

To the American people the Washington Conference of 1921–1922 appeared only as a triumph for peace. The Senate approved the naval treaty with a single dissenting vote—President Harding had profited from one of Wilson's most egregious errors at the Paris conference and appointed to the American delegation to the Washington Conference two senators, including Henry Cabot Lodge. There had been fear before the conference that the United States by engaging in a naval race would be acting the role of a militarist nation, not unlike imperial Germany under the kaiser and Admiral von Tirpitz. Instead the American government reaffirmed one of the doctrines of Mahan, that Anglo-American co-operation was the foundation of world order, and that policies antagonistic to Britain were the height of folly. It is noteworthy that the United States was willing to limit its naval armaments without attempting to solve the many questions of neutral rights which had so recently embroiled relations between Washington and London. The decisions of the Washington Conference much impressed the peoples of Britain and the United States, creating the somewhat questionable faith that great powers could confer successfully over their vital interests—that the conference method was one of the best ways of diplomacy. Moreover, many Americans came to believe that their country could most effectively make its contribution toward world peace by actions taken outside the League. The Republican Party announced modestly in its platform of 1924 that the Washington Treaty was "the greatest peace document ever drawn." Probably the conference was a success when one considers that battleships had a reduced part in the Second World War. A limit on their construction did not detract from the safety of the Allied nations.

The Washington Conference was not, of course, the end of naval rivalry among the great powers. A naval race developed after 1922 in the smaller categories of warships. From this cruiser race between Britain and Japan the United States abstained for several years, and early in 1927, President Coolidge called a new disarmament conference to discuss the competition. At a meeting which began in Geneva on June 20, 1927, and ended on August 4, there were representatives of Britain, the United States, and Japan. France and Italy did not attend, the French from pique because of the parity granted between them and Italy at the Washington Conference, the Italians because the French would not attend. The Geneva Conference of 1927 was a fiasco, for neither the British nor the Japanese were willing at that time to halt their cruiser race. The efforts of the Coolidge administration were embarrassing, for diplomatic rumors were set on foot in European capitals that President Coolidge had made "insufficient preparation" for the conference, which was equal to saying that Coolidge was an ignoramus in international affairs. In retaliation Congress in early 1929 passed an appropriation for fifteen heavy cruisers (10,-000 tons, 8-inch guns) and an aircraft carrier.

Here was the sort of language which nations understood, and after inauguration of President Herbert Hoover there were explorations by his ambassador to London, Charles G. Dawes, and the new British prime minister, Ramsay MacDonald. Hoover invited MacDonald to visit the United States, the visit in October 1929 proved a success, and the London Naval Conference assembled on January 21, 1930.

The London Conference addressed itself to limitation of naval categories not undertaken at the Washington Conference, and the result of a three-month deliberation was a limit on cruisers, submarines, and destroyers. There were no political questions on the agenda, such as had figured so prominently at Washington. The Japanese delegation nominally accepted a ratio of 3 in the lesser naval categories as compared with 5 for Britain and the United States, but Japan achieved parity for submarines and destroyers and virtual parity, through an involved provision, in heavy cruisers—at least until December 31, 1936, by which time the entire naval question was to be re-examined. The London Treaty was a three-power engagement, although France and Italy signed the document with the other powers on April 22, 1930. The two European nations pledged themselves to negotiate their differences, but after two years they gave up in disagreement.

With the London Conference the question of disarmament virtually ceased to have meaning for European and American diplomacy. Two further conferences were held—the League-sponsored General Disarmament Conference which met on February 2, 1932, at Geneva, and a second London Naval Conference which convened in 1935—but neither achieved any results. Although the conference at Geneva opened with several weeks of enthusiastic speeches, when the fifty-nine nations set to work there was no agreement. The conference enjoyed spurts of activity when various of the great-power delegations proposed limitation schemes. President Hoover on June 22, 1932, suggested an across-the-board reduction of one-third of all arms, but this idea died when seconded by Germany, the disarmed nation. German rearmament under Hitler ended the conference, which in 1934 adjourned "temporarily," never to meet again. As for the second London Conference, commencing in December 1935, it came to grief on the demands of the Japanese delegation for complete parity with Britain and the United States, but in the background was the increasing strength of the German navy. The signatories therefore invoked the so-called "escalator clause" of the London Treaty of 1930, by which signatories were released from their commitments when a nonsignatory threatened their national safety. The grand campaign for peace through disarmament, begun in 1921 with much hope and some minor achievement, disappeared in another naval race which terminated in war in 1939–1941.

Disarmament, the principal American alternative to membership in the League of Nations, hence proved of little value. So also did the other alternatives—the Kellogg, Root, and Bryan treaties, and the Kellogg Pact. The United States did little for the broad problems of world peace by supporting the noncontroversial health and other humanitarian activities of the League.

Even so, it is doubtful if American membership in the League of Nations could have halted the drift toward a Second World War. Most of the European nations were themselves unwilling to enforce peace after the armistice of 1918. France and its friends, especially Czechoslovakia under the inspiration of the Czech statesman Eduard Beneš, would have made of article 10 of the Covenant an ironclad guarantee against aggressors if they could have gained enough support for such a course, but this they were never able to do, because of the stand against enforcement of peace taken by Great Britain and the Dominions and the former neutral nations during the war—the Baltic countries and others.

As for any American initiative and success in the direction of enforcing peace (if the United States had joined the League), such would have been hardly imaginable. By the first anniversary of the armistice, the buoyant enthusiasm of the American people for making peace and justice prevail throughout the world, the enthusiasm which had carried the nation to victory in 1918, had begun to fasten itself to the almost hopeless ideas which dealt with world peace in terms of law rather than force, which offered the possibility of peace everywhere by signature rather than by continuing and ardent labor. Thereafter it was impossible to make Americans realize that a foreign policy had to be backed by military force rather than words. They wished to remain aloof from troubles outside the Western Hemisphere, and convinced themselves that they could do so by formulas.

The American people, one must conclude, had been improperly schooled for their sudden participation in the First World War. Having remained for nearly a century on the fringes of world international affairs—their last passing acquaintance being the overemphasized dangers of European intervention at the time of the Monroe Doctrine—they had forgotten the hard ways of international politics and, during the fighting of 1917–1918, had allowed their idealism such free rein that they were not mentally prepared for the rigors of peacemaking which followed. The disappointments of the Paris Peace Conference combined with the traditionally isolationist beliefs of the American people and helped the defeat of the Covenant and peace treaty in the Senate. From then on American diplomats did their best to assist the cause of peace without exciting the isolationist sentiments of their fellow citizens. It was an impossible task.

The greatest nation in the world could not remain apart from the main international current of the time. Its interests were too scattered geographically and too numerous not to become entangled in those of other nations. The international education of the American people, which had virtually ceased in the 1920's, was further neglected in the dangerous years after 1933, until it began once more with startling suddenness on December 7, 1941.

CONTEMPORARY DOCUMENTS

[Foreign Minister Briand in 1927 proposed a bilateral pact of perpetual peace between France and the United States, and it was from this proposition, together with shrewd advice from assistants in the state department, that Secretary Kellogg formulated what became the Kellogg-Briand Pact. Briand's initial suggestion arrived in the United States via the press cable from Paris, in the form of a newspaper message to the American people on the tenth anniversary of American entrance into the First World War. Source: *Foreign Relations of the United States: 1927* (3 vols., Washington, 1942), II, 611–613.]

The discussions over disarmament . . . have served at least to make clear, politically, the common inspiration and identity of aims which exist between France and the United States. . . . If there were any need between these two great democracies to testify more convincingly in favor of peace and to present to the peoples a more solemn example, France would be ready publicly to subscribe, with the United States, to any mutual engagement tending, as between those two countries, to "outlaw war," to use an American expression. The renunciation of war as an instrument of national policy is a conception already familiar to the signatories of the Covenant of the League of Nations and of the Treaties of Locarno. Any engagement subscribed to in the same spirit by the United States with another nation such as France would greatly contribute in the eyes of the world to broaden and strengthen the foundation upon which the international policy of peace is being raised. Thus two great friendly nations, equally devoted to the cause of peace, would give the world the best illustrations of the truth, that the accomplishment most immediately to be attained is not so much disarmament as the practice of peace.

[Briand submitted to the American government a draft treaty dated June 20, 1927, the very day the unsuccessful naval conference opened at Geneva—a conference France was refusing to attend. Source: *ibid.*, p. 616.]

Article 1. The high contracting powers solemnly declare in the name of the French people and the people of the United States of America that they condemn recourse to war and renounce it, respectively, as an instrument of their national policy towards each other.

Article 2. The settlement or the solution of all disputes or conflicts of whatever nature or of whatever origin they may be which may arise between France and the United States of America shall never be sought by either side except by pacific means.

[J. Theodore Marriner, chief of the division of Western European affairs of the department of state, prepared a memorandum on Briand's proposal, dated June 24, 1927. This memorandum set the course of the department away from the French bilateral proposition, toward what became the great multilateral Pact of Paris of August 1928. Source: *ibid*, pp. 617–618. Marriner was one of the most able members of the department of state in the years after the First World War. He was murdered in Beirut in 1937 by a crazed individual whose application for a visa had been turned down.]

The text of Mr. Briand's proposals for a Treaty . . . should be carefully considered from every point of view.

Mr. Briand's insistence that negotiations should begin at once without awaiting the arrival in this country of M. Claudel [Paul Claudel, the French ambassador] would seem to indicate that he was most anxious to keep this topic in the public eye most prominently during the meeting of the Naval Conference at Geneva in order to draw attention away from the fact that France is not there represented in a constructive step towards World Peace.

The vague wording and lack of precision in the draft seems also intended to give the effect of a kind of perpetual alliance between the United States and France, which would certainly serve to disturb the other great European Powers,—England, Germany and Italy. This would be particularly true as it would make the neutral position of the United States during any European war in which France might be engaged extremely difficult, since France might deem it necessary to infringe upon our rights as a neutral under this guaranty of non-aggression. A further point which Mr. Briand has not touched on is the question of France's obligations under the Covenant of the League of Nations to aid the League in the punishment of an aggressor state. It might likewise be used internally in France to postpone the ratification of the Debt Settlement and to create a feeling that payment was unnecessary.

In order to avoid this interpretation, it would be incumbent on the United States at once to offer a treaty in the same terms to England

and Japan, more especially as we are negotiating with them at the present moment [at the Geneva Naval Conference] and could hardly wish them to feel that we were entering into an alliance at the same time with another Power.

Certainly a single treaty of this nature, and, according to press despatches, France desires that it be an absolutely unique instrument, would raise the question of an alliance with a country outside the American hemisphere. A series of such agreements, unless it were absolutely world wide, would raise the same objections. All this tends to indicate that it would be best to keep the subject in abeyance at least until the conclusion of some agreement in Geneva. However, when the time comes actually to negotiate, it would seem that the only answer to the French proposition would be that, as far as our relations with France were concerned, adequate guarantees were contained in the Bryan Treaty, and that if any step further than this were required, it should be in the form of a universal undertaking not to resort to war, to which the United States would at any time be most happy to become a party. Before such a time, treaties of the nature which France suggests become practically negative military alliances.

ADDITIONAL READING

The best introduction to the diplomacy of the 1920's is L. Ethan Ellis's recently published *Republican Foreign Policy: 1921–1933* (New Brunswick, N.J., 1968). Allan Nevins, *The United States in a Chaotic World: 1918–1933* (New Haven, 1950), a volume in the Chronicles of America series, neatly brings together the leading issues of the time. *Selig Adler, *The Isolationist Impulse* (New York, 1957) sets out the presiding American philosophy toward international affairs. See also the same author's first-rate new book, *The Uncertain Giant: 1921–1941* (New York, 1965), a volume in the American Diplomatic History series. There are pertinent essays in Alexander De Conde, ed., *Isolation and Security* (Durham, N.C., 1957); together with the general accounts in *Jean-Baptiste Duroselle, *From Wilson to Roosevelt* (Cambridge, Mass., 1963); L. Ethan Ellis, *Frank B. Kellogg and American Foreign Relations: 1925–1929* (New Brunswick, N.J., 1961); and Robert H. Ferrell, *Frank B. Kellogg and Henry L. Stimson* (New York, 1962), vol. 11 in The American Secretaries of State and Their Diplomacy series edited by Samuel Flagg Bemis and R. H. Ferrell. For "atmosphere" see *Frederick Lewis Allen, *Only Yesterday* (New York, 1931).

Two books by Denna F. Fleming, *The United States and the League of Nations: 1918–1920* (New York, 1932) and *The United States and World Organization: 1920–1933* (New York, 1938) describe the course of American diplomacy toward the League and its organs. The definitive history of the League, in its technical aspects, is F. P. Walters, *A History of the League of Nations* (2 vols., London, 1952). Elihu Root's efforts on behalf of the World Court may be followed in Philip C. Jessup's *Elihu Root* (2 vols., New York, 1938) and *Richard W. Leopold, *Elihu Root and the Conservative Tradition* (Boston, 1954). For their special subjects see Harold G. Moulton and Leo Pasvolsky, *War Debts and World Prosperity* (New York, 1932) and *Herbert Feis, *The Diplomacy of the Dollar: First Era, 1919–1932* (Baltimore, 1950).

The diplomacy of the Kellogg Pact appears in *Robert H. Ferrell, *Peace in Their Time* (New Haven, 1952); John E. Stoner, *S. O. Levinson and the Pact of Paris* (Chicago, 1943), which deals with the efforts of a Chicago lawyer to rid the world of war; and J. Chalmers Vinson, *William E. Borah and the Outlawry of War* (Athens, Ga., 1957), concerning the lion of Idaho. See also David Bryn-Jones, *Frank B. Kellogg* (New York, 1937), an authorized work, together with the biographies of Senator Borah by Claudius O. Johnson and Marian C. McKenna mentioned at the end of the preceding chapter.

Disarmament as an avenue of American foreign policy in the 1920's and early 1930's has inspired a fairly large literature. For the Washington Naval Conference the best introduction is Harold and Margaret Sprout, *Toward a New Order of Sea Power* (2nd ed., Princeton, 1943), together with George T. Davis, *A Navy Second to None* (New York, 1940), both excellent accounts of American naval power during and after the First World War. See also Elting E. Morison, *Admiral Sims and the Modern American Navy* (Boston, 1942); Armin Rappaport, *The Navy League of the United States* (Detroit, 1962); and Gerald E. Wheeler, *Prelude to Pearl Harbor: The United States Navy and the Far East, 1921–1931* (Columbia, Mo., 1963). C. N. Spinks, "The Termination of the Anglo–Japanese Alliance," *Pacific Historical Review*, VI (1937), 321–340 is a first-rate article. Local color of the conference appears in Mark Sullivan, *The Great Adventure at Washington* (New York, 1922); Sullivan attended the meetings as a reporter. J. Chalmers Vinson, *The Parchment Peace* (Athens, Ga., 1956) defines in a most informative way the Senate's part in the Washington Conference—its influence on the treaties drawn up by Secretary Hughes. The secretary's work appears in detail in Merlo J. Pusey, *Charles Evans Hughes* (2 vols., New York, 1951), a fine biography, winner of the Pulitzer Prize; and briefly, in better perspective, in *Dexter Perkins's *Charles Evans Hughes and American Democratic Statesmanship* (Boston, 1956), a volume in the Library of American Biography series. A new book about Hughes is by Betty Glad, *Charles Evans Hughes and the Illusions of Innocence* (Urbana, Ill., 1966). Thomas H. Buckley has a forthcoming book on the United States and the Washington Conference, to be published by the University of Tennessee Press. Ernest R. May and Sadao Asada are preparing accounts of the conference. For the London Naval Conference of 1930 see the account in Henry L. Stimson and McGeorge Bundy, *On Active Service in Peace and War* (New York,

1948); Richard N. Current, *Secretary Stimson: A Study in Statecraft* (New Brunswick, N.J., 1954), a careful criticism; *Elting E. Morison, *Turmoil and Tradition: A Study of the Life and Times of Henry L. Stimson* (Boston, 1960), pro-Stimson; together with the remarks in *The Memoirs of Herbert Hoover: The Cabinet and the Presidency, 1920–1933* (New York, 1952). There is an account of the conference in *Robert H. Ferrell, *American Diplomacy in the Great Depression: Hoover–Stimson Foreign Policy, 1929–1933* (New Haven, 1957), corrected and enlarged in volume 11 of the American Secretaries series, cited above. A study of large merit is Raymond G. O'Connor, *Perilous Equilibrium: The United States and the London Naval Conference of 1930* (Lawrence, Kan., 1962). A survey of disarmament appears in Merze Tate, *The United States and Armaments* (Cambridge, Mass., 1948).

☆ **22** ☆

The Great Depression

The President . . . gave a summary of the attitude of the American man on the street. For a hundred and fifty years we had kept out of Europe; then in 1917 we had been dragged in in a great war. We had spent forty billions of dollars in the war, and we had added ten billions more in the shape of loans after the war. We were spending a billion dollars a year on our disabled men. And yet Europe was in a worse condition than she was before the war. This, he said, led to despair as to Europe and European affairs on the part of the ordinary American citizen, and now he just wanted to keep out of the whole business. This was the general attitude of the American public, and he did not see how the United States could take the leadership in any direction.

—memorandum by Secretary of State Stimson of a conversation between President Hoover and the Italian foreign minister, Count Dino Grandi, 1931

The United States after the First World War refused to join the League of Nations and instead elaborated an American policy for international peace consisting of two principal courses of action—signature of treaties of disarmament and signature of treaties for peaceful settlement of international disputes. These, one might say, were the American plans, the American nostrums, for world peace. In the 1920's they did not appear as nostrums but as entirely adequate measures, and American statesmen were inclined at times to dispute with the statesmen of Europe as to whether the League or, in reality, the American measures such as the Washington Conference treaties of 1921–1922 and the Kellogg-Briand Pact of 1928 had provided the basis for European and world peace after the First World War. In any event there was no serious challenge to the structure of peace in the 1920's, probably because the world was economically prosperous during that time, and because also the labors and rigors of the war had been so many and large that people everywhere wanted to forget about the very word "war." And so down to the year 1929, and for some time beyond it, Americans felt that they had discovered a satisfactory route to peace.

Unfortunately for such feelings, in the Great Depression decade of the 1930's the people of the United States as well as other nations discovered that world peace was not as secure as they had assumed. Treaties of disarmament and of peaceful settlement, or the League of Nations as it existed in the 1920's without American support, could provide a sense of international community during a quiet period, but these measures could not stand up when the going became rough in the 1930's. The Great Depression had a dual effect in undermining peace. It turned the attention of peoples of democratic countries to their own domestic economic welfare and made them reluctant to look at the broader problems of international peace, problems that lay beyond their national borders. The depression also persuaded the peoples of some countries that the most drastic sort of national leadership was the only way their personal condition might be bettered. It gave impetus to the institution of dictatorship, for the dictators could easily claim that they had the key to national solvency, that they knew how to take their countries out of the Great Depression. As a result of the preoccupation of democratic governments with what was hopefully called recovery, and of the rise of totalitarianism in Europe and Asia, the peace of the world fell apart. A series of major international events in the latter 1930's dealt terrible blows to international peace. By the end of the decade the nations of Europe, soon to be followed by nations outside of the Continent including the United States, found themselves in the Second World War.

A decade of American policy, and of work for peace by the League of Nations, proved ineffective when the shadow of totalitarian governments fell over large areas of Europe and Asia. Hitler became German chancellor in January 1933 and started at once to tear down the democratic Weimar Republic which during the 1920's had offered so much hope for the future of European politics. Sometime also in the worst years of the Great Depression, between 1929 and 1933, Mussolini adopted a policy of revision, by which he meant change, peaceful or otherwise, of the Treaty of Versailles. The Italian dictator ceased devoting himself to making the trains run on time and turned to serious pursuits, looking for diplomatic victories which would deflect the thoughts of his people from poverty and the drabness of post-1918 Italy. By the mid-1930's this policy led him into the arms of Hitler. Likewise the worst sort of nationalism seized Japan in the Far East. The Japanese army got out of hand in 1931 and occupied all of Manchuria, and this venture was followed by a full-scale Sino-Japanese War beginning in 1937. Trouble in the Far East brought sheaves of diplomatic protests from Washington, for ever since 1899 and the first Hay open door note, the United States had been pursuing a policy dedicated to friendship with Japan and to preservation of Chinese sovereignty. But it gradually became evident to Americans that nothing short of military defeat could deter the Japanese from further aggressive acts. It was a disillusioning experience during the 1930's to see thirty years of Far Eastern policy dissolve in war.

The other concerns of this chapter—the London Economic Conference, the Hull-Roosevelt reciprocal trade agreements, recognition of Soviet Russia, and the neutrality acts of 1935–1939—these represented no new crises in American foreign policy. They were only a continuation or attempted continuation of policies long adhered to by the republic's diplomats. The neutrality laws were an extension of the attempt in the 1920's to legislate war out of existence. Americans had always put their faith in law, and when the grand international statute of the 1920's—the Kellogg-Briand Pact—proved worthless, the people of the United States passed their own antiwar laws to keep war away from the Western Hemisphere. As for recognition of Soviet Russia in 1933, this accorded with the traditional American policy of recognizing the government *de facto* as the government *de jure*, whether or not the form of government was pleasing to the United States. The Reciprocal Trade Agreements Act of 1934 embodied the idea of trade reciprocity which occasionally had been employed, although never long enough to prove its merits, in American tariff acts. The London Economic Conference was in harmony with a traditional American diplomatic theory, infrequently practiced, according to which trade barriers wherever possible were to be lowered.

1. *Trouble in Manchuria, 1929–1933*

President Herbert Hoover and Secretary of State Henry L. Stimson directed American diplomacy in the years from 1929 to 1933, the most difficult years of the Great Depression. The president and his secretary were men of ability, yet different in temperament. Hoover believed in peace and disarmament. Stimson, a Long Island squire and ex-secretary of war under President Taft, was given to quick and not always careful judgments on international affairs and overestimated the martial ardor of the American electorate. One must say immediately, however, that Stimson, like his chief, Hoover, believed in the American postwar policies of disarmament and peaceful settlement, and despite occasional snap suggestions on foreign affairs, he almost always ended with the same views as the president. Under such leadership well-meaning caution was the key to

American policy, foreign and domestic.

During the Hoover administration the first entanglement of American diplomacy, the first test of the American ways to world peace, came in the Far East in 1929, when China and Russia challenged the Kellogg-Briand Pact by threatening to go to war, and then actually went to war, over the Chinese Eastern Railway in Manchuria. Here was an inkling of trouble in the future, and it occurred, oddly enough, before the world had descended into the Great Depression and before the dictatorships during the economic troubles of the 1930's took on power and strength.

The source of the Sino-Russian dispute over the Chinese Eastern deserves a short explanation. As was seen in previous chapters, Manchuria had been an issue between Russia and Japan ever since the Sino-Japanese War of 1894–1895, when at the end of that war the triple intervention led by Russia had forced Japan to disgorge territory in southern Manchuria which it had hoped to keep. Russia thereupon sought to take Manchuria for itself. After the Russo-Japanese War of 1904–1905, Manchuria was divided into Japanese and Russian spheres of influence, roughly along the lines of the two principal Manchurian railways, the South Manchuria and the Chinese Eastern. The two lines formed a sort of "T," the traverse being the CER and the stem the SMR.

Before the appearance of Chinese nationalism in Manchuria, the Russian and Japanese spheres bothered no one in the Far East or the capitals of Western nations. The United States halfheartedly consented to the Japanese sphere in Manchuria in the Root-Takahira agreement of 1908. But after the First World War, the American government at the Washington Conference obtained with considerable diplomatic skill a Japanese evacuation of the Shantung peninsula in central China, the peninsula dominating the approaches to Tientsin and Peking which had been taken from the Germans during the World War. This gave a new turn to the history of Far Eastern imperialism. The Chinese nationalists under Sun Yat-sen and Chiang Kai-shek foolishly believed that the Western powers would look with approval and joy upon the abolition of spheres of interest and foreign possessions and extraterritoriality in all China, including Manchuria. Pursuing this reasoning, the Chinese sought in 1919 to oust the Russians from the Chinese Eastern Railway and regain for China the Russian sphere of influence in northern Manchuria. Chinese politicians in Nanking reasoned that they should assert themselves first against the Russians, who were communists and not respected by the powers of the West. General Chiang and his supporters also hoped to gain a victory in foreign affairs which would turn Chinese thoughts away from the difficult and still unsolved, and perhaps insoluble, Chinese domestic problems.

The details of the Sino-Russian imbroglio over the Chinese Eastern in

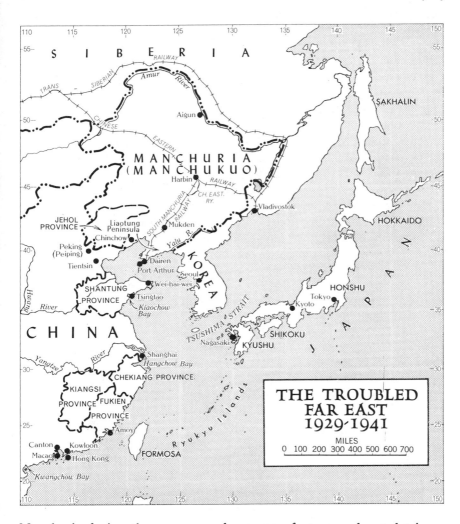

THE TROUBLED
FAR EAST
1929·1941

MILES
0 100 200 300 400 500 600 700

Manchuria during the summer and autumn of 1929 need not detain us.
The Chinese acted first by expelling the Russians from management of the
railway, and after violent expostulation the Soviet government beginning
in August 1929 sent troops against the foolhardy Chinese and forced the
Nanking regime to sue for peace. Unfortunately, after the initial seizure
of the Chinese Eastern Railway by the Chinese, Secretary Stimson in
Washington became excited and raised the subject of the Kellogg-Briand
Pact with both China and Russia. Although the Nanking and Moscow
governments promised to settle their dispute by peaceful means, the Russians in the autumn nonetheless invoked the right of self-defense and

began a military campaign against the Chinese. The Kellogg Pact, which to many Americans was the very foundation of pacific international relations, looked (to use the expression of an American diplomat) like thirty cents. Stimson made still another mistake near the end of the affair, actually after the Chinese had sued for peace, when in a circular note in late November 1929 he admonished the belligerents to cease fighting. The note was communicated to the Soviet Russian government, unrecognized by the United States since the Bolshevik revolution of 1917, by the French ambassador in Moscow. The result was an insulting unofficial communication via the public press from the Russian vice commissar of foreign affairs, Maxim Litvinoff, who told Stimson to mind his own business.

Litvinoff in 1929 thus had his small moment of triumph against the well-meaning but inexperienced Stimson. The latter soon turned to other international matters than Manchuria, particularly disarmament, with which he would have to deal at the London Naval Conference of 1930 and the General Disarmament Conference in 1932. The secretary of state's first two years of office were in fact largely concerned with disarmament, being only momentarily interrupted by the diplomatic fiasco over Manchuria. Stimson, however, learned in 1929 that quick action in Far Eastern matters, even if confined to verbal admonitions, could lead to grave embarrassment. The Kellogg-Briand Pact after its initial invocation in 1929 never looked the same and proved useless when a much more important conflict broke out between the Chinese and Japanese in Manchuria, beginning with a Sino-Japanese clash at Mukden on September 18, 1931. This conflict the Japanese liked to call the Manchurian incident; Stimson preferred, and rightly, to call it the Far Eastern crisis.

The crisis found part of its origin in the actions of the Chinese against the Russians in 1929. In their inept effort to seize Russian property in Manchuria, the Chinese managed to convince the Japanese that the South Manchuria Railway and all of Japan's other possessions in Manchuria, territorial and otherwise, which depended upon that railway, were endangered by the growing nationalism of the Chinese government. A second factor persuading Japan to move against China in Manchuria was the Great Depression, which struck with especial harshness in the Japanese islands, bringing misery to peasants and city workers. Among other difficulties for Japan, the bottom fell out of the silk market in the United States, and this catastrophe, combined with Chinese nationalist boycotts of Japanese cotton goods, meant a crisis in Japan's foreign trade, almost half of which was in cotton goods and silk with China and the United States. Manchuria, so it seemed, might provide under Japanese rule a safe area for Japan's trade, an area unaffected by foreign tariffs.

Added to these factors was increasing unrest in the Japanese army, a rebellious spirit among many of the younger officers. Until the decade of the 1920's, the Japanese officer corps was the preserve of the upper classes, who contributed the bulk of the higher-ranking officers. The army had always been a peasant army, and in the years after the First World War when democracy achieved a temporary popularity in Japan, the peasants began to rise into the officer corps, bringing into the army a new type of officer who was in reality half-educated—overly professional, ultrapatriotic, suspicious of Western ideas and intentions. These young officers, many of them old enough to know better, began in the latter 1920's to agitate and conspire against their elders, with vague ideas of overthrowing the government in Tokyo and establishing a "Showa restoration," a moral regeneration of Japan. Showa was the reign name of the Emperor Hirohito. The Meiji restoration of 1868 had rejuvenated the nation politically, they believed, by returning to the emperor the political powers usurped by the shoguns, and a Showa restoration would reform the nation's morals which had been debauched by the politicians. This was, to be sure, inexact historical reasoning, for the emperors in Japan have never enjoyed much real power, either in the early centuries before their domination by the shoguns or after the Meiji restoration. Still, the typical young officer believed in this restoration theory, and he had the courage of his ignorance. There was, one should add, a strong admixture of socialist thinking in this program of the young army officers. But after the Manchurian incident beginning on September 18, 1931, the older army officers gradually infiltrated the restoration movement of their younger confrères and in 1936 purged it of its socialist tendencies, leaving only its patriotism. This was a virulent residue. The younger officers eventually came back into control as their conservative superiors retired; the result was the attack on Pearl Harbor and a suicidal effort to achieve *Hakko Ichiu*, The Eight Corners of the Universe Under One Roof.

But to return to the incident of September 18, 1931, which inaugurated the Far Eastern crisis. That night, after alleging an explosion along the main line of the South Manchuria Railway a few miles north of Mukden and claiming that Chinese troops in the vicinity had sought to blow up the track of the South Manchuria Railway, the Japanese army in Manchuria, the so-called Kwantung Army, under leadership of its young officer elements, began occupying Manchuria. In a few days the Japanese spread out along the line of the SMR, and during the winter of 1931–1932 they audaciously took the Russian sphere of interest in Manchuria, the northern part of Manchuria bordering the line of the Soviet-controlled Chinese Eastern Railway. Manchuria was set up as an "independent" puppet empire called Manchukuo with Kang Teh (the boy emperor of China deposed in 1912;

also known by the names Hsuan T'ung and Henry Pu-yi) as "sovereign."
In Russia the Soviet regime was so busy collectivizing the farms and forwarding the second five-year plan that it could only watch the Kwantung
Army's movements in nervous fear, hoping that the Japanese would not
invade Siberia (there was sentiment in Japan for such an excursion). By
the spring of 1933, all Manchuria including the province of Jehol had
fallen, and the government in Tokyo temporarily persuaded the army to
follow a policy of relative moderation. For the next several years the

The Japanese take Manchuria, despite treaty pledges.

Japanese government was an unsteady coalition of bureaucrats and army
and navy officers. As time passed the bureaucrats of pacific inclination
dropped out of the government, the navy grew more warlike as it observed the successes of totalitarianism in Europe during the years 1935–
1939, and the army became supreme when in autumn 1941 the fire-eating
General Hideki (Razor Brain) Tojo, a sympathizer with the young officers, assumed the premiership.

The future did not stand revealed to American officials in Washington
in September 1931, and President Hoover and Secretary Stimson spent

the remainder of their time in office until March 1933, when the Manchurian affair came almost simultaneously to an end, attempting to halt Japan's aggression and if possible to persuade the Japanese to return the captured territory to China. The first policy adopted by Stimson and Hoover was one of inaction, for they remembered the fiasco over the Chinese Eastern in 1929. They hoped also that the League of Nations would take jurisdiction and persuade the Japanese to cease and desist. An American chargé d'affaires in Geneva in October 1931 sat at the League Council for a few days while Council members summoned up courage to invoke the Kellogg-Briand Pact. In November–December, Ambassador Dawes went over to Paris from his post in London and from the confines of a suite in the Ritz sought to inspire the League Council, then in session at the Quai d'Orsay. Not much came from Dawes's exhortations, except some additional feeling of American solidarity with the League during the Far Eastern crisis. This was more feeling than fact, for suspicion of the League dominated American relations with that organization throughout the interwar era. In Paris in 1931 Dawes had been careful to stay in his hotel, and never once did he cross the Seine to the Quai d'Orsay to meet with the League Council.

Shortly after this Paris meeting of the Council came further Japanese acts in Manchuria. The Japanese army occupied the South Manchurian town of Chinchow on January 2, 1932. This produced a statement of the American position toward aggression which became known as the Stimson Doctrine.

On January 7, 1932, Secretary Stimson announced that the United States could not "admit the legality of any situation *de facto* nor does it intend to recognize any treaty or agreement . . . which may impair the treaty rights of the United States or its citizens in China, including those which relate to the sovereignty, the independence, or the territorial and administrative integrity of the Republic of China, nor to the international policy relative to China, commonly known as the open door policy; and that it does not intend to recognize any situation, treaty, or agreement which may be brought about by means contrary to the covenants and obligations of the Pact of Paris of August 27, 1928, to which Treaty both China and Japan, as well as the United States, are parties."

The Stimson Doctrine, inspired in 1932 by Japan's conquest of Manchuria, was later applied by the United States to conquests by other nations in Europe. It has, however, obtained little support from other nations of the world and hence has failed to become a part of international law.

One might remark parenthetically, about the Stimson Doctrine, that authorship of the note of January 7, 1932, was afterward a subject of some controversy, or if not controversy then confusion, between Stimson and Hoover. Stimson had obtained the idea of such a declaration of non-recognition of the fruits of aggression from President Hoover in a cabinet meeting in November 1931, but the phrasing of the announcement was Stimson's. Hoover in the presidential election of 1932 took credit for the doctrine, saying in his acceptance speech, "I have projected a new doctrine into international affairs." The idea of nonrecognition so attracted him that despite defeat in November 1932 he afterward asked some cabinet members to prepare testimonial letters on the subject, which they did in the interest, as Hoover later put it, of "accuracy of historic fact." Stimson himself never claimed sole authorship of the idea of nonrecognition, but the idea nonetheless has taken his name.

It has been argued that there were two doctrines in 1932—a Stimson Doctrine and a Hoover Doctrine, the former implying sanctions of military force and the latter relying only on the sanction of international public opinion. This does seem contrary to the case in 1932, where there was not any essential difference of opinion between the president and the secretary of state. Stimson for a while in the autumn of 1931 had talked privately of military sanctions, but they were never within the realm of possibility and Stimson gradually came to understand as much. Public opinion in the United States would never have stood for them. Hoover, of course, a profoundly peaceful man, did not favor military sanctions or even economic sanctions (such as an embargo on war material) against Japan in 1931–1933.

The Stimson Doctrine, announced early in January 1932, had no effect on Japanese aggression, for it was late that same month that Japanese naval forces began an attack on the Chinese port of Shanghai; and Stimson on February 23, 1932, had to make a second statement of policy reinforcing his doctrine. The attack on Shanghai had little relation to the Japanese army's activities in Manchuria, despite what might seem to be the logic of Japan's military position in China: logic would indicate that the Japanese in 1931–1933 planned to take over all of China, and that the first move in Manchuria was to be followed by an attack on Shanghai, and if that were successful then attack elsewhere along the coast and eventually penetration into and occupation of the interior regions as well. In actual fact this was not the Japanese plan of conquest. There was no careful plan of conquest then or later. Japan's actions in China were an unco-ordinated series of movements, a crazy quilt of military campaigns. A Japanese admiral in Shanghai in early 1932 thought that because of some Chinese attacks on Japanese citizens residing in the port he was justified in occupying part of the city. He met unexpected resistance, and eventually, after the Japanese had brought in well over 50,000 regular army troops, the campaign was given up. But for a while in the spring of 1932 it looked to outside observers as if full-scale war was spreading over China. The Japanese air bombardment of a defenseless Chinese sector of Shanghai, the Chapei quarter, was an outrageous act that fired Western indignation. It persuaded Secretary Stimson that he should make another statement of the American diplomatic position relative to the Far East, and this he did in what has become known as the Borah Letter of February 23, 1932.

Conceived in the form of a public letter to the chairman of the Senate foreign relations committee (Stimson felt that if he sent a note to Japan he would receive a caustic reply), the Borah Letter restated eloquently the American stand against Japanese aggression. The secretary hinted that if Japan persisted in attacking China, the United States might abrogate the Five-Power Naval Treaty of Washington. At the end of his letter to Borah, Stimson placed a noble statement of American purposes toward China which showed the essentially humanitarian instincts of American Far Eastern policy: "In the past our Government, as one of the leading powers on the Pacific Ocean, has rested its policy upon an abiding faith in the future of the people of China and upon the ultimate success in dealing with them of the principles of fair play, patience, and mutual goodwill."

Afterward Stimson regarded the Borah Letter as the most important state paper of his career, and it was an eloquent statement of Japan's wrongdoings and the American position toward them, but neither it nor the Stimson Doctrine deterred the Japanese. World public opinion, which Stimson hoped to stir, remained occupied by the increasingly acute economic problems of the Great Depression. Stimson proved himself a competent lawyer and made a most careful summation to the jury, but the jury was not listening.

This was the public mood, in the United States and elsewhere, when the League of Nations on October 1, 1932, released a report on conditions in Manchuria. At the end of the Paris Council meeting in November–December 1931, the League had appointed a commission, and this body, headed by Lord Lytton of England and including Major General Frank R. McCoy as an unofficial American representative, had gone out to the Far East and interviewed government leaders and other individuals in China, Manchuria, and Japan. Laboring through the summer in Peking, the commission produced the famous review of Manchurian conditions known as the Lytton Report. It was written largely by two American assistants to the commission, George H. Blakeslee of Clark University and C. Walter Young of Johns Hopkins. The report sidestepped responsibility for the Mukden clash of September 18, 1931, but stated unequivocally that subsequent Japanese actions had gone far beyond any requirement of the original incident. The report found the Japanese claim of self-defense inadmissible. While fully recognizing Chinese delinquencies of administration in Manchuria prior to the Japanese attack, and granting the need of Japanese citizens in Manchuria for protection, the report put the blame for aggression on Japan. As for the Japanese puppet state, Manchukuo, the report said that it could not "be considered to have been called into existence by a genuine and spontaneous independence movement" as the Japanese claimed. The Japanese army, the commission discovered, was in full control.

The League of Nations adopted the Lytton Report with its recommendations, an autonomous Manchuria under Chinese sovereignty, on February 24, 1933, but it was too late by this time to do anything against Japan in Manchuria—and the League had never intended to, anyway. That same day, February 24, the first anniversary of publication of Stimson's letter to Senator Borah, the Japanese delegation at Geneva made a dramatic exit from the League. Japan announced permanent withdrawal from the League of Nations, taking as a souvenir the Pacific islands held under League mandate. The chief Japanese delegate at Geneva, Yosuke Matsuoka, told the League Assembly that as Christ had been crucified on the cross, so was Japan being crucified by the nations of the League. Privately Matsuoka explained that the powers had taught Japan the game of poker, but after they had acquired most of the chips they pronounced the game immoral and took up contract bridge.

This was the sad diplomatic end of the Manchurian affair. Hostilities in Manchuria petered out and were ended formally by the Tangku Truce of May 31, 1933. Secretary Stimson in Washington took satisfaction that the League in adopting the Lytton Report in February 1933 had endorsed the Stimson Doctrine of nonrecognition of Manchukuo. He at that moment could not know that in the future cases of Ethiopia, Austria, and Czechoslovakia, League members would forget about nonrecognition of the spoils of aggression. He did not realize that Japan in walking out of the League of Nations had set an easy example for other nations which did not wish to honor their international pledges—Germany left the League in October 1933, Italy in 1937. The American secretary of state in January 1933 conversed for a few hours with President-elect Franklin D. Roosevelt and hopefully sought to persuade FDR to continue the Hoover-Stimson policies in the Far East. With that the Hoover administration bowed out and the Roosevelt administration bowed in.

2. *The diplomacy of the New Deal*

During the first and second administrations of President Franklin D. Roosevelt, the American people continued largely to live apart from the realities of international relations. The diplomacy of the United States from 1933 to 1939 relied no longer on disarmament and treaties of peaceful settlement, for by the time the Hoover administration went out of office it was fairly clear that those American alternatives to the League of Nations had proved ineffective. Even so, the only new Rooseveltian device for world peace, reciprocal trade agreements, was no more effective than the policies of FDR's Republican predecessors. Roosevelt had no opportunity, of course, to return the country to the policies of his illustrious Democratic predecessor, Woodrow Wilson. At no time after the spring of 1920, least of all in 1933 and after, had it been possible to take the United States into the League. The temper of American opinion would never have allowed it. The memory of the clever anti-League propaganda of Senator Lodge and the Battalion of Death in 1919–1920 had solidified many ancient American prejudices, and an international body such as the League seemed to the average American citizen an impossible organization for his country to join. When William Randolph Hearst in February 1932 confronted the Democratic candidate for the presidency with the League issue, FDR came out flatly against membership. In the election of 1932 repeal of the eighteenth amendment was a far greater issue than any international matter.

But overreaching any issue of the 1932 campaign and dominating the policies of the first two Roosevelt administrations was the Great Depression, which had settled down over the country like an enormous blight. The depression, which lasted until 1941 and American entry into the Second World War, was the most calamitous domestic disaster in the history of the United States excluding only the Civil War. Roosevelt came into office with a mandate to do something about the depression, and from the outset of the New Deal foreign affairs took a place subordinate to economic and social reform. No one who can remember the grim depression days will assert that Roosevelt had any choice about his program. He had to take care of the immediate problem, which was to get the economy off dead center, the condition he found it in on the morning of his inaugural when every bank in the country had closed. It does not help to say with the advantage of hindsight that for Roosevelt foreign affairs, the rapidly expanding power of totalitarian regimes throughout the world, should have been more important than domestic matters. Roosevelt had to do something about the depression.

The London Economic Conference (June 12–July 24, 1933), where the United States together with sixty-three other nations was represented, offered a typical example of the influence of the Great Depression on American foreign policy during the first two Roosevelt administrations. Here, when an international measure was suggested that might have undermined the president's domestic economic program, Roosevelt did not hesitate to withdraw all American support. This conference had been called for the summer of 1933 to increase world trade through such measures as reduction of tariffs, stabilization of currencies, perhaps some agreement on war debts owed to the United States. The purpose of the conference—to increase trade—was always plain, although many proposals of the nations looking toward achievement of the purpose were uncertain. Roosevelt's secretary of state, Cordell Hull, acting in the midst of this confusion, produced a plan to facilitate world trade through tariff reciprocity, and Hull went off to London hoping to achieve a general treaty for lowering of tariffs. He hoped that the treaty would both help world trade and ensure world peace through the bonds of an international exchange of goods and services. But President Roosevelt, fearful of tariff reduction during the depression, deeply involved in the spring and early summer of 1933 in pushing through Congress the first measures of the New Deal, vetoed the proposal while the secretary was en route to the conference.

There then arose the question of currency stabilization, allowing the free exchange of one currency for another. When the conference began its deliberations, it appeared that many of the delegates at London wished currency stabilization via some sort of return to the gold standard by such leading financial nations as the United States and Great Britain, especially the United States. The British government in 1931 had gone off the gold standard, which meant that the pound sterling was no longer convertible easily into other currencies (a paper currency convertible at any time into gold could always be exchanged for other paper currencies). Many countries had followed the British off gold, including the United States under the Roosevelt administration in March and April 1933. World trade was thrown into an uproar, for without a gold standard the value of national currencies in world trade was tied to the value of national exports: if country A did not need the goods of country B, it was difficult to sell to country B; country A would not want B's currency, which was good only within country B; if A wished to sell its own goods to B, it had to find country C which wished B's goods; then A would take some of C's goods—or else work another deal between C and D, or on down the alphabet until A found some nation with goods which A needed. The intricacies of trade without the gold standard become readily understandable. The problem in the summer of 1933 was somehow to free the world's currencies, so that there would be no need for each nation desiring foreign trade to go suitoring to other nations, making detailed private arrangements for trade.

Currency stabilization, the nations believed, would have a tonic effect on world trade, but such a measure President Roosevelt would not allow. When a proposal was sent to the president, he vetoed it in a sharp message to the American delegation at London on July 2, 1933. This message, one should add, exploded the sole remaining hope of the London delegates, since the president had already forbidden a general treaty for American tariff reciprocity. FDR torpedoed the London Economic Conference, to use the figure of speech current at the time. He did it for domestic economic reasons, not because he did not wish to assist in the business of world peace. Roosevelt took a stand against stabilization because he feared that to make the dollar convertible upon demand, tying its value to the ups and downs of world trade, would jeopardize his recovery program. With the coming of the Great Depression the dollar had risen in value—a dollar would buy much more in 1933 than it had in 1929. This change placed debtors in the unenviable position of repaying loans contracted in the 1920's when the dollar had less value. The president wished to depreciate the dollar, at least to its level in the 1920's, and depreciating it would be difficult if the dollar's value were tied to world exchange conditions and, hence, out of his control.

Many individuals in 1933 and later believed that the collapse of the London Economic Conference was a catastrophe for world peace, that Roosevelt's action destroyed the last great hope for peace by conference before the Second World War. Certainly FDR's message of July 2, vetoing currency stabilization, not merely destroyed all hopes for the meeting but worsened world trade in addition, for it gave assurance that the United States would have nothing to do with the gold standard. Still, Roosevelt was taking the only possible course in 1933 when he put American economic recovery ahead of world recovery. "The world," he had remarked in his message, "will not long be lulled by the specious fallacy of achieving a temporary and probably an artificial stability in foreign exchange on the part of a few large countries only. The sound internal economic system of a nation is a greater factor in its well-being than the price of its currency in changing terms of the currencies of other nations." This declaration was hailed by FDR's countrymen in 1933 as an American financial declaration of independence. Few Americans in the depth of the depression would have supported international measures at the expense of the American economy.

The administration, however, soon showed something resembling contriteness for its behavior when in 1934 Secretary Hull announced a proposal to reduce tariff barriers all over the world. Hull's scheme was what he had hoped to offer at London the year before—tariff reciprocity.

Could Hull's reciprocal trade treaties have promoted international peace? One can only say that the tariffs of the world were lowest in the nineteenth century and that the nineteenth century marked the most warless period in modern history. It is difficult to know whether this was cause and effect (and which was which?), or coincidence, or the result of world dominance by British power in the form of the British navy; or perhaps the nineteenth century was a period of such phenomenal industrial growth, marking the spread through Western Europe and North America of the industrial revolution, that in such a time of physical development the nations of the world were too busy to fight each other often or for long.

Be that as it may, Secretary Hull was a firm believer in low tariffs. He was convinced that lower tariffs meant world peace. Roosevelt, with what appears to have been mild enthusiasm, sponsored reciprocity tariff legislation in accord with the wishes of his secretary of state, and the Hull-Roosevelt Reciprocal Trade Agreements Act passed Congress and received the presidential signature on June 12, 1934. It permitted executive lowering of the tariff to an extent of fifty per cent of any tariff schedule, providing that foreign nations would make similar adjustments in schedules in which the United States had an interest. Almost all concessions made would be extended automatically to other nations. The advantage of the Hull program was that tariffs could be adjusted without the express consent, on each schedule, of Congress, and hence adjustment could be made in the national interest and not that of some lobbyist.

As for the effects of the Hull-Roosevelt reciprocity program, they have been difficult to gauge, for the 1930's and 1940's proved extraordinarily disturbed years for foreign trade. The rearmament of Europe and coming of the Second World War and the perplexities of the postwar years obscured the results of American tariff reciprocity. Some individuals have ventured that American trade has increased greatly because of reciprocity. Cordell Hull in 1940 thought that the program was begun for "the express purpose of expanding our exports. . . . I submit that it has done so." Writing in the same year an economist, Grace Beckett, concluded (with perhaps undue caution) that reciprocity "seems to offer the only feasible program which will obtain some of the advantages of the international division of labor in a world filled with trade restrictions."

Another diplomatic act of the early New Deal period was recognition by the United States of the government of Soviet Russia. Because of the numerous outrages and horrors with which the Bolshevik Party had achieved and maintained power in Russia, and because the communist government represented expropriation and anticapitalism and had repudiated the debts of the tsarist regime and the short-lived provisional republic of 1917, the American government had refused recognition during the 1920's. The Bolsheviks did not increase their popularity by the constant emission of crude revolutionary propaganda which kept American officials stubborn. Nonetheless many businessmen in the United States and liberal leaders who considered communist Russia a social experiment rather than a dictatorship favored recognizing the Bolsheviks. This agitation grew in volume as the depression made businessmen sensitive to any, even remote, possibilities of foreign trade, and the result finally was diplomatic recognition.

How a nation such as Russia could have conducted any large-scale foreign trade with the United States should have been a mystery, for Americans needed nothing that Russia produced, and the Russians had no money (at this time they had not sent political prisoners in sufficient numbers into the Kolyma gold fields). Because of Bolshevik repudiation of the wartime debts, loans were out of the question. But in the lurid possibility of Russian trade, the dream was more important than reality. Here was another instance like China, where the existence of a large population in a large territory seemed without further explanation to mean enormous trade. The Roosevelt administration gave in to the economic arguments for recognition.

There were some other and minor reasons for recognizing communist Russia. For one, the increasing danger of a Japanese move against Russia in the Far East helped bring together the Soviet and American governments. Moreover, the American people had sickened of all the argument over recognition, pro and con, and remembered only that the now discredited Republican administrations of the 1920's had opposed relations with the Russians. Recognition of Soviet Russia by 1933 was a stale problem, tiresome and boring, and negotiations between Litvinoff, who had become Soviet commissar for foreign affairs, and President Franklin D. Roosevelt were completed with hardly a hitch.

In a formal exchange of notes on the day of recognition, November 16, 1933, Litvinoff promised that his country would (1) abstain from propaganda in the United States, (2) extend religious freedom to American citizens in the Soviet Union and negotiate an agreement to guarantee fair trial to Americans accused of crime in Russia, and (3) reopen the question of outstanding claims of both governments.

There followed a serious effort by the United States to improve relations with Russia. The president appointed as ambassador to Moscow the wealthy William C. Bullitt, who in a burst of enthusiasm departed for Russia to demonstrate his friendliness and that of his countrymen for the struggling socialists of the former tsarist empire. Between 1934 and 1936, at which latter date he was transferred to Paris, Bullitt made heroic efforts for American-Soviet friendship, including equipping of some Russian citizens with baseballs, bats, and gloves. American businessmen likewise did their best to obtain Russian orders. American private citizens, some of them of the most impeccably patriotic antecedents, demonstrated with effusion their friendship for Russia. Apropos this latter phenomenon of the 1930's, Eric F. Goldman has cited a news item in the Baltimore *Sun* for November 8, 1937: "Wearing a black ensemble with orchids at the shoulder, Mrs. William A. Becker, national president of the Daughters of the American Revolution, attended the reception at the Soviet Embassy last night to celebrate the twentieth anniversary of the Russian Revolution." Such camaraderie was to no avail. Moreover, American trade with Russia, so fondly anticipated, diminished after recognition instead of increasing. The Russians remained suspicious and difficult and forgot, if they had not from the beginning intended to ignore, their promises through Litvinoff in the prerecognition agreement. One can only conclude about this effort by the Roosevelt administration to improve relations with Soviet Russia that the Russians repulsed a sincere effort with as much hardness and disdain toward the well-intentioned American republic as they again would show after the Second World War.

A word remains about the neutrality acts of 1935, 1936, 1937, and 1939, which together with Secretary Hull's tariff-reciprocity agreements represented almost the sole discernible new moves by the United States toward the nations of Europe in the decade before the Second World War. A series of stark international events shook Europe to its foundations in the four years beginning with 1935. The first was the Italian conquest of Ethiopia, which began in 1935 and ended the next year. In 1936 came German reoccupation of the Rhineland, which made Germany militarily defensible against the French army by securing the approaches to the Rhine, and separated the French from their Czechoslovak allies. Occupation of the Rhineland broke down France's post-1918 alliances with the nations of Eastern Europe—Czechoslovakia, Rumania, and Yugoslavia (the Little Entente). The year 1936 saw the beginning of the Spanish Civil War, a death struggle between liberals and conservatives in Spain. The liberals drew in the radicals, and the reactionaries joined the conservatives. Germany and Italy sent help to the Franco regime, Russia to the Republicans. When peace came in 1939 it was a peace of exhaustion. The accession of General Francisco Franco to power in Spain, one should add, marked a sad deterioration in Western democratic fortunes, for the Spanish caudillo was a reactionary, opportunistic gentleman of the eighteenth century rather than the twentieth, who brought an intellectual, economic, and political blight to Spain during the years after the end of the civil war; during the Second World War the Allies had terribly difficult dealings with this Machiavel as he wavered between the German and Allied sides, waiting to see who would win the war. Meanwhile in March 1938, after rebuilding German military power, Hitler forced the *Anschluss* with Austria, and in September 1938 he took the Sudeten territory from Czechoslovakia after negotiation at Berchtesgaden, Godesberg, and Munich with the British prime minister Neville Chamberlain, the French premier Edouard Daladier, and the Italian dictator Mussolini. After having said in these conversations that the Sudetenland was his last demand, Hitler in March 1939 took most of the remainder of Czechoslovakia. Mussolini seized Albania in April. In midsummer the German Fuehrer precipitated the Danzig crisis with Poland, and on September 1, having waited until the crops had been harvested, he began the Second World War.

During these catastrophic four years of European history, the United States contented itself with enacting neutrality statutes. A special committee of the Senate headed by Gerald P. Nye of North Dakota had begun in 1934 to investigate profiteering in the United States during the First World War. The investigation lasted into 1936, and the Nye committee's voluminous testimony and exhibits helped condition the American people for staying neutral during Europe's new time of troubles. The Senate munitions investigating committee turned up little of a sensational nature, for it proved that many individuals had made sizable profits during the First World War, a conclusion which might have been evident without any investigation. Insofar as the committee showed that co-operation existed during the war between Wall Street banking firms (J .P. Morgan *et al.*), ammunition concerns (the "merchants of death"), and the Wilson administration, the American people in the mid-1930's became convinced that such co-operation was collusion, that sinister forces in 1917 had taken the nation into a war which it did not want. There would be no such nonsense again. In an act of Congress of August 31, 1935, hurried through both Houses just before the Italian attack in Ethiopia, the Roosevelt administration renounced some of the traditional rights of neutrals which had caused difficulty during the First World War, in the hope that the maritime troubles of that war which had led to American entry in 1917 would not repeat themselves in the Italian crisis. Mussolini had been making balcony speeches about Italy's destiny and gave the distinct impression that interference by anyone in the Ethiopian adventure would mean instant war. The Duce believed what he said. According to the Neutrality Act of 1935, an avowedly temporary affair, the president after proclaiming the existence of a state of war had to prohibit all arms shipments to belligerents and could forbid American citizens to travel on belligerent vessels except at their own risk. Roosevelt signed the neutrality act reluctantly and remarked in irritation that it was calculated to "drag us into war instead of keeping us out." This was unlikely, but after passage of the act the president and the state department could no longer bargain with Mussolini and could make no effective protests against the Italian bully's attack on a small tribal African state, because in advance the United States had given up any possible trump cards such as sending supplies to the Ethiopians. The president managed to obtain from Congress a six-month limit on the arms embargo. He had hoped that Congress would permit him to use the embargo only against aggressor nations, but Congress refused.

In following years the United States revised and refined its neutrality laws. The act of February 29, 1936, forbade loans to belligerents. A joint resolution of Congress on January 6, 1937, embargoed shipments to the opposing forces in the Spanish Civil War (the act of 1935 had applied only to war between nations and not to civil wars). A new act of May 1, 1937, brought together the provisions of previous legislation and added some new stipulations: travel on belligerent vessels was now forbidden, rather than allowed at the risk of the traveler; the president was authorized to list commodities other than munitions which belligerents might purchase in the United States and transport abroad in their own ships (this "cash and carry" provision of the act of May 1, limited to two years, expired by the time the European war began in September 1939). The act of May 1937 did give the president some discretion, for a tricky wording permitted FDR to move only when he could "find" a war. It stipulated that "Whenever the President shall find that there exists a state of war between, or among, two or more foreign states, the President shall proclaim such fact. . . ." When in July 1937 another war broke out—this time in China between Japanese and Chinese troops near Peking, the beginning of the long conflict which closed in 1945—Roosevelt refused to invoke the neutrality legislation on the technical ground that he did not find a war. The Sino-Japanese War of 1937–1945, like the "Manchurian incident" of 1931–1933, was an undeclared war, such being the fashion of the 1930's to get around the inconvenient promises of the Kellogg-Briand Pact. On technical ground Roosevelt could claim to find no war in China, and this technicality served his purpose of making munitions available to the beleaguered Chinese.

Thus the neutrality acts by 1937 had begun to appear not always in the national interest of the United States. Their invocation in the new Far Eastern war would have assisted the aggressor, not the victim. After the Second World War broke out in Europe, Congress in November 1939 revised the neutrality laws, repealing the embargo on arms and ammunition and authorizing "cash and carry" exports of war material to belligerent powers. Because this late revision of the neutrality regulations assisted the belligerents who controlled the high seas, that is, Britain and France, opponents of changing the laws argued that Congress was committing an unneutral act, unfavorable to Germany. Actually the act of November 4, 1939, reasserted the right of the United States to sell munitions of war to any nation which had the shipping to come and get them. Neutrality according to international law had never meant that a nation had to even up its trade with opposing belligerent nations. In any event the argument over the Neutrality Act of 1939 became academic when the United States in following months unmistakably demonstrated its sympathy for the Allies with such moves as the Lend-Lease Act of 1941. By this time the neutrality acts had been proved futile. They played no part whatsoever in keeping the United States at peace. It was absurd to pass legislation preventing American munitions trade with the European belligerents, to attempt to legislate the country "out of the First World War," for the causes of American entry into the first war differed markedly from those of entry into the second.

In the history of American diplomacy the decade of the 1930's, like the preceding decade, is a cheerless subject for analysis. The initial years of the Great Depression, from 1929 to 1933, passed in uncertainty, in expostulation to Japan but nothing more. Secretary of State Stimson and President Hoover were men of peace who did their best during an extraordinarily difficult domestic economic crisis. They realized that their measures were not altogether adequate, but they hoped that time would work for peace. It was impossible to imagine the course of history in the following years. The structure of peace arranged at Paris in 1919 had been challenged in the Far East by 1933, but it still appeared fairly secure in Europe. Almost all Americans, who did not realize that peace was indivisible, believed that Japan could enjoy a little aggression in Manchuria and that the Peace of Paris, buttressed by the Washington Conference treaties and the Kellogg-Briand Pact, would endure.

During the first two administrations of President Franklin D. Roosevelt, the people of the United States continued to think primarily in terms of the Great Depression, the effect of the depression on their own individual lives. Americans beginning in 1933 were preoccupied by the New Deal in domestic affairs, the grand effort to escape from the Great Depression, and they had little time or inclination to examine the course of international affairs. President Roosevelt in 1935 told Prime Minister Joseph A. Lyons of Australia that never again would the United States be drawn into a European war, regardless of circumstances. Representative Louis Ludlow of Indiana in 1935 first introduced his resolution in the House proposing a constitutional amendment that, except in the event of an invasion of the United States or its territorial possessions, the authority of Congress to declare war should not become effective until confirmed by a majority vote in a national referendum. The House of Representatives came close to voting the resolution out of committee in January 1938 and held back only because of a personal message from President Roosevelt to the speaker of the House. Pacifist feeling was much in vogue everywhere, in Europe as well as America, during these years. In England many young men were taking the Oxford Oath that they would never fight for king and country. Before the leading Western democracies—Britain, France, and the United States—understood what was going on outside their national borders, it was almost too late. The dictatorships of the world instituted the series of calamitous events: Ethiopia, the Rhineland, Spain, China, Austria, Czechoslovakia, Albania, Danzig. The time arrived when American diplomacy, as we see in retrospect, might have joined Britain and France in the stand against aggression. The United States, engrossed in the effort to achieve domestic economic recovery, renounced diplomacy in favor of neutrality.

Down to the end, confusion and inaction characterized American policy. Many prominent Americans had only the slightest notion of the holocaust that was preparing in Europe. Senator Borah in July 1939 declared that there would be no Second World War, and offered as authority his own private sources of information. When Hitler and Stalin on August 23, 1939, signed the Nazi-Soviet Pact, which gave Hitler a free hand in the West and was in a real sense the crucial diplomatic arrangement prior to outbreak of the war, the chairman of the House committee on foreign affairs, Representative Sol Bloom, called at the state department and told a department officer that the crisis was not serious and that he had "doped out" why Hitler had come to terms with Russia: to give himself an asylum when he should ultimately be thrown out by the Germans. No other country, Bloom said, would accept him. At the height of the crisis in August 1939 there was little that American diplomats could do except await its end. The brilliant state department career officer, Jay Pierrepont Moffat, wrote in his diary on August 26–27, 1939, "These last two days have given me the feeling of sitting in a house where somebody is dying upstairs. There is relatively little to do and yet the suspense continues unabated." Headlines and radio flashes at the beginning of the Second World War on September 1, 1939—GERMAN PLANES ATTACK WARSAW, ENGLAND AND FRANCE MOBILIZE—found the country almost as bewildered as it had been a quarter of a century earlier, in August 1914.

A CONTEMPORARY DOCUMENT

[The Borah Letter of February 23, 1932, was an eloquent statement of the American diplomatic position in regard to China. Source: *Foreign Rela-*

tions of the United States: Japan, 1931–1941 (2 vols., Washington, 1943), I, 83–87.]

You have asked my opinion whether, as has been sometimes recently suggested, present conditions in China have in any way indicated that the so-called Nine Power Treaty has become inapplicable or ineffective or rightly in need of modification, and if so, what I considered should be the policy of this Government.

This Treaty, as you of course know, forms the legal basis upon which now rests the "Open Door" policy towards China. That policy, enunciated by John Hay in 1899, brought to an end the struggle among various powers for so-called spheres of interest in China which was threatening the dismemberment of that empire. To accomplish this Mr. Hay invoked two principles, (1) equality of commercial opportunity among all nations in dealing with China, and (2) as necessary to that equality the preservation of China's territorial and administrative integrity. These principles were not new in the foreign policy of America. They had been the principles upon which it rested in its dealings with other nations for many years. In the case of China they were invoked to save a situation which not only threatened the future development and sovereignty of that great Asiatic people, but also threatened to create dangerous and constantly increasing rivalries between the other nations of the world. War had already taken place between Japan and China. At the close of that war three other nations intervened to prevent Japan from obtaining some of the results of that war claimed by her. Other nations sought and had obtained spheres of interest. Partly as a result of these actions a serious uprising had broken out in China which endangered the legations of all the powers at Peking. While the attack on those legations was in progress, Mr. Hay made an announcement in respect to this policy as the principle upon which the powers should act in the settlement of the rebellion. . . . He was successful in obtaining the assent of the other powers to the policy thus announced.

In taking these steps Mr. Hay acted with the cordial support of the British Government. In responding to Mr. Hay's announcement . . . Lord Salisbury, the British Prime Minister, expressed himself "most emphatically as concurring in the policy of the United States."

For twenty years thereafter the Open Door policy rested upon the informal commitments thus made by the various powers. But in the winter of 1921 to 1922, at a conference participated in by all of the principal powers which had interests in the Pacific, the policy was crystallized into the so-called Nine Power Treaty, which gave definition and precision to the principles upon which the policy rested. . . .

This Treaty thus represents a carefully developed and matured international policy intended, on the one hand, to assure to all of the contracting parties their rights and interests in and with regard to China, and on the other hand, to assure to the people of China the fullest opportunity to develop without molestation their sovereignty and independence according to the modern and enlightened standards believed to maintain among the peoples of this earth. At the time this Treaty was signed, it was known that China was engaged in an attempt to develop the free institutions of a self-governing republic after her recent revolution from an autocratic form of government; that she would require many years of both economic and political effort to that end; and that her progress would necessarily be slow. The Treaty was thus a covenant of self-denial among the signatory powers in deliberate renunciation of any policy of aggression which might tend to interfere with that development. It was believed—and the whole history of the development of the "Open Door" policy reveals that faith—that only by such a process, under the protection of such an agreement, could the fullest interests not only of China but of all nations which have intercourse with her best be served. . . .

It must be remembered also that this Treaty was one of several treaties and agreements entered into at the Washington Conference by the various powers concerned, all of which were interrelated and interdependent. No one of these treaties can be disregarded without disturbing the general understanding and equilibrium which were intended to be accomplished and effected by the group of agreements arrived at in their entirety. The Washington Conference was essentially a disarmament conference, aimed to promote the possibility of peace in the world not only through the cessation of competition in naval armament but also by the solution of various other disturbing problems which threatened the peace of the world, particularly in the Far East. These problems were all interrelated. The willingness of the American government to surrender its then commanding lead in battleship construction and to leave its positions at Guam and in the Philippines without further fortification, was predicated upon, among other things, the self-denying covenants contained in the Nine Power Treaty, which assured the nations of the world not only of equal opportunity for their Eastern trade but also against the military aggrandizement of any other power at the expense of China. One cannot discuss the possibility of modifying or abrogating those provisions of the Nine Power Treaty without considering at the same time the other promises upon which they were really dependent.

Six years later the policy of self-denial against aggression by a stronger against a weaker power, upon which the Nine Power Treaty had been based, received a powerful reinforcement by the execution by substantially all the nations of the world of the Pact of Paris, the so-called Kellogg-Briand Pact. . . .

On January 7th last, upon the instruction of the President, this Government formally notified Japan and China that it would not recognize any situation, treaty or agreement entered into by those governments in violation of the covenants of these treaties, which affected the rights of our Government or its citizens in China. If a similar decision should be reached and a similar position taken by the other governments of the world, a caveat will be placed upon such action which, we believe, will effectively bar the legality hereafter of any title or right sought to be obtained by pressure or treaty violation, and which, as has been shown by history in the past, will eventually lead to the restoration to China of rights and titles of which she may have been deprived.

In the past our Government, as one of the leading powers on the Pacific Ocean, has rested its policy upon an abiding faith in the future of the people of China and upon the ultimate success in dealing with them of the principles of fair play, patience, and mutual goodwill. We appreciate the immensity of the task which lies before her statesmen in the development of her country and its government. The delays in her progress, the instability of her attempts to secure a responsible government, were foreseen by Messrs. Hay and Hughes and their contemporaries and were the very obstacles which the policy of the Open Door was designed to meet. We concur with those statesmen, representing all the nations in the Washington Conference who decided that China was entitled to the time necessary to accomplish her development. We are prepared to make that our policy for the future.

ADDITIONAL READING

The Great Depression dominated American diplomacy for a decade after 1929, and so the proper introduction to the era is *John Kenneth Galbraith, *The Great Crash: 1929* (Boston, 1955), a witty account; together with *Harris G. Warren, *Herbert Hoover and the Great Depression* (New York, 1959), a fair and careful work. A general view of the period is Allan Nevins's *The New Deal and World Affairs: 1933–1945* (New Haven, 1950), a volume in the

Chronicles of America series; for the Hoover years see Nevins's *The United States in a Chaotic World* (New Haven, 1950) and the new account by L. Ethan Ellis, mentioned in the preceding chapter. Other general works are *Jean-Baptiste Duroselle, *From Wilson to Roosevelt* (Cambridge, Mass., 1963); *Robert A. Divine, *The Reluctant Belligerent: American Entry into World War II* (New York, 1965), a volume in the America in Crisis series; Selig Adler, *The Uncertain Giant: 1921–1941* (New York, 1965); and the fine new book by *John E. Wiltz, *From Isolation to War: 1931–1941* (New York, 1968). *Robert H. Ferrell, *American Diplomacy in the Great Depression* (New Haven, 1957) undertakes a detailed analysis of the Hoover years. For the two presidents, Hoover and FDR, one should consult *The Memoirs of Herbert Hoover: The Cabinet and the Presidency, 1920–1933* (New York, 1952); Frank Freidel's brilliant multivolume study *Franklin D. Roosevelt* (Boston, 1952–   ), of which the first three volumes take its subject to the inaugural in 1933—*Apprenticeship* (1952), *Ordeal* (1954), *Triumph* (1956); see also the beautifully written "life and times" by *Arthur M. Schlesinger, Jr., *The Age of Roosevelt* (Boston, 1957–   ), of which the first three volumes likewise have been published—*The Crisis of the Old Order* (1957), *The Coming of the New Deal* (1958), *The Politics of Upheaval* (1960); John Gunther, *Roosevelt in Retrospect: A Profile in History* (New York, 1950); *James M. Burns, *Roosevelt: The Lion and the Fox* (New York, 1956); together with *Dexter Perkins's excellent *The New Age of Franklin Roosevelt* (Chicago, 1956), a volume in the Chicago History of American Civilization series. The secretaries of state, Stimson and Hull, have each left their explanations—Stimson in his memoir written with the assistance of McGeorge Bundy, *On Active Service* (New York, 1948); and Hull's own *The Memoirs of Cordell Hull* (2 vols., New York, 1948), written just like the secretary's speeches, but laden with infomation together with asides on such subjects as the secretary's favorite game, croquet. For other volumes on Stimson see the titles at the end of the preceding chapter. For Hull the inquiring student should read the magisterial analysis in Julius W. Pratt, *Cordell Hull* (2 vols., New York, 1964), volumes 12 and 13 in the American Secretaries series. Accounts by or about subordinate state department officials are William Phillips, *Ventures in Diplomacy* (Boston, 1953); Joseph C. Grew, *Turbulent Era* (2 vols., New York, 1952); Waldo H. Heinrichs, *American Ambassador: Joseph C. Grew and the Development of the United States Diplomatic Tradition* (Boston, 1966), a magnificent biography; and Nancy Harvison Hooker, ed., *The Moffat Papers: Selections from the Diplomatic Journals of Jay Pierrepont Moffat* (Cambridge, Mass., 1956). The Moffat diary is a rare piece, deserving of a much more extensive publication; no student of the 1930's can afford to neglect this source.

For the Far Eastern crisis of 1931–1933, there is the personal account by Henry L. Stimson, *The Far Eastern Crisis* (New York, 1936), which should be supplemented by the small section in Stimson's memoirs and the accounts in the books, already cited, by Richard N. Current, Elting E. Morison, and the present author. Rodman W. Paul, *The Abrogation of the Gentlemen's Agree-*

ment (Cambridge, Mass., 1936) sets out a prime cause of Japanese dissatisfaction with the United States. Another cause of disagreement appears in Dorothy Borg, *American Policy and the Chinese Revolution: 1925–1928* (New York, 1947); the Japanese people and their government did not like any sort of American policy of concern for China, and there was a great deal of concern during this era. For the inside of Japanese politics, one of the motive forces of the trouble in the orient, see Delmer M. Brown, *Nationalism in Japan* (Berkeley, Calif., 1955); Yale C. Maxon, *Control of Japanese Foreign Policy: A Study of Civil-Military Rivalry, 1930–1945* (Berkeley, 1957); and Richard Storry, *The Double Patriots* (Boston, 1958), the title of which refers to the fact that as a double shot of whiskey has twice the strength of a single shot, so some Japanese citizens during the 1920's and 1930's and early 1940's sought to be double patriots. Armin Rappaport, *Henry L. Stimson and Japan* (Chicago, 1963) sets out that problem from an American point of view. Takehiko Yoshihashi, *Conspiracy at Mukden: The Rise of the Japanese Military* (New Haven, 1963); and Sadako N. Ogata, *Defiance in Manchuria: The Making of Japanese Foreign Policy, 1931–1932* (Berkeley, 1964), is the Japanese side. Akira Iriye, *After Imperialism: The Search for a New Order in the Far East, 1921–1931* (Cambridge, Mass., 1965) is a marvelous synthesis of the latest American and Japanese scholarship.

On American recognition of Russia one should consult the prior troubles in the United States at the end of the First World War, the *Red Scare: A Study in National Hysteria, 1919–1920* (Minneapolis, 1955) by Robert K. Murray. William A. Williams, *American-Russian Relations: 1781–1947* (New York, 1952) covers the entire span of relations with attention to the early twentieth century. Another general treatment is Thomas A. Bailey, *America Faces Russia* (Ithaca, N.Y., 1950). *Robert P. Browder, *Origins of Soviet-American Diplomacy* (Princeton, 1953) surveys the years before and immediately after recognition. Beatrice Farnsworth, *William C. Bullitt and the Soviet Union* (Bloomington, Ind., 1967) deals with that quixotic gentleman. *George F. Kennan, *Memoirs: 1925–1690* (Boston, 1967) considers this era, from the light of experience. See also *Kennan's *Russia and the West under Lenin and Stalin* (Boston, 1960).

For economics and diplomacy there is Herbert Feis, *1933: Characters in Crisis* (Boston, 1966), on the London Economic Conference of that year; and Lloyd C. Gardner, *Economic Aspects of New Deal Diplomacy* (Madison, Wis., 1964).

A general study of the neutrality legislation is *Robert A. Divine, *The Illusion of Neutrality* (Chicago, 1962). A balanced view of part of the neutrality period appears in the volume by *William L. Langer and S. Everett Gleason, *The Challenge to Isolation: 1937–40* (New York, 1952), the first of a two-volume study of American entrance into the Second World War, 1937–1941. See also *Selig Adler's *The Isolationist Impulse* (New York, 1957). An example of the antiwar agitation of the mid-1930's, with due attention to all the war-scare bogeys of the day, is H. C. Engelbrecht and F. C. Hanighen, *Merchants of Death* (New York, 1934). The little lady who started the Senate investigation, Dorothy Detzer, has sketched her activities in *Appointment on the Hill* (New York, 1948). Wayne S. Cole, *Senator Gerald P. Nye and American Foreign Relations* (Minneapolis, 1962) offers the career of that leading congressional exponent of isolation. John E. Wiltz, *In Search of Peace: The Senate Munitions Inquiry, 1934–1936* (Baton Rouge, La., 1963) puts the Nye committee in careful perspective, with the assistance of all available manuscript collections and the archives of the department of state.

☆ *23* ☆

To Pearl Harbor, 1939-1941

"My god! This can't be true! This must mean the Philippines."
"No, sir. This is Pearl."

> —Conversation between Secretary of the Navy
> Frank Knox and Admiral Harold R. Stark,
> December 7, 1941

One feels a sense of tragedy in watching a great nation enter a world war. The course of American diplomacy in the years before December 7, 1941, is a somber, melancholy spectacle. American arms had brought victory to the Allies in the First World War, but afterward the United States threw away the advantages of the victory and sought to retire into the safe and sane nineteenth century when foreign relations were one of the least concerns of the successive administrations in Washington. For a while during the post-Versailles decades, it appeared that the new American withdrawal—it was never complete isolation, for the American substitutes for the League indicated concern for world peace—would prove as successful as had the policies, or lack of them, of the nineteenth century. Especially in the golden period of the later 1920's, the tide of world prosperity supported a hope of washing away everywhere the rancors and antagonisms of the First World War. Instead, the Great Depression washed away prosperity and with it the hopes of the 1920's. By the time the United States had recovered its poise and, no longer preoccupied with domestic concerns, could look about—by the later 1930's—the peace of the world was almost irreparably lost.

American policy toward Europe in the later 1930's had little effect upon the course of events. The only discernible diplomatic action of the American government against the advance of aggression everywhere in the world was a series of personal communications which the president dispatched to the dictators during several of the European crises. President Franklin Roosevelt in a letter of September 27, 1938, counseled peace to the dictators at the time of the Munich crisis. On April 14, 1939, after the Nazi occupation of Prague, the president in an open letter asked the German and Italian leaders to avow friendly intentions toward a long list of thirty-one specified European and Middle Eastern nations. Hitler on both occasions denied warlike intentions and restated German grievances. On August 24, 1939, Roosevelt again appealed to the dictators, beseeching them to settle their problems by peaceful means rather than war. All this effort was to no avail.

When war broke out on September 1, the American government still had the Neutrality Act of 1937 on its statute books, making it impossible for friendly foreign nations to purchase arms and ammunition in the United States, even if they undertook to carry these war materials in their own ships. The Neutrality Act of 1937 was revised in an act of November 4, 1939, to accommodate the sorely pressed Allies who, unlike Hitler, had not prepared for war. This change in the neutrality laws of the United States, according to President Roosevelt's critics, was an unneutral act. One must doubt that it was unneutral. Its provisions were as permissible under international law as were those of the Neutrality Act of 1937. But there can be no doubt that as month succeeded month and the position of the Allies became more desperate, the policies of the American government underwent changes which were, in reality, unneutral. Finally in the autumn of 1941 a large-scale undeclared war broke out between Germany and the United States in the Atlantic: American naval vessels were convoying foreign ships and sinking German submarines on sight; the German U-boats were retaliating wherever possible by torpedoing American destroyers. Yet war, when it came, did not stem from American unneutrality in the Atlantic but came suddenly, despite the correct and careful policy of the United States in the Pacific. Detractors of the American president, claiming that Roosevelt purposely exposed the Pacific fleet to a Japanese attack, have since described the events of December 7, 1941, at Pearl Harbor as the back door to war.

1. *The war in Europe, 1939–1940*

When the war opened in September 1939, the Allies at once looked to American industry for assistance in building their supplies of war material, and in November the president signed the revised neutrality act which permitted assistance. Meanwhile, on September 5, two days after France and Britain declared war on Germany, Roosevelt had proclaimed American neutrality under the act of 1937. He announced on September 8 a limited national emergency, a rather unprecedented state of affairs which no American president had ever proclaimed before and which, presumably, FDR himself thought up in order to indicate American interest in the European conflict and yet at the same time avoid worrying Congress and the people by proclamation of an unqualified national emergency. Announcement of the latter might well have seemed like a prelude to American entry into the European war.

For the next few months little more of a concrete nature occurred to indicate the Roosevelt administration's essentially deep sympathy for the cause of the Allies in their fight against German aggression. In the early months of the war it appeared that a *Sitzkrieg*, a stalemate, had developed on the western front, and during the months until the spring of 1940 this "phony war" made the armament situation of Britain and France seem far less precarious than it was, even in the presence of much placing of arma-

Adolf Hitler

ment orders in American factories. In the winter of 1939–1940, President Roosevelt became ever more open in his castigation of the Nazi German government. Some of the utterances in his fireside chats were strong statements about the personalities in control of a government with which the United States was nominally at peace. But beyond verbal condemnation, and the general facilitating of Allied war material purchases, the United States did not go. It took the shattering events of the Nazi spring offensive of 1940 to bring the administration to an understanding of the power and danger of the German government and people under the demonic guidance of their Fuehrer.

The German offensive of 1940 had long been in preparation, and it came with the full fury of planning and purpose. First occurred the occupation of Denmark and the conquest of Norway. Then German troops pushed into the Netherlands, Belgium, and Luxembourg, down toward the French channel ports. Meanwhile the main German drive laced through the allegedly impassable Ardennes forest and moved via Sedan to the channel. Next followed the turning of France's Maginot line—the ponderous French fortifications were taken from the rear. The French and British infantry and light tanks, no match for the German Panzer divisions, were brushed aside like so much chaff. Soon it was a race with time, to see whether the British and some remnants of the French forces could escape over the channel from the encircled port of Dunkirk. By June 4, 1940, 338,226 troops, mostly British, had got across to England. They had lost all equipment excepting their side arms and their nerve. This latter quality proved far more important than anything else they could have taken with them. The new prime minister, Winston Spencer Churchill, the greatest statesman in British history, defiantly announced in Parliament that "we shall not flag or fail. We shall go on to the end . . . we shall fight in the seas and oceans, we shall fight with growing confidence and growing strength in the air, we shall defend our island, whatever the cost may be, we shall fight on the beaches, we shall fight on the landing-grounds, we shall fight in the fields and in the streets, we shall fight in the hills; we shall never surrender, and even if, which I do not for a moment believe, this island or a large part of it were subjugated and starving, then our Empire beyond the seas, armed and guarded by the British Fleet, would carry on the struggle, until, in God's good time, the New World with all its power and might, steps forth to the rescue and the liberation of the Old."

No American statesman at such an hour could have failed to see the stakes in the world conflict, and Franklin D. Roosevelt set to work with vigor to assist the beleaguered British government and people. In his annual budget message of January 1940, the president had already requested $1,800,000,000 for national defense, an unprecedented expenditure in time of peace, and he had asked for additional appropriations of $1,182,000,000. He called for production of 50,000 combat planes a year. He requested $1,277,000,000 more on May 31 for military and naval requirements, and in response to an urgent appeal from Prime Minister Churchill the war department on June 3 began releasing to Britain surplus or outdated stocks of arms, munitions, and aircraft. The war department turned stocks back to manufacturers, who sold them to the British. Over $43,000,000 worth went across the Atlantic in June 1940.

Other measures were quickly forthcoming. In a move not devoid of political overtones (Roosevelt was toying with the idea of a moratorium on domestic politics, much as Lincoln had sought a political truce in the early days of the Civil War), FDR appointed two prominent Republican leaders, Henry L. Stimson and Frank Knox, as secretaries of war and of the navy. It was possible also to interpret this move as an effort to silence Republican criticism of the administration's pro-Allied measures, although criticism of Roosevelt's actions was not always patterned on party lines. In any event, one must say that both appointees, Stimson and Knox, were strong and able men who served their country well in the emergency which began in June 1940 and continued for over five years. Knox died under the strain in 1944. Stimson, in an atmosphere of triumph and honor, returned to private life in 1945.

In addition to the bipartisan appointments of Stimson and Knox, the president undertook in other ways to prepare the country for the struggle which he felt was approaching. In early autumn of 1940, he discussed defense problems with Prime Minister W. L. Mackenzie King of Canada and agreed to establish a permanent joint board of defense. On August 31, with the consent of Congress, the first units of the national guard were inducted into federal service. On September 2 the president, in an executive agreement with the British government, traded fifty World War I destroyers in exchange for the right to 99-year leases on naval and air bases in Newfoundland, Bermuda, the Bahamas, Jamaica, St. Lucia, Trinidad, Antigua, and British Guiana. This he announced as "the most important action in the reinforcement of our national defense . . . since the Louisiana Purchase." Then on September 16, 1940, the Burke-Wadsworth Bill became law, providing for selective service, the first peacetime compulsory military-training program in the United States.

With these measures behind him the president went before the country as a candidate for a third term in the White House, running against the liberal Republican, Wendell Willkie. This campaign, one may say in retrospect, might have been used by both candidates—Willkie, like FDR, favored aid to the Allies—to educate the American people to the realities of international affairs. Unfortunately it was not. The presidential campaign of 1940 was a lost opportunity. Both candidates marred the campaign by a conscious trimming of foreign-policy issues. Willkie and FDR almost outdid each other in promising peace to the American electorate. It is true that the American people naively asked for, and were reassured by, such empty promises. It is also true that Willkie honestly, and despite the feverish injunctions of many of his political supporters, came out in favor of the Roosevelt administration's pro-Allied activities. Yet the rigors of electioneering finally drove Willkie into saying that "If you elect me president I will never send an American boy to fight in any European war." Not to be outdone, the president himself, at Boston on October 30, 1940, told American mothers, "I have said this before, but I shall say it again and again and again: Your boys are not going to be sent into any foreign wars." At Buffalo on November 2 he said: "Your President says this country is not going to war." It was only a few months after the campaign that American troops were en route to Greenland and Iceland; a little more than a year later the president had to take his promise back completely.

In a happy mood, President Roosevelt assures the nation that this country "is not going to war."

With the assurance of another four years of office, Roosevelt moved ahead in his plans for aid to Britain against Germany. In a fireside chat on December 29, 1940, he told the nation that it should become "the great arsenal of democracy." In his annual message to Congress on January 6, 1941, he enunciated the Four Freedoms—freedom of speech and expression, freedom of worship, freedom from want, freedom from fear. Then, having done all these things, having laid the moral and material basis of aid to Britain against the German tyranny, he turned to two new and pressing problems. British credit in the United States was running out, and the Johnson Act of 1934 prevented the floating of public loans. The requirements of British defense were so large that no private loans could possibly cover them. The president in his annual message of January 6, 1941, produced a new formula, "lend-lease." Then there was a second problem: a sudden increase in the effectiveness and rigor of German submarine warfare in the Atlantic made necessary some sort of naval protection for British ships transporting the American-made goods to England.

2. Lend-lease and its aftermath

Lend-lease was the first major policy of assistance toward Great Britain adopted by the Roosevelt administration. It was a massive contribution to the defeat of Nazi Germany. Previous measures, such as the Neutrality Act of 1939 and the destroyers-bases deal of 1940, had looked in the direction of an Allied victory, but lend-lease was a move of substance that reduced these other acts to insignificance.

Its inspiration lay in Britain's dire need, but more intimately it was a result of the increasing personal cordiality between the two leaders of Britain and the United States. Roosevelt had been corresponding with Winston Churchill since the beginning of the European war, and the delighted Churchill—who at the outbreak of the war was first lord of the admiralty—had replied over the mysterious signature of "Naval Person." Upon becoming prime minister in May 1940 he changed his signature to "Former Naval Person." Through the medium of this correspondence the two statesmen of the English-speaking peoples kept in contact, and the president was in a position to know quickly the difficulties of his British opposite. It was in response to Britain's needs, so persuasively and personally represented by Churchill, that Roosevelt in January 1941 proposed to Congress the Lend-Lease Act: "H.R. 1776"—so an official of Congress had numbered the epoch-making bill when it came before the House of Representatives. According to its terms the president could "lease, lend, or otherwise dispose of," to any country whose defense was vital to the United States, arms and other equipment and supplies to an extent of an initial appropriation of $7,000,000,000. Fiscally the Lend-Lease Act made history for the size of its original appropriation, which was more than ninety times the amount of the national debt which Secretary of the Treasury Alexander Hamilton had refunded in 1790. By the end of the war the United States had appropriated for lend-lease more than $50,-000,000,000, a gigantic sum which would have been incomprehensible to the nation's founding fathers. H.R. 1776 did not, to be sure, go through Congress without objection. There was a vociferous debate during the first three months of 1941 which for bitterness and passion has rarely been equaled in American history.

The reasons for the bitterness of the debate over lend-lease were not difficult to perceive. For one, it was clear that with the proposed Lend-Lease Act the Roosevelt administration was irreparably committing the United States to the Allied cause; from this act onward there could be no turning back. For another, the administration's opponents in Congress had been resisting the president's measures of help to Britain with the increasing conviction that such opposition was hopeless—and their despair translated itself easily into passionate outbursts on the floor of the Senate and House. For a third, there was much concern, part of it political but part of it utterly sincere, that the president, so recently re-elected to an unprecedented third term of office, was pushing his views too far in Congress and throughout the country, that he had an obedient congressional majority and was hoodwinking the people and moving steadily in the direction of a dictatorship. All this misgiving may seem nonsensical by hindsight, but many individuals in 1941 were agitated. Debate over lend-lease brought their feelings to the surface.

Probably the most outspoken accusation came from Senator Burton K. Wheeler, long an opponent of President Roosevelt, who in a remark which alluded to the Agricultural Adjustment Act of 1933 announced, "The lend-lease-give program is the New Deal's triple A foreign policy; it will plow under every fourth American boy." Roosevelt was outraged. He angrily denounced "those who talk about plowing under every fourth American child." He told his press conference that he regarded Senator Wheeler's remark as "the most untruthful, as the most dastardly, unpatriotic thing that has ever been said. Quote me on that. That really is the rottenest thing that has been said in public life in my generation."

Wheeler's crude metaphor was beyond question misplaced and inappropriate, and the president had reason to lose his temper. Nonetheless the administration did approach lend-lease, a momentous piece of legislation, in a not entirely candid way. Roosevelt, it has sometimes been said, was at his worst when moving indirectly, and in the case of lend-lease he came to the proposal's defense in a way which at the least might be described as inaccurate. He must have known that the measure would probably lead to war, and certainly that if it led to peace this end could come only after the United States for a long time had exposed itself to the danger of German retaliation while giving aid to the British. An administration official, Jesse Jones, said during the lend-lease debate, "We're in the war; at least we are nearly in it; we're preparing for it." This utterance FDR turned with the comment that lend-lease would be administered not as a war measure but, on the contrary, as a peace measure. Roosevelt denied that lend-lease contradicted the spirit, if not the terms, of the Neutrality Act of 1939.

The administration's supporters maintained vehemently that lend-lease would not lead to war. Senator J. W. Bailey of North Carolina remarked, "It is said that the passage of the bill will lead to war. I do not know whether it will or not. I think those who predict that it will lead to war are in a pretty safe position, because there is a great deal of probability that war is coming, either course we take, and, when it comes, those who say it will come on account of this proposed act will say, 'Now it has come on account of the act.' Those who take the affirmative have to take the responsibility for events. The man who takes the opposition side is always in a fortunate position; he is not responsible for anything; he can always say, 'I did not advocate it.' I question whether the passage of the pending bill will lead to war, and I say its object is to head off war."

Representative E. V. Izak of California said in the House, "I lost all patience with my people when they came to me during the last campaign and said: 'Please don't get us into war.' I said, 'Don't look at me. I am not getting you into war, but there is one man who has the power to do that, and that is Mr. Hitler. Look at him.' "

And so debate went on. As we have seen, the president under the proposed act could make any arrangements with other nations which he deemed satisfactory, which implied much congressional trust in the president's discretion,. Roosevelt did not have to report to Congress in any way on anything he did under the law. Because authorship of H.R. 1776 was unknown, many individuals believed (and they were right) that the proposed act had emanated from the White House; the anonymity and surmise lent an air of conspiracy to the debate in Congress. As Representative Karl E. Mundt of South Dakota remarked, "We find this piece of legislation—surreptitiously conceived, individually disclaimed, of unknown parentage—placed before us, like a baby in a basket on our doorstep, and we are asked to adopt it." Perhaps Representative Dewey Short of Missouri summed up this belief in lend-lease as a conspiracy when he said that "You can dress this measure up all you please, you can sprinkle it with perfume and pour powder on it, masquerade it in any form you please . . . , but it is still foul and it stinks to high heaven. It does not need a doctor, it needs an undertaker."

All this was to no avail. "An Act to Promote the Defense of the United States" became law on March 11, 1941. As a direct result of the act, with its enormous supplying of aid to Britain against Nazi Germany, a virtual state of war broke out in the autumn of 1941 along the Atlantic seaways.

The approach of President Roosevelt to this undeclared war was, like his approach to lend-lease, indirect, and it is fair to say that the president's incapacity for indirect action lent some color of untruthfulness to his words during the spring and summer and autumn of 1941. Congress, not altogether certain of presidential intentions with lend-lease, had written into the act a statement as follows: "Nothing in this Act shall be construed to authorize or to permit the authorization of convoying by naval vessels of the United States. Nothing in this Act shall be construed to authorize or to permit the authorization of the entry of any American vessel into a combat area in violation of section 3 of the Neutrality Act of 1939." The president denied for several months in 1941 that he had any intention of instituting convoys. Meanwhile he set on foot measures which in result if not in avowed purpose were equivalent to convoying.

After passage of the Lend-Lease Act the president began almost at once to feel out public opinion on convoys, through statements by himself and by friends and members of the administration. FDR on March 15 began a move toward convoying by a radio address in which he said he would maintain a bridge of ships to Britain. On March 16, Senator Carter Glass of Virginia said he favored convoys if the president intended to imply that in the radio address. Next day the Committee to Defend America by Aiding the Allies, a group of important private individuals with easy access to the White House, came out for convoys. In a press conference on March 18, Roosevelt parried questions on convoys. Secretary of the Navy Knox said on March 20 that the navy department had no plans for convoys. On March 27, Senator Glass again said he was in favor of convoys. Then on March 31, Senator Charles W. Tobey of New Hampshire and Representative Harry Sauthoff of Wisconsin introduced in the Senate and House a joint resolution against convoys.

Tobey made a speech in which he explored the convoy question. He found himself opposed by Senator Alben W. Barkley of Kentucky, the Senate majority leader, who argued that Germany already had the right to declare war on the United States because of America's violation of neutrality by aiding Great Britain with lend-lease. Barkley could not see any further danger from convoys. Tobey asked his opponent if he was defending convoys.

Barkley: "Oh, no; the Senator knows that I am not."

Tobey: "I am asking the Senator in good faith."

Barkley: "And I am answering the Senator in good faith; if we have violated international law in such a way as could result in a declaration of war against us by Germany, we have already done that, and the convoying of ships would be only an incident."

A little later Tobey observed, "there is always a straw that breaks the camel's back, and that straw in my judgment, will be when, as, and if we send convoys to transport goods to belligerent nations."

Barkley: "That will depend upon events that we cannot now foresee."

Tobey: "Does not the Senator feel so, too?"

Barkley: "I will express my views upon that subject when the occasion has arisen."

Tobey: "In the words of the advertisement, 'If eventually, why not now?'"

Barkley: "I do not think it is possible for anybody today, even including the wise Senator from New Hampshire, to foresee conditions that may exist."

The colloquy drifted off into irrelevancies, led by Barkley.

Such was the interesting exchange on the Senate floor between the president's spokesman and an opposition senator, and if no light emerged, it did serve to further interest in the proposition of convoys. Tobey, aroused over the matter, apparently gave information to the New York *Daily News*, published on April 17, 1941, to the effect that American naval vessels were giving assistance to the British far out into the Atlantic, doing patrols and reconnaissance, even sailing between opposing enemies on the high seas and daring one side to shoot. In reply the president's press secretary, Stephen Early, declared that American naval vessels were operating far out in the Atlantic "on neutrality patrol," flashing news of alien ships in uncoded messages that anyone could listen to. American ships were carrying out their original instructions, he said, "to observe and report," and they were "keeping war from our front doors." Early said that the president, after reading a morning paper, thought its account had woven the long-time and historic policy of the United States into a story which was a deliberate lie.

Shortly after this, on April 25, FDR made an explanation of the difference between a convoy and a patrol. There was the same difference between the two operations, he said, as between a cow and a horse ("if one looks at a cow and calls it a horse that is all right with the president, but that does not make a cow a horse"). Roosevelt recalled that in pioneer days the wagon trains going westward had armed guards and also scouts. The rule was, he explained, to keep the trains more than two miles from where the Indians were. He elaborated this pioneer example by saying that it was not safe to wait until the Indians got two miles away, but advisable to ascertain whether the Indians were 200 miles away.

Meanwhile on April 9 the president had signed an agreement with the Danish minister in Washington which included Greenland in "our sphere of co-operative hemispheric defense." Hitler launched his rash attack on the USSR in June. On July 7 there was an agreement with Iceland similar to that with Denmark. Under these arrangements United States military forces received convenient new bases for their "patrols" to protect their "security zone" and "patrol areas."

Two months passed after occupation of Iceland before there began to occur a perhaps not unexpected series of untoward incidents. The first, probably the most important, was the attack by a German submarine on the United States destroyer *Greer*, off Iceland, on September 4. The president took a strong view of this engagement. Roosevelt made a broadcast about the *Greer* on September 11 in which he said the vessel "was carrying American mail to Iceland. . . . She was then and there attacked by a submarine. . . . I tell you the blunt fact that the German submarine fired first upon this American destroyer without warning, and with deliberate design to sink her." He announced that he had given sink-on-sight orders to the navy, a decision which, he said, was the "result of months and months of constant thought and anxiety and prayer."

Without doubting the care that went into the president's decision, one should perhaps explain that the circumstances of the *Greer* attack were not altogether as the president described them. In his radio address he had, indeed, engaged in the time-honored diplomatic practice of *suppressio veri, suggestio falsi*. The *Greer* while en route to Iceland had been informed by a British plane of the presence of a submarine about ten miles directly ahead. The *Greer* gave chase, trailing the submarine and broadcasting its position for three hours and twenty-eight minutes, during which the British plane dropped four depth charges, when the submarine fired a torpedo which crossed the *Greer* about 100 yards astern. The destroyer answered with a pattern of eight depth charges; the submarine replied with another torpedo that missed the *Greer*. The chase went on for a while, with more depth charges, and the American ship finally gave up and proceeded to Iceland.

The sink-on-sight order came on September 11. The navy on September 16 announced convoying in the Atlantic as far as Iceland.

There followed a month later, on October 17, the torpedoing with severe damage of the destroyer *Kearny* by a German submarine west of Iceland, with loss of eleven American lives. FDR on October 27 delivered a long and vehement address, in the course of which he said,

"America has been attacked. The U.S.S. *Kearny* is not just a Navy ship. She belongs to every man, woman, and child in this Nation." The *Kearny* had also been attacking German submarines when she was torpedoed.

The tanker *Salinas* sank on October 30, 1941.

The destroyer *Reuben James* was torpedoed on the night of October 30, with loss of 96 officers and men.

The issue was clearly drawn between the United States and Germany —of that there could be no doubt. A series of unneutral acts had demonstrated the sympathies of the Roosevelt administration: lend-lease and convoying had put the case clearly enough. The leader of the German Reich knew in the autumn of 1941 that the government of the United States was his enemy.

In the course of events in the Atlantic there remained a touch of high principle, produced by President Roosevelt and Prime Minister Churchill during their dramatic meeting in Argentia bay off Newfoundland in mid-August 1941. It was during this meeting that they drew up the Atlantic Charter.

The Charter of August 14, 1941, was not a signed document, only a press release, a statement of principles agreed to by the participants at the Argentia meeting, but its informal nature did not lessen its importance. A document analogous to the Fourteen Points, it set out what were to be American and to some extent British aims for the remainder of the war years. It later was written into the United Nations Declaration of January 1, 1942, and adopted by all the Allies against Nazi Germany. In this joint declaration Roosevelt and Churchill pledged that their countries sought no aggrandizement, territorial or other; second, "they desire to see no territorial changes that do not accord with the freely expressed wishes of the peoples concerned"; third, they announced the right of all peoples to choose their own form of government; fourth, "access, on equal terms, to the trade and to the raw materials of the world"; fifth, economic collaboration among nations; sixth, freedom from fear and want; seventh, all men had the right "to traverse the high seas and oceans without hindrance"; eighth, disarmament of aggressors and limitation of the arms of peace-loving peoples. The Charter admittedly was not as explicit as the Fourteen Points—it was in fact downright vague in some of its pronouncements—but it did declare in rounded terms the war aims of the American and British peoples. As the war progressed, Churchill came to see that some of the Charter's provisions were visionary, and during a dinner at Yalta in 1945 he pointedly told Roosevelt that the Charter was not "a law, but a star." The American president, however, took the Charter seriously, and Churchill and the other Allies were therefore persuaded to take it into account.

Thus the United States had come in the Atlantic, through principle and practice, to virtually a state of belligerency against Germany, although in spite of these unneutral actions there was still no declared war in the Atlantic between the two nations. For the moment it suited the German dictator's purposes that there be no declaration of war. Hitler apparently believed that with the attack upon Russia in June 1941, an attack which at its outset came within a hair's breadth of victory, he could ensure his domination of the continent of Europe—afterward, he would settle scores with both England and the United States.

What would have happened had Russia collapsed in 1941 is an interesting subject for speculation. It is difficult to see how British and American power alone could have defeated a triumphant Germany, unless the war had gone on for years and perhaps decades. Roosevelt took a grave chance in coming to the defense of Britain when he did. Russia fortunately did not collapse in 1941, and history saved the reputation of an American president.

In retrospect it is easy to see where the German dictator made his mistakes. He could have nicely confused the American people in 1940–1941 by a magnanimous peace with France. He could have offered an olive branch to England and used every stratagem to convince the somewhat gullible Americans that he alone was holding back the Bolsheviks along the marches of Eastern Europe. Then, had he placated the Russian people in the captured areas of their country, instead of victimizing and enslaving and decimating them, he might have swept forward all the way across the steppes of Siberia in the guise of an anticommunist crusader. Doubtless the leaders of the American and British governments knew too much already about the bestial nature of the Nazi regime, but a careful propaganda effort might have caused trouble among the divided and confused American people. Luckily for the United States this historical nightmare never became real.

Thus far we have sketched the measures of the American government at the outbreak of the war in Europe and analyzed in some detail the mobilization of American resources which began after the successful German spring campaign against France in 1940. By the final month of the year 1941, the American navy was engaged in open although undeclared warfare with the German submarine fleets in the western Atlantic. Still, the event which plunged the United States into war derived from an entirely different development, the deterioration of American-Japanese relations in the summer and autumn of 1941.

3. Pearl Harbor

Ever since the Mukden incident of September 18, 1931, relations between Washington and Tokyo had been strained. For that matter, ever since the victory of Japan over Russia in 1904–1905 and the subsequent refusal of the Japanese to be houseboys for the open door, distrust had existed between the two Pacific nations, a distrust which on several occasions before 1931 had overcome the normal reticences of international discourse. At such moments as the segregation of Japanese school children in San Francisco schools in 1906, the Twenty-One Demands of 1915, and the exclusion of Japanese immigrants from the United States in the immigration act of 1924, Japanese anger at the American government rose to fever pitch. Long before the occupation of Manchuria, official relations between the two countries had become far from congenial.

The Manchurian affair initiated a precipitous decline in Japanese-American cordiality, and when in 1937 the Japanese army, having virtually taken over the civil government in Tokyo, went into China in a large way and began to seize China's main coastal cities and as much of the hinterland as could be easily held, relations between Japan and the United States sank lower and lower. The military operations of the so-called China incident were conducted on a ferocious scale. The Manchurian incident was marked by almost no atrocities by Japanese soldiers, but the China fighting in 1937 and thereafter was appallingly inhumane, perhaps as many as 100,000 Chinese soldiers and civilians being murdered in the sack of Nanking alone. In marked contrast to the doubted information about increasing Nazi brutalities in Europe, the American people quickly learned of this bloodletting in China, where the American missionary effort both Protestant and Catholic had for decades been large; the missionaries wrote home terrified letters about what was happening before their very eyes. President Roosevelt apparently believed at this time that public opinion was ready for some sort of positive policy. He proposed in a speech in Chicago on October 5, 1937, that there be an international quarantine of aggressors as the only means to preserve peace. He did not, it is true, pursue this policy at the Brussels Conference, held on November 3–24, 1937, by all the signatories (save Japan) of the Nine-Power Treaty. At Brussels the United States, along with the other nations, took a weak position and the conference broke up in despair. Still, the president was beginning to think of action. When on December 12, 1937, Japanese planes sank the United States river gunboat *Panay*, with loss of two American lives, the administration felt strong enough to demand from the

Japanese government an immediate apology, reparations, and guarantee against further incidents. The Tokyo regime, hardened though it was, made no effort to defend the act of its fliers.

Relations continued to deteriorate after 1937. When the Second World War commenced in Europe in 1939, the Japanese awaited events until after the fall of France in the early summer of 1940; then the Tokyo government on September 27, 1940, signed a Tripartite Pact with Germany and Italy. High government officials in Washington at once began to worry lest the three fascist powers were now concèrting their policies, and that while Japan alone of the three aggressor nations had not yet entered the lists against the Western democracies, it would enter in due time, presumably the worst possible time for Britain and America.

What, in truth, was the purpose of the Tripartite Pact of 1940? Did it as good as tell the world that Japan intended a new move of expansion in the Far East at the expense of American interests and therefore was enlisting Germany in event of a head-on collision with the United States? If Japan expanded further in the Far East, moved into territory other than China, it would be either (1) Siberia, or else (2) the much more attractive lands of the Dutch East Indies, French Indochina, British Malaya and Burma, perhaps Australia and New Zealand. It was axiomatic that the United States, while attempting to bolster England in the fight in Europe, could not allow Japan to knock down the British empire in Asia. An advance not into Siberia but into Southeast Asia, Australia, and New Zealand might well bring an American declaration of war. Even so, it was an error to construe the Tripartite Pact as aimed against the United States. Actually Germany in 1940 was seeking to enlist Japan in the forthcoming campaign against Soviet Russia, planned for the spring of 1941. The *Realpolitiker* in Berlin hoped that Japan would enter Siberia at the same time that the German army crossed the Russian borders in the west.

It was true, of course, that the Japanese were making up their minds to turn southward—but Allied diplomats in so reading the Tripartite Pact obtained the right conclusion from the wrong evidence.

The southward advance seemed necessary to the Japanese as the only solution of a crucial problem of military logistics. Japan's oil reserves were so small that they could not support a major and prolonged war. The Japanese depended upon imports from the United States for eighty per cent of their oil. As the military planners in Tokyo saw it, they must take the oil of the Dutch East Indies. The strategists of the Japanese army and navy were resigned to the fact that the southward advance meant a war with the United States. Hence they planned to destroy at the outset the principal American military force in the Pacific, the American fleet based on Pearl Harbor in Hawaii. From such a blow, they hoped, the American navy would require months and perhaps years to recuperate. During that period, Japan could so expand through the Far East as to become impregnable to American counterattack. Then, the United States having become involved in the war in Europe, American political leaders would negotiate a peace with Tokyo and allow Japan to keep the new "co-prosperity sphere."

Such a scheme of conquest may today seem foolhardy and irresponsible in the extreme, and perhaps it was. One might ask how the Japanese military, who were not complete fools, could have sponsored it. The minds of men, one can only conclude, are always capable of self-delusion. As for the leaders of the Japanese army and navy, they were mostly men of narrow background and intensely professional experience, incapable of making the large appraisals and informed guesses which are the rudiments of statesmanship. Japan's military planning was never the careful plotting and analysis which was later attributed to it. The Japanese military leaders really did not know where they were going. Japanese aggression was a jerry-built structure which moved uncertainly forward, one event leading crazily to another. It is easy to see now that the plan of the young officer enthusiasts led by General Tojo was an immense gamble. It would have been better for Japan in 1940–1941 to have obtained an agreement with the United States. The Japanese military, unfortunately, were unable to see a middle way out of their predicament. They could not see that honorable peace was an acceptable alternative to capitulation or war. Typical of Japanese reasoning was the contention of an admiral at an imperial conference—that because of the vulnerability of the Japanese military machine to a cutting off of foreign oil imports, Japan was like a patient who was certain to die if you did nothing but might be saved by a dangerous operation.

The southward advance was chosen instead of Siberia. The German government learned with surprise in the early spring of 1941 that Japan was negotiating a nonaggression pact with Russia. Foreign Minister Yosuke Matsuoka signed the pact in Moscow on April 13 with Foreign Minister Vyacheslav M. Molotov. The Russians already were anticipating the German attack which came on their western border in June, and they were happy to secure their eastern flank in Manchuria against the Japanese. Japan likewise secured its northern flank, and its armies could pursue the cherished southward advance.

The first move came quickly. The Japanese announced on July 25, 1941, that together with the Vichy French government of Marshal Henri-Philippe Pétain (the Vichy government controlled that part of France unoccupied by the Germans) they were undertaking a joint protectorate of Indochina. There was no reason why Japan should protect Indochina, except that Japanese troops could thereby menace the Philippines. Access to the airport at Saigon, acquired several months before, had already brought the British bastion of Singapore within easy range of Japanese bombing planes.

Not to be outdone, President Roosevelt on July 26, 1941, issued an executive order freezing Japanese assets in the United States. This ended all trade, forcing even those Japanese ships in American ports to depart in ballast. Among other things the president's executive order cut off all exports of oil.

Back in the summer of 1940 the United States had begun to embargo strategic materials to Japan—scrap iron, steel, and certain types of oil products—and in following months additional embargoes were placed until on January 27, 1941, Ambassador Joseph C. Grew in Tokyo warned, "There is a lot of talk around town to the effect that the Japanese, in case of a break with the United States, are planning to go all out in a surprise mass attack at Pearl Harbor." Actually this was the very time that Admiral Isoruku Yamamoto began planning the Pearl Harbor attack. When Grew's premonitions reached the United States, they were mulled over by the Office of Naval Intelligence, but ONI placed no credence in them. Between January and July 1941, much war material continued to go out from America to Japan. Only high-octane gasoline and aviation lubricating oil were openly forbidden in trade, and other types of petroleum products flowed in a stream across the Pacific to the Japanese army and navy. But on July 26 this trade came to a sudden end.

Both the United States and Japan began preparing for war. President Roosevelt in the summer of 1941 nationalized the Philippine forces and appointed the Philippine field marshal and former United States army chief of staff, Douglas MacArthur, as commanding general of army forces in the Far East. Meanwhile Japanese army planners drafted plans for major strikes against the Malay peninsula, the Philippines, and Pearl Harbor. Yet both nations needed time. The Japanese militarists needed a few months to train their carrier air groups to destroy the United States Pacific fleet, and America needed time for new naval construction and to reinforce the army in the Philippines.

There followed several months of last-minute diplomatic negotiations —which, let it be added, were sincere on both sides. On the American side President Roosevelt and Secretary of State Hull were anxious for peace if they could obtain it with honor. On the Japanese side the diplomats of the Tokyo government did not know what their military were up to. The Japanese ambassador in Washington, Admiral Kichisaburo Nomura, was an honorable man, a typical Japanese conservative, who knew that his poverty-striken country should not attempt to play the role of the frog which wanted to become a bull. Nomura with good reason was *persona grata* at the state department. He knew nothing of the plans of the militarists in his homeland.

Nomura's superior, Premier Prince Fumimaro Konoye, was a well-meaning individual but of weak tendencies, a person known in Japan as a liberal, yet as premier in 1937 he had said that China should be "beaten to her knees." Konoye in 1941 was window dressing for the militarists, and in early September they impatiently gave him six weeks to reach a settlement with the United States. The terms: America would have to turn China over to Japan. With this impossible proposal as his only program, Konoye sought a Pacific conference with Roosevelt. But the latter, well advised by Secretary Hull, who suggested that the Japanese be invited to detail their program in advance of any meeting, refused to meet the Japanese premier. The six-week deadline came and passed. Konoye, forced to resign, gave way to a new premier, General Tojo, the Razor Brain, in whose keeping events now lay.

The crisis moved rapidly toward a showdown. Ambassador Grew in Tokyo did not know exactly what was going on in the councils of the militarists, but in a cable of November 3 he warned Secretary Hull that Japan might resort to war measures with "dramatic and dangerous suddenness." Perhaps he recalled that all of Japan's modern wars, in 1894, 1904, and 1914, had begun without formal declaration of hostilities. Nomura in Washington on November 5 received instructions that it was "absolutely necessary" to come to an agreement with the United States by November 25. A special ambassador, Saburo Kurusu, another man of good will, made a hurried flight from Japan to assist Nomura in these negotiations. On November 20, the two Japanese ambassadors made what they regarded as their "absolutely final proposal," a rather immodest request for resumption of oil exports and noninterference by the United States in Japan's China incident. Secretary Hull realized that granting these terms was impossible, given the rising American popular temper. Americans might permit trimming on European matters, but they would allow their government no compromises with the Asiatic Axis partner, Japan. The American people did not realize how close their country was to war, but it is doubtful if in 1941 they would have permitted a Munich in the Far East, even had they known the seriousness of affairs.

For a short time Washington officials did consider some sort of *modus vivendi*. Military preparations were in a perilous state—an army contingent was at sea near Guam, the marines were just pulling out of Shanghai where for years they had been protecting American commercial interests, and 21,000 troops were scheduled to sail from the United States for the Philippines on December 8. Secretary Hull prepared a three-month *modus*

Secretary Hull escorts Japanese ambassador, Nomura (L.) and special ambassador, Kurusu (R.) to the White House.

vivendi, which included some concessions on oil, and submitted it to representatives of China, Great Britain, Australia, and the Netherlands in Washington. The Chinese government violently opposed the idea. Winston Churchill described it as "thin diet for Chiang Kai-shek." And, in any event, a *modus vivendi* would have been unacceptable to the Japanese. Premier Tojo in Japan already had rejected any compromise along the lines of Hull's draft, and so when the state department dropped the matter, nothing was lost.

Hull then presented the Japanese with a long document dated November 26, which among other requests asked the Japanese to get out of China. At the Tokyo war crimes trial after the end of the war, General Tojo admitted that the note of November 26 was little more than a restatement of the Nine-Power Treaty of Washington, to which Japan had been a party, but twenty years after the Washington Conference the Nine-Power Treaty was unacceptable to Japan's rulers. On December 1 a cabinet council met in the imperial presence in Tokyo and ratified General Tojo's decision to make war on America, Great Britain, and the Netherlands. The Pearl Harbor striking force, which had already sailed, was notified that X-day was December 7. Nomura and Kurusu, unaware that the die had been cast, were instructed to present the Japanese reply to the November 26 proposal at 1:00 P.M. Washington time, December 7, which was twenty minutes before the striking hour at Pearl Harbor.

The intensely interesting details of the Pearl Harbor attack have been carefully described from both the Japanese and American sides in a number of books and essays easily available to serious readers. Briefly, the Japanese attack force of six carriers, escorted by two battleships and a full complement of cruisers, destroyers, and submarines, sailed undetected through high seas and fog. When the fleet changed course toward Hawaii, on the final lap of the voyage, one of the carriers hoisted to its masthead the identical flag which the revered Admiral Togo had displayed on his flagship before the battle of Tsushima strait in 1905. It was a great moment in Japanese history when on Sunday morning, "the day that will

Pearl Harbor—*Downes* and *Cassin* in the foreground, *Pennsylvania* at the rear.

live in infamy" (as President Roosevelt would describe it in his war message), the attacking Japanese planes roared over Pearl Harbor and found the battleship fleet exactly where it was expected, tied up to the mooring quays along the southeast shore of Ford Island.

The valor and heroism of the surprised and trapped seamen will long live in the annals of American naval warfare. More than 2,300 lives were lost that terrible Sunday morning. Eight battleships capsized or were otherwise put out of action. Fortunately for the United States, Admiral William F. Halsey was away with a carrier striking force on a special mission, and his precious ships escaped the disaster in the harbor. Fortunately too, the Japanese in their attack virtually ignored the installations and fuel tanks at Pearl Harbor, destruction of which would have presented grave logistic problems and perhaps forced a removal of the fleet's remaining ships to the American west coast. Still, the Japanese attack on Pearl Harbor, despite such miscalculations, was appallingly successful. American entry into the Second World War occurred after an unprecedented naval disaster.

4. *The theory of the back door*

Was Pearl Harbor the back door to war?

This question was to trouble many Americans for years to come. Debate over the circumstances of American entry into the Second World War had to await the end of the war itself, but in 1945 it rose to the surface of public discussion and raged for the next four or five years—until the loss of China to the communists in 1949 and its sequel in 1950, the Korean War, turned attention to what seemed an even more serious kind of skulduggery than Pearl Harbor.

While it lasted, the controversy over Pearl Harbor was an acrimonious affair. John T. Flynn, the well-known journalist, blew the lid off the Pearl Harbor controversy in 1945 when immediately after V-J Day he published his pamphlet *The Final Secret of Pearl Harbor*. He showed that the American government in the months before entry into the war had cracked the highest Japanese secret code, the so-called purple cipher, and had been reading Japan's innermost diplomatic and military secrets long before the attack of December 7, 1941. Pressure for a congressional investigation became overwhelming, and Congress authorized a special joint committee which sat from November 15, 1945, to May 31, 1946. Its record of hearings encompassed approximately 10,000,000 words, and this mountain of evidence was published in October in 39 volumes. But the joint committee came to no agreement as to the meaning of its evidence and publicly registered its uncertainty in a report containing dissenting majority and minority views.

Argument continued, with the key question being why the Pearl Harbor disaster had occurred if the government was so well-informed on Japanese intentions. Some individuals chose to believe that there had been an intelligence lapse before the fleet disaster—that plenty of warnings had come from the decoded intercepts but they were not properly evaluated. The intercepts (according to this view) came in bits and pieces to the desks of leading administration officials, military and civil, and these busy people did not have time enough to evaluate them. Another interpretation of the Pearl Harbor disaster, however, was that the intercepts and other important pieces of information were ignored, purposely left unassembled, because President Roosevelt had "planned it that way." He had determined to expose the fleet to the Japanese so as to force the reluctant American nation into the Second World War. This latter belief produced a veritable school of "revisionist" historians led by the historian and sociologist Harry Elmer Barnes. As Barnes pointed out in a book entitled *Perpetual War for Perpetual Peace*, Pearl Harbor was a dastardly plot. "The net result of revisionist scholarship applied to Pearl Harbor," he wrote, "boils down essentially to this: In order to promote Roosevelt's political ambitions and his mendacious foreign policy some three thousand American boys were quite needlessly butchered. Of course, they were only a drop in the bucket compared to those who were ultimately slain in the war that resulted, which was as needless, in terms of vital American interests, as the surprise attack on Pearl Harbor."

What can one make out of this sort of accusation? Have the revisionists ever succeeded in proving their case about Pearl Harbor? In actual fact they have not, for an enormous amount of scholarship, revisionist and antirevisionist, has been expended on the subject of Pearl Harbor, and no one has emerged with clear proof, even a trace of proof, that the American president in 1941 purposely exposed the Pacific fleet to achieve his goals in foreign policy. For the revisionists, apparently, a wish has been father to the thought. Many of them wanted to believe that President Roosevelt was a villain, and by a quick leap or two of the imagination they managed to turn wishes into conviction.

Admittedly a circumstantial case can be constructed in support of revisionist history. It is true that the authorities in Washington prior to December 7, 1941, badly bungled some warning messages to the various Pacific commands, messages based on information derived from the Japanese intercepts. These messages employed customary military circumlocution in an effort to seem mindful of all occasions and eventualities; the Pearl Harbor commanders interpreted the messages as a warning against sabotage—and among other precautions they bunched their planes on the runways where they made convenient targets for Japanese attack. Likewise it is true that Roosevelt at the very moment of Pearl Harbor was contemplating a message to Congress warning that in the event of a Japanese move into the Southwest Pacific the United States would take appropriate action, and the Japanese attack saved him the trouble of arguing with skeptical congressmen.

The back-door theorists have borrowed support from the treatment of the army and navy commanders at the unfortunate Hawaii base, Admiral Husband E. Kimmel and Lieutenant General Walter C. Short. They were hastily—and, the present writer believes, most unfairly—cashiered after the Japanese attack; their treatment by the Washington administration was so ungenerous as to suggest that they were needed as scapegoats to remove suspicion from higher authorities. General Short died in 1949, but Admiral Kimmel lived to publish a book in 1955 hinting broadly that Short and he were scapegoats for the president of the United States. One of Kimmel's friends, Rear Admiral Robert A. Theobald, who was in command of fleet destroyers at the time of the Japanese attack, wrote a book with the same title as the pamphlet by Flynn, *The Final Secret of Pearl Harbor,* and openly accused the late president of exposing the fleet and thereafter sacking the military commanders at Hawaii.

But no one has really proved any untoward acts at Pearl Harbor, and the burden of proof must rest with Roosevelt's detractors. Nearly all the records of the United States government have been opened to public or congressional scrutiny, and no proof of a presidential plot has yet appeared.

It ought to be possible, therefore, to settle the argument for revisionism by an argument drawn from what might be termed common sense. What man, one might ask, having risen to the presidency and enjoyed two successful terms in office, would jeopardize his life's reputation, not to speak of the fate of his country, to engage in a plot so crude that it sounds as if it came out of the sixteenth century, the era of Niccolo Machiavelli? Common sense refuses to believe in the possibility of such a course. Moreover, in so large and unwieldy an establishment as the government of the United States it is enormously difficult to set a conspiracy on foot without someone revealing it. Many people must be privy even to the highest secrets of state, and it is inconceivable that conspiracy could advance in such a situation. Even if he were thwarted by the German government's refusal to declare war against the United States because of American aid to Britain in supplies and convoying, it defies common sense to believe that President Franklin D. Roosevelt would have constructed in diabolical cleverness a Pacific back door to war.

Personalities and recriminations aside, the fact is that the Japanese attack in 1941 on the Pearl Harbor battleship fleet united the American nation as no other single event could have done and at last took the country into the Second·World War at the side of Britain and Russia. Once again, as Churchill had hoped a year and a half before, "in God's good time, the New World, with all its power and might," came to "the rescue and the liberation of the Old." The American people finally realized that a generation of diplomatic error had to be redeemed in war. They and their leaders had been well intentioned. The mistakes of the post-Versailles years had been partly their own fault, partly that of others, partly a conjunction of unfortunate circumstances. But the error of the times, wherever the responsibility, had to be redeemed. When the signal towers at Pearl Harbor on Sunday morning, December 7, 1941, messaged the United States the stupefying news,

AIR RAID PEARL HARBOR THIS IS NO DRILL

there began the first of what proved to be 1,351 days of war.

A CONTEMPORARY DOCUMENT

[Secretary Hull on November 26, 1941, gave the Japanese government a stiff proposal. In retrospect, of course, the Japanese should have accepted it. Source: *Foreign Relations of the United States: Japan, 1931–1941* (2 vols., Washington, 1943), II, 769–770.]

The Government of the United States and the Government of Japan propose to take steps as follows:

1. The Government of the United States and the Government of Japan will endeavor to conclude a multilateral non-aggression pact among the British Empire, China, Japan, the Netherlands, the Soviet Union, Thailand and the United States.

2. Both Governments will endeavor to conclude among the American, British, Chinese, Japanese, the Netherland and Thai Governments an agreement whereunder each of the Governments would pledge itself to respect the territorial integrity of French Indochina and, in the event that there should develop a threat to the territorial integrity of Indochina, to enter into immediate consultation with a view to taking such measures as may be deemed necessary and advisable to meet the threat in question. Such agreement would provide also that each of the Governments party to the agreement would not seek or accept preferential treatment in its trade or economic relations with Indochina and would use its influence to obtain for each of the signatories equality of treatment in trade and commerce with

French Indochina.

3. The Government of Japan will withdraw all military, naval, air and police forces from China and from Indochina.

4. The Government of the United States and the Government of Japan will not support—militarily, politically, economically—any government or regime in China other than the National Government of the Republic of China with capital temporarily at Chungking.

5. Both Governments will give up all extraterritorial rights in China, including rights and interests in and with regard to international settlements and concessions, and rights under the Boxer Protocol of 1901.

Both Governments will endeavor to obtain the agreement of the British and other governments to give up extraterritorial rights in China, including rights in international settlements and in concessions and under the Boxer Protocol of 1901.

6. The Government of the United States and the Government of Japan will enter into negotiations for the conclusion between the United States and Japan of a trade agreement, based upon reciprocal most-favored-nation treatment and reduction of trade barriers by both countries, including an undertaking by the United States to bind raw silk on the free list.

7. The Government of the United States and the Government of Japan will, respectively, remove the freezing restrictions on Japanese funds in the United States and on American funds in Japan.

8. Both Governments will agree upon a plan for the stabilization of the dollar-yen rate, with the allocation of funds adequate for this purpose, half to be supplied by Japan and half by the United States.

9. Both Governments will agree that no agreement which either has concluded with any third power or powers shall be interpreted by it in such a way as to conflict with the fundamental purpose of this agreement, the establishment and preservation of peace throughout the Pacific area.

10. Both Governments will use their influence to cause other governments to adhere to and to give practical application to the basic political and economic principles set forth in this agreement.

ADDITIONAL READING

For the years 1939 to 1941 see the general works cited in previous chapters, by Duroselle, Divine, Wiltz, Pratt, Adler, and Nevins. There also are the excellent volumes by *William L. Langer and S. Everett Gleason, *The Chal-*

lenge to Isolation: 1937–40 (New York, 1952) and *The Undeclared War: 1940–1941* (New York, 1953). This account of American entrance into the Second World War, published by the Council on Foreign Relations, was based on exhaustive study of available manuscript and printed sources. The eminence of its authors and sponsorship has ensured an account that will stand for some time to come. A shorter study dealing with the same period is Donald F. Drummond, *The Passing of American Neutrality: 1937–1941* (Ann Arbor, Mich., 1955). Two bibliographical surveys are Louis Morton, "Pearl Harbor in Perspective," *United States Naval Institute Proceedings*, LXXXI (1955), 460–468; and Wayne S. Cole, "American Entry into World War II: A Historiographical Appraisal," *Mississippi Valley Historical Review*, XLIII (1956–1957), 595–617.

Events in Europe during 1939–1941 can be traced in many memoirs and special works. The plight of Europe appears poignantly in *Winston S. Churchill, *The Gathering Storm* (Boston, 1948), *Their Finest Hour* (1949), and *The Grand Alliance* (1950), the first three volumes of *The Second World War* (6 vols., Boston, 1948–1953). A book of enduring interest is John F. Kennedy's *Why England Slept* (New York, 1940), a remarkable production from a then slightly-known young man. For the European temper of the time see also Harold Butler's *The Lost Peace: A Personal Impression* (London, 1941); *A. L. Rowse, *All Souls and Appeasement* (London, 1961); Anthony Eden, *Memoirs: Facing the Dictators* (Boston, 1962); and Elizabeth Wiskemann, *The Europe I Saw* (New York, 1968). The fall of France, one of the most dramatic and saddening events of the early part of the war, appears in the brilliant memoir by Edward Spears, *Assignment to Catastrophe* (2 vols., New York, 1954–1955), by a key British official and confidant of Churchill.

On the American side there is a new study of the United States and Germany in the 1930's by Arnold Offner, *American Appeasement* (Cambridge, Mass., 1969), a first-rate volume; Robert Dallek, *Democrat and Diplomat: The Life of William E. Dodd* (New York, 1968), a biography of the American ambassador in the early 1930's; Hans L. Trefousse, *Germany and American Neutrality: 1939–1941* (New York, 1951), still useful; Saul Friedlaender, *Prelude to Downfall: Hitler and the United States, 1939–1941* (New York, 1967); and James V. Compton, *The Swastika and the Eagle: Hitler, the United States, and the Origins of World War II* (Boston, 1967). The activities of American diplomats in Paris and London have been examined critically by William W. Kaufmann, "Two American Ambassadors: Bullitt and Kennedy," in *Gordon Craig and Felix Gilbert, eds., *The Diplomats* (Princeton, 1953). R. H. Dawson has treated *The Decision to Aid Russia: 1941* (Chapel Hill, N.C., 1959). Theodore H. Wilson has published a nostalgic account of the Argentia Conference—the Atlantic Charter Conference—of 1941, the first wartime meeting between Roosevelt and Churchill, entitled *The First Summit* (Boston, 1969). There is a section on this era of American history in *George F. Kennan, *Memoirs: 1925–1950* (Boston, 1967). Wayne S. Cole, *America First* (Madison, Wis., 1953), the history of the America First Committee, complements Walter Johnson, *The Battle Against Isolation* (Chicago, 1944), an account of the Committee to Defend America by Aiding the Allies. See also Manfred Jonas, *Isolationism in America: 1935–1941* (Ithaca, N.Y., 1966), and Warren I. Cohen, *The American Revisionists: The Lessons of Intervention in World War I* (Chicago, 1967). There are memoirs by Stimson and by Hull, cited earlier, and the biographies by Elting E. Morison, Richard N. Current, and Julius W. Pratt. *Robert E. Sherwood's *Roosevelt and Hopkins* (New York, 1948) is a wonderfully lucid history written from the Hopkins papers by the well-known playwright.

An accounting of a special subject is Raymond A. Esthus's *From Enmity to Alliance: United States-Australian Relations, 1931–1941* (Seattle, 1964).

For American-Japanese relations prior to the Pearl Harbor crisis consult Joseph C. Grew, *Ten Years in Japan* (New York, 1944). Grew's later memoir, *Turbulent Era*, does not include the diary extracts printed in *Ten Years*. Waldo H. Heinrichs, *American Ambassador* (Boston, 1966) sets out Grew's activities. See also Dorothy Borg's prize-winning work, *The United States and the Far Eastern Crisis of 1933–1938* (Cambridge, Mass., 1964) which is highly reliable, an excellent treatment; Manny T. Koginos, *The "Panay" Incident: Prelude to War* (Lafayette, Ind., 1967); and *Robert J. C. Butow, *Tojo and the Coming of the War* (Princeton, 1961). Paul W. Schroeder has examined *The Axis Alliance and Japanese-American Relations: 1941* (Ithaca, N.Y., 1958). See also Frank W. Iklé, *German-Japanese Relations: 1936–1940* (New York, 1957).

Pearl Harbor has inspired a large literature, much of it based on the voluminous *Pearl Harbor Attack: Hearings before the Joint Committee on the Investigation of the Pearl Harbor Attack* (39 vols., Washington, 1946); together with the summary *Report on the Investigation of the Pearl Harbor Attack* (Washington, 1946). The best summary of this material, beautifully written, is Walter Millis, *This Is Pearl!* (New York, 1947). See also Basil Rauch, *Roosevelt: From Munich to Pearl Harbor* (New York, 1950); and Toshikazu Kase, *Journey to the* Missouri (New Haven, 1950). The naval side of the surprise appears in Samuel Eliot Morison's *The Rising Sun in the Pacific: 1931–April 1942* (Boston, 1948), a volume in Morison's *History of United States Naval Operations in World War II* (15 vols., 1947–1962). *Walter Lord, *Day of Infamy* (New York, 1957) is a "the day when . . . " approach, of a type briefly in vogue. *Herbert Feis, *The Road to Pearl Harbor* (Princeton, 1950) is a carefully researched study, probably the most authoritative yet published. Since the mid-1950's the Pearl Harbor literature has not enlarged much, with the notable exception of the excellent book by *Roberta Wohlstetter, *Pearl Harbor: Warning and Decision* (Stanford, Calif., 1962), which examines the intelligence failure in December 1941.

The "back door to war" books are numerous, but most of the nuances of this interpretation appear in Harry Elmer Barnes, ed., *Perpetual War for Perpetual Peace* (Caldwell, Idaho, 1953). See also the first of the genre, John T. Flynn, *The Final Secret of Pearl Harbor* (New York, 1945); together with Charles A. Beard, *American Foreign Policy in the Making: 1932–1940* (New Haven, 1946) and *President Roosevelt and the Coming of the War, 1941: A*

Study in Appearances and Realities (New Haven, 1948); George Morgenstern, *Pearl Harbor: The Story of the Secret War* (New York, 1947); Charles C. Tansill, *Back Door to War* (Chicago, 1952); Rear Admiral Robert A. Theobald, USN (ret.), *The Final Secret of Pearl Harbor: The Washington Contribution to the Japanese Attack* (New York, 1954); Husband E. Kimmel, *Admiral Kimmel's Story* (Chicago, 1955). Antidotes to the above are the review of Morgenstern's book by Samuel Flagg Bemis, "First Gun of a Revisionist Historiography for the Second World War," *Journal of Modern History*, XIX (1947), 55–59; and the review of Beard's second volume by Samuel Eliot Morison, *By Land and By Sea* (New York, 1953), chapter fifteen, "History through a Beard," pp. 328–345. Richard N. Current, "How Stimson Meant to 'Maneuver' the Japanese," *Mississippi Valley Historical Review*, XL (1953–1954), 67–74, ably explains a difficult quotation from Stimson's diary. On November 25, 1941 the secretary of war dictated to his diary the remark, "The question was how we should maneuver them [the Japanese] into the position of firing the first shot . . . ." Interpreted by Roosevelt's detractors as proof that the administration was planning to sink the Pacific fleet, this quotation indicated nothing of the sort. Everyone, Current contends, expected the Japanese to be smart enough not to attack American territory, and Stimson hoped that FDR, perhaps through a message to Congress, could convince the American people that a Japanese move against Siam or the Netherlands Indies or Malaya—even though it was not directly against American territory—was proper cause for a declaration of war. The Japanese move, when made (and if the ground had been properly prepared for it in America), could be announced as "firing the first shot."

☆ 24 ☆

The Second World War

Russian entry will have a profound military effect in that almost certainly it will materially shorten the war and thus save American lives. . . . The concessions to Russia on Far Eastern matters which were made at Yalta are generally matters which are within the military power of Russia to obtain regardless of U.S. military action short of war.

—Henry L. Stimson to Joseph C. Grew, May 21, 1945

The two world wars of the twentieth century have been fought by coalitions, in 1914–1918 by the Triple Entente and Dual Alliance, during 1939–1945 by the Axis powers and the Allies, and in gathering and holding the several parts of the coalition, the diplomat was in both periods a truly important individual. In the Second World War, maintenance of the Allied coalition of the United States, Great Britain, and Russia required exacting exercise of the art of diplomacy. There was no serious trouble in fusing the war efforts of America and Britain. After December 7, 1941, the hard-pressed British were eager to work with their new ally, the United States. Not that there never was dissension between the two English-speaking allies, for there was plenty, but in every large question no doubt ever existed that a compromise sooner or later could be made. Maintenance of the coalition with Russia was far more difficult. Sometimes relations trembled in the balance over arrangement of the smallest matter. Mutual trust was a perennial problem between the English-speaking nations and the Russians. Even in the period of extreme military hazard, the years 1941–1942, the communist regime was sometimes difficult and unco-operative. Fortunately diplomacy managed to hold the coalition together to the end of the war.

The implementing of the coalition—it is almost impossible to treat the Second World War without lapsing into its jargon—became the special business of conferences between the Allies. There were meetings between the British and the Americans, and between the British and the Russians. There were conferences of the Big Three: Teheran (November–December 1943); Yalta (February 1945); Potsdam (July–August 1945). These last conferences occupied an especially prominent place in operation of the Allied coalition. How much did the spectacular meetings of the Big Three accomplish? Was it not true that lower-level diplomacy, coupled with the exigencies of the war, took the coalition through to victory? Meetings of the leaders during the Second World War, it seems fair to say, if they accomplished little else, must have produced some bonhomie which helped carry forward the war effort. There doubtless were, moreover, a number of decisions of a delicate, highly political nature which were far easier to take during a face-to-face conference than through the toils of the lower-level conferences. Administratively there were problems difficult for subordinates to solve, and when issues became pointed and were of importance, a personal conference of leaders was an expeditious way of reaching decisions.

1. *The time of emergency*

The period of emergency in the conduct of the war was beyond doubt the years 1941–1942. In the summer of 1941, Germany had attacked Russia, and it was on December 4, 1941, that a German task force reached the gates of Moscow and momentarily breached the city's outer defenses. The exhausted German soldiers of the army group of Field Marshal von Kluge gazed off into the distance, for a day or two, and saw the towers of the Kremlin. At this moment of crisis, the Japanese government rushed precipitately into the war with a successful attack on the American fleet at Pearl Harbor.

During ensuing weeks and months, it often seemed that the Allies could not survive. To Americans, reading the wordy optimism of their newspapers, the full crisis was never quite evident, but to military planners in Washington there came during the winter and spring of 1942 a cold feeling of the imminence of defeat. The late official historian of the American army, Kent Roberts Greenfield, has written that the winter and spring of 1942 was a period of "terrific stress and anxiety." American experts gave the Russians little chance of survival. Nor did it seem that the Japanese were going to be stopped easily in the Pacific. Twenty years of Pacific diplomacy collapsed in the weeks after Pearl Harbor when the Japanese army and navy spread out to the island possessions of the United States, the Netherlands, and Great Britain, reaching southward toward an almost defenseless New Zealand and Australia.

Small wonder that when the American government arranged for a ceremony in Washington on January 1, 1942, at which representatives of the twenty-six Allied warring countries signed the United Nations Declaration, there was not much quibbling about any of the principles of the Atlantic Charter, which document had been included *in toto* in the declaration. The Russians adhered to the Charter with the reservation that "the practical application of these principles will necessarily adapt itself to the circumstances, needs, and historic peculiarities of particular countries." The American government did not question what measure of acceptance the Russians were offering. The military picture of the moment dominated all diplomatic considerations.

Throughout the year 1942 military necessity kept interallied dissension to a minimum, and if there was ever a time when coalition diplomacy proved relatively easy, this was it. The United States welcomed the Russians as allies, as had the British the previous summer. There was little skepticism in America's welcome to Russia. There was no undertone of opportunism such as characterized Churchill's private remark, "If Hitler invaded Hell, I would make at least a favorable reference to the Devil in the House of Commons." The hope in the United States, a hope which the circumstances of the moment would seem to have supported, was that under wartime pressure Russian patriotism had supplanted communism as the motive force of the government of the USSR. It seemed entirely possible that Russia would drop its communist theories and return to traditional friendships in the West. The Soviets, for example, in 1943 announced dissolution of the Comintern, the international propaganda arm of the Communist Party which had caused so much strife in the 1920's and 1930's. This at the time seemed an act of signal importance—although unfortunately the Comintern would reappear in 1947 under the name of Cominform.

America's first year in the war, the time of peril, saw little Allied dissension, but it did mark some considerable American embarrassment vis-à-vis the Russians over the question of a second front in France. The Soviets wished to draw German divisions from the Russian front and pressed the issue of a second front in every possible way. It worried American planners, who knew that even if the United Nations cause could survive the trials of the first year of the coalition, at least another year would have to pass before the United States could marshal its resources and build its military power to a level where a large-scale second front in France—anything larger than a small bridgehead—was a possibility. Opinion swayed to and fro in the spring and early summer of 1942. It was embarrassing that the troops of the United States and Great Britain were not engaged in fighting the Germans at this crucial time, except for some British activity against General Erwin Rommel's mixed force of Italians and Germans in North Africa. This Anglo-American inactivity was an embarrassing fact. Almost the full weight of German power was falling on Soviet Russia. American military planners wished ardently to make a move in 1942, to open a small bridgehead in France with Operation Sledge-hammer and follow it the next year with the big drive, Operation Roundup. In May 1942 President Roosevelt, during a conversation with the Russian foreign minister Molotov, promised a second front within the year. Prime Minister Churchill in conferences with Roosevelt at Hyde Park and Washington (June 18–27) argued against a cross-channel attack that year, and in July the British flatly refused to support it. Roosevelt persisted in believing that an attack should be made somewhere, and out of the confusion, and the embarrassment of not providing the Russians with support, came the proposal of an invasion of North Africa.

The political situation in North Africa was such as to welcome an Allied invasion, so the British and Americans believed. Parts of North Africa were French protectorates, and one portion, Algeria, was an actual department of France. When the French had met defeat at the hands of the Germans in June 1940, they had reconstituted a feeble government at the southern French city of Vichy, and the Vichy regime had retained allegiance of the North African provinces of Tunis and Morocco and the department of Algeria. The Vichy government was headed by the aged Pétain, assisted by Admiral Jean François Darlan and Pierre Laval. It was in many ways a defeatist regime and seemed on occasion much too pro-German. Its political vulnerability provided the Western Allies, Britain and the United States, with an opportunity to occupy French North Africa. The Allies believed that the army and civil officers in this area would welcome British and American troops, and from North Africa the invasion of Europe might eventually be launched. In the event, this turned out to be a fond hope. The Allied landings in North Africa actually almost miscarried. In the invasion of November 1942, co-operation was obtained from the French only because Admiral Darlan happened to be in North Africa and was able to persuade the local French army commanders to welcome the Allies. One should add that co-operation with Darlan, an individual of mixed character, later led to much soul-searching by some Allied publicists and writers, and after the war there was a heated argument over whether such co-operation was justified on grounds of military necessity; the present writer believes it was justified—though many of his readers will disagree.

But to return to the subject of the North African invasion. This invasion, it should be remarked, was essentially a compromise move. Secretary of War Stimson argued vigorously with the president against the operation. Stimson believed that the North African invasion, decided upon in July 1942, delayed the eventual cross-channel attack for an entire year. Still, what could the Americans do in 1942 without co-operation from their British ally? The British had been fighting Hitler for three years and urged their superior wisdom in matters of strategy. Indeed, the then chief of the imperial general staff, Sir Alan Brooke, in memoirs published a dozen years after the war, argued that the Americans were strategic morons and that only through British and especially his own superior wisdom was disaster averted in 1942. Sir Alan in that year comforted the Americans by telling them they could still have Operation Roundup in 1943, and that the North African affair would be preliminary. The chief of staff of the American army, General George C. Marshall, and his naval opposite, Admiral Ernest J. King, predicted that North Africa's Operation Torch would kill Roundup, which it did. Sir Alan in his memoirs confessed that he intended it to do so. The North African affair was in truth a political decision, rather than a matter of strategy. Perhaps it had to be. President Roosevelt was convinced that American troops had to become engaged somewhere, and the only feasible move—lacking support from the British for Sledgehammer—was Torch. General Marshall years after the war told the distinguished naval historian Samuel Eliot Morison that "the great lesson he learned in 1942 was this: in wartime the politicians have to do *something* important every year. They could not simply use 1942 to build up for 1943 or 1944; they could not face the obloquy of fighting another 'phony war.' The 'something' . . . was Operation Torch . . . ."

The difficulty over supporting the Russians in 1942 and the decision to go into North Africa raised in peculiarly sharp form a fundamental conflict in strategy between the British and Americans which was not adjourned for two years thereafter, namely, whether it was better to make a frontal invasion of the Continent via France, or to move northward into Europe from the Mediterranean via Italy and Yugoslavia. This issue had come to American attention for the first time during the conference between Roosevelt and Churchill at Argentia bay in 1941, when American military planners accompanying the president were appalled at the gingerly nature of British strategy. By the year 1944, when American troops came to constitute a preponderance of the strength of the Western Allies, it was possible to insist on American strategy, and the Allies thereupon went into France. But the strategic argument of France v. the Balkans persisted throughout the war, and some postwar literary strategists have flayed the American frontal strategy in much the same manner as did Sir Alan Brooke in his memoirs. So perhaps this controversy is worth examination at this point.

The British view of proper Anglo-American strategy for the Second World War is not difficult to state. Churchill and the British government had devoutly desired the invasion of North Africa in 1942, albeit for reasoning different from that of the American president. Churchill had always in mind such military butcheries as Passchendaele and the Somme during the First World War, when hundreds of thousands of British soldiers died in a series of dreadful and futile offensives. Apropos of British reluctance to fight again on the Continent, Morison in a published lecture has recalled the simple inscription on a tablet erected by the British government in Nôtre Dame de Paris: "To the glory of God and to the memory of one million men of the British Empire who fell in the Great War, 1914–1918, and of whom the greater part rest in France." When General Marshall, in England for staff conversations, was arguing vehemently for a cross-channel invasion of Europe, the late Lord Cherwell said to him, "It's no use—you are arguing against the casualties on the Somme." Churchill was not going to risk more such massacres simply because the Russians were crying for help and the Americans were eager to assist them.

There were two further reasons which may have prompted the British to oppose a cross-channel invasion. For one, British strategists and especially Churchill bore in mind the political purpose of the war—to defeat Hitler's Germany without bringing down the structure of Western civilization on the Continent. For this reason it appeared desirable to adopt toward Europe a strategy resembling that employed against Napoleon in the war of a century earlier, a strategy of beleaguerment, of probing at the periphery of the Continent, of feeling one's way cautiously, and perhaps moving through the Balkans and Central Europe to the Ruhr and Rhineland, North Germany and Berlin. Churchill may also have had in mind a campaign to open a route of supply to Russia through the Dardanelles and Bosporus, which if successful would have vindicated the ill-fated effort that he had sponsored during the First World War, an unsuccessful campaign that for years had clouded his political career. The British for such reasons as this elaborated their policy of cautious containment, a first step of which could be the taking of North African bases.

What can one conclude about this Anglo-American argument? Perhaps it is correct to say that Torch, the compromise of 1942, was a wise preliminary for the cross-channel invasion in 1944—that establishing a bridgehead in France in 1942 and a full-scale second front in 1943, as hoped for by General Marshall and Admiral King and President Roosevelt and Secretary Stimson and many other American leaders, would have been too dangerous, given the strength of German forces in France in those years, given Allied, especially American, inexperience in warfare, given the need for time to beat down the German submarine fleets in the Atlantic and time also to produce landing ships and tanks and the innumerable other requirements of land warfare on a vast scale. Some of the Mediterranean operations which followed the Torch landings, especially the Italian campaigning of the last year or so of the war, were strategically questionable, but the initial North African occupation did have justification pending the build-up of Allied strength to a point where the cherished cross-channel invasion was likely to succeed. It would have been a terrible blow to the Western Allies if in 1942 they had attempted Operation Sledgehammer, the proposed bridgehead operation, and been hurled off the Continent in a repetition of the British debacle at Dunkirk in 1940.

But is it not true that the cross-channel strategy which eventually prevailed in 1944 proved an unwise move from a political point of view, just as Churchill in 1942 had been sensing it would be? Did not the Allies lose Central Europe and the Balkans to the Russians because they chose the cross-channel attack in 1944, rather than an invasion up through Italy and the historic Ljubljana gap into Europe's (to use Churchill's phrase) "soft underbelly"? Actually there is little to be said for this argument, so frequently presented in the years after the Second World War. The compromise of 1942, the Torch operation, made sense at the moment, but by 1944, British strategy had become outmoded. Once the Allies had the requisite strength, there were many more advantages in an attack across France than up through Yugoslavia. It was fortunate that the Allies did not pursue the British peripheral strategy after 1943. Had they done so, it is possible that the American and British forces could have obtained control of Belgrade, Bucharest, Budapest, Prague, and Vienna, instead of those capitals passing to the Russians. It is also possible, even probable, that an American-British advance through the Balkans and Central Europe might have bogged down in the difficult terrain of that region, with the consequence that the Russian armies, rolling across the North German plain, would have reached the Ruhr and Rhineland and passed on into the Low Countries and France—with results for the postwar political organization of the Continent which can readily be calculated. Even in its strictly political possibilities, not to speak of its military difficulty, British strategy was less effective than the opposing American strategy. It was far better to give Russia the Balkans and Central Europe rather than the Continent's vastly more valuable northern and western areas.

So Churchill's losing out on his peripheral strategy, after an initial success in 1942, was all for the best. He fought to the bitter end. At one point in 1943 he put up a terrific argument for a landing on the island of Rhodes and was still arguing after Roosevelt and Stalin at the Teheran

Conference in December 1943 tried to dissuade him. At Algiers in January 1944, during an informal meeting with the Americans, he announced with full Churchillian rhetoric, holding onto the lapels of his coat as if making a speech in the House of Commons: "His Majesty's government cannot accept the consequences if we fail to make this operation against Rhodes!" General Marshall, present at the meeting, told the prime minister, "No American is going to land on that goddam island!"

2. From Casablanca to Quebec

With the year 1943, the tide of war turned in favor of the Allied coalition, and there could no longer be any serious cause for worry, after the victories of that year and the triumphs of the year that followed. The only question concerned the time necessary to defeat an enemy who was imaginative, brave, tenacious, even fanatical. By the beginning of 1943, the German and Italian troops in North Africa, numbering about 250,000, were falling into a hopeless position and would be forced to surrender on May 13, 1943. Meanwhile the beginning of a new phase of the war in Russia came with the German surrender at Stalingrad, February 2, 1943. This victory, in which twenty-two German divisions, including a galaxy of German generals, were made prisoners, was followed in the summer of 1943 by the complete failure on the Russian front of a German general offensive.

Although the crucial points in a conflict seldom become visible until after the fighting has ceased, it began to be evident in 1943 that a change for the better had come in the Pacific war as well. In the Pacific the United States first had suffered the disaster at Pearl Harbor; not too long after that had come the inevitable surrender in the Philippines, on May 6, 1942. But then in the summer of 1942 the first good news arrived from the Pacific: the Japanese were driven back from Midway on June 3–6, in a victory of naval aviation that forbade further Japanese advances. A year later, by mid-1943, United States forces in the Pacific were on the offensive everywhere.

When victory thus came into sight—and it was visible at the beginning of 1943—there appeared a need for a statement of Allied policy toward the enemy, some statement that would hold the coalition together until the end of the war. The squabbling over spoils that had broken so many coalitions must not occur. The embarrassment of not being able to provide a second front in France in either 1942 or 1943 must be relieved; there was the bare possibility that the Russians in disgust might make an arrangement with the Germans, as they had done under other circumstances in

August 1939. With these purposes in mind, Roosevelt and Churchill, meeting in a conference at Casablanca, January 14–24, 1943, announced the doctrine of unconditional surrender.

The doctrine was carefully premeditated and was no off-the-cuff pronouncement as Roosevelt later liked to make out. The president, as Robert Sherwood has remarked, "often liked to picture himself as a rather

Roosevelt and Churchill at Casablanca.

frivolous fellow who did not give sufficient attention to the consequences of chance remarks," and so he made light of the calculation that went into his new doctrine, unconditional surrender. He talked carefully from notes that day at Casablanca. He had just managed to get two bickering French generals—Henri H. Giraud and Charles de Gaulle—to shake hands, and this, according to FDR's fanciful recollection, brought to mind a chain of ideas: "We had so much trouble getting those two French generals together that I thought to myself that this was as difficult as arranging the meeting of Grant and Lee—and then suddenly the press conference was on, and Winston and I had had no time to prepare for it, and the thought popped into my mind that they had called Grant 'Old Unconditional Surrender' and the next thing I knew, I had said it."

Whatever the incidental errors that attached to it, the new doctrine of unconditional surrender was singularly important for Allied diplomacy during the Second World War. This policy, along with that of the Balkan *v.* cross-channel strategy, has stirred much debate among postwar analysts and writers. Was unconditional surrender a wise policy? Is not every surrender, by definition, a surrender on conditions? The diary of the Nazi propaganda minister, Josef Goebbels, reveals the joy with which that functionary presented to the German people the choice between fighting or groveling before the Allies. The Allied declaration of unconditional surrender appeared to him as a godsend, for it would, he thought, spark the German people to fight for an honorable peace. It proved what he had always told them, that surrender to the Allies could only be dishonorable. The military analyst of the New York *Times*, Hanson W. Baldwin, wrote that unconditional surrender was one of the blunders of American diplomacy during the war. It prolonged the war, Baldwin believed, and encouraged the Germans to fight to the last man, leaving for the Allies in 1945 a country which was the most complete shambles ever seen by conquering soldiers.

Elmer Davis, who conducted the Office of War Information and to whom in 1942–1945 fell much of the burden of explaining to the American people the nation's wartime policy, has defended this policy of unconditional surrender. Davis argued that the policy served notice on our allies, in particular the Russians, that there would be no premature peace with Germany. Moreover, so Davis contended, "the unquestionably good effect of unconditional surrender—an effect which was its primary purpose," was upon the Germans themselves. It prevented them from telling again the story they told after 1918, that they had not been defeated militarily in the field but had been stabbed in the back by civilian revolutionists in Berlin. To the argument that the policy of unconditional surrender left no responsible government in Germany with which the Allies could negotiate, Davis answered that there never was any chance for a government to arise with which the Allies could have negotiated. The Germans could not, certainly did not, unseat the Hitler regime. Their random wartime conspiracies against Hitler were heroic but naive affairs, easily put down by the Gestapo. Even the conspiracy to assassinate Hitler which miscarried on July 20, 1944, with such tragically terrible results for thousands of the conspirators and their relatives and friends, was an amateurish plot with little chance of success. To crush the regime required an absolute military defeat.

Certainly it was impossible to negotiate with the Hitler regime, which was the most bestial government known since the statistically clouded times of the medieval Huns and the fabled slaughters of the ancient oriental satrapies. No negotiated peace was possible with the regime that had slaughtered literally millions of people, men and women and children, by machine guns and starvation camps and efficient gas ovens, giving to the world's languages a new word, *genocide.*

But whatever the virtues—or defects—of unconditional surrender, it does seem true that the doctrine, for perhaps twenty months after its enunciation in January 1943, held off the making of wartime commitments that would have prejudiced the postwar settlement. The principle of "no predetermination," a rather jawbreaking idea, was finally abandoned, and with questionable results, in a conference at Moscow on October 9–18, 1944, when Churchill and Stalin agreed to divide the Balkans into spheres of interest. According to one version—there has been no official confirmation of these figures—Russia was assigned a 75/25 or 80/20 preponderance in Bulgaria, Rumania, and Hungary, while in Yugoslavia the ratio was 50/50. It was agreed also that the Curzon Line, a roughly ethnographic line in Eastern Poland proposed as a boundary in 1919, would be the new postwar Polish boundary, and that Poland, having thereby lost territory to Russia in the east, would be given a western boundary along the Oder, obtaining compensation at the expense of Germany. The American government, not a party to these arrangements, let it be known that it would not be bound by them. It was American policy to refrain from division of spoils until the peace conference at the end of the war. Divisions of territory, so the United States maintained, were one of the prime methods of disrupting a coalition prior to the end of a war. The British government agreed with such reasoning in the period of emergency, the year 1942, but underwent a change of mind, if not of heart, when as victory approached it became evident that the Russians could make their own pleasure prevail in Eastern Europe, with or without agreement with the English-speaking Allies. Britain felt that an agreement might at least confirm British interests in Yugoslavia and especially in Greece (where, according to Churchill's memoirs, the ratio of Russian–British influence was to be 10/90, in favor of Britain). Perhaps Churchill thought it was better to anticipate the inevitable in Eastern Europe, with the hope of getting something in the process.

Having set forth the doctrine of unconditional surrender at Casablanca in January 1943, the leaders of the United States and Britain communicated it to the Russians, who for the moment accepted it. For the rest of the year the attention of the two English-speaking governments was occupied with the North African campaign, the seizure of Sicily (July 10–August 17), and the invasion of Italy (September 3). Forcing the retirement of Mussolini—who afterward escaped to North Italy and founded another Italian government under German sponsorship—the Allies began the slow movement up the boot of Italy toward Rome. They also prepared for the cross-channel invasion.

Throughout the year 1943, arguments over strategy raged between the British and American governments. The question again was whether to enter the Continent through the Balkans and Central Europe or by crossing the channel. This time the British, despite the tireless importunities of Churchill, lost to the Americans, who possessed more troops and equipment and were in a position to dictate strategy. By the end of the year there was no longer doubt as to the cross-channel operation. Planning it, however, required, in Western eyes, some co-ordination with the Russian front, and there followed the Teheran Conference, November 28–December 1, 1943.

Stalin, Roosevelt, and Churchill at Teheran.

Held at the capital of Iran, the conference was attended by Roosevelt, Churchill, and Stalin. It was the first three-power meeting on the highest level. The Russians promised at this conference to co-ordinate their campaigns with the projected invasion of France. The conference also produced a plan for an international organization to keep the peace, an idea of the Americans which was accepted with some enthusiasm by the British and with less interest by the more skeptical Russians. Stalin at Teheran reiterated a promise made at the Moscow Conference of foreign ministers (October 19–30, 1943) to enter the war against Japan after hostilities ended in Europe.

Before going to Teheran, Roosevelt and Churchill had a meeting at Cairo with Generalissimo and Mrs. Chiang Kai-shek. The meeting was apart from the Teheran proceedings because the Russians had not yet entered the Far Eastern war and did not desire to antagonize the Japanese. At the Cairo Conference (November 22–26, 1943), the United States,

Chiang Kai-shek, Roosevelt, Churchill, and Madame Chiang at Cairo, accompanied by their staffs.

Britain, and China promised to prosecute the war against Japan until the Japanese surrendered unconditionally. Japan was to be deprived of all Pacific islands acquired since 1914. Manchuria, Formosa, and other territories taken from China by Japan were to be restored to China. The three powers were "determined that in due course Korea shall become free and independent." At a second Cairo conference (December 4–6, 1943), the president and prime minister met the president of Turkey, Ismet Inönü, and received and gave pledges of support in the war against Germany —albeit without Turkish hostilities, not declared until February 23, 1945.

In concluding this account of the era when the coalition, having passed through the emergency, stood in sight of victory, there remains the year 1944, a year of campaigning and heavy fighting. Diplomacy languished during 1944.

Churchill and Roosevelt did meet again in the late summer at Quebec (September 11–16, 1944), where the two leaders heard Secretary of the Treasury Henry Morgenthau offer a plan for postwar Germany. On September 15, 1944, the president and the prime minister initialed an abbreviated version of the Morgenthau Plan, under which Russia and other devastated countries could "remove the machinery they require" from Germany, the heavy industry of the Ruhr and Saar to be "put out of action and closed down" and these two German provinces placed under indefinite international control. The plan initialed at Quebec, phrased in Churchill's own words, included a much-quoted statement that the measures for the Ruhr and Saar "looked forward to" conversion of Germany into a country "primarily agricultural and pastoral in character." This was, beyond question, a silly proposition. Morgenthau's scheme ignored the fact that the German people could not live without the industrial complex erected in their country, the center of economic life on the Continent. Whatever the intentions of its author, the Morgenthau Plan was a starvation plan. President Roosevelt rejected the proposal later that year, and Churchill eventually admitted that initialing it had been an error. Churchill seems to have been willing to accept the Morgenthau Plan tentatively because at the time he needed a large postwar American loan and the chief exponent of the plan was secretary of the treasury. When news of the scheme leaked out, it had an unfortunate effect in Germany, playing into the hands of Propaganda Minister Goebbels. Hitler in a New Year's message to the German people drew attention to what he described as a plot of the British, Americans, Bolsheviks, and "international Jews," which he said would result in the "complete ripping apart of the German Reich, the uprooting of 15 or 20 million Germans and transport abroad, the enslavement of the rest of our people, the ruination of our German youth, but, above all, the starvation of our masses." In the years after the war, much was made in the United States of the fact that the Morgenthau Plan as originally drawn gave virtual control of Germany to Soviet Russia (the Russians along with other nations of the Continent were to control Germany), and that the plan had been worked out by Morgenthau's chief assistant at the treasury, Harry Dexter White, who after his death in the early postwar years was accused of Communist Party affiliations. No one, let it be added, has proved that the Morgenthau Plan was Soviet in origin. Perhaps one should simply remark, in conclusion, that the proposal and its temporary and partial adoption at Quebec in September 1944 was an unfortunate but small chapter in American diplomatic history. The scheme of the secretary of the treasury was an amateur proposal, typical of many in American diplomacy.

3. *Yalta*

The Yalta Conference (February 4–11, 1945) properly began the third and final period in the history of the wartime coalition, the period of disintegration, of dissolution and disillusion. By the time the conference met, the wartime coalition had outlived its military usefulness. Germany was a doomed country by 1945, with many of its cities in rubble from Allied bombing, with its eastern and western areas ravaged by the encroaching Allied armies—the Russians coming from the east, the British and Americans from the west. Americans at the beginning of 1945 were preparing to cross the Rhine. Hordes of Russian soldiers had approached to within a hundred miles of Berlin. Soviet armies had concluded a victorious peace with Finland, occupied Rumania, Bulgaria, most of Poland, and driven deeply into Hungary, Yugoslavia, and Czechoslovakia. Understandably, when the war's end was near, there was no longer serious need for the Allied coalition, which was beginning, although ever so imperceptibly, to dissolve. A conference meeting under such circumstances was bound to encounter trouble.

The Yalta Conference, held at what had been the Crimean resort of the last tsar of Russia—the Livadia Palace built by Nicholas II in 1911 some two miles from the town of Yalta—did not at the time seem to be a meeting of despair and cynicism, a conference during which the hopes of the world disappeared in an orgy of secret agreement and bickering, with the evil genius of Moscow receiving benefits and giving none. The American nation did not at the time receive the impression of Yalta which has tempted many later writers to believe that the fruits of the war were lost in an eight-day meeting. Churchill buoyantly sent a message to Roosevelt on January 1, 1945, in advance of a preliminary Anglo-

The Big Three and their foreign ministers at Yalta (Eden, Stettinius, and Molotov).

American meeting at Malta (held January 30–February 2, 1945): "No more let us falter! From Malta to Yalta! Let nobody alter!" A few days later, in a telegram of January 8, the prime minister was becoming gloomy: "This may well be a fateful Conference, coming at a moment when the Great Allies are so divided and the shadow of the war lengthens out before us. At the present time I think the end of this war may well prove to be more disappointing than was the last." Still, this was a momentary reaction, and it never infected the spirits of the Americans at Yalta. Roosevelt and his advisers concluded their labors in the Crimea in a spirit close to exaltation. They felt that the postwar world was going to be safe—that the world had been saved for freedom and peace in a way which would have gladdened the heart of Woodrow Wilson. There was to be, verily, a new world. It would have been unbelievable to leaders of the American government in early 1945 had they been told that their hopes were not merely to be dashed, but the meeting in which they had seen their vision of a New Jerusalem would soon be described by many of their countrymen as a conference of blunder and surrender.

What is the truth about Yalta? The Yalta Conference was the most controversial of the wartime diplomatic meetings, and in the light of later argument it deserves a close and sharp look. It dealt with essentially four issues: (1) voting arrangements in the new United Nations; (2) general policy toward the liberated governments of Eastern Europe, and specific policy toward the postwar government of Poland; (3) the immediate postwar governance of Germany; (4) Russia's joining the war against Japan.

Of these issues at Yalta, arrangements pertaining to the UN were probably of minor importance. Steps toward formation of the United Nations had already been taken before Yalta, notably at the Moscow Conference of foreign ministers in October 1943, when a joint declaration by Great Britain, the United States, the USSR, and China projected "a general international organization, based on the principle of sovereign equality of all peace-loving states, and open to membership by all such states, large and small, for the maintenance of international peace and security." It was after return from this conference that Secretary Hull declared extravagantly that, if the provisions of the Moscow Declaration were carried out, there would be no need for "spheres of influence, for alliances, for balance of power or any other of the special arrangements through which, in the unhappy past, the nations strove to safeguard their security or to promote their interests." At Yalta the date was set—Wednesday, April 25, 1945—for opening of the San Francisco Conference to work out the constitutional details of the UN. The three great powers at Yalta were in perfect agreement on their need for a right of veto in the UN. Stalin favored a veto even on discussion of matters at the UN, but Churchill and Roosevelt prevailed on him to allow the right of free speech in the new Parliament of the World. With this issue resolved, the Soviet dictator lost interest in the proposed world organization and turned to other matters.

In the meantime he had asked for and received Assembly seats for Byelorussia and the Ukraine, a concession by the Western statesmen which later brought much criticism of the Yalta Conference. The Russian argument was that the British empire was well represented in the Assembly, and that to confine a great power like Russia to one seat was unfair. The Russians at first asked for sixteen seats, one for each of the Soviet republics. The Russian ambassador to the United States, Andrei Gromyko, argued that any of the Soviet republics was more important than Guatemala or Liberia. To the query as to whether the Russian republics had been given control of their foreign relations Gromyko had answered that they soon would have such control. Finally the Russians compromised on three seats, and it was agreed that the United States also might request three seats. The American government has never asked for this bonus representation. The multiple-seat concession to Russia at Yalta has provoked a good deal of criticism from American public opinion—although it is difficult to see what advantage the Russians gained by their increased Assembly representation.

In the matter of Eastern Europe the Yalta Conference has also been criticized. Here attack frequently has been directed to the Yalta Declaration on Liberated Europe, drafted by the state department and accepted almost *in toto* by the conferees, which specified free elections and constitutional safeguards of freedom in the liberated nations. It was employed as a propaganda device by the Soviets, who never seriously considered putting it into effect. In retrospect the pledges of the Soviets in the declaration appear almost grotesque: "By this declaration," the United States, Britain, and Russia announced, "we reaffirm our faith in the principles of the Atlantic Charter, our pledge in the Declaration by the United Nations, and our determination to build in co-operation with other peace-loving nations world order under law, dedicated to peace, security, freedom and general well-being of all mankind." The Yalta Declaration on Liberated Europe had the immediate result of lending to the activities of the Soviet occupation authorities in Eastern Europe a certain sanctity and authority conferred by the democratic allies. Conspicuous posting of the text of the declaration throughout the liberated areas made the task of occupation easier. What followed is now well-known. The Soviets pursued their own brand of democracy in the liberated countries, first by means of coalition governments. The communist members of the coalition, supported by the red army, then infiltrated every position of responsibility in the government. Even so, the Yalta Declaration did some good, for without it the Russians might have omitted the coalition stage of their takeover of Eastern Europe in favor of a brutal takeover without attempt at legality. In this respect the Yalta Declaration may have given the East European peoples two or three years in which they had some freedom. Moreover, the declaration is the one Russian promise for this area of the Continent with which the United States and Britain have been able to reproach the Russians. It is a contractual arrangement which Russia violated.

But then one comes to the case of Poland as decided at Yalta, another matter about which the West has felt uneasy. Germany's attack on Poland had brought on the war in 1939. The British and Americans both felt during the war that an independent Polish government was essential in any acceptable postwar organization of Europe. Great Britain had guaranteed Polish national existence in 1939, and in the United States six million Americans of Polish descent laid constant and heavy political pressure upon President Roosevelt. The Western Allies at Yalta did the best they could for Poland and spent more time at the conference discussing Poland's postwar frontiers and government than any other subject. Churchill described the Polish question as "the most important question" before the conference. Still, Poland by February 1945 had been almost completely occupied by the red army, and any arrangements made at Yalta in regard to Poland had to be made out of hope rather than with certainty that they would be put into effect.

The Polish boundary question was straddled at Yalta—after much discussion—with tentative agreement on the Curzon Line as the eastern boundary but disagreement over the western boundary. Roosevelt and Churchill were not averse to a line along the Oder River, but as for continuing it southward along the Western Neisse, that was something else, and the decision was that "the final delimitation of the Western frontier of Poland should thereafter await the Peace Conference." This decision was reaffirmed at the Potsdam Conference of July–August 1945. The peace conference for Poland never met, and the Russians made their own bilateral arrangement with Poland of the Curzon Line in the east and the Oder-Western Neisse in the west.

The Western Allies reserved their consent to Poland's boundaries, but in the matter of Poland's postwar government the Americans and British at Yalta made what with hindsight appears to have been an ill-advised concession. The Russians received clearance to expand the so-called Lublin Committee, a Soviet-sponsored group of Polish-Russian communists, by including representatives of the Polish government-in-exile then domiciled in London. The government-in-exile in London had far more right to claim the postwar government of Poland than did the cardboard Lublin Committee, propped as the latter was by the Russian army and Russian funds. The Soviets knew that their Polish organization was a fraud, and they were willing to "broaden" it and dress it in legitimacy by inclusion of members from the London Polish government. Not long afterward, all the noncommunists were squeezed out of the newly organized Warsaw government. The Western powers sensed the danger of trying to combine oil and water, Lublin and London, but they felt that they could do little more than accept Russian promises. At Yalta there was still hope that the Russians had changed their spots, that it would be possible to live amicably with the communist regime, and in that hope and possibility the agreement on postwar Poland was consummated. In retrospect it appears that it would have been far better to have championed the London Poles, even at the risk of the government of Poland going to the Lublin Committee. It went to the committee anyway.

But perhaps this was the best that could be done. Roosevelt's adviser, Admiral William D. Leahy, said to the president at the time that the Polish agreement was so elastic that the Russians could "stretch it all the way from Yalta to Washington without ever technically breaking it." Roosevelt agreed: "I know, Bill—I know it. But it's the best I can do for Poland at this time."

There thus was a certain inevitability at Yalta in regard to the postwar government and boundaries of Poland. The provisions at Yalta for extra Russian seats at the UN Assembly, while not inevitable, were unimportant. Division of Germany into zones of occupation was an easier part of the Yalta proceedings and was done with success because the war map of the moment, while giving Eastern Germany to Russia, gave the Western Allies the rich industrial complex of West Germany. This was no even division, but the Russians had to accept it because of the war map.

Planning for the division of Germany had preceded the Yalta Conference by a number of months, and when the Western Allies met Stalin in the Crimea, they were fairly certain of what they desired in the way of occupation zones. A European Advisory Commission met in London in 1944 and recommended that Russia receive the eastern third of Germany, and that the southeastern zone go to the United States and the northwestern zone to Britain. There was to be joint control of Berlin and an Allied Control Commission for Germany. These proposals came before Churchill and Roosevelt at the Quebec Conference in September 1944, and the two statesmen agreed, Roosevelt reserving control by the United States over Bremen and Bremerhaven as enclaves within the British zone for purposes of supplying American troops in Bavaria. At Yalta this was essentially the arrangement for German occupation, with Roosevelt and Churchill persuading Stalin to allow to liberated France an occupation zone "within the British and American zones." The Russian leader was at the outset against the idea of a French role in the occupation of Germany. Overlooking his own delinquency in the Nazi-Soviet Pact of August 1939, he said that France had "opened the gate to the enemy" in 1940 and "contributed little to this war." Churchill cagily remarked that "every nation had had their difficulties in the beginning of the war and had made mistakes." Stalin gave in, and France obtained not merely

OCCUPATION ZONES IN GERMANY AND AUSTRIA

an occupation zone but a place on the Allied Control Commission.

In the matter of German reparations agreed upon at Yalta in a hedged and general way, it was decided that a reparations commission should be set up, with instructions that "the Soviet Union and the United States believed that the Reparations Commission should take as a basis of discussion the figure of reparations as twenty billion dollars and fifty per cent of these should go to the Soviet Union." The British opposed naming any reparations figure and managed also to write into the instructions a statement of purpose, "to destroy the German war potential," rather than the more broadly phrased Russian statement, "for the purpose of military and economic disarmament of Germany." All in all—so a student of this complicated subject, John L. Snell, has concluded—"the reparations decisions at Yalta constituted a thinly disguised defeat for the Russians and a clear-cut rejection of the Morgenthau plan and the Quebec agreement of September, 1944."

But it was not chiefly its provisions for Germany or its stipulations for Eastern Europe or the UN that later gave the Yalta Conference notoriety. Rather it was the provisions for Russia to enter the Far Eastern war. Here one comes to the nub of the Yalta controversy. Agitation over the Far Eastern provisions of Yalta became a political matter in the United States, with the Democratic Party, in power in 1945, generally defending Yalta's Far Eastern terms, and the Republicans characterizing them as a "betrayal of a sacred trust of the American people." Entrance of Russia into the war against Japan was unnecessary—so ran the accusation—and it was not merely obtained at Yalta, it was bought, at an outrageous price.

The reason for the Yalta concessions to obtain entrance of Russia into the Far Eastern war was, simply, that President Roosevelt's military advisers told him they needed Russian help. The military situation appeared downright difficult for the United States. American military leaders estimated that the war in Europe would last until July 1, at least, and that the Pacific war would require (and this with Russian help) another year and a half, that is, until December 1946. How long the war would take without Russian help, no one knew. Japanese troop strength at the time of Yalta was impressive, in terms of men (but ignoring armaments, which it later turned out that they did not have). The Japanese had 2,000,000 to 2,500,000 troops in Japan 1,000,000 in China, and 1,000,-000 in Manchuria and Korea. The United States by the end of the war had sent only about 1,459,000 army troops and 187,500 marines into the Pacific and scattered them from Australia to Alaska. Casualties were high in operations against the Japanese. Shortly after the Yalta Conference came the costly attack on Iwo Jima, an island two and one-half miles wide by four and two-thirds miles long, on which the marine corps lost nearly 7,000 dead and 20,000 wounded. Okinawa, invested soon afterward, cost 11,260 dead and 33,769 wounded. At Okinawa the Japanese sank 36 ships and damaged 368 others. It is understandable that Roosevelt and his advisers at Yalta wanted Russian entrance into the Far Eastern war. American military leaders estimated that an invasion of Japan would cost at least half a million American casualties, even if Japanese forces in China, Manchuria, and Korea stayed on the mainland. Douglas MacArthur, who later described as "fantastic" the Yalta concessions for Russian entrance into the Pacific war, told a Washington staff officer in early 1945 that Russian support was essential for the invasion of Japan. According to a memorandum of a conversation of February 25, 1945, sent by Brigadier General George A. Lincoln to General Marshall, "General MacArthur spoke of the strength of the opposition to be expected in invading the Japanese home islands. He declared that planning should start at once, that heavy firepower would be needed to cover the beachheads, and that as many Japanese divisions as possible should first be pinned down on the mainland, principally by Soviet forces." When Russia on August 8, 1945, invaded Manchuria, MacArthur declared flatly, "I am delighted at the Russian declaration of war against Japan. This will make possible a great pincers movement that cannot fail to end in the destruction of the enemy." Such was the feeling of Roosevelt's advisers at the time of Yalta, and it explains a number of the Yalta concessions to Russia.

As everyone now knows, the military estimate of Japan's strength was inaccurate. Actually Japan was on its last legs at the time of Yalta. In the summer of 1944 the marines had captured Saipan, and this defeat spelled the beginning of the end of Japan's will to fight. The cabinet of General Tojo resigned on July 18, 1944, in shame and disgrace, and from that moment onward it was a matter not of *if* but of *when* Japan would surrender. Russian assistance was not needed when, by the early summer of 1945 (after the Yalta Conference, and before the Russians entered the Far Eastern war), United States submarines sank ferry boats passing between the islands of Japan, and when the American fleet engaged with impunity in offshore bombardments. The taking of bases other than Saipan—Iwo Jima, Okinawa—secured air strips within easy bombing range of every part of Japan. The huge B-29 bombers in their fire raids wreaked havoc upon the island empire. Even before the dropping of the atomic bombs at Hiroshima (August 6, 1945) and Nagasaki (August 9), the dreadful daily bombing raids had proved roughly comparable in deadliness to the atomic explosions. At Hiroshima between 91,233 and 423,263 people died as a result of the atomic bombing (the figures are highly uncertain). In the conventional raids on Japan the total of deaths ran apparently to 241,000. It was an apocalyptic end for the Japanese. Their government ceased hostilities on August 14, and surrendered formally on September 2. No intervention by Russia in Manchuria (August 8) was necessary to bring down the bamboo edifice that had once been the center of the Japanese empire.

At Yalta the Russians agreed to join the war against Japan in "two or three months" after defeat of Germany, and when Germany fell on V-E Day, May 8, 1945, it was presumed that the Russians would join the Far Eastern war sometime in August. In return for this dubious service (which at the time seemed necessary), the Russians received the territory and privileges in China and the Pacific region that they had enjoyed prior to the Russo-Japanese War of 1904–1905: Southern Sakhalin and the Kurile Islands, railroad concessions throughout Manchuria (disguised as a joint Sino-Russian venture in railroading), and Port Arthur and Dairen (the latter was internationalized, meaning that it was free for Russian use).

It was embarrassing, but necessary, to obtain Chiang Kai-shek's acquiescence to these territorial infringements on Chinese sovereignty, and this necessity has since agitated some of the critics of Yalta. Even so, anyone conversant with the wartime military situation in China must grant that Chiang had done virtually nothing to expel the Japanese from his country. In 1945 he was still in his miserable and remote capital at Chungking. His troops had no control of any sort in Manchuria, not to speak of the seacoast, which had passed to the Japanese in 1937–1938. For Chiang to give Russia rights in territory which he did not possess was no concession. True, the Western Allies at the Cairo Conference in 1943 had promised complete restoration of Chinese sovereignty. Yet there had been no real Chinese control over Manchuria since the end of the nineteenth century when Russia received the first large concessions, and a restoration of Chinese sovereignty did not preclude restoration of Russian privileges. It is technically possible for a nation to exercise sovereignty at the time that its territory is encumbered by servitudes. Extraterritoriality had been a commonplace in the orient in the nineteenth century, and the United States had not relinquished its extraterritorial privileges in China until 1943. Admittedly this is a bit of a technical argument in favor of the Yalta agreement on Russian privileges in China. There is something to be said for the broad, more equitable interpretation of international arrangements. The difficulty in 1945 was the seeming necessity of getting Russia into the Far Eastern war. This meant obtaining an ally for Chiang Kai-shek, which the latter statesman, in view of his own minuscule contribution to the war, should have welcomed. Chiang signed a treaty with the Russians in August 1945. The unfortunate aspect of the matter was that he was not consulted in the Yalta arrangement—but again, had he been consulted there almost certainly would have been a leak to the Japanese of the imminence of Russian intervention. As Roosevelt said at Yalta to Stalin and Churchill, anything told to the Chinese "was known to the whole world in twenty-four hours."

Yalta was beyond dispute the climax of coalition diplomacy. It was the moment when the issues of the war, in all their complexity, came to focus.

Most of these issues were not decided at Yalta, for they already had been decided in one way or another. Stalin had twice promised, informally at the Moscow foreign ministers' meeting of October 1943, formally at Teheran, to enter the war against Japan. Arrangements for the postwar Polish government, over which so much bitterness later would appear, had been anticipated during the October 1944 meeting in Moscow of Stalin and Churchill. Eventual settlement of the problem of Eastern Europe, despite the promises at Yalta, was also set forth at the Moscow Conference of 1944. Other illustrations could be cited to show how the Yalta Conference in most cases focused issues rather than "settled" them.

The conference was memorable, too, because it was the second and last meeting of the wartime Big Three. Something seemed strange about Stalin sitting later for formal Big Three pictures with Clement Attlee and Harry S. Truman. By the time of the Potsdam Conference, the war in Europe was over and the war against Japan almost won, and the new faces at the Potsdam conference table symbolized the end of an era. During the war there had been high emotion and drama of a sort that would have pleased a Shakespeare. A coalition mastered the world and the triumvirs of that coalition, Stalin, Churchill, and Roosevelt, lent grandeur to what in every sense was a crucial point in history—the Second World War.

A CONTEMPORARY DOCUMENT

[With but a few weeks to live, President Roosevelt on March 1, 1945, addressed a joint session of Congress to report on the results of the Yalta Conference. Contrary to his custom, he made his address while seated. His face was worn and even haggard. The speech, however, had the old ring—and a few of the old asides—of the happy warrior. Source: *Department of State Bulletin*, March 4, 1945.]

Mr. Vice President, Mr. Speaker, members of the Senate and of the House of Representatives:

It is good to be home.

It has been a long journey. I hope you will agree that it was a fruitful one.

Speaking in all frankness, the question of whether it is to be entirely fruitful or not lies to a great extent in your hands. For unless you here in the halls of the American Congress—with the support of the American people—concur in the decisions reached at Yalta, and give them your active support, the meeting will not have produced lasting results.

That is why I come before you at the earliest hour after my return. I want to make a personal report to you—and, at the same time, to the people of the country. Many months of earnest work are ahead of us all, and I should like to feel that when the last stone is laid on the structure of international peace, it will be an achievement for which all of us in America have worked steadfastly and unselfishly—together.

I return from this trip—which took me as far as 7,000 miles from the White House—refreshed and inspired. The Roosevelts are not, as you may suspect, averse to travel. We thrive on it! . . .

There were two main purposes at the Crimean Conference. The first was to bring defeat to Germany with the greatest possible speed and with the smallest possible loss of Allied men. That purpose is now being carried out in great force. The German Army, and the German people, are feeling the ever-increasing might of our fighting men and of the Allied Armies. Every hour gives us added pride in the heroic advance of our troops over German soil toward a meeting with the gallant Red Army.

The second purpose was to continue to build the foundation for an international accord which would bring order and security after the chaos of war, and which would give some assurance of lasting peace among the nations of the world. . . .

It was Hitler's hope that we would not agree—that some slight crack might appear in the solid wall of Allied unity which would give him and his fellow gangsters one last hope of escaping their just doom. That is the objective for which his propaganda machine has been working for months.

But Hitler has failed.

Never before have the major Allies been more closely united—not only in their war aims but in their peace aims. And they are determined to continue to be united with each other—and with all peace-loving nations—so that the ideal of lasting world peace will become a reality. . . .

The German people, as well as the German soldiers, must realize that the sooner they give up and surrender, by groups or as individuals, the sooner their present agony will be over. They must realize that only with complete surrender can they begin to reestablish themselves as people whom the world might accept as decent neighbors.

We made it clear again at Yalta, and I now repeat—that unconditional surrender does not mean the destruction or enslavement of the German people. The Nazi leaders have deliberately withheld that part of the Yalta declaration from the German press and radio. They seek to convince the people of Germany that the Yalta declaration does mean slavery and destruction for them—for that is how the Nazis hope to save their own skins and deceive their people into continued useless resistance. . . .

Of equal importance with the military arrangements at the Crimean Conference were the agreements reached with respect to a general international organization for lasting world peace. The foundations were laid at Dumbarton Oaks. There was one point, however, on which agreement was not reached at Dumbarton Oaks. It involved the procedure of voting in the Security Council.

At the Crimean Conference, the Americans made a proposal on this subject which, after full discussion, was unanimously adopted by the other two nations.

It is not yet possible to announce the terms of that agreement publicly, but it will be in a very short time.

When the conclusions reached at the Crimean Conference with respect to voting in the Security Council are made known, I believe you will find them a fair solution of this complicated and difficult problem. They are founded in justice and will go far to assure international cooperation in the maintenance of peace.

A conference of all the United Nations of the world will meet in San Francisco on April 25, 1945. There, we all hope, and confidently expect, to execute a definite charter of organization under which the peace of the world will be preserved and the forces of aggression permanently outlawed.

This time we shall not make the mistake of waiting until the end of the war to set up the machinery of peace. This time, as we fight together to get the war over quickly, we work together to keep it from happening again.

I am well aware of the constitutional fact—as are all the United Nations—that this charter must be approved by two thirds of the Senate of the United States—as will some of the other arrangements made at Yalta.

The Senate of the United States, through its appropriate representatives, has been kept continuously advised of the program of this government in the creation of the international security organization.

The Senate and the House of Representatives will both be represented at the San Francisco conference. The congressional delegates to the San Francisco conference will consist of an equal number of Republican and Democratic members. The American Delegation is —in every sense of the word—bipartisan.

World peace is not a party question—any more than is military victory. . . .

As the Allied Armies have marched to military victory, they have liberated peoples whose liberties had been crushed by the Nazis for four years, and whose economy had been reduced to ruin by Nazi despoilers.

There have been instances of political confusion and unrest in these liberated areas—as in Greece and Poland and Yugoslavia and other places. Worse than that, there actually began to grow up in some of them vaguely defined ideas of "spheres of influence" which were incompatible with the basic principles of international collaboration. If allowed to go unchecked, these developments might have had tragic results.

It is fruitless to try to place the blame for this situation on one particular nation or another. It is the kind of development which is almost inevitable unless the major powers of the world continue without interruption to work together and to assume joint responsibility for the solution of problems which may arise to endanger the peace of the world.

We met in the Crimea, determined to settle this matter of liberated areas. I am happy to confirm to the Congress that we did arrive at a settlement—a unanimous settlement.

The three most powerful nations have agreed that the political and economic problems of any area liberated from the Nazi conquest, or of any former Axis satellite, are a joint responsibility of all three governments. They will join together, during the temporary period of instability after hostilities, to help the people of any liberated area, or of any former satellite state, to solve their own problems through firmly established democratic processes. . . .

One outstanding example of joint action by the three major Allies in the liberated areas was the solution reached on Poland. The whole Polish question was a potential source of trouble in post-war Europe, and we came to the conference determined to find a common ground for its solution. We did.

Our objective was to help create a strong, independent, and prosperous nation, with a government ultimately to be selected by the Polish people themselves.

To achieve this objective, it was necessary to provide for the formation of a new government much more representative than had been possible while Poland was enslaved. Accordingly, steps were taken at Yalta to reorganize the existing Provisional Government in Poland on a broader democratic basis, so as to include democratic leaders now in Poland and those abroad. This new, reorganized Government will be recognized by all of us as the temporary Government of Poland.

However, the new Polish Provisional Government of National Unity will be pledged to holding a free election as soon as possible on the basis of universal suffrage and a secret ballot.

Throughout history, Poland has been the corridor through which attacks on Russia have been made. Twice in this generation, Germany has struck at Russia through this corridor. To insure European security and world peace, a strong and independent Poland is necessary.

The decision with respect to the boundaries of Poland was a compromise, under which, however, the Poles will receive compensation in territory in the north and west in exchange for what they lose by the Curzon Line. The limits of the western boundary will be permanently fixed in the final peace conference. It was agreed that a large coastline should be included. . . .

The Crimean Conference was a meeting of the three major military powers, on whose shoulders rest the chief responsibility and burden of the war. Although, for this reason, France was not a participant in the conference, no one should detract from the recognition there accorded of her role in the future of Europe and the world.

France has been invited to accept a zone of control in Germany and to participate as a fourth member of the Allied Control Council of Germany.

She has been invited to join as a sponsor of the international conference at San Francisco.

She will be a permanent member of the International Security Council together with the other four major powers.

And, finally, we have asked that France be associated with us in our joint responsibility over the liberated areas of Europe.

Agreement was also reached on Yugoslavia, as announced in the communiqué, and is in process of fulfilment.

Quite naturally, the Crimean Conference concerned itself only with the European war and with the political problems of Europe— and not with the Pacific war.

At Malta, however, our Combined British and American Staffs made their plans to increase the attack against Japan.

The Japanese warlords know that they are not being overlooked. They have felt the force of our B–29's and our carrier planes; they have felt the naval might of the United States and do not appear very anxious to come out and try it again.

The Japs know what it means to hear that "the United States Marines have landed". And we can add, having Iwo Jima in mind:

"The situation is well in hand".

They also know what is in store for the homeland of Japan now that General MacArthur has completed his magnificent march back to Manila and Admiral Nimitz is establishing his air bases right in the backyard of Japan itself—in Iwo Jima.

It is still a tough, long road to Tokyo. The defeat of Germany will not mean the end of the war against Japan. On the contrary, America must be prepared for a long and costly struggle in the Pacific.

But the unconditional surrender of Japan is as essential as the defeat of Germany—if our plans for world peace are to succeed. For Japanese militarism must be wiped out as thoroughly as German militarism.

On the way home from the Crimea, I made arrangements to meet personally King Farouk of Egypt, Haile Selassie, Emperor of Ethiopia, and King Ibn Saud of Saudi Arabia. Our conversations had to do with matters of common interest. They will be of great mutual advantage because they gave us an opportunity of meeting and talking face to face, and of exchanging views in personal conversation instead of formal correspondence. . . .

The Conference in the Crimea was a turning point in American history. There will soon be presented to the Senate of the United States and to the American people a great decision which will determine the fate of the United States—and of the world—for generations to come.

There can be no middle ground here. We shall have to take the responsibility for world collaboration, or we shall have to bear the responsibility for another world conflict.

I know that the word *planning* is not looked upon with favor in some quarters. In domestic affairs, tragic mistakes have been made by reason of lack of planning; and, on the other hand, many great improvements in living, and many benefits to the human race, have been accomplished as a result of adequate, intelligent planning—reclamations of desert areas, developments of whole river valleys, provision for adequate housing.

The same will be true in relations between nations. For a second time, this generation is face to face with the objective of preventing wars. To meet that objective, the nations of the world will either have a plan or they will not. The groundwork of a plan has now been furnished and has been submitted to humanity for discussion and decision.

No plan is perfect. Whatever is adopted at San Francisco will doubtless have to be amended time and again over the years, just as our own Constitution has been.

No one can say exactly how long any plan will last. Peace can endure only so long as humanity really insists upon it, and is willing to work for it—and sacrifice for it.

Twenty-five years ago, American fighting men looked to the statesmen of the world to finish the work of peace for which they fought and suffered. We failed them then. We cannot fail them again and expect the world again to survive.

The Crimean Conference was a successful effort by the three leading nations to find a common ground for peace. It spells the end of the system of unilateral action and exclusive alliances and spheres of influence and balances of power and all the other expedients which have been tried for centuries—and have failed.

We propose to substitute for all these a universal organization in which all peace-loving nations will finally have a chance to join.

I am confident that the Congress and the American people will accept the results of this conference as the beginnings of a permanent structure of peace upon which we can begin to build, under God, that better world in which our children and grandchildren— yours and mine, the children and grandchildren of the whole world —must live.

ADDITIONAL READING

The Second World War, like the war of 1914–1918, has produced a spate of memoirs and scholarly studies, and in sketching out this literature it is difficult to know where to start and stop. In addition to the more general works such as those by Nevins and Duroselle, there are books dealing only with the diplomacy of the war, notably *Gaddis Smith, *American Diplomacy during the Second World War: 1941–1945* (New York, 1965), a volume in the America in Crisis series. Smith's book has proved of much interest to college and university readers because of its good scholarship and sprightly prose. *John L. Snell, *Illusion and Necessity: The Diplomacy of Global War, 1939– 1945* (Boston, 1963) is another book of great merit. William L. Neuman, a distinguished scholar, recently has published *After Victory: Churchill, Roosevelt, Stalin and the Making of the Peace* (New York, 1967), which sets out the arguments over the postwar world as they arose in wartime. An older multivolume history of American wartime diplomacy is by Herbert Fels, a former economic advisor to the Department of State, who has a penchant for detail but writes from long experience: *The Road to Pearl Harbor* (Princeton, 1950); *The China Tangle: The American Effort in China from Pearl Harbor to the Marshall Mission* (1953); *Churchill, Roosevelt, Stalin* (1957); *Between War and Peace: The Potsdam Conference* (1960); and *Japan

Subdued: The Atomic Bomb and the End of the War in the Pacific[*] (1961), which in revised edition (1967) bears the title *The Atomic Bomb and the End of World War II*. A critical account of political-military strategy appears in Hanson W. Baldwin, *Great Mistakes of the War* (New York, 1950). *Samuel Eliot Morison, *Strategy and Compromise* (Boston, 1958) is a brilliant analysis, countering the assertions in Baldwin and also in Arthur Bryant, *The Turn of the Tide* (New York, 1957), the first volume of the diaries of Lord Alanbrooke. *Paul Kecskemeti, *Strategic Surrender: The Politics of Victory and Defeat* (Stanford, Calif., 1958) considers among other topics the unconditional-surrender formula of the Casablanca Conference. See also the account by Anne Armstrong, *Unconditional Surrender: The Impact of the Casablanca Policy upon World War II* (New Brunswick, N.J., 1961). Any study of unconditional surrender, one should add, is now open to reassessment because of the state department's recent publication of the Casablanca Conference documents in the series *Foreign Relations of the United States*.

No one can study the war of 1939–1945 without appreciating the influence of Winston Churchill, the great British prime minister. Churchill's importance historically has not lessened—and probably has greatly increased—with the writing of his memoirs, the last three volumes of which consider the war from 1942 to 1945: *The Hinge of Fate* (Boston, 1950); *Closing the Ring* (1951); and *Triumph and Tragedy* (1953). An investigation of Churchill's strategic views is Trumbull Higgins, *Winston Churchill and the Second Front 1940–1943* (New York, 1957). The best biography is Alan Moorehead's *Winston Churchill: In Trial and Triumph* (Boston, 1955), a model of brevity, judgment, and literary skill.

For titles about Roosevelt, see books listed at the end of chapter twenty-two. The vast literature on FDR ranges from volumes about "that man in the White House"—such as John T. Flynn, *The Roosevelt Myth* (New York, 1948)—to such defenses as Arthur M. Schlesinger, Jr., "Roosevelt and His Detractors," in E. N. Saveth, ed., *Understanding the American Past* (Boston, 1954).

The memoir output for the Second World War has been prodigious. In addition to the titles on Cordell Hull and Henry L. Stimson listed in preceding chapters are Edward R. Stettinius, Jr., *Lend-Lease: Weapon for Victory* (New York, 1944) and *Roosevelt and the Russians* (Garden City, N.Y., 1949); Forrest C. Pogue, *George C. Marshall: Education of a General* (New York, 1963) and *Ordeal and Hope, 1939–1942* (New York, 1966), two excellent volumes of a biography not yet finished; Ernest J. King and Walter M. Whitehill, *Fleet Admiral King* (New York, 1952); William D. Leahy, *I Was There* (New York, 1950), by a man who as FDR's military aide saw as much high-level diplomacy as any official of the American government save the president; Walter Millis and Eugene S. Duffield, eds., *The Forrestal Diaries* (New York, 1951), diary jottings, letters, and memoranda; John M. Blum, *From the Morgenthau Diaries: 1928–1945* (3 vols., Boston, 1959–1967), a mine of information, edited with authority; the books by the undersecretary of state until 1943, Sumner Welles, *The Time for Decision* (New York, 1944), *Where*

Are We Heading? (New York, 1946), and *Seven Decisions that Shaped History* (New York, 1951); Fred L. Israel, ed., *The War Diary of Breckenridge Long* (Lincoln, Nebr., 1966), by another leading official of the state department; *Robert E. Sherwood, *Roosevelt and Hopkins* (New York, 1948); *Dwight D. Eisenhower, *Crusade in Europe* (Garden City, N.Y., 1948); Harry C. Butcher, *My Three Years with Eisenhower* (New York, 1946), by the general's naval aide.

For American diplomacy toward specific countries, two notable books deal with Germany: Henry Morgenthau, *Germany Is Our Problem* (New York, 1945), by the author of the Morgenthau Plan; and Allen W. Dulles, *Germany's Underground* (New York, 1947), an account of the tragic uprising on July 20, 1944, by the German opposition to Hitler. See the same author's *The Secret Surrender* (New York, 1966), an account of the end of the war in Italy. Dulles was the representative in Switzerland of the Office of Strategic Services, the American wartime intelligence organization. Relations with Vichy France appear in *William L. Langer, *Our Vichy Gamble* (New York, 1947), a defense of the department of state's policy; and Paul Farmer, *Vichy— Political Dilemma* (New York, 1955). See also Milton Viorst, *Hostile Allies: FDR and Charles de Gaulle* (New York, 1965). Russian relations are set down by the American wartime ambassador, William H. Standley, *Admiral Ambassador to Russia* (Chicago, 1955), written with Arthur A. Ageton; the military head of lend-lease, Major General John H. Deane, *The Strange Alliance* (New York, 1947); and *George F. Kennan, *Memoirs: 1925–1950* (Boston, 1967). Spain's diplomatic dealings for the prewar period are in Claude G. Bowers, *My Mission to Spain* (New York, 1954), by the ambassador during the latter 1930's; and Richard P. Traina, *American Diplomacy and the Spanish Civil War* (Bloomington, Ind., 1968), a new study. For the wartime era see the books by the then ambassador, the well-known historian Carlton J. H. Hayes, *Wartime Mission to Spain* (New York, 1945); and the state department's economic advisor *Herbert Feis, *The Spanish Story* (New York, 1948).

The question of Yalta—whether Yalta was a sell-out—has agitated publicists and the American public ever since the Yalta apportionment of territory and influence between the Western Allies and Soviet Russia. A special congressional request to the state department resulted in the United States government's publication in 1955 of the Yalta conference papers in a special volume in the series *Foreign Relations of the United States*. That volume has been carefully digested and compared with other memoir and documentary publications in the excellent book edited by *John L. Snell, *The Meaning of Yalta* (Baton Rouge, La., 1956). General MacArthur's allegations on the subject of Yalta led the department of defense to take the extraordinary step of releasing from its records 105 pages of documents entitled *The Entry of the Soviet Union into the War Against Japan: Military Plans, 1941–1945* (Washington, 1955); this report shows that MacArthur approved of the Yalta arrangements for Soviet assistance against Japan. Helpful articles on Yalta are Rudolph A. Winnacker, "Yalta—Another Munich?" in *Virginia Quarterly Review*, XXIV (1948), 521–537; Ellis M. Zacharias, "The Inside Story of Yalta,' *United*

Nations World, III (1949), 12–16, arguing that erroneous intelligence estimates brought the Yalta effort to enlist Russia against Japan; Louis Morton, "The Military Background of the Yalta Agreements," *The Reporter*, April 7, 1955; and Raymond J. Sontag, "Reflections on the Yalta Papers," *Foreign Affairs*, XXXIII (1954–1955), 615–623, defending the Yalta agreements as the only agreements that could have been made, given the temper of the times. Sontag believes that in the light of what happened in the following decade it was entirely proper that the United States made a sincere effort to get along with the Soviet Union, for otherwise we would have uneasy consciences today.

*Robert J. C. Butow, *Japan's Decision to Surrender* (Stanford, 1954) is the best book on its subject. See also Joseph C. Grew, *Turbulent Era* (2 vols., New York, 1952); and Toshikazu Kase, *Journey to the "Missouri"* (New Haven, 1950). On the decision to drop the atomic bombs on Japan, there is Louis Morton, "The Decision to Use the Atomic Bomb, 1945," in Kent R. Greenfield, ed., *Command Decisions* (New York, 1959); Feis, *Japan Subdued* (Princeton, 1961); Len Giovannitti and Fred Freed, *The Decision to Drop the Bomb* (New York, 1965); and the controversial volume by Gar Alperovitz, *Atomic Diplomacy: Hiroshima and Potsdam* (New York, 1965). Alperovitz contends that the highest officials of the American government sanctioned use of the bomb in Japan not so much to save the lives of American soldiers, sailors, and airmen, as to impress Soviet Russia with American strength and thereby obtain a better relationship with Russia during the forthcoming difficult era of peace.

Books on American wartime relations with China appear at the end of chapter twenty-seven.

Europe, 1945-1950

I remember, when I was Secretary of State, I was being pressed constantly, particularly when in Moscow, by radio message after radio message to give the Russians hell . . . . When I got back I was getting the same appeal in relation to the Far East and China. At that time, my facilities for giving them hell—and I am a soldier and know something about the ability to give hell—was 1⅓ divisions over the entire United States. This is quite a proposition when you deal with somebody with over 260 and you have 1⅓. We had nothing in Alaska. We did not have enough to defend the air strip at Fairbanks . . . .

> —George C. Marshall, address to an audience at the Pentagon, 1950

After every one of the major wars in American history—the revolution, the Civil War, the First and Second World Wars—there has been a letdown, a time when people relaxed from wartime trials and enjoyed peace with unaccustomed vigor and abandon. The greater the war the greater the letdown, and the first few months after 1945 were a relaxed, loose, and frivolous time; the nation enjoyed itself as never before in its history. The end of gas rationing came in 1945, and soon afterward the end of other rationing; "the boys" came home; the cars moved out on the roads; the night clubs expanded their seating capacities. The United States in 1945 and 1946 in no sense experienced what occurred in postwar Britain —continued rationing, and a general tightening of belts. Neither did it experience the troubles of continental nations—dropping production, rising unemployment, and lack of food and fuel by large segments of the population. Americans enjoyed themselves in a burst of postwar spending and self-indulgence, which when compared to the austerity of other nations, victor and defeated alike, seems in retrospect almost callous.

This letdown, the wonderful feeling of relaxation after the war, accounts largely for the aimlessness of American diplomacy in the first year or two after V-E and V-J days. The purposes of American diplomacy understandably became lost in the general hubbub. After all, who wanted to think about diplomacy when the nation had just won the largest war in human history? Peace was to be enjoyed; meanwhile, let the diplomats play their private games—so Americans thought.

There were other, if less important, reasons for the course of American diplomacy after 1945. For one, the leadership of the republic's diplomacy was not all that it might have been. When Vice President Harry S. Truman on April 12, 1945, was elevated to the presidency by the death of President Roosevelt, he had little knowledge of foreign affairs. He had been vice president for a few weeks and had had almost no briefing on the conduct of American foreign relations. Nor could he receive assistance from James F. ("Jimmy") Byrnes, his inexperienced appointee as secretary of state (Byrnes replaced Edward R. Stettinius, Jr., in July 1945; Stettinius had replaced Hull in December 1944). Jimmy Byrnes was an able politician who during the war had made himself almost indispensable to President Roosevelt as a troubleshooter, ferreting out problems and their solutions with admirable efficiency, but when translated into the state department he discovered himself in a milieu different from American domestic politics. For some months, perhaps for most of the time that he held the secretaryship (until January 1947), he moved slowly, attempting to take the measure of his responsibilities.

The nation's diplomacy, thus in trouble, was further crippled by the precipitous demobilization of the American armed forces. During the war the enormous military power of the United States had given a strength to the country's diplomacy that it had not possessed since the time of the First World War, when for a fleeting moment there had been another large army in being. If only some of American wartime military power could have been retained, if the draft could have continued to feed into the army and navy and air force just a part of its wartime levies of young men, the series of defeats that befell American diplomacy in the postwar years might not have occurred. Hindsight makes this easy to see. At the time no one worried. There was a compelling pressure for demobilization, and the Washington government had little choice except to let the complicated war machine of May 1945 disintegrate within half a dozen months under a ruinous point system that released first the armed forces' most experienced members.

But the overwhelming desire for letdown, for return to normal ways of behavior and thought, was the chief cause of our woes after the Second World War. Desire for relaxation carried everything before it. Few individuals looked for trouble in foreign affairs, and almost everyone chose to enjoy the postwar domestic prosperity to the limit. The United Nations, President Roosevelt had believed, would care for future international rivalries. There would be few problems from Soviet Russia. The Russians, almost all Americans thought in 1945, would be peaceful and easy to get along with. General Dwight D. Eisenhower concluded after a trip to Moscow that "nothing guides Russian policy so much as a desire for friendship with the United States," and this was the prevailing view. When in 1946 and 1947 Soviet intentions became all too clear, written in actions and verbiage that everyone could understand, it was nearly too late to do anything. Americans found that they were without the means to make their will prevail, short of a preventive atomic war, which was humanely unthinkable. There was no conventional military machine to back the nation's diplomacy, and two or three years were necessary to rebuild the military forces. Besides, the country was repelled by the idea of turning again to military pressure in foreign relations. It sought for a while with considerable success to institute a program of economic aid to Europe and the Middle East and Asia. Part of that program, the Marshall Plan, resuscitated the faltering economies and wrought startling improvements in the material well-being of the Continent. Even so, the threatened subversion of pro-Western regimes in Greece and Turkey, the need to buttress them militarily, as was recognized in the Truman Doctrine of 1947, and the continuing use of strong-arm methods by the Russians in such cases as the Berlin blockade of 1948–1949, all gave indication of trouble ahead. Something more than economic measures was necessary to stop communism. The nation in 1950 woke with a start when the communist invasion of South Korea demonstrated the importance of a military as well as an economic policy. For five years the United States had sought, with growing distraction, to pursue its own national prosperity, and in 1950, on June 25 to be exact, the postwar letdown came to an end.

1. *The United Nations*

In the months after victory, probably nothing characterized the times more hopefully for Americans than did creation in 1945 of the United Nations. The UN would provide, its American supporters believed, a solvent for national rivalries. It would be the Parliament of the World of which poets long had sung. An American president in 1919 had revealed a vision of world government which failed to obtain popular support. Woodrow Wilson, his supporters were saying while the Second World War was still being fought, had been "ahead of his time." By 1945, time had caught up with the prophecy, and many Americans were approaching the new world organization with a childlike faith that within a few years was humbling to recall. The UN was to be the government of the brave new world; the mistakes of 1919 would not be repeated. Because of the United Nations, so carefully established before the war had ended, there would be no muddle and descent into international anarchy such as had marked the two decades after the armistice of 1918.

The intention of the United States to establish and participate in a new world organization had become obvious well before the end of the Second World War. In the year 1943 both houses of Congress passed resolutions —the Fulbright Resolution in the House (September 21, 1943), the Connally Resolution in the Senate (November 5, 1943)—stipulating, as Representative J. William Fulbright put it, "creation of appropriate international machinery with power adequate to establish and to maintain a just and lasting peace, among the nations of the world." The Senate, with due attention to its traditions, added in the Connally Resolution that the "general international organization" should be "based on the principle of the sovereign equality of all peace-loving states." A year later, in 1944, the United States invited Britain, Russia, and China to meet in Washington to plan for the new organization, a meeting held from August 21 to October 7, at a mansion known as Dumbarton Oaks—the meeting thereby becoming known as the Dumbarton Oaks Conference. Its draft proposals became the basis of the UN Charter when the latter was drawn up at the San Francisco Conference of the following year.

Delegates of fifty nations attended the grand conference at San Francisco which opened on April 25, 1945. President Truman gave the speech of welcome. The resultant UN Charter was signed on June 26 and established a General Assembly of all member nations to meet periodically, each nation with a single vote, together with a Security Council of eleven members in continuous session. There were to be such other organs as an Economic and Social Council, an International Court of Justice (sitting at The Hague, replacing the old and similarly titled League organization, the Court of International Justice), a Trusteeship Council, and a Secretariat. The Senate of the United States advised and consented to the UN Charter on July 28, 1945, by a vote of 89 to 2. Other nations quickly added their assents, and the Charter went into effect on October 24, 1945. The first meeting of the General Assembly was held in London on January 10, 1946; the Security Council convened the same month. The headquarters of the new organization was not to be in the location of the discredited League—Geneva, Switzerland—but in the metropolis of the Western Hemisphere, New York City, in a new skyscraper along the Manhattan range. This splendid slim tower of steel and glass, sumptuously appointed, has since been visited by (to use the skeptical description of Reinhold

Stettinius signs the U.N. Charter for the United States as Truman looks on.

Niebuhr) multitudes of Americans prompted by piety or school principals or women's clubs. These Americans seemed to regard the UN as a kind of supergovernment that could guarantee peace if only devotion to it were absolute. Viewing the UN's headquarters in their own country, Americans apparently believed that this time the world organization, the UN, would work.

Had they examined the UN Charter with greater care they might have found in it reason for skepticism, or at least for reservation, because in some ways the new organization was a less imposing institution than the old League of Nations. The preamble to the Charter was impressive enough, though rather bittersweet when read in the light of the world's history after 1945. "We the peoples of the United Nations," it began in a vein reminiscent of the constitution of the United States,

determined to save succeeding generations from the scourge of war, which twice in our life-time has brought untold sorrow to mankind, and to reaffirm faith in fundamental human rights, in the dignity and worth of the human person, in the equal rights of men and women and nations large and small, and to establish conditions under which justice and respect for the obligations arising from treaties and other sources of international law can be maintained, and to promote social progress and better standards of life in larger freedom, and for these ends to practice tolerance and live together in peace with one another as good neighbors, and to unite our strength to maintain international peace and security, and to ensure, by the acceptance of principles and the institution of methods, that armed force shall not be used, save in the common interest, and to employ international machinery for the promotion of the economic and social advancement of all peoples, have resolved to combine our efforts to accomplish these aims.

Such was the auspicious beginning. But as one read further in the Charter, into the substantive articles, he discovered some qualifications in its detailed constitutional arrangements. The very length of the Charter—the Covenant of the League of Nations had 26 articles; the UN Charter required 111—gave it an air of uncertainty, recalling the manner in which state constitutions in the United States frequently have been drawn to great length so that the governments inaugurated under them would not merely be precisely informed of their duties but limited in their powers. Perhaps, however, the length of the Charter was a scheme to hide the inevitable reservations of national sovereignty—the "loopholes," as the two express reservations of the Covenant of the League had been known. There were two similar loopholes in the Charter, just as all-encompassing as those in the Covenant. Part 7 of the UN Charter's article 2 reserved to member nations "matters which are essentially within the domestic jurisdiction of any state." Article 51 thoughtfully set forth, "Nothing in the present Charter shall impair the inherent right of individual or collective self-defense . . . ." Taken together, the provisions for domestic jurisdiction and self-defense would allow any scheming nation to wiggle out of its UN commitments, if it so desired. An additional loophole was the veto power over any UN actions held by the five permanent members of the Security Council, the United States, Great Britain, the USSR, France, and China. Every possible contingency thus was fenced in, in advance.

If one analyzed the Charter carefully, he found that it bound its membership to little more than good behavior. It certainly was no stronger than the League of Nations. And it was positively weaker when one considered that the Charter showed a startling lack of the procedures and regulations for members in event of international trouble that had marked the Covenant of the League of Nations. The Covenant specified procedures in case of war or threat of war. The Charter did little except declare "breaches of the peace" (the word "war" does not appear in the articles of the Charter, except twice in the phrase "Second World War") as the proper business of the membership, without stating what should thereafter be done. A skeptic or a cynic might have asked what was gained by the 111 new articles, other than the admission to membership of Soviet Russia. The Russians, having been expelled from the League in 1939 during the war with Finland, would have nothing to do with the old world organization and insisted upon a completely new one. Now there was the new one, weaker organizationally than the old.

Quite apart from its constitutional inadequacies, the UN developed a special functional weakness in the years after 1945, a weakness which deserves some mention. This was the unanticipated rise of the General Assembly to a position of importance within the UN organization, accompanied by the decline in prestige of the Security Council. The increased role of the Assembly was not, as said, anticipated by the UN's founders. The San Francisco Conference had established the Security Council in a belief that in this select body of eleven members, dominated by five great powers possessing permanent seats and the right to veto any action deemed detrimental to their interests, the work of watching over the world could easily be accomplished. In the springtime of 1945, there was little anticipation, at least on the American side, that American-Russian relations would soon deteriorate to a point where the Council could hardly function at all. The Americans in drawing up their list of powers for permanent membership in the Council also did not anticipate how drained of energy the British were in 1945, how Great Britain's stature in a year or two or three would decline to that of a virtually second-class power. France also had appeared to the United States as a far more important nation than postwar events proved. Likewise it was, apparently, a mistake to have included China among the permanent members of the Council, for neither was China a great power in 1945, nor could Nationalist China fairly represent the Chinese people after 1949, when the Kuomintang was driven from the mainland to Formosa. The Security Council, as constituted in 1945, was crippled from the start. This most important policy determining arm of the UN did not in any major respect represent the true distribution of strength, military and diplomatic, throughout the world.

The idea behind organization of the Security Council as a body dominated by the great powers was essentially a good one, for this meant, if the idea worked as planned, that nations holding dominant power in the UN were also the nations truly responsible for maintenance of peace throughout the world. The UN structure, as conceived in this way, contained the prime requisite for any well-planned political organization—a linking of power and responsibility. But the idea went awry in the unforeseen diminution of power of Britain, France, and China, and the new antagonism between the United States and the Soviet Union. This development soon led to confusion within the UN; then the United States confounded the confusion by adopting a policy of taking major political questions, many of them with profound implications for the controversy between the two superpower groups, to the General Assembly. The Assembly, the planners of the UN had assumed, was to be a talking place, a kind of town meeting with extremely limited powers, a forum where the smaller nations of the world could have representation without power. The United States for its own reasons decided that it would be good to have "decisions," resolutions of support, from the General Assembly and went to the Assembly for such notable decisions as that to gain the UN's co-operation in the Korean War after the North Korean invasion of South Korea in June 1950.

By soliciting support from the Assembly, the United States placed itself in a delicate position. It would not always be convenient for the American government to solicit Assembly support. But the Assembly, having been solicited by the United States, began to take its support seriously, as something to be given or withheld as the case might require. The Assembly was a large and unwieldy organization, including the numerous new nations of Southeast Asia and the Middle East and—in the 1960's—Africa. Hence, whenever the Assembly gave or withheld support in the form of a resolution, many nations voted—nations other than the United States, Great Britain, Western Europe, and the British Commonwealth—and it was difficult to be sure of the votes. If the United States was not constantly on guard, the Asian-Arab bloc could team up with the Latin American nations and secure an Assembly majority. The African bloc became so strong by the latter 1960's—by 1968 it contained forty nations—that it could join with Latin America and almost obtain a majority. Assembly majorities frequently did not have the faintest correspondence to world power. But for better or worse, a modicum of power passed to the Assembly, after the abdication of the Security Council, and how the United States would handle this new development was a matter for time to tell. Some thoughtful people, observing the irresponsibility of the Assembly and the difficulty of reaching decisions in the Security Council, were beginning to believe that the UN was finished so far as constructive work was concerned. It was, they believed, a place of passion, of unreason, frequently of utter confusion, with little regard for the problems of the great powers of the world.

An especially confused polarization developed in the UN, often discussed as a division between "East" and "West." These two terms have probably become inextricably imbedded in the language, but they need comment, even if in a digression. They are ihaccurate if only in that the "West" division includes such eastern nations as the Philippines and Japan, and would also like fervently to enroll India and many other Asiatic countries. It is unfortunate that the language of discussion in western countries thus tends to concede all eastern countries to the communist bloc.

In the first years after the war the confusions of the UN's organization, structural and functional, were only in part apparent. The UN in its first days was a forum of deadlock, with the *nyet* of Russian representatives echoing through the meetings of the Security Council, with the two superpowers at odds over all kinds of international proposals. It was, perhaps, unfortunate that the new world organization should have been asked to help solve at this time one of the most difficult problems ever presented to any government, national or international—the problems of limitation and reduction of atomic arms.

It was on January 24, 1946, two weeks after its opening meeting, that the UN Assembly created a commission to study the control of atomic energy. The American elder statesman, Bernard M. Baruch, on June 14, 1946, proposed an international atomic development authority to which the United States would turn over its atomic bomb secrets, provided that there was an international control and inspection of bomb production not subject to big-power veto, and that further manufacture of bombs would cease and existing stocks be destroyed. "We are here," Baruch told the UN's Atomic Energy Commission, "to make a choice between the quick and the dead. That is our business. Behind the black portent of the new atomic age lies a hope which, seized upon with faith, can work our salvation. If we fail, then we have damned every man to be the slave of Fear. Let us not deceive ourselves: We must elect World Peace or World Destruction." The Soviet Union, unfortunately, was not willing to accept the Baruch proposals, balking in particular at the American elder statesman's demand for international control and inspection. The Russian representative in the Security Council, Andrei A. Gromyko, in a speech on March 5, 1947, remarked, "Logic tells us that any thought may be reduced to an absurdity. This applies even to good thoughts and ideas. The transformation of atomic-energy control into an unlimited control would mean to reduce to an absurdity the very idea of control of atomic energy in order to prevent its use for military purposes. Unlimited control would mean an unlimited interference of the control and controlling organ—or organs—in the economic life of the countries on whose territories this control would be carried out, and interference in their internal affairs. . . . the authors of the so-called Baruch plan completely ignore national interests of other countries and proceed from . . . the interests actually of one country; that is, the United States of America."

The issue of atomic limitation and control by the UN thereupon deadlocked. Testimony to this saddening fact was the McMahon Act of 1946, reorganizing the American domestic atomic program under a new civilian five-man Atomic Energy Commission. There were two atomic tests at Bikini in July 1946. The UN had proved incapable of halting the atomic armaments race.

2. The nadir of American diplomacy

In the early postwar period of 1945–1946, faith in the UN was coupled, as we have seen, with a dominant American mood of letdown, relaxation —which insofar as it expressed itself in policy was marked by a desire to "get out of" Europe and "get out of" Asia. Troops and military forces in those distant places should come home. The world should return to its prewar habits, nations "standing on their own feet" without American aid and sustenance. The nations should "get off the U.S. taxpayer's back." If this were done, so Americans thought, everything would be just fine. In the merry chase at home, the effort to get caught up in cars and refrigerators and deep-freezers and all the other items that had gone out of production during the war, there was enough to do without thinking of foreign countries.

Despite the popular mood, diplomacy could not come to a stop. International relations continued, whether most Americans saw any value in them or not. In the initial postwar period, accommodation with Russia was the purpose and goal of American diplomats. This turned out to be largely a negative rather than positive effort, to preserve a wartime alliance that the Russians found no longer useful. The wartime alliance had begun to break, even before the end of the war in Europe, and the stresses and strains had been visible at the Yalta Conference, but for some time thereafter the West sought futilely to arrange some kind of friendly settlement with the East. Everyone in 1945 hoped for one world, a family of nations. The UN "*has* to work," people said. One world or none. The atomic bomb would unify or destroy the world. Such ideas as coexistence, containment, and cold war, utterly foreign to American wartime hopes, were not talked of by the people and statesmen of the United States until 1947 and thereafter.

There were rumblings of trouble as early as the spring of 1945, but they were unknown to the American public. President Roosevelt a short time before his death had admitted to Senator Arthur Vandenberg, "Just between us, Arthur, I am coming to know the Russians better . . . ." President Truman had discovered shortly after entering the White House that American dealings with Russia had been a "one-way street," and the new president talked turkey to the Russian foreign minister, Molotov, when the latter visited Washington a few days before the opening of the San Francisco Conference. "I have never been talked to like that in my life," Molotov said. "Carry out your agreements," Truman answered, "and you won't get talked to like that."

Uneasiness over Russian relations continued. On May 12, four days after V-E Day, Prime Minister Churchill sent a memorable telegram to President Truman: "What is to happen about Russia?" he asked. "What will be the position in a year or two, when the British and American Armies have melted and the French has not yet been formed on any major scale, when we may have a handful of divisions, mostly French, and when Russia may choose to keep two or three hundred on active service? An iron curtain is drawn down upon their front. We do not know what is going on behind. There seems little doubt that the whole of the regions east of the line Lübeck-Trieste-Corfu will soon be completely in their hands. To this must be added the further enormous area conquered by the American armies between Eisenach and the Elbe, which will, I suppose, in a few weeks be occupied, when the Americans retreat, by the Russian power. . . . Thus a broad band of many hundreds of miles of Russian-occupied territory will isolate us from Poland. . . . Surely it is vital now to come to an understanding with Russia, or see where we are with her, before we weaken our armies mortally. . . ."

This magnificent advice went unheeded. It came too soon to be followed. The American government prepared hopefully for the Potsdam Conference, held on July 17–August 2, 1945. As an earnest of good will toward Russia, President Truman ordered American troops to begin withdrawal from the advanced positions they held in central Germany. In the final rush of the war, the Western Allied troops had penetrated beyond their Yalta-allotted zones of occupation on a front 400 miles in length and at one point 120 miles in depth. Despite Churchill's plea, the United States gave up this territory, beginning the withdrawal on June 21. Americans hoped that at Potsdam no force or threats of force would be necessary, that the good work begun so auspiciously at Yalta, the work of establishing the hopes of peoples everywhere for a lasting peace, would be carried forward decisively to a settlement of European problems and, perhaps, a preliminary settlement of Far Eastern affairs. (Japan was a secret subject for discussion at Potsdam, as at Yalta, for the Soviet Union had not yet entered the Far Eastern war.) And it was one of the ironies of history that the British statesman who so recently had given the American government such a good piece of advice was forced to attend Potsdam while the results

The triumvirs at Potsdam. The surrender of Germany seemed to require yet another conference of the victorious powers. On July 17 Joseph Stalin, Winston Churchill, and Harry S. Truman, who had succeeded Franklin D. Roosevelt, met in Potsdam, a suburb of Berlin. Before the conference had finished its work, Churchill was replaced by Clement Attlee, the new Labor Prime Minister of Great Britain.

of an election in his home country were still in doubt. Churchill brought to Potsdam the leader of the British Labour Party, Clement Attlee, and when it became known during the meetings of the conference that Attlee had won the election, he replaced Churchill at the closing sessions.

The diplomacy of accommodation with the Russians was pursued at the Potsdam Conference amid the gardens and brownstone splendor of the Cecilienhof, once the country estate of the last Crown Prince William of Hohenzollern. Surrounded by history, the conference had every inspiration for success, but what had gone before—the eagerness to please the Soviets, the withdrawal by the Western Allies into their zones of occupation, the disavowal of Churchill's leadership by the British people, the uncertainties of American leadership—these were the decisive factors at Potsdam, together, of course, with Russia's vast army in possession of all Eastern Europe: East Germany, Czechoslovakia, Poland, Yugoslavia, Bulgaria, Rumania, Albania. The decisions of Potsdam, like those of the preceding wartime conferences, were foreordained. The Russians admitted that they had made a private deal with the Polish Provisional Government of National Unity (dominated by the Lublin Committee) whereby Poland received a slice of Germany, the line of the Oder and Western Neisse Rivers, in compensation for Poland's loss to Russia of the territory east of the Curzon Line. The Western Allies at Potsdam could do nothing about this accomplished fact, the new Polish border drawn within Russia's zone of East Germany, except to vow in the conference's protocol that "the final delimitation of the western frontier of Poland should await the peace settlement."

There were two other, and minor, developments at Potsdam. President Truman proposed that the principal waterways of the world—Panama, the Bosporus, Kiel, Suez, the Rhine-Danube waterway from the North Sea to the Black Sea—be opened to trade and passengers of all the world. This scheme was perfectly agreeable to the British, Churchill declaring it "remarkable and important," but it meant in effect, through opening the Rhine-Danube waterway, an opening up of the iron curtain, and this the Russians would not allow. The proposal slipped into oblivion. The other development worthy of notice at Potsdam was the so-called Potsdam Declaration, a statement by Britain and the United States that the Japanese should give up the fighting in the Far East. "We call upon the government of Japan," Truman and Churchill announced on July 26, 1945, "to proclaim now the unconditional surrender of all Japanese armed forces, and to provide proper and adequate assurances of their good faith in such action. The alternative for Japan is prompt and utter destruction." Had the Japanese known that the words of the declaration were barbed by the test explosion of the first atomic bomb on July 16 at Alamogordo,

New Mexico, they might have heeded the warning from Potsdam, but they did not know of the successes of Allied science.

After the Potsdam Conference came the interminable meetings in Europe and America of the Council of Foreign Ministers, in which nothing seemed to be accomplished. There were four meetings of the foreign ministers during the first year of peace, and the meetings went on and on. The ministers talked and argued but could come to no agreement. The apogee of disagreement was reached at the Moscow meeting in the spring of 1947, when there were forty-four sessions devoted to economic and political problems in Germany and Austria.

The regular meetings of the Council of Foreign Ministers, as had been the case with the Potsdam Conference, were disappointing in their results. Nor was the Paris Peace Conference of 1946, a series of special meetings of the foreign ministers of Great Britain, France, the Soviet Union, and the United States, held between the dates of April 25 and October 15, a triumph for American diplomacy. It gave a short-lived independence to Hungary, Rumania, and Bulgaria, which the Russians soon snatched away. It provided for Finnish independence, which Finland somehow maintained, perhaps because as an independent country Finland was able to pay more reparations to Russia than would have been the case if the Finns had not received their independence. As for the conference's deliberations on Italy, that nation was a province of the Western Allies, Britain and the United States, and they could have controlled Italian destinies with or without a Paris Peace Conference. The Paris meetings ratified the Western decision to give Italy independence. The conference had the effect, although the democratic allies at the outset had fervently hoped that this would not be, of confirming the military settlement made in Europe at the end of the war in 1945. Indeed, after one combined the results of the Paris Peace Conference with the results of the various regular meetings of the foreign ministers during 1945–1946, together with the accomplishments of the Potsdam Conference, he discovered that the settlements might have been predicted by any neophyte: where the red armies stood, there the Russians organized and manipulated governments to their own taste; wherever the West had stationed its forces, it retained local political control.

Despite what in retrospect appears to have been an obvious situation, the loss of Eastern Europe to the communists was at the time an unnerving experience for the Western powers. At the end of the war there had been high hope that the Russians in their preserve of Eastern Europe— Hungary, Rumania, and Bulgaria, together with the already nominally free Yugoslavia, Poland, and Czechoslovakia—would maintain political freedom in the occupied nations, in accord with the Yalta Declaration on

Liberated Europe. There would be, so Americans hoped, free elections in Eastern Europe, after which the reconstituted governments would continue to allow political freedom. It was one of the most disillusioning experiences of the postwar era to see the Russians ignore the Yalta Declaration and subvert the East European governments to communism. At the Potsdam Conference in 1945, Stalin had made the Soviet position clear when he said, "any freely elected government would be anti-Soviet and that we cannot permit." Western statesmen did not think the Soviet dictator would follow such a course of open domination as he did in Eastern Europe, for it seemed impossible that he would stoop to such outrageous behavior.

As mentioned briefly in the preceding chapter, conversion of the small countries of Eastern Europe into Soviet satellites was in each case, including even that of Czechoslovakia (February 25, 1948), a legal affair, accomplished by infiltrating the postwar coalition governments. In these war-devastated nations it had proved extremely difficult at the war's end to establish any kind of democratic government. Before the war, when conditions had been far more favorable, most of these countries had succumbed, in one form or another, to totalitarian regimes. In 1945 it was necessary to begin anew. Still, these nations were making the effort to fulfill the promises of the Yalta Declaration on Liberated Europe, and it appeared quite probable that the humiliations and trials of the war years had invigorated a spirit of democracy that had always been latent. Old and new political parties began to appear, and there was some sign of life politically, but at that moment the communist parties in Eastern Europe through a devious process of force, intimidation, and assimilation took over the other political parties. The favorite communist gambit was to form a coalition government, a practical necessity in the first postwar months, and then to obtain for their own party the key cabinet portfolio, the ministry of the interior, which in most European countries controls the police. From this vantage point a communist minister could institute measures of a sort that members of other parties, seeking political freedom, discovered stifling to party effort and initiative. From the ministry of the interior the communists in the former Axis satellite nations reached out to the government bureaucracies, and before the usually somewhat naive democratic leaders realized what was happening, the jig was up. Once a communist premier and cabinet took over, dissident politicians found themselves silenced and, in many instances, with one-way tickets to Siberia.

The communization of Hungary was a typical case of Russian postwar behavior behind the iron curtain. As is related by Stephen D. Kertesz in his fascinating volume *Diplomacy in a Whirlpool,* after the end of hostilities in Hungary there appeared a National Independence Front, a coalition established during the German occupation by underground leaders of the Smallholder, Social Democrat, and Communist parties. Later three other parties were admitted to the Front. The Hungarian Communist Party was careful at first to disguise its intentions, announced to the weary Hungarian people that democracy was the best policy, and even went so far as to pose as protectors of religion, affirming that the Christian churches were worthy of support. As for the Russians, the Hungarian communists said, they were interested only in annihilating fascism and had no intention of interfering with Hungarian domestic politics.

There followed the organization of a Hungarian government by the Independence Front with co-operation of the communists. Members of the provisional government were chosen with care, to give the populace confidence. The new prime minister and two other cabinet members were generals of the old prewar regime of the conservative Admiral Nicholas Horthy. But the new minister of the interior was a crypto-communist, and he at once set about organizing the police all over the country.

Then, in March 1946, came an attack against the largest noncommunist party, the Smallholders, by a left-wing bloc under communist leadership. The bloc gave ultimatums to the Smallholders in the name of the progressive Hungarian people, asking for expulsion from the national assembly of "reactionary" deputies. The Smallholders under pressure expelled twenty-one deputies, but after this step toward self-liquidation the party still held a parliamentary majority. Soon afterward, however, the Hungarian police discovered a plot and arrested the secretary-general of the Smallholder Party, Béla Kovács, whose "confessions" made to interrogators under duress implicated other members of the party including the prime minister, Ferenc Nagy. Nagy was in Switzerland on vacation when the crisis culminated at the end of May, and he could resign in personal safety. The Smallholder speaker of the national assembly, Monsignor Béla Varga, fled Hungary to avoid arrest, and eventually came, as did Nagy, to the United States. The collapse of the Smallholders was followed by annihilation of the other parties and establishment of a "people's republic" on the approved Moscow model.

Observing this process of communization, American diplomatic representatives in Eastern Europe, in Budapest and Bucharest and Sofia and Belgrade and Warsaw and Prague, protested without end, but to no avail. It was humiliating and frustrating to watch the subversion to communism of so large and important an area, without being able to do a thing about it. The diplomacy of the United States in 1945 and 1946 reached a nadir. Never in the twentieth century had American prestige in Europe fallen so low. And this within two years of the tremendous victory of 1945.

Some at the time and later would believe that Soviet actions in 1945–1946 were shrewdly calculated and that the undoubtedly low estate of American diplomacy by the end of the year 1946 was a masterly piece of work achieved by the genius of the Soviet dictator. Here, it might have seemed, was diplomacy worthy of Bismarck, Talleyrand, or Vergennes. Stalin had accomplished everything he wished, and without war.

One must take exception to this view that Russian postwar actions were, as examples of the diplomatic art, masterpieces of calculation and achievement. Soviet diplomacy was beyond doubt shrewd, but it was a cheap kind of shrewdness, a petty, narrow shrewdness that gained short-term advantages while losing long-term advantages of far greater value. First of all, one must say that many of the Soviet actions in the early postwar years were unnecessarily irritating to the West. The Russians could have accomplished the subversion of the East European governments with much greater finesse. Indeed, subversion of those governments, from the Russian point of view, should not have been necessary. An independent government can be subservient without enslavement, and subservience might have sufficed for Russia's purpose of economic exploitation. Few military advantages were to be gained from control of the satellites. Militarily the positions of the red army in the satellite countries were of doubtful value in 1945 and subsequent years, and with achievement of parity in atomic bombs between Russia and the United States, the value of those positions declined further. The satellite armies, so carefully trained, have proved politically unreliable. The only gain that the Soviets could have realized from the satellites was economic.

There were other Soviet blunders in the years immediately following the war. At Yalta and Potsdam, the Russians had agreed to a demarcation of occupation zones in Germany that gave the West the most valuable part of the country, the industrial portion that later became the heart of the West German state. The setting up of the German Democratic Republic made this a permanent division of territory. Moreover, when in Great Britain the Churchill government lost the election in 1945 and gave way to the Labor Party, an avowedly socialist party, there was opportunity for the Soviets to flatter this new Labor government, and perhaps try to separate it from its ally, the United States. Instead the Russians rebuffed the British Laborites. They chose to treat the British Labor Party with the same contempt that they had shown the Churchill regime. There was similarly shabby treatment of the French government. Already, during the war, the Russians had refused to consider the French a great power, and it was with difficulty that Britain and the United States persuaded Stalin to permit the French to supervise a zone in Germany and a section of the Anglo-American area in Berlin. In such manner the new

Fourth Republic of France found itself insulted by the Eastern colossus at a time when honeyed treatment might have drawn France into the communist camp. In somewhat similar fashion the Russians frightened the smaller nations of Western Europe into association with the Western Allies. By these tactics—shrewd in the short term, erroneous over the long run—the USSR by its own ineptitude unified the West instead of dividing it, creating by its actions that which it most feared. Soviet tactics by 1947 produced the Western policy of containment. The following year the Soviets, by forcibly taking over Czechoslovakia in the so-called Czech coup, made possible the passage of the Marshall Plan through Congress.

A famous article, "The Sources of Soviet Conduct," appeared in the American journal *Foreign Affairs* in 1947. Written by a "Mr. X," later identified as George F. Kennan of the state department, the article made a classic plea for a new Western policy toward Russia. Kennan, incidentally, when chargé d'affaires in Moscow the previous year, had sent a long cable to the department in which he had sketched many of the points of his *Foreign Affairs* article. Russian wartime and postwar expansion, he now argued publicly, was only another example of the migrations westward of barbaric peoples from the recesses of the Asiatic heartland, a migration similar to that of the Mongol conqueror of the thirteenth century, Genghis Khan. The best diplomacy for the United States, the persuasive Kennan said, was containment, a policy less than war itself, but a policy of opposing force with force, of drawing a line, a defense perimeter (as the military men liked to describe it), and warning the Russians "Thus far shall you go, and no farther." It was clear, Kennan wrote, "that the main element of any United States policy toward the Soviet Union must be that of a long-term, patient but firm and vigilant containment of Russian expansive tendencies. . . . such a policy has nothing to do with outward histrionics: with threats or blustering or superfluous gestures of outward 'toughness.' . . . demands on Russian policy should be put forward in such a manner as to leave the way open for a compliance not too detrimental to Russian prestige." Kennan's article ended with an apostrophe to manifest destiny: ". . . the thoughtful observer of Russian-American relations will find no cause for complaint in the Kremlin's challenge to American society. He will rather experience a certain gratitude to a Providence which, by providing the American people with this implacable challenge, has made their entire security as a nation dependent on their pulling themselves together and accepting the responsibilities of moral and political leadership that history plainly intended them to bear."

Shades of 1898! And in the enormously troubled era of fifty years later!

3. *The Truman Doctrine*

It was in the early spring of 1947, with Western Europe in economic and military peril, with the nations of Eastern Europe falling like ninepins under complete communist control, that the United States turned to a policy of containment. Early in the year the government of Great Britain had found itself unable to guarantee further support to the pro-Western governments of Greece and Turkey. The British on February 21 communicated this intelligence privately to Washington, with the advice that if after April 1 the United States could not pay the bill, economically and militarily, for these two nations, then Greece and Turkey would have to shift for themselves, presumably falling to communism. It was a difficult situation. President Truman took the only acceptable course in the face of this threatened disaster and prevented it by a program of economic and military aid to Greece and Turkey and other nations willing to resist aggression, a program that in its sweeping general justification of aid took the appellation of the Truman Doctrine.

Senator Arthur Vandenberg, the Republican Party's leading expert on foreign affairs, urged that Truman make his proposal of aid in a speech before Congress, and in accord with this advice the president went before a joint session on March 12 and asked for $400,000,000 for military and economic aid to the Greek and Turkish governments. In a message notable for its frank and forthright approach, he estimated that the United States had contributed $341,000,000,000 toward winning the Second World War. He pointed out that the assistance he was recommending to Greece and Turkey amounted to little more than $\frac{1}{10}$ per cent of the wartime investment. "I believe," the president said, "that it must be the policy of the United States to support free peoples who are resisting attempted subjugation by armed minorities or by outside pressures." Great responsibilities, the president remarked, had been placed upon the United States by the swift movement of events, and he was confident that Congress would face these responsibilities squarely.

Congress proved decisively in favor, and the aid bill passed by a vote in the Senate of 67–23 (April 23) and in the House of 287–107 (May 9). This first appropriation under the Truman Doctrine, signed by the president on May 15, was a relatively small program, in view of the outlays that followed under the Marshall Plan and the North Atlantic Treaty Organization, but it was a beginning, and as such marked an upward turn in American diplomatic fortunes. If Greece and Turkey had succumbed to the increasing pressure—Greece was almost surrounded by Albania,

Yugoslavia, and Bulgaria, all communist states; Turkey had a long border with the USSR—Western Europe might have followed in the wake of such a disaster. The two eastern Mediterranean nations had never before been associated with the American national interest, and it was a novel procedure for President Truman to convince the national legislature and the American people that two such foreign localities had now, perforce, come within the American defense perimeter.

Opposition to the Truman Doctrine nonetheless was voluble and sharp. One of the arguments against the program was that the Greek government was undemocratic, corrupt, and reactionary, that Turkey was not a democracy and had been neutral during most of the war. Why (so ran the argument) attempt to defend the free world by aiding such questionable governments? Or, why not let Greece and Turkey pass into the communist orbit, since those two nations merely would be exchanging one form of undemocratic government for another? The Truman administration could only argue that in matters of foreign policy it was not always possible to choose between white and black. Then too, the government of Greece might evolve toward more democratic ways if it could be economically buttressed. The government of Turkey was already moving from its era of tutelage under Mustafa Kemal toward an era of fuller democratic government. Future governments in Ankara and Athens might turn out to be different from the governments of the moment. Under noncommunist regimes the future was at least hopeful, whereas under communist regimes it would become disastrous.

Some opponents of the Truman Doctrine in Congress and in the public press during the spring of 1947 raised the argument that the doctrine by-passed the United Nations. The UN, they claimed, was the place to develop plans for economic assistance on such scales as were required in Greece and Turkey. This argument appeared frequently in the speeches and pronouncements of members of Congress and others whose friendship for the UN had never been warm, and whose sudden stand in favor of handing over the fate of Greece and Turkey to the UN sounded suspiciously like buck-passing.

During the debate over the Truman Doctrine, Representative Walter H. Judd, a former medical missionary to China, drew a comparison between American aid to Greece and Turkey and American aid to China which was momentarily embarrassing to the Washington administration. Judd wanted to know why the United States in 1947 was urging the communists in one country—China—to co-operate with China's accredited regime, and opposing communists in other countries with arms and economic aid. Here was a sincere argument, using an analogy not easy to refute. Undersecretary of State Dean Acheson hedged in his answer to

Judd, saying that the situation was different. China was a place unlike Turkey and Greece. The point, of course, was that despite the global implications of the Truman Doctrine it was difficult to aid such a large country as China. Later, in the 1960's, it turned out that it was almost too late to assist even such a small Asian country as South Vietnam. The Truman Doctrine in its practical effect was limited to Western and Mediterranean Europe.

It was a noble gesture, the Truman Doctrine, but it came too late to suffice by itself for containing Russian expansion. Immediately after the appropriation for Greece and Turkey passed Congress, indeed while it was in passage, it became evident that more than just aid to Greece and Turkey was necessary to stem the rise of communism. In the spring of 1947 Americans began to realize that all Europe was sick, and that something had to be done quickly, some measure of relief to Europe undertaken on a grand scale, or else the Continent would fall irresistibly under the sway of Moscow. Hanson W. Baldwin in the New York *Times* of March 2, 1947, reviewed the "plague and pestilence, suffering and disaster, famine and hardship, the complete economic and political dislocation of the world." He remarked that the United States was "the key to the destiny of tomorrow; we alone may be able to avert the decline of Western civilization, and a reversion to nihilism and the Dark Ages." The economic situation in all Europe in the spring of 1947 was desperate. With support from the temporary relief organization, the United Nations Relief and Rehabilitation Administration (UNRRA), due to end (UNRRA was launched late in 1943 and came to an end on March 31, 1947), Poland, Hungary, Greece, Italy, Austria, and Yugoslavia found themselves in a bad way. It was at this time that Winston Churchill described Europe as "a rubble heap, a charnel house, a breeding ground of pestilence and hate." Everywhere in Europe people lacked sufficient food, clothing, and shelter. Drought had killed most of the 1946 wheat crop, and the severe winter of 1946–1947 cut the prospects for the crop of 1947. In France, between three and four million acres of wheat planted in the autumn were destroyed in January and February 1947. In England at this time, a coal shortage became so serious that London found its electric power shut off for hours every day. What would the United States do about a Europe on the verge of economic breakdown? Would it pursue a do-nothing policy and let the pro-Western governments in Britain, France, and elsewhere pass out of office, to be succeeded by less friendly and, in some instances, by communist cabinets?

Having already taken a step in the direction of economic aid to Greece and Turkey, the Truman administration found the way clear to a more general and ambitious program of aid to all Western Europe. President

Truman on January 21, 1947, had replaced Secretary of State Byrnes by General George C. Marshall. The new secretary in a commencement address at Harvard in June 1947 announced the program that was to bear his name, the Marshall Plan.

4. *The Marshall Plan*

In conceiving the Marshall Plan, the American secretary of state brought together various ideas and opinions of his subordinates in the state department, linked them to the eagerness of President Truman to arrest the progress of world communism, and contributed his own decisive and forthright approach. The resultant plan as the secretary elaborated it tentatively before the Harvard assemblage on June 5, 1947, was pre-eminently the result of staff work in the department of state. It was the kind of work that the department had not done for a long time, since fifteen years before when Henry L. Stimson was secretary of state. When Marshall had taken over the state department he had told his undersecretary, Acheson, to straighten out the lines of command, and to set the unwieldy organization on the kind of footing that would enable it to function and would prevent the suffocation of every idea that sought to make its way from desk officers through the hierarchy to the office of the secretary. When the Truman Doctrine injected a new note of decision into American diplomacy, the already reorganized department sprang to life and produced a ferment of ideas that set the secretary to thinking about a general plan of European economic assistance. The original impetus for the Marshall Plan came from a series of extraordinary memoranda by Marshall's able undersecretary of state for economic affairs, the Texas cotton merchant William L. Clayton. If anyone truly was the "father" of the Marshall Plan, it was "Will" Clayton, who reported in detail to Marshall not merely about Europe's economic problems but about the need for a massive injection of American public funds. About this time, George F. Kennan, as head of the department's new policy-planning staff, produced an able memorandum sometimes cited as the beginning of the Marshall Plan, but one must say that Clayton's memoranda were the force behind the new policy. Charles ("Chip") Bohlen, a department career officer who later became ambassador to Russia and to France, then proceeded to draft Marshall's Harvard speech.

The secretary of state himself produced two ideas which went into his speech and were of high importance in the resulting proposal. In his speech Marshall called upon the European governments to help themselves by drafting a program of mutual economic aid, to which the United States would make a substantial contribution. He told the European nations that instead of bringing their various shopping lists to the United States, as had been the case with lend-lease and UNRRA, the nations should get together and decide among themselves the best allocation of resources. Only after such decision would the United States contribute. "It is already evident," he said, "that before the United States Government can proceed much further . . . there must be some agreement among the countries of Europe as to the requirements of the situation and the part those countries themselves will take. . . . The initiative, I think, must come from Europe. . . . The Program should be a joint one, agreed to by a number, if not all, of the European nations."

Secondly, there was apparently no stipulation in Marshall's original proposal that it should include only the nations of Western Europe. The secretary apparently defined his offer of aid to Europe as everything up to the Urals. The Marshall Plan encompassed Russia and satellites in Eastern Europe, and the Soviets could participate if they wished.

In this provision for an all-European program there might have been the death of the Marshall Plan, even before it passed beyond the stage of proposal. If the Russians had participated in the plan, they could have wrecked it, either through their devious activities or else by their mere entrance. For it was almost inconceivable that Congress would have voted the appropriations necessary to put the Marshall Plan in business if the Russians had chosen to join in Secretary Marshall's proposed program. Fortunately the Russians did not join.

They certainly had their opportunity, as Foreign Secretary Ernest Bevin arranged for a planning meeting in Paris of the European foreign ministers—Britain, France, and Russia. The Paris meeting of foreign ministers opened on June 27, with Molotov present. Bevin dominated the proceedings. After two or three days of desultory conversation, he took a proposal by the French foreign minister Georges Bidault, reduced it to a single page by taking out the extra words, and sent this page to Bidault and Molotov on the morning of July 1. Bevin was urging that the three foreign ministers draw up a proposition for the American government. Molotov had been saying that each nation should send its own shopping list. Bevin coolly told Molotov that the Russians wanted a blank check from the Americans, and what would happen if he, Bevin, went to Moscow and asked for a blank check from the Russians? The meeting of July 1 adjourned on this note. The final meeting, next day, brought a clean break. Bevin presided. Molotov repeated his arguments and finished by saying that any joint Anglo-French action without Russian consent might have very grave consequences. Bidault said the French would go with the British. Bevin said that he, like Bidault, proposed to carry on. The following day, July 3, the British and French governments invited all European states to meet in Paris and draw up a proposal for the American government.

Molotov departed the Paris meeting without a sign that his government would co-operate. The Russians foolishly turned against the Marshall Plan and announced their own bogus program of economic aid to Eastern Europe, known as the Molotov Plan.

Before the Russian policy of obstruction became clear, there was an attempt by two of the satellites, Poland and Czechoslovakia, to accede to the Marshall Plan. Both nations expressed willingness to attend the general planning session scheduled to open in Paris. The party line immediately went out from Moscow, and the Polish foreign minister had the unenviable task of explaining to the American ambassador why his country was turning down participation in the Marshall Plan. When he made his explanations, the foreign minister refused to look the ambassador in the face, and his discomfiture was perfectly clear. In the case of the Czechoslovaks the embarrassment was far worse, as they had shown more interest than the Poles. A delegation from Prague was summoned to Moscow, and Stalin thereupon conversed with Prime Minister Klement Gottwald. The Czechoslovak leader met Stalin alone and came back to his hotel visibly shaken, saying he had never seen the Russian dictator so angry. After a second conference of the Czechoslovaks and Russians, a general meeting in which the Russians more politely set out their objections to the Marshall Plan, the Prague government took back its words and sent back the Paris invitation.

The way was open for action by the American Congress, and action was forthcoming. Debate on Marshall's proposal of June 1947 had begun during the autumn and early winter, and in January 1948 the time of decision arrived. By this date it was apparent that Congress would not balk. Senator Robert A. Taft believed that there was not much good that could come out of helping foreigners, for it would only spread bankruptcy from Europe to America, but he said he would vote for the European Co-operation Act. Anguished left-wingers such as Henry A. Wallace, the former secretary of agriculture and of commerce, denounced the proposed aid program as a wanton attack on the Soviet Union, a "Martial Plan." But Wallace had little support in Congress. The Marshall Plan passed easily and was signed by President Truman on April 3. The initial appropriation, aid for the fifteen months from April 3, 1948, through fiscal 1949 (ending June 30, 1949), amounted to $5,850,100,000. China received Marshall Plan aid, through fiscal 1949, of $275,000,000, and there also was $125,000,00 for military aid. This gesture—and it could be nothing more, for China was fast going down the drain, the country passing to the communists—was to quiet the "China first" members of Congress.

Sixteen European nations, together with the zones of West Germany and the Free State of Trieste, gathered in Paris in March 1948 and formed the Organization for European Economic Co-operation, or OEEC, an international co-ordinating body that would represent all European partners in the plan. To these states the United States, via the Marshall Plan, gave through the Economic Co-operation Administration, or ECA (and its successor at the end of 1951, the Mutual Security Administration), between April 3, 1948, and June 30, 1952, the sum of $13,348,800,000. Three nations took over half this amount. The United Kingdom obtained $3,189,800,000, France $2,713,600,000, West Germany $1,390,600,000. Italy (including Trieste) received $1,508,800,000, the Netherlands $982,-100,000. Iceland took the smallest amount, $29,300,000. Such was the Marshall Plan in operation.

It was a noble effort by the United States, and in its effect upon the European economy it showed itself vastly worthwhile, for European production in 1950 was 45 per cent higher than in 1947, 25 per cent higher than in 1938, the last prewar year; in 1952 production was 200 per cent over 1938. By the end of the Marshall Plan in 1952, there was an economic base in Europe, a solid foundation on which the United States could build an alliance against the USSR. An effective military alliance would have been impossible in 1947.

All this for the reasonable expenditure of $13,348,800,000, a negligible sum compared to the near $1,000,000,000,000 income of the American economy during that same period. The Marshall Plan expenditures were only a fraction of America's liquor bill over the same period. Unconvincing were the claims of some political leaders in 1947 and thereafter that European aid was bankrupting the nation, that the billions sent to Europe would force the United States treasury into fiscal chaos, ending the American way of life. The country in 1947–1952 enjoyed an unprecedented prosperity and hardly felt the expenditures of the Marshall Plan.

When the plan ended in 1952 after the beginning of the Korean War, with production in Europe still rising in a manner most encouraging to the people and government of the United States, there were perhaps two problems that Marshall aid had undertaken to solve without complete success. If the plan had hoped to make Europe more efficient in production and marketing techniques, and if it had sought to capture the sympathy of European workers so as to wean them away from communism, it had been something of a failure, for those two goals were not altogether achieved. Europe by 1952 was still inefficient economically. Much of its trade was throttled by cartels, if not by trade barriers at national borders. As for the workers of Europe, in Italy and France (although not in England, Scandinavia, Germany, Austria, Luxembourg, the Netherlands, and Belgium) they had failed in the early years of the Marshall Plan to receive much benefit from the new production that the plan achieved. The poor in Italy and France had not become poorer, but the rich grew richer. Italian and French workers were dissatisfied with their lot and not unwilling to express their feelings by voting communist in national elections. Even so, despite such difficulties, the Marshall Plan provided a healthy economic base in Europe from which reforms, economic and democratic, might be made in the future. This was no ordinary accomplishment.

The Korean War eventually brought an end to the Marshall Plan, an end to exclusively economic aid to the countries of Western Europe. There had been a stipulation that not a cent of Marshall Plan aid should go into military supplies. Early in 1951 the United States informed Europeans that further American assistance would have to be allotted for defense purposes. (This, incidentally, was not as large a blow as it appeared, for Europe and chiefly Germany benefited hugely from the "Korean boom" in the world market.) By 1952 the United States was giving eighty per cent of its aid to Europe in military weapons and the other twenty in defense support. By 1952 the plan, the Economic Co-operation Administration or ECA, merged with its competitor, the Military Defense Aid Program of MDAP, in the Mutual Security Administration, MSA (in 1953 rechristened the Foreign Operations Administration or FOA; in 1955 rechristened the International Co-operation Administration or ICA; in 1961 rechristened the Agency for International Development or AID).

5. *The Berlin blockade*

A crisis of more than momentary importance in the first half-decade after the war was the Berlin blockade of 1948–1949, which for a time appeared to be a prelude to a Third World War. Prior to the Korean War, no crisis looked so dangerous as this Russian attempt in 1948 to seal off Berlin from Western access by rail or road and to force the Western Allies thereby into a change of their German policy. The blockade took its origin in the efforts of the Western Allies to unify their zones in Germany, once the honeymoon period with the Russians was over. The Western Allies, Britain and France, led by the United States, felt that they had to do something in the years 1946 and 1947 and early 1948 to bring the collapsed German economy to its feet again. This effort involved a series of moves toward a West German government which the Russians construed as a challenge to their own occupation policy in Eastern Germany.

Prior to the reforms instituted by Allied authorities in Germany—

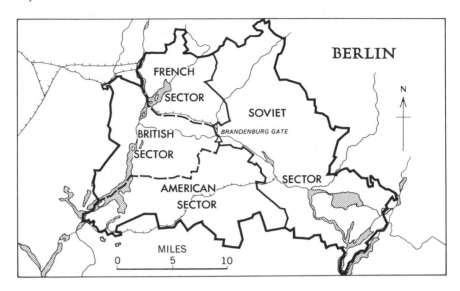

reforms led by the imaginative American military governor, General Lucius D. Clay—the West Germans had lived on the "cigarette economy," in which the American cigarette had replaced the inflated Reichsmark as a standard of value. Food rations in the Allied zones were set at 1,500 calories daily, well below the normal requirement. Steel production in Germany in the year 1946 was down to 2.6 million tons. There was little incentive to work, Communist Party memberships began to increase, the American army was spending $1,000,000,000 a year in relief funds to feed the hungry Germans, and there was a compelling pressure from the United States to get the Germans off the American taxpayer's back. There was, in truth, every reason for the Allies to attempt to get their zones organized economically.

These moves antagonized the Russians and led to the showdown over Berlin. General Clay at first had persuaded the British to fuse their zone in Western Germany with the American zone, and the result was "Bizonia," which with addition of the French zone became "Trizonia." In the spring of 1948, a conference of the Western powers in London invited the Germans to elect delegates to a constitutional convention which would create a new government for West Germany. In June 1948 the Allies instituted a drastic currency reform in Western Germany, repudiating 90 per cent of the Reichsmarks then circulating and substituting a new and soundly controlled money. Almost at once the sparks of economic life began to flare up throughout the cities and countryside of Allied-occupied Germany. There commenced such a renaissance of

The Berlin blockade—"The Big Push of '48."

economic life as has hardly been seen during the course of modern history. The Russians, doubly disturbed by this economic-political revival under Western capitalist auspices, moved to stop it with the Berlin blockade beginning April 1, which became total on June 24, 1948.

That there could have been such a thing as a Russian blockade of Berlin and an Allied airlift would have seemed incredible to Americans in 1945. The United States had been uninterested in Berlin in 1945. In the closing days of the war, General Eisenhower's victorious Western armies had moved far into Germany. Troops were not far from Berlin, but they were not in force. The Russians had hundreds of thousands of troops massed close to the city and wanted to take it anyway. Since it was plain that the taking of the city would be costly in lives, Eisenhower advised against the Western Allies' taking Berlin with or ahead of the Russians. As he informed Washington, "May I point out that Berlin is no longer a particularly important objective." The chiefs of staff in Washington agreed, and President Truman concurred, and Berlin was conquered by the Russians, who allowed the Allies to occupy specified sectors within the city. Access to those sectors was through Russian-held territory. But few individuals worried in 1945 over the security of the Western Allies' position in Berlin, over the fact that the Soviets could blockade at will the Western sectors of the city.

The only thing that saved West Berlin in 1948–1949 was the Allied right to air corridors to the city across the Soviet zone of East Germany. Fortunately, on November 30, 1945, the Allied Control Council in Berlin had approved a paper providing three corridors of commuication between Berlin and West Germany, and flights through these three corridors could proceed without notice. The powers including Russia established a four-power Berlin Air Safety Center in February 1946. This center continued to operate through the Berlin blockade of 1948–1949, with Russian members coming daily to their offices as if everything were normal.

The only alternative means of supplying West Berlin with food and fuel was to push through armed road convoys, or an armored train.

An airlift seemed at the outset impossible in 1948, but the Allies were determined to stay in Berlin. The odds appeared impossible for democracy, but General Clay had informed the Pentagon on April 10, 1948,

When Berlin falls, Western Germany will be next. If we mean . . . to hold Europe against communism, we must not budge. . . . If we withdraw, our position in Europe is threatened. If America does not understand this now, does not know the issue is cast, then it never will and communism will run rampant. I believe the future of democracy requires us to stay.

The challenge, therefore, was taken up. The Allied air forces by dint of quick work and improvisation brought together enough planes from all over the world to accomplish what by any standard was a gigantic task. General Clay had estimated that by the winter of 1948–1949 it would be necessary for the Allies to bring in 4,500 tons of food and fuel a day. By October 1948 the average daily airlift haul was approaching 5,000 tons. One day in April 1949, 1,398 Allied planes landed a record 12,941 tons. The planes came in every 61.8 seconds. Altogether, from June 24, 1948, until May 12, 1949, Allied planes ferried 1,592,787 tons, over half a ton apiece, for each of the 2,250,000 Berliners in the Western sectors.

In the course of the blockade there was a bit of humor in Berlin. The American commandant, Brigadier General Frank L. Howley, in his *Berlin Command* (1950) has recounted the Russians' difficulty in constructing a war memorial at Pankow during the blockade. The Soviets had contracted to a West German builder for a large statue of Lenin, and the German thoughtfully sent over all the material except Lenin's head, which he kept as security until he should receive payment for his work in the more valuable West marks. The Russians wanted to pay in East marks and appealed to Howley.

"But we must have the head!" wailed General Kotikov. "How can we unveil the monument next week without it?"

The Berlin airlift.

"Too bad," was Howley's reply.

The Russians paid in West marks.

Once during the blockade Howley was compelled to invite Kotikov to a lunch conference. Chicken was served, and the Russian commandant complained that it was tough.

"It ought to be," Howley pointed out, "it had to fly all the way from Frankfurt."

On another occasion, after a meeting between the city's four commandants, including the Russian, the discussants were having the usual post-conference refreshments. Kotikov suffered from ulcers and ate with care. A waiter brought a tray of drinks. Howley indelibly remembered the result:

"Champagne?" someone asked.

Kotikov puffed out his cheeks and shook his head. "Makes me belch," he said.

"Have a Martini," I said shrewdly.

"What is a Martini?" Kotikov asked.

I pointed to the lethal drink on the tray. Innocently, Kotikov picked it up. I took champagne. Kotikov raised his glass.

. . . We all drank. To my astonishment, Kotikov gulped the entire contents of his glass—Martini, olive, and all. A look of wonder crossed his face. I proposed a toast. Another Martini clanked down to the Russian's ulcers. There were two more toasts and two more rapid Martinis for Kotikov.

I looked at him curiously. His disarmingly cherubic face was twisted. Obviously his stomach was on fire.

I nodded toward another Martini.

"Nyet!" he gasped.

At the outset of the blockade the Americans caught the Soviet commander for Germany, Marshal Sokolovsky, in a speed trap on an autobahn, and the marshal—whose bodyguard had jumped out to face the Americans with guns—cooled his heels for an hour, with an American gun in the pit of his stomach, until an officer came along and identified him. And there were two other episodes involving Sokolovsky. One related to his house, where Howley discovered the heating arrangements were via a gas main which ran through the American sector. Howley turned off the gas. Sokolovsky had to move. The marshal's assistants then foolishly put his furniture in a van and tried to truck it surreptitiously through the American sector, and Howley captured the furniture.

But to return to the more highly diplomatic, and serious, aspects of the Berlin blockade. Not merely, of course, did the Western powers supply the people of their sectors in Berlin. The airlift produced in Berlin and throughout Europe a tremendous wave of pro-Allied enthusiasm. Sight of the hundreds of giant transports circling down over Tempelhof airdrome was an indication of Western power that thrilled Berliners, and the morale of the inhabitants of that embattled city rose to such heights that the Russians in disgust called off their blockade on May 12, 1949. The way was clear for a West German government. The way was clear in all Europe for the Marshall Plan. And with the Marshall Plan, Americans hoped, would come sufficient economic power that the Europeans in a not too distant future might be able to participate in defense of their countries against a possible Russian invasion.

In this chapter nothing has been said about the origin and development of the North Atlantic Treaty Organization which occurred in 1949 and subsequent years. NATO was a logical accompaniment of the Marshall Plan: the plan prepared the economic base from which a European military plan could be constructed. NATO, however, remained subordinate to the Marshall Plan until 1950 and the Korean War, and so it is perhaps better to put off discussion of it until a subsequent chapter dealing with Europe from 1950 onward.

As for President Truman's program of Point 4, the fourth of a series of suggestions that the president elaborated in his inaugural address of January 1949, this in a sense was a world counterpart to the Marshall Plan.

It promised technical assistance—American agricultural, mechanical, medical, and administrative knowledge—to the so-called underdeveloped countries (incidentally, those countries heartily disliked the word "underdeveloped" with its unintended meaning of American superiority). In financial outlay it has never come near equaling the expense of the Marshall Plan, and generally one can say that Point 4 has been much more promise than fulfillment. Only here and there have efforts at amelioration been made, at places where either a small amount of money could do a large amount of good, or where "pilot projects," demonstrations of effectiveness of aid, could hope to bring in further assistance from other quarters. Appropriation for Point 4 in its first year amounted to $35,000,-000, and outlays since then have not been large. Perhaps the chief difficulty with the program was that the United States, despite its vast wealth, could not underwrite the economies of all the poorer nations of the world. And it was difficult to obtain public support in the United States for Point 4; Americans in the war and postwar years already had paid out a great deal for foreign assistance and were disinclined to finance economic development indefinitely for no more precise purpose than developing underdeveloped countries. Many were ready to hear ridicule; the head of the International Co-operation Administration, in charge of Point 4 work, was accused of various absurdities and delinquencies: providing striped pants for Greek undertakers and bathtubs for Egyptian camel drivers; supplying wild grass seed for sowing along Lebanese highways; flying Arabs to Mecca; building roads for the royal Cadillacs in Saudi Arabia; and—that ancient political accusation!—iceboxes for Eskimos (there was "absolutely no trace of iceboxes for Eskimos," the harassed administrator protested, "nor are we in the business of furnishing aid to the Eskimos").

The first five years of peace in Europe after the Second World War, one might conclude, marked a period of numerous trials and troubles, and by 1950, when recovery was at last in sight, the Far East erupted in the Korean War, spelling new trouble. The course of power and politics on the Continent had proved far different from what Americans had expected in the rosy haze of V-E Day 1945. Europeans and Americans by 1950 had nonetheless come together against the menace of Russian communism. Matters were not yet out of danger, but the worst, so Americans hoped, was over.

A CONTEMPORARY DOCUMENT

[President Truman's address to Congress on March 12, 1947, in which he announced what became known as the Truman Doctrine, was a notable declaration of principle. Source: *Public Papers of the Presidents of the United States: Harry S. Truman, 1947* (Washington, 1963), 176–180.]

The gravity of the situation which confronts the world today necessitates my appearance before a joint session of the Congress.

The foreign policy and the national security of this country are involved.

One aspect of the present situation, which I wish to present to you at this time for your consideration and decision, concerns Greece and Turkey.

The United States has received from the Greek Government an urgent appeal for financial and economic assistance. Preliminary reports from the American Economic Mission now in Greece and reports from the American Ambassador in Greece corroborate the statement of the Greek Government that assistance is imperative if Greece is to survive as a free nation.

I do not believe that the American people and the Congress wish to turn a deaf ear to the appeal of the Greek Government. . . .

The British Government, which has been helping Greece, can give no further financial or economic aid after March 31. Great Britain finds itself under the necessity of reducing or liquidating its commitments in several parts of the world, including Greece.

We have considered how the United Nations might assist in this crisis. But the situation is an urgent one requiring immediate action, and the United Nations and its related organizations are not in a position to extend help of the kind that is required. . . .

No government is perfect. One of the chief virtues of a democracy, however, is that its defects are always visible and under democratic processes can be pointed out and corrected. The government of Greece is not perfect. Nevertheless it represents 85 percent of the members of the Greek Parliament who were chosen in an election last year. Foreign observers, including 692 Americans, considered this election to be a fair expression of the views of the Greek people.

The Greek Government has been operating in an atmosphere of chaos and extremism. It has made mistakes. The extension of aid by this country does not mean that the United States condones everything that the Greek Government has done or will do. We have condemned in the past, and we condemn now, extremist measures of the right or the left. We have in the past advised tolerance, and we advise tolerance now.

Greece's neighbor, Turkey, also deserves our attention.

The future of Turkey as an independent and economically sound state is clearly no less important to the freedom-loving peoples of the world than the future of Greece. The circumstances in which Turkey finds itself today are considerably different from those of Greece. Turkey has been spared the disasters that have beset Greece. And during the war, the United States and Great Britain furnished Turkey with material aid.

Nevertheless, Turkey now needs our support. . . .

The British Government has informed us that, owing to its own difficulties, it can no longer extend financial or economic aid to Turkey. . . .

One of the primary objectives of the foreign policy of the United States is the creation of conditions in which we and other nations will be able to work out a way of life free from coercion. . . .

I believe that it must be the policy of the United States to support free peoples who are resisting attempted subjugation by armed minorities or by outside pressures.

I believe that we must assist free peoples to work out their own destinies in their own way.

I believe that our help should be primarily through economic and financial aid which is essential to economic stability and orderly political processes. . . .

I therefore ask the Congress to provide authority for assistance to Greece and Turkey in the amount of $400,000,000 for the period ending June 30, 1948. . . .

In addition to funds, I ask the Congress to authorize the detail of American civilian and military personnel to Greece and Turkey, at the request of those countries, to assist in the tasks of reconstruction, and for the purpose of supervising the use of such financial and material assistance as may be furnished. I recommend that authority also be provided for the instruction and training of selected Greek and Turkish personnel. . . .

This is a serious course upon which we embark.

I would not recommend it except that the alternative is much more serious.

The United States contributed $341,000,000,000 toward winning World War II. This is an investment in world freedom and world peace.

The assistance that I am recommending for Greece and Turkey amounts to little more than $\frac{1}{10}$ of 1 per cent of this investment. . . .

Great responsibilities have been placed upon us by the swift movement of events.

I am confident that the Congress will face these responsibilities squarely.

ADDITIONAL READING

The years between 1945 and 1950 were an era of disillusion when the wartime gospel preached by Wendell Willkie, *One World* (New York, 1943) dissolved into a highly dangerous Russian-American rivalry. Such a volume as that edited by Raymond Dennett and Joseph E. Johnson, *Negotiating with the Russians* (Boston, 1951) would have seemed impossible to Americans in 1941–1945 in view of the motif of the period expressed in the title of Walter Lippmann's *The Cold War* (New York, 1947).

General books on the era and afterward, dealing in whole or part with American diplomacy, are such volumes as Dexter Perkins, *The American Approach to Foreign Policy* (rev. ed., Cambridge, Mass., 1962); Robert E. Osgood, *Ideals and Self-Interest in America's Foreign Relations: The Great Transformation of the Twentieth Century* (Chicago, 1953); Eric F. Goldman, *The Crucial Decade: America, 1945–1955* (New York, 1956), with an updating under the title *The Crucial Decade and After* (1960), a lucid, witty, intelligent sketch after the fashion set by Frederick Lewis Allen's social history of the 1920's, *Only Yesterday* (New York, 1931); *Hans W. Gatzke, *The Present in Perspective* (Chicago, 1957); *Herbert Agar, *The Price of Power: America since 1945* (Chicago, 1957), a book in the Chicago History of American Civilization series; *William A. Williams, *The Tragedy of American Diplomacy* (Cleveland, 1959); Stephen D. Kertesz, ed., *American Diplomacy in a New Era* (Notre Dame, Ind., 1961), a group of essays; Denna F. Fleming, *The Cold War and Its Origins: 1917–1960* (2 vols., New York, 1961); *Norman A. Graebner, *Cold War Diplomacy: American Foreign Policy, 1945–1960* (Princeton, 1962), an interesting narrative with documentary annexes; *John W. Spanier, *American Foreign Policy since World War II* (3d ed., New York, 1968); *William G. Carleton, *The Revolution in American Foreign Policy: Its Global Range* (New York, 1963); *Walter La Feber, *America, Russia, and the Cold War: 1945–1966* (New York, 1967), an able volume in the America in Crisis series. A book of much merit is *Dexter Perkins, *The Diplomacy of a New Age: Major Issues in U.S. Policy since 1945* (Bloomington, Ind., 1967); this work is short, readable, sensible.

In the era since 1945 there has been an enormous publication by participants and contemporary observers, and the reader may wish to examine carefully selected excerpts from this literature. A book now is available, by *Lawrence S. Kaplan, *Recent American Foreign Policy: Conflicting Interpretations* (Homewood, Ill., 1968), containing fifteen chapters, each with editorial introduction, documents, views of participants, and views of observers.

For American statesmen there are *Harry S. Truman, *Memoirs* (2 vols., Garden City, N.Y., 1955–1956); William Hillman, ed., *Mr. President* (New

York, 1952), a volume compiled with Mr. Truman's active assistance; James F. Byrnes, *Speaking Frankly* (New York, 1947), in which Truman's second secretary of state looked carefully over his career; the same author's *All in One Lifetime* (New York, 1958), with a different time-perspective; Richard L. Walker and George Curry, *Edward R. Stettinius, Jr. and James F. Byrnes* (New York, 1965), volume 14 in the American Secretaries series; Robert H. Ferrell, *George C. Marshall* (New York, 1966), volume 15 in the same series; Dean Acheson, *Sketches from Life of Men I Have Known* (New York, 1961); and *The Pattern of Responsibility: Edited by McGeorge Bundy from the Records of Secretary of State Dean Acheson* (Boston, 1952), a compilation of speeches and papers.

The United Nations commenced functioning before the cold war got seriously under way, and the American beginnings of the UN appear in Robert A. Divine, *Second Chance: The Triumph of Internationalism in America during World War II* (New York, 1967).

Recent students have taken new interest in the origins of the cold war, for which see Arthur M. Schlesinger, Jr., "Origins of the Cold War," *Foreign Affairs*, XLVI (1967–1968), 22–52. John Gaddis is considering this problem in a forthcoming study.

The important subject of Germany appears in John L. Snell, *Wartime Origins of the East-West Dilemma over Germany* (New Orleans, 1959); *Philip E. Mosely, *The Kremlin and World Politics* (New York, 1960), containing an inside account of the European Advisory Commission; *Stephen E. Ambrose, *Eisenhower and Berlin, 1945: The Decision to Halt at the Elbe* (New York, 1967), which argues that the Americans had almost no opportunity to get to Berlin ahead of the Russians; Hajo Holborn, *American Military Government* (Washington, 1947); Marshall Knappen, *And Call It Peace* (Chicago, 1947), a firsthand account of the early years of occupation, written in bitterness or, at the least, exasperation; Harry L. Coles and Albert K. Weinberg, *Civil Affairs: Soldiers Become Governors* (Washington, 1964); Eugene Davidson, *The Death and Life of Germany* (New York, 1959), a first-rate analysis of the occupation down to West German independence in 1955; John Gimbel, *The American Occupation of Germany: Politics and the Military, 1945–1949* (Stanford, Calif., 1968). The American military governor, Lucius D. Clay, offers his accounting in *Decision in Germany* (Garden City, N.Y., 1950). W. Phillips Davison, *The Berlin Blockade: A Study in Cold War Politics* (Princeton, 1958) is best for that subject. See also William M. Franklin, "Zonal Boundaries and Access to Berlin," *World Politics*, XVI (1963–1964), 1–31. The purging of the Nazi war criminals has given rise to a large literature, but a book which supersedes all the books on this subject is Eugene Davidson's *The Trial of the Germans: An Account of the Twenty-Two Defendants Before the International Military Tribunal at Nuremberg* (New York, 1966), dedicated to the men and women of July 20, 1944. Davidson shows the extraordinary guilt of the defendants but is uncertain about the business of judgment.

For its special subject see Stephen D. Kertesz, ed., *The Fate of East Central Europe* (Notre Dame, Ind., 1956), essays by a dozen or so experts; together with Kertesz's own excellent volume, *Diplomacy in a Whirlpool* (Notre Dame, 1953).

The turning point in American policy toward Europe is set out philosophically in George F. Kennan, "The Sources of Soviet Conduct," *Foreign Affairs*, XXV (1946–1947), 566–582; the same author's *Memoirs: 1925–1950* (Boston, 1967); and *Joseph M. Jones, *The Fifteen Weeks (February 21– June 5, 1947)* (New York, 1955), by a speechwriter at the department of state. A special study is Harry B. Price, *The Marshall Plan and Its Meaning* (Ithaca, N.Y., 1955).

The actions of leading American officials—diplomats, military men, administration figures—appear in *Dwight D. Eisenhower, *Crusade in Europe* (Garden City, N.Y., 1948); Arthur Bliss Lane, *I Saw Poland Betrayed* (Indianapolis, 1948), by the American ambassador to Poland; W. Bedell Smith, *My Three Years in Moscow* (Philadelphia, 1950), by the American ambassador; Arthur H. Vandenberg, Jr., ed., *The Private Papers of Senator Vandenberg* (Boston, 1952); Walter Millis and Eugene S. Duffield, eds., *The Forrestal Diaries* (New York, 1951); John P. Armstrong, "The Enigma of Senator Taft and American Foreign Policy," *Review of Politics*, XVII (1954–1955), 206–231, a trenchant analysis of the isolationist senator's meandering views on foreign policy.

☆ **26** ☆

Europe in Recent Years

Ich bin ein Berliner.

—President John F. Kennedy, Berlin, 1963

In the first dozen or so years after the end of the Second World War, the forward movement of Russian communism, politically and militarily, was distressingly rational in its large outlines, and the organization of the later chapters of this book, one hopes, displays this fact. The initial Soviet move was toward the nations of Western Europe, where the troubles of the war had brought military, social, and economic ills of a seemingly insoluble sort and where, according to communist dogma, the contradictions of the capitalist system were about to deliver these nations into the hands of the revolutionary workers of the world. This move was stopped largely by American policy—the Truman Doctrine, the Marshall Plan, and the North Atlantic Treaty Organization (NATO).

Blocked at this point, the USSR allowed the North Koreans to start a war in the Far East, which if successful might have spread communism throughout Asia and made Russian satellites of the weak governments in that part of the world. Again the United States responded, this time with military force, and if the UN-US successes in Korea of 1950–1953 did not prevent the partition of Indochina in 1954, they at least brought proof that there would be no easy conquest of Asia by the USSR if the United States could help it.

At this moment the Russian government turned to the Middle East (for which see chapter twenty-nine) and stirred up trouble.

When the Middle Eastern nations failed to fall like a row of nine-pins there was Africa, and Latin America.

During all the movements of what one must consider to have been Russian policy, the continent of Europe remained the most important part of the world, and both the Russians and the Americans understood this continuing fact of international relations. If the Soviet Union moved its pawns around the corners of the board, the important pieces were in Europe.

1. *The strengthening of NATO*

The North Atlantic Treaty was signed in Washington on April 4, 1949, by representatives of the United States and eleven European powers. NATO's original members were, in addition to the United States, the nations of Benelux (Belgium, the Netherlands, and Luxembourg), France, Britain, Canada, Italy, Portugal, Denmark, Norway, and Iceland. Greece and Turkey joined NATO in February 1952, and West Germany joined in 1955, making a total of fifteen countries. By article 5 of the treaty the signatories agreed that an attack upon one would be an attack upon all, to be followed by individual or collective resistance under the stipulations of the UN Charter's article 51, the "collective self-defense" article. For the United States, membership in NATO was an epoch-making proposition, for not since the Treaty of Mortefontaine of the year 1800, when the United States disengaged itself from its French alliance, had the American government been bound in peacetime by a treaty of alliance. Signature of the North Atlantic Treaty in 1949 indicated clearly that the era of isolation had ended.

Three Russian moves of strength—the communist coup in Czechoslo-vakia in February 1948, the Berlin blockade of 1948–1949, and the Korean War of 1950–1953—had led first to the creation and thereafter to the buildup of NATO. The communist seizure of power in Czechoslo-vakia aroused the West and led to talk of military action to counter such Russian moves. During the turmoil in Prague, the Czech foreign minister Jan Masaryk, son of the founder of the republic and well known in the West, died in an apparent suicide under circumstances suggesting that the communists pushed him out of a window. Soon afterward came the Berlin blockade, which made the West wonder how far the Russians were will-ing to go in violating the war's territorial settlement—to move the iron curtain westward to the Atlantic Ocean? NATO was organized while the blockade was in progress.

If there were any uncertainties as to Russian intentions, these were resolved by outbreak of the Korean War in 1950. Thereafter the Allies set out in earnest to construct a strong military force in Western Europe, for it seemed that only by opposing force with force could the position of the West against Russia be made tenable. General Eisenhower, the American military commander of the Second World War, went to Europe in 1951 to establish the Supreme Headquarters, Allied Powers in Europe, known as SHAPE, and his command received the available standing forces in Western Europe which at the time consisted of 15 army divisions together with a handful of planes.

Eisenhower's presence in Europe galvanized the NATO powers, and large plans were drawn for a NATO force that on the ground, would be almost able to defend Western Europe against the red army divisions in East Germany and the satellite nations. At the NATO Council meeting in Lisbon in February 1952, a plan issued to raise in Western Europe (not counting Italian, Greek, and Turkish troops) a force of 50 divisions, ready and reserve, and 4,000 aircraft by the end of that year. At the defined time, the plan was largely met: 25 divisions were to be ready for combat, and all were on hand by December 1952; 25 more divisions in reserve were to be avilable in thirty days, and all but three or so were ready. The aircraft goal fell short by between 200 and 300 planes.

This achievement came at a time when the Korean War was drawing to an end, and in the year 1953 the European powers, surveying the better prospects for peace in the Far East, began to reconsider their NATO goals. The goal for 1953 in Western Europe had been 75 divisions (ready and reserve) and 6,500 aircraft; this figure was revised downward to 56 divisions and 5,500 aircraft. For the following year, 1954, the provisional goal had been 100 divisions; this goal was reset at 60, with 30 ready divisions.

The goal of NATO in Western Europe in the latter 1950's and the 1960's was kept at 30 ready divisions, but it is easy to see that the original hopes of the United States and the other nations never came to maturity. After admission into NATO in 1955, the West German government promised 12 divisions and eventually supplied them, although they were not well backed by supply troops in the manner of American divisions. The United States contributed 5 divisions, with a total force in West Germany of 225,000 troops. Britain had 3 ready divisions, the Netherlands 2, Belgium 2, Canada a brigade. The French contingent to NATO never amounted to much, about two understrength divisions, as troops were siphoned off to Indochina and Algeria. The ready strength of NATO in Western Europe hence amounted to about 25 divisions, far short of the original goal but a considerable force nonetheless. The Italians, Greeks, and Turks possessed ready troops, but they were not on the spot in Western Germany and the Low Countries, where trouble might occur.

How did the NATO troops appear in strength as compared with those of the Soviet Union and its allies? It is a curious fact that at the present writing, 1969, the Warsaw Pact forces are smaller than the NATO forces in the latter's Division Forces in the Center Region, 619,000 troops as compared to NATO's 677,000. The Soviets, however, get twice as many effective divisions from their manpower as do the NATO forces. It is, indeed, an extraordinary situation, the seemingly built-in inefficiency of NATO. As Malcolm W. Hoag of the RAND Corporation has written in a recent study, "NATO outspends and outmans the Warsaw Pact, but it has never converted this potential for conventional superiority into actuality." NATO troops luxuriate in extra vehicles, expensive equipment, complex supply organization, whereas the Warsaw Pact nations organize fighting divisions. The RAND Corporation's analyst, mentioned above, has recommended that the United States government adopt the Soviet Union's divisional structure. This is unlikely, despite the military advantages; the commanders of the American army and the West European NATO contingents, accustomed to their comfortable ways, would not willingly give them up.

In connection with the buildup of NATO—whatever the inefficiency of the resultant forces—the new state of West Germany was able to increase its bargaining power with the Western Allies by obtaining a grant of full sovereignty on May 5, 1955, exchanging as a *quid pro quo* a contribution of German troops to NATO. The West German government found itself in the enviable position where both the *quid* and the *quo* were to its advantage, although the Western powers, especially the United States, felt rewarded by the German troop contribution. Ten years after the defeat of 1945, a German government received full sovereignty in Europe, a remarkable event which few individuals would have predicted. In view of the French preoccupation in the mid-1950's with the rebellion in Algeria, a relatively small German rearmament was enough to bring to being on the Continent a German army larger than the French.

The issue of Germany's troop contribution to NATO was complicated and is worth some comment, although with passage of time it has begun to take on the appearance of a detail within the larger scene of diplomacy in Europe and the world. At the beginning of the Korean War, the United States was anxious to include a German contingent within NATO and without much finesse impressed this sentiment upon its NATO Allies. The French were disturbed by this notion of German rearmament within so short a time after the recent troubles and not unnaturally became cautious. In October 1950 the French premier of the moment, René Pleven, pulled a special rabbit out of his hat, the Pleven Plan, which by 1952 was called the European Defense Community (EDC). This scheme was readily understandable as a linked expression of French dislike of German rearmament and concession to the need for German troops in NATO. EDC was a compromise by which German contingents would be included within NATO but in a military organization no larger than the divisional level: the divisions of members of EDC would be mixed at the corps and army level. This was the chief point of EDC, and there were subsidiary provisions for a joint military budget for the multi-national European defense force, the budget to be raised by assessing each member country a share based on its national income.

EDC commended itself to American diplomats in 1952 because of their desire for haste in bringing together a European force to oppose the red army. The Americans thrust it upon Pleven's successors until the French, who had repudiated Pleven, scuttled EDC by a rousing vote in the National Assembly in August 1954. This despite Secretary of State Dulles's pronouncement of December 1953 that if EDC did not pass the Assembly, the United States might have to make an agonized reappraisal of its European commitments.

The Germans soon afterward were admitted to NATO by another stratagem, more involved if less soothing to French fears of a new German army. The solution was to refurbish a treaty concluded between Britain, France, and Benelux in 1948: the Brussels Pact alliance known also as Western Union. In its revised form, christened Western European Union or WEU, its original signatories offered membership to West Germany and Italy, which the two former enemy nations accepted. WEU was not an organic union like EDC, but an alliance, and it allowed Germany to keep more control over its armed forces than would have been the case under EDC. After joining WEU, West Germany was invited to become a member of NATO, and all armed forces of WEU were to be subject to the NATO supreme commander, who now was referred to as the Supreme Allied Commander, Europe, or SACEUR. The French assembly approved WEU on December 30, 1954.

In any discussion of West Germany's entry into NATO, one should point out that this move had an economic as well as military basis which was well understood by the European powers, especially Great Britain. The trouble was that the West Germans, with their defense problems taken care of by their erstwhile enemies, had been able prior to 1955 to have a special advantage in competition for foreign markets—they had no production facilities tied up in military work and could produce goods for export at an advantage over their Western European competitors. The British in particular felt the competition of West Germany during the Korean War boom and after, and when nine per cent of Britain's total national product and fifteen per cent of its metal and two-thirds of its scientific brain power was being consumed in the armament race, this business of German competition was no laughing matter.

Even after the Germans were persuaded to take up the burden of their own defense, Britishers were inclined to point out how the Germans were still the leading war profiteers of Europe. The American army in the latter 1950's was spending so many dollars annually in West Germany that this expenditure helped the West Germans keep ahead nicely in dollar exchange. One British statesman was moved to say plaintively to an American colleague that it might be advisable for Scotland to threaten an attack on England so the English could have a rich American army stationed in their midst.

In addition to the issue of a German contingent within NATO, another aspect of the alliance—concerning a choice of weapons—is worth some attention. The organization's weakness in firepower led the United States in 1954, even before securing the inclusion of West German forces, to introduce "tactical" atomic weapons into the armament of the American divisions in NATO. This was a fateful decision. Perhaps it was necessary because of NATO's weakness, but it was a serious move. United States military forces in Europe in December 1954 received delivery of a number of 280-millimeter atomic cannon—"Atomic Annie," as the new gun was affectionately named. Shortly thereafter, the American army in West Germany announced acquisition of field artillery battalions equipped with Corporal and Honest John missiles. It became known that atomic bombs were stockpiled in Germany. In public speeches the leaders of the American armed forces announced that their cannon and missiles would see use in any future war with Russian forces in Europe. The impression they gave was that atomic cannon and missiles were just a little more powerful than ordinary artillery and represented only one more and rather minor miracle of American science. Magazines in the United States published army press releases with pictures extolling the virtues of the huge new cannon, and the cannon looked like a cannon, which was reassuring.

What most people failed to understand were the consequences if armies in the field used such small atomic weapons for tactical purposes. An atomic explosion was an atomic explosion whether propelled out of cannon or by missiles or dropped from planes, and equipment of American armies in Europe with these small atomic weapons meant conversion of the armed forces to atomic strategy. And in any future war, tactical use of atomic cannon and missiles would be a signal, so many informed commentators in the United States and Europe believed, for all-out use of atomic weapons. The tactical use of atomic weapons was impossible. Who could tell when tactical employment shaded into strategic employment? No military writer or practitioner has ever been able to draw a clear line between tactics and strategy. Choice of atomic weapons for

America's NATO forces was a fateful and perhaps fatal step. Viscount Sir Bernard Montgomery put the case frankly: "The reason for this action is that we cannot match the strength that could be brought against us unless we use nuclear weapons." He said that with this decision "we have reached the point of no return as regards the use of atomic and thermonuclear weapons in a hot war." Bluntly, the use of tactical weapons in the field meant hydrogen bombs on the homeland.

2. *Russian embarrassments*

One of the most momentous developments for American foreign policy in recent years, an event for which the United States was decidedly not responsible, was the death on March 5, 1953, of Joseph Stalin. The headlines came suddenly. On March 4 they announced: STALIN GRAVELY ILL AFTER STROKE. On March 5: STALIN SINKING: LEECHES APPLIED. Then on March 6: STALIN DEAD. A grand state funeral took the tyrant to his public tomb—at least for a while his public tomb—alongside the body of the great Lenin, and there were muffled reports that Stalin had been quietly eliminated by his associates in the Kremlin. The world turned to the more important speculation of how the leader's decease would affect Russian foreign policy. That it would no one doubted.

The first trouble for the successors came when they loosened some of the controls over the Russian and satellite peoples that had marked the last years of the old dictator. Even a small measure of freedom was dangerous and led to an uprising in East Berlin in June 1953 that spread throughout East Germany. In the Stalin Allee, the grand avenue of East Berlin that was to be the showplace of the workers' paradise, some German construction workers quit their jobs in protest over an increase of work requirements, their so-called norms, and paraded down the street, calling upon other workers to join them. The parade turned into a riot and then a demonstration of almost the entire populace of East Berlin against the Russians. Workers attacked Russian tanks with stones and paving bricks. The officials of the East German government, in a state of mind close to terror, pleaded with their fellow countrymen to go back to work. The revolt spread to other cities in East Germany; there were mass meetings throughout West Berlin and the cities of West Germany; the riots did not subside until Soviet troops broke up the demonstration and until it was certain that there would be no armed assistance from the Western-occupied part of Germany. Clearly, these events showed that Russian rule of the East Germans after eight long years had been unsuccessful; that the young men and women of the East zone who had been painstakingly indoctrinated with communism were the first to throw it over; that probably the East-zone military units being organized and trained by the Russians would be unreliable adjuncts of any Soviet army invading the West.

The East German revolt of 1953, if unsuccessful for the Germans, gave Western observers reason to feel heartened. There was no question but that the cause of the West was looking up in the hitherto supposedly lost areas behind the iron curtain.

One might have thought that because the relaxation of Stalinist bonds had produced riots in East Germany, the new Soviet leaders would have been careful thereafter. But three years later on February 24–25, 1956, the Russian leader Nikita S. Khrushchev (for reasons as yet not altogether divined in the West) denounced his former master Stalin to a secret gathering of the Twentieth Congress of the Soviet Communist Party in Moscow. This speech, soon leaked and since famous, gave new hope and led to new revolts of the East European peoples. Some eight months later Moscow's two satellites Poland and Hungary were in open rebellion, and the Poles by a combination of fortune and discretion managed to obtain from the Russians a large measure of freedom. The Hungarians went too far and brought about a communist terror and re-imposition of the communist puppet government by force of Russian

The Hungarian Revolt.

arms. The Khrushchev speech, coupled with relaxation of secret-police measures in the satellites, appears to have had this remarkable effect.

The speech of Khrushchev in early 1956 constituted one of the most important documents of the twentieth century. It was leaked to the West apparently by officials of the Polish government, and the department of state in Washington became Khrushchev's publisher when it released the text in April 1956. The speech well rewarded close reading and was published in book form by the Columbia University Press. In this impassioned address, punctuated by frequent and tumultuous applause and other sounds of approval or astonishment throughout the great hall in Moscow, Khrushchev set down many, though presumably not all, of his former chief's delinquencies. It turned out that Stalin was enormously vain, given to faking his own biography both by claiming authorship of books he did not write and by interpolating whole sections favorable to himself and his genius. He was enormously suspicious, and even came to believe that one of his oldest associates, Klementi Voroshilov, was an English agent— he had microphones planted in Voroshilov's house. Stalin was enormously jealous of his military achievements and during the war was accustomed to sit in his office tracing the front lines on a globe. He lost his composure when the Germans pressed close to Moscow in 1941 and for days was unable to take hold of his government duties. But more important than these delinquencies were his hatreds and deceits; he personally sent thousands of innocent people to their deaths in the latter 1930's and by his example led to purging and liquidation of hundreds of thousands and perhaps millions of Russians. As late as 1951 Stalin arranged the execution of a member of the politburo, Nikolai Voznesensky. Khrushchev disclosed that the politburo had little power of decision and had operated in the late Stalin years mostly in fragmented committees—quartets, quintets, septets.

The cult of the individual, the impassioned Khrushchev declaimed, had to be destroyed, and if he did not tell all the evils of Stalinism, he told enough. His sincerity was sufficiently obvious to give his speech the ring of truth. His revelations shook communist parties in all nations of the world and led to personal reassessments of the sort that had occurred in 1939 when Stalin had taken Russia temporarily, via the Nazi-Soviet Pact, into the camp of the Germans.

Beyond question this speech was important and appears to have led traceably to the outbreaks in Hungary and Poland in October 1956.

A history of American diplomacy is no place to set down these internal developments of Soviet government and politics in their full details, but because the two revolts of 1956 did have meaning for Russian strength— or weakness—in Eastern Europe and because this weakness in satellite territories subtracted from Russian military strength and political prestige, it deserves recounting in outline.

The Polish revolt was the more interesting because it was successful and presented a model for other satellites seeking independence. The Poles, it should be noted, had managed to preserve some independence during their years under communism. Poland never had been completely in the hands of the Stalinists and even the Polish Stalinist leader Boleslaw Bierut appears to have advised subordinates against too draconian measures in his country. When after Stalin's death the word came down from Moscow that destalinization was the order of the day, the Poles could argue that their quiet opposition had been politically correct. Then in the summer of 1956 came riots in Poznan by workers who had tired of exploitation by the Soviet Union. These riots had been observed by Westerners who were in Poznan visiting an international fair and hence were fit subject for advice from Moscow, but the rioters were treated gingerly by the Polish Communist Party and let off without much chastisement after surprisingly fair trials. The Poznan riots and their careful settlement, as events turned out, were a straw in the wind giving indication of larger developments, in the course of which Wladyslaw Gomulka moved from the status of a disgraced and imprisoned former functionary to become chief of the Communist Party in Poland.

Gomulka appears to have been a shrewd operator. Having experienced the rigors of a Polish communist prison, he was guided by caution and a sense of what might happen to him and his collaborators in event they failed. He managed to marshal the support of the Polish people, and with this he set out to follow his own course. On October 19 when he was suddenly confronted in Warsaw with an august Moscow delegation consisting of Khrushchev, Molotov, Anastas Mikoyan, and the politburo member Lazar Kaganovich, he threatened an armed uprising against any Soviet-inspired military coup. At this point Khrushchev backed down, realizing that it was better to have a national communist in charge of Poland than start a civil war between Russian and Polish communists, to the ruin of Soviet prestige throughout the world. Gomulka on his own side was careful to prevent excesses by Polish patriots anxious to abandon not merely the Russian tie but communism. He seems to have realized that the hope of his leadership, the opportunity for achieving Poland's national independence, lay in the foundation of a Titoist regime, a government modeled on that of Marshal Tito of Yugoslavia, who had managed through control of his army and party apparatus to maintain independence against Moscow. Tito had come to power in Yugoslavia with communist help during the Second World War. Although himself a Moscow-trained communist, he was too spirited a person to be a Moscow puppet, and gathering about him the patriotism of the Yugoslav people he had cut loose from Russian direction in 1948. By adroit maneuvering—economic assistance from both West and East, but especially from the West—Tito had managed to create and maintain an independent communist government. The example of Yugoslavia lay at hand, and Gomulka seized it. He moved carefully but surely. He was willing to break up premature strikes by Polish students and dispersed a student demonstration on October 22, 1956. In this uneasy position, halfway between two worlds, the Polish leader managed to gain control over his country.

The outburst in October in Budapest was a different affair from its beginning, for the Hungarians discovered no resting place between satellite and independent status. The communist leader Imre Nagy sought, as had Gomulka, to hold his countrymen from excess, but students and army officers leading the revolt found themselves on an irresistible popular wave; communists were turned out of power, many were pursued and killed; Cardinal Joseph Mindszenty, Roman Catholic primate of Hungary, entered Budapest in triumph to the ringing of all the city's church bells broadcast for the world to hear. This was too much for the Russians, already humiliated by the triumph of national communism in Poland, and after some initial confusion it became clear that the revolt in Hungary would be snuffed out. It was. The Soviet army feigned a withdrawal from Budapest on October 30 but on November 4 reappeared and, city block by city block, reconquered the capital from its own people.

The deaths of the rebels could not obliterate the meaning of their country's revolt—that in Hungary as in Poland, Russian communism had been rejected, however firmly imposed; that despite a decade or more of indoctrination, the youth of satellite nations was unwilling to forgo nationalism for communism.

3. *Alarms and excursions*

Soviet policy toward Europe in recent years has been gingerly and sometimes oblique as compared with the crudities of the early years after 1945. For a while in the latter 1950's and early 1960's it seemed as if the Russian leaders were willing largely to let the successes of Soviet space science speak for their nation's power. The first *sputnik* went up in 1957, and the world, not merely Europe, looked agog as the scientific marvel glided silently around the globe. Other sputniks quickly followed, and eventually manned flights. All the while the American government appeared far behind in what became known as the space race. The result was predictable for European politics. Many Europeans began to ask how the American government could continue to shield them against Russian aggression, considering the scientific superiority of the institutes in Moscow and Leningrad.

The race for space that began in 1957 between Russia and the United States never had large understanding by the American public, not to mention the publics of Western and Eastern Europe and of the many other nations of the world. For years, in relating its spectacular feats in space, the Soviet government was able to bank on popular ignorance. The problem may have been that Americans and other peoples thoroughly understood the political meaning of a race—a trial between two nations or a kind of Olympic game—and this ordinary understanding conveniently covered the ignorance of what space feats meant in the scientific, not to mention the real power races between the United States and Russia or any other nation attempting a space race.

The truth of the space race was that from the outset the Russians acted from weakness, not strength. Back in 1954 the United States government had exploded its first hydrogen bomb at Bikini (at Eniwetok in 1952 it had fired a device, not a bomb), and this huge bomb was not merely a triumph of explosive power—the Russians required seven years to fire a bigger one—but a triumph of American scientific ingenuity. American scientists had taken the sixty-odd-ton device of 1952—it was so heavy, J. Robert Oppenheimer said, that it would have to be hauled to its target in an oxcart—and reduced it to a small size in the bomb of 1954. Because of this reduction, American intercontinental ballistic missiles no longer needed the tremendous thrust for which the country's experts were designing them. The government immediately abandoned its plans, already well toward completion, to build a huge missile to carry hydrogen warheads into the Soviet Union. It turned to much smaller missiles, with smaller thrust, which easily could lift the miniaturized H-bomb of 1954. The result became embarrassingly obvious in 1957 when the Russians, who apparently had been unable to miniaturize their H-bombs and hence had developed huge-thrust missiles, threw their sputnik into the air. The principal requisite to put a satellite in orbit was thrust, not a large amount of scientific know-how.

For some years after 1957 the American government was embarrassed before its own public and those of other nations, friends and foes, because its small-thrust missiles could not easily lift satellites. There were several well-publicized failures, inducing clowns in the Moscow circus to enter the ring bearing balloons, to announce to their audiences that the balloons were American sputniks, and then to stick pins in the balloons. The first American satellites were small, and for manned flights the United States had to miniaturize its space capsules, keeping the weight down by painful compromises and extremely costly lightweight metals. Of course, a decision was made to build missiles with huge thrust, not merely enough to send aloft earth satellites with larger scientific payloads, or more space observers, but to hurl unmanned and manned capsules into flights to the moon and to Mars. A "man on the moon" was no longer a joke. It was no joke either that a Russian might get there first.

The American space probes have been models of scientific experiment and have kept the United States far ahead of Russian experiments. The Soviets have preferred propaganda victories, and this preference has led them to send up astronauts when, so many American scientists contended, instruments could do the work much better. There is an open argument, continuing to the present day, as to whether it is at all advantageous to place a man on the moon or on Mars when an instrument can do much more. It has proved impossible, though, for a great nation to avoid the space race, and the American government by 1968 had sunk a total of $44,000,000,000 in the race. The department of defense had spent about a third of this amount. The National Aeronautics and Space Agency (NASA) had spent the rest. At its peak of operations in 1966, NASA was employing 35,000 people at fifteen scattered centers, plus some 400,000 scientists, engineers, and workers among its thousands of contractors.

For the first two or three years after 1957, the space race remained the clear preserve of the Soviet Union, and the Russians derived immense propaganda victories, including the feeling of many Europeans, as mentioned, that their nations were virtually defenseless, despite the presence of NATO troops and the United States's often-remarked willingness to defend Western Europe whatever the cost. In these initial space-race years the feeling increased that the United States was suffering from a "missile gap"—that Soviet sputniks were proof of the extreme vulnerability of the continental United States to Soviet missiles, and hence that the Americans would not risk Russian nuclear retaliation by fighting to protect Western Europe. There was great psychological insecurity in Europe in the latter 1950's.

Then, early in May 1960, just before a scheduled "summit meeting" of the leaders of the United States, Britain, France, and Russia in Paris, the so-called U-2 affair gave additional evidence of American weakness and Soviet strength—or at least it seemed to give such evidence.

What happened in May 1960 is common knowledge and needs no long recital. Ever since the beginning of the cold war, the United States had been spying on the Soviet Union with fast-flying reconnaissance planes, which often flew along the coast of Soviet territory carrying cameras that could photograph far inland. Once in a while the Soviets would violate international waters and shoot down one of these planes to discourage the operation. There were fourteen known incidents prior to the U-2 affair. The Soviets, on their side, had been overflying Alaska and Canada. In 1957 there were reports that the United States air force was flying a remarkably efficient jet reconnaissance plane, and these planes by 1960 had been making "milk runs" over the Soviet Union for four years. The Soviets knew the United States was violating their airspace but could not shoot down the American planes and did not like to admit inability to defend their territory. Then on May 1, 1960, the pilot of one of the new spy planes used by the Central Intelligence Agency, the Utility-2, as it was known, Francis Gary Powers, had some sort of trouble with his jet plane as it was sailing 65,000 feet over the Soviet Union and crashed near Sverdlovsk, the Soviet Pittsburgh. Through a series of stupidities understandable in all large organizations (governments, businesses) the United States government tried to cover up what had happened, and Premier Khrushchev was able to trap the Americans in a whole series of lies. The American government then lost its nerve (when lying is necessary, one should do a thorough job) and President Eisenhower admitted personal responsibility for the U-2 flights.

Not least of the hardly reassuring aspects of the U-2 affair was that the pilot, Powers, was being paid $2,500 take-home pay a month and obviously was to have blown up himself and his plane when he got into trouble. A deplorable choice for the job, he had lacked the nerve. He was a country boy from Jenkins, Kentucky. Everything about his life was mediocre (except for skill in flying), prior to his descent into Russia, which was a disaster. What, for example, were the CIA's academic qualifications for the job which Powers took? In high school in Grundy, Virginia, across the border from Jenkins, Powers ranked twenty-second among sixty-nine graduating seniors. At Milligan College, 110 miles away from Grundy, at Johnson City, Tennessee, he compiled a strong B-minus average and graduated in 1950 likewise twenty-second in his class, this time of fifty-nine graduates. He possessed none of the qualities set out some years later by Arthur T. Hadley as those necessary for a good spy:

. . . a psychologically well-balanced individual—not ordinary, but so well-balanced as to appear normal. He needs the same deep, introspective knowledge of himself that the ideal psychiatrist needs. He should have looked perceptively at himself and the world around him and come up with his own philosophy. His balance must be self-sustaining, an internal gyroscope. The man who needs praise, fellowship, coaching or even understanding cannot maintain the pace. Nor will the shibboleths of conventional wisdom sustain the agent in his dark hour. Conventional wisdom does not recognize the occasional necessity of murder or suicide.

Francis Gary Powers at the opening of his trial on espionage charges in Moscow. At his left is defense counsel Mikhail Griniev.

In Russian captivity Powers admitted to being a spy and said he was sorry. His wife, sister, father, mother, his wife's mother, a doctor, and a family friend came to the public Moscow trial and lent melodrama to it, replete with tears. The CIA in 1962 exchanged Powers for the Soviet spy Colonel Rudolf Ivanovitch Abel (a far more interesting person, captured in New York City after the defection of Abel's assistant, Lieutenant Colonel Reino Hayhanen). The CIA saw to it that Powers disappeared into anonymity.

The American embarrassment over the U-2 affair came to a small crisis during the Paris summit meeting, which Khrushchev "wrecked" by allowing it to convene just long enough to accuse the president of the United States of hypocrisy and then go back to Moscow in a huff, although not before making other angry pronouncements while on French soil and holding a press conference at which he harangued a roomful of reporters while his defense minister, Marshal Malinovsky, sat glowering at his side.

The intelligence achievement of the U-2 flights was almost completely lost from view during the hullaballoo over the downing of Powers's plane and the failure of the summit, and during the American presidential election of that same year, in which there was much uninformed talk about a missile gap in Russia's favor. By 1960, however, and the cessation of the flights by order of the president, the American government had closed an intelligence gap of major proportions. The U-2's high-resolution, long-range aerial cameras, which could photograph ground features in fantastic detail, literally showing golf balls on greens, had produced an almost microscopic analysis of Russian territory. The photos indicated that Russian intercontinental ballistic missile strength had been vastly overrated as compared to that of the United States. The missile gap was in favor of the United States. It was a marvelous piece of intelligence which no indignation of Khrushchev or embarrassment even of the president of the United States could affect.

After the Cuban missile crisis, which was an attempted "quick fix" of the Russian missile inferiority (see chapter thirty), the Soviets and Americans in the limited Test-Ban Treaty of 1963 agreed to cease atmospheric tests of nuclear weapons. The Soviets turned to other interests in foreign policy and said little more about sputniks and U-2's. The true scientific and military balance, if not the propaganda balance, had been too much in favor of the United States.

American policy toward Europe in the 1960's also turned to other problems—notably the sallies of an unexpected antagonist, General Charles de Gaulle.

A large concern of the state department in these latter years was the waywardness of French national policy under De Gaulle's presidency of the Fifth Republic. During the Second World War, Churchill had quipped that the greatest cross which he had to bear was the cross of Lorraine. By the 1960's, De Gaulle was at it again.

At one point in the developing antagonism between the United States and Cuba after the advent of Premier Fidel Castro, President Eisenhower had said to a press conference that he did not understand what was "eating" Castro. The same might well have been said about De Gaulle. Some psychology was at work there which did not reduce easily to logic. The French economy had come into prosperity. De Gaulle in 1962 managed to give Algeria to the Algerians. Eight years earlier France had given Indochina to the Americans. At last a French government had obtained economic and military stability. De Gaulle put through a new constitution which ensured his control of the government and ended the kaleidoscopic ins and outs of cabinets and premiers. With these accomplishments one might have thought that *le grand Charlie* would have been content. It is possible that his malevolence toward the United States and Britain came from memory of the slights by Churchill and Roosevelt during the war years. There may also have been some psychic delight in discomfiting people who spoke English. For his own good reasons the general in 1967 forced all American NATO installations out of France, making the supply routes to the troops in Germany pass through Antwerp and German ports, forcing American fighter planes to other and sometimes more vulnerable fields. De Gaulle vetoed British participation in the Common Market, the European plan for lower tariffs and freer trade which had grown out of the Marshall Plan and was beginning to rationalize the Continent's economy. The British were in economic trouble because of disappearance of their imperial markets and other problems too numerous to mention, but De Gaulle would not give his erstwhile ally the slightest assistance.

The French president offered a stream of advice to the United States, advice on Vietnam, NATO, how to get along with the Russians, how to solve the German problem. He was acting like a European Nehru.

All the while he maintained a foolish *force de frappe*, a plane-carried nuclear strike force. Americans believed that his *force de frappe*, slow-moving, probably bearing only A-bombs (France exploded its first hydrogen device in 1967), would not get off the ground in event of any future nuclear war.

At last, on April 28, 1969, De Gaulle gave up the presidency of France, having lost a national referendum in which he had staked his political future. What the future government of France would be became, once more, an open question, put perhaps better than the answers the General had been providing the American government.

In the picture of power and politics in Europe in the later years after 1945, the United States and the Soviet Union tried their best to preserve their interests. Despite difficulties, both nations seemed to be doing so. It is interesting to observe that as the United States received the gratuitous advice of General de Gaulle, so the Soviet Union in its own sphere east of the iron curtain had to tolerate unpleasantness. Europe, even Eastern Europe, was reasserting its independence. Liberalization of the regime in Russia after the death of Stalin loosened beyond repair some of the bonds in Eastern Europe. The Albanians got out of line and stayed out of line, their tiny economy and insignificant military power supported by the Chinese communists, who were glad to create trouble for the Russians. At times the faithlessness of the Albanians provoked Russian leaders to lose their tempers. "Comrade Hodza," Khrushchev said to the premier of Albania during a great public reception in Moscow, "you have just poured a bucket of dung over my head, and I don't like it." But it was necessary to overlook the ungracious behavior of the Albanians. The Rumanians began to pursue an independent policy in the mid-1960's, and the Soviets could do little short of sending troops into the country. Wherever Russian troops were encamped, there was, of course, relative co-operation by the local governments—as in East Germany, Poland, Hungary, and Bulgaria.

The Russians found themselves forced in the 1960's into two further rigorous moves in Eastern Europe which created momentary uproars in the West, and by which the Soviets undoubtedly lost face in the European and world propaganda battle. The one, of course, consisted of the raising of a barrier along the border between East Berlin and the city's Western sectors. So many East Germans were escaping over the border, attracted partly by the political freedom but more by the opportunities in the bustling West German economy—a quarter of a million able-bodied East Germans were crossing annually—that the Russians had to do something or else see their East German state bleed to death. The result was the Berlin wall, put up after the closing of the frontier on August 13, 1961. By that time the East German regime had lost three millions of its population, with sixteen million persons remaining, as compared to West Germany's fifty-three millions. Despite the outcry in the West about this wall, the barrier was not such a bad proposition in a broader diplomatic sense, for it stabilized what was becoming an impossible situation laden with disaster for European peace. In the latter 1960's the East German economy made strides toward equaling that of West Germany, and unrest in the East zone quieted.

The Czechoslovak invasion of August 1968 was a Russian move of similar nature. The Prague regime of the Slovak leader Alexander Dubček had begun to democratize almost in entirety, all the while professing communism. Such an example of liberalism was too much for the Soviets. Suddenly, under the provisions of the Warsaw Treaty of 1955 (NATO's analogue) to which the Czechoslovaks had subscribed, the Soviets together with contingents from East Germany, Poland, Hungary, and Bulgaria took over Czechoslovakia. They imprisoned Dubček, but popular feeling rose so high that they had to treat with his regime, infiltrating it with his enemies, laying down demands for return to the *status quo ante* liberalization, requiring the Czechoslovaks to permit a permanent garrison of Russian troops on their soil.

There was not much the United States could do about Russia's actions east of the iron curtain. Former President Eisenhower wrote in his memoirs that during the Hungarian invasion of 1956 the American government could not do a thing, because Hungary was as remote from American power as was Tibet. President Kennedy in 1961 told his adviser Walt

Whitman Rostow, shortly before the raising of the Berlin wall, that the United States was powerless in East Berlin and in the Soviet areas of Eastern Europe generally—that these places were beyond the reach of American military might. In August 1968 the United States government was the more embarrassed because it needed Russian help in ending the Vietnam War. Notes passed back and forth, but there was no action. The Russians in 1968 said that they had the right to invade West Germany if necessary. The American government repeated its pledges to NATO, that the invasion of a member of the alliance, such as West Germany, would take the United States to war. Talk arose of increasing NATO's strength, which for fifteen years had languished at about 25 divisions. An increase in NATO strength, though, was doubtful, as in the latter months of 1968 the Czechoslovak situation began to return to what one might describe as "iron curtain normal."

A CONTEMPORARY DOCUMENT

[President Kennedy made some remarks in West Berlin on June 26, 1963, which Berliners long will remember, if only because in his brief address he said that he considered himself one of them. Just a few months afterward the handsome young president met his tragic end. But apart from the meaning of the speech for the people of Berlin, and the fact that it was given in the shadow of tragedy, it is worth reading today because Kennedy in his felicitous way expressed the sentiments of European and world freedom. Source: *Department of State Bulletin*, July 22, 1963.]

I am proud to come to this city as the guest of your distinguished Mayor, who has symbolized throughout the world the fighting spirit of West Berlin, and I am proud to visit the Federal Republic with your distinguished Chancellor who, for so many years, has committed Germany to democracy and freedom and progress, and to come here in the company of my fellow American, General Clay, who has been in this city during its great moments of crisis and will come again if ever needed.

Two thousand years ago the proudest boast was *"Civitas Romanus sum."* Today, in the world of freedom, the proudest boast is *"Ich bin ein Berliner."* (I appreciate my interpreter translating my German.)

There are many people in the world who really don't understand, or say they don't, what is the great issue between the free world and the Communist world. Let them come to Berlin. There are some who say that communism is the wave of the future. Let them come

John F. Kennedy addresses crowds of Berliners.

to Berlin. And there are some who say in Europe and elsewhere we can work with the Communists. Let them come to Berlin. And there are even a few who say that it is true that communism is an evil system but it permits us to make economic progress. *Lasst sie nach Berlin kommen.*

Freedom has many difficulties and democracy is not perfect, but we have never had to put a wall up to keep our people in, to prevent them from leaving us. I want to say, on behalf of my countrymen, who live many miles away on the other side of the Atlantic, who are far distant from you, that they take the greatest pride that they have been able to share with you, even from a distance, the story of the last 18 years. I know of no town, no city, that has been besieged for 18 years that still lives with the vitality and the force and the hope and the determination of the city of West Berlin. While the wall is the most obvious and vivid demonstration of the failures of the Communist system, for all the world to see, we take no satisfaction in it for it is, as your Mayor has said, an offense not only against history but an offense against humanity, separating families, dividing husbands and wives and brothers and sisters, and dividing a people who wish to be joined together.

What is true of this city is true of Germany—real, lasting peace in Europe can never be assured as long as one German out of four is denied the elementary right of free men, and that is to make a free choice. In 18 years of peace and good faith, this generation of Germans has earned the right to be free, including the right to unite their families and their nation in lasting peace, with good will to all people. You live in a defended island of freedom, but your life is part of the main.

So let me ask you, as I close, to lift your eyes beyond the dangers of today to the hopes of tomorrow, beyond the freedom merely of this city of Berlin, or your country of Germany, to the advance of freedom everywhere, beyond the wall to the day of peace with justice, beyond yourselves and ourselves to all mankind. Freedom is indivisible, and when one man is enslaved all are not free. When all are free, then we can look forward to that day when this city will be joined as one and this country and this great continent of Europe in a peaceful and hopeful glow. When that day finally comes, as it will, the people of West Berlin can take sober satisfaction in the fact that they were in the frontlines for almost two decades.

All free men, wherever they may live, are citizens of Berlin, and, therefore, as a free man, I take pride in the words *"Ich bin ein Berliner."*

ADDITIONAL READING

A general book on the temper of Europe—and American opinion about Europe's capabilities—is *Theodore H. White, *Fire in the Ashes: Europe in Mid-Century* (New York, 1953), a volume which because of its keen insights and high literary quality is still good reading. George F. Kennan, *Realities of American Foreign Policy* (Princeton, 1954) sought to set out the course of "realism" as he saw it at that time. A group of essays which ably catches the basis of American optimism about Europe and the world in the early 1950's is *David M. Potter, *People of Plenty* (Chicago, 1954); after all, in the postwar era the American people were living better than ever before in their history. *Henry L. Roberts, *Russia and America: Dangers and Prospects* (New York, 1956) sums up the view of expert opinion within the Council on Foreign Relations—Roberts wrote from the vantage point of seminar discussions at the Council. Dexter Perkins, *America's Quest for Peace* (Bloomington, Ind., 1962) offers the views of a well-known and much admired specialist on American foreign relations.

Books by and concerning the leading figures in the American government in the 1950's and 1960's are Dwight D. Eisenhower, *Mandate for Change* (New York, 1963) and its sequel, *Waging Peace* (New York, 1964). Robert J. Donovan, *Eisenhower: The Inside Story* (New York, 1956) obtained access to minutes of cabinet meetings and other high-level papers of the Eisenhower administration. *Sherman Adams's *Firsthand Report* (New York, 1961) offers the views of the era's "assistant president," which may not be altogether reliable on issues of foreign policy, since Adams handled mostly domestic matters. Secretary Dulles, of course, has had much attention from biographers, as he was a stirring subject. Andrew H. Berding, *Dulles on Diplomacy* (Princeton, 1965) offers the recollections of one of his principal assistants and commentary by Dulles on all sorts of foreign affairs. Louis L. Gerson, *John Foster Dulles* (New York, 1967), volume 17 in the American Secretaries series, is the best book published to date about the secretary and contains a good deal of new information from interviews and manuscript collections. G. Bernard Noble, *Christian A. Herter* (in press), volume 18 in the same series, presents the Herter regime at the department, 1959–1961, again with much new material and firsthand interpretation.

For the Kennedy era an easy resort is the massive memoir by *Arthur M. Schlesinger, Jr., *A Thousand Days* (New York, 1965), written by an historian who was a White House assistant and took part in many of the events he describes. *Theodore C. Sorensen, *Kennedy* (New York, 1965), by the president's principal assistant, lacks the literary quality of Schlesinger's volume but may be even more reliable.

The chairman of the Senate committee on foreign relations during much of this time, J. William Fulbright, has published *Old Myths and New Realities* (New York, 1964), which is a vaguely critical account, rather a querulous book, indicative of the impractical views often offered to presidents and other individuals wielding power in government, by people who have the power to criticize and reject. See also the same author's *The Arrogance of Power (New York, 1967).

The Johnson administration's critics and prognosticators have tended to focus on policy toward Vietnam, for which see the titles at the end of chapter thirty-one.

For its special subject see the book by *Herbert Feis, Foreign Aid and Foreign Policy (New York, 1964). As the era of the Marshall Plan has slipped back into history, public criticism of foreign aid has increased. Aid often seemed wasted, or at least the recipients were not grateful; and at home there was the need of aid to the slums of American cities and, abroad, the massive cost—in the latter 1960's—of the war in Vietnam.

For persons interested in American foreign policy the best way to keep up with the rush of events, without succumbing to the daily speculations of the television commentators, is to read the daily and weekly New York Times, especially the Sunday section entitled "The News of the Week in Review." If one takes only the Sunday Times, this sort of reading is not more expensive, and it is far more rewarding, than reading the magazines of news opinion, Time, Newsweek, and US News and World Report, all of which have their editorial points of view. Excellent journals are Foreign Affairs, the Economist (British), Reporter (unhappily defunct in 1968), Harper's, and Atlantic. Annually the Council on Foreign Relations publishes, a year or so behind events, The United States in World Affairs, and each annual volume is available in paperback a year after publication of the hardcover edition.

For the North Atlantic Treaty Organization an excellent beginning point is the article by Lawrence S. Kaplan, "NATO and Its Commentators: The First Five Years," International Organization, VIII (1954), 447–467, a bibliographical survey. Robert E. Osgood re-examines the treaty organization in NATO: The Entangling Alliance (Chicago, 1962), a book with an intriguing title. The British scholar Alastair Buchan offers his view in NATO in the 1960's (rev. ed., New York, 1963). NATO is constantly under survey, predictions of its end occurring annually, and a typical survey is *Ronald Steel, The End of Alliance: America and the Future of Europe (New York, 1964).

Khrushchev's speech to the Twentieth Party Congress appears in *The Anti-Stalin Campaign and International Communism (New York, 1956), a translation published by the Russian Institute of Columbia University, which includes the responses of communist leaders and organs in other countries. For its subject see Paul E. Zinner, ed., National Communism and Popular Revolt in Eastern Europe: A Selection of Documents on Events in Poland and Hungary, February–November 1956 (New York, 1957); and Report of the Special Committee on the Problem of Hungary (New York, 1957), the official, factual report on the Hungarian revolution submitted to the United Nations General Assembly.

Julius W. Pratt, "De Gaulle and the United States: How the Rift Began," The History Teacher, I (1968), 5–15, reviews the disagreement between the general and United States officials during the Second World War. Edward Weintal and Charles Bartlett, *Facing the Brink* (New York, 1967) has a section on the virtual withdrawal of France from NATO.

As for the U-2 affair, the best present source—overwritten, and of course from open materials—is *David Wise and Thomas B. Ross, *The U-2 Affair* (New York, 1962). Arthur T. Hadley, "Complex Query: What Makes a Good Spy?", *The New York Times Magazine*, May 29, 1960, contains the description of a spy quoted in the present text. Ovid Demaris, "Going to See Gary," *Esquire*, May 1966, is a slightly flip account of an interview with the former U-2 pilot, who in 1966 was a test pilot at the Lockheed plant in Burbank, California. Powers by this time had divorced his wife and remarried, his second wife being a former Central Intelligence Agency psychometrist. In the interview he described how back in May 1960 during his excursion over the Soviet Union everything suddenly had turned orange in the cockpit, "all I could see was just the eyes on the faceplate about an inch or so in front of my face," and he was afraid he could not get out. The plane seemed to have lost its wings and was plunging down, but he managed to get out without using the ejection seat (which may have been wired for an explosion immediately, rather than after a delay), and his parachute opened. He landed in a field and was surrounded by a group of people.

On cloak-and-dagger operations, of which the U-2 was only one, there is an increasingly large literature. *Alan Moorehead, *The Traitors* (New York, 1952) describes the atomic spies of the early postwar period, especially the most damaging Russian agent of them all, the British physicist Klaus Fuchs. An excellent little book is Dan T. Moore and Martha Waller, *Cloak and Cipher* (Indianapolis, 1962). See also the authoritative commentary in *Allen Dulles, *The Craft of Intelligence* (New York, 1963) and Christopher Felix, *A Short Course in the Secret War* (New York, 1963). A popular account appears in *David Wise and Thomas B. Ross, *The Invisible Government* (New York, 1964); the same authors have written *The Espionage Establishment* (New York, 1967). An autobiographical sketch of unusual interest, by the renegade Britisher who so embarrassed both the British and American intelligence services, is *Kim Philby, *My Silent War* (New York, 1967). Philby composed these memoirs in the Soviet Union, where he now is residing, and it is a nice question as to whether he receives his royalties or whether they go to Soviet intelligence.

☆ *27* ☆

China

Nothing that this country did or could have done within the reasonable limits of its capabilities could have changed that result; nothing that was left undone by this country has contributed to it. It was the product of internal Chinese forces, forces which this country tried to influence but could not. A decision was arrived at within China, if only a decision by default.

—Dean Acheson, letter of transmittal of the China White Paper, 1949

Americans in the years since the end of the Second World War have heard more about Far Eastern affairs than ever before in their history. In magazines and newspapers, from public rostrums and private platforms, information and misinformation about the Far East has poured forth in flood proportions, and there is no indication that the flood is in any way receding. The years since 1945 have been an era of intense interest in the orient. John Hay could announce a policy of the open door at the beginning of the twentieth century and hear polite applause from certain interested segments of the American people, but even a minor pronouncement on Far Eastern policy from Dean Acheson or John Foster Dulles, not to mention Dean Rusk, at once touched off long, sharp, and acrid debate.

One easily understandable reason for public interest in the Far East has been the vast extent of American involvement in the area during and after the war of 1941–1945. After fighting and winning the war against Japan, the United States was forced to occupy the Japanese Islands, half of Korea, parts of the Chinese mainland, and island groups off the Asian coast: Ryukyus, Bonins, Volcanoes, Marshalls, Carolines, Marianas. Then came two events in the orient of large importance for American diplomacy, the communization of China and the Korean War. In the confused debate about these events, punctuated by President Truman's dismissal of the popular General MacArthur as American commander in the area, there ensued more controversy than Americans had heard since President Franklin D. Roosevelt led the country to adopt measures assisting the European Allies against Germany in the crucial years 1939–1941. And the problems that followed the Korean cease-fire, such matters as Japan's resumption of a place in world affairs, disposal of the Matsu, Quemoy, and Tachen island groups, the place of Formosa in world affairs, the crisis of Vietnam, likewise have engaged Americans of both political parties in argument and debate.

There also has been in recent years a new intellectual attraction of Americans toward the Far East, which has accompanied the diplomatic-military events and further increased American interest in the orient. During the Hay era at the turn of the century, people in the United States considered the East a strange place, quaint and backward. There was from earliest times little inclination to welcome orientals into the Western Hemisphere; it was all right to take Western civilization to them, but it was not right if Chinese, Japanese, Indians, or Southeast Asians wished to leave their own area of the world. In the years after 1945 American views changed drastically. There was a new conviction that the East was an undeniable fact of life, that it was a part of the world whether the West cared to admit it or not, and that in the interests of world peace it would be a good idea to be friendly to Eastern states and statesmen. Among many Americans there was belief that the nations of Europe had bungled Far Eastern problems and allowed a conflict to develop there in 1931–1933 that spread some years later to Europe and the entire world. Had the Europeans taken more pains with the orientals, so ran popular feeling in the United States, the train of calamities that came after the Manchurian incident might have been stopped at the outset. It was now necessary, many Americans thought, to have some kind of meeting intellectually of East and West; there had to be intellectual rapport between the two major divisions of the human race, or confusion of purposes might be followed by incidents that would lead to another world war. When, shortly after the end of the Second World War, the American philosopher F. S. C. Northrop published a book entitled *The Meeting of East and West*, carrying the good tidings that the cultures and civilizations of East and West could meet in the undifferentiated esthetic continuum, Americans bought thousands of copies of the book. Perhaps they did not read beyond the first chapters, but they were expressing their hope that somehow, in some way, the hundreds of millions of human beings in the orient might come into some kind of spiritual communion, and perhaps thereby international co-operation, with the peoples of the Western world.

As for the idea long held by American businessmen that the East contained illimitable markets for the products of the nation's industry, that notion had died in the experience of the past forty or so years, and it had little to do with American concern over the Far East after 1945. After the Second World War, one heard little about four hundred million customers or the other old-time cries for commercial expansion. At the turn of the century the markets of Asia had seemed enormously attractive because *fin de siècle* businessmen were expecting a depression, some kind of permanent blight on the national economy, if they could not dispose of their goods to such buyers as the people of Asia. The American businessman eventually discovered to his sorrow that the Asians had no capacity to pay. And during the Second World War had come realization that the American domestic market was capable of far greater consumption than anyone had suspected, that if the American worker were paid a high wage he would turn his wage into purchases. One of the principal impulses to American relations with the Far East in the nineteenth century and in the heyday of imperialism at the end of the century, the attraction of trade, was largely absent in the years after the Second World War.

1. *Nationalist China prior to 1945*

Probably the communization of China was the single event that, more than any other happening in the orient, has bothered Americans in the years since the end of the Second World War. Why did China go communist in the first four years of the postwar era? How could China, after a century of friendship for the United States, since the Cushing Treaty of 1844, turn on its good friend and benefactor at a moment when Americans faced in Soviet Russia the most implacable and dangerous foe they had ever had?

This, in truth, is not an easy question to answer. The victory of the Chinese communists was no simple proposition, and to understand what happened to China in the years after the war one must look back to the events of Chinese history in the 1920's and 1930's and early 1940's.

China, as mentioned in previous chapters, had undergone a time of troubles near the beginning of the twentieth century because of the breakdown of the Manchu dynasty's control over large areas of the Chinese subcontinent. The Manchus had been governing China ever since the mid-seventeenth century, and their power, as had held true of the dynasties before, was in a decline following an initial era of some vigor. In the mid-nineteenth century serious trouble had come with the Taiping rebellion and the Nien Fei uprisings, and by the turn of the century there was no question but that a new regime was due. The Western powers and Japan sought momentarily to partition the empire themselves, but because of the imminence of war in Europe—not, incidentally, because of the American open door policy—the powers abandoned this effort, and matters rocked along uncomfortably until, almost without effort, the Chinese themselves overthrew the Manchu dynasty in 1911.

The next dozen years was a swirling period when government after government assumed power in a nominal way in Peking, and when in the provinces there was competition for place and power by a large number of local warlords. This competition was not greatly different from what had been practiced during the last years of the Manchus, but it became more apparent once the traditional central authority disappeared. For a while one of the leading functionaries of the Manchu court, Yuan Shih-kai, ruled from Peking, and he would have liked to have changed his rule, which was described to the European nations as republican, into another empire with himself as the first monarch of the new dynasty. His efforts came to naught, and Yuan died in 1916, according to a Chinese phrase, "from eating bitterness." Confusion continued, the warlords ruled in their satrapies throughout China, and whatever warlord was the most powerful and closest geographically to Peking took over the Chinese government and acted as if he were the government. This confusion was all very frustrating to Chinese diplomatic representatives abroad, but they tried as best they could to maintain the fiction that their government was united and powerful, and frequently they managed to put a rather respectable face upon what was in truth a chaotic situation at home.

As events gradually revealed the course of the future, a revolutionary movement in the south of China proved the most important intellectual and military movement in China for the 1920's and 1930's and the first years of the 1940's, for it was from Canton that the Kuomintang or Nationalist Party took its origin and in time moved northward to assume the rule of China in the name of the Chinese people. The Kuomintang was the creation of Dr. Sun Yat-sen, who in 1924 elaborated his Three Principles of the People: People's Nationhood (nationalism); People's Power (democracy); People's Livelihood (variously translated as livelihood, socialism, or communism). Dr. Sun had long been a revolutionary, and it was his custom to foment revolution from the French concession of Shanghai, where he lived in a house on the Rue Molière—a convenient location, for when revolutions were unsuccessful, he scurried to the safety of French extraterritoriality and escaped the revenge of his enemies. Later he was to proclaim that foreign concessions were one of the chief causes of China's difficulties, but for a while he was glad to use their facilities. At any rate, Dr. Sun was not too successful as a revolutionist until some Russian communist agents came into China and, beginning in

1923, assisted him in organizing both his party and his army. The autocratic nature of the Kuomintang Party owes much to the inspiration of Dr. Sun's Russian communist advisers in the early 1920's, who taught the doctor—Sun was a medical doctor, not a doctor of philosophy—how to establish a party with unswerving obedience to its leader. The Nationalist army likewise was modeled most profitably on the advice of Sun's communist assistants, and some of his officers (including the young Chiang Kai-shek) even had been to Moscow and studied the organization of the red army so as to understand communist military theories at first hand. By the mid-1920's everything was ready in South China for the march north, and Dr. Sun set out with his party and his army to take over the Chinese government.

The takeover was successful, although two events of importance occurred during the move of the Nationalists northward which changed the character of the revolution. First Dr. Sun, who had suffered from cancer, died in Peking in 1925, the leadership of the Kuomintang Party passing to his chief general, Chiang Kai-shek. Second, General Chiang discovered that the communists in his entourage were not as amenable to his advice as he may originally have hoped. In 1927 Chiang put them down and thereby established his authority over the party as leader and interpreter of the revolution. The move of the Nationalists northward, having met with these events, concluded in triumph in 1927 when Chiang occupied Nanking and in 1928 when he took Peking. The seat of the National government was kept at Nanking rather than at the traditional location, Peking, because the latter city was too close to Manchuria and thus subject both to attack by the Manchurian warlord and also to domination by the Manchurian powers, Japan and Russia.

The years between 1927 and 1937, from the Kuomintang taking of Nanking to the Japanese attack on China, in which Japan occupied Nanking and began forcing the Nationalist regime into the Chinese hinterland, were the era when Chiang Kai-shek tried as best he could to secure his control over China, present a united front toward the foreign powers and, generally, convert the Chinese peasantry to the Three Principles of the People as laid down by his mentor Dr. Sun Yat-sen. There was hope among the Western nations that Chiang would be able to introduce into the Nanking regime not merely nationalism but some considerable elements of democracy, the second of Dr. Sun's principles. There was hope that the Chinese, if given Western support, would be able for the first time since the heyday of the Manchu dynasty in the eighteenth century to put their nation's house in order. For a time, it must be admitted, success seemed to be coming to the Nationalists. The control of the regime stretched out from Nanking, taxes began to flow toward the Nationalist

Dr. Sun Yat-sen (seated) and his chief general, Chiang Kai-shek.

treasury, and in 1928 the warlord of Manchuria, General Chang Hsueh-liang, announced his allegiance to the Kuomintang; everything looked as if, with luck, China would convert itself into a unified national state on the model of Western nations. There was talk early in this era of relinquishment of extraterritoriality by the Westerners and Japan. Then the Chinese went too far—first with the Russians in the Chinese Eastern Railway affair of 1929, next when, in a fit of idiocy, they began to tinker with Japanese prerogatives in the South Manchuria Railway, precipitating in 1931 the Manchurian incident by which Japan seized, within two years, all of Manchuria. Pressure thereafter mounted against the Nationalist regime, and Chiang's government tottered on several occasions. In 1937 the Japanese, observing the preoccupation of the Western nations with the series of untoward events in Africa and Europe, decided that the time had come, as Premier Konoye put it, to beat the Chinese to their knees. The Japanese attack on China's coastal cities in 1937 began a new and miserable era for the Nationalist regime.

It was the Sino-Japanese War of 1937 and thereafter which at last brought in the Americans and involved them in the politics of China. The war began with a series of horrible massacres of Chinese civilians and soldiers by the Japanese troops, at Nanking and other places, and the character of the war, thus established in ferocity, never changed during the years that followed. The Japanese were angered that the regime of Chiang Kai-shek retreated to Chungking and there received American support. Their anger and frustration resulted finally in an alliance with Germany and the attack on Pearl Harbor. But American aid to the Chinese only increased after this catastrophic event, and by the years 1943 and 1944 the American government was virtually propping up the Nationalist regime in Chungking—the regime might well have fallen otherwise—by shipping over the hump of the Himalayas supplies and instructors for the Chinese army, and by maintaining in Chinese territory Major General Claire L. Chennault's Fourteenth Air Force. General Joseph W. Stilwell established himself in Chungking not merely as American commander of the China-Burma-India theater, the CBI, but also as military adviser and chief of staff to Chiang Kai-shek. Stilwell thereupon sought to galvanize the Chinese armies to resistance against the Japanese.

Part of Stilwell's endeavors consisted of trying to obtain the military cooperation, perhaps with American supplies, of the Chinese communist armies; and this effort by the American high command during the Second World War raises the question of the strength of Chinese communism by this time. The communists in China by the war years were a strong group but not the dominant group, and as late as 1945 (when Stalin on August 14 made a treaty with the Nationalist regime, apparently in the belief that the Nationalists would remain the dominant group in China), it did not seem possible that mainland China within a short period could pass under communist control. Communism in China had been a faltering affair, and whatever strength the communists possessed by 1945 had come only after years of labor and some serious setbacks. Russian communists had attempted in the early 1920's to spread the revolution to China, but they had sought to do it by revolutionizing the views of city workers, an effort that failed miserably. According to the accepted party line, communism was to make its first conquests intellectually in the cities of China, the workingmen were then to be made communists, and their efforts, according to Russian theory imported into China, would promote and eventually realize the revolution. The city communists in the mid-1920's attached themselves to the Nationalist movement of Dr. Sun Yat-sen and his successor Chiang Kai-shek, and perhaps their leaders hoped that with time they could control that movement. But Chiang surprised them and put them out in 1927 at Hankow. Communism in China languished after its defeat by the Nationalists, and until a deviationist named Mao Tse-tung undertook to revolutionize the peasantry rather than the city workers, achieving the revolution by a means other than that prescribed by the doctrinaires of Moscow, there was no success at all. When attacked by the Nationalists, the country communists resisted heroically, and in 1934 they set out on the long roundabout trek from Kiangsi province to remote Shensi in China's northwest, where they sought to establish themselves for a revolution which they foresaw distant in the unknown future. The coming of the war between the Japanese and the Nationalists in 1937 was a heaven-sent boon to the Chinese communists, who because of united front tactics were enabled for a while to pose as patriots against the Japanese and in the meantime were relieved of Nationalist military pressure. Gradually they improved their position in their capital city of Yenan and established areas of control behind Japanese lines throughout China, but their power by the end of the Second World War was by no means strong.

During the war, naturally, they feared entering any coalition with Chiang Kai-shek, remembering the draconian measures he had taken against them nearly twenty years before in 1927 at Hankow and the many years required before communism had again gained any strength in China. When Stilwell tried to get the communists and Nationalists together, he doubtless misguessed the situation.

Stilwell's main effort in China, however, was not so much to bring the communists and Nationalists together as to reorganize and invigorate the troops of Chiang Kai-shek. Here, surely, was a heroic proposition. And as the one problem—mixing communists and Nationalists—proved intractable, so did the other, larger problem. The chief factor in Stilwell's failure in this latter regard was a personal incompatibility between the American commander and Chiang Kai-shek. Stilwell was also undercut from at least two other directions: General Chennault believed that airpower alone would save China and had many private channels through which he sent these views to Washington; and there were many wellwishers of China in the United States who thought that whatever General Chiang desired it should be given to him and not with advice as to how to use it. But the largest difficulty that developed was the dislike of Stilwell for Chiang and vice versa. The two men could not get along. Chiang did not like to be told the truth with bluntness, and "Vinegar Joe" Stilwell could tell the truth only in such a way. One of the semihumorous aspects of the war in the Far East—and it would have been a downright hilarious business if so much had not been at stake—was Stilwell's private-diary treatment of Chiang Kai-shek. The American commander referred to the generalissimo of China as "Peanut" and "a crazy little bastard." And at one point in their relations, when Stilwell had presented to Chiang what appeared to be virtually an ultimatum from President Roosevelt that he reform his armies, Vinegar Joe repaired to his quarters and wrote out a bit of doggerel, the "Peanut Poem," which must go down as a wartime classic:

> I've waited long for vengeance—
> At last I've had my chance.
> I've looked the Peanut in the eye
> And kicked him in the pants.
>
> The old harpoon was ready
> With aim and timing true,
> I sank it to the handle,
> And stung him through and through.
>
> The little bastard shivered,
> And lost the power of speech.
> His face turned green and quivered
> As he struggled not to screech.
>
> For all my weary battles,
> For all my hours of woe,
> At last I've had my innings
> And laid the Peanut low.
>
> I know I've still to suffer,
> And run a weary race,
> But oh! the blessed pleasure!
> I've wrecked the Peanut's face.

This masterpiece was very probably read by General Chiang, whose agents constantly were about Stilwell's quarters in Chungking and made every effort to read his correspondence and dispatches.

But very probably Stilwell did not care, for he had observed the miserable morale of Chinese troops in the field, the corruption that ran rampant through the entire Nationalist government and down through the Nationalist army command to the junior officers, and he saw that if the endless manpower of China were ever to be marshalled effectively in a military way there would have to be the most serious sort of reform of the Chinese armies and probably the Chinese government. General Chiang's face, if saved at the moment, would only be lost later.

Stilwell had the faithful backing of his military superiors in Washington, General Marshall and Secretary of War Stimson. Even so, the dissatisfaction of various of General Chiang Kai-shek's supporters once their monetary and other interests promised to be affected by Stilwell's proposed reforms turned into a veritable campaign against the doughty American commander, and this, linked to the insubordination of Chennault and the opinions of important Americans who made flying visits to China, resulted in President Roosevelt's ordering Stilwell relieved in 1944.

Stilwell's successor, Lieutenant General Albert C. Wedemeyer, did not take a strong stand against the military and other delinquencies of the Nationalist government. The efforts of the American government became more diplomatic than military thereafter.

Wedemeyer was assisted by Major General Patrick J. Hurley, who in November 1944 was appointed American ambassador to Chungking and sought to help Nationalist China through the war. Just what the effect of Hurley's mission was, beyond a general pouring of oil on troubled waters, is difficult to measure, though the general, whom no one could ever accuse of the slightest communistic leanings, tried as had Stilwell to bring the Nationalists and communists together in a coalition government. His work in this regard must have amused or amazed the Chinese, for Hurley (who had been born in Choctaw Indian country) liked to demonstrate a blood-curdling Comanche yell. He chose to loose this salutation to the Chinese communists at Yenan—Mao Tse-tung, Chu Teh, Chou En-lai, and others—when he first met them on an official ambassadorial visit at the airport of their city. He admittedly did not like the Chinese communist leaders. He referred to them as Mouse Dung and Joe N. Lie. He nonetheless did his best in China. His was not an easy mission, and he found himself crossed by his nominal subordinates in the foreign service accredited as observers at Yenan and elsewhere, such highly talented and trained foreign service officers as John Stewart Service and John Paton Davies, who naturally thought he did not know much about China. At

Mao Tse-tung confers with Patrick J. Hurley. (Between them is Army observer Col. I. V. Yeaton.)

any rate Hurley's disgust mounted to a point where, after recall to the United States in the autumn of 1945, he resigned in a huff in November of that year. He charged publicly that his work had been sabotaged, and he engaged thereafter in a crusade against disloyal Americans that eventually found much sympathy among his fellow countrymen.

Such was the condition of American diplomacy toward China in 1945 when—through few efforts either by the Nationalists or the communists, though admittedly more by the Nationalists—the Pacific War on August 14 came to a sudden end after the explosions at Hiroshima and Nagasaki and the declaration of war by Russia on Japan.

2. *The communization of China*

In the years that followed, down through 1949, the communists achieved control of China. This diplomatic defeat, if not the greatest suffered by the United States in the postwar era, was certainly one of the most dramatic and disheartening turns of events. For a century the United States had acted *in loco parentis* to the Chinese, and in four short years the work of a century disappeared with little left to show for it except a small enclave of Free China on Formosa and, on the continent, a heated outpouring of diatribe and accusation of American imperialism tinged with sarcastic description of the United States as a paper tiger. When the Chinese treated their good friends the Americans in this way, it was difficult to take, and when such treatment occurred at the moment when, throughout the world, the American government was being attacked by the Soviet communists, it was almost too much to bear.

What was the course of American diplomacy in the crucial years for China following V-J Day? By autumn of 1945, Ambassador Hurley was recalled, and he was replaced in 1946 by a long-time Presbyterian missionary in China, the distinguished president of Yenching University in Peking, Dr. John Leighton Stuart, who remained ambassador to China until his resignation in 1952. Ambassador Stuart presided at the American embassy in Nanking during the downfall of the Nationalist regime, and his brilliant and touching memoir, *Fifty Years in China*, is one of the best accounts available on why China went communist.

The ambassador watched a succession of American special missions to China and saw them fail, one after the other. The Chinese problem was too much for them. The essential difficulty, as he wrote in his memoirs, was "a gigantic struggle between two political ideologies with the overtones of democratic idealism perverted by bureaucratic incompetence on the one side, succumbing to a dynamic socialized reform vitiated by Communist dogma, intolerance and ruthlessness on the other. And the great mass of suffering inarticulate victims cared for neither but were powerless to do anything about it." "The party members on both sides were a mere fraction of the huge, disorganized, inarticulate, amorphous population." The Chinese people "were neither Kuomintang nor Communist but merely Chinese, desiring to be allowed to live their own lives with a minimum of government interference or oppression." Given this difficulty, given the struggle between the two political factions in China, the fight to the end for leadership of the Chinese nation, there was little that the United States was able to do unless by a considerable intervention in Chinese affairs, and this neither the American nor the Chinese people wanted.

At the end of the war, the Americans did do a large favor for the Nationalist Chinese by ferrying, both by boat and plane, thousands upon thousands of Nationalist troops into the Japanese-occupied areas so that they could take over those localities ahead of the Chinese communists. Likewise the Nationalists received huge amounts of American surplus military equipment. By such heroic efforts the Nationalist regime was saved at least temporarily, and this move offset the advantage accruing to the communists when, at the close of the war, they either captured from the Japanese or received from Russian troops in Manchuria stocks of Japanese arms and equipment.

The first and major diplomatic attempt by the United States to assist Nationalist China in the postwar years was the mission of General Marshall, who went out to the Far East as special ambassador in December 1945, following Ambassador Hurley's resignation, to attempt to bring together the communists and Nationalists in the tradition of Stilwell and Hurley. After a year Marshall gave up the job as lost and returned to the United States to become secretary of state, replacing James F. Byrnes in January 1947. The hope of the Marshall mission was, first, to obtain a truce in fighting between the communists and Nationalists and, second, to persuade the two sides to join in a coalition government. They were then to disband their armies except for a small number of troops of both sides which were to be brought into a single Chinese army and trained by American advisers. The Joint United States Military Advisory Group, JUSMAG, some 1,000 officers and men, was brought to Nanking to advise on organization of the coalition force of the coalition government, neither of which, unfortunately, ever came into being. A truce between the Nationalists and the communists did, however, continue spasmodically through part of the year 1946.

The hopes of the Marshall mission were bright at first; Ambassador Stuart later believed that the two sides came close to agreement. In retrospect, given what apparently was the detached view of Stalin at this time —the Russian dictator seems to have advised the Chinese communists to make peace with the Nationalists, believing that the Nationalists were the winning side in China—there may have been some possibility of bringing the two sides into a rough and tentative agreement. Still, most of the leaders of both sides, Nationalist and communist, were the same individuals who had taken part in the arguments of the 1920's and 1930's, and there was a personal feud between the two groups, quite apart from their intellectual and other differences. Animosities long ago had gotten out of control on both sides. Chiang, for instance, had said publicly that "the

Japanese are only lice on the body of China, but Communism is a disease of the heart." The communists in like vein criticized the Nationalists. Moreover, the communists quickly recognized the weakness of the Nationalists when the latter came back to the coastal regions after the war. Many of the Nationalist leaders in the coastal cities behaved in the most shameful fashion, and grafting in connection with the Chinese version of UNRRA, CINNRA, reached heights unknown before even in China. Thus the only hope for the Nationalist government, namely keeping the political support and sympathy of city businessmen and the students and intellectuals, was dashed by this conquistador spirit of the Nationalists' return. The communists knew this.

General Marshall later said, apropos his efforts to form a coalition government, that the communists favored the idea because they "felt the Kuomintang was just an icing on the top and all its foundations of public support had become almost nonexistent or at least hostile, so if they could ever get the thing in the political arena they would win . . . it would not have been hard but a rather easy thing for the Communists to dominate the government." The general also understood the reluctance of the Nationalists to let in the communists: "I read yesterday [these remarks were made privately in October 1949 at a special meeting of Far Eastern experts in the state department] of the death of Hannegan, the former Chairman of the Democratic National Committee. He came out to China and I asked him: 'Did you ever know anybody in political life that gave up something unless he just had to?' He said, no, offhand he couldn't think of anyone. Well, here was a whole party being asked to give up the position they were in and admit a two-party procedure of government. Now, when I say 'give-up' you see, it differs from the ordinary two-party situation in this country, because the man held sort of a double office. He might be a General in the army but he is also, well, he is also the National Committee which really determines laws, and he was enjoying the preferment of pay and everything of that sort."

After the smoke began to clear in China, following the Japanese surrender, the weakness of the Nationalist regime became apparent. When both sides violated the Marshall truce, and when the Nationalists in 1947 began a full-scale military campaign against the communists in Manchuria, the fate of the Chiang Kai-shek government was sealed.

Ambassador Stuart told General Marshall when the latter left early in January 1947 that there were three courses for American policy in China: (1) sufficient aid to the Nationalist government together with advice and controls so that it could defeat the communists; (2) a halfhearted course; and (3) complete withdrawal of the United States from efforts to bolster any regime in China. Stuart preferred the first course to the

other two, and the third course to the second. The United States followed
the second. Perhaps, however, it was the only possible course for the
American government, considering the postwar letdown among the
American people and the increasing difficulties with the Russians in the
years 1946 and 1947 culminating in the Truman Doctrine and the Marshall Plan of the latter year. The United States throughout the early postwar era was busy looking at Europe, and it is worth noting that the
Berlin blockade began in 1948 at the crucial time of the Chinese revolution and ended in 1949 when the communists had almost taken over
mainland China. Stepping in, full-scale, in China might have involved
committing several divisions of American troops, perhaps as many as
twenty or thirty, which was an impossible policy at the time, short of a
general mobilization, which neither Congress nor the American people
would ever have supported.

If one were to assess the relative contribution to the fall of Nationalist
China on the mainland, the chief portion would lie with the Chiang regime, the second with the communists, the third with the Russians who
supported the Chinese communists at least spiritually (there is little or no
proof of any Russian material support to the Chinese revolution), and the
least portion with the United States.

The Chiang regime was nearly hopeless. General Chiang himself contributed to the debacle because, despite his willingness to pursue any
course that was for the good of China, he had become accustomed
through years of power and command to construing the welfare of China
in terms of his own welfare. Not that the general was a grafter, for he was
not; but he was inclined to believe that only he could rule China properly. As for his advisers, they were often corrupt and incompetent or both.
The result was a bureaucratic mess, from the top down, that could
hardly have been worse.

Moreover, through the long years of war the regime's supporters gradually had disappeared. The war had destroyed Chinese industry or else
placed it under occupation in the coastal cities, and Chiang thus lost support of the small but important group of Chinese businessmen. Another
group of supporters, the students, dwindled in numbers because of the
wartime dislocation. The regime gradually came to depend upon the
landlord class. But here was a weak foundation, susceptible to destruction
by the propaganda of the Chinese communists. Land reform—an aspect
of the People's Livelihood set forth by Sun Yat-sen as the third of his
principles—was one of the most pressing demands of the peasant Chinese,
a demand to which Chiang could not afford to listen and which played
straight into the hands of the communists, who posed as agrarian reformers. While Chiang was reorganizing his regime in the cities after the

war, the communists revolutionized the countryside. The Nationalist government, as we have seen, was also extraordinarily inept in the manner of its return to the coastal cities of China. This was no way to win friends and influence people. Thus Chiang tidied up the job of self-destruction.

The United States sought to shore up the Nationalist regime, but with no good results; in fact many American measures became propaganda for the communists. The Marshall mission, and even more the useless military mission in Nanking, JUSMAG, gave the communists their rallying cry that the Americans were pitting Chinese against Chinese, supporting the Nationalists in their war against the communists. General Wedemeyer suddenly reappeared in China in 1947 with a staff of investigators and without much finesse drew together a brutally frank report which criticized the Chinese government and further alienated support, both American and Chinese, from the Chiang Kai-shek regime. In the same year, 1947, such private Americans as William C. Bullitt and Congressman Walter H. Judd came out on junketing tours of China and after a quick reconnaissance made speeches or allowed statements to be published in China and in their homeland which told Americans what was wrong with the Chinese and vice versa, again to the embarrassment of people in the field such as Ambassador Stuart, who were trying as best they could to help the Chinese people. Meanwhile the Nationalist campaign in Manchuria drew off the best of Chiang's troops, and thereafter it was a matter of time until his defeat.

Government affairs by early 1949 were in utter confusion. Chiang Kai-shek had quit the Nanking regime and was in nominal retirement at his native village in Chekiang, although he was apparently giving orders to his troops by long-distance telephone. The highest officers of the government, including the acting president, Li Tsung-jen, were in Nanking; the administrative and other officials were in Canton. Everyone was looking obliquely at Formosa, considering the possibility of retreat to that haven of safety. The Nanking troops were unpaid (or paid in so-called gold yuan, Nationalist paper, which was equivalent to being unpaid). Their pay was set at four Chinese dollars silver a month, worth two American dollars, and this pay in silver would have made them willing to fight. Ambassador Stuart, seeking to devise ways to use unspent ECA funds to pay the troops, learned that for several months the top ranking Nationalist generals had been holding 30,000,000 silver dollars. They continued to hold them. Nanking fell, and the government moved to Canton, which fell, and Chungking, which fell, and then to Formosa. On December 9, 1949, the Kuomintang cabinet began to function in Taipei, the capital of Formosa (which the Nationalists had renamed Taiwan).

Until the last, incompetence was the order of the day. The Nationalists sought to stop the wild inflation of their final months by instituting on August 19, 1948, a new currency, the gold yuan already mentioned, equal to four United States dollars, which was handled not by their own treasury officials but by a private and respected group of Shanghai citizens who were to publish statements each month of the issues and backing of the currency. Despite brutal measures taken by Chiang Kai-shek's eldest son, Chiang Ching-kuo, against speculators in Shanghai, by the end of September 1948 the gold yuan had lost 98 per cent of its value. The generally increasing scarcity of goods could not help but prove inflationary, and the fall of Tsinan in Shantung province at this time—the communists were advancing on Nanking—helped the yuan along toward worthlessness. Ambassador Stuart discovered after this gold yuan fiasco that the Nationalists had nearly $300,000,000 in bullion. He estimated that $10,-000,000 would have bought up all the gold yuan in circulation, then worth $75,000,000,000 at face value.

All the money that the United States had put into China between 1937, the beginning of the Sino-Japanese War, and the departure of the Nationalists from the mainland in 1949 had gone down the drain, so far as concerned shoring up the Nationalist regime. The $275,000,000 in Marshall Plan funds appropriated in the spring of 1948 had proved of doubtful value, for such aid was too little and too late; economic projects could not save the Nationalist government in 1948. The $125,000,000 simultaneously voted by Congress for military aid had no effect affirmatively on the situation. Because of the slowness in filling Chinese orders for weapons, the United States was more criticized for its assistance than praised. And what weapons arrived in China were mostly wasted by troops unable to use them or else fell into the hands of the communists through desertions by individual soldiers or sellouts by their generals. Communist forces taking over Tientsin in January 1949 were completely supplied with American equipment. The communists entered Peking during the same month with a long retinue of American tanks.

Grants and credits in the twelve-year period 1937–1949 had come to the large total of $3,523,000,000. About 40 percent had been authorized before V-J Day and the remainder thereafter. This did not include so-called sales, virtually gifts, to the Chinese government of American military- and civilian-type surplus property made since V-J Day, material with a procurement cost of over $1,078,000,000. Nor did such totals include large quantities of ammunition left by American forces in China and transferred by the United States to the Chinese government at the end of the war, or the cost of special missions to China, or relief contributions through such agencies as the World Health Organization.

It is a strange commentary on United States policy toward China that in the postwar years 1945–1949 the American government contributed about $2,000,000,000 in grants and credits to the Chinese, while at the same time the Russians before their retirement from Manchuria took $2,000,000,000 worth of machine tools and other booty, stripping many factories bare, hauling off to Siberia everything that was portable; it is also strange that the net result of this subtraction and addition by the two powers was the almost universal impression among the Chinese people that the Russians were their benefactors and the Americans their oppressors.

Perhaps the dislike arose from the United States having too suddenly exerted its power in the Far East, from the old criticism which had focused on the British and the French as imperialists and colonial exploiters becoming unfairly but all too easily attached to the United States. General Marshall, in describing our difficulties in the Far East after the war, not particularly in China, remarked that on one occasion "One of our Generals said 'good morning' to somebody and that was reflected in all the papers as a hideous example of our duplicity."

On October 1, 1949, the Central People's Government of the People's Republic of China was formally inaugurated at Peking and began to seek recognition from foreign governments. The Soviet Union recognized it the next day, October 2. The Nationalist government severed relations with the USSR on October 3, and the following day the United States announced that it would continue to recognize the Chiang Kai-shek government. The Chinese communist regime quickly stabilized the currency and set about stopping corruption among the officialdom. The revolution was over—or perhaps it had just begun.

3. *Free China and Communist China*

At the outset of the era beginning in 1949 after the communization of the mainland, there came the Korean War, and this in the United States gave inspiration to a debate of impressive proportions, which will be treated in the next chapter, about American Far Eastern policy and general military strategy.

The war and the debate led to some changes of American policy toward Taiwan—toward Free China—which are worth setting down at this point. When the Korean War broke out, President Truman ordered the Seventh Fleet to protect Chiang Kai-shek against any aggression from the mainland, and this order was coupled with a directive forbidding Chiang's armies from crossing the Formosa strait to mainland China. But during the presidential election of 1952, there was much criticism of the order restraining Chiang: the president of Nationalist China had been leashed, so the cry went, and if he were unleashed he might reconquer China. Leading members of the Republican Party in the United States were determined to free Chiang for the mainland invasion, and so President Dwight D. Eisenhower gave Chiang the go-ahead in his first state-of-the-union address on February 2, 1953. The new policy lasted for about a year and a half, during which Chiang did not move an inch from the position he had been in while on leash. Finally, in a treaty between the United States and Free China concluded on December 2, 1954, both countries guaranteed each other's security, pledged alliance, and promised that either country before taking action toward communist China would concert its measures with those of the other country. This latter provision effectively re-leashed President Chiang, for he thereafter could not move without permission from the United States.

In the autumn of 1954, and again in 1958, trouble occurred in connection with Nationalist-occupied islands—the Tachen, Quemoy, and Matsu island groups—off the coast between Taiwan and the mainland. The two Quemoy islands lie about five miles off the Chinese mainland, about 105 miles west of Taiwan. On September 3, 1954, the communist Chinese —who from their moment of triumph in 1949 onward had been proclaiming their intention of liberating Taiwan from the Nationalists, and made an explicit announcement to that effect in the summer of 1954—began shelling with coastal batteries some of the Tachen Islands. The Nationalists replied with their own artillery and with announcements of a fight to the finish. The New York *Times* published grim pictures of Nationalist soldiers huddled in scooped-out holes and caves with their rifles at the ready. With the fall of the island of Yikiangshan in January 1955, the situation looked dangerous, and President Eisenhower obtained from Congress an extraordinary resolution giving him authority "to employ the armed forces of the United States as he deems necessary for the specific purpose of securing and protecting Formosa [Taiwan] and the Pescadores [these latter islands were occupied by the Nationalists] against armed attack, this authority to include the security and protection of such related positions and territories of that area now in friendly hands and the taking of such other measures as he judges to be required or appropriate in assuring the defense of Formosa and the Pescadores." The fall of Yikiangshan made evacuation of the Tachen group a military necessity, but the two other island groups involved in the controversy, Matsu and Quemoy, which commanded the approaches to important harbors in the Fukien province of mainland China and were possible staging points for a Nationalist invasion of communist China, were retained by the Nationalists. Whether the United States would support Chiang Kai-shek in defending

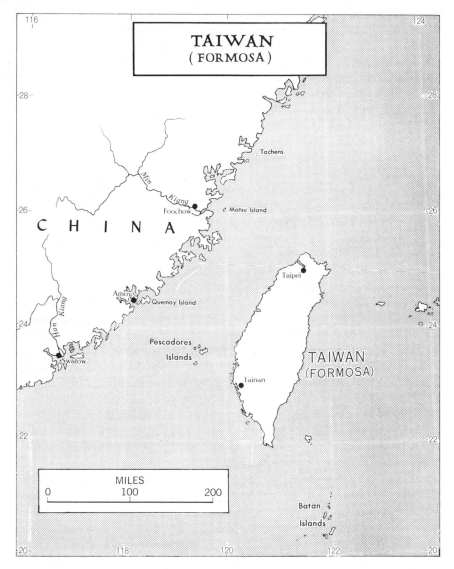

these islands was never made clear at the time or thereafter by the American government, on the theory that it was good policy to keep the communist regime in China guessing.

This island fracas might have been a small affair except for the possibility of irresponsible action by the Nationalists, who were all the while looking in the direction of assistance from the United States Seventh Fleet. Further, because the affair occurred immediately after the tragic

French disaster at Dienbienphu in Indochina, there was much sentiment for stern action against the communists, perhaps using American planes to bomb Fukien on the mainland and any possible marshalling places for ships for the supposed Taiwan invasion. Happily the affair quieted down.

In 1958, when the communists again bombarded the Quemoys, they seemed to be trying primarily to embarrass the United States. At one point they were firing only on even-numbered dates; supplies could thus reach the garrison on alternate days. When Secretary of State Dulles visited Formosa in October 1958, the shelling resumed during his stay, stopped after he left. No military decision was reached, and the ticklish offshore-islands question lingered on in uncertainty.

What, however, had been happening in the meantime in communist China, the home of all but a small fraction of the Chinese people, now governed by the regime of Mao Tse-tung in Peking? China, in the words of Mao (who, actually, used the expression for all of Asia), "stood up" beginning in 1949. The power of communist China, as exhibited first in the intervention in the Korean War in 1950–1953, more lately in the development of atomic weapons and their carriers, and in support of the North Vietnamese, became one of the large question marks of the world.

The face of China could not be changed overnight, and undoubtedly many aspects of the old, corrupt, inept China remained in the new, yet there was from the first a sharp break with the old China in the administrative practices of the new. In ways totally unknown to former Chinese governments the new communist state was efficient bureaucratically, and the efficiency was applied in a terroristic regime over the Chinese people which likewise was something new among Chinese governments. Not that there had been no massacres and terrible vengeances of governments and leaders on the hapless Chinese people in the past, but these had been inefficient uses of terror, mostly illogical and of short duration. The new use of terror was unprecedented. Executions of opponents of the regime may well have numbered into the millions. Against the background of these novel uses of bureaucracy and terror, the Chinese communists put forth a claim to great-power status among the powers of the world.

What was the precise strength and weakness of this new regime? It was easy to speak in general, rather than particular, about China. Just precisely what was going on in the new Red China was not easy to discover, though enough became known through escapees and through unconscious disclosures in communist publications to enable makers of policy in the West gradually to perceive certain stresses and strains of the regime. During an initial period of honeymoon, everything had seemed to be going well, and many Chinese everywhere, not merely in mainland China, were proud that their country at last was unified under what gave every evidence of being a strong government. The intervention in Korea gave more support to the belief that China had stood up. But in the years since the Korean truce there have been signs that all is not so well in China, though this is not to say that revolution against the regime is around the corner or will occur in the foreseeable future. Some such signs have been perceived in the incessant propaganda campaigns among the Chinese people by the government, a technique necessary for communicating with an illiterate peasantry. The Chinese have been sloganed to death, so it might seem, with such campaigns as the three-anti movement—anti-corruption, anti-waste, anti-bureaucratism. There was also the five-anti movement (anti-bribery, anti-tax-evasion, anti-fraud, anti-stealing state property, and anti-theft of state economic secrets). A momentary relief was the Rectification Campaign announced by Mao Tse-tung in February 1957 in terms of a Chinese classic, "Let the hundred flowers bloom." The government invited criticism and obtained a large amount of it, whereupon it clamped the lid down and began a new campaign known as "weeding the garden."

The communist Chinese regime in the 1960's seemed to be in the throes of a factional fight over the succession to Chairman Mao. President Liu Shao-chi was in an altogether unenviable position, for Mao's designated—could one be sure?—successor Lin Piao was publicly vilifying the nation's chief executive. "China's Khrushchev," Liu was called, together with "traitor, renegade and scab," and "lackey of imperialism, modern revisionism and the Kuomintang." The Central Committee of the Chinese Communist Party announced on November 1, 1968, that it had expelled President Liu from the party. In the political swirl Chairman Mao's wife, once an actress, suddenly became active. The position of Premier Chou En-lai was not always clear, although he appeared to be an effective mediator and always managed to keep close to the center of power. The militia-like red guards, young communists whose idol was Chairman Mao and who hence could be appealed to in terms of devotion to Mao, occasionally ran amok in Peking and other of the large cities. Sometimes the workers, to whose factories the red guards went to propagandize, beat them up. The governments of some cities declared allegiance to President Liu, and the Peking government was forced to send emissaries to treat with them. The army gave the appearance of being loyal to Lin Piao, but it was difficult to be certain. There thus was a welter of factionalism, and yet it was something more. Whether it would break communist China apart was difficult to say.

Whether the political confusion and the succession to Chairman Mao, whenever it should come, would have any meaning for international relations was also hard to say. The political uncertainty did not seem to affect in any way the striking successes being obtained in China's laboratories for design of nuclear weapons, both atomic and hydrogen. The Chinese were developing advanced missiles, and by the latter 1960's their weaponry had frightened the United States government into constructing a limited anti-ballistic-missile screen. This screen would be a very expensive piece of construction and might easily cost more than all the aid given Nationalist China from 1937 to 1949.

China by the latter 1960's was itself giving aid—to the North Vietnamese in their war against the United States.

Americans could comfort themselves to a minor extent by observing that the Chinese were becoming aware of their appalling population problem. The United Nations' *Demographic Yearbook* for 1967, published in 1968, estimated the Chinese population at 720,000,000, up 11,000,000 from 1966. If these figures were roughly accurate, the annual rate of growth was 1.5 per cent, not far above that of the United States (1.3) or the Soviet Union (1.2), and a long way from the top rate of growth in Central America (3.5) or the lowest, in Europe (.8). But it was far too high for China's slender economic resources. What this meant in terms of China's economy was clear, for despite the most strenuous program of industrialization, the population would be growing more rapidly than the capacity to care for it. The gloomy predictions of the early nineteenth-century philosopher of population, Thomas Malthus, may have come true in China.

By imitation of Russian methods, the Chinese sought to escape this vicious population spiral, but probably to no avail. There were two five-year plans, the first beginning in 1953 and the second in 1958. Results of these were impossible for outsiders to measure. but in no case could they have been startling, because China was terribly poor in the major requirements for industrialization, coal and steel and oil. A necessary concomitant to the five-year plans, again taking a page from the experience and doctrine of Stalin, was collectivization of agriculture—because of the need to place the Chinese peasantry under close supervision so that the state could extract the last ounce in agricultural production to obtain capital to build industry, since capital obviously was not going to come in large amounts from outside China. Spectacular results numerically were announced for Chinese collectivization, and by the end of the year 1955 and out of a peasant population that (accepting the official Chinese statistics) numbered about 480,000,000, supposedly 60 per cent were turned into agricultural producer co-operatives. In June 1956 the total, precise enough to be suspicious, was 91.7 per cent. Rumor and some verification coming from communist China was to the effect that this collectivization functioned according to the Russian experience: that is, was ineffective. Agriculture is an occupation that requires numerous careful and personal tasks, and close supervision is impractical if attempted contrary to the will of the agriculturist. The Chinese peasant discovered that the produce of collectivized farms went to the state at starvation prices. Collectivization appeared to have lowered agricultural output, rather than raised it, and probably took innumerable peasants to the edge of existence or beyond.

The meaning of all this domestic turmoil and supposed reform in communist China was fairly clear for American diplomacy, namely, that China was not the great power in terms of long-run economic strength and inherent capability that Americans had come to think it was. Mao was strong, but China was weak. The communist government of China was distinctly a second-class dragon as compared to the first-class dragon to the north. Communist claims to the contrary, there were still flies in China.

If the United States waited long enough and meanwhile built up the other Asian countries economically and militarily, might it eventually be able to reduce the intransigence of the new Peking government and bring the communists to their senses? Could Taiwan, the present domicile of Chiang Kai-shek, be made into another West Berlin, or West Germany? Could Taiwan become a showcase at the front door of communist China, proof that the democratic way, reliance on the dignity of man and his own resourcefulness if left to go his way without inhuman pressures, was the best course for Asia as well as for Western Europe?

In this respect one should state that Taiwan, since the establishment there of Chiang, had beyond question proved an island of some intellectual freedom for the million or more of mainland Chinese who went there with Chiang. While there was not complete freedom of speech in Taiwan, and while some individuals feared that if the government of that island passed under control of Chiang Ching-kuo a tight dictatorship would ensue, still there was a large freedom of behavior in Taiwan if contrasted to the mental confinement of mainland China. And economically Taiwan had progressed under Chiang's rule. The standard of living there was not high, but it was high for an Asian economy. Much money had been poured into Formosa by the United States, there had been a large-scale land reform, and the general economic picture was fairly bright.

So one could conclude that the scene of two Chinas, recognized and unrecognized, had some contrasts favorable to the West. True, matters were unsettled, and perhaps with eventual relinquishment of the Taiwan government by Chiang Kai-shek they would worsen.

The record of American relations with China, one might conclude, had been one of co-operation and friendship for a hundred years until in 1949 it fell to pieces, and at least for the next two decades it was not put together again. Perhaps it never would be, although any honest observer of the American scene would at once have remarked the hearty good will present among people of the United States toward the people of China, the fervent hope of Americans that somehow the Chinese people, with all their virtues and the tragedies of their history, might come at last into national and individual happiness. The regime in Peking, if it accepted in friendship the good will of Americans and the willingness to help that it surely implied, had opportunity to become the greatest government in all Chinese history, instead of pursuing the old Manchu oppressive tradition albeit with a twentieth-century bureaucracy, terror, and ideology.

A CONTEMPORARY DOCUMENT

[The department of state in August 1949 published a voluminous compilation of documents entitled *United States Relations with China: With Special Reference to the Period 1944–1949*, the so-called China White Paper. This book of 1054 pages consists of two approximately equal parts, a detailed chronology and documentary annex. That it was compiled *ex parte* the United States against Nationalist China admits of no doubt. Ambassador Stuart felt that it was a serious matter for the government to publish confidential conversations of its diplomats within a very few years of the event and contended that because of the possibility of such publication, diplomats in the future will become guarded in their reports to Washington. This seems an admissible criticism, although in recent years there has been hurried declassification of all manner of materials, and publication of the White Paper initiated what for better or worse is now an American pattern. Stuart believed that some of the documents compromised Chinese and other individuals who thought they were speaking to him in private, and this delicate problem may well have been neglected in publication of the White Paper. Whatever one thinks of the White Paper, it has been a boon to historians and will continue to be, until the annual documentary publication, *Foreign Relations of the United States*, comes to the year 1949, which may be the year 1975 or later, given its present (1969) 24-year lag, and the fact that annually it is dropping behind a year. When the department of state published the White Paper, Secretary Acheson introduced the volume with a letter of transmittal to President Truman in which he set out authoritatively and eloquently the administration's policy toward China. Extracts from that letter follow. Source: *op. cit.*, pp. iii, x, xiv, xvi.]

Department of State
Washington, July 30, 1949

The President: In accordance with your wish, I have had compiled a record of our relations with China, special emphasis being placed on the last five years. This record is being published and will therefore be available to the Congress and to the people of the United States.

. . . This is a frank record of an extremely complicated and most unhappy period in the life of a great country to which the United States has long been attached by ties of closest friendship. No available item has been omitted because it contains statements critical of our policy or might be the basis of future criticism. The inherent strength of our system is the responsiveness of the Government to an informed and critical public opinion. It is precisely this informed and critical public opinion which totalitarian governments, whether Rightist or Communist, cannot endure and do not tolerate. . . .

When peace came [in 1945] the United States was confronted with three possible alternatives in China: (1) it could have pulled out lock, stock and barrel; (2) it could have intervened militarily on a major scale to assist the Nationalists to destroy the Communists; (3) it could, while assisting the Nationalists to assert their authority over as much of China as possible, endeavor to avoid a civil war by working for a compromise between the two sides.

The first alternative would, and I believe American public opinion at the time so felt, have represented an abandonment of our international responsibilities and of our traditional policy of friendship for China before we had made a determined effort to be of assistance. The second alternative policy, while it may look attractive theoretically and in retrospect, was wholly impracticable. The Nationalists had been unable to destroy the Communists during the 10 years before the war. Now after the war the Nationalists were . . . weakened, demoralized, and unpopular. . . . We therefore came to the third alternative policy whereunder we faced the facts of the situation and attempted to assist in working out a *modus vivendi* which would avert civil war but nevertheless preserve and even increase the influence of the National Government.

The reasons for the failures of the Chinese National Government . . . do not stem from any inadequacy of American aid. Our military observers on the spot have reported that the Nationalist armies did not lose a single battle during the crucial year of 1948 through lack of arms or ammunition. The fact was that the decay which our observers had detected in Chungking early in the war had fatally sapped the powers of resistance of the Kuomintang. Its leaders had proved incapable of meeting the crisis confronting them, its troops had lost the will to fight, and its Government had lost popular support. The Communists, on the other hand, through a ruthless discipline and fanatical zeal, attempted to sell themselves as guardians and liberators of the people. The Nationalist armies did not have to be defeated; they disintegrated. History has proved again and again that a regime without faith in itself and an army without morale cannot survive the test of battle. . . .

It must be admitted frankly that the American policy of assisting the Chinese people in resisting domination by any foreign power or powers is now confronted with the gravest difficulties. The heart of China is in Communist hands. The Communist leaders have foresworn their Chinese heritage and have publicly announced their subservience to a foreign power, Russia, which during the last 50 years, under czars and Communists alike, has been most assiduous in its efforts to extend its control in the Far East. In the recent past, attempts at foreign domination have appeared quite clearly to the Chinese people as external aggression and as such have been bitterly and in the long run successfully resisted. Our aid and encouragement have helped them to resist. In this case, however, the foreign domination has been masked behind the facade of a vast crusading movement which apparently has seemed to many Chinese to be wholly indigenous and national. Under these circumstances, our aid has been unavailing.

The unfortunate but inescapable fact is that the ominous result of the civil war in China was beyond the control of the government of the United States. Nothing that this country did or could have done within the reasonable limits of its capabilities could have changed that result; nothing that was left undone by this country has contributed to it. It was the product of internal Chinese forces, forces which this country tried to influence but could not. A decision was arrived at within China, if only a decision by default. . . .

ADDITIONAL READING

An excellent introduction to the present chapter is *John K. Fairbank, *The United States and China* (rev. ed., Cambridge, Mass., 1962), a volume in the American Foreign Policy Library series, by the professor of Chinese history at Harvard. Books on Asia dealing in part with China, by acknowledged scholars, are by Paul H. Clyde and Burton F. Beers, Claude A. Buss, Fred Greene, George E. Taylor and Franz H. Michael, Kenneth S. Latourette, and

Harold M. Vinacke. For its important subject see Paul A. Varg, *Missionaries, Chinese, and Diplomats* (Princeton, 1958). Worth any student's attention for readability and shrewd generalization is *Guy Wint's now rather old *Spotlight on Asia* (London, 1956).

Two accounts of American policy, with conflicting points of view, are *Tang Tsou, *America's Failure in China: 1941–1950* (Chicago, 1963); and Anthony Kubek, *How the Far East was Lost: American Policy and the Creation of Communist China, 1941–1949* (Chicago, 1963). Tang Tsou believes American policy hardly a success, and indeed a failure, but does not endorse the conspiracy theory which appears in Kubek's book.

For the background of postwar American relations with China see titles at the end of chapters 10, 16, 22, 23. Wartime relations appear in Herbert Feis, *The China Tangle* (Princeton, 1953), a scholarly account based on all available printed and manuscript materials. A fine piece of journalism reflecting the authors' disgust with Kuomintang China is *Theodore H. White and Annalee Jacoby, *Thunder Out of China* (New York, 1946). See also Theodore H. White, ed., *The Stilwell Papers* (New York, 1948), published after the general's untimely death, with an introduction by Mrs. Stilwell, containing Vinegar Joe's plain thoughts on some highly political subjects. The diary is a mixture of letters, diary jottings, and commentary by the editor. The most detailed and authoritative work on American military policy—which had large political meaning—in the China-Burma-India theater during the Second World War is by Charles F. Romanus and Riley Sunderland, *Stilwell's Mission to China* (Washington, 1953); *Stilwell's Command Problems* (Washington, 1956); and *Time Runs Out in CBI* (Washington, 1960).

The years of China's fall to communism, 1945–1949, appear in colorful detail in Pierre Stephen Robert Payne, *The Marshall Story* (New York, 1951); Don Lohbeck, *Patrick J. Hurley* (Chicago, 1956); Albert C. Wedemeyer, *Wedemeyer Reports* (New York, 1958); and more authoritatively, with equal attention to color, in John Leighton Stuart's excellent *Fifty Years in China* (New York, 1954). See also the China White Paper, already mentioned, which is available in a paperback edition.

Anyone reading the White Paper will be interested in the stenographic report of the proceedings of a conference of Far Eastern experts held at the department of state on October 6, 7, and 8, 1949. This report contains statements by General Marshall and other participants and appears in the fifth volume of US Sen., 82d Cong., 1st Sess., *Institute of Pacific Relations: Hearings before the Subcommittee to Investigate the Administration of the Internal Security Act and Other Internal Security Laws of the Committee of the Judiciary* (15 vols., Washington, 1951–1953).

On communist China one should consult the colorful account by Derk Bodde, *Peking Diary: A Year of Revolution* (New York, 1950), which sets out the communist occupation of Peking. See also such travel books as those by Frank Moraes (editor of *The Times of India*), *Report on Mao's China* (New York, 1953); and Robert Guillain, *600 Million Chinese* (New York, 1957). Richard L. Walker, "Guided Tourism in China," *Problems of Com-*

munism, vol. 6 (Sept.–Oct. 1957), 31–36, gives the standard tourist's itinerary. At one point, Walker writes, the tourist visits Mao Tse-tung's birthplace and talks to an uncle of his; and it has been discovered that the "uncles" work in shifts.

Studies of communist China include W. W. Rostow, *The Prospects for Communist China* (New York, 1954); and Richard L. Walker, *China under Communism: The First Five Years* (New Haven, 1955), a lively and interesting book. For Sino-Russian relations see David Dallin, *Soviet Russia and the Far East* (New Haven, 1948); Robert C. North, *Moscow and Chinese Communists* (Stanford, 1953); and Howard Boorman *et al.*, *Moscow-Peking Axis: Strengths and Strains* (New York, 1957), a study by four experts for the Council on Foreign Relations which saw no prospect in the foreseeable future that the ties between Russia and communist China would weaken because of any possible American action, either by continuing or by changing our China policy. Of course, in the years after publication of Boorman's book, those ties not merely weakened of their own accord, but snapped.

An exciting intellectual excursion into the problems of Asia, still relevant, is Edwin O. Reischauer's *Wanted: An Asian Policy* (New York, 1955).

☆ **28** ☆

Japan, the Korean War, Southeast Asia

Now, the tradition of which he wrote—that of meeting force with maximum counter-force—is in itself not one that exists outside military textbooks. To be sure, it is a good rule for the employment of troops, but it has no bearing on the relations between governments or between peoples. The American people have accomplished much and attained greatness not by the use of force but by industry, ingenuity, and generosity. Of course the third paragraph of Mac-Arthur's letter [to Representative Joseph W. Martin] was the real "clincher." I do not know through what channels of information the general learned that the Communists had chosen to concentrate their efforts on Asia—and more specifically on his command. Perhaps he did not know just how much effort and how much sacrifice had been required to stem the Communist tide in Iran—in Greece—at Berlin. . . . But then MacArthur added a belittling comment about our diplomatic efforts and reached his climax with the pronouncement that "there is no substitute for victory." . . . there is a right kind and a wrong kind of victory, just as there are wars for the right thing and wars that are wrong from every standpoint. . . . The kind of victory MacArthur had in mind—victory by the bombing of Chinese cities, victory by expanding the conflict to all of China—would have been the wrong kind of victory.
—Harry S. Truman, *Memoirs: Years of Trial and Hope* (1956)

The relations of the United States toward China have beyond doubt been the most exigent American concern in the Far East in the years after 1945, and for this reason they have been dealt with separately in the preceding chapter. They were not, however, the only question in the orient to occupy the attention of the American public, for there were many questions of diplomacy in regard to the occupation of Japan, the Korean War, and the new nations of Southeast Asia, including the two succession states of British India—India and Pakistan.

An especially detailed analysis of American relations with the two most important succession states of French Indochina—North and South Vietnam—will appear in chapter thirty-one.

1. *The occupation and democratization of Japan*

Of the many unexpected events and strange occurrences in the Far East in the past two decades, none was more spectacular than the occupation of Japan by the United States armed forces and the democratization of that country under the rule of General Douglas MacArthur. At the end of the war, MacArthur set himself up in Tokyo and began to order the course of Japanese affairs. The American general became a latter-day shogun, something of an emperor, a dictator. Who in 1941 could have foretold such a turn of affairs?

MacArthur proved a happy choice for the job in Japan. His critics would always describe him as a little larger than life, as an ambitious man who had done everything in his career with a success more complete than he deserved, but no matter how one felt about the general there could be no doubt that in his first years in Tokyo he lent a prestige and authority to the occupation that no other American could have given it. When MacArthur's limousine drove up to his office, a respectful crowd of Americans and Japanese was always on hand. When the general left Tokyo on his homeward trip in 1951, recalled in the atmosphere of censure by President Truman, Japanese lined the route to the airport. MacArthur in Japan became a strange kind of democratic autocrat who ordered the new Japanese constitution to be composed by his underlings, apparently writing in a few phrases himself, and then presented the constitution to the Japanese people with such commanding presence that they ratified it and were thankful. When he finished his work at Tokyo, the Japanese were largely governing themselves, the economy of the nation was booming, the Japanese government was on the high road to independence and foreign recognition.

The occupation left many marks on Japanese life. American occupation authorities promoted a revived labor movement, land reform, freedom of the press, women's suffrage, educational reform, and efforts to give the average Japanese some protection against what had been an oppressive and brutal police. These measures acquainted all classes of Japanese society with ideas of freedom and liberty. When the Japanese received their national independence in the Japanese Peace Treaty Conference held at San Francisco on September 4–8, 1951, and when the occupation came to an end with ratification of the peace treaty early the next year, it proved impossible to turn the clock back, impossible to repudiate all the occupation reforms.

Admittedly, some American measures during the occupation were not altogether successful. The Americans sought to "humanize" the emperor, and in a New Year's rescript of January 1, 1946, Emperor Hirohito repudiated (as he described it) "the false conception that the Emperor is divine." How much change this announcement could make in Japanese attitudes was difficult to say. Likewise, American efforts failed to break up the concentration of business enterprise in Japan. Ever since the industrialization of Japan in the later nineteenth century, business enterprise had concentrated in the hands of a small group of wealthy families, the *zaibatsu* such as the Mitsui and Mitsubishi, and it was the hope of American occupation authorities that decartelization might create economic democracy. Despite an active program of decartelization, it proved an ex-

General Marshall and General MacArthur in Tokyo.

traordinarily difficult task to change the pattern of an economy. To play safe, to avoid risking a collapse of the Japanese economy through perhaps economically dangerous methods of cartel control, it was finally decided to keep the cartels, to follow a policy of "putting the cartel before the hearse."

What direction has Japan taken since independence in 1952? Will the reformation of the postwar years continue into the future? These are difficult questions to answer, for perhaps there has not been enough time to judge Japan's reorientation carefully and intelligently. Some matters are fairly clear. It appears certain that the spirit of militarism in Japan has almost disappeared. Too many Japanese were killed in the war: the battle losses among soldiers, sailors, and airmen, the casualties from the American air force's fire bombings in Tokyo and elsewhere, and the holocausts at Hiroshima and Nagasaki, were terribly costly. The tragedy of the Second World War was by 1945 so omnipresent in Japan that militarism could no longer have had its old attraction. The so-called MacArthur constitution contained a clause renouncing war that was reminiscent of the Kellogg-Briand Pact of 1928 and sounded for this reason altogether American in expression, but the Japanese apparently accepted this remarkable clause in good faith, glad to be excused from further fighting. According to the constitution the Japanese people "forever" renounced "war as a sovereign right of the nation and the threat or use of force as a means of settling international disputes." To carry out that hope, the constitution continued, "land, sea, and air forces, as well as other war potential, will never be maintained." When these provisions of American military government first appeared they evoked little or no criticism. Later, during and after the Korean War when it seemed necessary that Japan establish defense forces of strength and size, the general public antipathy in Japan toward military men and measures had hardly lessened.

One may fairly conclude that the new Japan has thus far proved worthy of American confidence. Under MacArthur the Japanese nation was not remade in six years. "The Japanese people since the war," MacArthur told Congress in 1951, "have undergone the greatest reformation recorded in modern history." There could be some doubt about this. Still, the new Japan is a nation far different from the one that upset the peace of Asia in the years before and immediately after Pearl Harbor.

2. The Korean War

American occupation of Korea, unlike that of Japan, encountered grave troubles of an unexpected sort which led not to peace but to further war.

The difficulties in Korea were caused in general by the post-1945 antagonism between the United States and the Soviet Union. In particular they stemmed from the division of Korea in 1945 into two zones of occupation, Soviet and American, separated by the thirty-eighth parallel.

Choice of the thirty-eighth parallel was a military decision, of the peculiarly military-diplomatic variety that occurred in several areas in Europe and Asia at the end of the war. The thirty-eighth parallel was a fair dividing line, for it left more territory and less population above the line, and the reverse below. A division had to take place because at the time of V-J Day the American commander in the area was unable to move his troops into Korea until September 8. Japan surrendered suddenly, and it took some time to bring up troops for occupation duty. Had there been no such arrangement as the thirty-eighth parallel, the Russians could have moved down from Manchuria and occupied the entire peninsula. Later critics of American policy might have remembered that. No one at the time, certainly not the military commanders on the spot, anticipated a division of the world between communists and noncommunists, and the consequently unfortunate results for Korea.

After this division of Korea in 1945, the events that led to the Korean War are not difficult to trace. In September 1947, when East-West tensions were in evidence, the United States informed the USSR that it was referring the question of Korean reunion and independence to the United Nations. In January of the next year, the Russians announced that the UN commission scheduled to visit Korea would not be permitted to enter North Korea. Elections were held in South Korea in May 1948. The government of the American-sponsored leader in South Korea, Syngman Rhee, in December 1948 signed an agreement with the United States for economic and military assistance. A People's Republic meanwhile had been set up in North Korea in September.

At this juncture came some unfortunate pronouncements by American government and military leaders. In a speech in January 1950, Secretary of State Dean Acheson declared that South Korea was outside the American defense perimeter and its defense was a matter for the United Nations, and other statements by Acheson and by General MacArthur indicated that the American government did not consider South Korea, or for that matter Taiwan, among the territories in the Far East that it would defend against attack. South Korea, the strategists said, was not within the American defense perimeter. General MacArthur at this time stated that only a lunatic would fight on the mainland of Asia. These announcements of military lack of interest in Korea later became the subject of wide criticism, and during the campaign that preceded the presidential election of 1952 it was said that Secretary Acheson in January 1950 had virtually announced to the communists that Korea could be taken without American interference.

Actually, the communists could have read American intentions from the condition of the American army, for unless the army made a strenuous effort, it was too weak to engage in any war in Korea. It was unprepared for war. The secretary of defense in 1949–1950 was Louis Johnson, an able appointee but dedicated to the proposition that the defense budget of about $14,000,000,000 was large enough to defend American interests abroad. The atomic bomb, he believed, would make up for the weakness of the United States army's total ground forces of approximately ten under-strength and ill-equipped divisions. American military unpreparedness, rather than any such factor as public statements by the secretary of state or General MacArthur, probably accounts for the willingness of the USSR to permit the North Koreans to invade South Korea in 1950. The American people and their leaders allowed the military forces of the United States to disintegrate after the Second World War, and there was almost nothing to stop the North Koreans when the invasion started. Lack of military preparation was, incidentally, no party matter in the United States. It was a national policy. If the Democratic Party, which was then in power, failed to provide for the army, there was little pressure from the Republican opposition to increase appropriations. Indeed there was the reverse. So the cause of the Korean War has appeared in retrospect.

The United States was therefore at considerable disadvantage at the outset of the war. When the North Koreans attacked on June 25, 1950, and caught the defending forces of the South Koreans off guard, American forces based in Japan could give little support; there was only the weak occupation garrison, and it was well understood that the American strategic plan in the Far East contemplated defense of Japan and Okinawa and the Philippines but not Korea. Korea and also Taiwan were quickly brought within the American line of defense. President Truman on June 27 instructed the Seventh fleet to patrol Formosa strait and authorized use of the navy and air force in Korea; on June 29 he gave MacArthur permission to use army combat and service troops "to insure the retention of a port and air base in the general area of Pusan."

Several reasons were advanced, officially and unofficially, to justify the decision to send troops into Korea, although the purpose of preserving American prestige in Asia and throughout the world was paramount. In some authoritative quarters it was suggested that by allowing the North Koreans to attack, the Russians were feeling out a soft spot in American defenses. There was another theory, somewhat corollary, that the Russians were seeking to give the world a demonstration of Soviet strength and American weakness. A third hypothesis was that the USSR was testing our resolution. This hypothesis urged that the North Korean invasion was analogous to Hitler's reoccupation of the Rhineland in 1936, and that if the United States in 1950 did not stand up to Russia there would only occur—as after 1936—further aggressions and ultimately a major war. A fourth view, advanced by John Foster Dulles, then in charge of preparations for the Japanese peace treaty, was that the Korean aggression was an attempt by Russia to block American efforts to make Japan a full member of the free world. A fifth view was that the attack would halt the American attempt to create in South Korea an Asian republic, a "hopeful, attractive Asiatic experiment in democracy."

Militarily the commitment of American troops to the Korean peninsula was undesirable. Korea was a minor threat to Japan, and in the high noon of the age of imperialism when Japan coveted Korea, it had often been said that the Korean peninsula was a dagger pointed at the heart of Japan. Military strategy had changed considerably by the mid-twentieth century; bases in Korea were not much more advantageous for invasion of Japan than bases in Manchuria or China or the Kamchatka peninsula. Korea had outlived whatever military importance it may have had. For American strategists in 1950 it was a military liability, a useless appendage of Asia, vulnerable to attack from all sides. American military strength in 1950 was so small—at the height of the Korean War after a hasty partial mobilization it was only twenty-four divisions—that to commit six of them to a minor Asian peninsula was strategically most undesirable. In the tense and taut months of the Korean War, the ideal place for those troops was in Europe, where in numbers and equipment the Soviet army held an immense advantage over NATO troops. In terms of broad military strategy there was no advantage in sending troops to Korea, but for several nonmilitary reasons this had to be done.

By great good fortune it was possible for the United States to obtain the sanction of the United Nations for its military action in Korea, and this eventually had some military—though far more diplomatic—advantage. The USSR had been boycotting meetings of the UN Security Council since January 1950 when its delegate, Jacob Malik, had walked out in protest against continued Western recognition of the diplomatic envoys of Nationalist China. Malik was unable to obtain instructions to re-enter the Security Council until August 1, 1950, by which time the United States had received UN support for the Korean War. On June 27 the Council, its Russian colleague absent, called upon UN members to "furnish such assistance to the Republic of Korea as may be necessary to repel the armed attack and to restore international peace and security in the area." It was the same day that Truman ordered air and naval forces into Korea, two days before he authorized ground troops. The UN voted a unified UN command in Korea under a commander to be designated by

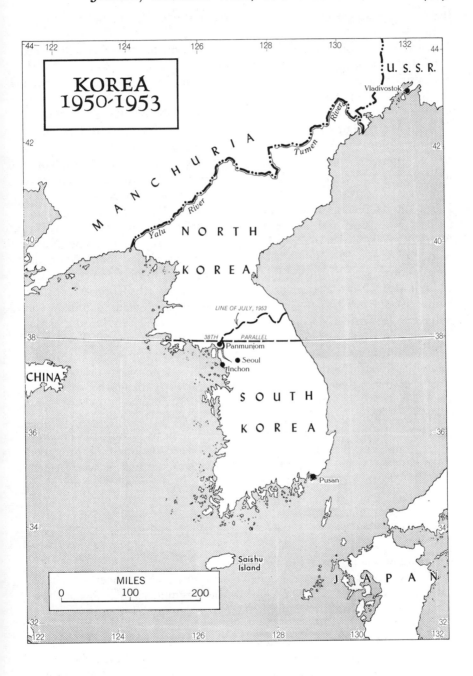

KOREA
1950-1953

the United States, and General MacArthur was so designated on July 8, 1950.

In view of its diplomatic and military consequences, perhaps the most debatable episode in the conduct of the war was the UN invasion of North Korea undertaken in October 1950. Invasion of a Russian satellite marked the high point of American post-1945 strategy and diplomacy. It never has been attempted since. And the invasion of North Korea, following General MacArthur's brilliantly conceived Inchon landings in September, brought Chinese intervention on a massive scale. Although he had taken few precautions, MacArthur was certain the invasion of North Korea would prove successful. Leaders in Washington, diplomatic and military, approved the thrust because they felt it would be a hopeless task to put Korea on its feet if either Chinese or North Korean communists remained in control of the dams and power stations along the Yalu River, North Korea's northern boundary with Manchuria. In invading North Korea, a communist country, MacArthur appears to have counted on the same boldness that had stood him in such good stead in Japan. He apparently hoped that a determined move to the North Korea-Manchuria border would not bring Chinese intervention. He failed to reckon the difference between the demoralized people of a defeated Japan and the high-spirited Chinese communists who had just won a long civil war.

The Chinese intervention brought a second American retreat down the peninsula toward Pusan (this time during the cold Korean winter). Then, after recouping their strength, the Americans began another push upward, a sort of slow-but-sure "meat grinder" advance known in army parlance as Operation Killer, followed by a tactic picturesquely named Operation Ripper. Encountering this new American power, the communists through the Russian delegate on the Security Council, Malik, raised the subject of a truce. After a frustrating two years of talk between American and North Korean representatives meeting most of the time in an improvised "truce tent" at Panmunjom, the truce went into effect on July 27, 1953.

Meanwhile had come a great debate in the United States over the conduct of American diplomacy in the Far East—one of the most vociferous arguments in many years.

The great debate mainly was over Korea, but it also concerned notable and specific events: the loss of China to the communists in 1949 and President Truman's abrupt dismissal of MacArthur in 1951. It was at its climax in the presidential election of 1952, an election held, unfortunately, while the Korean War still was in course.

The war bothered many American citizens. Korea seemed the wrong place for the United States to fight, after failing to fight communism in China. The Korean War, unlike other American wars, did not proceed toward any discernible conclusion; it seesawed indecisively up and down the Korean peninsula, moving strangely from one almost unpronounceable place name to another. The war seemed a thoroughly unsatisfactory affair.

The loss of China to the communists also had been a most difficult event for Americans to endure. China had been the focus of American interests in the orient since 1784. China had been the hope of American traders and businessmen. It had been the center of American missionary activity since the days when young students went out to the East to work for "the evangelization of the world in this generation." Partly as a result of China's expenditure of the Boxer indemnity for educational purposes, more Chinese students had come to America than had the nationals of any other Far Eastern country. The Kuomintang government had consisted in large part of American-educated Chinese. When in so severe a period of international tension as the years after 1945 China went over to the camp of America's enemy, it was a signal for more soul-searching by makers of United States policy and by the general public than had occurred in generations. Someone, so it seemed, had lost China.

In the presence of such dissatisfaction came the dismissal of General MacArthur. President Truman removed the general from command because he had flagrantly disobeyed a presidential order against pronouncements on foreign policy by government officials without prior clearance from the state department. MacArthur had disagreed with some of the strategic and diplomatic views of the Truman administration, and with little regard for the consequences and perhaps as a direct challenge to the president, the general had talked openly to reporters and sent communications to friends at home, one of them a letter to the Republican leader of the House of Representatives, Joseph W. Martin, which was an open invitation to President Truman to dismiss him or acquiesce in the general's judgment. With the unanimous support of the joint chiefs of staff in Washington, Truman dismissed MacArthur from all Far Eastern commands.

This was almost too much for the American people to take, at least at the moment. Many Americans were beginning by 1951 to air their perplexities. Was there not something wrong with the administration in Washington? There had been revelations of spy activities in the United States, a conspicuous instance having involved Alger Hiss, a former state department official and New Deal appointee. The department of state was vulnerable to partisan attack because Secretary of State Acheson had been friendly with Hiss. Democratic administrations had been in power in Washington since 1933, and it was not difficult to argue that any disasters of foreign policy since that time, including Korea, had been the result of their errors, unpremeditated or intentional, inspired by "leftist" views or perhaps allegiance to communism. As Senator Joseph R. McCarthy of

Wisconsin was reported to have said, "How can we account for our present situation, unless we believe that men high in this government are concerting to deliver us to disaster? This must be the product of a great conspiracy on a scale so immense as to dwarf any previous venture in the history of man."

The American people, irritated over Korea and China, used the occasion of MacArthur's relief to give the discharged general a welcome the like of which had not been seen since the Lindbergh enthusiasm of 1927 and Admiral Dewey's reception in 1899.

MacArthur came home in triumph. San Francisco, New York, and innumerable other localities went wild for the general. After MacArthur Day in New York City, the department of sanitation reported that the MacArthur litter weighed 16,600,000 pounds; the previous record had been 3,600,000. It was the general's first visit to his country since a short trip from the Philippines in 1937, and the homecoming may have been warmer for this reason, perhaps also because he and the nation were to each other such unknown quantities. But whatever the ingredients of his welcome, it could have been construed only as a demonstration against the Truman administration. The president did not greet the general on the steps of the White House, but MacArthur achieved the next best recognition in being invited to address a joint session of Congress, with his speech broadcast over the national radio and television networks.

The dismissal of MacArthur and the general's reception in the United States faded from public memory, and American diplomacy and politics continued in their accustomed courses. President Truman, who sat out the storm, guessed correctly that MacArthur's star would come down almost as quickly as it went up. The MacArthur hysteria provided an occasion, however, for a careful public statement by the Truman administration of the basic principles and purposes of American diplomacy during the Korean War, and this statement deserves some attention. When the general's greeting had run its course, two senatorial committees in May and June of 1951 held "an inquiry into the military situation in the Far East and the facts surrounding the relief of General of the Army Douglas MacArthur from his assignments in that area."

The MacArthur hearing, for those American citizens who followed its stenographic reports closely, was extremely enlightening. After the Chinese had intervened in North Korea in late November 1950, MacArthur had spoken out in favor of attacks on the Chinese mainland. The general had been giving the impression that the slow pace of the war, the moving up and down the Korean peninsula, had derived entirely from strategic blunders by politicians and political generals in Washington. Such allegations were major political attacks in the pre-presidential campaign atmos-

MacArthur addressing a joint session of Congress, wherein he made his famous statement, "Old soldiers never die, they just fade away."

phere of the capital in 1951–1952, and the Truman administration's answer to its deposed proconsul may have taken some inspiration in the political need for a defense. Certainly much of the great debate of 1951–1952, defense and offense, carried implications for the presidential campaign. Even so, the administration's response had a ring of sincerity. General Omar Bradley, chairman of the joint chiefs of staff, put the administration's reasoning succinctly. "Taking on Red China," Bradley said at the hearings, would have led only "to a larger deadlock at greater expense." "So long," Bradley said, "as we regarded the Soviet Union as the main antagonist and Western Europe as the main prize," the strategy advanced by MacArthur "would involve us in the wrong war at the wrong place at the wrong time and with the wrong enemy."

Nothing could have been clearer than Bradley's statement of the American position. It was a position that derived not from blunders by politicians and political generals, but from careful consideration of all the factors in the United States's politico-military policy. MacArthur had failed to understand the many responsibilities of his government and had advocated a policy in the Far East that was exclusively military in nature. He had been so ill-advised as to push his views in the public press and in letters to congressmen, rather than keep his opinions in proper military channels. After the controversy over his dismissal had cooled, the Bradley-Truman view of strategy and diplomacy seemed sensible.

There remained the presidential campaign, toward which much of the great debate over foreign policy, as mentioned, had been directed. The Korean War became perhaps the prime issue of the campaign, although it was accompanied on the Republican Party's side by two others, corruption in the government and communism in the government. The GOP's formula for victory was K^1C^2. The Republican platform argued that Allied morale in Asia was crumbling because Russia's "Asia first" policy contrasted so markedly with the American policy of "Asia last." The Republican nominee for president, General Eisenhower, eventually was moved to declare that if elected he would "go to Korea" and straighten things out. For this reason among others, Eisenhower was elected. Soon after his inauguration, and perhaps because of his trip to Korea, the Korean War came to an end with the armistice of July 1953. The great debate ended with it.

The Truman administration's views on Korean strategy had prevailed. Eisenhower in his short period of office during the war did not change the Korean strategy of limited war—of war for a limited purpose, the containment of Soviet-inspired aggression in Korea—and achievement of this purpose, one can fairly say, marked the basic achievement of the Korean War. This was a large success of American policy, this turning into victory of what on all sides in June 1950 and again in November–December of that year had looked like imminent defeat.

Other events of diplomatic importance followed from the Korean conflict. The war encouraged the United States to a far larger rearmament than it had begun in 1948 and 1949. The United States roused its allies in Europe and made a heroic effort to put teeth into NATO, engineering the appointment of General Eisenhower as supreme commander of NATO forces.

Likewise there were some marked economic effects of the Korean War. It seems fairly certain that although the Korean War did not pull the United States out of an economic recession—the downward economic trend that had begun in 1949 had reversed itself well prior to the

North Korean invasion—it did give an impetus to the American economy that sent it spinning ahead to what over the next years proved ever higher levels of production, wages, and employment. Two months after the Korean War began, employment crossed the 62,000,000 mark, two million beyond the fondest dreams of New Dealers at V-J Day. And there was even a sort of mental fillip that came with the Korean War. Many of the post-1945 worries about an economic depression, memories of the Great Depression that had only been temporarily stilled by the prosperous years of the Second World War, were laid to rest during the Korean boom. With release from this fear, the economy moved ahead with un-heard-of confidence.

The facts set out above do not make a triumph of the tragedy of Korea. No one in the United States is soon going to forget the casualties during that conflict: 33,629 young men killed in action. And the cost of the war was many billions of dollars. Perhaps this price in men and treasure was not too great for the major benefit of Korea, the limit that the war placed, at least temporarily, upon Soviet aggression throughout the world.

In regard to American diplomacy toward Korea in the post-1945 years, one should not end the present account without mentioning the capture of the United States navy ship *Pueblo* in January 1968 by the naval forces of the North Korean government, and the problems and questions that the so-called "*Pueblo* case" raised for more than a year thereafter. The *Pueblo* case was a strange postscript to the Korean War, and if it did anything it raised once again the debates of 1950–1953—in particular, the issue of whether a limited war was a sufficient solution to aggression in the Far East. The lessons of the Korean War, nonetheless, were brought to bear upon the *Pueblo* case, for the government of the United States chose not to make a retaliatory attack on North Korean military installa-tions or cities, took the long, tedious route into negotiation, and actually issued an abject apology for violation of North Korean rights. Then upon release of the *Pueblo's* crew it made the remarkable assertion that the statement of apology had been offered under duress. After release of the *Pueblo's* crew, the case almost immediately focused upon the conduct of the captain, Lloyd Bucher, who had surrendered the ship and crew with-out a fight, and the conduct of all crew members who, while in jail in North Korea, violated the military service's injunction that after capture every member of the armed forces is restricted by the pledge, "I am bound to give only name, rank, service number and date of birth." There followed a long, inconclusive trial of the captain, and the American public was treated to an extraordinary recital of North Korean brutality and American suffering. The real issue, however, was not the fate of the crew

Commander Lloyd Bucher, Captain of the U.S.S. *Pueblo*, crossing the "Bridge of No Return," dividing North and South Korea, after being freed by the North Koreans.

but the course of American policy, the fact that the government of the United States, despite the passage of years, was not willing to give up the lesson of the war of 1950–1953, namely, that a limited war had to be kept limited. Even when the North Koreans on April 14, 1969, shot down an American reconnaissance plane in international waters off the North Korean coast, a lumbering, propeller-driven Super Constellation carrying 31 Americans, all of whom were killed, the government of the United States did no more than protest through diplomatic channels. As of the present writing, May 1969, the *Pueblo* remains in North Korean custody.

3. *Southeast Asia, India, and Pakistan*

For the years from the end of the Korean War until the heating up of the Vietnam War in the mid-1960's, the history of American diplomacy in the Far East was relatively uneventful. The ebb and flow of daily diplomatic communication with the capital cities and the statesmen of the Asian countries continued without let-up, but by the end of the war in Korea, Americans hoped (until the Vietnam War flared), the basic settlement of territories and peoples in the orient had been made. There remains for the present chapter some account of American diplomacy toward Far Eastern nations other than China, Japan, and Korea—namely, Southeast Asia, India and Pakistan.

In Southeast Asia the United States played a part during the post-World War II years in the attainment of Indonesian independence. The agreement between the Netherlands government and the Republic of Indonesia, by which both parties concluded a truce and the Netherlands agreed to Indonesian independence, was concluded by a UN team, including the American representative Frank P. Graham, abroad the USS *Renville* on January 17, 1948. After this agreement the Dutch in November 1949 transferred sovereignty over the Netherlands East Indies (except Dutch New Guinea) to the Republic of the United States of Indonesia.

It is another story, impossible to detail here, of how the Indonesians under the patriotic but utterly irresponsible leadership of President Sukarno came within a hair's breadth of economic collapse and a communist takeover. A slightly premature coup launched against the Indonesian army in 1965 forced the army's generals in self-defense to turn upon the communists—with the result that the Indonesian Communist Party, which had been a flourishing organization, was wiped out. Several hundred thousand people in Indonesia were murdered in a horrible orgy of patriotic revenge, many of the victims being Chinese suspected of communist leanings. A new president, General Suharto, replaced "the father of Indonesia," Sukarno, who was relegated to a quiet private life with his concubines and friends. Sukarno had known about and supported the communist uprising and was fortunate to have escaped death at the hands of his avenging generals.

In regard to the Philippine Islands, so long a charge upon American patience and funds, Congress fulfilled its promise under the Tydings-McDuffie Act of 1934 by granting the islands independence on July 4, 1946, despite the interruption and chaos of the Japanese occupation from 1941 to 1945. The results of independence were at first unfortunate. General

MacArthur had advanced the candidacy of Manuel Roxas as president of the Philippines; Roxas, who died in 1948, was succeeded by Elpidio Quirino. Under the administrations of these two statesmen, affairs in the islands reached a state of crisis. By 1950, when the American government found itself embroiled in Korea, government in the Philippines had so deteriorated that there was grave doubt whether the commonwealth could survive. An economic commission sent out to Manila in that year, headed by a former undersecretary of the treasury, Daniel Bell, found that much of the $1,500,000,000 given the Filipinos between the years 1945 and 1950 as economic aid and payments of various kinds had found its way into the hands of grafters, profiteers, and high officials of the government. Meanwhile the insurrectionary activity of the communist-led Hukbalahaps (Huks) was attracting many of the poverty-stricken country people, who had received no relief from their government and saw relief in communism. It was a serious situation, which fortunately was retrieved in the nick of time by election in 1953 of the reforming Philippine leader Ramón Magsaysay, under whose enlightened administration order was restored, especially in the ranks of the Philippine army and bureaucracy. His successors managed to keep Philippine politics in fairly decent order, at least by modest standards. American pride was restored in the Philippine Islands as a "showcase of democracy" in Asia. It had been a close call.

A word remains about American relations with India and Pakistan, those two new and important powers that replaced British India in 1947. Was the transfer of government from Britain to two independent nations of any consequence for the foreign relations of the United States? There were some consequences, though none was drastic. In the case of India the United States was soon to discover a leader of neutralist sentiment in the United Nations. The independent government of India, led at the outset by Jawaharlal Nehru as both prime minister and foreign minister, took the stubborn view that security came from peace rather than peace from security, that creation of military blocs against the Soviet Union and its satellites could result only in creation of counterblocs, that—in other words—the way to end the cold war was not through aligning nation against nation but through finding areas of agreement between the United States and its friends and the Soviet Union and its friends. The Indians thought Americans obsessed by communism. The government of India was friendly to communist China. Nehru took a cautious line toward Russia's suppression of the Hungarian uprising in 1956 at the very time when he was castigating Britain (the former colonial power) for military intervention in Egypt. The Indians flirted with the communists in other ways that bothered the Americans. The Americans felt that Indian neutralism was a result of India's sheer inexperience with Russian communism, that the Indians had been too busy with securing their national independence from the British before and after 1947 to understand how the Soviets during the same period had abandoned pledges and turned world peace upside down. American diplomats told the Indians these facts and views. They were answered by more neutralist arguments and with requests for large loans to import wheat. The combination was all that some Americans could stand, and a little more.

It seemed so impossible for Americans to do anything of lasting value for India and Indians, given the problems of the country. Escape from British rule only had brought those problems to the surface. Nehru had clung to power long after he had ceased to be an efficient leader. Indeed, his talents within India had been largely devoted to freeing the country from the British; after 1947 he hardly knew what to do. Although for seventeen years he was able to exert much influence abroad, not all of it was positive and helpful. Under his successors, Lal Bahadur Shastri and Mrs. Indira Gandhi (Nehru's daughter), India appeared incapable of national advance, capable only of remaining on dead center. American visitors to India returned with foreboding, feelings of oppression from the mass of people, from the stench, from the arid intellectual arguments, from the general futility of life. Nothing had changed since E. M. Forster had published *A Passage to India* in 1924, except that there now were 525,000,-000 Indians, far more than the country decently could support. In Calcutta, a sinkhole of humanity, more than 100,000 of the 7,500,000 inhabitants of India's largest and most culturally alert city lived on the sidewalks, sleeping there each night. Some Americans believed that the best way to defeat the Russians would be to give them India, an embrace with death. Others felt that sometime, perhaps in the twenty-first century, the masses of India would emerge from the middle ages. Indians themselves were appalled at the staleness of Congress Party politics—the party of independence no longer had an issue. Madame Pandit's leadership inspired little confidence. The language issue was flaring, and it was possible that rejection of the English language (in India, English was the only possible language of education, considering the impossible number of national languages) would force a breakup of the country into linguistic regions.

If these difficulties of Indian-American relations were not enough, there was American policy toward Pakistan and (as Indians believed) toward Kashmir. The Indians watched with intense misgivings the signing of a military agreement in 1954 between the United States and Pakistan, by which Karachi received economic credits and military supplies. Pakistan joined the Baghdad Pact and SEATO (for which see chapters twenty-nine, thirty-one). These moves had a double effect upon India:

they showed India's Muslim rival following an independent line in foreign policy, vying for leadership perhaps with India; and they foreshadowed an arms race between the two successionist states. They had been at active and bitter issue over Kashmir, the large province to the north of the Indian subcontinent which, under a Hindu maharaja, requested accession to India in October 1947. But Pakistan claimed Kashmir, and the Indian case was weakened by the fact that three-fourths of the province's population of four million was Muslim. Civil war broke out in Kashmir. There followed several futile UN efforts to arrange a plebiscite. And then, in 1954, came the arms agreement between the United States and Pakistan. This the Indians interpreted as American support for Pakistan in Kashmir.

The thorny problems of American relations with India and Pakistan will not probably meet solution for some years to come, though one should hasten to add that in general there are far more points of agreement than of disagreement between the United States and India and that Indian leaders have recognized this fact on unemotional occasions. Whatever difficulties have existed in American relations with India and Pakistan, one might conclude, have been underlaid by a large amount of mutual good will. Certainly between the peoples of India and the United States, or Pakistan and the United States, there is no enmity—if only because most Americans know little about either. And as the United States in the nineteenth century had gone through an era of national bumptiousness, so might India in the twentieth, if only from weakness and despair rather than a heady belief in manifest destiny. India, and Pakistan too, have a long road to travel before the pressure of population upon extremely thin economic resources lessens. Their main tasks lie in domestic reconstruction, each nation solving its problems and, internationally, learning first to get along with each other. This is the logic of the situation. But no Indian, of course, can be expected to foreclose his sovereign right to a large foreign policy. And given the US-USSR frictions, US-China frictions, USSR-China frictions, it is perhaps useful to hear an independent voice in world affairs.

Thus while American policy in Asia is having successes and failures by the latter twentieth century, no wise man will venture predictions of its course for even so short a time as five or ten years. The United States faces many problems in the orient. It is obvious that what is happening in the Far East is a drastic, rapid awakening of the native peoples to currents of thought that have been common in the Western world for a century and more. Nationalism is the chief of these ideas to emerge after the Second World War. There had been Indian nationalism and Chinese nationalism and Japanese nationalism for many years before the era 1939–

1945, and nationalism had been nascent in other of the countries of Asia, but during the war the last of the colonial ties snapped, and peoples in Asia saw the future increasingly a matter for their own making. The peculiar brand of Asian nationalism championed by the Japanese was short-lived in its effect upon Japanese-occupied countries, but it encouraged a genuine native nationalism that appeared with force and vigor as soon as the Japanese left and the former occupying powers sought to return. The French and Dutch learned this truth far later than the British, with the result that in the Netherlands East Indies and in Indochina there were vicious civil wars before the occupying powers relinquished control. None of these developments had been foreseen by American diplomacy in 1945.

The Harvard historian Edwin O. Reischauer, who was ambassador to Japan in the early 1960's, had pointed out in a brilliant book, *Wanted: An Asian Policy*, published in 1955, that the United States and other Western nations had three resources of policy toward Asia: military, economic, and ideological. Reischauer appreciated the occasional need to apply military power, the necessity for the West to maintain in the orient as in the occident a respectable military capacity, but he believed that Americans and Europeans had erred by pursuing in the main a military policy. Ten years of experience with military policy—incidentally the most costly choice of policy—had proved it largely futile, for coercion failed in the Netherlands East Indies, and in Indochina and it succeeded only under special conditions in Korea. The policy of economic support and maneuver which the Western powers had engaged in desultorily was so slow and uncertain in action that it could not hope to have much immediate influence upon day-to-day, pressing needs of Western diplomacy. The industrialization that was attempted in the East could not increase productivity to keep up with the increase of population. The average Indian was likely to find himself no better off despite new industrial techniques and experiments.

The level on which the West could reach the East, Reischauer believed, was intellectual or ideological. By urging approach at this level, he was not advocating the popular but vague American view of the late 1940's, a "meeting of East and West," but a concrete, serious effort by Americans and other Westerners to present democracy to Asians as an active, serious, immensely practical way of life. The ideological was the cheapest line of approach, he argued, far cheaper than military or economic assistance. Democracy, so presented, would be attractive to Asians, who found its ideas enticing and its theories interesting. In this regard, he counseled, we should not be disturbed if ideological debates in Asia veered from one extreme to another. We should not worry if our ideas were accepted only to be juxtaposed with impractical ideas—more likely than not, communist ideas. Economic debates especially, he pointed out, were far more theoretical in the East than in the United States, because the crude economies of most of the new Asian countries had given so little experience against which to measure theory.

In the course of time and with good fortune democracy may win out in the East. It is up against grave difficulties, when even the more democratic Eastern nations have only a handful of people competent to staff, lead, and control the governments, an elite leadership exercising some kind of tutelage and experiencing little enlightened restraint from the bulk of the citizenry. In any economic program of large proportions it is possible that in the East the totalitarian methods of communism may prove momentarily more effective than the vacillations of a primitive and precarious democracy. Communism has an undeniable ideological appeal in Asia, and in the latter third of the twentieth century the diplomats of the United States find themselves hard put to defend their system of government against the spurious claims of the Bolshevik and Chinese revolutions. The state department, confronting the post-1945 difficulties and disasters in the Far East, can only hope that time will work in favor of democracy, the cause of the United States.

CONTEMPORARY DOCUMENTS

[General MacArthur early in 1951 was in open rebellion against the civil leadership of the American government, and his letter to Congressman Martin provoked President Truman to recall him. The congressman had written MacArthur for advice and received plenty of it. Martin at first did not quite know what to do with the MacArthur letter. He had asked the general to write "either on a confidential basis or otherwise," and MacArthur had not labeled the response as confidential. "At that period of my life," Martin later observed, "I used to take walks at night, particularly if something was weighing on my mind. When I was worried, I could think better while walking. It was not unusual for me to tramp the streets for a mile or so before retiring, and when I had the MacArthur letter on my hands, I know I covered a few extra blocks each night for good measure." Then Senator Tom Connally, the chairman of the foreign relations committee, declared his belief that there would be no world war that year, 1951. On the same day the speaker of the House of Representatives, Sam Rayburn, warned, "I think that we stand in the face of terrible danger and maybe the beginning of World War III." Martin found this Democratic confusion "intolerable" and released the MacArthur letter, reading it to the House. The correspondence between Martin and the general appears in *My First Fifty Years in Politics* (New York, 1960), pp. 203–205.]

March 8, 1951

PERSONAL

My dear General:

In the current discussions on foreign policy and overall strategy many of us have been distressed that although the European aspects have been heavily emphasized we have been without the views of yourself as Commander-in-Chief of the Far Eastern Command.

I think it is imperative to the security of our nation and for the safety of the world that policies of the United States embrace the broadest possible strategy and that in our earnest desire to protect Europe we not weaken our position in Asia.

Enclosed is a copy of an address I delivered in Brooklyn, N.Y. February 12, stressing this vital point and suggesting that the forces of Generalissimo Chiang-Kai-shek on Formosa might be employed in the opening of a second Asiastic front to relieve the pressure on our forces in Korea.

I have since repeated the essence of this thesis in other speeches and intend to do so again on March 21 when I will be on a radio hookup.

I would deem it a great help if I could have your views on this point, either on a confidential basis or otherwise. Your admirers are legion and the respect you command is enormous. May success be yours in the gigantic undertaking which you direct.

Sincerely yours,
Joseph W. Martin jr.

[In two weeks Martin received his information]

GENERAL HEADQUARTERS
SUPREME COMMANDER FOR THE ALLIED POWERS
Office of the Supreme Commander
Tokyo, Japan
20 March 1951.

Dear Congressman Martin:

I am most grateful for your note of the 8th forwarding me a copy of your address of February 12th. The latter I have read with much interest, and find that with the passage of years you have certainly lost none of your old time punch.

My views and recommendations with respect to the situation created by Red China's entry into the war against us in Korea have been submitted to Washington in most complete detail. Generally these views are well known and clearly understood, as they follow the conventional pattern of meeting force with maximum counterforce as we have never failed to do in the past. Your view with respect to the utilization of the Chinese forces on Formosa is in conflict with neither logic nor this tradition.

It seems strangely difficult for some to realize that here in Asia is where the Communist conspirators have elected to make their play for global conquest, and that we have joined the issue thus raised on the battlefield; that here we fight Europe's war with arms while the diplomats there still fight it with words; that if we lose the war to Communism in Asia the fall of Europe is inevitable, win it and Europe most probably would avoid war and yet preserve freedom. As you point out, we must win. There is no substitute for victory.

With renewed thanks and expressions of most cordial regard, I am,

Faithfully yours,
Douglas MacArthur

ADDITIONAL READING

For general books on the Far East, see authors listed at the end of the previous chapter. An able introduction to Japan is Edwin O. Reischauer, *The United States and Japan* (rev. ed., Cambridge, Mass., 1965), a volume in the American Foreign Policy Library series. In addition see *William L. Neumann's *America Encounters Japan* (Baltimore, 1963). For their special subjects three interesting books are Jonathan B. Bingham, *Shirt-Sleeve Diplomacy: Point 4 in Action* (New York, 1954); Eugene Staley, *The Future of Underdeveloped Countries* (New York, 1954); and Merle Curti and Kendall Birr, *Prelude to Point Four: American Technical Missions Overseas, 1838–1938* (Madison, Wis., 1954).

Many books deal with the American occupation of Japan. Elizabeth Gray Vining, *Windows for the Crown Prince* (Philadelphia, 1952), by a well-known writer of children's books who became private tutor to Crown Prince Akihito, tells a touching story of its author's efforts—successful, we must hope—to instruct "Jimmy" (the crown prince) in democratic ways. The premier during the occupation era, Shigeru Yoshida, published *The Yoshida Memoirs: The Story of Japan in Crisis* (Boston, 1962). For its special subject see Chitoshi Yanaga, *Big Business in Japanese Politics* (New Haven, 1968), by a professor of political science at Yale. Harry E. Wildes's *Typhoon in Tokyo* (New York, 1954), criticizes the "occupationnaires," although it is written by one of them. Another book on the occupation is E. J. Lewe Van Aduard, *Japan: From Surrender to Peace* (New York, 1954). Another, by a Japanese newspaperman, is Kazuo Kawai, *Japan's American Interlude* (Chicago, 1960). For the peace treaty see Bernard C. Cohen, *The Political Process and Foreign Policy: The Making of the Japanese Peace Settlement* (Princeton, 1957); and Frederick S. Dunn, *Peace-Making and the Settlement with Japan* (Princeton, 1963). Herbert Feis sets out the struggle between the United States and the Soviet Union, 1945–1952, over the right to direct the occupation of Japan, in *Contest over Japan* (New York, 1967).

On the subject of the American shogun, General Douglas MacArthur, consult such biographies as John Gunther, *The Riddle of MacArthur* (New York, 1951); Charles A. Willoughby and John Chamberlain, *MacArthur: 1941–1951* (New York, 1954), by the general's intelligence chief; and Louis Morton, "Willoughby on MacArthur: Myth and Reality," *The Reporter*, Nov. 4, 1954, a rebuttal; Courtney Whitney, *MacArthur: His Rendezvous with History* (New York, 1956), a fulsome account; Frazier Hunt, *The Untold Story of Douglas MacArthur* (New York, 1954), sheer hero worship; and Richard H. Rovere and Arthur M. Schlesinger, Jr., *The General and the President and the Future of American Foreign Policy* (New York, 1951), the "meat axe" approach to MacArthur's reputation, by a writer for the *New Yorker* magazine and the well-known historian, reissued with some revision under the title *The MacArthur Controversy and American Foreign Policy* (New York, 1965). More recent studies are Trumbull Higgins, *Korea and the Fall of MacArthur* (New York, 1960), and *John W. Spanier, *The Truman-MacArthur Controversy and the Korean War* (Cambridge, Mass., 1959). In his last years MacArthur wrote his *Reminiscences* (New York, 1964), some parts of which are identical with General Whitney's book cited above; presumably MacArthur had ghosted sections of his aide's volume. Then, within hours after the general's death, three newspaper correspondents published interviews with MacArthur, given some years before under the injunction that the correspondents were not to publish until the general had died. The interviews contained scurrilous references to former President Truman and extraordinary advices on how the Korean War should have been brought to an end—by the sowing of a cobalt belt across the upper part of Korea, which would have meant death by radioactivity to anyone who stepped into it. These interviews again raised questions as to MacArthur's judgment.

For the Korean War a good place to begin is Arthur L. Grey, Jr., "The Thirty-eighth Parallel," *Foreign Affairs*, XXIX (1950–1951), 482–487, on how the country was divided in 1945. Analysis of contemporary theories about the cause of the war is in Alexander L. George, "American Policy-making and the North Korean Aggression," *World Politics*, VII (1954–1955), 209–232. A new study of the decision to intervene is by *Glenn D. Paige, *The Korean Decision* (New York, 1968). A dramatic event in the war appears in *Allen S. Whiting, *China Crosses the Yalu: The Decision to Enter the Korean War* (New York, 1960). The best contemporary account of the fighting probably is S.L.A. Marshall, *The River and the Gauntlet* (New York, 1953), by the distinguished military commentator. See also the book by one of the American military commanders, Mark W. Clark, *From the Danube to the Yalu* (New York, 1954); after the war in Europe, Clark served in the Allied occupation of Austria. The best retrospective account is by another of the military commanders, *Matthew B. Ridgway, *The Korean War* (Garden City, N.Y., 1967). Admiral C. Turner Joy, *How Communists Negotiate* (New York, 1955) contains the experiences of one of the American negotiators of the Korean truce. The Council on Foreign Relations has published L. M. Goodrich, *Korea: A Study of United States Policy in the United Nations* (New York, 1956).

The great debate of 1951–1952 appears in the "MacArthur hearings," the *Military Situation in the Far East: Hearings before the Committee on Armed Services and the Committee on Foreign Relations* (5 vols., Washington, 1951). Only in a democracy could such an outpouring of information and allegation be published so soon after events, for all the world to read and ponder. A notable book by a member of the United States Senate at this time is Joseph R. McCarthy, *America's Retreat from Victory: The Story of George Catlett Marshall* (New York, 1951). See also Norman A. Graebner, *The New Isolationism: A Study in Politics and Foreign Policy since 1950* (New York, 1956); *Richard H. Rovere, *Senator Joe McCarthy* (Cleveland, 1960), a friendly account, indicating how the senator's drinking and gaming habits took over after McCarthy received the criticism of the Senate; and Earl Latham, *The Communist Controversy in Washington: From the New Deal to McCarthy* (Cambridge, Mass., 1966).

George McT. Kahin, *Nationalism and Revolution in Indonesia* (Ithaca, N.Y., 1952) discusses a nation about which many Americans have been ill-informed. More recently, with the retirement of Sukarno, Indonesia has drifted into the news. Garel A. Grunder and William E. Livezey, *The Philippines and the United States* (Norman, Okla., 1951) is an able survey of its subject. Alvin H. Scaff, *The Philippine Answer to Communism* (Stanford, Calif., 1955) relates the suppression of the "Huks." A first-class piece of research and writing— on a subject where research is difficult—is Theodore Friend, *Between Two Empires: The Ordeal of the Philippines, 1929–1946* (New Haven, 1965). Concerning a nation not mentioned in this present text, Edwin F. Stanton's *Brief Authority* (New York, 1956) is an admirable account of a career diplomat's service in—among other places—postwar Thailand. Francis B. Sayre, *Glad Adventure* (New York, 1957), a most interesting autobiography, also contains observations on Thailand, by an American long familiar with the country.

American diplomacy toward India has been set down in Chester Bowles, *Ambassador's Report* (New York, 1954). Excellent pieces of reporting are Robert Trumbull, *As I See India* (New York, 1956); and Carl T. Rowan, *The Pitiful and the Proud* (New York, 1956), about a tour through India by an American Negro journalist. Selig S. Harrison, ed., *India and the United States* (New York, 1961) has some interesting essays, although the book generally speaking seems to show the difficulty of assembling a volume about India with an American authorship—unless that authorship is joint. *Barbara Ward, *India and the West* (rev. ed., New York, 1964) treats that subject with all the authority and speculative intensity of which its author is so capable.

A book of prospect, like *Wanted: An Asian Policy* published some years before and mentioned in the preceding chapter, is *Edwin O. Reischauer, *Beyond Vietnam: The United States and Asia* (New York, 1967).

☆ **29** ☆

The Middle East and Africa

"When is it to happen?" I asked.

"October 29; next Monday," Lloyd answered. "Israel will attack through Sinai that evening and the following morning we and the French will issue our ultimatum to her and Egypt to clear the Canal Zone for us to move our troops in. Egypt will, presumably, refuse, and directly she does so we shall start bombing Egyptian airfields."

—Anthony Nutting, *No End of a Lesson* (1967)

The involvement of the United States in the Middle East and Africa has been essentially a phenomenon of recent world politics, occurring almost entirely since the end of the Second World War. The First World War weakened everywhere the bonds and customs of generations. As we now can see, profound changes were in the making after 1918. Somehow, perhaps through an initial inertia or the slow beginnings of all large changes, for many years not much happened in the areas remote from Europe, and superficial observers in the Middle East and Africa, especially the latter, might well have concluded in 1945 that the quietness of generations had found no disturbance. The gospel of Woodrow Wilson, of national self-determination, nonetheless was spreading to the ends of the earth. Nor would the coming of industry to the extra-European peoples fail to affect their social structures and politics. In the Middle East in particular, the increasing extraction of oil was bound to make enormous changes in everyday life. The appearance of change, economic, social, political, diplomatic, seemed somehow to await the end of the Second World War when, like a cyclone, it burst upon the consciousness of the area's peoples and upon the awareness of peoples and statesmen everywhere. The end of the Second World War opened a new chapter in the history of the Middle East and Africa, a chapter in which the policy of the United States figured prominently.

1. *The beginnings of American interest in the Middle East*

For a century and a half after the founding of the great republic of the New World, citizens of the United States took only sporadic interest in the problems of what variously was described as the Near East or the Middle East. The contacts of Americans with that crossroads of three continents were scarcely worth chronicling. Trade with the lands around the southern and eastern Mediterranean and eastward to Iran, from Syria south to Saudi Arabia, was slight. As early as 1785, American vessels made voyages to the area, seeking commerce in places not under the domination of Great Britain, as in the same era vessels went out to establish trade with China. In the years down to 1815, there were the disputes with the Barbary pirates over the capture of American trading vessels and enslavement of the crews, leading to the final defeat of the pirates in 1815–1816. After the War of 1812, Americans began to enjoy freer trade in the lucrative European markets. The trade with the Middle East continued but never became large. As for other contacts of the Middle East and the United States, emigration to America was virtually nonexistent, except for some Lebanese who for religious and economic reasons made the long journey. American visitors from time to time went to Palestine or Egypt, from piety or curiosity. There was a trickle of missionaries and educators. Many persons in the United States learned about the Holy Land from their Bibles, scanning the strange pictures of oddly square houses set down on rounded, rocky hills. Beyond Biblical study, beyond contacts of a few traders, tourists, missionaries, teachers, American knowledge and concern did not go.

Theodore Roosevelt and John Hay produced a fuss over Perdicaris and Raisuli in 1904, and in 1905–1906 Roosevelt participated in the high politics of Europe at the Algeciras Conference. This involvement was over a country at the far end of the Middle East, by some definitions belonging rather to Africa. TR's interest, anyway, was either domestic politics in the United States or the politics of Europe: for him, Morocco was not itself important.

At the end of the First World War, at the Paris Peace Conference of 1919, a strange assortment of suitors and suppliants came before the committees of the victor nations, and from some of these princes and princelings Americans began to learn about national problems in the Middle East. It was a confusing babel, and although representatives at the conference, President Wilson not least, listened courteously to the cases and pretensions, they hesitated to put credence in them. The president permitted a committee of investigation, the King-Crane Commission, named after the president of Oberlin College, Henry C. King, and the plumbing magnate Charles Crane, to go out to the area and look into the national claims, but not much came from this American group other than a report which disappeared in the paper accumulations of the Paris Conference. In the apportioning of mandates at the conference the United States was spoken of in connection with Armenia. The plight of the Armenians had been a staple of international conversation for decades, and the moral indignation of Americans had fastened on their sufferings. Armenians had come to the United States as immigrants. Americans, though, had never thought of any serious political assistance to the suffering Armenians, unlike the British people, who permitted a large politique toward Turkey in the years prior to the First World War. When the question of an American mandate for Armenia arose at Paris, it never got to a serious stage, to the point where its acceptance or rejection became a matter of American politics. When the Senate turned down the Treaty of Versailles, all thought of an Armenian mandate went with it.

A major American interest in missions in the Middle East flourished beginning in the nineteenth century and continued long into the twentieth century, until the years of turmoil after the Second World War when nationalism made missions increasingly difficult and in some places, such as Egypt, almost impossible. Missionaries went to the Middle East frequently under direction of the Presbyterian Church. They established Robert College in Istanbul, and the American University at Beirut, with far higher standards than the local schools. A much smaller university was founded in Cairo, the American University at Cairo. The missionaries created medical stations which saved many thousands of lives. Sometimes these ministrations, medical and educational, led to converts. For the most part the missionaries found proselytizing possible only among the native Christian sects, such as the 4,000,000 Copts in Egypt. Muslims were willing to accept the educational and medical wisdom of the missionaries but not their religion.

Of American political interest in the area up to the entrance of the United States into the Second World War there was almost none. The only political interference of record, which may have been more of an act of mercy, was an episode in 1941 in Iraq when the American minister connived the escape of the regent, Abdel Illah, then in danger of his life from pro-Axis countrymen. The minister took the regent out of Baghdad in his automobile, hiding him under some rugs in the back seat.

During the war the politics of the region went into eclipse as masses of British and American troops came into the area. The British were there to

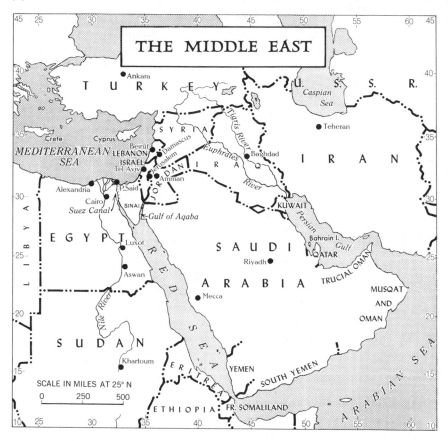

prevent the capture by German troops of the Suez canal. The Americans came in early 1942 as headquarters and logistic support for the Ninth Air Force stationed in Libya and Tripolitania, and to co-ordinate the huge supplies sent to British forces in the Middle East by American ships sailing around the Cape of Good Hope and up into the Red Sea. Many individual Americans thereby discovered the Middle East's fascination as a place of history as well as a cauldron of native politics kept below boiling point by the presence of troops and the war's economic opportunities.

At the end of the war the American government watched in some confusion as the British expelled the French from the area, though not from Algeria, where they most needed expelling. In Algeria in 1827 the ruler had slapped the French consul with a fly swatter, and three years later troops landed at Sidi Ferruch, not to leave until the early 1960's. In the years prior to the First World War, the French had obtained protectorates in Lebanon and Syria. During that war and at the peace conference, they consolidated their position and arranged a sharing of influence with the British, who themselves had been in Egypt since 1882. In the interwar years, the French and British had dominated Middle Eastern politics from their embassies and legations in the capitals of the supposedly independent native kingdoms and principalities. After 1945 the British remained—except for the French in Algeria. Everything otherwise seemed the same.

To Americans only gestures thereafter appeared important. They did not anticipate new developments in the Middle East other than the gradual retirement of the British and an increasing democratization of the area under native governments. The American government raised its legation in Cairo to the status of an embassy in 1946. Creation of the Sixth Fleet in that same year was largely a gesture toward Russian ambition in Iran and pressure upon Turkey and Greece, rather than a response out of fear of the politics of the area south of Turkey, the politics of the Arabic-speaking Middle East.

By this time the United States had become involved in Middle Eastern economics if not politics. In the years immediately prior to the Second World War, the American navy had become fearful of the exhaustion of oil reserves in the United States, and during the war the navy had sought to exploit the reserves—which turned out to be fantastically large—of Saudi Arabia. By 1945 the American consortium of oil companies in Arabia, the Arabian-American Oil Company (Aramco), was the largest single private American investment overseas. In immediate postwar years Americans invested in other oilfields, and jointly with the British they operated the fields of Kuwait, which now have exceeded in production those of Saudi Arabia. They exploited the Bahrain fields in British-supervised territory and obtained a substantial cut in the Iraqi, Irani, and Qatari fields (Qatar was a tiny territory on the eastern fringe of Arabia; like Kuwait and Bahrain it was British-controlled through a native potentate). The American share in Middle East oil production had been 13 per cent in 1939, and the British had been 60 per cent—the balance going mostly to French and Dutch companies. By 1956 the American share was 65 per cent and the British 30 per cent.

What a marvelous bounty the oil revenues could have been for the peoples of the Middle East! Usually a flat fifty per cent of total revenues went to local rulers or governments. The trouble with the distribution of the revenues, however, was two-fold. For one thing, the countries of the Middle East with the largest and most turbulent populations, notably Egypt, but also Jordan and Syria, had almost no oil, and despite the fact that their populaces were largely Arabic-speaking, and that their boundaries were artificial creations of the First World War and other historical developments which had nothing to do with economic or ethnic realities, these oil have-not nations had to stand by and watch geographical nullities like Kuwait and Qatar grow obscenely rich. For another, the rulers and governments of the oil-rich nations used the revenues scandalously. The Saudis lived in absurd pleasure. By the 1950's the younger Saud—who in 1969 would die in exile in Athens, pried off the throne in 1964 by his younger brother Feisal—was maintaining an enormous palace in Riyadh, reputed to have cost $50,000,000. In Kuwait an air-conditioned yacht lay in the harbor, a gift by an American oil company. This remarkable vessel contained a throne room, a sheep pen on the upper deck, and a galley designed for the roasting of three whole sheep at a time. Around Lake Geneva in Switzerland lay the villas of the Middle Eastern rulers, and they and their retinues were constantly coming and going to the Geneva railway station in processions of Cadillacs. All the while their people were living in rags and walking the hard, hot pavements of their cities in bare feet. In Egypt a majority of the people lived in tumbledown mud-brick rabbit warrens, and the young girls daily went down to the river bank or the canals to fill their clay jugs and gasoline tins with the polluted water. The river and canals contained the snails that carry the parasites causing bilharziasis, a disease which caused slow debilitation and death among 95 per cent of Egyptian villagers. In the old imperial days, the British had referred to Egyptians derisively as "wogs," worthy oriental gentlemen, and had been certain that Egyptians by nature were lazy. Anyone, even a Britisher, would have been lazy with bilharziasis.

It was so easy to poke fun at Middle Easterners, especially Egyptians. Ambassador Stanton Griffis, who presided over the embassy in Cairo in 1948–1949, considering it a way station to Madrid, where he wished to go and eventually did, enjoyed the diplomatic social season which began with a round of visitation by the forty local ministers and ambassadors. He counted 479 cups of Turkish coffee, 84 cups of French coffee, 306 Coca Colas, 4 cups (sic) of Arabian coffee, and 76 other national drinks from slivovitz to vodka and arak. He saw Luxor—the greatest collection of antiquities in the entire Middle East—from his ambassadorial plane, and decided that was enough ("I have seen so much of archeology around Cairo that I had no great ambition to tramp around more ruins, and I see one every day at shaving time . . . ."). As for the military situation of the Arab countries in the Middle East, Griffis found it ridiculous. When he asked his senior military attaché to tell him the size and strength of the army of one of the smaller countries, the answer was that "they have about five thousand men under arms, about half of them are usually absent without leave, and the other half are looking for them. When they find them they change places."

2. Israel

The independence of the State of Israel marked the first large political concern of the United States in the Middle East and set American diplomacy on a course which has not always proved in the national interest. If one could have excised the problem of Israel from the Middle East there still would have been plenty of trouble for the United States. No one could assert that without Israel everything in the area would have been plain sailing. Nonetheless, in the eyes of the offended and humiliated Middle Eastern Arab nations, the independence of Israel has so mortgaged American diplomacy that almost any resort, even welcoming the Russians to the area, has seemed to them justified. The Arab nations believe that Israeli imperialism is much more of a danger to them than Russian imperialism; the largest problem in the world at the present time is the State of Israel.

The exact nature of American political interference in the Middle East in support of Israeli independence is not easy to determine, even with retrospect of twenty or more years. One can contend that creation of this alien (so the Arabs would say) state was not an act of the United States but the act of Hitler, who so threatened world Jewry that many members of what hitherto had been a religion felt the need for a political state. One can contend also that after the Second World War the creation of Israel was an act of private individuals in Palestine, assisted by private American citizens—that the American government itself was fairly neutral and at one crucial point in the last months of 1947 and first months of 1948 actually hostile. It is an open question whether the president of the United States in the months immediately prior to May 1948, Harry S. Truman, had any large part in the creation of a new Middle Eastern state. Only later did it appear that Truman had assisted Israel. Surely the president was not playing domestic politics. He was as nonpartisan in foreign affairs as he was partisan in domestic affairs and never would have sponsored trouble for the United States abroad to obtain his election to the presidency at home. In the actual event, New York State went for Thomas E. Dewey in the presidential election of 1948, and Truman won anyway. One must doubt whether the American government sponsored Israel, as both Arabs and Israelis have asserted.

As for an American promise to uphold Israeli independence, an American "commitment" to Israel akin to American support in 1947 of Greece and Turkey, there was none prior to May 1948 and there has been none since: talk of a commitment in later years is an inexactitude, to put it mildly.

It is easy, though, to understand how the American government was willing to stand by and see the appearance of the Israeli state, given the American concerns in other areas of the world in the same era, especially Europe and China. The creation of Israel occurred at a time also when the politics of the Middle East had not been infected by Russian intrigue. At the end of the war, the Soviets had asked for territory in Libya, the erstwhile colony of defeated Italy. They had interfered in northern Iran in 1945–1946 and put heavy pressure upon Greece and Turkey .They otherwise had not entered into Middle Eastern politics at this time and did not do so until, as we now can see, they had failed in their effort to overwhelm Western Europe in the late 1940's and turned to the Far East, which simmered down by 1954–1955. Only then did they take interest in the crossroads of continents, an area characterized by a rising Arab nationalism, the economy of oil, some of the world's worst social inequalities, and the loosening imperial hold of Great Britain.

The course of events leading to the independence of Israel is of interest in the present pages only insofar as it showed interference by the United States government. Admittedly there was some diplomacy. At the very end of the Second World War, President Roosevelt had sought to "sweet talk" Ibn Saud into supporting the admission of more Jewish refugees into Palestine, then a British mandate. In a meeting aboard the cruiser *Quincy*, anchored in Great Bitter Lake in the Suez, the president and king explored the subject. Roosevelt gave Ibn Saud, like himself an invalid, a wheel chair, and the conversation auspiciously began. The Arab king ruffled at mention of more Jews in Palestine and said that the Jews should have German territory, considering what Roosevelt said Hitler had done to the Jews. The Arabs, said Saud, had done nothing to the Jews. The aging Saud, first of his royal line, was implacable.

There followed under President Truman an effort of statesmanlike proportions to put the Jewish problem in Palestine into the hands of two committees, but each of these committees refused to recommend the independence of a Jewish regime in Palestine.

But the year 1946, in which both committees reported, was a congressional election year, and Eliahu Epstein (later Elath), the Washington representative of the international Zionist movement, known as the Jewish Agency, arranged for a statement by the president on Yom Kippur, October 4, 1946, favoring 100,000 immigrants for Palestine. Several days later, Governor Dewey said that several hundred thousand should be admitted. Epstein remarked in a private letter to a confederate in London how, some years before, candidates for the House and Senate had to remind many Jews of the existence of Palestine in order to win their votes. Now, he said, things were different, although the British were mobilizing their "stooges" in the United States, such as James Reston of The New York *Times*, who just had published a "vicious" article.

The British government, the mandatory power, was not happy with any use of the Palestine issue in American domestic politics, and Foreign Secretary Bevin was incensed, for after the war the lid had come off of terrorism in what was still a British-governed area. The Haganah, the largest and most moderate of the Jewish political groups in Palestine, was not doing much to prevent the excesses of the Irgun Zvai Leumi and the "Stern gang," whose extremists were taking British troops as prisoners and executed two sergeants in barbaric fashion after the British had executed Jewish terrorists. The British public was outraged and deeply resented what appeared to be gratuitous advice from the American government. In these circumstances the British government on April 2, 1947, gave the Palestine mandate to the United Nations. In 1947 the British, afflicted by a floundering domestic economy, abandoned India, Greece, and Turkey, and with good reason decided to get rid of the Holy Land.

The question of what the American government had to do with the independence of Israel depends upon how one interprets American action during the crucial year after the British turned over the future of Palestine to the UN, and particularly on what the United States did or did not do during the era from November 1947, when the Palestine issue came to a crisis in the United Nations, to May 1948, when Israel declared its independence. The issue at the United Nations was at first unclear: the UN sent another committee to Palestine, and it reported much in the vein of the two previous American committees, that Palestine should not be divided into two independent states but should contain two autonomous communities, Arab and Jewish, bound in economic union, with Jerusalem under direct UN trusteeship. The Jewish Agency at first was hostile to this proposal but then came to see that the issue was not the report of the UN committee but rather which of the two communities in Palestine would be able to dominate the area militarily once the British withdrew. If any single act created the State of Israel, it was the UN decision of November 29, 1947. Immediately afterward the British announced that they were relinquishing the mandate, their forces leaving Palestine, on May 15, 1948. No such thing as a UN force existed which could occupy Palestine in place of the British and enforce the UN decision. The American government by itself certainly was not able to send troops to Palestine to enforce the UN decision. A debate within the cabinet, set forth clearly in Secretary of Defense Forrestal's memoirs, shows that the American army of the time could not have sent more than a division to Palestine without a partial mobilization, which was impossible in an election year, 1948, and impossible anyway, given the temper of public opinion so soon after the end of the Second World War. The helpless British had quartered nearly 60,000 troops in Palestine, without result. The US army estimate of troops necessary to enforce the UN decision was a minimum of 80,000 and a maximum of 160,000. Again, in the hiatus of power created by the UN decision, the Jewish Agency received an opportunity to take over as much of Palestine as its troops, already well trained (many having served under the British in the Second World War), could occupy.

It is interesting that during the crucial months prior to Israeli independence, when the Jewish Agency desired only the slightest nod from the United States, President Truman was anything but friendly to the cause of the Jews in Palestine. He had become incensed by the pressure upon small-state delegations to the UN, and upon the American government, during the voting in the General Assembly over the resolution of November 1947, when the Firestones were dragooned to get the vote of Liberia, when the Philippine delegate was exposed to indignities, when the little Caribbean and Central American states found themselves under intense private influences. The president put on the red light, as Dean Acheson once characterized Truman's behavior when angered. According to Acheson, when the red light goes on there is nothing to do but wait for the green light. Truman told his staff that he would see no one on the subject of a Jewish state in Palestine. Chaim Weizmann, soon to become president of the new state, waited impatiently in New York at the Waldorf-Astoria but could not get to see the president. Truman's secretary referred all inquiries to the United Nations.

It was at this crucial time that the national executive vice president of B'nai B'rith, Maurice Bisgyer, and the president of the organization, Frank Goldman, put Truman's old haberdashery partner and First World War buddy, Eddie Jacobson, up to calling at the White House. There was nearly a row. "In all the years of our friendship," Jacobson remembered, "he never talked to me in this manner." Jacobson argued tenaciously that Truman at least should talk to Weizmann. Truman abruptly turned around in the presidential swivel chair and started looking out the window. "All of a sudden he swiveled around again, faced his desk, and looked me straight in the eyes and said the most endearing words I ever heard: 'You win, you baldheaded . . . I will see him.' " Unnerved, Jacobson fled to the Hotel Statler and downed two double bourbons before talking to Bisgyer and Goldman, who were awaiting him. During a meeting on March 18, 1948, the president assured Weizmann (who entered the White House undetected, by a roundabout way) that he, Truman, would go forward with the UN partition plan.

This, in truth, was all the United States government did prior to the announcement of Israel's independence on May 15.

After the event the Truman administration did recognize the new state with a slight haste. Midnight, May 15, Palestine time, was 6:00 P.M., May 14, Washington time. Eleven minutes later, when the new regime had not even had time to cable its existence, basing his action only on a request from Epstein of the Jewish Agency in Washington, Truman extended presidential *de facto* recognition. This recognition in eleven minutes, compared with the three days necessary to recognize Panama in 1903, the eleven months necessary after San Jacinto to recognize Texas in 1836–1837.

At the time it was not possible to see that Israeli independence would unsettle the entire Middle East and raise political problems of an explosive nature. An Israeli-Arab war at once began which went on inconclusively for a year and ended with an uneasy armistice still in existence. Weaknesses of the Arabs, apparent in the war, brought a revolution in Egypt in 1952. A caravan of Middle Eastern calamities, beginning in the mid-1950's with the appearance in the area of Russian arms purchased by Egypt, led to nationalization of the Suez canal in 1956 and gravely embarrassed the North Atlantic Treaty Organization. Suez produced a spectacle in the UN of the United States and Russia siding against Britain and France. The Suez crisis left a heritage of distrust between the United States and Britain and France that lasted for years, at least to the end of the 1960's. Among the Arabs the confusions of Suez begat the Lebanon crisis of 1958, when a division of American troops landed in the eastern Mediterranean after murderous revolts in Lebanon and Iraq and the near breakup of the Western alliance structure in the Middle East, the Baghdad Pact. These events are fit subjects for discussion in the pages that follow. In large part they stemmed from dissensions incident to creation of the State of Israel in 1948. Americans, troubled with disorder all over the globe, could take little comfort in the burning antagonism of the Arabs for Israel. A million and more Arab refugees would sit sullenly in their tents and hovels ringed about Israel, mulling over the iniquities of their displacement. The United States bore most of the economic burden of paying for their food and lodging, health and education, $433,418,000 for the years 1950 through June 30, 1968 (the total disbursal to the refugees from all sources was $629,053,000), and received in return their hostility. The United States, they concluded, had sponsored this malignant and malevolent (they believed) foreign state on their ancestral soil. If the Jews were entitled to Palestine because of residence there in the pre-Christian era, then the Indians surely owned the United States. In their myopic righteousness the displaced Arabs, and their relatives miserably placed in Egypt, Syria, and the other oil-have-not nations, regarded the Jews as their prime enemies. Anyone else who gave the Arab nations help, such as the Russians in the mid-1950's, could become their friends.

3. *The Suez crisis*

The Suez crisis of 1956 occurred at the same time as Russian troubles in Eastern Europe, a moment which could not have been better so far as the Soviets were concerned. The Suez fiasco in the Middle East showed the disunity of the Western Allies in a glaring way and drew the world's attention from Russia's defeat in Poland and grisly triumph over the revolution in Hungary.

This 1956 crisis over the Suez had been long in preparation, and it might be well to look back into its origins, for only in its historical context can it be understood.

Here one could write in long detail of the background of British and French policy in the Middle East, and such detail would be entirely relevant, although too extensive for inclusion in the present account. French interest in the Middle East went back to the nineteenth century, when the French government had acted as protector of the Christians in Lebanon against the Turks. British interests likewise reached back into the nineteenth century: Benjamin Disraeli in 1875 had managed the purchase of the khedive of Egypt's 44-per cent share in the Suez Canal Company; the British had bombarded and subdued Alexandria in 1882 and had maintained a temporary occupation of Egypt for forty years, until 1922. In that year Britain unilaterally terminated the protectorate, leaving details for future negotiation, which were finally settled in an Anglo-Egyptian treaty of 1936. Meanwhile the British and French during the First World War had managed by military action against the Turks to become heirs to the Middle Eastern fragments of the former Turkish empire. The two European powers secured their new hegemony by mandates from the League of Nations, and during the 1920's and 1930's it was the word from London or Paris that came down to the Middle Eastern capitals and made or unmade prime ministers and chiefs of staff. During the Second World War, large bodies of Allied troops maintained peace in the area, and only in 1945 and thereafter did a new basis of government become possible.

The new regimes, as they set themselves up with their grants of freedom from Britain and France after the Second World War, were in many ways shadow governments, tribal arrangements that had little relation to the geographical realities of the Middle East. It has often been pointed out that such cartographical monstrosities as Iraq, Jordan, or Syria could not have expected to continue indefinitely in their original shapes. In the early years after 1945, everyone hoped against hope that the Middle East would remain quiet or semi-quiet while the greater problems of Europe and Asia were attended to. The appearance of the State of Israel in 1948, when the British abandoned the Palestine mandate, did not represent any large calculation by Western statesmen. Few Americans or citizens of Britain and France had time to give much thought to the Middle East in that hectic year 1948, the year of the Marshall Plan's first operations, of the Berlin

'TICK TOCK'

The crisis of 1956 had been long in preparation.

blockade, and of communist successes in China. That area of the world rattled along, so to speak, and the new nations of the Middle East went their new ways with apparent stability and little attention. In the year 1950, Britain, France, and the United States concluded a Tripartite Declaration under which they promised, among other things, to prevent any border changes by the Arab states or Israel: "The three Governments, should they find that any of these States was preparing to violate frontiers or armistice lines, would, consistent with their obligations as members of the United Nations, immediately take action, both within and outside the

United Nations, to prevent such violation." Although this part of the declaration proved later to be a dead letter, another part provided for a virtual arms embargo, a careful measuring of requests for arms by the Arab nations or Israel, so that there would be no arms competition by these small nations. In such fashion everything continued in fairly good order until February 1955, when Israeli troops, in retaliation for border incidents by the Egyptians, made a large raid against Egyptian army forces in the so-called Gaza strip area adjoining Israel. Thereupon, the Egyptian government, under its new nationalist leader Gamal Abdel Nasser, announced negotiation in September 1955 of an arms deal with Russia and Czechoslovakia. This was the thin entering wedge for serious trouble.

There had been troubles even before 1955. The prime minister of Iran, Dr. Mohammed Mossadegh, had precipitously nationalized the Anglo-Iranian Oil Company in 1951 and raised a large row with Great Britain. But eventually things came back under control in Iran, the shah abdicating in August 1953, then returning and appointing a new prime minister who jailed Dr. Mossadegh. The new government negotiated a settlement with the British oil company.

There also had been difficulty over Britain's withdrawal from the Suez canal zone, which finally was arranged in an Anglo-Egyptian agreement of 1954. Then when Britain, after terminating the Anglo-Egyptian condominium of the Sudan, managed to set up a free government in the Sudan, there was much Egyptian dissatisfaction, for the Egyptians wanted to annex the Sudan. Other than such difficulties, and Britain's troubles with Cyprus, where Greeks and Turks competed for the island with acts of terrorism against each other and their British rulers, all was fairly quiet in the Middle East until the Russian-Czech arrangement to sell arms in exchange for Egyptian cotton.

This action alarmed the Israelis and led them to seek arms and support for what they knew would be an easy military operation against the Egyptians. The Israelis numbered something over a million and a half souls and they saw around them forty million Arabs. Anti-Israel propaganda came night and day from the Cairo radio which blanketed the Middle East. Many of the Israelis who had known Hitler were not unwilling to believe that President Nasser of Egypt was another Hitler. The government of Israel in 1948, when it was just a few weeks old, had decisively defeated the combined armies of the Arab states in war. The Israelis were eager to do it again.

In July 1956 President Nasser complicated his position (as well as everyone else's position) by nationalizing the Suez canal, an act which won him the enmity of the British government. He had been negotiating with the Western powers to obtain funds to raise the level of the Nile by a higher dam at Aswan in upper Egypt, which would generate electricity to promote Egypt's industrialization, in addition to increasing the area of cultivable land. The failure of this effort was his avowed reason for nationalizing the canal. He announced that he would use the income from the canal to build the dam. For the British, who had been treated to many humiliations since the end of the Second World War, to be thus humiliated by the Egyptians seemed at the moment unbearable. President Nasser engaged the intense dislike of Prime Minister Anthony Eden, who had made a reputation in the 1930's for being willing to stand against Hitler and had broken from the Neville Chamberlain government over this issue.

Meanwhile the French, who like the British owned a large amount of stock in the Suez canal, had become more particularly angered at Egypt because of the Egyptians' support for the rebels in Algeria.

The makings of trouble were at hand. In the summer of 1956 the French commenced an intrigue with the Israelis, who wanted to have a whack at Nasser. The British joined the intriguers. The agreement was that Israel would attack Egypt, and Anglo-French forces then would take over the canal area, with the British air force meanwhile neutralizing the Egyptian air force. The Anglo-French would enter the canal zone under the guise of an intervention to keep the Israelis and Egyptians apart.

In the subsequent military operations, between October 29 and November 2, 1956, the forces of Israel brilliantly finished off all Egyptian troops in the Sinai peninsula and could have cut straight to Cairo and taken all Egypt if they had not been stopped by their prior arrangement with Britain and France. The two Western powers gave both the Israelis and Egyptians an ultimatum on October 30 that they refrain from military operations within ten miles of the canal. This phrasing of the ultimatum allowed the Israelis to occupy a hundred miles of Egyptian territory. When the Egyptians ignored the ultimatum, the British and French brought their forces into the canal area, shelled and occupied Port Said. The Egyptians blocked the canal with wrecks. There followed a diplomatic, military, and economic impasse at Suez until the United Nations at the instance of Canada created a UN Emergency Force, UNEF, which beginning in mid-November arrived in the Middle East and by Christmas 1956 had replace the British and French, with the Israelis retreating to their home base.

In the course and sequels of this complex crisis the United States joined with Russia in opposing Britain and France, the Russians threatened to shoot missiles into the Western capitals and to send "volunteers"—that is, troops—to the Middle East; the United States said that volunteers meant war, the Egyptians in effect held the blocked canal as a hostage, there was sabotage of the Iraq oil pipeline through Syria, the British pound sterling came within an ace of devaluation, two British ministers resigned, there was indication that India and Pakistan might withdraw from the Commonwealth and join forces with a new international African-Arab-Asian bloc; the United States and especially Secretary of State Dulles received an exceedingly bad press in Britain and France, the Israelis were angry because they did not receive a chance to destroy Nasser; Nasser rose in stature to be the most powerful and attractive of all the Arab leaders, Prime Minister Eden lost the Nobel Peace Prize for which before the Suez operation he had been a candidate, went to Jamaica for three weeks to recuperate from what could not have been a more maladroit piece of diplomacy, and not long afterward relinquished the seals of his office to Harold Macmillan.

The lesson of Suez was plain for everyone to read: use of armed force by the Western powers could no longer secure their interests in the Middle East. As Guy Wint and Peter Calvocoressi wrote in an excellent little book, *Middle East Crisis:* "The fundamental British error has been to persist too long in a policy that has been overtaken by events. . . . The alternative to staying is going away. In 1947 the British left India lock, stock, and barrel. . . . Withdrawal may be repugnant and is certainly risky, but once the facts dictate it, it needs to be made sharply. Failure to realize this in the Middle East led to . . . an achievement for which it would be hard to find a parallel in the history of British diplomacy."

An especial sadness of the British fiasco over nationalization of the Suez canal was that the whole operation on the Anglo-French side, the intervention in Egypt after the Israelis had attacked, was shadowed in collusion. This was not an appropriate aura for twentieth-century British diplomacy, even if it had enveloped French diplomacy on innumerable occasions. What about the British idea of the behavior of a gentleman, the notion of fair play? Not without reason had Sir Harold Nicolson in his well-known manual on diplomacy set out as a prime attribute of the good diplomat the telling of the truth. Suez inspired many official half-truths. And two notable falsehoods had been uttered in the British government's holy of holies, the House of Commons. Randolph Churchill pointed out in *The Rise and Fall of Sir Anthony Eden,* published soon after the debacle, that only a fool would believe that the British government had not conspired with the French and Israelis to arrange for the Israeli attack followed by the Franco-British intervention. He recalled the famous remark of the Duke of Wellington on another occasion, "If you can believe that, you can believe anything." Not, however, until a decade later, when the number two man in the British foreign office at the time of Suez, Anthony Nutting, published a little volume entitled *No End of a Lesson,* did the full truth come out. Nutting related the inner workings of British diplomacy prior to Suez. He told how the French and British and Israelis had conspired against the Egyptians. When he had protested to Foreign Secretary Selwyn Lloyd, the latter said, employing a facetious joke, "There's only one worse thing than having a yes-man on one's team, and that's having a no-man like you." When Nutting suggested to Eden a consultation with the foreign office's legal adviser, Sir Gerald Fitzmaurice, he met the flattest of negatives: "Fitz is the last person I want consulted. The lawyers are always against our doing anything. For God's sake, keep them out of it. This is a political affair." The Eden government then used Israel as a stalking horse against Egypt. The British, of course, had to come in after Israel attacked, because the Israelis had insisted upon neutralization of the Russian-equipped Egyptian air force, and only the British had enough planes in the area to do this job. After the debacle, Lloyd lied in Parliament, albeit one could interpret his words as technically correct: "It is quite wrong to state that Israel was incited to this action by Her Majesty's Government. There was no prior agreement between us about it." Eden did worse, by saying simply that "there was not foreknowledge that Israel would attack Egypt." In British politics it is unforgiveable to deceive the Commons, whatever deception a leader or member must employ outside. When in 1963 the secretary of state for war, Sir John Profumo, falsely told the House that he had no connection with a London prostitute, he was disgraced and forced to resign.

Because of what was known and suspected of the Suez affair, British and French prestige vanished from the Middle East. Arab resentment was for a moment deflected from the United States because of the undeniably firm American stand against the Suez venture of its allies. But the Americans were susceptible to the same illusions, if not the same methods, as the British and French, and two years later, in a not exactly analogous situation, they also made a show of armed force in the Middle East and focused upon themselves the hostility of the Arab world.

4. *The Lebanon and Iraq crisis of 1958*

The crisis of 1958, like that of two years before, represented a move by the West—this time the United States—to stop by force the power of Arab nationalism. In 1957, after the Suez fiasco, the two Arab states of Egypt and Syria formed a union (which however lasted only a few years), turning themselves into a United Arab Republic under the presidency of Gamal Abdel Nasser. The small sheikdom of Yemen allied itself with this new combine. Nasser set out to unite the entire Middle East by feeding the fires of Arab nationalism. He could thus inspire internal revolts in Arab countries, promote their union with the United Arab Republic, and nationalize the oil-producing properties. If successful, he not merely would have a more powerful position from which to confront the Western Allies and also Soviet Russia, but he could help solve the internal problems of Egypt and some of the other poor Arab states by obtaining control over the oil revenues of the region. By nationalizing the canal in 1956, he had taken control of the most important means of transport, and this move had not yet been offset by Western construction of large oil tankers which could profitably make the run around South Africa. This all made sense from a Middle Eastern point of view, and the only courses open to the West were to retire from the area, or to come to an accommodation with the United Arab Republic, or (and this was a poor alternative) to seek alliance with the few anti-Nasser leaders in the Middle East who still had some control over their governments. This latter course, which was the one taken by the West, meant Western military support to the regimes in Jordan and Iraq and Lebanon.

The government of Premier Nuri es-Said in Iraq, with its seat in Baghdad, had long been as pro-Western as Nuri could make it and at the same time retain power, and so Iraq became the foundation of this Western policy. Iraq in February 1955 had made an alliance with Turkey, the Baghdad Pact, and the two nations had then been joined by Pakistan and Iran and Great Britain. The purpose of this alliance was to form a group with NATO in Europe, SEATO in the Far East, and the Rio Pact allies in the Western Hemisphere. On paper these various regional alliances against communism looked impressive; unfortunately, the Baghdad Pact was a fragile creation because it pivoted on the government of Nuri es-Said in Iraq. This government was doing its best after Suez to contain what the West was beginning to call Nasserism in the Middle East, but this undertaking was difficult when the enthusiasm for Arab unity was running so high, fanned day after day as the Cairo radio talked of a united Arab people. Abruptly, on July 14, 1958, a revolt erupted in Baghdad, led by the Iraqi army. Troops occupied the capital in the early morning, and King Feisal of Iraq, his uncle the crown prince Abdel Illah, and Premier Nuri es-Said were all murdered. The new army "republican" government was at once recognized by President Nasser's United Arab Republic, the Baghdad Pact seemed to cave in, and the position of the West in the Middle East looked insecure in the extreme.

The Eisenhower administration at once moved to ensure the independence of Lebanon, threatened also with Nasserism. Before the nationalist coup in Iraq, there had been a civil war in Lebanon, a confused struggle of political factions embittered by a Christian-Arab antagonism, the pro-Nasser and anti-Nasser feeling of the Lebanese, and a general division of the tiny country between its westernized city dwellers in Beirut and the inhabitants of the small towns and the hill areas. After the murders in Baghdad, the pro-Western president of Lebanon, Camille Chamoun, a Maronite Christian, asked for immediate military support from the United States. President Eisenhower sent American marines into Lebanon. The forces of protection, welcomed enthusiastically by President Chamoun, soon numbered 14,000, almost equivalent to an army division. They landed under protection of the United States Sixth fleet, much in evidence in the Mediterranean at this time, whose publicity officers announced that it was ready for all eventualities.

Simultaneously British troops, crossing Israeli territory en route, were flown from Cyprus to Amman, the capital of Jordan, where the anti-Nasser leader King Hussein was in dire straits with a near-bankrupt treasury, an unreliable army, the example of Iraq, and a noisy pro-Nasser sentiment among his citizenry. These troops, to the number of 3,000, were received by Hussein, who had asked for them, and were stationed at the airport at Amman, presumably to protect the Jordanian capital in event of revolution.

Here, then, was a new move by force into the Middle East, with American and British troops instead of British and French. It was a dangerous move, considering the force of Arab nationalism and the willingness of the Soviet Union to pose as the friend of the Arabs. Newspapers in the United States proclaimed a time of crisis and peril. In the days after the Iraq revolution and the British and American military moves, there was a heated verbal exchange between the West and Soviet Russia, with Khrushchev indulging in hints of open warfare, branding the Americans as fascist aggressors and enemies of the Arab people. President Nasser spoke out strongly against the United States. President Eisenhower in a statement after the marines entered Lebanon said that they were going there to protect the little country against communism and the terroristic tactics of the president of the United Arab Republic. During the remainder of July and through August, the controversy wore on, with proposals by Khrushchev of another summit meeting and counterproposals by Eisenhower and Prime Minister Macmillan and talk of what the UN could do or should do. By the end of the summer, a new regime took office in Lebanon under the Lebanese army commander Fuad Chehab. Jordan eventually straightened out, after the United States and Britain engaged in a frantic operation to bring in oil and other supplies to bolster its economy and secure Hussein against Nasser.

It was no easy matter for the Americans to decide what to do about the Middle East, after the measures of the summer of 1958. Americans had the distinct feeling that short of Russian invasion of the area, with all that could mean for the extension of communism into Africa and Asia, there was no national interest of the United States in the Middle East that was worth a war.

The United States, as became clear during the Lebanon and Iraq crisis, had two hostages to fortune in the Middle East: oil and the State of Israel. For the moment the problem of Israel was not pressing and hence was largely a theoretical matter. Israel at the moment was strong enough militarily to resist all the Arabs in combination. But if Arab nationalism were to invigorate the armies of the Arab states and make them a little more efficient, Israel would be in serious trouble, and what would the American government do?

The problem of oil was more pressing (even with the United States still by far the world's largest producer), for Europe vitally needed the oil of the Middle East, without which its economy would collapse. And the United States vitally needed Europe. Only if the United States were willing drastically to cut down its own domestic oil requirements, probably moving the majority of Americans' cars off the highways, could enough oil come from the Western Hemisphere to care for Europe and make the Western Allies secure against Middle Eastern oil blackmail.

It appeared that the best course for American diplomacy in the Middle East was to re-examine carefully the extent of American interests in the area and to design a policy to fit those interests. This course would require examination of the oil contracts by American and other Western companies with the Middle Eastern governments. It would probably also involve an honest bargaining over the contracts between the West and the Arab nationalists, with willingness to do business even under nationalization so long as the terms were fair, but with determination to pull out and to refuse to buy Middle Eastern oil if the terms were unfair. In pursuit of this course, the United States would necessarily take an interest in spreading oil revenues from the "have" nations such as Iraq and Saudi Arabia and Kuwait (170,000 people; one-seventh of the world's known oil reserves) to the "have-not" nations of Egypt, Syria, Jordan, and Lebanon. This course would also mean an open discussion diplomatically of the problem of Israel, which since the Arab military defeats of 1948 had appeared in Arab eyes as the largest problem in the Middle East, more important than the "colonial" schemes of the United States, Britain, and France. In this regard it would be essential somehow for Western statesmen to convince both the Israelis and the Arabs that the two peoples could live together, to their mutual benefit, and "living together" would mean some arrangement by the Israelis to settle the status of the Arabs who during establishment of Israel had left the country. An accommodation on such matters as the above would have to be arrived at. An imaginative American diplomacy could accomplish it.

President Eisenhower in 1957 obtained congressional approval of a resolution which became known as the Eisenhower Doctrine, expressing the determination of the United States to use its armed forces in behalf of any Middle Eastern state which requested "aid against overt armed aggression from any nation controlled by international communism." Accompanying this new doctrine was a crash program of economic assistance totaling $200,000,000. Inspired by the Lebanon and Iraq crisis, the president in August 1958 spoke before the UN and offered a plan for economic development in the area. Whether these measures were well thought out, whether they reached to the root of Middle Eastern troubles, was difficult to say. At least they were efforts, and the latter two—the economic plans —seemed to be moving in the right direction.

In the 1960's, as in the 1950's, but fortunately without the great international crisis of the mid-1950's, the United States tried valiantly to keep the lid on Middle Eastern politics, adjusting differences and disagreements of the nations of the area short of war. It was heavy going and was not assisted by the little six-day war which the Israelis conducted against Egypt in June 1967, when in a lightning stroke they expelled Egyptian troops from the Gaza strip and from the straits controlling entrance to the Red Sea port of Eilat. They even chased the Egyptians back to the western side of the Suez canal and occupied the Sinai peninsula up to the great ditch itself. They forced Jordanian troops out of Jerusalem, not merely regaining the Wailing Wall but taking the Mosque of Omar. The latter is a very sacred place to Muslims, second only to Mecca, because it contains the rock from which Mohammed, the Prophet of Allah, ascended into heaven (the rock has a hole in it, marking the place where Omar was standing before he and a roughly circular piece of the rock went to heaven). The Israelis also occupied a small portion of Syria. Books about this new desert war appeared on American newsstands within a week or two of the event. Newsreels showed millions upon millions of dollars of Russian equipment strewn in the desert sands. The Israelis refurbished some of it and sold some to Western military representatives, who took it home to analyze. The United Nations solemnly condemned this war of 1967 and resolved that the Israelis should evacuate their new imperial holdings. The State of Israel remained in possession, however, and gave no sign of retreat or remorse. In a world in which the two superpowers, Russia and the United States, had their own hostages to public relations, Czechoslovakia and Vietnam, there was not much more to say except to deplore the violence which again had inflamed the Arabs, perhaps at a time when they were beginning to forget their humiliations of 1948-1949

General Moshe Dayan enters the old city of Jerusalem. With him are Brigadier General Uzi Narkiss (L.) and Major General Izhak Rabin (R.).

and 1956. Passions in the Middle East now might not simmer down until the year 2000. Some individuals asked uncertainly whether the economy of Israel, in straits with the ending of West German reparations, and with bonds coming due, would be able to stand a long boycott by its neighbors who might have been its customers. A letter to the New York *Times* in the summer of 1968 suggested that all the Israelis who wished might be invited into the United States as permanent residents, and the state liquidated. An answering letter said that after the victory of 1967 no patriotic Israeli would consider such a denouement.

5. *Africa*

Turning briefly to the subject of Africa—the dark continent of Henry M. Stanley and Dr. David Livingstone, as it was known a century ago—one must say that American relations until recent times have been desultory and almost inconsequential, as compared to relations with the Far East and even the Middle East. It is true that the most important ship ever to arrive on American shores was the unknown Dutch vessel of 1619 that bore the first African slaves. More than ten per cent of the present American population has descended from those unknown immigrants aboard that unknown ship and the slave vessels that followed. Other than this heartbreaking chapter of American (for the most part colonial) history, now far into the past, American-African relations until recent years have not been eventful.

Relations until the time of the Civil War were nonetheless almost entirely concerned with the problem of slavery. An increasing legitimate trade existed in these years, a trade of American tobacco, rum, lumber, and foodstuffs, in exchange for hides (for New England's shoe factories), peanuts, gum copal (a resinous substance from tropical trees, used for varnishes and lacquers), palm oil, ivory. But the illegitimate trade in slaves flourished, even though the slave trade was forbidden to American citizens beginning in 1807. The American squadrons stationed off the African coast as a result of the Webster-Ashburton Treaty proved in the main ineffective in preventing this illicit trade, in which slaves were carried not merely to the South but to the Caribbean. The United States refused to allow the British navy to assist in suppressing the slave trade at its source, for fear of permitting undue interference with American commerce. The right of visit and search anywhere, Americans maintained, could apply only to wartime. This unsatisfactory situation continued until the Civil War brought a more sensible attitude by the federal government. Then the British squadrons received permission to stop suspected American slavers, and the African slave trade came to an abrupt end. Meanwhile Liberia had been founded in the 1820's, and 15,000 American freemen went there, to be joined by 5,000 Africans taken from captured American slavers and returned to the continent of their birth.

The half-century after Appomattox saw the rise of other issues with regard to Africa. The United States government sent representatives to the Berlin Conference of 1884–1885, called to deal with problems of the Congo. These representatives helped persuade the European powers to accept provisions for freedom of trade in Central Africa, outlawing the slave traffic, and providing for neutralization of the area in time of war. Then a change of administrations, from President Arthur to President Cleveland, brought caution, and Secretary of State Bayard announced that the United States, declining to ratify the treaty of 1885, could not "join in the responsible political engagements in so remote and undefined a region as that of the Congo Basin." Many years later another American president, Wilson, showed more concern for Africa than had his predecessor Cleveland, even though Wilson in American domestic politics proved no defender of Negro rights. At the Paris Peace Conference of 1919, he required the Allies to institute the mandate system for Africa, providing for the open door and some international accountability and control, as a price of their obtaining Germany's colonies of Tanganyika, Togo, Cameroons, Ruanda-Urundi, and Southwest Africa.

The state department in 1938 got around to recognizing the need for American diplomats to know something about Africa. A desk was set aside for a department officer to concentrate exclusively on the problems of Africa. The appointee designated by Secretary of State Hull was Henry S. Villard, who nearly thirty years later, when Africa had become an object of intensive study, recalled his experience. Before 1938, he wrote in his memoir *Affairs at State*, our policy toward the colonized African continent was—to quote Lewis Carroll—"a perfect absolute blank." Upon taking over the African desk, he was reminded of a story about Governor Alfred E. (Al) Smith when the latter was running for president in 1928. " 'Tell 'em all you know,' " yelled a heckler in the audience, " 'it won't take long.' " " 'I'll tell 'em all we both know,' " replied Al amiably, " 'it won't take any longer.' "

Despite the state department's recognition of Africa, not much happened in American-African relations until the latter 1950's. And even in the last third of the twentieth century, the continent of Africa has yet to prove an important arena of world affairs, as compared to all the other continents except Australia. Potential trouble is there, but it has not developed, despite fears that Africa is ready to burst into flames. American policy toward Africa, as opposed to that for the Middle East, has had to deal with no exigent crises. The reader will protest that the problems incident to independence in the Congo in 1960–1963, the oppression of *apartheid* in the Union of South Africa in recent years, the confusions of Rhodesian independence, the starvation in separatist Biafra—that these troubles, to mention only a few, have been of concern in this country. True enough, and yet these difficulties, whatever dangers they hold for the future, are not yet of the proportion of the Suez crisis of 1956 or even the two other Israeli wars of 1948–1949 and 1967.

In Africa, as in the Middle East, the Second World War and its aftermath compressed half a century of economic change and political evolution into little more than a decade. During the war, the fighting nations of Europe conducted a few minor operations in Africa. The United States government built airfields at Dakar and in Liberia and depended on uranium from the mines of the Belgian Congo. Liberia and Ceylon were the only remaining sources of natural rubber after the fall of the East

Indies to the Japanese early in the war. More important than the war itself was the immediate postwar economic development of Africa. Between the first discovery of diamonds at Kimberley in 1871 and the beginning of the Second World War, the total external investment in Africa south of the Sahara has been estimated at $6,000,000,000, but nearly as much was pumped in during the initial postwar decade. Prices of the products of Africa went up and remained up, seven or eight times higher than the prewar level, until a drop in prices in 1957. Foreign capital poured in, even if most of it went to the already-developed white portion of the continent, to the Union of South Africa and to the Rhodesias. The colonial powers in their last years, the decade or so after the war, showed an awakening social conscience, doubtless in part because of the imminent loss of their empires. They appreciated the returns from their investments, in primary· products either sent to the metropolises or sold elsewhere, *e.g.*, to the United States (cocoa from the British-ruled Gold Coast—present-day Ghana—was a big dollar-earner). Britain, France, Belgium, even Portugal began to put money into the colonies rather than, as had been the prevailing view prior to 1939, taking money out. Perhaps one should say that prior to 1939 there had been more of an insistence on a pay-as-you-go development in colonies; after the Second World War, the idea of pump priming arose. After the war, the French rarely spent less than $250,000,-000 a year in Africa, and virtually every British colony evolved its ten-year development plan with annual subsidies from the mother country of at least $70,000,000. American economic interest in Africa increased too in these years. On the eve of the Second World War, the total direct annual imports to the United States from all of Africa were about $50,000,-000, approximately two per cent of total imports. Adding the imports of African commodities processed in Europe, the total was less than four per cent. American exports to Africa in that period slightly exceeded $100,000,000 in value. By 1955, imports from Africa came to $618,702,-000, or 5.4 per cent of total imports; exports were up to $587,577,000, or 3.8 per cent of total exports. Of the estimated total direct investment of the United States abroad of about $22,000,000,000 at the end of the year 1956, African investment exclusive of Egypt and the Sudan was $836,-000,000. The largest single country of investment was Liberia, but the Liberian figure included over $250,000,000 of "flag of convenience" American shipping, mostly tankers. Meanwhile, from July 1945 through December 1955, the American government gave away a total of $71,-595,000 in Africa, which, however, was only 0.15 per cent of the total American government largesse in that period of more than $46,000,000,000 spent in foreign aid. Much of the $71,595,000 for Africa was military materials.

American interests in Africa were growing by the later 1950's. Some 4,500 American missionaries were helping with the more than 20,000,000 Christian converts in Africa. In non-Muslim Africa most of the people were followers of tribal African religions, and conversion was not as difficult as elsewhere, either in the Middle or Far East. But other than the missionary influence, difficult to evaluate because it included educational and medical assistance, and other than the increasing economic interest, there were not many signs that Africa was going to engage the national interest of the United States in any serious way. As late as October 1957, according to the *Foreign Service List,* the foreign service had only 248 officers in its 33 African posts, whereas it had 256 officers in the single nation of West Germany alone. The African posts concerned themselves largely with American citizens resident in or visiting the localities, and with the colonial rulers. Chester Bowles, well-qualified as an observer of American foreign relations, passed through Africa in 1955 and visited four American consulates, and only one had ever had an African to dinner. Of the 680 book borrowers registered in 1955 in the United States Information Agency in Leopoldville, Belgian Congo, Bowles found that only twelve were Africans. He discovered that the library contained 4,020 books in English and 280 in French. He asked how many people in Leopoldville could read or speak English. "Perhaps 1800, all but a few of them Belgians," was the answer. The library was doing almost nothing to improve American-Congolese relations.

In the latter 1950's the independence movement gained irresistible momentum in Africa, and the United States had to adjust its diplomatic actions to what turned out to be a considerably different political situation. The American government had hesitated to offend the colonial powers in Africa—Portugal, Belgium, France, and Britain—for all were NATO allies. Moreover, it was comforting to believe that Africa stood apart from the cold war as a safe area. Anyway, the United States was so hectically busy in the years after 1945 that, if some alarmist had cried from the rooftops about Africa (and some did), it still would have been difficult to do much. But then came the first announcements of independence: the Sudan (1956), Ghana (1957), Guinea (1958). Gingerliness began to prove costly. The American government waited a month after the Guineans left the French Community before recognizing the fact of their independence —this despite the precedent of eleven minutes in recognizing the State of Israel. Seven months proved necessary before appointment of an American ambassador, and ten before taking the risk of offending General de Gaulle by discussing financial aid with President Sékou Touré. Meanwhile the Soviet Union sent assistance and a large diplomatic and technical mission.

Things no longer could be what they once were. In the old days, and long after 1945, the Soviet Union had almost no opportunity to penetrate Africa. The colonial powers refused to allow the establishment of Russian consulates. Shortly after 1945 the South Africans turned hostile. The Liberians were wary of offending their mentor, the United States. Only Ethiopia had a permanent Russian diplomatic mission prior to the independence of the Sudan. The Soviets were reduced to sponsoring lavish trips to Moscow for African students in Western European universities. Then

The "Twentieth-Century Dilemma."

the flood of newly independent countries gave opportunity to them, and also to Chinese communists. The African nations affected world politics in other ways. As African states began to multiply almost without end, until by 1968 there were a total of forty (not counting Rhodesia, which unilaterally declared its independence in 1965), block voting began in the United Nations. The African group rivaled and then doubled that of Latin America in size, and it became obvious that there was a new and highly sensitive interest of Assembly members in colonial questions, human rights, economic co-operation. The American delegation became more obviously anticolonial as the African states supported by the Soviet Union pushed that touchy issue. Aid and technical assistance began to pour into Africa from all sides—Chinese, Russian, American. Some American tax-payers began to notice that this assistance was costing money, which was true enough. But as a Liberian citizen piquantly said, "You Americans need friends in Africa to support you against the Communists and that kind of friendship costs money."

Every kind of question tended to involve a protest to the United States, and for a while it appeared as if the Congo—which prematurely achieved independence in 1960—was going to be the cross on which American policy was crucified. The Congo trouble was in essence Belgian, not American. The Congo had been a colony ruled by Belgians from *Belgium*. There were no political parties, and no one voted, not even the Belgians who lived there—a condition which, the Belgians pointed out to visitors, proved the absence of racial discrimination. In all the years of their rule the Belgians had prevented the education of Congolese beyond grade school, thinking that this course would prevent the appearance of nationalism. They thereby created a near chaos soon after independence, when the independent government of the Congo almost broke up. In the province of the Congo known as Katanga, the great Belgian copper mining corporation, the Union Minière du Haut Katanga, employing 50,000 workers, paid taxes of several million dollars a month to a local government which under leadership of Moise Tshombe declared independence of the Leopoldville regime. The Union Minière, incidentally, had been doing very well indeed prior to independence, paying annual dividends to its stockholders amounting to thirty per cent of the total income earned by the 1,200,000 African workers in the Congo. Some ob-servers believed that the mining corporation had inspired as well as financed Katanga's secession. The United Nations sought to solve the Katanga dispute, in the course of which occurred the tragic death of Secretary General Dag Hammarskjold in a plane accident in the Congo in 1962. His successor, U Thant, excoriated the secessionist government of Katanga. "Mr. Tshombe," he said,

is a very unstable man, he is a very unpredictable man. The same can be said of his two colleagues, Mr. [Godefroid] Munongo, who pretends to be the interior minister of Katanga, and Mr. [Evariste] Kimbe, who pretends to be the foreign minister. I have tried to get Tshombe and the central Government to negotiate but without any results. I don't know what I can do with such a bunch of clowns.

President Tshombe reacted sharply. "Just yesterday," he told reporters, "Mr. Gardiner, a high United Nations official, proposed to me that I become Vice President of the Congo—me, the clown." Contingents of UN troops eventually enforced unity by breaking up the Katangese government, defeating Tshombe's white mercenaries and miscellaneous African troops. The United States airlifted the UN operation. Several American missionaries were killed, and many Belgian nationals. At last peace settled down on the erstwhile Belgian colony. The United States and the UN had paid dearly for the deficiencies of Belgian colonial rule.

For a brief moment in October 1962, Africa entered the highest American diplomatic-strategic calculations when the government of the United States realized during the Cuban missile crisis that, despite the blockade of Cuba by the American navy, the Soviet government still might be able to fly atomic warheads into Cuba if Soviet planes could refuel in North Africa. The two countries with sufficiently large airports and refueling facilities were Guinea and Senegal. President Kennedy hastily dispatched his local ambassadors to see the leaders of those African nations, and Presidents Sékou Touré and Leopold Senghor at once gave assurance that the Russians could not use the airfields at Conakry and Dakar.

Other than this strange piece of diplomacy, no major questions seem to emerge between the United States and the nations of Africa. As the Congo and the other newly independent countries adjust to new responsibilities, the United States government and its citizens try to be helpful where they can. Investment keeps rising, and by the end of the year 1967 the total United States direct investment in Africa was $2,300,000,000, which represented two and one-half times the book value of such investment at the beginning of the decade. Trade goes up. In 1965 the exports of the United States to Africa crossed the $1,000,000,000 mark. United States exports to Africa (including Egypt) for 1968 were projected to have approached the 1966 record of $1,300,000,000. Hopes go up, too, that African nationalism in the latter twentieth century will not have to experience all of the travail of earlier nationalisms in other parts of the world. The world has become such a dangerous place for that sort of thing.

A CONTEMPORARY DOCUMENT

[American diplomacy toward the Middle East has produced no illustrious state papers—a fact difficult to reconcile with the rhetorical possibilities of an area so full of religious meaning to the average American. President

Lyndon B. Johnson's address of June 19, 1967, to a department of state foreign policy conference for educators is unexciting reading, and not much has been heard about it since its enunciation and automatic publication in the *Department of State Bulletin*, July 10, 1967. The points made in that speech, however, are still American policy as of the present writing, 1969.]

. . . Now, finally, let me turn to the Middle East—and to the tumultuous events of the past months [in particular, the six-day war of early June 1967]. Those events have proved the wisdom of five great principles of peace in the region.

The first and greatest principle is that every nation in the area has a fundamental right to live and to have this right respected by its neighbors.

For the people of the Middle East the path to hope does not lie in threats to end the life of any nation. Such threats have become a burden to the peace, not only of that region but a burden to the peace of the entire world.

In the same way, no nation would be true to the United Nations Charter or to its own true interests if it should permit military success to blind it to the fact that its neighbors have rights and its neighbors have interests of their own. Each nation, therefore, must accept the right of others to live.

This last month, I think, shows us another basic requirement for settlement. It is a human requirement: justice for the refugees.

A new conflict has brought new homelessness. The nations of the Middle East must at last address themselves to the plight of those who have been displaced by wars. In the past, both sides have resisted the best efforts of outside mediators to restore the victims of conflict to their homes or to find them other proper places to live and work. There will be no peace for any party in the Middle East unless this problem is attacked with new energy by all and, certainly, primarily by those who are immediately concerned.

A third lesson from this last month is that maritime rights must be respected. Our nation has long been committed to free maritime passage through international waterways; and we, along with other nations, were taking the necessary steps to implement this principle when hostilities exploded. If a single act of folly was more responsible for this explosion than any other, I think it was the arbitrary and dangerous announced decision that the Strait of Tiran would be closed. The right of innocent maritime passage must be preserved for all nations.

Fourth, this last conflict has demonstrated the danger of the Middle

Eastern arms race of the last 12 years. Here the responsibility must rest not only on those in the area but upon the larger states outside the area. We believe that scarce resources could be used much better for technical and economic development. We have always opposed this arms race, and our own military shipments to the area have consequently been severely limited.

Now the waste and futility of the arms race must be apparent to all the peoples of the world. And now there is another moment of choice. The United States of America, for its part, will use every resource of diplomacy and every counsel of reason and prudence to try to find a better course.

As a beginning, I should like to propose that the United Nations immediately call upon all of its members to report all shipments of all military arms into this area and to keep those shipments on file for all the peoples of the world to observe.

Fifth, the crisis underlines the importance of respect for political independence and territorial integrity of all the states of the area. We reaffirmed that principle at the height of this crisis. We reaffirm it again today on behalf of all. This principle can be effective in the Middle East only on the basis of peace between the parties. The nations of the region have had only fragile and violated truce lines for 20 years. What they now need are recognized boundaries and other arrangements that will give them security against terror, destruction, and war. Further, there just must be adequate recognition of the special interest of three great religions in the holy places of Jerusalem.

These five principles are not new, but we do think they are fundamental. Taken together, they point the way from uncertain armistice to durable peace. We believe there must be progress toward all of them if there is to be progress toward any. . . .

On the basis of peace we offer our help to the people of the Middle East. That land, known to every one of us since childhood as the birthplace of great religions and learning, can flourish once again in time. . . .

ADDITIONAL READING

The American Foreign Policy Library series (published at Harvard) appears to have produced more volumes for the Middle East than for any other section of the world: Lewis V. Thomas and Richard N. Frye, *The United States and Turkey and Iran* (Cambridge, Mass., 1952); Nadav Safran, *The United States and Israel* (1963); Charles F. Gallagher, *The United States and North Africa:*

Morocco, Algeria, and Tunisia (1963); William R. Polk, *The United States and the Arab World* (1965). A general work is *John C. Campbell, *Defense of the Middle East* (rev. ed., New York, 1960). John A. De Novo, *American Interests and Policies in the Middle East: 1900–1939* (Minneapolis, 1963) is a masterly accounting. The British influence in the region has been of importance, and for this subject see M.A. Fitzsimons, *Empire by Treaty: Britain and the Middle East in the Twentieth Century* (Notre Dame, Ind., 1964). Special studies are David H. Finnie, *Pioneers East: The Early American Experience in the Middle East* (Cambridge, Mass., 1967); Joseph L. Grabill's analysis of American missionaries and Middle Eastern diplomacy before, during, and after the First World War, now in press; D. Van der Meulen, *The Wells of Ibn Saud* (New York, 1957), about the development of Saudi Arabia; William A. Eddy, *F.D.R. Meets Ibn Saud* (New York, 1954), by the American minister in the early postwar years who interpreted for President Roosevelt during the meeting of the two heads of state; Stanton Griffis, *Lying in State* (Garden City, N.Y., 1952), the book with the admirable title, by the one-time ambassador to Egypt.

The literature about Israel is large and impossible to set out here. The present author has a chapter on the independence of Israel in his *George C. Marshall* (New York, 1966), and the bibliographical essay of that volume contains explanation of the literature on independence. William Phillips, *Ventures in Diplomacy* (Boston, 1952) contains a chapter on the joint Anglo-American commission. James G. McDonald, *My Mission in Israel: 1948–1951* (New York, 1951), is an outspokenly partisan account by the late ambassador, filled with criticism of the department of state. The well-known crusader, one might say, against Israel, Alfred M. Lilienthal, has published three books hostile to the creation of the new nation: *What Price Israel* (Chicago, 1953); *There Goes the Middle East* (New York, 1957); *The Other Side of the Coin* (New York, 1965). The present writer recalls speaking with an Arab student who without much thought had attempted to pass through customs at Alexandria with one of Lilienthal's books in her luggage; after a seemingly interminable explanation she was allowed through. Edward H. Buehrig is completing a book on the United Nations Relief and Works Agency, presently caring for the displaced Arabs of former Palestine.

An excellent book on the Suez crisis is by *Guy Wint and Peter Calvocoressi, *Middle East Crisis* (London, 1957), a Penguin Special. Sir John Bagot Glubb, knighted after his expulsion from Jordan, has written many books about the region, notably *A Soldier with the Arabs* (New York, 1958). On the Suez crisis, see especially the accounting in Louis L. Gerson, *John Foster Dulles* (New York, 1967). Anthony Eden's *Memoirs: Full Circle* (Boston, 1960) is an intriguing explanation which circles around the question of Great Britain's collusion with the Israelis. Among recent books on the Suez crisis, Herman Finer's *Dulles over Suez* (Chicago, 1964) caused a furor because it purported to be based on conversations with many of the participants. Finer is intensely hostile to Dulles, and his long book sometimes turns into an harangue. Anthony Nutting's *No End of a Lesson: The Inside Story of the*

Suez Crisis (New York, 1967) at last reveals the sorry behavior of the British government under Sir Anthony Eden.

For the Lebanon crisis of 1958 see Leila M. T. Meo, *Lebanon: Improbable Nation* (Bloomington, Ind., 1965). There also is an account in the opening chapters of Charles W. Thayer, *Diplomat* (New York, 1959); and in the recent memoir by *Robert D. Murphy, *Diplomat among Warriors* (New York, 1963).

On the United States and Africa the literature is scattered and sparse, reflecting the slightness of those relations until after the Second World War. J. Gus Liebenow, "United States Policy in Africa South of the Sahara," in Stephen D. Kertesz, ed., *American Diplomacy in a New Era* (Notre Dame, Ind., 1961) is a competent survey, by an acknowledged expert in the new field of African studies. Raymond W. Bixler, *The Foreign Policy of the United States in Liberia* (New York, 1957) is best for that subject. George E. Brooks and Norman R. Bennett, eds., *New England Merchants in Africa: A History through Documents, 1802 to 1865* (Brookline, Mass., 1965) is a thorough accounting. W. E. B. DuBois was one of the first scholars to investigate the history of the African slave trade, and his book has become a classic: *The Suppression of the African Slave Trade* (New York, 1896). See also Peter Duignan and Clarence Clendenen, *The United States and the African Slave Trade: 1619–1862* (Stanford, Calif., 1963), a short account. Hugh G. Soulsby, *The Right of Search and the Slave Trade in Anglo-American Relations: 1814–1862* (Baltimore, 1933) is exhaustive and exhausting. Samuel Eliot Morison, *"Old Bruin"* (Boston, 1967) treats Commodore Perry's experiences on the African station in the 1840's. Parthenia E. Norris in a thesis at Indiana University, "The United States and Liberia," sets out the effort of the Liberians to enslave the natives of the back country, and the investigation of this scandalous situation by the League of Nations in the early 1930's. Chester Bowles, *Africa's Challenge to America* (Berkeley, Calif., and Los Angeles, 1957) was one of the first books to call attention to the emergence of African nationalism in our own times, and what this might mean for the United States. Since then there has been a flood of books, most of them the work of publicists and special pleaders. The best recourse for the student is the journal *Africa Report*, which among other things gives accounting of the new books.

☆ *30* ☆

Good Neighbor in Latin America

No state has the right to intervene in the internal or external affairs of another.
—Article 8 of the Convention on the Rights and Duties of States, adopted by the Seventh International Conference of American States at Montevideo, 1933

President Franklin D. Roosevelt in the early 1930's presided over a marked change in the diplomacy of the United States toward Latin America—the adoption of a policy of the good neighbor, and the abandonment of the role of colossus of the north. This "good neighbor policy" has characterized American relations with the twenty independent republics of the Western Hemisphere down to the present day. At the outset the good neighbor policy contained a certain ambivalence, for to the government in Washington the phrase meant that it would behave with more care and punctilio, whereas to Latin American governments it meant that the United States was subscribing openly, making a public testimony, in favor of nonintervention in their internal or external affairs. The Roosevelt administration was not keen on a pledge of total abstention and never really committed itself to keeping its hands off Latin America. Nonetheless, as time passed it became apparent that the United States no longer was going to play the part of instructor and chastiser of the hemisphere. Despite three interventions in the 1950's and 1960's, of which one was fully the most important world crisis of the entire era after the Second World War, the government in Washington accepted the view of its Latin American friends as to the true, inner meaning of good neighborliness.

821

The phrase "good neighbor," incidentally, was not original with Roosevelt when in his inaugural address of March 4, 1933, he declared, "In the field of world policy, I would dedicate this nation to the policy of the good neighbor . . . ." It was a phrase which in Latin American relations went back at least to the early nineteenth century, and was assuredly one of the most familiar clichés in the language of international intercourse. Roosevelt, indeed, used it in regard to the entire world in his address of 1933. President Herbert Hoover, his predecessor, in 1928–1929 used the phrase on several occasions during a preinaugural tour of Latin America. But it was in Roosevelt's time that American policy obviously changed to that of the good neighbor, and the phrase has become associated, perhaps unjustly, with his name.

1. *Pan-Americanism*

The relations of the United States with Latin America in an organized, international sense, a sense of Pan-Americanism, which led naturally to the policy of the good neighbor, began as early as 1826 when the liberator Simon Bolívar called the Congress of Panama as a convention of the states newly independent of Spain. The United States sent two representatives, who failed to arrive in time for the meeting. Decades later, in 1881, Secretary of State Blaine undertook to revive Pan-Americanism. He primarily wished to halt the War of the Pacific then raging between Chile, Peru, and Bolivia. And there were other troubles. Argentina was in danger of entering this conflict. Mexico and Guatemala were at odds. Costa Rica and Colombia were engaged in a boundary dispute. Largely to preserve peace in the hemisphere, Blaine invited the nations to a conference at Washington scheduled for November 1882. With the death of President Garfield, he left office and his successor as secretary of state, Frederick T. Frelinghuysen, canceled the invitations. Cleveland's secretary of state, Bayard, renewed them for a conference in 1888. In the following year, under Benjamin Harrison, Blaine again became secretary of state and had the pleasure of presiding over the first Pan-American Conference, which met from October 1889 until April 1890. Seventeen Latin American states attended, all except the Dominican Republic. Although the goal of the United States, formation of a customs union, was defeated, and although no machinery was set up for arbitration of disputes—another of Blaine's purposes—the International Bureau of American Republics was established. Later it became known as the Union of American Republics (with its secretariat, the Pan-American Union), and since 1951 as the Organization of American States (so phrased that it might include Canada; the

Pan-American Union is now known as the Secretariat).

There followed three Pan-American Conferences in the early twentieth century—Mexico City in 1901–1902, Rio de Janeiro in 1906, and Buenos Aires in 1910—but little came from them. The fifth Pan-American Conference met at Santiago de Chile in 1923, again with few notable results. The sixth conference, at Havana in 1928, was notable not for the results of the meeting but because of the way in which the affair turned into a virtual rebellion of the Latin American nations against the power and influence of the United States. It was at this meeting that the envoy of El Salvador introduced a resolution against intervention, "that no state has a right to intervene in the internal affairs of another," a proposal directed, of course, against the interventions by the United States. President Coolidge's special representative at the meeting in Havana, Charles Evans Hughes—Coolidge himself had opened the conference by a visit and speech in the Cuban capital—finally could contain himself no longer and stood up in the assemblage to speak impromptu about what he denominated the "interposition" of the United States in the affairs of its neighbors. Hughes's speech, the last defense by American representatives of the policy of intervention, was terse and to the point. The distinguished former secretary of state asked the representative of El Salvador what the United States was to do "when government breaks down and American citizens are in danger of their lives? Are we to stand by and see them butchered in the jungle . . . ?" After this reply the Salvadorean withdrew his motion and the conference turned to other matters, less politically sensitive.

Hughes had made the final defense of the old policy, and even in the year he made it the United States recognized that the old method of intervention was neither effective nor necessary. Both the appearance of Coolidge at Havana and the appointment of Hughes to head the American delegation showed a new policy toward the Latins. The president's old college friend, Dwight Morrow, had gone to Mexico the year before, in 1927, and Morrow's appointment too showed the fear of the Coolidge administration that something needed to be done with Latin American relations. President-elect Hoover undertook his tour of Latin America in November 1928, and although some individuals claimed that he did this to get away from office seekers in the United States, one must guess that there were less strenuous ways of escaping them than making 25 speeches and traveling for ten weeks in ten Latin countries. His tour, like the moves of Coolidge that same year, showed a change of policy.

Hoover in 1930 established through Secretary Stimson the new recognition policy. He tried also, without too much success, to settle a boundary controversey in the Chaco between Paraguay and Bolivia and the Leticia affair between Peru and Colombia (Peru had taken Leticia from Colombia). He also permitted publication of a long memorandum drawn up in 1928 by Undersecretary of State J. Reuben Clark, which after an exhaustive exegesis of 236 pages showed that the Roosevelt Corollary of 1904 had no reason to be attached to the Monroe Doctrine. In a seventeen-page covering letter to Secretary of State Kellogg, Clark explained, in authentic department of state passive-voice style, that "it is not believed that this corollary is justified by the terms of the Monroe Doctrine, however much it may be justified by the application of the doctrine of self-preservation." Clark thus did not deny that the United States possessed the right in Latin American affairs of "interposition of a temporary character" (so Hughes liked to describe American intervention policy), but he denied that the Monroe Doctrine justified intervention. This notable memorandum received reinforcement by statements from Stimson and Undersecretary of State William R. Castle. Stimson declared that the Monroe Doctrine was "a declaration of the United States versus Europe —not of the United States versus Latin America." Castle explained that the Monroe Doctrine "confers no superior position on the United States." The era of tutelage and instruction by force was plainly over.

The good neighbor policy was really a nonintervention policy, and this policy, announced by both Hoover and Franklin D. Roosevelt, was made formal in resolutions of the several Pan-American Conferences that have met since 1933: Montevideo in 1933 (the seventh regular conference), Buenos Aires in 1936 (a special meeting), Lima in 1938 (eighth conference), Mexico City in February-March 1945 (special meeting), and, since the Second World War, Rio de Janeiro in 1947 (special meeting), Bogotá in 1948 (ninth), and Caracas in 1954 (tenth).

The conferences of 1933 and 1936 were probably crucial in obtaining from the United States specific expressions of intention not to interfere any more in Latin America. At Montevideo in 1933 the Latins, having seen the signs of change of policy, rose to the occasion with speech after speech. The distinguished historian of Cuba, Dr. Herminio Portell-Vilá, told the conferees: "Delegates, perhaps no other country has as important and special reason as Cuba for presenting a point of view on the very important problem of intervention or nonintervention. . . . Intervention is not only the 'curse of America,' but as a Cuban internationalist has said, it is the 'curse of curses' of any country, the cause of all evils of the Cuban Republic. Cuba was born with the congenital vice of intervention. . . . I wish to say . . . that the Platt Amendment and the Permanent Treaty have the evil of compulsion, for the people of Cuba did not accept either one freely, due to the fact that the country was full of North American bayonets."

The foreign minister of Argentina, Dr. Carlos Saavedra Lamas, said that any intervention, regardless of the reasons, was bad (Lamas in the mid-1930's received the Nobel Peace Prize for a grand project for peace which many of the Latin nations signed and which virtually duplicated several treaties already concluded for Latin America and the Kellogg-Briand Pact for world peace sponsored in 1928 by the United States).

The Haitian delegate (the Americans were still unwelcome guests in his country) said that American marines and the American government had brought to his nation "indescribable anguish."

To such arguments, based not entirely on history, the United States representatives at Montevideo made no effort to reply, but instead accepted, to the surprise of the other delegates, the crucial part of the Convention on the Rights and Duties of States: "No state has the right to intervene in the internal or external affairs of another." The chief of the American delegation, Secretary of State Hull, added a reservation mentioning "the law of nations as generally recognized and accepted," a broad enough hole to crawl through if the occasion demanded. International law, the secretary knew, was sufficiently obscure about intervention so that to invoke it was to invoke uncertainty.

The Montevideo pledge, Hull nonetheless announced, marked "the beginning of a new era." To effect its resolution for a new course, the United States evacuated Nicaragua in 1933, and the marines left Haiti in 1934. The Platt Amendment for Cuba was abrogated by a treaty between the United States and Cuba in 1934, and a similar treaty abandoned the American protectorate of the Dominican Republic in 1940.

At the special Buenos Aires Conference of 1936 called by the United States, the American government made a strenuous effort to better its friendships in Latin America. President Roosevelt journeyed to the Argentine capital on a cruiser to open the conference in person, and the United States agreed to an undertaking of nonintervention more inclusive than that of Montevideo: "The High . . . Parties declare inadmissible the intervention of any one of them, directly or indirectly, and for whatever reason, in the internal or external affairs of any of the Parties." The text did not define intervention, thus leaving a useful loophole for the United States. Seeking to close this gap, the Latin states invited the Roosevelt administration to sign at Buenos Aires a Declaration of Principles of Inter-American Solidarity and Co-operation, in which the signatories "proclaim their absolute juridical sovereignty, their unqualified respect for their respective sovereignties and the existence of a common democracy throughout America." But this was put in the form of a declaration, rather than a convention which after ratifications by the several states would have been binding. Undersecretary of State Sumner Welles, referring to the nonbinding declaration, said diplomatically that it was a Magna Carta of American freedom and collective security.

The last two words of Welles's pronouncement, which appeared in international verbiage about this time, indicated that the purposes of the United States in the Western Hemisphere were changing. The good neighbor policy had begun at the end of the 1920's as a reaction to the policy of intervention, a policy which was no longer necessary to protect the canal—matters in Europe seemed peaceful enough in 1928—and which had raised much ill will in Latin America. Intervention policy needed to be replaced by a policy more in line with Latin American nationalism and *amour propre*. By the year 1936, Nazi Germany was moving actively in Europe to effect revision of the Treaty of Versailles, with the plan that soon emerged of tearing up the treaty and creating a new order in Europe and perhaps the world. Because of this new exigency, the United States at the Buenos Aires Conference began to speak in terms of collective security, which thereafter became the theme of Pan-American meetings. When war came in Europe, the Declaration of Panama of 1939, a result of a meeting of foreign ministers of the American republics, established a security zone around the Americas south of Canada, which by 1941 was patrolled in vital areas by warships of the United States. The Declaration of Havana in 1940, made by another meeting of the foreign ministers, transformed into a Pan-American task what had long been a part of United States foreign policy, the No-Transfer Principle, that territory held in the Western Hemisphere by a non-American power could not be transferred to another non-American power. The declaration of 1940 was designed to prevent Dutch and French territories in the New World from passing under German control after the fall of those nations in the Nazi spring offensive of 1940.

In the war of 1941–1945 against Germany and Japan, the United States found that the Latin American republics all came to its support in one form or another. Eventually all of them declared war, and two of the republics, Brazil and Mexico, sent military contingents abroad—Brazil sent a division to Italy and Mexico an air squadron to the Far East. The Cuban navy co-operated against German submarines in the Gulf of Mexico. The American government obtained military bases on the soil of Brazil, Cuba, Ecuador, and Panama. In exchange for this assistance the United States gave all the republics except Argentina and Panama (Argentina did not declare war until March 24, 1945) $491,456,432.64 in lend-lease supplies.

Argentina proved difficult until almost the end of the war—a "bad neighbor," Secretary Hull called that country in his memoirs—and the United States used practically every means except severe economic sanctions and war to bring the Argentines into line. Most of the other Latin

American nations gave lip service to the efforts by the United States to coerce Argentina. They were afraid of Argentina and also did not wish a principle of coercion introduced into their relations when with so much trouble they had just rid themselves, they hoped, of American intervention.

The Argentines, declaring war on Germany in March 1945, were able to take part at the United Nations Conference in San Francisco when it met in April 1945. But after the war as during the war, the Argentines refused their co-operation to the United States, and in the immediate postwar era the fascist government of President Juan D. Perón in Argentina probably caused more concern in the United States than did any other development in Latin America. In its policy toward Argentina during Perón's rise and rule, the United States government seems to have been thoroughly unsuccessful. In 1943–1945 it exerted heavy pressure to prevent Perón's rise to power, and in 1946 at the time of Perón's candidacy for president of Argentina the department of state published a Blue Book virtually denouncing as a Hitler satellite the government of a country with which the United States maintained diplomatic relations. Perón enlisted the indignation of his countrymen at this interference and was handily elected president. Later the United States made an uneasy peace with his regime in return for measures taken in Argentina against former Nazis and communists. By 1955 the United States was beginning to give the dictator financial support. Thereupon his countrymen rose up and threw him out. After his fall and exile, Perón was seen to have been a naive, childish individual who had succeeded in almost ruining Argentina's economy and bankrupting its government.

American diplomacy toward most of the Latin republics other than Argentina was not nearly so eventful after 1945 as in the years before the war. President Harry S. Truman in April 1945, upon assuming the presidency, said that he would continue the good neighbor policy. But there were no large gestures of the sort made by his predecessor at Montevideo and at Buenos Aires. Since the end of the Second World War the problems of the United States in Latin America usually—with three notable exceptions set forth in the following pages—have seemed small compared with those in other areas of the world. For this reason, perhaps, and because in essentials the good neighbor policy had been accomplished by 1945, there was a lapse of diplomacy in the region.

The only international act in Latin American relations after the war which has had any considerable importance is the Inter-American Treaty of Reciprocal Assistance (the "Rio Pact") of September 2, 1947, concluded at the special conference held expressly for the purpose in Rio de Janeiro that year. This treaty, under article 51 of the UN Charter, which allows regional agreements for collective security, set forth that in case of a dangerous "fact or situation" short of armed attack, the parties would hold a special consultation and decide what to do. And under the new treaty there was not merely a right but an obligation of every American state to help meet an armed attack upon another American state or its territory until the UN Security Council should take effective measures to repel the aggression. The nature of the action to be taken by the American states was to be determined by a two-thirds vote in a meeting of foreign ministers of the Western Hemisphere, parties to the dispute not voting. No state could be required to use armed force without its consent —hence the United States by vote of the foreign ministers might have to cut diplomatic relations with another state, or cut trade, but it did not have to use (without its consent) armed force. The treaty went into effect after ratification by two-thirds of the signatories in December 1948 (it became effective, of course, only among the signatories who had ratified). In due time all twenty-one republics adhered. This was the principal formal diplomatic act of the postwar era.

2. *Guatemala*

It might appear curious that in the 1950's, when the Rio Pact presumably was working, the United States government intervened in Guatemala, and that in the next decade it intervened in Cuba and the Dominican Republic. Shades of Theodore Roosevelt! Was the era of the 1950's and 1960's, then, a throwback to the older ways of behavior? Actually the three interventions of recent times, such apparent contradictions of Pan-Americanism, of the policy of the good neighbor, all had their separate rationales and, considered individually, made sense. They were not deviations from the policy of inter-American co-operation to which the United States had turned after the First World War. Each of these interventions concerned international communism, and for reasons peculiar to the inter-American movement and the countries which were parts of it, the United States believed that it had to act unilaterally, one might say under the Monroe Doctrine, to protect its vital interests. The members of the Organization of American States did not greatly question these interventionist moves by the United States, which seems to say that they covertly approved of them.

The first of the interventions, in Guatemala, involved mainly the rise to power of a talented local troublemaker, Jacobo Arbenz Guzmán, who wished to succeed President Juan José Arévalo. Arévalo had been in office since the late 1940's and constitutionally could not succeed himself. Arbenz's supporters in 1949 arranged the assassination of their leader's principal rival for the presidency, the chief of the armed forces, Francisco Javier Arana. Arbenz in January 1953 was inaugurated president of the republic. Thereupon difficulties arose. The country seemed to be turning toward communism. The communists in Guatemala came out in the open and were extremely active. Trouble broke out in Honduras, where Arbenz seemed to be causing strikes by labor organizations. A Swedish freighter, the *Alfhem*, sailing from Stettin, brought into Puerto Barrios a cargo of 15,424 cases of Czechoslovak-made military equipment, totaling 2,000 tons of arms, which were unloaded in the presence of the minister of defense.

At Caracas in March 1954, at the Tenth Inter-American Conference, Secretary Dulles had an experience which showed which way the wind was blowing and what the United States might do about it. Dulles was seeking to obtain a resolution against communist subversion and came to see that such a resolution would prove attractive to the Latin American nations because it would provide a basis for intervention by the United States in the affairs of a state threatened by communism but, at the same time, would allow the other states of the hemisphere to stand aside and preserve the purity of the nonintervention doctrine while the United States did the dirty work. It was awkward for the Latin states themselves to intervene, even for a good reason like getting rid of communism. Communism was entering Latin America under the guise of democratic nationalism, and the communists would be the first to raise the banner of nonintervention. The nations were willing for Dulles to take the lead, and the vote on his resolution proved extremely interesting: 17–1; two states abstained—Argentina and Mexico; Costa Rica was absent; the objector was Guatemala.

The Guatemalan crisis came to white heat early in June 1954 when Arbenz proclaimed a dictatorship, in the course of which there was cold-blooded killing of opponents. In mid-June a force of a few hundred revolutionists led by Colonel Carlos Enrique Castillo Armas invaded from Honduras and within two weeks gained control of the country. Arbenz went to Czechoslovakia. Guatemala returned temporarily to peaceful ways, but Castillo was assassinated some months later.

Who in the United States government took the leading role in this first postwar intervention? This point is of interest, because it was commonly said at the time that the Central Intelligence Agency had masterminded the Guatemalan revolution. Was the CIA pursuing a private foreign policy? Did it have the active support of President Eisenhower? It is surprising to relate that the leading part in the government's decision in favor of Castillo was not taken by CIA Director Allen W. Dulles, supposedly Castillo's *éminence grise*, but by the chief executive of the United

States. According to the first volume of Eisenhower's memoirs, published in 1963, in the midst of the crisis the assistant secretary of state for inter-American affairs, Henry F. Holland, armed with three large law books, one day joined a small group in the presidential office. The rebels in Guatemala had lost two of their three old bombing planes, and the question was whether the United States government should replace them. Holland was against any American action.

"What do you think Castillo's chances would be without the aircraft?" Eisenhower asked Allen Dulles.

The answer was unequivocal: "About zero."

"Suppose we supply the aircraft. What would the chances be then?"

Again the CIA chief did not hesitate: "About 20 per cent."

Eisenhower considered the matter carefully, knowing about the blame that always descended upon the United States in any cases or supposed cases of intervention in the affairs of Latin America. But he "knew from experience the important psychological impact of even a small amount of air support. In any event, our proper course of action—indeed my duty —was clear to me. We would replace the airplanes."

It was a small affair, and no blame appears to have come to rest upon Eisenhower's action, which after all he did not reveal until nine years later. By that time it did not seem like an intervention at all.

3. *Cuba—the real crisis*

Tad Szulc and Karl E. Meyer, reporters respectively for the New York *Times* and Washington *Post*, have written that there is "a curious contrast in American relations with Cuba, Puerto Rico and the Philippines—the three territories whose destiny was determined by the Spanish-American War." In the Philippines and Puerto Rico, which became American colonies, the United States established a series of reforms which if not altogether successful seem to have been modestly so. At any rate, in both of these places a large pro-American sentiment appeared which has flourished down to the present day. In Cuba the Americans arranged for independence in 1902. American lighthanded supervision in Cuba appears to have produced a veritable hive of anti-Americanism. All of which seems to say, The more imperialism the better.

In seeking to understand how Cuban-American relations reached their tangled state of the early 1960's, one also should remember the condescension of such early American diplomatic representatives as Norval Richardson, mentioned in chapter seventeen. Moreover, Cuba boasted a fairly large society and culture at the time of the Spanish-American War, whereas Puerto Rico and the Philippines were more backward. Could it be that Cuban sensibilities were therefore more easily offended?

The turns and twists of international affairs are difficult to analyze, and it may be that, as in so many cases, the plunging of Cuban-American affairs into the abyss of 1961–1962 and the enmity which has continued for the rest of the decade had no roots in logic, and that it was the chance appearance of a "maximum leader," Fidel Castro, who has raised anti-Americanism into an article of faith for his fellow Cubans. When Castro departs from his authority, as sometime he must, perhaps a resurgence of friendly feeling for the United States will follow his exit, although by that time the Cuban educational system may have twisted the minds of a generation of his countrymen.

Castro, one must say, did not come to power because of anti-Americanism, but because of the revulsive dictatorships of his two principal predecessors, Gerardo Machado and Fulgencio Batista, whose names together were synonymous with Cuban politics for thirty and more years, from the mid-1920's through the 1950's. Machado entered the presidency in 1925. His dictatorship became oppressive when the world-wide Great Depression descended upon Cuba after 1930. At last he promised genuinely free elections for the year 1934; but in August 1933 a violent general strike paralyzed the island and Machado was forced to retire. The maker of governments thereafter, until the appearance of Castro, was Colonel Batista, whose rule, like that of Machado, became ever more oppressive until he too was forced from office.

In discussing Castro's rise to power and the American intervention which followed, it is of some interest to point out that years before, in 1933, just after Machado had gone, a considerable discussion occurred within the American government as to whether the United States should intervene against the successor regime. Had the United States intervened and remained, Castro today might be an American citizen. There was fear in 1933 that Cuba was turning unduly radical, perhaps communist. Ambassador Sumner Welles in Havana asked for the marines. Ambassador Josephus Daniels in Mexico—secretary of the navy during President Wilon's intervention there a generation earlier—argued vociferously with his former assistant secretary who had become president, Franklin D. Roosevelt, that the United States should not intervene in Cuba. In the summer of 1933 Daniels wrote the president a pointed letter:

You know that the things we were forced to do in Haiti was [sic] a bitter pill to me, for I have always hated any foreign policy that even hinted of imperialistic control. Frank Lane knew my feeling, and during the Haitian direction, with mock seriousness, he would rise at the Cabinet meeting and say to our colleagues "Hail the King of Haiti." The danger of that pivotal country, so near our shores, falling into the control of some European nation, added to the business of assassinating presidents, made it imperative for us to take the course followed. . . . I never did wholly approve of that Constitution of Haiti you had a hand in framing or the elections we held by which our hand-picked President of Haiti was put in office. I expect, in the light of experience, we both regret the necessity of denying even a semblance of "self-determination" in our control of Haiti, when we had to go in and end revolutions or see some European government do so. Your "Good Neighbor" policy will not, I hope, be subjected to any such emergency as we were up against.

Roosevelt saw the light. He deprecated any talk of armed intervention in Cuba. He told reporters on September 6, 1933, that the United States was not sending any massive naval forces to Cuba, but only "three, four, five little fellows." He told them to "Lay off on this intervention stuff. As you know, that is absolutely the last thing we have in mind. We don't want to do it." At his press conference two days later, he reminded them that the American naval forces in Cuban waters were "little bits of things." Early in 1934, after Batista had replaced an objectionable president with a more acceptable leader, the American government recognized the new Cuban regime.

Batista's rule in Cuba lasted for twenty-five years, and during this long era the American government tried to allay tensions between the two countries. It gave up the Platt Amendment in 1934. That same year it concluded a reciprocity treaty under which Cuban sugar obtained a price in the United States of approximately two cents above the price in the world market. Some people believed that this bounty only kept Cuban sugar noncompetitive with domestic cane and beet sugar. True enough, but the American government had singled out Cuban sugar for this advantage in the domestic market and could just as well have placed a tariff on all foreign sugar. The critics also said that the bounty helped American sugar companies in Cuba. Likewise true. It also helped make Cuban sugar workers the highest paid in the world, except for those in the United States and its possessions. Labor costs in Cuba were so high that the island's sugar had to sell at cost on the world market.

As Batista's mandate began to run out in the 1950's, the American government made some efforts to persuade him to step down. These efforts tended to be countered by the friendliness of Ambassador Earl E. T. Smith. There did not seem to be great danger whether Batista stayed or left. The state department assumed that the American-equipped Cuban army would prevent too far a swing to the left. Secretary of State Dulles paid little attention to Latin America. President Eisenhower likewise was concerned with European and Asian problems, unlike his brother Milton, the president of Johns Hopkins University, who undertook several Latin American missions and later wrote a book entitled *The Wine is Bitter* (1963).

Then Batista, together with his entourage, departed by plane on January 1, 1959, for the Dominican Republic, and Cuba suddenly belonged to a young man who for two years had been carrying on an insurrection from the Sierra Maestra Mountains. Castro and a few followers had holed up there, issued pronouncements, given interviews to American correspondents. The Cuban government collapsed into the hands of this then thirty-two-year-old bearded revolutionary, over six feet tall, dressed in fatigues, riding in a jeep, and carrying a submachine gun.

The first months of Castro's rule probably were confusing to him, but they were more confusing to the government of the United States. The Eisenhower administration recognized the Castro regime six days after the fall of Batista, and American firms in Cuba hastened to pay their taxes in advance to show their approval. In February 1959, Castro became premier, preferring not to take the title of president. Already, however, the executions had begun, circus-like affairs, for the trials were held in stadiums and other public places. Cuba had no tradition of executions, and the constitution of 1940 which Castro said he would restore had prohibited the death penalty. Americans, and many Cubans, were horror-struck. President Eisenhower was understandably angry when, in that spring of 1959, the American Society of Newspaper Editors invited Castro to the American capital to give a speech. Eisenhower would have liked to have denied him a visa. He did not invite him to the White House. Castro nonetheless went to the capital of the erstwhile colossus of the north, now the good neighbor, and made the speech. It was a neighborly address, in which he denied any communist influence in his government.

It was after his American trip that relations rapidly deteriorated. Shortly after his return to Cuba the revolution began to pick up speed and become not merely a Cuban affair but one for all of Latin America, even the world. In 1959, the Castro-styled Year of the Revolution, Cuban propaganda began to spread leaflets in Spanish and English in the American South and in New York's Harlem urging Puerto Ricans and American Negroes to rise against oppression. The Cubans made contact with the American Indians too, and in July 1959 the premier received Mad Bear, an Iroquois nationalist, as a guest in Havana. The next year, 1960, was the Year of the Agrarian Reform, and before that year ended Castro had seized the approximately one billion dollars of American-owned property in Cuba. The United States was organizing an invasion. That autumn he came again to the United States, this time to New York to attend the Assembly of the United Nations in company with many other foreign leaders, including Nikita Khrushchev, Jawaharlal Nehru, and Marshal Tito. This was the occasion on which Castro and company at first resided in a midtown New York hotel and then moved uptown to the Theresa in Harlem, leaving behind the litter of cigar butts, chicken feathers, uncooked steaks, and towels with shoeshine stains. When he spoke at the UN, Castro took four and one half hours to present his case. His most memorable remark was that the two American presidential contenders of that year, John F. Kennedy and Richard M. Nixon, lacked "political brains," for which comment he was reprimanded by the chair. At this UN Assembly session he met Khruschchev and physically embraced him. Khrushchev feigned delight at the encounter, and probably was delighted, although the Russian leader afterward told Nehru privately that Castro was a "romantic."

Early in 1960 the Central Intelligence Agency surreptitiously began to move against Castro, and one thing led to another and eventually to the ill-fated invasion effort of April 17, 1961. As planning matured, the CIA (known jocularly to the co-operating Cuban exiles as the Cuban Invasion Authority) mounted its forces in Guatemala, the locale of its successful effort against communism a few years before. The plans for invasion were approved by the US joint chiefs of staff. Their execution then was delayed until after the inauguration of the Kennedy administration. The new

The CIA fails in Cuba.

president approved the invasion project because it seemed so far along and because it had such august backing, not merely by Director Dulles but by the joint chiefs. He did put a condition on the invasion, that the United States forces must not be directly involved—that is, there would be no air cover. When the 1,500 Cuban exiles went ashore into the marshy Bay of Pigs, this condition proved sufficient to ensure their defeat. One should point out, though, that Castro could have pitted 250,000 militia against the invaders, a force which, whether or not the invaders had airpower, would have overwhelmed them. One result of this fiasco was that President Kennedy never afterward placed full faith in the advice of the joint chiefs and that he thereafter maintained a command post in the White House from which to watch over the projects of the sprawling United States government.

A fiasco is itself bad enough for a large and prestigious government, but it is forgivable. This fiasco, however, led directly into the most frightening international crisis since the end of the Second World War—the Cuban missile crisis of October 1962.

The essential point of contention in the missile crisis was that, as President Kennedy subsequently said, the Soviet leaders were trying to change materially the balance of power and were seeking to do it on territory in the Western Hemisphere. The Soviet Union's difficulty vis-à-vis the United States in 1962, which impelled them into this Cuban adventure, was the same trouble that had plagued the USSR ever since the Russians had exploded their first atomic weapon in 1949, namely, that the Americans had been staying far ahead in the atomic weapons race. The Soviets seemed much stronger than they were. They held a local superiority in Europe and had threatened the French and British with missiles during the Suez crisis of 1956—safe in the knowledge that the United States did not approve of the diplomacy of its NATO allies. In the next year, 1957, the Soviets had been able—as mentioned in chapter twenty-six —to put up their first sputnik, evidence of their superiority in the space race. To undiscerning peoples of the world it seemed as if the Russians, given their actions in 1956–1957, were ahead in the atomic race. Such was hardly the true state of affairs. By the end of the Eisenhower administration, the Americans held a commanding lead not merely in nuclear weapons but in ability to take those weapons into Russian territory. In brief, the Soviet Union knew that the missile gap—so ignorantly talked about by Kennedy supporters in the 1960 presidential race in the United States—was not in its favor. The new administration soon recognized its power and openly asserted it. The Soviets were embarrassed and appear to have been looking for a "quick fix" for their position, a short-term arrangement of missiles on Cuban soil until they could install hard-site solid-fueled intercontinental ballistic missiles in great numbers on their own soil, and until they could construct missile-launching nuclear submarines.

Premier Castro's quarrel with the United States became Soviet Russia's grand opportunity. Castro's apparent fear of the United States might make the emplacement of Russian missiles seem a sensible reaction to American power, justifying to the world's innocents what was a sheer power play by the Soviet Union. For it is evident now that the kinds of missiles almost emplaced in Cuba by Premier Khrushchev would have far exceeded in quantity and quality the requirements of Castro—if such there were— for protection against the United States. After all, Castro only needed one nuclear-armed missile with a range sufficient to get to Miami. He did not need the capacity to blanket the United States as far as the Mississippi River. And who knows what kind of weaponry the Soviets would have brought into Cuba if President Kennedy had failed to react against the weapons the Russians did cart in? By the time the president acted against the Russians (with Castro, of course, by that time unwittingly in the middle) there were at least 42 Il-28 light bombers and an equal number of strategic missiles in Cuba. Technicians were readying nine missile sites. Six of them had four launchers each for so-called medium-range ballistic missiles (range: 1,100 miles), and three of them were fixed sites for intermediate-range missiles (range: 2,200 miles). The three fixed sites each had four launching positions.

The Kennedy administration through U-2 reconnaissance discovered precisely what the Soviets were up to, and after an extraordinary series of conferences and consultations at the White House, state department, and Pentagon, the president decided upon a careful course. He recently had read Barbara Tuchman's *The Guns of August*, an account of how the major powers of Europe had been drawn into the First World War largely out of miscalculation. He vowed to his intimates that if some future historian were to consider his acts in the missile crisis it would be understood that "we made every effort to find peace and every effort to give our adversary room to move"; he was not going to have anyone write, at a later date, a book entitled "The Missiles of October" and say that the United States had failed to do all it could to preserve peace. The president already had given the Russians a warning, to no avail. On September 4 he had said that he would not permit installation in Cuba of surface-to-surface missiles. The Soviet news agency Tass had disclaimed such an intention, and Ambassador Anatoly Dobrynin in private had denied flatly that the Russian government contemplated such a course. The Soviets, however, had refused to take Kennedy seriously, presumably because of the maladroit invasion of the year before, perhaps also because Khrushchev had underestimated Kennedy's nerve during a meeting in Vienna in the summer of 1961 when the president had confessed to the Russian leader that the Cuban invasion had been a mistake, perhaps partly because Khrushchev had been able to make such a fiesta of the U-2 affair of 1960, inspiring many Americans to feelings of remorse. Khrushchev had ignored Kennedy's first warning and displayed every evidence of belligerency. The president therefore gave the Russians a public warning which no one, in or out of government, in the United States or the Soviet Union, could mistake. There would be no miscalculation by the Russian government in 1962.

On October 22, Kennedy in a television "spectacular"—of a sort which no one on this earth wishes to see again—announced his policy about the missiles in a manner that not merely Khrushchev but anyone listening and watching could understand. ". . . it shall be the policy of this nation," he said, "to regard any nuclear missile launched from Cuba against any nation in the Western Hemisphere as an attack by the Soviet Union on the United States requiring a full retaliatory response upon the Soviet Union."

The unnerving, frightening aspect of this public message was not its content but the fact that it was public. It was a facedown. It was eyeball-to-eyeball, to use a current graphic expression. Kennedy raised up the national interest of the United States in a public showdown with the Russians. There always is danger that the extreme publicity in such a move will produce equal intransigence on the other side. In October 1962 there then could have been no recourse except Armageddon.

The president, one should add, believed that he had no choice, and that if he did not act he would be impeached. "It looks really mean, doesn't it?," he said to his brother Robert. "But then, really there was no other choice. If they get this mean on this one in our part of the world, what will they do on the next?"

Two days after the address of October 22, the government of the United States, with unanimous support of the Organization of American States, inaugurated a blockade of Cuban waters, and the grand question became whether the Soviet ships then approaching, laden with military hardware, would try to run the blockade. On that Wednesday morning, October 24, an intelligence report stated that two Russian vessels, the *Gagarin* and the *Komiles*, accompanied by a Soviet submarine, were nearing the 500-mile blockade barrier. They were within an hour of interception. The aircraft carrier *Essex* was to signal the submarine by sonar and ask it to surface and identify itself, and if the Russian craft refused then the Americans would drop depth charges with small explosives until the

The Executive Committee meets in the White House during the Cuban missile crisis. The President is bending over the table at the right, next to Secretary of State Rusk. Robert Kennedy is standing to the far left.

sub surfaced. Robert Kennedy in his book *Thirteen Days* remembered his brother sitting in a White House conference room during this dreadful moment of waiting:

His hand went up to his face and covered his mouth. He opened and closed his fist. His face seemed drawn, his eyes pained, almost gray. We stared at each other across the table. For a few fleeting seconds, it was almost as though no one else was there and he was no longer the President. Inexplicably, I thought of when he was ill and almost died; when he lost his child; when we learned that our oldest brother had been killed; of personal times of strain and hurt. The voices droned on . . . .

Tension in the room that dread morning was broken when a messenger brought a note to Director John A. McCone of the CIA disclosing that some Soviet ships approaching the quarantine line had stopped dead in the water, a sign that Moscow was not going to offer an immediate confrontation.

The crisis wore on for several days as messages went back and forth between Kennedy and Khrushchev. Russian technicians in Cuba were hurriedly uncrating and assembling the Il-28 bombers, and working frantically to ready the missile sites. On Friday night, October 26, Khrushchev sent an emotional message which showed how far the relations between Russia and the United States had deteriorated:

If you have not lost your self-control, and sensibly conceive what this might lead to, then, Mr. President, we and you ought not now to pull on the ends of the rope in which you have tied the knot of war, because the more the two of us pull, the tighter that knot will be tied. And a moment may come when that knot will be tied so tight that even he who tied it will not have the strength to untie it, and then it will be necessary to cut that knot, and what that would mean is not for me to explain to you, because you yourself understand perfectly of what terrible forces our countries dispose. Consequently, if there is no intention to tighten that knot, and thereby to doom the world to the catastrophe of thermonuclear war, then let us not only relax the forces pulling on the ends of the rope, let us take measures to untie that knot. We are ready for this.

But the end of the crisis was no easy matter, even after the Soviet premier had sent his message of Friday, October 26. The next day, Saturday, the president received another message, not so emotional, indeed rather stiff in tone, presumably composed in the Soviet foreign office. By this time the president's advisers had analyzed and reanalyzed the Soviet position so much that they were becoming confused. Any course of action seemed fraught with danger. No action at all was impossible; time was running out, what with the Soviet technicians in Cuba hurrying their work. The president's brother, Robert, and the president's counsel, Theodore C. Sorensen, suggested a solution. They recalled that an important official of the Soviet embassy in Washington had approached a reporter for the American Broadcasting Company, John Scali, and proposed that the Soviet Union would remove the missiles in Cuba, under United Nations supervision and inspection, if the United States would lift the blockade and give a pledge not to invade Cuba. The Soviet official had asked Scali to transmit this proposition to the American government, which Scali had done. Robert Kennedy and Sorensen contended that the president should "accept" this proposal, even though it was unofficial and Khrushchev could have disavowed it. In forty-five minutes that Saturday afternoon the two men wrote a draft of a note. The president worked on it, had it typed, and signed it.

At last, on Sunday, October 28, Khrushchev backed down and agreed to take the missiles out of Cuba. He had received far more of a confrontation than he had anticipated. In his behavior there was something of an analogy to the confusion of Talleyrand many, many years before, during the crisis over "XYZ." But how high the stakes had risen since that eighteenth-century misunderstanding over a few million dollars!

Shortly after the premier's decision the Soviets dismantled their bases and hoisted their missiles into the holds of waiting ships. The American

A Soviet missile-laden ship leaving Cuba, accompanied by a U.S. Navy vessel. Visible overhead is the wing of a U.S. Navy patrol plane.

navy convoyed the Soviet vessels out of Cuban waters and watched them slowly sail off into the Atlantic, back to their distant bases in the USSR.

For students who wished to learn lessons from the Cuban missile crisis, insofar as one could learn from an affair in which the full truth may never be known, a notable fact was that many well-meaning Americans had not understood that the Soviet Union had made a large aggressive move in the cold war. To a remarkable extent the Soviets were able to hoodwink people. There was a considerable feeling that Castro needed protection against the United States, however wrong Castro was. Some individuals also believed that, after all, the United States maintained missiles abroad, and why should not the Soviet Union have its overseas missile bases? Letters appeared in newspapers asking for a mutual missile withdrawal, that the Soviet Union should take its weapons out of Cuba in exchange for removal of the squadron of fifteen American Jupiter missiles then on Turkish soil.

The Jupiter issue was a fairly complicated proposition, and public opinion easily could have misunderstood it—and of course did so, to the benefit of the Soviet Union. Here, surely, was one more evidence of how a considerable amount of American opinion sometimes can be led by the nose. In retrospect it is disquieting to see how the Soviet Union was able to exploit public ignorance during a tremendous international crisis. At one point during the 1962 crisis, Khrushchev requested an exchange of the American Jupiters in Turkey for his own country's missiles then in Cuba. The Russian leader knew what he was doing. He was putting an outrageously plausible face upon what had been a great act of aggression. The Americans who argued for an exchange had no idea that the 1,100-mile Jupiter system was equal only in part to the Russian delivery system being established in Cuba. The United States had no missiles in Turkey or anywhere else equivalent to the intermediate-range, 2,200-mile missiles Khrushchev had shipped into Castro's island. Moreover, because of the near-certain American ability to strike the Soviet Union with atomic weapons carried from within the continental United States, or by submarines, and the USSR's then very weak delivery capability beyond intermediate ranges, the emplacement of Soviet missiles in Cuba was a far more important military advantage than was a comparable American base in Turkey. Also, if the Russians had wished only to force the United States into withdrawing the missiles from Turkey, there were easier ways to do that than to emplace missiles in Cuba. In previous months President Kennedy had been anxious to get the Jupiters out of Turkey, for the stationing of Polaris submarines in the Mediterranean had made the liquid-fueled, "soft"-sited Jupiters virtually useless. Secretary of State Rusk had approached the Turkish government in the spring of 1962, but the Turks had balked about removal of the missiles. The president had instructed the state department to go ahead anyway, negotiating withdrawal of the missiles whether the Turks liked it or not. The state department made another approach. The Turks balked again. Nothing more happened, though Kennedy assumed that everything was being arranged. During the Cuban missile crisis the president then discovered to his consternation that his own government, through the state department's inefficiency, had given the Russians a plausible justification for the Cuban affair, permitting them to argue that they were only doing in Cuba what the United States had done in Turkey. The state department's failure also had given the Russians an opportunity, if the United States had attacked Cuba, to attack Turkey and thereby challenge the whole structure of NATO (would the predominantly European NATO allies respond to an attack on the Turks?). And would the United States, with or without NATO support, thereupon fire the Jupiters at the Soviet Union? It was a complex situation, and no one who understood the Jupiter question could allow it to enter the Cuban equation. But public opinion, not being privy to the United States government's conversations with the Turks, not understanding how obsolete were the Jupiters, or what the United States would do with the Jupiters if the Russians attacked Turkey, tended to fall in with the barefaced Russian suggestion of a trade. Even the American ambassador to the United Nations, Adlai Stevenson, usually a man of judgment, argued in a presidential staff meeting that the United States should withdraw its Jupiters from Turkey and its missiles from Italy, plus give up the Guantanamo naval base, in exchange for a withdrawal of the Russian missiles from Cuba.

Another instructive—and also, one should add, more reassuring—facet of the crisis was the fact that Berlin had not become a part of the crisis. A previous chapter has shown how much of American diplomacy toward Europe in the 1940's and 1950's was conducted with concern for the exposed American position in Berlin—deep in the Russian zone, a hostage for American good behavior, just like the Philippines in the Far East after 1898. President Kennedy was on the lookout for trouble, remarking: "We must expect that they will close down Berlin—make the final preparations for that." But when the crisis came over Cuba, Berlin did not enter the conversations. Berlin would have complicated an already too-complex equation. It might have made the Cuban crisis too dangerous. Russian action in Berlin could have triggered the American missile forces. Soviet Foreign Minister Gromyko said to the Supreme Soviet in December 1962 that the Cuban crisis "made many people think how the whole matter might have developed if yet another crisis in Central Europe had been added to the critical events around Cuba."

After the Cuban crisis, American prestige, so hurt by the invasion effort of 1961, was not merely restored but mightily increased. President Kennedy did not threaten a rain of American atomic weapons on the Soviet Union to raise American prestige, but his successful resolution of the crisis served as such a threat.

Parenthetically one should note that Kennedy gave orders to all of his officials never to claim a victory over the Soviet Union. "He respected Khrushchev for properly determining what was in his own country's interest and what was in the interest of mankind," the president's brother recalled. "If it was a triumph, it was a triumph for the next generation and not for any particular government or people."

It is also of interest that some years later, after Kennedy's assassination, and after Khrushchev's fall from power, the ex-premier in moody retirement was interviewed by an enterprising American reporter and said that, of all the Americans he had known, the one he respected most was John F. Kennedy.

In the shaking out of positions and reputations that occurred after the crisis of October 1962, no one emerged with a more pathetic appearance than the premier of Cuba. Castro with his jeep and submachine gun had become almost irrelevant to the great scene he had helped create. He did not seem to know what had happened, once the diplomacy left his feeble grasp. When everything was over, he did not even have a pledge from President Kennedy not to invade Cuba. Kennedy had made such a pledge contingent upon on-site verification of the removal of Soviet weapons—which the United States never obtained. The Russians claimed that the president had made an out-and-out pledge. Castro complained to the United Nations that "officials of the U.S. Government declare that they do not consider themselves bound by any promise."

4. *The Dominican Republic*

After the missile crisis had blown over, the Dominican crisis blew up —but it was almost a relief compared to the problems and prospects which had opened over Cuba. From beginning to end the intervention of the United States in the Dominican Republic, which arose after the assassination of President Trujillo, was a small affair, compared to what had preceded it.

The Trujillo dictatorship had lasted from 1930 until the shooting of the Dominican president in 1961 and beyond question had constituted one of the worst dictatorships ever to have flourished in Latin America. If there was any single explanation for the untoward political events which followed after Trujillo's death, it was the excesses of his regime, which so poisoned all of Dominican life—society, economics, politics—that it may well be that the rest of the twentieth century will not see peace and quiet, not to mention true democracy, in the Dominican Republic. The dictator's follies have now become public knowledge in the United States. During his regime the mastheads of newspapers and the country's license plates celebrated his virtues with such legends as "Twenty-fifth Year of the Era of Trujillo." He changed the name of the capital city from Santo Domingo to Ciudad Trujillo. Signs everywhere read *"Dios y Trujillo,"* and it apparently is true that the dictator wished to change the signs to read *"Trujillo y Dios."* The dictator was not always president; he sometimes inaugurated other individuals and for a short time appointed himself ambassador to the United Nations and ascended into New York. He was, however, the country's only five-star general, the *Generalísimo.* (After his death he was called the *Difuntísimo*, the Most Defunct.) He was careful to provide for his relatives, of whom there were many, including six brothers and four sisters. His son, Ramfis, became a colonel at the age of three and a general at the age of nine. As a juvenile-adult Ramfis spent some time at one of the U.S. Army's war colleges but left under a cloud.

He was accustomed to living luxuriously aboard his father's yacht off California waters, where he entertained assorted movie stars. No one will ever know how much money the Trujillo family accumulated, or what happened to it. Much of the Dominican Republic belonged personally to the Trujillos, and those holdings at least were confiscated after the dictator was assassinated. Estimates of funds sent abroad to numbered accounts in Swiss banks range wildly up toward a billion dollars. A former American ambassador, John Bartlow Martin, has related that one conservative estimate published in Europe in 1962 put the total Swiss account at $800,000,000. Martin himself estimated the total at only between $150,000,000 and $200,000,000.

The frightful cost of the dictatorship was due not so much to the amounts of money sent abroad or the inanities of the dictator and his family, but to what all this meant for the everyday life of Trujillo's countrymen. For them the cost of his rule was enormous. The assassinations, the tortures, the degradations were beyond calculation, and some of them beyond description—they rivaled the worst of the Nazi atrocities. It is difficult to realize that one man could do all these things to the poverty-stricken people of the Dominican Republic, many of whom Ambassador Martin in the early 1960's found living almost outside of the money economy, people in the *barrios* with virtually nothing, no past and no future. And Trujillo's rule affected not merely his countrymen. In the first days of October 1937, Dominican troops killed an estimated 12,000 Haitians inside the Dominican Republic (no one knows the total, which may have been as high as 30,000) in a mad orgy, the purpose of which is difficult to imagine.

Contrary to common interpretation, Trujillo did not have much support from the United States government, although he managed to get along. He had obtained his start in politics by entering the marine-trained constabulary during the occupation. Years later he arranged an end to the customs supervision, and he traded heavily on this treaty of 1940 with the United States. The good neighbor policy became odious to his countrymen, and after Trujillo's fall the statue of Cordell Hull was one of the first to be pulled down. Nonetheless the American government was wary of the dictator and from the beginning of foreign aid in 1946 down to the time of Trujillo's death gave the republic only some $5,000,000, no large amount considering that in 1962–1963 alone the Americans gave or lent some $70,000,000.

The dictator's excesses at last became too much. In a 1956 plot, the full details of which are still unknown and perhaps always will be, he had arranged the disappearance from the Columbia University campus of Jesús María Galíndez, an exiled critic who had written a doctoral dissertation hostile to the regime. Ambassador Martin believed Galíndez's body, never discovered, was thrown to the sharks, together with that of Gerald Murphy, the pilot who reportedly ferried the kidnapped professor to the Dominican Republic. There was an uproar in the United States over this affair, and Trujillo retained an eminent New York law firm to make an impartial investigation, which it did and gave the regime a fairly good bill of health. In the year 1960, though, Trujillo went too far when he arranged for an automobile containing explosives to be parked along the route of a parade in Caracas, Venezuela, so that the president of that republic, Rómulo Betancourt, would be blown up. Something went wrong; the person sitting next to Betancourt was killed, and only the president's hands were burned. Betancourt was furious and took his case to the Organization of American States. In an unprecedented move the OAS imposed diplomatic and economic sanctions on the Dominican Republic. The dictator's position began to weaken, and at that point his enemies gunned him down.

The assassins failed to organize immediately after the dictator's death, and Ramfis presided over a bloodbath. Slowly the republic got back on its feet, expelled the Trujillo family, and in 1962 elected a president, Juan Bosch, who had been an exile for twenty-five years.

Ambassador Martin, already mentioned, a free-lance writer from Indiana who for a while was a Kennedy speechwriter, has published a brilliant, huge volume of 743 pages, *Overtaken by Events* (1966), setting out an almost day-by-day account of Dominican politics from the time he came as ambassador in 1962 until after he returned in 1965 during the wild military melee of that year. Martin has written of how he sometimes felt that the Dominicans received the governments they deserved. He liked the citizens of the island republic, yet was repelled, he said, by their impracticality, their laziness, their extremism—traits which together meant they could not seize the opportunity that presented itself with the death of Trujillo. Bosch was almost an incarnation of the good and bad qualities of his countrymen and during his seven months in office managed to do little. As Martin relates, he did avoid political persecutions or killings, and for that short time the Dominican Republic knew freedom. Martin did his best to support Bosch, even though the president was his own worst enemy and had a genius for alienating people whom he needed. It was slow, uphill work, even for an able ambassador such as Martin, surely one of the best representatives the United States government has sent abroad in many a day. President Kennedy backed him up, and sometimes kidded him, as when after one White House conference Martin was walking out of the presidential office. The president followed and said loudly for his outer-office assistants to hear: "There he goes—the Earl E. T. Smith of this Administration." Martin, startled, could only reply, "What a thing to say."

Like Mazzini, the nineteenth-century revolutionary, Bosch inflamed a generation he could not lead, and in 1963 he was ousted in a military coup led by a military man by the name of Elias Wessin y Wessin, a deeply religious, fanatical anticommunist, born of middle-class Lebanese parents, a man completely honest, politically naive, seeing no difference between the noncommunist revolutionary left and communism, seeing only black and white.

Then two years later, in 1965, a coup occurred against the military regime. This latter revolt soon turned into a serious business, as arms were distributed to the citizens, who took up the weapons for an enormous variety of purposes. Extremism was loosed. The heritage of Trujillo had triumphed. "Men and women like this," Martin afterward wrote, "have nowhere to go except to the Communists." The rebel leader, Colonel Francisco Caamaño Deño, had all the makings of a Dominican Castro.

President Johnson brought in the marines, a total of 22,000 troops and 8,000 sailors manning some 40 ships. The marines set up a neutral zone between the fighting Dominicans. The Organization of American States voted 14 to 5 to send an inter-American force to the Dominican Republic, commanded by a Brazilian general. United States forces eventually were withdrawn. The new president of the troubled republic became Joaquin Balaguer, a former appointee of Trujillo who presumably had turned over a new leaf. It was an unsatisfactory solution, achieved with far more expense than the American government had put out in the Dominican Republic for economic and other aid. The cost of American military intervention in the Dominican Republic in 1965 was $150,000,000.

What by this time was the prospect for relations with Latin America? Whether there will be trouble in the future with Latin America is difficult to say at present, although it may well be that the spectacular growth of population, which is increasing at an annual rate of 2.9 percent (and in Central America at the highest rate in the world, 3.5), may bring a time when population will outrun resources and governments of these regions will be tempted once more to follow adventuresome foreign policies. That moment has not yet arrived. Population pressure has not reached such a degree as to raise fears in the minds of American makers of foreign policy, although in two of the small countries, El Salvador and Haiti, and in the United States commonwealth of Puerto Rico, population is already making much difficulty.

Problems may also arise out of the extremely unequal distribution of wealth and position in Latin America. The United States as a true democracy has become a sort of showcase to all Latin America, and many of the Latins with the increased advantages of education are going to ask questions about the medieval social structures in some of their nations. Getting these structures adjusted to modern twentieth-century realities may bring considerable political trouble, perhaps international trouble.

It has always been so difficult to help the peoples and nations of Latin America. In this respect the inquiring and hopeful student had only to look at the fate of a project of the Kennedy administration, the Alliance for Progress. In 1960 the United States had joined with other nations of the hemisphere in the Act of Bogotá, based on a proposal by former President Juscelino Kubitschek of Brazil, pledging a mutual effort to promote social justice and economic progress. President Kennedy then proclaimed the Alliance for Progress, and in 1961 the nations of the hemisphere signed the Charter of Punta del Este, committing the United States to specific economic and social goals. The American government undertook to provide "a major part" of the $20,000,000,000 needed for the alliance, including more than $1,000,000,000 the first year.

The Latin American nations also had responsibilities, which they found difficult to meet. Much of the outside money for Latin American development was to come from private investment, and private investors were likely to be frightened off by the instability which surely would be promoted by the Punta del Este social and economic goals. The Latin countries, moreover, did not have the pool of skilled manpower such as Europe possessed on the eve of the Marshall Plan. After several years the Alliance for Progress appears to be petering out, going the way of so many other projects and dreams for the betterment of the Western Hemisphere.

In Latin America, as in other places, the United States has seemed constantly to be coming up against dead ends, but no better policy has appeared, to date, than that of the good neighbor.

A CONTEMPORARY DOCUMENT

[President Kennedy on Saturday afternoon, October 27, 1962, sent a letter to Premier Khrushchev "accepting" the Soviet leader's proposal to remove the missiles from Cuba under UN supervision and inspection, in return for which the United States government would lift the blockade and give a pledge not to invade Cuba. As mentioned, this proposition was only an unofficial suggestion by a member of the Soviet embassy in Washington, advanced to the ABC reporter John Scali. The suggestion, however, proved the key that unlocked the puzzle; Khrushchev accepted the proposal the next day. It is interesting that the president's technique in this case—advocated, of course, by his brother Robert and by Theodore Sorensen—had been employed before in American diplomacy. It was no new technique to base a diplomatic move on an assumption which either was incorrect or, at least, lacked authoritative expression. Secretary of State Stimson in 1929 blandly assumed that the other powers which had signed the Kellogg-Briand Pact were in agreement with his own policy toward the governments of China and Russia, which were then quarreling over control of the Chinese Eastern Railway and, indeed, engaging in an undeclared war. Stimson sent a note to the belligerents in November 1929 in which he claimed to represent all the powers of the Pact of Paris. He knew that, even if the other signatories of the Kellogg Pact objected to his diplomacy, they would hesitate to state their objections openly. A second instance of this rather sly sort of diplomacy, the assumption of somewhat more than other parties had intended, occurred under Secretary of State Hay, who in 1899 thanked the great powers of Europe for their support of the first open door note, although he knew they had not supported it. A somewhat similar instance, and perhaps the most perfect analogy to what President Kennedy did on October 27, 1962, occurred at the time of the XYZ affair. Foreign Minister Talleyrand sent an unofficial proposal for peace to the French chargé at The Hague, Louis Pichon, who then spoke with the American minister there, William Vans Murray. The American minister sent this information to President John Adams, who thereupon accepted Talleyrand's offer, although Adams knew that Talleyrand might disavow what, after all, was only a private note to the French chargé in the Netherlands. To be sure, this sort of diplomacy holds dangers. But the resolution of the Cuban missile crisis in this manner proved a stroke of genius. Source: Robert F. Kennedy, *Thirteen Days* (New York, 1969), pp. 102–104.]

Dear Mr. Chairman:

I have read your letter of October 26th with great care and welcomed the statement of your desire to seek a prompt solution to the problem. The first thing that needs to be done, however, is for work to cease on offensive missile bases in Cuba for all weapons systems in Cuba capable of offensive use to be rendered inoperable, under effective United Nations arrangements.

Assuming this is done promptly, I have given my representatives in New York instructions that will permit them to work out this weekend—in cooperation with the Acting Secretary General and your representative—an arrangement for a permanent solution to the Cuban problem along the lines suggested in your letter of October 26th. As I read your letter, the key elements of your proposals—

which seem generally acceptable as I understand them—are as follows:

1. You would agree to remove these weapons systems from Cuba under appropriate United Nations observation and supervision; and undertake, with suitable safeguards, to halt the further introduction of such weapons systems into Cuba.

2. We, on our part, would agree—upon the establishment of adequate arrangements through the United Nations to ensure the carrying out and continuation of these commitments—(a) to remove promptly the quarantine measures now in effect, and (b) to give assurances against an invasion of Cuba. I am confident that other nations of the Western Hemisphere would be prepared to do likewise.

If you will give your representative similar instructions, there is no reason why we should not be able to complete these arrangements and announce them to the world within a couple of days. The effect of such a settlement on easing world tensions would enable us to work toward a more general arrangement regarding "other armaments," as proposed in your second letter, which you made public. I would like to say again that the United States is very much interested in reducing tensions and halting the arms race; and if your letter signifies that you are prepared to discuss a detente affecting NATO and the Warsaw Pact, we are quite prepared to consider with our allies any useful proposals.

But the first ingredient, let me emphasize, is the cessation of work on missile sites in Cuba and measures to render such weapons inoperable, under effective international guarantees. The continuation of this threat, or a prolonging of this discussion concerning Cuba by linking these problems to the broader questions of European and world security, would surely lead to an intensification of the Cuban crisis and a grave risk to the peace of the world. For this reason, I hope we can quickly agree along the lines outlined in this letter and in your letter of October 26th.

John F. Kennedy

ADDITIONAL READING

Pan-Americanism has inspired a considerable literature, for which see J. B. Lockey, *Pan-Americanism: Its Beginnings* (New York, 1920), concerning the nineteenth century; Samuel Guy Inman, *Inter-American Conferences 1826–1954: History and Problems* (Washington, 1965), an uncritical run-through of dates and places and resolutions; Russell H. Bastert, "Diplomatic Reversal:

Frelinghuysen's Opposition to Blaine's Pan-American Policy in 1882," *Mississippi Valley Historical Review*, XLII (1955–1956), 653–671, together with the same author's "A New Approach to the Origins of Blaine's Pan American Policy," *Hispanic American Historical Review*, XXXIX (1959), 375–412, two fine pieces of scholarship; J. L. Mecham, *The United States and Inter-American Security: 1889–1960* (Austin, Tex., 1961); Gordon Connell-Smith, *The Inter-American System* (New York, 1966). The movement of American policy away from intervention appears in Alexander De Conde, *Herbert Hoover's Latin American Policy* (Stanford, Calif., 1951); the present author's "Repudiation of a Repudiation," *Journal of American History*, LI (1964–1965), 669–673, relating how the Roosevelt administration was not keen about the Clark Memorandum and refused to give it official recognition as the policy of the United States; E. O. Guerrant, *Roosevelt's Good Neighbor Policy* (Albuquerque, N.M., 1950); *Bryce Wood, *The Making of the Good Neighbor Policy* (New York, 1961), excellent; the same author's *The United States and Latin American Wars: 1932–1942* (New York, 1966); Donald M. Dozer, *Are We Good Neighbors?: Three Decades of Inter-American Relations, 1930–1960* (Gainesville, Fla., 1961), arguing that Latin Americans distrust us; Alton Frye, *Nazi Germany and the American Hemisphere: 1933–1941* (New Haven, 1967); and O. E. Smith, Jr., *Yankee Diplomacy: U.S. Intervention in Argentina* (Dallas, Tex., 1953).

For the Guatemala intervention about the only source of reliability is Dwight D. Eisenhower, *Mandate for Change* (Garden City, N.Y., 1963).

For Cuba there is a large group of titles. E. David Cronon, "Interpreting the New Good Neighbor Policy: The Cuban Crisis of 1933," *Hispanic American Historical Review*, XXXIX (1959), 538–567 is best for its subject, now almost forgotten in view of the later crises. See also Cronon's *Josephus Daniels in Mexico* (Madison, Wis., 1960), which relates the work of an apostle of neighborliness who perforce went to Mexico with a reputation for the opposite —gained as Woodrow Wilson's secretary of the navy. Earl E. T. Smith, *The Fourth Floor* (New York, 1962) refers cryptically in its title to the floor of the state department building in Washington where Cuban affairs are handled; Smith was ambassador during the Batista era in the late 1950's. Ruby Hart Phillips, *The Cuban Dilemma* (New York, 1963) offers the views of the New York *Times* correspondent. *Karl E. Meyer and Tad Szulc, *The Cuban Invasion* (New York, 1962) gives all the detail known to correspondents, which was a great deal. For the missile crisis of 1962 see Arthur M. Schlesinger, Jr., *A Thousand Days* (New York, 1965); Theodore C. Sorensen, *Kennedy* (New York, 1965); Edward Weintal and Charles Bartlett, *Facing the Brink* (New York, 1967); Arnold L. Horelick, "The Cuban Missile Crisis," *World Politics*, XVI (1963–1964), 363–389; *Elie Abel, *The Missile Crisis* (Philadelphia, 1966); and the posthumously published book by Robert F. Kennedy, *Thirteen Days* (New York, 1969), a remarkable volume, judicious, highly informative, written out by its late author in longhand on legal-size sheets, as clear and straightforward an account as any professional writer might have given.

The Dominican crisis has had a good deal of journalistic attention. Best for background is Sumner Welles, *Naboth's Vineyard: The Dominican Republic, 1844–1924* (2 vols., New York, 1928). John Bartlow Martin, *Overtaken by Events: The Dominican Crisis from the Fall of Trujillo to the Civil War* (New York, 1966) is by the former American ambassador and is a detailed accounting. Dan Kurzman, *Santo Domingo: Revolt of the Damned* (New York, 1965) is good journalism.

The future of Latin America appears in the appraisals of Milton S. Eisenhower, *The Wine Is Bitter: The United States and Latin America* (Garden City, N.Y., 1963); Samuel Shapiro, *Invisible Latin America* (Boston, 1963); Ernest R. May, "The Alliance for Progress in Historical Perspective," *Foreign Affairs*, XLI (1962–1963), 757–774.

Vietnam

The United States is in clear danger of being left naked and alone in a hostile world . . . . American foreign policy has never in its history suffered such a stunning reversal . . . . What is American policy in Indochina? All of us have listened to the dismal series of reversals and confusions and alarms and excursions which have emerged from Washington over the past few weeks. . . . We have been caught bluffing by our enemies. Our friends and allies are frightened and wondering, as we do, where we are headed. . . . This picture of our country needlessly weakened in the world today is so painful that we should turn our eyes from abroad and look homeward.

—Senator Lyndon B. Johnson, 1954

To an American of the 1960's, Vietnam has been a name to conjure with. The foreign policy of the United States has had many worries and concerns since the end of the Second World War, but in no case has there been so much confusion and travail as over the fate of this little country which, in 1945, and indeed for several years thereafter, most Americans had hardly heard of and could not have placed upon their maps of the world within hundreds or thousands of miles of its true location. The war in Vietnam has led to the garrisoning of 540,000 American troops, with perhaps 300,000 more men backing up the supply lines from the United States. Annual costs are running to $30,000,000,000. The annual rate of sacrifice is more than 10,000 American lives. The loss of life in Vietnam has outrun the death toll in the Korean War (33,629); between December 22, 1961 (when the first American soldier was killed in Vietnam), and April 1969, the same number of lives were lost in Vietnam. And there have been other costs of the war. When President Lyndon B. Johnson took office following the assassination of President Kennedy, he announced with assurance that there would be victory in the war on poverty, and that other domestic conflicts would be solved. The Vietnam

War has delayed these developments. As a result of Vietnam, all sorts of unusual notions are abroad, which have not strengthened the country's political (and, some people would say, moral) fiber. Churches such as the new United Methodist Church are telling their members that civil disobedience, a tactic hardly talked about since Henry Thoreau had taken to making pencils and not paying his taxes, is perfectly all right as a rule of personal conduct, so long as church members know what they are doing. Civil disobedience has, in turn, inspired violence, not merely in the ghettos of American cities but (stupidity of stupidities) in the administration buildings of American colleges and universities. The American army also has had troubles, not only with draft resisters but with Vietnam resisters in its own midst—men and officers who refuse to serve in Vietnam, or who appear in uniform at protest meetings. It is a strange set-to, or comedown, or whatever it is, after the hopes and dreams of the Second World War and its victory in 1945, not to mention the hopes and dreams which President Woodrow Wilson had enunciated so hauntingly so many years before.

Not least of the confusions of Vietnam is that the Vietnamese, the inhabitants of the places known by the year 1969 as North Vietnam and South Vietnam, probably do not care a hoot about their position in the cold war or about the general problems of American domestic policy. All they wish for is peace in their native land. They doubtless have some other claims and desires but generally would be satisfied with peace and the ability to live decently and quietly without foreign intervention. The war which the French began in 1945 and took through a long nine-year trial into defeat at the strangely named place of Dienbienphu has been picked up by the Americans and translated into a much larger conflict which has meant no more to the Vietnamese than the so-called First Indochinese War of 1945–1954. The Vietnamese certainly have wanted independence, but by 1969 even that desire is an uncertainty as so many of the people of Vietnam stand on the political fence and want only the opportunity to hop off without someone trying to kill them.

1. *The heritage*

Involvement in Vietnam came from a combination of French and American actions, no doubt, together with the acts of national and international communism, although Americans like to believe that it was either the communists or the French who brought them into the Vietnamese morass.

Consider then, at the outset, the acts of the French. How much do the

VIETNAM

CHINA

NORTH VIETNAM

Hanoi
Haiphong
Nam Dinh

GULF OF
TONKIN

HAINAN

LAOS

Vientiane

CEASE FIRE LINE

Hue

Da Nang

THAILAND

Bangkok

CAMBODIA

Mekong River

SOUTH VIETNAM

Que Nhon

Phnom Penh

Saigon

GULF
OF
SIAM

MILES

0   100   200   300

French have to answer for, in terms of what the Vietnam War is doing to American lives, treasure, politics, perhaps morality—not to mention the lives, treasure, politics, and morality of the Vietnamese people? The government of France, nearly a century ago, entered the Far East at a time when imperialism was not a dirty word. French moves into Asia came at a time when the French nation, defeated in the short war of 1870–1871 with Germany, thought that some *gloire* might be available outside France and even outside Europe. Prince Bismarck, the wily practitioner of *Realpolitik*, and France's nemesis in Europe, encouraged the French to exercise their ambitions outside Europe. Bismarck had good reason: he did not want the French to intrigue against the new Second Reich and arrange a war of revenge. The French for a while took up this inferential advice from Bismarck, and what in the latter half of the twentieth century is known as Vietnam, and before that was known as Indochina, was one of the pieces of stray territory which the French government in Paris and the French people began to cherish.

The usual things, for Asian imperialism, happened in Indochina—present-day Vietnam, together with the neighboring present-day states of Laos and Cambodia—and there is not much point in detailing them. Suffice to say that settlers moved out there, not so much to settle on land as to settle on the backs of natives who would themselves work the land. Other French fortune-seekers were going out to Africa, notably Algeria, at this time, and it was the sort of trekking which went on everywhere, conducted by the nationals of all the imperial states. The French fortune-hunters went ahead with their fortunes, protected by law and diverted by the morality of the native peoples, the customs of the locality in Indochina that one took as much from opportunities as possible; and by the time of the World War of 1914–1918 the French had done handsomely for themselves and their descendants. Their only failure was in political knowledge, a sense of how far they might go in personal ways without encountering political forces which would end their personal prosperity. One can hardly blame them for failing to sense the incipient nationalism of the Indochinese and believing instead that the doctrines of President Wilson were all right for Europe, and maybe for the United States since, after all, those doctrines came from there; but—so the *colons* thought—Wilsonian doctrines could never have any currency in the Far East, among possessors of that strange entity, the oriental mind.

This mistake of the French in failing to see the growing nationalism in Indochina was not apparent even at the end of the World War in 1918, when one Ho Chi Minh, not long before a pastry cook for the renowned chef in London, Escoffier, went to the Paris Peace Conference and consorted with equally odd characters, such as a young man named Syngman

Rhee from Korea, and tried to argue his national cause in the anterooms and coffee places of the French capital. Ho's was an impossible mission, as was that of Rhee. Like so many other of the individuals whom the American journalist Philip Bonsal, an official at the conference, described as "suitors and suppliants," Ho went back to his native land with a feeling that there was not much of a future. That is, not much of a future except intrigue and patience, a long time ahead during which it would be necessary to dodge the French police and try slowly to galvanize the special interests of his countrymen—many of whom did not even realize that they had a country.

This Ho Chi Minh, who by the latter 1960's has had the intense attention of the American government and people, whose every move would find interpretation, whose obscure writings are now searched and double-checked for turns and twists of logic which Ho perhaps never intended, spent the interwar years in intrigue, with some attention to the writings and thoughts of the Russian communists, and did not become an important personage (except to the French Indochinese police) until the time of the Second World War. During the latter stages of that war, some American troops were dropped to accompany Ho's peregrinations, and they gave Ho advice of a minor sort and such encouragement as they could offer. Then the war was over, and Ho suddenly found himself, as head of the resistance to the Japanese, a national hero. He also discovered a major opportunity which, but for French stupidity, he might have seized and which in retrospect would have offered perhaps the best solution to what now has distinctly become the problem of Vietnam.

When the Japanese surrendered, a vacuum of power opened in Saigon and Hanoi, the two major cities of Indochina. Ho and his supporters realized that nature abhorred such a situation. They were tempted to establish a government in Hanoi, which they proceeded to do, with the ministries of the new regime assigned to an assortment of individuals, not all of whom were communist. All the French then had to do, if they would, was recognize the Hanoi government.

The decision of the French government in Paris, in all its immediate postwar weakness, to hold firm in so outlandish a place as Indochina was one of the major miscalculations of French politics in the twentieth century, and in the memory of this decision, twenty and more years later, it seems an almost equal miscalculation of the American government to have permitted the French to return. President Roosevelt at several of the wartime conferences had urged some sort of trusteeship for Indochina and stood strongly against French imperialism, which had given evidences of being unable to control colonial peoples except by misgovernment—by terror and brutal police measures, as in North Africa and in the Middle

East. Roosevelt must have known that there had been a veritable blood bath in Indochina in 1931 when the Foreign Legion had put down an insurrection. The country of Indochina had received the president's close attention in 1941 when the Japanese had taken it over, threatening Singapore from the airport at Saigon. That Japanese move had led Roosevelt to a countermove, the cutting off of Japan's oil supplies from the United States, the single most important American move leading to the attack on Pearl Harbor and the entire involvement in the Second World War. Had the weak French not been in Indochina, it was possible that the United States would not have entered the war. And the French, Roosevelt knew, were not merely weak but despicable in their behavior with native peoples. Why let them return, to cause more trouble? Unfortunately the wartime president had many things on his mind, and not least of them was General de Gaulle's pride, which was likely to make trouble for all kinds of things connected with the supposed *gloire* of France. After the president of the United States died in April 1945 and his power passed to President Truman, so many other issues arose that Indochina got lost in the shuffle. With our present-day experience, it is easy to say that it should not have been thus lost. But how can one blame Roosevelt and Truman for letting this little domino, the Smaller Dragon, as Joseph Buttinger has described it, pass back into French hands, while the Americans, busy everywhere, tried at least to prop up a decent regime in the territory of the Big Dragon to the north.

If the French came back in a vacuum of power, or in forgetfulness, they did not waste time in mulling over their loss of power in Europe and what it meant for Asia. They did not waste time in contemplating the immediate postwar behavior of other European nations, such as Britain in India and Ceylon and Burma, or the Dutch, if belatedly, in Indonesia. The willingness of these European imperial powers, notably Britain, to give up their empires was lost on the French, who decided to keep theirs. One might thereby advance a thesis that the less one has the more important it is to him.

People sometimes ask why the postwar French governments in Paris—there were fifteen of them between 1945 and 1954—did not recognize the futility of trying to hold Indochina, and why they instead began a series of actions against the native Vietnamese which commenced with the expulsion of Ho's government from Hanoi in 1946 and ended, eight years later, in the mud and death of Dienbienphu. Could not some of the Socialist governments of France have taken hold of the Vietnam problem and solved it, to the everlasting credit of France and the betterment of the history of the United States? It so happened that the policy of the French Right triumphed in Indochina because the Left failed to comprehend what was going on outside of Europe. The Right had its mind and attention on what was going on in Hanoi and Saigon, whereas the Left was concerned about the economic problems of France in Europe. It was ever so easy to make mistakes in Indochinese policy, as, for example, to take the line pursued by Léon Blum,who was premier at the crucial time in December 1946 when the French government moved in force against the Hanoi government of President Ho. Blum took the point of view that it was necessary to restore order in Indochina before dealing with the Ho regime; and to the people in Indochina doing the restoration, restoring order meant using the French police and army against the resistance. The native forces under Ho, known as the Vietminh, moved slowly out of Hanoi and into inaccessible portions of Indochina. They began to construct networks—infrastructures, as they were known—of secret supporters and saboteurs in all the provinces, meanwhile bringing together their own troops and organizing them with whatever weapons were at hand. The French governments changed in Paris like a kaleidoscope and sent sometimes good administrators and sometimes bad, pursuing the policy of force which eventually failed.

In the tangled history of French political mistakes in Indochina after 1945, it is necessary also to mention the second string to the French bow, namely, intrigue. French representatives on the spot, even such personally well-intentioned individuals as the priest-admiral, Georges Thierry d'Argenlieu, who was high commissioner in the first postwar months, thought that local customs being what they were, it might be possible to bribe the Indochinese into co-operation, on the principle that the means might not merely be acceptable locally but would justify the ends of civilized France. The military measures of the French did not prove successful, and when shot through with intrigue the whole position in Indochina collapsed. Eventually the Americans took it over, whereafter an even graver situation arose.

The problem of the French in Indochina was aptly characterized by the former American ambassador-turned-newspaperman, William C. Bullitt, who went to Indochina in 1947. In an article for *Life* magazine, he wrote of the Vietnamese desire for independence, saying that Ho, then in hiding in the northern part of Indochina, wanted independence. From this truth Bullitt then moved to oversimplification, remarking that the French could train the Indochinese in independence and should be allowed to do this with the help of the Americans, who could furnish arms. Bullitt thought, too, that it would be necessary for the French first to defeat Ho but that this was easily possible during the training period for independence.

The French hated the idea of independence and tried to hoodwink the Indochinese. The Indochinese knew it, and this was the impossibility of the Bullitt policy, which, however, seemed so briskly sensible to Americans. Americans followed this policy of helping the French—until the French by 1954 clearly were beyond help. The French were sure of themselves. That false prophet, Charles de Gaulle, out of power in the early postwar years, remarked confidently at a press conference on November 17, 1948, that time was working for France. "The true rule to observe at this moment in Indochina is not to rush anything. We must know how to take our time. . . . Sooner or later the French solution [that is, a military solution, followed by independence perhaps in the year 2000] will have to be accepted." French policy blindly pursued the defeat of the Indochinese (by this time they were beginning to be described as the Vietnamese, meaning those peoples of Indochina who did not live in Laos and Cambodia). General Jean Leclerc, possessor of a truly Napoleonic megalomania, was sent out in 1950 to straighten out the situation and contributed instead to its failure. Leclerc could not even take disagreement from Frenchmen and surely was prepared to hear no advice from the Vietnamese. He was followed by General Henri Navarre, who had a "plan" (as most military men must have plans). The Navarre Plan was that France slowly should build its military strength until there were enough troops for large-scale action against the Vietnamese; meanwhile the available forces would conduct offensive operations to the limit of their power. The Navarre Plan failed to work, except to the advantage of the Vietnamese, who trapped large numbers of French troops.

The French continued to follow this fatuous policy of military measures accompanied by intrigue—quite apart from its immorality, intrigue is always fatuous, because sooner or later it rebounds. At the center of the policy was the former Emperor Bao Dai, whom the French sought to make the focus of Vietnamese patriotism, in opposition to Ho Chi Minh's Vietminh, hitherto almost the sole resort of patriotism. Bao Dai was no large figure on the pages of history. He was a descendant of a noble Indochinese family, whatever that lineage meant. He was a shrewd man and an undoubted Indochinese patriot. But he could not stand up to adversity or to debauchery. When something went wrong with his political fortunes, his custom was to drown his sorrows in nightclubbery and whatever else of an entertaining nature stood available. After a while his well-known trips to Paris and the Riviera affected his image, as Americans later would have said, for he became known as the nightclub emperor. His role in Indochina was tragic, but he was too much of a comedian and laughed at the wrong lines. Withal he was politically shrewd, as mentioned, and for a long time gave the French a difficult run for their money—which eventually, in 1949, he took.

The hope of the French was to bring the innumerable anticommunist factions of Vietnam behind the figurehead of Bao Dai, but instead they managed only to bring all the native fortune-seekers; and the more of these "supporters" the ex-emperor had, the lower he sank in the estimation of his countrymen. When he returned to Saigon under heavy police guard in 1949, after an agreement with the French, he was as dispirited as the populace that watched his arrival. The individuals then appointed to the ministries were a series of unmitigated disasters, until in 1954 he dismissed his premier of the moment and took on the biggest disaster of all, Ngo Dinh Diem.

2. *The Geneva Conference and SEATO*

The debacle of the French forces in 1954 hardly needs recital. The French under General Navarre conceived the idea of an outpost at Dienbienphu which would prevent infiltration into Vietnam from Laos. The Vietminh then undertook to invest and seize this fortress with its sixteen battalions of French Union forces, first ringing the surrounding hills with carefully hidden Chinese artillery pieces, then making the French airstrip at the camp unusable, then tunnelling and ditching their way up to the French lines and slowly overwhelming the French strong points. It was high time for negotiation when, in early March 1954, the Vietminh forces at enormous cost in lives (some estimates say that 2,500 men entombed themselves in the mud in this initial action) took the strong points Gabrielle and Béatrice, and artillery pounded the third strongpoint into submission. The French decided to negotiate. Indeed, there is some evidence that General Vo Nguyen Giap's investing of Dienbienphu was timed carefully so as to enable the Vietminh to seize the fortress on May 7, 1954, the day before the question of Vietnam came before the conference which had assembled in Switzerland to examine the entire issue of Vietnamese independence.

The plight of France in Vietnam was of course closely linked to the plight of France in Europe, and it was this fact which at first had so bothered the Americans and helped lead to the Geneva Conference of 1954. So long as the French were maintaining 150,000 troops in Vietnam, their army could not be of much use in Europe. It seemed necessary somehow to give the French a respite in the Far East, so that they could consider quietly their behavior toward the plans which after 1950 were maturing to bring the West German Republic into the defense arrangements of the North Atlantic Treaty Organization. The United States government, in the calling of the Geneva Conference, was not altogether happy with the meeting which would arrange Vietnam, but by that time the pressures of diplomacy in Europe had brought the British and Russians into a willingness to do something for France, if for different reasons, albeit all connected with Europe. The British wanted to help the French get back on their feet and support NATO through the French-originated scheme of the European Defense Community, so strongly championed also by Secretary of State Dulles in 1954. The Russians thought that they saw a chance to defeat EDC, highly unpopular in the French parliament, through helping the French in Indochina as a *quid pro quo*. The Russians apparently were also interested in supporting the French Communist Party, which was the largest communist party in Europe and was much concerned over the effect of the Indochinese imbroglio upon its political fortunes in France. The European situation, then, at first agitated by the United States, then acted upon by the British and Russians, helped produce the Geneva Conference.

The Chinese Communists likewise were willing to see peace of some sort in Indochina, not to help the French, but to enable the Peking regime to get international recognition. The purposes of Peking have often been obscure, but it does seem probable that in 1954, one year after the end of

It was feared Dulles would lead us into the French-Indochina war in 1954, but Eisenhower refused to intervene.

the war in Korea, the Communists in Peking wished to become more internationally respectable and perhaps get recognition from the European governments if not the American. Co-operation in an arrangement for Indochina would help. Perhaps it even would be possible for the Chinese Communists to join what the Russians in the first post-Stalin months were trumpeting as the Big Five—the wartime Big Three plus France and China. Contrary to American suppositions, then, especially contrary to the thoughts of Secretary Dulles, who felt sure that the Chinese in 1953–1954 were aching to intervene somewhere in Asia now that Korea had quieted down, the Chinese in 1954 actually co-operated with the Russians and British, against the regime of President Ho.

The mechanics of calling the conference were veiled through the convening, at Russian request, of a conference of foreign ministers of the Big Four, held in Berlin in January–February 1954. This conference set up a meeting in Geneva, allegedly to study the Korean situation, but actually as an opportunity to put Indochina on the agenda. The Indochinese item of the agenda came up on May 8, 1954, two weeks or so after the conference opened, a day after the French surrender at Dienbienphu. The two Vietnamese sides were present, North and South, as well as Chinese Communist representatives, together with the Big Four.

The resulting agreements were, most of them, not "finalized" in Geneva, and the only documents signed there were by military representatives of France and the Vietminh providing for armistices in Laos, Cambodia, and Vietnam. Subsequent arrangements, entered into by the other conferees but not by the United States (which for most of the time had an observer mission), provided for the partitioning of Vietnam at the seventeenth parallel, for no foreign bases in either part of Vietnam, North or South; for neither of the new, supposedly temporary, states to join a military alliance; for country-wide elections leading to unification by July 20, 1956 (two years after the formal conclusion of the Geneva Conference), and for an International Control Commission composed of Canadian, Polish, and Indian representatives, with the Indian representative as chairman. There also was provision for repatriation, within about a year, of refugees.

What precisely was American policy during the Geneva Conference? In the course of these drawn-out conversations at Geneva, which ran true to form for conferences in that the conversation began on April 26 and ended on July 20 (actually July 21; see below), the United States faltered and nearly fell, for the conference was not an American idea and the result was not much to the taste of Secretary Dulles, who believed that democratic nations defeated communists instead of negotiating with

them. According to one critic, Dulles was like a global insurance salesman, signing up nations against communism—no man to like Geneva:

John Foster Dulles [wrote the witty Richard Rovere] raised anti-Communism
from ideology to theology. Moreover, he was the first true globalist to become
Secretary of State. He did not complain of the lack of specificity in the
Truman Doctrine. He wanted us to smite the devil everywhere—or so at least
he said—even in those provinces, such as the satellite states of Eastern Europe,
where Satan's rule had been a *fait accompli* for several years. He traveled the
world like a possessed insurance salesman, offering bargains in American protection to any nation whose leaders would give him their word that they, too,
despised Communism.

Dulles therefore played with alternatives to the Geneva surrender, or
accommodation (as the British, Russians, and Chinese would have described it). When General Paul Ely, one of the highest-ranking French
officers, came to Washington late in March on special mission to say that
he hoped the Americans would give enough support to French forces in
Indochina so that the French could hang on somehow until after the
Geneva Conference and thereby get better terms at that meeting, Dulles
apparently allowed the chairman of the American joint chiefs of staff,
Admiral Arthur W. Radford, to propose an American airstrike in support
of the garrison at Dienbienphu. Radford may have made this proposition
on his own, although that seems doubtful. Anyway, Ely went back to
Paris and got consent of the cabinet, and then the American government
reneged on its own proposition after Dulles had offered it to a group of
congressmen who strongly advised him to consult with the allies and also
Congress. An airstrike might have embroiled the United States in Indochina ten years before it did. Dulles's frustration with negotiation of the
dispute, rather than a military decision, almost led him up this garden
path, but he vacillated and turned another way. American policy thereupon changed from the domino theory, which had a brief popularity
(President Eisenhower had announced early in April 1954 that Indochina
was like the first in a series of dominoes that could fall to communism in
rapid succession), to belief that the division of Indochina into North and
South, with the communists confirmed in possession of the North, would
provide a bastion of democracy for the free world in the South and eventually a chance to take the North and return things to where they ought
to have been under French rule.

Perturbed by the drift of negotiation, which was out of his hands,
Dulles hit on the idea of a security organization for the Far East, which he
created in a conference held at Manila. On September 8, 1954, the United

States, France, Australia, New Zealand, the Philippines, Thailand, and Pakistan agreed to a Southeast Asia Treaty Organization (SEATO). Dulles looked upon this new organization as more an enactment of words than a military organization. He preferred the title MANPAC, for Manila Pact, rather than SEATO, which sounded too much like NATO. He said to the conferees at Manila that the pact was not anything like the European analogue, but more of a statement. It specified only consultation among the signatories, and action in accord with their constitutional processes, which could mean much or little. It excluded from its purview the potential "hot spots" of Hong Kong, Taiwan, and all territories to the north, such as the former French Associated States, although a special protocol attached to the treaty included Cambodia, Laos, and South Vietnam by assuring them protection without requiring any obligation, and also specifying that there would be no action except by invitation or consent.

Meanwhile the French government under Premier Pierre Mendès-France had gotten out of Indochina—almost. Mendès-France had asked for the premiership on June 17, 1954, by promising the Chamber that if they chose him he would get the nation out of Indochina by July 20. The Geneva Conference fulfilled his mandate on July 21, backdating the necessary documents to allow him the triumph of his deadline. The idea was that France would grant independence to the three Associated States, and help them toward national survival. The United States government shortly afterward announced to the French that it would deal separately with the Associated States, considering them independent entities available for grants and foreign assistance. This intelligence persuaded the French government to drop all vestiges of support for the erstwhile colonies, allowing the Americans, who seemed to want the job, to take over.

3. *Sink or swim with Ngo Dinh Diem*

Bao Dai shortly after the debacle of Dienbienphu had appointed the Catholic leader Ngo Dinh Diem as premier, and a year later, having consolidated this office into a position of almost unrivaled power, Diem dumped Bao Dai. South Vietnam became a republic with Diem as president. A new era opened which the New York *Times* correspondent Homer Bigart later would characterize with the unhappy catch phrase "sink or swim . . . ."

Diem soon gave some evidence of being a swimmer. As a Catholic he could gain support in the United States and managed good relations with Francis Cardinal Spellman of New York City, one of the nation's most influential clerics. To all appearance he was personally incorruptible, although this said nothing for his relatives. It seems now, in retrospect, that he was a traditional official, a conservative, a mandarin. His only "revolutionary" quality was a desire to have independence from the French. His only "miraculous" quality was his ability in his first few years of power to consolidate his rule. Helping him in the consolidation were his brother-in-law Ngo Dinh Nhu, and his brother's wife, known in the West as Madame Nhu (as Arthur Schlesinger would describe her, "the lovely and serpentine Madame Nhu"). Another brother was the leading bishop of Vietnam. There was still another brother. It was a family enterprise.

One of the points of consolidation about which much has since been written, Diem's refusal to allow elections in his part of Vietnam as stipulated in the Geneva agreement of 1954, deserves some explanation, if only because the United States government backed him in this refusal, and it now has become a source of some embarrassment. President Ho of North Vietnam duly invoked the agreement that elections should occur sometime before July 20, 1956. Diem refused, which he technically could do because South Vietnam was not party to the agreement about elections. Should Diem and the United States government have sponsored elections? The result, if honest, might have given the country to Ho. The latter statesman would have received the unanimous support of the people of North Vietnam; Ho would not have allowed a free election there (President Johnson later would ask who had elected Ho president of North Vietnam, pointing out that Ho never had run for election in his life). And Ho would have had a good deal of support in the South, where most of the people had not yet experienced his rule and his name had become a legend because of his opposition to the Japanese and his long-time nationalism. Diem, on his part, could have worked a crooked election, as he had done in 1955 in displacing Bao Dai, but that would have been difficult with foreign observers all over the country. And surely an election in such a semiliterate country as Vietnam would have to be a farce, whether free or managed. After Diem refused to conduct an election in 1956, the British and Russians, two signatories of the Geneva agreements, issued a halfhearted appeal. The USSR was not anxious for a precedent for East Germany and the other satellites.

As Diem set to work, the prospect economically was not, one should add, poor. At the time of the partition in 1954, the south might have had a better prospect economically than the north. There soon would be a large rice surplus for export. The rubber plantations had not suffered greatly during the First Indochinese War, and rubber could produce foreign exchange. Even if the industry of the country, what little there was of it, was mostly in the north, the south was clearly viable economically.

It was necessary, however, that Diem do something serious about the land problem in the south, and, as we now see, it was a pity that he did not. The south had plenty of land available for distribution among the peasants, for a good deal of land had been abandoned, having gone out of cultivation during the First Indochinese War. The land problem cried out for solution. About 2.5 per cent of the landlords in the Mekong delta owned half the cultivated land, and 80 per cent of the land was tilled by tenants, with the usual high rents, irrigation fees, uncertain tenure, and scandalously high interest rates for small loans. The large landowners, Vietnamese and French, had supported Diem's predecessors. There were some land successes under his regime, notably a large project sponsored by the Americans to resettle Catholic refugees from the north. But then the land reform began to stagnate, becoming ever more nominal. It did not help when provinces changed hands back and forth from Vietcong (that is, Ho's partisans in the south) to South Vietnamese loyal to the Saigon government. The troops of the latter always seemed to bring along the landlords, whose minds were bent on collecting back rents. Diem also worked out an arrangement to have tenants who bought land pay for it in too few years, such a short time that the cost became a hardship. It would have been better to have given the land away, as the northerners were advocating. There also was a problem of enforcing the laws about the maximum amount of land retainable by South Vietnamese landlords, and of enforcing the maximum rents by tenants as established by the Diem regime at 25 per cent of the crops.

The hope of the regime in addition to land reform lay in securing a decent officialdom, but Diem possessed the mandarin feeling that the peasants were stupid—one American said that nowhere had he found a government official who liked the peasants—and refused to send out understanding officials, and instead counted on the grasping type. If an official was honest, Diem and Nhu would tend to distrust him and send him out to an insecure district where the communists would kill him. The communists were trying anyway to kill the better officials. This co-operation between Diem and his enemies for different reasons was almost unbeatable as a system to destroy the regime. As it became more and more rotten, reforming the officialdom proved more difficult; because of the rising strength of the communists in the south, the corrupt officials tended to be the only support the regime had left. When the Americans talked about government reform, Diem smiled and made promises.

The two most important Americans in the early 1960's were Ambassador Frederick E. Nolting, Jr., and General Paul Harkins, and both of these well-meaning men believed that it would be unwise to press Diem. They considered that it might be possible to steer him gently and gradually toward reform, but to press him, they said, would be self-defeating. They seemed to ignore the fact that otherwise Diem would defeat not merely himself but the Americans. The theory of Nolting and Harkins, in retrospect, could hardly have been worse. And so economic and social reform failed, having never really started, and Diem continued to receive a procession of foreign visitors who first heard from subordinates of Diem about the miracle of Vietnam and then listened politely to the president's monologues. The people of Saigon lined the streets and greeted the distinguished foreigners coming and going because Nhu had told them to get out there and wave.

It was in this period that what Arthur Schlesinger aptly has described as the politics of inadvertence occurred—the decision symbolized by the Taylor-Rostow mission of 1961 to increase military assistance. The initial decision to give military aid, taken eleven years before, had seemed entirely sensible. President Truman on June 27, 1950, when everything in Korea was caving in, announced that the United States would increase military assistance "to the forces of France and the Associated States in Indochina," and sent a military mission. Sums jumped from $119,000,000 in Mutual Security Program funds in the summer of 1951 to $815,000,000 for fiscal 1954 (July 1, 1953 through June 30, 1954). The numbers of American troops went up slowly. By the end of Eisenhower's presidency there were a mere 800. Then in October 1961 two able advisers of President Kennedy, General Maxwell Taylor and Walt W. Rostow, went out on a mission to Vietnam, and returned to urge enlargement of the military role to include military advisers to improve the level of local action by the South Vietnamese army; American troops in Vietnam increased from 1,364 by the end of 1961 to 15,500 by November 1963 at the time of President Kennedy's death.

As it turned out, November 1963 was a crucial month, as it witnessed the assassinations of Presidents Kennedy and Diem. In subsequent months, as cliques of politicians and generals shuttled in and out of power in Saigon, and President Ho and his partisans began a massive effort to seize all South Vietnam, President Johnson in desperation ordered in large contingents of American troops. American army and marine forces in Vietnam rose to 400,000, and then to 540,000, plus supporting troops in Japan and elsewhere, plus supporting air force units in Guam and elsewhere, plus US navy forces in Vietnamese waters. The maximum number of troops committed at any one time by the United States in Korea in 1950–1953 had been 470,000. By the year 1969 the Vietnamese were tying down more than 40 per cent of American combat-ready divisions, more than 50 per cent of American air power, more than a third of American naval strength.

By that late date it seemed unfortunate that President Johnson had not taken a declaration of war against North Vietnam, or declared a national emergency, or somehow obtained a more clear mandate for the use of massive armed force than he had received in the so-called Tonkin Resolution by Congress after two incidents in August 1964 involving American destroyers in the Gulf of Tonkin. The destroyers had been in the gulf on an intelligence mission, and because their electronic gear was picking up North Vietnamese radio traffic, and because the Americans ingeniously were translating this traffic and knew exactly what the North Vietnamese were doing, there was no large surprise aboard the American vessels when North Vietnamese torpedo boats attacked them. The attacks took place in international waters—the attack of August 2 occurred 28 miles off the coast, and the attack of August 4 occurred 60–65 miles off the coast. The president informed Congress of the attacks and received a congressional blank check to use the armed forces to protect the country's national interests. This, then, together with the precedent of the undeclared Korean War, and the fact that the president even in peacetime is commander in chief of the armed forces, constituted the legal basis of the massive American military intervention in Vietnam beginning in 1965.

In extenuation of President Johnson's actions after the Tonkin Resolution, one must say that without massive American intervention South Vietnam would have passed under control of President Ho. President Johnson's critics should understand also that, even if in retrospect this result might not have been an impossible solution, it would have produced a bloodbath of Ho's opponents in South Vietnam. Would the citizens of the United States, after encouraging—however ill-advisedly—the anti-Ho groups in South Vietnam wish to stand by and see them butchered in the jungle? The choice before President Johnson in 1965 was not easy. Moreover, it is one thing to be in charge of a great government and have to make decisions, and another to sit back, wait for some dust to settle, and point out mistakes. If one makes no decisions he makes no mistakes. Certainly (and one can almost behold the rhetoric of Vietnam unfolding, tempers rising, even in the present pages) the holder of high office must stand responsible for his mistakes. President Johnson never argued to the contrary. One might ask, then, whether charity should extend to the president of the United States if he makes a mistake, and whether Americans anyway should not understand that their government, like the governments of other peoples, makes mistakes.

In afteryears the Iwo Jima flag raising inspired such cartoons as these. Left: "Flag Raising in Central Park." Right: "Ky's Cabinet," referring to a momentary Vietnamese cabinet headed by Nguyen Cao Ky.

Whatever the logic or rationale, mistake or mistakes, the deed was done, the people of the United States by the time of the presidential election of 1968 found that they had a large problem on their hands and an opportunity to express their pleasure or displeasure with candidates Eugene J. McCarthy, Robert F. Kennedy, and Hubert H. Humphrey in the Democratic Party primaries, later with George McGovern at the party's Chicago convention, and, after that dismal assemblage, with the three candidates in November—Humphrey, Richard M. Nixon, and George C. Wallace.

4. *Prospect*

As this chapter is being written, it is difficult to know what will happen with American policy toward Vietnam. All of us live in our own time and not merely look back upon events—history, as we like to describe our interpretations—but anticipate events with the predilections and emotions of the moment. The beginning of the year 1969 is a bewildering time to be alive. History is repeating itself with the age-old spectacle of the younger generation repudiating the older, with the old bemoaning the young, with the alternations in politics, economics, society, intellect, of hope and despair, expansiveness and conservatism. But is there more to the present day than repetition? The pace of life, of course, has increased dramatically. How different the momentum of diplomacy now is from the time, more than a century and a half ago, when President Jefferson wrote plaintively to one of his envoys in Europe that he had not heard from him for two years, and trusted that this would be remedied before another year was out. But how does the historian analyze the present-day swirl? Does he fasten his gaze upon some blob floating upon the sea of history, and watch the blob float off toward nothingness, meanwhile predicting for it a great future? Vietnam may prove to be such a patch floating upon history; or it may prove to be something far larger and deeper, causing the downfall of the American republic; or it may be neither so big nor so small, neither dire nor meaningless. The present writer cannot be sure of the course of events anywhere, perhaps least of all in Vietnam. He can only set out tentatively, from the prospect of the present day, where he thinks events are moving.

By the beginning of the Nixon presidency, certain facts—one might call them—have become evident about Vietnam.

The first is that military power, of the traditional sort exerted by all great nations on the ground, has not done the trick, has not managed to control the revolutionary situation in South Vietnam.

The second is that air power likewise has not worked as anticipated. Huge amounts of explosives have been dumped in Vietnam, with dubious results. It is difficult to be accurate in bombing, flying in with fast-moving planes, for sometimes just a few feet make the difference. If spotter planes drop smoke bombs marking the target, the wind may blow the smoke off course before the devastation can arrive. Military objectives are difficult to find, and often it is the same old wooden bridge. The American air force has spent several billion dollars to knock out perhaps three or four hundred millions worth of North Vietnamese industry, most of which is not useful to the North Vietnamese military effort. Even if the purpose of the bombing is to "increase the quotient of pain," it begins to be doubtful who is hurting the most.

A third fact is that bombing does not prevent men and supplies from moving increasingly into the south, wherever the North Vietnamese want them. The numbers of men passing over the infiltration routes have increased from an estimated 12,400 in the years before the bombing to 26,000 in 1965, the year the bombing began, and to 54,800 in 1966. As for supplies, former Secretary of Defense Robert McNamara has testified that North Vietnam's total imports, of all kinds, are only 5,800 tons a day. Knocking out the docks and piers at Haiphong would not matter much, because the North Vietnamese could bring in 8,400 tons a day by road and rail from China. Of these imports, an estimated 550 tons a day are military supplies. Former Assistant Secretary of State Roger Hilsman has contended that the north requires only 85 of these tons in the south. Hilsman has worked out an equation for the transport necessary to get this material southward: one small steel-hulled coastal trawler, four or five junks, fourteen army-type 6 x 6 trucks, 85 jeeps, 225 elephants, 340 reinforced bicycles, 1,135 quarter h.p. prime movers (men with packs). The area of interdiction is the size of Connecticut.

A fourth fact is that the north is showing no manpower shortage, and hence the business of the kill rate, so much talked about, does not work well. In addition to the insurgents in the south, the Vietcong, President Ho can call on the quarter of a million of young men in the north who reach the age of seventeen each year and spend them as the United States is spending dollars. As for the half million North Vietnamese manning the anti-aircraft defenses, they are no drain on resources, and there are more hundreds of thousands available as "volunteers" from Red China.

A fifth and last fact is that the troops of the Republic of Vietnam, the ARVN forces, are of little help even for holding the cities of their own country. The ARVNs lean forward in their foxholes and call it a patrol. They are given to siestas and vacations—when the lunar New Year, or Tet, offensive began early in 1968, many ARVN troops were on leave. They have little incentive to fight, as for many of them the army is just a job, or something they have been forced into.

Presented with such a dismal array of facts, what is the richest country of the world to do, since it is being made a fool of by one of the poorest? Some Americans believe their country is readying itself for a fall that would make the fall of Rome seem like a quiet and rather simple-minded thud, compared to our crash. Some citizens recall the proposed strategy of General MacArthur during the Korean War, that the United States should bomb everything in China, exchanging Chinese lives for American safety. On the other side of the spectrum of opinion about Vietnam is a feeling akin to the pacifism of the 1920's and 1930's, the Kellogg-Briand Pact, a world without war or even evil, and, if war did exist, of turning the other cheek.

In truth, the three possible strategies logically open to the government of the United States at the moment seem fairly clear. They are: (1) escalation; (2) a long negotiation accompanied by military forcefulness; (3) immediate withdrawal.

Consider the extremes, (1) and (3). Not merely is the American way usually not extremism, but these all-or-nothing solutions do appear over-logical. Besides, they are politically impossible. The American people have rejected escalation; of that President Johnson became certain in 1968. As for withdrawal, the cost in American lives and treasure has been too high in Vietnam to allow for pulling the plug, cutting the cord, leaving the scene carrying lock, stock, and barrel, or else dropping those items for the

Vietnamese to quarrel over.

The remaining strategy, then, the one which the Nixon administration is pursuing at the present time, is to negotiate, all the while continuing to press the North Vietnamese forces and the Vietcong forces in South Vietnam.

Negotiation presents, of course, many difficulties. A long negotiation accompanied by military forcefulness is no easy strategy for a nation brought up on Gettysburg, regarding that battle as more decisive than Vicksburg. The negotiation is likely to be long, and in the course of it the American people may become impatient. Any talk with the communists, however promising, takes not merely weeks but months, perhaps years, as at Panmunjom, the Geneva Conference of 1954, the Laos Conference of 1961–1962 designed to bring peace to that little state. American goals in Vietnam are extremely limited, but it is not certain that the American public, perhaps basically impatient, sensitive also to the large commitment there, would be content with a slow putting down of the North Vietnamese revolution in South Vietnam, when all the while the nation had to put up with negotiation talk. This raises the possibility of a future escalation.

In a negotiation, can the North Vietnamese get away from the influence of Peking? The Chinese communists are distinctly hostile to the United States, looking to the defeat of what they consider a paper tiger. Hanoi has a boundary with communist China. Despite the traditional Vietnamese dislike for the Chinese, it does appear as if the Hanoi regime might have trouble—out of the geographic nearness—if it tries to act too independently of the Chinese.

Can the Russians be of help at Paris? The Russians seem to have been interested in helping, but it is questionable how much help they could give—even if they wished. They might have some leverage, in that they have provided the North Vietnamese with the world's most modern anti-aircraft screen. But the northerners have that screen, and possession would make it difficult for the Russians to put a price on something already sold and out of hand.

British experience with a communist insurgent movement in Malaya after the Second World War indicates that it may be better not to negotiate with insurgents. It is interesting to note that the government of Malaya made no offer to negotiate but only held out generous surrender terms for individuals. When the Malayan communists saw that they were losing, they offered to surrender arms in exchange for recognition as a legal political party (which would have maintained their infrastructure). This offer was not accepted, and it required five more years to put them down, to Malaya's great advantage.

A general view of the first meeting between the United States and North Vietnam delegations in Paris.

Negotiation holds undoubted dangers, and among them is the possibility of losing everything through some clever North Vietnamese talk. Secretary of Defense Clark Clifford in 1968 narrated to a press conference, albeit not concerning the problem of Vietnam, what he described as the parable of the hunter and the bear:

A hunter was in the forest one day and came upon a clearing and he saw a large bear in the middle of the clearing. As he raised his rifle and took aim, the bear said, "Wait a minute, friend. Don't shoot." The hunter lowered his rifle and the bear said, "What do you want?" The hunter said, "I want a fur coat." The bear said, "Well, that is reasonable. What I want is a full stomach. Let's sit down and negotiate." So they sat down and they negotiated. After a while, the bear left alone.

Despite the above parable, and all the other quandaries of negotiation, it does appear as if the peace talks in Paris are worth undertaking. The Paris talks are worth their wear and tear on the patience of the American negotiators, for who can tell, say, when a live-and-let-live agreement might emerge from the peace conference, some agreement in which loose ends could be left for the future to tie?

During the negotiation it may be possible for the United States to cut down its troop strength in Vietnam, as McGeorge Bundy recently proposed in a speech at De Pauw University in Greencastle, Indiana. In two or three years that strength might come down to 150,000 or 100,000 men —which is no small military force, and a body of troops sufficient to deny to North Vietnam a military victory in South Vietnam.

Trusting, meanwhile, to the chapter of accidents, Americans might then discover that time had worked for their purposes. Richard Rovere in a recent book, *Waist Deep in the Big Muddy*, has eloquently pointed out the need for time. He recalls that the late secretary of state and chief of staff of the US army, George C. Marshall, seems once to have said that if we could just hold on for twenty or thirty years without starting a nuclear war, we could be sure of one thing and one thing only: the world would be a different place. This was a restatement of the old Greek maxim, Rovere recalls, that in walking in a flowing stream one never steps into the same water twice. Solomon once said that our time is a very shadow that passes away, and Justice Holmes said that time has upset many fighting faiths. Jefferson, as we have seen, trusted to time for many things, including a solution to the problem of Louisiana. Americans need to be patient as their government negotiates, and perhaps cuts down its troop strength in Vietnam, in hope of better days and more profitable occasions.

A CONTEMPORARY DOCUMENT

[When the war in Vietnam heated up, when the United States poured a huge army into South Vietnam, and when, early in 1968, the conflict was going against the forces of the United States and South Vietnam, the Tonkin Resolution of 1964—the congressional resolution authorizing the president to use the armed forces of the United States to attack North Vietnamese territory—came in for severe criticism. About this time the chairman of the Senate committee on foreign relations, J. William Fulbright of Arkansas, received a letter, from someone either inside the armed services or having access to their records, offering alleged details of how the Johnson administration had provoked the destroyer incidents of August 1964 so as to escalate the Vietnam War. Fulbright did not reveal the authorship of this letter, but acting partly on the basis of its allegations, partly from other information which he had gathered, he invited Secretary of Defense McNamara to testify before the committee, which McNamara did on February 20. The grueling interrogation of that day ran in print to 110 pages. The result of this investigation, one must say, was largely unsatisfactory to both sides—if one may describe the Johnson administration and some of the senators on the committee as constituting sides. The result was a considerable confusion, rather than enlightenment. Senator Fulbright even came to wonder if there had been an attack. The hearing did show that there had been complexities, not easily analyzed, in the engagements of the destroyers *Maddox* and *Turner Joy* with North Vietnamese naval forces on August 2 and 4, 1964. The North Vietnamese at the time had possibly confused the mission of the American destroyers with some simultaneous operations by South Vietnamese naval craft and thought the American vessels were supporting the South Vietnamese operations (although the North Vietnamese surely knew that they were attacking American vessels). The American ships, on their part, knew before the attack on August 4 that they were going to be attacked. Classified intelligence information, the sources of which were not revealed at the hearing of February 1968, gave a clear warning. It is possible to believe that the *Maddox* had itself picked up the attack warning, from the North Vietnamese radio traffic. Meanwhile, the United States government had warned the North Vietnamese government in unequivocal terms that dire consequences would follow any such attack. It was possible therefore to argue, and this contention was heard during the hearing of February 1968, that the American vessels should have left the scene so as to avoid an incident. The American ships were, so it seems, probably outside of North Vietnamese territorial waters; the committee hearing spent much time on this problem, and one can at least argue that the ships were outside North Vietnamese waters. Perhaps the most confusing issue in the hearing related to the intelligence mission of the American ships. Secretary McNamara said that intelligence was not the primary mission of the *Maddox*. The American vessel nonetheless was picking up a great deal of information through its electronic devices. Could one then justify the North Vietnamese attack on the *Maddox?* Ever since the end of the Second World War, as mentioned in a previous chapter, intelligence missions have created much international trouble. The Russians periodically have attacked American aircraft flying along the Russian coast—craft admittedly outside territorial limits, but engaging in surveillance with long-range cameras and other gear. The hearing of February 1968 was conducted in the memory of two notable recent naval incidents involving intelligence-gathering ships. In June 1967, during the six-day war, the Israelis had bombed and sunk the American intelligence ship *Liberty* and killed thirty-four American sailors. Then in January 1968 the North Koreans had attacked and captured the intelligence ship *Pueblo*. Both the *Liberty* and *Pueblo* incidents occurred on the high seas. It was evident that Chairman Fulbright and some of his committee believed that the United States government had been very unwise in choosing a North

Vietnamese attack on intelligence vessels as an occasion for obtaining so far-reaching a congressional authorization as the Tonkin Resolution, virtually a declaration of war against North Vietnam. Some of the committee members also appeared disturbed that the White House staff had prepared a draft resolution, in the form of a "working paper," some time before the Tonkin Gulf incidents. The thought seemed to be that the administration had been anticipating an incident. Senator Fulbright had supported the Tonkin Resolution in 1964, and during the hearing of February 1968 publicly recanted his position. Source: 90th Cong., 2d Sess., *Hearing Before the Committee on Foreign Relations of the United States Senate* (Washington, 1968), pp. 79–81.]

. . . The Chairman. Well, I don't think anyone, I don't believe anyone, certainly myself, entertained the idea this was a plot or a conspiracy.

The point really is, and I think there is evidence sufficiently to justify an inquiry as to whether or not the decision-making process, with all these conflicting reports coming in, is sufficiently accurate and reliable to justify taking such a decision to declare war on another country, which was the immediate outgrowth of this particular series of events.

Secretary McNamara. I didn't comment on that.

The Chairman. I think this committee, and certainly as chairman of the committee I think it was very unfair to ask us to vote upon a resolution when the state of the evidence was as uncertain as I think it now is, even if your intercepts are correct. Of course, none of those intercepts were mentioned to us, I don't believe, in the testimony on August 6 [, 1964]. Your statement and General Wheeler's [General Earle G. Wheeler, chairman of the joint chiefs in 1964] was without any doubt, any equivocation that there was an all-out attack.

I submit that even if you give the most favorable interpretations to these reports that it was far less than positive and unequivocal as your statement before the committee indicates.

This has been very serious to me and all members of this committee and the Senate.

We have taken what is called the functional equivalent of a declaration of war upon evidence of this kind, and action as precipitate as this was. Even the commander, that is one of the crucial cablegrams from the commander of the task force [the two destroyers], recommended that nothing be done until the evidence was further evaluated. I read it this morning, I won't read it again.

But that alone almost, if I had known of that one telegram, if that had been put before me on the 6th of August [1964], I certainly don't believe I would have rushed into action.

We met, if you will recall for 1 hour and 40 minutes, in a joint meeting of the Armed Services and this committee and we accepted your statement completely without doubt. I went on the floor to urge passage of the resolution. You quoted me, as saying these things on the floor. Of course all my statements were based upon your testimony. I had no independent evidence, and now I think I did a great disservice to the Senate. I feel very guilty for not having enough sense at that time to have raised these questions and asked for evidence. I regret it.

I have publicly apologized to my constituents and the country for the unwise action I took, without at least inquiring into the basis. It never occurred to me that there was the slightest doubt, certainly on the part of Commander Herrick who was in charge of the task force that this attack took place. He obviously had doubts, his own cablegram so states. That is the reason for it. I feel a very deep responsibility, and I regret it more than anything I have ever done in my life, that I was the vehicle which took that resolution to the floor and defended it in complete reliance upon information which, to say the very least, is somewhat dubious at this time.

Well, I just wanted to make that for the record. . . .

If I had had enough sense to require complete evaluation I never would have made the mistake I did. . . . I must say this raises very serious questions about how you make decisions to go to war.

I mean, this is not a small matter that we are in, in Vietnam, and I think for the future, the least I can do and the committee can do, is to alert future committees and future Senates that these matters are not to be dealt with in this casual manner. . . .

Well, I delivered myself. . . .

ADDITIONAL READING

The best book is by Joseph Buttinger, *Vietnam: A Dragon Embattled* (2 vols., New York, 1967). This author's analysis is fairminded without the special pleading and the bitterness which marks so much of the Vietnam literature.

C. Turner Joy, *How Communists Negotiate* (New York, 1955) offers the experience of an American negotiator in Korea, worth perusing when thinking about the chances of negotiation over Vietnam. James Shepley, "Three Times at the Brink of War: How Dulles Gambled and Won," *Life* (Jan. 16, 1956) is the famous interview in which Dulles reportedly said that the important point in diplomacy was to know how to go to the brink without falling over.

According to Dulles, there were three episodes of what his detractors quickly described as brinkmanship (in imitation of a then popular word, gamesmanship, given currency by the British humorist Stephen Potter): Korea, Indochina, and Taiwan. Ellen J. Hammer, *The Struggle for Indochina: 1940–1955* (Stanford, Calif., 1955) is an early account, written before the subject warmed up. For the diplomacy of Secretary Dulles see Louis L. Gerson, *John Foster Dulles* (New York, 1967).

The Second Vietnamese War appears in * Denis Warner, *The Last Confucian: Vietnam, Southeast Asia, and the West* (Baltimore, 1964), a Penguin Special. The title of Warner's book refers to Ngo Dinh Diem. In 1965, with the strengthening of American forces, the books on Vietnam began to reach flood proportions, of which *Robert Shaplen, *The Lost Revolution* (rev. ed., New York, 1966) is one of the best. Arthur M. Schlesinger, Jr., took sections from his memoir of President Kennedy and updated and enlarged them into * *The Bitter Heritage* (Boston, 1967); Schlesinger's book places no blame on Kennedy, and implicitly considers President Johnson the inventor of the Vietnam disaster, but in many respects it is a model of scholarship and understanding, and its judgments are holding up remarkably well. Edward Weintal and Charles Bartlett, *Facing the Brink* (New York, 1967) considers this brink among others. *George McTurnan Kahin and John W. Lewis, *The United States and Vietnam* (New York, 1967) is an account by two scholars at Cornell. The leaders of North Vietnam are now having their minds plumbed, and it is something of a novelty to Americans, perhaps, to learn that individuals such as General Vo Nguyen Giap, one of those persons whom former Undersecretary of State George Ball was thinking of when he said that their names looked like typographical errors, has had something worthwhile to say about warfare; for Giap's opinions see *People's War, People's Army* (New York, 1967), and also *Big Victory, Great Task* (New York, 1968). *Foreign Affairs*, XLVI (1967–1968), 425–475 contains four articles on Vietnam by Roger Hilsman, Sir Robert Thompson, Chester L. Cooper, and Hamilton Fish Armstrong. Richard Rovere, *Waist Deep in the Big Muddy* (Boston, 1968) is a small volume of acute analysis which almost concludes that everything is hopeless, and was predicated upon the re-election of President Johnson; the president rearranged this situation by announcing his withdrawal from the race at the time *Waist Deep* was published; which seems to say that things are not always as bad as they seem.

☆ *32* ☆

The Diplomatic Revolution: The New Weapons and Diplomacy

> In a world atmosphere already extremely sensitive to power, the introduction of this weapon has profoundly affected political considerations in all sections of the globe. . . . To put the matter concisely, I consider the problem of our satisfactory relations with Russia as not merely connected with but as virtually dominated by the problems of the atomic bomb.
>
> —Memorandum by Henry L. Stimson for President Truman, September 11, 1945

1. *The brooding omnipresence*

Until recent years, the art of diplomacy, it is fair to say, has rested on the possibility of war. From time out of mind, diplomats have proceeded on the assumption that, should their missions fail, should the nations to which they are accredited prove contentious rather than peaceful, there was always the recourse of war. Often this possibility, intimated in a veiled and delicate diplomatic hint, was sufficient to bring intransigent nations around to the point of sweet reasonableness. There have been many historic occasions when hints of war, backed by undoubted willingness and ability to wage war if necessary, have settled international disputes. The historian can say with confidence that if the possibility of war had suddenly been removed from the diplomatic arena, the result would have been virtually a revolution in the conduct of diplomacy.

This possibility has in truth been removed in the years since 1945, for invention of the atomic bomb has made war so unbearably destructive that none of the possessors of atomic weapons has been willing to open hostilities on a large scale. There is indeed a sort of balance of terror between the United States and the Soviet Union. According to Secretary of Defense Clifford in a revealing announcement of October 25, 1968, the American nuclear force level as of that date consisted of 1,000 Minuteman intercontinental ballistic missiles, 54 Titan-2 ICBM's, 566 Polaris missiles, and 656 bombers of the Strategic Air Command (SAC). Clifford said—it would be fascinating to know how he had learned this—that the Russians as of that moment in history possessed 900 ICBM's (up from 720 a year before), 75-80 submarine missiles (more than double the figure of a year before), and 150-155 long-range bombers. The United States, he announced, possessed 4,206 "deliverable" nuclear weapons, either missiles or bombs, against 1,200 for the Russians. Hence the Americans had a four-to-one edge (at least if one counts numbers of deliverable weapons, apart from their TNT equivalents). On the Russian side there understandably has been clear appreciation that in an atomic war the gains of all of the slow, painful, immensely costly five-year plans could disappear in radioactive dust. But the Americans also have been fearful that a Russian attack on the United States, even a second-strike attack, might be just as effective as any American attack on Russia. The United States has well over 150 metropolitan areas with more than 50,000 inhabitants each, and their locations are well known. For many years the Americans have published detailed maps of their country, freely available to all comers at the corner gas station. The Russians have considerably fewer such areas of concentration of industry and people, and there are no corner gas stations.

International hatreds today are as implacable as any since the beginning of the modern era, since the Renaissance and Reformation at the end of the Middle Ages. Yet there is no general war. The intense reluctance of the powers to engage in war, their continuing refusal to submit their rivalries to what our nineteenth-century ancestors were wont to describe as the arbitrament of the sword, is the fundamental diplomatic fact of our time. In the words of former Secretary of State Dean Acheson, nuclear war has become "the brooding omnipresence, under the shadow of which the nation-states impinge on one another." The technical feasibility of nuclear war, the insufferable human consequences of a nuclear Armageddon, has shifted the foundations of diplomacy and caused a diplomatic revolution.

In the years after 1945, the great powers have tried to adapt their thinking and talking to the new picture of power and politics in the world. During the years of American atomic monopoly, from 1945 to 1949, Soviet Russian diplomats felt keenly their country's lack of atomic weapons and apparently chose to adopt as a kind of defense mechanism a provocative verbiage, a ferocity of language previously unknown in diplomatic intercourse. It is true that, from the time of the Russian revolution of 1917, negotiation with the Soviets usually has lacked the amenities and politesse traditional to diplomacy, but in the immediate post-1945 years there was a new virulence in the language of Russian negotiators, caused in part by embarrassments of the atomic arms race. Russian diplomatic talk continued its sharpness for a few years after 1949 when there was atomic inferiority. As for American diplomats in the initial post-1945 era, they talked in the accustomed politeness of diplomacy but sometimes gave a tone to their negotiation that carried a reminder of the existence, in American possession, of a weapon of unprecedented strength. Realizing that for several years after the end of the war their country possessed little military strength from which to negotiate, other than the bomb, diplomats of the United States were forced to remind their opponents on occasion of the existence of this special ace in the hole. After the Soviet Union obtained the bomb, the American government toned down its statements. And as for the allies of the United States (among whom only Great Britain and France possess the bomb, as of the present writing, 1969), they often betrayed what might for lack of a better phrase be described as psychological insecurity. America's allies felt that they were too close to the seat of Russian power, too exposed to quick retaliation, to play as forthright a role in diplomacy as the Americans, and they resented any veiled remarks by diplomats that the United States possessed an arsenal of bombs which it would, if necessary, use. This reluctance by weak allies to follow the American diplomatic lead became especially apparent in the years after 1949 when the Russians were building bombs. "No annihilation without representation" was the plea of the British, who did not obtain their own bomb until 1952.

2. *Theory and practice in a revolutionary era*

The initial periods of the atomic era, the years from 1945 to 1949 when the United States possessed a monopoly of nuclear weapons, and then the period from 1949 to 1953 when the United States held a clear superiority, were much easier times for the conduct of foreign relations than were the years which followed. As seen in previous chapters, James F. Byrnes, George C. Marshall, and Dean Acheson all had to wrestle with extremely difficult questions and crises and met with success and with failure. But the fact of monopoly, and after that, until 1953, of superiority, gave a security, however tenuous, to the conduct of American policy. Then, because the Russians by about 1953 had obtained enough atomic bombs to devastate most of the continental United States, even if they did not possess a nuclear arsenal as large as American bomb stocks, the diplomatic revolution began to affect almost every large action of American statesmen. Commencing with the secretaryship of John Foster Dulles, appointed by President Eisenhower in 1953, diplomacy became truly difficult.

In its opening years the Eisenhower-Dulles team hopefully announced several new policies, or new courses announced as new policies. There was talk of liberation of the captive nations of Eastern Europe, of an agonizing reappraisal of America's relations with its allies, of a new look in American military defenses based on a decision to meet Russian aggressive military moves with "massive retaliation." Each of these policies was born under the exigencies of the diplomatic revolution and took its course under the compulsions which attached to that revolution in 1953 and thereafter, the virtual equality of Russian and American atomic power.

In the present pages it is unnecessary to repeat some of the comments about these policies made in previous chapters, except to point out how in each case diplomatic choices narrowed markedly because of the new weapons in the hands of an adversary. Consider the policy of liberation, so boldly announced during the presidential campaign of 1952. By that year containment had begun to wear a little thin, just from being around for five years. The time had come for a new proposition. Logically, liberation also made sense. There was a logical problem with the slogan of 1947, containment. in that it was negative: everyone knows that positive teaching is far more valuable than negative; no one wishes to be negative, at least not for five years. Containment also appealed to many American citizens whose ancestors had come from behind the iron curtain and who habitually voted Democratic. For the Republican Party, liberation was politically irresistible. And it had great philosophic possibilities. As the historian Louis L. Gerson has shown, John Foster Dulles prior to appointment as secretary of state had been philosophizing about how dynamic forces always prevail over static, active over passive; that nonmaterial forces have a more powerful effect than material; that moral or natural law, not made by man, determines right or wrong, and that in the long run only those nations conforming to this law escape disaster; vigor, confidence, sense of destiny, belief in mission, all had led to the growth of the American republic; there needed to be a second American revolution; by conduct and example the United States could project its political, social, and economic ideas which were, he said, "more explosive than dynamite"; America was once the conscience of mankind, and it was foolish to let Marx replace the American thinkers of the eighteenth century; ideas were weapons. Dulles wanted "genuine independence in the nations of Europe and Asia now dominated by Moscow." The United States, he said, should not be a party to any "deal" confirming Soviet rule over the satellites. Dulles wrote the foreign relations planks of the Republican Party platform for 1952 and remarked brightly in one of them:

We shall again make liberty into a beacon light of hope that will penetrate the dark places. It will mark the end of the negative, futile and immoral policy of "containment" which abandons countless human beings to a despotism and godless terrorism, which in turn enables the rulers to forge the captives into a weapon of our destruction. . . . The policies we espouse will revive the contagious, liberating influences which are inherent in freedom. They will inevitably set up strains and stresses within the captive world which will make the rulers impotent to continue in their monstrous ways and mark the beginning of the end.

But when all this platform promising had led the Republicans into power, what happened? The only discernible results of the epoch-making policy of liberation were the establishment of an annual celebration in the United States known as Captive Nations Day, and the sending of balloons over Eastern Europe bearing cheery messages of good will from the United States to the peoples of the satellite nations. The American government did absolutely nothing when the workers of East Berlin and other East German cities revolted in June 1953, nor during the Hungarian and Polish revolts of 1956. At these critical moments the Eisenhower-Dulles policy of liberation became indistinguishable from the Truman-Acheson policy of containment. The United States could not risk driving the USSR into atomic war to liberate the captive peoples of the satellite nations between Western Europe and Russia. It is worthy of note that the Western spokesmen of the captive peoples, leaders of the East European emigration to the West after 1945, did not favor forcible liberation, and for the same reason that deterred the American government—the terrible nuclear vengeance that Russia might wreak on all Europe in event of an attempted Western military liberation of Eastern Europe.

The second item on the list of Eisenhower-Dulles diplomatic pronouncements, the projected agonizing reappraisal of 1953, was the attempt to scare France—recounted in chapter twenty-six—into co-operating with NATO when the United States was doing its best to incorporate West Germany in the military alliance against Russia. One well can understand why Dulles had lost patience with the shuffling of French politics in 1953, which was much worse than during most of the political eras of the French republics. He felt that only a blunt announcement would move the wayward French. On a visit to France that year, he twice announced the possibility of an agonizing reappraisal, once at the NATO Council meeting and then at a press conference in Paris. The language of the mid-twentieth century, he perhaps believed, had to be dramatic to cut through the world's great daily outpouring of oratory and words in general.

It was unfortunate that he resorted to this kind of statement that the United States might pull out of Europe if the European Defense Community failed, because by such talk he said the very thing that the Russians might well have wanted. His talk of agonizing reappraisal was a double failure, short-range and long. The immediate result of the pressure was to touch the *amour-propre* of the French Assembly, which voted down the proposed European Defense Community that would have brought German divisions into NATO. In this immediate sense the threat of a new American policy failed. The more long-range effect of it was that Dulles was reinforcing false and even dangerous worries and concerns in the minds of the sensitive Western European allies. For the United States, the less such reinforcement the better. The Western European nations were exposed to Russian nuclear vengeance; if the United States pulled out of Europe they would come immediately under Russian dominance. The threat of an American departure in 1953, combined with the actions of the United States three years later during the Suez crisis in which the Americans sided with Russia against Britain and France, gave a chancey aspect to American policy of the 1950's, tending in subtle ways to erase the affirmations of the late 1940's. Europeans always have been slightly cynical about American policy. They distrust big policy shifts and have a tendency to underrate the major moves of American opinion by taking seriously the constant minor statement-making in the press and in Congress. They have had trouble believing in what Americans, at least, knew was a major shift of policy in 1947–1949. They think that sooner or later we will crawl back into our holes, go back to the wisdom of 1796 and the Farewell Address. Dulles's statement of a possible American policy was a dangerous remark during the tensions of the diplomatic revolution when the Western Europeans could not maintain an independent policy. Here, and this is the point of the commentary above, was another evidence of how the diplomatic revolution had interfered with what in the old days would have been a straightforward result, in itself good or bad, of an American pronouncement. The diplomatic revolution impinged upon Dulles's pronouncement, colored it luridly, producing a set of ideas quite different from what he intended.

The new look, another Eisenhower-Dulles principle, better known as a military policy of massive retaliation, was an attempted return to an atomic strategy rather than continuance of the combined atomic-conventional strategy which the United States had adopted after the opening of the Korean War in 1950. This sort of reshaping of the American military establishment was in the cards at this time, as the testing of hydrogen devices and bombs by both the Americans and Russians was tending to stress atomic warfare. The Russians were making great claims of their new atomic prowess, and it probably was necessary for the American government to announce its own atomic ability if only for diplomatic reasons, both with the publics of the United States, Britain, and France and with the many flighty publics of the neutral nations. It was hard to say the right thing here, but something needed to be said in 1952–1953–1954, what with the changing atomic picture. Then there was the problem of changing the American army, which just had finished fighting the Korean War on the old-time, Second-World-War basis. It was clear that the army had to be reorganized, but no one knew how. There was need to cut military expenditures from the level of the Korean War's last year, $53,000,000,000 —but how far? The $15,000,000,000 budget of pre-Korea years? The new Republican administration needed to demonstrate ability with money, after the profligacy of the Democrats, and so the Eisenhower administration looked to the sinkhole of most of the budget, the military expenditures. Perhaps here there was an unfamiliarity of President Eisenhower

John Foster Dulles, the exponent of massive retaliation and brinkmanship, assures Uncle Sam, "Don't be afraid—I can always pull you back."

with the novelties of military budgeting in a nuclear age; his last acquaintance with military budgets had been as chief of staff immediately after the war when the individual services were cutting the budget pie in crudely equal slices, not even facing up to the problems of atomic warfare. President Eisenhower in 1953 may also have been willing to cut the conventional military budget because, though a military man (and often known during his presidency as General Eisenhower), he needed to impress his civilian side on the American people. There was a melange of reasons behind the proposed new policy of massive retaliation, including the fact that Eisenhower early in 1953 had threatened the Chinese in Korea with nuclear war if they did not stop fighting. The war somehow had stopped. Early in 1954 trouble was looming in Indochina, perhaps another Chinese intervention. Secretary Dulles said on September 2, 1953, "The Chinese Communist regime should realize that such a second aggression could not occur without grave consequences which might not be confined to Indochina." Dulles in January 1954, in a famous address to members and guests of the Council on Foreign Relations in New York, announced a basic government decision "to depend primarily on a great capacity to retaliate by means and at places of our own choosing." With this, he later said, "you do not need to have local defense all round the 20,000-mile perimeter of the orbit of the Soviet World." In March 1954, Vice President Richard M. Nixon announced a corollary, the "nibble-to-death doctrine": "We have adopted a new principle. Rather than let the Communists nibble us to death all over the world in little wars, we will rely in future on massive mobile retaliatory powers." This strategy was defined visibly about this time when there were hair-raising revelations of a thermonuclear device exploded by the United States at Eniwetok in November 1952. A three-megaton (equivalent to 3,000,000 tons of TNT) hydrogen force had ripped a mile-wide crater in the ocean's floor and devastated an area of six miles in diameter. On March 1, 1954, the United States exploded a large H-bomb at Bikini, with a force of fifteen megatons. A radioactive cloud swirled far out from the explosion area, much farther than anticipated, down on the Japanese tuna trawler *Lucky Dragon*, which was seventy miles away, bringing sickness to the crew and eventual death by a collateral cause to one crew member.

The new look, massive retaliation, had its own contemporary inspirations, but as a theory of foreign relations it did not fit well into the military requirements of the nuclear age, and it came to grief. "More bang for the buck" sounded good, the slogan was compelling, until the administration realized that reductions in conventional military power would have an automatic effect on the conduct of American diplomacy. "Diplomacy without armaments," Frederick the Great once said, "is like music without instruments." If this aphorism has needed qualification in the latter twentieth century, it still carries truth. A wide range of armaments was necessary in the day of limited war (for limited war was the only feasible kind of armed conflict after invention of the new weapons; total war had become almost too repulsive for practical consideration). The years 1953–1954 were no time to reduce the military establishment and rely primarily on atomic weapons when the type of war to be anticipated was limited war, totally unsuited to atomic strategy.

Eventually massive retaliation yielded to a more long-range view of American armaments, and most of the proposed cuts in conventional military power were abandoned.

A fourth principle of diplomacy advanced to the publics of Europe and America in the middle 1950's deserves some mention here, because while this proposition did not become part of American foreign policy (for reasons which, one must assume, showed a more mature thinking by policy makers than earlier in the decade), it had much attraction and for a while dominated public forums on foreign policy. This proposed principle, like its official predecessors outlined above, came a cropper because it ignored the perils of the diplomatic revolution, even while trying to solve them. In this respect, perhaps, it showed that almost any policy other than a cautious maintenance of the *status quo* was a dangerous adventure in the era of the diplomatic revolution.

The proposed policy was called "disengagement," and any student who undertakes to plumb its rise and fall in the American and European discussion of the 1950's can measure accurately the nuclear and other problems of world politics at that time and, indeed, down to the present time. At the outset, disengagement seemed so attractive. It took its origin out of the attempts by the Soviet Union early in the decade to prevent West Germany from joining NATO, in the course of which the Soviets proposed the unification of Germany as a neutralized state. There could be no German alliances within German unity so conceived. This initial blandishment held attraction, although any careful observer would have noted the cantonments of Russian troops in the nearby Eastern European nations, notably Poland, and hence the exposed nature of any Germany so unified. The West German government of Chancellor Konrad Adenauer was hardly taken in by such a proposition, and the idea quietly lapsed. Gradually, though, the original Soviet suggestion was transmuted into a proposal, or set of proposals, never clearly elaborated, for a nuclear-free zone in Eastern Europe which might include only Germany, or some of the Eastern European countries, or all of them. In the minds of its proponents such a zone might be all of Europe. It might include the British Isles. In the latter case the Russians would be back within their borders and the Americans within theirs. The only difficulty was that the Russians would be much closer than the Americans.

The temporarily retired American diplomat-turned-historian, George F. Kennan (Dulles had retired him in 1953 by refusing to give him an ambassadorial or other high appointment) took up disengagement and advocated it in a series of broadcasts over the British Broadcasting Corporation in 1957, the Reith lectures, which were published next year under the title of *Russia, the Atom and the West.* Kennan went so far as to advocate American disengagement from some of the developing nations of the world, telling those nations (in event that they were seeking to blackmail the United States for more aid) that they could give themselves to the Russians if they wished.

The doctrine of disengagement, so enchantingly portrayed, evoked a furious response in the journal *Foreign Affairs* by former Secretary of State Acheson, who said that the only disengagement possible in this world was disengagement from life, which was death. He remarked that the passage of time, twenty years from 1918, had brought the errors of 1938, and after another twenty years the errors, distressingly similar, of 1958. Disengagement, it was now called. It was the same futile and lethal attempt to crawl back into the cocoon of history. Such doctrine would undo all the work of 1947–1949 which had produced a livable, prosperous situation in Western Europe.

Kennan like any good debater resorted to metaphor in meeting the arguments of his former chief. He said that the very purpose of containment was creation of a position of strength from which to negotiate, not construction of a blockhouse. Containment presumed eventual compromise, not the crushing of Soviet power. Hence the link between containment and disengagement. He believed that if the Russians moved five hundred miles to the east, behind their own borders, only the most dire of circumstances, general war, would bring them back. They had to watch for the requirements of public opinion in their own and in the free areas. Through their propaganda, he said, the Russians had mortgaged themselves to such notions as peace and noninterference. He referred to an "overmilitarization of thought" about the cold war.

Disengagement gradually disappeared as a talked-about theory, and little was heard from it after the year 1959. The reason, so it now seems, was not so much the arguments of its proponents or adversaries but the enormously difficult business of taking a new diplomatic step in so complicated an era as that of the diplomatic revolution. The sides of policy, the unforeseen results, complexities, counterforces, were almost too many to calculate. One preferred to stay where he was, to live with what he knew. The British military analyst and historian Michael Howard summed up the problem well when he wrote at the time that "The frying-pan is hot, but where will we land if we jump out of it?"

3. *The problems of deterrence*

What, then, are the diplomatic possibilities for the United States in the new and strange age after 1945? How can American diplomacy so estimate the possibilities of each moment in the era of the diplomatic revolution that it can maintain the national interest in a world at peace?

The word most commonly used by strategists of the West to describe the purpose of Western policies is deterrence. The West hopes to deter the Soviet Union—to maintain sufficient military strength and diplomatic agility to persuade the USSR to refrain from either limited or atomic war, to keep roughly the post-1945 balance of territory and peoples throughout the world, to avoid the unknown but obviously dangerous possibilities of full-scale war. This is Western policy: to avoid war, to keep peace with honor, until in some distant and wonderful future the suspicions of Russian leaders will cool and the world can turn with full attention to the problems of peaceful living.

And it is not merely a matter of deterring the Russians. As the 1960's draw to an end, a new and perplexing adversary is entering the lists, quite possibly against the preservation of peace: the People's Republic of China. The Chinese have tested nuclear bombs and are readying intercontinental ballistic missiles. Both the Russian and American governments worry incessantly about this malevolent regime which, though communist, is through its newspaper press and official spokesmen inviting plagues on both their houses. It is unnerving to contemplate the political confusion in communist China over the succession to Chairman Mao, for one knows that a government in such confusion might confuse foreign policy as well. If it has done nothing else, the entrance of communist China into the politics of the diplomatic revolution has vastly complicated the equations of peace and war. The Americans and Russians, united in this one situation, wish the best of luck to the Chinese people in their strivings for a better life and hope that time will prove a solvent for the Chinese government's ill will.

Deterrence might give the world time to cool down. The two major atomic powers will have to hope that the Chinese would not resort to some irrational act. They will have to hope that the British and French as atomic powers also would preserve world peace (a far easier thing to do). Meanwhile the two major powers will have to remain roughly equal in their nuclear armaments, the chief runners approximately abreast, neither

The diplomat in the atomic age.

tempted to take advantage of some large lead. The peace might be in danger if one of the two major powers, or perhaps the Chinese, should happen on some scientific discovery which would allow it to neutralize its opponent's nuclear strike force. A working antiballistic-missile system might do this. One of the continuing concerns of United States military men and scientists has been that the Russians through high-altitude test explosions prior to the Test-Ban Treaty of 1963 might have managed to learn a good deal about the jamming of electrical systems. If employed in an attack, such knowledge might destroy the electronics, hence the effectiveness, of the American missile system. Senator Henry M. Jackson, the Senate's expert on this sort of thing, was raising this very question in the autumn of 1968. The hunch of most American specialists, a hunch not certified by specific knowledge of Russian knowledge, is that the Russians do not yet know enough to be sure of their ability to jam the American missile system and hence make the United States defenseless before a Soviet attack. Meanwhile a recent technological advance, the MIRV (multiple independently targeted re-entry vehicle) warhead, a missile warhead containing multiple bombs, including decoy bombs along with "the real McCoy," has probably made antiballistic-missile defense much more difficult.

Diplomats have calculated their national advantages with more unsureness in the latter twentieth century than ever before. There has been an almost miraculous, or diabolic, invention of new weapons in the years since Hitler in 1939, an almost forgotten date, invaded Poland and began the Second World War. The diplomats' task requires almost more information than intelligence can comprehend. One could hope that they will not turn to guessing instead of rational investigation, that they will not proceed on a day-to-day basis hoping that today's decision would ensure the possibility of another decision tomorrow, that by no chance in some large enemy country will decisions pass into the hands of such an irrational individual as another Hitler or Stalin, who in his warped intelligence might find justification for nuclear war and plunge the world over the brink.

The nearest American diplomatic analogy to these problems was offered by the problems of the early years of independence, when the nation's diplomats learned to counter the tricks and dissimulations of Europe's professional diplomats. The analogy is none too close when one realizes that diplomacy in the latter eighteenth century, despite its deceits, was still a profession of gentility and mutual respect. That wisest of eighteenth-century Americans, Benjamin Franklin, could negotiate with men of common background and some trustworthiness, a Vergennes or a Richard Oswald. He never had to deal with statesmen who lived according to a totally different ethic. The worst a diplomat could expect in those days, an unwanted war, could in no way be as destructive as war in the 1970's. Franklin did not have to make daily surveys of the prospects for existence.

A mass of problems confront a present-day secretary of state. There is the problem of the United States's allies, whether the country could count on their assistance in crisis. Our allies can be frightened away by our diplomatic ineptitude. As a close student of our atomic diplomacy, William W. Kaufmann, has put it, the United States must be extremely careful of its allies, displaying "a willingness to act as the leader of a coalition rather than as the principal of a kindergarten." (But perhaps, some devotees of one-solution atomic strategy believe, allies are not necessary when the ICBM is removing the need for overseas bases for the American strategic air force and even the necessity for that air force itself.)

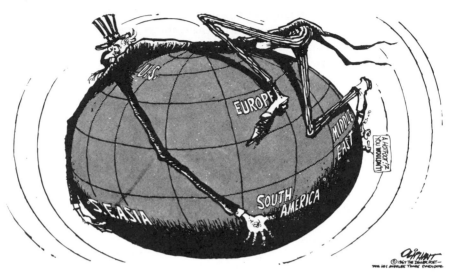

Sam's responsibilities.

There is the problem of keeping the American government free of military domination when so much diplomacy is of a military nature and subject to the supposed expert knowledge of military men. What might have happened if President Kennedy had listened to his military advisers during the Cuban missile crisis of 1962! With the notable exception of General Maxwell Taylor, the president believed, these advisers were full of bad advice, if nonetheless in an eminent position to offer it. The president's brother Robert remembered that the leading military advisers in 1962

seemed to give so little consideration to the implications of steps they suggested. They seemed always to assume that the Russians and the Cubans would not respond or, if they did, that a war was in our national interest. One of the Joint Chiefs of Staff once said to me he believed in a preventive attack against the Soviet Union. On that fateful Sunday morning when the Russians answered they were withdrawing their missiles, it was suggested by one high military adviser that we attack Monday in any case. Another felt that we had in some way been betrayed.

There is the problem of keeping a large conventional military establishment ready for eventualities and of justifying this conventional establishment to the American people. Many Americans are concerned that their friends and relatives are confined unwillingly within the air force or army or navy. The secretary of state must convince the nation of the unpalatable truth that the conventional military establishment is his only hope for conducting a sane foreign policy, that without armaments of all kinds, conventional as well as atomic, the diplomacy of the United States might well become ineffective because it would be unbelievable—a foreign enemy would know that it could push us to the very end of our patience, since at no stage short of that end would the American nation be willing to use its atomic weapons and risk thereby its own destruction.

There is the cost of atomic weaponry, piled onto that of the conventional military establishment, a large problem for Americans to reckon with. Military costs are so high that they encourage searches on the part of both government and citizenry for cheaper solutions, easy formulas for difficult problems. There is always the question of whether the American taxpayer may fail to understand why each year his income tax is so high. The bulk of the tax goes for national defense, and the cost of that defense is astonishingly high. The military budget for fiscal 1970 (July 1, 1969, through June 30, 1970) may run as high as $85,000,000,000. During the war of 1941–1945 submarines cost between $5,000,000 and $7,000,000. Nuclear-powered submarines cost between $45,000,000 and $78,000,000. In late 1968 the department of defense decided to authorize construction of a "quiet" nuclear-powered submarine which would cost an estimated $150–200,000,000. By the end of the 1960's the United States was planning for a total of 111 missile-firing or attack submarines (minimum total cost: approximately $5,000,000,000). Technological breakthroughs in production of weaponry could make expensive plant investment useless or nearly useless overnight. It has been necessary frequently to initiate weapons projects in several ways, employing different theoretical approaches until experiment could show the correct course. On February 25, 1958, the "last of the Navahos," the last of the unsuccessful and obsolete Navaho missiles, was fired at the missile proving ground on Cape Canaveral, closing a program that had cost about $700,000,000 but was canceled in the summer of 1957. It was necessary, defense officials argued, to have expensive "booboos" of this sort. But if the demands of an economy-minded public should override informed strategic thinking, the result might well be a cutting down of experiment that prevented quick results. Especially there might be a reduction of "pure science" in the universities and private laboratories, research which often did not lead immediately to anything but in the long run could produce breakthroughs. Will the people support their armament program to an extent necessary to keep up with the Russian and Chinese programs, which do not depend on popular support?

There is, lastly, the problem of education. The people will have to learn the requirements of their country's contemporary diplomacy and this learning is difficult without careful study of the nation's diplomatic history. But to what use? Education was the vain hope of eighteenth-century philosophers and nineteenth-century liberal reformers, and in the twentieth century the best-educated country in Europe, Germany, adopted a foreign policy full of error and mistake, precipitating the world into its present difficult position.

One thing is certain, that foreign relations by the latter twentieth century had become the central problem of the great republic of the New World.

A CONTEMPORARY DOCUMENT

[In recent months the Soviet Union has been drawing abreast of the United States in the missile race, and it is of interest that President Nixon in his first press conference on January 27, 1969, gave evidence that he is willing to allow this closing of what hitherto has been a large American lead. The president said he hoped to gain a political *quid pro quo* for allowing the Russians to close the gap, and said he believed also that a nuclear nonproliferation treaty would help ensure any United States-Soviet missile arrangement. Source: The New York *Times*, January 28, 1969.]

. . . Q. Mr. President, on foreign—foreign policy, nuclear policy in particular, could you give us your position on the nonproliferation treaty and on the starting of missile talks with the Soviet Union?

A. I favor the nonproliferation treaty. The only question is the timing of the ratification of that treaty. That matter will be considered by the National Security Council by my direction during a meeting this week. I will also have a discussion with the leaders of both sides in the Senate and the House on the treaty within this week and in the early part of next week.

I will make a decision then as to whether this is the proper time to ask the Senate to move forward and ratify the treaty. I expect ratification of the treaty and will urge its ratification at an appropriate time and I would hope an early time.

As far as the second part of your question with regard to strategic arms talks, I favor strategic arms talks. Again it's a question of not only when but the context of those talks.

The context of those talks is vitally important because we're here between two major, shall we say, guidelines. On the one side there is the proposition which is advanced by some that we should go forward with talks on the reduction of strategic forces on both sides.

We should go forward with such talks clearly apart from any progress on political settlement and on the other side the suggestion is made that until we make progress on political settlements, it would not be wise to go forward on any reduction of our strategic arms even by agreement with the other side.

It is my belief that what we must do is to steer a course between those two extremes. It would be a mistake, for example, for us to fail to recognize that simply reducing arms through mutual agreement, that failing to recognize that that reduction will not in itself assure peace. The war which occurred in the Mideast in 1967 was a clear indication of that.

What I want to do is to see to it that we have strategic arms talks in a way and at a time that will promote, if possible, progress on outstanding political problems at the same time, for example, on the problem of the Mideast, on other outstanding problems in which the United States and the Soviet Union acting together can serve the cause of peace. . . .

Q. Mr. President, back to nuclear weapons—both you and Secretary Laird [Secretary of Defense Melvin R. Laird] have stressed, quite hard, the need for superiority over the Soviet Union. But what is the real meaning of that, in view of the fact that both sides have more than enough already to destroy each other, and how do you distinguish between the validity of that stance and the argument of Dr. Kissinger [Henry A. Kissinger, the president's principal White House assistant for foreign affairs] for what he calls "sufficiency."

A. Here again, I think the semantics may offer an inappropriate approach to the problem. And, I would say that with regard to Dr. Kissinger's suggestion of sufficiency that that would meet, certainly, my guideline—and I think Secretary Laird's guideline—with regard to superiority.

Let me put it this way: When we talk about parity, I think we should recognize that wars occur, usually, when each side believes it has a chance to win. Therefore, parity does not necessarily assure that a war may not occur.

By the same token, when we talk about superiority, that may have a detrimental effect on the other side, in putting it in an inferior position, and therefore giving great impetus to its own arms race. Our objective in this Administration—and this is a matter that we're going to discuss at the Pentagon this afternoon, and it will be a subject of a major discussion in the National Security Council within a month—our objective is to be sure the United States has sufficient military power to defend our interests and to maintain the commitments which this Administration determines are in the interests of the United States around the world. I think sufficiency is a better term, actually, than either superiority or parity. . . .

ADDITIONAL READING

For what has become a strange new subject since 1945, that of atomic weapons and diplomacy, there is a large literature, and although some of it is trivial and some of it has become dated, there are books of lasting value to which the student can turn. There is no single book that deals generally with what might be described as atomic diplomacy, but several volumes together provide an excellent introduction. One might begin by reading the brilliant work by *Walter Millis, *Arms and Men* (New York, 1956), which sets out in historical perspective the military history of the United States and its connection with high policy from 1775 onward. Millis's last chapters, "The Hypertrophy of War" and "The Future of War," are among the best essays he has ever published. See also * Dean Acheson, *Power and Diplomacy* (Cambridge, Mass., 1958), and Stephen D. Kertesz's penetrating new book, *The Quest for Peace through Diplomacy* (Englewood Cliffs, N.J., 1967). Reading of these works might be followed with Richard G. Hewlett and Oscar E. Anderson, Jr., *The New World: 1939–1946* (University Park, Pa., 1962), the first volume in an official history of the Atomic Energy Commission, written by two expert historians; *Lansing Lamont, *Day of Trinity* (New York, 1965), a popular account of the same subject; *Fletcher Knebel and Charles W. Bailey III, *No High Ground* (New York, 1960), on the explosion of the first atomic weapons, which General Carl Spaatz said disposed of all high ground (referring to the old military injunction to "seize the high ground"); *David Bradley's *No Place to Hide* (Boston, 1948) by a naval doctor present at the Bikini explosions in 1946; and the several books by the physicist and science-writer Ralph E. Lapp, such as *Atoms and People* (New York, 1956) and *The Voyage of the Lucky Dragon* (New York, 1958). A narrative for sleepless nights is Herman Kahn, *On Thermonuclear War* (2d ed., Princeton, 1961), and the same author's *Thinking about the Unthinkable* (New York, 1962). Reassuring is William W. Kaufmann, *The McNamara Strategy* (New York, 1964), drawn from the speeches and other public papers of the then secretary of defense. See also Bernard Brodie, *Escalation and the Nuclear Option* (Princeton, 1966).

Personal accounts of work with the atom are Arthur H. Compton, *Atomic Quest* (New York, 1956), by the Nobel Prize laureate in physics; Gordon Dean, *Report on the Atom* (New York, 1954), by the late former chairman of the Atomic Energy Commission; Lewis L. Strauss, *Men and Decisions* (New York, 1962), by another chairman of the AEC; and especially *The Journals of David E. Lilienthal* (3 vols., New York, 1964–1966), the second volume of which considers the years during the Truman administration when Lilienthal was the first chairman of the AEC, years when he often wondered how peace might prevail. The Lilienthal diary ranks with the diaries of Henry L. Stimson and Edward M. House—the three most important diaries of American public men in the first half of the twentieth century. A commentary on the world of atomic physics, with oblique views into the personal rivalries among physicists and into the debates of the Atomic Energy Commission on such large questions as whether to build the H-bomb, is the fascinating publication of the AEC, *In the Matter of J. Robert Oppenheimer: Transcript of Hearing before Personnel Security Board* (Washington, 1954). *Haakon Chevalier, *Oppenheimer: The Story of a Friendship* (New York, 1965) shows some of the sides of the Oppenheimer case. The latest work about this enigmatic man, comparing him with another physicist of equal if not greater influence, the late Ernest O. Lawrence, is Nuel Pharr Davis, *Lawrence and Oppenheimer* (New York, 1968).

Turning to military problems and atomic weaponry, there are the works by the British air marshal and strategist, Sir John Slessor, *Strategy for the West* (New York, 1954) and *The Great Deterrent* (London, 1957). Slessor's American opposite, the former secretary of the air force Thomas K. Finletter, has written *Power and Policy* (New York, 1954), together with *Foreign Policy: The Next Phase* (New York, 1958). See James M. Gavin, *War and Peace in the Space Age* (New York, 1958). When General Matthew B. Ridgway retired from the army, he published an able memoir, *Soldier* (New York, 1956), criticizing the Eisenhower administration's reliance on air-atomic power at the cost of the army's ability to defend the nation in nonatomic wars. In this regard see Robert E. Osgood, *Limited War: The Challenge to American Strategy* (Chicago, 1957). Also *Bernard Brodie, *Strategy in the Missile Age* (Princeton, 1959). Disengagement appears in George F. Kennan, *Russia, the Atom, and the West* (New York, 1958), and in summary in *Michael Howard, *Disengagement in Europe* (Baltimore, 1958), a Penguin Special. Two opposing views are Dean Acheson, "The Illusion of Disengagement," *Foreign Affairs*, XXXVI (1957–1958), 371–382; and George F. Kennan, "Disengagement Revisited," *Foreign Affairs*, XXXVII (1958–1959), 187–210.

Books on nuclear disarmament are increasing, and among recent titles are Joseph L. Nogee, *Soviet Policy toward International Control of Atomic Energy* (Notre Dame, Ind., 1961); *John W. Spanier and Joseph L. Nogee, *The Politics of Disarmament: a Study in Soviet-American Gamesmanship* (New York, 1962), a readable survey; Walter Millis, *An End to Arms* (New York, 1965), a scenario, one might say, of what is necessary to reduce world tensions and create a warless world, by an expert military historian; Arthur H. Dean, *Test Ban and Disarmament: The Path of Negotiation* (New York, 1966), by a leading negotiator along this path; Harold K. Jacobson and Eric Stein, *Diplomats, Scientists and Politicians: The United States and the Nuclear Test Ban Negotiations* (Ann Arbor, Mich., 1966); Stephen D. Kertesz, ed., *Nuclear Non-Proliferation in a World of Nuclear Powers* (Notre Dame, Ind., 1967), the report of a meeting of the American Assembly.

On the question of civil control of the government of the United States see Arthur Ekirch, *The Civilian and the Military* (New York, 1956); *Samuel

P. Huntington, *The Soldier and the State* (Cambridge, Mass., 1957); Ernest R. May, ed., *The Ultimate Decision: The President as Commander in Chief* (New York, 1960), the problem as seen through the experiences of several of the presidents down to and including Eisenhower; Edgar E. Robinson, Alexander De Conde, Raymond G. O'Connor, and Martin B. Travis, Jr., *Powers of the President in Foreign Affairs: 1945–1965* (San Francisco, 1966); and Marcus Cunliffe, *Soldiers and Civilians: The Martial Spirit in America, 1775–1865* (Boston, 1968). Raymond G. O'Connor has edited an able collection of documents, *American Defense Policy in Perspective: From Colonial Times to the Present* (New York, 1965).

Scientists are becoming thoroughly aware of how the world of physics now impinges on the world of politics. Two recent books on this subject are *Robert Gilpin, *American Scientists and Nuclear Weapons Policy* (Princeton, 1962), and Alice Kimball Smith, *A Peril and a Hope: The Scientists' Movement in America, 1945–47* (Chicago, 1965). Well worth attention is the *Bulletin of the Atomic Scientists,* edited by the distinguished biophysicist Eugene Rabinowitch, and dedicated to the social aspects of their work by the atomic scientists of the United States.

Secretaries of State

John Jay (*1745–1829*)—1784–1790—The Continental Congress

Thomas Jefferson (*1743–1826*)—1790–1793—*President* George Washington

Edmund Randolph (*1753–1813*)—1794–1795—*President* George Washington

Timothy Pickering (*1745–1829*)—1795–1800—*Presidents* George Washington *and* John Adams

John Marshall (*1755–1835*)—1800–1801—*President* John Adams

James Madison (*1751–1836*)—1801–1809—*President* Thomas Jefferson

Robert Smith (*1757–1842*)—1809–1811—*President* James Madison

James Monroe (*1758–1831*)—1811–1817—*President* James Madison

John Quincy Adams (*1767–1848*)—1817–1825—*President* James Monroe

Henry Clay (*1777–1852*)—1825–1829—*President* John Quincy Adams

Martin Van Buren (*1782–1862*)—1829–1831—*President* Andrew Jackson

Edward Livingston (*1764–1836*)—1831–1833—*President* Andrew Jackson

Louis McLane (*1786–1857*)—1833–1834—*President* Andrew Jackson

John Forsyth (*1780–1841*)—1834–1841—*Presidents* Andrew Jackson *and* Martin Van Buren

Daniel Webster (*1782–1852*)—1841–1843 *and* 1850–1852—*Presidents* William Henry Harrison, John Tyler, *and* Millard Fillmore

Abel Parker Upshur (*1791–1844*)—1843–1844—*President* John Tyler

John Caldwell Calhoun (*1782–1850*)—1844–1845—*President* John Tyler

James Buchanan (*1791–1868*)—1845–1849—*President* James K. Polk

John Middleton Clayton (*1796–1856*)—1849–1850—*President* Zachary Taylor

Daniel Webster (second service)

Edward Everett (*1794–1865*)—1852–1853—*President* Millard Fillmore

William Learned Marcy (*1786–1857*)—1853–1857—*President* Franklin Pierce

Lewis Cass (*1782–1866*)—1857–1860—*President* James Buchanan

Jeremiah Sullivan Black (*1810–1883*)—1860–1861—*President* James Buchanan

William Henry Seward (*1801–1872*)—1861–1869—*Presidents* Abraham Lincoln *and* Andrew Johnson

Elihu Benjamin Washburne (*1816–1887*)—1869—*President* Ulysses S. Grant

Hamilton Fish (*1808–1893*)—1869–1877—*President* Ulysses S. Grant

William Maxwell Evarts (*1818–1901*)—1877–1881—*President* Rutherford B. Hayes

James Gillespie Blaine (*1830–1893*)—1881 and 1889–1892—*Presidents* James A. Garfield, Chester A. Arthur, *and* Benjamin Harrison

Frederick Theodore Frelinghuysen (*1817–1885*)—1881–1885—*President* Chester A. Arthur

Thomas Francis Bayard (*1828–1898*)—1885–1889—*President* Grover Cleveland

James Gillespie Blaine (second service)

John Watson Foster (*1836–1917*)—1892–1893—*President* Benjamin Harrison

Walter Quintin Gresham (*1832–1895*)—1893–1895—*President* Grover Cleveland

Richard Olney (*1835–1917*)—1895–1897—*President* Grover Cleveland

John Sherman (*1823–1900*)—1897–1898—*President* William McKinley

William Rufus Day (*1849–1923*)—1898—*President* William McKinley

John Hay (*1838–1905*)—1898–1905—*Presidents* William McKinley *and* Theodore Roosevelt

Elihu Root (*1845–1937*)—1905–1909—*President* Theodore Roosevelt

Robert Bacon (*1860–1919*)—1909—*President* Theodore Roosevelt

Philander Chase Knox (*1853–1921*)—1909–1913—*President* William H. Taft

William Jennings Bryan (*1860–1925*)—1913–1915—*President* Woodrow Wilson

Robert Lansing (*1864–1928*)—1915–1920—*President* Woodrow Wilson

Bainbridge Colby (*1869–1950*)—1920–1921—*President* Woodrow Wilson

Charles Evans Hughes (*1862–1948*)—1921–1925—*Presidents* Warren G. Harding *and* Calvin Coolidge

Frank Billings Kellogg (*1856–1937*)—1925–1929—*President* Calvin Coolidge

Henry Lewis Stimson (*1867–1950*)—1929–1933—*President* Herbert C. Hoover

Cordell Hull (*1871–1955*)—1933–1944—*President* Franklin D. Roosevelt

Edward Reilly Stettinius, Jr. (*1900–1949*)—1944–1945—*Presidents* Franklin D. Roosevelt *and* Harry S. Truman

James Francis Byrnes (*1879–   *)—1945–1947—*President* Harry S. Truman

George Catlett Marshall (*1880–1959*)—1947–1949— *President* Harry S. Truman

Dean Gooderham Acheson (*1893–   *)—1949–1953—*President* Harry S. Truman

John Foster Dulles (*1888–1959*)—1953–1959— *President* Dwight D. Eisenhower

Christian Archibald Herter, Jr. (*1919–1966*) —1959–1961— *President* Dwight D. Eisenhower

Dean Rusk (*1909–   *)—1961–1969—*Presidents* John F. Kennedy *and* Lyndon B. Johnson

William Pierce Rogers (*1913–   *)—*President* Richard M. Nixon

Index